Autodesk Inventor 2026 For Beginners

Tutorial Books

Table of Contents

Table of Contents ... iv

Topics covered in this Book ... xvi

Chapter 1: Getting Started with Autodesk Inventor 2026 ... 1

Introduction to Autodesk Inventor 2026 ... 1

Starting Autodesk Inventor 2026 ... 3

File Types ... 4

User Interface ... 4

Environments in Autodesk Inventor ... 5

Part environment ... 5

Assembly environment ... 5

Drawing environment ... 6

Sheet Metal environment ... 6

File Menu ... 6

Quick Access Toolbar ... 7

Graphics Window ... 8

Status Bar ... 8

View Cube ... 8

Dialogs ... 9

Changing the display of the Ribbon ... 10

Marking Menus ... 12

Shortcut Menus ... 12

Starting a new document ... 12

The Create New dialog ... 13

Application Options dialog ... 14

Changing the Color Scheme ... 14

Autodesk Inventor Help ... 15

Questions ... 16

Chapter 2: Sketch Techniques ... 18

Sketching in the Sketch environment ... 18

Sketch Commands ... 18

The Line command ... 19

Creating Arcs ... 20

The Arc Three Point command ... 20

The Arc Tangent Command ... 20

The Center Point Arc command ... 22

- Creating Circles 22
  - Center Point Circle 22
  - Tangent Circle 22
- Creating Rectangles 23
  - Two Point Rectangle 23
  - Three Point Rectangle 23
  - Two Point Center Rectangle 24
  - Three Point Center Rectangle 24
- Creating Slots 25
  - Center to Center Slot 25
  - Overall Slot 25
  - Center Point Slot 26
  - Three Point Arc Slot 26
  - Center Point Arc Slot 26
- The Polygon command 27
- The Ellipse command 28

The Dimension command 29
- Linear Dimensions 29
- Angular Dimensions 30
- Adding Dimensions to an Arc 30
  - Adding a Radius or Diameter or Arc Length dimension 31
  - Adding a Linear dimension to the Arc 31
  - Adding an Angular dimension to an Arc 31

Over-constrained Sketch 32

Constraints 32
- Coincident Constraint 32
- Horizontal Constraint 33
- Vertical Constraint 33
- Concentric Constraint 34
- Equal Constraint 34
- Collinear Constraint 35
- Tangent Constraint 35
- Parallel Constraint 36
- Perpendicular Constraint 36
- Symmetric Constraint 36

Constraint Settings......37
  The Inference tab......37
  Show/Hide All Constraints......38
Adding Dimensions and Constraints Automatically......38
The Construction Command......39
The Centerline Command......39
The Fillet command......40
The Chamfer command......40
The Extend command......41
The Trim command......42
The Offset command......42
The Move command......42
The Copy command......43
The Rotate command......43
The Scale command......44
The Stretch command......44
Circular Sketch Pattern......45
Rectangular Sketch Pattern......46
The Mirror command......47
Creating Splines......47
  Control Vertex Spline......47
  Interpolation Spline......48
Examples......48
  Example 1 (Millimeters)......48
    Starting a Sketch......49
    Adding Constraints......51
    Adding Dimensions......52
    Finishing the Sketch and Saving it......55
  Example 2 (Inches)......56
    Starting a Sketch......56
  Example 3 (Millimeters)......62
    Starting a Sketch......63
Questions......68
Exercises......69
  Exercise 1......69
  Exercise 2......69

Exercise 3....69

Chapter 3: Extrude and Revolve Features....71

Extruded Features....71

Revolved Features....72

Project Geometry....73

Planes....74

Offset from Plane....74

Parallel to Plane through Point....74

Midplane between Two Planes....75

Midplane of Torus....76

Angle to Plane around Edge....76

hree Points....76

Two Coplanar Edges....77

Coplanar Lines....77

Coplanar Edges....77

Tangent to Surface through Edge....78

Tangent to Surface through Point....78

Tangent to Surface and Parallel to Plane....78

Normal to Axis through Point....79

Normal to Curve at a Point....80

UCS....80

Additional options of the Extrude command....81

Boolean....81

Join....81

Cut....81

Intersect....81

New Solid....81

Behavior....82

Match Shape....85

Adding Taper to the Extruded Feature....85

View Modification commands....87

Examples....89

Example 1 (Millimeters)....89

Creating the Base Feature....90

Creating the Extrude Cut throughout the Part model....91

Creating the Extruded Cut up to the surface next to the sketch plane 93
Extruding the sketch up to a Surface 96
Example 2 (Inches) 98
Creating the Revolved Solid Feature 98
Creating the Revolved Cut 100
Adding a Revolved Feature to the model 101
Questions 104
Exercises 104
Exercise 1 (Inches) 104
Exercise 2 (Millimetres) 105
Exercise 3 (Inches) 105
Exercise 4 (Millimetres) 106
Chapter 4: Placed Features 107
Hole 107
Simple Hole 108
Extend Start 110
Saving the Hole Settings 111
Counterbored Hole 111
Countersink Hole 112
Tapped Hole 113
Taper Tapped Hole 113
Thread 114
Fillet 115
Smooth Fillet 116
Inverted Fillet 116
Selection Modes 117
Solids 118
Variable Radius Fillet 120
Corner Setback 121
Face Fillet 122
Full Round Fillet 123
Chamfer 123
Distance and Angle chamfer 124
Two Distances chamfer 124
The Face Draft command 125

Fixed Edge ...125
Fixed Plane ...125
Shell...126
Examples ...128
Example 1 (Millimeters)...128
Questions...137
Exercises ...137
Exercise 1 (Millimetres) ...137
Exercise 2 (Inches) ...138
Chapter 5: Patterned Geometry...140
Mirror...141
Mirror Solids ...142
Create Patterns ...143
Rectangular Pattern...143
Using the Compute options...145
Creating a Pattern Along a Path ...146
Patterning the entire geometry ...147
Suppressing Occurrences...147
Circular Pattern...148
Sketch Driven Pattern ...150
Examples ...150
Example 1 (Millimeters)...150
Example 2 (Millimeters)...158
Example 3 (Millimeters)...165
Questions...171
Exercises ...171
Exercise 1 (Millimetres) ...171
Chapter 6: Sweep Features...172
Path sweeps ...173
Profile Orientation...175
Twist ...176
Path and Guide Rail Sweeps ...176
Path and Guide Surface Sweeps ...178
Swept Cutout...178
Coil ...179
Helical Cutout...184

Examples 184
Example 1 (Inches)....184
Questions....190
Exercises 190
Exercise 1....190
Exercise 2....191
Chapter 7: Loft Features 192
Loft 192
Loft sections....192
Conditions 193
Direction Condition 193
Tangent Condition 194
Smooth (G2) Condition 194
Rails 194
Closed Loop....196
Center Line Loft....197
Area Loft 198
Loft Cutout....200
Examples 200
Example 1 (Millimetres)....200
Example 2 (Inches)....204
Questions....225
Exercises 226
Exercise 1....226
Chapter 8: Additional Features and Multibody Parts....227
Rib 227
Applying Draft to the Rib Feature 228
Adding a Boss to the Rib feature....229
Offset....229
Diameter 229
Draft Angle....229
Bend Part....230
Multi-body Parts 230
Creating Multibody Parts....231
The Split command 231
Join 233

Intersect 234
Cut 234
Emboss 234
Decal 236
Mark 236
Marking a Sketch using the Project Method 237
Marking a Sketch using the Wrap Method 237
Using the Derive tool 238
Using the Finish tool 240
Examples 241
Example 1 (Inches) 241
Example 2 (Millimetres) 247
Questions 253
Exercises 253
Exercise 1 (Millimeters) 253
Exercise 2 (Millimeters) 255
Exercise 3 (Inches) 256
Chapter 9: Modifying Parts 257
Edit Sketches 257
Edit Feature 258
Suppress Features 258
Resume Suppressed Features 259
Examples 265
Example 1 (Inches) 265
Example 2 (Millimetres) 268
Questions 270
Exercises 270
Exercise 1 270
Chapter 10: Assemblies 272
Starting an Assembly 272
Inserting Parts 273
Moving and Rotating Components 276
Free Move 276
Free Rotate 277
Applying Constraints 277
Mate Constraint 277

The Mate Solution 277
The Flush Solution 278
Aligning Axes or Edges using the Mate Constraint....................278
Insert Constraint 280
Angle Constraint....................281
Tangent Constraint....................281
Symmetry Constraint....................282
Joints 282
Ball Joint....................282
Rotational Joint 283
Rigid Joint....................283
Cylindrical Joint....................284
Planar Joint 285
Slider Joint 285
Analyze Interference....................287
iMates....................288
Editing and Updating Assemblies....................289
Editing Constraints....................290
Replace Components....................291
Pattern Component....................292
Mirror Components....................293
Copy Components 295
Sub-assemblies 296
Rigid and Flexible Sub-Assemblies....................297
Demote 297
Promote....................298
Assembly Features....................299
Top-Down Assembly Design 302
Create Component....................302
Exploding Assemblies....................304
Taking a Snapshot 307
Examples 307
Example 1 (Bottom-Up Assembly)....................307
Example 2 (Top-Down Assembly) 315
Example 3 (Presentations) 324
Starting a New Presentation File....................325

Creating a Storyboard Animation 325
Taking the Snapshot of the Explosion....327
Questions....328
Exercise 1....328
Chapter 11: Drawings....330
Starting a Drawing....331
Create a drawing from an already opened Part or Assembly file....332
Creating a Base View....333
Projected View....333
Auxiliary View....334
Section View....334
Detail View....337
Break a View....339
Break Out....340
Exploded View....341
View Style....341
View Alignment....342
Parts List....344
Adding Balloons....345
Using the Auto Balloon command....345
Dimensions....345
Baseline Dimension....346
Baseline Dimension Set....347
Ordinate Dimensions....348
Ordinate Set....348
Changing the Origin....349
Hole Table....349
Hole Table - Selection....350
Hole Table - View....350
Hole Table - Feature....351
Center Marks and Centerlines....351
Centerlines....352
Centerline Bisector....352
Automated Centerlines....353
Centered Pattern....354
Creating Hole and Thread Notes....354

Chamfer Notes....355

Examples....356

Example 1....356

Making the Styles Library Editable....356

Starting a New Drawing File....357

Editing the Title Block and Borders....357

Editing the Styles and Standards....361

Starting a New File using Custom Template....364

Retrieving Dimensions....368

Example 2....372

Questions....375

Exercises....375

Exercise 1....375

Exercise 2....376

Chapter 12: Surface Design....377

Extruded Surface....377

Loft....379

Creating a Transition Surface using the Loft command....380

Creating the lofts using Guide Rails....381

Creating a Centerline Loft....382

Sweep....382

Path + Guide....384

Path + Guide Surface....384

Patch....385

Trim....386

Creating Ruled Surfaces....387

Normal to Surface....387

Tangent to Surface....387

Ruled Surface along a Vector....388

Replacing Face....389

Extend....389

Sculpt....390

Stitch Surfaces....391

Thicken/Offset....392

Converting a Surface to Solid....392

Deleting Faces....393

Unwrap....394

Example 1....394

Drawing the layout sketch....395

Creating the Front Surface....399

Creating the Label surface....400

Creating the Back surface....402

Sculpting the Surfaces....402

Creating the Handle Surface....404

Blending the Handle with Surface Model....405

Blending the Bottom handle....408

Creating the Neck and Spout....415

Filleting the Label and Bottom Surfaces....417

Adding thickness to the model....418

Creating the Emboss on the Label Face....420

Mirroring the Emboss feature....421

Embossing the bottom face....422

Filleting the Embosses....423

Adding Threads....425

Example 2....429

Questions....437

Index....438

Introduction

Welcome to the *Autodesk Inventor 2026 For Beginners* book. This book is written to assist students, designers, and engineering professionals in designing 3D models. It covers the essential features and functionalities of Autodesk Inventor using relevant examples and exercises.

This book is written for new users, who can use it as a self-study resource to learn Autodesk Inventor. Also, experienced users can use it as a reference. The focus of this book is part modeling, assembly modeling, drawings, and surface design.

Topics covered in this Book

- Chapter 1, "Getting Started with Autodesk Inventor 2026", gives an introduction to Autodesk Inventor. The user interface and terminology are discussed in this chapter.
- Chapter 2, "Sketch Technique," explores the sketching commands in Autodesk Inventor. You will learn to create parametric sketches.
- Chapter 3, "Extrude and Revolve features," teaches you to create basic 3D geometry using the Extrude and Revolve commands.
- Chapter 4, "Placed Features," covers the features which can be created without using sketches.
- Chapter 5, "Patterned Geometry," explores the commands to create patterned and mirrored geometry.
- Chapter 6, "Sweep Features," covers the commands to create swept and helical features.
- Chapter 7, "Loft Features," covers the Loft command and its core features.
- Chapter 8, "Additional Features and Multibody Parts," covers additional commands to create complex geometry. Also, the multibody parts are covered.
- Chapter 9, "Modifying Parts," explores the commands and techniques to modify the part geometry.
- Chapter 10, "Assemblies," explains you to create assemblies using the bottom-up and top-down design approaches.
- Chapter 11, "Drawings," covers how to create 2D drawings from 3D parts and assemblies.
- Chapter 12, "Surface Design," covers how to create complex models using surface design tools.

Chapter 1: Getting Started with Autodesk Inventor 2026

Introduction to Autodesk Inventor 2026

Autodesk Inventor is a parametric and feature-based system that allows you to create 3D parts, assemblies, and 2D drawings. The design process in Autodesk Inventor is shown below.

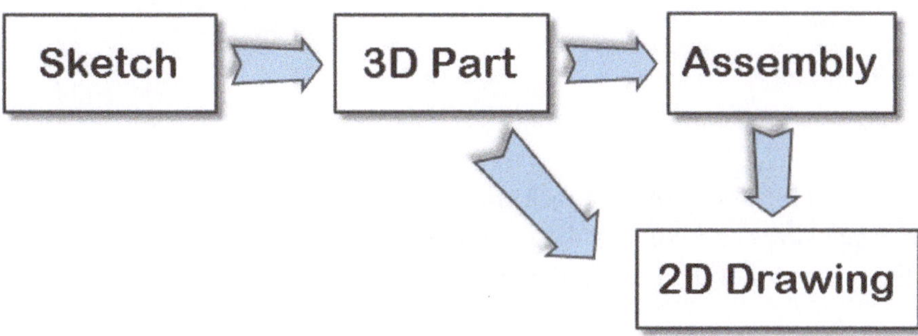

In Inventor, everything is controlled by parameters, dimensions, or constraints. For example, if you want to change the position of the hole shown in the figure, you need to change the dimension or relation that controls its position.

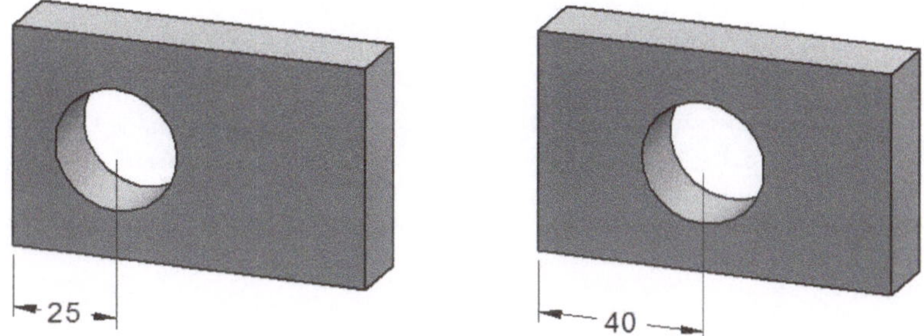

The parameters and constraints that you set up allow you to have control over the design intent. The design intent describes the way your 3D model will behave when you apply dimensions and constraints to it. For example, if you want to position the hole at the center of the block, one way is to add dimensions between the hole and the adjacent edges. However, when you change the size of the block, the hole will not be at the center.

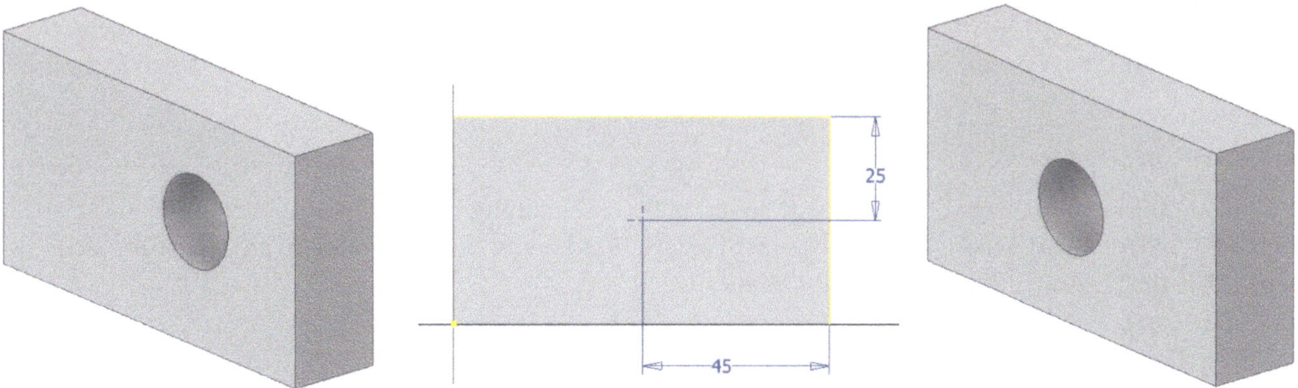

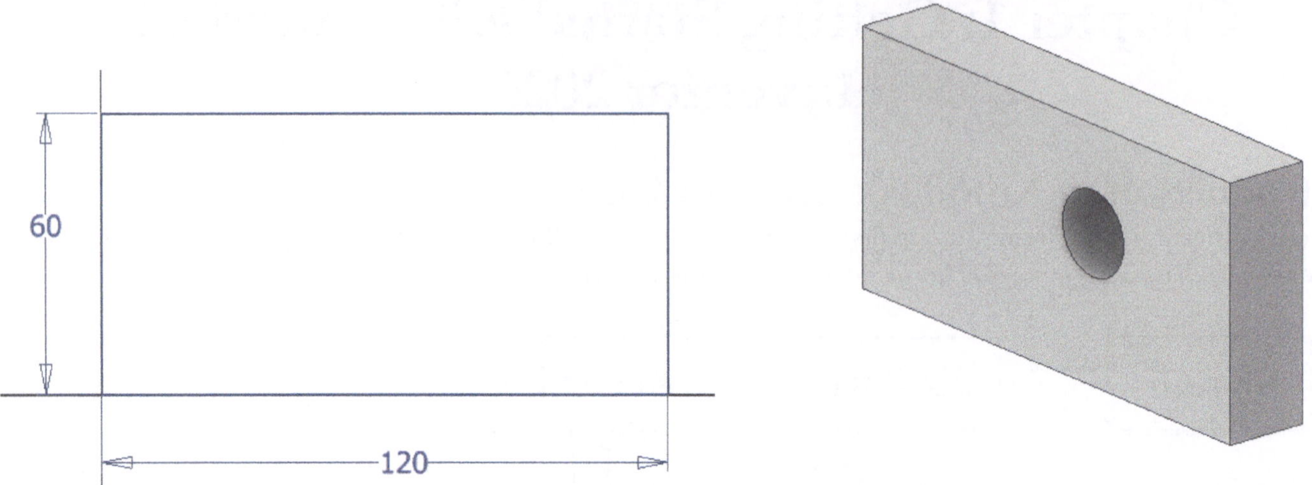

You can make the hole to be at the center, even if the size of the block changes. To do this, click on the hole feature and select **Edit Sketch**. Next, delete the dimensions and create a diagonal construction line. Apply the Coincident constraint between the hole point and the midpoint of the diagonal construction line. Next, click **Finish Sketch** on the Ribbon.

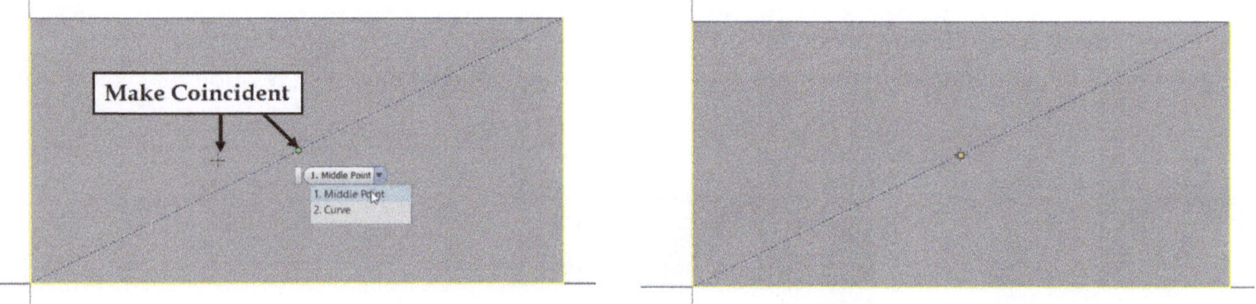

Now, even if you change the size of the block, the hole will always remain at the center.

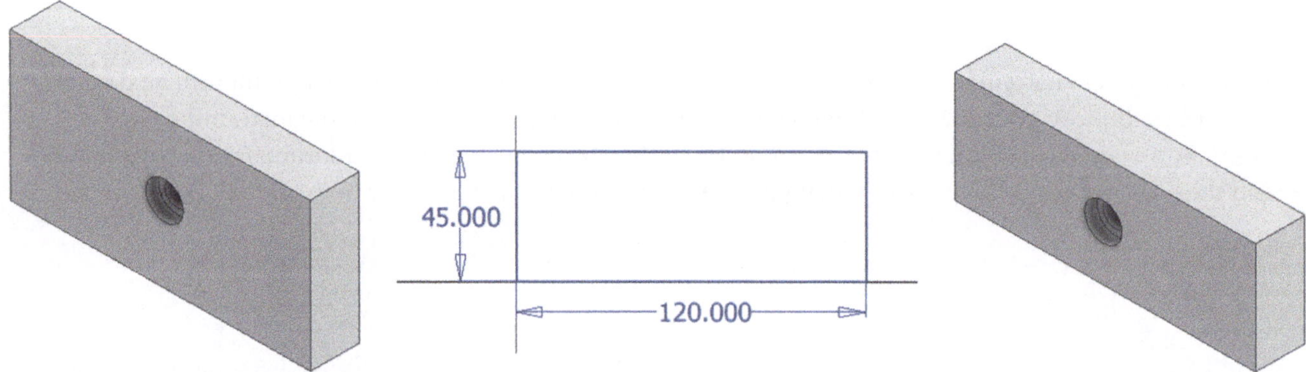

The other significant advantage of Autodesk Inventor is the associativity between parts, assemblies, and drawings. When you make changes to the design of a part, the changes will take place in any assembly that it is a part of. Also, the 2D drawing will update automatically.

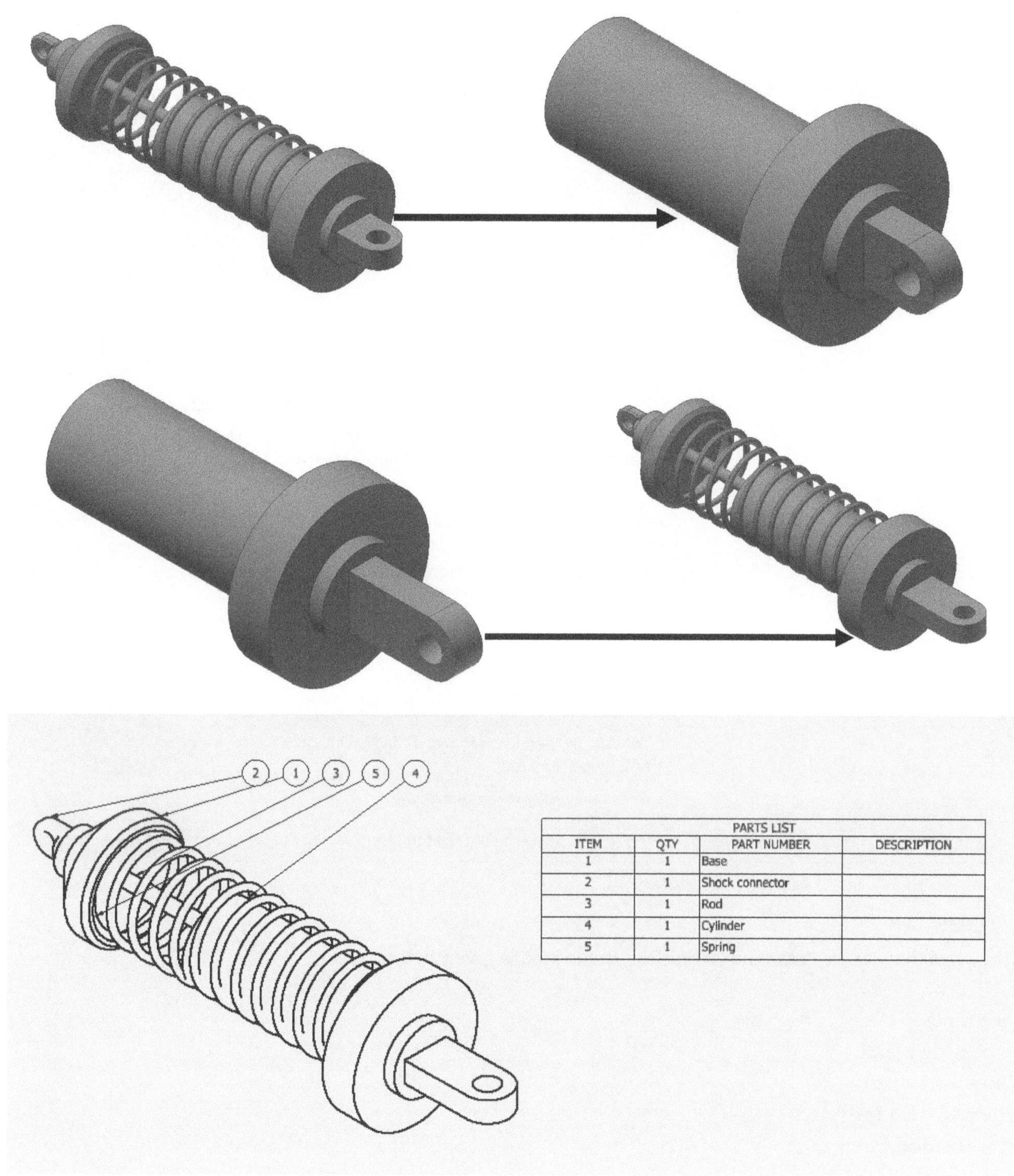

PARTS LIST			
ITEM	QTY	PART NUMBER	DESCRIPTION
1	1	Base	
2	1	Shock connector	
3	1	Rod	
4	1	Cylinder	
5	1	Spring	

Starting Autodesk Inventor 2026

To start **Autodesk Inventor 2026**, click the **Autodesk Inventor 2026** icon on your computer screen. To start a new part or assembly or drawing file, then click the **New** option from the **New** drop-down on the **Home** screen. Click **Metric** under the **Templates** folder on the **Create New File** dialog to start a new part document. Then, click **Standard(mm). ipt** under **Part - Create 2D and 3D objects**, and then click the **Create** button.

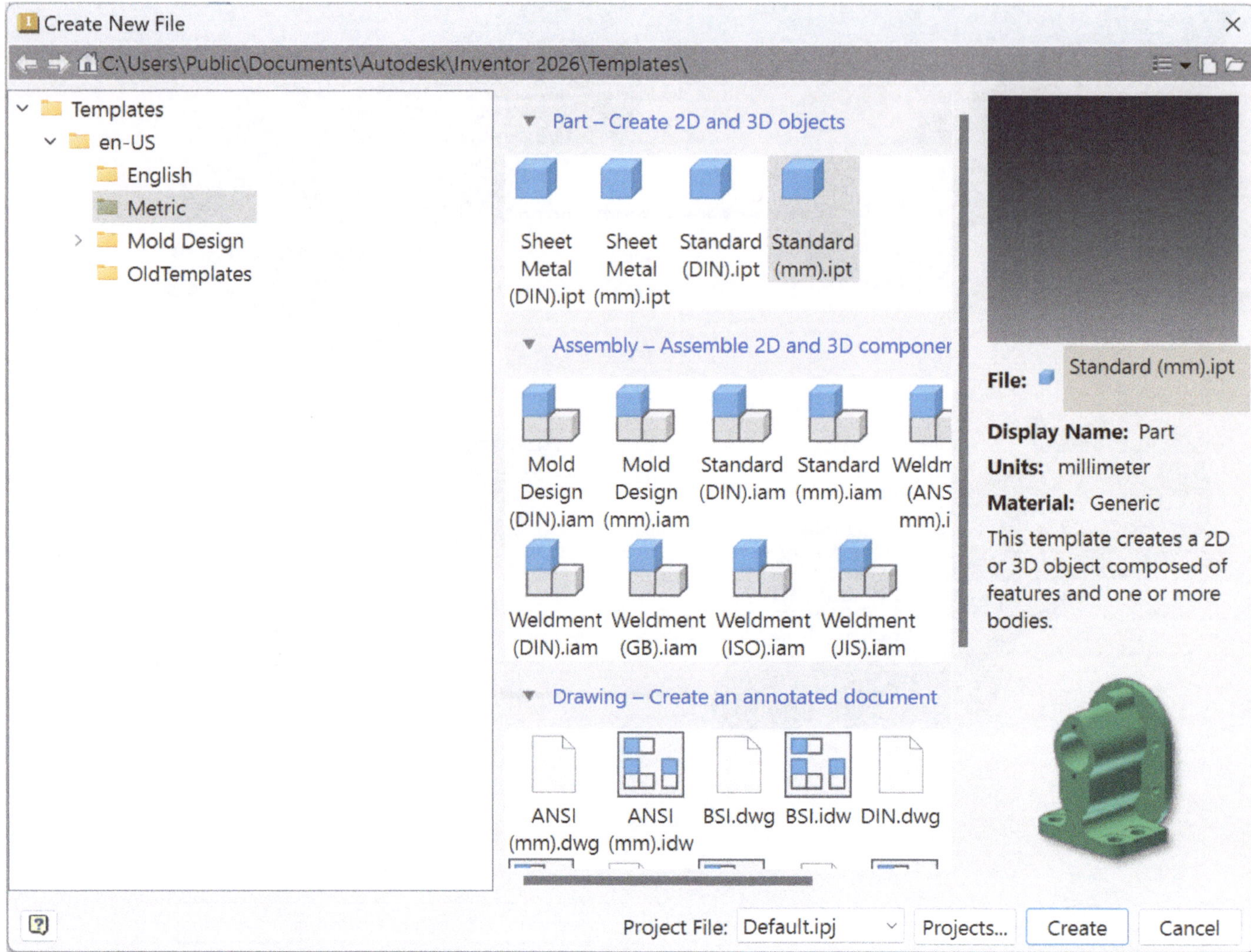

File Types

Various file types that can be created in Autodesk Inventor are given below.

- **Part (.ipt)**
- **Assembly (.iam)**
- **Drawing (.dwg)**
- **Sheet Metal (.ipt)**
- **Presentation (.ipn)**

User Interface

The following image shows the **Autodesk Inventor** application window.

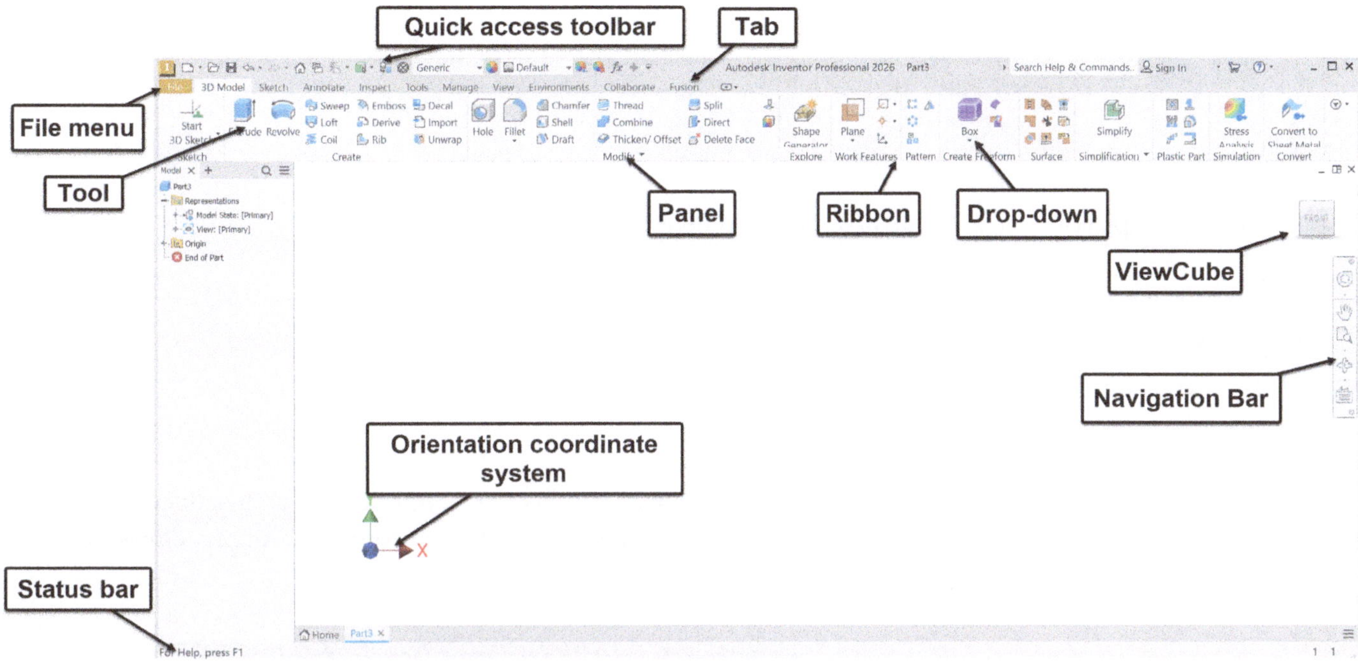

Environments in Autodesk Inventor

There are five primary environments available in Autodesk Inventor: **Part**, **Assembly**, **Drawing**, **Presentation**, and **Sheet Metal**. Also, there are some additional environments to create exploded views, renderings, and simulations.

Part environment

This environment has all the commands to create a 3D part model. It has a ribbon located at the top of the screen. The Ribbon is arranged in a hierarchy of tabs, panels, and commands. Panels such as **Sketch**, **Create** and **Modify** consists of commands, which are grouped based on their usage. Panels, in turn, are grouped into various tabs. For example, the panels, such as **Sketch**, **Create**, and **Modify** is located in the **3D Model** tab.

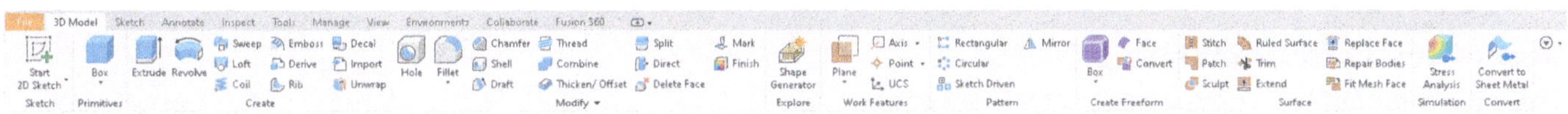

Assembly environment

This environment is used to create assemblies. The **Assemble** tab of the Ribbon has various commands, which will allow you to assemble and modify the components.

The **3D Model** tab in the Assembly environment has commands, which will help you to create holes, fillets, and other features at the assembly level.

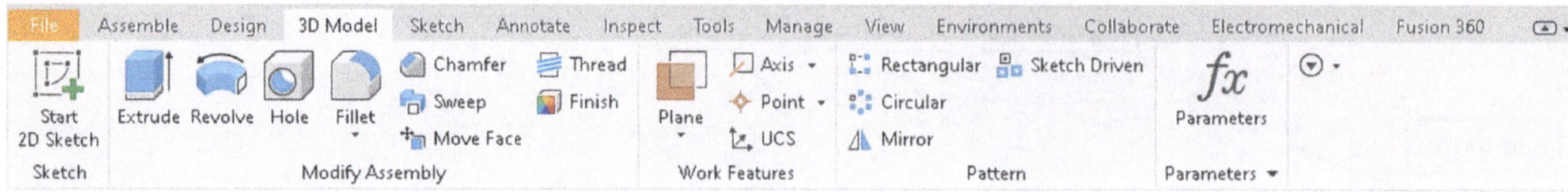

The **Inspect** tab helps you to inspect the assembly geometry.

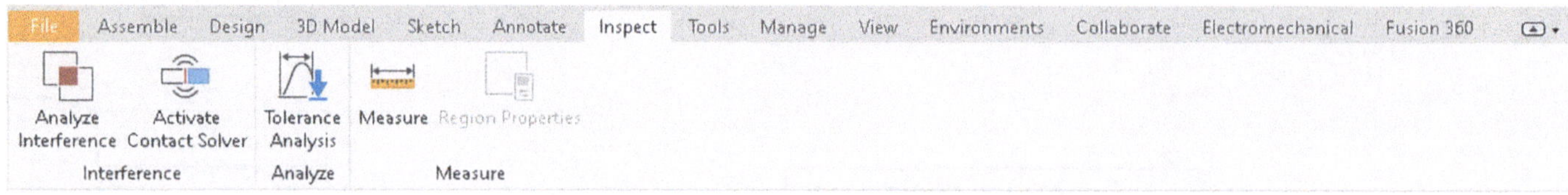

The **Tools** tab has some advanced commands, which will help you to access application options, document settings, and appearance options. In addition to that, you can customize the environment, automate processes, and add external apps.

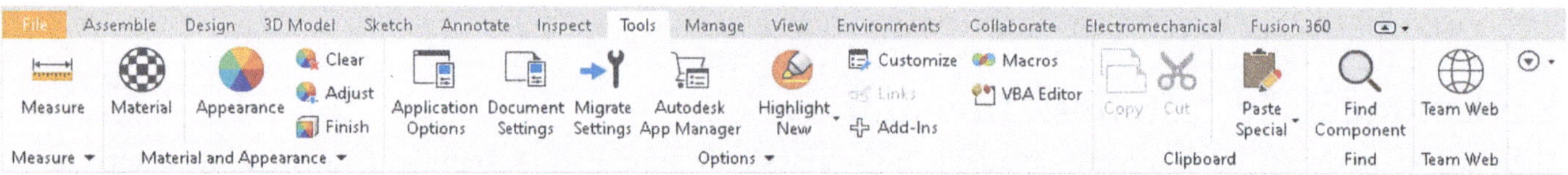

Drawing environment

This environment has all the commands to generate 2D drawings of parts and assemblies.

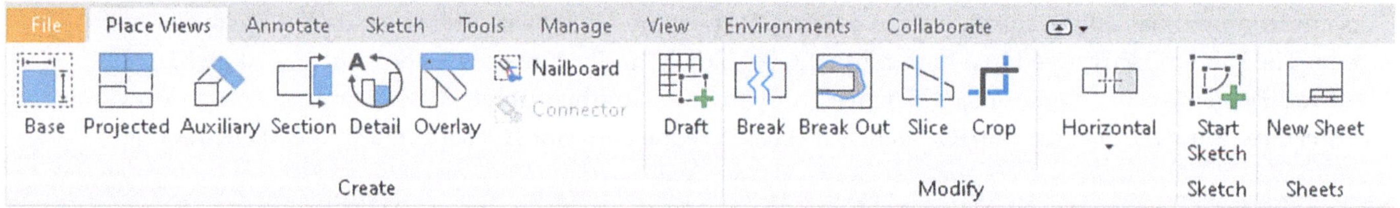

Sheet Metal environment

This environment has commands to create sheet metal parts.

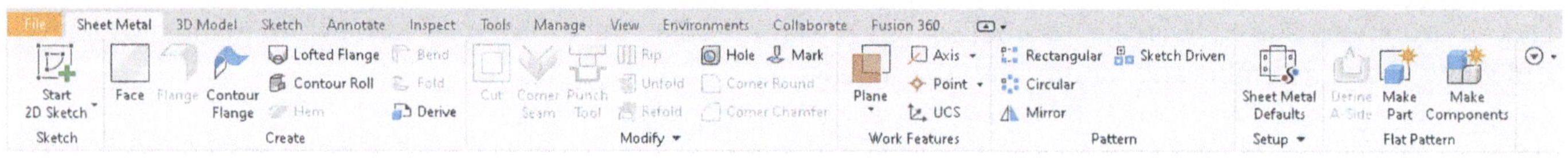

The other components of the user interface are discussed next.

File Menu

The **File Menu** appears when you click on the **File** tab located at the top left corner of the window. The **File Menu** consists of a list of open menus. You can see a list of recently opened documents under the **Recent Documents** menu located on the right side.

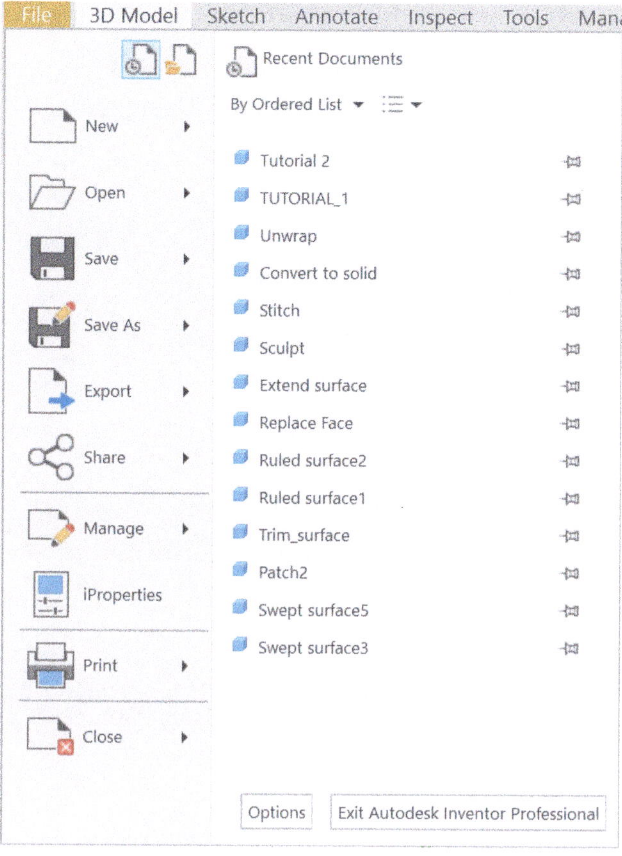

Quick Access Toolbar

The Quick Access Toolbar is located at the top left corner of the window. It consists of commonly used commands such as **New**, **Save**, **Open**, and so on. You can add more commands to the **Quick Access Toolbar** by clicking on the down-arrow next to the **Design doctor** icon, and then selecting them from the pop-up menu.

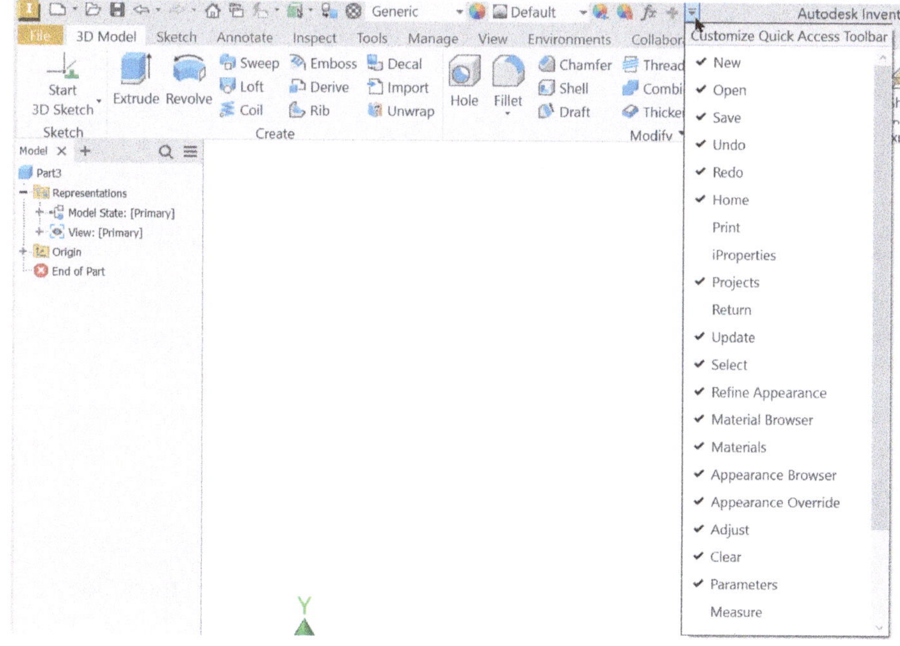

Graphics Window

The Graphics window is the blank space located below the Ribbon. You can draw sketches and create 3D geometry in the Graphics window. The left corner of the graphics window has a **Model window**. Using the **Model window**, you can access the features of the 3D model.

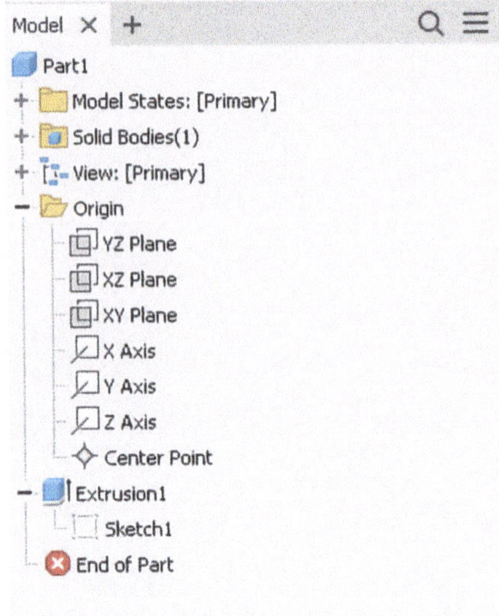

Status Bar

Status Bar is located at the bottom of the Autodesk Inventor window. It is useful when you activate a command. It displays various prompts while working with any command. These prompts are a series of steps needed to create a feature successfully.

The **Search Help & Commands** bar is used to search for any command available in Autodesk Inventor 2026. It is located at the top right side of the title bar. You can type any keyword in the **Search Help & Commands** bar and find a list of commands related to it.

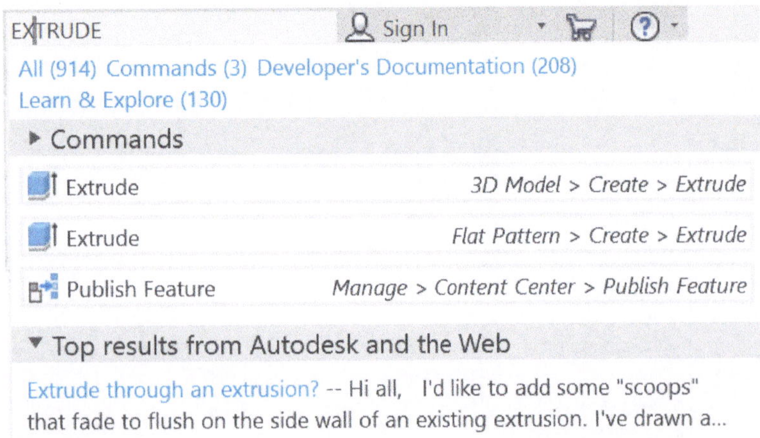

View Cube

It is located at the top right corner of the graphics window and is used to set the view orientation of the model.

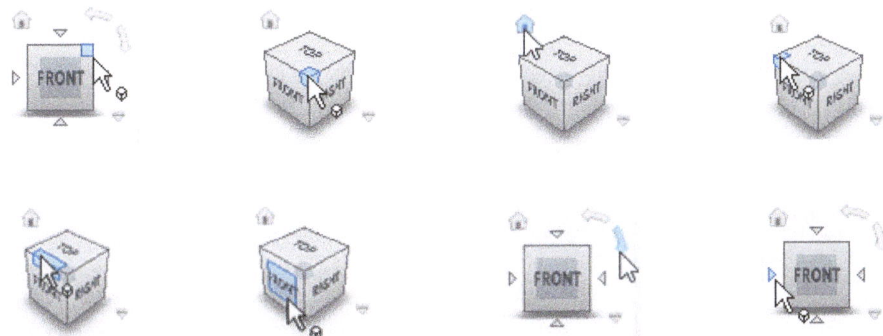

Dialogs

Dialogs are part of the Autodesk Inventor user interface. Using a dialog, you can easily specify many settings and options. Various components of a dialog are shown below.

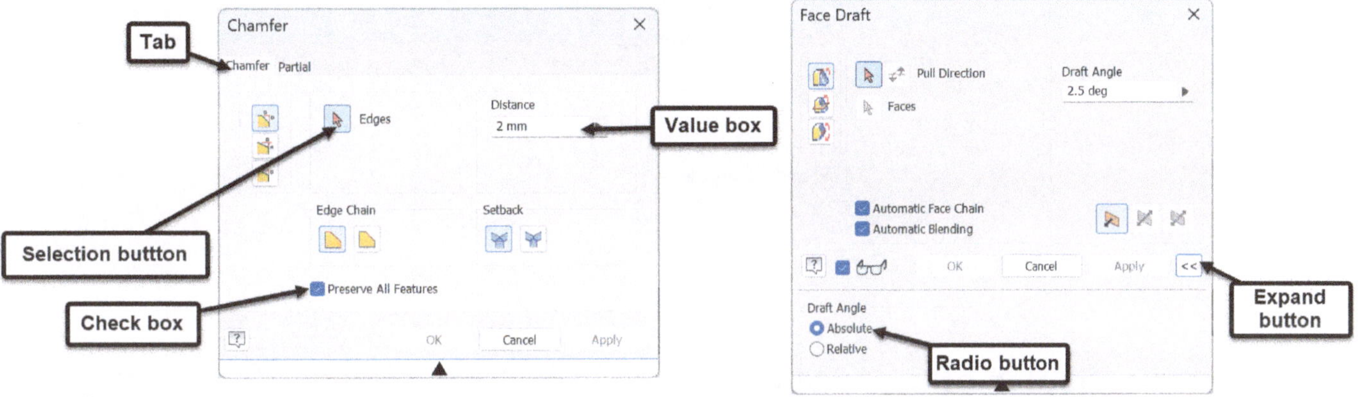

The Properties panel

When you activate most commands in Inventor, the software automatically shows interface elements related to that command. Similar to dialog boxes, the **Properties panel** appears. This panel gives you immediate control over the settings and options for the active command, allowing you to adjust them as you work.

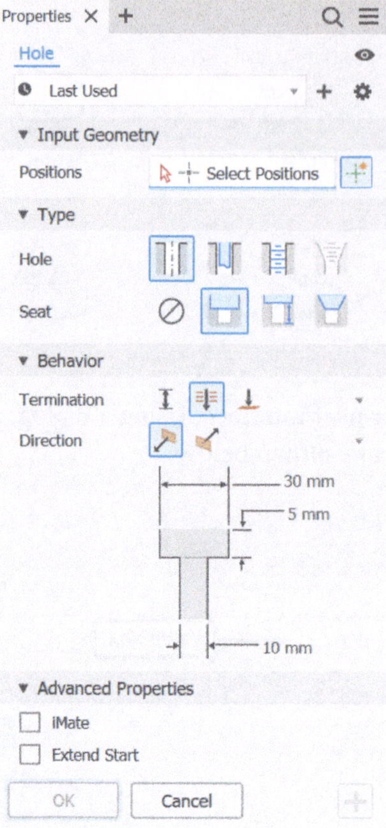

Changing the display of the Ribbon

You can add or remove commands from the Ribbon by clicking the right mouse button on it and then selecting **Customize User Commands**. On the **Customize** dialog, click on the commands in the list box located at the left side, and then click **Add** >>; the command is added to the Ribbon. If you want to remove the command from the Ribbon, then select it from the list box located on the right side. Next, click the **Remove** << button. After making the required changes, click **OK** to save the changes.

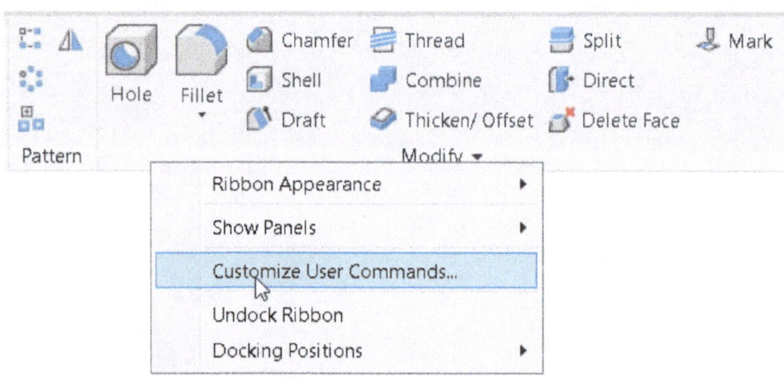

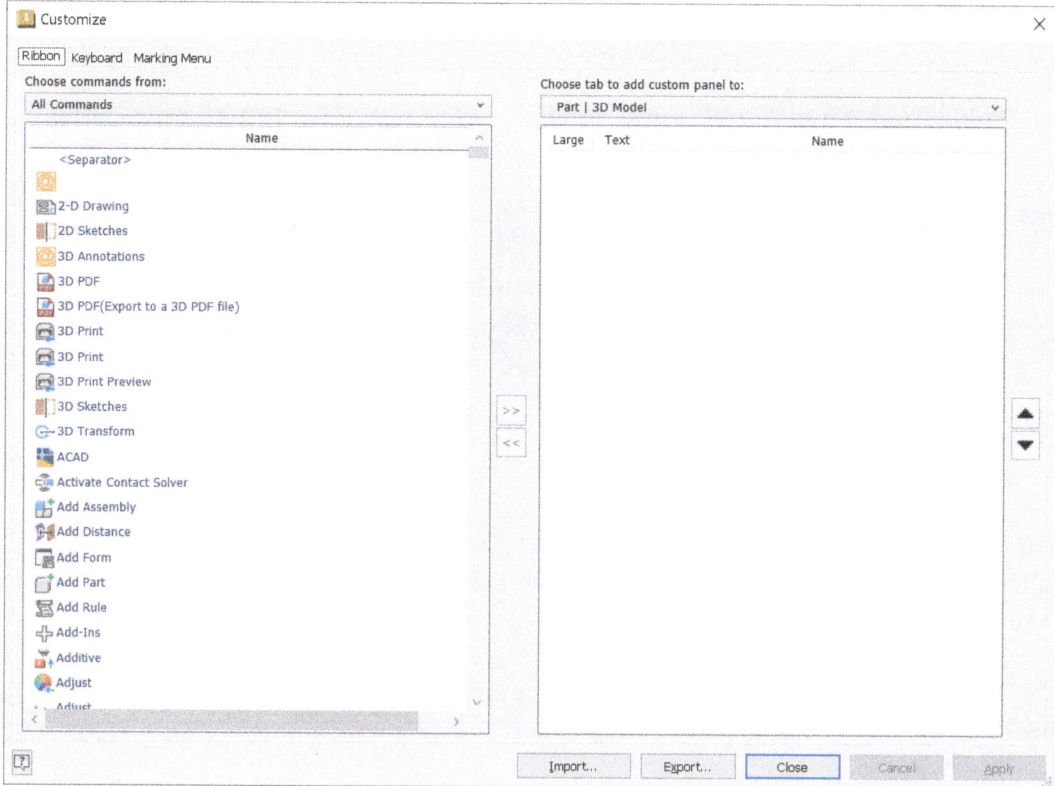

You can minimize the Ribbon by clicking on the **Minimize to Panel Buttons** down arrow. It lists three different options: **Minimize to Tabs, Minimize to Panel Titles,** and **Minimize to Panel Buttons**.

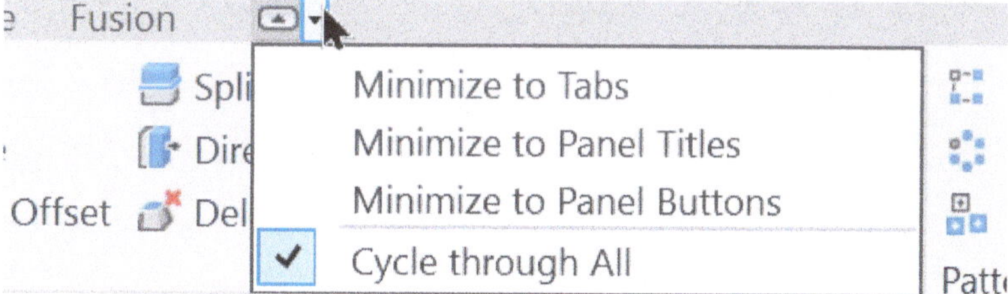

Select the **Minimize to Tabs** option to display only tabs.

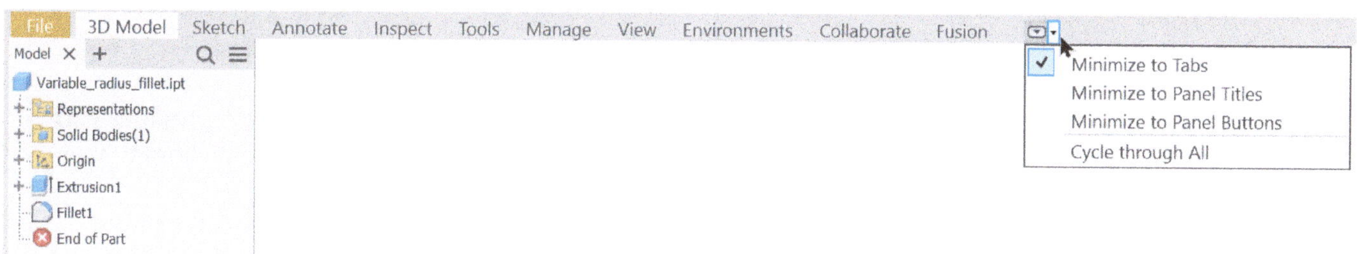

Select the **Minimize to Panel Titles** option to display both tabs and panel titles.

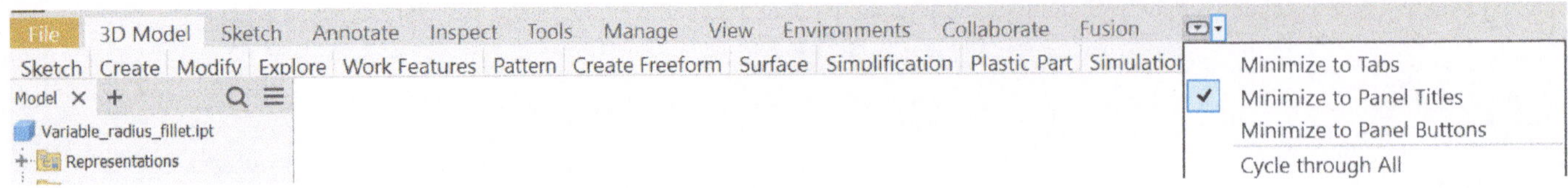

Select the **Minimize to Panel Buttons** option to display both tabs and panels.

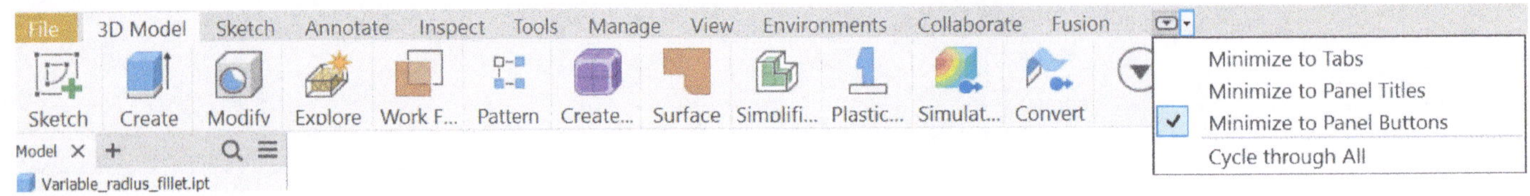

Marking Menus

Marking Menus provide you with another way of activating commands. You can display Marking Menus by clicking the right mouse button. A Marking Menu has various commands arranged radially. You can add or remove commands to the Marking Menu by using the **Customize** dialog.

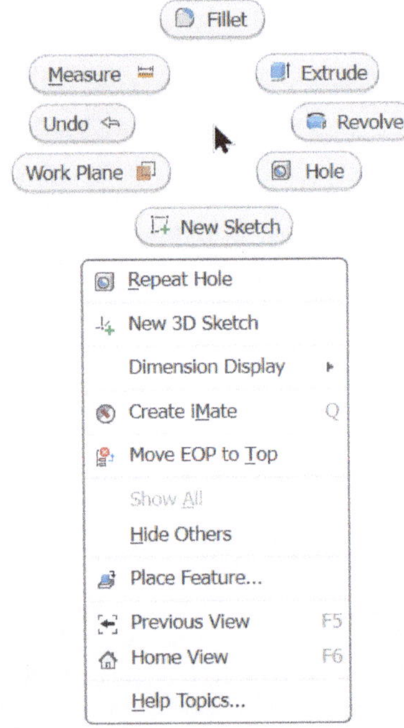

Shortcut Menus

Shortcut Menus are displayed when you right-click in the graphics window. Autodesk Inventor provides various shortcut menus in order to help you access some options very easily and quickly. The options in shortcut menus vary based on the environment.

Starting a new document

You can start a new document directly from the **Home** screen or by using the **Create New** dialog. On the **Home** screen, select the required option from the **New** drop-down to start a part, assembly, drawing, or a presentation document.

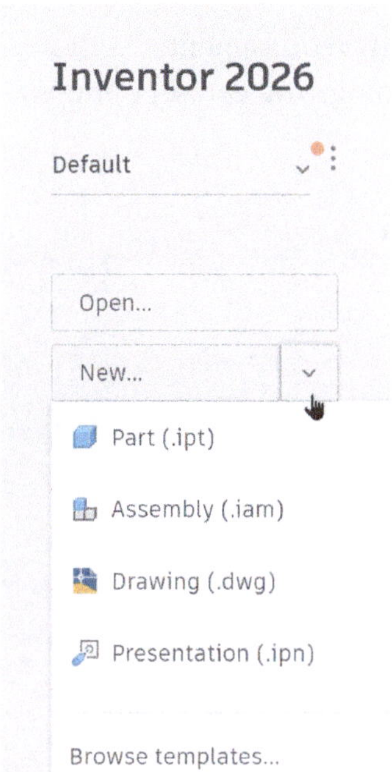

The Create New dialog

To start a new document using the **Create New** dialog, click the **New** button on any one of the following:

- **Quick Access Toolbar**
- **File Menu**
- **New** drop-down on the **Home** screen

The **Create New File** dialog appears when you click the **New** button. In this dialog, select the required standard from the **Templates** section. The templates related to the selected standard will appear. Select the. iam, .dwg, .ipt, or .ipn templates to start an assembly, drawing, part, or presentation file, respectively.

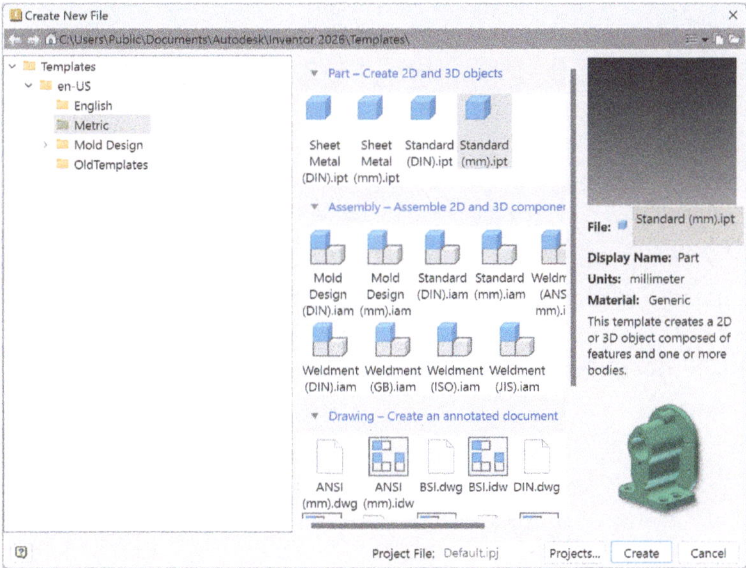

Application Options dialog

You can use the **Application Options** dialog to customize Autodesk Inventor as per your requirement. On the **File Menu**, click the **Options** button to open the **Application Options** dialog. In this dialog, you can set options on each of the tabs.

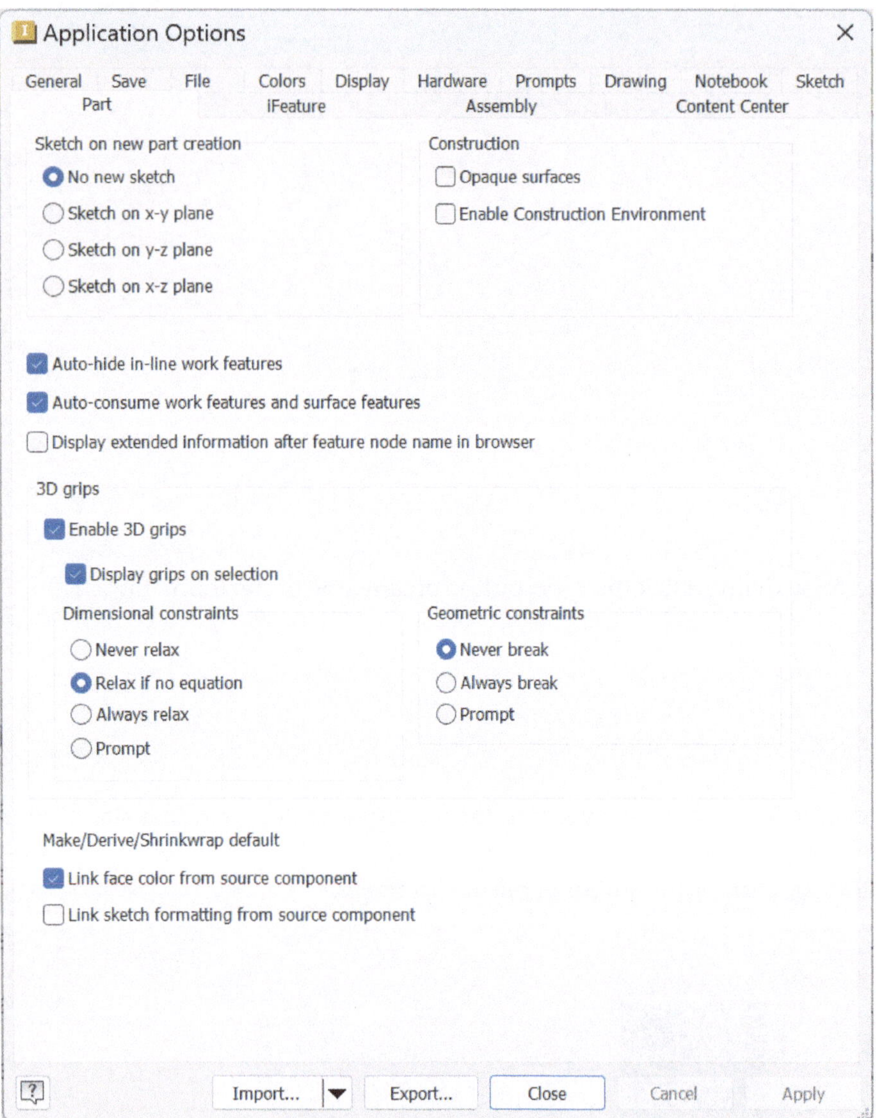

Changing the Color Scheme

The **Colors** tab of the **Application Options** dialog helps you to change the background color, reflection environment, and Color Theme. On the ribbon, click **Tools > Options > Application Options** to open this dialog. On this dialog, click the **Colors** tab and set the **Color scheme** to **Presentation**. Next, select **Background > 1 Color**, and then click **OK**; the background color changes to white.

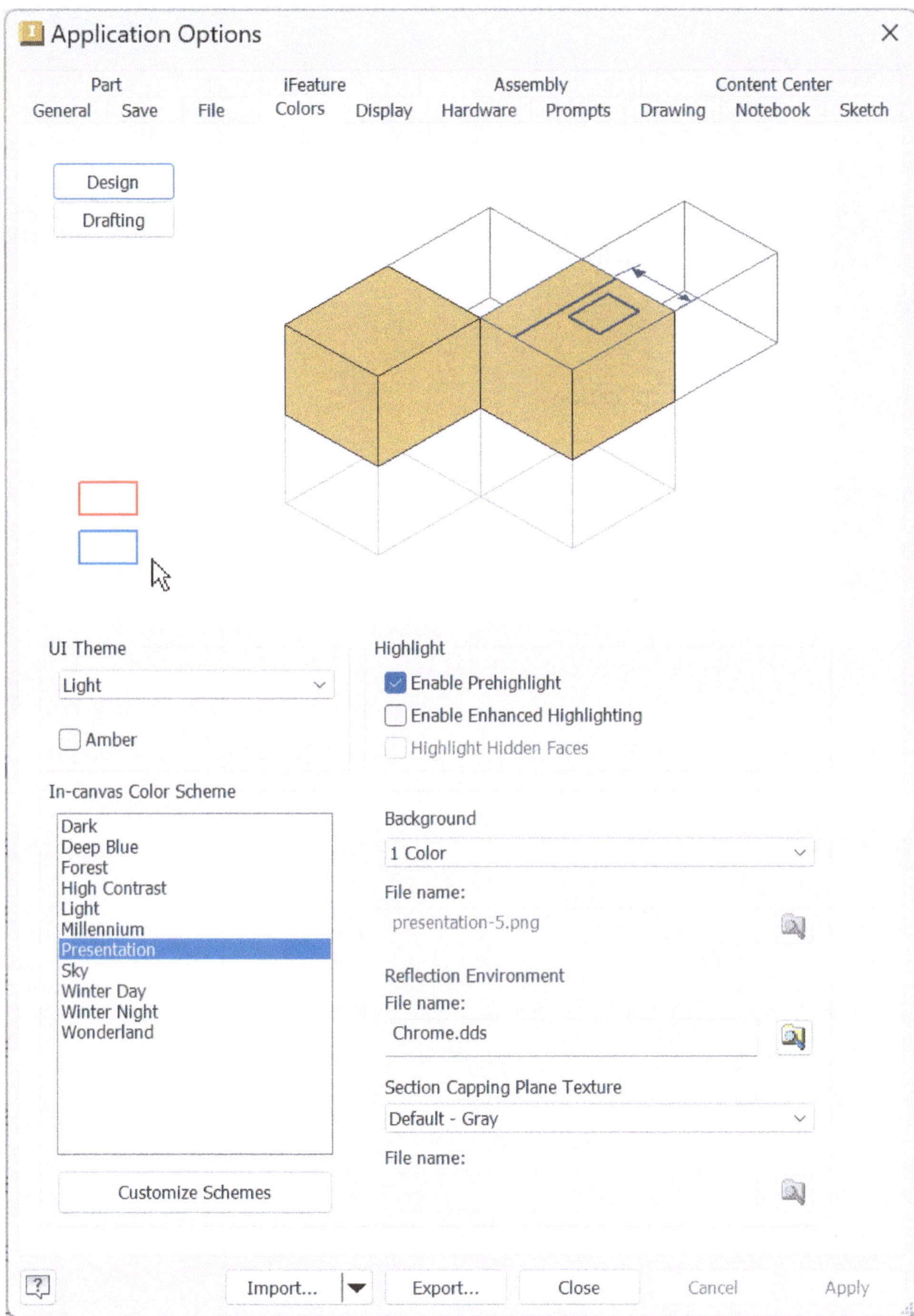

Autodesk Inventor Help

Autodesk Inventor offers you the help system that goes beyond basic command definition. You can access Autodesk Inventor help by using any of the following methods:

- Press the **F1** key.
- Click on the **Autodesk Inventor Help** option on the right side of the window.

Questions

1. Explain how to customize the Ribbon.
2. What is the design intent?
3. Give one example of where you would establish a relationship between a part's features.
4. Explain the term 'associativity' in Autodesk Inventor.
5. List any two procedures to access Autodesk Inventor Help.
6. How to change the background color of the graphics window?
7. How to activate the Marking Menu?
8. How is Autodesk Inventor a parametric modeling application?

Chapter 2: Sketch Techniques

This chapter covers the methods and commands to create sketches in the part environment. The commands and methods are discussed in the context of the part environment. In Inventor, you create a rough sketch, and then apply dimensions and constraints that define its shape and size. The dimensions define the length, size, and angle of a sketch element, whereas constraints define the relations between sketch elements.

In this chapter, you will:

- Create sketches in the Sketch Environment
- Use constraints and dimensions to control the shape and size of a sketch
- Learn sketching commands
- Learn commands and options that help you to create sketches easily

Sketching in the Sketch environment

Autodesk Inventor provides you a separate environment to create sketches. It is called the Sketch environment. To activate this environment, click **3D Model > Sketch > Start 2D Sketch** on the ribbon. Next, click on any of the Planes located at the center of the graphics window. The **Sketch** tab appears on the Ribbon. On this tab, you can find different sketch commands. You can use these commands and start sketching on the selected plane. After creating the sketch, click **Sketch > Exit > Finish Sketch** on the Ribbon to finish the sketch.

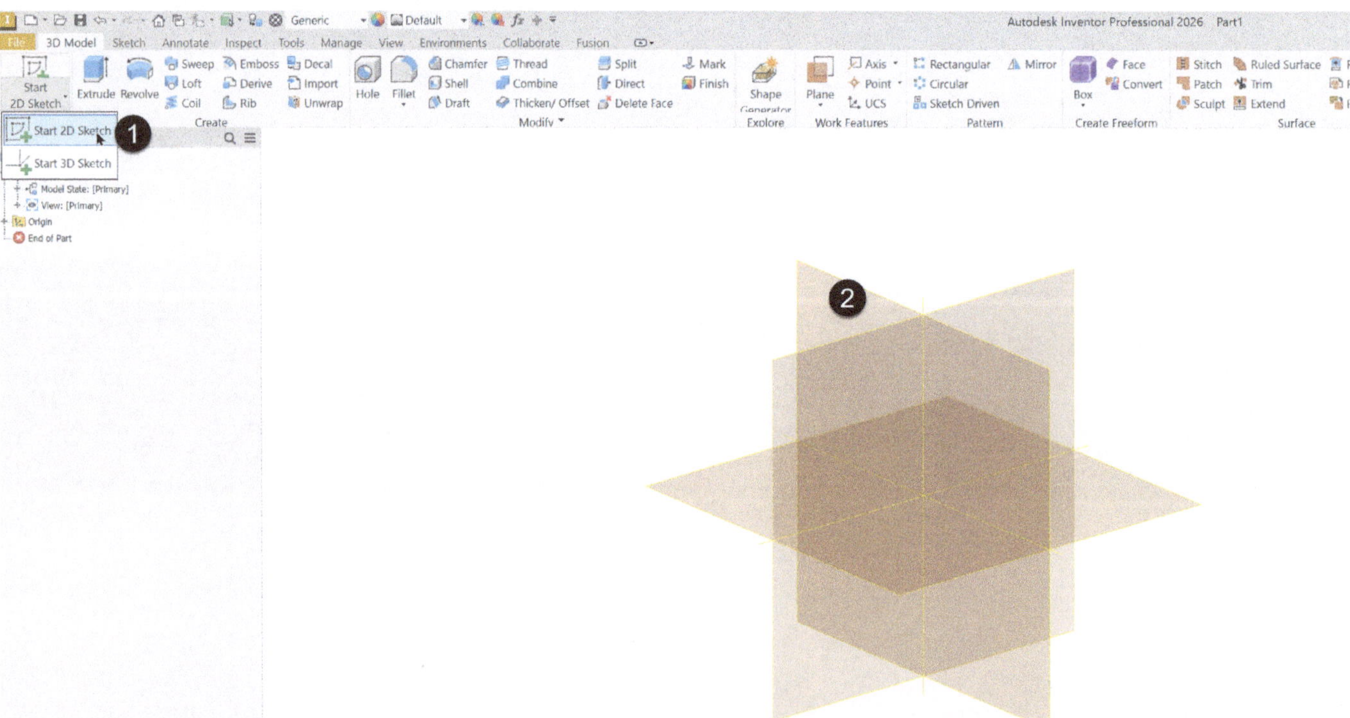

Sketch Commands

Autodesk Inventor provides you with a set of commands to create sketches. These commands are located on the **Create** panel of the **Sketch** ribbon.

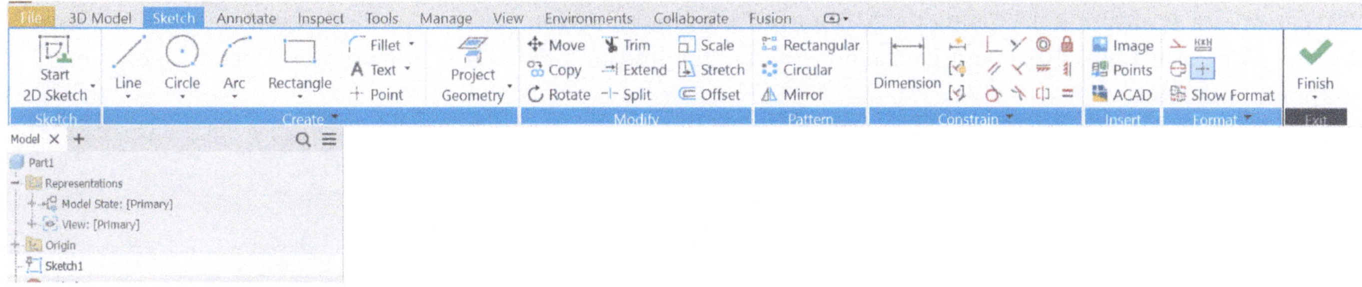

The Line command

The Line command is the most commonly used while creating a sketch. To activate this command, click **Sketch > Create > Line** on the Ribbon. As you move the pointer in the graphics window, you will notice that a box is attached to it. It displays the X and Y coordinates of the pointer. To create a line, click in the graphics window, move the pointer and click again. After clicking for the second time, you can see that an endpoint is added, and another line segment is started. It is a convenient way to create a chain of lines. Continue to click to add more line segments. You can right-click in the graphics window and click **Restart** if you want to end the chain. Now, start creating a separate line chain. Right click and select **OK** or press **Esc** to deactivate the **Line** command.

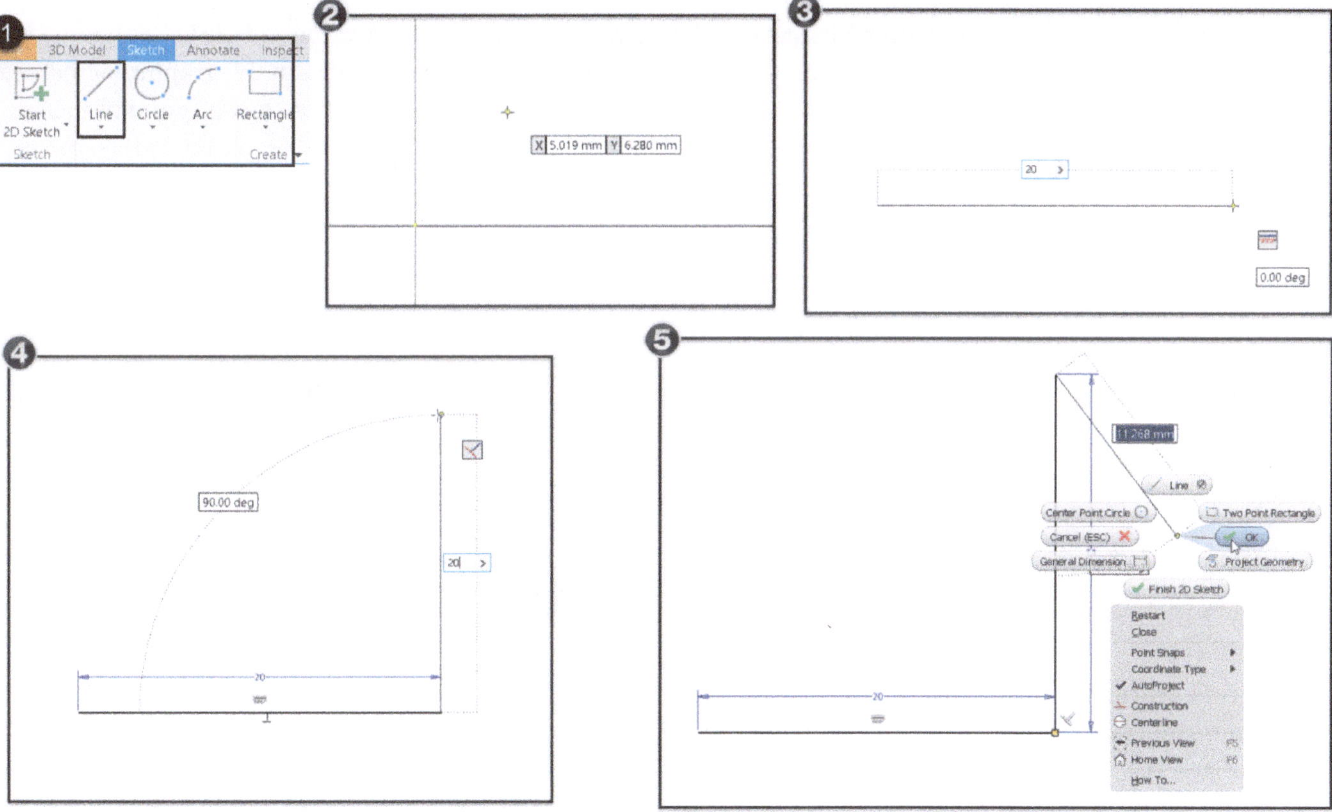

Tip: To create a horizontal line, specify the start point of the line and move the pointer horizontally; the Horizontal constraint glyph appears next to the pointer. Click to create a horizontal line. Also, the Horizontal constraint is applied to the line. You will learn about constraints later in this chapter. Likewise, you can create a vertical line by moving the pointer vertically and clicking.

Creating a Midpoint Line

You can create a midpoint line using the **Midpoint Line** command (on the ribbon, click **Sketch** tab > **Line** drop-down > **Midpoint Line**). Next, specify the midpoint of the line, and then move the pointer. Click to specify the endpoint of the line.

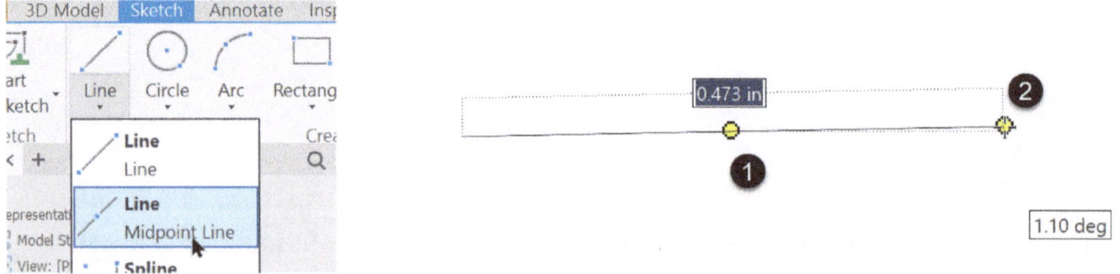

Creating Arcs

Autodesk Inventor allows you to create an arc using three commands: **Arc by Three Point, Arc by Tangent**, and **Arc by Center Point.**

The Arc Three Point command

This command creates an arc by defining its start, end, and radius. Activate the **Arc Three Point** command, by clicking **Sketch** tab **> Create** panel **> Arc** drop-down > **Arc Three Point** on the Ribbon. In the graphics window, click to define the start point of the arc. Next, move the pointer and click again to define the endpoint of the arc. After defining the start and end of the arc, you need to define the size and position of the arc. To do this, move the pointer and click to define the radius and position of the arc.

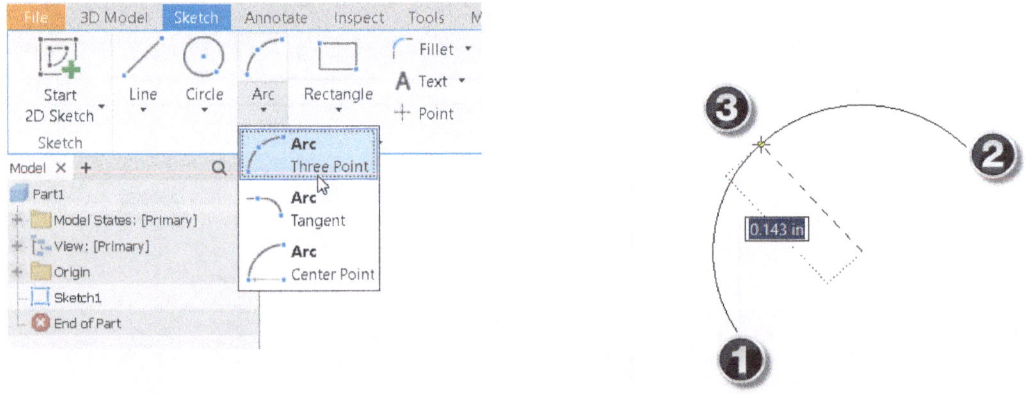

The Arc Tangent Command

This command creates an arc tangent to another entity. To activate this command, click **Sketch > Create > Arc** drop-down **> Arc Tangent** on the ribbon. Click on the endpoint of the entity to start the arc. The arc is tangent to the starting entity. Move the pointer and click to define the radius and position of the arc.

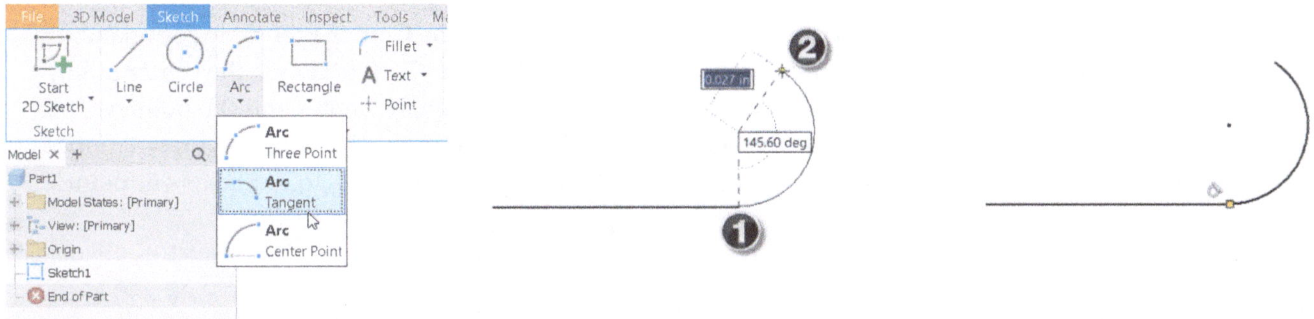

Autodesk Inventor allows you to create an arc tangent to the line without activating the **Tangent Arc** command. To do this, activate the **Line** command and create a line. Next, move the pointer away, and then take it back to the endpoint of the line. Now, press and hold the left mouse button and drag the pointer in-line with the existing line. Next, drag the pointer to either side of the existing line to specify the size and direction of the arc. After dragging up to the required distance, release the left mouse button to specify the endpoint of the arc.

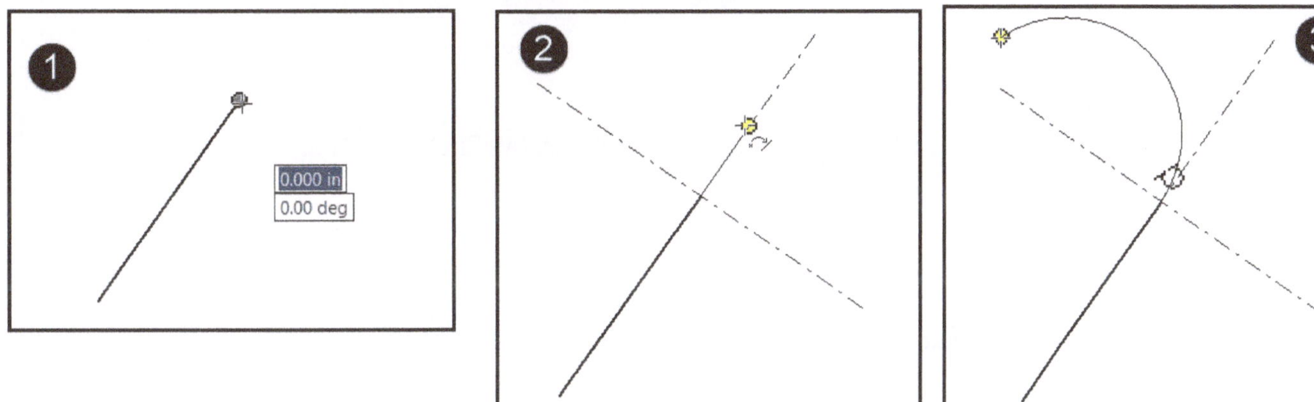

If you want to create a normal arc using the **Line** command, then first create a line. Next, move the pointer away from the endpoint, and then move it back. Press and hold the left mouse button and drag the pointer along the dotted line displayed perpendicular to the existing line. Next, drag the pointer on either side of the dotted perpendicular line to specify the size and direction of the normal arc. After dragging up to the required distance, release the left mouse button to define the endpoint of the arc.

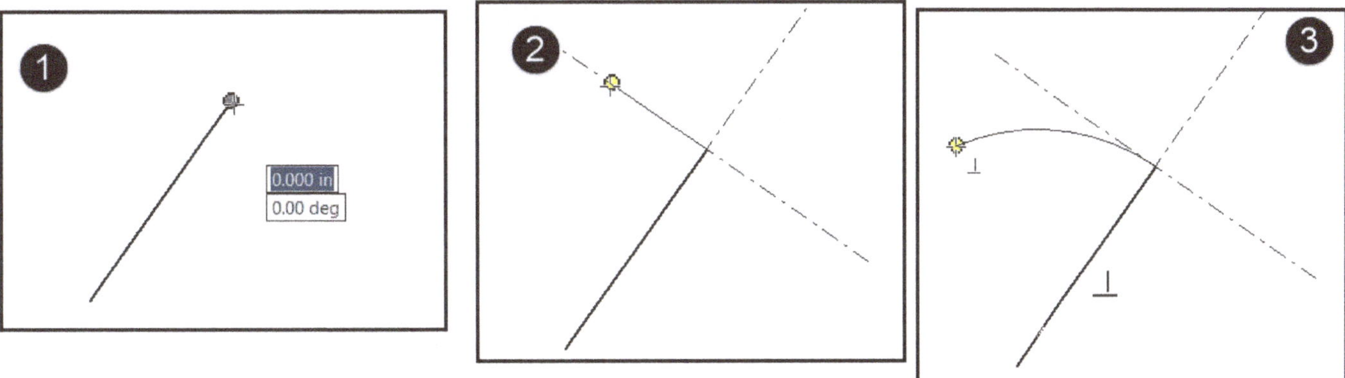

The Center Point Arc command

This command creates an arc by defining its center, start, and end. Activate the **Center Point Arc** command, by clicking **Sketch > Create > Arc** drop-down **> Arc Center Point** on the Ribbon. Click to define the center point. Next, move the pointer, and you will notice that a dotted line appears between the center and the pointer. This line is the radius of the arc. Now, click to define the start point of the arc and move the pointer; you will notice that an arc is drawn from the start point. Once the arc appears the way you want, click to define its endpoint.

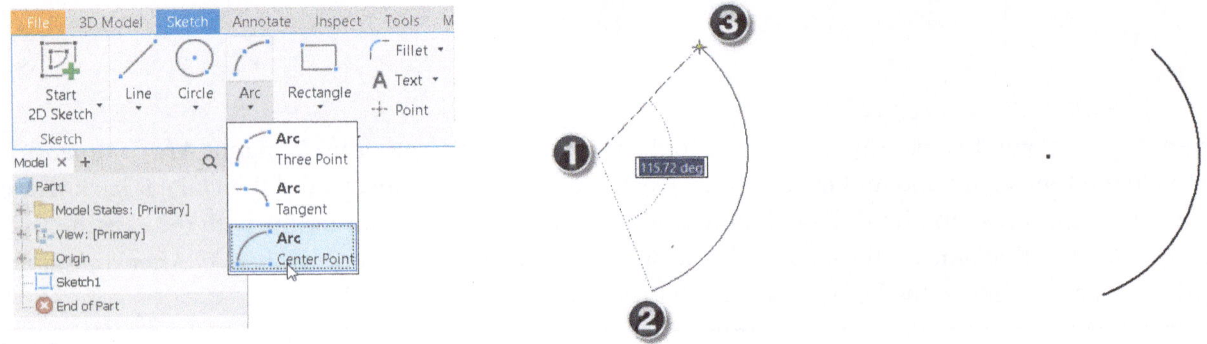

Creating Circles

Inventor allows you to create a circle using two commands: **Center Point Circle** and **Tangent Circle**.

Center Point Circle

This is the most common way to draw a circle. Activate the **Center Point Circle** command, by clicking **Sketch > Create > Circle** drop-down **> Circle Center Point** on the Ribbon. Click to define the center point of the circle. Drag the pointer, and then click again to define the diameter of the circle.

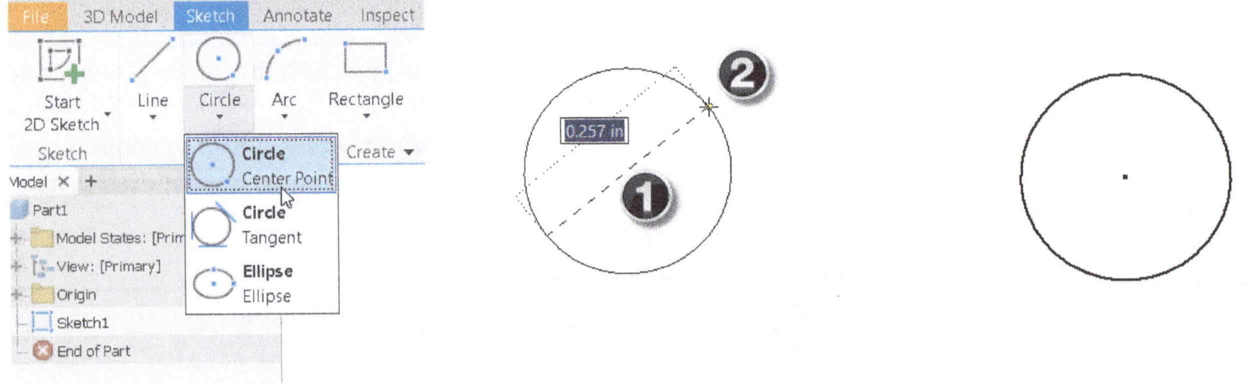

Tangent Circle

This command creates a circle tangent to three lines. Activate this command by clicking **Sketch > Create > Circle** drop-down **> Circle Tangent** on the Ribbon. Select three lines from the graphics window; a circle is created tangent to the selected lines.

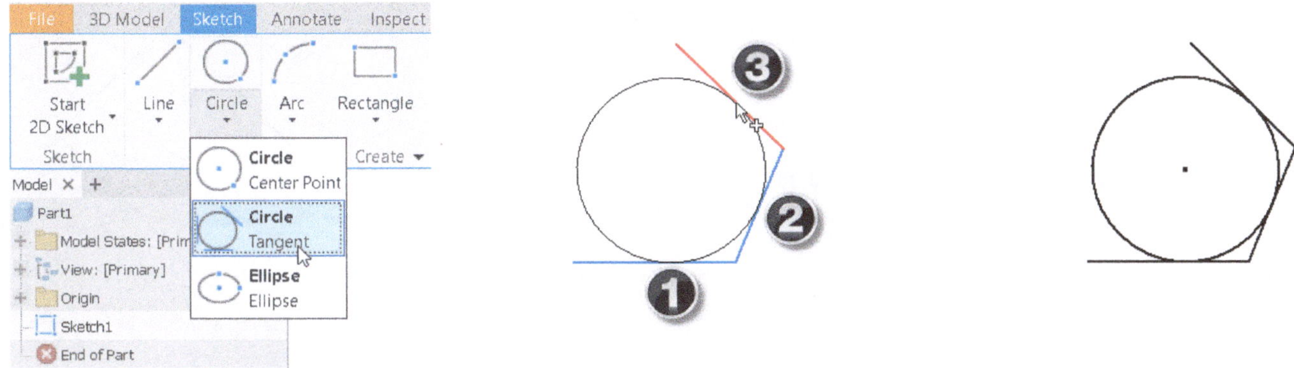

Creating Rectangles

Inventor allows you to create a rectangle using four different commands: **Two Point Rectangle, Three Point Rectangle, Two Point Center Rectangle**, and **Three Point Center Rectangle**.

Two Point Rectangle

This command creates a rectangle by defining its diagonal corners. Activate the **Two Point Rectangle** command (On the Ribbon, click **Sketch > Create > Rectangle** drop-down > **Rectangle Two Point**). In the graphics window, click to define the first corner of the rectangle. Move the pointer and click to define the second corner. You can also type in values in the boxes attached to the pointer.

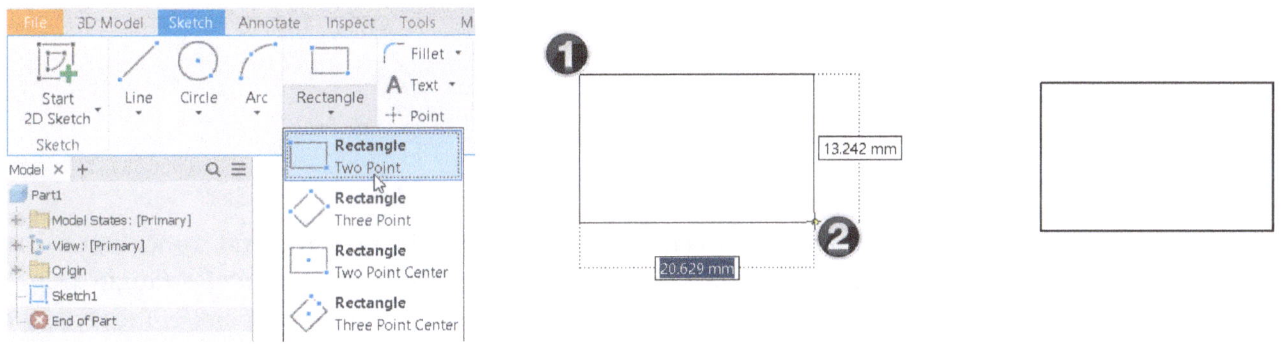

Three Point Rectangle

This command creates an inclined rectangle. Activate the **Three Point Rectangle** command (On the Ribbon, click **Sketch > Create > Rectangle** drop-down > **Rectangle Three Point**). Specify the first two points to define the width and inclination angle of the rectangle. You can also enter width and inclination angle values in the value boxes displayed in the graphics window. Next, specify the third point to define the height of the rectangle.

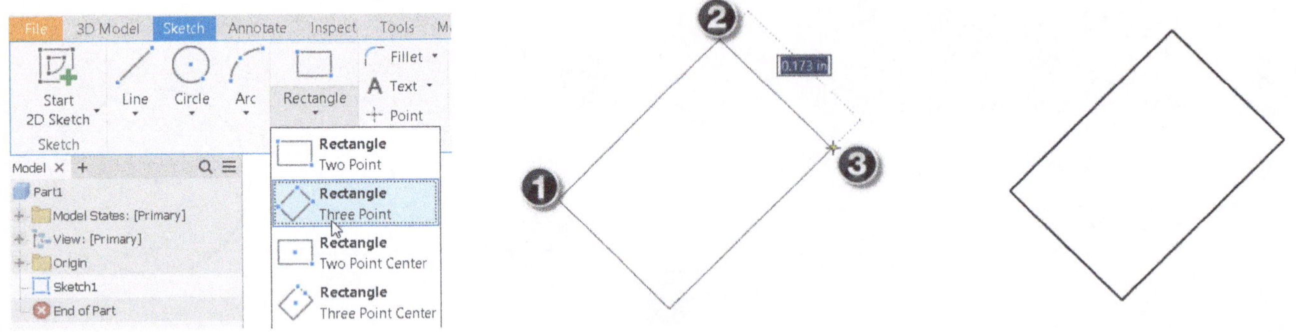

Two Point Center Rectangle

This command creates a rectangle using two points: center and corner points. Activate the **Rectangle Two Point Center** command (On the Ribbon, click **Sketch > Create > Rectangle** drop-down > **Rectangle Two Point Center**). In the graphics window, click to define the first point as a center of the rectangle. Next, specify the corner point to define the width and height of the rectangle. You can also type in the values in the value boxes displayed in the graphics window.

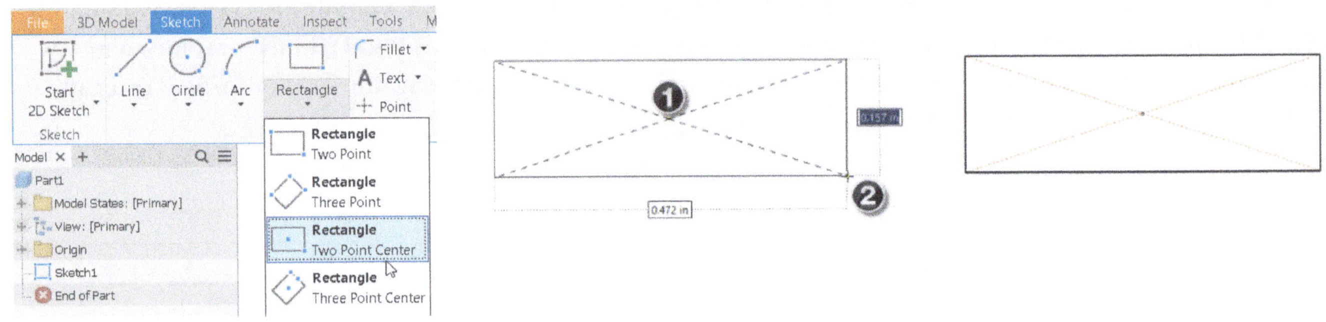

Three Point Center Rectangle

This command creates a rectangle using three points: center, the midpoint of the first side, and corner point. Activate the **Three Point Center Rectangle** command (On the Ribbon, click **Sketch > Create > Rectangle** drop-down > **Rectangle Three Point Center**). In the graphics window, click to specify the center point of the rectangle. Move the pointer and click to specify the midpoint of the first side. Also, the specified point defines the direction and distance of the second side. Next, specify the corner point to define the distance of the first side. This command creates the inclined as well as the horizontal rectangle.

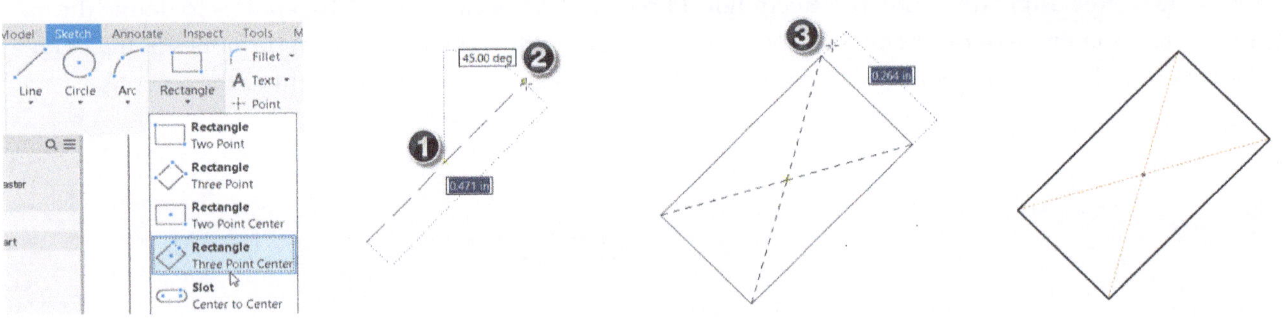

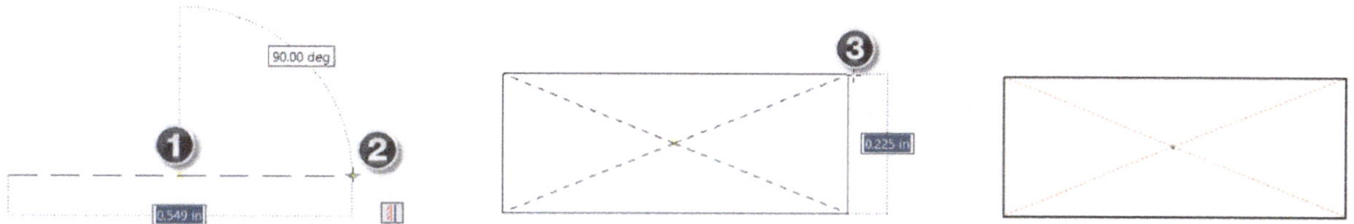

Creating Slots

In Inventor, you can create a straight and arc slots using five different commands: **Center to Center Slot, Overall Slot, Center Point Slot, Three Point Arc Slot, Center Point Arc Slot**.

Center to Center Slot

This command creates a straight slot by defining the centers of start and endcaps of the slot and then defining its width. Activate this command (on the ribbon, click **Sketch > Create** > **Rectangle** drop-down > **Slot Center to Center**). Click to specify the start point of the slot. Next, move the pointer and click to specify the endpoint; the length and orientation of the slot are defined. Now, move the pointer outward and click to define the slot width.

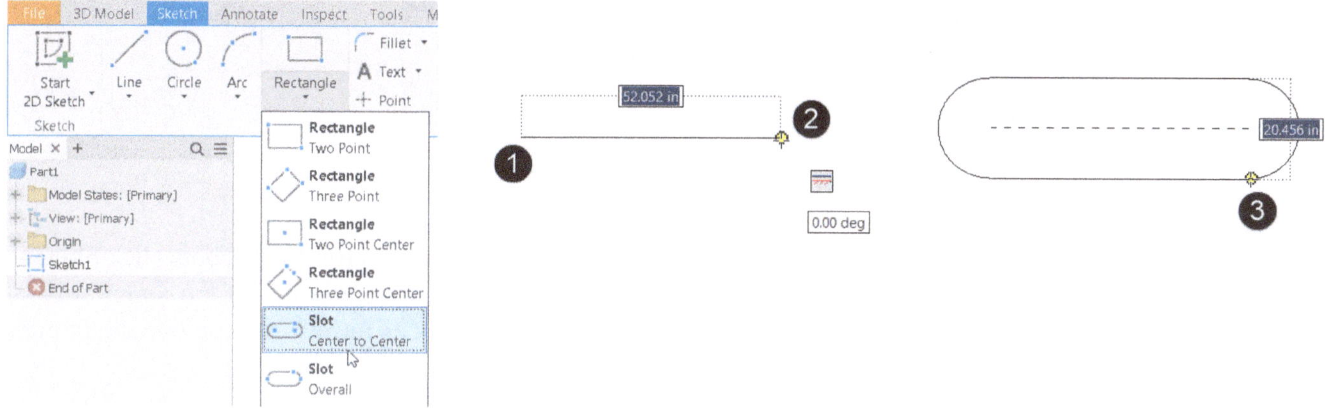

Overall Slot

This command creates a straight slot by defining its start, end, and width. Activate this command (on the ribbon, click **Sketch > Create** > **Rectangle** drop-down > **Slot Overall**). Specify the start and endpoints of the slot. Next, move the pointer and click to specify the slot width.

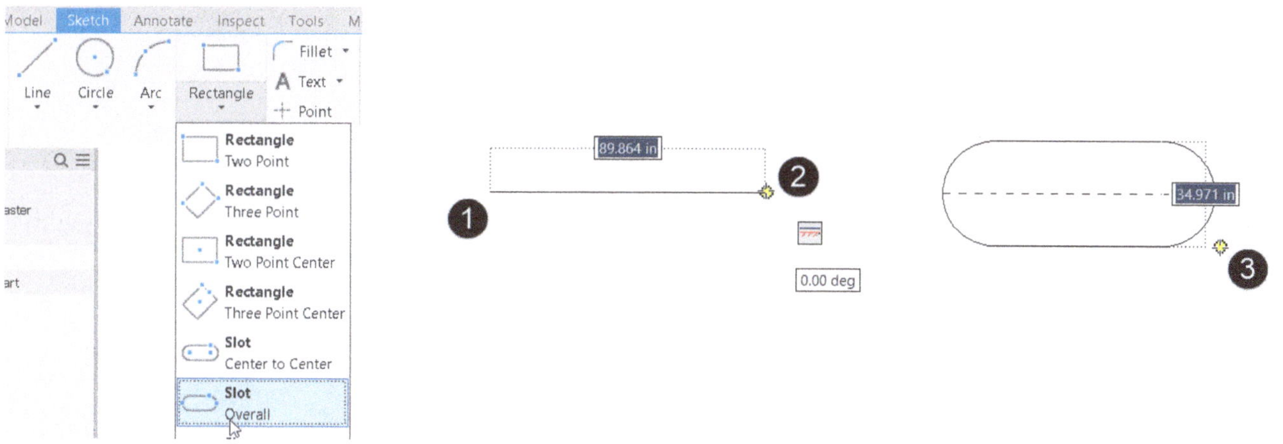

Center Point Slot

This command creates a straight slot by defining its centerpoint, endpoint, and width. Activate this command (on the Ribbon, click **Sketch > Create > Rectangle** drop-down > **Slot Center Point**) and click to specify the centerpoint of the slot. Next, move the pointer and click to specify the centerpoint of the endcap; this defines the length and orientation of the slot. Now, move the pointer outward and click to define the slot width.

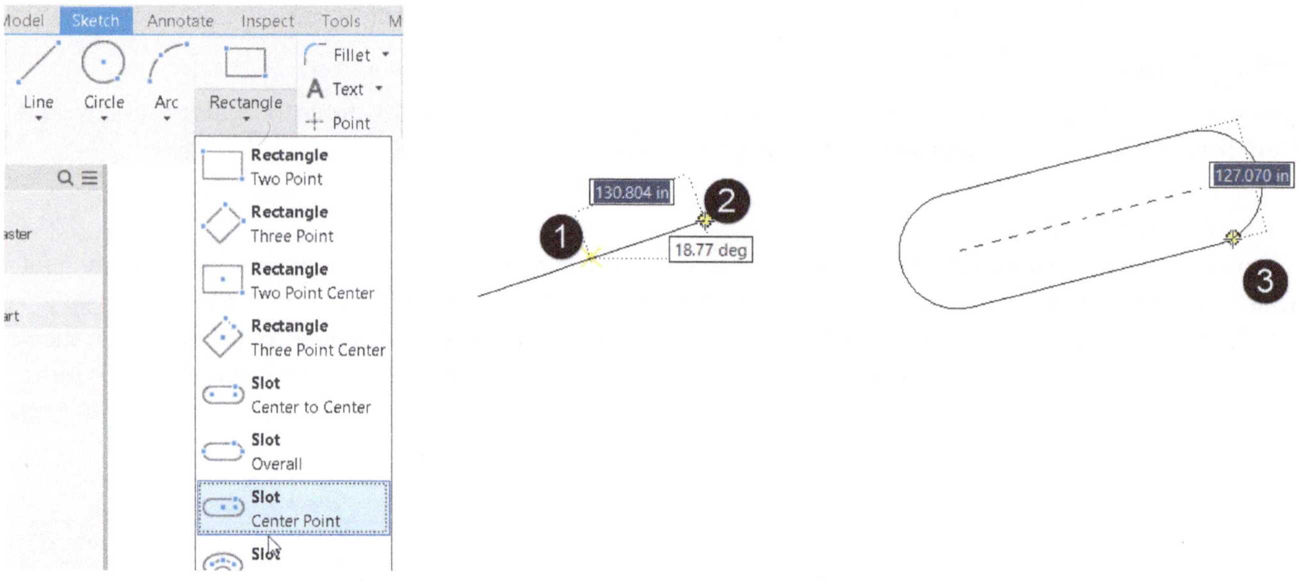

Three Point Arc Slot

This command is similar to the **Three Point Arc** command. Activate this command (on the Ribbon, click **Sketch > Create > Rectangle** drop-down > **Slot Three Point Arc**) and specify the start and endpoints of the center arc of the slot. Next, you need to specify the third point of the center arc; this defines its radius. Now, move the pointer outward and click to define the slot width.

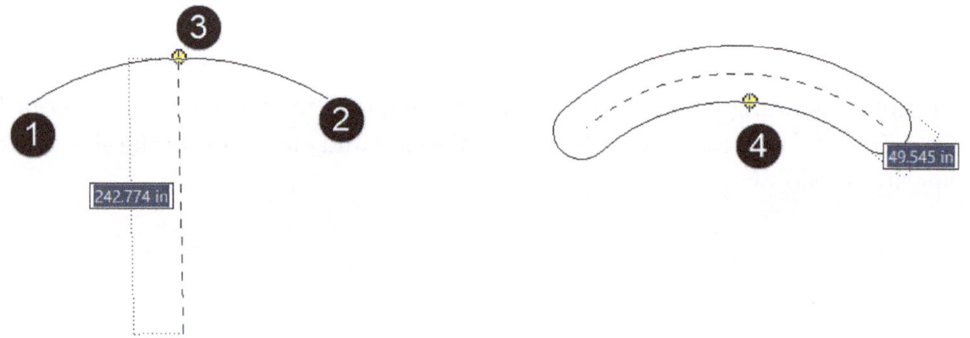

Center Point Arc Slot

This command works on the same principle as that of the **Center Point Arc** command. Activate this command (on the Ribbon, click **Sketch > Create > Rectangle** drop-down > **Slot Center Point Arc**) and specify the center of the arc slot. Next, specify the start and endpoints of the center arc. Now, move the pointer outward and click to define the slot width.

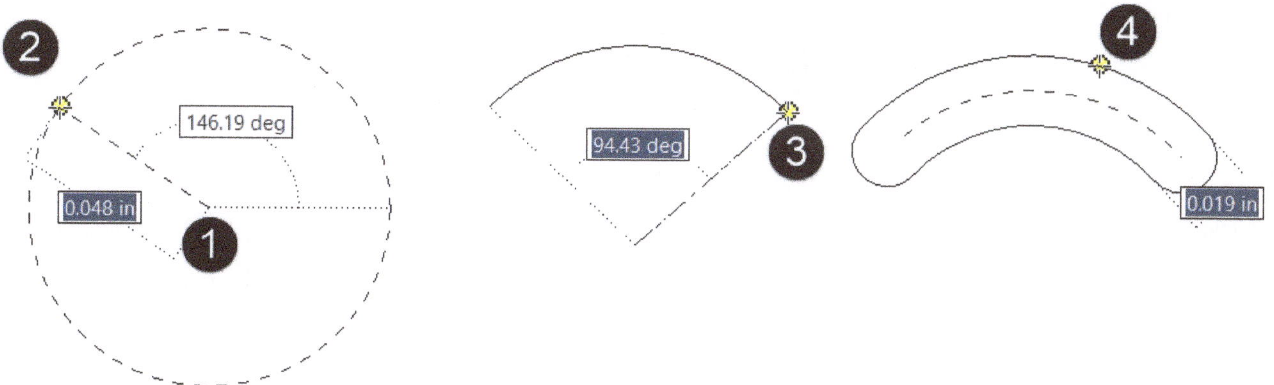

The Polygon command

This command provides a simple way to create a polygon with any number of sides. Activate this command (On the Ribbon, click **Sketch > Create > Rectangle** drop-down **> Polygon**) and click in the graphics window to define the center of the polygon. As you move the pointer away from the center, you will see a preview of the polygon. To change the number of sides of the polygon, just click in the **Number of Sides** box on the dialog and enter a new number; the preview is updated.

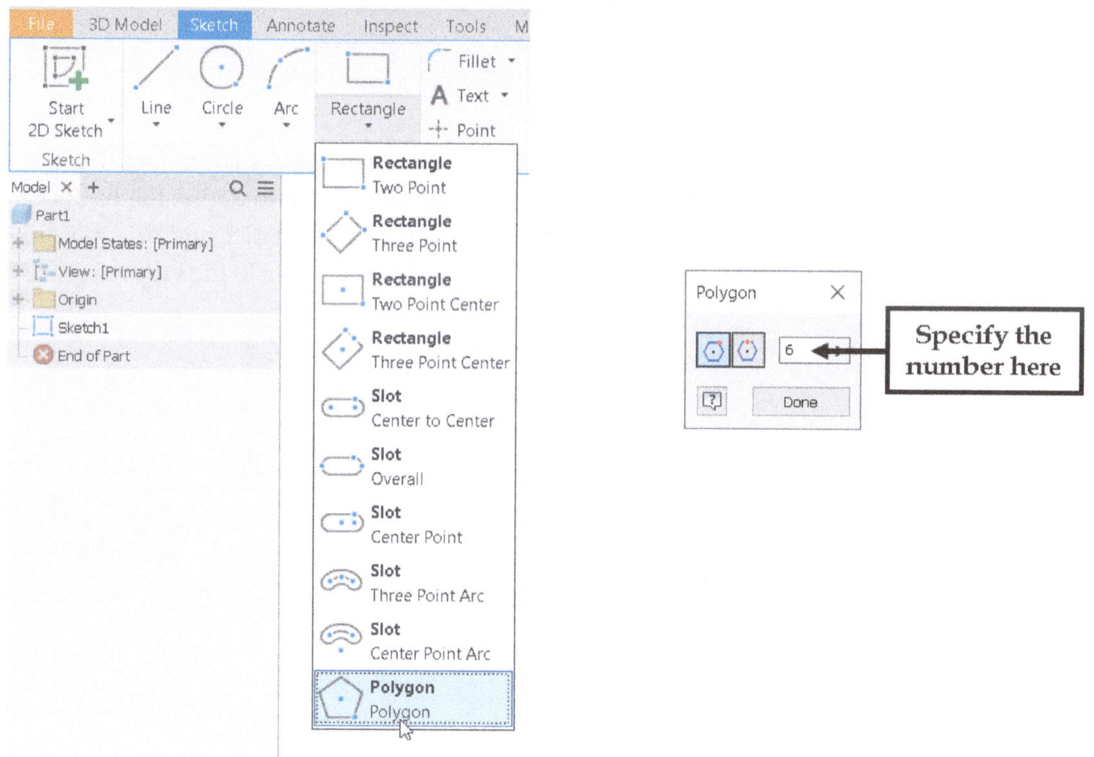

Now, you have to define the size of the polygon. On the **Polygon** dialog, there are two options to define the size of the polygon: **Inscribed** and **Circumscribed.** If you click the **Inscribed** option, a vertex of the polygon will be attached to the pointer. If you select **Circumscribed**, the pointer will be on one of the flat sides of the polygon. Click in the window to define the size and angle of the polygon. Click **Done** on the **Polygon** dialog to create a polygon.

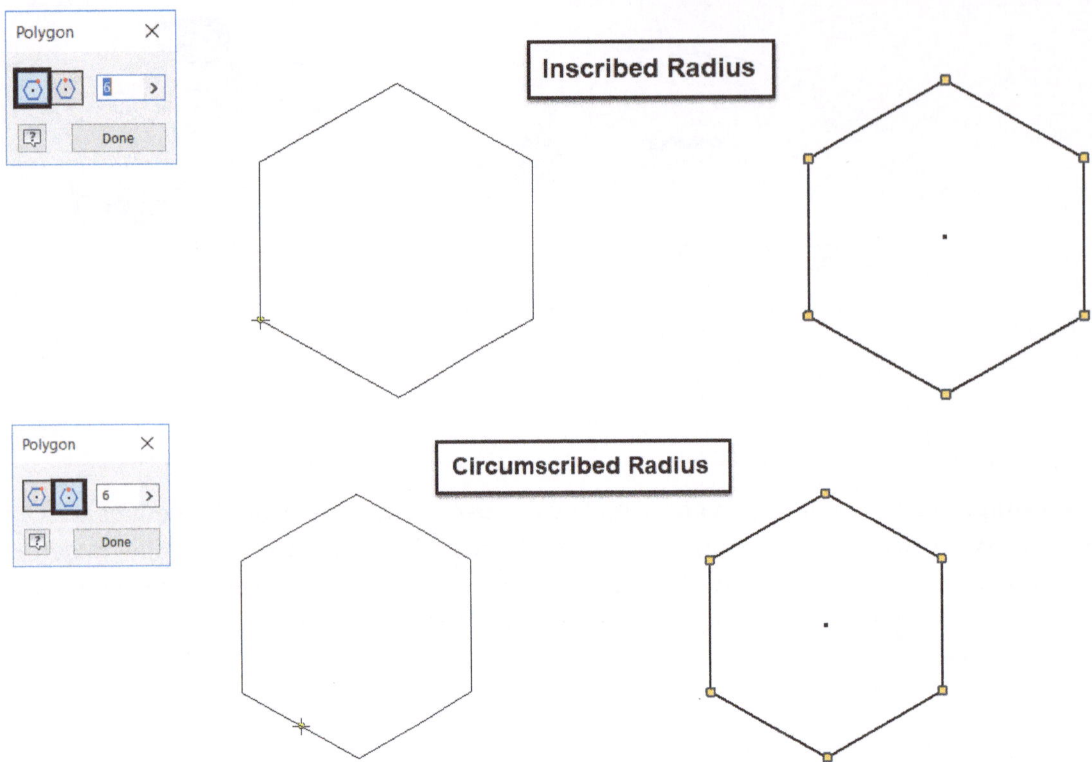

The Ellipse command

This command creates an ellipse using a center point, and major and minor axes. Activate this command (On the ribbon, click **Sketch > Create > Circle** drop-down **> Ellipse**). In the graphics window, click to define the center point of the ellipse. Move the pointer away from the center point and click to define the distance and orientation of the first axis. Next, move the pointer in the direction perpendicular to the first axis and click; the ellipse is created.

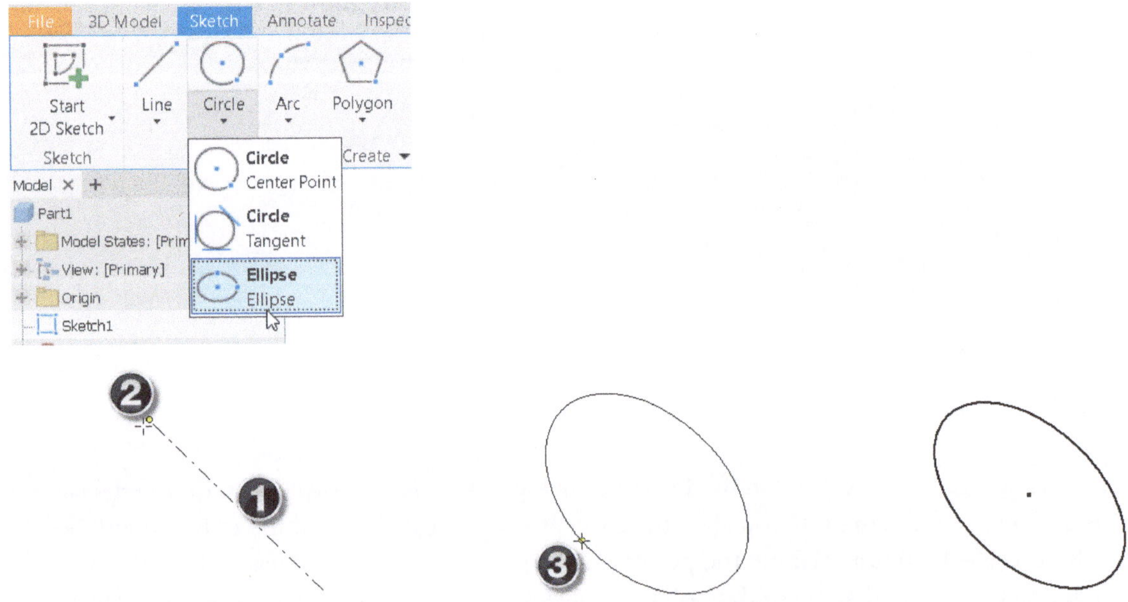

The Dimension command

It is generally considered good practice to ensure that every sketch you create is fully constrained before creating solid features. The term 'fully-constrained' means that the sketch has a definite shape and size. You can fully-constrain a sketch by using dimensions and constraints. You can add dimensions to a sketch by using the **Dimension** command. You can use this command to add all types of dimensions, such as length, angle, and diameter, and so on. This command creates a dimension based on the geometry you select. For instance, to dimension, a circle, activate the **Dimension** command (On the Ribbon, click **Sketch > Constrain > Dimension**), and then click on the circle. Next, move the pointer and click again to position the dimension; you will notice that the **Edit Dimension** box pops up. Type-in a value in this box, and then press Enter to update the dimension.

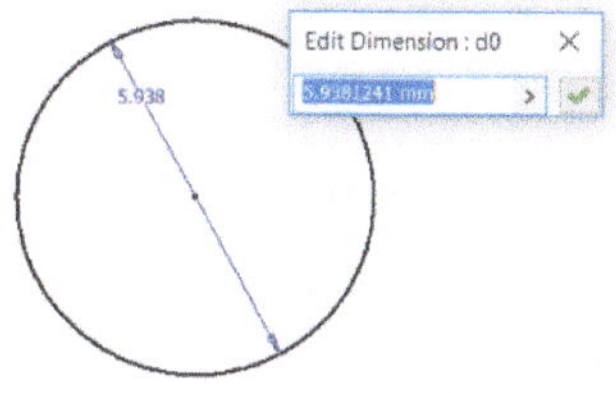

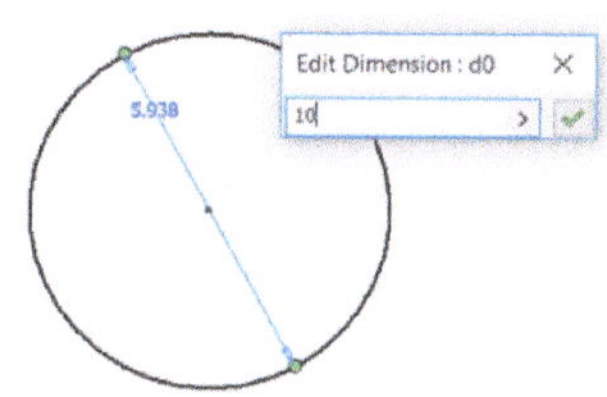

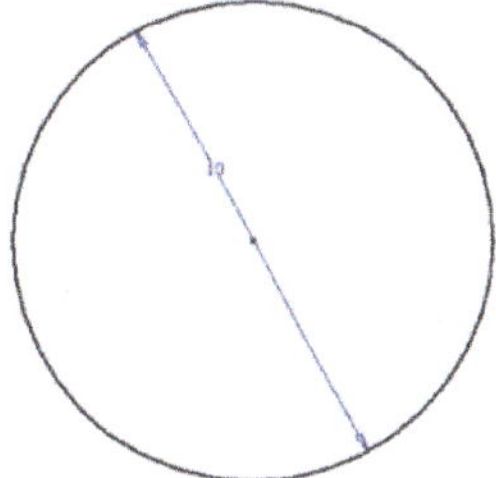

Linear Dimensions

To add dimension to a line, activate the **Dimension** command, and select the line. Next, move the pointer in the vertical direction (or) right-click and select **Horizontal** from the menu; the horizontal dimension is created. Click to position the dimension.

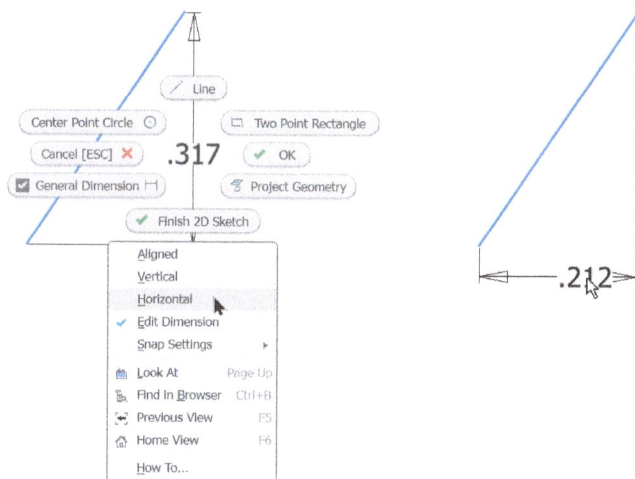

To create a vertical dimension, activate the **Dimension** command, and select a line. Move the pointer in the horizontal direction (or) right-click and select **Vertical** from the shortcut menu; the vertical dimension is created. Click to position the dimension.

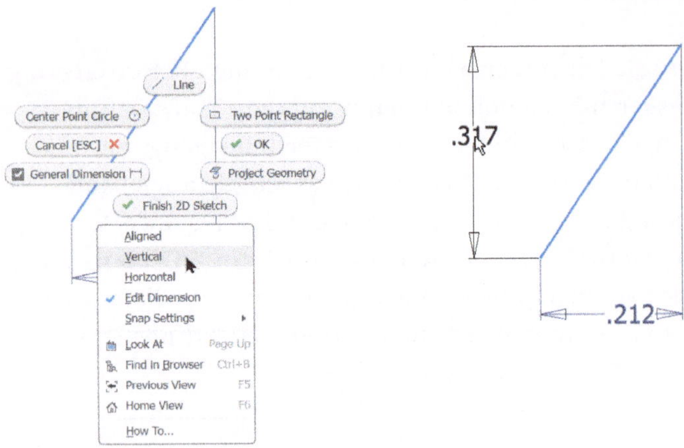

To create a dimension aligned to the selected line, right click and select **Aligned** from the shortcut menu. Next, position the dimension and edit its value.

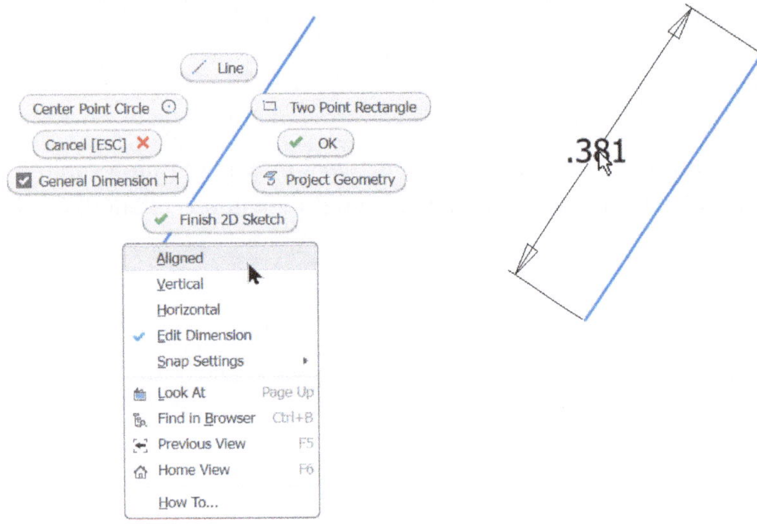

Angular Dimensions

Click the **Dimension** command on the **Constrain** panel of the **Sketch** tab, and then select two lines that are positioned at an angle to each other. Move the pointer between the selected lines and click to position the dimension. Next, type in a value, and click the **OK** button.

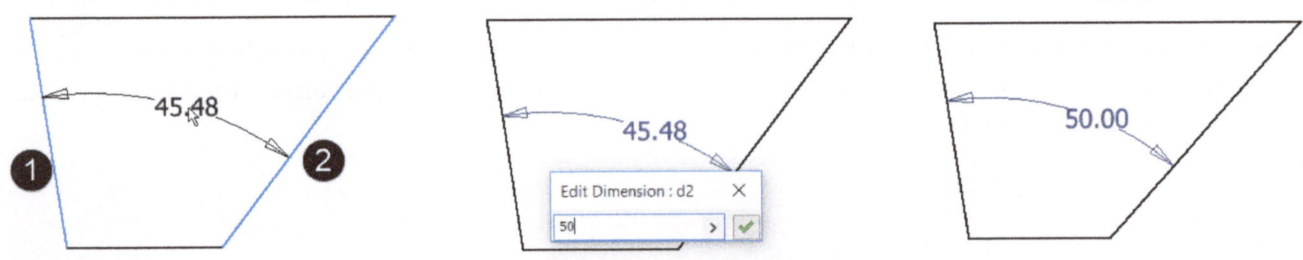

Adding Dimensions to an Arc

Inventor allows you to add five types of dimensions to an arc: Radius, Diameter, Arc Length, Arc angle, and Linear dimension.

Adding a Radius or Diameter or Arc Length dimension

To add a radius or diameter or arc length dimension to an arc, activate the **Dimension** command and select the arc. Next, right click and select **Dimension Type > Radius** or **Diameter** or **Arc Length**. Position the dimension and edit the dimension value.

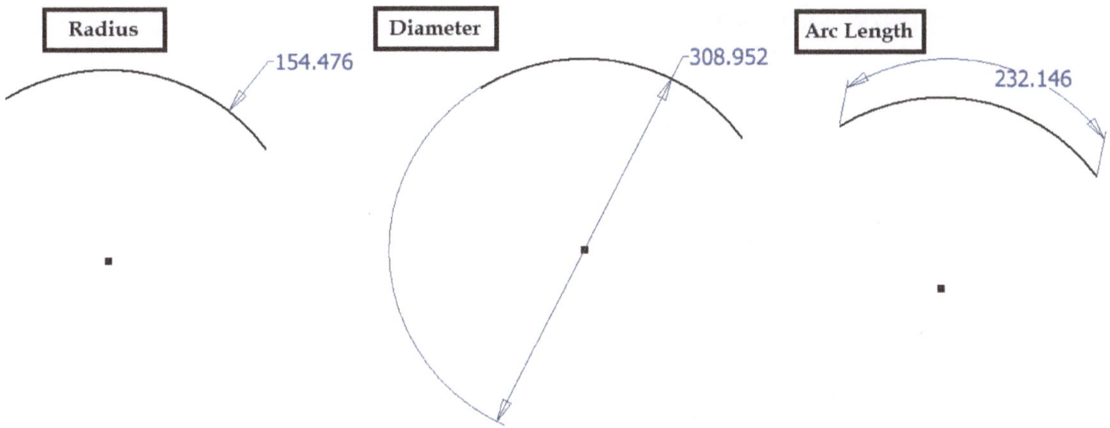

Adding a Linear dimension to the Arc

To add a linear dimension to an arc, activate the **Dimension** command, and select its endpoints. Next, select the arc and position the linear dimension.

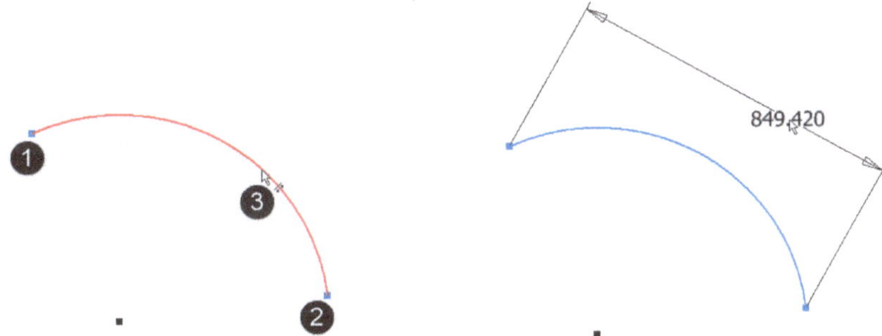

Adding an Angular dimension to an Arc

To add an angular dimension to an arc, activate the **Dimension** command and select the center point of the arc. Next, select the arc and position the angular dimension.

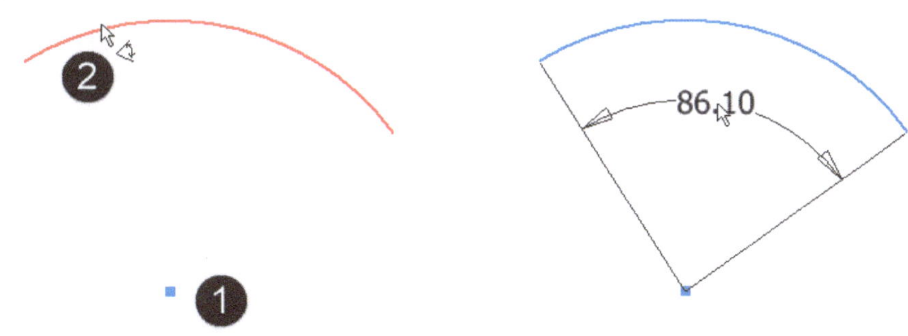

Over-constrained Sketch

When creating sketches for a solid or surface feature, Autodesk Inventor will not allow you to over-constrain the geometry. The term 'over-constrain' means adding more dimensions than required. The following figure shows a fully constrained sketch. If you add another dimension to this sketch (e.g., diagonal dimension), the **Create Linear Dimension** message pops up. It shows that the dimension over constrains the sketch. If you click **Accept**, then the dimension in the sketch will be displayed in brackets.

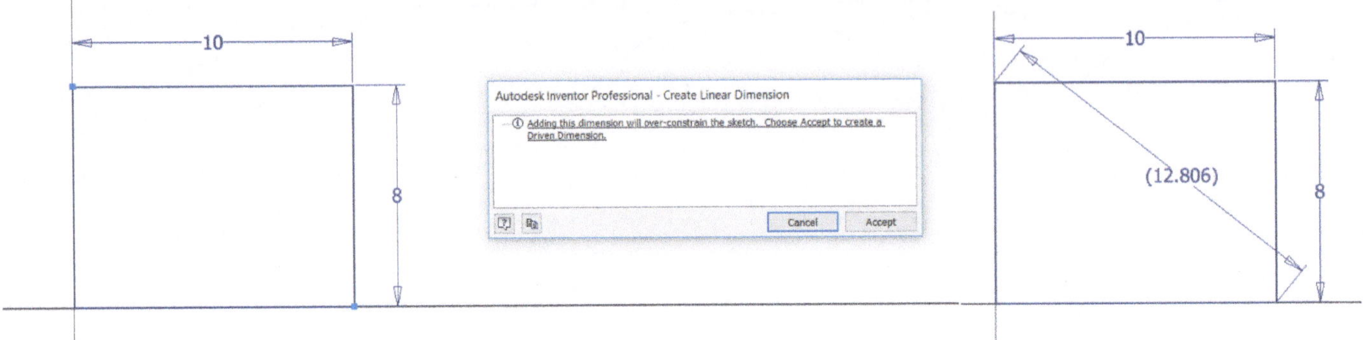

Constraints

The constraints are used to control the shape of a drawing by establishing relationships between the sketch elements. You can apply constraints to a sketch using the commands available on the **Constrain** panel of the **Sketch** ribbon.

Coincident Constraint

This constraint connects a point with another point. Click the **Coincident Constraint** button on the **Constrain** panel of the **Sketch** tab and select the points to be made coincident to each other. The selected points will be connected.

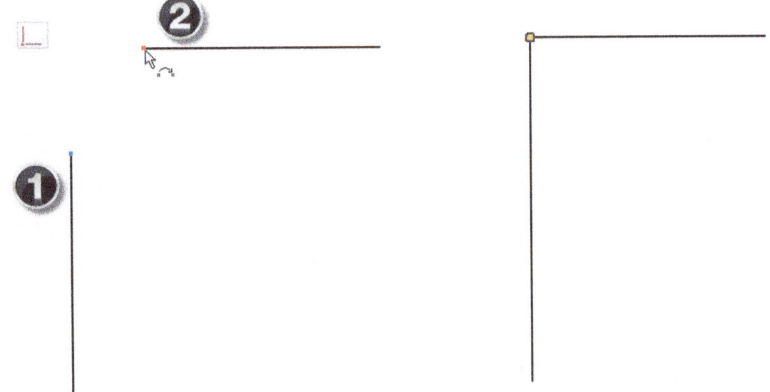

In addition to that, this constraint makes a vertex or a point to be on a line, curve, arc, or circle. Click the **Coincident Constraint** button on the **Constrain** panel and select a line, circle, arc, or curve. Next, select the point to be made coincident. The point will lie on the selected entity or its extension.

The **Coincident** constraint also forces a point or vertex to be aligned with the midpoint of a line. Activate the **Coincident Constraint** command and click on a point or vertex. Next, click on the midpoint of a line; the point will coincide with the midpoint of the line.

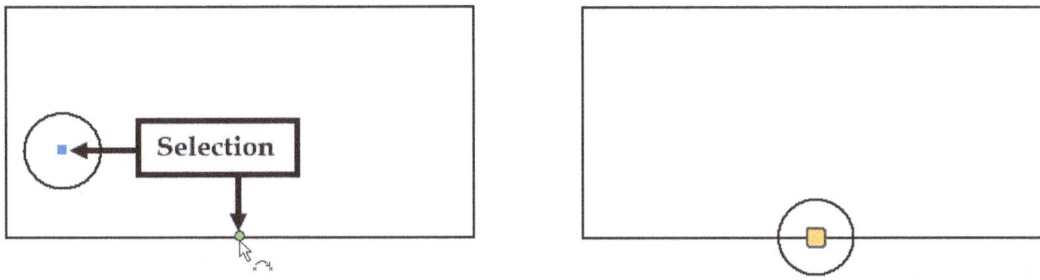

Horizontal Constraint

This constraint makes a line horizontal. Click the **Horizontal Constraint** button on the **Constrain** panel and select a free-to-move line; the line is made horizontal.

The **Horizontal Constraint** also aligns the two selected points horizontally. Click the **Horizontal Constraint** button on the **Constrain** panel and then select the points to align them horizontally.

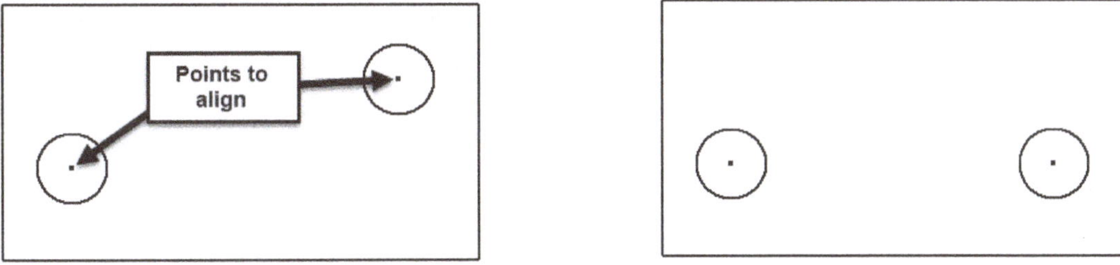

Vertical Constraint

This constraint makes a line vertical. Click the **Vertical Constraint** button on the **Constrain** panel and select an under-constrained line; the line is made vertical.

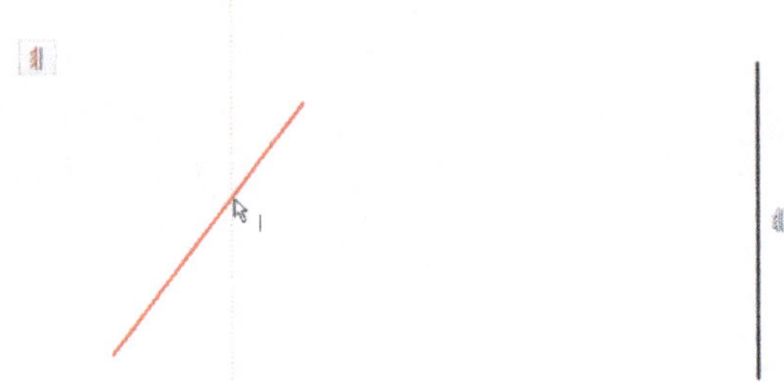

The **Vertical Constraint** also aligns the two selected points vertically. Click the **Vertical Constraint** button on the **Constrain** panel and then select the points to align vertically.

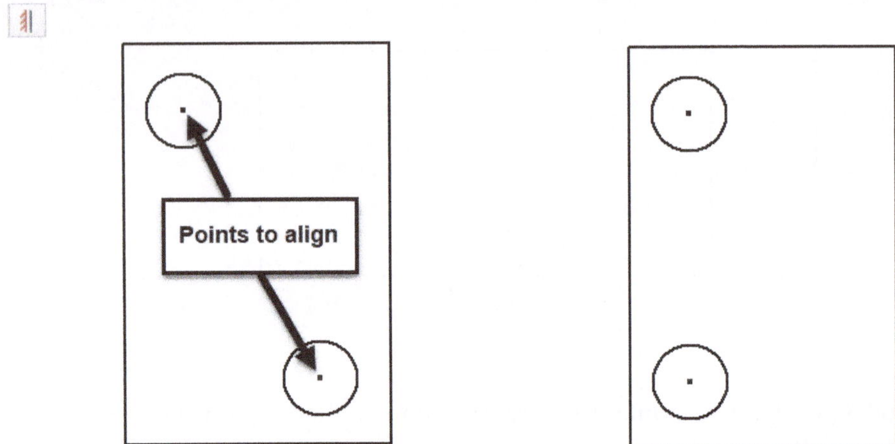

Concentric Constraint

This constraint makes the center points of two arcs, circles, or ellipses coincident with each other. Click the **Concentric Constraint** button on the **Constrain** panel and select a circle or arc from the sketch. Select another circle or arc. The circles/arcs will be concentric to each other.

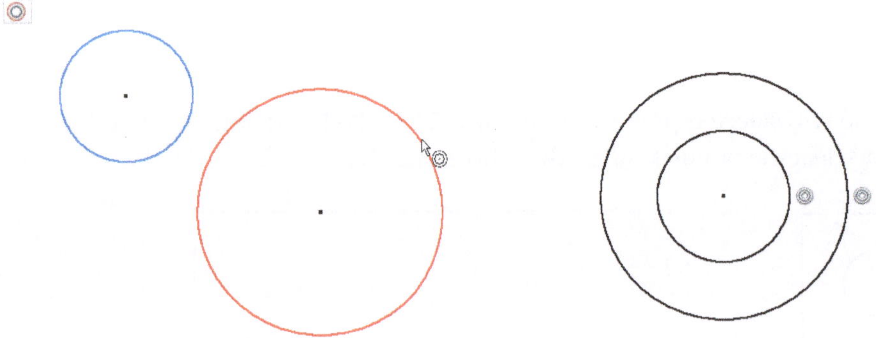

Equal Constraint

This constraint makes two lines equal in length.

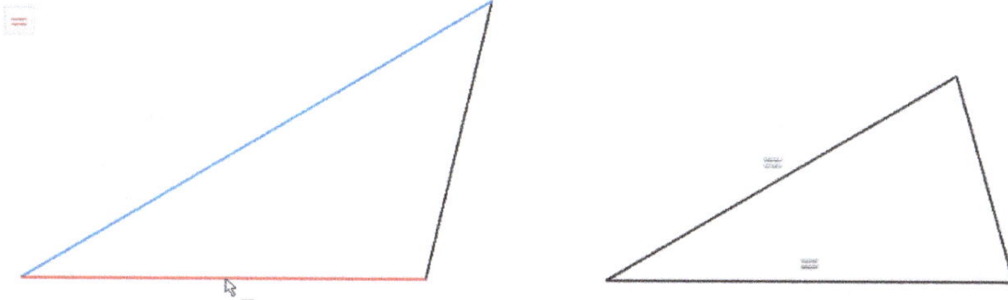

In addition to that, this constraint makes two circles or arcs equal in size.

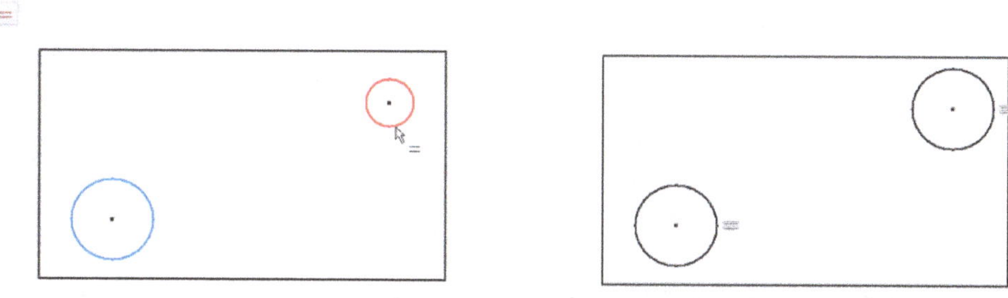

Collinear Constraint

This constraint forces a line to be collinear to another line. The lines are not required to touch each other. On the ribbon, click **Sketch > Constrain > Collinear Constraint**. Select the two lines, as shown. The second line will be collinear to the first line.

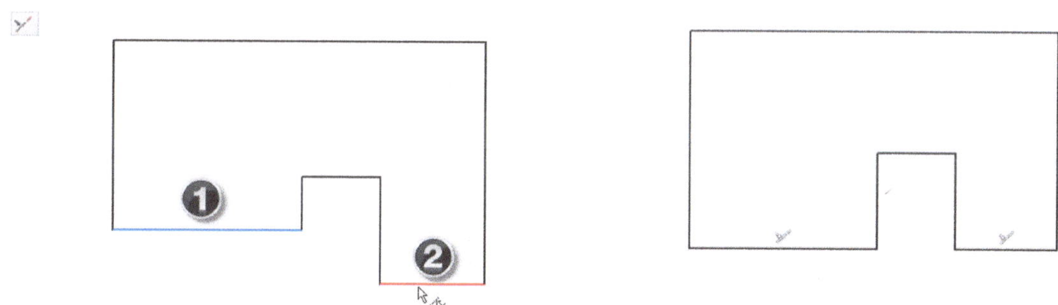

Tangent Constraint

This constraint makes an arc, circle, or line tangent to another arc or circle. On the **Constrain** panel, click the **Tangent** button and select a circle, arc, or line. Select another circle, arc, or line; both the elements become tangent to each other.

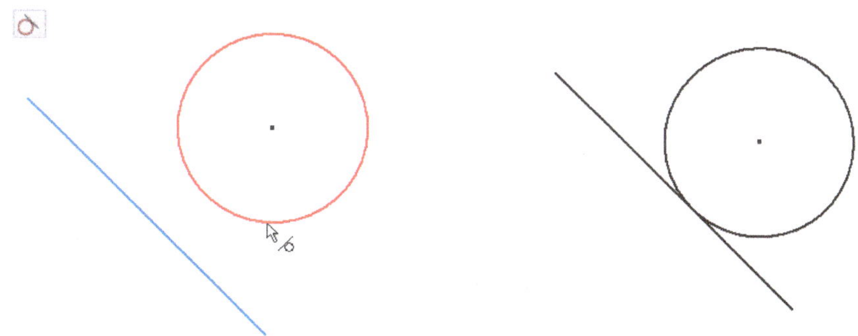

Parallel Constraint

This constraint makes two lines parallel to each other. Click the **Parallel Constraint** button on the **Constrain** panel and select two lines from the sketch. The under-constrained line is made parallel to the constrained line. For example, if you select a line with the **Vertical Constraint** and a free-to-move line, the free-to-move line becomes parallel to the vertical line.

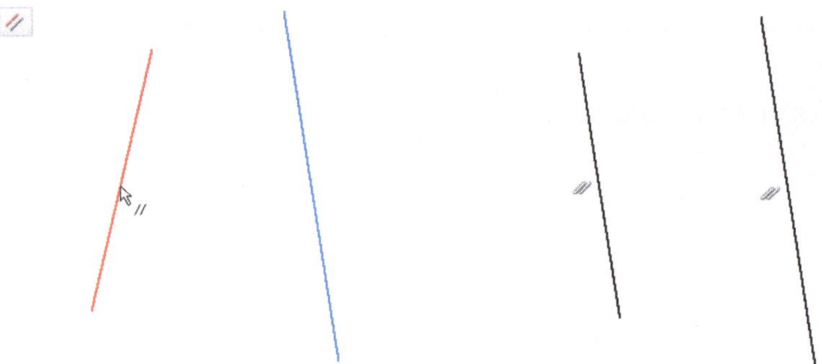

Perpendicular Constraint

This constraint makes two lines perpendicular to each other. Click the **Perpendicular Constraint** button on the **Constrain** panel and select two lines from the sketch. The two lines will be made perpendicular to each other.

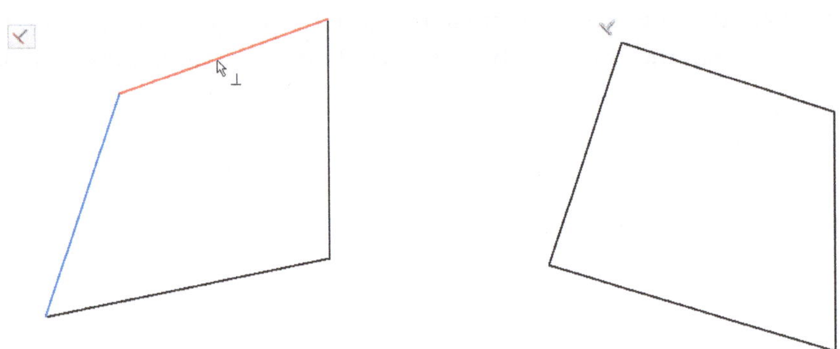

Symmetric Constraint

This command makes two objects symmetric about a line. The objects will have the same size, position, and orientation about a line. Activate this command (on the Ribbon, **Sketch > Constrain > Symmetric)** and click on the first object. Next, click on the second object, and then select the symmetry line. The two objects will be made symmetric about the symmetry line.

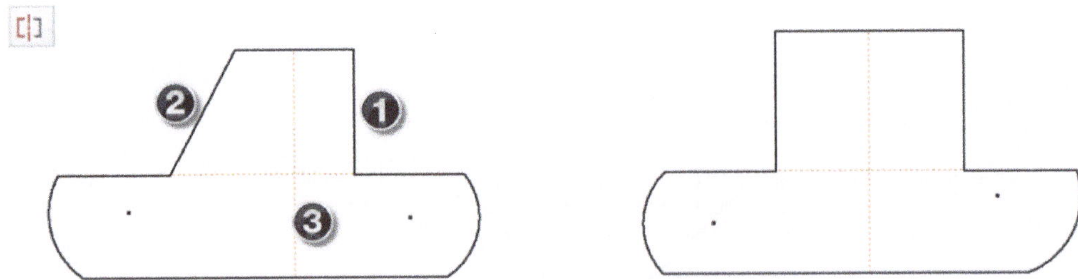

You can continue selecting the objects to be made symmetric about the previously selected symmetry line.

Constraint Settings

The **Constraint Settings** dialog helps you to specify settings related to infer constraints and dimensions. Infer constraints are applied between the sketch elements immediately after they are created. The type of constraints applied between the sketch elements depends on their position and orientation. To open the **Constraint Settings** dialog, click **Sketch > Constrain > Constraint Settings** on the Ribbon.

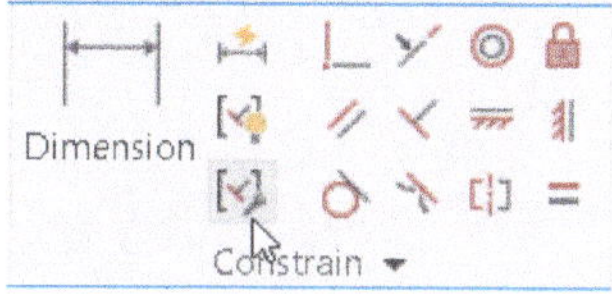

The Inference tab

The inference options are available on the **Inference** tab of the **Constraint Settings** dialog. Click this tab on the **Constraint Settings** dialog and check the **Infer Constraints** option, if not already checked. Next, check the constraints in the **Selection for Constraint Inference** section that is to be created while creating the sketch. By default, all the constraints are checked.

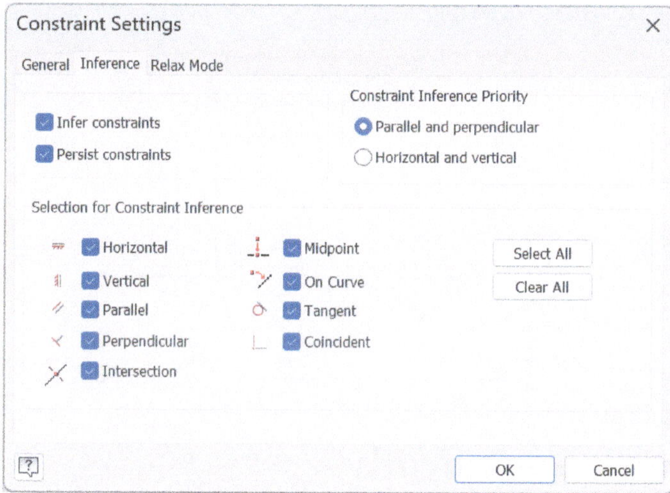

Under the **Constraint Inference Priority** section, specify the priority of the constraints to be created between two sketch elements. For example, check the **Parallel and Perpendicular** option from the **Constraint Inference Priority** section. Next, create a horizontal line and move the pointer vertically upward. Notice that Inventor tries to create the **Perpendicular** constraint between the horizontal line and the new line. However, if you check the **Horizontal and vertical** option, Inventor will create the **Vertical** constraint between the horizontal line and the new line.

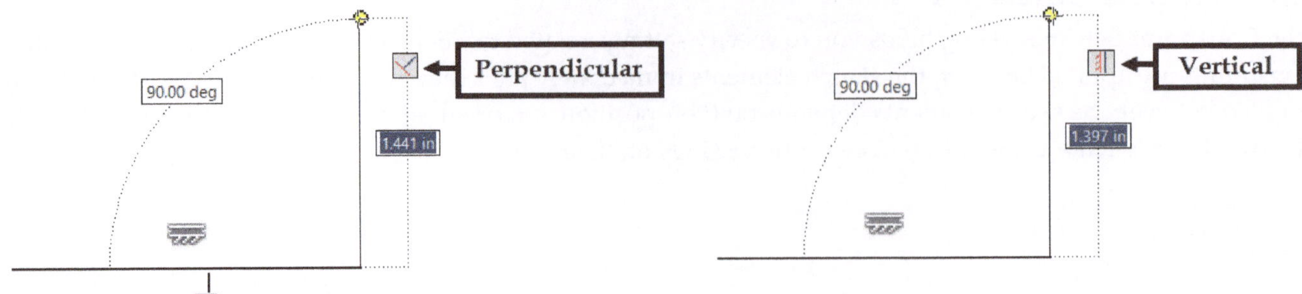

Click **OK** to close the dialog.

Show/Hide All Constraints

As constraints are created, they can be viewed using the **Show All Constraints** option. To view all the constraints of a sketch, right click in the graphics window and select **Show All Constraints**. When dealing with complicated sketches involving numerous relations, you can turn off all the constraints. To do this, right click in the graphics window and select **Hide All Constraints**.

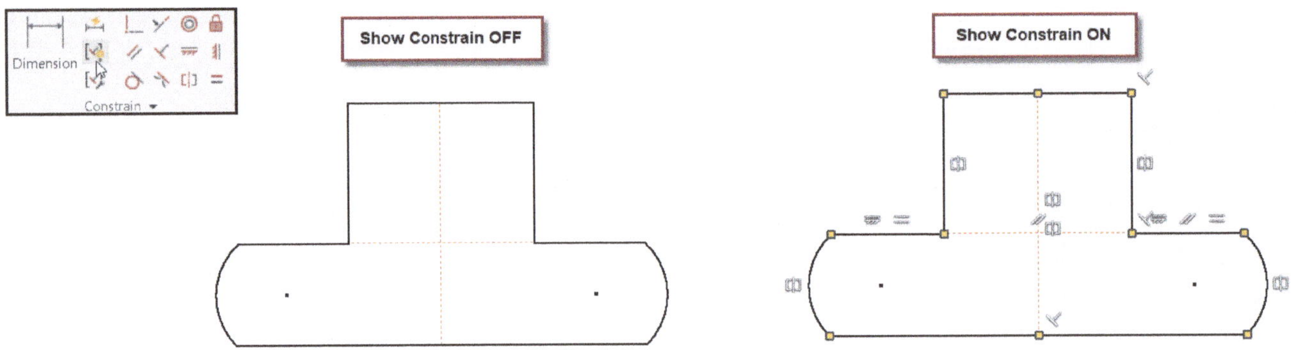

Adding Dimensions and Constraints Automatically

Autodesk Inventor has a command to add dimensions and constraints to the sketch automatically. On the ribbon, click **Sketch > Constrain** panel > **Automatic Dimensions and Constraints**. On the **Auto Dimension** dialog, the number of dimensions required to fully-constrain the sketch is displayed. Click **Apply** on the **Auto Dimension** dialog to apply the dimensions. Click **Done** if you are satisfied with the dimension. Otherwise, click **Remove** to erase all the automatic dimensions.

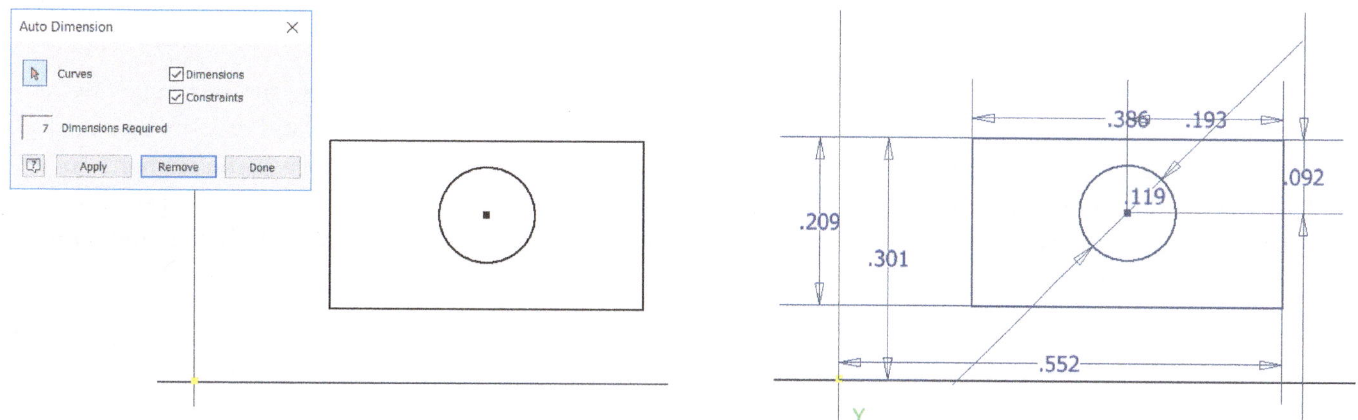

The Construction Command

This command converts a sketch element into a construction element. Construction elements support you to create a sketch of desired shape and size. To convert a sketch element to a construction element, click on it and click **Sketch > Format > Construction** on the Ribbon. You can also convert it back to a sketch element by clicking on it and deselecting the **Construction** button on the **Format** panel.

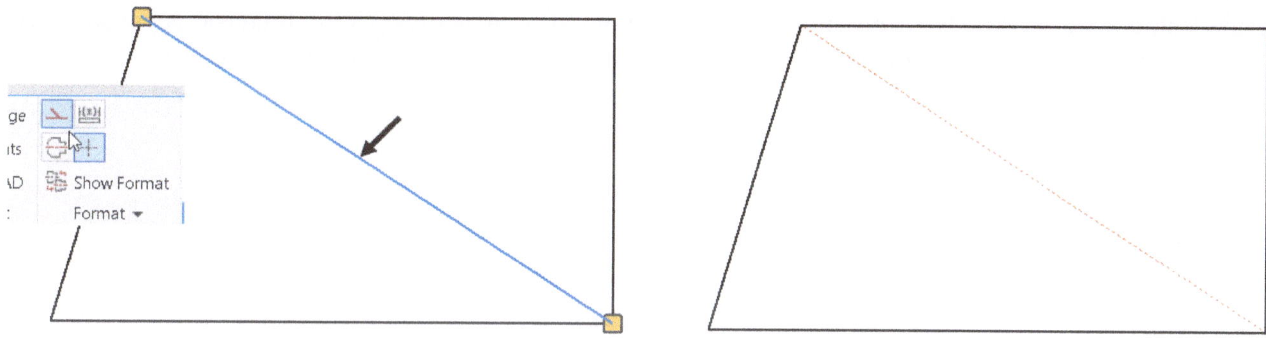

The Centerline Command

This command converts a line into a centerline. The centerline can be used as the axis of revolution while creating a revolved feature. Select a line to convert it into a centerline and click the **Centerline** button (on the Ribbon, click **Sketch > Format > Centerline**). You can also create centerlines directly by activating the **Centerline** command.

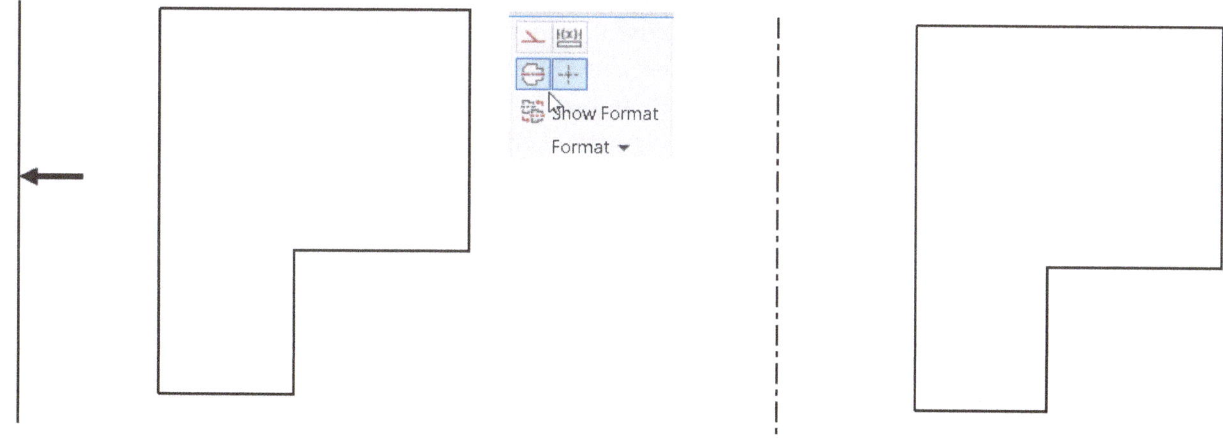

The Fillet command

This command rounds a sharp corner created by the intersection of two lines, arcs, circles, and rectangle or polygon vertices. Activate this command (On the Ribbon, click **Sketch > Create > Fillet)** and type-in a radius value in the **Radius** box on the **2D Fillet** dialog. Next, select the elements' ends to be filleted. The elements to be filleted are not required to touch each other. Keep on selecting the elements of the sketch; the fillets are added at the corners at which two selected elements intersect. Also, notice that the fillets are created with an equal radius, and a dimension is added to only one fillet.

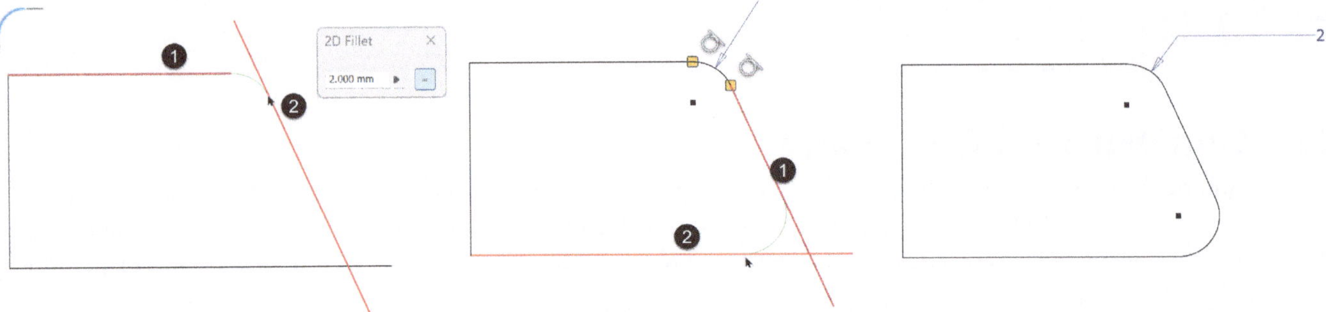

If you want to create a fillet with a different radius, then deselect the **Equal** icon on the **2D Fillet** dialog. Next, type in a new value in the **Radius** box, and then select the corners to be filleted. Separate dimensions are added to each of the fillets. You can change the fillet radii individually by double-clicking on the dimensions.

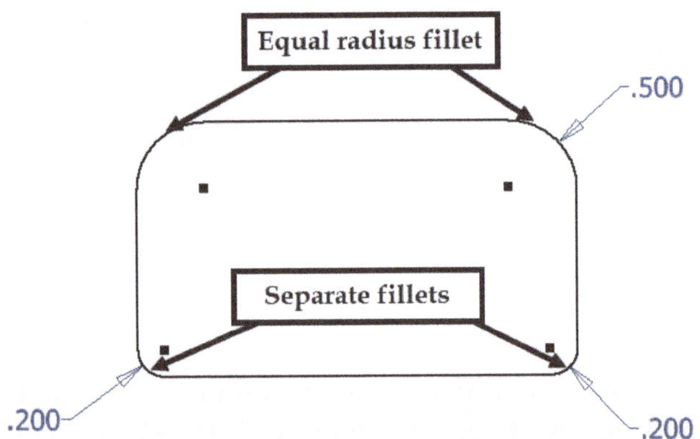

The Chamfer command

This command places an angled line at the intersection of two nonparallel lines. It can create a chamfer using any one of three different options: **Equidistant**, **Two distances**, and **Distance and Angle**. Activate this command (On the Ribbon, click **Sketch > Create > Fillet** drop-down **> Chamfer**) and select the elements' ends to be chamfered. By default, the **Equidistant** icon is selected to define the chamfer. Type-in the chamfer distance in the **Distance** box and click **OK**. By default, the **Dimension** icon is selected on the **2D Chamfer** dialog. As a result, the dimensions are added to chamfer. Deselect this icon if you do not want to add a dimension.

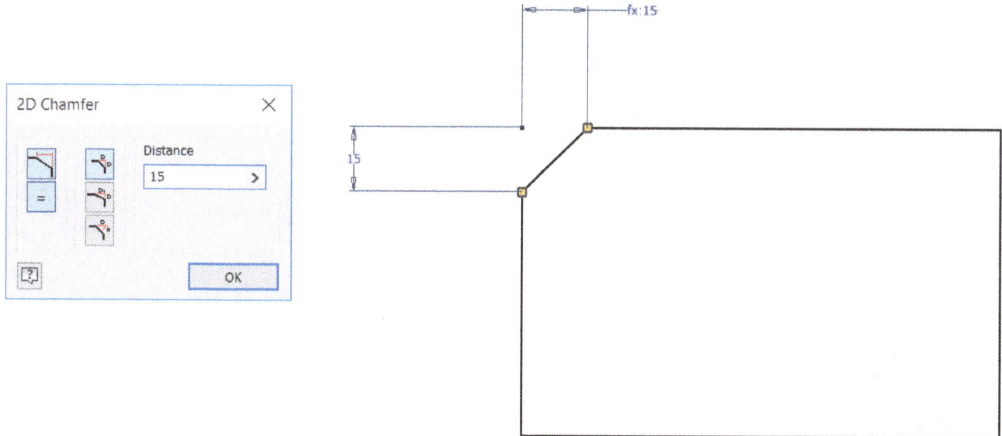

On the **2D Chamfer** dialog, click the **Two Distances** icon and type-in the chamfer distances in the **Distance1** and **Distance2 boxes**. Next, select the corner to be chamfered and click **OK**.

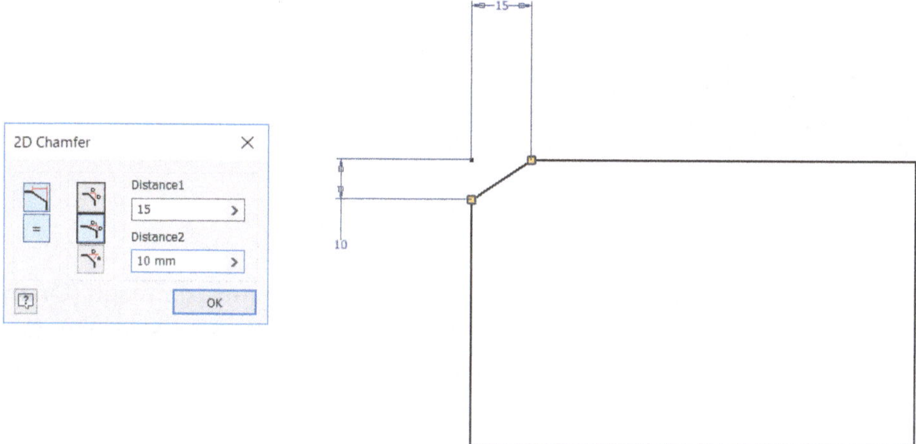

On the **2D Chamfer** dialog, click **Distance and Angle** icon and type-in the chamfer distance and angle in the **Distance** and **Angle** boxes, respectively. Next, select the corner to be chamfered and click **OK**.

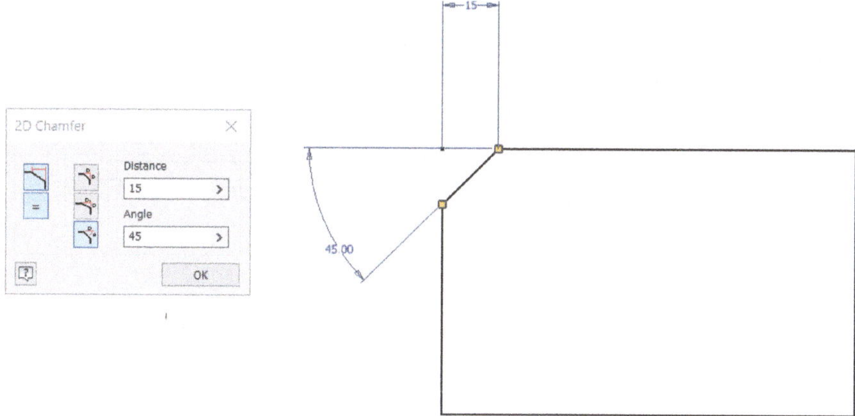

The Extend command

This command extends elements such as lines, arcs, and curves until they touch another element called the boundary edge. Activate this command (On the Ribbon, click **Sketch > Modify > Extend**) and click on the element to extend. It will extend up to the next element.

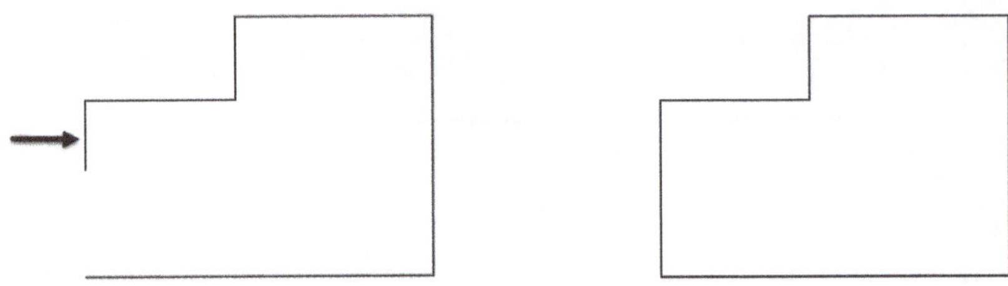

The Trim command

This command trims the end of an element back to the intersection of another element. Activate this command (On the Ribbon, click **Sketch > Modify > Trim**) and click on the element or elements to trim. You can also drag the pointer across the elements to trim.

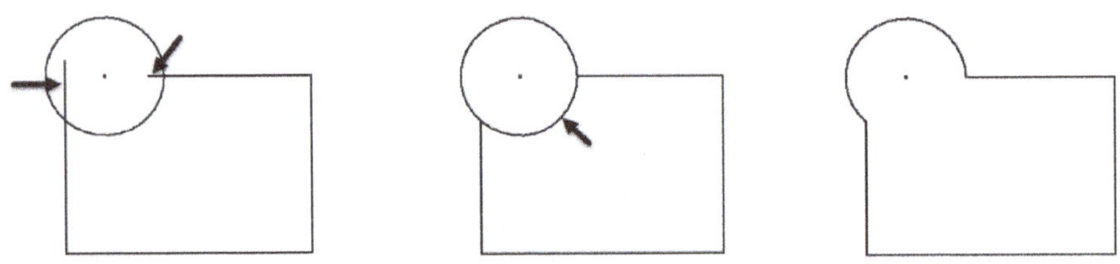

The Offset command

This command creates a parallel copy of a selected element or chain of elements. Activate this command (On the ribbon click **Sketch > Modify > Offset**) and select an element or chain of elements to offset. After selecting the element(s), move the pointer in the outward or inward direction, type in a value in the **Distance** box, and press Enter. The parallel copy of the elements will be created.

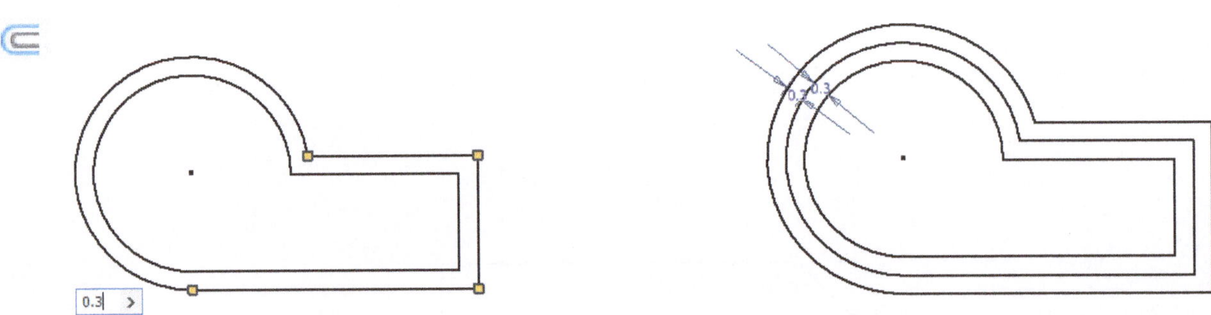

The Move command

This command relocates one or more elements from one position in the sketch to any other position that you specify. Activate this command from the **Modify** panel, and then click on the elements to move. Next, click the **Base Point** button and select a base point; a message box appears if there are any constraints or dimensions associated with the selected sketch element. Click **Yes** to relax the dimensions and constraints associated with the object. Move the pointer and click at a new location. Click **Done**.

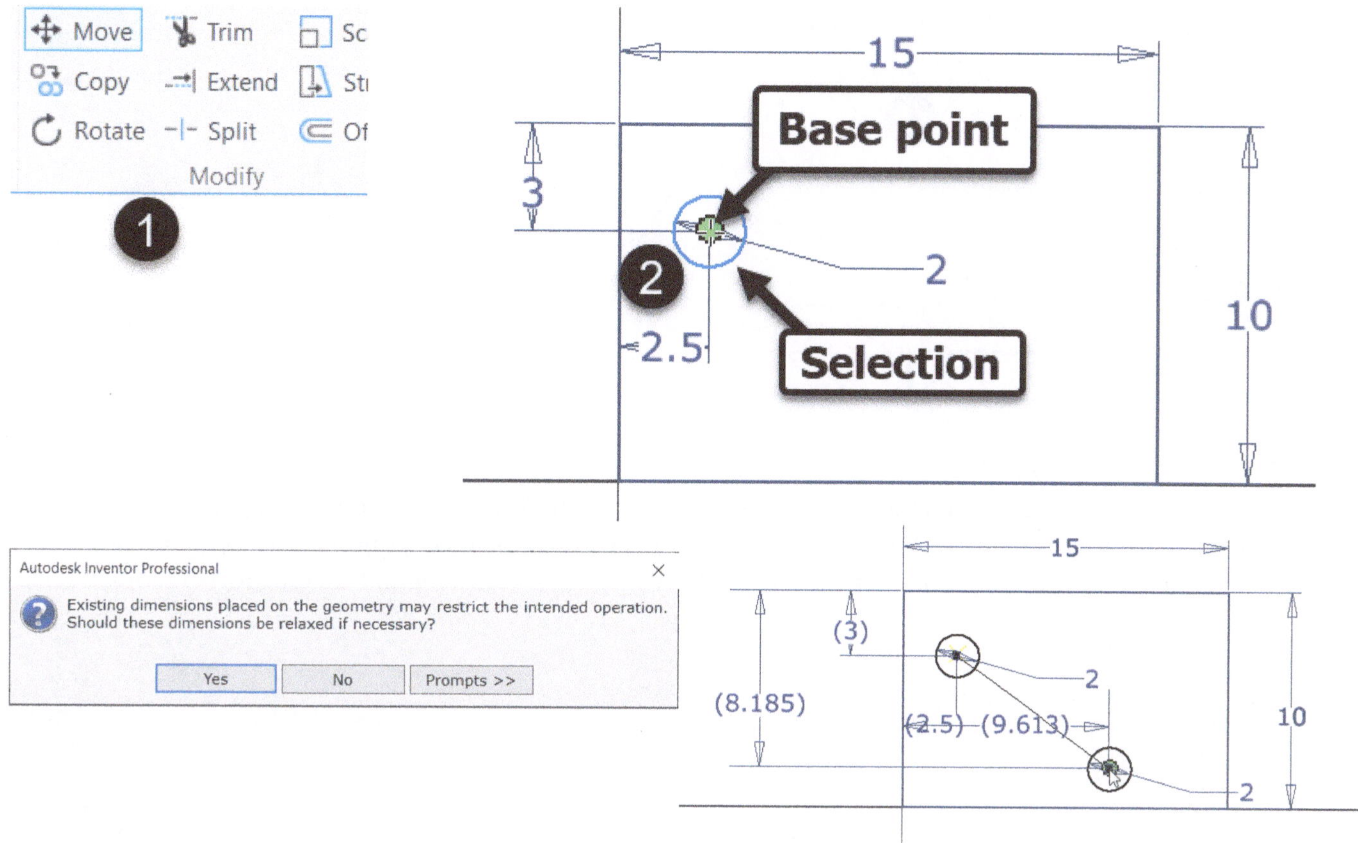

The Copy command

The **Copy** command can be used to copy and move the selected elements.

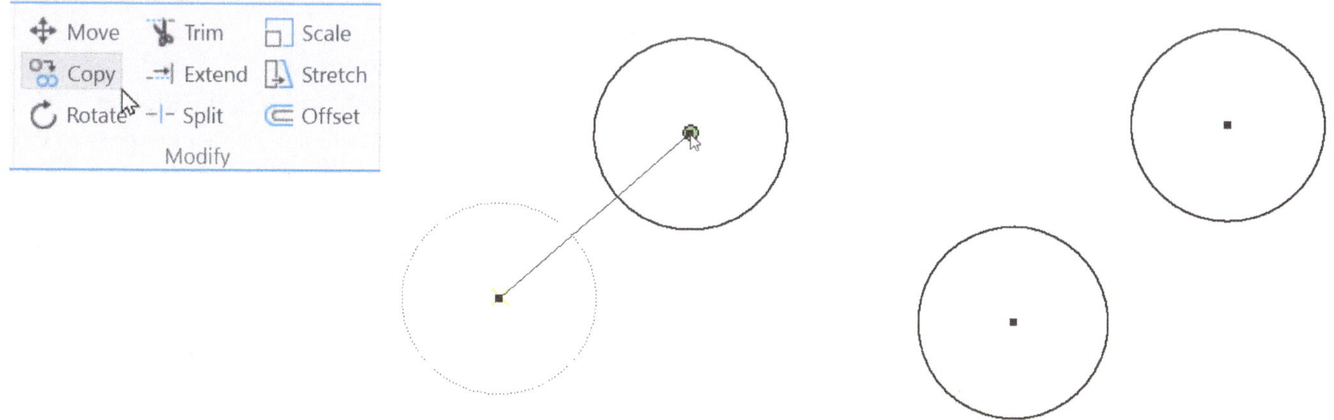

The Rotate command

This command rotates the selected elements to any position. Activate this command from the **Modify** panel, and then select the elements to rotate. Next, you must define a center point and a point from which the object will be rotated. Move the pointer and click to define the rotation angle. You can use the **Copy** option on the **Rotate** dialog to copy and rotate the selected elements. Click **Done**.

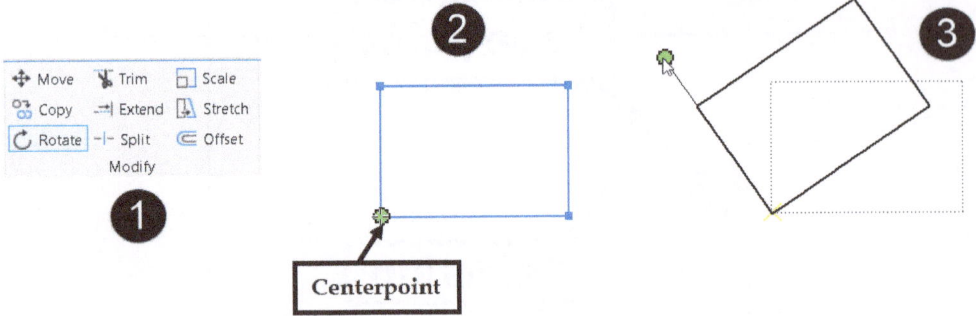

The Scale command

This command increases or decreases the size of elements in a sketch. Activate this command from **Modify** panel, and then select the elements to scale. After selecting the elements, click the **Base Point** button and select a base point. You can then scale the size of the selected elements by moving the pointer and clicking (or) entering a scale factor value in the **Scale Factor** field on the dialog.

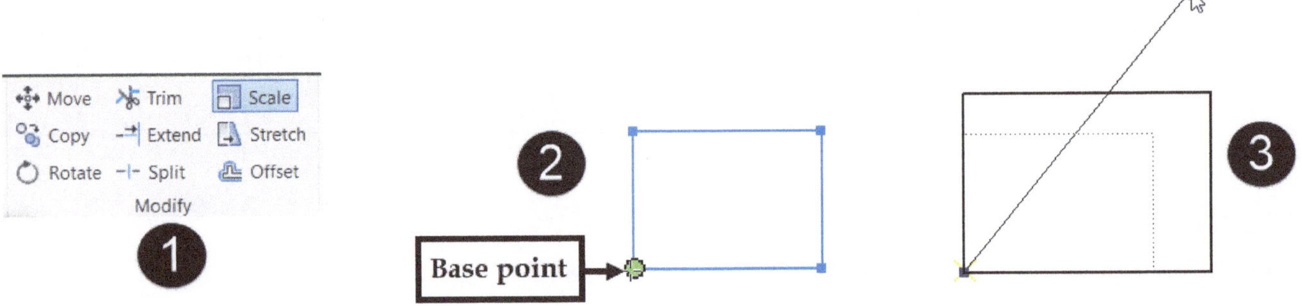

The Stretch command

This command stretches the selected geometry using a base point. Activate this command (On the Ribbon, click **Sketch > Modify > Stretch**), click the **Select** selection button on the **Stretch** dialog, and select the elements to be stretched. Next, click the **Base Point** selection button on the **Stretch** dialog and select the point, as shown. Autodesk Inventor pops-up a dialog, showing, "The geometry being edited is constrained to other geometry. Would you like those constraints removed?". Click the **Yes** button, drag the base point, and then click to stretch the part geometry. Click **Done** after stretching.

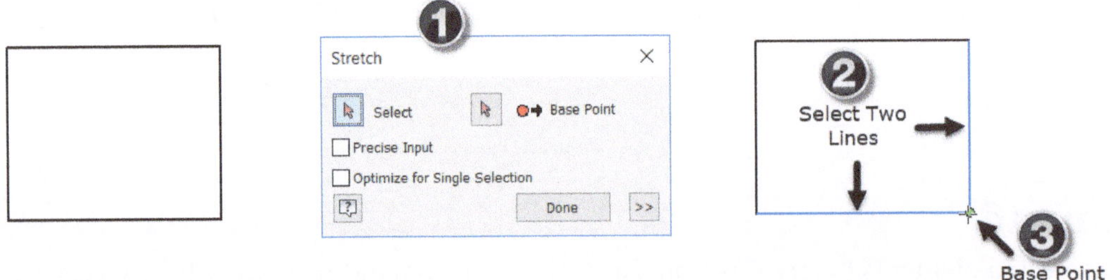

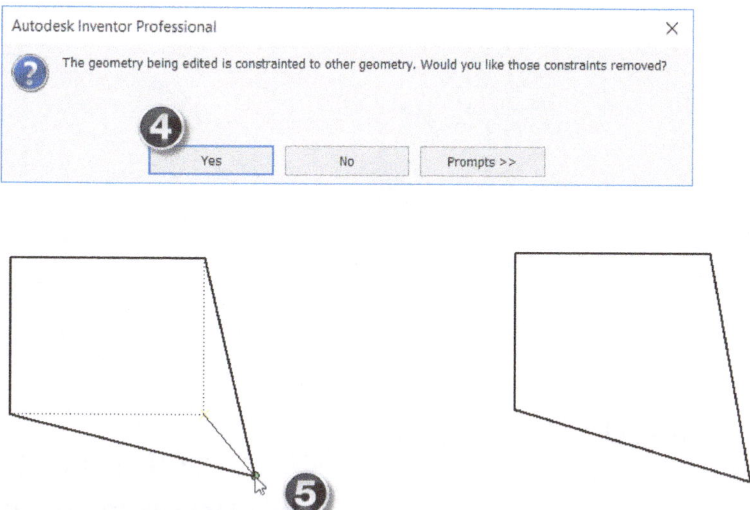

Circular Sketch Pattern

This command creates a circular pattern of the selected sketch elements. Activate the **Circular Pattern** command (on the Ribbon, click **Sketch > Pattern > Circular**) and select the sketch elements to be patterned circularly. On the **Circular Pattern** dialog, click the **Axis** button and select a point around which the sketch elements will be patterned. Next, type in a value in the **Count** box to define the instance count of the pattern. Next, specify the total angle in the **Angle** box. By default, it is 360-degrees, and you can change its value as per your requirement.

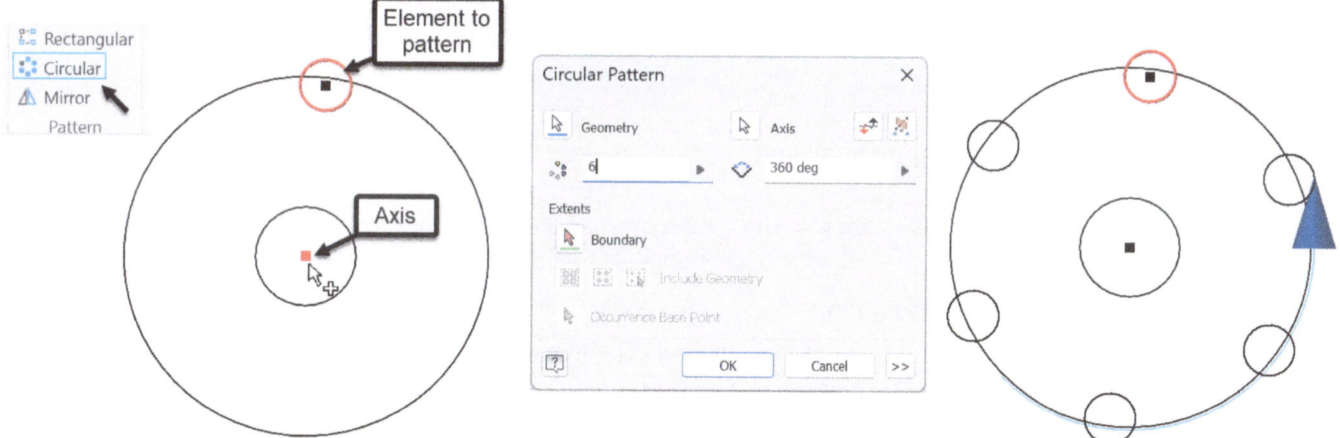

The **Extents** section controls pattern boundaries. Use **Boundary** to select a closed sketch that defines the pattern's containment region. **Include Geometry** automatically includes any occurrence fully inside this boundary. For partial overlaps, **Include Centroids** adds occurrences whose center point lies within the boundary, while **Include Using Occurrence Base Points** evaluates inclusion based on each occurrence's manually defined base point - if this point falls within the boundary, the entire occurrence is included.

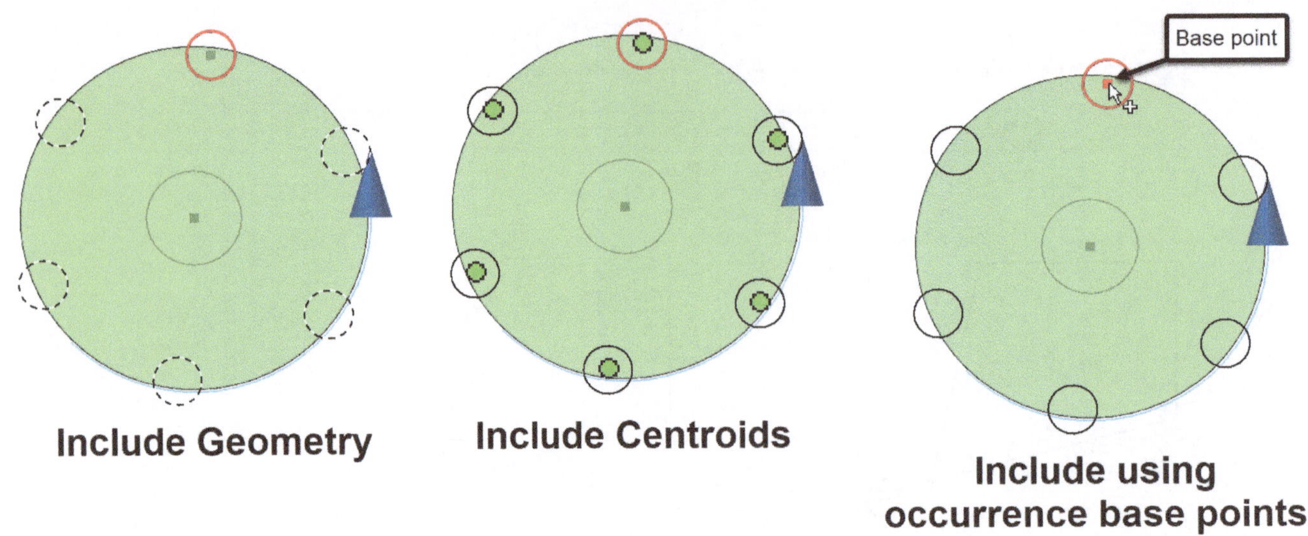

Click the expand << button located at the bottom right corner of the dialog and notice the three options: **Suppress**, **Associative**, and **Fitted**.

The **Fitted** option helps you to specify the total angle of the circular pattern. If you uncheck this option, the value that you enter in the **Angle** box will be taken as the angle between the instances.

The **Associative** option creates a link between the source object and the patterned instances. If you modify the source object, the patterned instances will be modified automatically. In addition to that, you cannot delete the instances of the pattern.

The **Suppress** option helps you to suppress instances.

Click **OK** to create a circular sketch pattern. Use the **Trim** command to erase the unwanted portions of the sketch.

Rectangular Sketch Pattern

This command creates a rectangular pattern of the selected sketch elements. Activate the **Rectangular Pattern** command (on the Ribbon, click **Sketch > Pattern > Rectangle**), and select the sketch elements to the pattern. On the **Rectangular Pattern** dialog, click the cursor icon in the **Direction 1** section and select a line to define the first direction. You can click the **Flip** icon to reverse the direction in which the pattern is created. Next, type-in values in the **Count** and **Spacing** boxes. Likewise, specify the **Direction 2** settings and click **OK**.

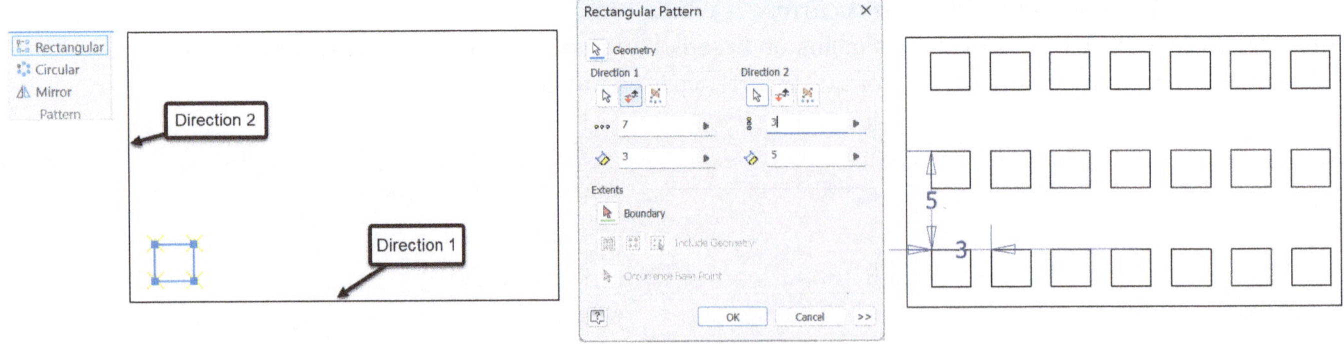

The Mirror command

This command creates a mirror image of the selected elements. It also creates the **Symmetric** constraint between the original and mirrored elements. Activate this command from the **Pattern** panel, and then select the elements to mirror. Next, click the **Mirror Line** button and select a line to define the mirror-line. Click **Apply** and **Done** on the **Mirror** dialog.

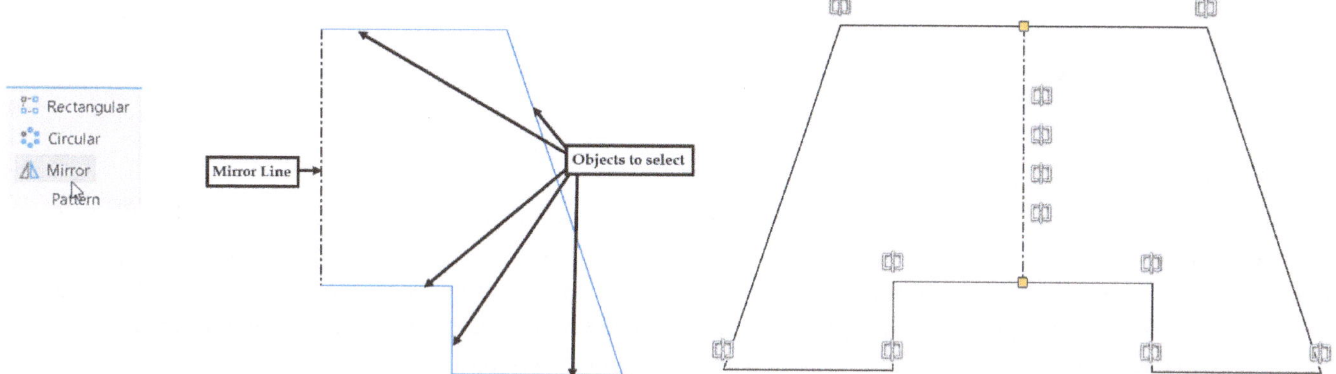

Creating Splines

Splines are non-uniform curves, which are used to create smooth shapes. In Inventor, you can create a smooth spline curve using two commands: **Control Vertex Spline** and **Interpolation Spline**.

Control Vertex Spline

The **Control Vertex Spline** command helps you to create a spline by defining various points called as control vertices. Activate this command (on the ribbon, click **Sketch > Create > Line** drop-down **> Spline Control Vertex**). In the graphics window, click to specify the first control vertex. Move the pointer and specify the second vertex. Likewise, specify the other control vertices. As you define the control vertices, dotted lines are created connecting them. Also, the spline will be created. Press Enter to complete the spline.

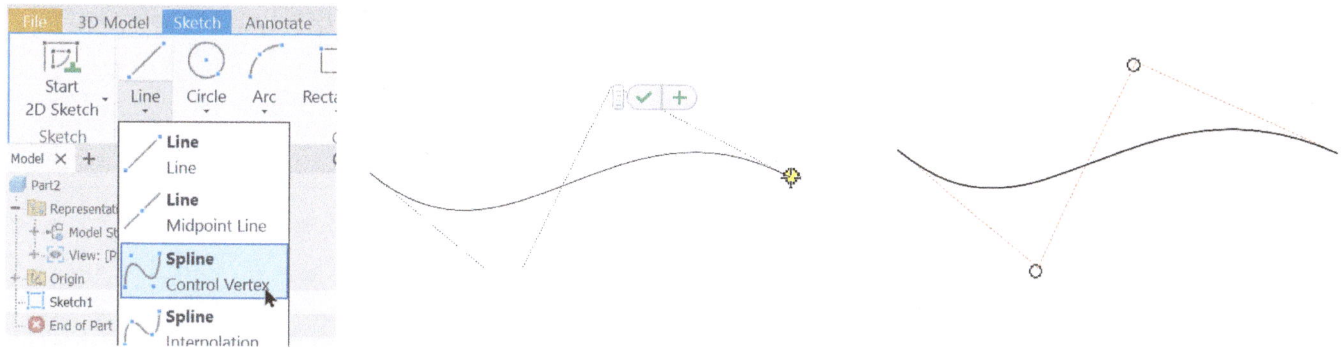

You can also add new control vertices to the spline. To do this, right-click on the spline and select **Insert Vertex** from the menu. Click on the desired position to place the new vertex. Now, you can modify the shape and size of the spline by dragging the control vertices. You can also add dimensions and constraints to the control vertices and dotted lines.

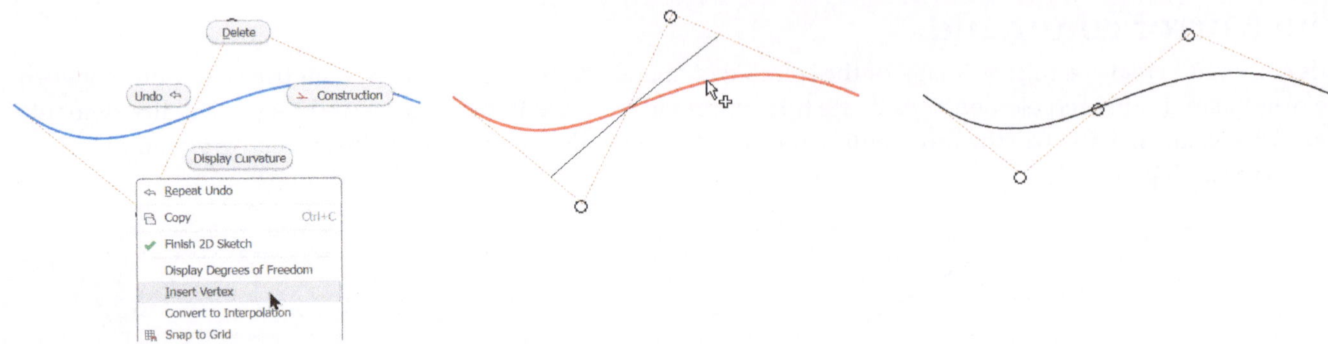

Interpolation Spline

The **Interpolation Spline** command creates a smooth spline passing through a series of points called fit points. Activate this command, by clicking **Sketch > Create > Line** drop-down **> Spline Interpolation**. In the graphics window, click to specify the first point of the spline. Move the pointer and specify the second point of the spline. Likewise, specify the other points of the spline, and then press Enter to create the spline. The endpoints are square-shaped, whereas the fit points along the curve are diamond shapes.

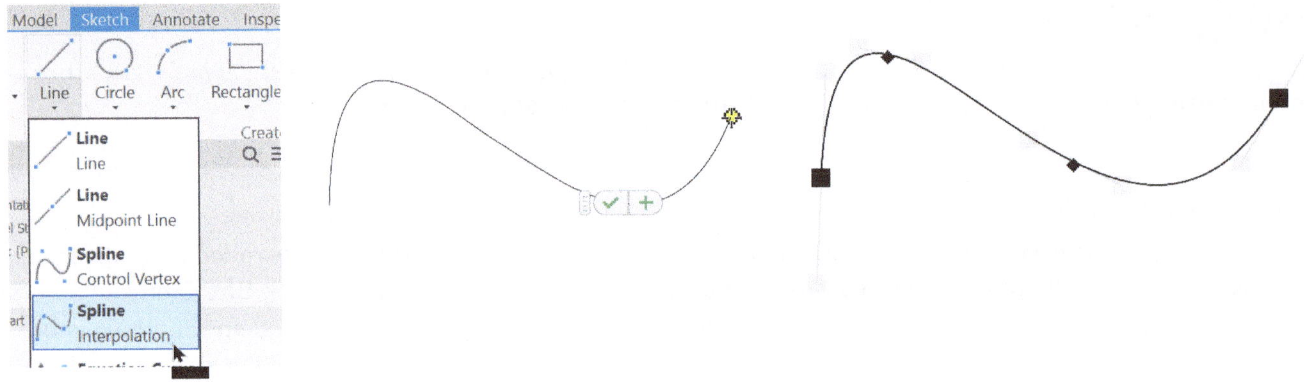

You can add a new fit point on the spline. To do this, right-click on the spline and select **Insert point** from the menu. Click on the desired position to place the new point. You can click and drag the fit points to reposition them. Also, it changes the shape of the spline.

Examples

Example 1 (Millimeters)

In this tutorial, you will draw the sketch shown below.

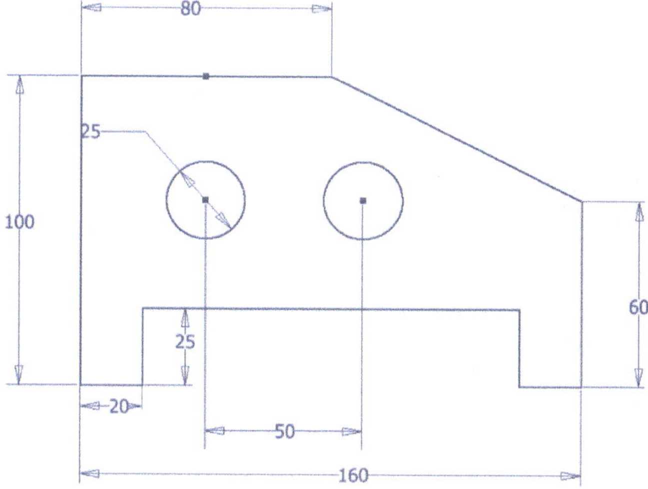

1. Start **Autodesk Inventor 2026** by double-clicking the **Autodesk Inventor 2026** icon on your desktop.
2. To start a new part file, click **New** drop-down > **New** on the **Home** screen.
3. On the **Create New File** dialog, click the **Metric** folder under **Templates**.
4. Click the **Standard(mm).ipt** icon under the **Part – Create 2D and 3D Objects** section.

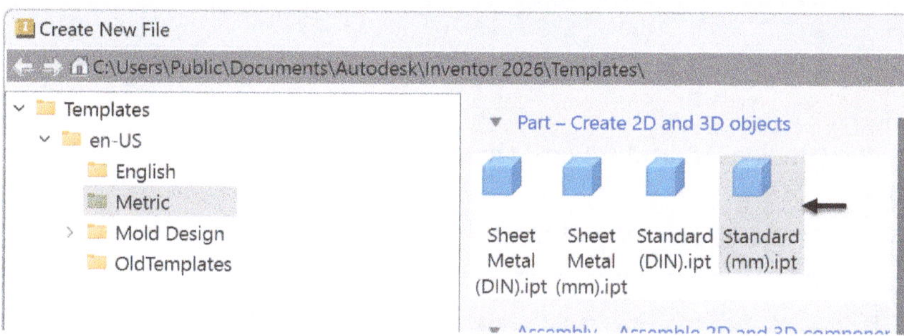

5. Click the **Create** button on the **Create New File** dialog.

A new model window appears.

Starting a Sketch

1. To start a sketch, click **3D Model > Sketch > Start 2D Sketch** on the ribbon. Click on the XY plane. The sketch starts.

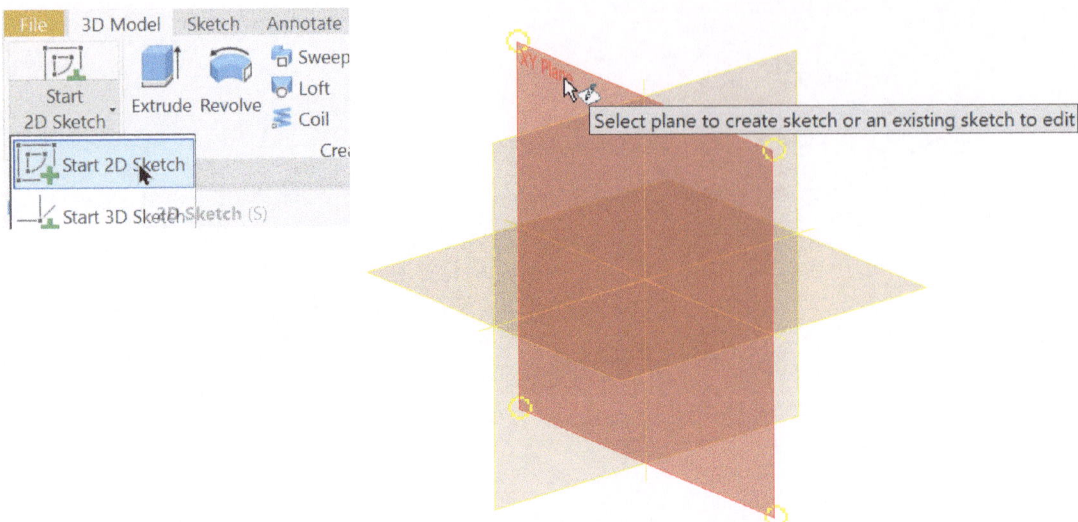

2. Click **Sketch > Create > Line** on the ribbon. Click on the origin point to define the first point of the line.

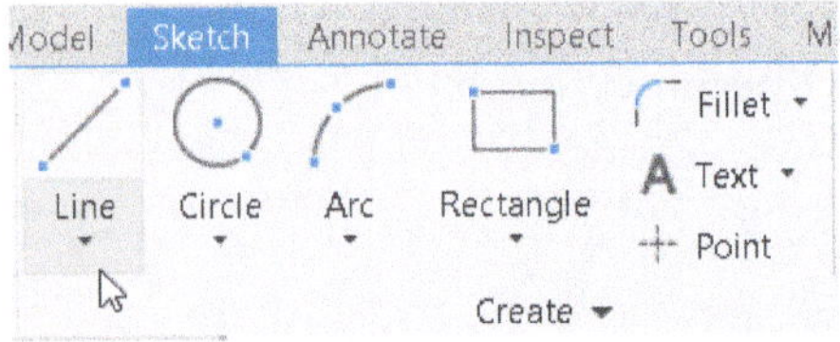

3. Move the pointer along the horizontal axis (thick axis) and toward the right.
4. Click to define the endpoint of the line.
5. Move the pointer vertically upwards. Click to create the second line.

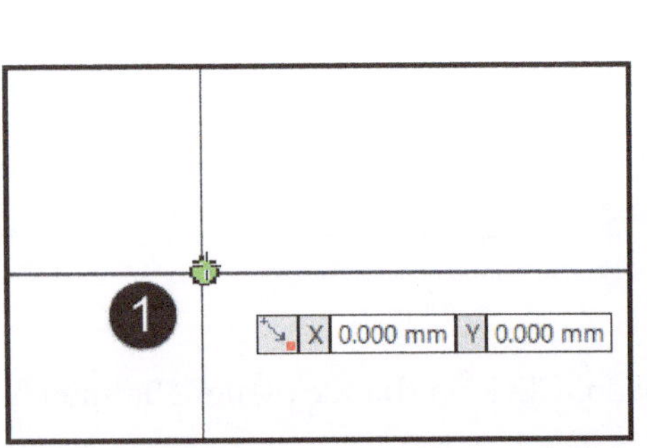

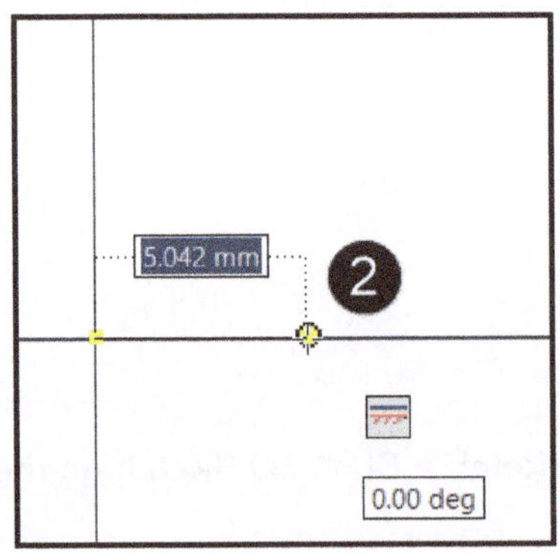

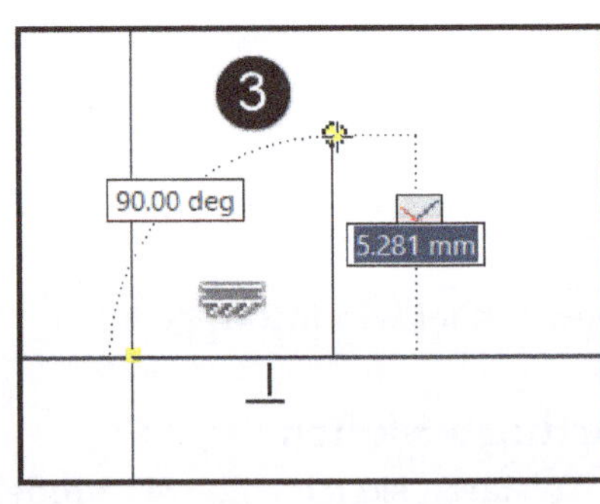

6. Create a closed-loop by selecting points in the sequence, as shown below.

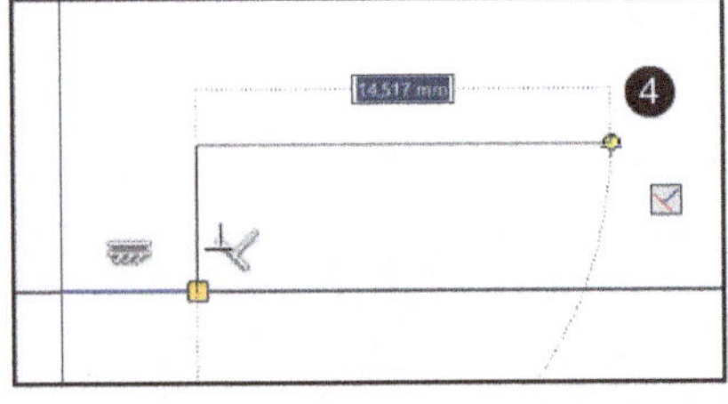

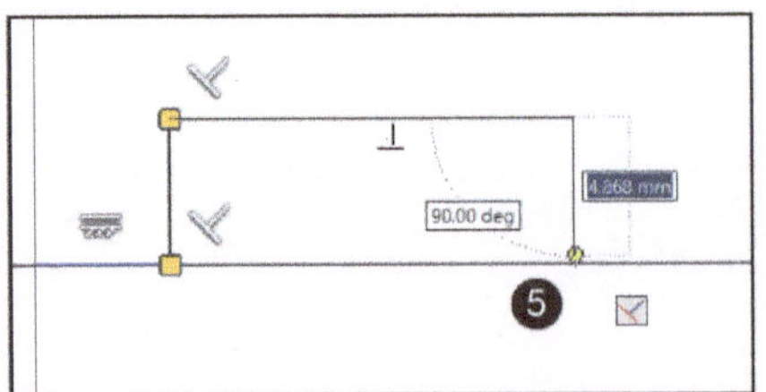

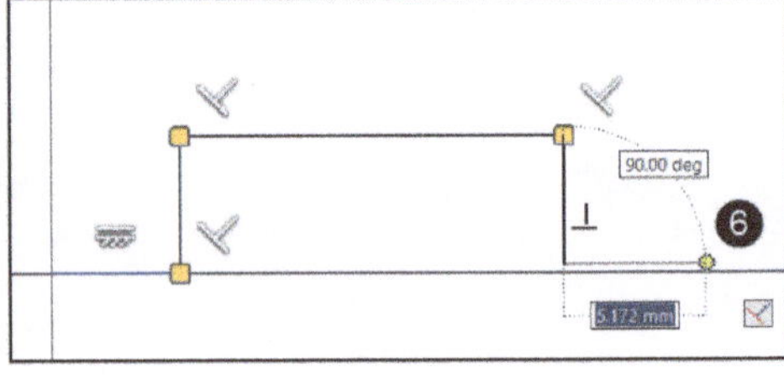

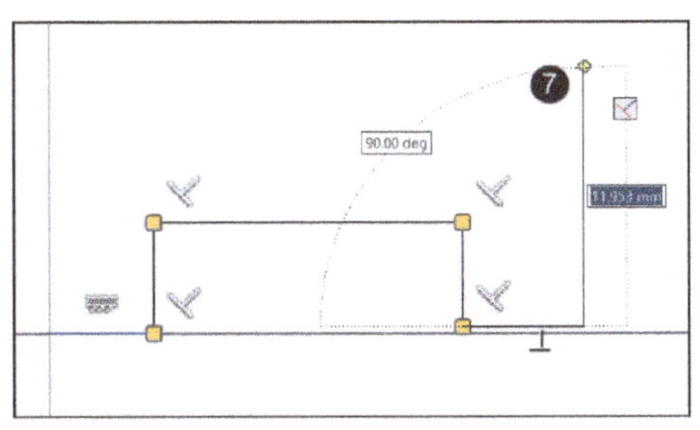
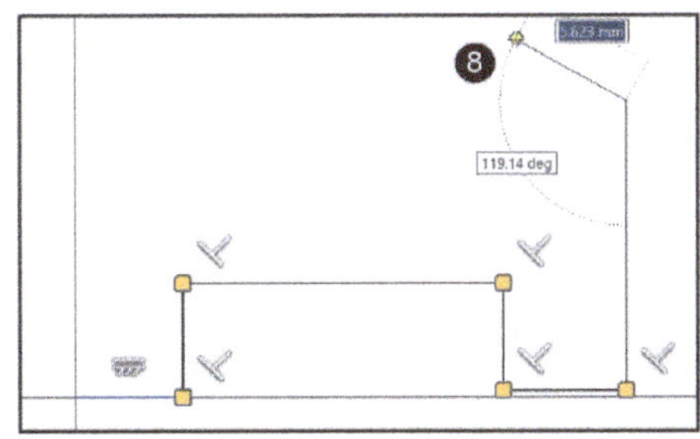
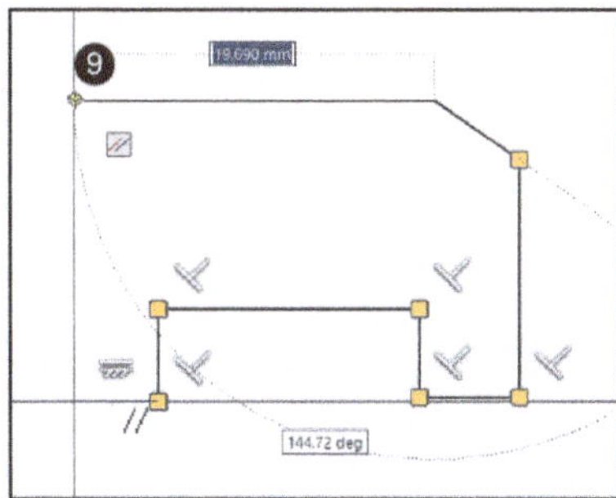
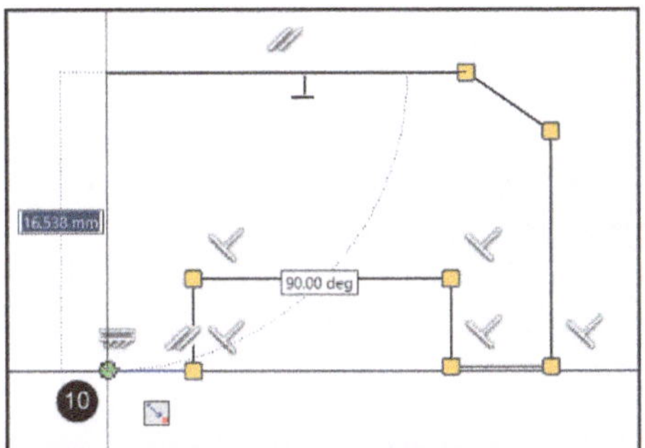

Adding Constraints

1. Click **Sketch > Constrain > Collinear Constraint** on the Ribbon, and then click on the two horizontal lines at the bottom; they become collinear.

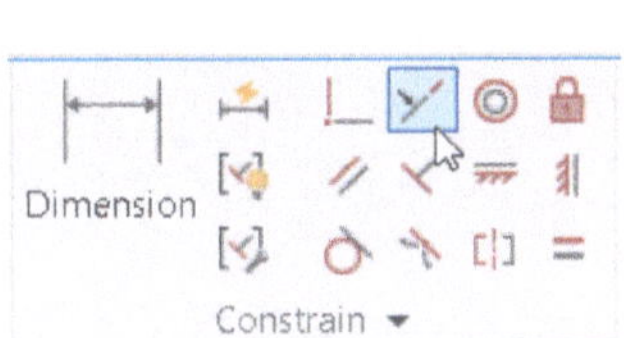

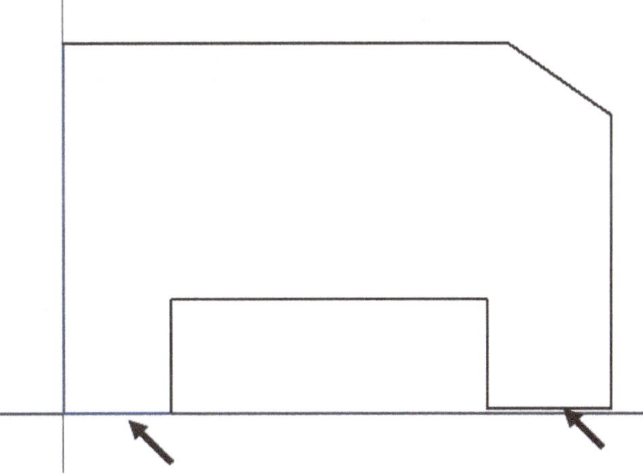

2. Click **Sketch > Constrain > Equal** on the Ribbon and click on the two horizontal lines at the bottom; they become equal in length.

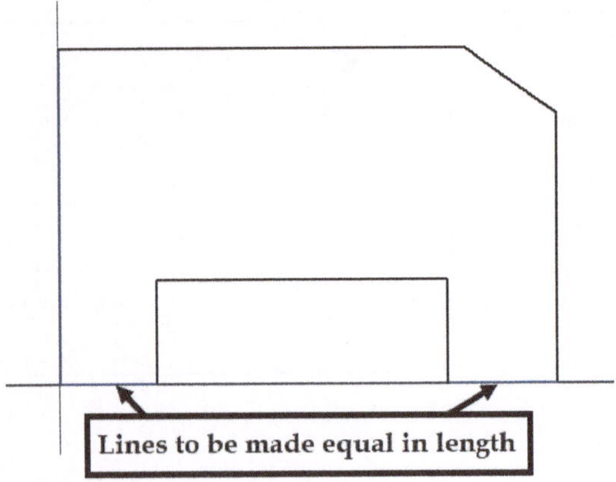

Adding Dimensions

1. On the ribbon, click **Sketch > Constrain > Constraint Settings**. On the **Constraint Settings** dialog, click the **General** tab and check the **Edit dimension when created** option. Click **OK** to close the dialog.

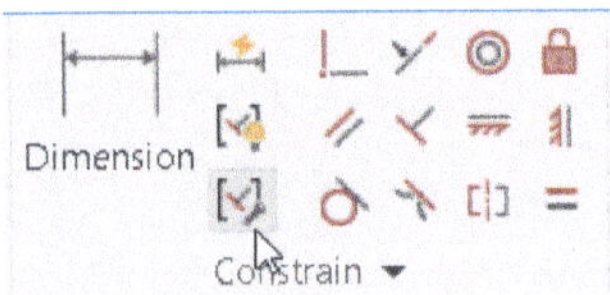

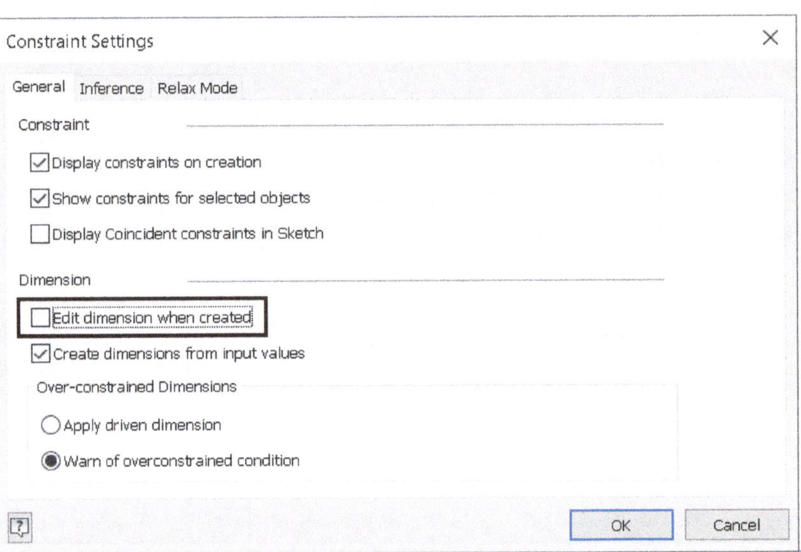

2. Click **Sketch > Constraint > Dimension** on the Ribbon and click on the left and right vertical lines. Move the mouse pointer downward and click to locate the dimension.
3. Type-in **160** in the **Edit dimension** box and press Enter.

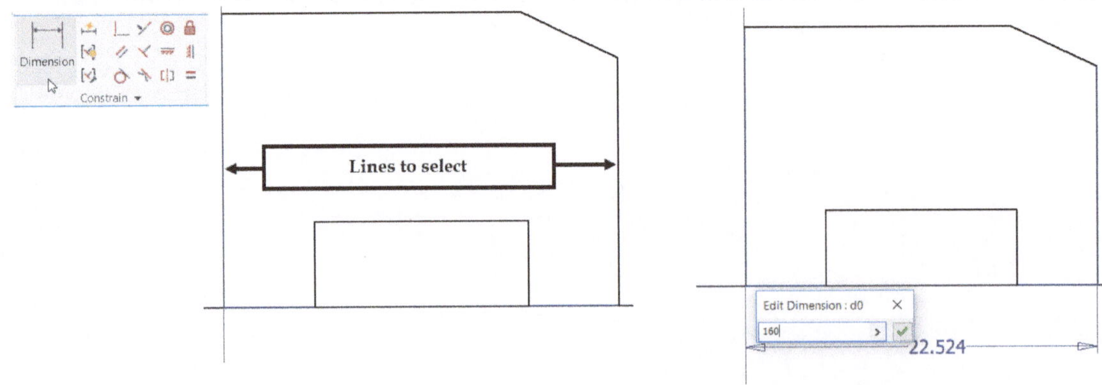

4. On the Navigate Bar, click **Zoom > Zoom All**; the sketch is fit in the graphics window.
5. Click on the lower-left horizontal line. Move the mouse pointer downward and click to locate the dimension.
6. Type-in **20** in the dimension box and press Enter.

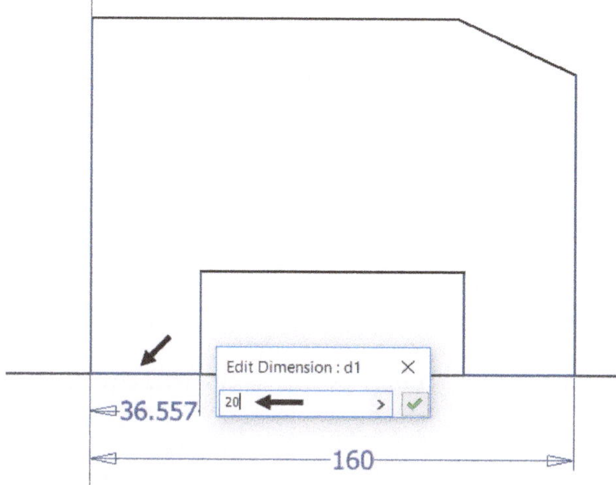

7. Click on the small vertical line located at the left side. Move the mouse pointer towards the right and click to position the dimension.
8. Type-in **25** in the dimension box and press Enter.

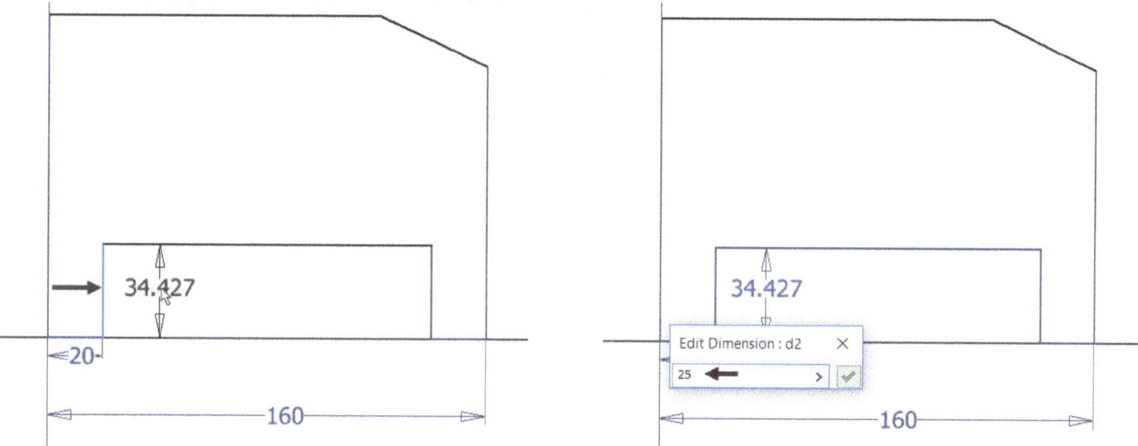

9. Create other dimensions in the sequence, as shown below. Press Esc to deactivate the **Dimension** command.

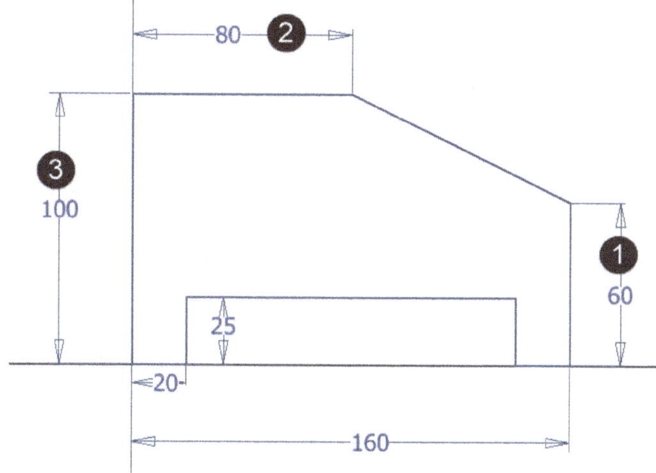

10. On the ribbon, click **Sketch > Create > Circle Center Point** . Click inside the sketch region to define the center point of the circle. Move the mouse pointer and click to define the diameter. Likewise, create another circle.

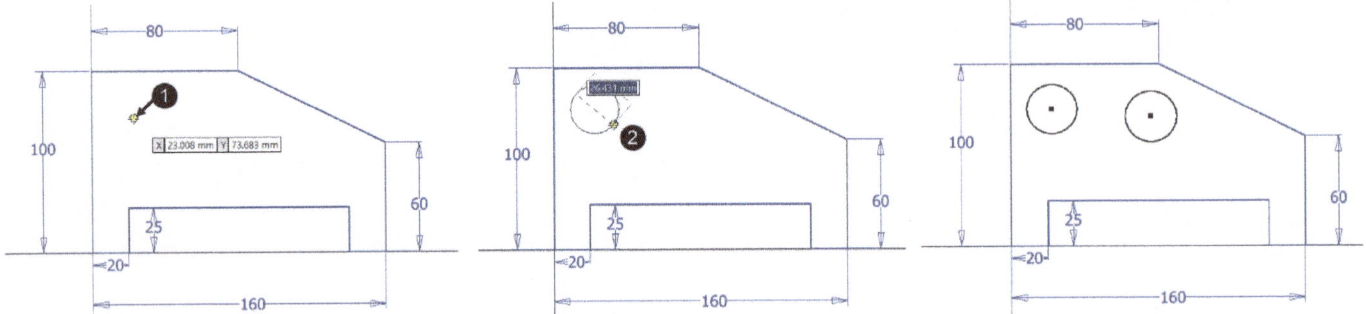

11. On the ribbon, click **Sketch > Constrain > Horizontal** . Click on the center points of the two circles to make them horizontally aligned.

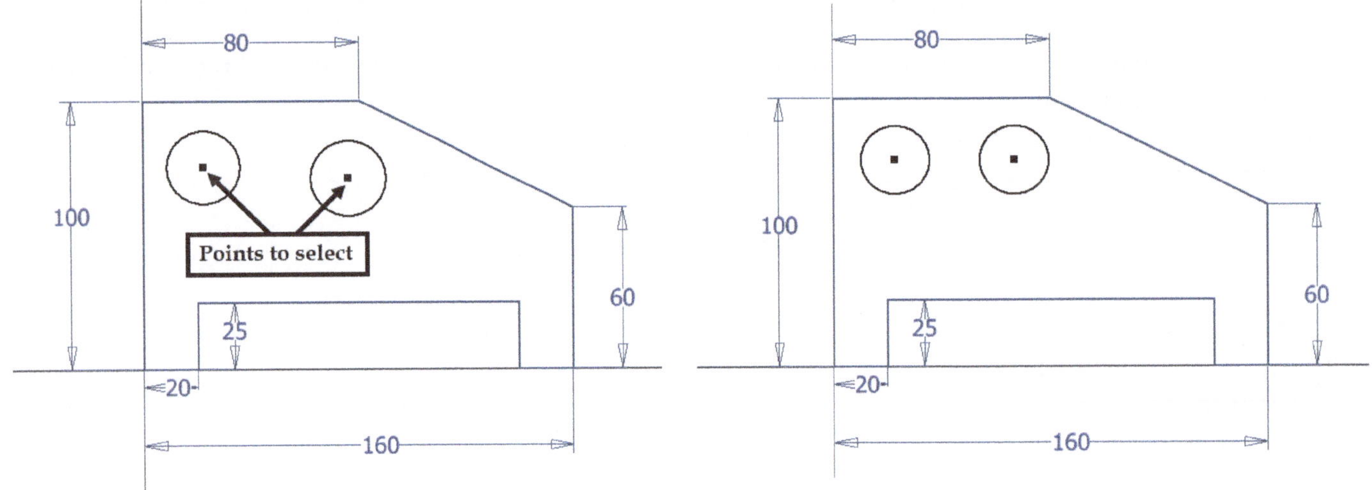

12. Select the center point of any one of the circles and the corner point, as shown; the circles are aligned horizontally with the corner point.

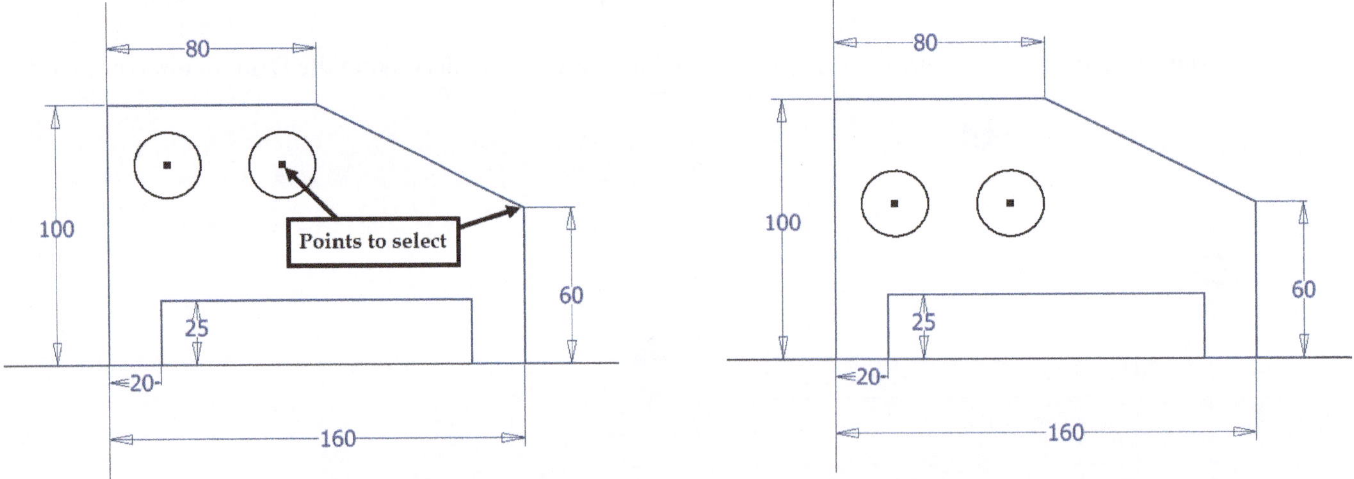

13. On the ribbon, click **Sketch > Constrain > Vertical**. Click on the center point of the left circle and the midpoint of the top horizontal line; the left circle is aligned vertically with the midpoint of the top horizontal line.

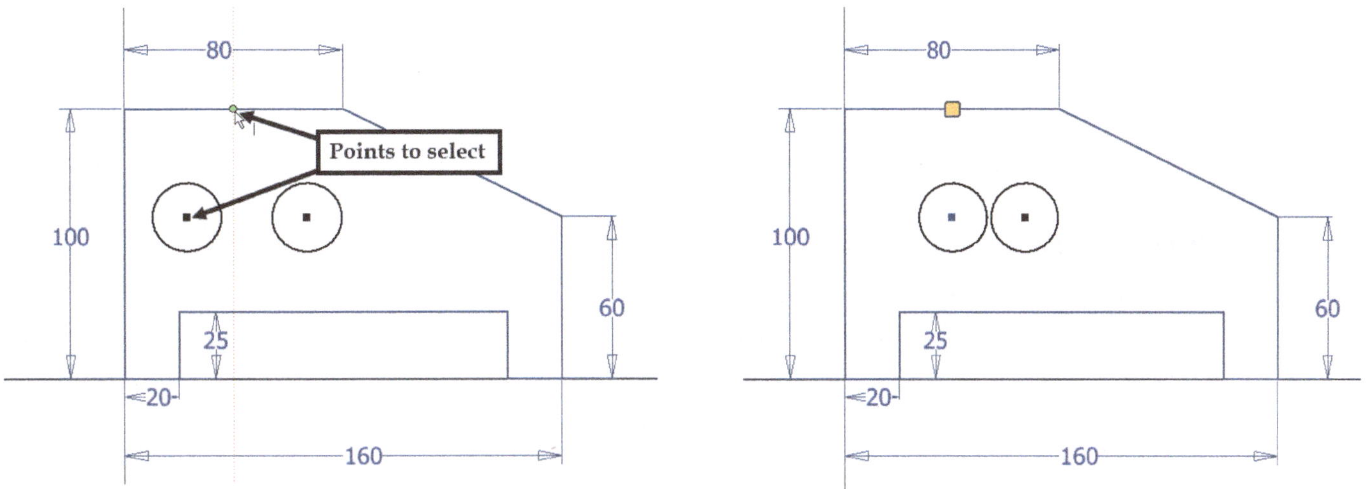

14. On the Ribbon, click **Sketch > Constrain > Equal**, and then click on the two circles. The diameters of the circles will become equal.
15. Activate the **Dimension** command and click on any one of the circles. Move the mouse pointer and click to position the dimension. Type **25** in the dimension box and press Enter. Create a dimension between the circles, as shown below.

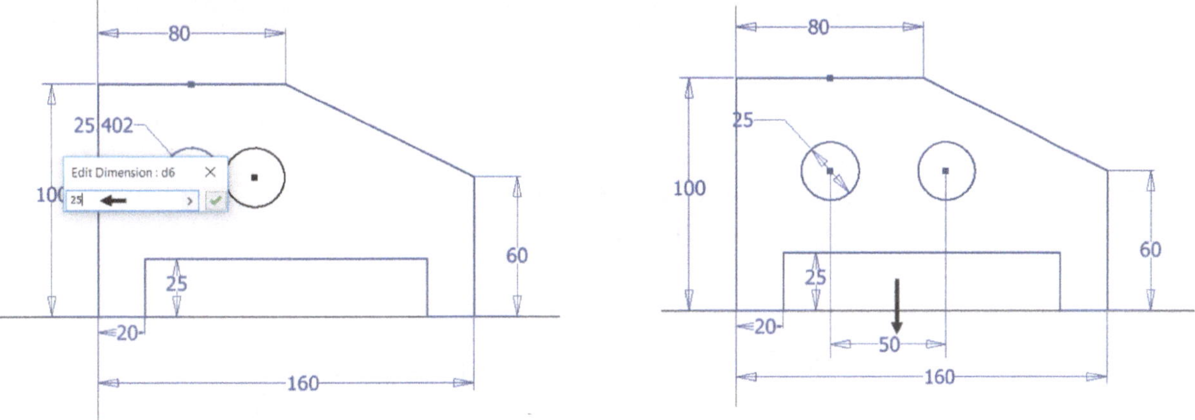

Finishing the Sketch and Saving it

1. On the Ribbon, click **Sketch > Exit > Finish Sketch** to complete the sketch.
2. Click the **Save** icon on the **Quick Access Toolbar**. Define the location and file name and click **Save** to save the part file.

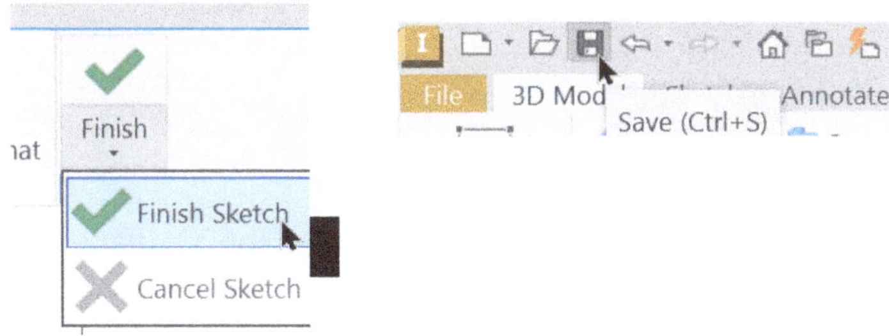

3. Click **Close** on the top right corner of the graphics window to close the part file.

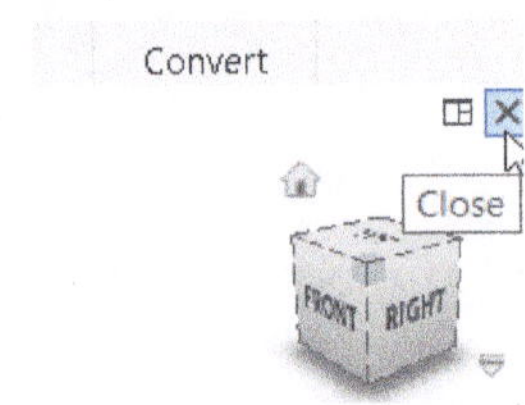

Example 2 (Inches)

In this tutorial, you will draw the sketch shown next.

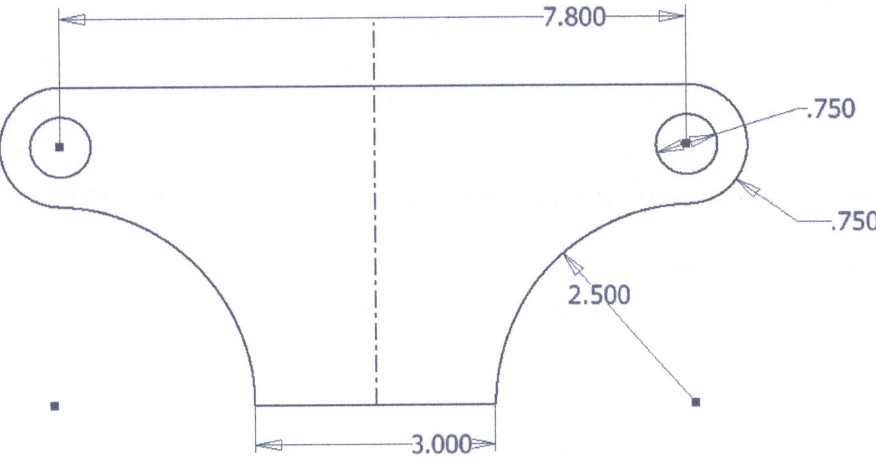

1. Start **Autodesk Inventor 2026** by double-clicking the **Autodesk Inventor 2026** icon on your desktop.
2. To start a new part file, click **New** drop-down **> New** on the **Home** screen.
3. On the **Create New File** dialog, click the **Templates > en-US** folder.
4. Click the **Standard.ipt** icon under the **Part – Create 2D and 3D objects** section.

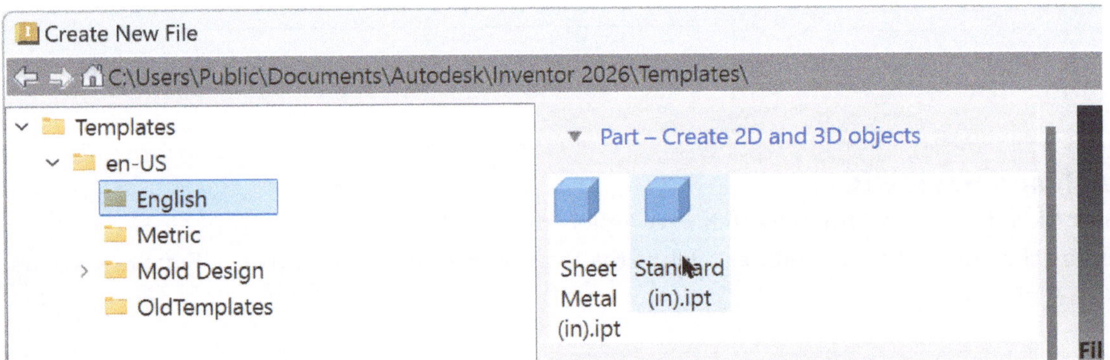

5. Click the **Create** button on the **Create New File** dialog.

Starting a Sketch

1. To start a sketch, click **3D Model > Sketch > Start 2D Sketch** on the ribbon. Click on the XY plane. The sketch starts.

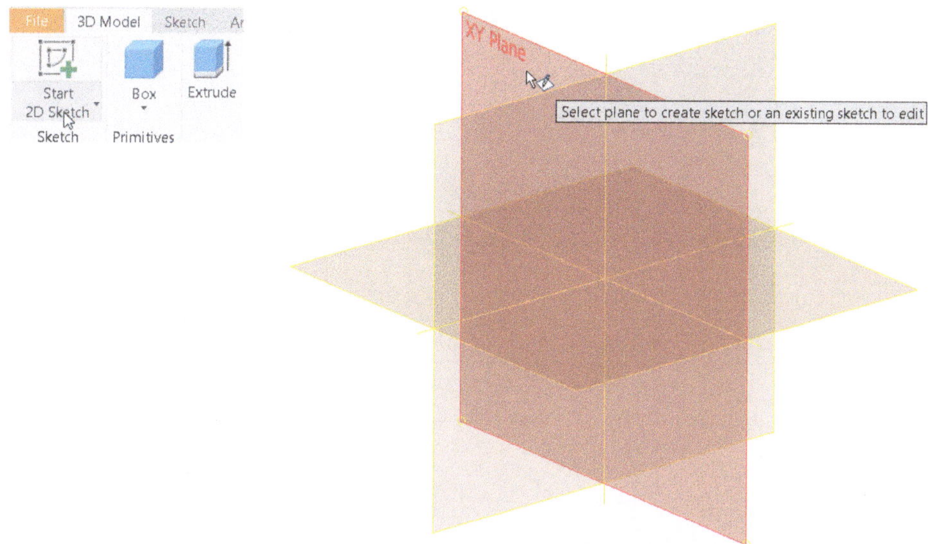

2. Activate the **Line** command (On the Ribbon, click **Sketch > Create > Line**).
3. Click on the second quadrant of the coordinate system to define the start point of the profile. Drag the pointer horizontally and click to define the endpoint.

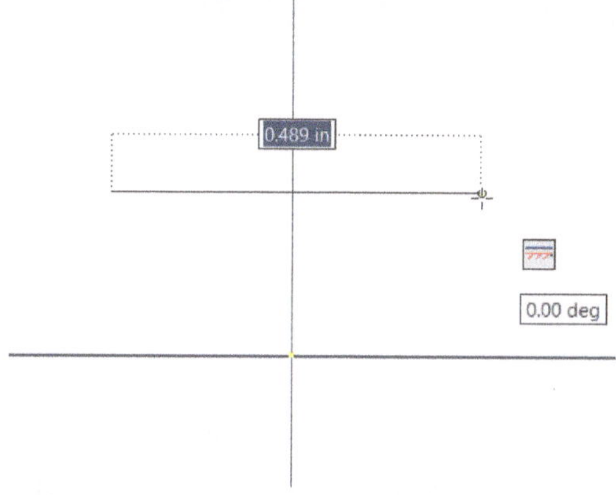

4. Take the pointer to the endpoint of the line. Next, press and hold the left mouse button and drag the pointer along the vertical dotted line. Move the pointer towards the right, as shown. Release the left mouse button to create an arc normal to the horizontal line.

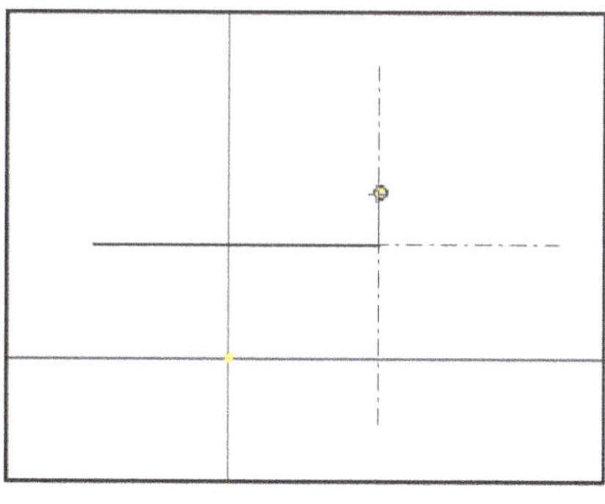

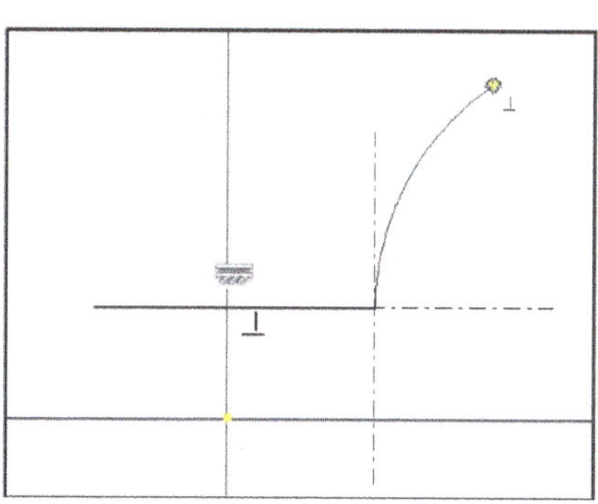

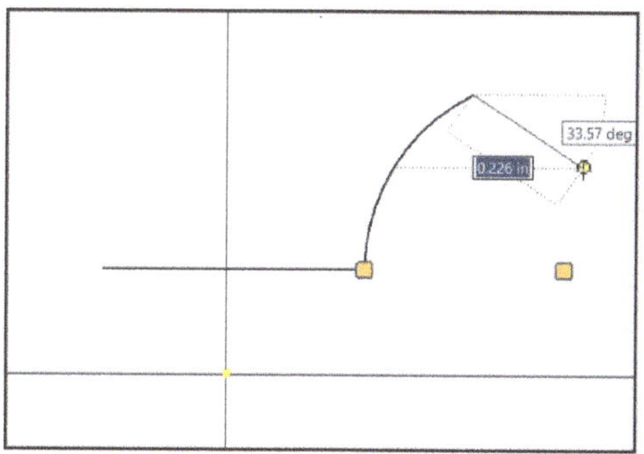

5. Take the pointer to the endpoint of the arc. Next, press and hold the left mouse button and drag it towards the right and then upwards. Release the left mouse button when a vertical dotted line appears, as shown.

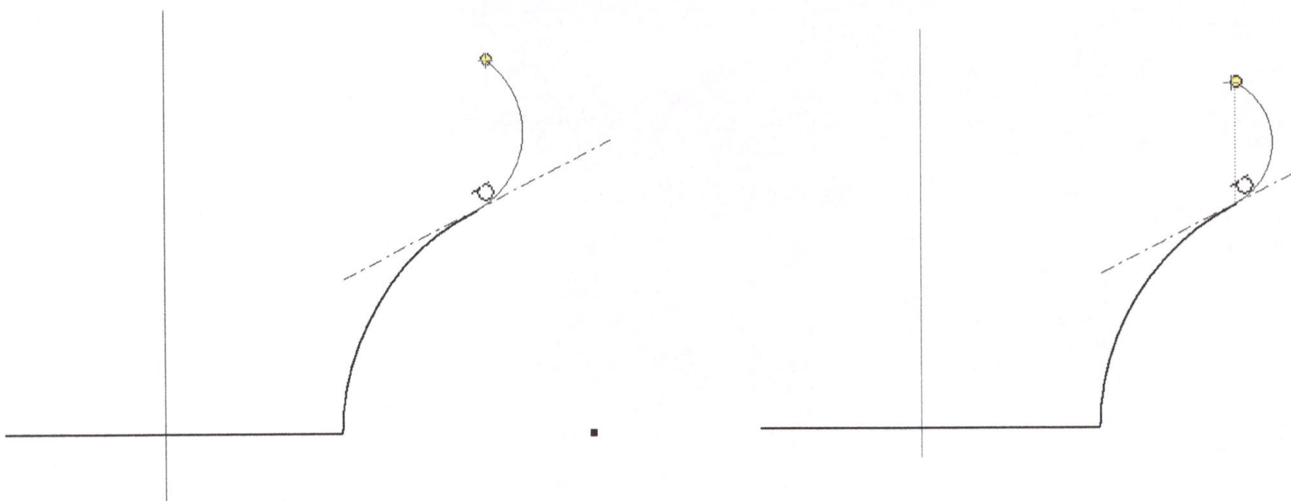

6. Move the pointer toward the left and click to create a horizontal line.

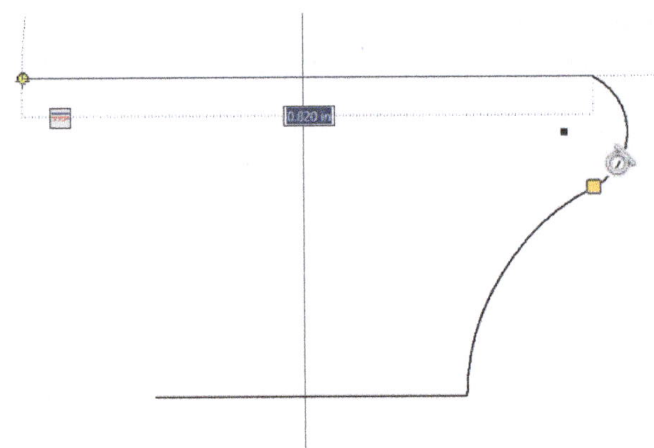

7. On the ribbon, click **Sketch > Create > Arc drop-down > Arc Three Point** . Select the endpoint of the line and move it downward and click when a vertical dotted line appears, as shown. Move the pointer towards the left and click when the Tangent constraint symbol appears.

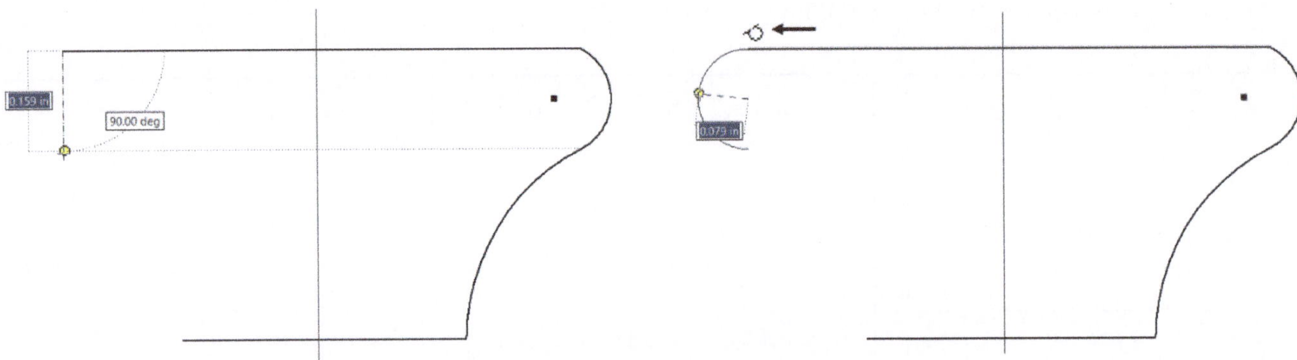

8. Make sure that the **Arc** command is active. Select the endpoint of the last arc and move the pointer downward and click on the start point of the lower horizontal line. Move the pointer upward right, and then click to close the sketch. Click the right mouse button and click **OK**.

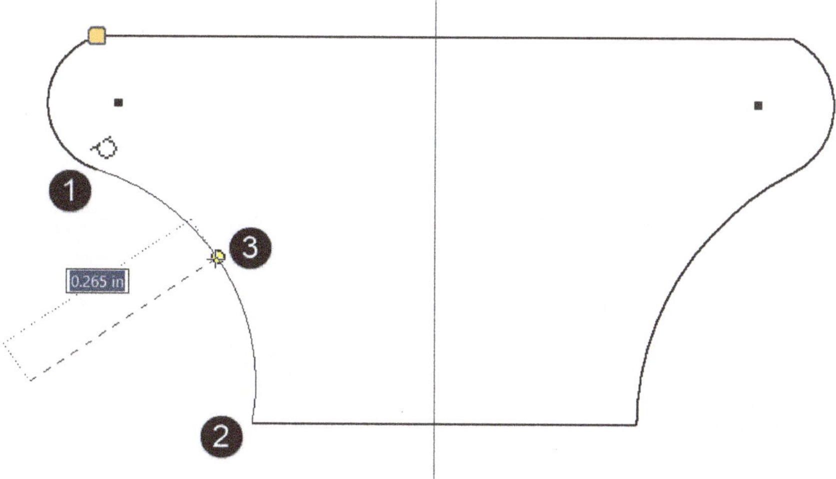

9. Click **Sketch > Create > Circle Center Point** on the Ribbon. Draw a circle inside the closed sketch, as shown.

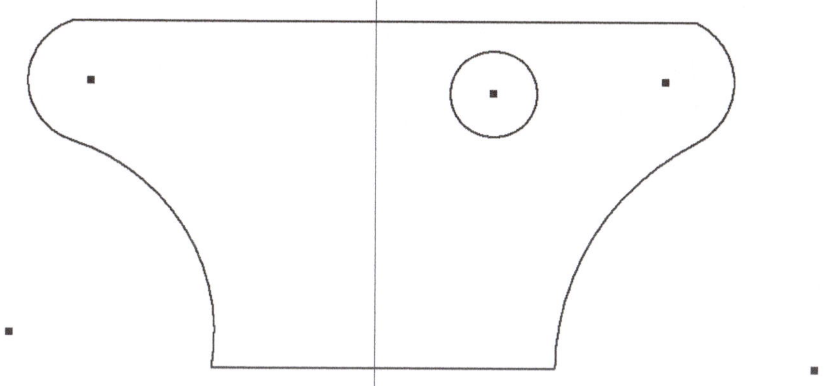

10. Click **Sketch > Constrain > Concentric Constraint** on the ribbon.

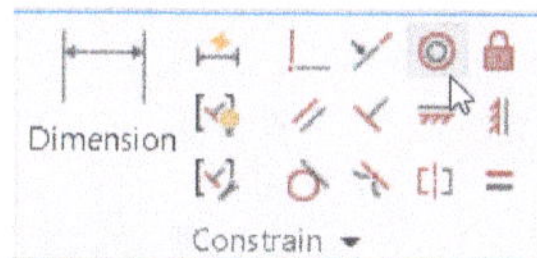

11. Click on the circle and small arc on the upper right. The circle and arc are made concentric.

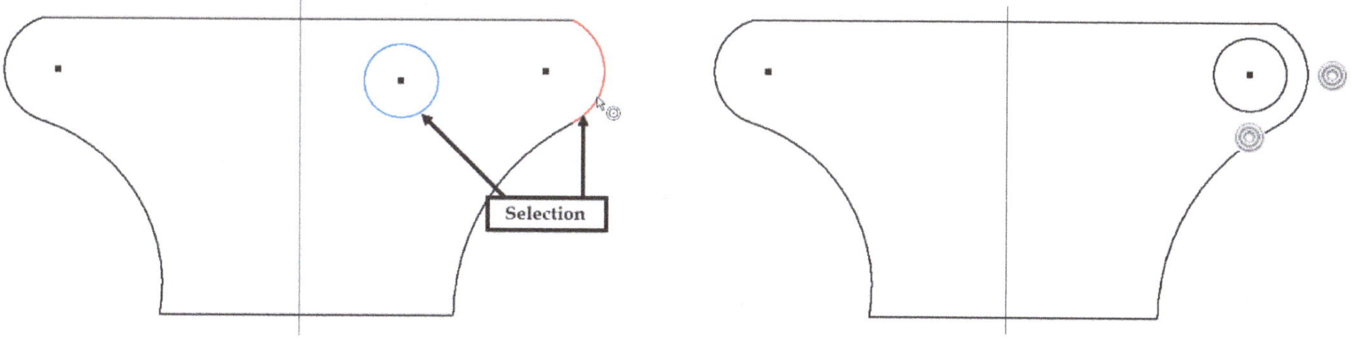

12. Likewise, create another circle concentric to the small arc located on the left side.

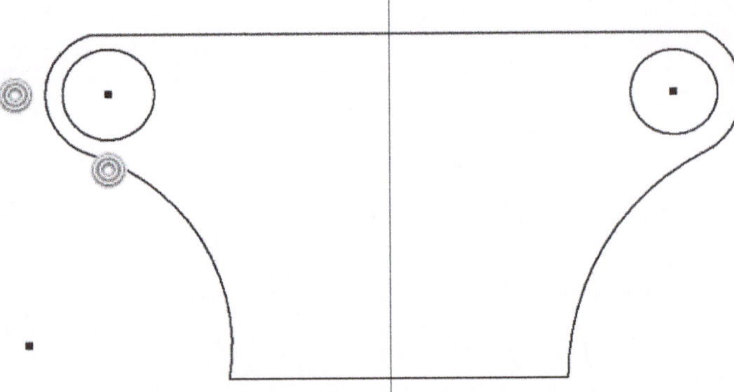

13. On the ribbon, click **Sketch > Format > Centerline**. Next, activate the **Line** command and create a vertical line starting from the sketch origin.

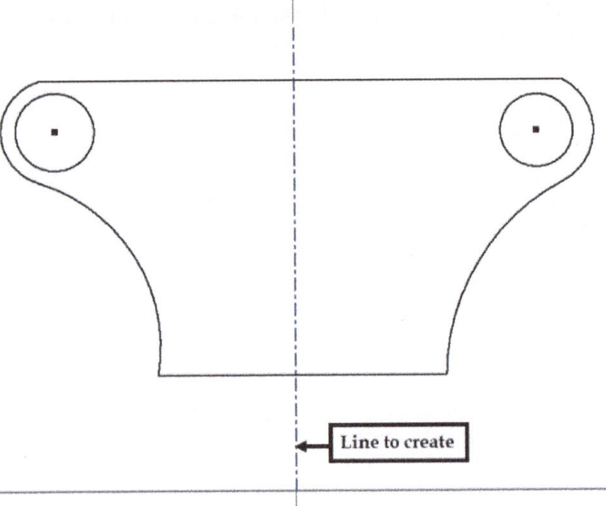

14. On the ribbon, click **Sketch > Constrain > Symmetric**.

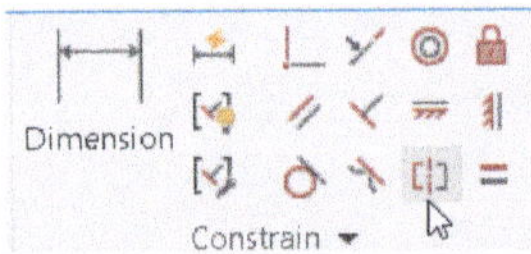

15. Click on the large arcs on both sides of the centerline. Next, select the centerline; arcs are made symmetric about the centerline.

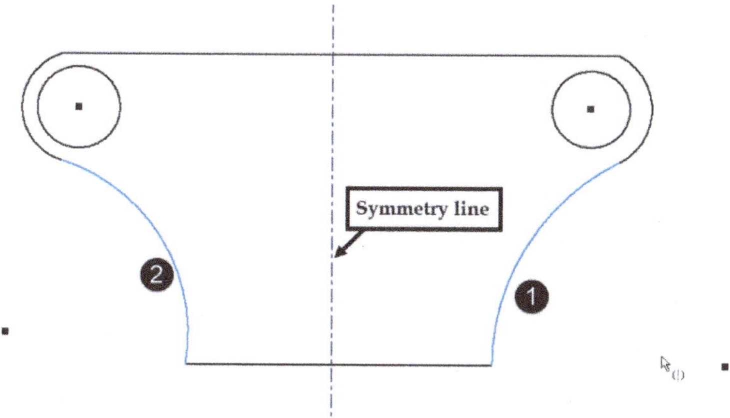

16. Likewise, make the small arcs and circles symmetric about the centerline.

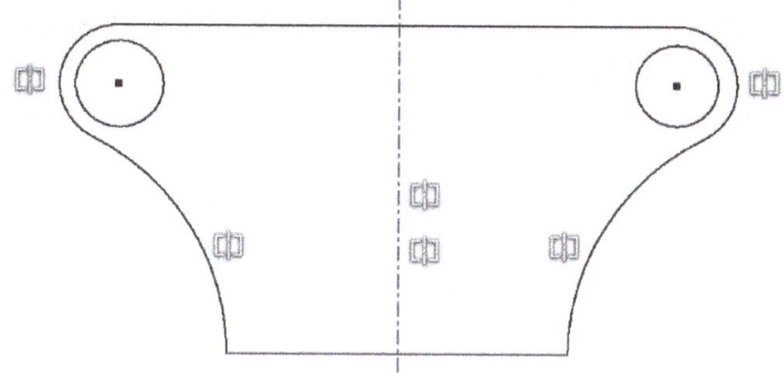

17. On the Ribbon, click **Sketch > Constraint > Coincident Constraint**, and then select the bottom horizontal line and sketch origin.

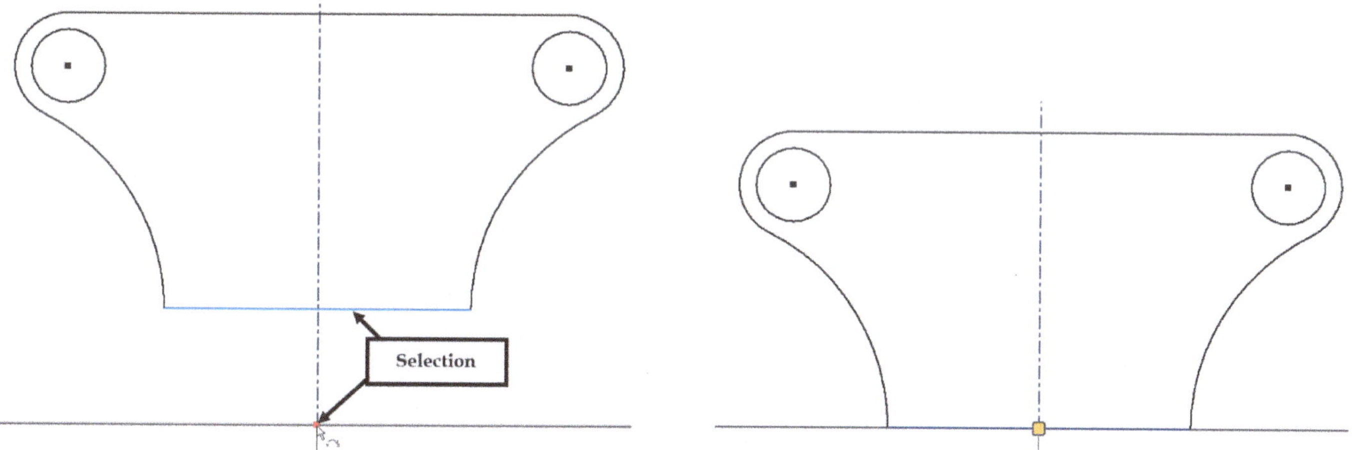

18. Activate the **Dimension** command and apply dimensions to the sketch in the sequence, as shown below.

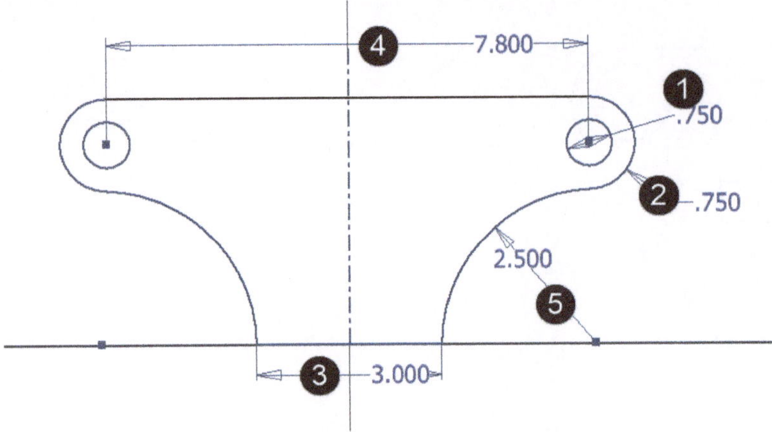

19. On the Navigation pane, click **Zoom > Zoom All** to fit the drawing in the graphics window. The sketch is fully constrained, and all the sketch elements are displayed in blue color.
20. Click **Finish Sketch** on the Ribbon to complete the sketch.
21. To save the file, click **File > Save**.
22. On the **Save As** dialog, specify the location of the file and type-in **C1_Example2** in the **File name** box and click the **Save** button.
23. To close the file, click **File > Close > Close All**.

Example 3 (Millimeters)

In this tutorial, you will draw the sketch shown below.

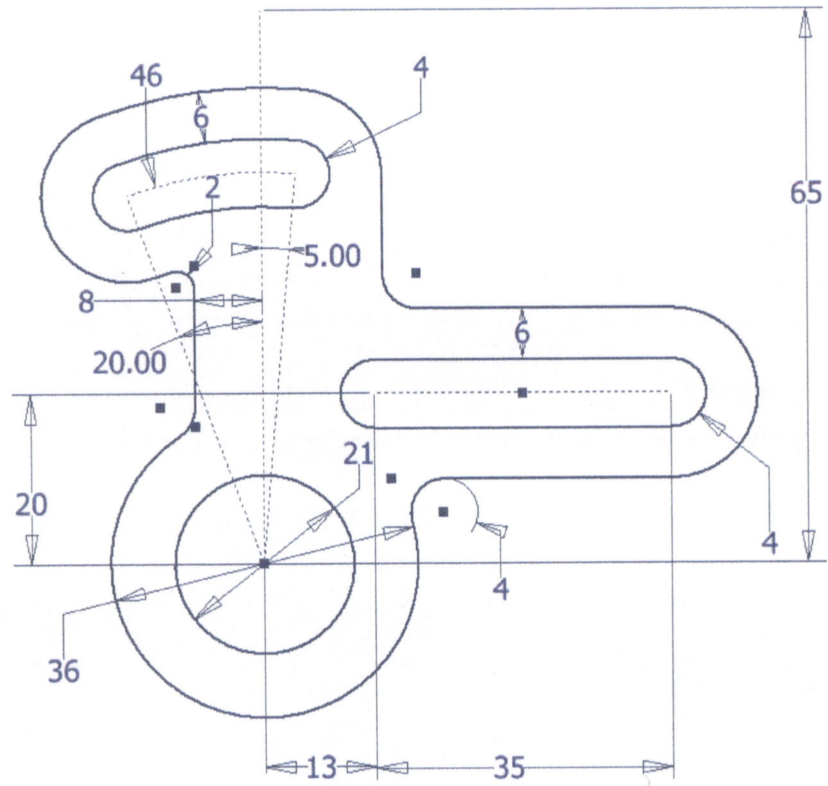

1. Start **Autodesk Inventor 2026** by double-clicking the **Autodesk Inventor 2026** icon on your desktop.
2. To start a new part file, click **New** drop-down **>** **New** on the **Home** screen.
3. On the **Create New File** dialog, click the **Metric** folder under **Templates**.
4. Click the **Standard(mm).ipt** icon under the **Part - Create 2D and 3D Objects** section.
5. Click the **Create** button on the **Create New File** dialog.

A new model window appears.

Starting a Sketch

1. To start a sketch, click **3D Model > Sketch > Start 2D Sketch** on the ribbon. Click on the XZ plane. The sketch starts.

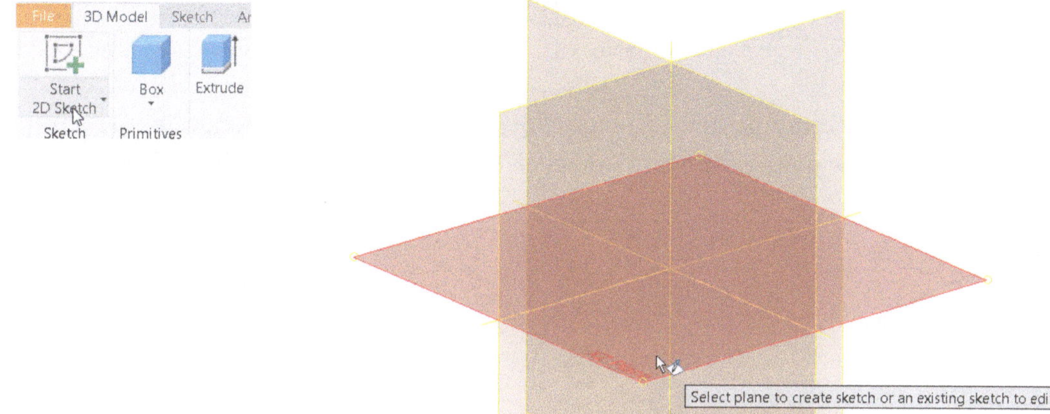

2. Click **Sketch > Create > Circle Center Point** on the Ribbon. Click on the origin point to define the center point of the circle. Move the pointer outward and click to create a circle.
3. Likewise, create another circle with the origin point as its center.
4. On the Ribbon, click **Sketch > Constrain > Dimension** and select the inner circle. Place the dimension and type in **21** in the **Edit Dimension** box. Click the green check; the size of the outer circle is adjusted automatically.
5. On the **Navigate Bar**, click **Zoom**, press and hold the left mouse button, and drag the pointer upward; the sketch is zoomed out. Right click and select **OK**.
6. On the ribbon, click **Sketch > Create > Rectangle** drop-down > **Slot Center Point Arc** . Select the sketch origin to define the center point of the arc, and then define the start and endpoints of the arc, as shown. Move the pointer outward and click to define the slot width. Right click and select **OK**.

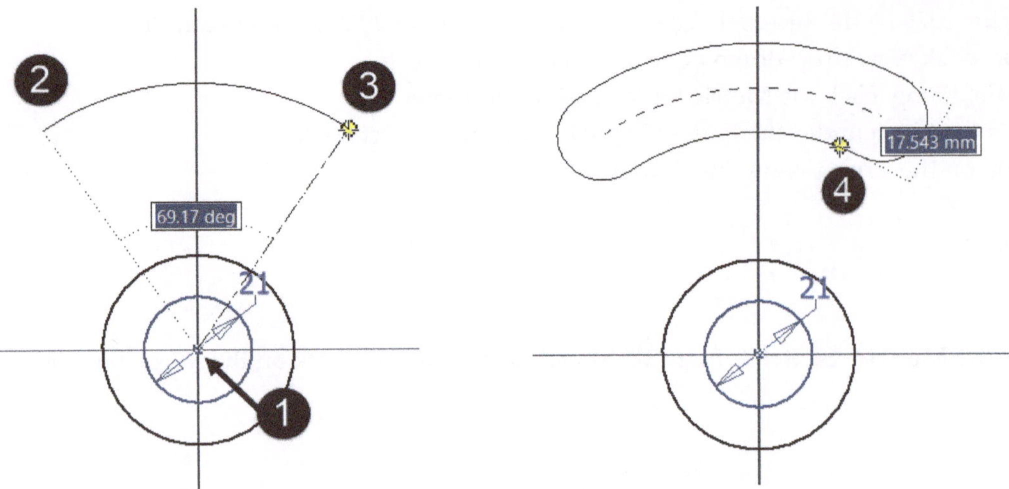

7. On the ribbon, click **Sketch > Create > Rectangle** drop-down **> Slot Center to Center** . Specify the center points of the endcaps, and then move the pointer outward and click to define its width. Right click and select **OK**.

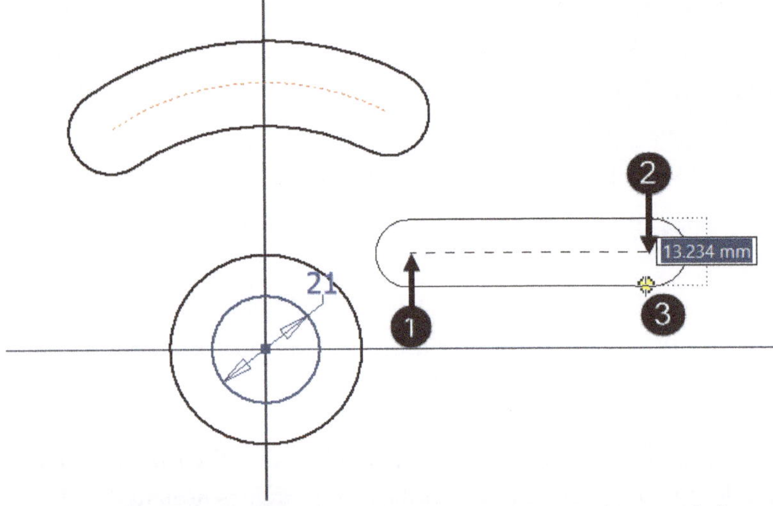

8. On the Ribbon, click **Sketch > Format > Construction**, and then create a vertical line starting from the sketch origin. Likewise, create two more lines passing through the center points of the slot. Click on the **Construction** icon on the **Format** panel to deactivate it. Make sure that both the construction lines coincide with the origin point.

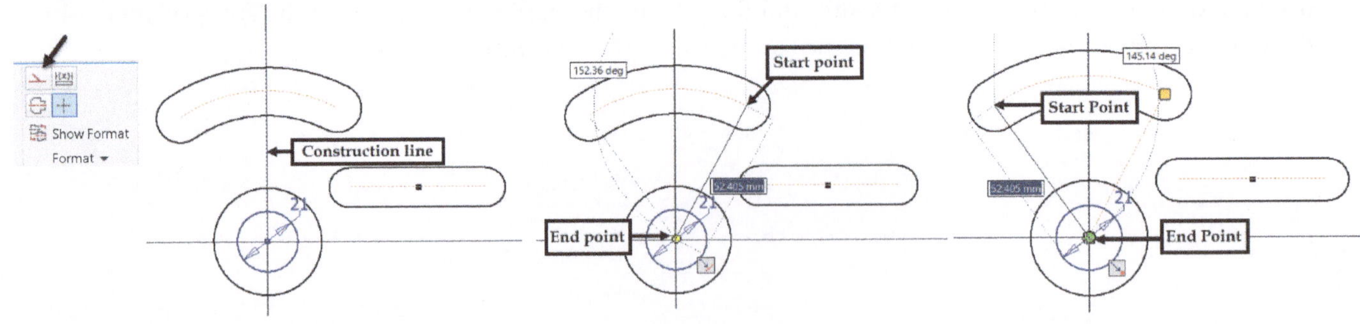

9. On the ribbon, click **Sketch > Constrain > Dimension**. Select the vertical construction line and the right construction line. Move the pointer between the two lines and click to place the dimension. Type-in **5** in the Edit dimension box, and then click the green check.
10. Likewise, create another angled dimension between the vertical and left construction lines, as shown.

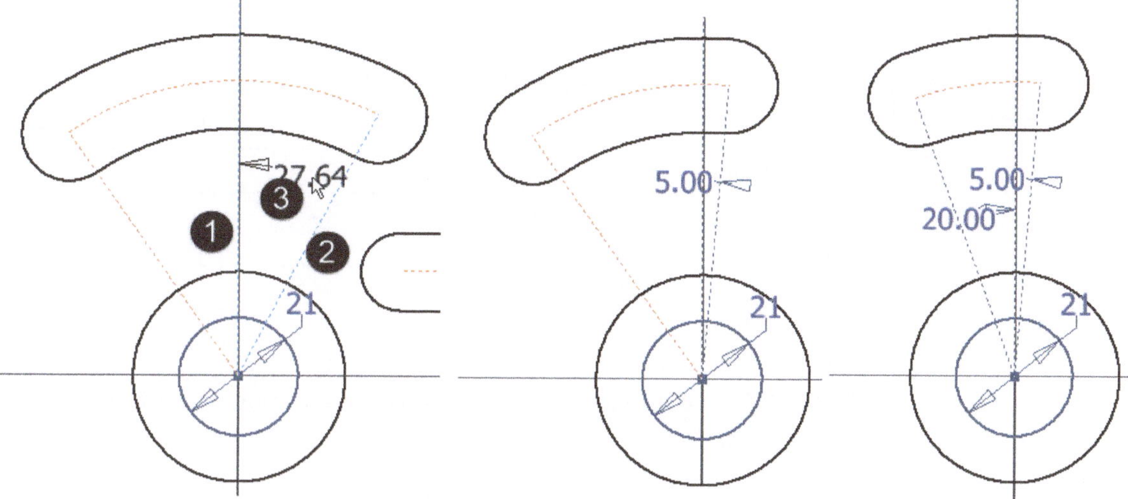

11. Add remaining dimensions to the sketch, as shown.

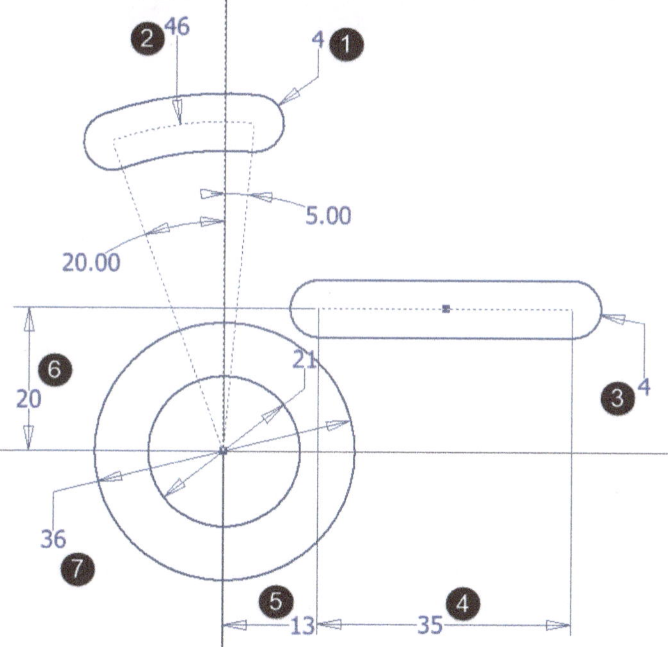

12. On the ribbon, click **Sketch > Modify > Offset** . Select the arc slot, move the pointer outward, type **6**, and press Enter. Likewise, offset the straight slot by **6** mm distance.

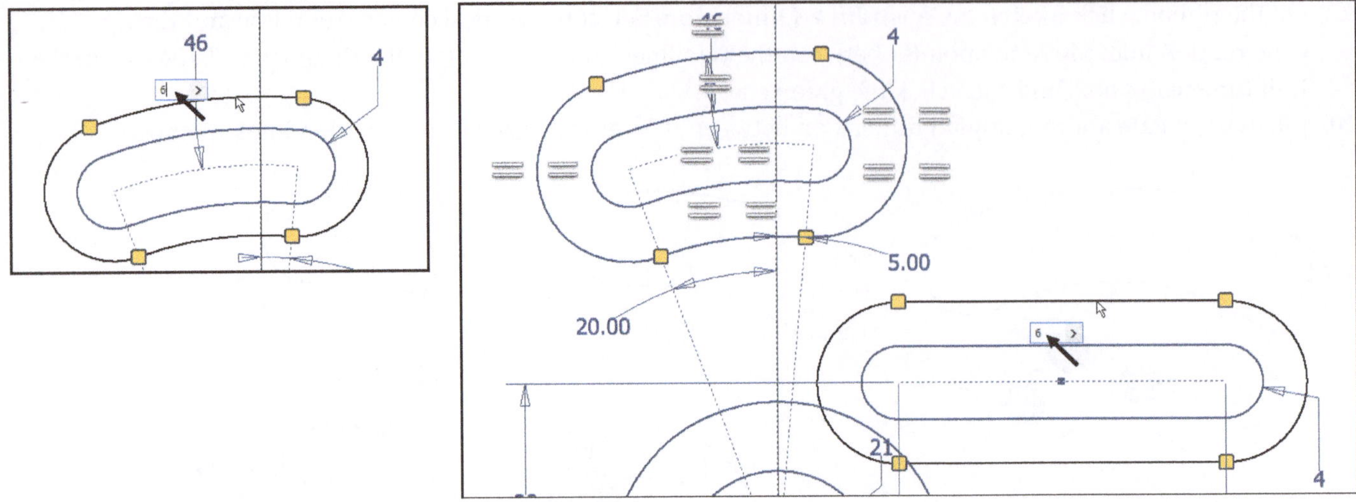

13. Select the vertical construction line with the **Offset** command still active. Move the pointer toward the left, type **8**, and press Enter. Right click and select **OK**.

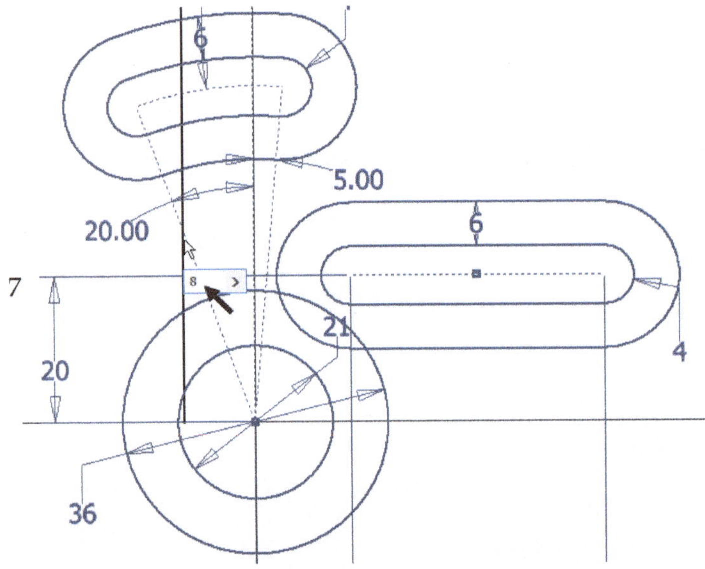

14. On the ribbon, click **Sketch > Create > Line**. Specify the start point on the offset of the arc slot, as shown. Move the pointer vertically downward and click on the offset of the straight slot.

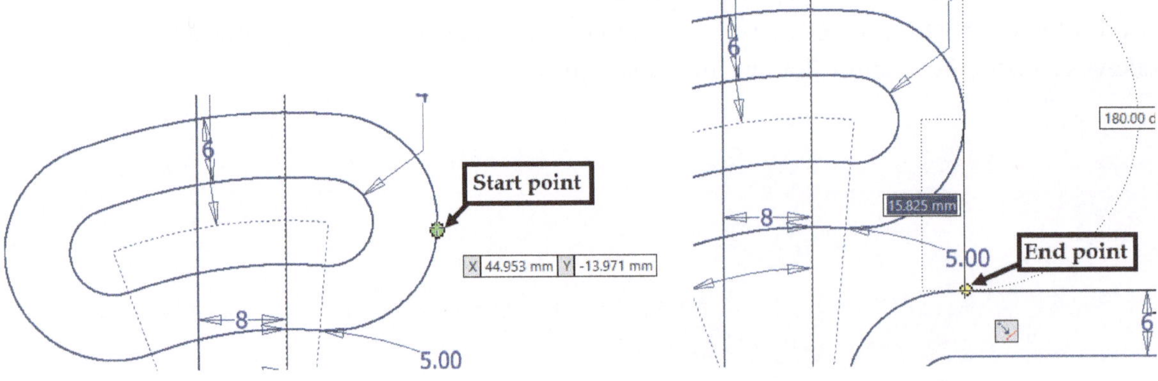

15. On the Ribbon, click **Sketch > Modify > Trim** and click on the portions of the sketch, as shown. Right click and select **OK**.

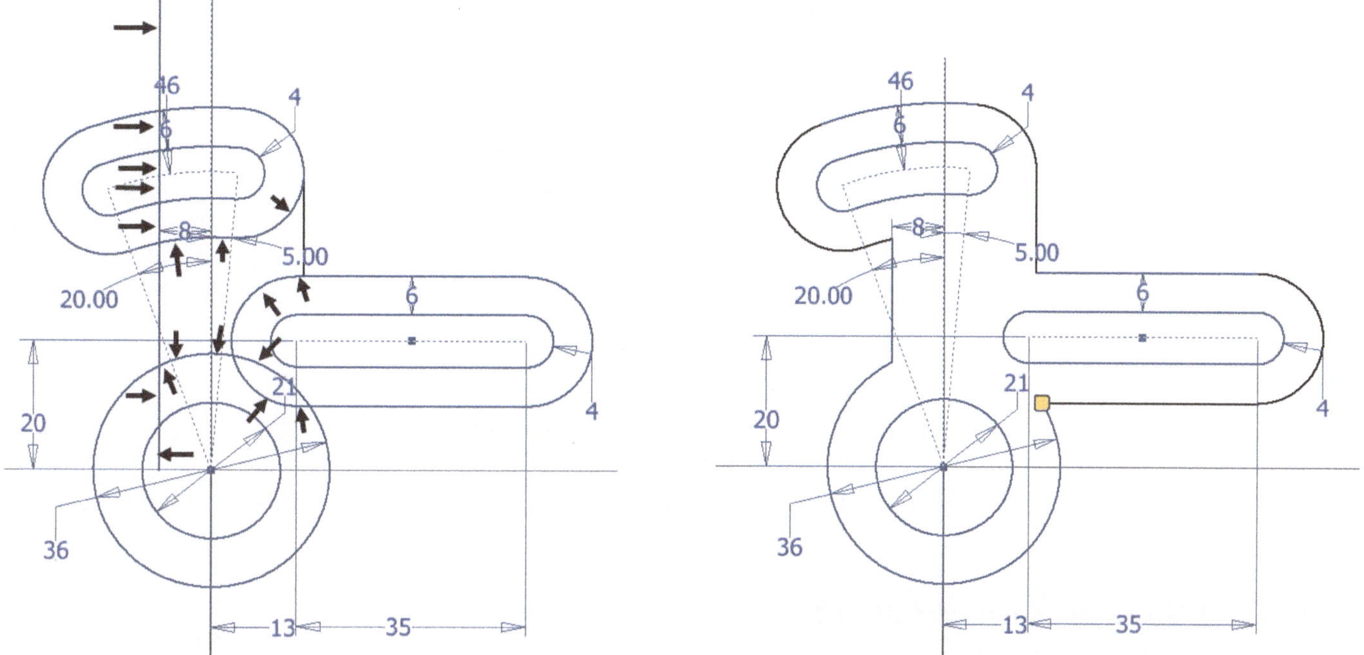

16. On the ribbon, click **Sketch > Create > Fillet** . Type **4** in the **Radius** box of the **2D Fillet** dialog. Select the entities at the three corners, as shown.
17. Type **2** in the **Radius** box and select the entities forming the corner, a shown.

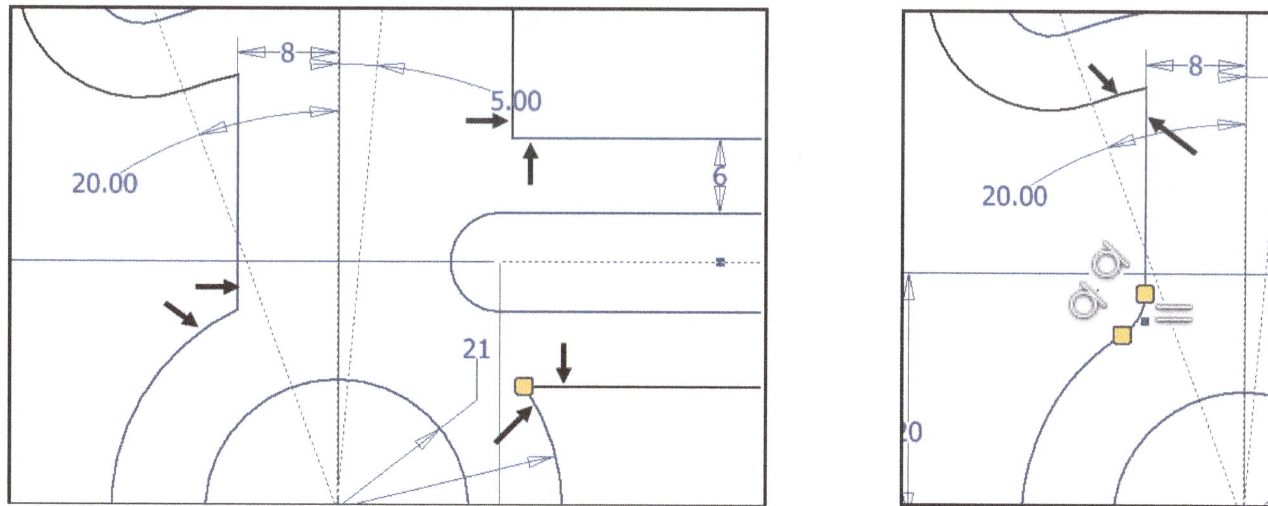

18. On the ribbon, click **Sketch > Constrain > Tangent**. Apply the tangent constraint between the set of entities, as shown.

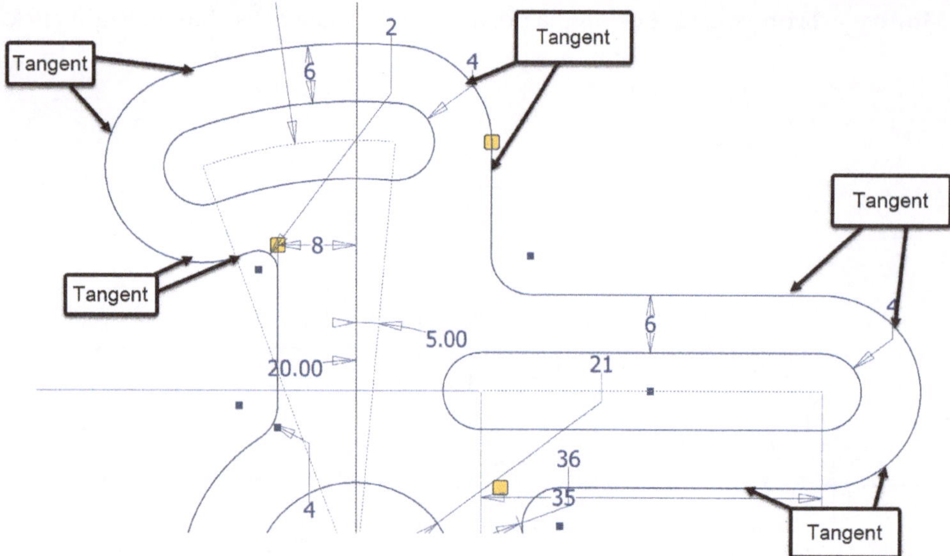

The sketch turns blue, which means that it is fully defined. However, the status shows that 1 dimension is still needed to define the sketch fully.

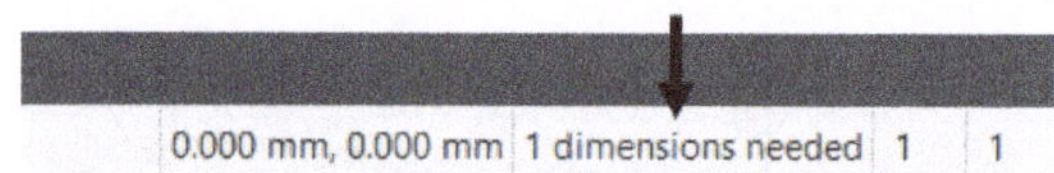

19. Add dimension to the vertical construction line; the status bar now displays the **Fully Constrained** message.
20. Click **Finish Sketch** on the Ribbon to complete the sketch.
21. To save the file, click **File > Save.**
22. On the **Save As** dialog, specify the location of the file and type-in **C1_Example3** in the **File name** box and click the **Save** button.
23. To close the file, click **File > Close > Close All.**

Questions

1. What is the procedure to create sketches in Inventor?
2. List any two sketch *Constraints* in Inventor.
3. Which command allows you to apply dimensions to a sketch automatically?
4. Describe two methods to create circles.
5. How do you define the shape and size of a sketch?
6. How do you create a tangent arc using the **Line** command?
7. Which command is used to apply multiple types of dimensions to a sketch?
8. List the commands to create arcs?
9. List the commands to create slots?
10. What are inferred constraints?

Exercises

Exercise 1

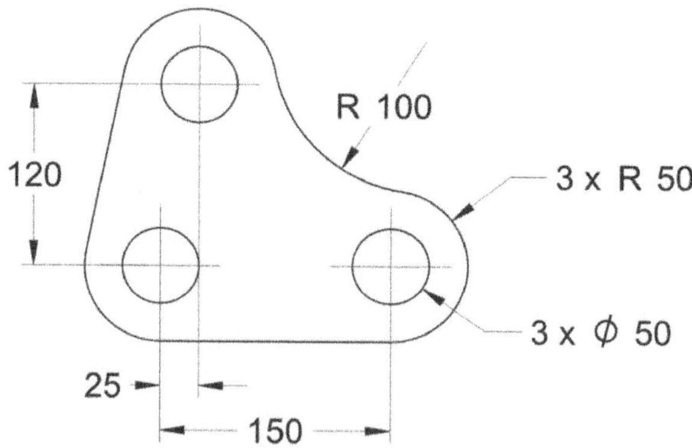

Exercise 2

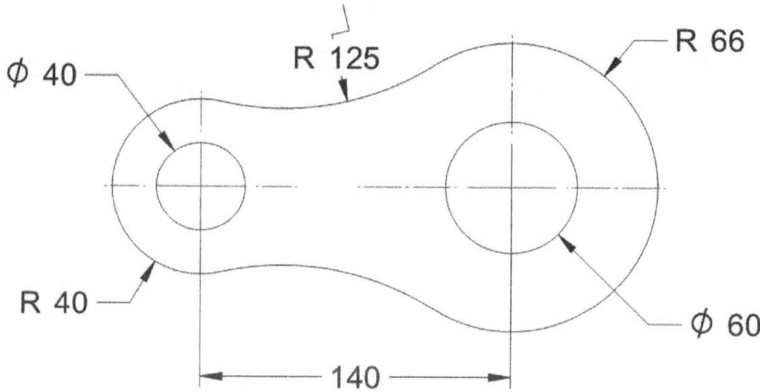

Exercise 3

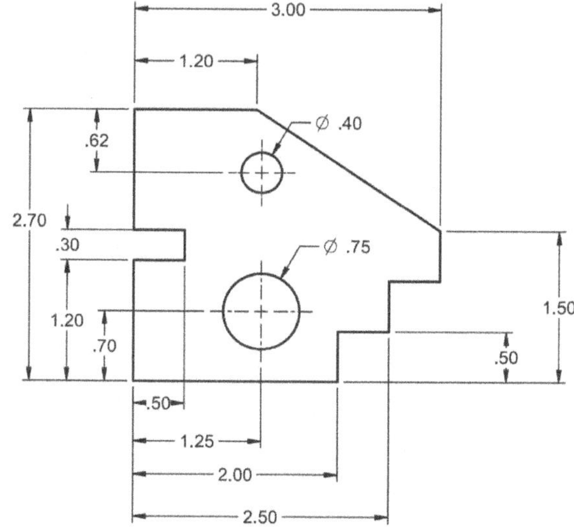

Chapter 3: Extrude and Revolve Features

Extrude and revolve features are used to create basic and simple parts. Most of the time, they form the base for complex parts as well. These features are easy to create and require a single sketch. Now, you will learn the commands to create these features.

In this chapter, you will learn to:

- Create *Extrude* and *Revolve* features in the part model
- Create Work Planes
- Work with additional options in the *Extrude* and *Revolve* commands

Extruded Features

Extruding is the process of taking a two-dimensional profile and converting it into a 3D model by giving it some thickness. A simple example of this would be taking a circle and converting it into a cylinder. Once you have created a sketch profile or profiles you want to *Extrude*, activate the **Extrude** command (On the ribbon click **3D Model > Create > Extrude**); the sketch is selected automatically. Click inside the sketch profile, if not already selected. Type-in a value in the **Distance A** box to specify the thickness of the *Extruded* feature.

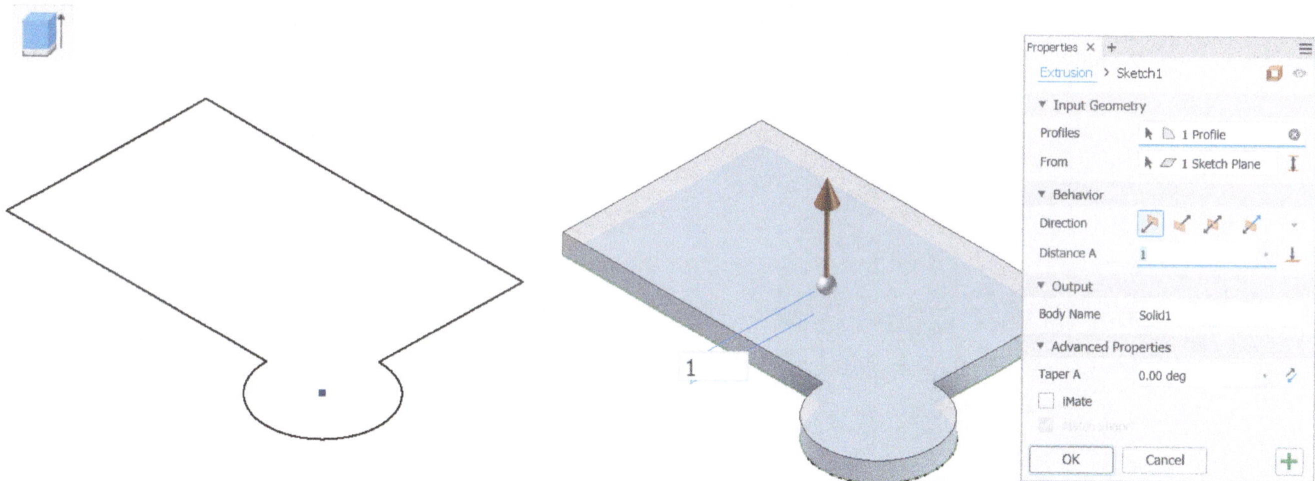

You can click the **Symmetric** icon on the dialog to add equal thickness on both sides of the sketch.

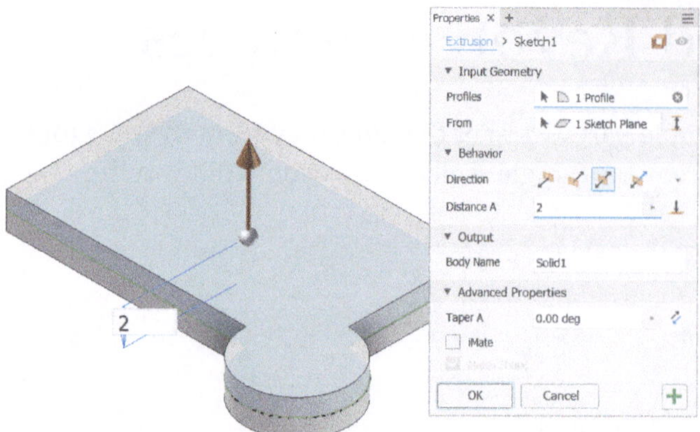

On the **Extrude Properties** panel, enter a name in the **Body name** box under the **Output** section. Next, click **OK** to complete the *Extruded* feature.

Revolved Features

Revolve is the process of taking a two-dimensional profile and revolving it about a centerline to create a 3D geometry (axially symmetric shapes). While creating a sketch for the *Revolved* feature, it is essential to think about the cross-sectional shape that will define the 3D geometry once it is revolved around an axis. For instance, the following geometry has a hole in the center. This could be created with a separate *Extruded Cut* or *Hole* feature. However, in order to make that hole part of the *Revolved* feature, you need to sketch the axis of revolution so that it leaves a space between the profile and the axis.

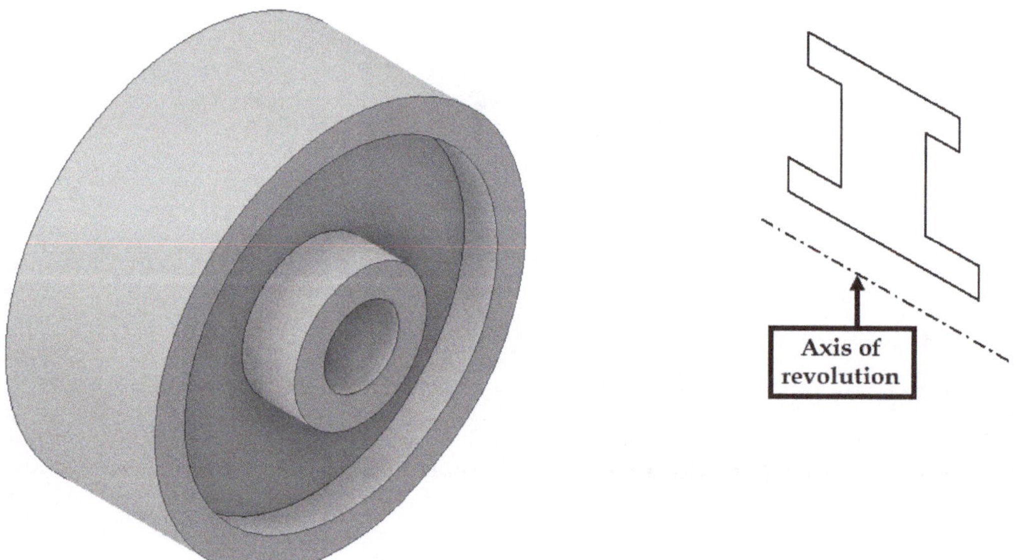

After completing the sketch, activate the **Revolve** command (On the Ribbon, click **3D Model > Create > Revolve**); the sketch profile is selected, automatically. Click on the sketch to define the section of the *Revolved* feature, if the sketch is not already selected. Also, notice that the axis of revolution is selected if you have sketched the axis using the **Centerline** command. You need to click the **Axis** button on the dialog and select the axis if you have created it using the simple **Line** or **Construction** command.

On the **Revolve Properties** panel, select **Full** icon under the **Behavior** section; the sketch will be revolved by full 360 degrees. You can also specify an angle in the **Angle A** box under the **Behavior** section. If you click the **To** icon, then the sketch will be revolved up to the selected face. In addition to that, you need to specify the revolution direction using the **Direction** options: **Default** , **Flipped** , **Symmetric** , and **Asymmetric** . On the **Revolve Properties** panel, enter a name in the **Body name** box under the **Output** section. Next, click **OK** to complete the *Revolved* feature.

Project Geometry

This command projects the edges of a 3D geometry onto a sketch plane. Activate the Sketch environment by selecting a plane or model face. On the **Sketch** tab of the Ribbon, click **Create** panel > **Project** drop-down **> Project Geometry**. Click on the edges of the model geometry to project them on to the sketch plane. Press **Esc** to deactivate the command.

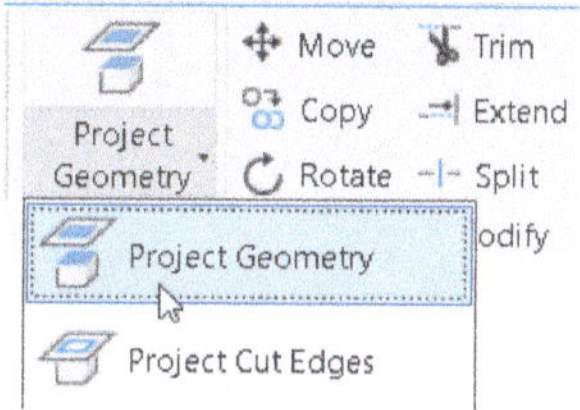

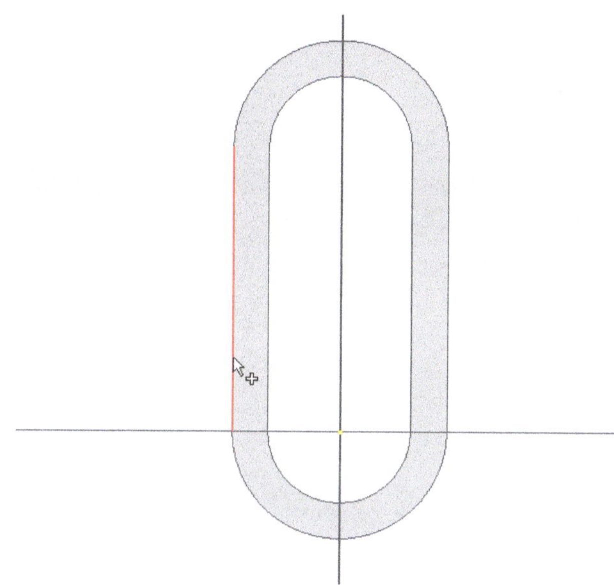

The projected element will be yellow in color and fully constrained. If you want to convert it into a typical sketch element, then right click on it and select **Break Link**.

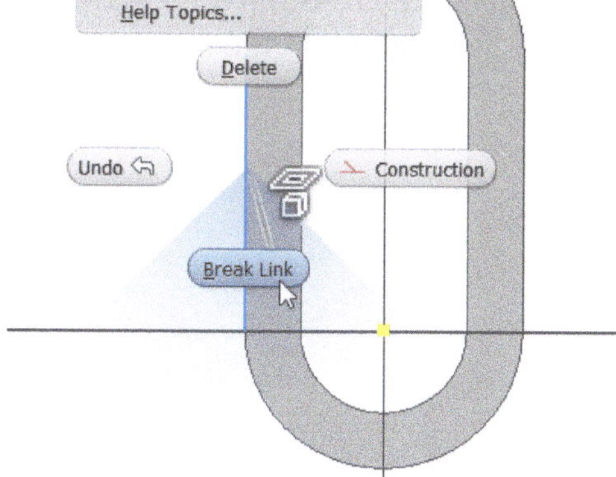

Tip: However, the projected geometry will be broken if the exiting geometry is deleted. You can select the broken projections by right-clicking selecting the **Select Broken Projections** option.

Planes

Each time you start a new part file, Inventor automatically creates default work planes. Planes are a specific type of element in Inventor, known as Work Features. These features act as supports to your 3D geometry. In addition to the default work features, you can create your additional planes. Until now, you have learned to create sketches on any of the default planes (XY, YZ, and XZ planes). If you want to create sketches and geometry at locations other than default planes, you can create new work planes manually. You can do this by using the commands available on the **Plane** drop-down of the **Work Features** panel.

Offset from Plane

This command creates a plane, which will be parallel to a face or another plane. Activate the **Offset from Plane** command (click **3D Model > Work Features > Plane** drop-down **> Offset from Plane** on the ribbon). Click on a flat face and drag the arrow that appears on the plane (or) type-in a value in the **Distance** box on the **Mini toolbar**.

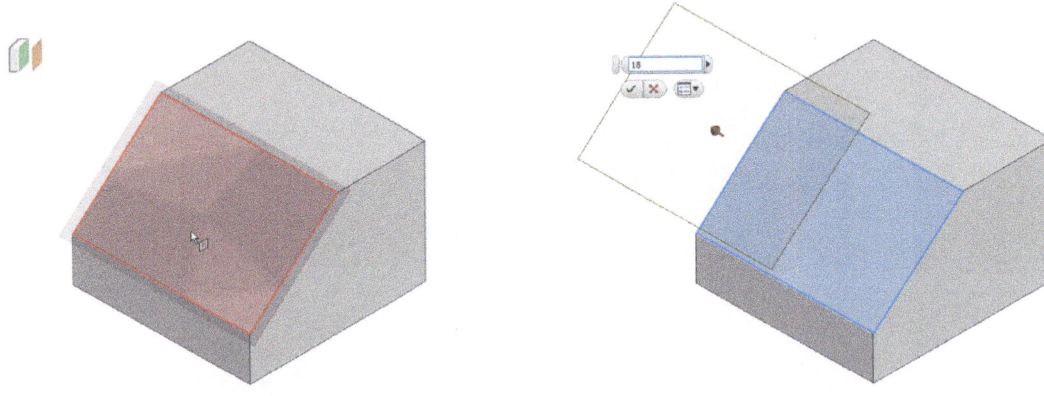

Click **OK** on the **Mini toolbar** to create the offset plane.

Parallel to Plane through Point

This command creates a plane, which will be parallel to a selected point, face, or plane through a point. Activate the **Parallel to Plane through Point** command (click **3D Model > Work Features > Plane** drop-down **> Parallel to Plane through Point** on the Ribbon) and Select a planar face or work plane. Next, select a point on the part geometry.

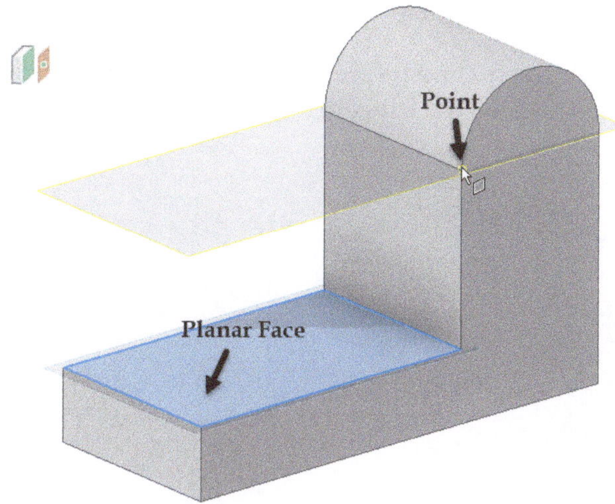

Midplane between Two Planes

This command creates a plane, which lies at the midpoint between two selected planes. You can also create a plane passing through the intersection point of the two selected faces. Activate the **Midplane between Two Planes** command (click **3D Model > Work Features > Plane** drop-down **> Midplane between Two Planes** on the Ribbon) and click on two faces of the model geometry. Click **OK** to create the Midplane.

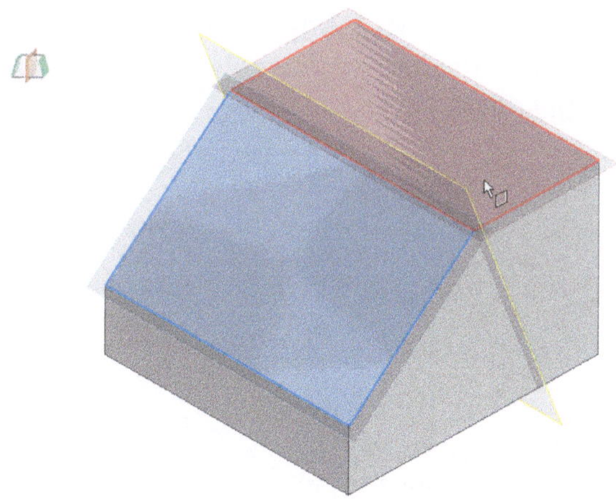

Another example of Midplane Between Two Planes.

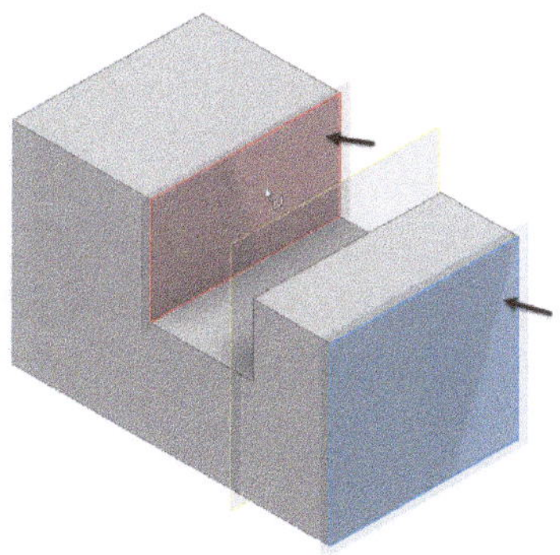

Midplane of Torus

This command creates a plane through the midplane of a torus. Activate the **Midplane of Torus** command (click **3D Model > Work Features > Plane** drop-down **> Midplane of Torus** on the Ribbon) and select a torus to create the midplane.

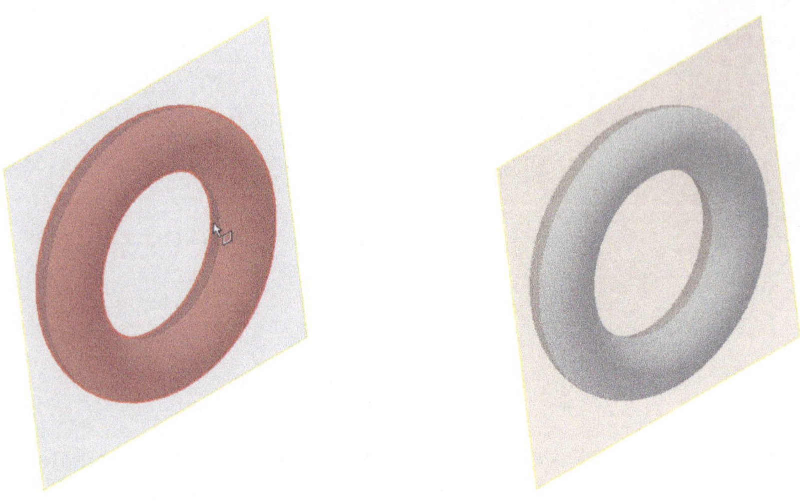

Angle to Plane around Edge

This command creates a plane, which will be positioned at an angle to a face or plane. Activate the **Angle to Plane around Edge** command (click **3D Model > Work Features > Plane** drop-down **> Angle to Plane around Edge** on the Ribbon) and select a flat face or plane. Next, click on the edge of the part geometry to define the rotation axis. Type-in a value in the **Angle** box and click **OK** to create the plane.

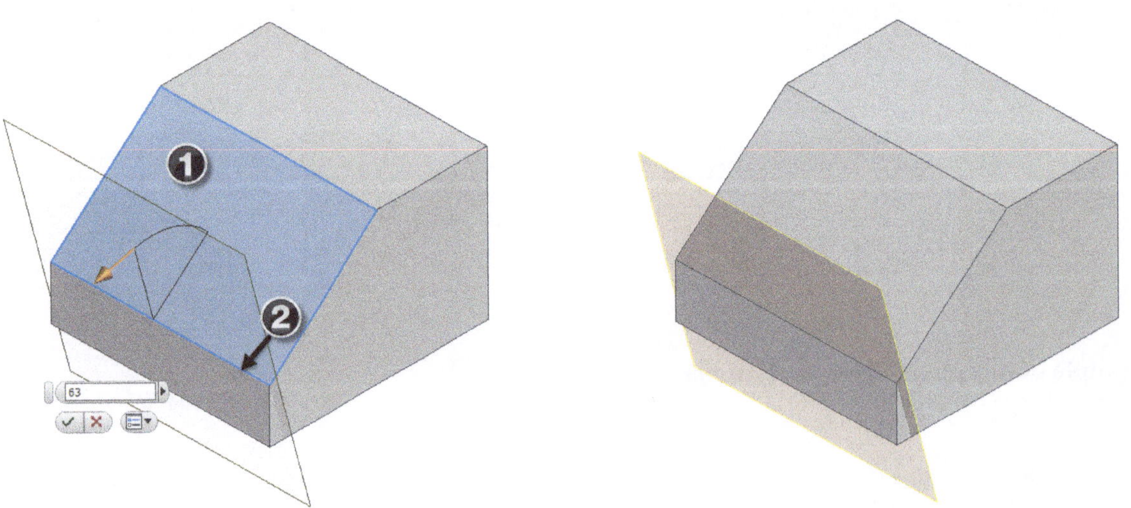

Three Points

This command creates a plane passing through three points. Activate the **Three Points** command (click **3D Model > Work Features > Plane** drop-down **> Three Points** on the Ribbon) and select three points from the model geometry. A plane will be placed passing through these points.

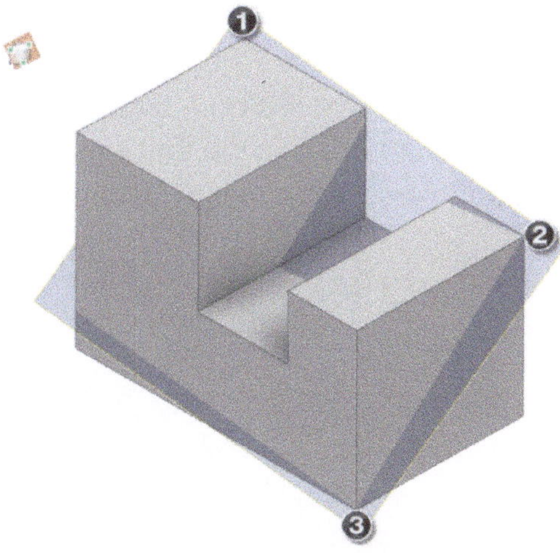

Two Coplanar Edges

This command creates a plane passing through two coplanar axes, edges or lines. Activate the **Two Coplanar Edges** command (click **3D Model > Work Features > Plane** drop-down **> Two Coplanar Edges** on the Ribbon) and select two coplanar axes or edges or lines.

Coplanar Lines

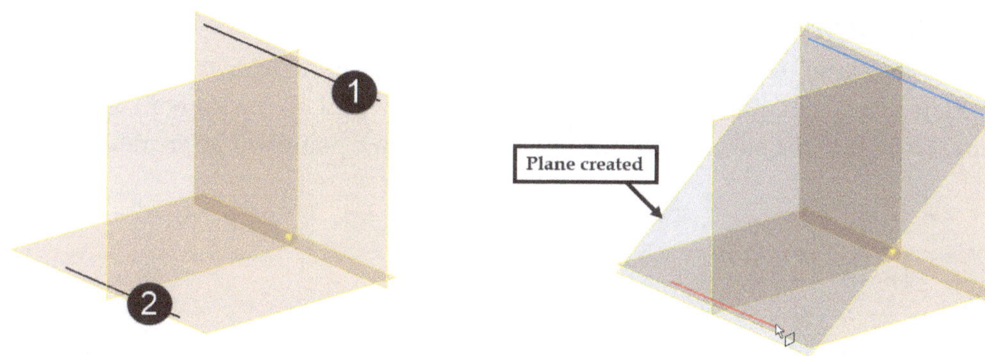

Coplanar Edges

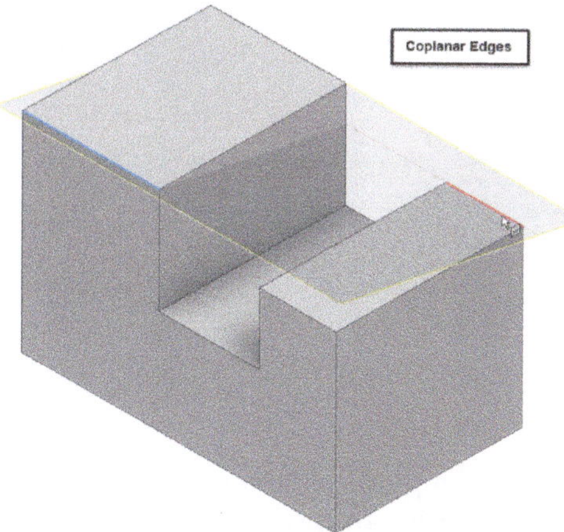

Tangent to Surface through Edge

This command creates a plane tangent to a curved face and passing through an edge. Activate this command (click **3D Model > Work Features > Plane** drop-down **> Tangent to Surface through Edge** on the Ribbon) and select a curved face and a straight edge. A plane tangent to the selected face and passing through the edge appears.

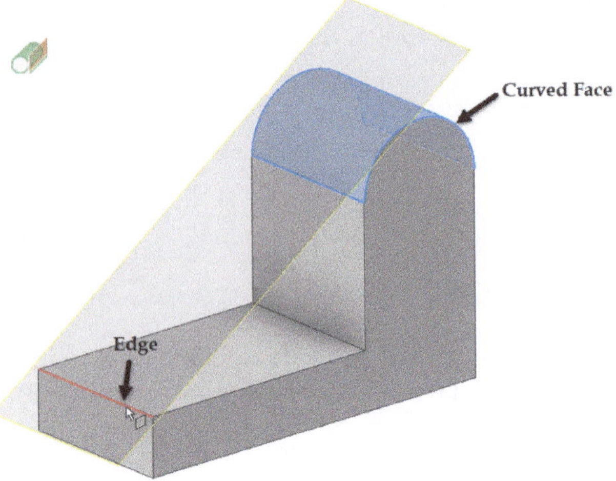

Tangent to Surface through Point

This command creates a plane passing through a point and tangent to a curved face. Activate this command (click **3D Model > Work Features > Plane** drop-down **> Tangent to Surface through Point** on the Ribbon) and select a curved face and a point. A plane tangent to the curved face and passing through a point will be created.

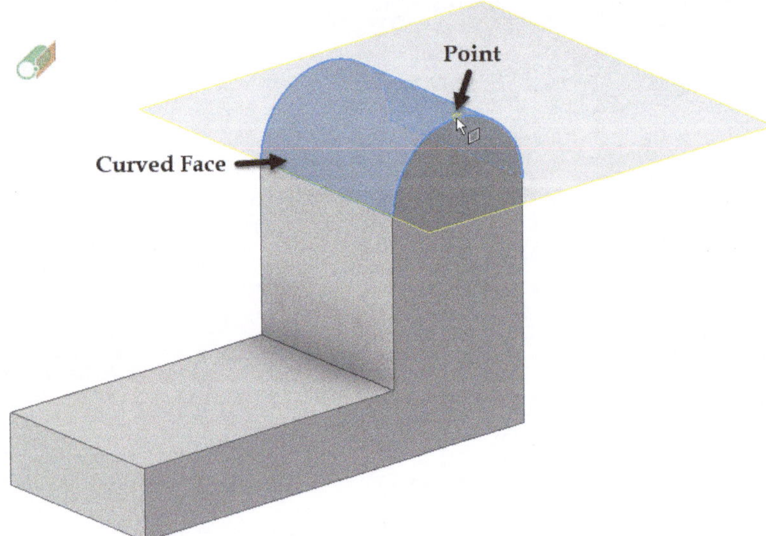

Tangent to Surface and Parallel to Plane

This command creates a plane, which is tangent to a curved face and parallel to a plane. Activate this command (click **3D Model > Work Features > Plane** drop-down **> Tangent to Surface and Parallel to Plane** on the Ribbon) and select a curved face. Next, select a planar face or a plane; a plane tangent to the selected curved face and parallel to the plane appears.

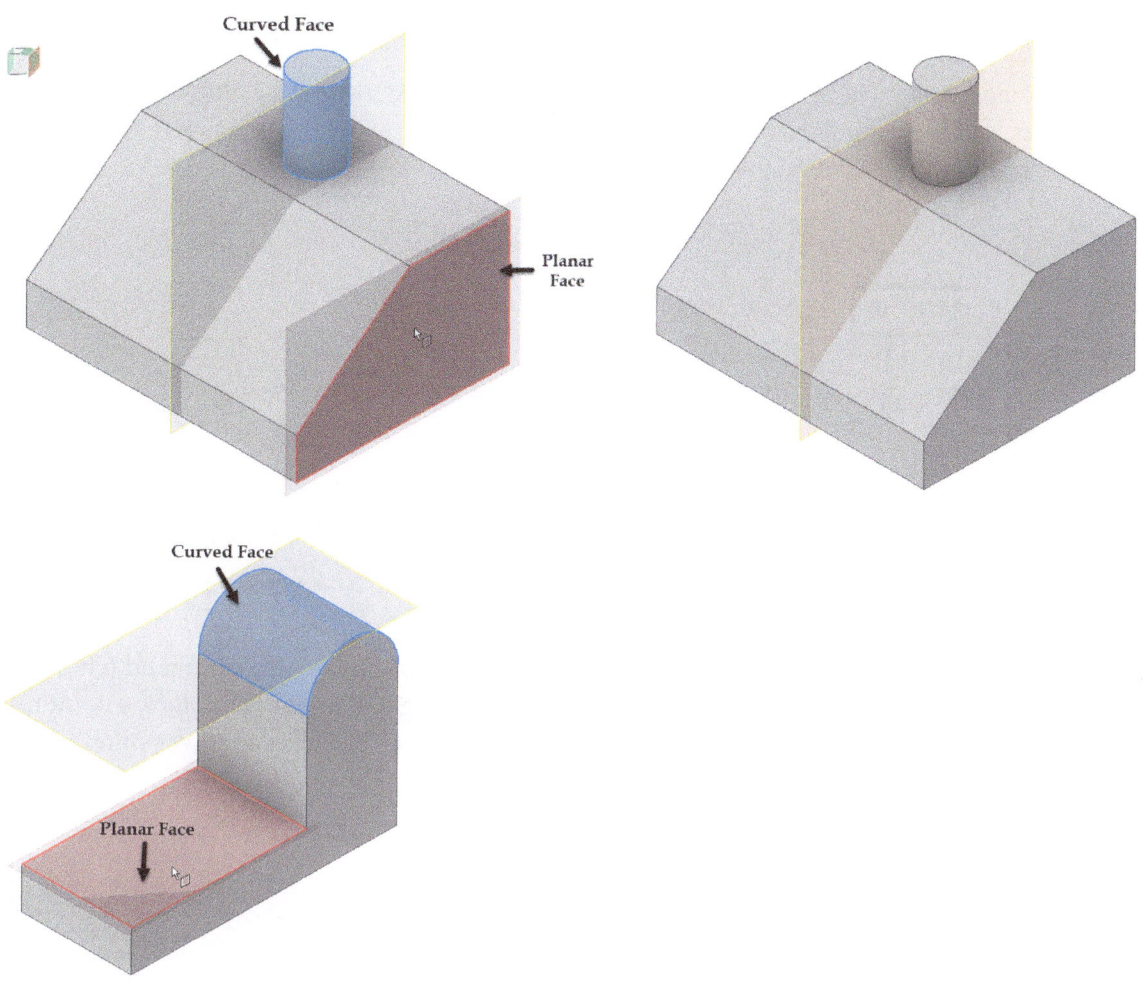

Normal to Axis through Point

This command creates a plane, which will be normal to an axis or edge and at a point. Activate this command (click **3D Model > Work Features > Plane** drop-down **> Normal to Axis through Point** on the Ribbon) and select an axis or edge. Next, click on a point to define the location of the plane.

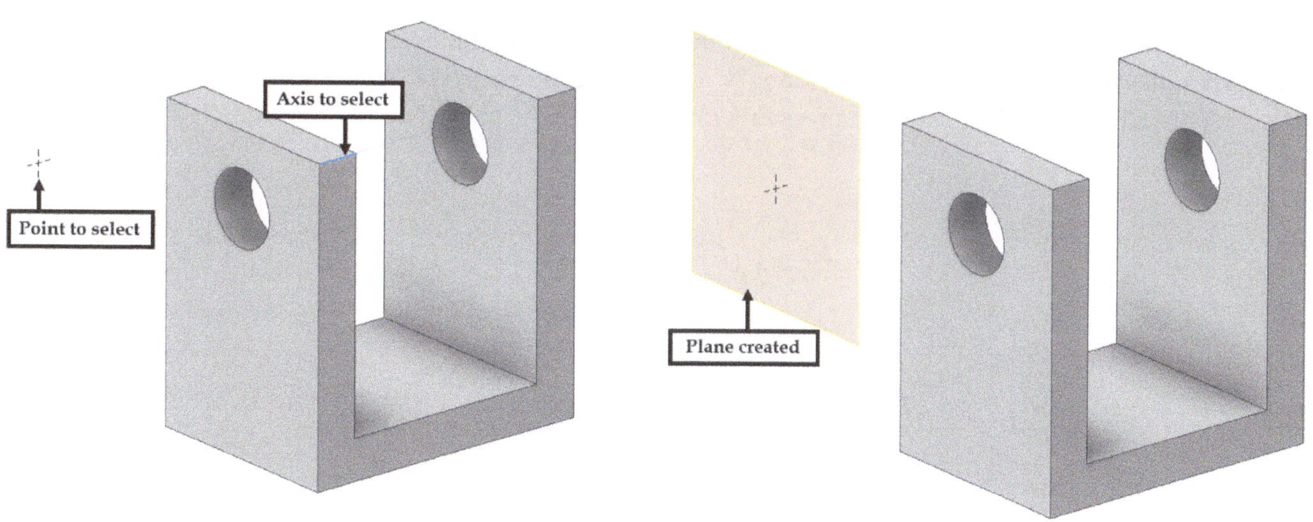

Normal to Curve at a Point

This command creates a plane, which will be normal to a line, curve, or edge. Activate this command by clicking **3D Model > Work Features > Plane** drop-down **> Normal to Curve at a Point** on the Ribbon. Select an edge, line, curve, arc, or circle. Next, pick a point to define the location of the plane.

UCS

This command creates a new coordinate system in addition to the default one. Activate this command (click **3D Model > Work Features > UCS** on the ribbon). The UCS triad appears on the graphics window. Pick a point to specify the origin of the UCS. Next, select the point to specify the X-axis of the UCS. Select another point to specify the Y-axis; the UCS will be created.

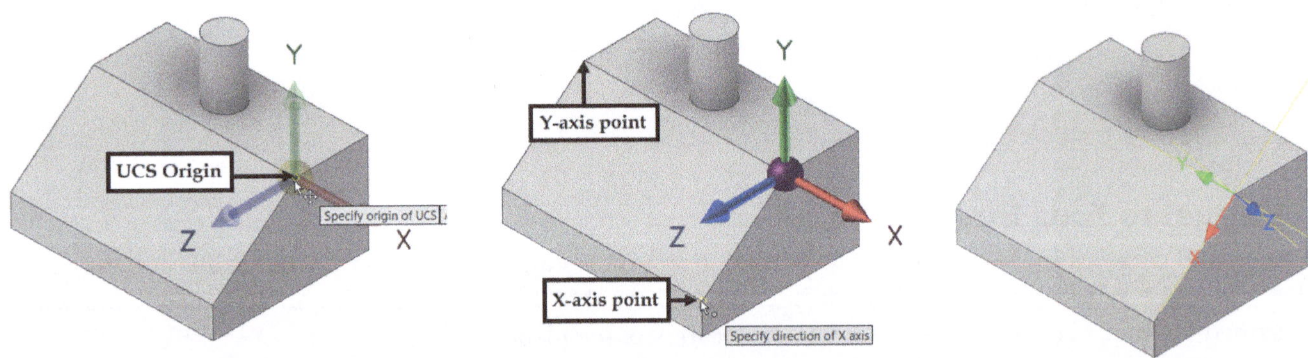

If you want to edit the UCS, you can double-click on any one of the axes of the UCS. Next, click and drag the X, Y, or Z arrow handles to translate the UCS triad along X, Y, or Z-axis, respectively. You can also click on the arrow handles, type-in a distance value, and then press Enter; the UCS will be moved up to the specified distance along the selected axis.

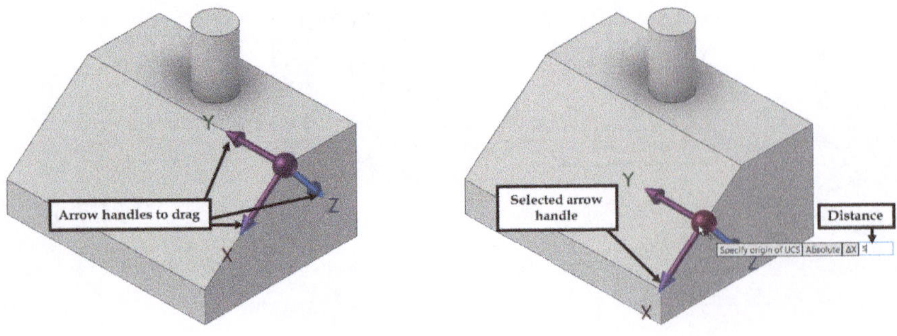

If you want to change the orientation of the UCS, you can rotate it about any one of the axes. To do this, click on the shaft portion of an axis. Next, press and hold the left mouse button and drag the pointer; the UCS is rotated about the selected axis. You can also click on the shaft portion of the axis, and then specify the angle in the angle box.

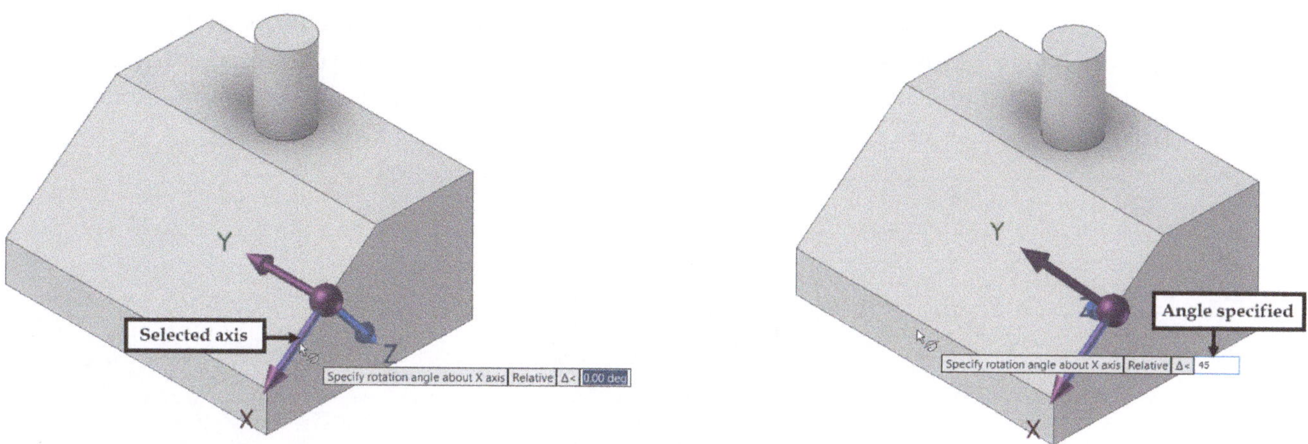

Additional options of the Extrude command

The **Extrude** command has some additional options to create complex features of a 3D geometry.

Boolean

When you extrude a sketch, the **Boolean** options determine whether the material is added, subtracted, or intersected from an existing solid body.

Join

This option adds material to the geometry.

Cut

This option removes material from the geometry.

Intersect

This option creates a solid body containing the volume shared by two separate bodies.

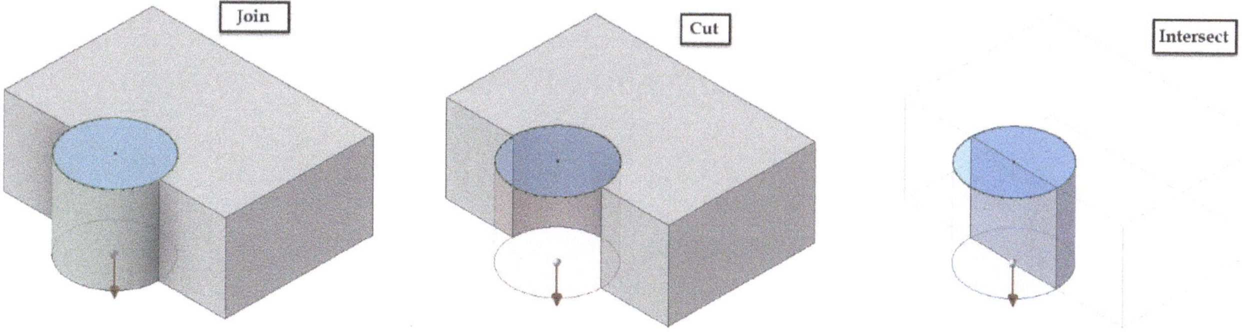

New Solid

This option creates a separate solid body. It will be helpful while creating multi-body parts.

Behavior

On the **Extrude Properties** panel, the **Behavior** section has various options to define the start and end limits of the *Extrude* feature. These options are **Distance, To Next, To, Between, All,** and **Distance from face.**

The **Distance** option extrudes the sketch up to the specified distance. On the **Extrude Properties** panel, select **Distance** from the **Behavior** section. Specify the distance in the **Distance A** box and click on the required direction icon. There are four types of **Direction** icons: *Default, Flipped, Symmetric,* and *Asymmetric* icons.

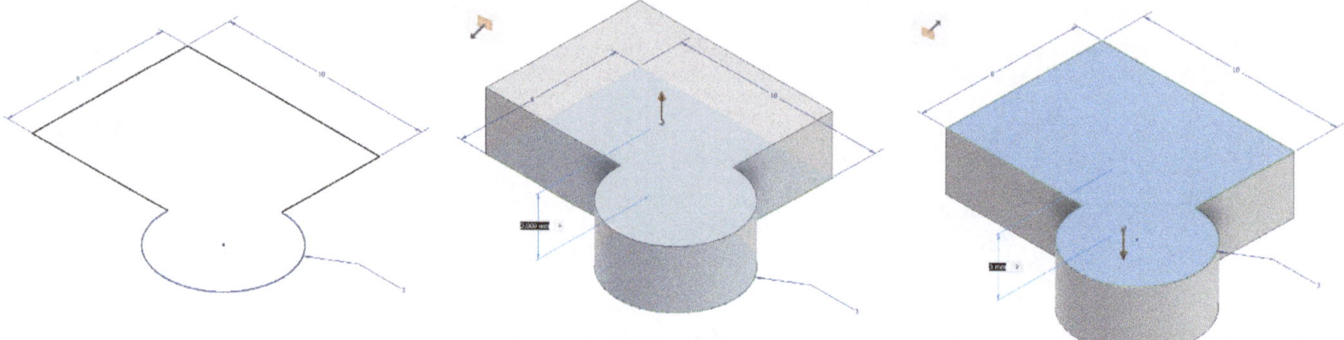

When you select the **Asymmetric** icon, you must specify the two distances in the **Distance A** and **Distance B** boxes, respectively.

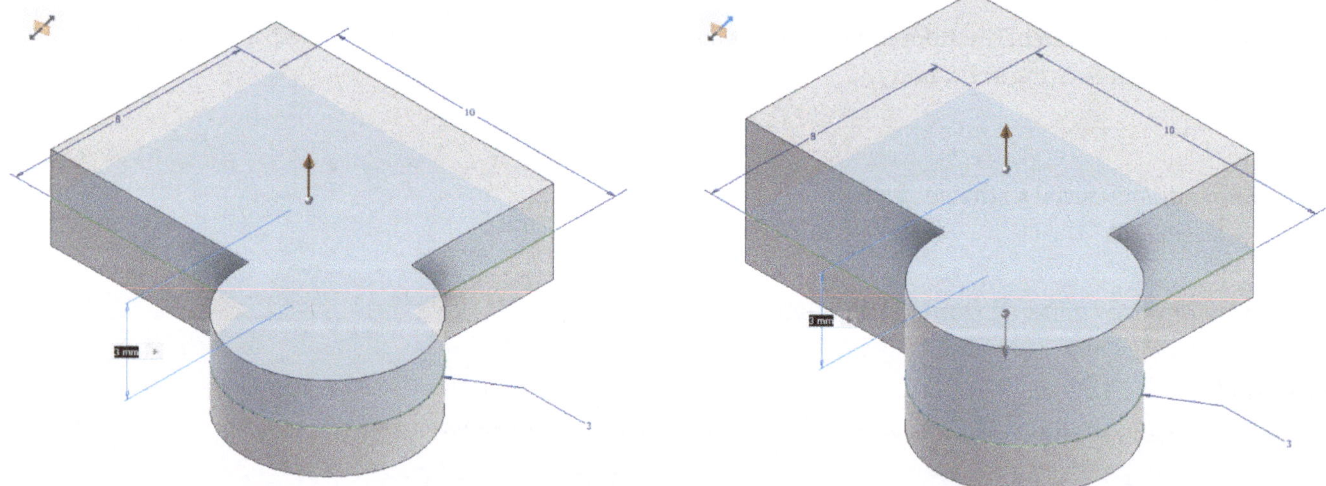

The **To Next** option extrudes the sketch through the face next to the sketch plane.

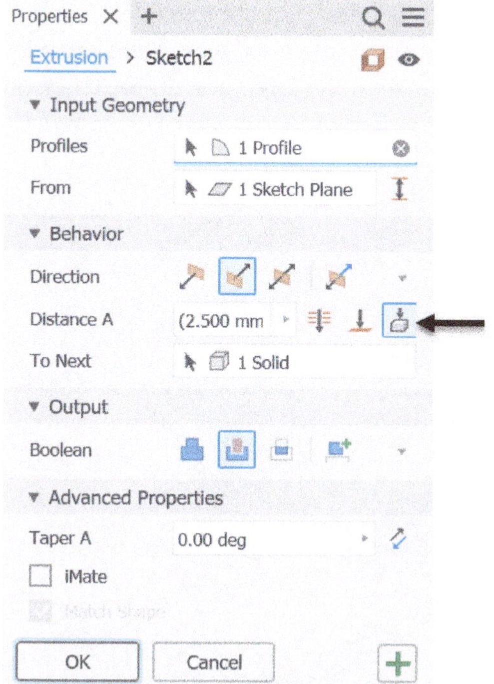

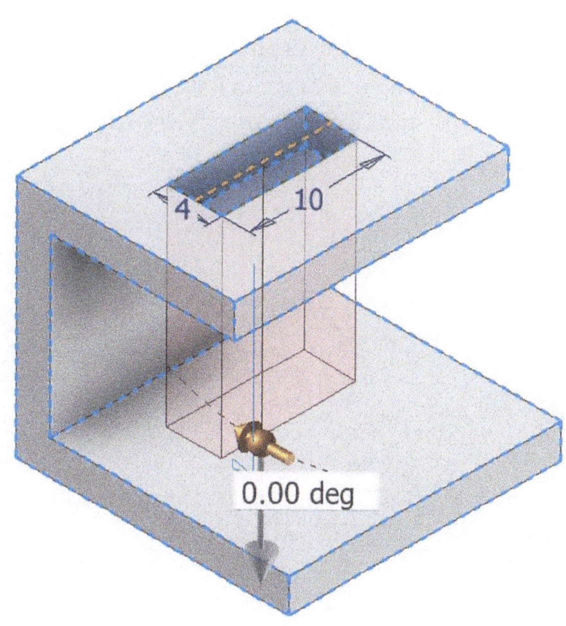

The **To** option extrudes the sketch up to a selected face. Ensure that the sketch will lie on the selected face if projected. On the **Extrude Properties** panel, click on the **Join** icon to add material to the part and select **To** from the **Behavior** section. Next, select the face or plane; the sketch will be extruded up to the selected face or plane.

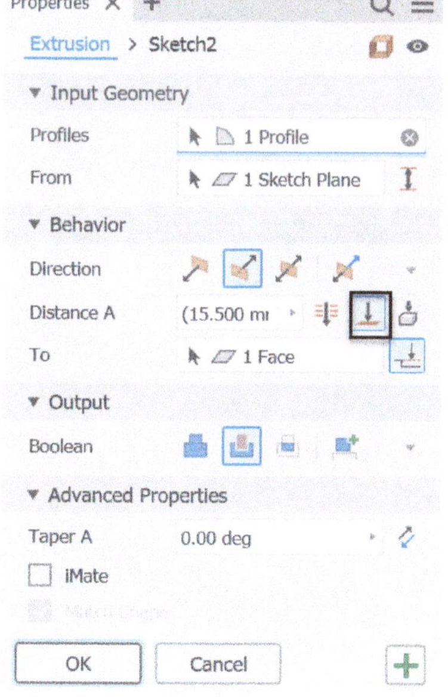

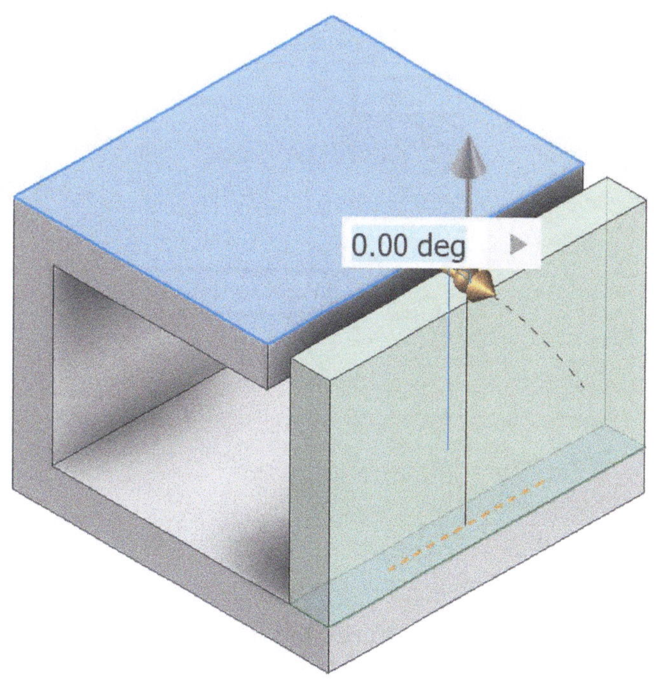

The **From** option extrudes the sketch from the selected face up to the specified distance. On the **Extrude Properties** panel, click in the **From** box under the **Input Geometry** section and select the *From* face. The sketch is select by default as you activate the **Extrude** command. Next, specify the distance in the **Distance A** box. Click on any one of the direction icons to specify the direction.

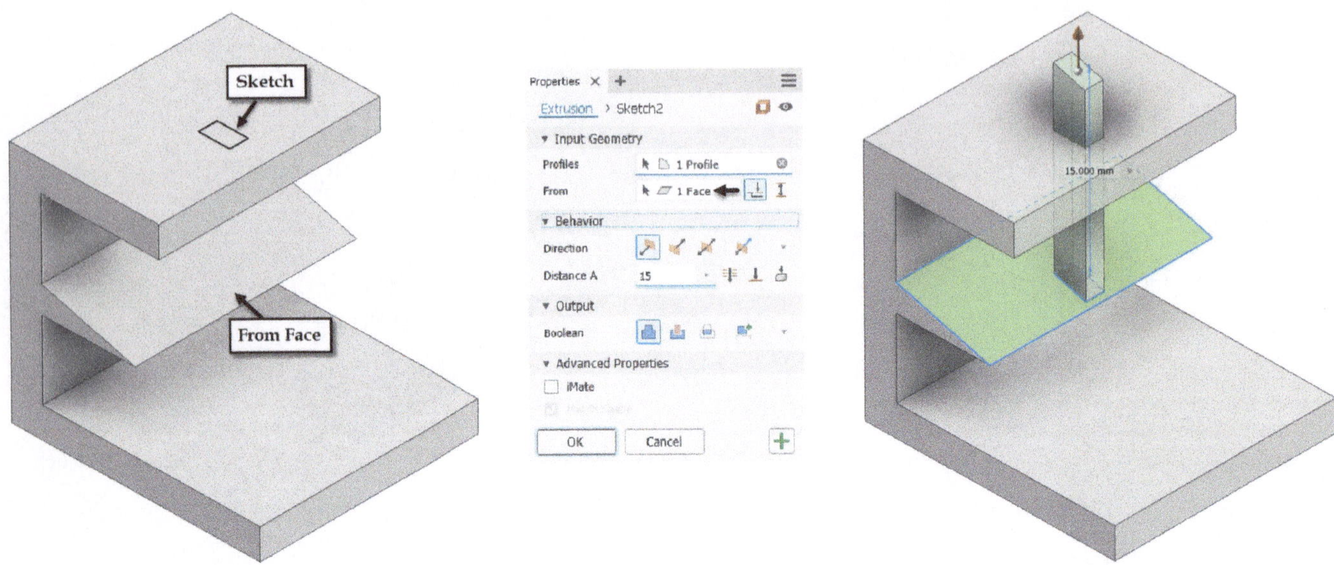

Autodesk Inventor allows you to extrude the sketch between the two selected faces. On the **Extrude** Properties panel, click in the **From** selection box and select the starting face of the extruded feature. Next, click the **To** icon in the **Behavior** section and select the face up to which the sketch is to be extruded; the sketch is extruded between the two selected faces.

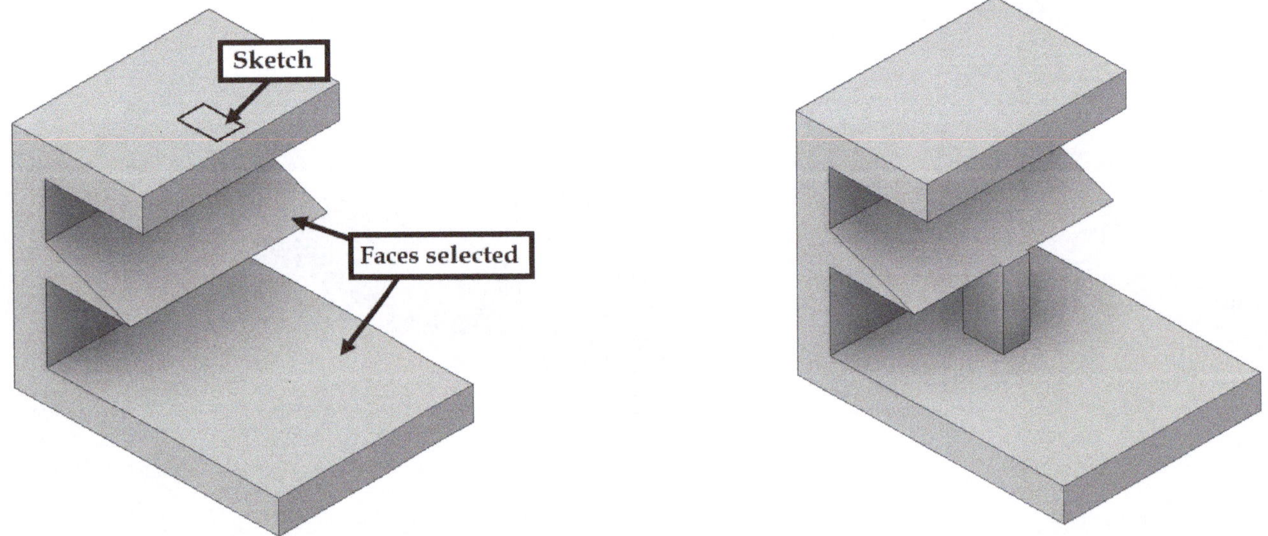

The **Through All** option extrudes the sketch throughout the 3D geometry. On the **Extrude Properties** panel, select **Through All** from the **Behavior** section. Click on any one of the direction icons to specify the direction.

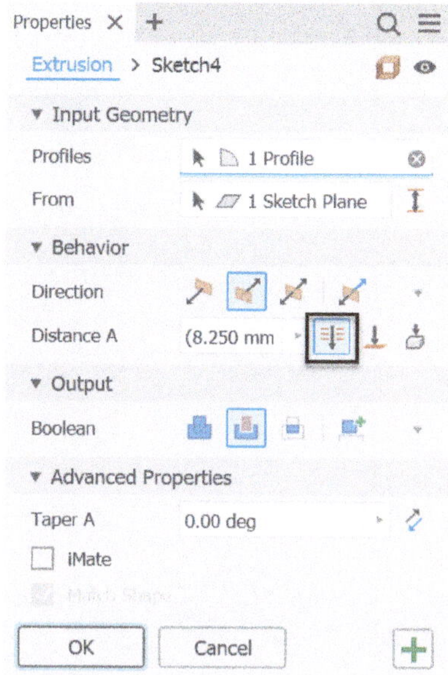

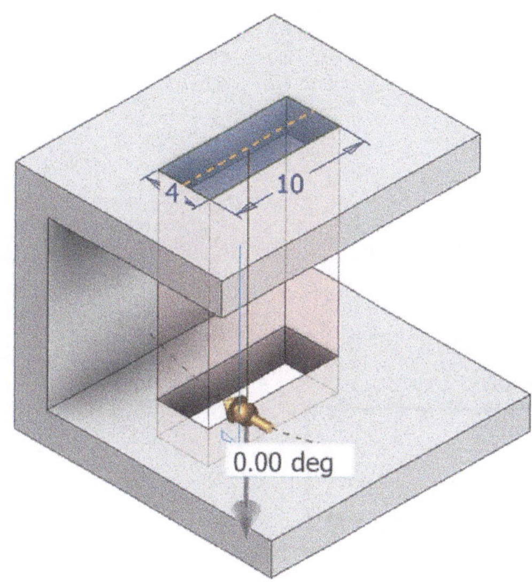

Match Shape

This option adds an *Extrude* feature to an existing feature using an open profile. It extends the profile to meet the adjacent edges. Activate the **Extrude** command, and then click on the open profile. On the **Extrude Properties** panel, check the **Match Shape** option at the bottom. Notice that a rectangle boundary appears enclosing the entire geometry. Click on a region of the rectangle to specify the material side. Next, select the **Boolean** and **Behavior** type. Click **OK** to create the extruded feature.

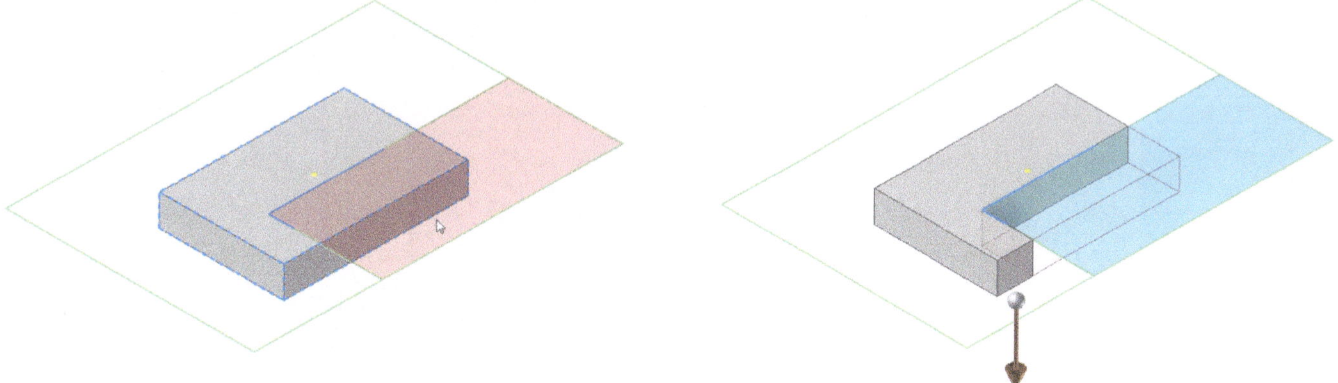

Adding Taper to the Extruded Feature

The **Taper** option will help you to apply a draft to the extrusion. On the **Extrude Properties** panel, expand the **Advanced Properties** section and enter the angle value in the **Taper** box. You can apply the taper in the four directions: *Default, Flipped, Symmetric,* and *Asymmetric.*

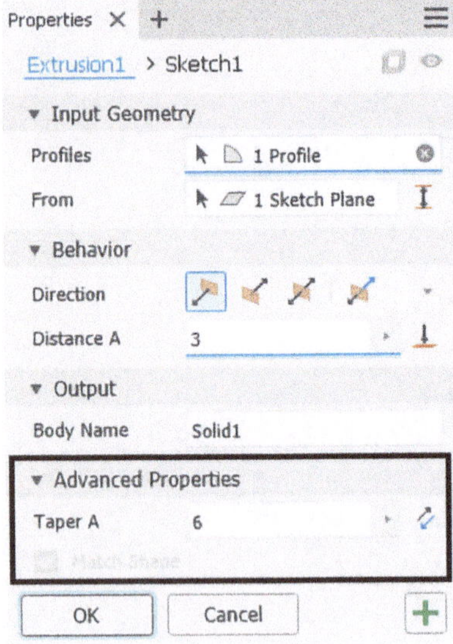

Click the **Flip direction** icon under the **Advanced Properties** section to reverse the taper direction.

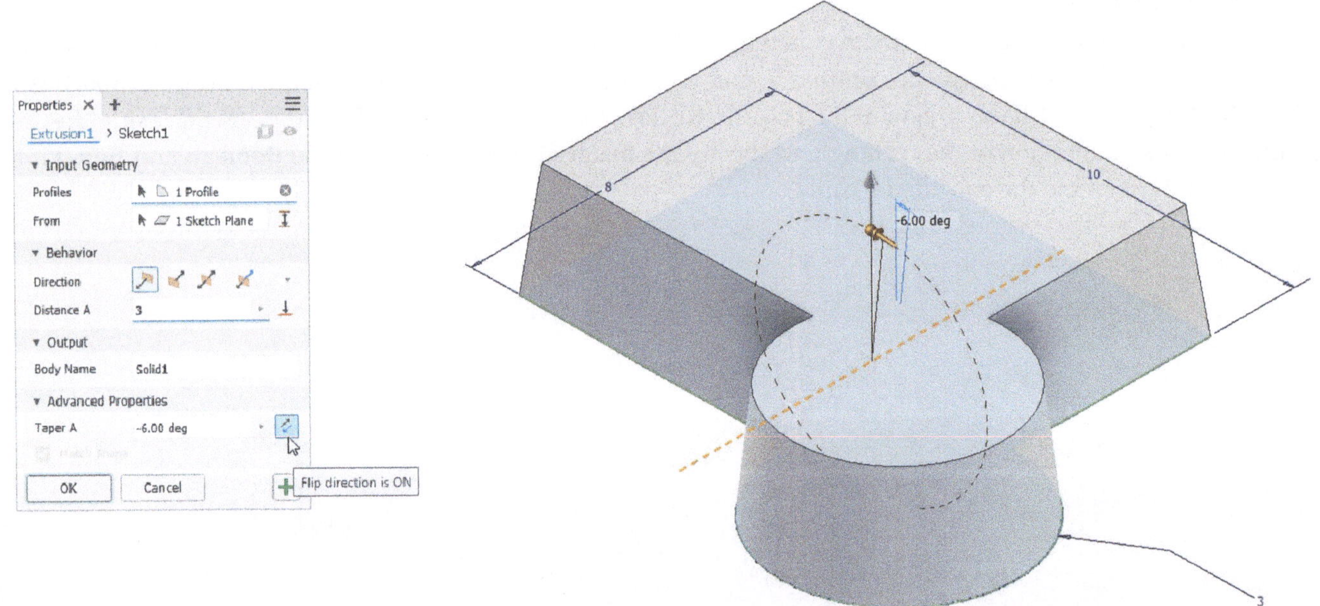

After specifying the draft angle, click on any one of the direction icons under the **Behavior** section.

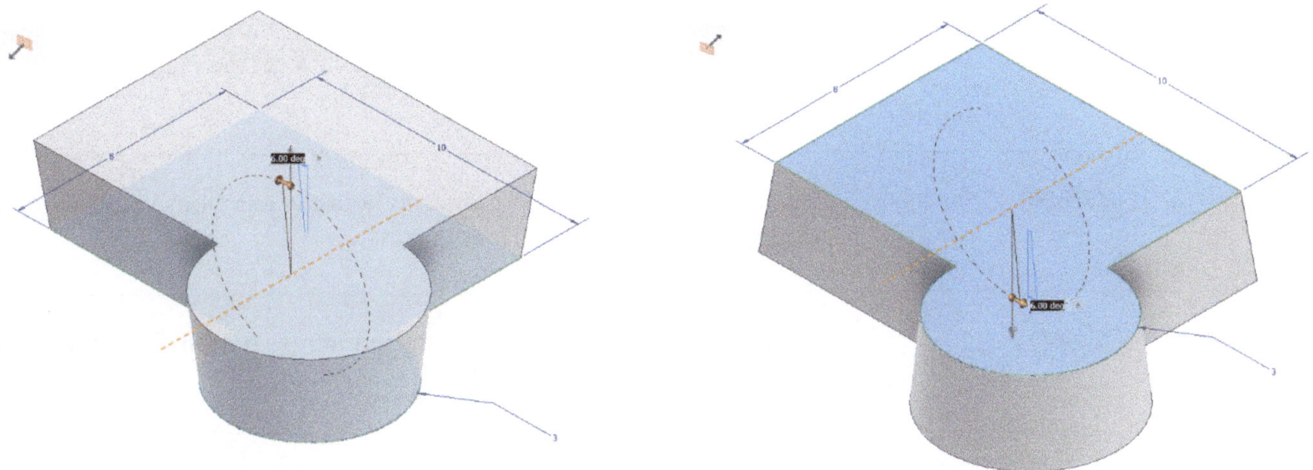

The draft angle can be changed dynamically using the arrow that appears on the geometry. A positive angle applies an inward draft, and a negative angle applies an outward draft.

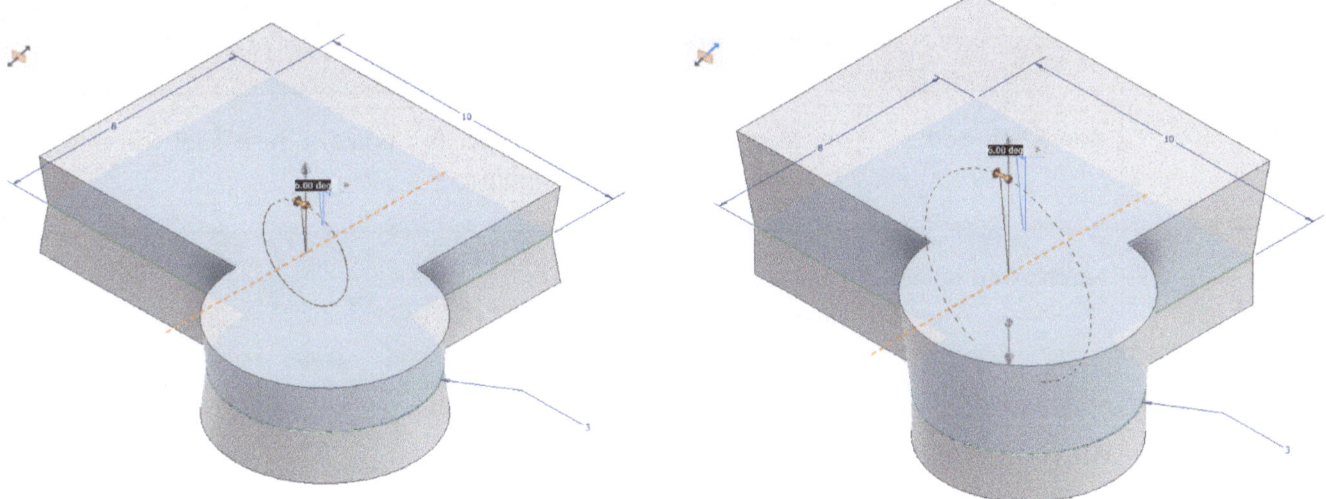

Click **OK** to complete the Extruded Feature.

View Modification commands

The model display in the graphics window can be changed using various view modification commands. Most of these commands are located on the **View** tab on the ribbon. These commands can also be accessed from the **Navigation bar** in the graphics window. The following are some of the main view modification commands:

	Zoom All	The model will be fitted in the current size of the graphics window so that it will be visible completely.

	Pan	Activate this command, press and hold the left mouse button, and then drag the pointer to move the model view on the plane parallel to screen.	
	Orbit	Activate this command and press and hold the left mouse button. Drag the pointer to rotate the model view.	
	Zoom	Activate this command and press the left mouse button. Drag the mouse to vary the size of the objects accordingly.	
	Look At	This command positions a selected planar face parallel to the screen. You can also select an edge to make horizontal to the screen.	
	Zoom window	Activate this command and drag a rectangle. The contents inside the rectangle will be zoomed.	
	Zoom Selected	Activate this command and specify a point of the model; the view is zoomed in at the selected point.	
	Navigation wheel	This wheel has various navigation options such as **Zoom**, **Pan**, **Orbit**, and **Rewind**.	ZOOM CENTER WALK ORBIT REWIND LOOK UP/DOWN PAN
	Shaded with Edges	It represents the model with shades along with visible edges.	

	Shaded	It represents the model with shades without visible edges.	
	**Wireframe**	It represents the model in wireframe along with the hidden edges	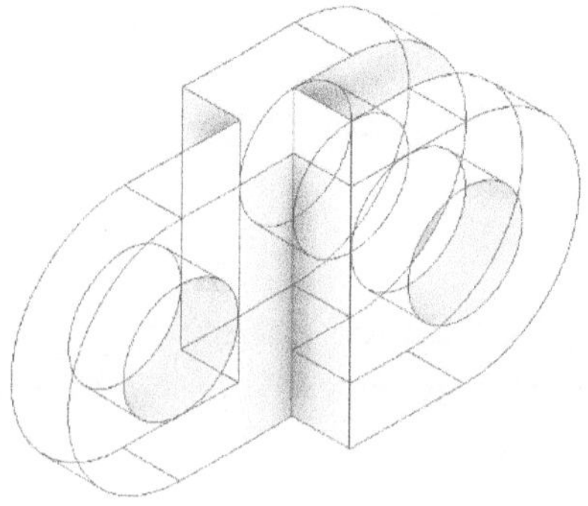
	**Wireframe with hidden edges**	It represents the model in wireframe. The hidden edges are displayed in dashed lines.	
	**Wireframe with Visible edges only**	It represents the model in wireframe. The hidden edges are not shown.	

Examples

Example 1 (Millimeters)

In this example, you will create the part shown below.

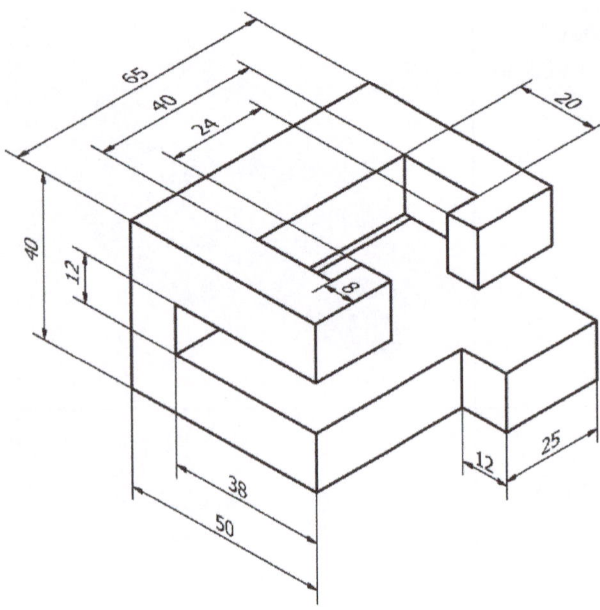

Creating the Base Feature

1. Start **Autodesk Inventor 2026** by double-clicking the **Autodesk Inventor 2026** icon on your desktop.
2. To start a new part file, click **File menu > New**.
3. On the **Create New File** dialog, click the **Metric** folder under **Templates**.
4. Click the **Standard(mm).ipt** icon under the **Part – Create 2D and 3D Objects** section.
5. Click the **Create** button on the **Create New File** dialog.
6. To start a sketch, click **3D Model > Sketch > Start 2D Sketch** on the ribbon. Click on the XY plane. The sketch starts.

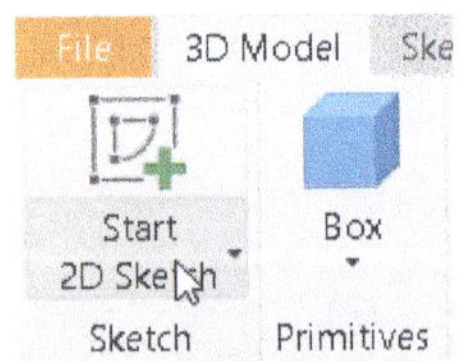

7. Click **Sketch > Create > Rectangle Two Point** on the ribbon. Click the origin point to define the first corner of the rectangle. Next, move the pointer toward the top right corner and click to define the second corner.
8. Click **Sketch > Constrain > Dimension** on the ribbon.
9. Select the horizontal line of the rectangle, move the pointer upward, and then click to position the dimension.
10. Type **50** in the **Edit Dimension** box and click the green check.
11. Select the vertical line of the rectangle, move the pointer horizontally, and then click to position the dimension.
12. Type **40** in the **Edit Dimension** box and click the green check.
13. Press **Esc** to deactivate the **Dimension** command.

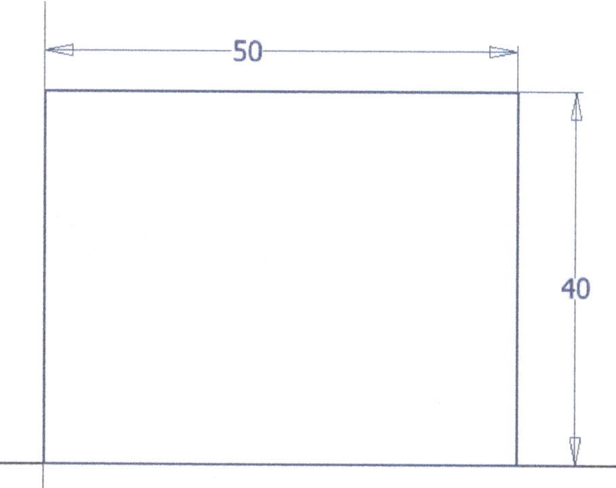

14. On the ribbon, click **Sketch > Exit > Finish Sketch.**
15. Click on the **Home** icon located at the top left corner of the ViewCube.

16. On the ribbon, click **3D Model > Create > Extrude**; the sketch is selected automatically.
17. On the **Extrude Properties** panel, under the **Behavior** section, click **Direction > Symmetric** icon.
18. Type-in **65** in the **Distance A** box.
19. Click **OK** on the **Extrude** dialog to complete the *Extrude* feature.

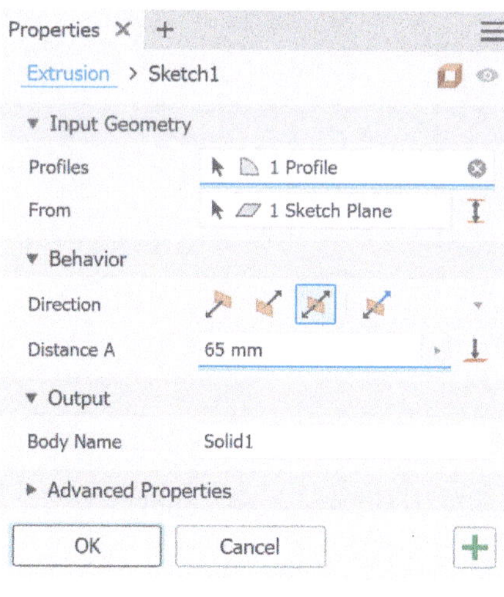

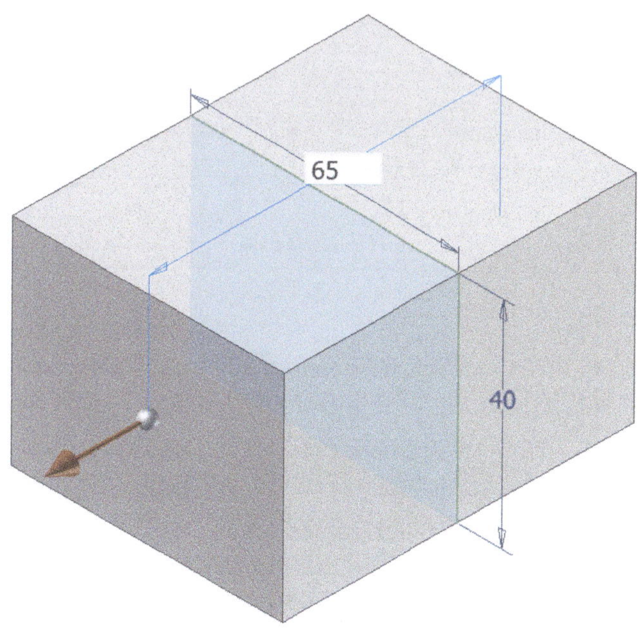

Creating the Extrude Cut throughout the Part model

1. To start a sketch, click **3D Model > Sketch > Start 2D Sketch** on the ribbon.
2. Click on the front face of the part geometry.

3. Click **Sketch > Create > Rectangle Two Point** on the ribbon.
4. Click near the upper portion of the right vertical edge.
5. Move the pointer diagonally toward the bottom-left corner, and then click.

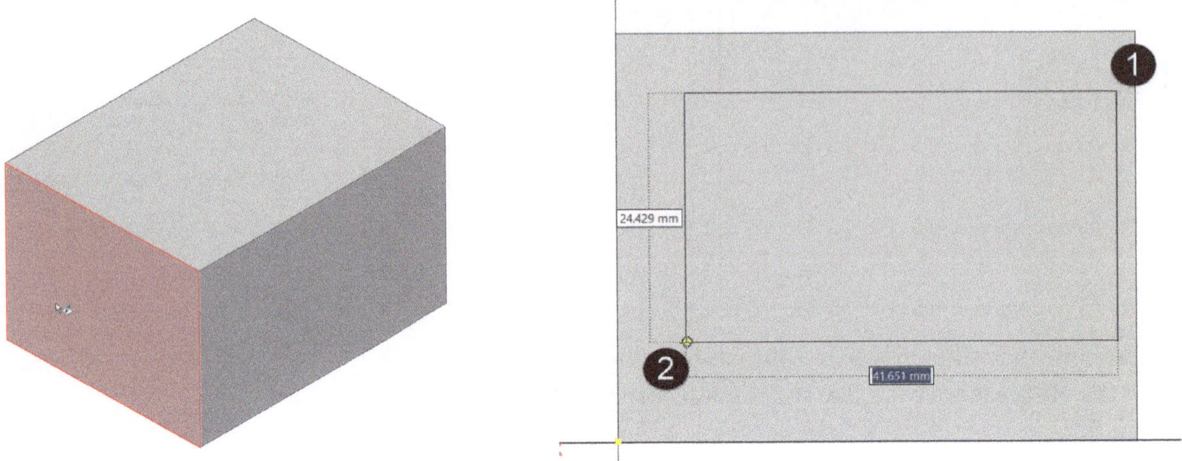

6. On the ribbon, click **Sketch > Constrain > Coincident Constraint**, and then select the midpoint of the right vertical line. Next, select the midpoint of the right vertical edge of the model; the two points are made coincident to each other.

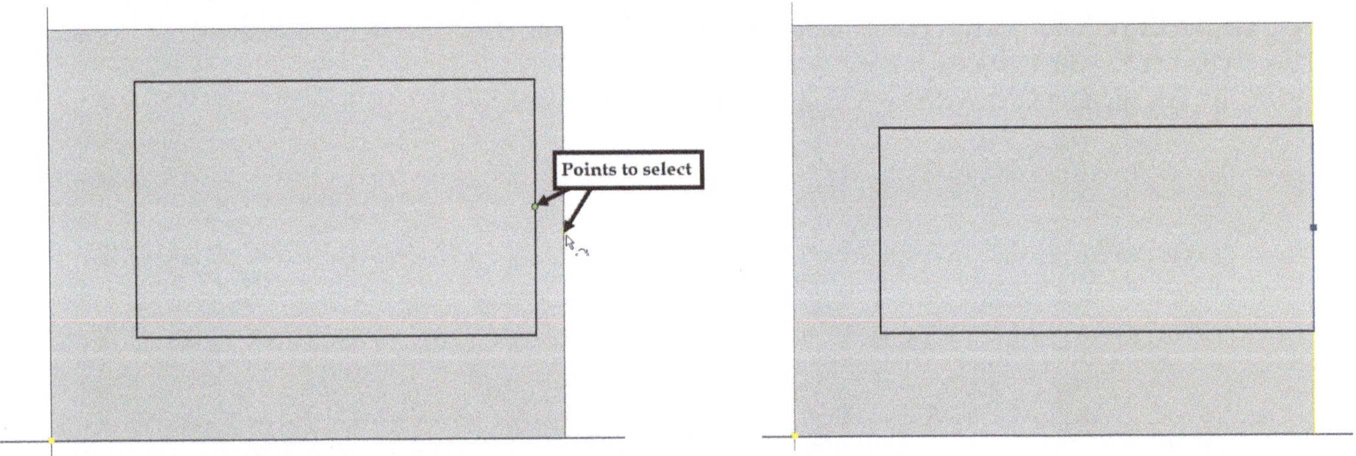

7. On the ribbon, click **Sketch> Constrain > Dimension** .
8. Select the horizontal line of the sketch; move the pointer vertically downward and click.
9. Type **38** in the **Edit Dimension** box and click the green check.
10. Select the vertical line of the sketch, move the pointer horizontally, and click to position the dimension.
11. Type **12** in the **Edit Dimension** box and click the green check.
12. Press **Esc** to deactivate the **Dimension** command.
13. Click **Sketch > Exit > Finish Sketch** on the ribbon.
14. On the ribbon, click **3D Model > Create > Extrude**. On the **Extrude Properties** panel, click the **Boolean > Cut** icon under the **Output** section.
15. Next, click the **Through All** icon under the **Behavior** section.

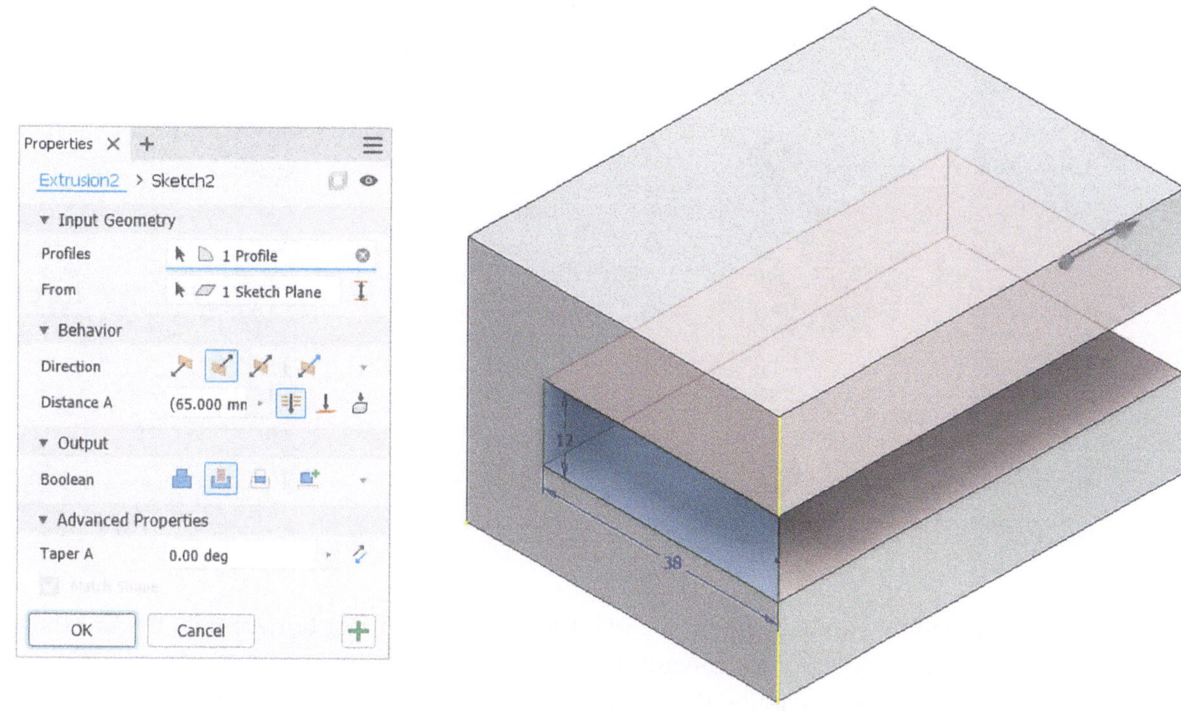

16. Click **OK** to create the cut throughout the part model.

Creating the Extruded Cut up to the surface next to the sketch plane

1. Click **3D Model > Sketch > Start 2D Sketch** on the ribbon and click on the top face of the part model, as shown.

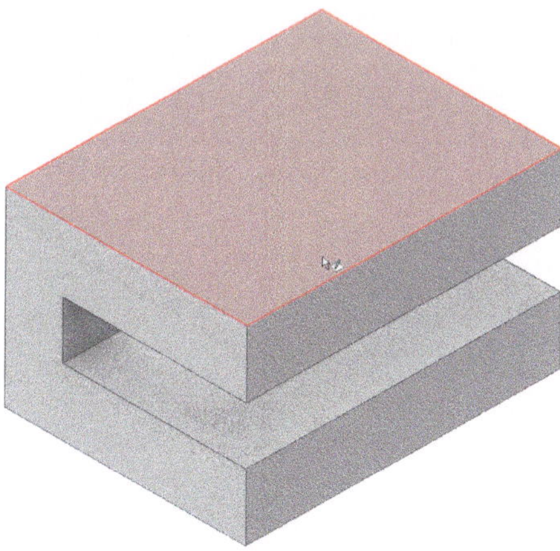

2. Activate the **Line** command (**Sketch > Create > Line** on the ribbon).
3. Click on the lower right portion of the model face to define the start point of the line. Move the pointer vertically upward and click.
4. Move the pointer horizontally toward left and type **8** in the length box attached to the pointer. Press Enter to create a horizontal line with a dimension.

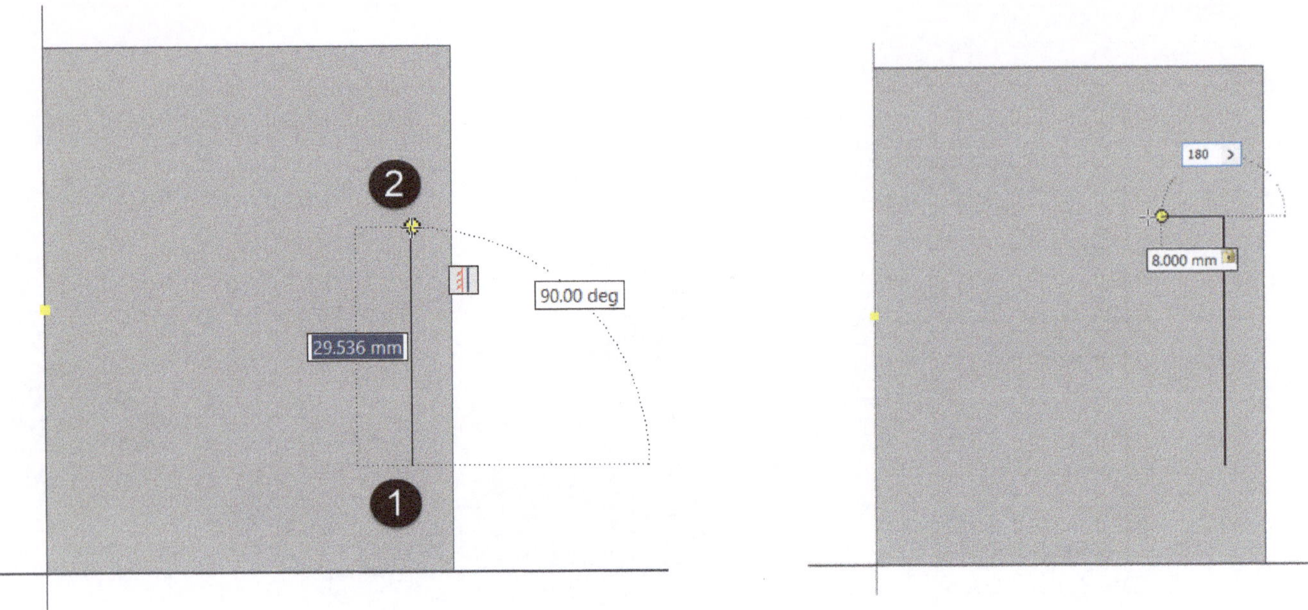

5. Move the pointer vertically upward and click. Move the pointer horizontally toward the left, type **20**, and press Enter. Move the pointer toward down and click.
6. Likewise, create the remaining three lines, as shown. Press **Esc** to deactivate the Line command.

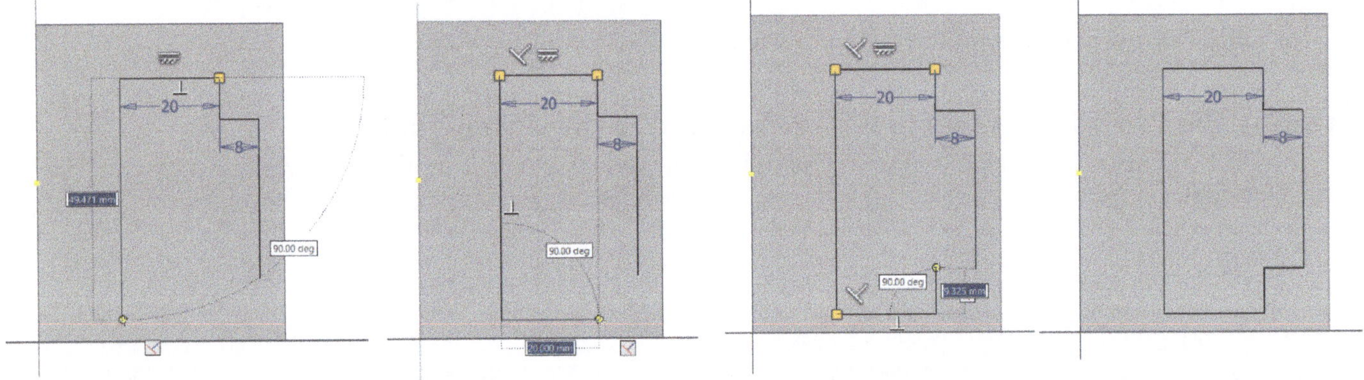

7. Click **Sketch > Constrain > Equal** on the ribbon.
8. Select the two vertical lines, as shown.
9. Select the two horizontal lines, as shown.

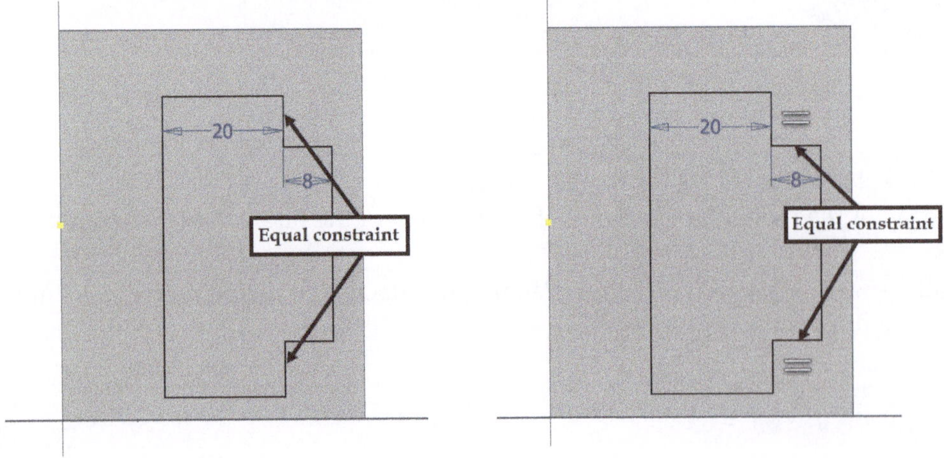

10. On the ribbon, click **Sketch > Constrain > Coincident Constraint**.
11. Select the midpoints of the right vertical line and right vertical edge; the selected points are made coincident to each other.
12. On the ribbon, click **Sketch > Constrain > Dimension**. Select the right vertical line of the sketch; move the pointer towards the right and click – type **24** in the **Edit Dimension** box and press Enter.
13. Likewise, apply the other dimensions, as shown. Press **Esc** to deactivate the **Dimension** command.

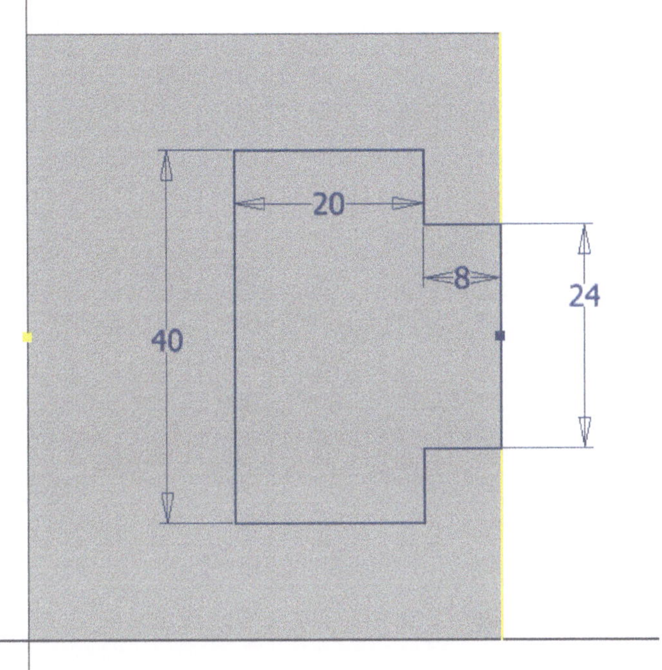

14. On the ribbon, click **Sketch > Exit > Finish Sketch**.
15. Click **3D Model > Create > Extrude** on the ribbon.
16. On the **Extrude Properties** panel, click the **Boolean > Cut** icon under the **Output** section.
17. Click the **To Next** icon under the **Behavior** section, as shown.

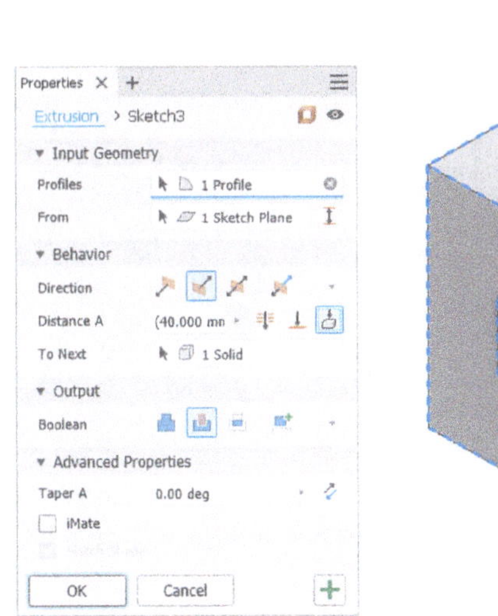

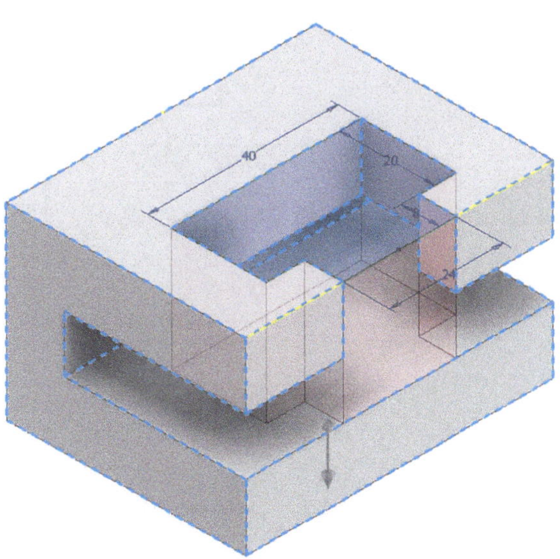

18. Click **OK** to create the *Extruded Cut* feature up to the surface next to the sketch plane.

Extruding the sketch up to a Surface

1. Click **3D Model > Sketch > Start 2D Sketch** command and click on the flat face, as shown.

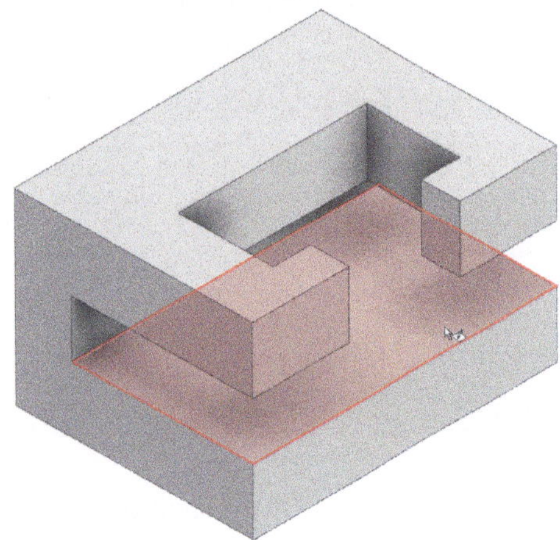

2. Draw a rectangle. Apply the coincident constraint between the top left corner of the rectangle and the top right corner of the model. Add dimensions and finish the sketch.

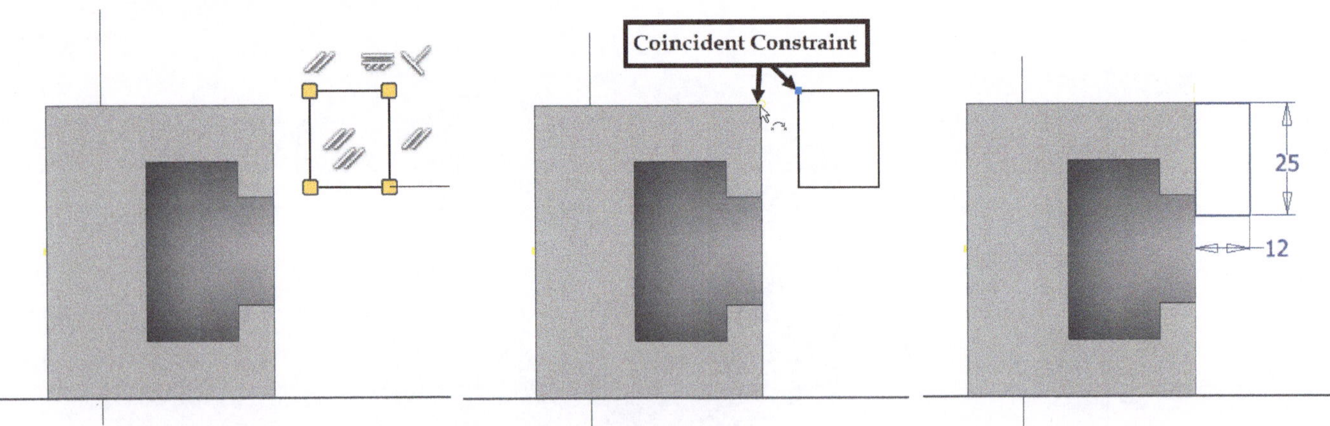

3. On the ribbon, click **3D Model > Create > Extrude**. On the **Extrude Properties** panel, click the **To** icon under the **Behavior** section.
4. Select the bottom face of the part model, as shown.

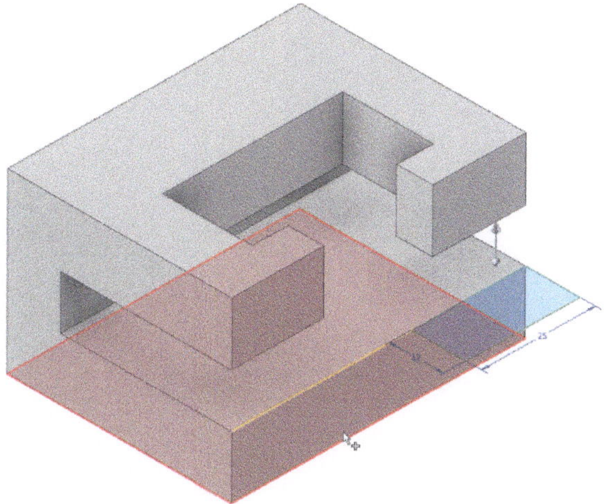

5. Make sure that the **Extend face to end feature** is active under the **Behavior** section.

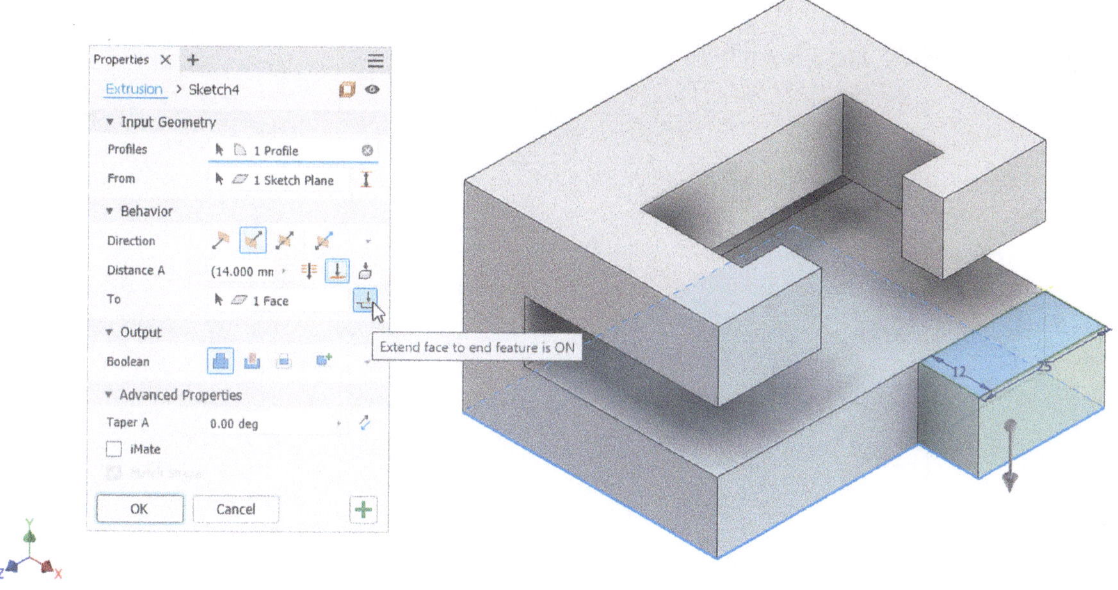

6. Click **OK** to complete the part model.

7. Save and close the file.

Example 2 (Inches)

In this example, you will create the part shown below.

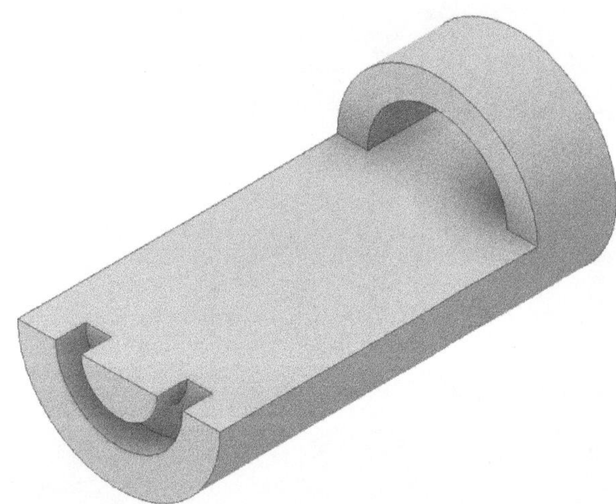

Creating the Revolved Solid Feature

1. Start **Autodesk Inventor 2026** by double-clicking the **Autodesk Inventor 2026** icon on your desktop.
2. To start a new part file, click the **New** button on the Quick Access Toolbar.
3. On the **Create New File** dialog, click the **Templates > en-US** folder.
4. Click the **Standard.ipt** icon under the **Part - Create 2D and 3D Objects** section. Click **Create** to start a new part file.
5. On the ribbon, click **3D Model > Sketch > Start 2D Sketch**. Click on the **XZ** plane.
6. On the ribbon, click **Sketch > Create > Rectangle > Rectangle Three Point Center** and specify the three points of the rectangle, as shown. Press **Esc** to deactivate the Rectangle command.

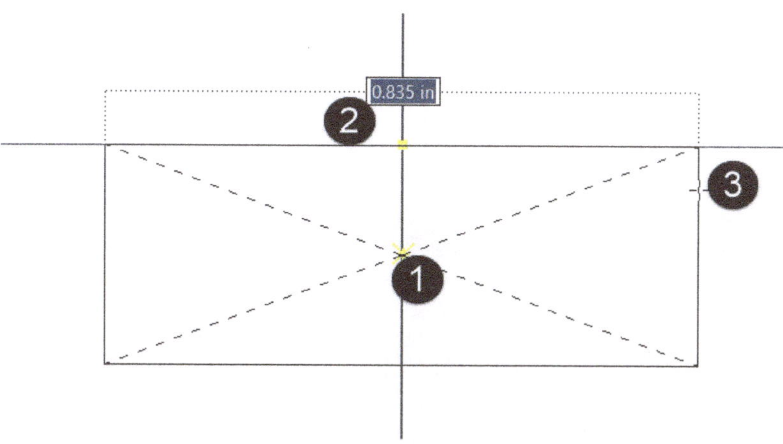

7. Click **Sketch > Constrain > Dimension** on the ribbon and apply dimensions, as shown.
8. On the ribbon, click **Sketch > Constrain > Coincident Constraint**, and then select the midpoint of the top horizontal line. Next, select the sketch origin. Press **Esc**.

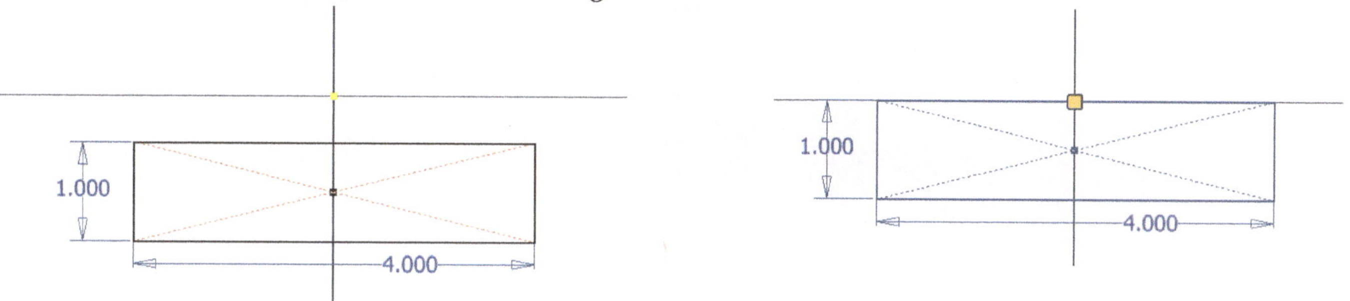

9. Click **Sketch > Exit > Finish Sketch** on the ribbon.
10. Click the **Home** icon located at the top left corner of the ViewCube.

11. Activate the **Revolve** command (click **3D Model > Create > Revolve** on the ribbon); the sketch profile is selected, automatically.
12. On the **Revolve Properties** panel, click in the **Axis** selection box and select the axis line, as shown.
13. Deselect the **Full** icon under the **Behavior** section and enter **180** in the **Angle A** box.
14. Click **Direction > Default** icon and click **OK** to create the *Revolve* feature.

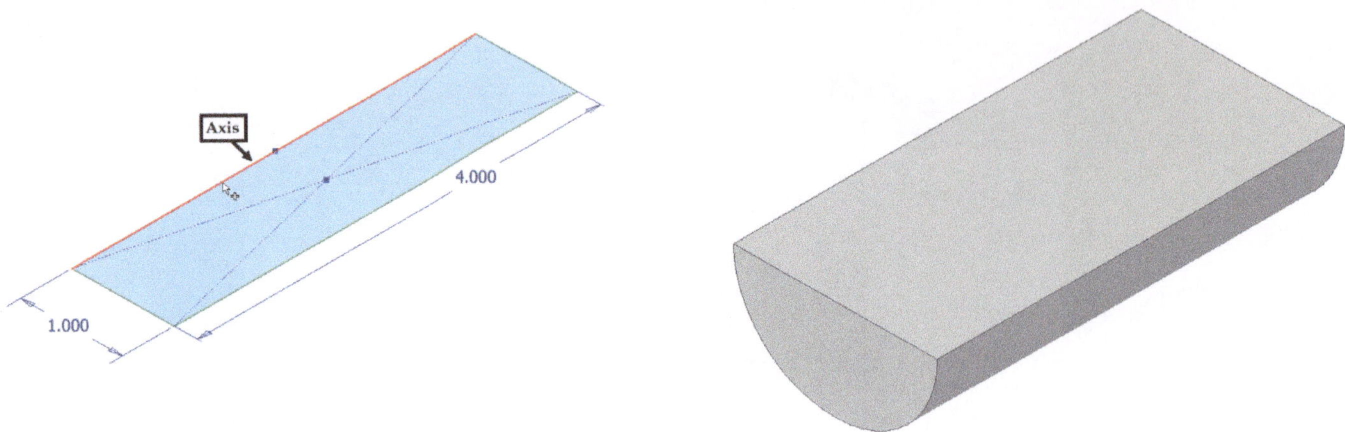

Creating the Revolved Cut

1. On the ribbon, click **3D Model > Sketch > Start 2D Sketch**. Click on the top face of the part model, as shown.

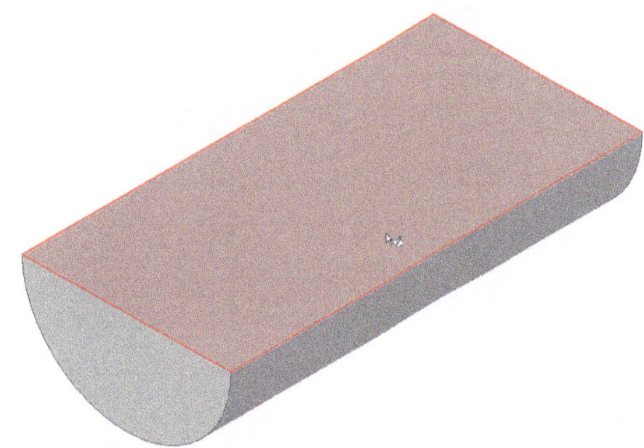

2. Draw the sketch and apply the dimensions, as shown.
3. On the ribbon, click **Sketch > Constrain > Collinear Constraint** and select the left vertical line of the sketch. Next, select the left vertical edge of the model. Click **Finish Sketch**.

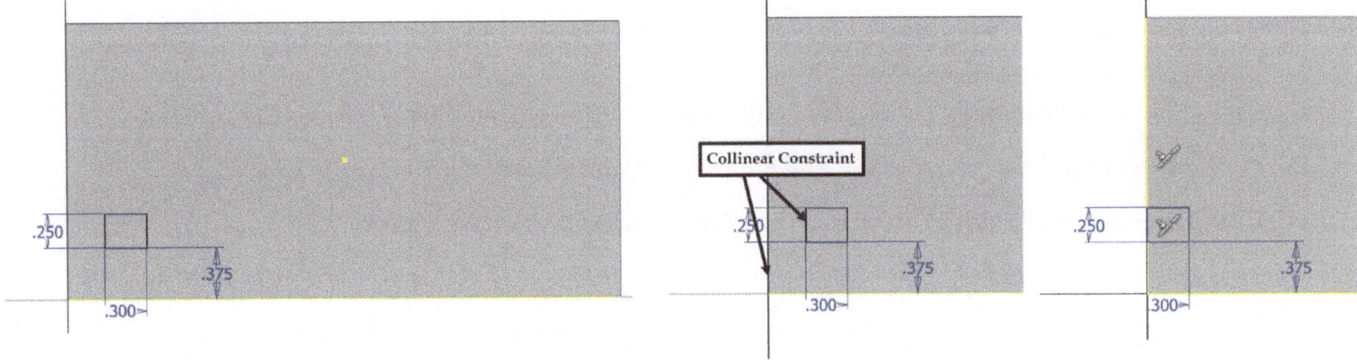

4. Click **3D Model > Work Features > Axis** on the ribbon. Next, click the curved face of the *Revolved* feature.
5. Activate the **Revolve** command and click in the region of the sketch.
6. On the **Revolve Properties** panel, click in the **Axis** selection box and select the newly created axis from the **Model** tab of the Browser window. (leave this step if the axis is already selected).

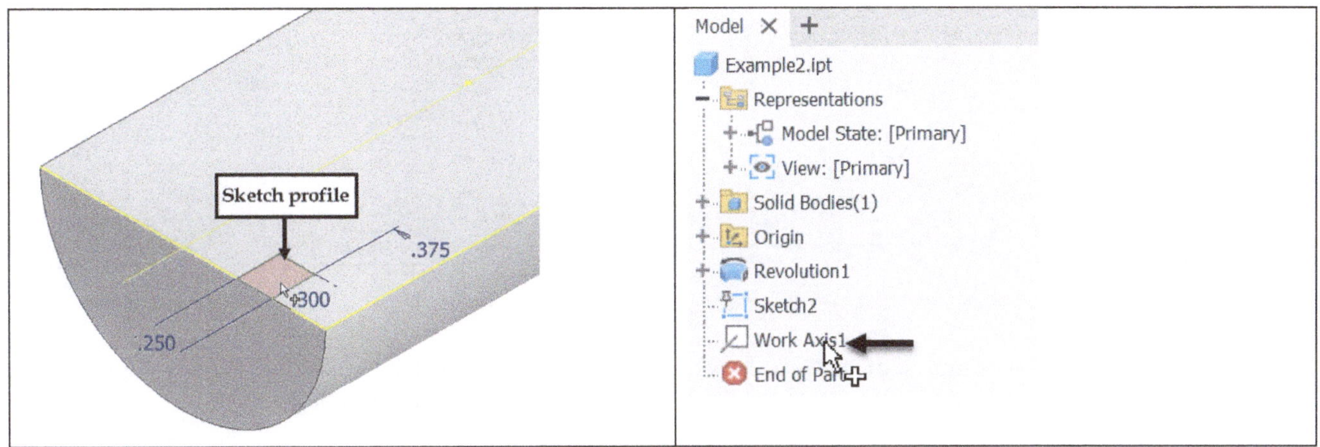

7. Click the **Cut** icon under the **Output** section on the **Revolve Properties** panel.
8. Click the **To Next** icon under the **Behavior** section. Click the **Direction > Default** icon and click **OK** to create the *Revolved Cut* feature.

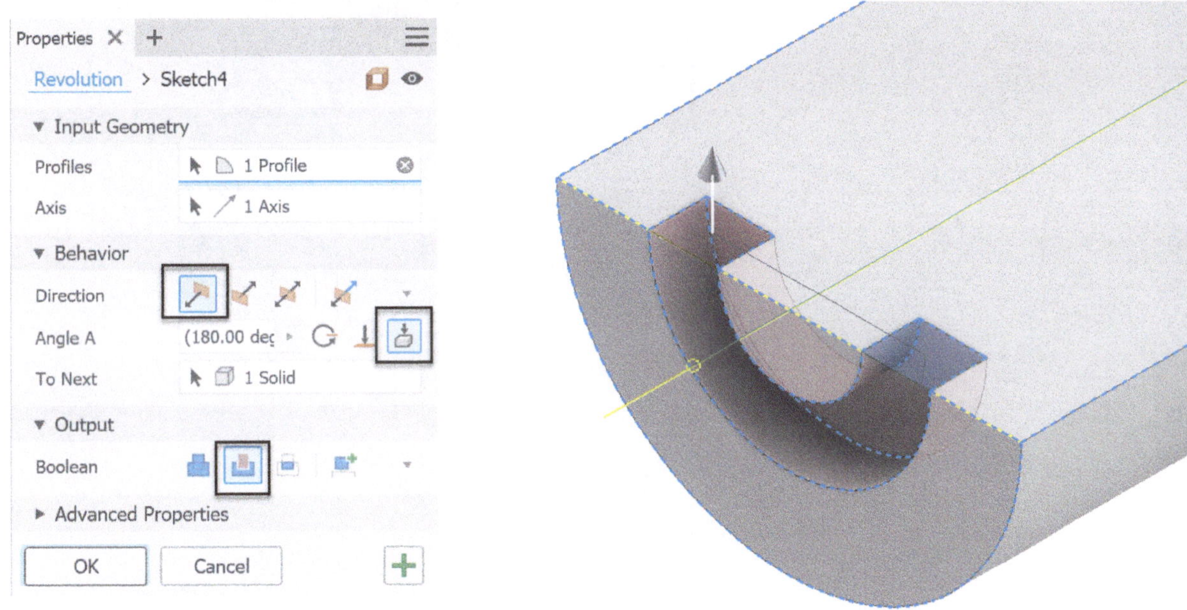

Adding a Revolved Feature to the model

1. Activate the **Start 2D Sketch** command and click on the top face of the part model.
2. Draw the sketch and apply dimensions and constraints, as shown. Finish the sketch.

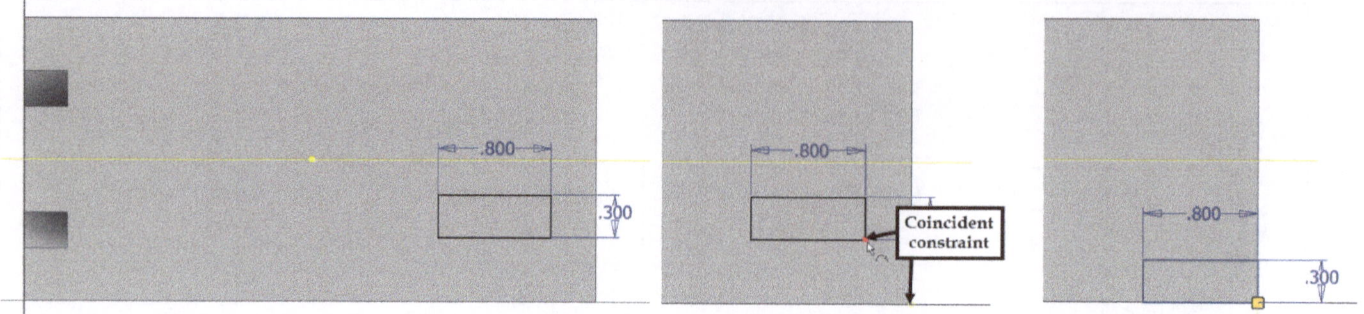

3. Activate the **Revolve** command and select the sketch from the part model.
4. On the **Revolve Properties** panel, click in the **Axis** selection box and select the axis, as shown. Make sure that the **Join** icon is selected.
5. Click **Angle A** > **To** icon in the **Behavior** section and select the top face of the model geometry.

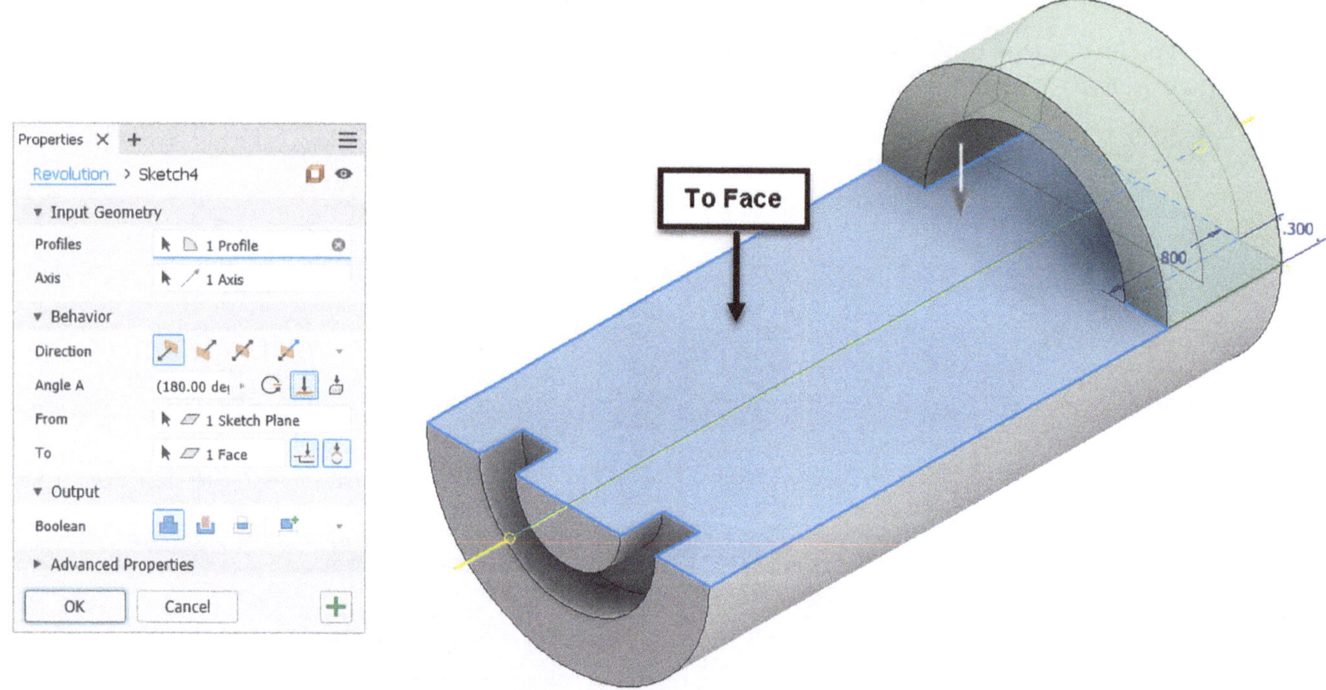

6. Click **OK** to add the *Revolved* feature to the part model.

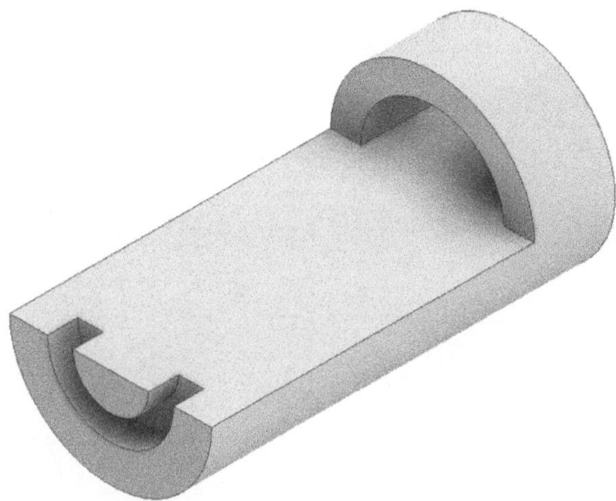

7. Save and close the file.

Questions

1. How to create parallel planes in Inventor?
2. What are the **Direction** options available on the **Extrude Properties** panel?
3. List the options to specify the extents of the extruded feature.
4. How do you extrude an open profile in Inventor?
5. List the Boolean operations available on the **Extrude Properties** panel.
6. How to create angled planes in Inventor?

Exercises

Exercise 1 (Inches)

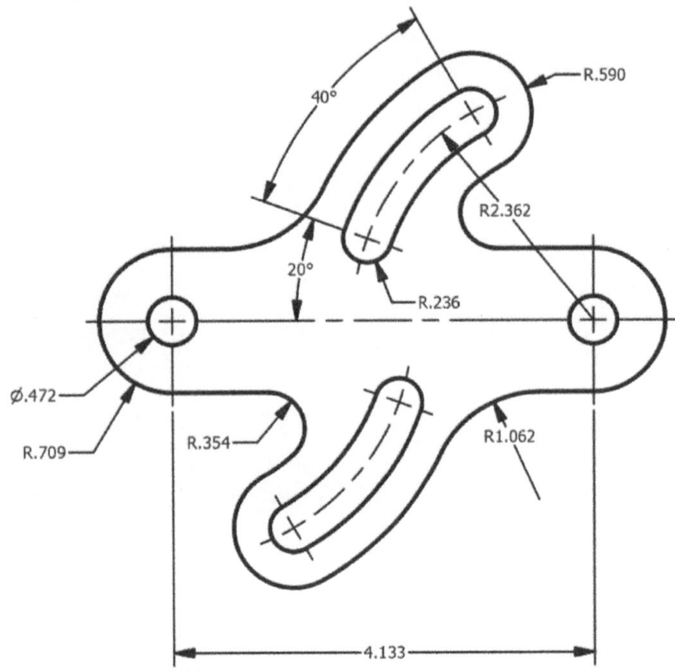

Exercise 2 (Millimetres)

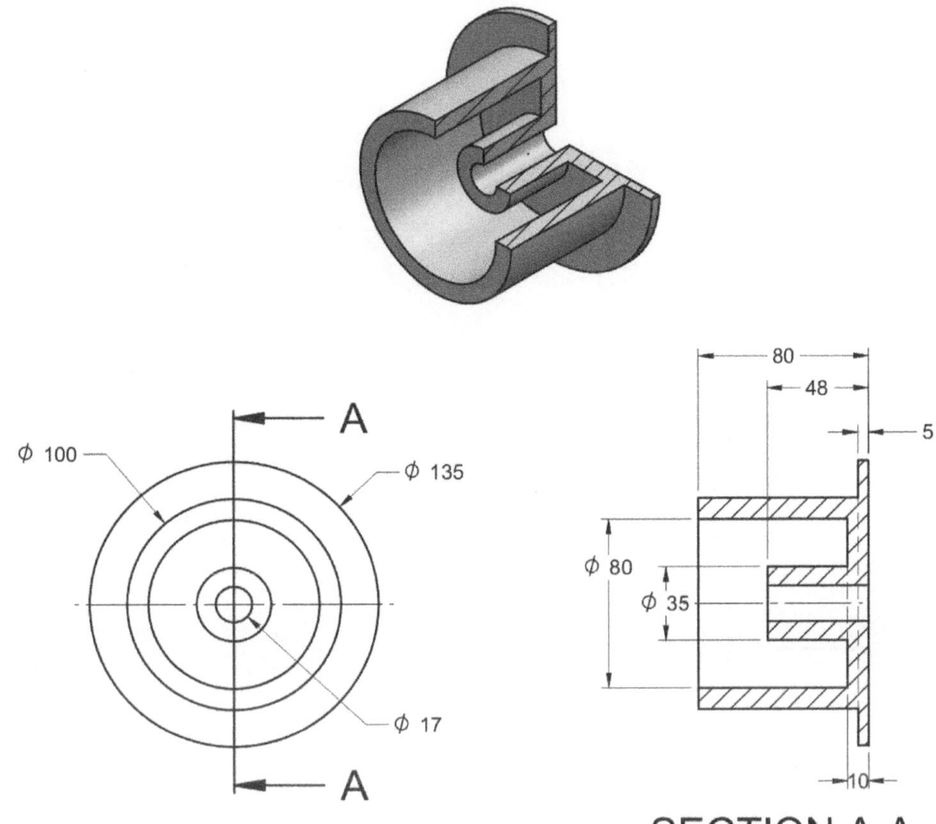

Exercise 3 (Inches)

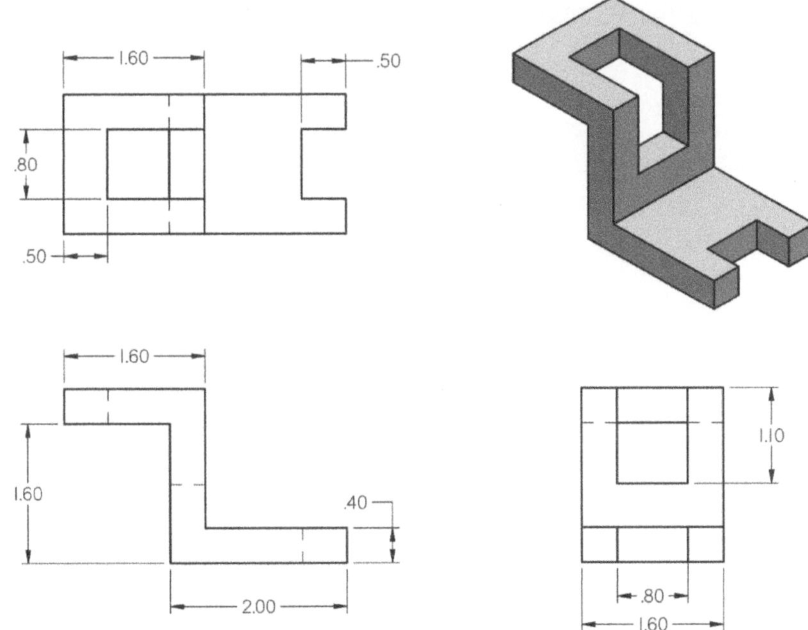

Exercise 4 (Millimetres)

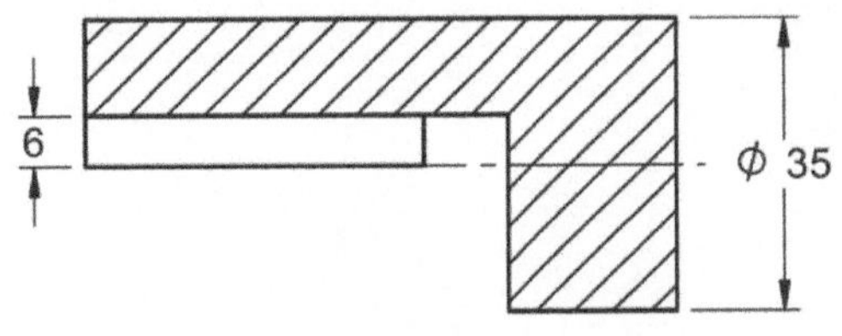

SECTION A-A

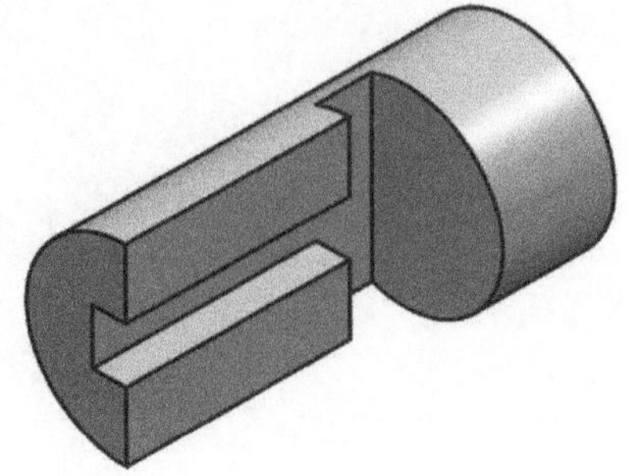

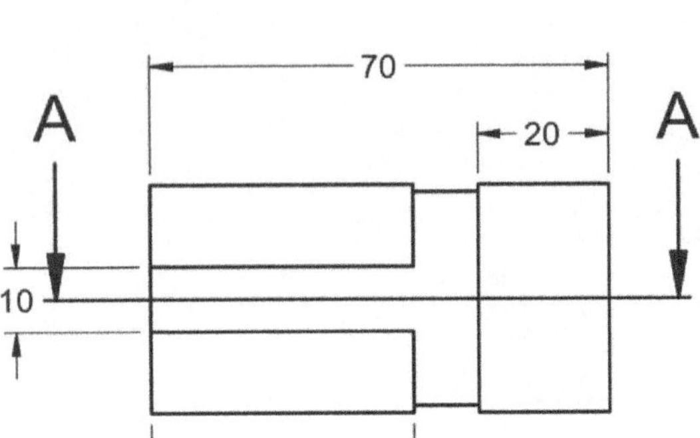

Chapter 4: Placed Features

So far, all of the features that were covered in the previous chapter were based on two-dimensional sketches. However, there are certain features in Inventor that do not require a sketch at all. Features that do not require a sketch are called placed features. You can simply place them on your models. However, to do so, you must have some existing geometry. Unlike a sketch-based feature, you cannot use a placed feature for the first feature of a model. For example, to create a *Fillet* feature, you must have an already existing edge. In this chapter, you will learn how to add placed features to your design.

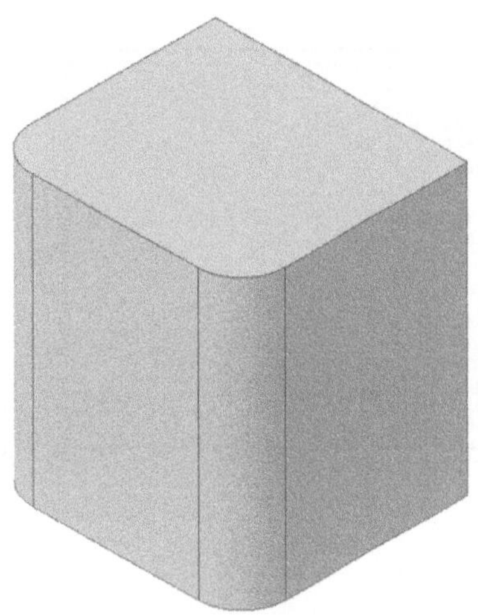

The topics covered in this chapter are:

- *Holes*
- *Threads*
- *Fillets*
- *Chamfers*
- *Drafts*
- *Shells*

 Hole

As you know, it is possible to use the *Extrude* command to create cuts and remove material. However, if you want to drill holes that are of standard sizes, the **Hole** command is a better way to do this. The reason for this is that it has many hole types already predefined for you. All you have to do is choose the correct hole type and size. The other benefit is when you are going to create a 2D drawing, Inventor can place the correct hole annotation automatically. Activate this command (Click **3D Model > Modify > Hole** on the ribbon), and you will notice that the **Properties** panel appears on the screen. The components of the **Properties** panel are shown in the figure below. There are options in this panel that make it easy to create different types of holes.

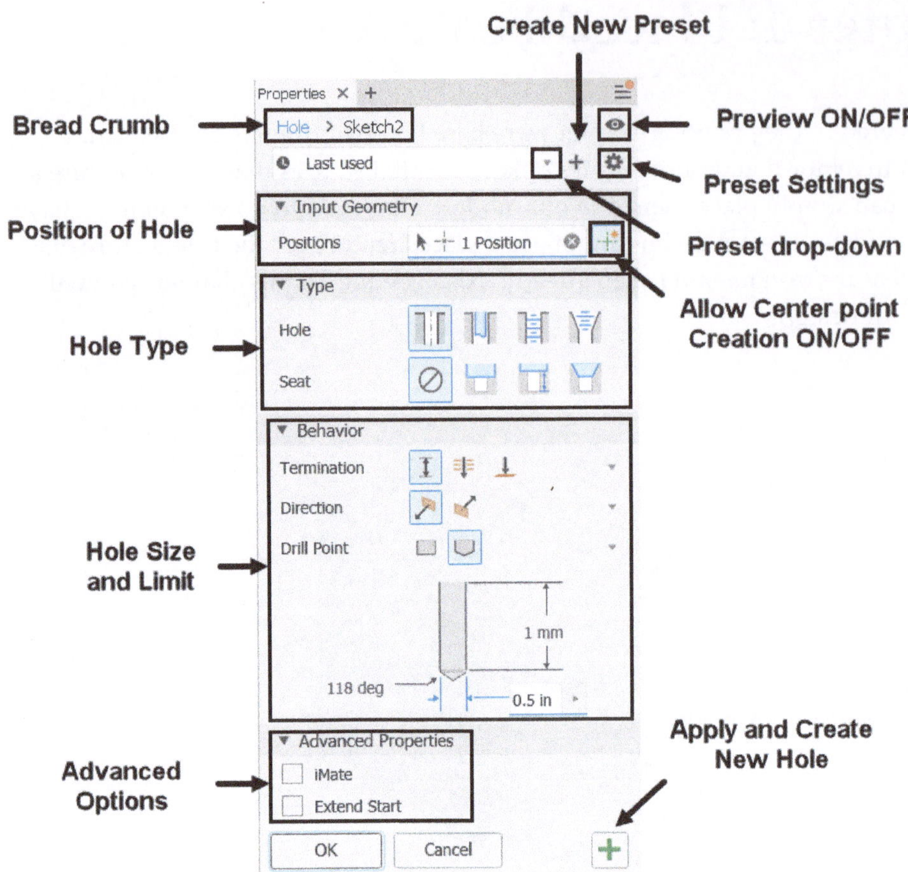

Simple Hole

To create a simple hole feature, select **Type > Simple Hole** on the **Properties** panel. Type-in a value in the **Diameter** box attached to the hole image in the **Size** section.

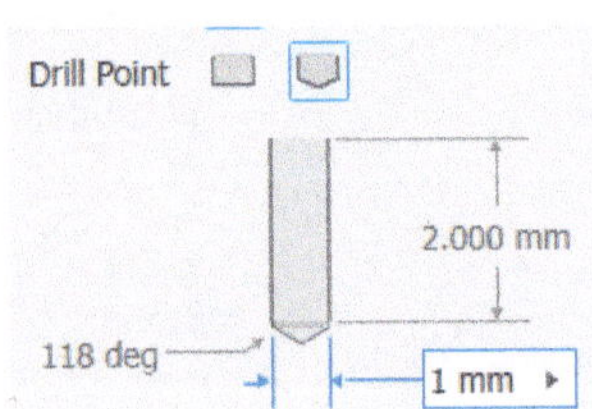

Next, select the **Termination** type. If you want a *Through-hole*, select **Termination > Through All**. If you want the hole only up to some depth, then select **Termination > Distance**, and then type in a value in the **Hole Depth** box attached to the hole image.

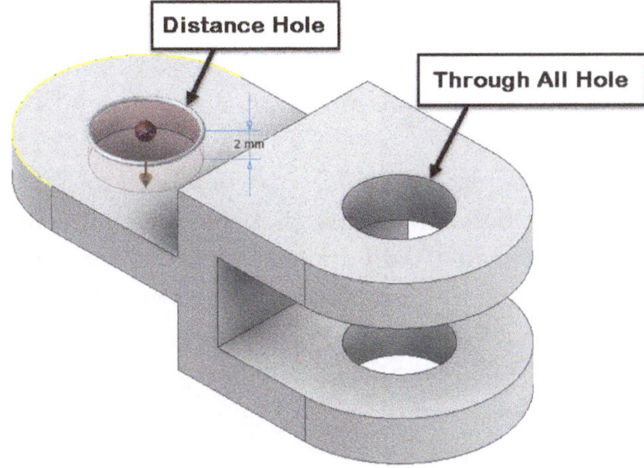

If you want the hole only up to a surface, then select **Termination > To** and select a face or surface on the graphics window; the hole will be created up to the selected surface.

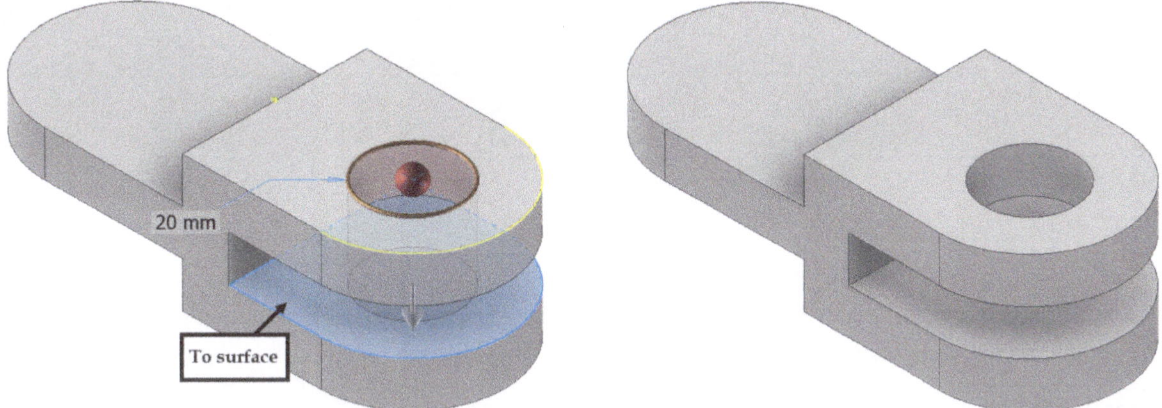

The **Drill Point** section has two options to define the depth of the hole: **Flat**, **Angle, Flat W, Angle V,** and **Angle Y**. The **Flat** option creates a hole with a flat bottom. The **Angle** option creates a hole with an angled bottom. The **Drill Point Angle** box defines the angle of the cone tip at the bottom.

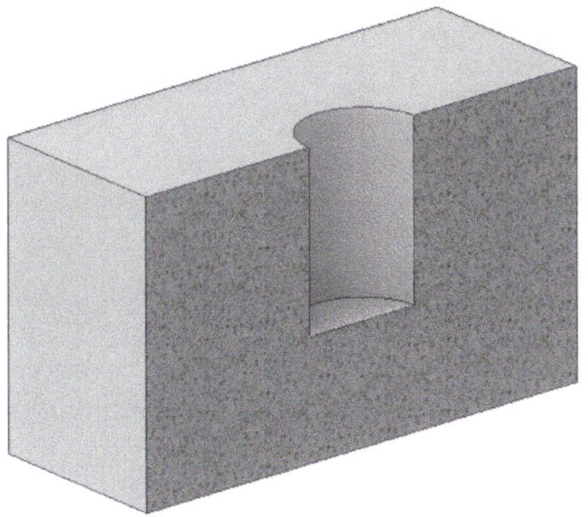

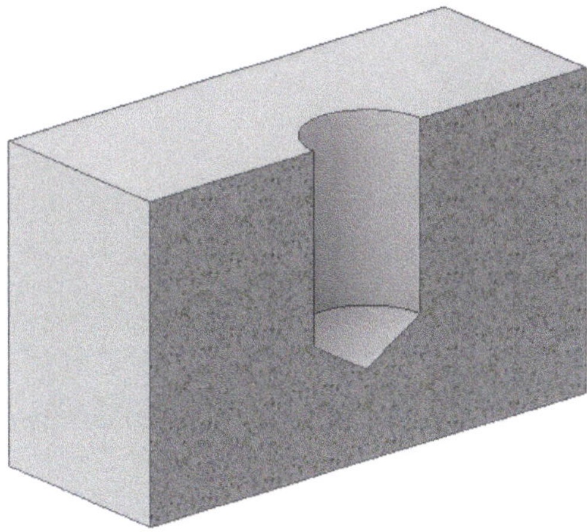

The **Flat W** option also creates a flat-bottomed drill point but is used specifically for 2D and 3D annotations. It ensures that the drilling tool is represented according to the ISO standard in drawings.

The **Angle V** option functions like the **Angle** option, providing additional flexibility for defining angles through manual input or geometry selection on the model.

The **Angle Y** option creates a unique drill point shape that is part of the hole's depth parameter.

After specifying the settings on the **Properties** panel, click on a face to place the hole. Next, you need to specify the exact location of the hole by adding constraints or dimensions or both. To do this, click the **Sketch** link in the Bread Crumbs of the **Properties** panel; the **Sketch** environment is activated. Add dimensions and constraints to define the hole position. You can also add multiple hole points by using the **Point** command (on the ribbon, click **Sketch > Create > Point**). Next, click the **Hole** link in the Bread Crumbs area of the **Properties** panel.

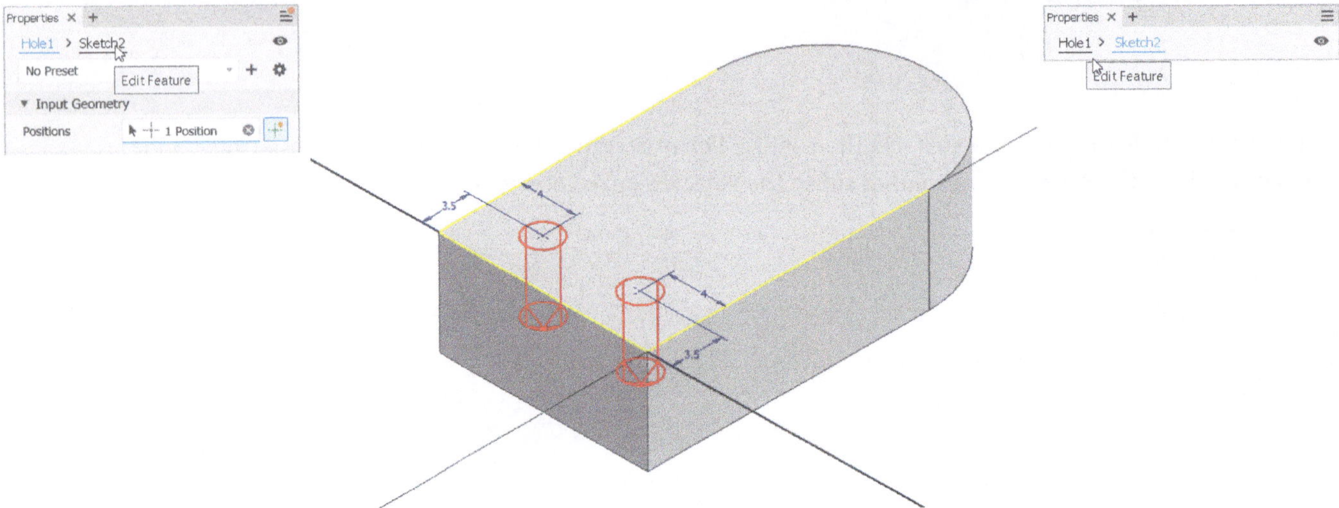

If you want to create a hole concentric to a circular edge, click on a face to place the hole. Next, select a circular edge; the hole will be concentric to it. Click **OK** to complete the hole feature.

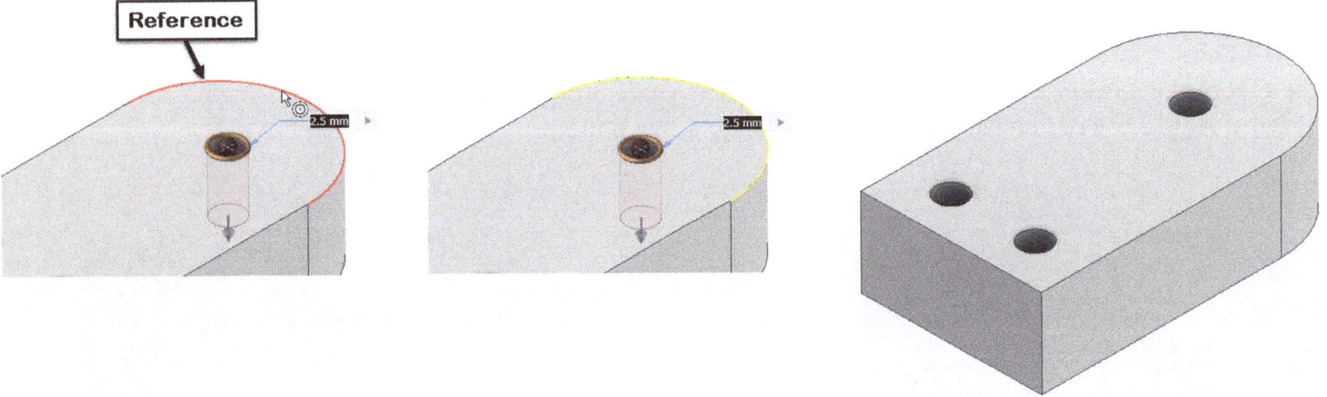

Extend Start

The **Extend Start** option is available in the **Advanced Properties** section and is used to extend the hole beyond its starting point. Select this option to remove any portion of the model geometry that blocks the starting point of the hole, as shown.

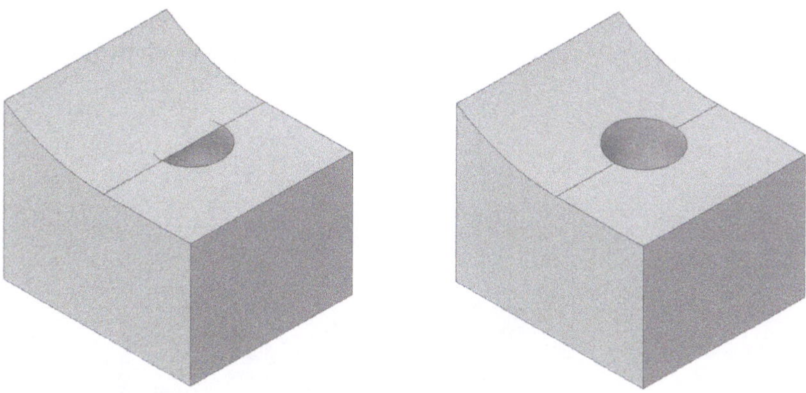

Saving the Hole Settings

While creating a hole, Inventor allows you to save the settings specified on the **Properties** panel for future use. You can use these settings to create a hole with the same specifications multiple times. On the **Properties** panel, click the **Create new preset** icon next to the **Preset** drop-down. Next, type a name for the preset and click the blue check; the settings are saved. You can access the saved settings from the **Preset** drop-down.

You can make changes to the preset settings and save it using the **Save Current** option available on the **Preset Settings** drop-down. Likewise, you can rename or delete the preset using the **Rename Current** and **Delete Current** options, respectively.

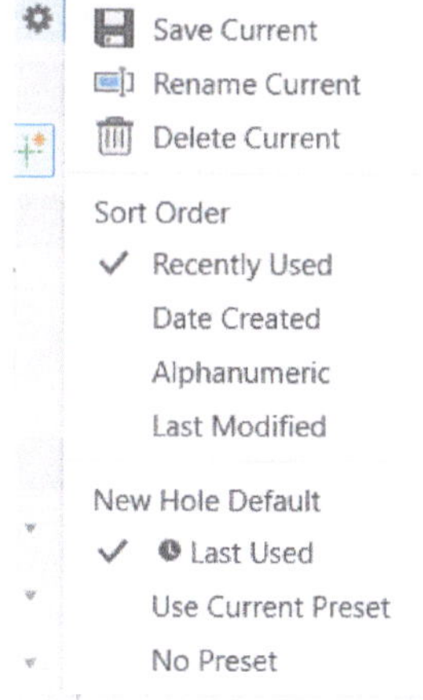

Counterbored Hole

A counterbore hole is a large diameter hole added at the opening of another hole. It is used to accommodate a fastener below the level of the workpiece surface. To create a counterbore hole, select **Type > Seat > Counterbored**. Next, specify the Counterbore Diameter, Counterbore Depth, and Diameter. Specify the desired

Drill Point option (**Flat, Angle, Flat W, Angle V, or Angle Y**). If you click the **Flat** or **Flat W** option, then you need to specify only the **Hole Depth** value. If you click the **Angle, Angle V**, or **Angle Y** option, then specify the **Hole Depth** and **Drill Point Angle** value.

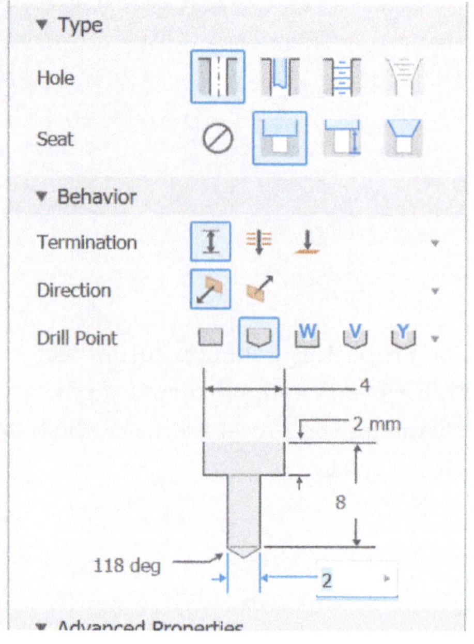

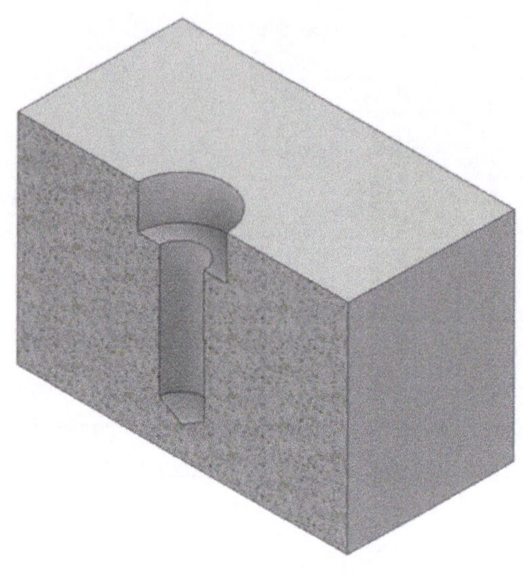

Countersink Hole

A countersunk hole has an enlarged V-shaped opening to accommodate the fastener below the level of the workpiece surface. To create a countersink hole, select **Type > Seat > Countersink**. Type-in values in the **Diameter, Countersink Diameter**, and **Countersink Angle** boxes. Set the hole depth and end condition.

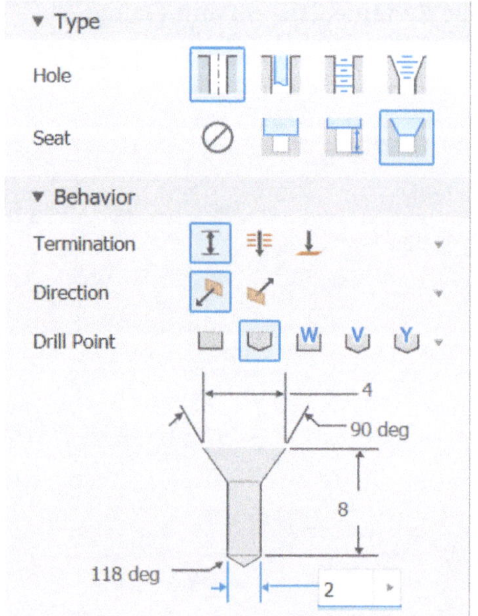

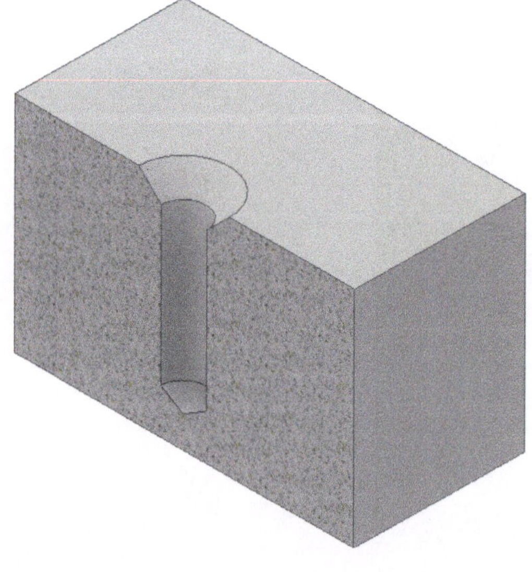

Tapped Hole

To create a tapped hole feature, select **Type > Hole > Tapped Hole**. Under the **Threads** section, select the thread standard from **Type** drop-down and also select the **Size, Designation,** and **Class**. Check the **Full Depth** option to create threads for the full depth of the hole. If you uncheck this option, you need to specify the thread depth in the **Thread Depth** box. Specify the desired thread direction from the **Thread** section. Specify the remaining hole options that are similar to the simple hole feature. Click **OK** to create the Tapped Hole.

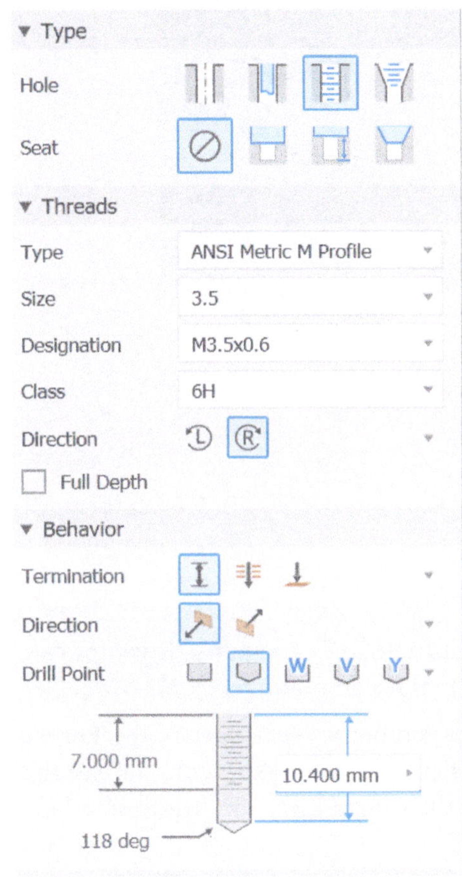

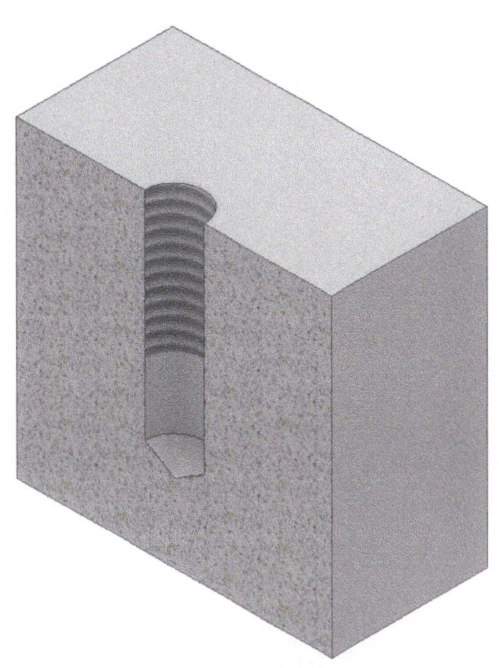

Taper Tapped Hole

Tapering is the process of decreasing the hole diameter toward one end. A tapered tapped hole has a thread, and the diameter gradually becomes smaller towards the bottom. To create a tapered tapped hole, select **Type > Hole > Taper Tapped Hole**. Next, you need to specify the thread **Type** and **Size**. The tapered thread types and sizes are different from the regular threads. Next, you need to specify the thread **Direction** and thread depth. Click **OK** to create the Taper Tapped Hole.

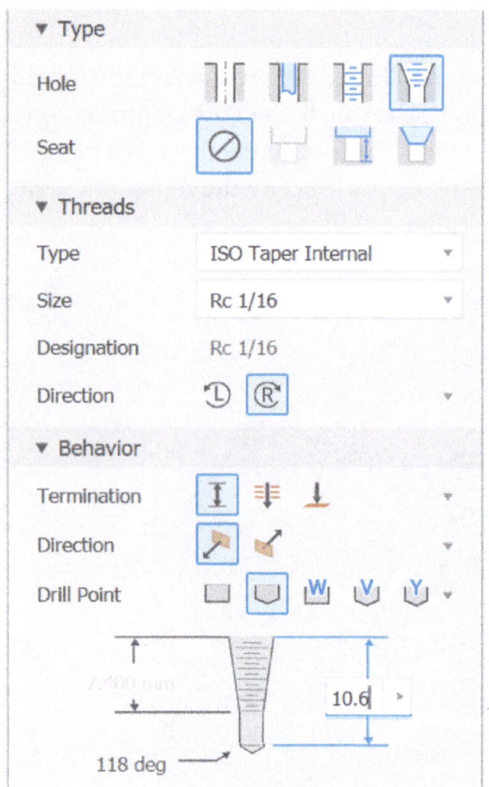

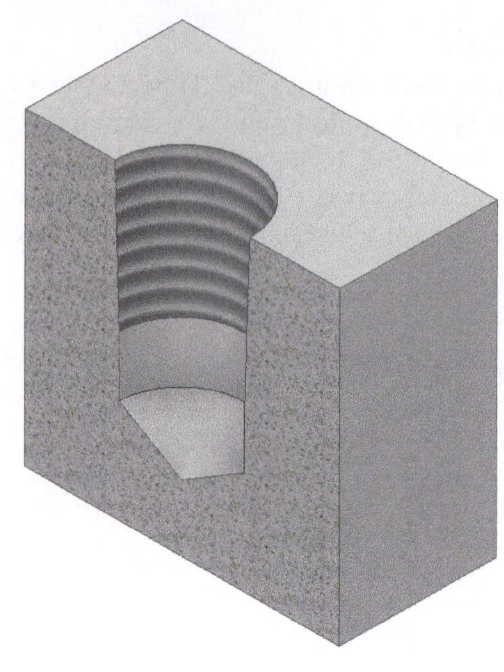

Thread

This command adds a thread feature to a round face. If you add a thread feature to a 3D geometry, Inventor can automatically place the correct thread annotation in the 2D drawing. Activate this command (click **3D Model > Modify > Thread** on the ribbon) and click on a cylindrical face of the part geometry. Next, specify the **Thread Type** on the **Thread Properties** panel. The **Size** is automatically selected as per the size of the circular face of the part geometry. Next, specify the **Designation** and **Class** values. Also, select the thread direction (**Right hand** or **Left hand**).

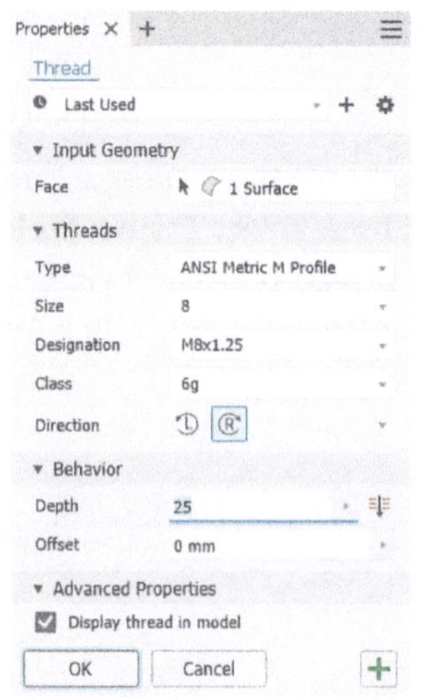

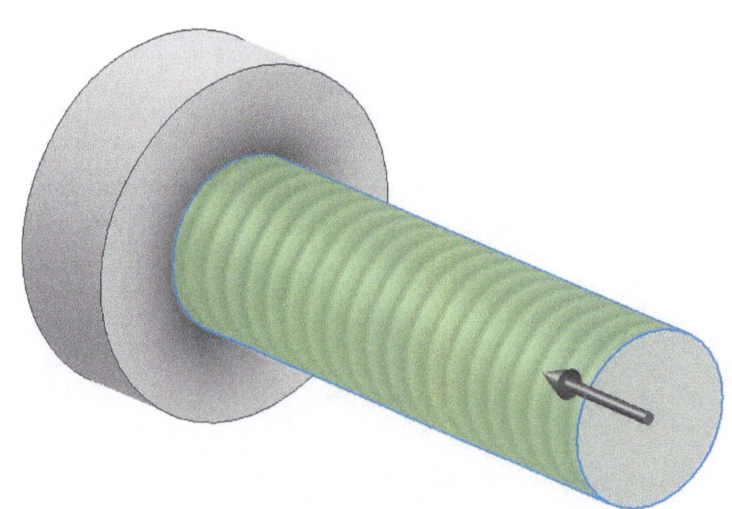

The **Full Depth** option is activated by default under the **Behavior** section on the **Thread Properties** panel. It creates the thread up to the entire depth of the round face. Turn off the **Full Depth** icon, if you want to specify the depth of the thread in the **Depth** box. Next, enter a value in the **Offset** box, if you want to create a thread at a distance from the start face of the cylinder.

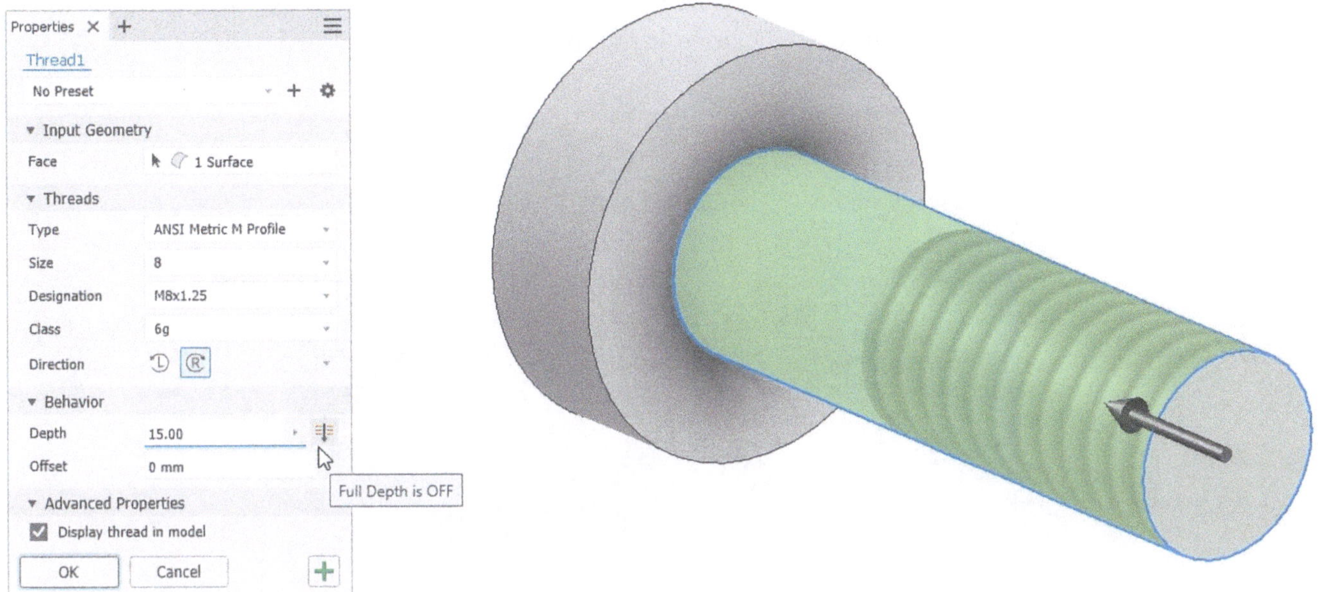

Select the **Display thread in model** option to view the thread in the part geometry. Note that if you deselect this option, the thread will not be displayed in the part geometry. However, you can view the thread in the 2D Drawing. Click **OK** to complete the thread feature.

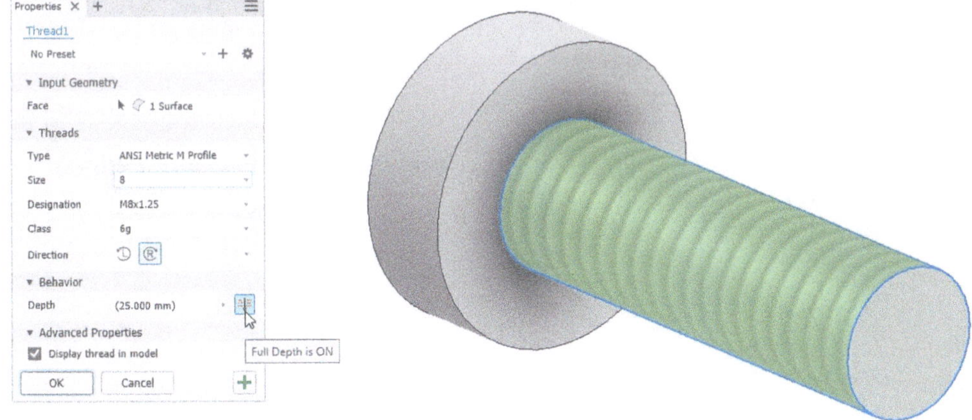

Fillet

This command breaks the sharp edges of a model and blends them. You do not need a sketch to create a blend. All you need to have is model edges. To activate this command, click **3D Model > Modify > Fillet** on the ribbon and select the edges to fillet. As you start selecting edges, you will see a preview of the geometry. Inventor allows you to select the edges, which are located at the back of the model without rotating it. By mistake, if you have selected the wrong edge, you can deselect it by holding the Shift key and selecting the edge again. You can change the radius by typing a value in the **Fillet Constant Radius** box. As you change the radius, all the selected edges will be updated. It is because they are all part of one instance. If you want the edges to have different radii, you must create fillets in separate selection sets. To do this, click the **Add constant radius edge set** icon in the **Selection Sets** section. Next, select the edges to be added to set. Type the radius value in the **Fillet Constant Radius** box displayed next to the newly selected edge set. Select the **Tangent** option from the drop-down located next to the **Fillet Constant Radius** box to create fillets that are tangent to the adjacent faces. Next, click **OK** to complete the fillet feature. The *Fillet* feature will be listed in the **Model Window**.

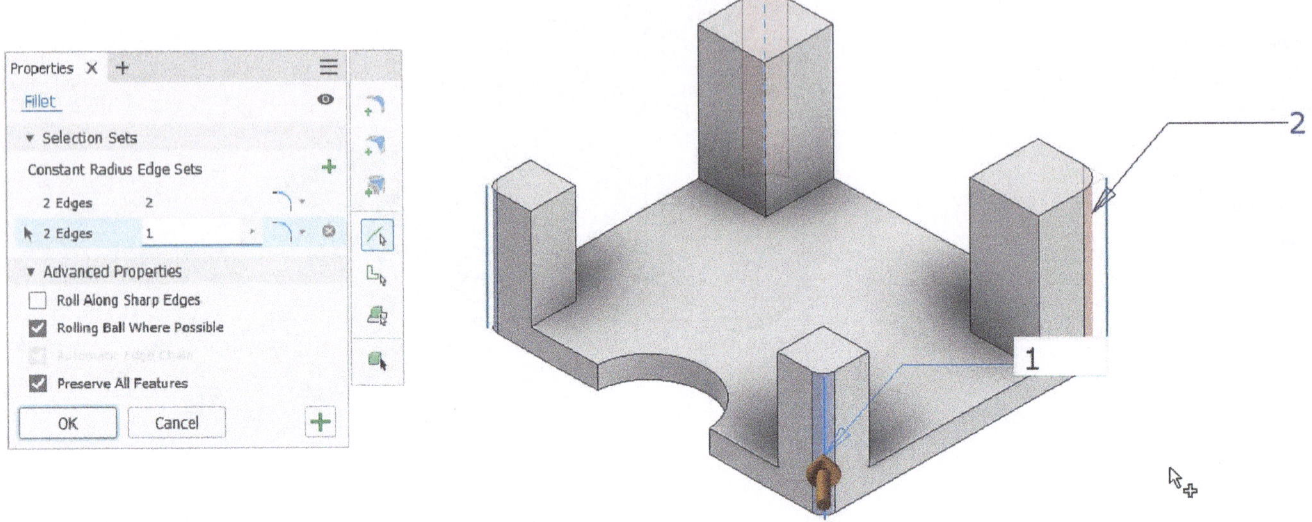

Smooth Fillet

By default, the edge fillets are tangent to the adjacent faces. However, if you want to create a smooth fillet that is curvature continuous with the adjacent faces, then select the **Smooth G2** option from the drop-down located next to the **Fillet Constant Radius** box.

Inverted Fillet

The **Inverted** option helps you to create convex or concave fillets. Convex fillets are created on exterior edges. Whereas, the concave fillets are created on interior edges.

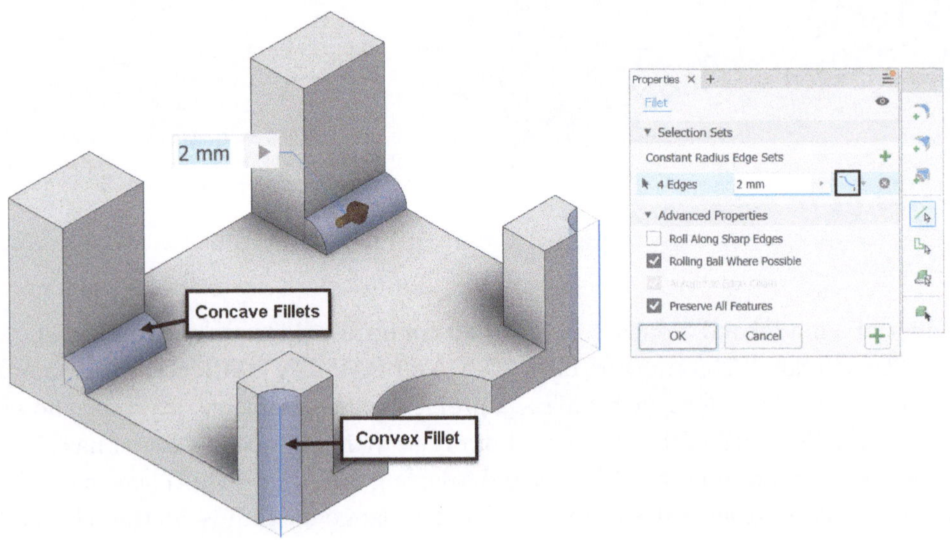

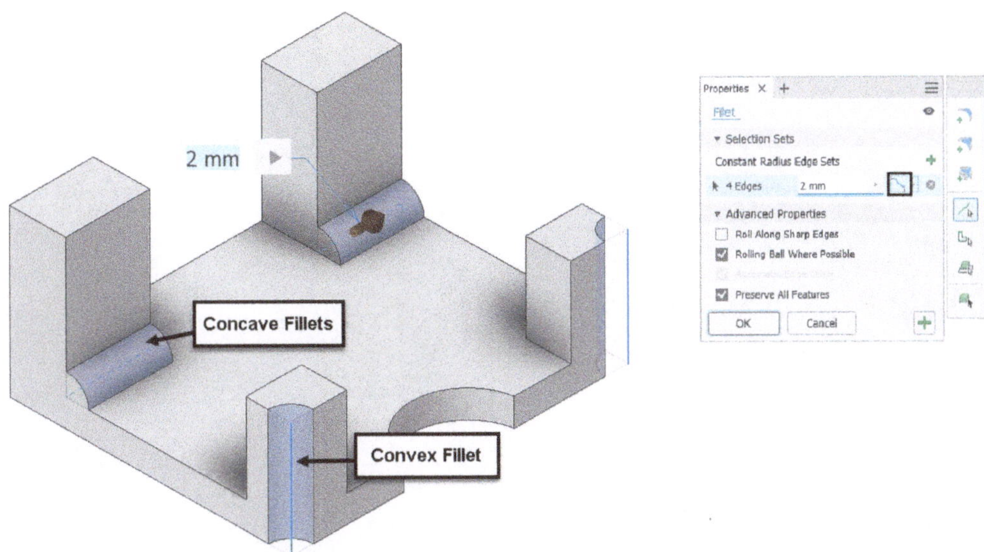

If you want to create the inverted fillet, then select the **Inverted** option from the drop-down located next to the **Fillet Constant Radius** box. Next, type in the radius value and click **OK** to create the inverted fillet.

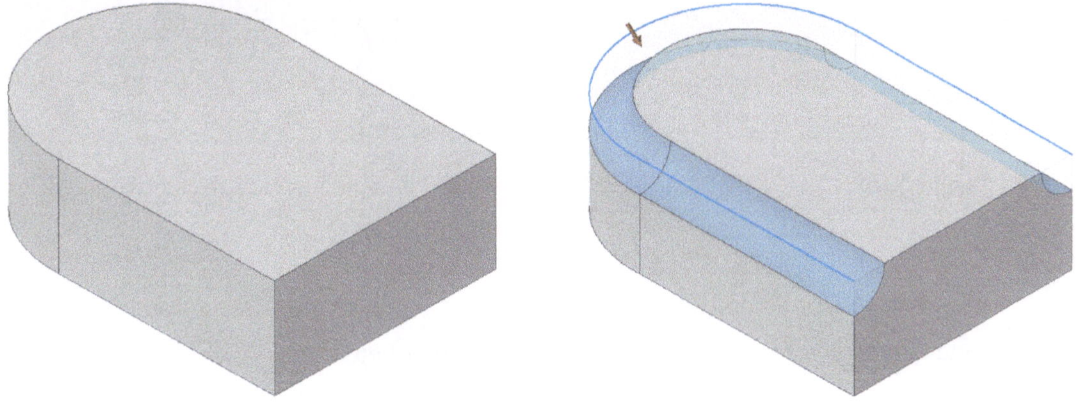

Selection Modes

The **Fillet** command allows you to select the edges to be filleted using three selection modes: **Edge**, **Loop**, and **Feature**.

The **Edge** selection mode allows you to select individual edges.

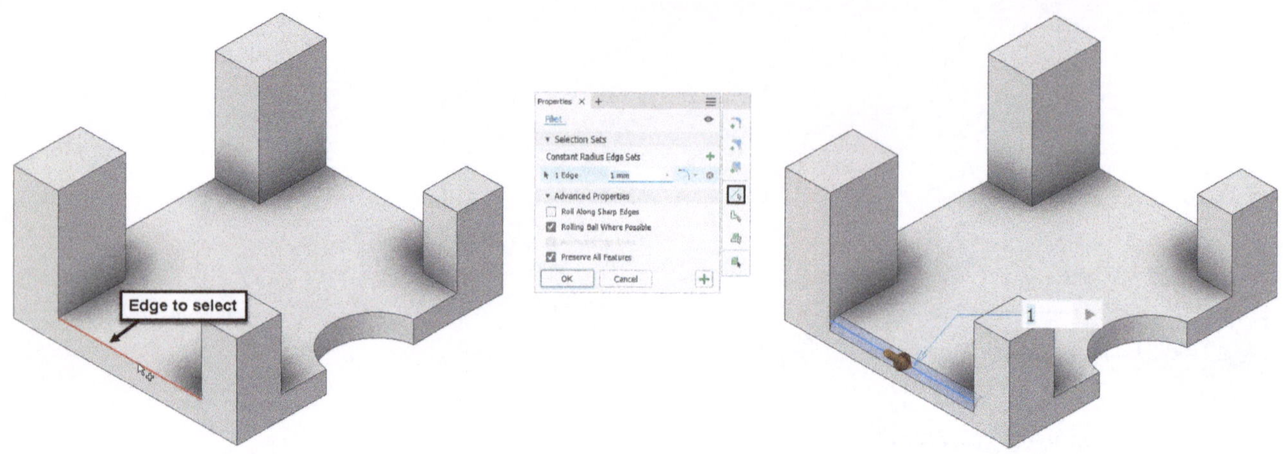

The **Loop** selection mode allows you to select a loop of edges.

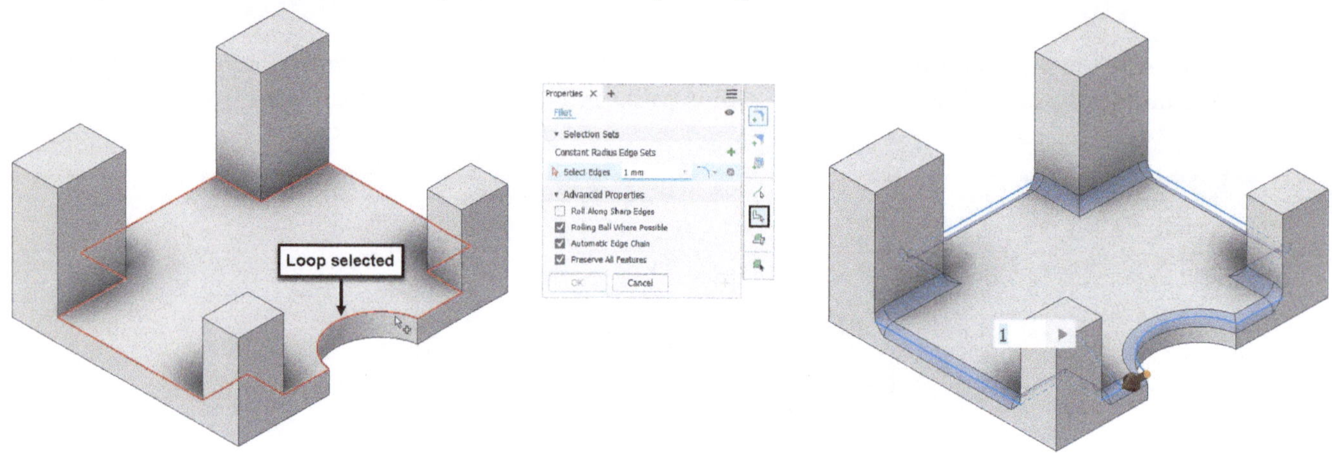

The **Feature** selection mode allows you to select the entire feature to be filleted.

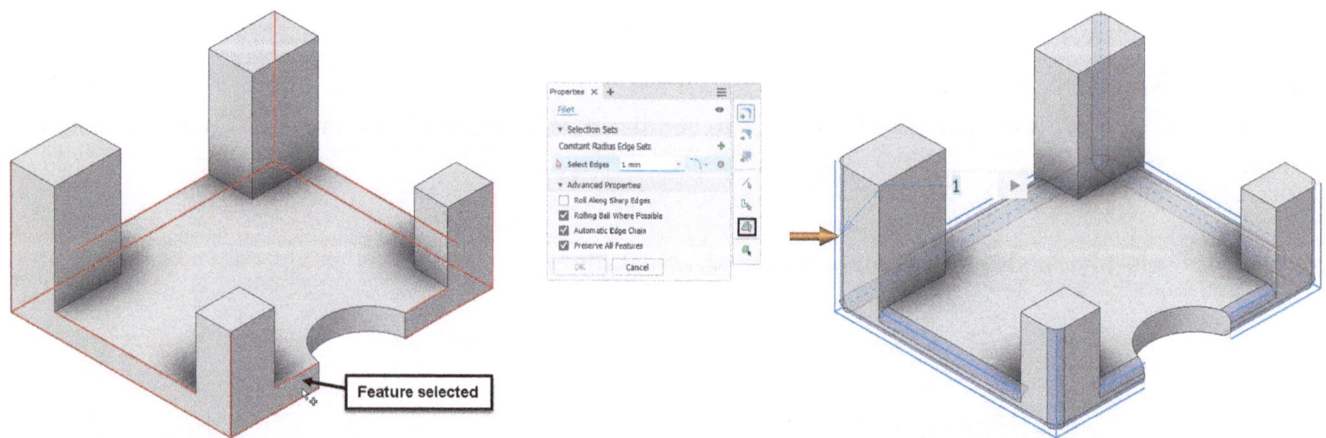

Solids

The **Fillet** command has options to create fillets or rounds without selecting the edges individually. To do this, click the **Solids** icon on the left side of the **Fillet** Properties panel. Next, select an option from the drop-down available in the **Solids** section.

The **All Edges** option adds fillets to all edges of the select solid. Select this option from the drop-down available in the Solids section. Next, type-in values in the radius boxes of the Fillets and Rounds.

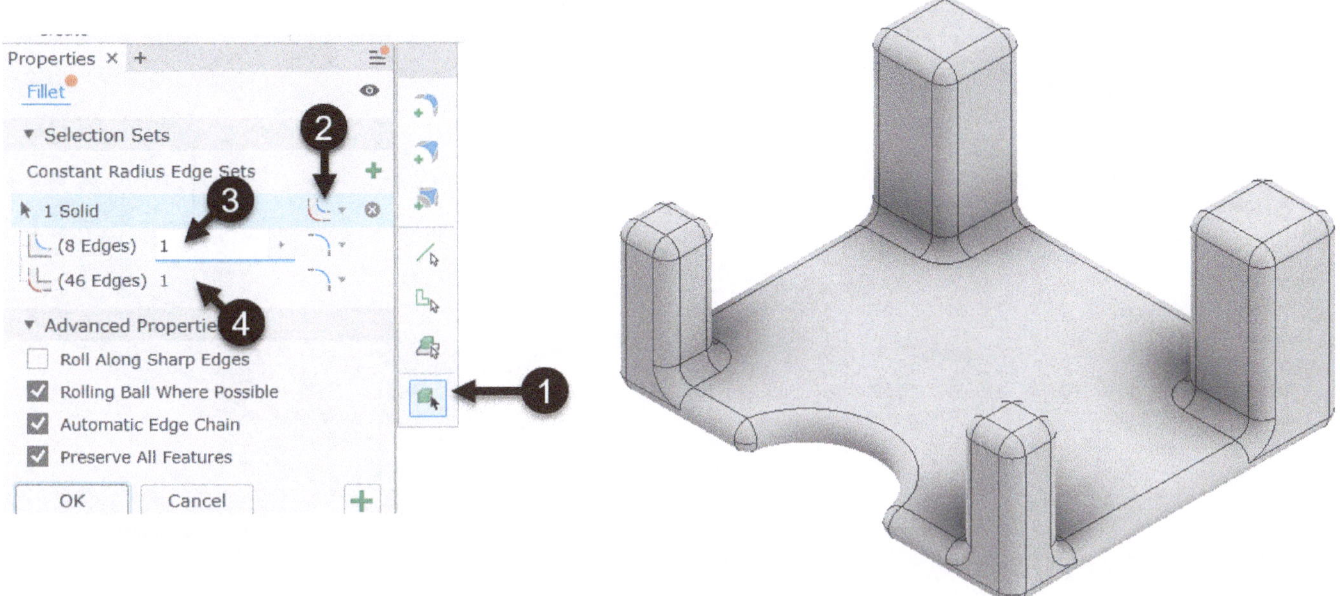

The **All Fillets** option creates fillets on the interior edges of the model, automatically.

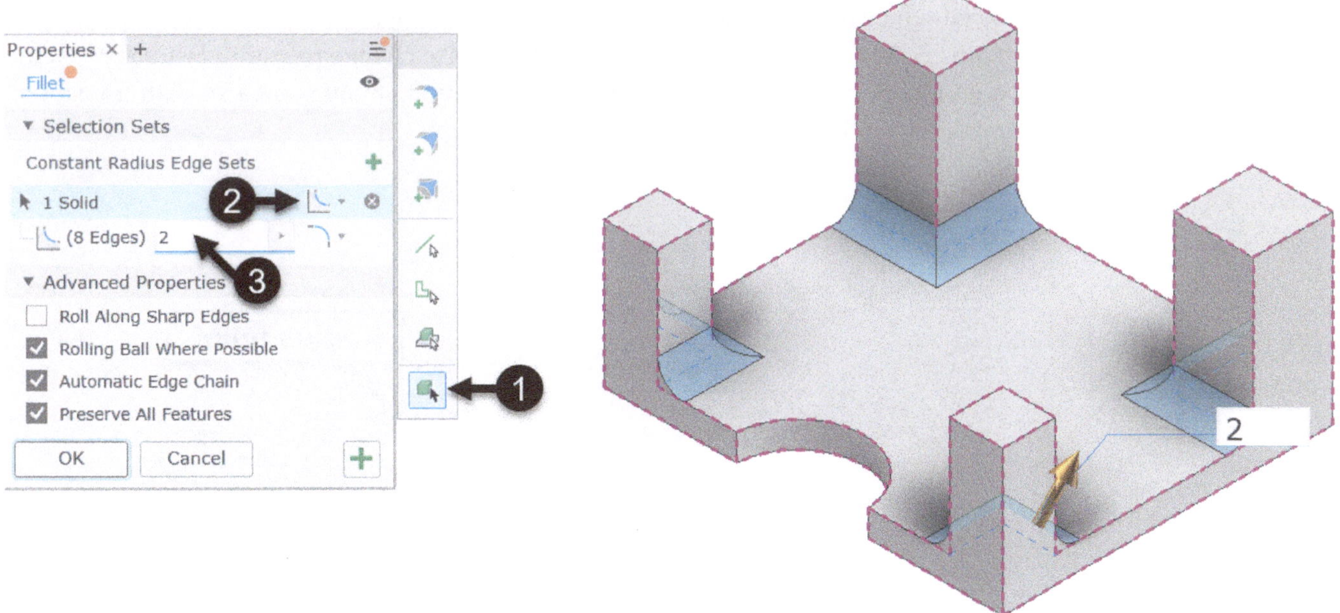

The **All Rounds** option creates rounds on the exterior edges of the model, automatically.

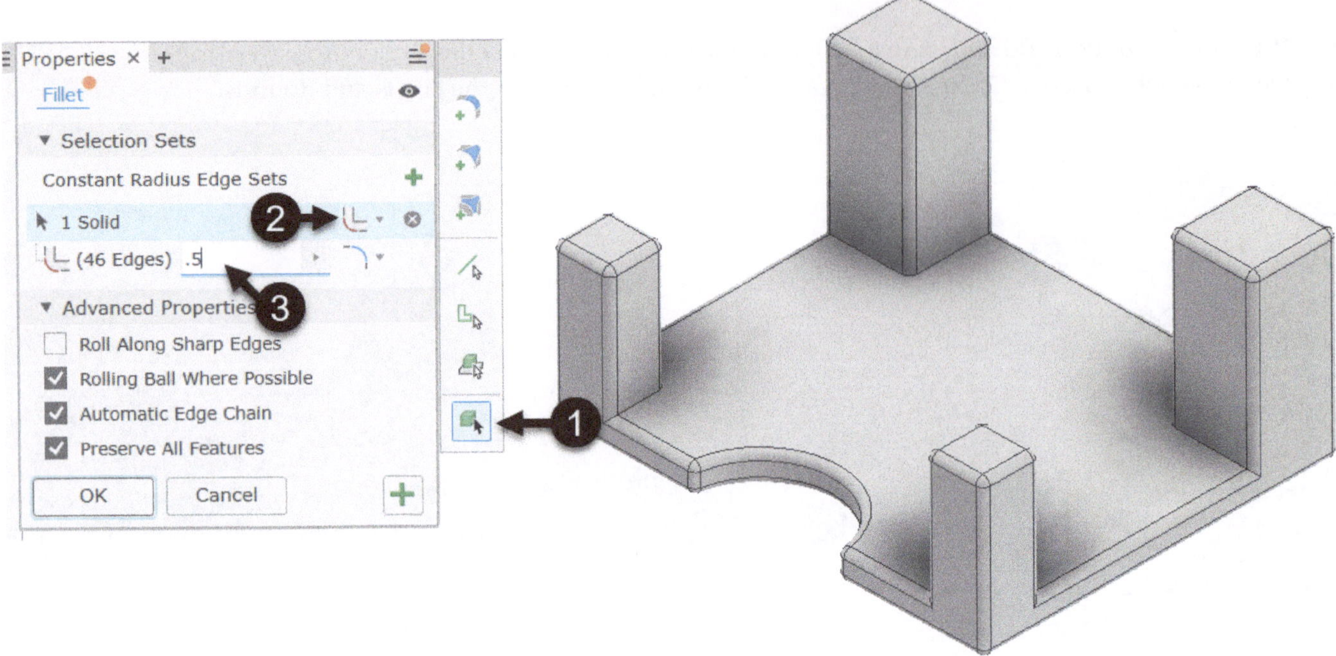

Variable Radius Fillet

Inventor allows you to create a fillet with a varying radius along the selected edge. Activate the **Fillet** command to create a variable fillet. On the **Fillet** properties panel, click the **Add Variable Radius Fillet** icon, and then select the edge to add a fillet. Specify the variable radius points on the selected edge. Next, double-click on the dimensions displayed on the radius points and change the values. You can also change the radius values of each point in the **Fillet** properties panel. Check the **Smooth Radius Transition** option, if you want a smooth transition between the variable radius points. Click **OK** to create the variable radius fillet.

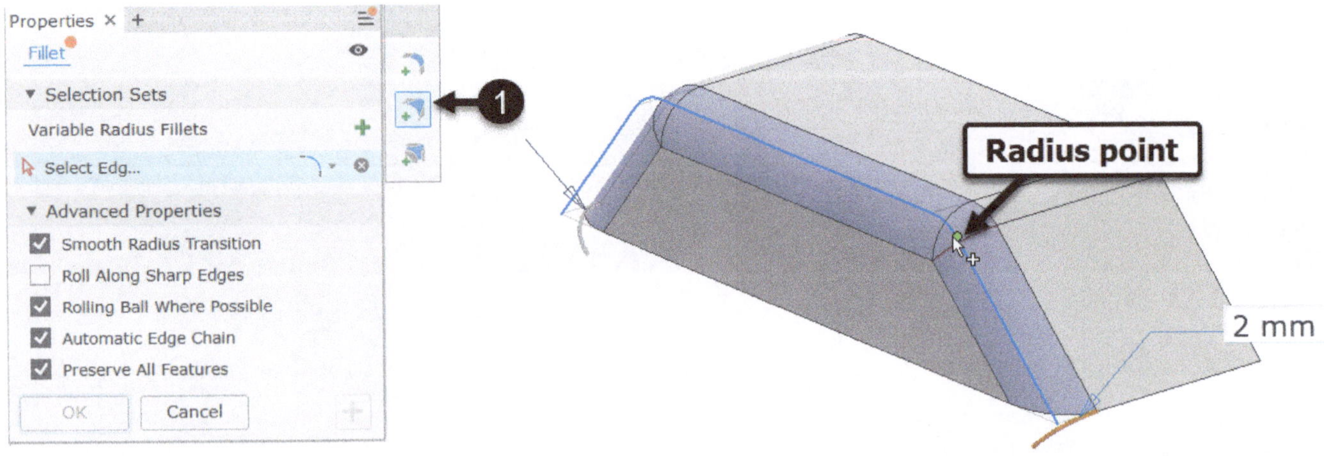

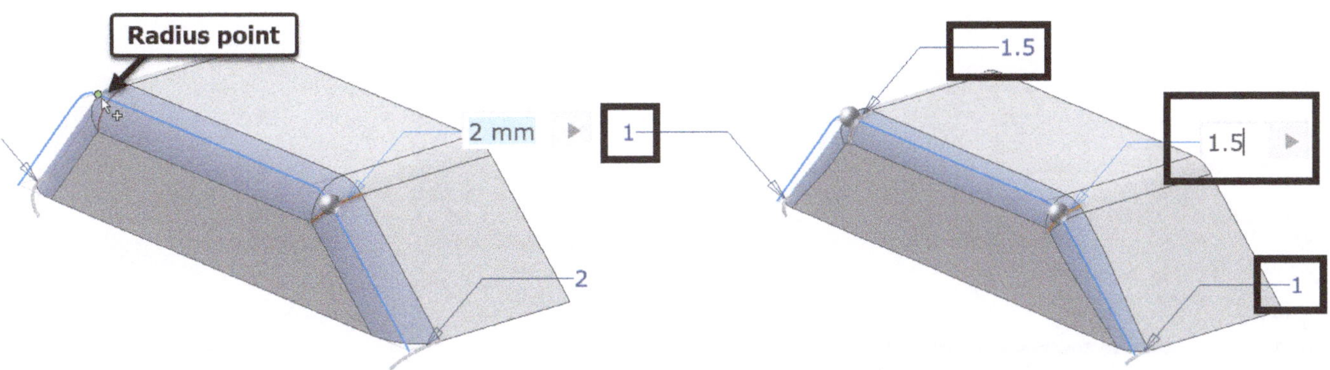

Corner Setback

If you create fillets on three edges that come together at a corner, you have the option to control how these three fillets are blended. Activate the **Fillet** command and select the three edges that meet together at a corner. Next, click the **Add corner Setback** icon on the **Fillet** Properties panel, and then click on the vertex where the three fillets meet; the three edges and setback values appear on the dialog. Under the **Corner Setback Behavior** section, click in the **Setback Distance** boxes of the individual edges, and then change their values. Check the **Minimal** option if you do not want to apply the setback.

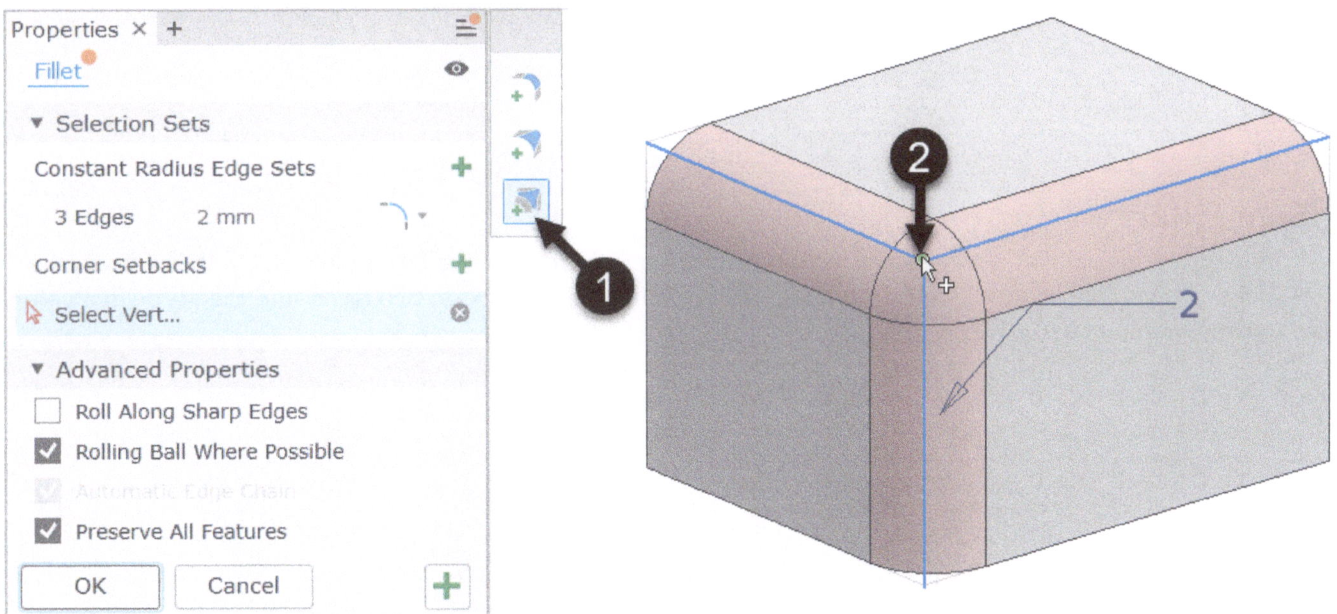

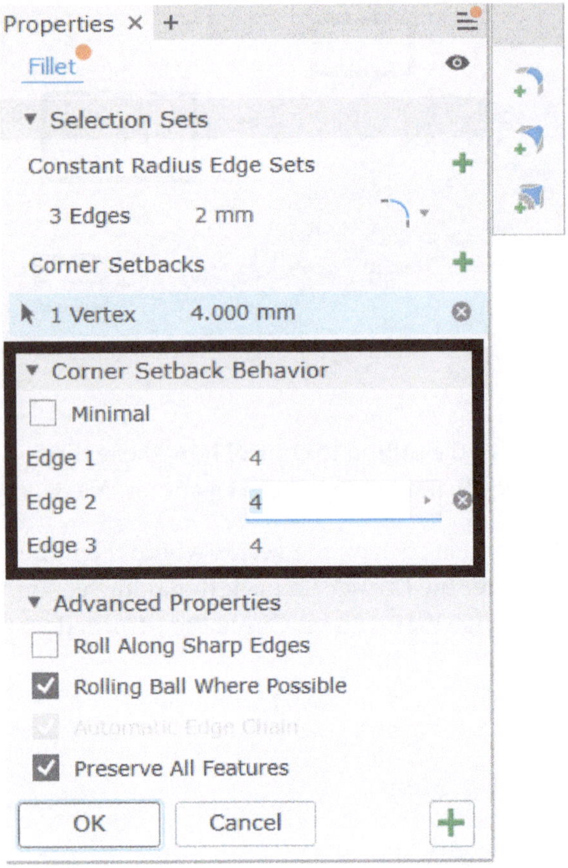

Properties × +
Fillet
Selection Sets
Constant Radius Edge Sets
3 Edges 2 mm
Corner Setbacks
1 Vertex 4.000 mm
Corner Setback Behavior
Minimal
Edge 1 4
Edge 2 4
Edge 3 4
Advanced Properties
Roll Along Sharp Edges
Rolling Ball Where Possible
Automatic Edge Chain
Preserve All Features
OK Cancel

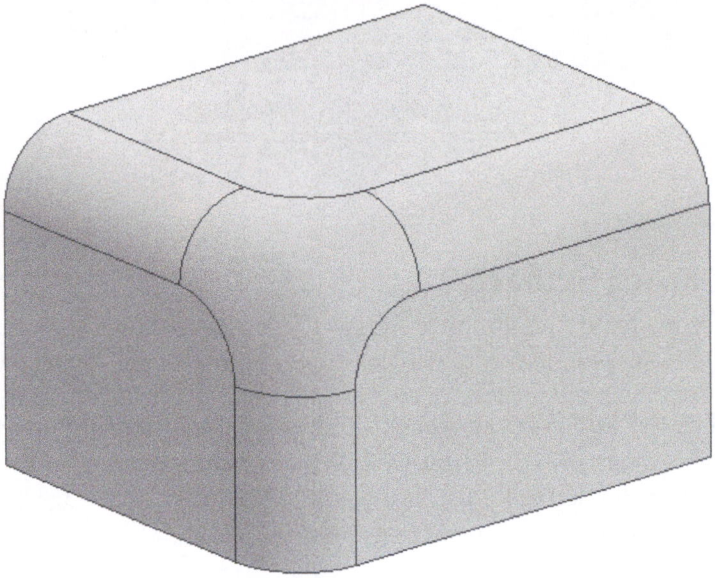

Face Fillet

This command creates a fillet between two faces. The faces are not required to be connected. On the ribbon, click **3D Model** tab > **Modify** panel > **Fillet** drop-down > **Face Fillet**. Next, click on two faces, and then type in a value in the **Radius** box and click **OK**.

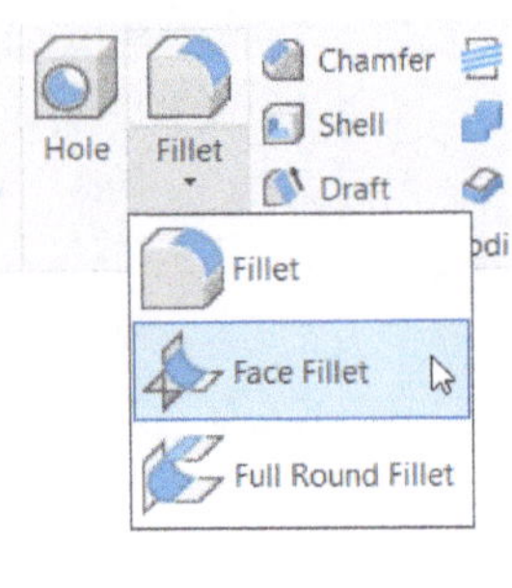

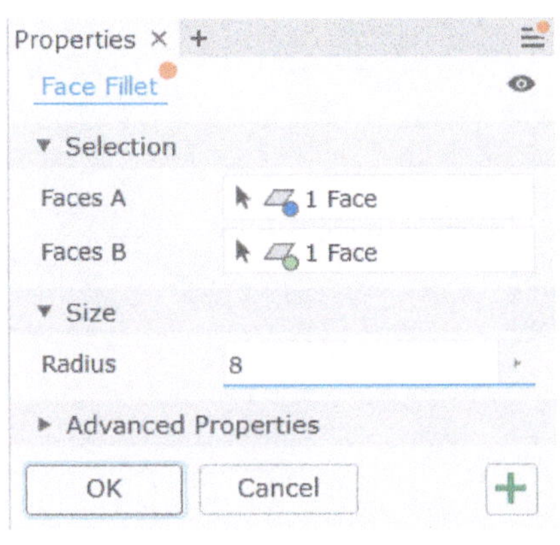

Full Round Fillet

This command creates a fillet between three faces. It replaces the middle face with a fillet. On the ribbon, click **3D Model** tab > **Modify** panel > **Fillet** drop-down > **Full Round Fillet**. Next, click on three faces of the model geometry. Click **OK** to replace the middle face with a fillet.

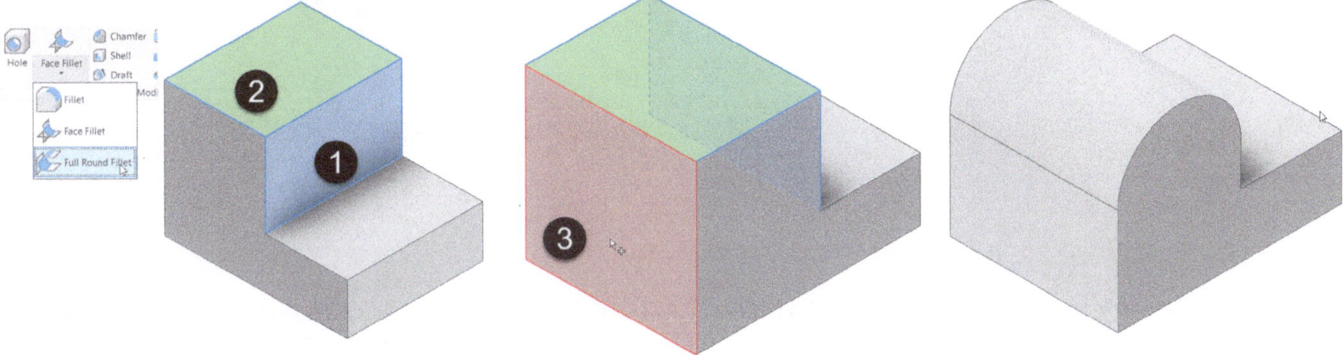

Chamfer

The **Chamfer** and **Fillet** commands are commonly used to break sharp edges. The difference is that the **Chamfer** command adds a beveled face to the model. A chamfer is also a placed feature. Activate this command (click **3D Model > Modify > Chamfer** on the ribbon) and click the **Distance** icon on the top left corner of the **Chamfer** dialog. Select the edge to chamfer and type in a value in the **Distance** box. Click **OK** to complete the chamfer.

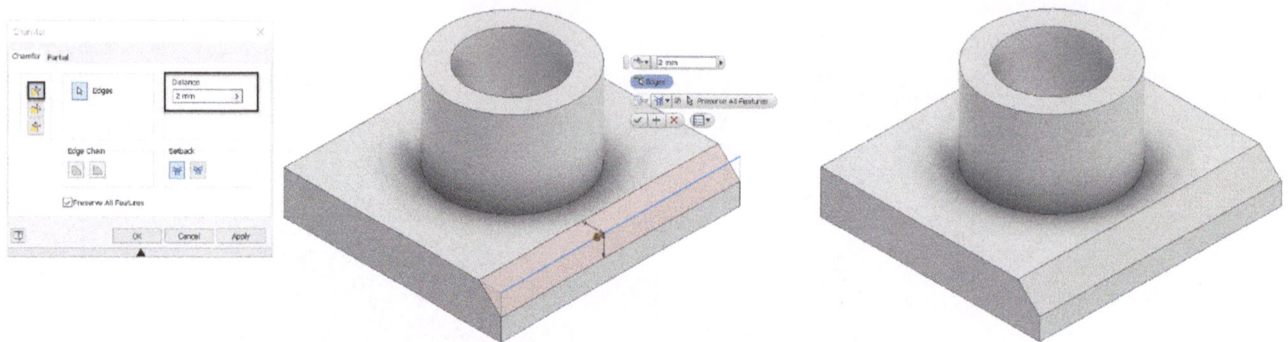

Distance and Angle chamfer

This option lets you create a chamfer by defining its distance and angle values. On the **Chamfer** dialog, click the **Distance and Angle** icon. Select a face from the part geometry, and then select the edge that is coincident with it. Type-in values in the **Distance** and **Angle** boxes; the distance and angle values are measured from the selected face. Click **OK** to complete the feature.

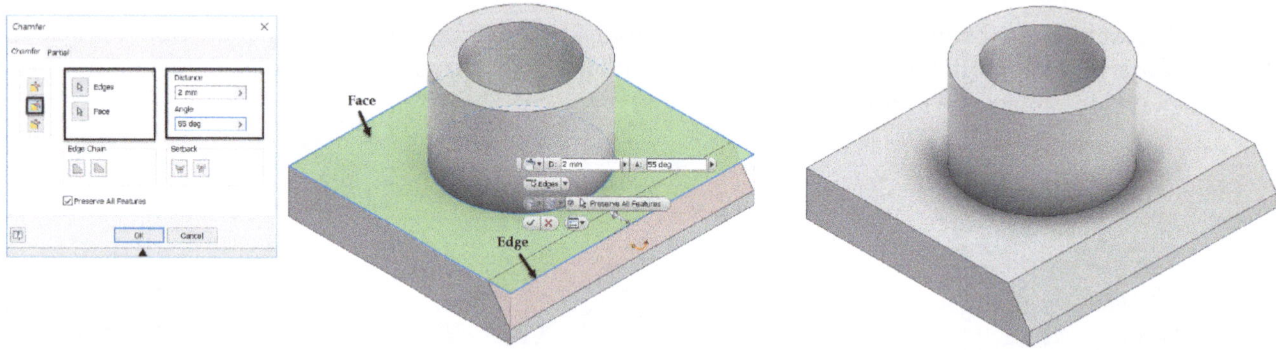

Two Distances chamfer

If you want a chamfer to have different setbacks on both sides of the edge, then click the **Two Distances** icon on the **Chamfer** dialog and click on edge to chamfer. Type-in values in the **Distance 1** and **Distance 2** boxes on the dialog. If you want to switch the setback distance, then click the **Flip Distances** button on the dialog. Click **OK**.

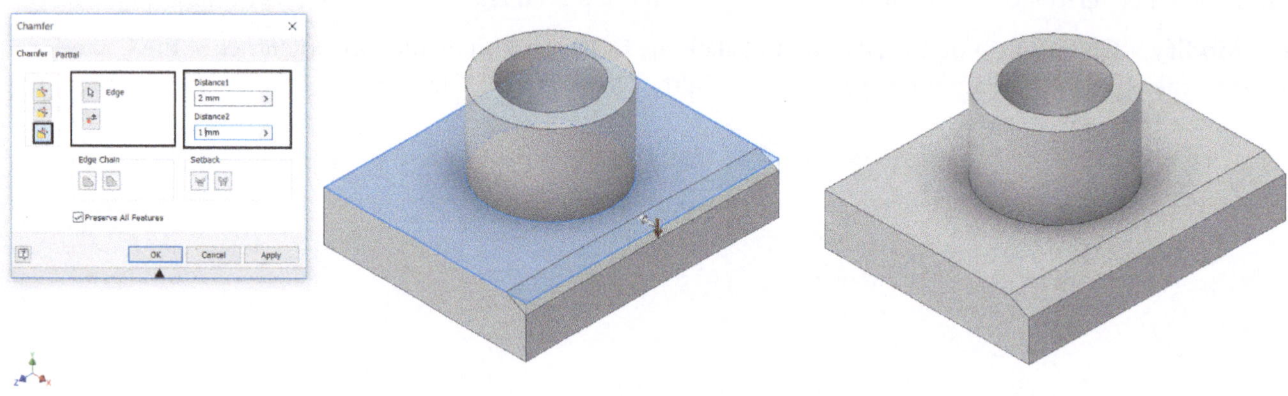

The Face Draft command

When creating cast or plastic parts, you are often required to add a draft on them so that they can be molded easily. A draft is an angle or taper applied to the faces of components so that they can be removed from the mold easily. The following illustration shows a molded part with and without a draft.

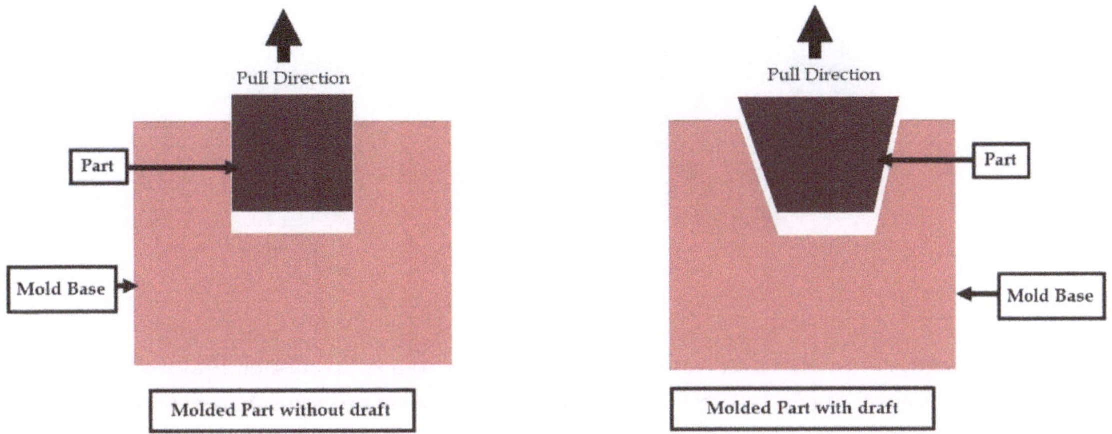

The **Face Draft** command will help you to apply a draft to the model geometry. To activate this command, click **3D Model > Modify > Draft** on the ribbon. There are three draft options in the **Face Draft** dialog: **Fixed Edge**, **Fixed Plane**, and **Parting Line**.

Fixed Edge

The **Fixed Edge** option uses an edge to define the pull direction of the draft. Click the **Fixed Edge** icon on the **Face Draft** dialog and select an edge from the model geometry; the pull direction is defined. Next, click on the **Faces to draft** selection button and select the faces to draft. Specify the angle in the **Draft Angle** box. To reverse the direction of the draft, click the **Flip Pull Direction** icon. Click **OK** to create the draft feature.

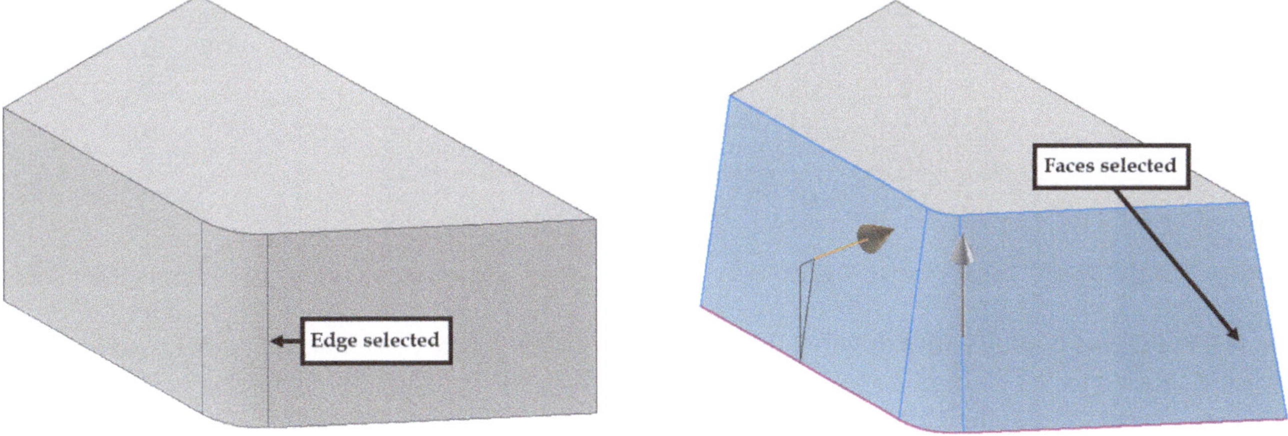

Fixed Plane

On the **Face Draft** dialog, click the **Fixed Plane** icon, and then select a face, which will act as a reference plane (fixed face) for the draft. The draft angle will be measured with reference to this face. After selecting the reference plane (fixed face), click the **Faces to Draft** selection button, and select the faces to draft. Next, type in a positive or negative value in the **Draft Angle** box. If you want to flip the draft direction, then click the **Flip Pull Direction** icon. Click **OK** to apply a draft to the model.

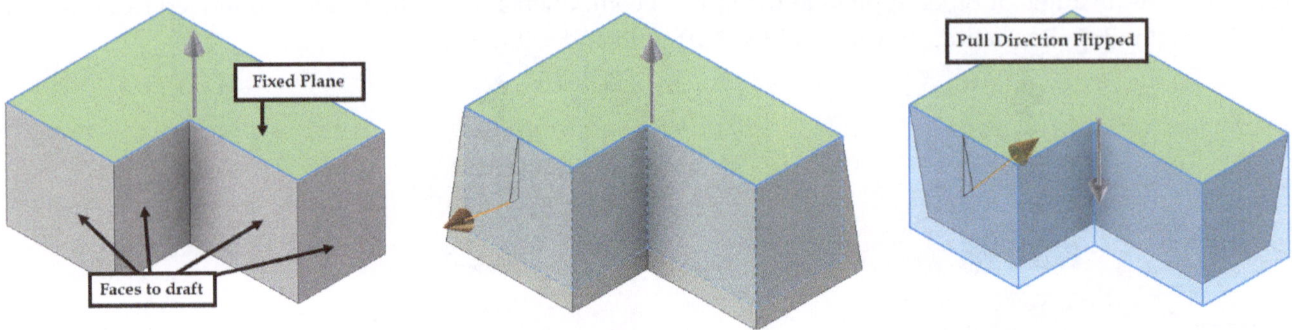

Shell

The **Shell** command is another useful command that can be applied directly to a solid model. It allows you to take a solid geometry and make it hollow. It can be a powerful and timesaving technique when designing parts that call for thin walls such as bottles, tanks, and containers. This command is easy to use. You should have a solid part to use this command. Activate this command from the **Modify** panel (On the ribbon, click **3D Model > Modify > Shell**) and select the faces to remove. Enter the wall thickness in the **Thickness** box. Click the **Inside** , **Outside** , or **Both Sides** button to specify whether the thickness is added inside or outside or both sides of the model.

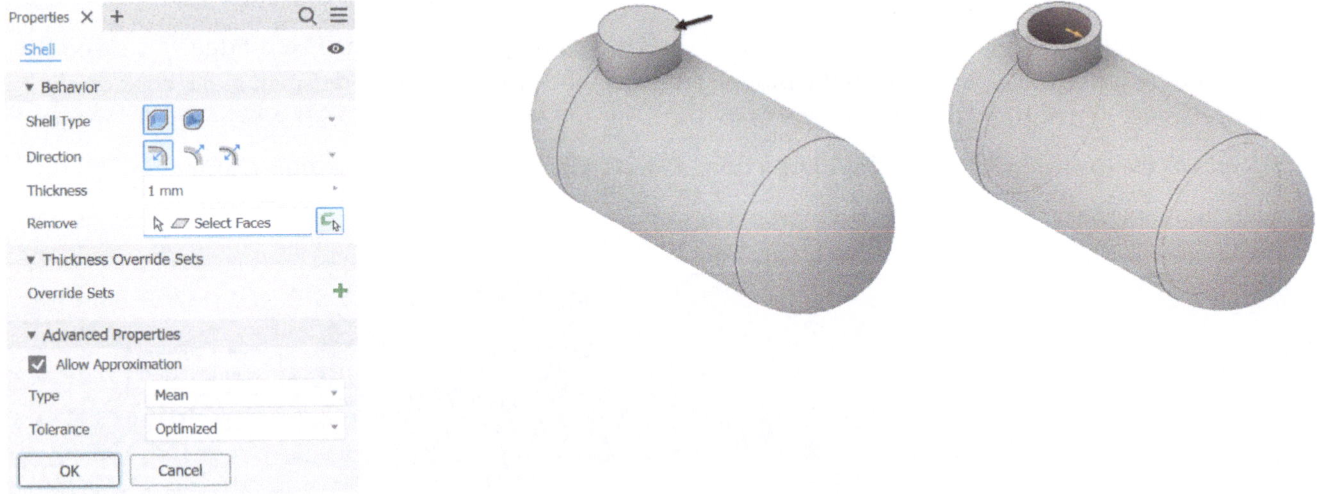

If you want to shell a portion with a different thickness value, click the **Add Shell Set** icon under the **Thickness Override Sets** section. Select the outer face of the portion to which you want a different thickness value. Type the alternate thickness value in the **Thickness** box under the **Thickness Override Sets** section.

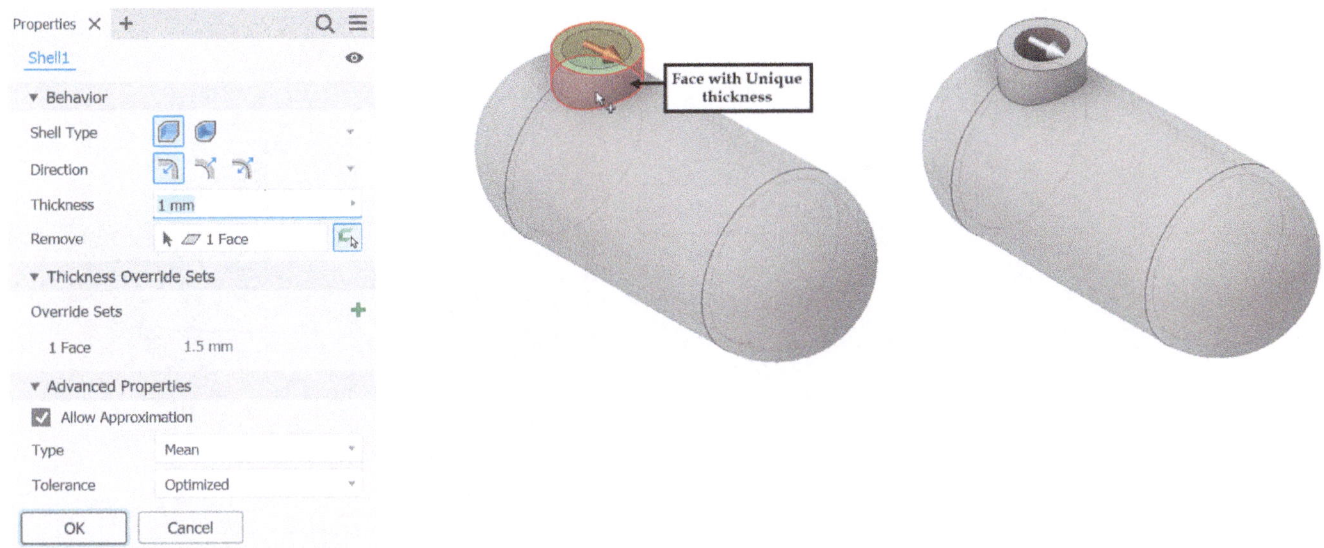

If you want to shell the solid body without removing any faces, then simply type in a value in the **Thickness** box and click **OK**. This creates the shell without removing the faces. Change the **Visual Style** to **Wireframe** or **Shaded with Hidden Edges** to view the shell.

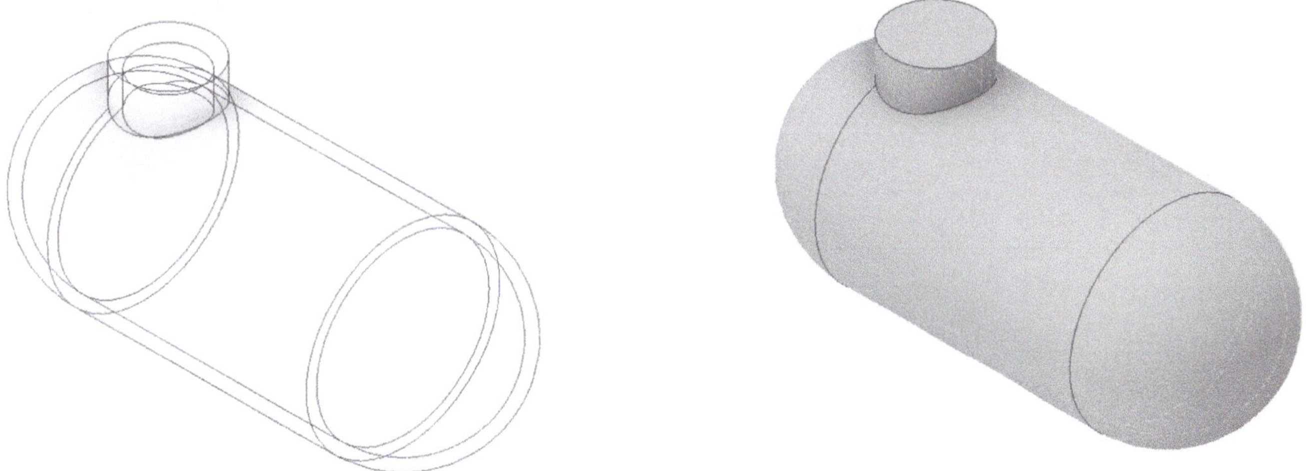

Creating the Shell with Rounded Corners

The **Rounded Corners** option creates a hollow model with smooth external edges instead of sharp ones. To apply this feature, select **Shell type > Rounded Corners**, sets the desired wall thickness, specify the thickness direction, and select the faces to remove for openings. Note that this option will not create a shell with rounded edge if you select **Direction > Inside**.

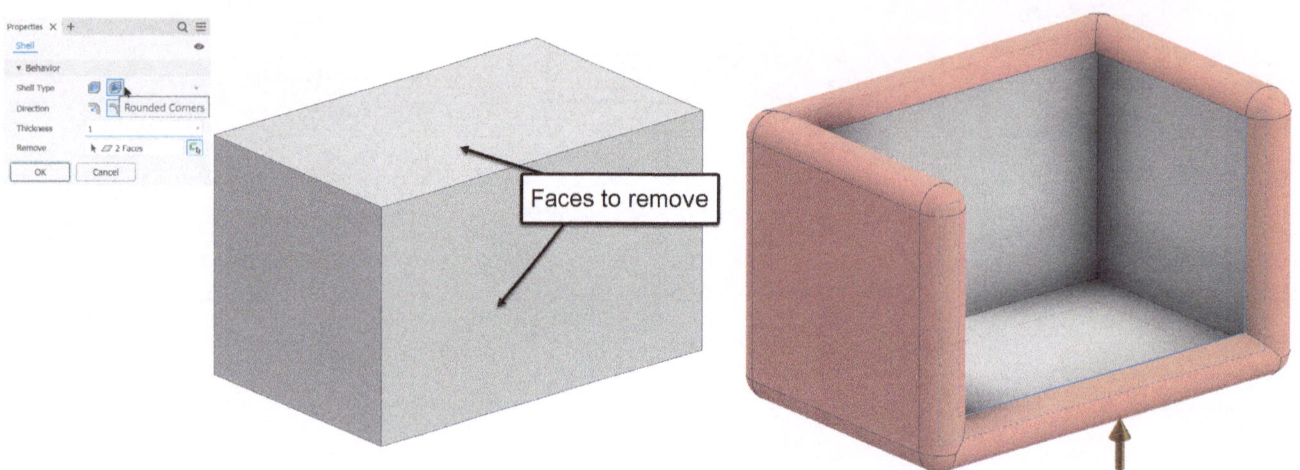

Examples

Example 1 (Millimeters)

In this example, you will create the part shown below.

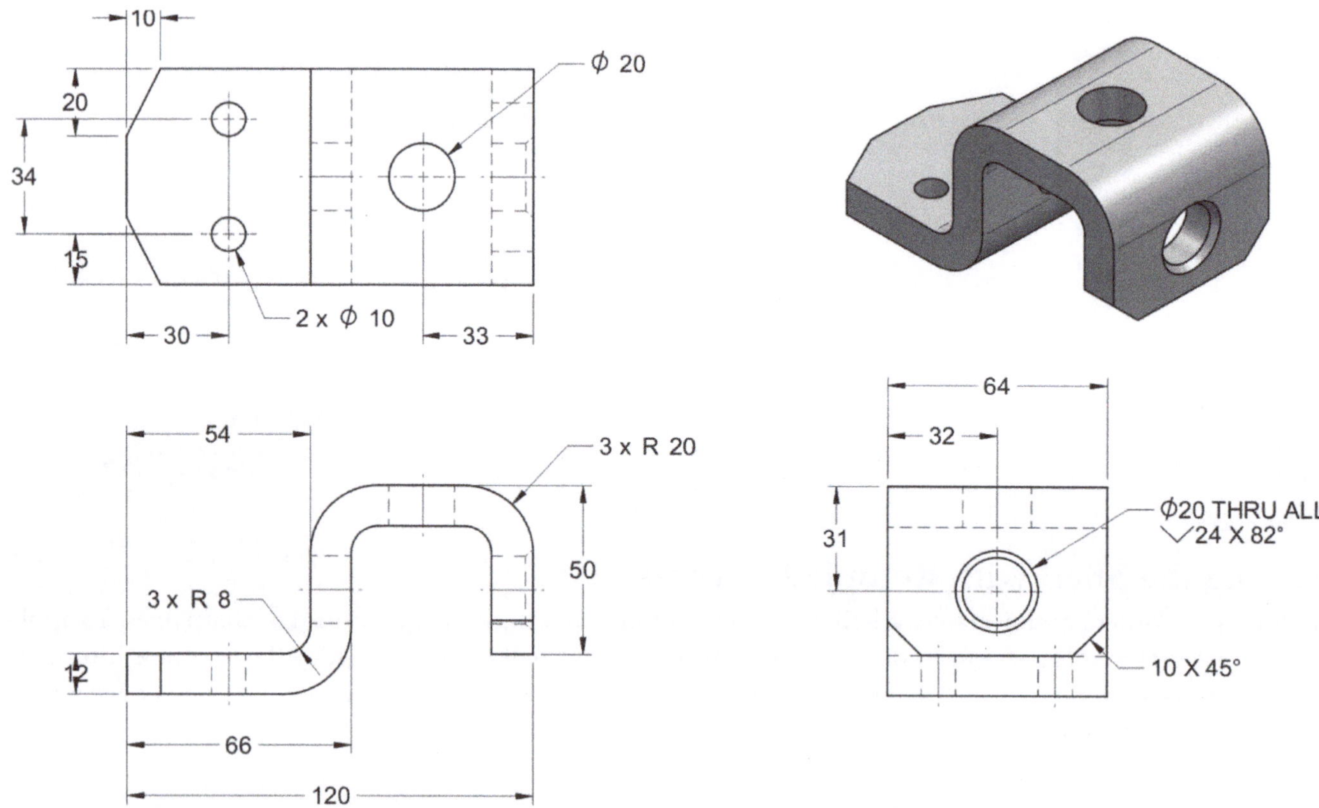

1. Start **Autodesk Inventor 2026** by double-clicking the **Autodesk Inventor 2026** icon on your desktop.
2. To start a new part file, click the **New** button on the Quick Access Toolbar.
3. On the **Create New File** dialog, click the **Metric** folder under **Templates**.
4. Click the **Standard(mm).ipt** icon under the **Part – Create 2D and 3D Objects** section.
5. Click the **Create** button on the **Create New File** dialog.

6. To start a sketch, click **3D Model > Sketch > Start 2D Sketch** on the ribbon. Click on the **XY** plane.

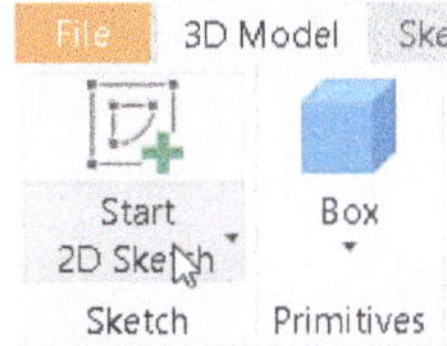

7. Click **Sketch > Create > Line**, on the ribbon. Draw a sketch and offset it up to **12** mm distance. Next, close the ends of the sketch using the **Line** command. Add dimensions to constrain the sketch fully. Click **Finish Sketch** on the ribbon.

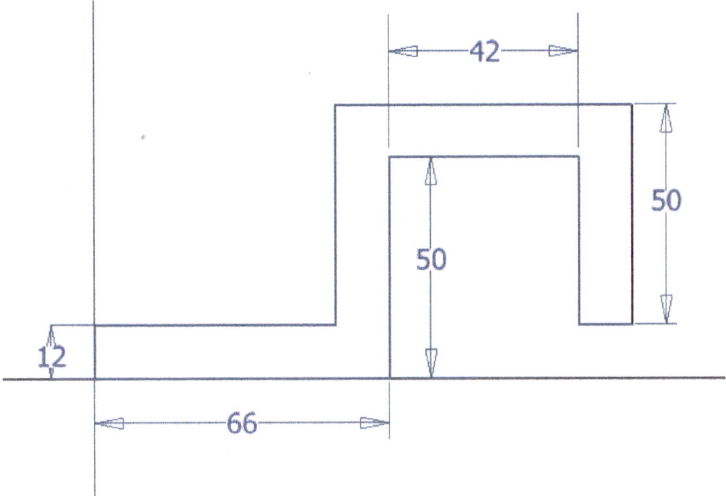

8. Activate the **Extrude** command (on the ribbon, click **3D Model > Create > Extrude**). On the **Extrude Properties** panel, type **64** in the **Distance A** box and click the **Symmetric** icon. Click **OK**.

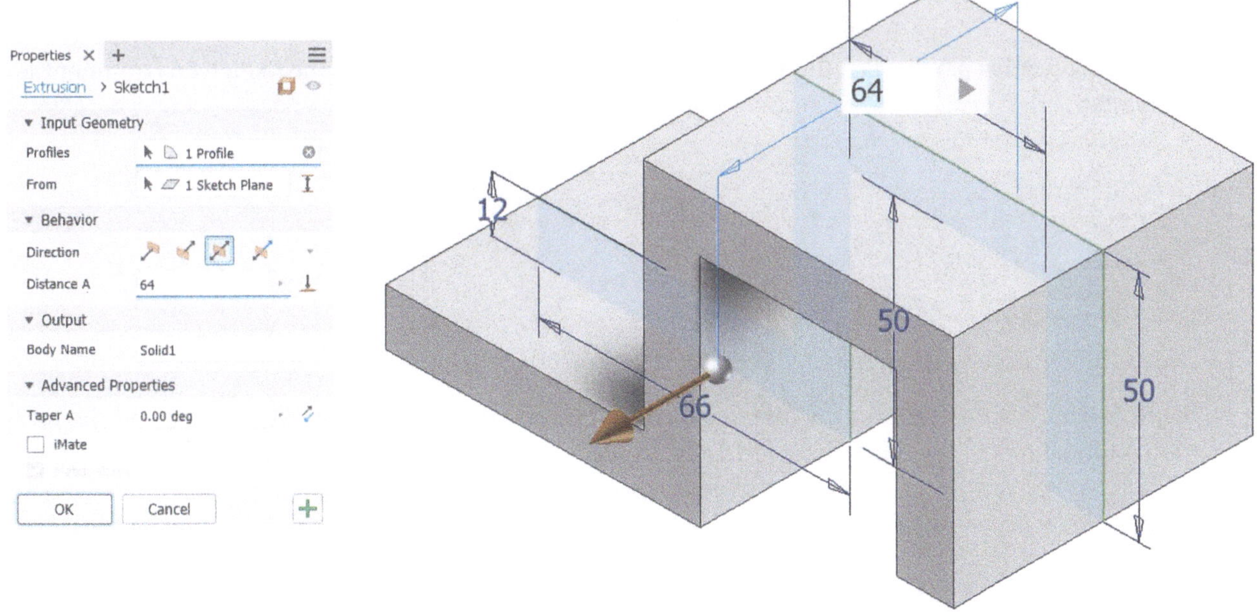

9. On the ribbon, click **3D Model > Modify > Hole**. Click on the right-side face of the part model, as shown.

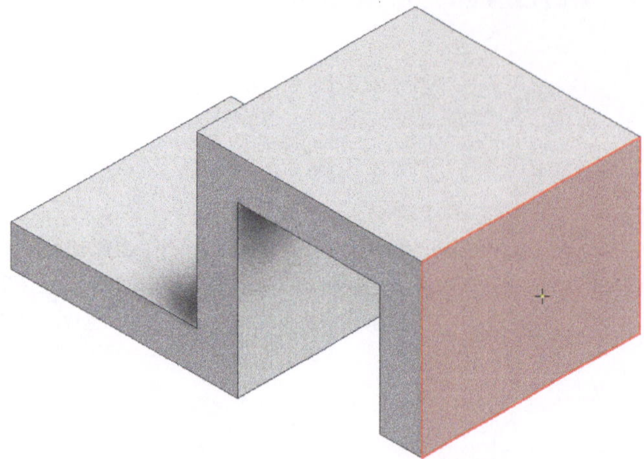

10. On the Properties panel, click **Type > Hole > Simple Hole** . Also, select **Type > Seat > Countersink**
11. Under the **Behavior** section, set the **Countersink Diameter** and **Countersink Angle** values to **24** and **82**, respectively. Set the **Diameter** value to **20** mm. Also, select **Behavior > Termination > Through All.**

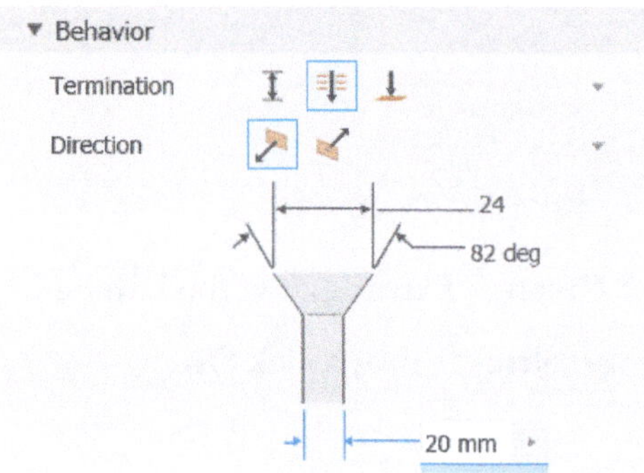

12. On the **Properties** panel, click the **Sketch2** link in the Breadcrumbs area; the Sketch environment is activated.

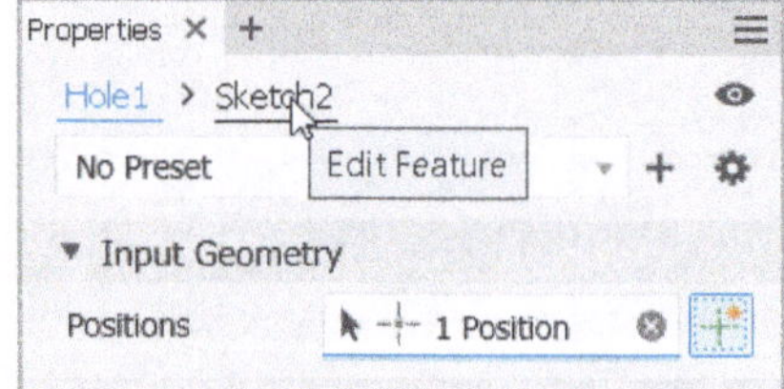

13. Add a dimension between the hole point and the top edge, as shown.
14. Click **Sketch > Constrain > Vertical Constraint** on the ribbon. Select the hole point and the midpoint of the top edge; the two points are vertically aligned.

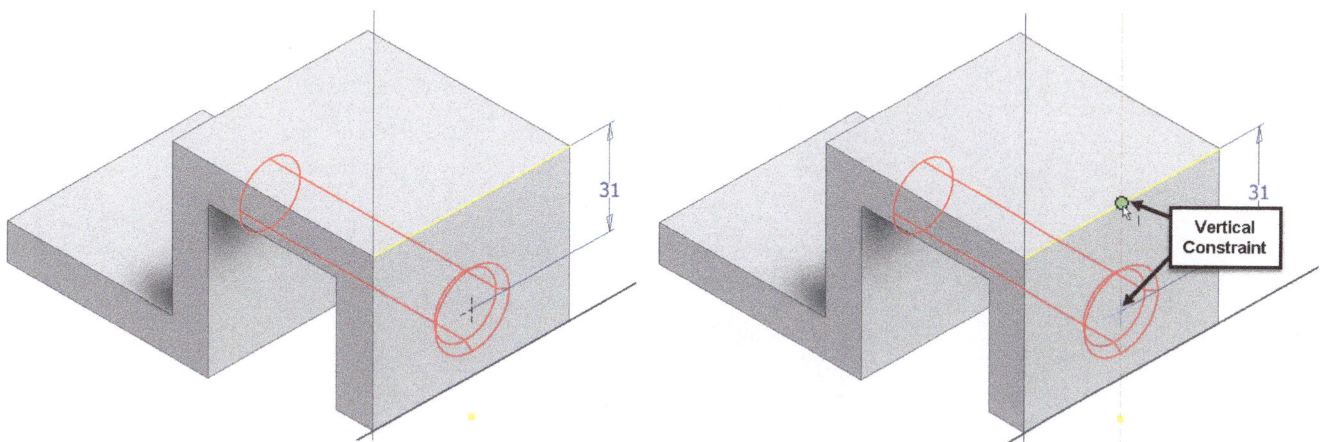

15. Click the **Hole** link on the **Properties** panel, and then click **OK** to complete the hole feature.

16. Activate the **Hole** command and click on the top face of the part model.
17. On the **Properties** panel, select **Preset** drop-down **> Last used**. Next, select **Type > Seat > None**.
18. On the **Properties** panel, click the **Sketch3** link in the Breadcrumbs area; the Sketch environment is activated.
19. On the ribbon, click **Sketch > Constrain > Horizontal Constraint** . Select the center point of the hole and the midpoint of the right edge; the two points are aligned horizontally.
20. On the ribbon, click **Sketch > Constrain > Vertical Constraint** . Select the center point of the hole and the midpoint of the back edge; the two points are aligned vertically.

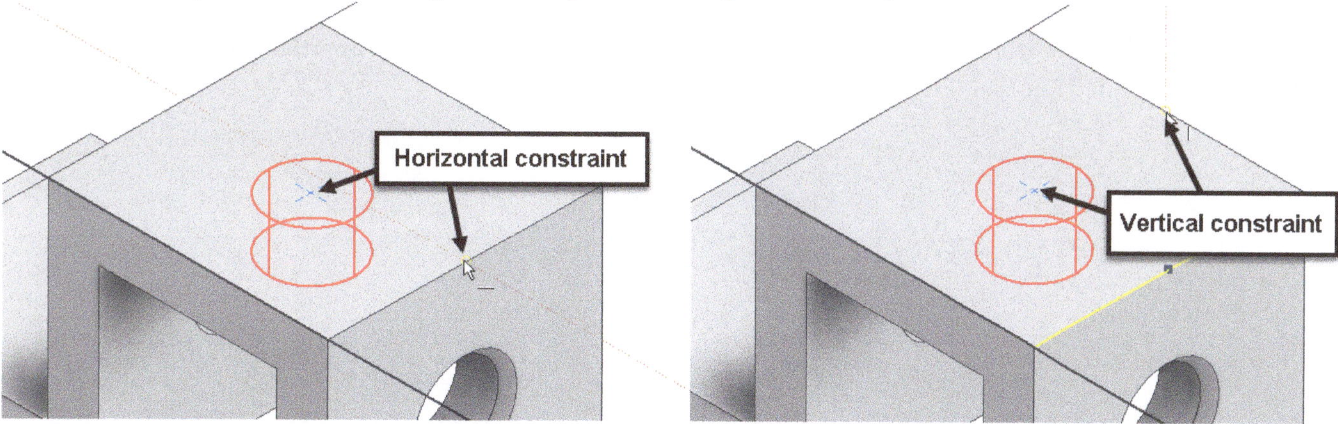

21. Click **Finish Sketch** on the ribbon to complete the hole feature.

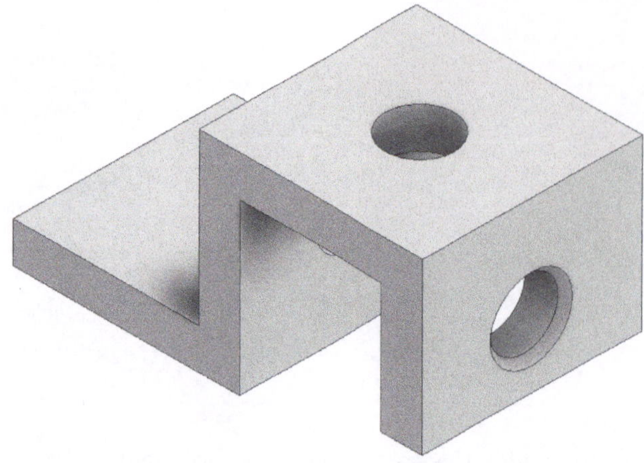

22. Click the top-left corner point of the ViewCube, as shown; this changes the view orientation of the part model.

23. Activate the **Start 2D Sketch** command and click on the lower top face of the part model. Place two points and add dimensions to define the hole location, as shown. Click **Finish Sketch** on the ribbon.

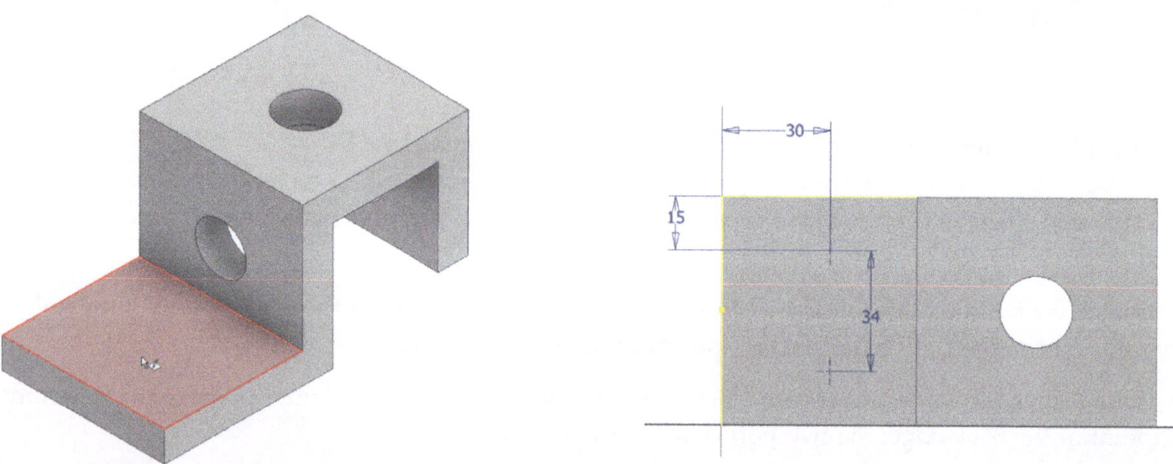

24. Click **3D Model > Modify > Hole** to activate the **Hole** command. On the **Properties** panel, select **Type > Hole > Simple Hole**. Set the **Diameter** value to 10mm.

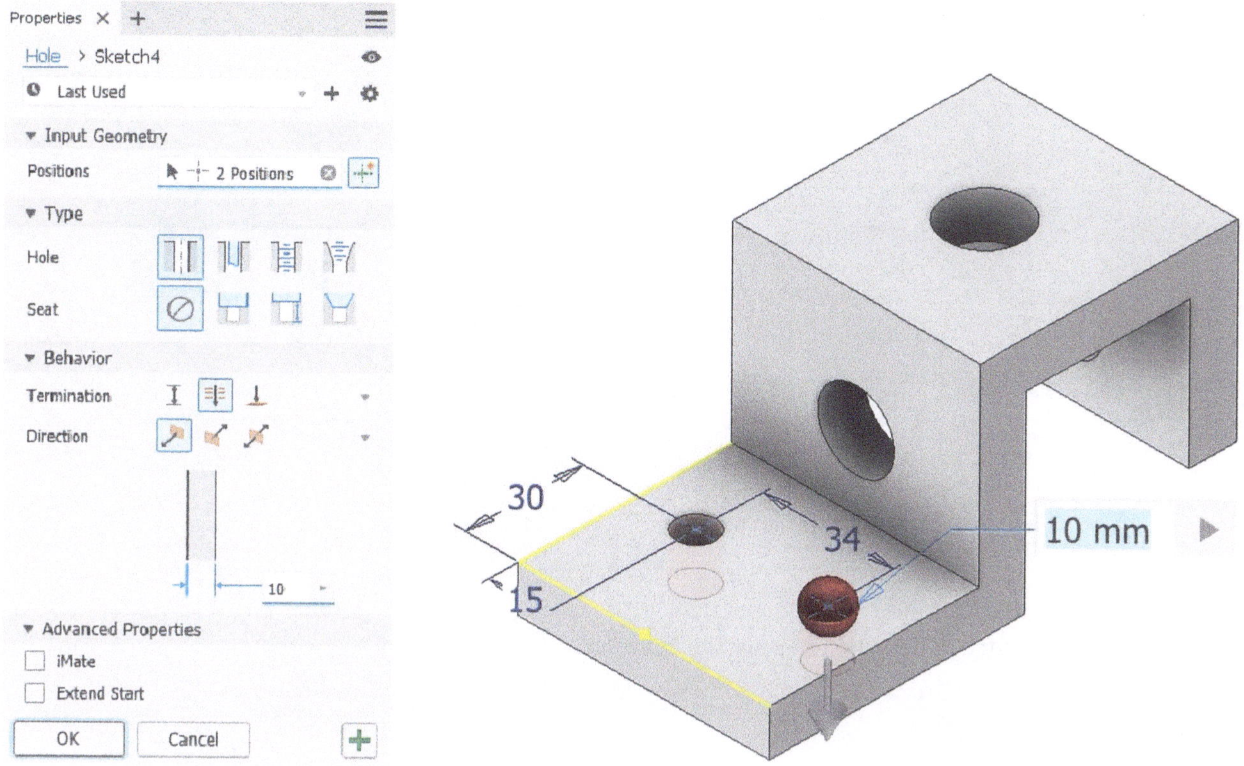

25. Click **OK** to complete the hole feature.

26. Click **3D Model > Modify > Chamfer** on the ribbon. On the **Chamfer** dialog, click the **Two Distances** icon. Set the **Distance 1** and **Distance 2** values to **10** and **20**, respectively.
27. Click on the right corner edge, as shown in the figure.

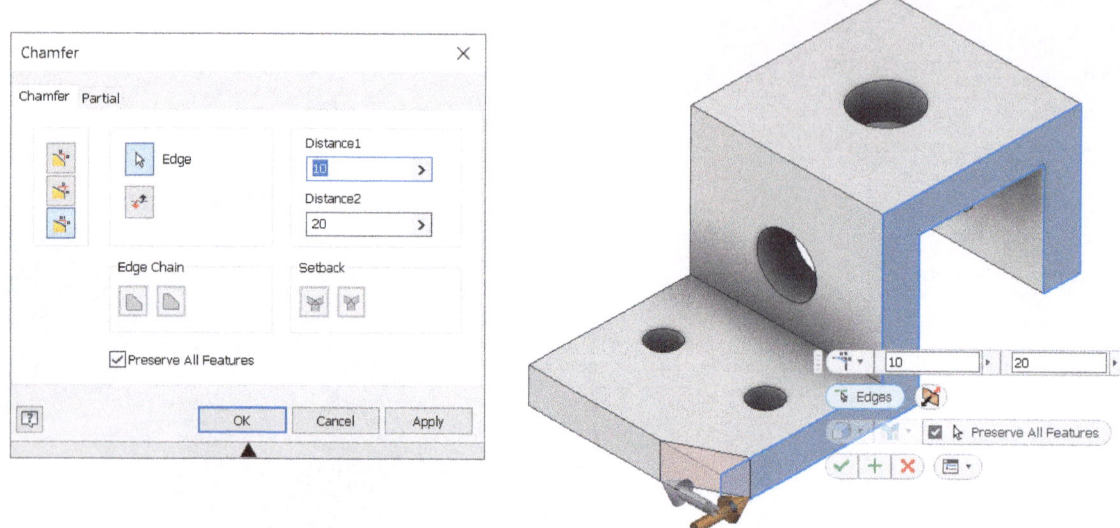

28. Click **Apply** on the dialog.
29. Click on the left edge. Click **OK** to apply the chamfer.

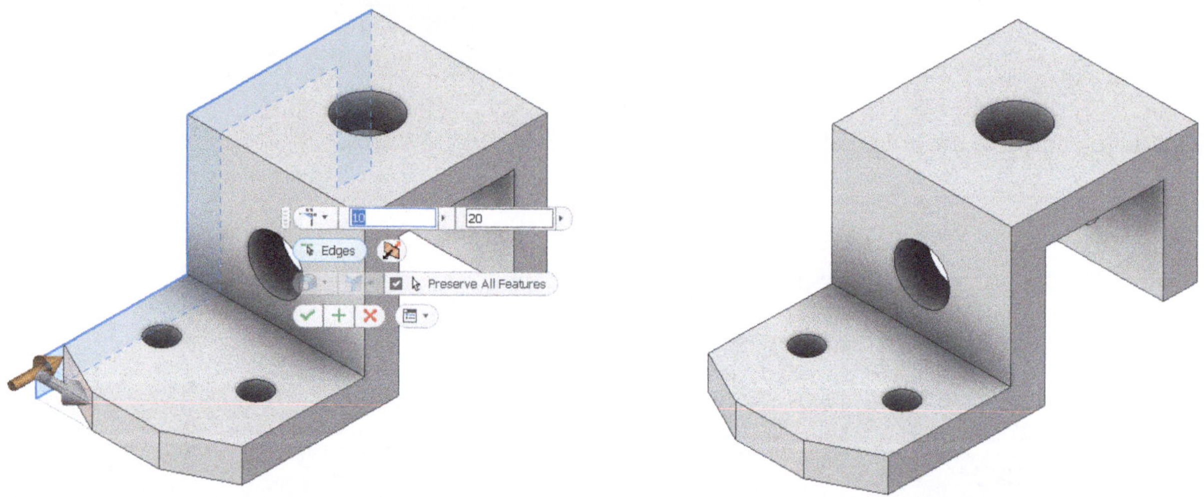

30. Click **3D Model > Modify > Fillet** on the ribbon. On the **Fillet** Properties panel, click the **Add Constant radius edge set** icon. Under the **Selection Sets** section, set the **Fillet Constant Radius** value to **8** mm and select the **Tangent** option from the drop-down located next to the **Fillet Constant Radius** box.

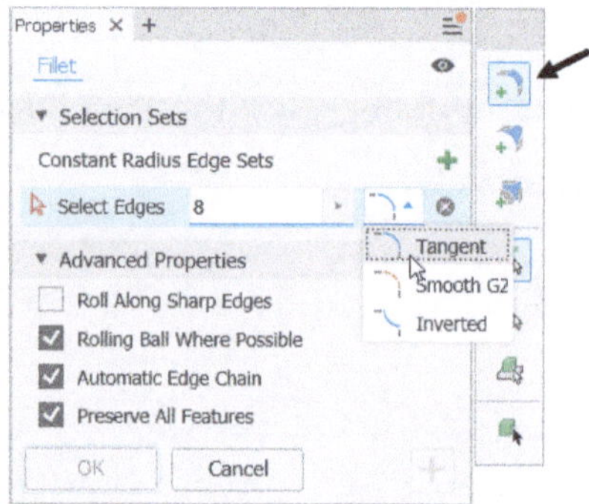

31. Click the **Sets selection priority to edges** icon.
32. Click on the horizontal edges of the part model, as shown below.

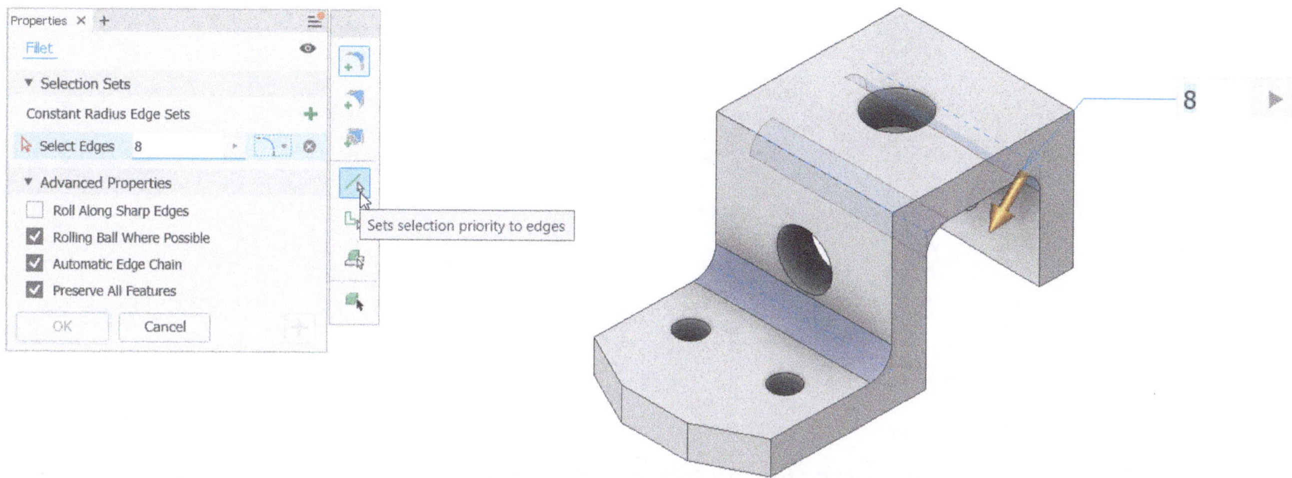

33. Click the **Add Constant radius edge set** icon on the **Fillet** Properties panel.
34. Set the **Fillet Constant Radius** value to **20** mm under the **Selection Sets** section.
35. Click on the outer edges of the part model, as shown below. Click **OK** to complete the fillet feature.

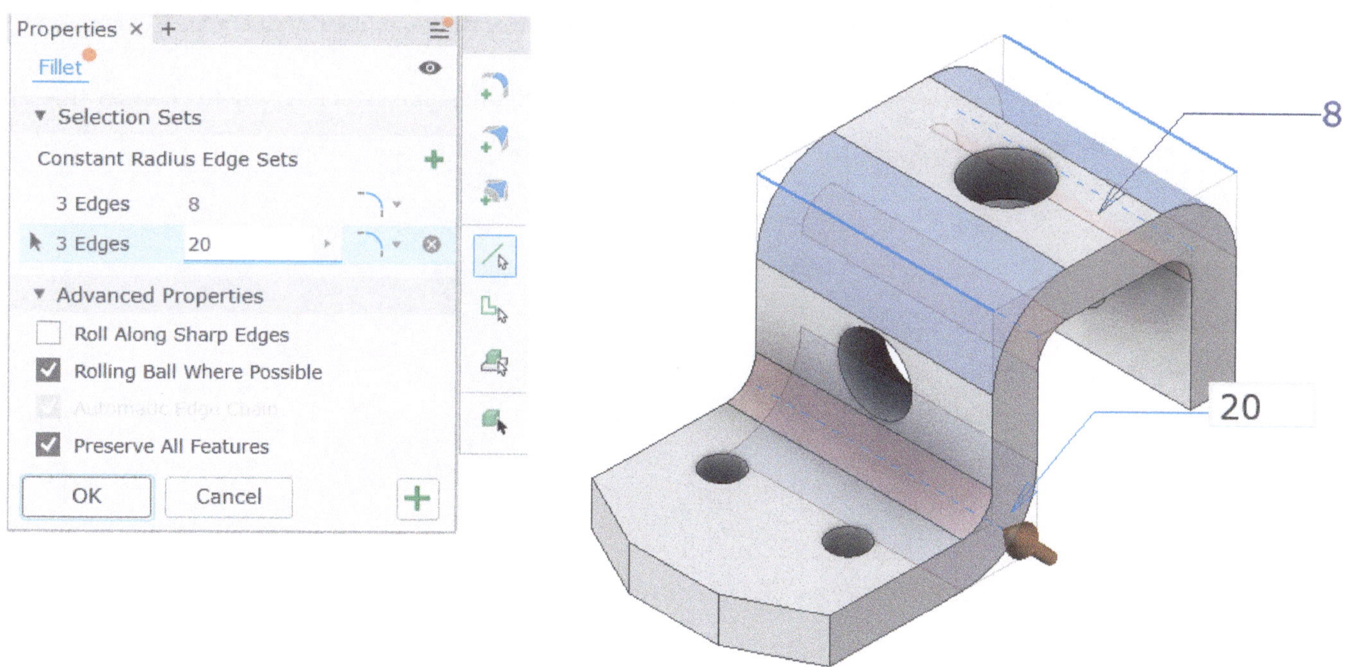

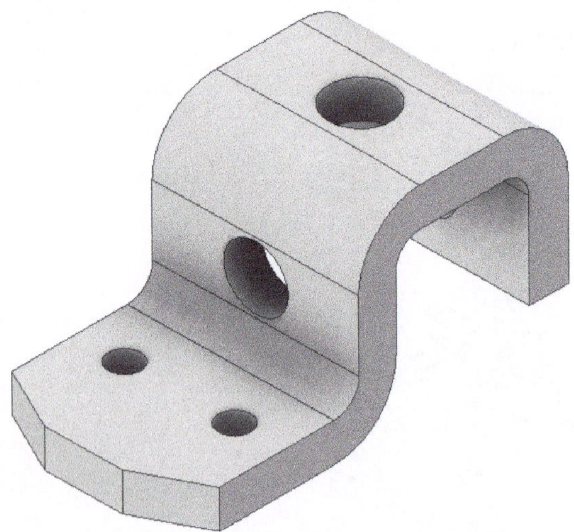

36. Click on the **Home** icon located at the top left corner of the ViewCube.

37. On the ribbon, click **3D Model > Modify > Chamfer**. On the **Chamfer** dialog, click the **Distance** icon on the left.
38. Click on the lower corner of the part model and type in **10** in the **Distance** box. Click **Apply** to chamfer the edge.

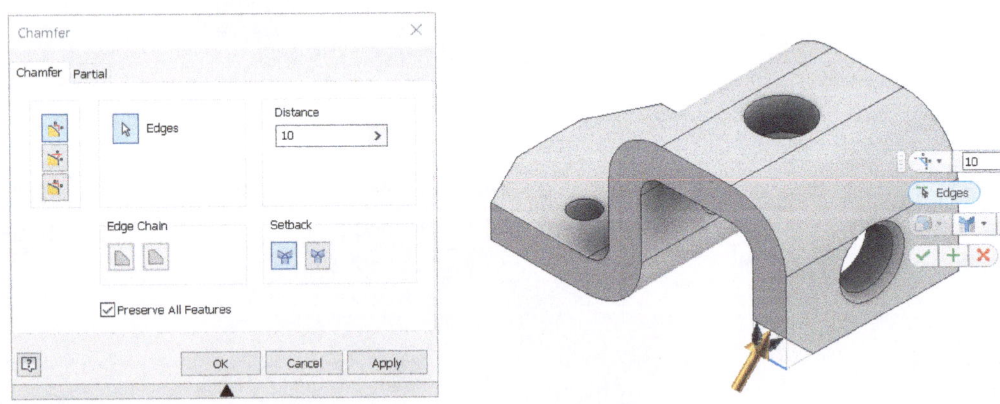

39. Likewise, select the other edge and enter **10** mm in the **Distance** box.
40. Click **OK** to chamfer the selected edge.

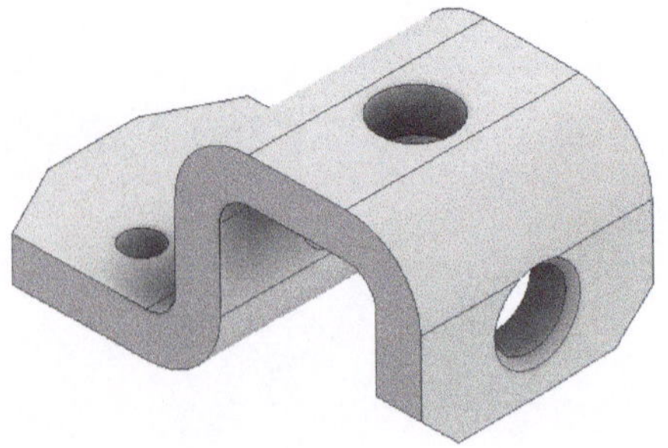

41. Save and close the file.

Questions

1. What are the placed features?
2. How to create a counterbored hole?
3. Which option allows you to create chamfer with unequal setbacks?
4. Which option allows you to create a variable radius blend?
5. How is the size of the external thread defined?
6. How to create a Smooth Fillet?
7. How to add an alternative thickness to a shell feature?
8. What is the difference between the Tapped and Taper Tapped Holes?
9. What is the use of the **Preset** drop-down of the Properties panel?
10. What is the purpose of the **Rounded Corners** option in **Shell** Properties panel?

Exercises

Exercise 1 (Millimetres)

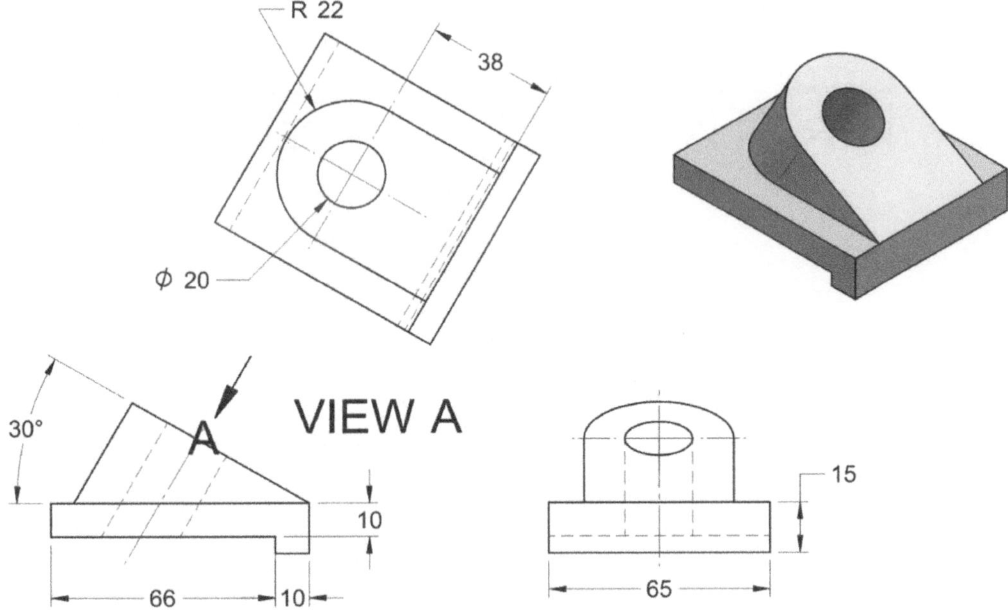

Exercise 2 (Inches)

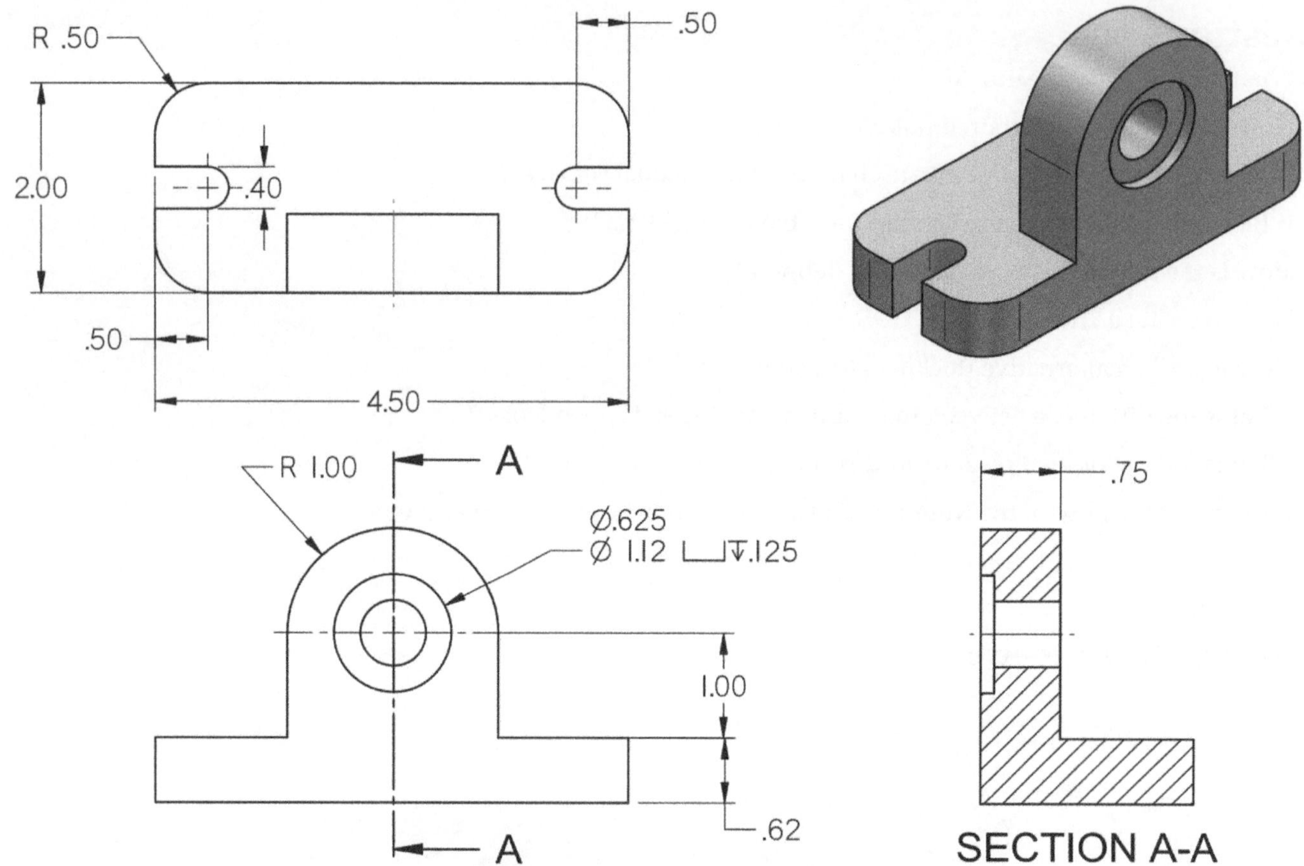

Chapter 5: Patterned Geometry

When designing a part geometry, most of the time, there are elements of symmetry in each part, or there are at least a few features that are repeated multiple times. In these situations, Autodesk Inventor offers some commands that save your time. For example, you can use mirror features to design symmetric parts, which makes designing the part quicker. It is because you only have to design a portion of the part and use the mirror feature to create the remaining geometry.

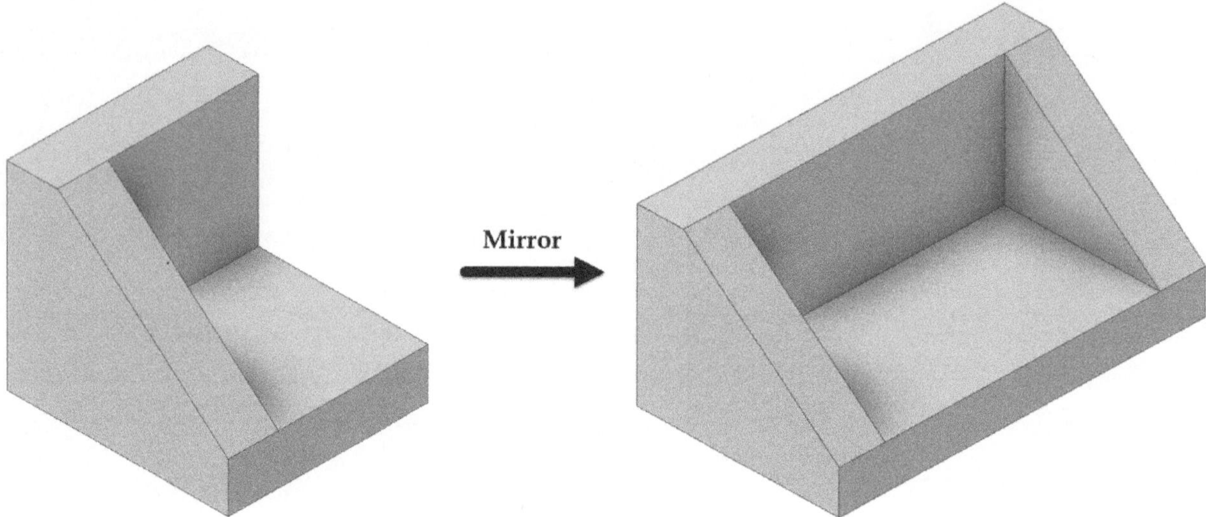

Also, there are some pattern commands to replicate a feature throughout the part geometry quickly. They save you time from creating additional features individually and help you modify the design easily. If the design changes, you only need to change the first feature; the rest of the pattern features will update automatically. In this chapter, you will learn to create mirrored and pattern geometries using the commands available in Inventor.

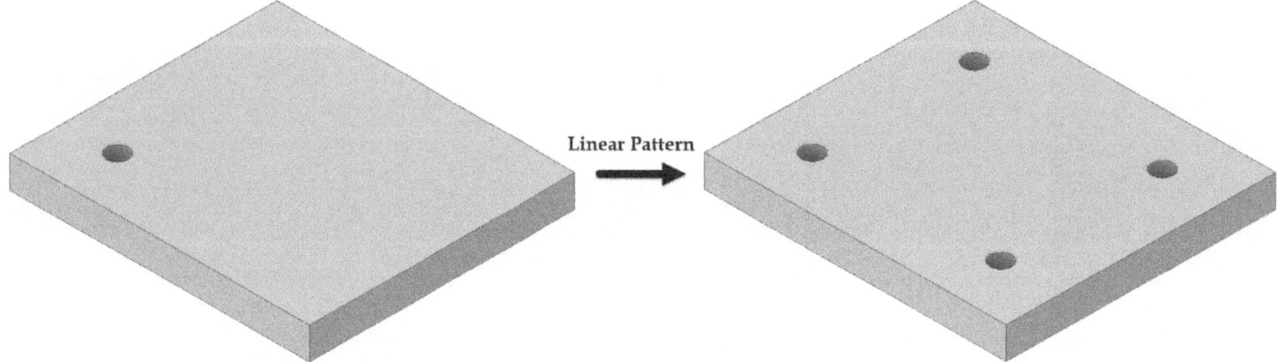

The topics covered in this chapter are:

- *Mirror* features
- *Rectangular Patterns*
- *Circular Patterns*
- *Sketch Driven Patterns*

Mirror

If you are designing a symmetric part, you can save time by using the **Mirror** command. Using this command, you can replicate the individual features of the entire body. To mirror features (3D geometry), you need to have a face or plane to use as a reference. You can use a model face, default plane, or create a new plane if it does not exist where it is needed.

Activate the **Mirror** command (click **3D Model > Pattern > Mirror** on the ribbon). On the **Mirror** dialog, click the **Mirror Individual Features** icon on the left. On the part geometry, click on the features to mirror, and then click the **Mirror Plane** selection button on the **Mirror** dialog. Now, select the reference plane about which the features are to be mirrored.

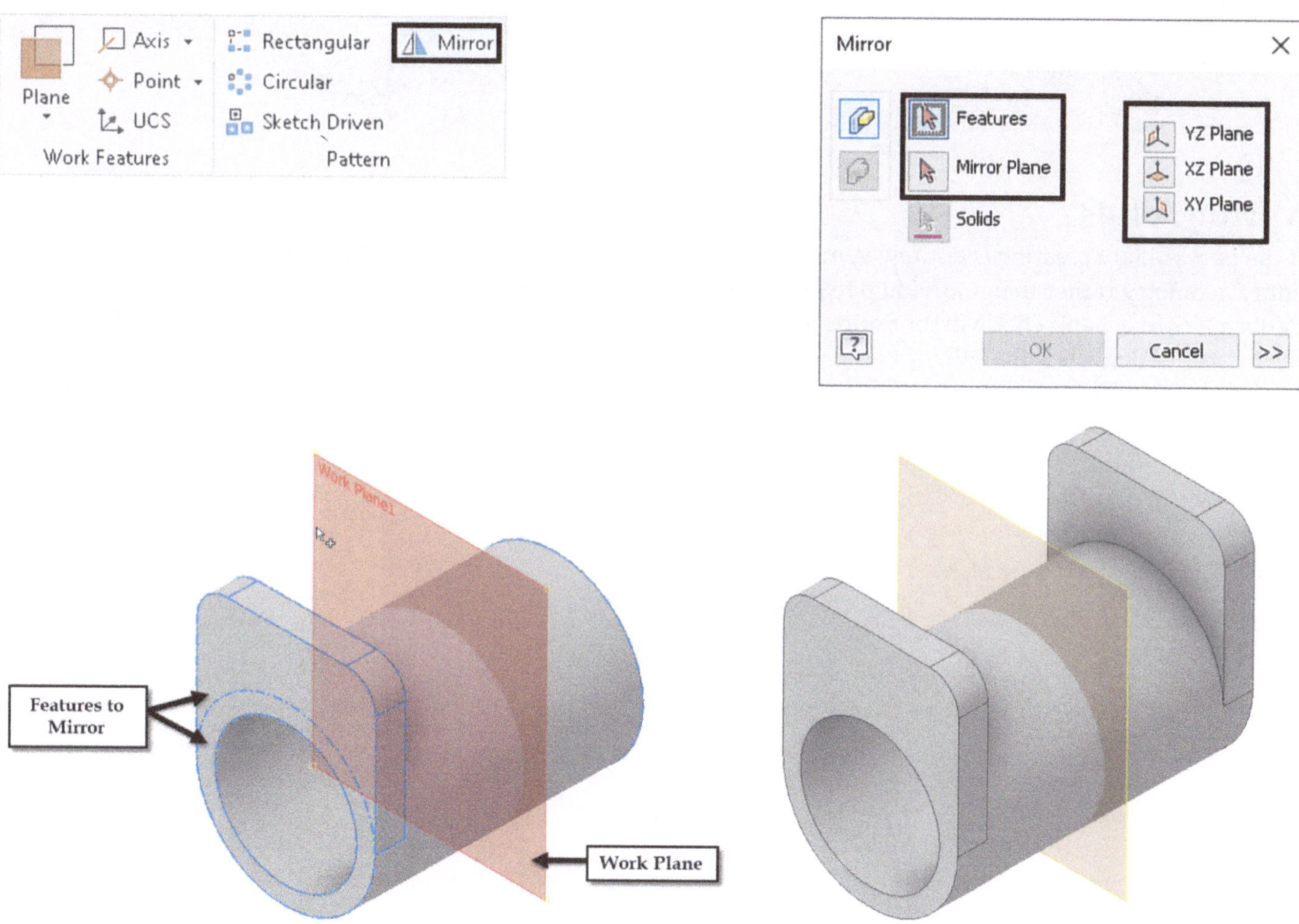

Now, if you make changes to the original feature, the mirrored feature will be updated automatically.

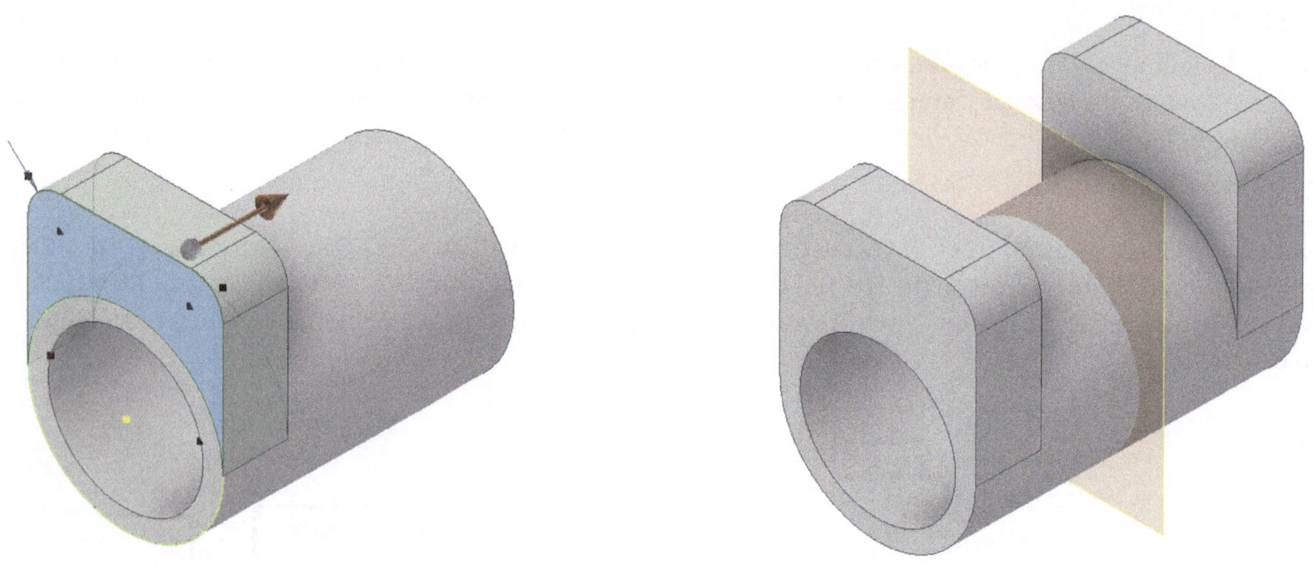

Mirror Solids

If the part you are creating is entirely symmetric, you can save more time by creating half of it and mirroring the entire geometry rather than individual features. Activate the **Mirror** command (On the ribbon, click **3D Model > Pattern > Mirror**) and click **Mirror Solids** icon on the **Mirror** dialog; the solid part is selected automatically. On the **Mirror** dialog, click the **Mirror Plane** selection button and select the face about which the geometry is to be mirrored. To include other features like planes, axes, work points, and surfaces in the mirror feature, click the **Include Work/Surface Features** selection button and select the features. Inventor allows you to specify whether the mirrored body will be joined with the source body or to create a separate body. Click **OK** to complete the mirror geometry.

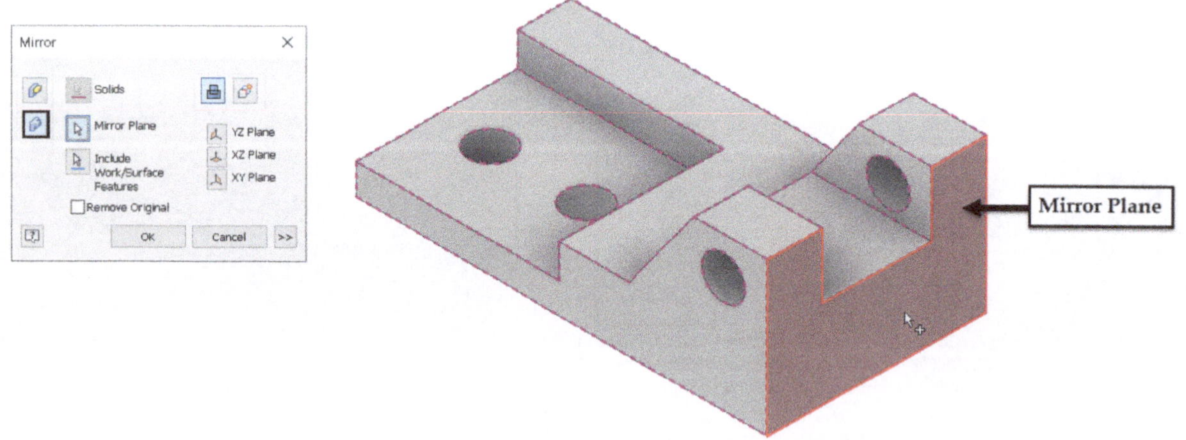

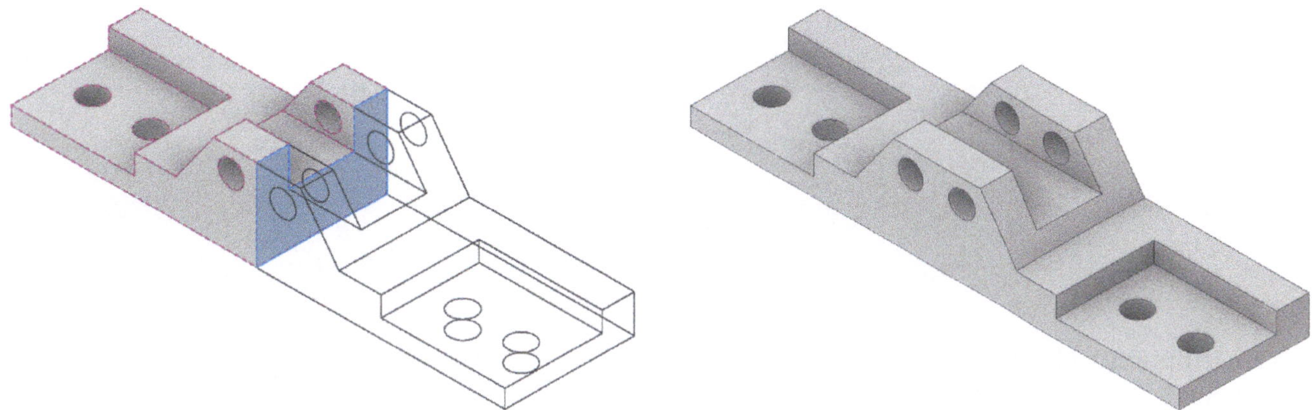

Create Patterns

Inventor allows you to replicate a feature using the pattern commands **Rectangular Pattern**, **Circular Pattern**, and **Sketch Driven**. The following sections explain the different patterns that can be created using the three pattern commands.

Rectangular Pattern

To create a pattern in a rectangular fashion, you must first activate the **Rectangular Pattern** command (On the ribbon, click **3D Model > Pattern > Rectangular Pattern**). On the **Properties** panel, click the **Pattern Individual Features** icon on the right side, and then select the feature to pattern from the model geometry. Click the selection button in the **Direction A** section and select an edge, face, or axis to define **Direction A** of the pattern. Next, select **Distribution > Incremental**. You will notice that a pattern preview appears on the model. Enter a value in the **Number** and **Distance** box. Click the **Flip** icon, if you want to reverse the pattern direction. Click the **Midplane** icon to create the pattern on both sides of the source feature.

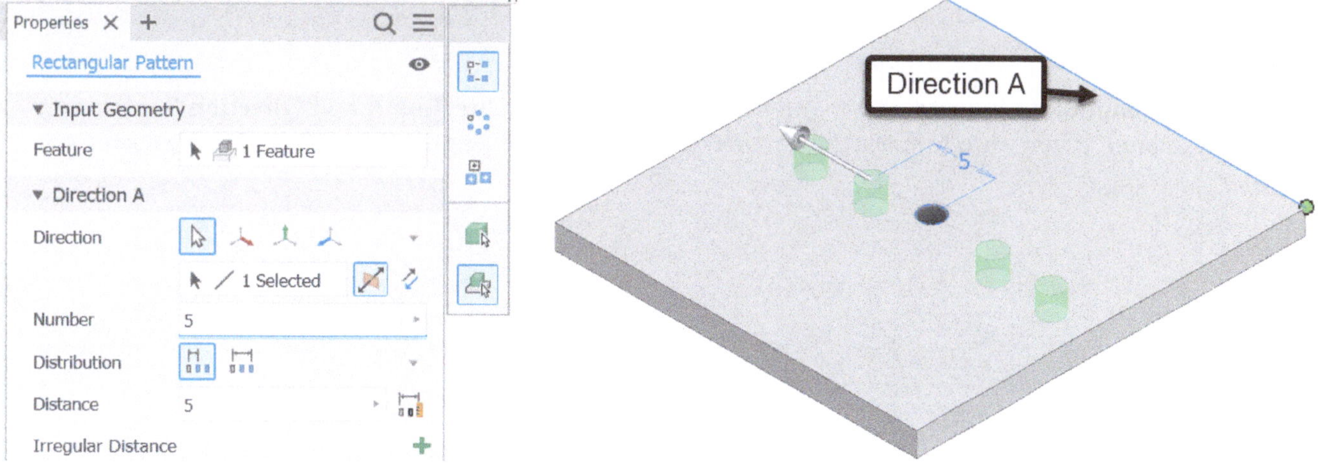

Click the selection button in the **Direction B** and select an edge, face, or axis to define the second direction of the pattern. Set the parameters (**Number** and **Distance**) of the pattern in direction B. Next, click **OK** to complete the pattern.

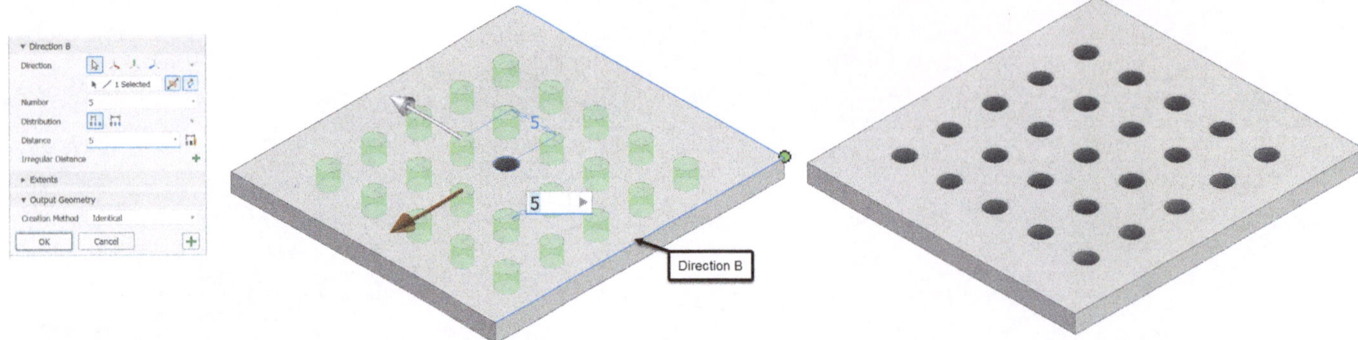

Select **Distribution > Fitted** from the **Properties** panels, if you want to enter the occurrence count and total length values along the direction A or direction B.

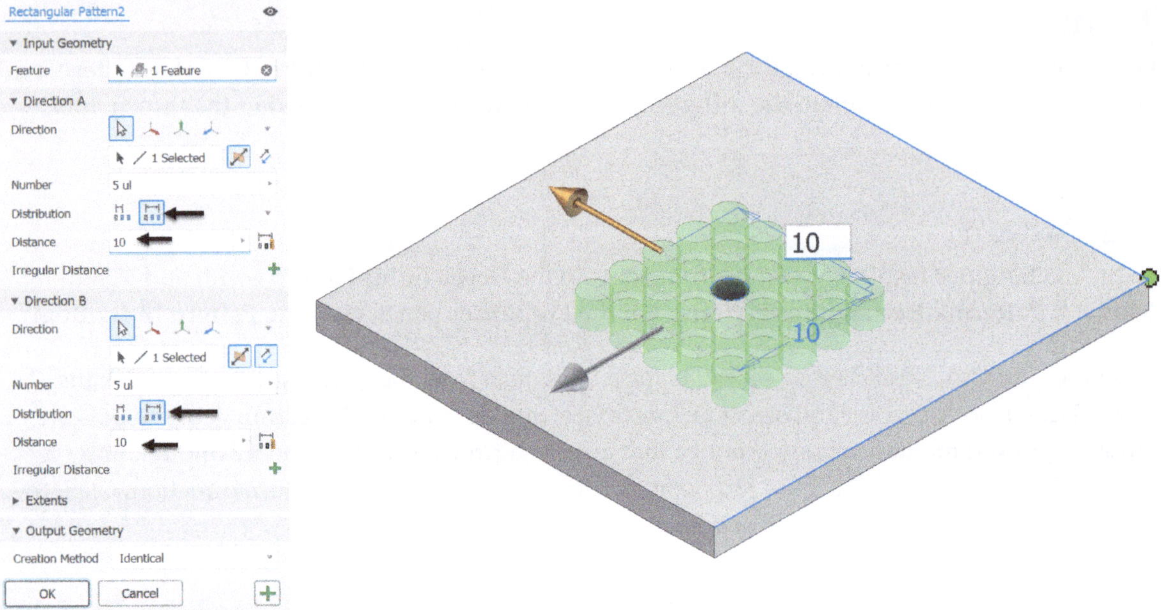

Click the **Curve Length** icons located next to the **Distance** boxes in the **Direction A** and **Direction B** section on the **Properties panel**, If you want to space the pattern based on the total length of the selected curve used for direction.

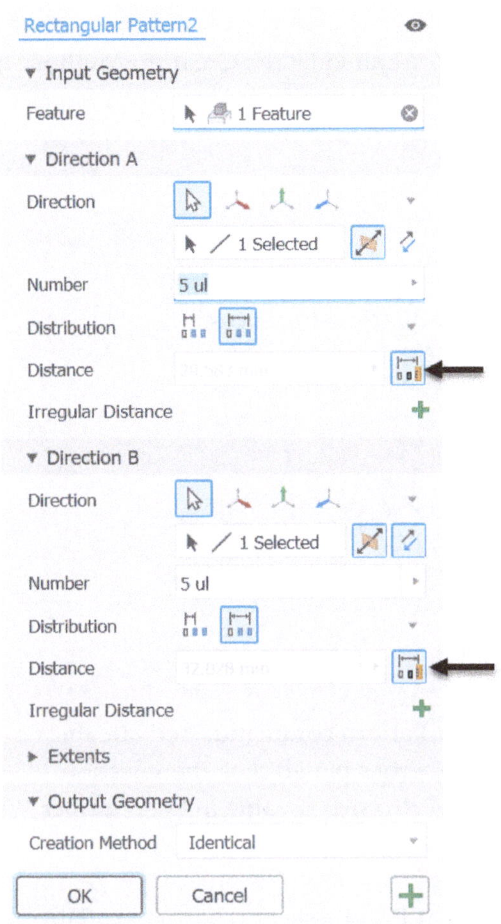

Rectangular Pattern2

▼ Input Geometry

Feature — 1 Feature

▼ Direction A

Direction — 1 Selected

Number — 5 ul

Distribution

Distance

Irregular Distance

▼ Direction B

Direction — 1 Selected

Number — 5 ul

Distribution

Distance

Irregular Distance

▸ Extents

▼ Output Geometry

Creation Method — Identical

OK Cancel

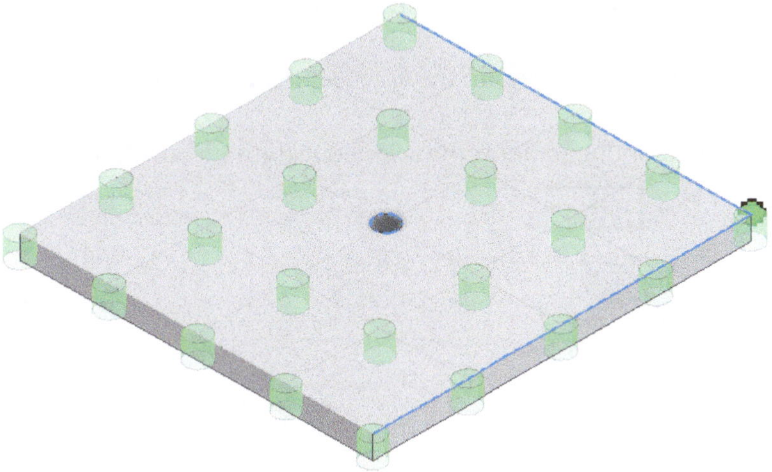

Extents

The **Extents** section controls pattern boundaries. Use **Boundary** to select a closed sketch that defines the pattern's containment region. There are three **Inclusion** options: **Include Geometry fully enclosed by boundary, Include Geometry whose centroid is inside the boundary, Include Geometry whose base point is inside the boundary.** The **Include Geometry fully enclosed by boundary** option automatically includes any occurrence fully inside this boundary. For partial overlaps, the **Include Geometry whose centroid is inside the boundary** option adds occurrences whose center point lies within the boundary, while the **Include Geometry whose base point is inside the boundary** options evaluates inclusion based on each occurrence's manually defined base point - if this point falls within the boundary, the entire occurrence is included.

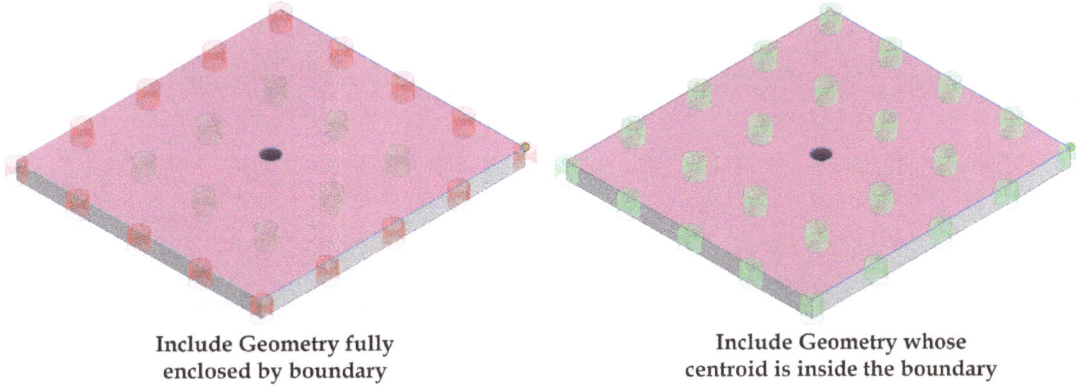

Include Geometry fully enclosed by boundary

Include Geometry whose centroid is inside the boundary

Using the Creation Methods

The **Creation Method** has three options: **Optimized, Identical**, and **Adjust**. You can view the **Creation Method** drop-down in the **Output Geometry section** on the **Properties** panel.

The **Optimized** option patterns the faces of the selected feature.

The **Identical** option creates the exact copies of the feature.

The **Adjust** option patterns the selected feature by calculating the extents of individual instances.

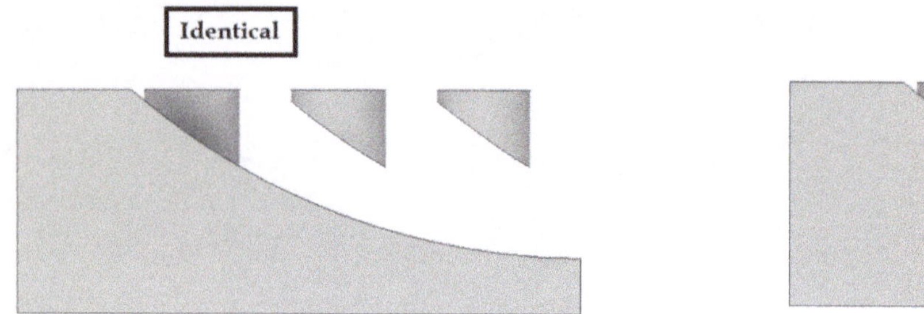

Creating a Pattern Along a Path

You can create a pattern along a selected curve or edge using the **Rectangular Pattern** command. Activate the **Rectangular Pattern** command and click on the feature to pattern. On the Properties panel, click the selection button in the **Direction A** section and select a curve, edge, or sketched path. Next, enter a value in the **Number** box. Select the Distribution option, and then specify the **Distance** value.

Next, you need to specify the start of the pattern. To do this, first, slick the **Start Point** selection button available in the **Direction A** section and select a point or vertex to define the start point.

Select an option from the **Creation Method** drop-down from the **Output Geometry** section. The options in this section are discussed earlier.

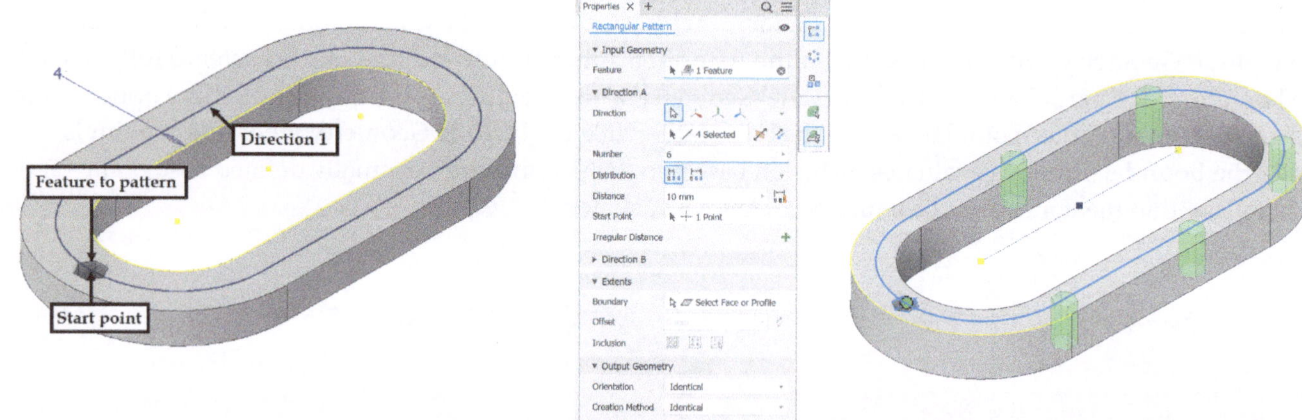

Specify the orientation using the **Orientation** drop-down in the **Output Geometry** section, which has two options: **Identical** and **Direction1**. The **Orientation** options are explained in the figure, as shown next. Click **OK** to create the pattern along the path.

Patterned Geometry

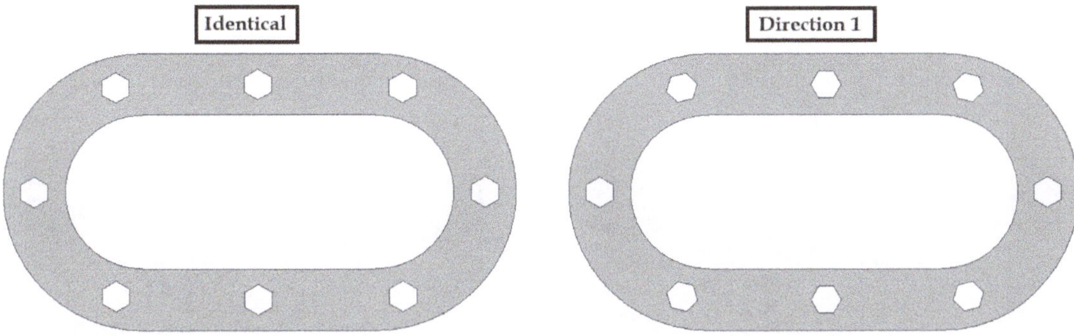

Patterning the entire geometry

The **Pattern Solids** option allows you to pattern the entire part geometry. Activate the **Rectangular Pattern** command and click the **Patter Solids** icon on the Properties panel. Next, define the direction, occurrence count, and spacing between the instances. There is no need to select the geometry as the entire body is selected by default.

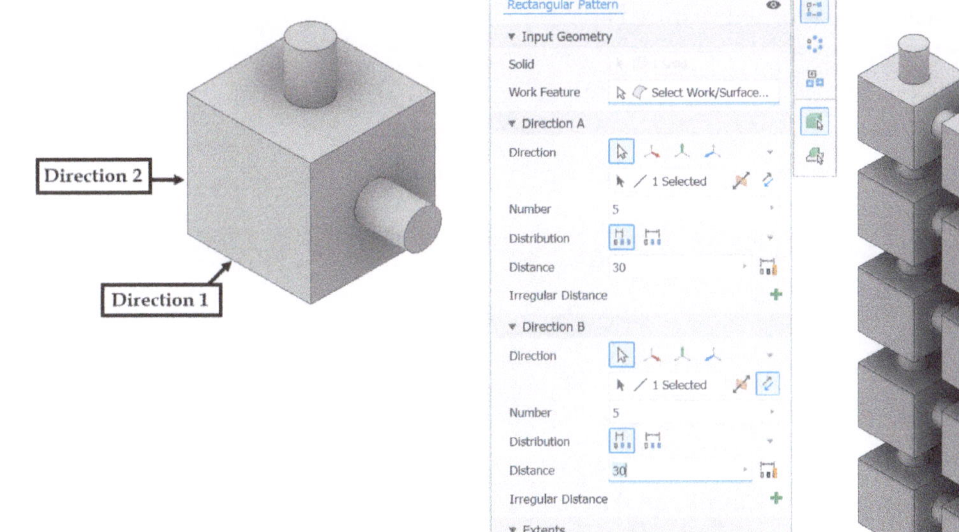

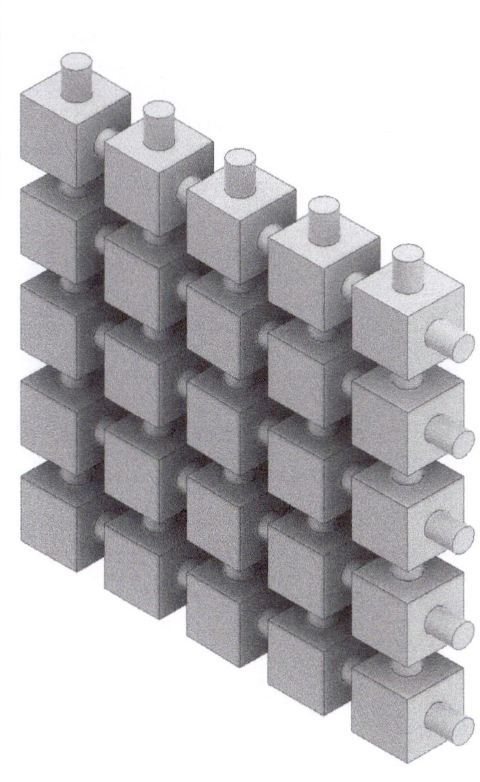

Suppressing Occurrences

If you want to suppress an occurrence of the pattern, then expand the **Rectangular Pattern** feature in the Model window. Next, place the pointer on an occurrence; it is highlighted in the graphics window. Likewise, identify the occurrence to be suppressed. Next, right-click on it and select **Suppress**.

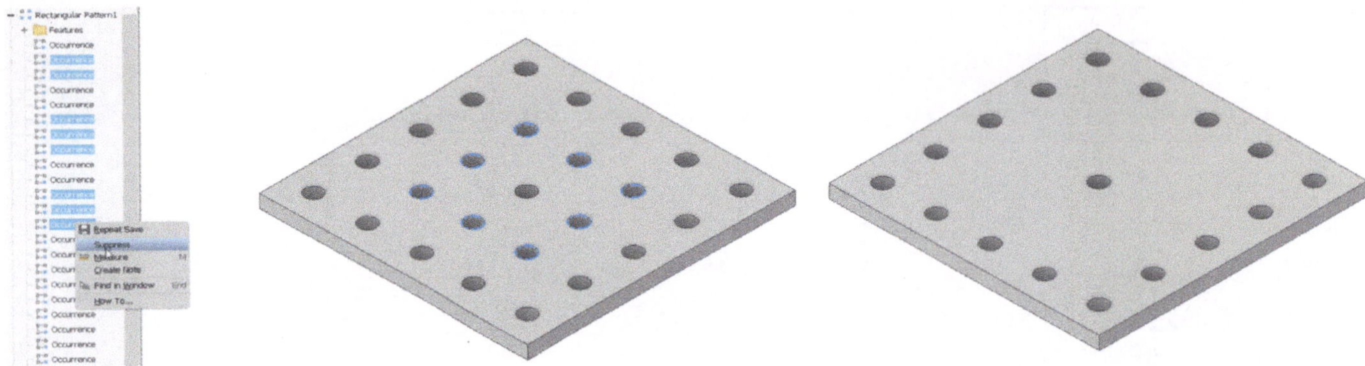

Circular Pattern

The circular pattern is used to pattern the selected features circularly. Activate the circular pattern command (click **3D Model > Pattern > Circular Pattern** on the ribbon) and select the feature to pattern from the model geometry. Click **Direction** > **Custom Direction** button in the **Orientation** section and select the axis from the model geometry or click on a round face; the axis of the rotation is defined. Usually, the axis of rotation is perpendicular to the plane/face on which the selected feature is placed.

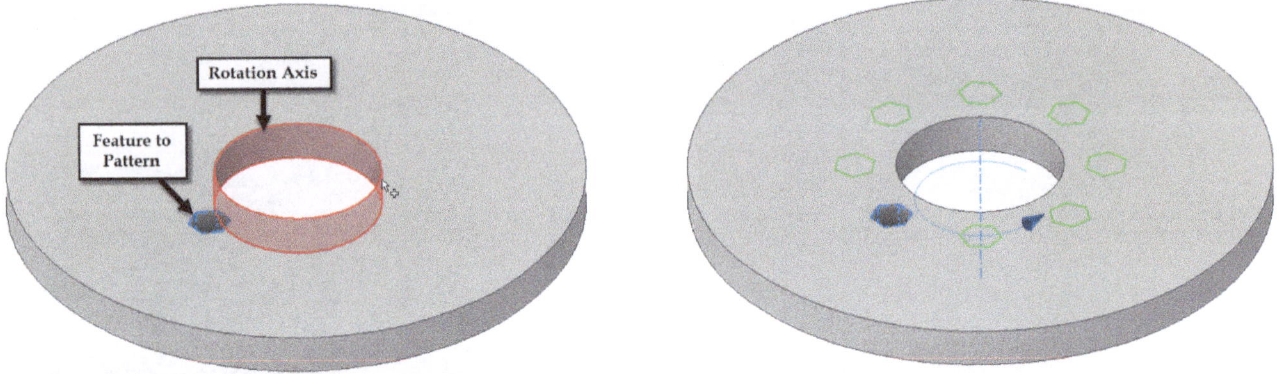

Select **Distribution** > **Fitted**. Type-in values in the **Count** and **Angle** boxes of the **Orientation** section. The total number of occurrences you specify will be fitted in the occurrence angle.

Patterned Geometry

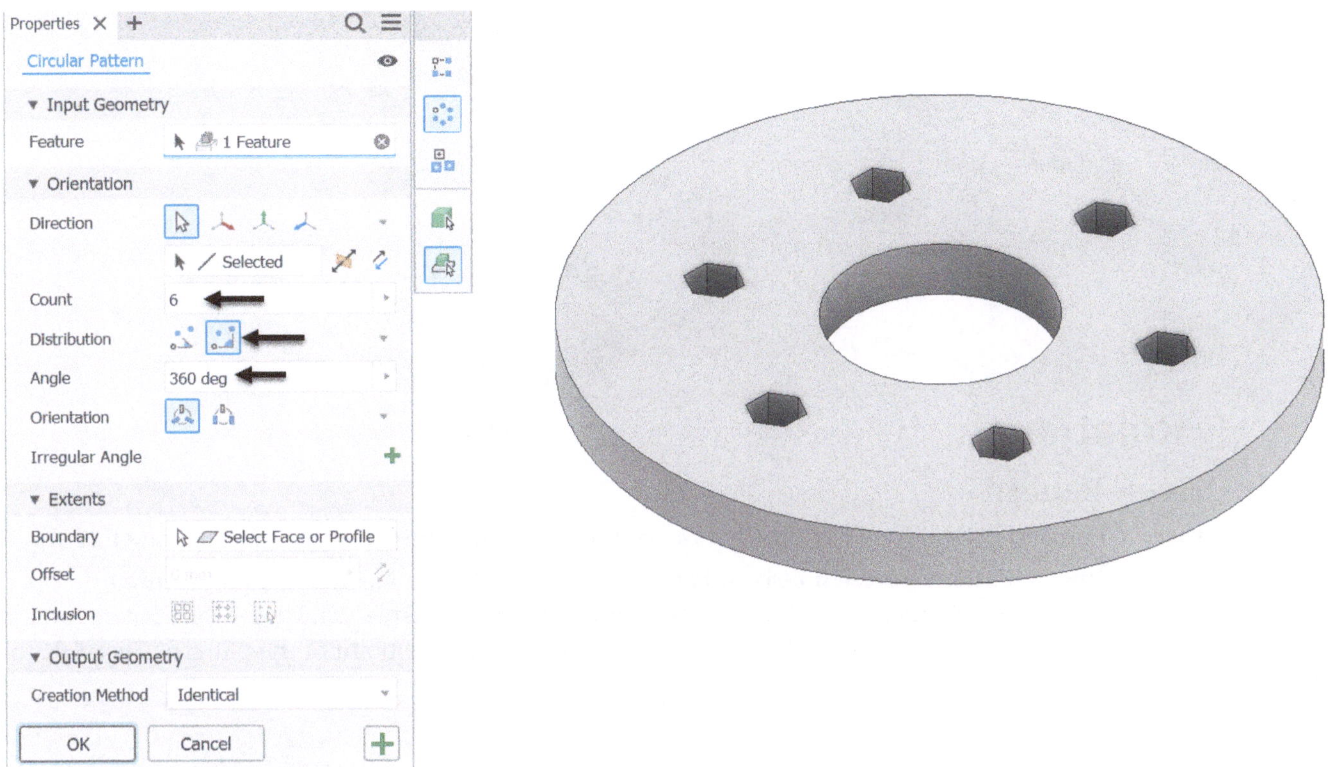

Select **Distribution > Incremental**, if you want to type-in the count and the angle between individual instances.

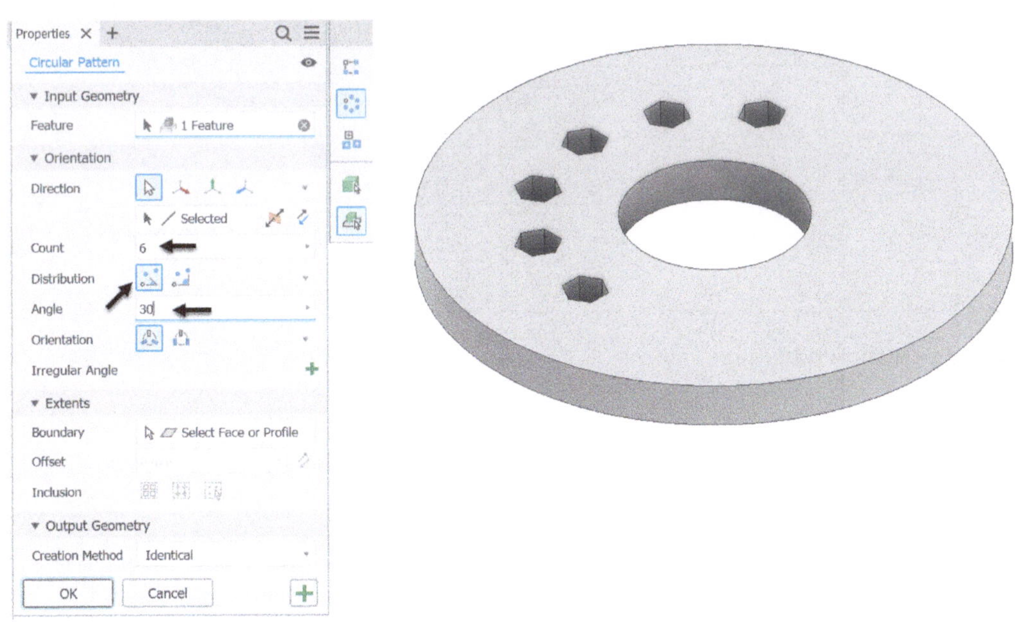

Under the **Orientation** section, click the **Rotational** icon to change the orientation of the instances, as they are patterned in the circular fashion. Click the **Fixed** icon, if you want to pattern the feature with the original orientation.

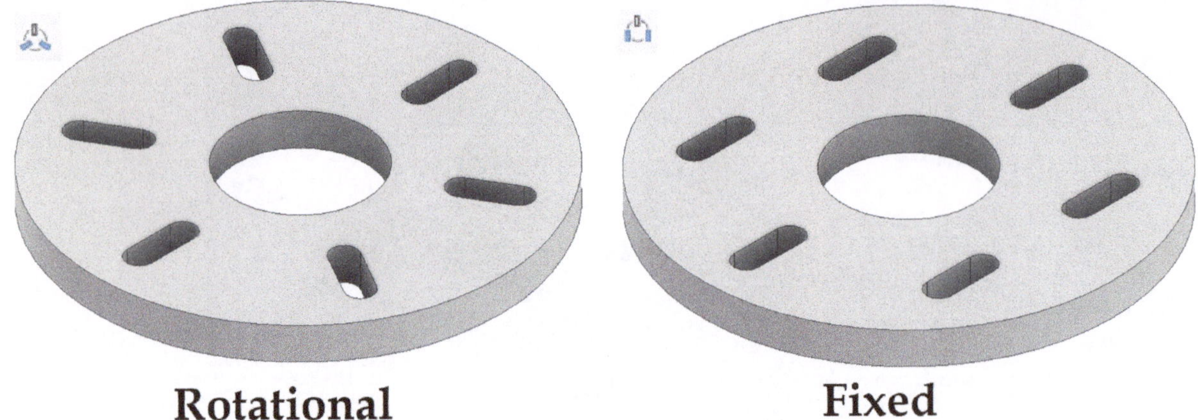

Sketch Driven Pattern

The **Sketch Driven** command is used to pattern the feature or body by using the sketch points. Activate this command (click **3D Model > Pattern > Sketch Driven Pattern** on the ribbon). Next, select the feature to pattern; the sketch is selected automatically, and the preview of the pattern is displayed. Under the **Placement** section, click the **Base Point** selection button and select a point to define the base point of the pattern. Click **OK** to create the pattern

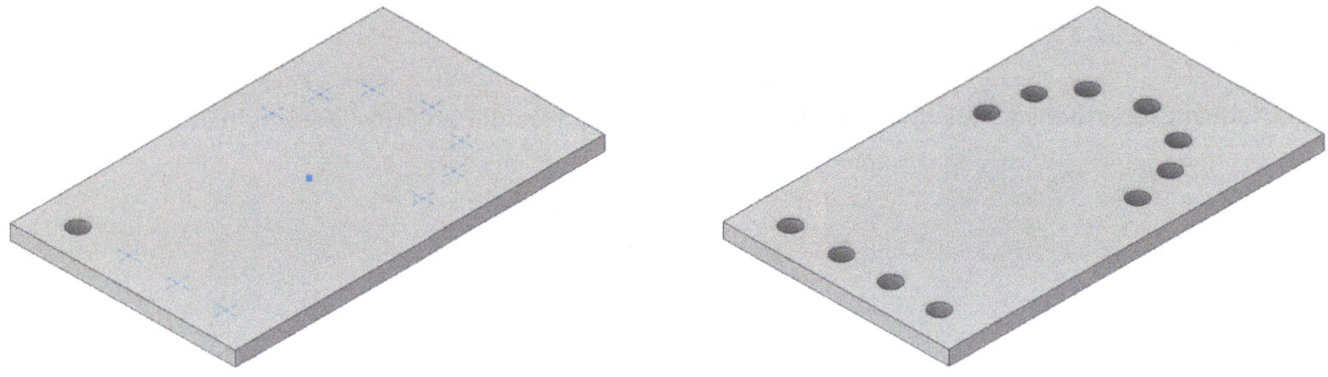

Examples

Example 1 (Millimeters)

In this example, you will create the part shown below.

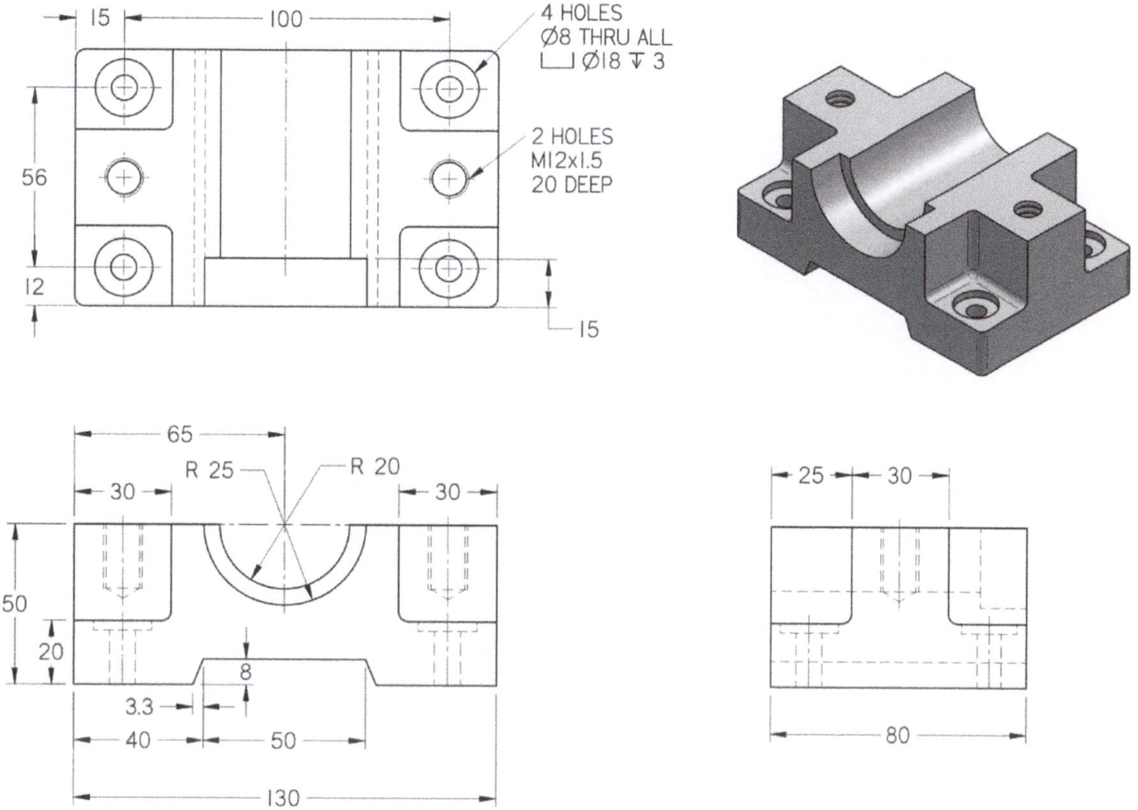

1. Start **Autodesk Inventor 2026.**
2. Open a new file using the **Standard (mm).ipt** template.
3. To start a sketch, click **3D Model > Sketch > Start 2D Sketch** on the ribbon. Click on the **XY** plane.
4. Create a rectangular sketch, add dimensions as shown, and click **Finish Sketch** on the ribbon.

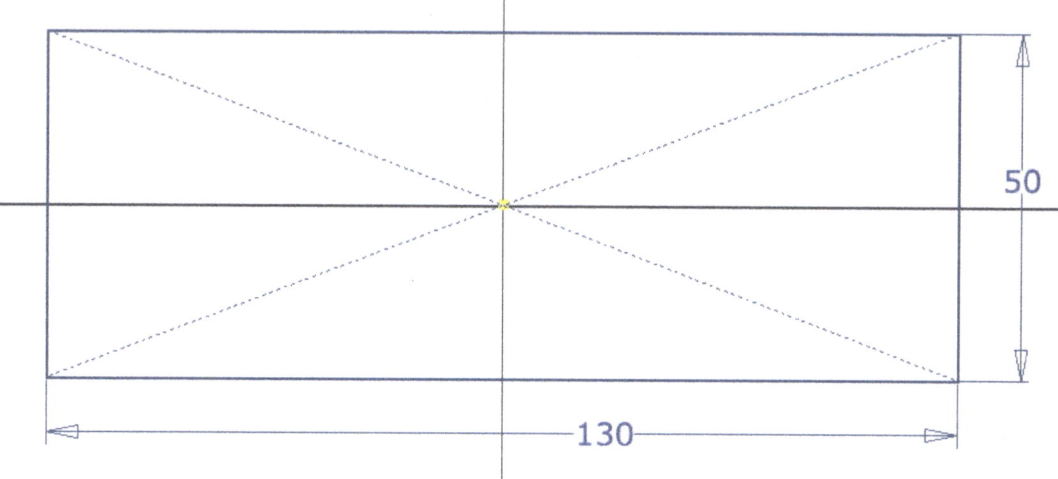

5. Activate the **Extrude** command.

6. On the **Extrude Properties** panel, click the **Symmetric** icon under the **Behavior** section and type in **80** in the **Distance A** box. Click **OK** to complete the Extrude feature.

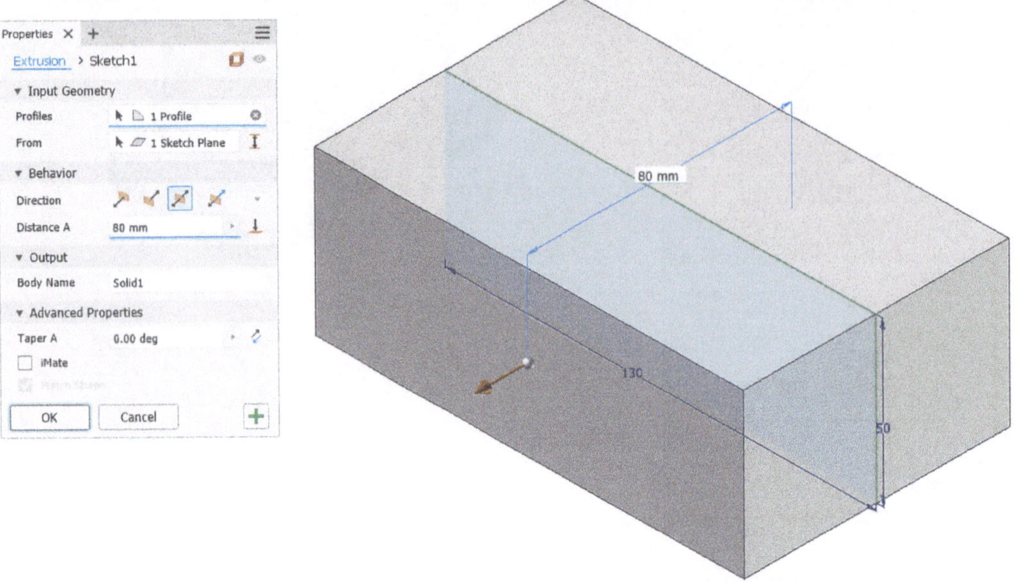

7. Click **3D Model > Sketch > Start 2D Sketch**, on the ribbon.
8. Click on the top face of the part model, as shown in the figure. Next, the draw sketch, as shown. Click **Sketch > Exit > Finish Sketch**, on the ribbon.

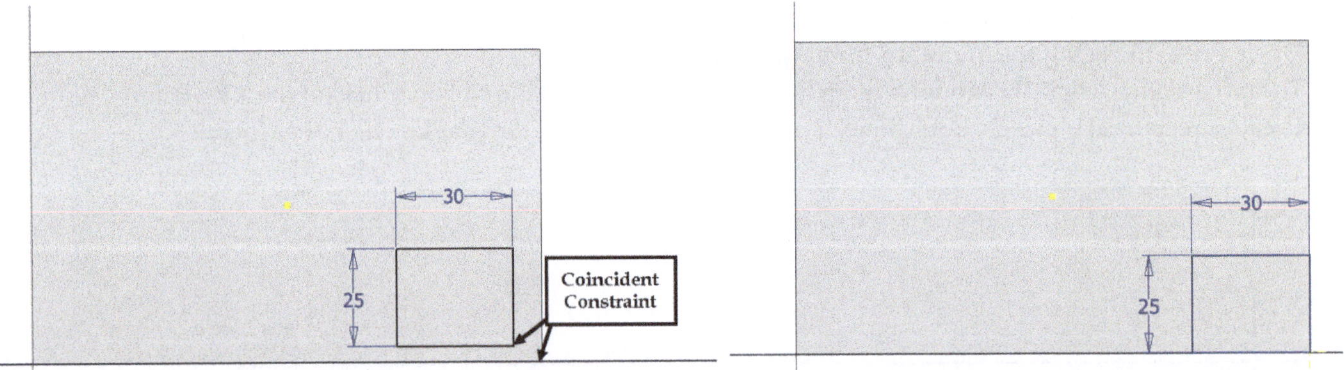

9. Activate the **Extrude** command from the ribbon.
10. On the **Extrude Properties** panel, click the **Boolean > Cut** icon under the **Output** section.
11. Type-in **30** in the **Distance A** box under the **Behavior** section and click **OK** to create the *Cutout* feature.

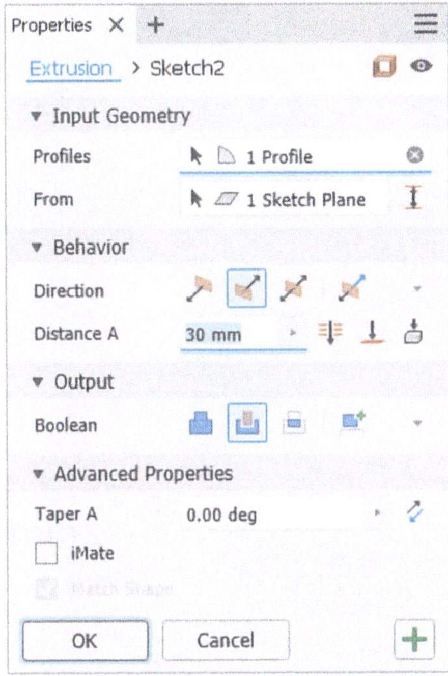

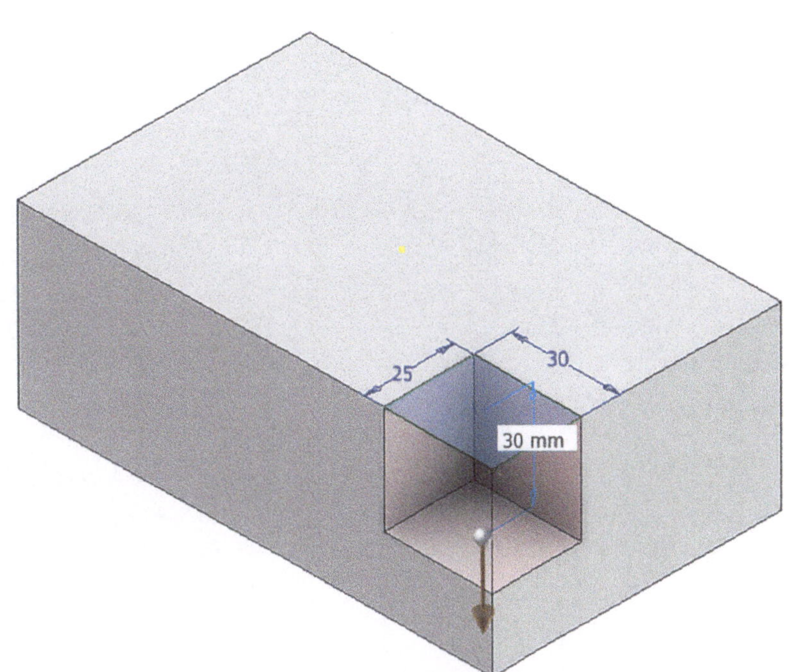

12. Activate the **Start 2D Sketch** command and click on the top face of the *Cutout* feature.
13. Click **Sketch > Create > Point** on the ribbon and place the point.
14. On the ribbon, click **Sketch > Constrain > Horizontal Constraint** . Select the point and the midpoint of the right vertical edge; the selected points are aligned horizontally.
15. On the ribbon, click **Sketch > Constrain > Vertical Constraint** . Select the point and the midpoint of the bottom horizontal edge of the cutout; the selected points are aligned vertically.

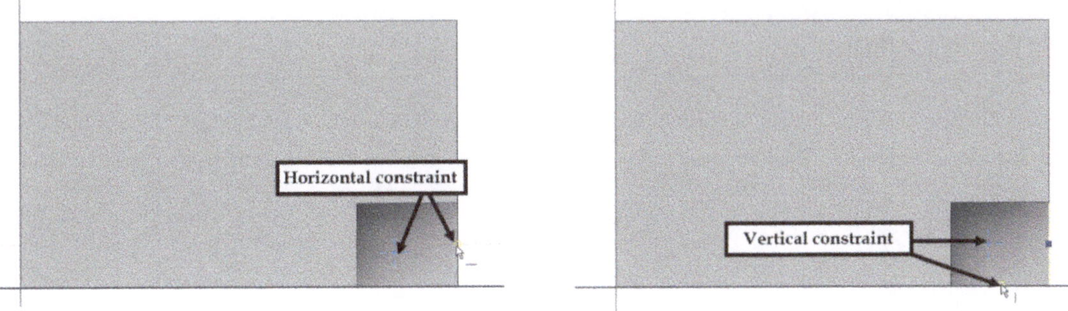

16. Click **Finish Sketch** on the ribbon.
17. Activate the **Hole** command and place the counterbore hole on the *Cutout* feature.

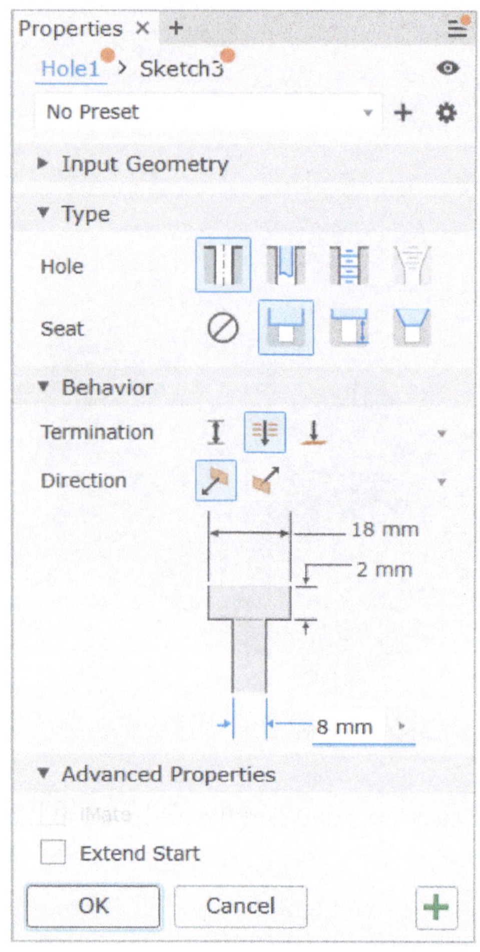

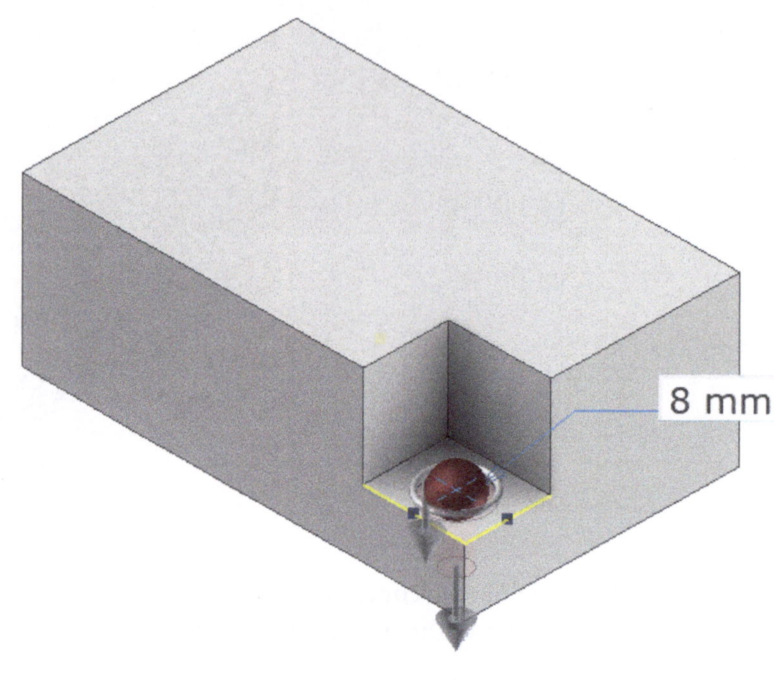

18. Click **OK** to complete the *Hole* feature.

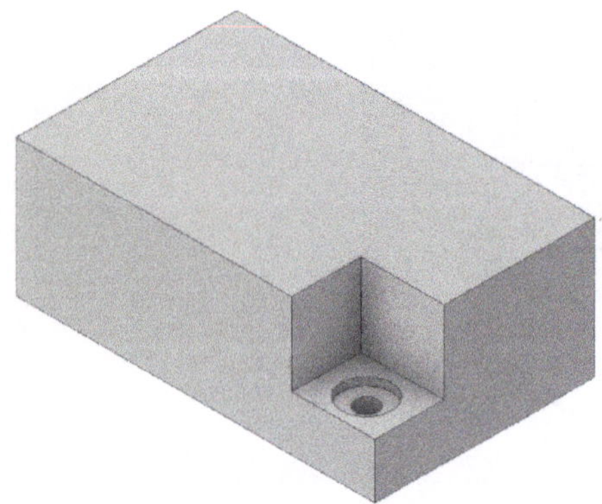

19. Click **3D Model > Pattern > Rectangular Pattern**, on the ribbon.
20. On the **Properties panel**, click the **Features** selection button and select the *Hole* and *Cutout* features.
21. Click the **Direction > Custom Direction** selection button in the Direction A section, and click on the top front edge of the part model.
22. Type in **2** and **100** in the **Number** and **Distance** boxes, respectively.

23. Click the **Direction > Custom Direction** selection button in the **Direction B** section, and click on the top side edge of the part model.
24. Type in **2** and **55** in the **Number** and **Distance** boxes, respectively.
25. Click the **Flip** button next to the **Direction** selection box in the **Direction B** section, if the preview of the rectangular pattern is displayed outside the model. Click **OK** to complete the pattern feature.

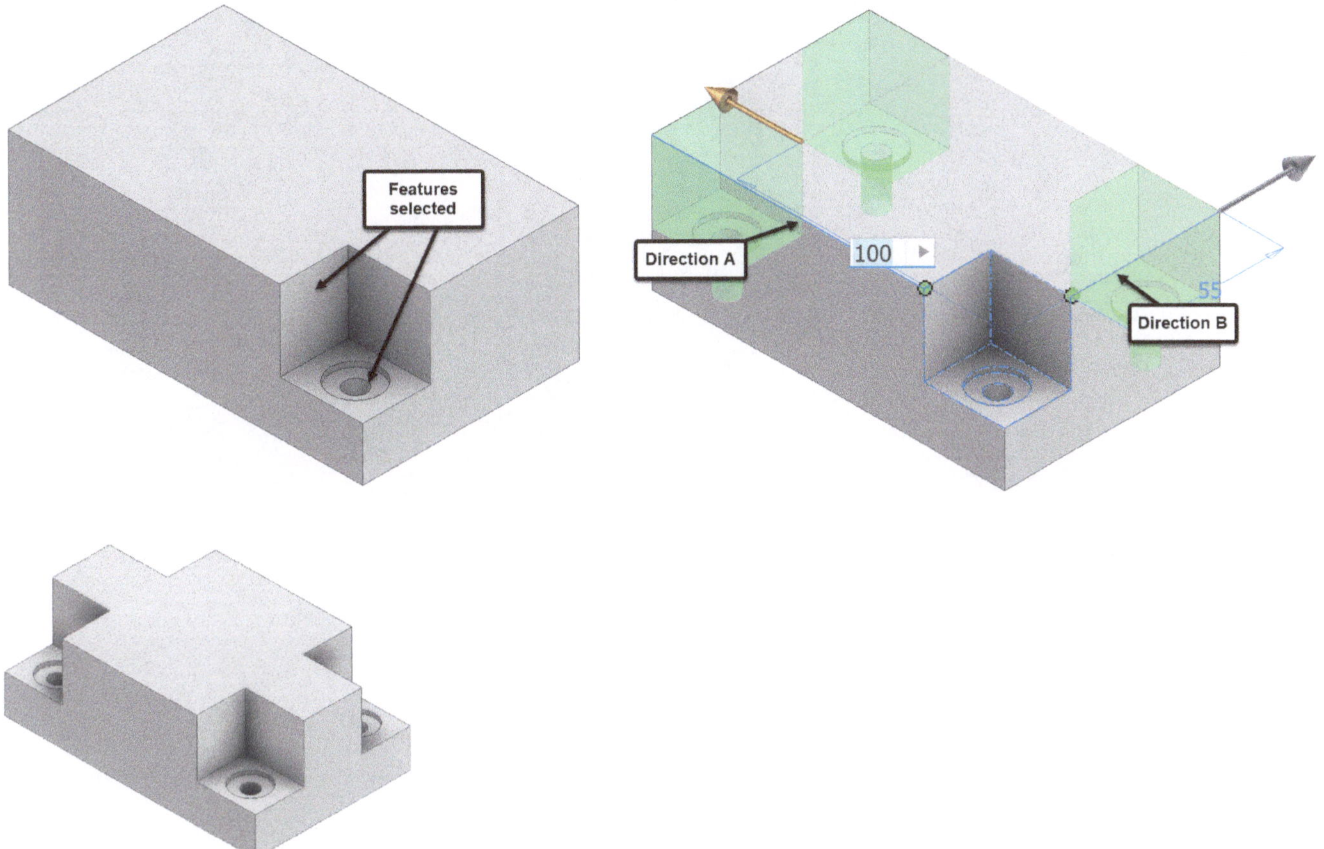

26. Click **3D Model > Sketch > Start 2D Sketch**, on the ribbon. Click on the front face of the part model.
27. Click **Sketch > Create > Point**, on the ribbon. Place a point and apply the **Coincident Constraint** between the point and the midpoint of the top edge, as shown. Click **Finish Sketch** on the ribbon.

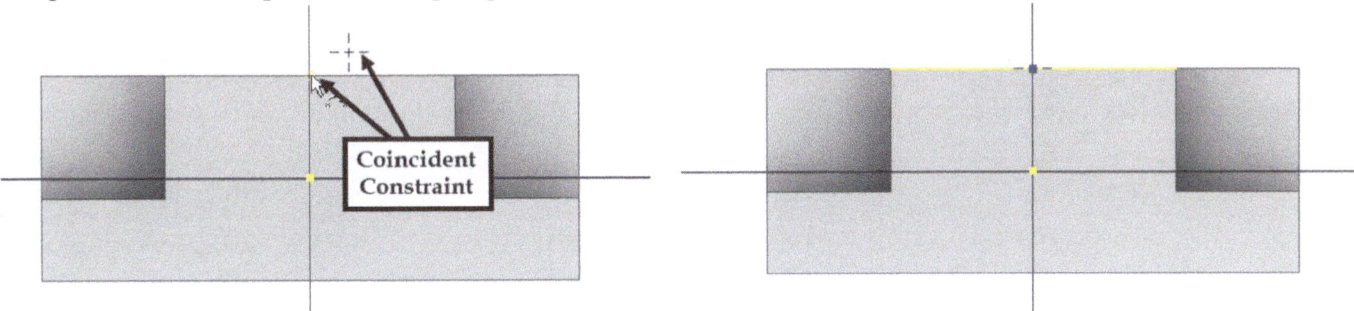

28. Click **3D Model > Modify > Hole**, on the ribbon.
29. On the **Properties panel**, click **Type > Hole > Simple Hole.**
30. Click **Type > Seat > Counterbore** on the **Properties** panel.
31. Click **Behavior > Termination > Through All**. Set **Direction** to **Default.**
32. Type-in **50** and **15** mm in the **Counterbore Diameter** and **Counterbore Depth** boxes, respectively.

33. Set the **Diameter** value to **40** mm and click **OK** to create the counterbore hole.

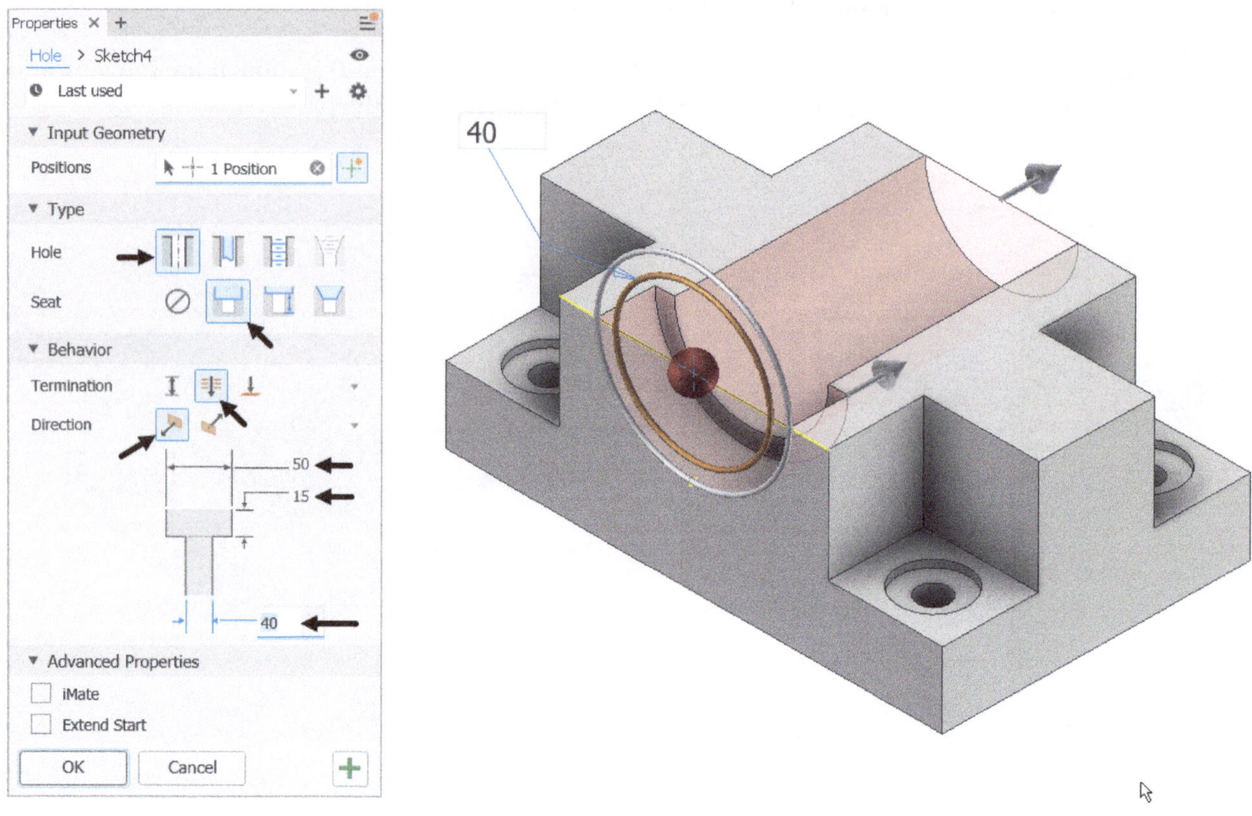

34. Click **3D Model > Modify > Hole**, on the ribbon and click on the top face of the part model, as shown.
35. On the **Properties** Panel, click **Type > Hole > Tapped Hole**, and set the parameters, as shown in the figure.

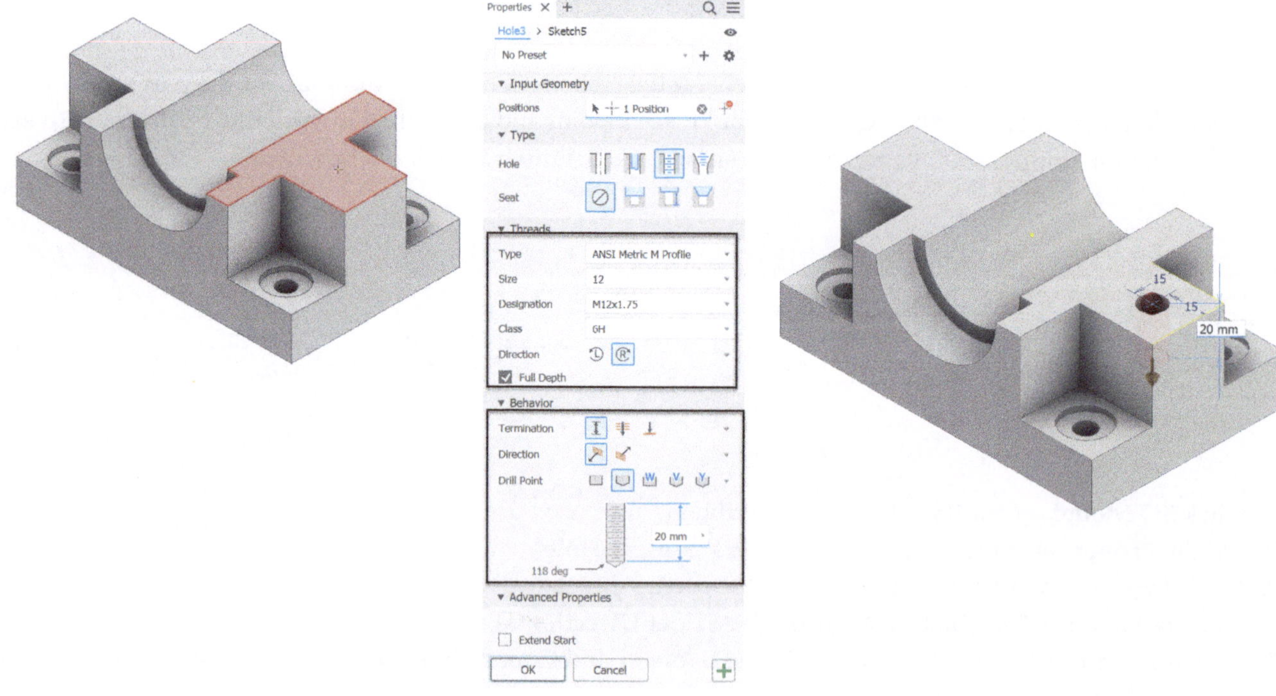

36. Click the **Sketch5** link in the Breadcrumbs area of the **Properties** panel. Add dimensions to the point and click **Finish Sketch**.

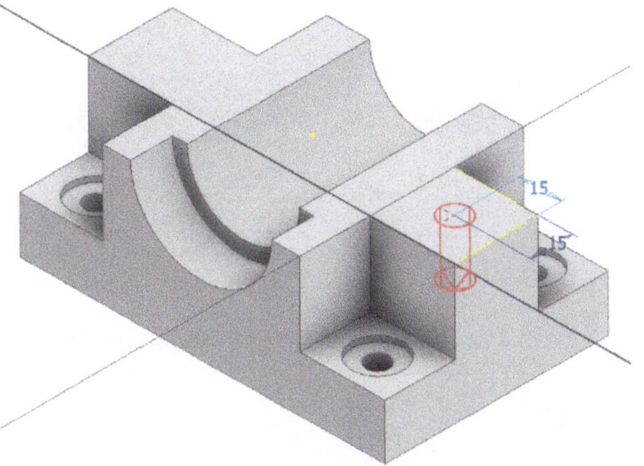

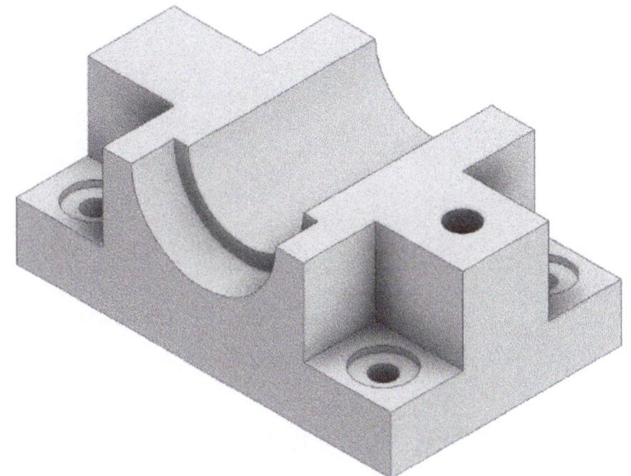

37. On the ribbon, click **3D Model > Pattern > Mirror** .
38. On the **Mirror** dialog, click the **Features** button and select the threaded hole feature from the part model.
39. Click the **Origin YZ plane** icon on the **Mirror** dialog. Click **OK** to complete the mirror feature.

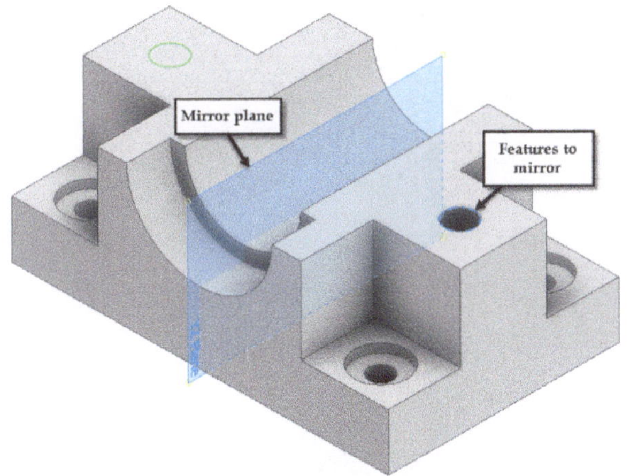

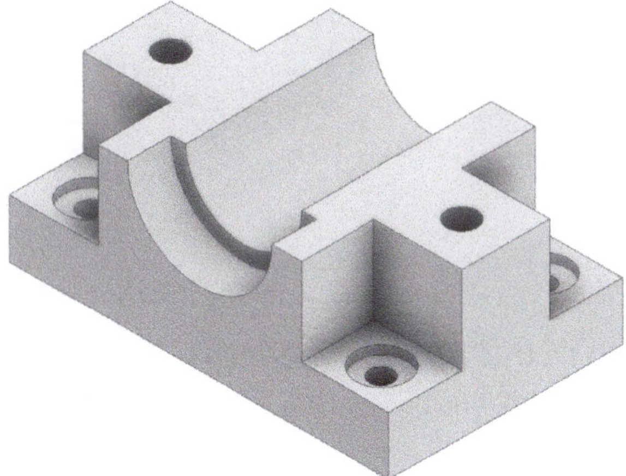

40. Activate the **Start 2D Sketch** command and click on the front face of the part model.
41. Draw the sketch and add dimensions, as shown in the figure. Note that you should apply the **Symmetric** constraint between the two inclined lines. Click **Finish Sketch** on the ribbon.
42. Create a *Cutout* throughout the part model, as shown.

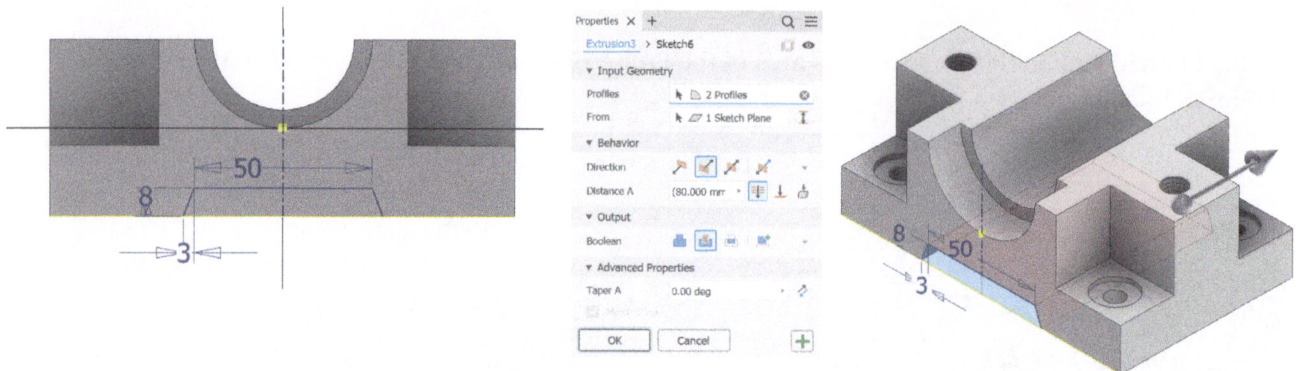

43. On the ribbon, click **3D Model > Modify > Fillet**.
44. Click on the edges of the cutout feature; the edges are filleted — type **2** in the **Radius** box available on the **Fillet** dialog.
45. Likewise, select the edges of the remaining cutout features. Click **OK**.

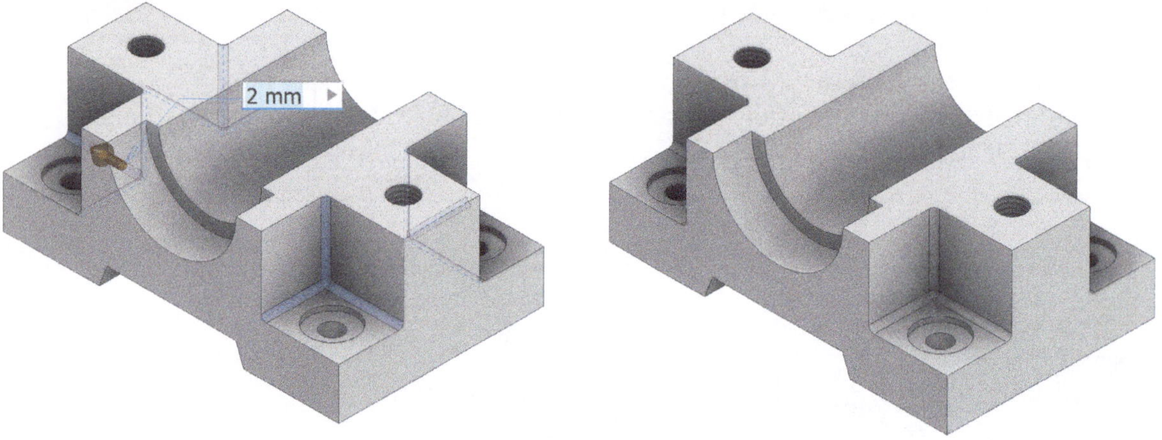

46. Save and close the part file.

Example 2 (Millimeters)

In this example, you create the part shown next.

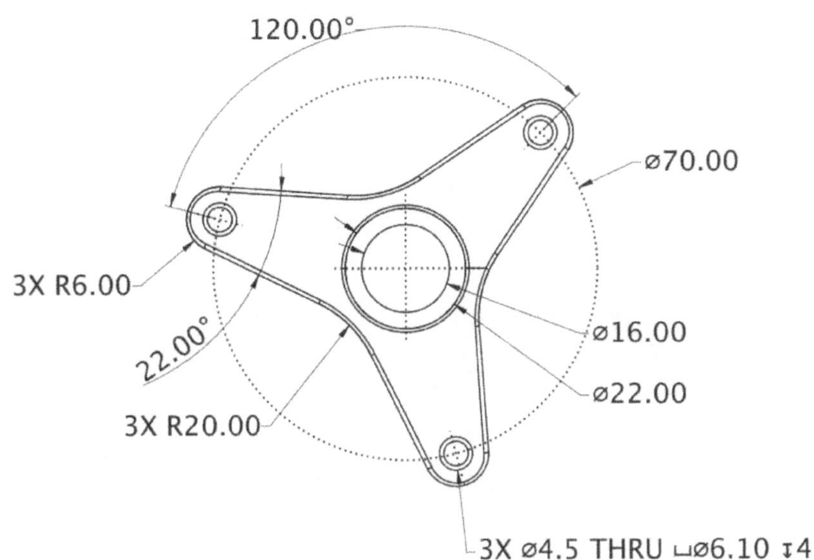

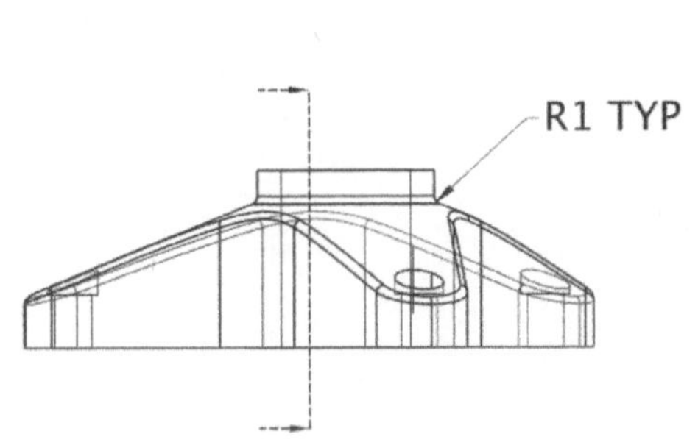

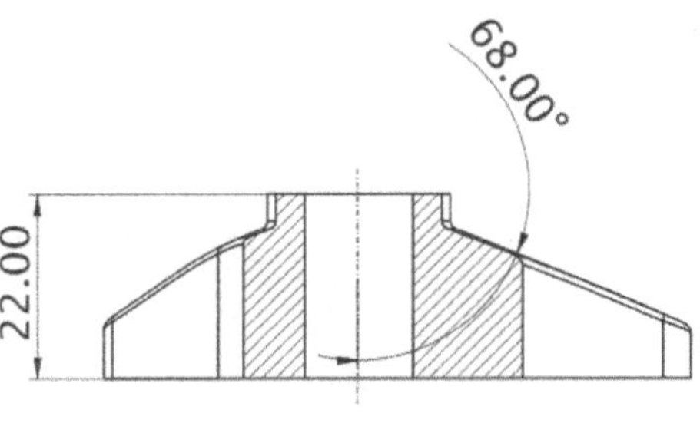

Creating a New document

1. Click **Autodesk Inventor 2026** on the desktop to start the application.
2. To start a new part file, click **Get Started > Launch > New** on the Ribbon.
3. On the **Create New File** dialog, click the **Metric** folder under **Templates.**
4. Click the **Standard(mm).ipt** icon under the **Part – Create 2D and 3D Objects** section.
5. Click the **Create** button on the **Create New File** dialog.

A new model window appears.

Creating the Extruded feature

1. To start a sketch, click **3D Model > Sketch > Start 2D Sketch** on the ribbon. Click on the XZ plane. The sketch starts.
2. Click **Sketch > Create > Line** on the ribbon. Next, click in the graphics window, move the pointer downward and click.
3. Click on the horizontal axis of the sketch. Next, move the pointer and select the start point of the vertical line.
4. On the ribbon, click **Sketch > Create > Fillet** . Type **6** in the **Radius** box of the **2D Fillet** dialog. Select corner point, as shown.

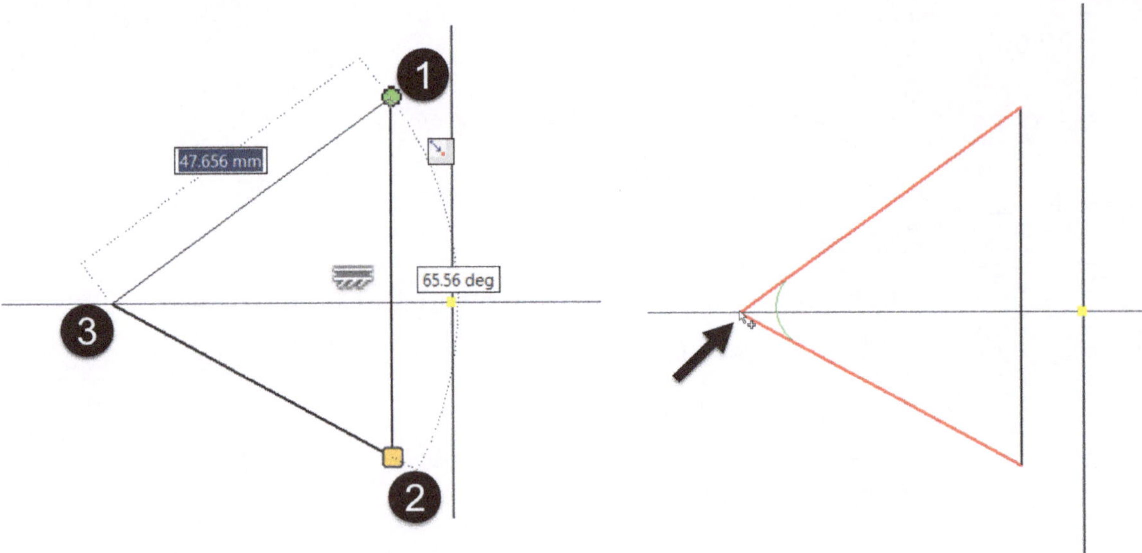

5. Click **Sketch > Constrain > Equal** on the ribbon. Select the two inclined lines.

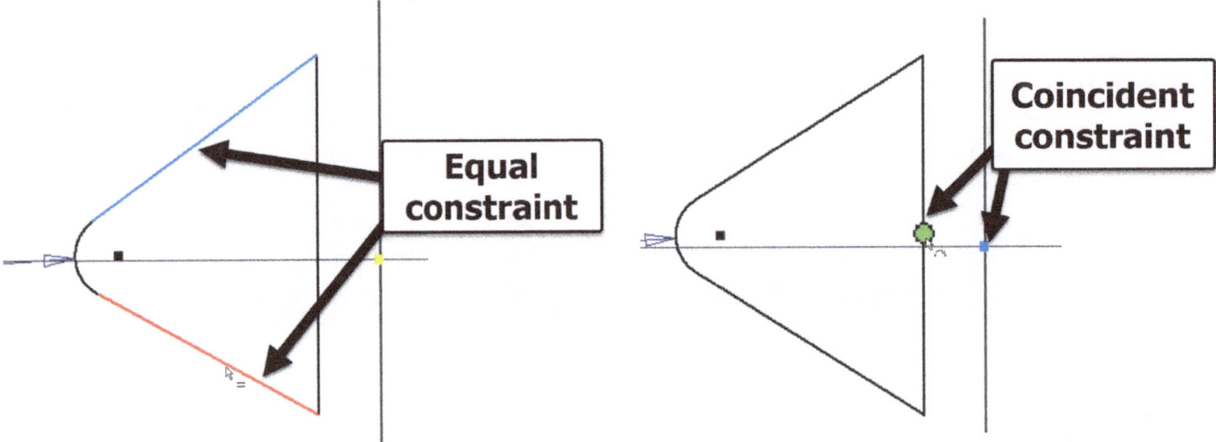

6. Create the angle dimension between the two inclined lines.
7. Create the horizontal constraint between the sketch origin and the centerpoint of the fillet.
8. On the ribbon, click **3D Model > Create > Extrude**; the sketch is selected automatically.
9. Type-in **22** in the **Distance A** box.
10. Click **OK** to complete the *Extrude* feature.

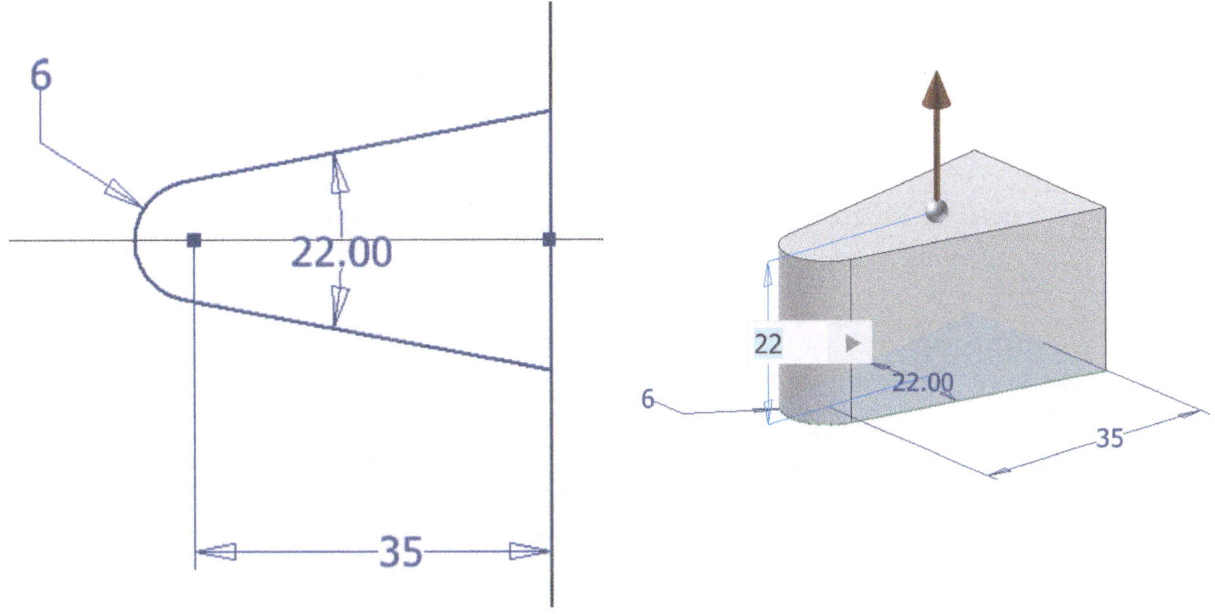

Creating the Counterbore Hole

1. Click **3D Model > Modify > Hole**, on the ribbon.
2. On the **Properties panel**, click **Type > Hole > Tapped Hole**.
3. Under the **Threads** section, select **Type > ISO metric profile**. Next, select **Size > 4**.
4. Select **Designation > M4x0.7**. Next, check the **Full Depth** option.
5. Click **Type > Seat > Counterbore** on the **Properties** panel.
6. Click **Behavior > Termination > Through All**. Set **Direction** to **Default**.
7. Type-in **6.1** and **17** mm in the **Counterbore Diameter** and **Counterbore Depth** boxes, respectively.
8. Click on the horizontal face of the *Extruded* feature.

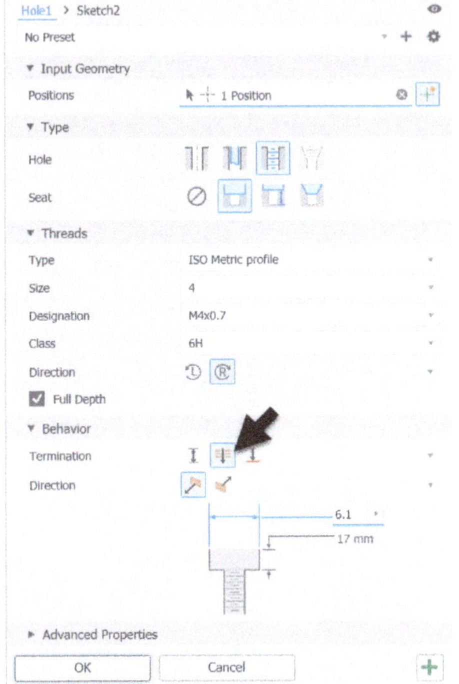

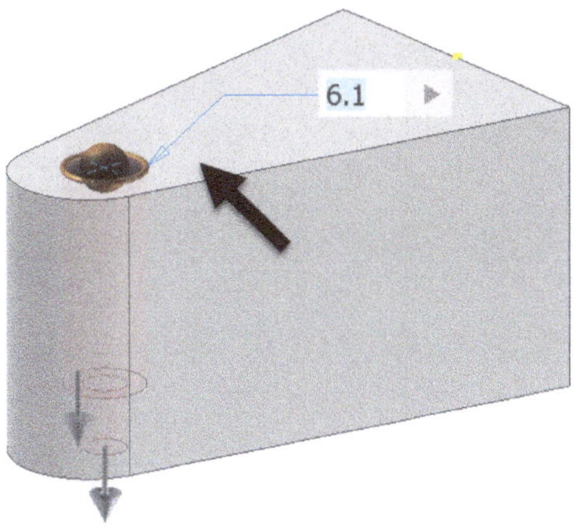

9. Click **Sketch2** on the top of the **Properties** panel; the Sketch environment is activated.
10. On the ribbon, click **Sketch > Create > Project Geometry**. Click on the circular edge.
11. Click the **Sketch > Constrain > Coincident Constraint** icon and select the center point of the projected geometry.
12. Select the center point of the hole. Next, click the **Return to Hole** icon on the ribbon.

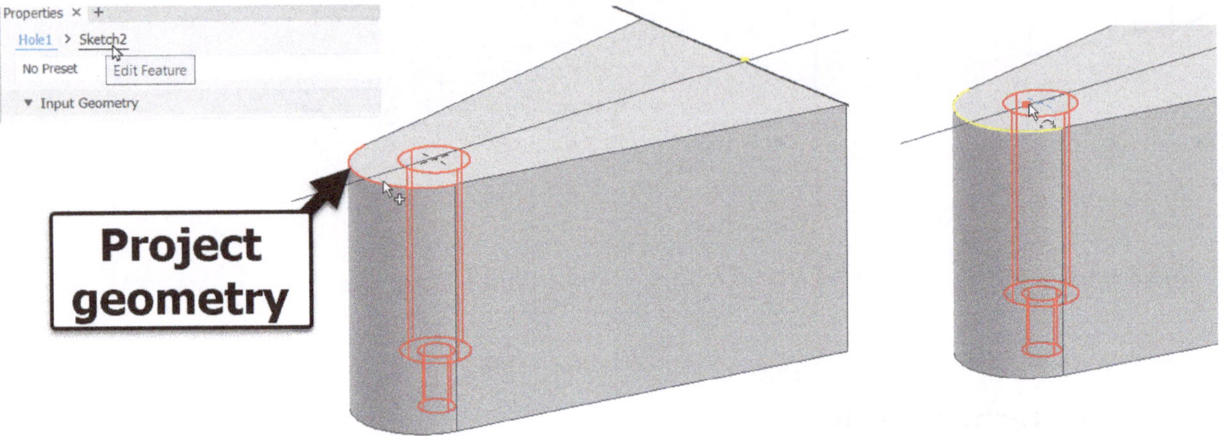

13. Click **OK** on the **Properties** panel.

Creating the Circular Pattern

1. On the ribbon, click **3D Model > Pattern > Circular Pattern**. Click the **Features** icon and select the extruded and hole features. Now, you have to define the axis of the circular pattern.
2. Click **Direction > Y axis** from the **Orientation** section on the **Properties** panel. It defines the pattern axis.
3. Select **Distribution > Fitted** and type-in **3** and **360** in the **Count** and **Angle** boxes, respectively.
4. Select **Orientation > Rotational**. Click **OK** on the Properties panel.

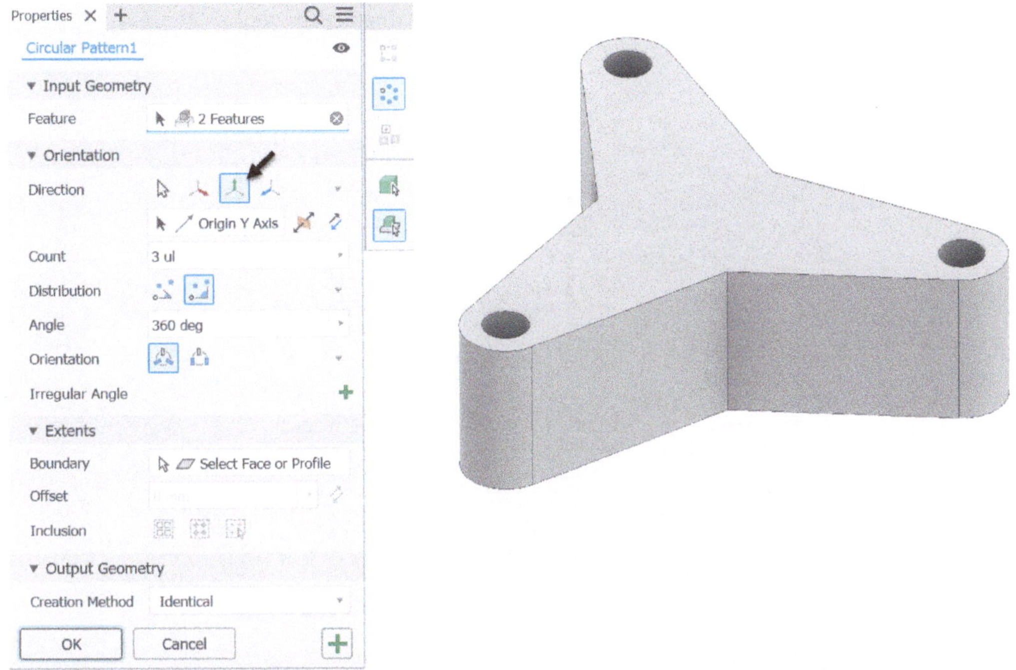

Creating a Revolved Cut

1. Click the **Create 2D Sketch** icon on the ribbon and select the YZ plane.
2. Click the **Slice graphics** icon at the bottom of the graphics window.
3. Create the sketch, as shown. Next, apply constraints and dimensions to the sketch and click **Finish Sketch**.
4. Activate the **Revolve** command and click in the region of the sketch.
5. On the **Revolve Properties** panel, click in the **Axis** selection box and select the Y-axis from the Browser window.
6. Click the **Intersect** icon under the **Output** section on the **Revolve Properties** panel.

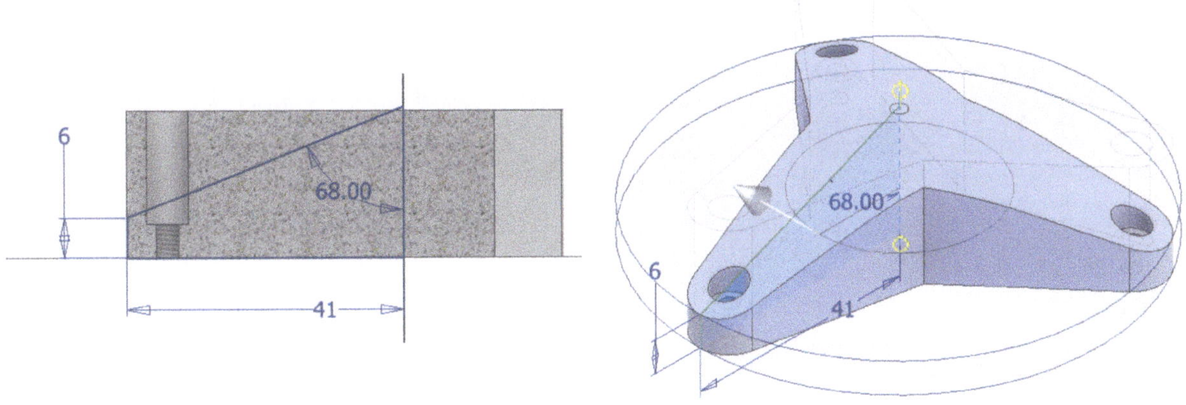

Creating Cylindrical Feature and Hole at the center

1. Click the **Create 2D Sketch** icon on the ribbon and select the XZ plane.
2. Click the **Slice graphics** icon at the bottom of the graphics window.

3. Create a circle at the center of the model and add dimension to it. Next, click **Finish Sketch**.
4. On the ribbon, click **3D Model > Create > Extrude**; the sketch is selected automatically.
5. Type-in **22** in the **Distance A** box.
6. Click the **Join** button under the **Boolean** section.
7. Click **OK** to complete the *Extrude* feature.

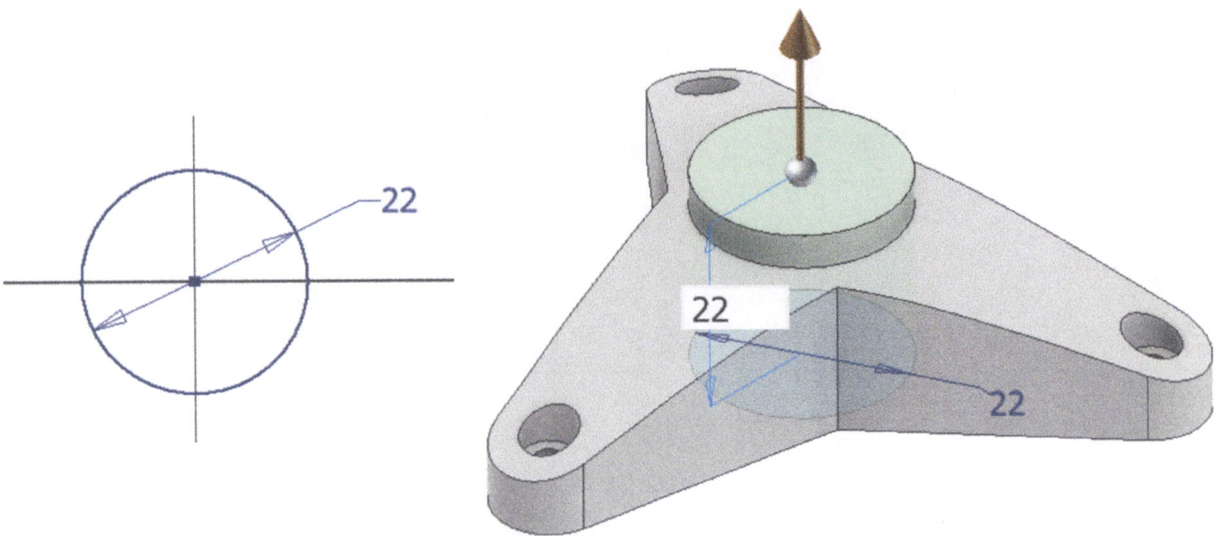

8. Click **3D Model > Modify > Hole**, on the ribbon.
9. Click on the horizontal face of the *Extrude* feature. Next, select the cylindrical face of the model, as shown.
10. On the **Properties** panel, click **Type > Hole > Simple Hole**.
11. Select **Seat > None**. Next, type **16** in the **Diameter** box.
12. Select **Termination > Through All**. Next, click **OK** on the **Properties** panel; the hole is created.

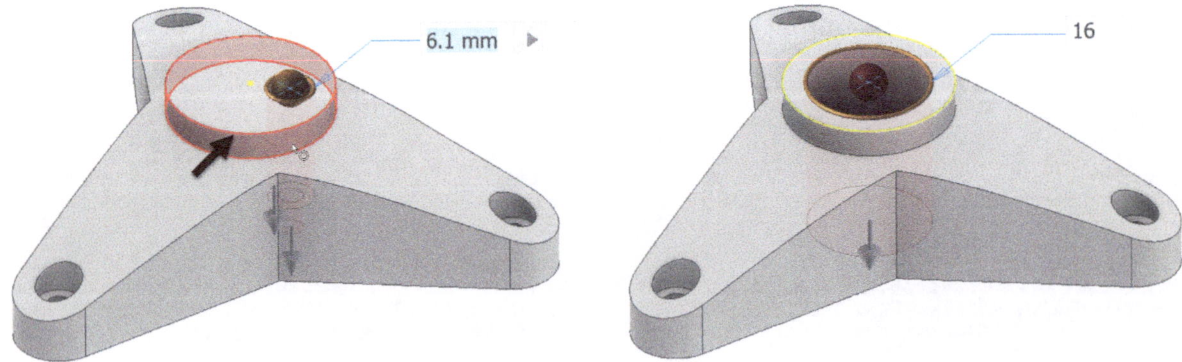

Creating Fillets

1. Click **View > Appearance > Visual Style > Wireframe** on the ribbon.
2. Click **3D Model > Modify > Fillet** on the ribbon. On the **Fillet** Properties panel, under the **Selection Sets** section, set the **Fillet Constant Radius** value to **20** mm.
3. Select the edges, as shown. Next, click **OK**.
4. Click **View > Appearance > Visual Style > Shaded with edges** on the ribbon.

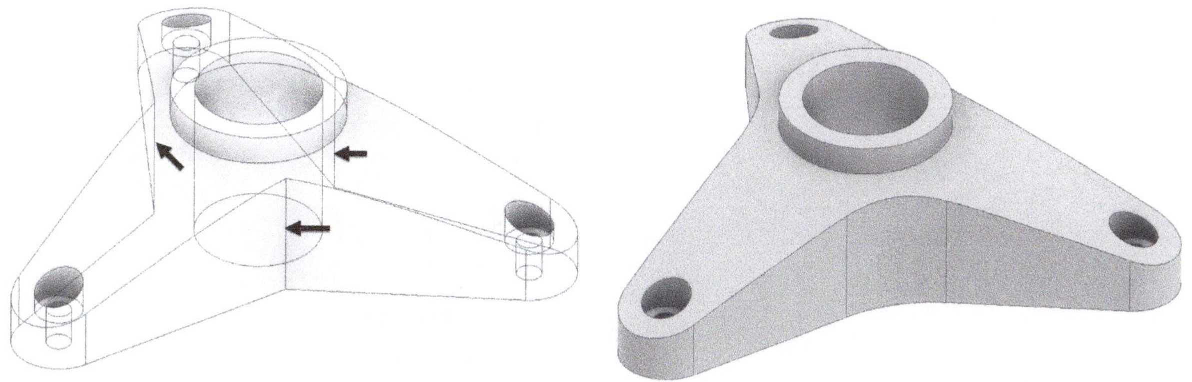

5. Click **3D Model > Modify > Fillet** on the ribbon. On the **Fillet** Properties panel, under the **Selection Sets** section, set the **Fillet Constant Radius** value to **1** mm.
6. Select the edges, as shown. Next, click **OK**.

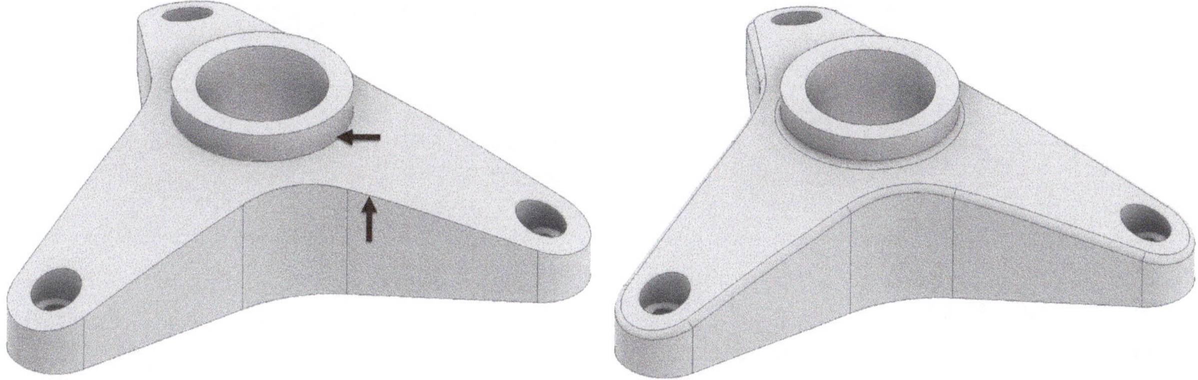

7. Save and close the design file.

Example 3 (Millimeters)

In this example, you create the part shown next.

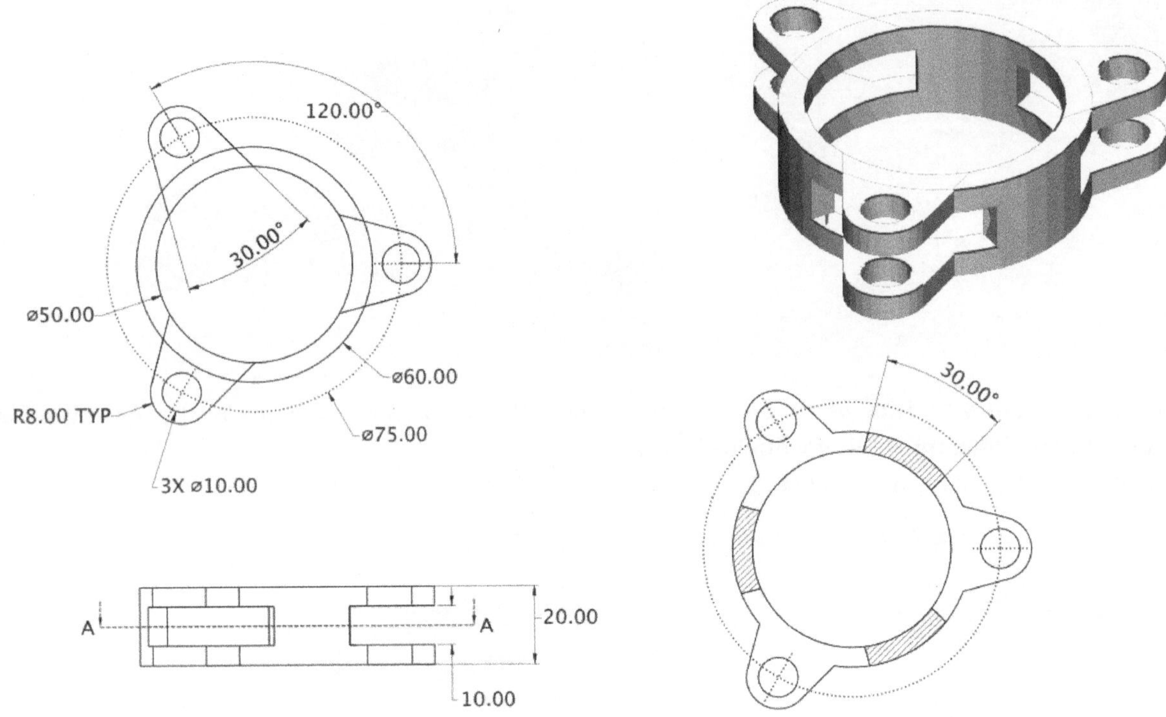

Creating a New document

1. Click **Autodesk Inventor 2026** on the desktop to start the application.
6. To start a new part file, click **Get Started > Launch > New** on the Ribbon.
7. On the **Create New File** dialog, click the **Metric** folder under **Templates**.
8. Click the **Standard(mm).ipt** icon under the **Part - Create 2D and 3D Objects** section.
9. Click the **Create** button on the **Create New File** dialog.

Creating the Cylinder

1. On the ribbon, click **3D Model** tab > **Primitives** panel > **Primitives** drop-down > **Cylinder**.
2. Select the XZ Plane from the graphics window. Next, select the sketch origin.
3. Move the pointer outward. Next, type 60 and press ENTER.
4. On the **Properties** panel, enter **20** in the **Distance A** box. Next, click the **Symmetric** button and click **OK** to create the cylinder.

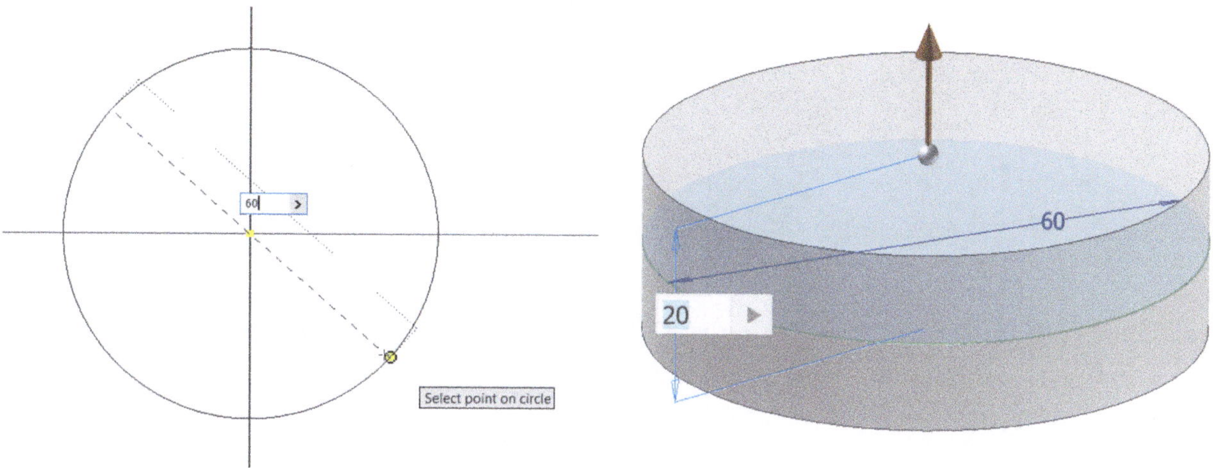

Adding the Extruded feature

1. Click the **Create 2D Sketch** icon on the **Sketch** panel and select the top face of the model.
2. Create a sketch using the **Line** tool, as shown. Next, create the fillet and add dimensions to the sketch.

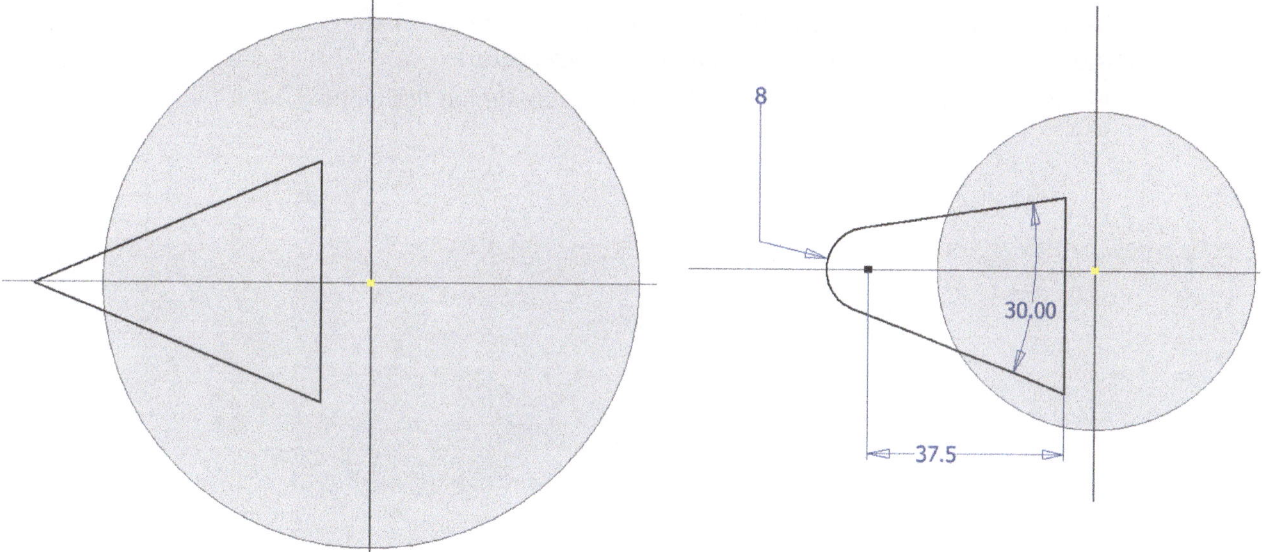

3. Apply the **Equal** constraint between the inclined lines. Next, apply the Coincident constraint between the midpoint of the vertical line and the sketch origin.

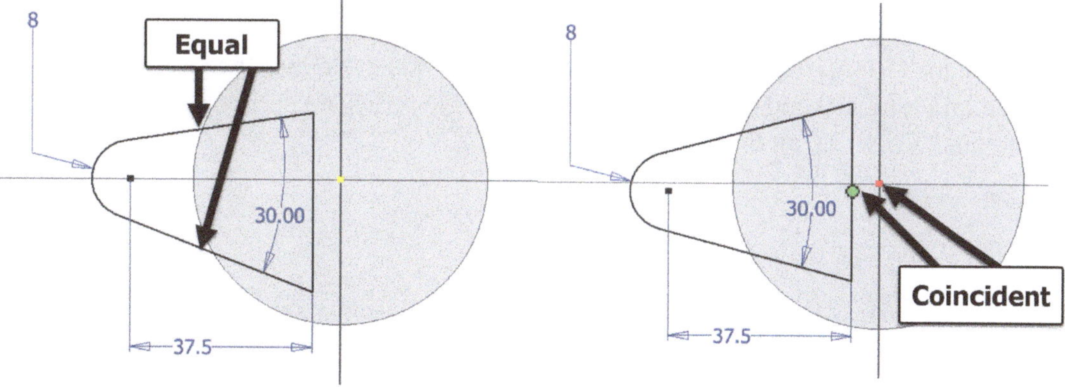

4. Create a circle coincident to the center point of the arc. Next, add the Diameter dimension to it.

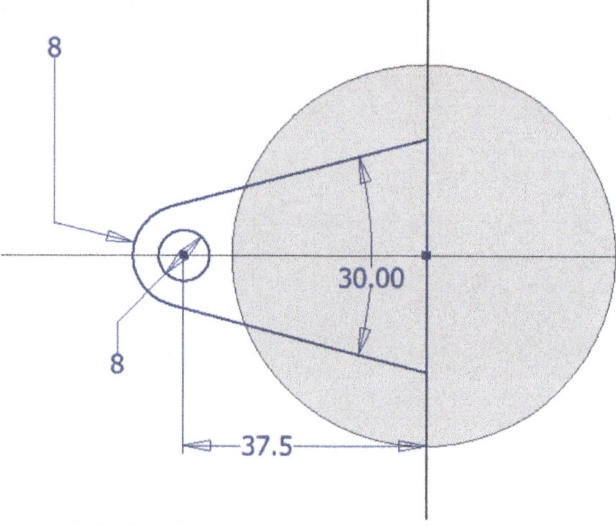

5. Click the **Finish Sketch** button.
6. Activate the **Extrude** command and click in the region enclosed by the sketch. On the **Extrude Properties** panel, click the **Flipped** icon under the **Behavior** section to extrude upward.
7. Type **20** in the **Distance A** box and click **OK** to create the *Extrude* feature.
8. Click the **Join** button under the Boolean section. Click **OK** to create the *Pad* feature.

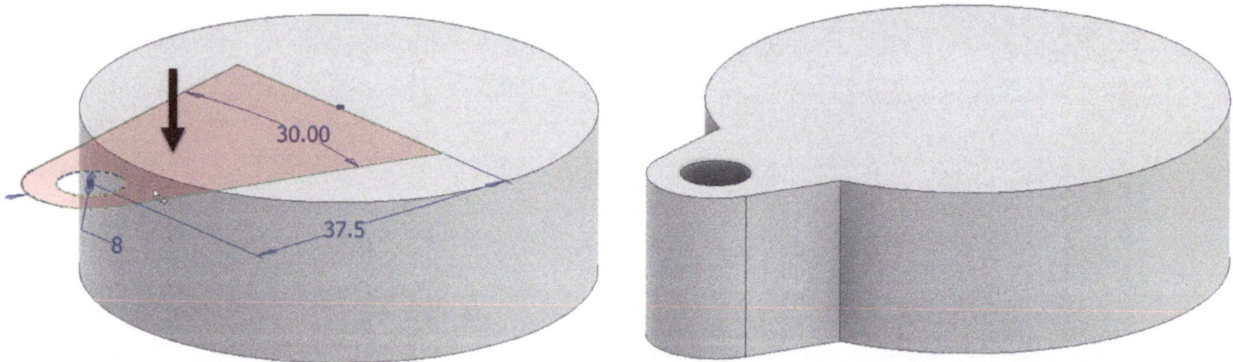

Creating the Circular Pattern

1. On the ribbon, click **3D Model > Pattern > Circular Pattern**. Click the **Features** icon and select the second extruded feature. Now, you have to define the axis of the circular pattern.
2. Click **Direction > Y axis** from the **Orientation** section on the **Properties** panel. It defines the pattern axis.
3. Select **Distribution > Fitted** and type-in **3** and **360** in the **Count** and **Angle** boxes, respectively.
4. Select **Orientation > Rotational**. Click **OK** on the dialog.

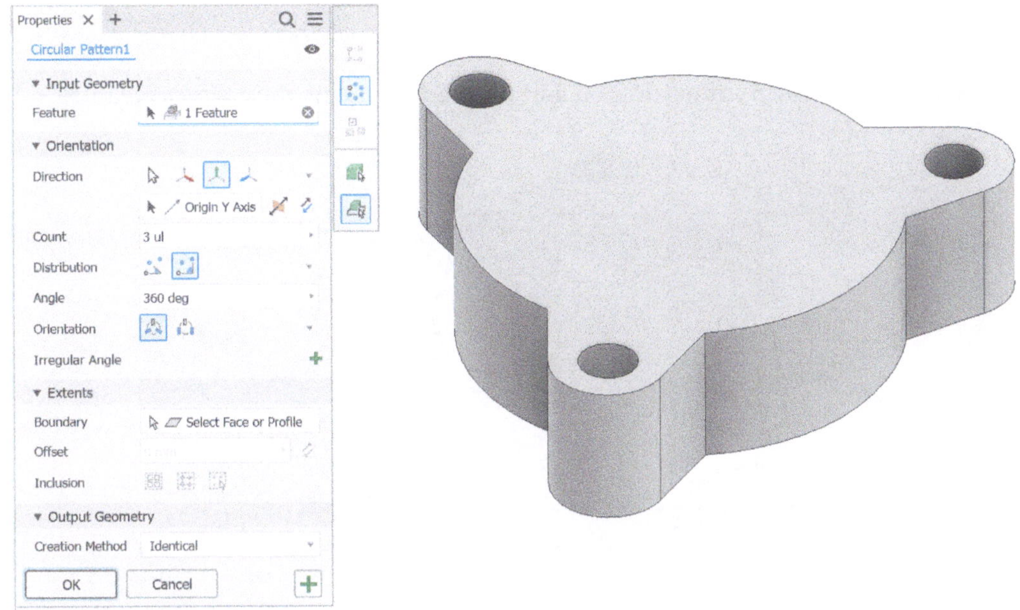

Creating the Extruded Cut Features

1. Activate the **Extrude** command and click on the top face of the model.
2. Activate the **Circle** command. Next, select the origin point of the sketch, move the pointer outward and click.
3. Add the diameter dimension to the circle and click **Finish Sketch** on the ribbon.
4. Click the **Cut** icon on the **Properties** panel.
5. Click the **Through all** icon, and then click **OK**.

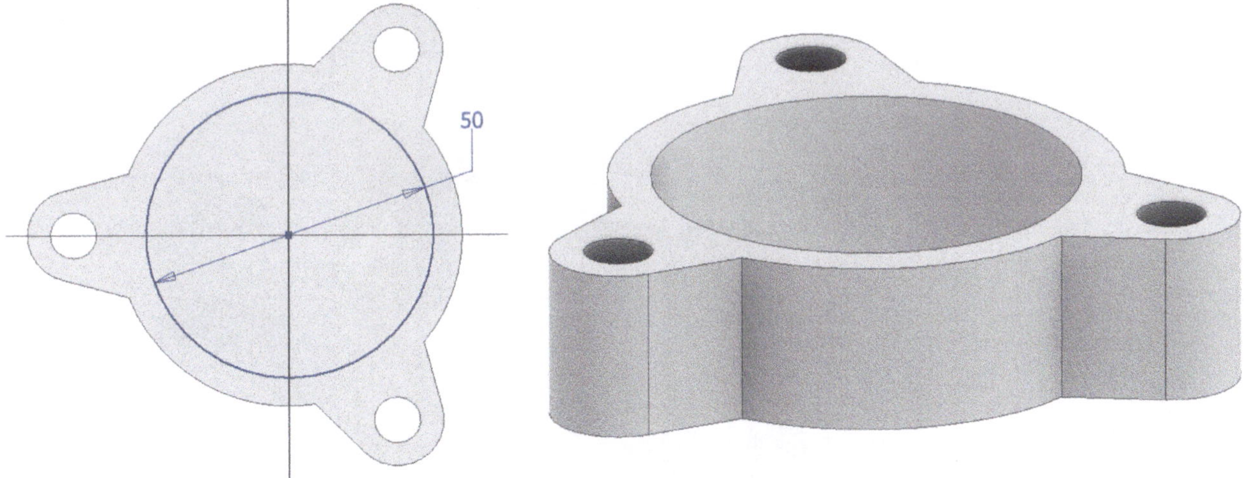

6. Activate the **Extrude** command and select the XZ Plane from the Browser window.
7. Click **Sketch > Create > Line** on the ribbon. Next, click on the horizontal axis of the sketch, move the pointer to top-left corner and click.
8. Move the pointer vertically downward and click to create a vertical line.
9. Move the pointer and select the start point of the sketch.
10. Apply the **Equal** constraint between the two inclined lines. Next, create the angular dimension between the two inclined lines.
11. Create the horizontal dimension between the endpoint of the vertical line and the sketch origin.
12. Create the horizontal dimension between the start point of the sketch and the sketch origin.

13. Click **Finish Sketch** on the ribbon.
14. Click the **Cut** icon on the **Properties** panel.
15. Enter **10** in the **Distance A** box. Next, click the **Symmetric** icon and click **OK** to create the *Extruded* feature.

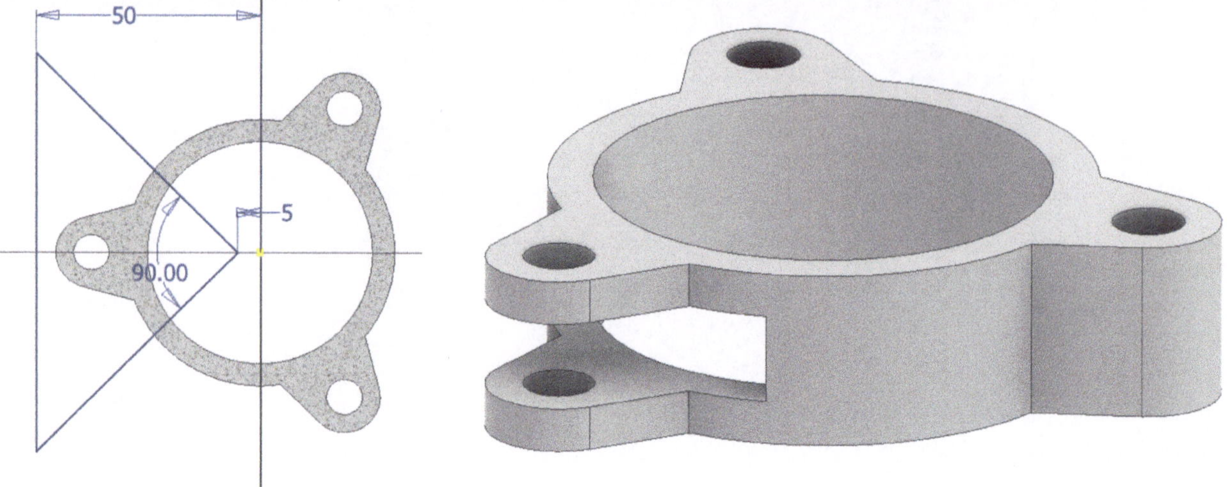

Creating a Circular Pattern

1. On the ribbon, click **3D Model > Pattern > Circular Pattern**. Click the **Features** icon and select the newly created extruded cut feature. Now, you have to define the axis of the circular pattern.
2. Click **Direction > Y axis** from the **Orientation** section on the **Properties** panel. It defines the pattern axis.
3. Select **Distribution > Fitted** and type-in **3** and **360** in the **Count** and **Angle** boxes, respectively.
4. Select **Orientation > Rotational**. Click **OK** on the dialog.

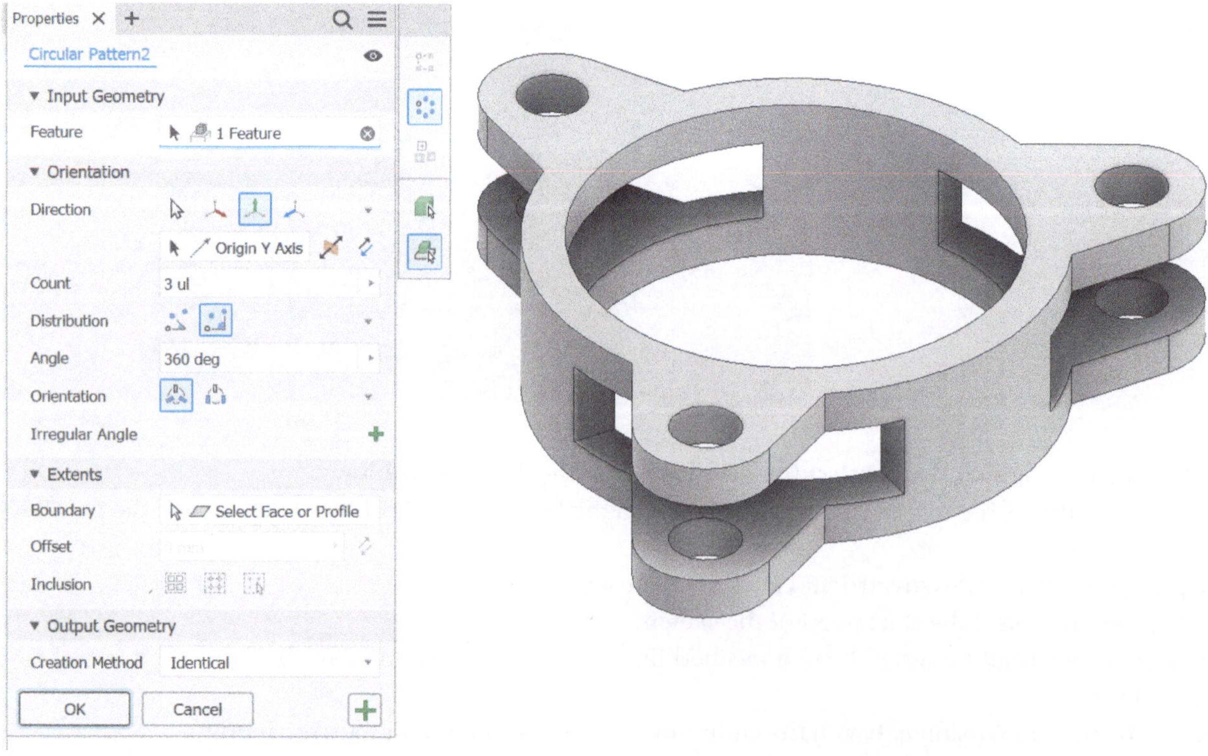

5. Click **OK**.

6. Save and close the design file.

Questions

1. Describe the procedure to create a mirror feature.
2. List any two pattern types.
3. Describe the procedure to create a pattern along a curve.
4. List the methods to define spacing in a Rectangular pattern.

Exercises

Exercise 1 (Millimetres)

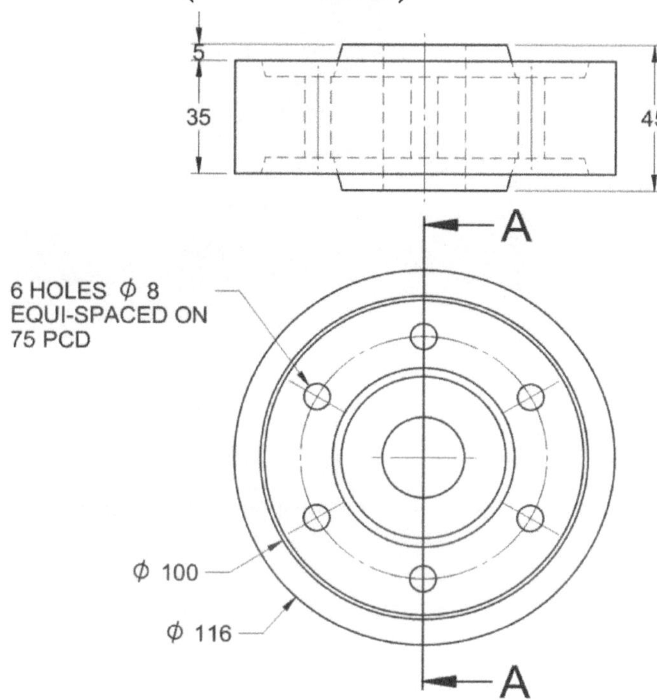

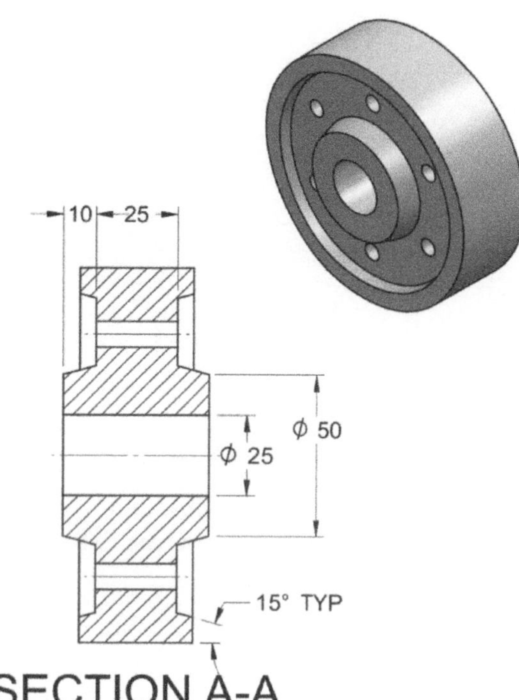

Chapter 6: Sweep Features

The **Sweep** command is one of the basic commands available in Inventor that allow you to generate solid geometry. It can be used to create simple geometry as well as complex shapes. A sweep is composed of two items: a cross-section and a path. The cross-section controls the shape of the sweep while the path controls its direction. For example, take a look at the angled cylinder shown in the figure. It is created using a simple sweep with the circle as the profile and an angled line as the path.

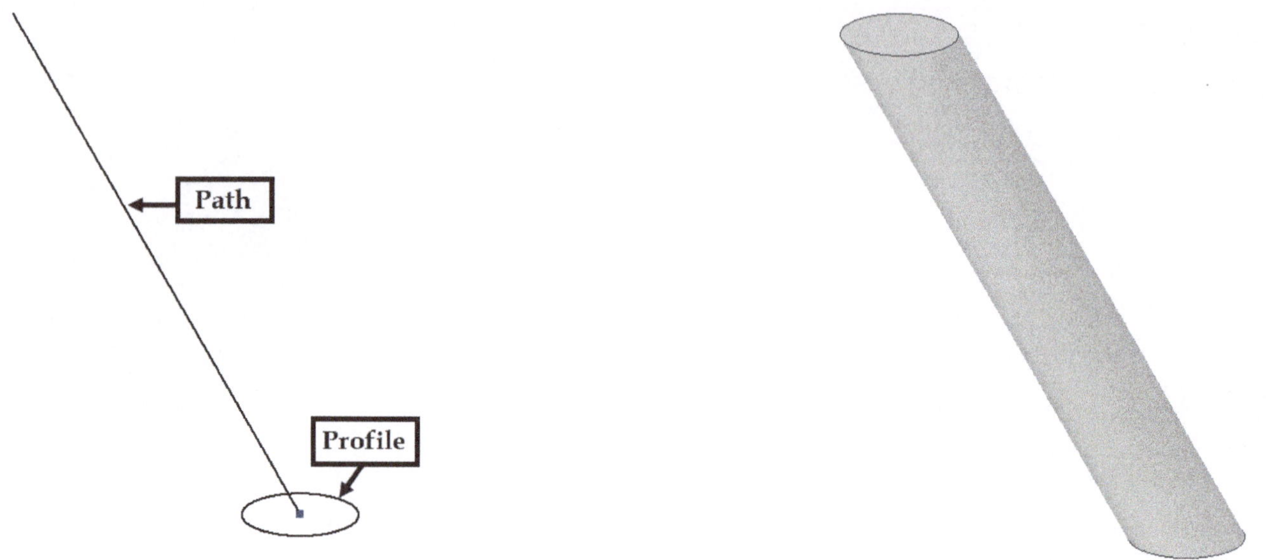

By making the path a bit more complicated, you can see that a sweep allows you to create shapes you would not be able to create using commands such as Extrude or Revolve.

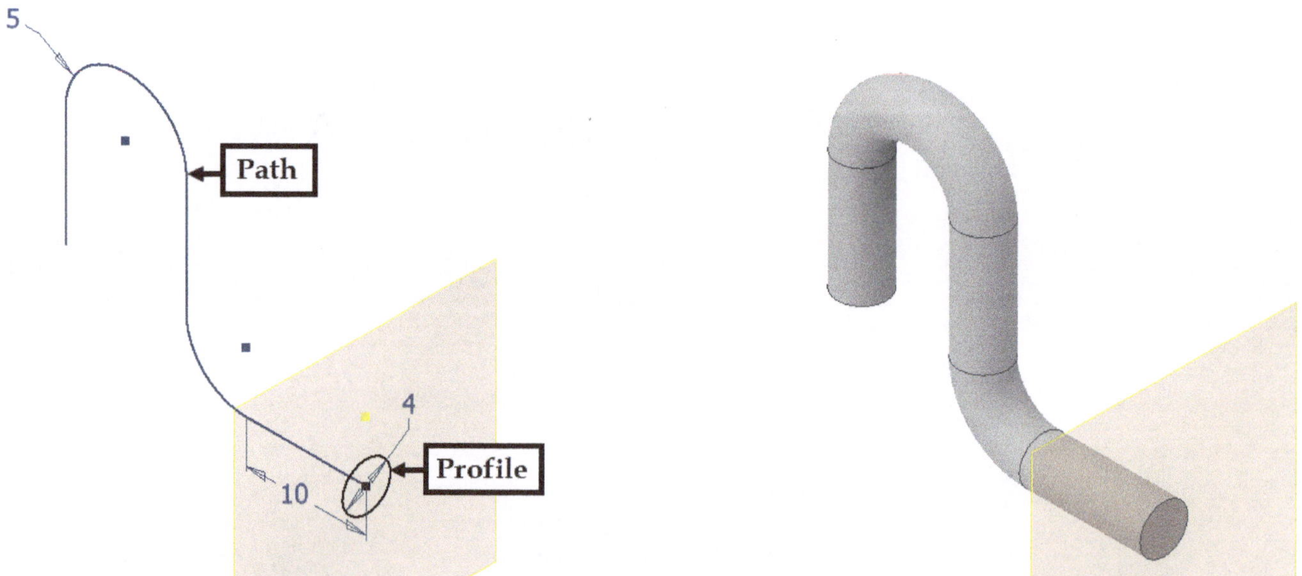

To take the sweep feature to the next level of complexity, you can add guide rails and guide surface. By doing so, the shape of the geometry is controlled by guide rails and surface. For example, the circular cross-section in the figure varies in size along the path because a guide rail controls it.

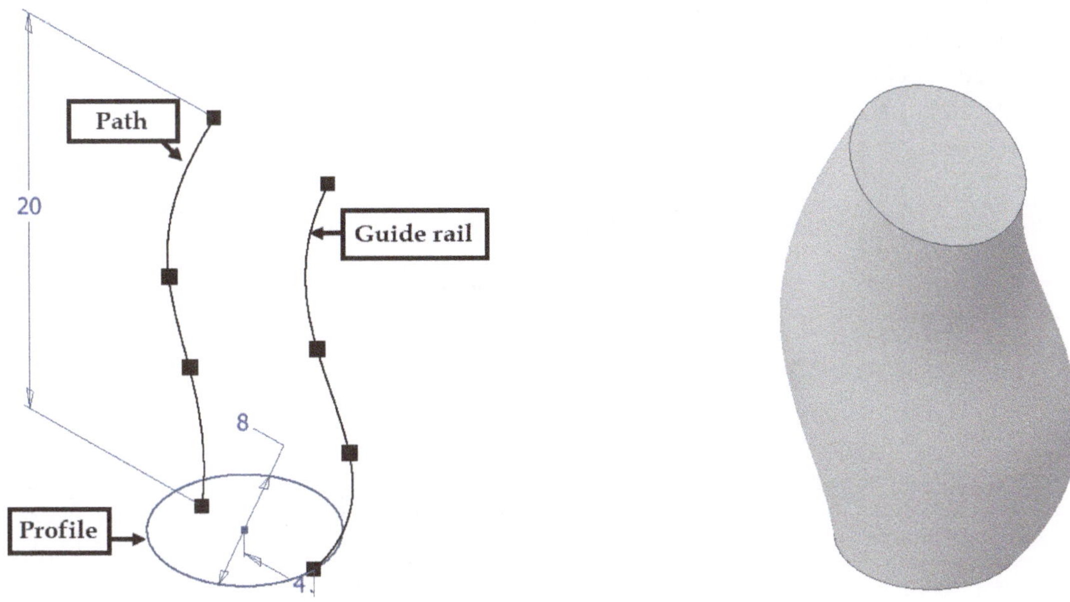

The topics covered in this chapter are:

- *Path sweeps*
- *Path and Guide rail sweeps*
- *Path and Guide Surface sweeps*
- *Scaling and twisting the cross-section along the path*
- *Swept Cutouts*
- *Coils*

Path sweeps

This type of sweep requires two elements: a path and profile. The profile defines the shape of the sweep along the path. A path is used to control the direction of the profile. A path can be a sketch or an edge. To create a sweep, you must first create a path and a profile. Create a path by drawing a sketch. It can be an open or closed sketch. Next, click **3D Model > Work Features > Planes drop-down > Normal to Curve at Point** on the ribbon, and then create a plane normal to the path. Sketch the profile on the plane normal to the path.

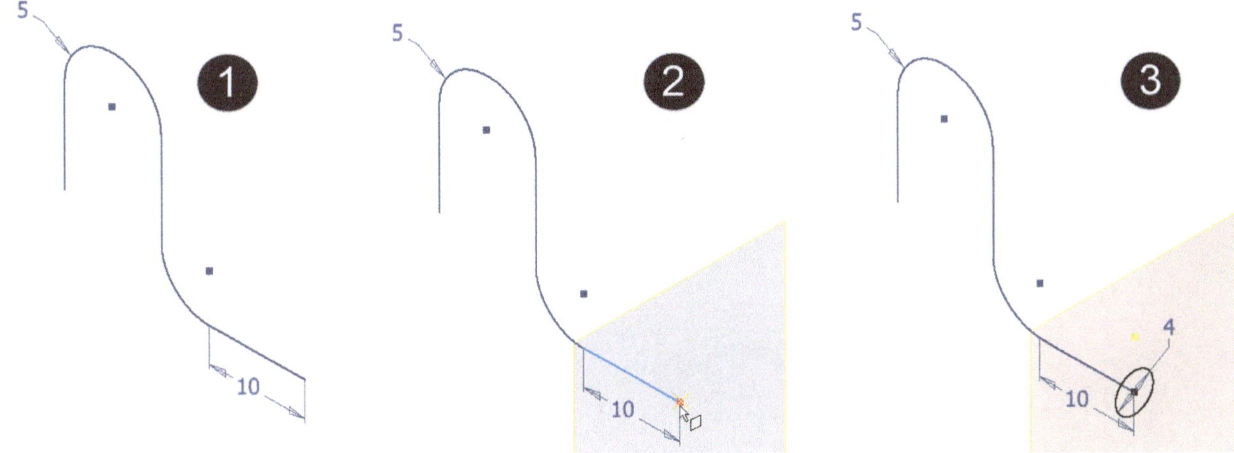

Activate the **Sweep** command (click **3D Model > Create > Sweep** on the ribbon). As you activate this command, the **Sweep Properties** panel appears showing different options to create the sweep. Click on the **Path** selection box under the **Input Geometry** section and select the path from the graphics window. If there is any closed sketch in the graphics window, it will be selected as the profile automatically. Next, click **OK**.

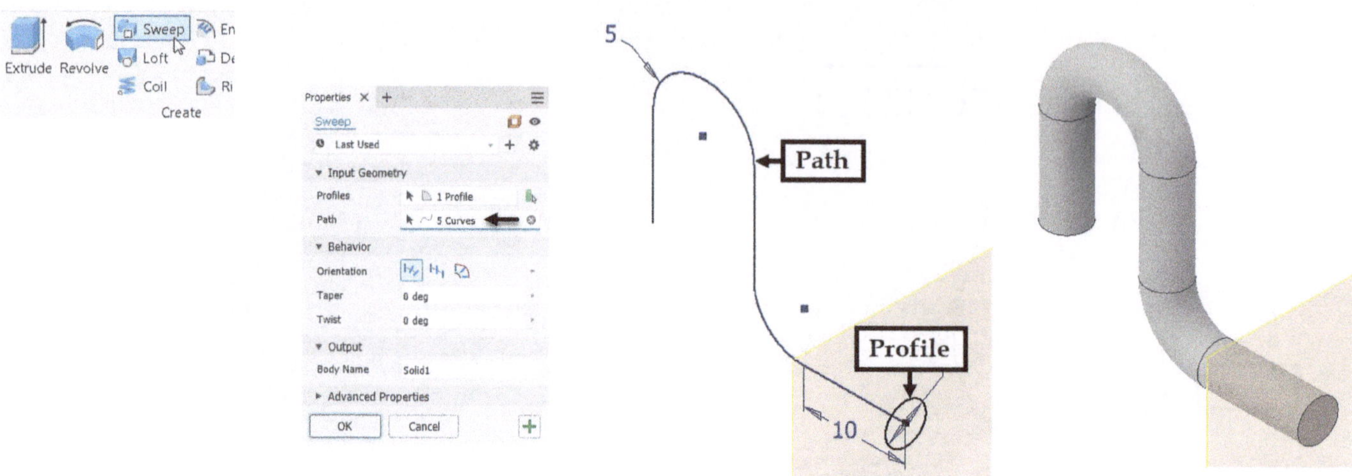

Autodesk Inventor will not allow the sweep to result in a self-intersecting geometry. As the profile is swept along a path, it cannot come back and cross itself. For example, if the profile of the sweep is larger than the curves on the path, the resulting geometry will intersect, and the sweep will fail.

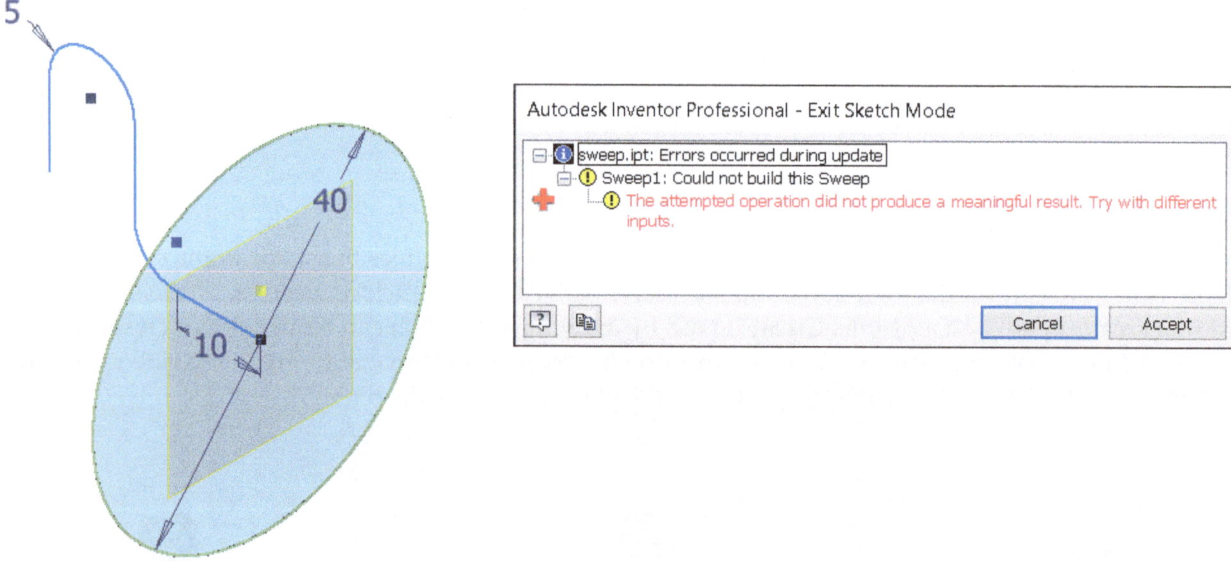

A sweeping profile must be created as a sketch. However, a path can be a sketch or an edge. The following illustrations show various types of paths and resultant sweep features.

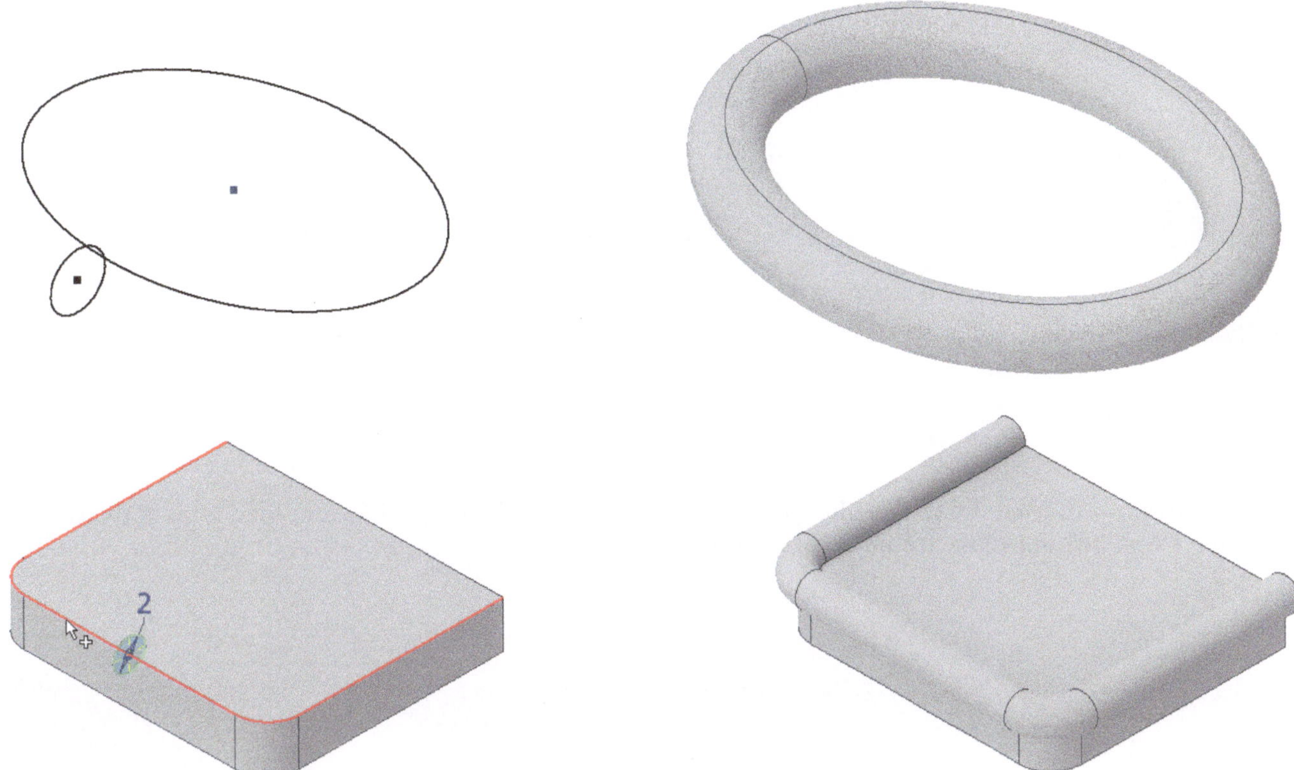

Profile Orientation

The **Orientation** options define the orientation of the resulting geometry. The **Follow Path** option sweeps the cross-section in the direction normal to the path. The **Fixed** option sweeps the cross-section in the direction parallel to itself.

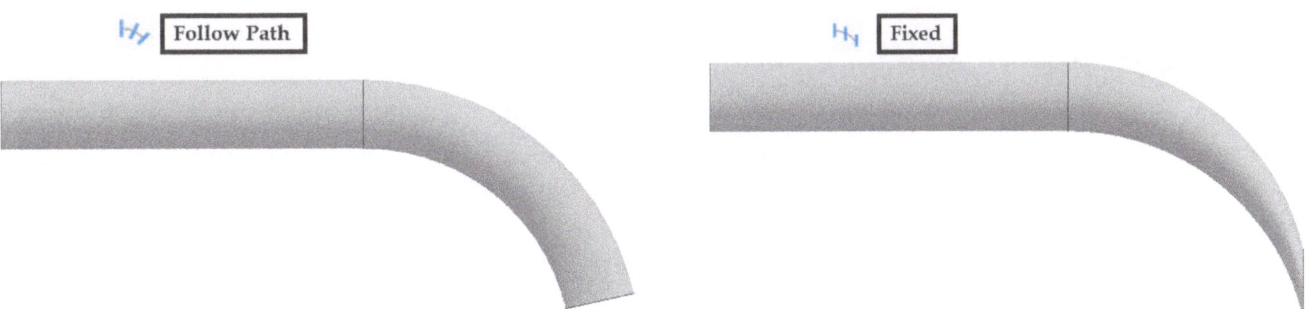

Taper

Inventor allows you to taper the sweep along the path. Select the profile and path, and then type in a value in the **Taper** box under the **Behavior** section. Click **OK** to create the tapered sweep feature.

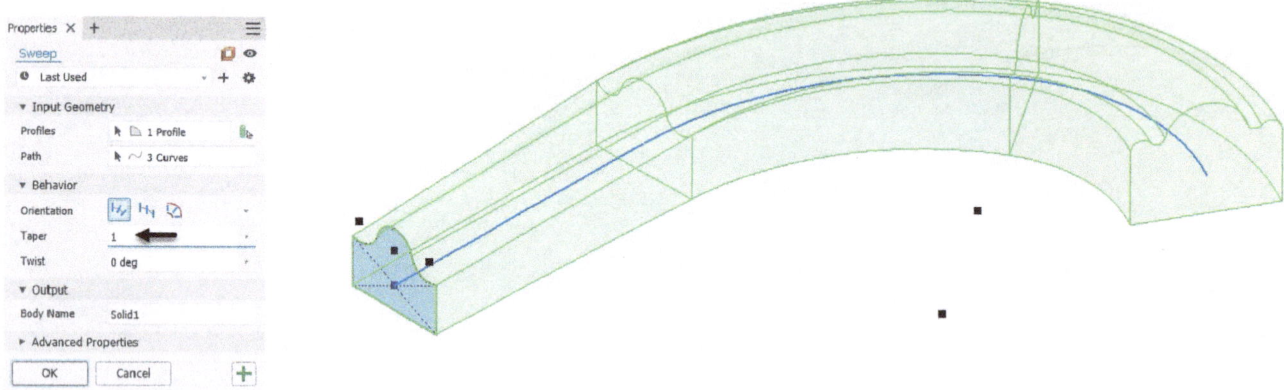

Twist

Inventor allows you to twist the profile along the path. Define the path and profile, and then type-in the twist angle in the **Twist** box; the twist is applied to the profile.

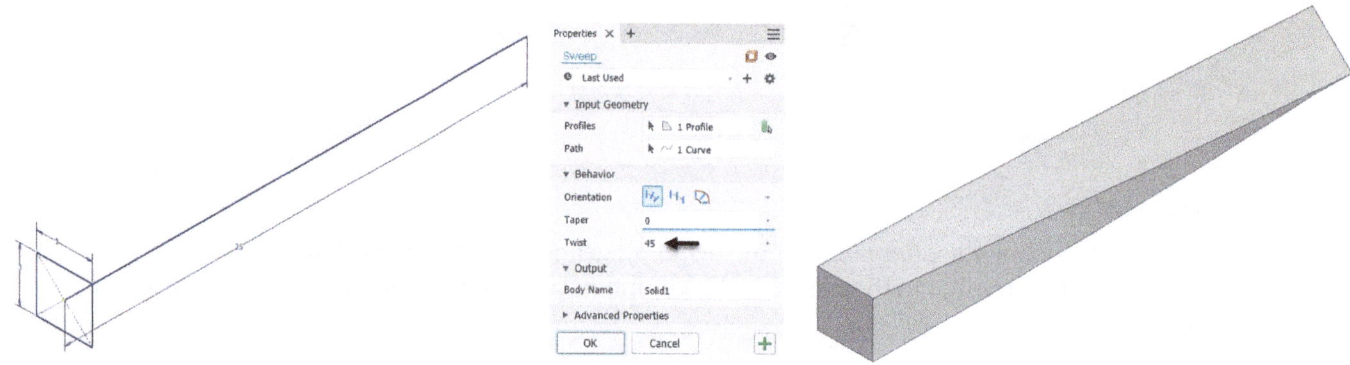

Path and Guide Rail Sweeps

Inventor allows you to create sweep features with path and guide rails. It can be useful while creating complex geometry and shapes. To create this type of sweep feature, first, create a path. Next, create a profile and guide rail, as shown in the figure. Activate the **Sweep** command and select **Orientation > Guide** on the **Sweep** Properties panel; the profile is selected, automatically.

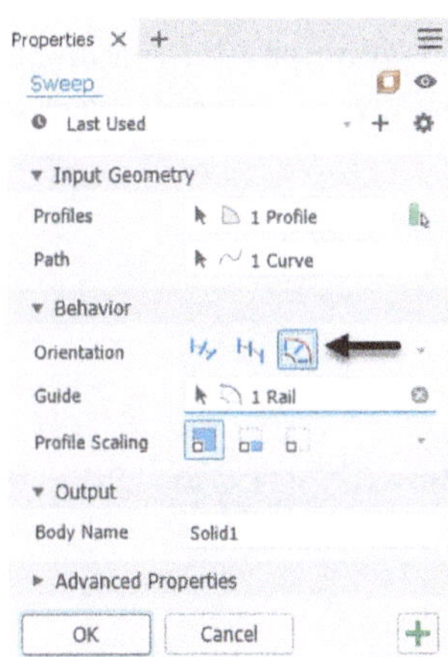

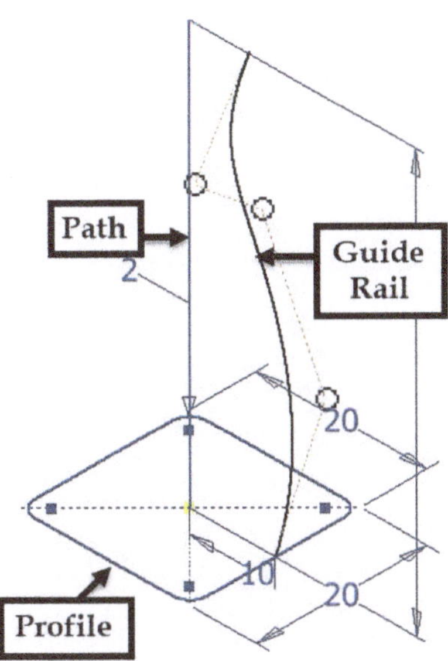

Click the **Path** selection button and select the path. Next, click on the **Guide** selection box and select the guide rail. The preview of the geometry will appear. Select an option from the **Profile scaling** section. The **X &Y Scaling** option scales the geometry in both X and Y directions. The **X Scaling** option scales the geometry in the **X** direction only. The **No Scaling** option just sweeps the profile along the path without considering the guide rail. Click **OK** to complete the feature.

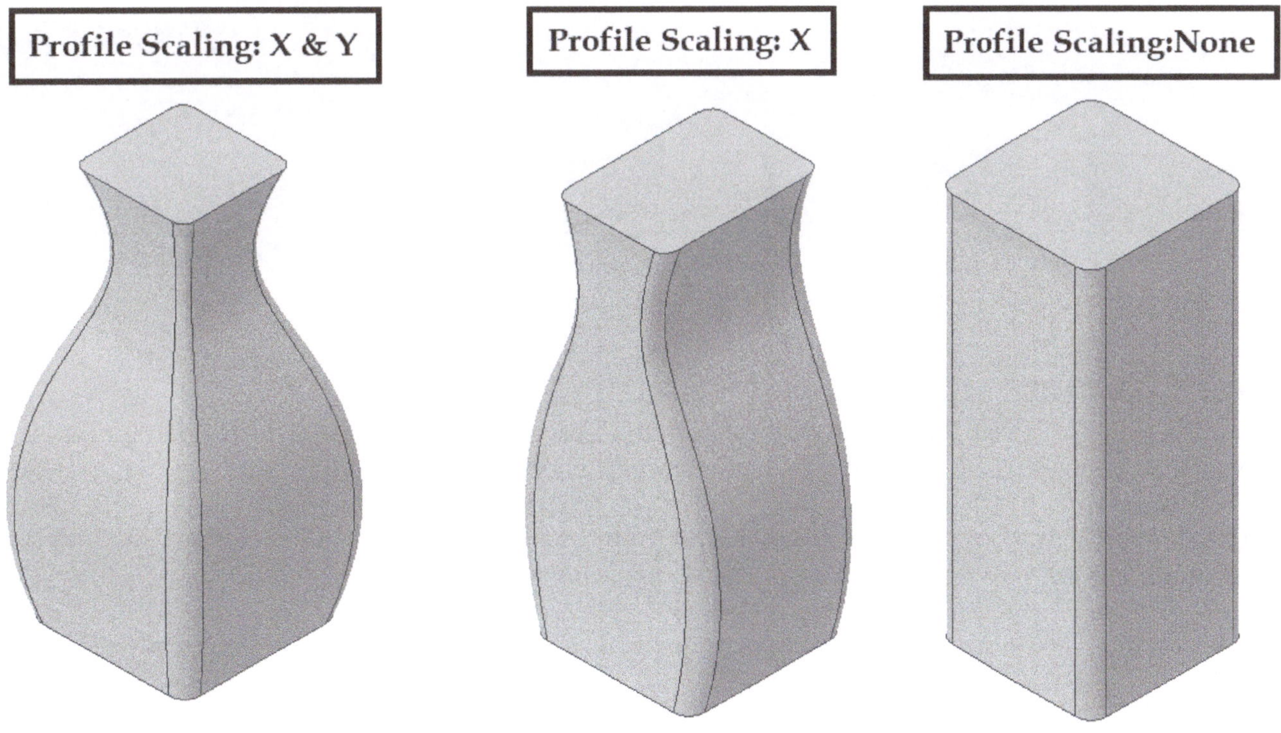

Path and Guide Surface Sweeps

The **Guide** option on the **Sweep Properties** panel will be useful while sweeping a profile along a non-planar path. For example, create a path and profile similar to the one shown in the figure. Next, create a sweep feature using the **Follow Path** option; the sweep is not attached to the cylindrical surface.

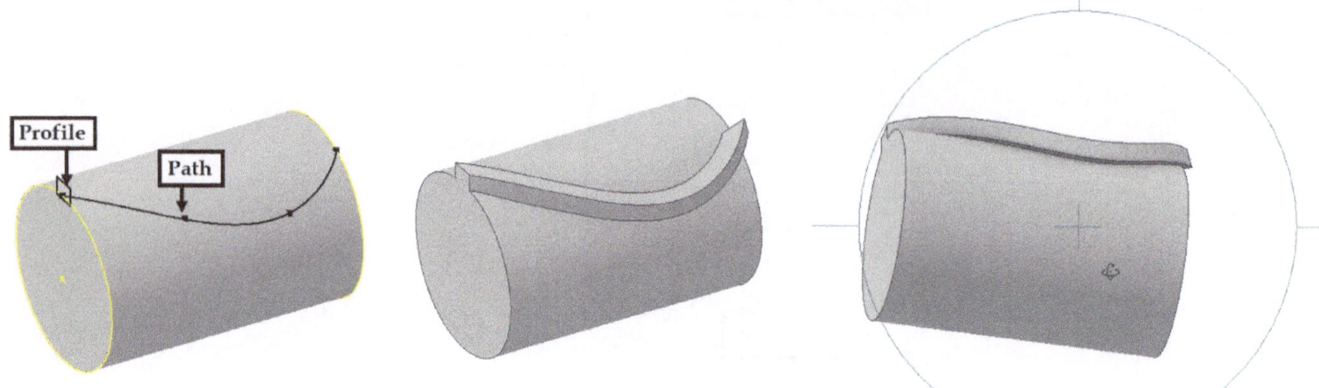

Now, right click on the **Sweep** feature in the **Model** window and select **Edit Feature**. On the **Sweep** Properties panel, select **Orientation > Guide** , and then select the cylindrical surface to define the guide surface. Click **OK** and notice that the sweep feature is attached to the surface.

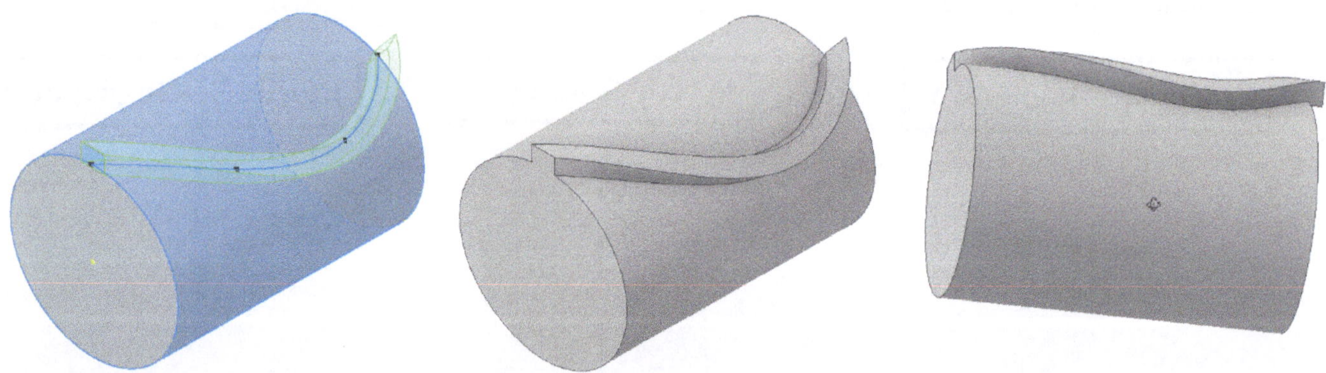

Swept Cutout

In addition to adding swept features, Inventor allows you to remove geometry using the **Sweep** command. Activate this command (click **3D Model > Create > Sweep** on the ribbon); the profile is selected automatically. On the **Sweep Properties** panel, click in the **Path** selection box under the **Input Geometry** section and select the path from the part geometry. Click the **Orientation > Follow Path** icon under the **Behavior** section. Click the **Cut** icon under the **Output** section. Click **OK** to create the swept cutout.

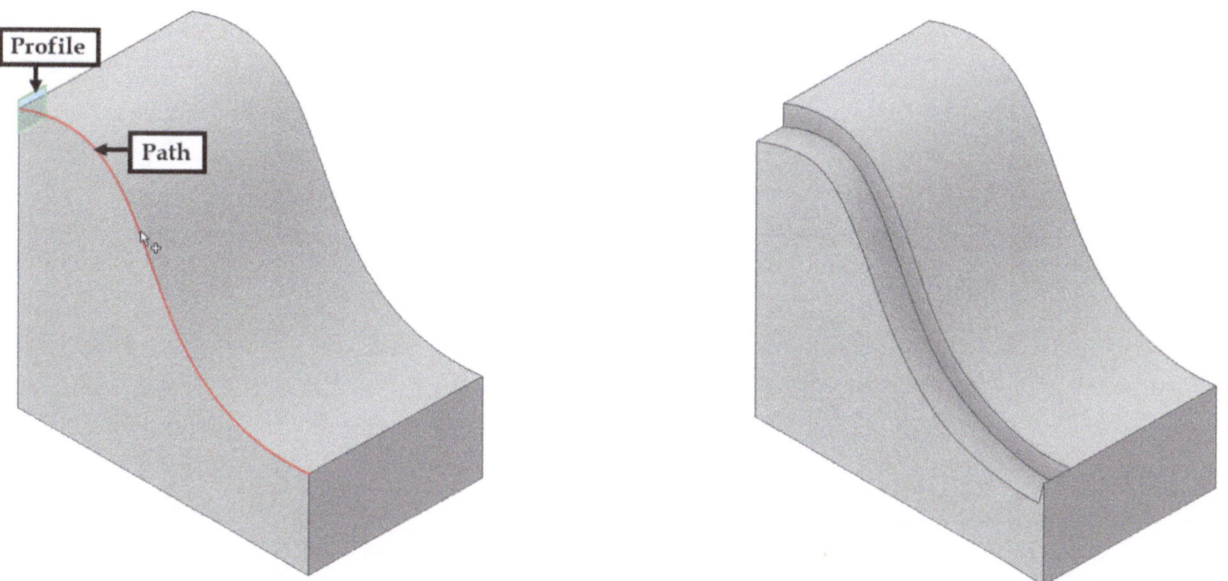

You will notice that the swept cutout is not created throughout the geometry. It is because the profile is swept only up to the endpoints of the path. In this case, you must edit the path such that it extends beyond the geometry. Expand the **Sweep** feature in the **Model** window and notice that a 3D sketch is created from the selected model edge. Right click on the 3D sketch and select **Edit 3D Sketch**. Next, create a line that is continuous and collinear with the path. Click **Finish Sketch** on the ribbon. Now, right click on the **Sweep** feature in the **Model** window and select **Edit Feature**. Click the **Path** selection button on the **Sweep Properties** panel, and then select the newly created line. Click **OK** to complete the feature. The resultant swept cutout will be throughout the geometry.

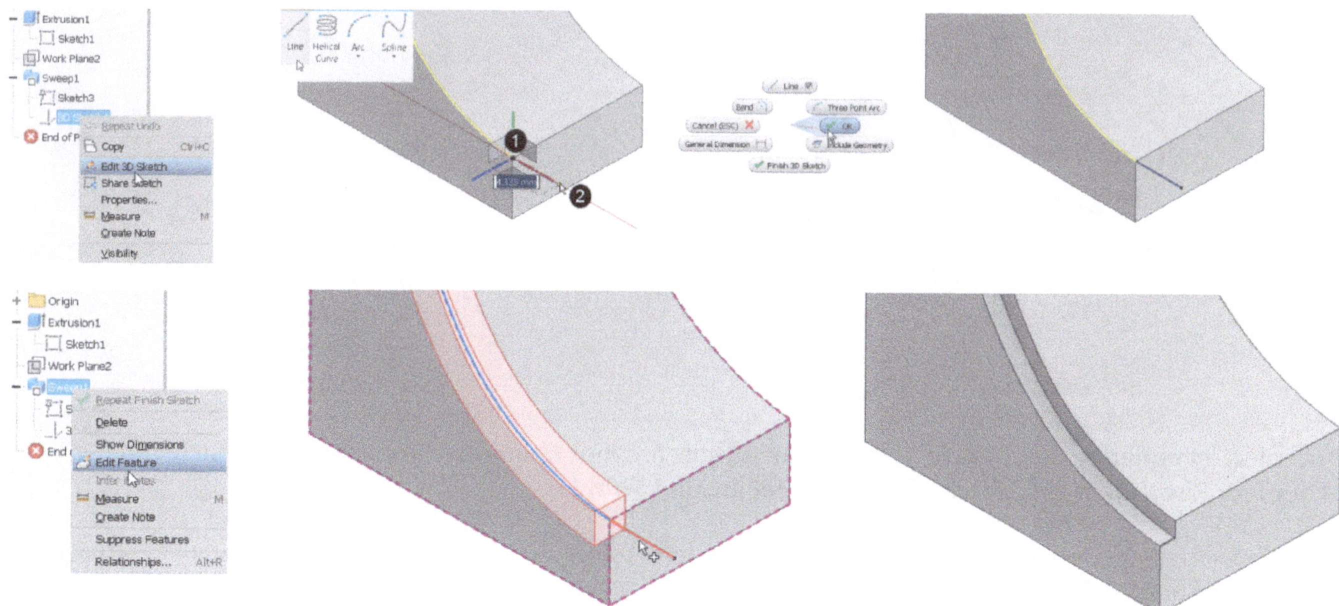

Coil

This command creates a spring or spiral-shaped feature. To create this type of feature, you must have a profile and a line (axis). They can be on the same plane or different planes. Activate the **Coil** command (click **3D Model > Create > Coil** on the ribbon); the profile is selected, automatically. Click the **Axis** selection button and select a line or axis; the preview of the coil appears on the screen.

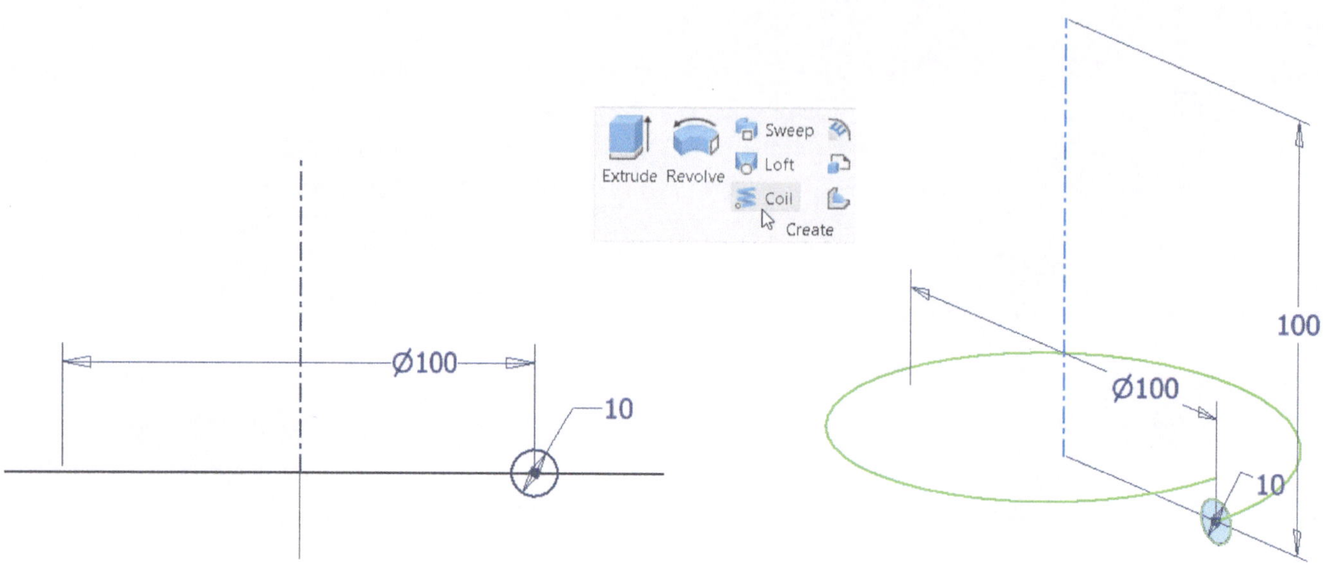

Click any one of the icons available in the **Rotation** section; this defines the coil direction.

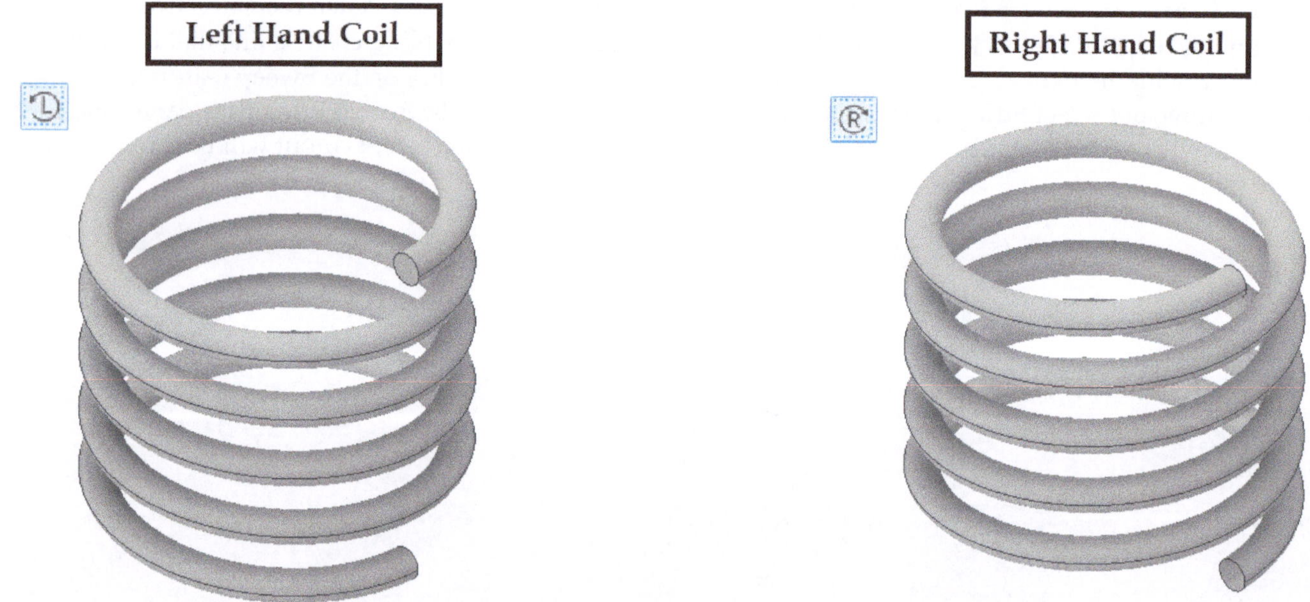

Now, select an option from the **Method** drop-down. There are four options in this drop-down: **Pitch and Revolution**, **Revolution and Height**, **Pitch and Height**, and **Spiral**.

The **Pitch and Height** option creates a helical coil by using the total height of the coil and the distance between the turns. You need to specify the **Height** and **Pitch** values.

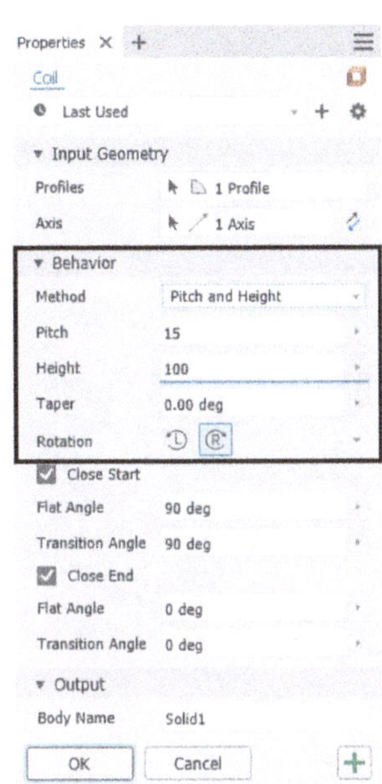

The **Revolution and Height** option creates a helical coil by using the total height of the coil and number of turns.

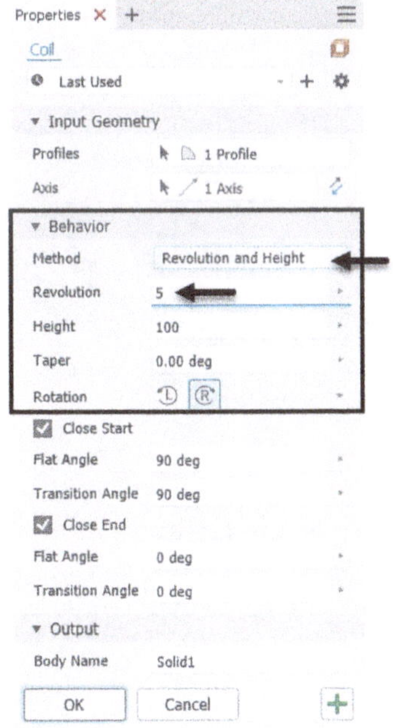

The **Pitch and Revolution** option use the pitch and number of revolutions you specify to create the coil.

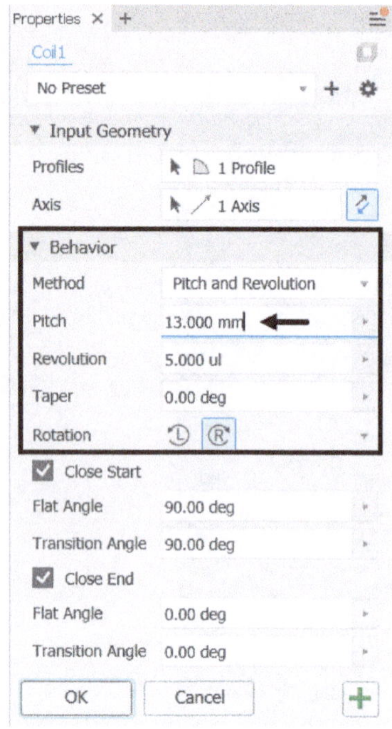

The **Spiral** option creates a spiral-shaped feature.

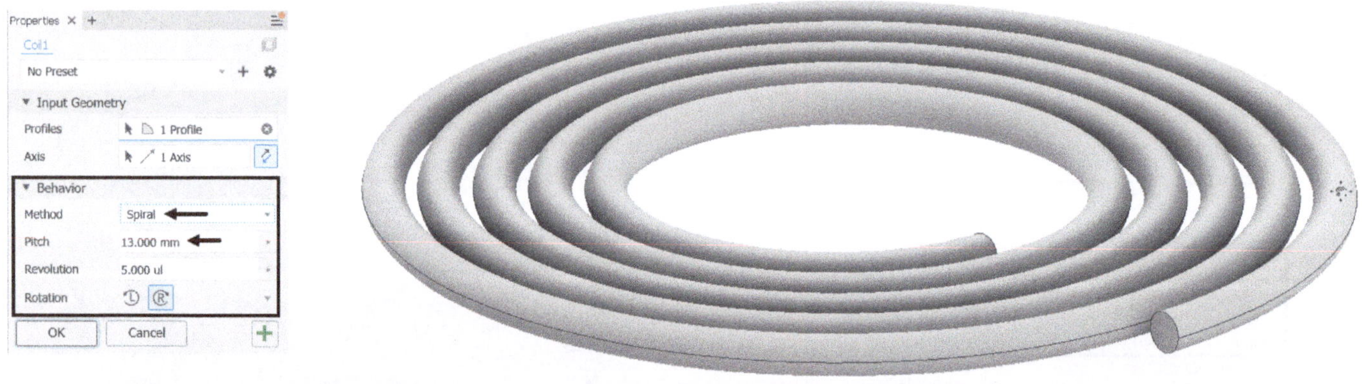

The **Taper** box helps you to apply taper to the coil. You can apply a taper to a coil by entering the angle. The positive or negative angle values define the taper direction.

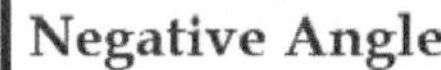

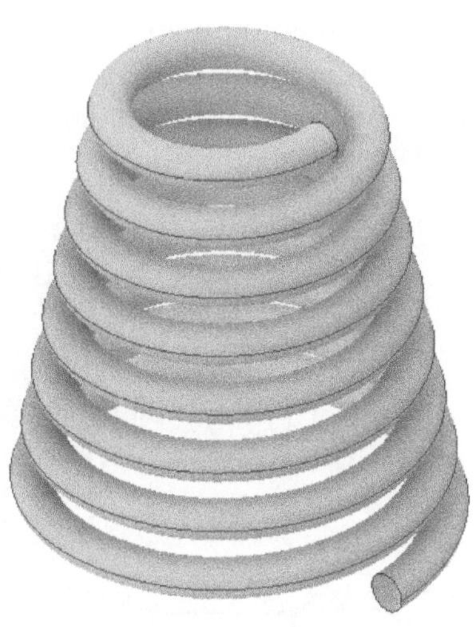

The **Close start** and **Close end** options help you to specify the transition type for the start and end of the coil. Leave these options unchecked if you want to create a coil without any transition. Check these options if you want to create a flat transition so that the coil can stand upright on a flat surface. The **Transition Angle** box is used to specify the transition distance beyond the coil. The transition distance will be less than one revolution. The **Flat Angle** box is used to specify the distance of the flat portion that extends beyond the transition.

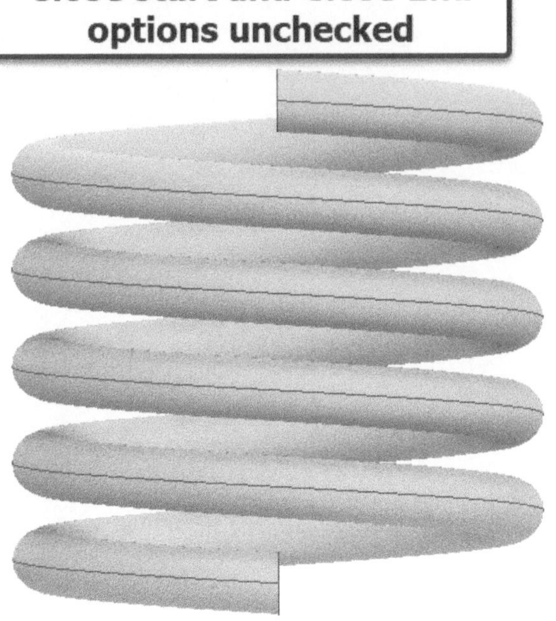

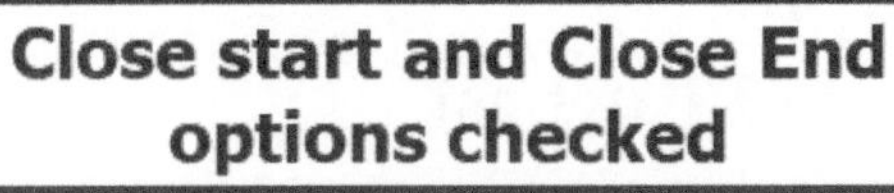

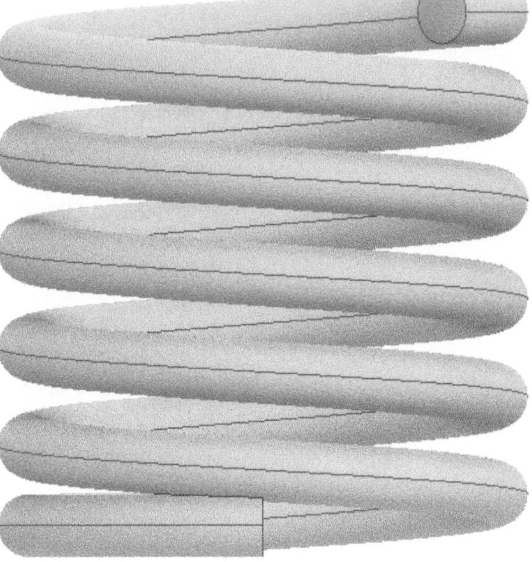

Click **OK** on the **Coil** Properties panel to create the coil.

Helical Cutout

The **Coil** command can also be used to remove material from the part geometry (cylindrical feature) by creating a helical feature. To create this feature, first, you must have an existing geometry and the sketches of the profile and axis. Activate this command (click **3D Model > Create > Coil** on the ribbon) and select the profile. Click the **Axis** selection button under the **Input Geometry** section and select the axis. Click the **Cut** icon from the **Boolean** options under the **Output** section. Select Revolution and Height from **Method** drop-down under the **Behaviour** section. Define the number of revolutions and height, and then click **OK** to create the helical cutout.

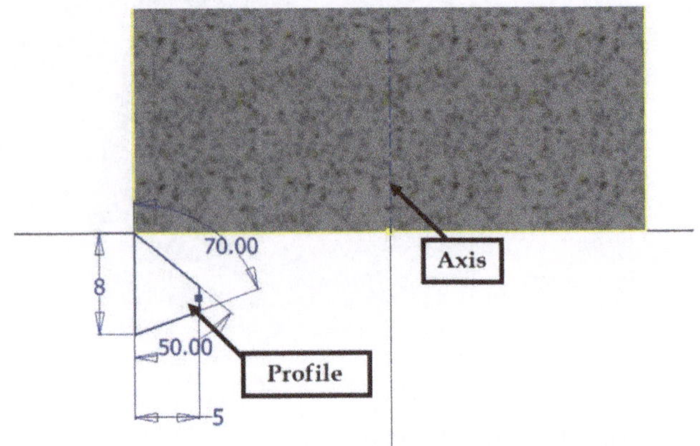

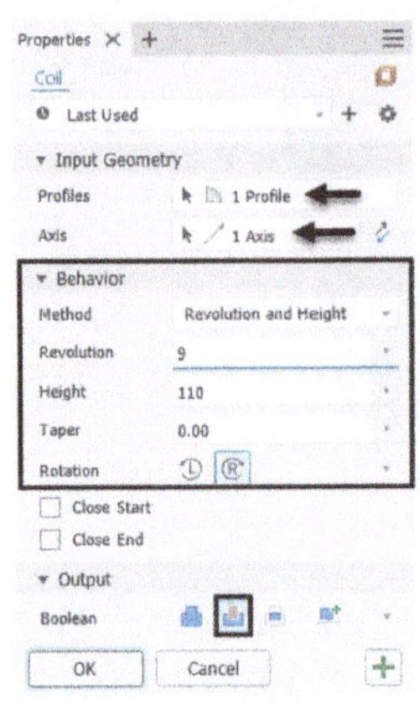

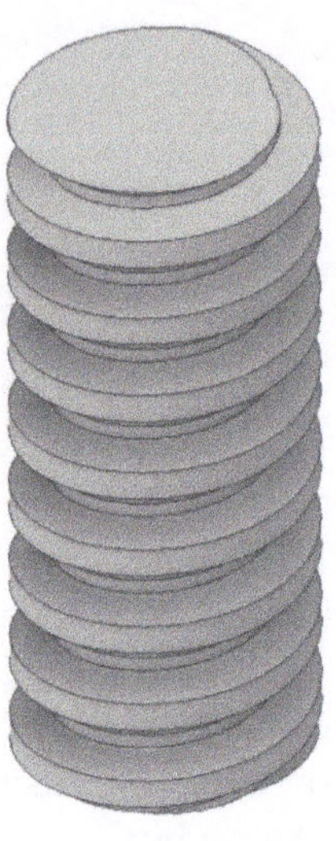

Examples

Example 1 (Inches)

In this example, you will create the part shown below.

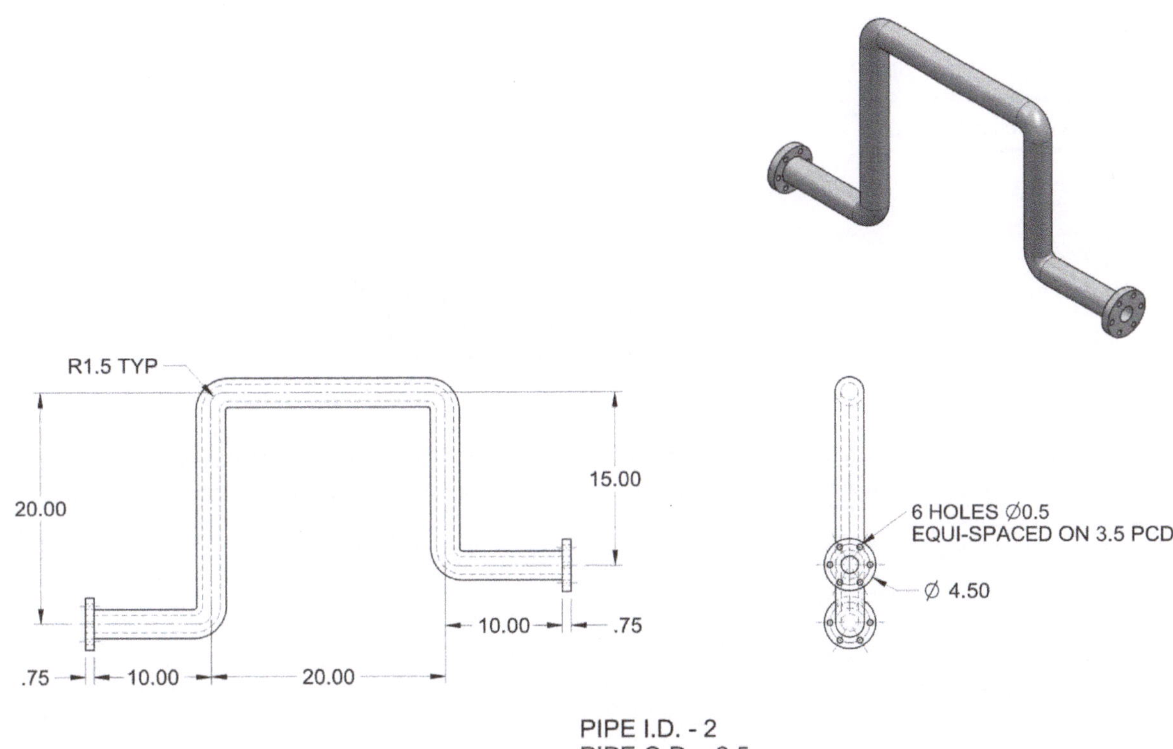

1. Start **Autodesk Inventor.**
2. On the **Quick Access Toolbar**, click **New**; the **Create New File** dialog pops up.
3. On this dialog, click **Templates > en-US**. Select the **Standard.ipt** template and click **Create.**
4. On the ribbon, click **3D Model > Sketch > Start 2D Sketch** and draw the sketch on the **XY** plane, as shown below.

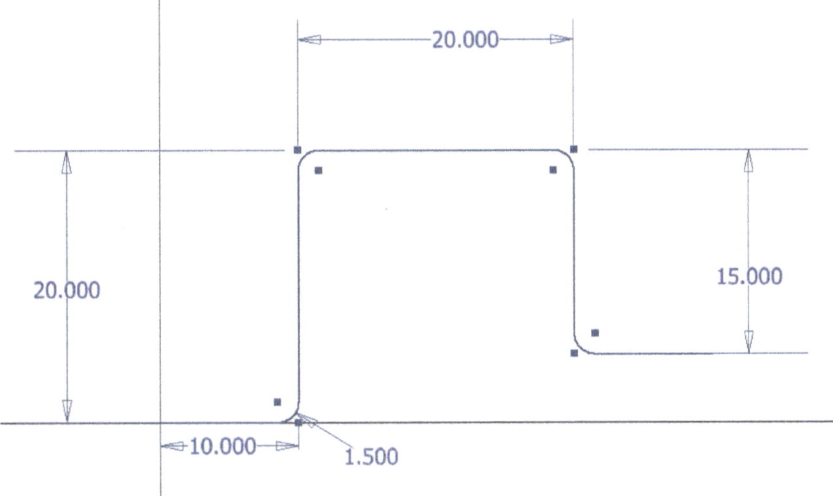

5. Click **Finish Sketch** on the ribbon.
6. On the ribbon, click **3D Model > Work Features > Planes** drop-down > **Normal to Curve at Point** and click on the lower horizontal line.
7. Click on the endpoint of the line to locate the plane.

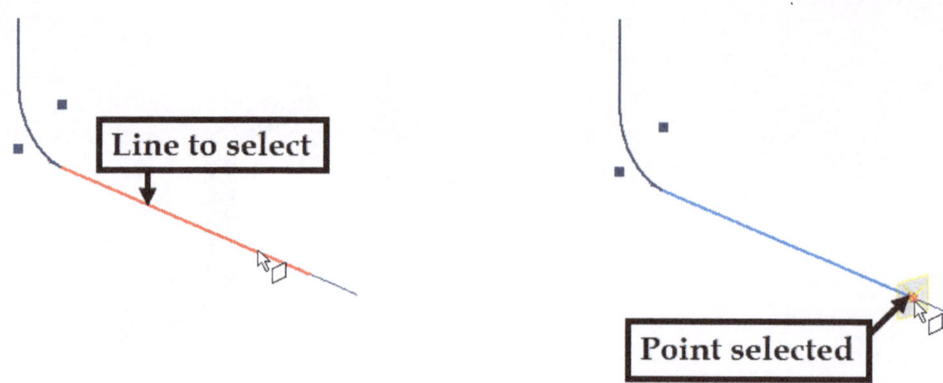

8. On the ribbon, click **3D Model > Sketch > Start 2D Sketch**, and then select the plane normal to the curve.
9. On the ribbon, click **Sketch > Create > Circle Center Point** and draw a circle of **2.5**-inch diameter. Click **Finish Sketch**.

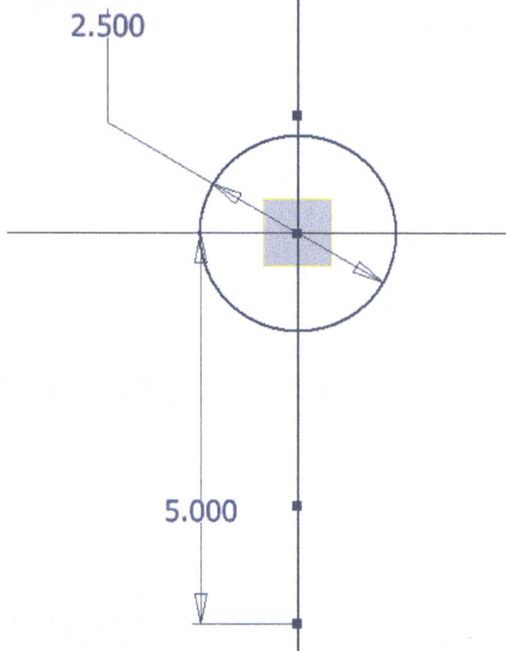

10. On the ribbon, click **3D Model > Create > Sweep**; the **Sweep Properties** panel pops up. On this panel, click **Orientation > Follow Path** under the **Behavior** section.
11. Click in the **Path** selection box under the **Input Geometry** section, and then click on the first sketch to define the path of the *Sweep* feature. Click **OK** to complete the *Sweep* feature.

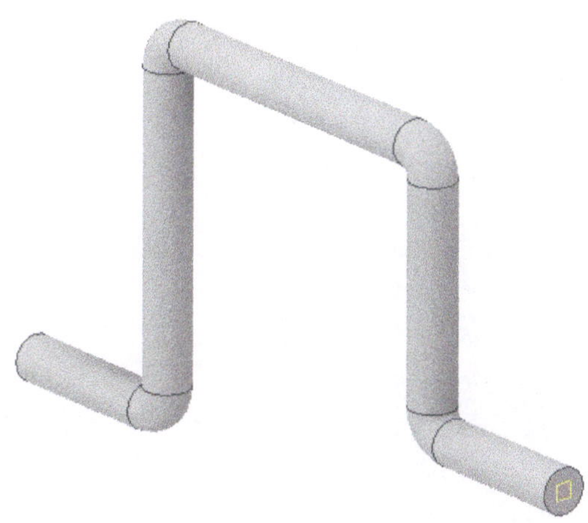

12. On the ribbon, click **3D Model > Modify > Shell**. Click on the end face of the *Sweep* feature.
13. Rotate the part geometry and click on the end face on the other side.
14. Select **Shell Type > Sharp Corners**. Select **Direction > Inside**.
15. Type-in **0.5** in the **Thickness** box. Click **OK** to shell the *Sweep* feature.

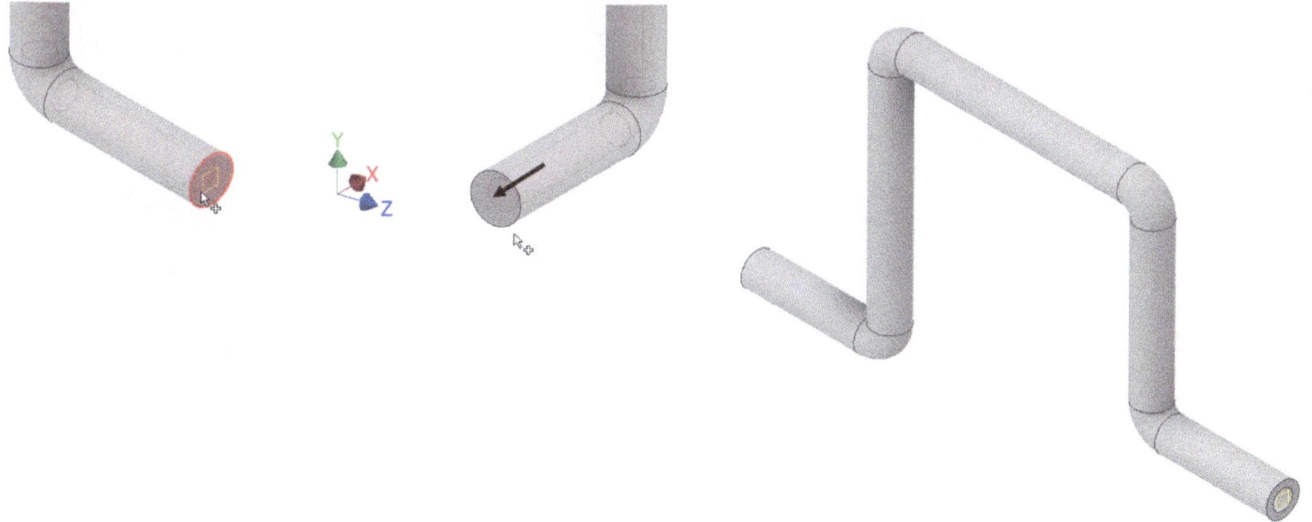

16. On the ribbon, click **3D Model > Sketch > Start 2D Sketch** and click on the front-end face.
17. On the ribbon, click **Sketch > Create > Project Geometry**. Click on the inner edge of the end face to project it.
18. Draw a circle of **4.5** in diameter. Click **Finish Sketch** on the ribbon.

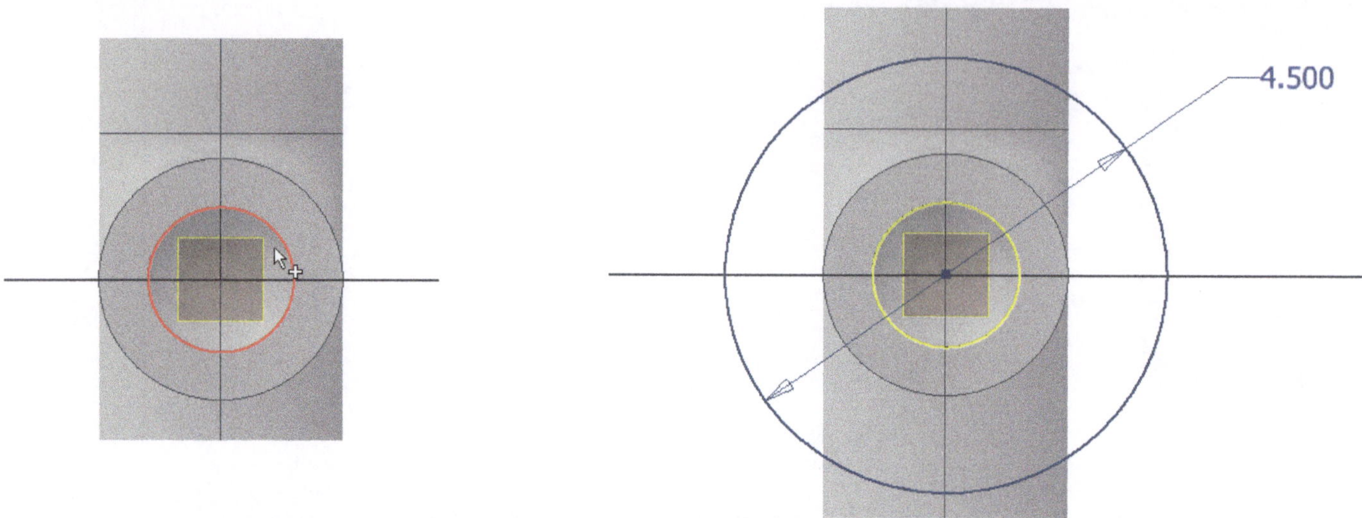

19. Activate the **Extrude** command and click inside the sketch region, as shown. Type-in **0.75** in the **Distance A** box. Click **OK** to create the flange.

20. Create a simple hole of a **0.5**-inch diameter on the extruded face.

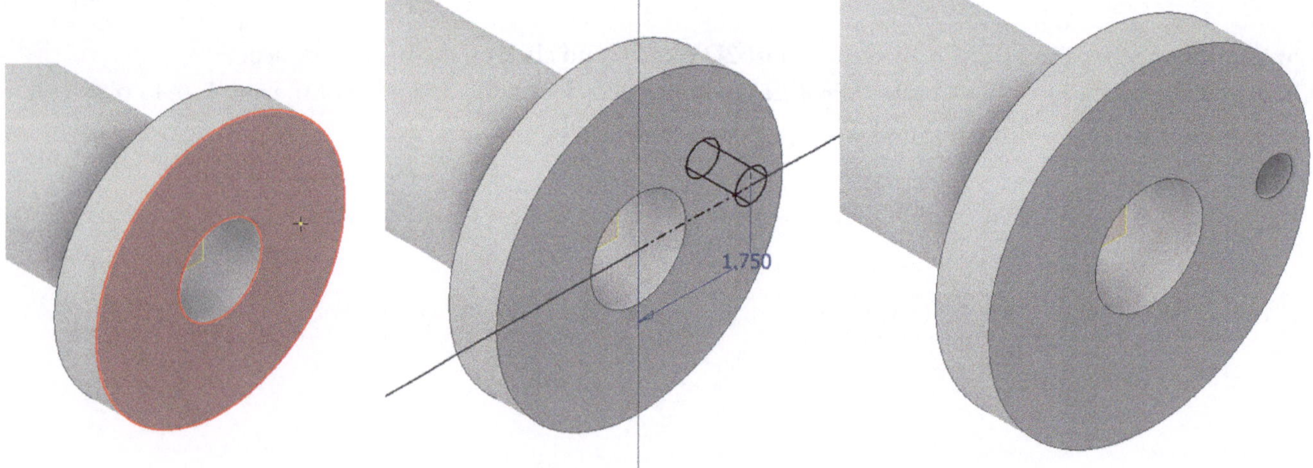

21. On the ribbon, click **3D Model > Pattern > Circular Pattern** . Click the **Pattern Individual Features** icon and select the hole feature from the geometry. Now, you have to define the axis of the circular pattern.
22. Click the **Rotation Axis** selection button and select the cylindrical face of the extruded feature. It defines the pattern axis.
23. Type-in **6** in the **Occurrence Count** box and click **OK** on the dialog. The hole is patterned circularly.
24. On the ribbon, click **3D Model > Pattern > Circular Pattern** . Click the **Features** icon and select the hole feature from the geometry. Now, you have to define the axis of the circular pattern.
25. Click **Direction > Y axis** from the **Orientation** section on the **Properties** panel. It defines the pattern axis.
26. Select **Distribution > Fitted** and type-in **6** and **360** in the **Count** and **Angle** boxes, respectively.
27. Select **Orientation > Rotational**. Click **OK** on the Properties panel.

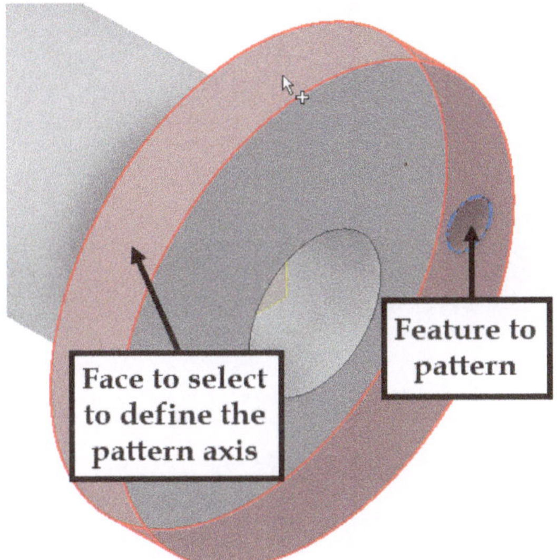

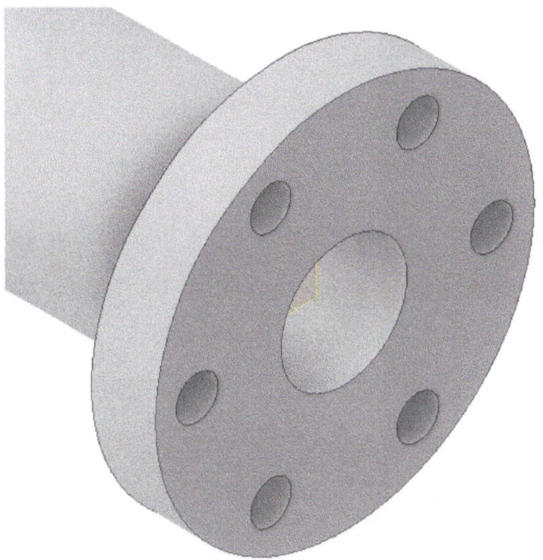

28. Change the model view orientation, as shown. Start a sketch on the end face of the *Sweep* feature, and then create a sketch point, as shown. Next, click **Finish Sketch** on the ribbon.

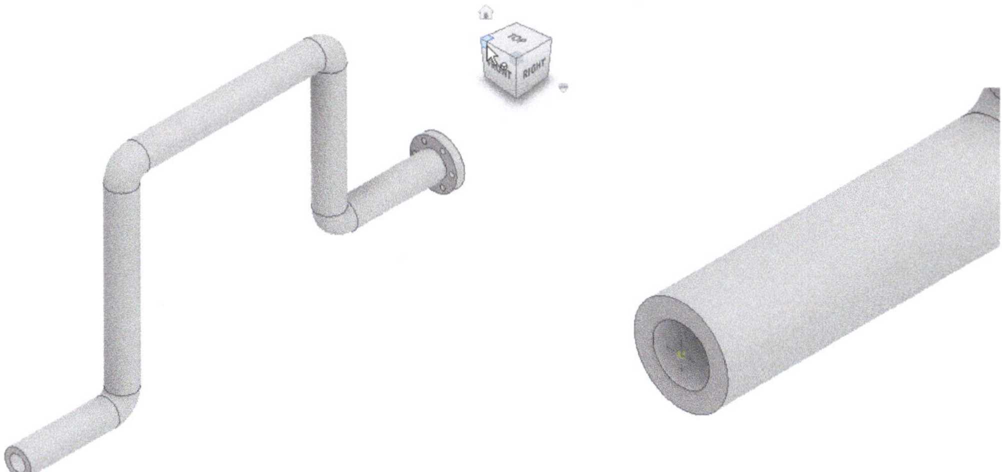

29. On the ribbon, click **3D Model > Pattern > Sketch Driven** ; the sketch point is selected, automatically.
30. Select the extruded feature and the circular pattern.

31. Click the **Base Point** selection button on the **Sketch Driven Pattern** dialog. Select the circular edge of the extruded feature, a shown. Its center point is selected as the base point.
32. Click **OK** to create sketch driven pattern.

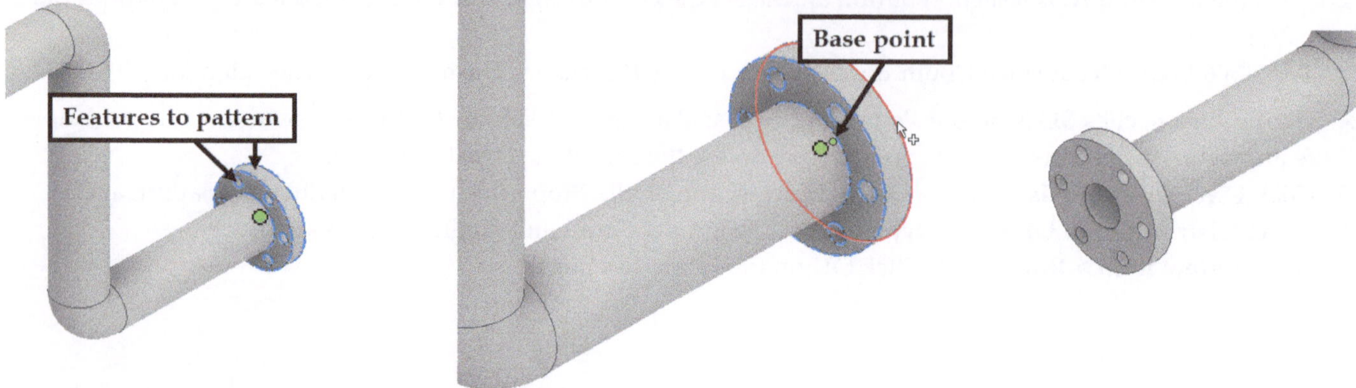

33. Save and close the part file.

Questions

1. List the methods to create the *Sweep* features.
2. How to apply twists and turns to *Sweep* features?
3. How is the **Guide** option useful?
4. List any two options to define the size of the coil features.

Exercises

Exercise 1

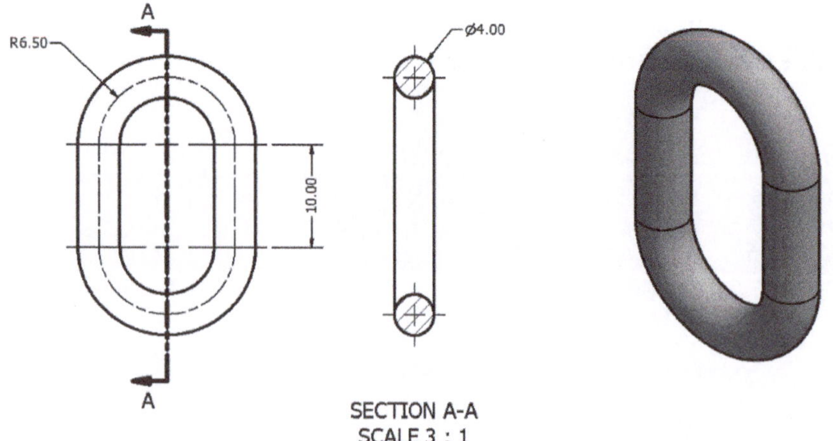

Exercise 2

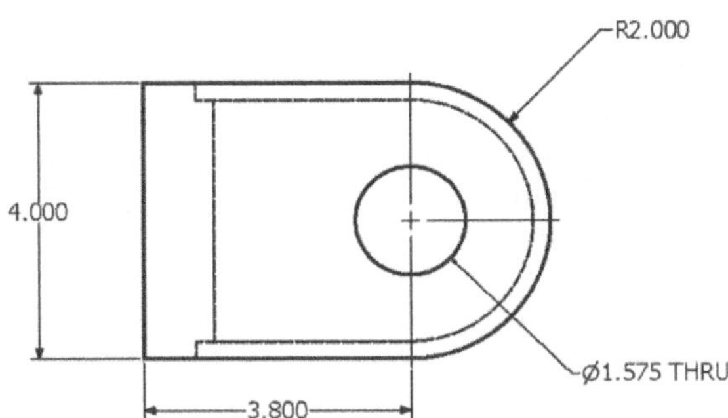

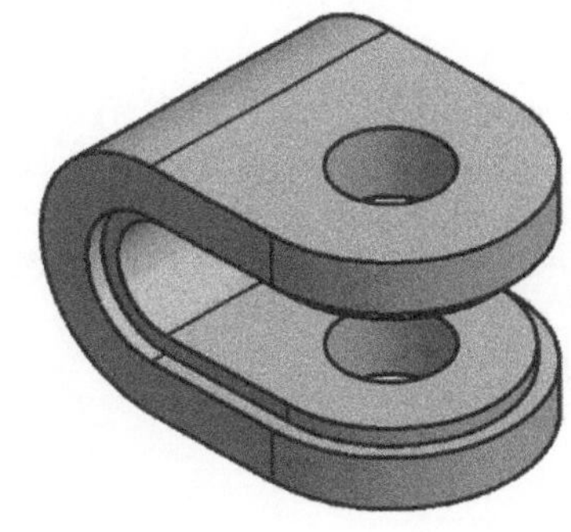

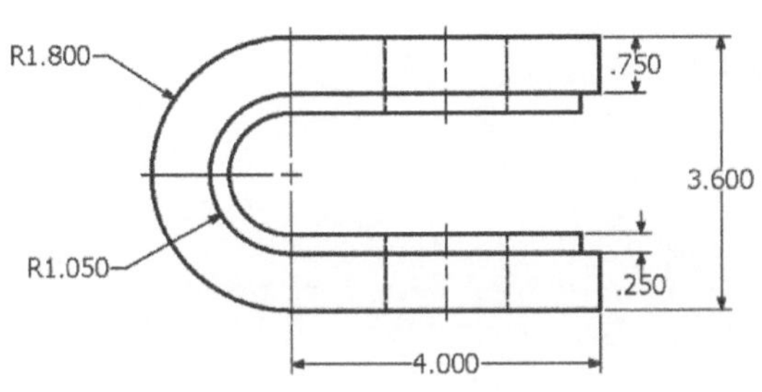

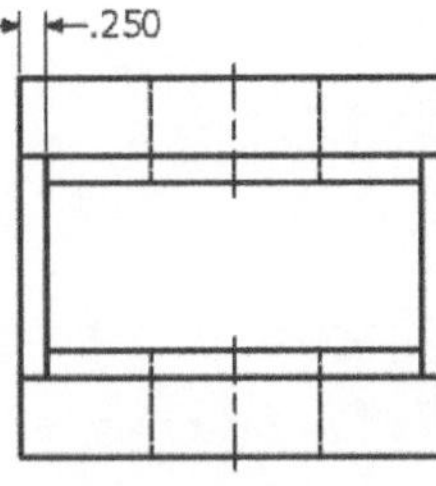

Chapter 7: Loft Features

The **Loft** command is one of the advanced commands available in Inventor that allows you to create simple as well as complex shapes. A basic loft is created by defining two cross-sections and joining them together. For example, if you create a loft feature between a circle and a square, you can easily change the cross-sectional shape of the solid. This ability is what separates the loft feature from the sweep feature.

The topics covered in this chapter are:

- *Basic Lofts*
- *Loft sections*
- *Conditions*
- *Rails*
- *Closed Loop*
- *Center Line Loft*
- *Area Loft*
- *Loft Cutouts*

Loft

This command creates a loft feature between different cross-sections. To create a loft, first, create two or more sections on different planes. The planes can be parallel or perpendicular to each other. Activate the **Loft** command (click **3D Model > Create > Loft** on the ribbon); the **Loft** dialog appears. Now, you need to select two or more cross-sections that will define the loft. On the dialog, click in the **Sections** area, and then select the cross-sections from the graphics window. Click **OK** to create the loft.

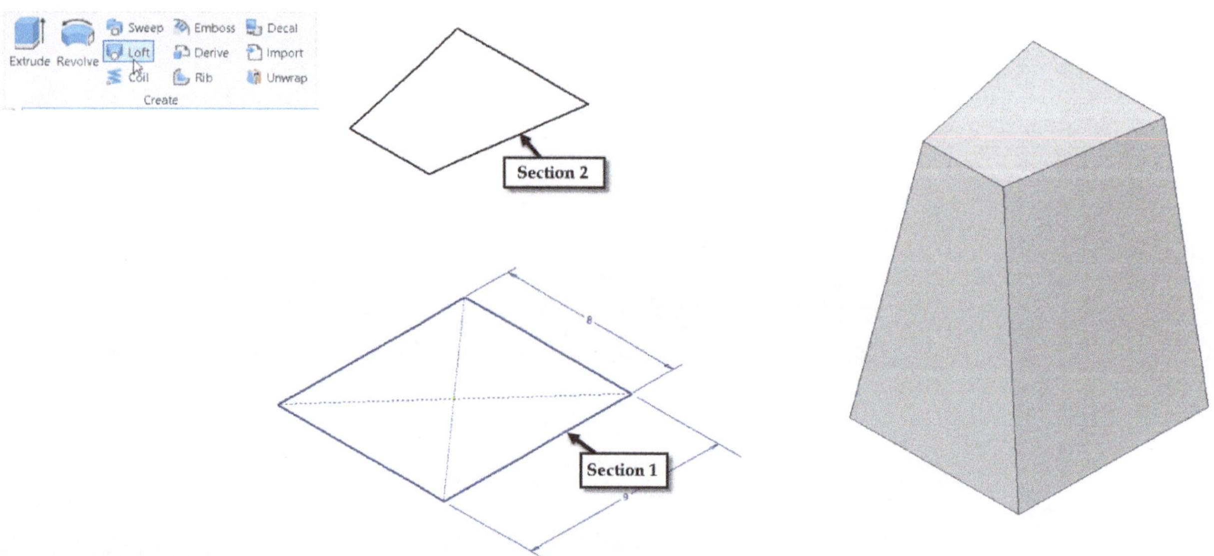

Loft sections

In addition to 2D sketches, you can also define loft cross-sections by using different element types. For instance, you can use existing model faces, surfaces, and points. The only restriction is that the points can be used at the beginning or end of a loft.

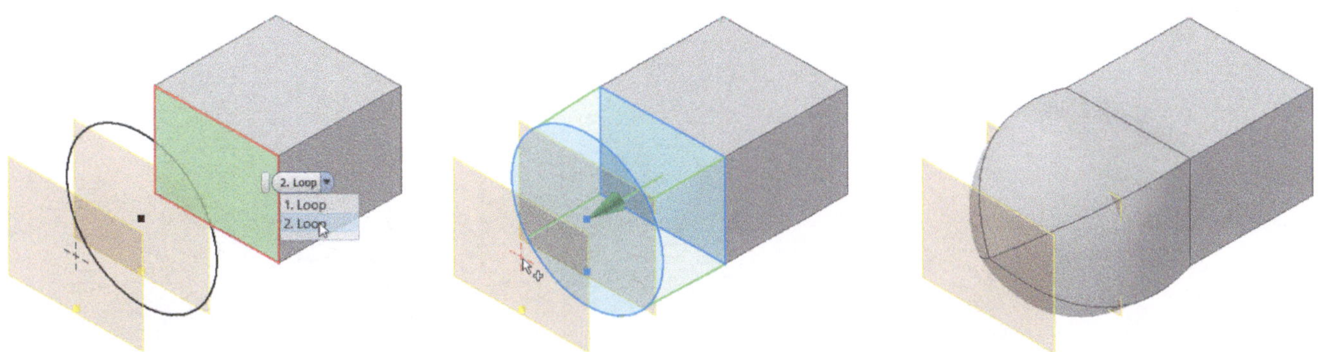

Conditions

The cross-sections and the plane location control the shape of a simple loft. However, the **Conditions** tab options can control the behaviour of the side faces. If you would like to change the shape of the side faces, you can use the **Conditions** tab options either at the beginning of the loft, the end of the lofts, or both.

Direction Condition

Click the **Conditions** tab and select **Direction Condition** from the drop-down located next to the first section. Next, enter 60 in the **Angle** box; the preview of the loft updates. You can notice that the beginning of the loft starts at an angle of 60 degrees to the cross-section. You can control how much influence the angle will have by adjusting the parameter in the **Weight** box. A lower value will have a lesser effect on the feature. As you increase the value, the more noticeable the effect will be, eventually. If you increase the number high enough, the direction angle will lead to self-intersecting results.

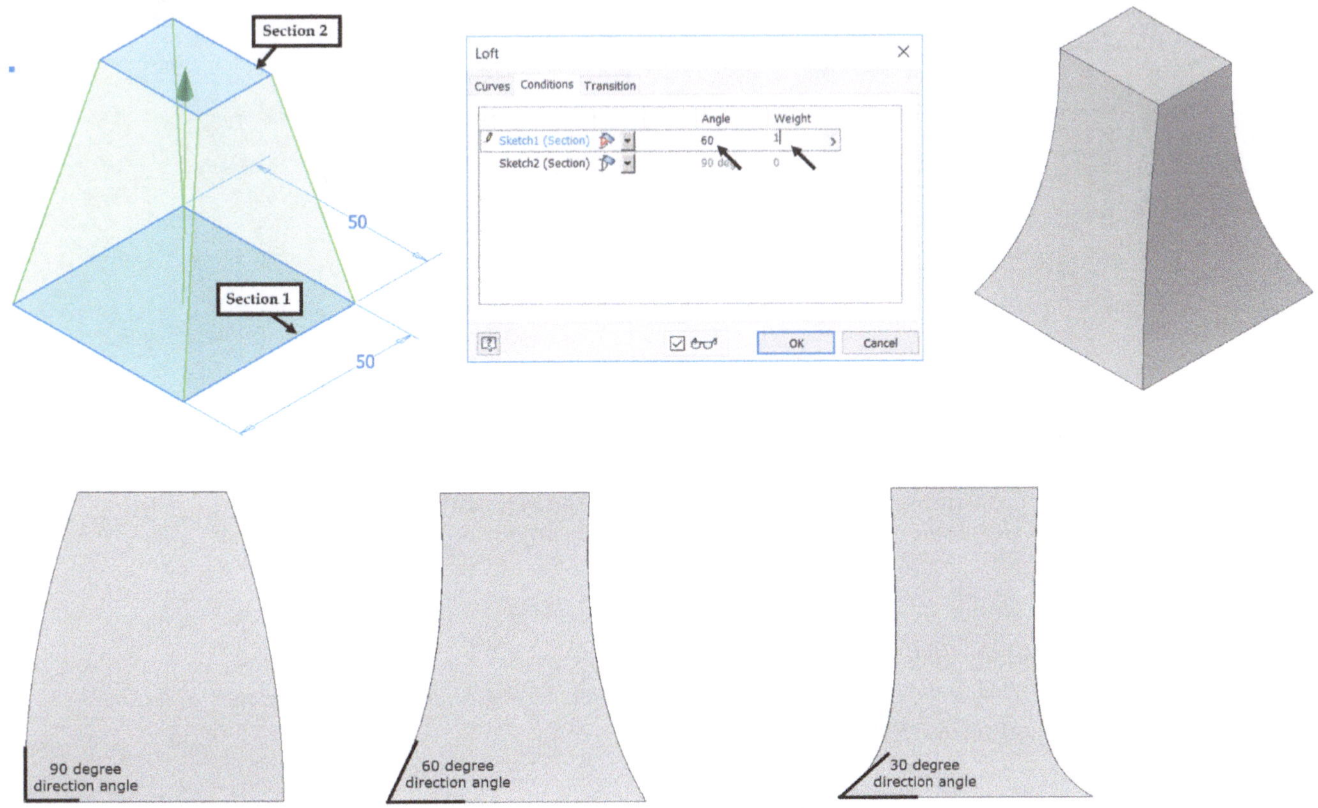

Likewise, you can also apply the direction condition to the second cross-section of the loft.

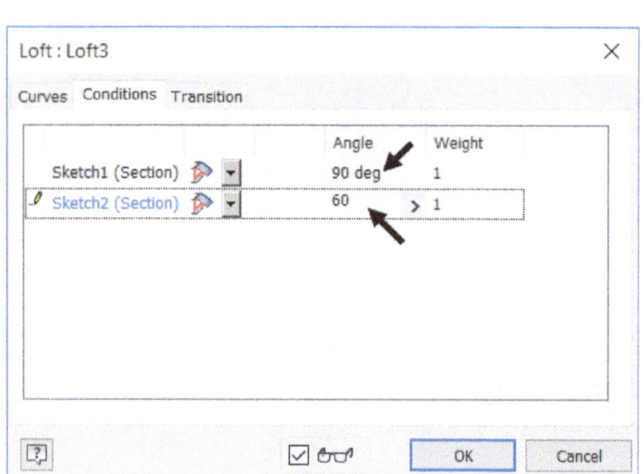

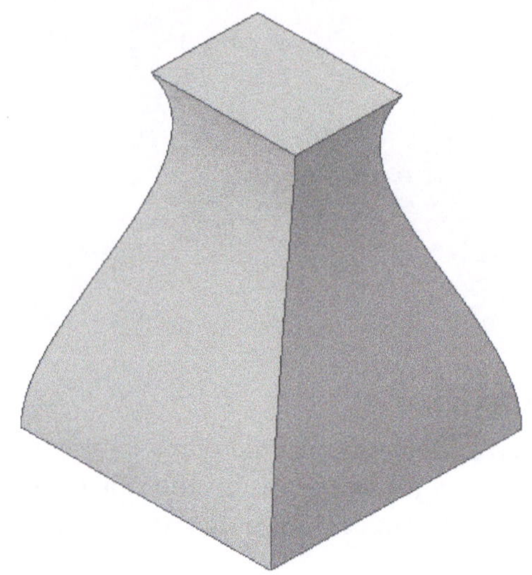

Tangent Condition

The **Tangent Condition** option is available when you select an existing face loop as one of the cross-sections. This option makes the side faces of the loft feature tangent to the side faces of the existing geometry.

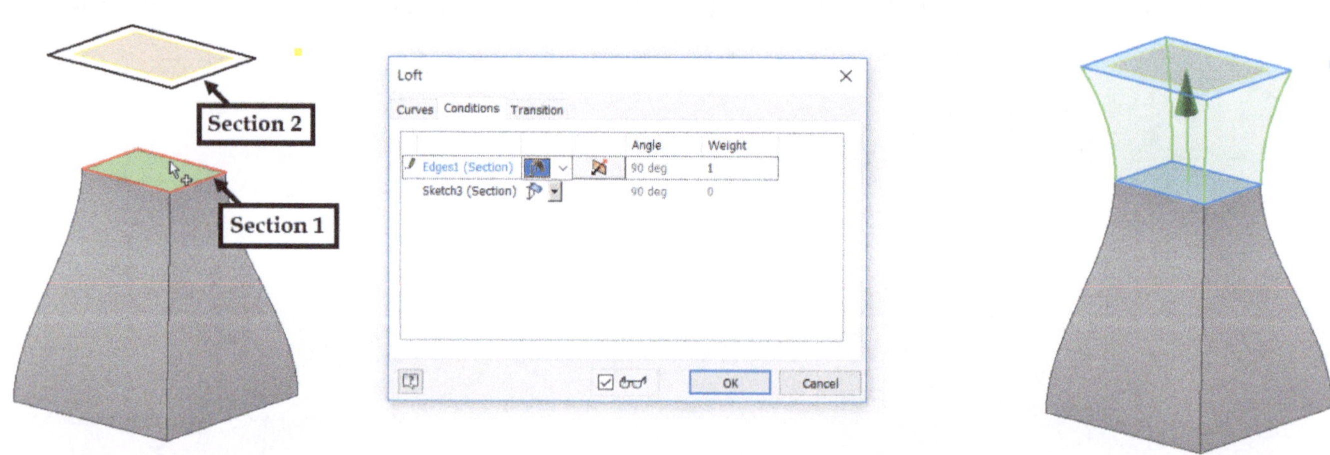

Smooth (G2) Condition

The **Smooth (G2) Condition** option is available when you select an existing face loop as one of the cross-sections. This option makes the side faces of the loft feature curvature continuous with the side faces of the existing geometry.

Rails

Similar to the **Condition** options, rails allow you to control the behavior of a loft between cross-sections. You can create rails by using 2D or 3D sketches. For example, start a sketch on the plane intersecting with the cross-sections, and then create a spline, as shown.

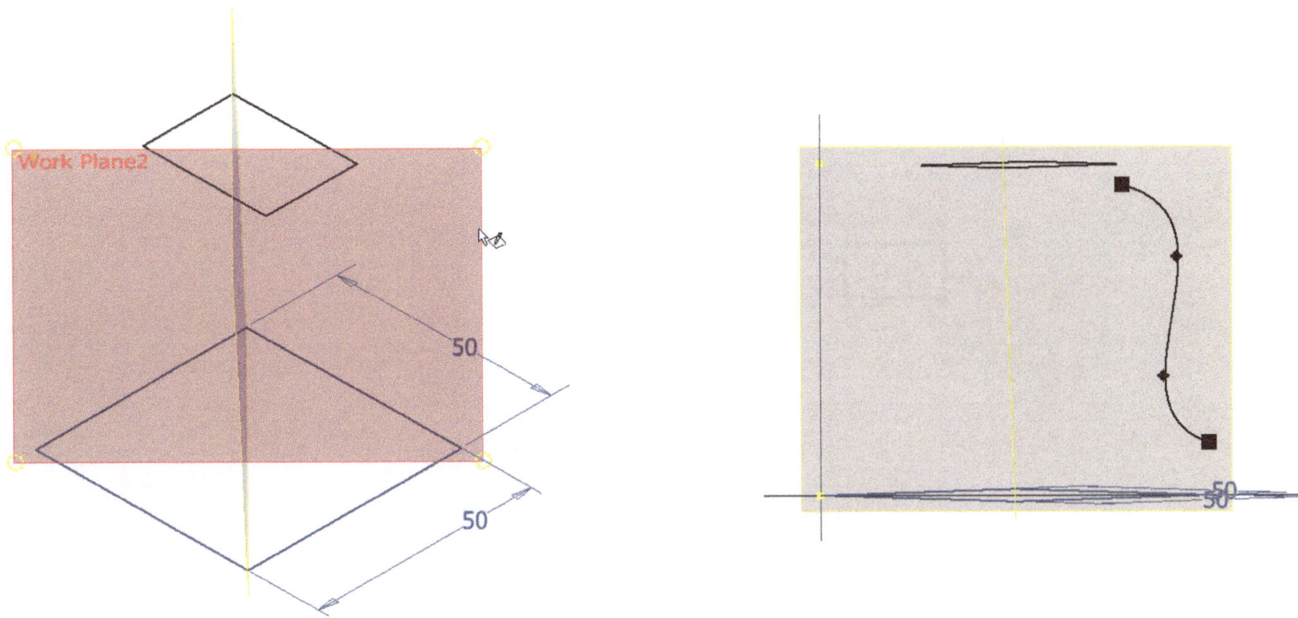

Next, you need to connect the endpoints of the spline with the cross-sections. To do this, click **Sketch > Create > Project Geometry** on the ribbon, and project the endpoints of the cross-sections onto the sketch plane. Next, apply the **Coincident Constraint** between the endpoints of the spline and the projected elements. Click **Finish Sketch** on the ribbon.

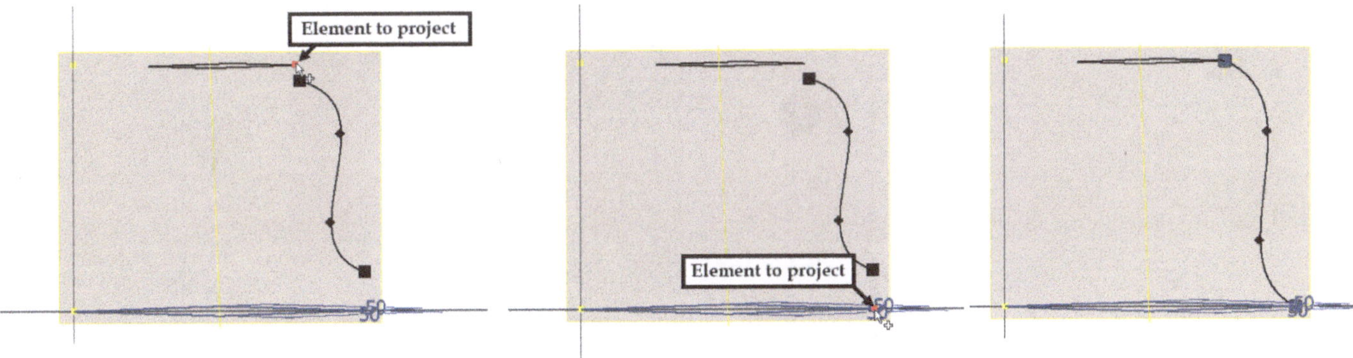

Likewise, create a sketch on the other plane, as shown. Next, click **Finish Sketch**.

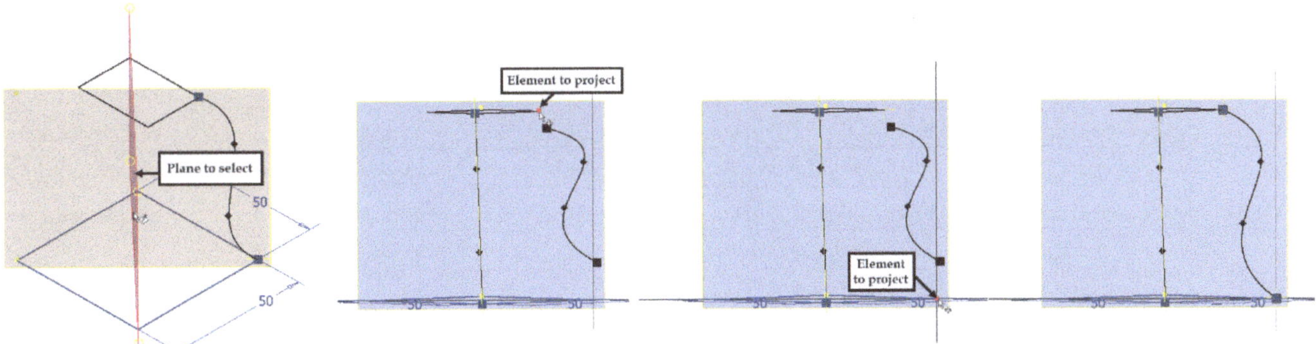

Now, activate the **Loft** command and select the cross-sections. To select rails, click in the **Rails** section and select the first rail. Next, click the **Click to add** option in the **Rails** section and select the other rails; you will see that the preview updates. Notice that the edges with rails are affected.

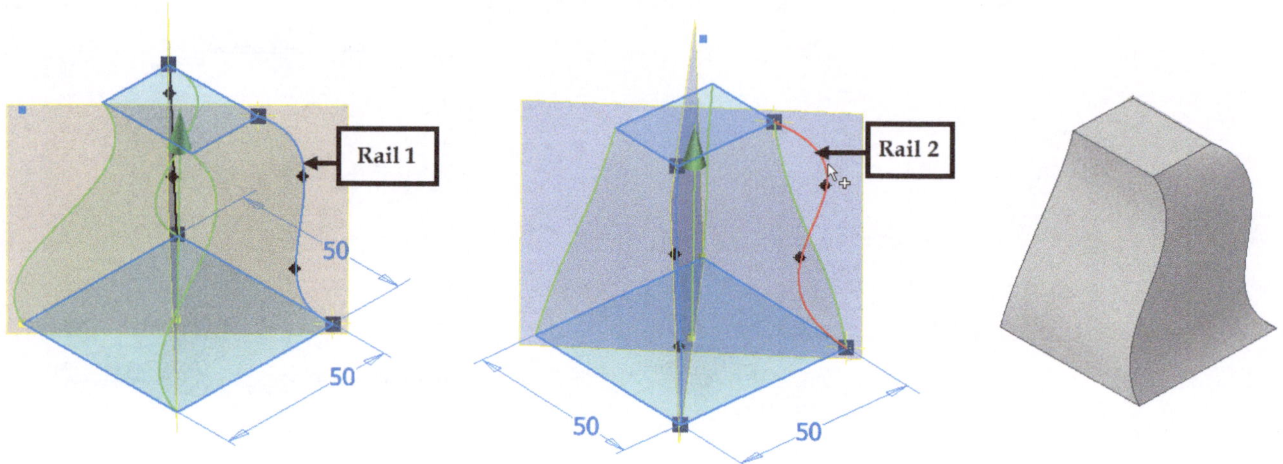

Closed Loop

Inventor allows you to create a loft that closes on itself. For example, to create a model that lofts between each of the shapes, you must select four sketches as shown in the figure, and then check the **Closed Loop** option on the dialog. Next, click **OK**; this will give you a closed loft.

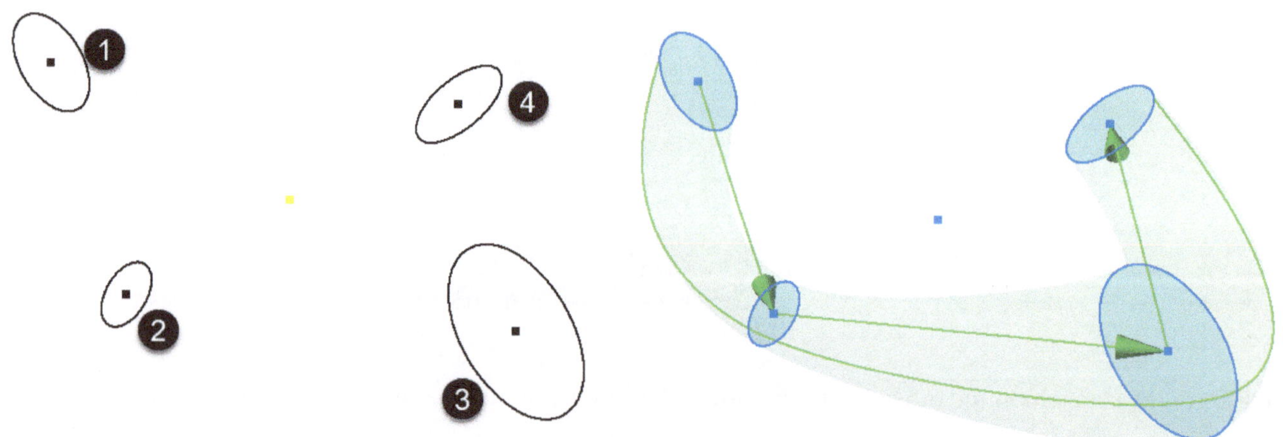

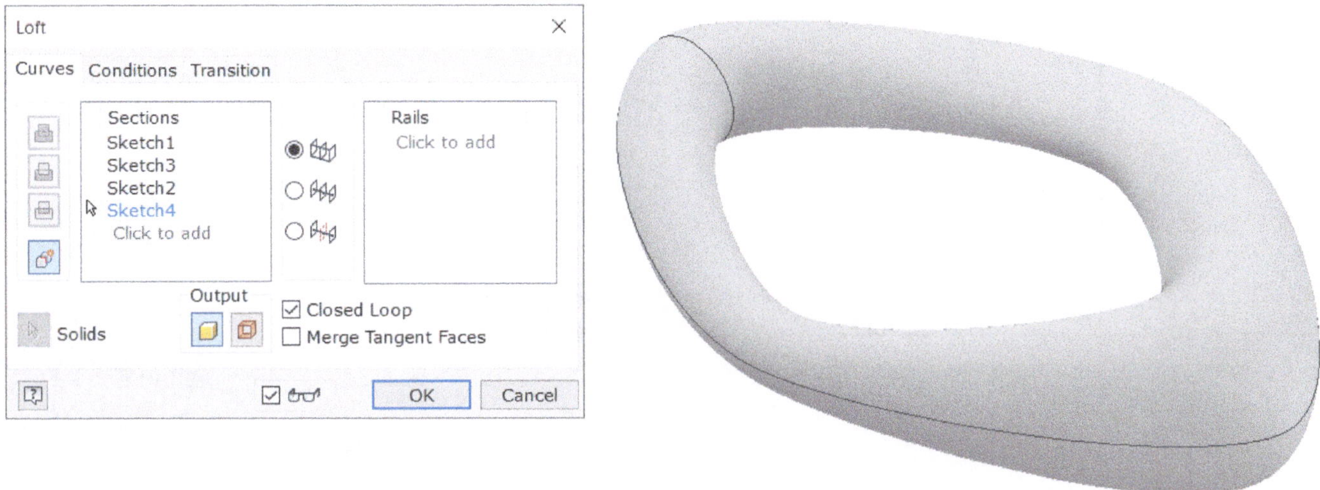

Center Line Loft

In the previous section, you have created a closed loft using four sections. However, the transition between the sections was not smooth. The **Center Line** option helps you to create a smooth transition between the sections. First, create a centerline passing through all the sections, as shown. Next, activate the **Loft** command and select the **Center Line** option, and then select the centerline. Click on the **Section** area and select the loft sections; the preview of the loft appears. Check the **Closed Loop** option, if you want to create a closed-loop, and then click **OK**.

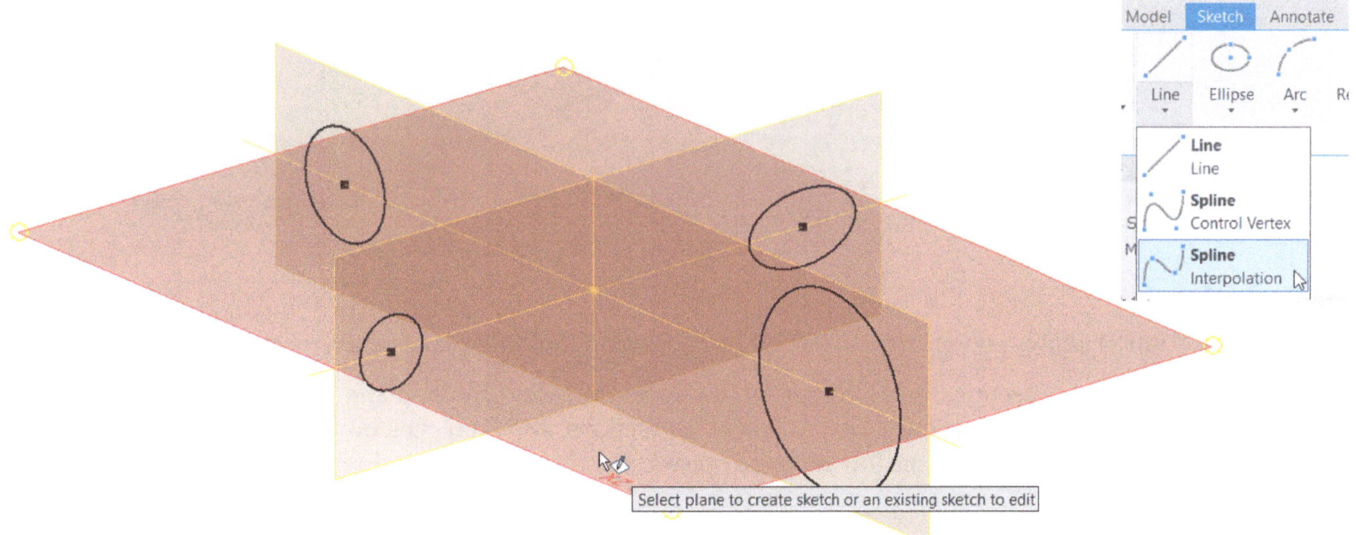

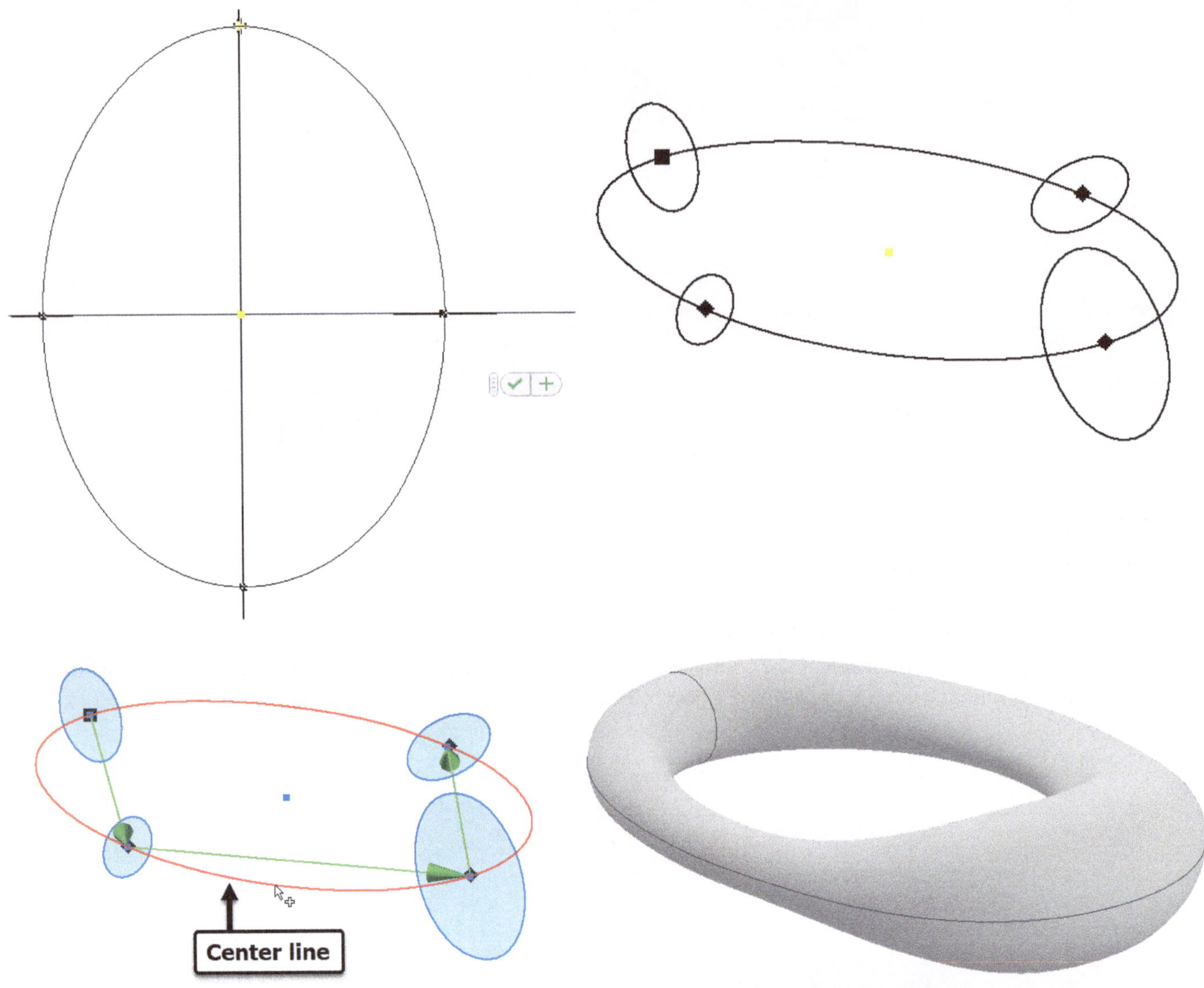

Area Loft

The **Area Loft** option allows you to create a loft without creating multiple planes and cross-sections. You need to have a start and end cross-sections, and a centerline. Activate the **Loft** command and select the **Area Loft** option from the **Loft** dialog. Select the start and end cross-sections, and then click on the **Center Line** area and select the centerline; the preview of the loft feature appears.

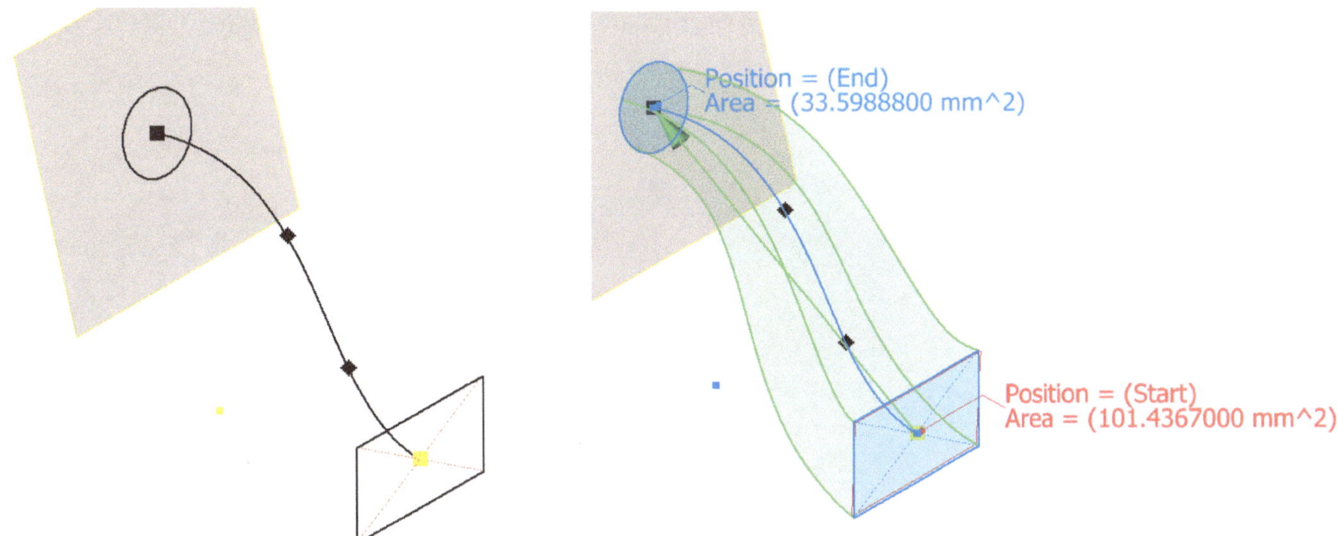

Click in the **Placed Sections** area and click on the centerline to place a section; the **Section Dimensions** dialog appears. On this dialog, specify the section position using the **Section Position** options: **Proportional Distance** and **Absolute Distance**. The **Proportional Distance** option allows you to specify the location by entering a value between 0 and 1. The zero value specifies the location at the start point of the centerline. In contrast, the 1 value places the section at the endpoint. The **Absolute Distance** option allows you to enter the exact distance at which the section will be positioned. In this case, select the **Proportional Distance** option and enter **0.5** in the box.

The **Driving Section** option allows you to place a section and specify its size. The **Driven Section** option allows you only to place the section. The size of the placed section will be driven by the start and end sections. In this case, select the **Driving Section** option.

Next, select an option from the **Section Size** section. The **Area** option allows you to enter the area of the placed section. Whereas, the **Scale Factor** option allows you to enter the scale factor. The area of the placed section is scaled by the value that you enter. For example, if you enter 0.9 in the **Scale Factor** box, the area of the placed section will be scaled by 0.9 times. In this case, select the **Scale Factor** option and enter 0.9 as the scale factor. Click **OK** to apply the position and size values of the placed section. You can change the values of the placed section by double-clicking on the values displayed on it.

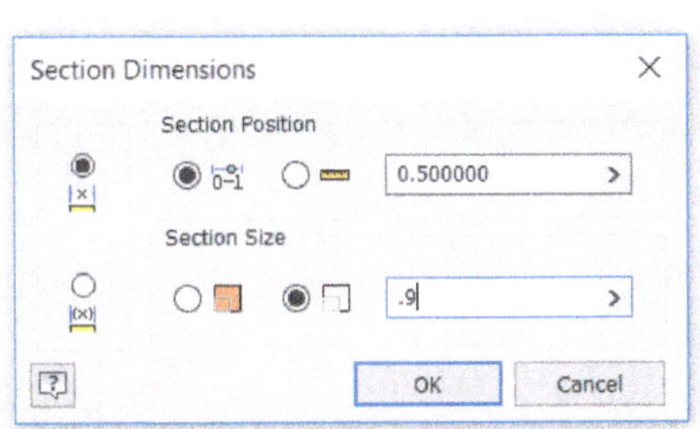

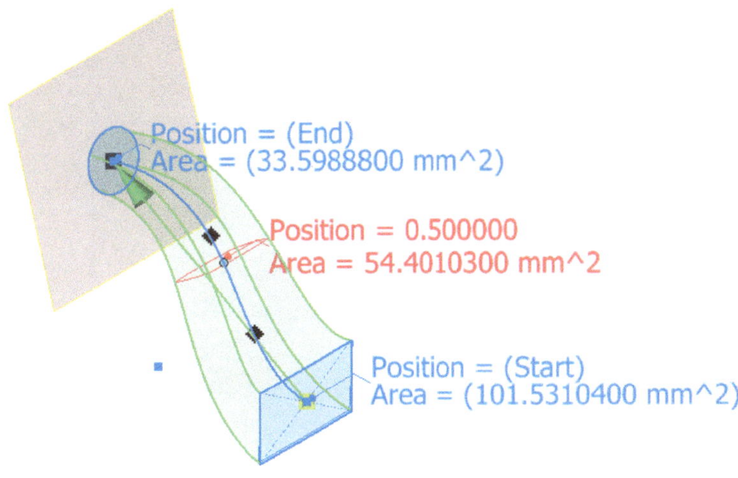

Likewise, click the **Click to add** option in the **Placed Section** area, and then add another section. Click **OK** to complete the feature.

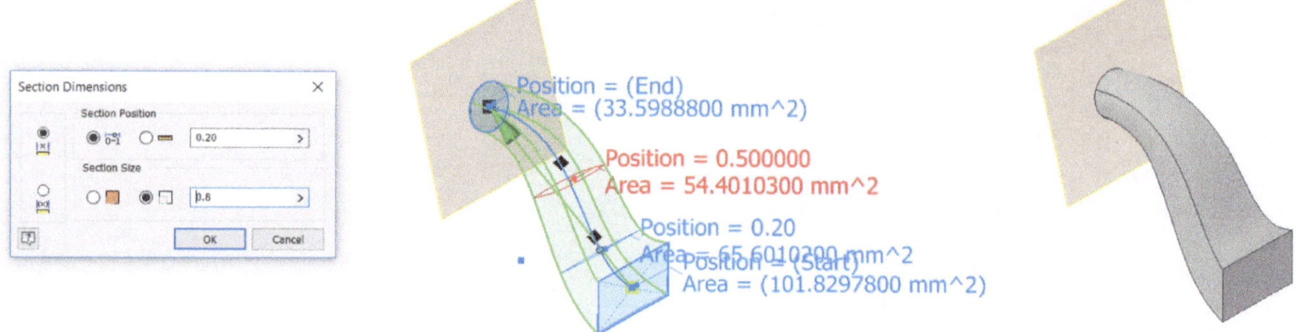

Loft Cutout

Like other standard features such as extrude, revolve and sweep, the loft feature can be used to add or remove material. You can remove material by using the **Loft** command. Activate this command (click **3D Model > Create > Loft** on the ribbon) and select the cross-sections. Click **Cut** and **OK** to create the loft cutout.

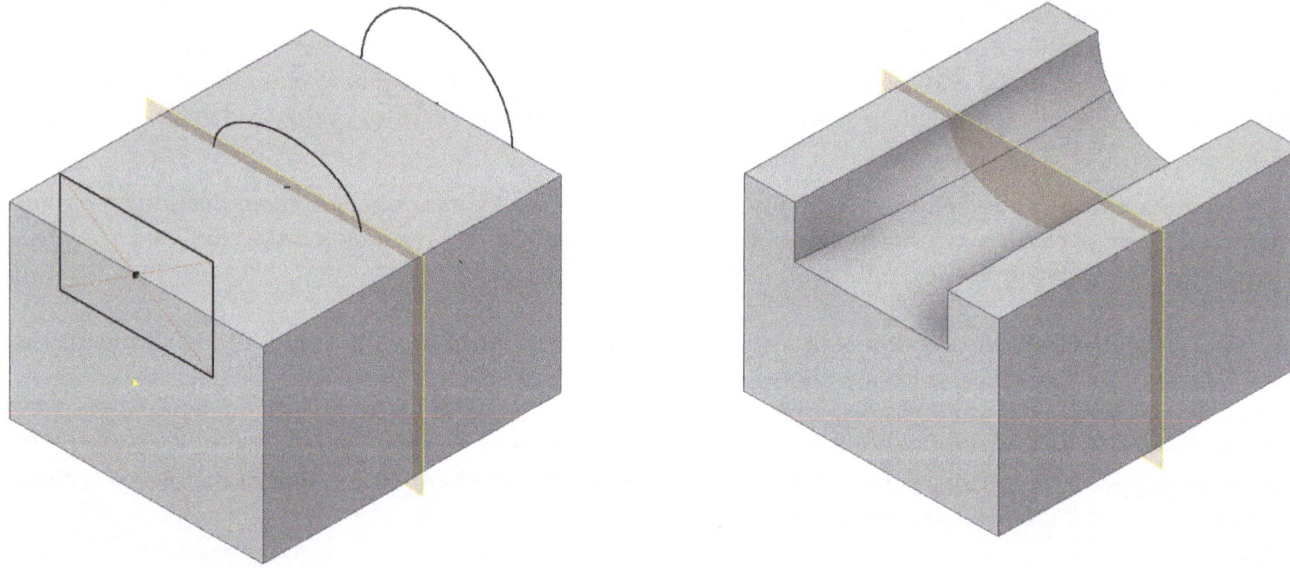

Examples

Example 1 (Millimetres)

In this example, you will create the part shown below.

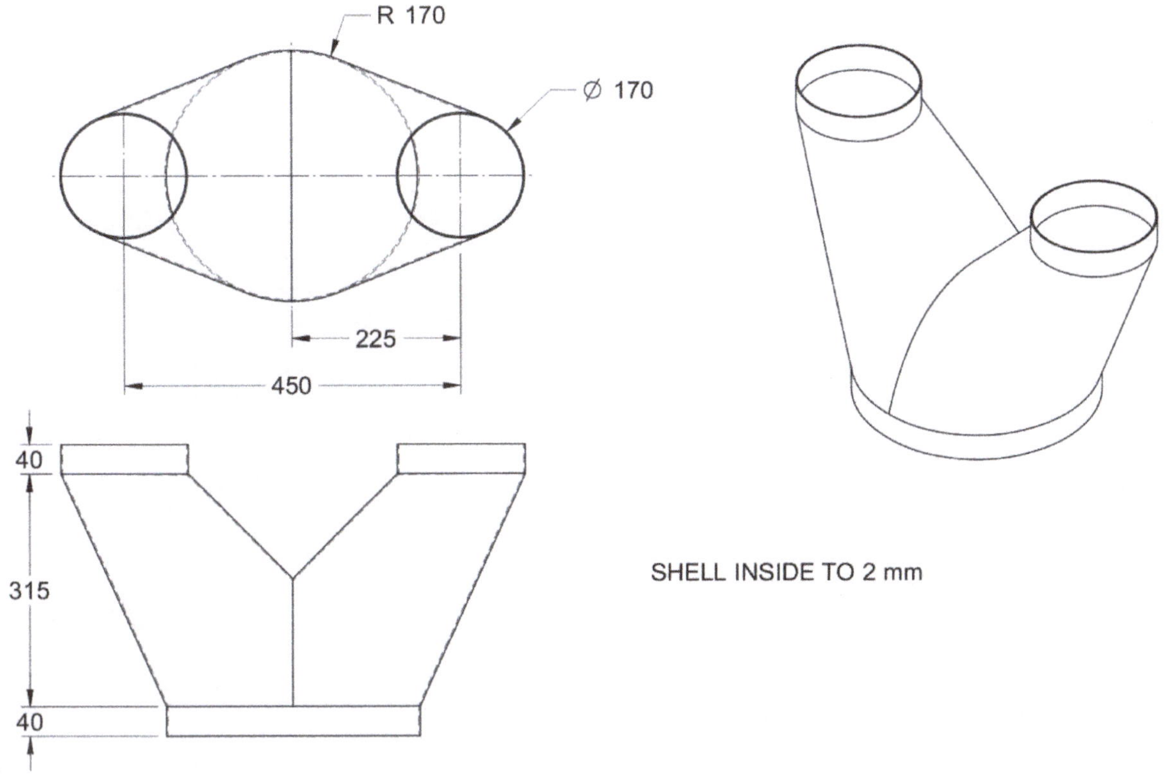

1. Start **Autodesk Inventor**.
2. On the **File** menu, click the **New** icon; the **Create New File** dialog appears. On this dialog, click **Templates > en-US > Metric**, and then click the **Standard (mm).ipt** template. Click **Create**; a new part file is opened.
3. To start a new sketch, click **3D Model > Sketch > Start 2D Sketch** on the ribbon.
4. Select the **XZ Plane** and draw a circle of **340 mm** in diameter. Click **Finish Sketch** on the ribbon.
5. Create the *Extrude* feature with a **40 mm** thickness.

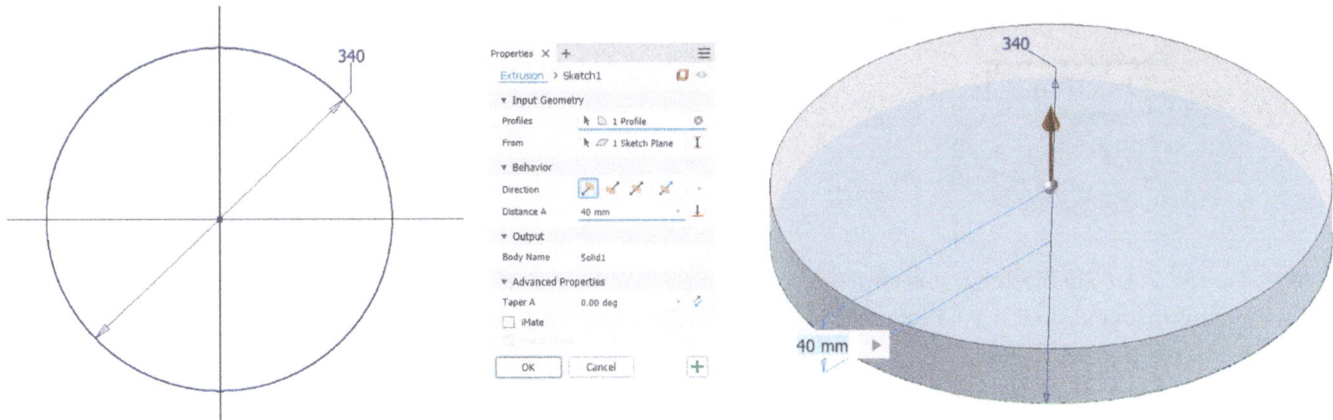

6. On the ribbon, click **3D Model > Work Features > Plane** drop-down **> Offset from Plane** .
7. Click on the top face of the geometry – Type-In **315** mm in the **Offset** box and press Enter.
8. On the ribbon, click **3D Model > Sketch > Start 2D Sketch**, and then select the newly created plane.
9. Activate the **Circle Center Point** command and draw a circle of **170** mm in diameter. Also, add dimensions and constraints to the circle, as shown. Click **Finish Sketch** on the ribbon.

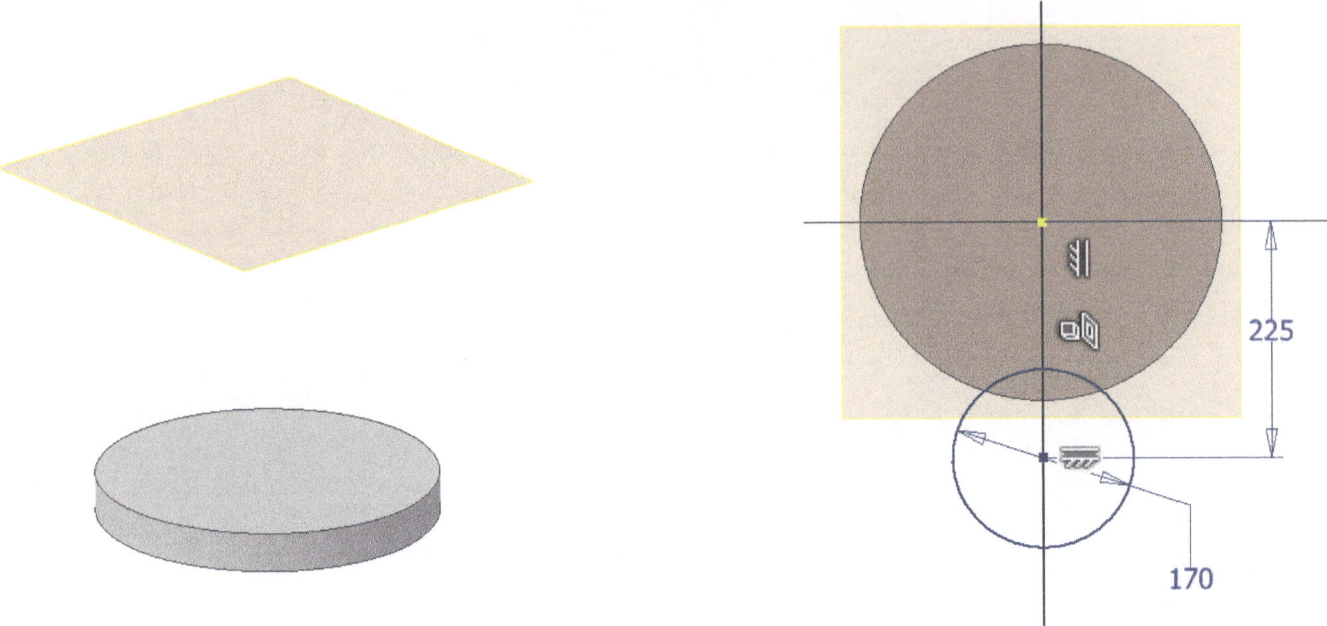

10. On the ribbon, click **3D Model > Create > Loft** .
11. Click on the circle and the top circular edge of the *Extrude* feature. Click **OK** to complete the *Loft* feature.

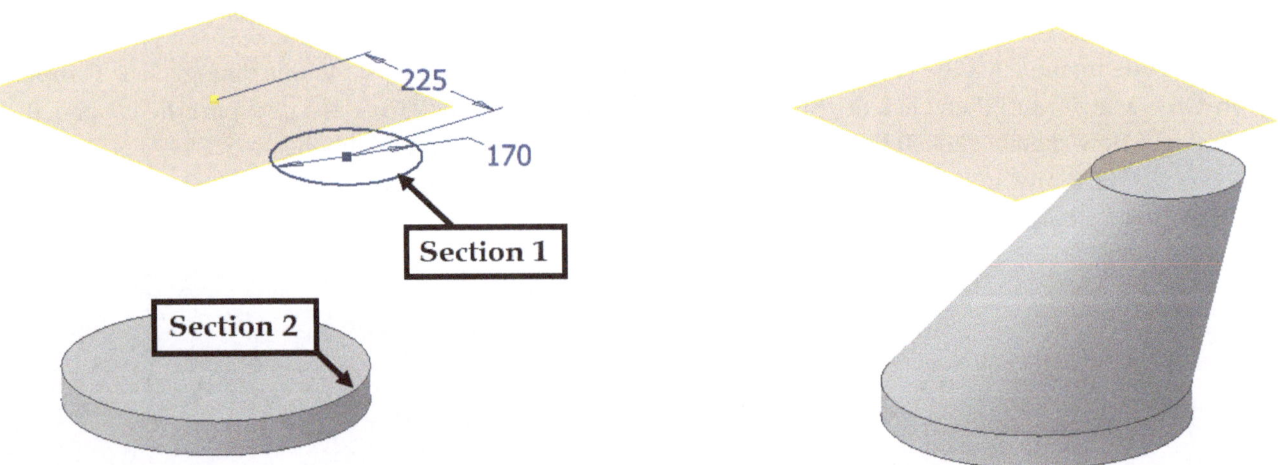

12. Activate the **Start 2D Sketch** command and click on the top face of the *Loft* feature.
13. On the ribbon, click **Sketch > Create > Project Geometry**, and click on the circular edge of the top face. Click **Finish Sketch** on the ribbon.
14. Activate the **Extrude** command and type **40** in the **Distance A** box. Press Enter.

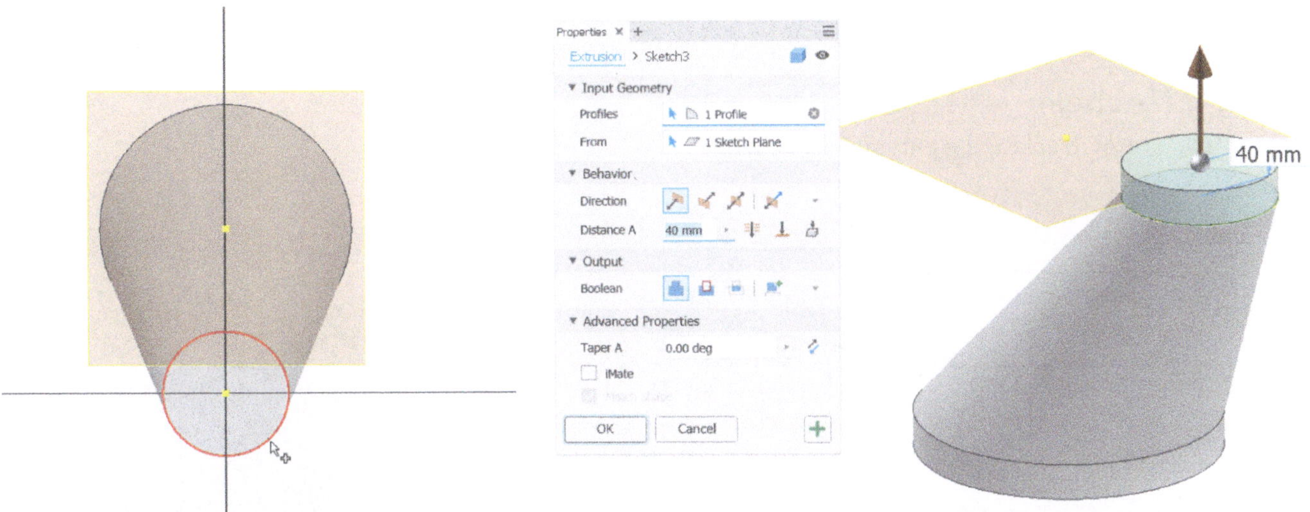

15. On the ribbon, click **3D Model > Pattern > Mirror**. Select the loft feature and the extruded feature on top of it.
16. Click the **Origin YZ Plane** icon on the **Mirror** dialog. Click **OK** to mirror the selected features.

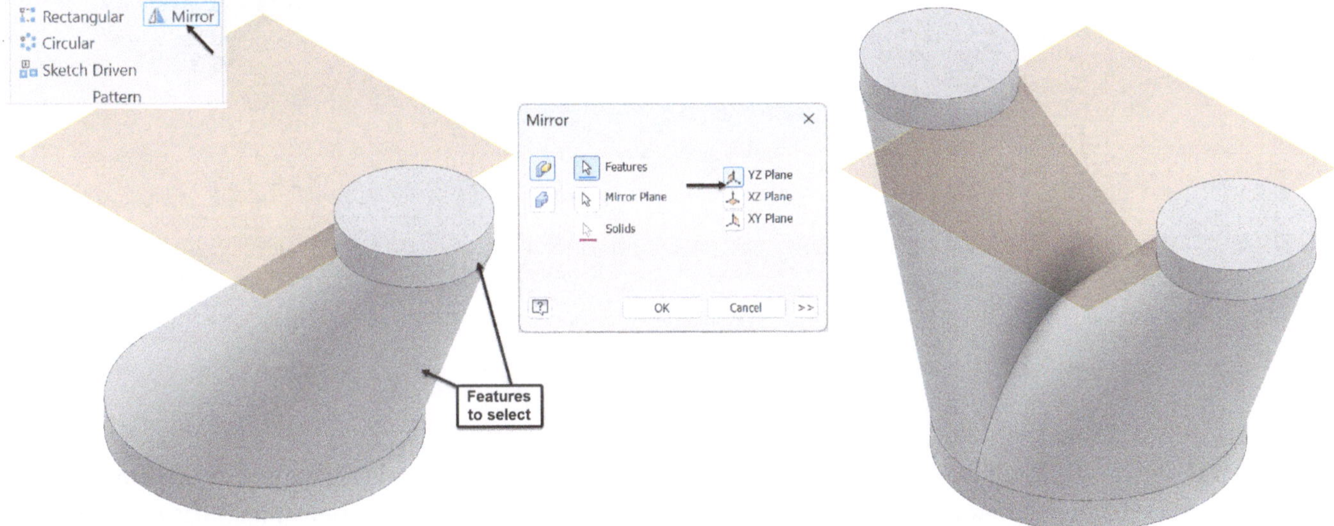

17. On the ribbon, click **3D Model > Modify > Shell** and click on the flat faces of the part geometry.
18. Type **2** in the **Thickness** box and press Enter. The part geometry is shelled.

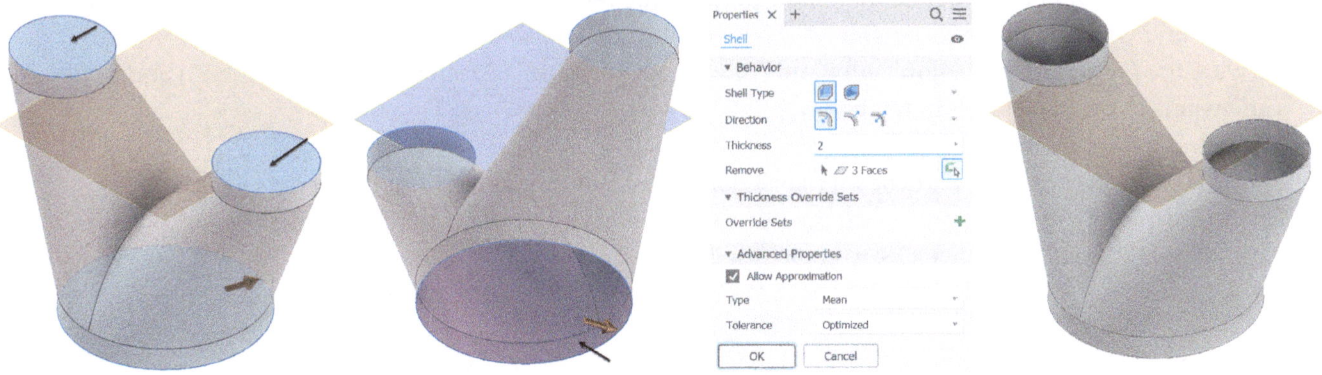

19. Save and close the part file.

Example 2 (Inches)

In this example, you will create the part shown below.

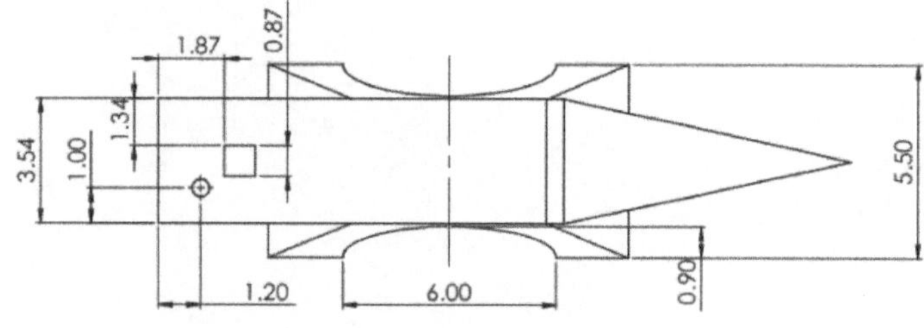

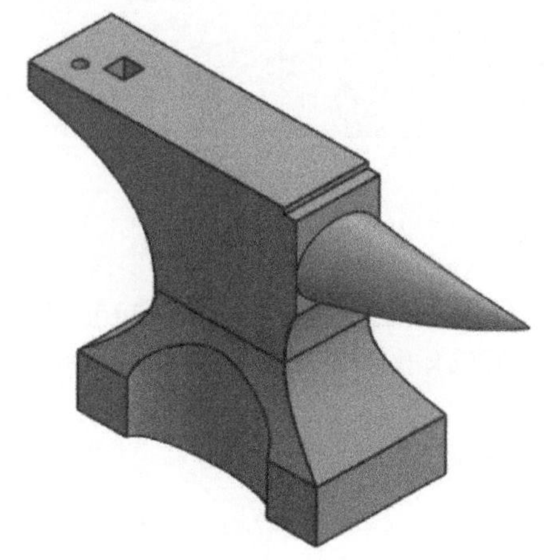

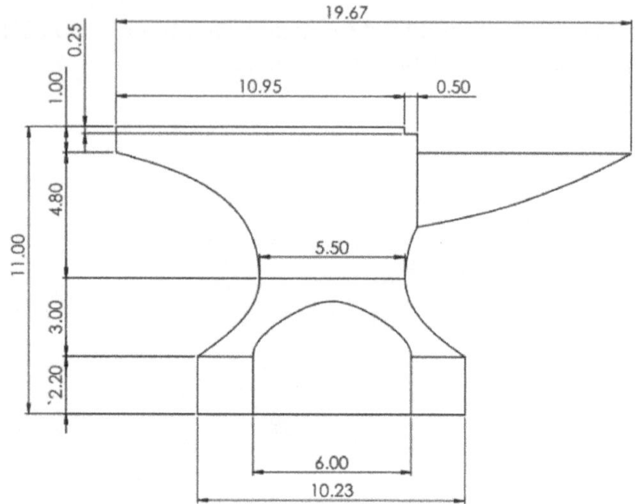

1. Start **Autodesk Inventor 2026**.
2. On the **File** menu, click the **New** icon; the **Create New File** dialog appears. On this dialog, click **Templates > en-US**, and then click the **Standard.ipt** template. Next, click the **Create** button; a new part file is opened.
3. To start a new sketch, click **3D Model > Sketch > Start 2D Sketch** on the ribbon.
4. Select the **XZ** plane to start the sketch.
5. Click **Sketch > Create > Rectangle > Two Point Center Rectangle** on the ribbon.
6. Click on the origin point to define the center point of the rectangle. Move the mouse pointer diagonally upward and click to draw a rectangle.
7. Activate the **General Dimension** command (**Sketch > Constrain > Dimension** on the ribbon) and apply dimensions to the sketch, as shown below.
8. Click **Finish Sketch** on the ribbon.
9. Click **3D Model > Create > Extrude** on the ribbon and select the sketch (if not already selected).
10. On the **Extrude Properties** panel, click the **Direction > Default** under the **Behavior** section and type in **2.2** in the **Distance A** box. Next, click **OK** to create the *Extrude* feature.

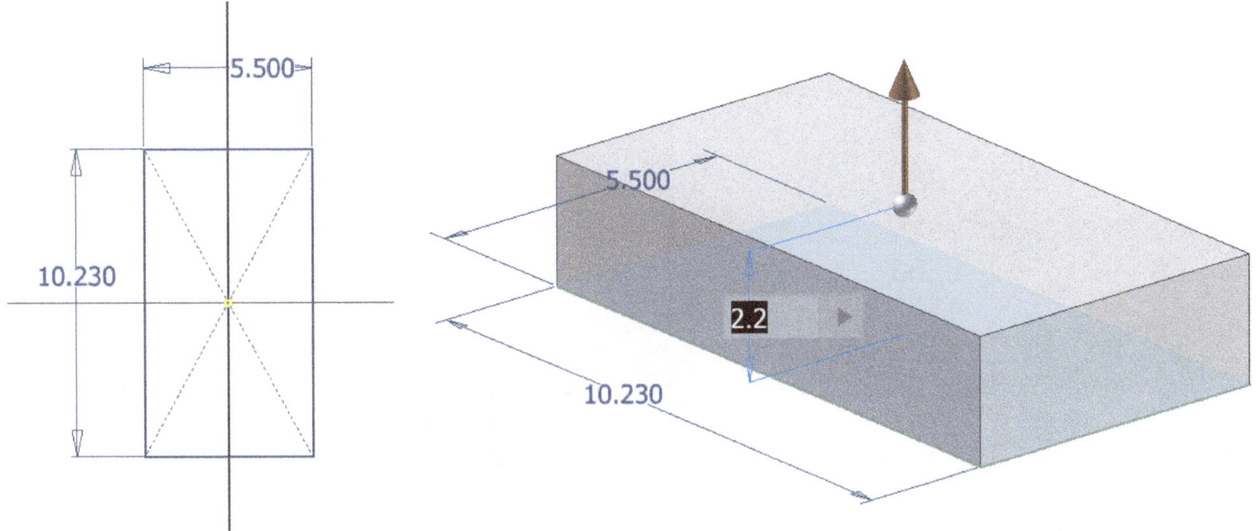

11. Click **3D Model > Work Features > Plane > Offset from Plane** on the ribbon and click on the top face of the model.
12. Type-in **3** in the **distance** box of the mini toolbar and click **OK** to create an offset plane.

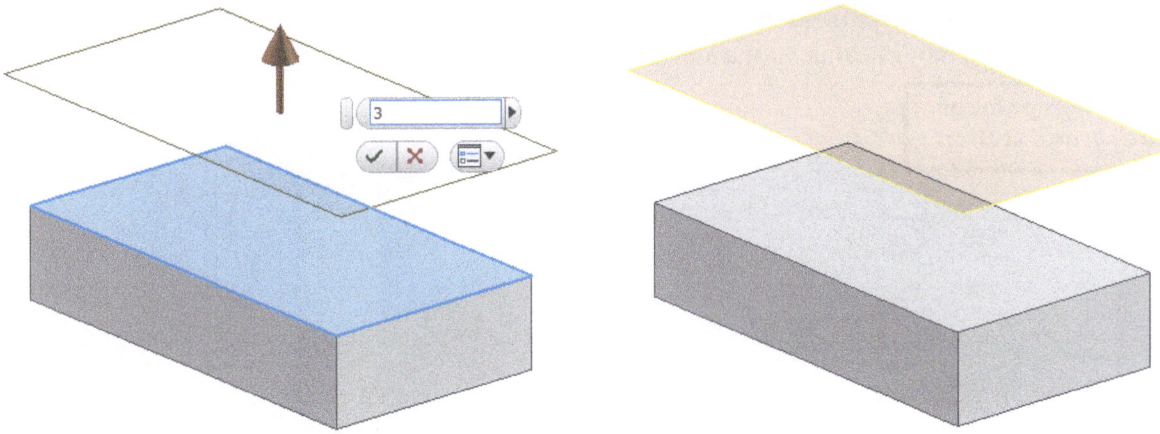

13. Click **3D Model > Sketch > Start 2D Sketch** on the ribbon and click on the newly created plane.
14. Click **Sketch > Create > Rectangle > Two Point Center Rectangle** on the ribbon.
15. Click on the origin point to define the center point of the rectangle. Move the pointer upward and click to draw a rectangle.
16. Activate the **General Dimension** command and apply dimensions to the sketch, as shown in the figure.
17. Click **Finish Sketch** on the ribbon.

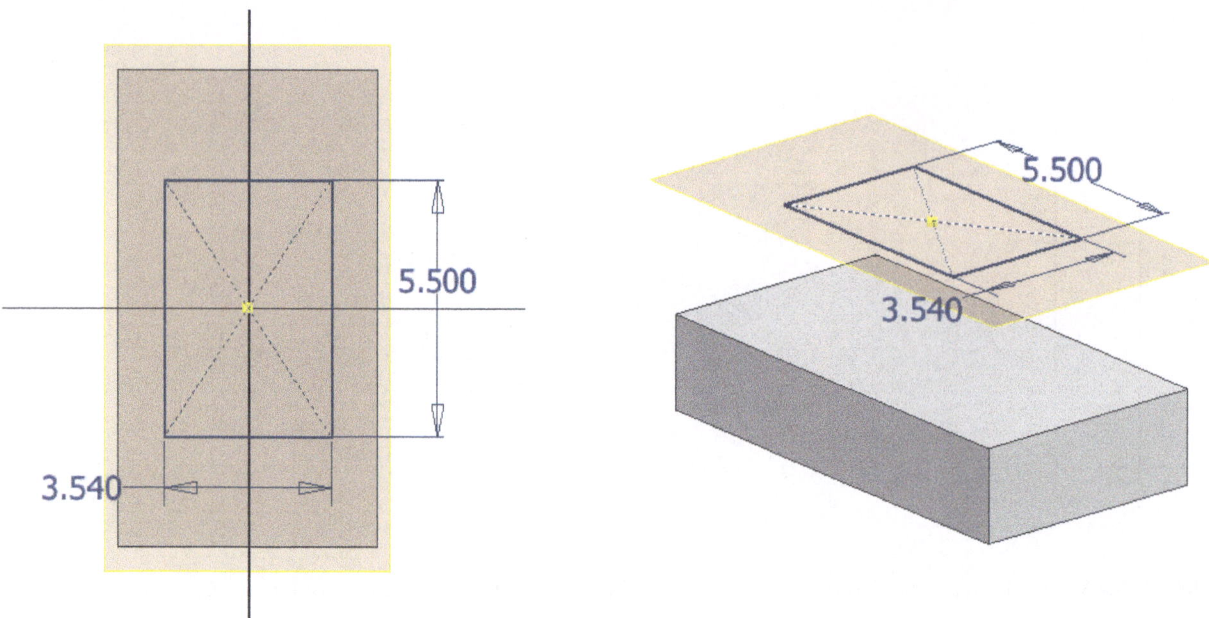

18. Click **3D Model > Create > Loft** on the ribbon; the **Loft** dialog appears on the screen.
19. On the **Loft** dialog, click **Curves > Sections > click to add** to select the sections.
20. Click on the top face of the first feature at the left corner, as shown.
21. Select the rectangular sketch by clicking on the left corner, as shown.

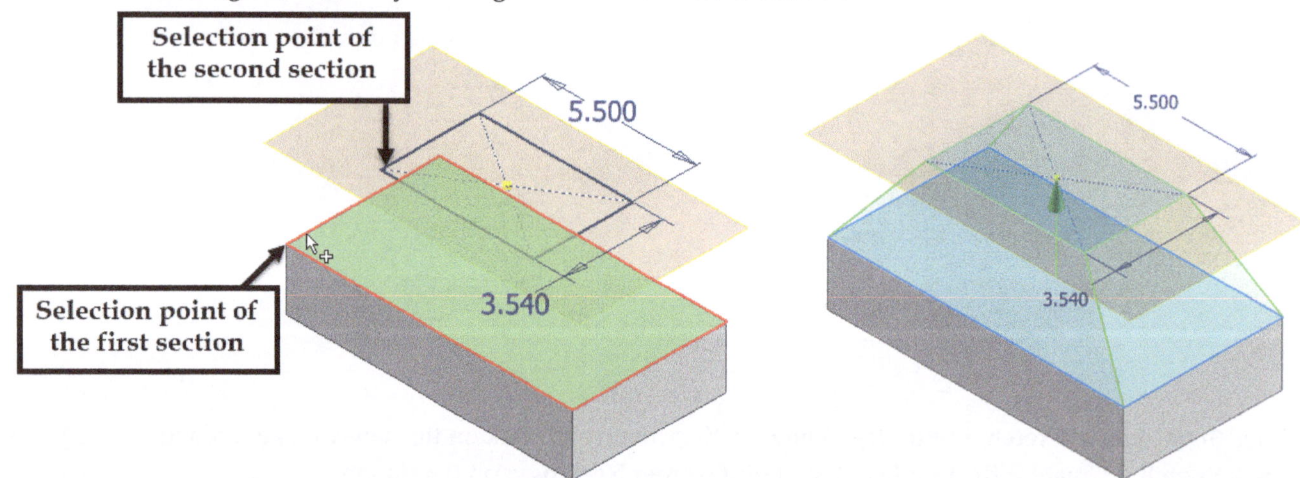

22. On the **Loft** dialog, click the **Conditions** tab.
23. Set the end condition of the first section to **Free Condition**.
24. Set the end condition of the second section to **Direction Condition**.
25. Set the **Weight** of the second section to 1.
26. Type-in **90** degrees in the **Angle** of the second section. Click **OK** on the **Loft** dialog to create the *Loft* feature.

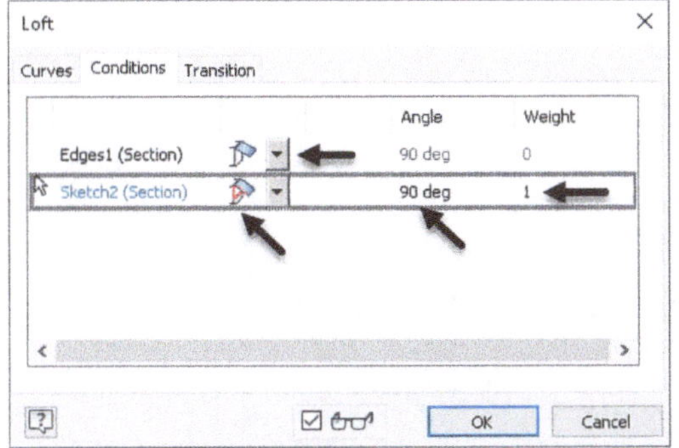

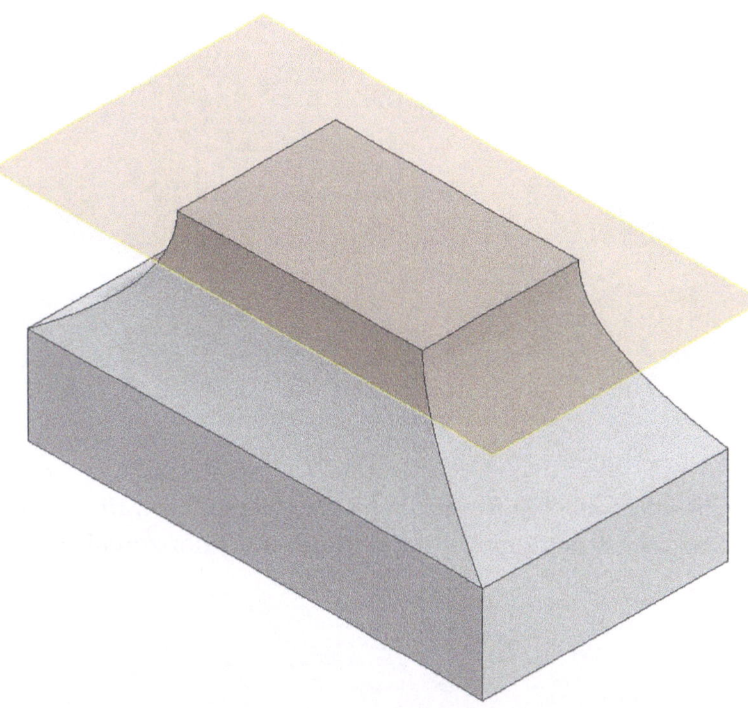

27. Click **3D Model > Sketch > Start 2D Sketch** on the ribbon, and then select the top face of the loft feature.
28. Click **Sketch > Create > Circle** drop-down **> Ellipse** on the ribbon.
29. Click in the graphics window to specify the center point of the ellipse.
30. Move the mouse pointer vertically upward and notice the **Vertical Constraint** glyph. Now, click to specify the first axis of the ellipse.
31. Move the pointer horizontally toward the right click to create the second axis of the ellipse.

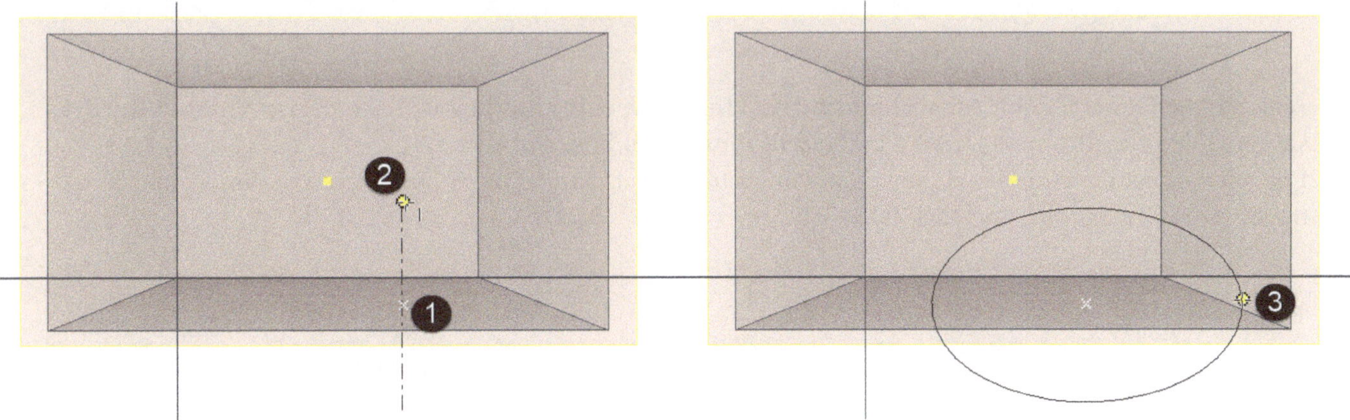

32. Click the **Sketch > Constrain > Vertical Constraint** icon and select the center point of the ellipse.
33. Select the center point of the rectangular edge, as shown.

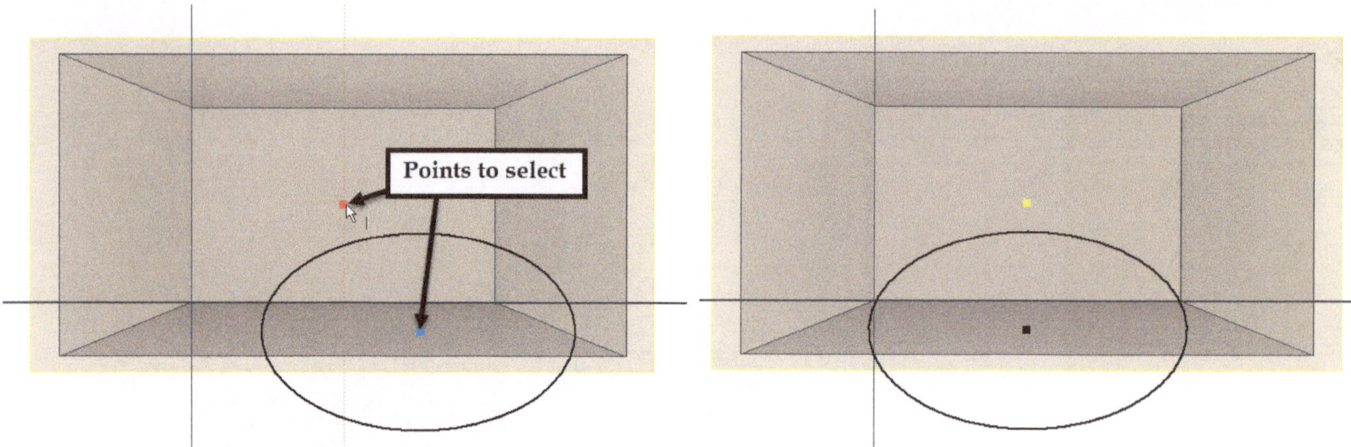

34. Click the **Sketch > Constrain > Coincident Constraint** icon and select the center point of the ellipse.
35. Select the center point of the ellipse and the horizontal edge of the model, as shown.

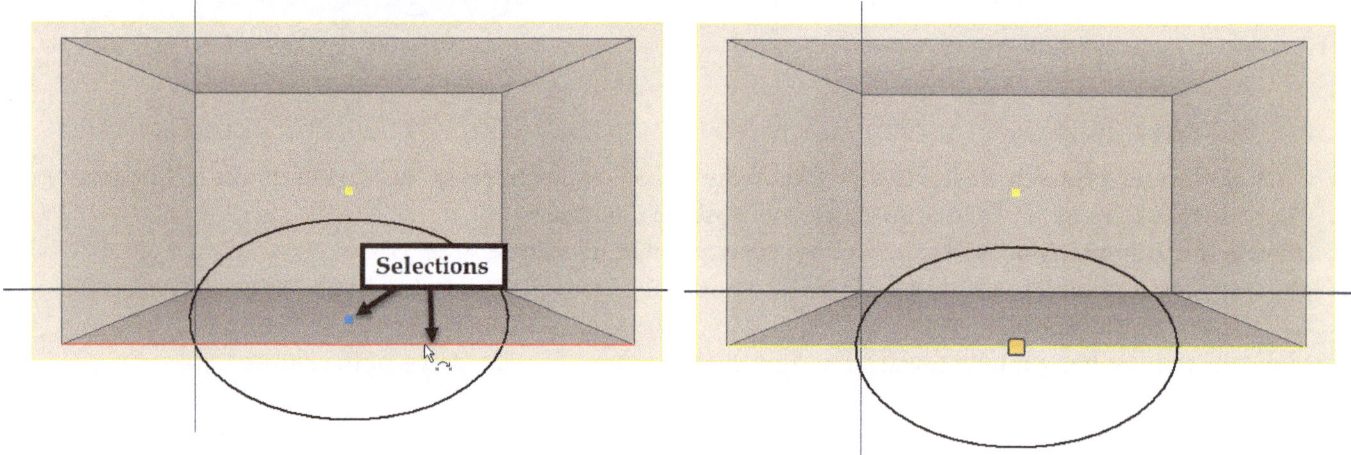

36. Activate the **General Dimension** command and select the ellipse and move the mouse pointer upward, as shown. Place the dimension, type **3** in the **Edit dimension** box, and click **OK**.
37. Likewise, select the ellipse and move the pointer towards the right, as shown. Place the dimension, type **0.9** in the **Edit dimension** box, and click **OK**.

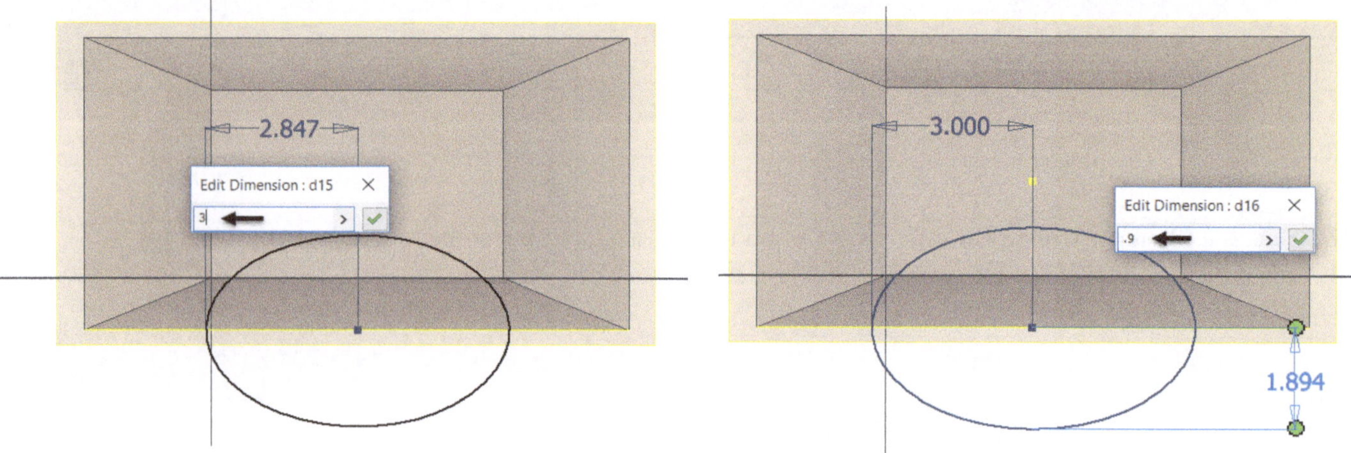

38. Click **Finish Sketch** on the ribbon.

39. Click **3D Model > Create > Extrude** on the ribbon and select the ellipse.
40. On the **Extrude Properties** panel, click the **Output > Boolean > Cut** icon.
41. Click the **Through all** icon under the **Behavior** section on the **Extrude Properties** panel. Click **OK** to create the extruded cut feature.

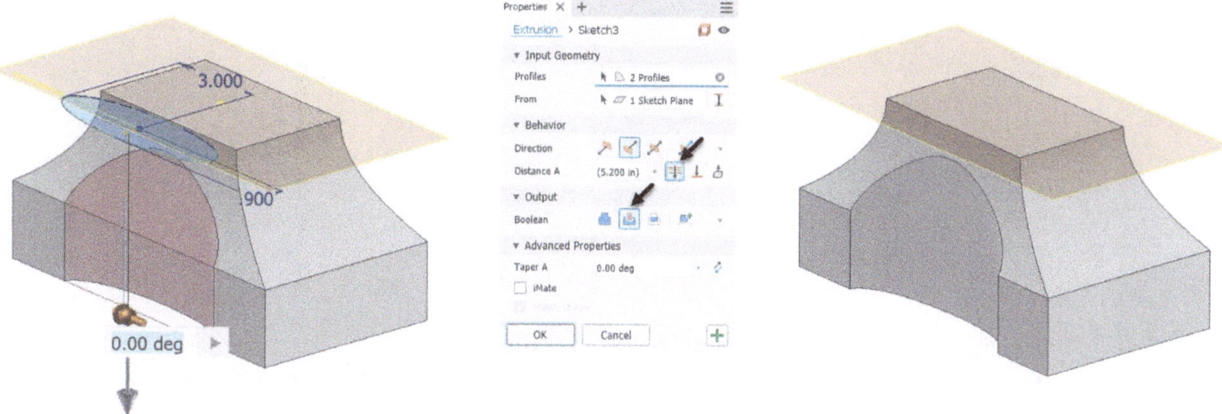

42. On the ribbon, click **3D Model > Pattern > Mirror** ; the **Mirror** dialog appears on the screen.
43. On the dialog, click the **Features** button and select the *Extruded cut* feature from the **Model** window.
44. Next, click the **Mirror Plane** button and select the **Origin XY Plane** icon on the dialog. Click **OK** to create the *Mirror* feature.

45. Click **3D Model > Work Features > Plane** drop-down **> Offset from Plane** on the ribbon and click on the top face of the loft feature. Type-in **4.8** in the **distance** box and click **OK**.

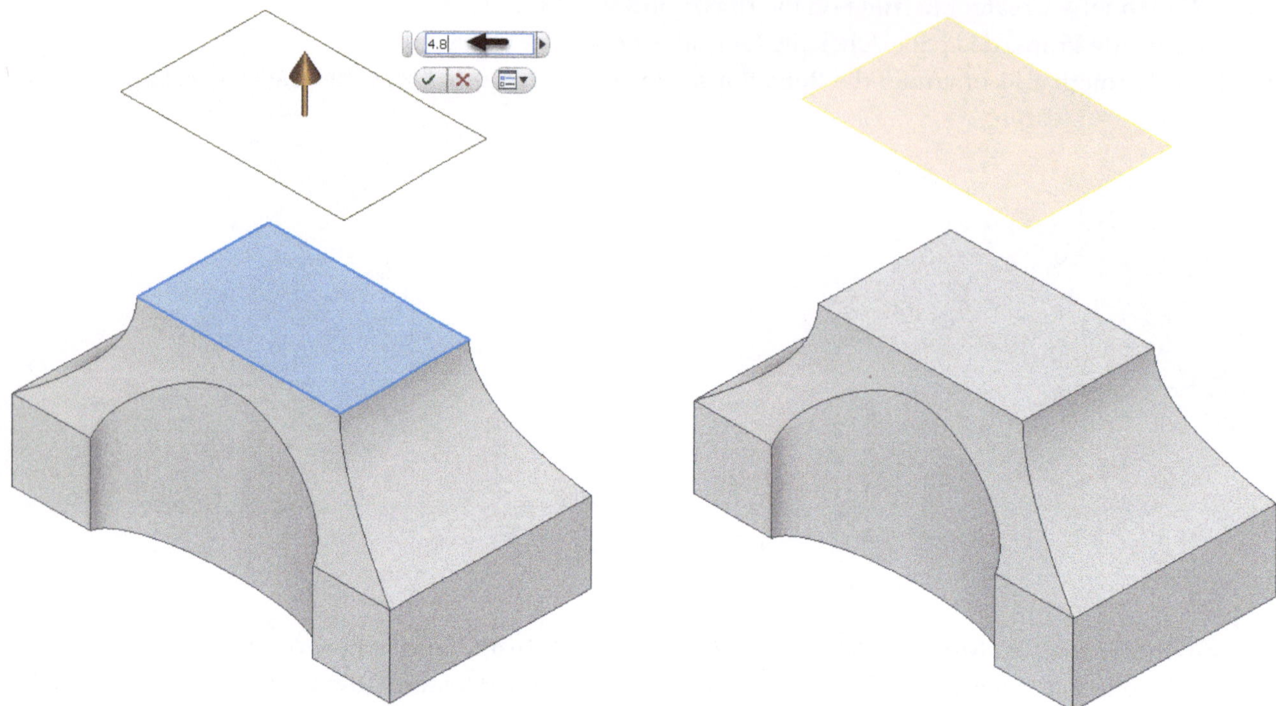

46. Click **3D Model > Sketch > Start 2D Sketch** on the ribbon and click on the newly created work plane.
47. Create a rectangle and add dimensions to it, as shown.

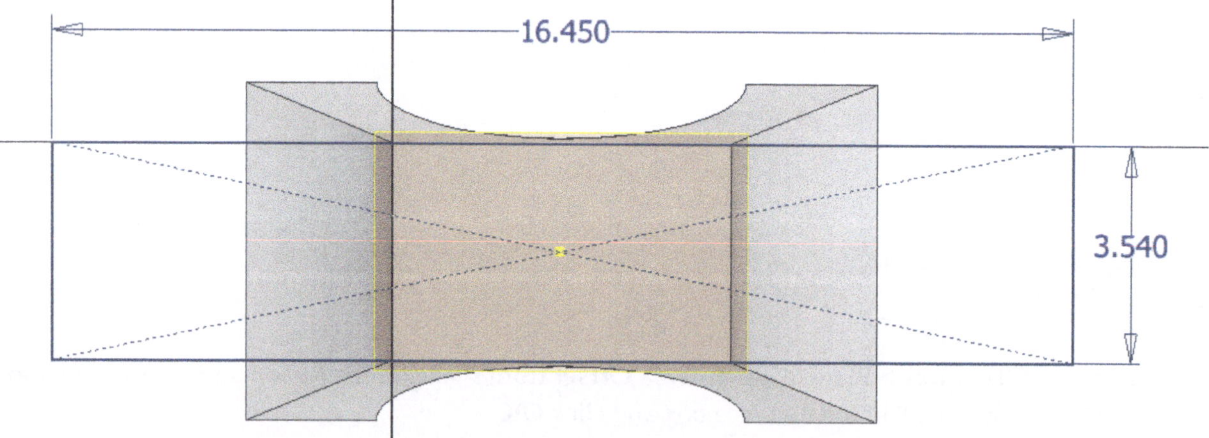

48. Click **Finish Sketch** on the ribbon.
49. Click **3D Model > Work Features > Plane** drop-down **> Parallel to Plane through point** on the ribbon. Next, expand the **Origin** folder in the **Model** window and select the **XY Plane**.
50. Click on the top corner of the loft feature, as shown.
51. Likewise, create another parallel plane at the backside.

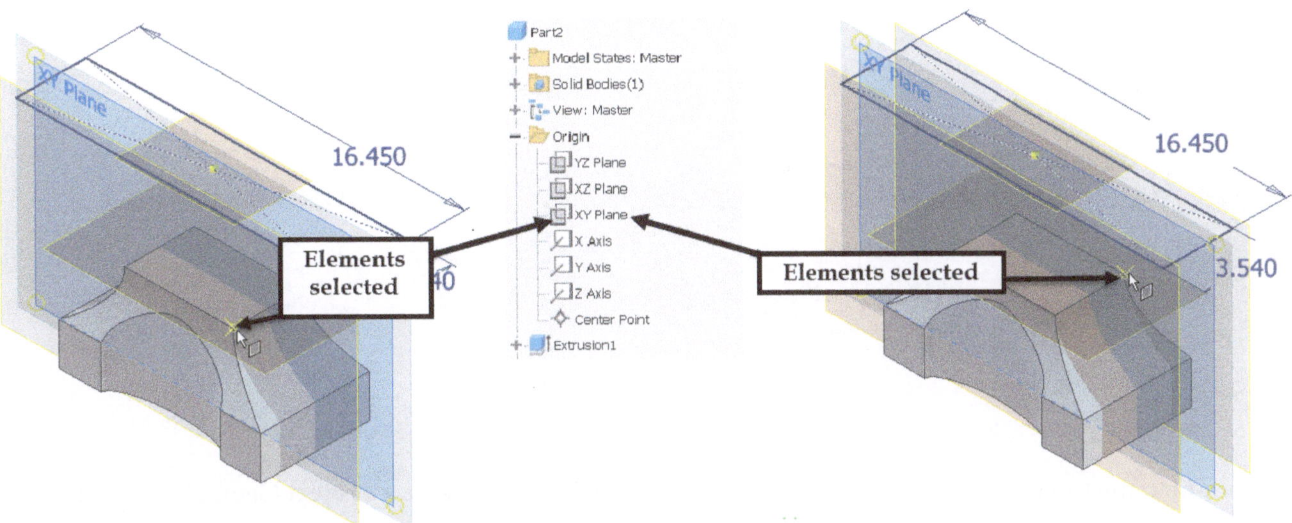

52. Click **3D Model > Sketch > Start 2D Sketch** on the ribbon and select the plane created on the front side.

53. Click **Sketch > Create > Project Geometry** on the ribbon and click the edge, as shown. Right-click and select **OK**.

54. Click **Sketch > Create > Line** drop-down **> Spline Interpolation** on the ribbon, as shown. Next, right-click and select **Create**.

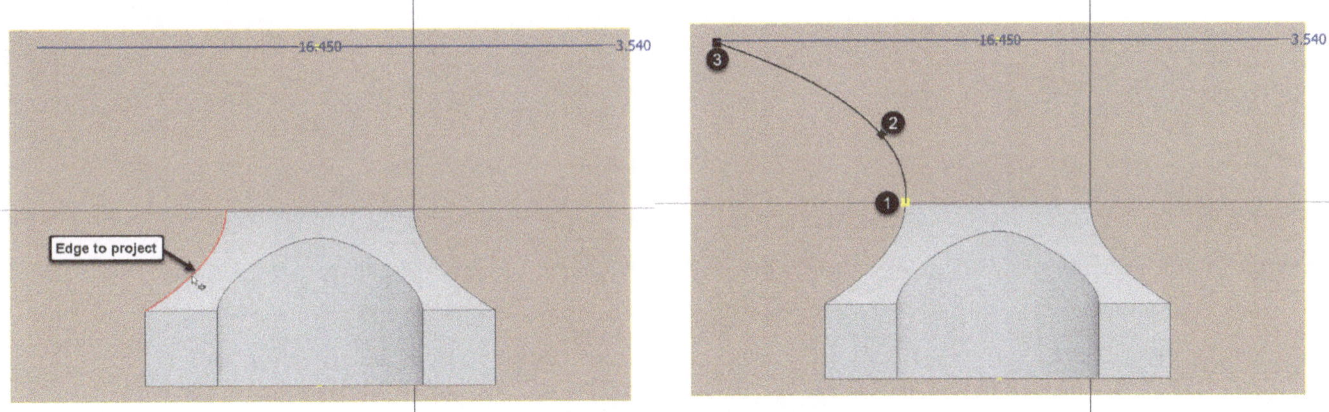

55. Click the **Sketch** tab **> Constrain** panel **> Tangent** icon on the ribbon.

56. Select the projected edge and the spline; the spline will become tangent to the projected edge. Right-click and select **OK**.

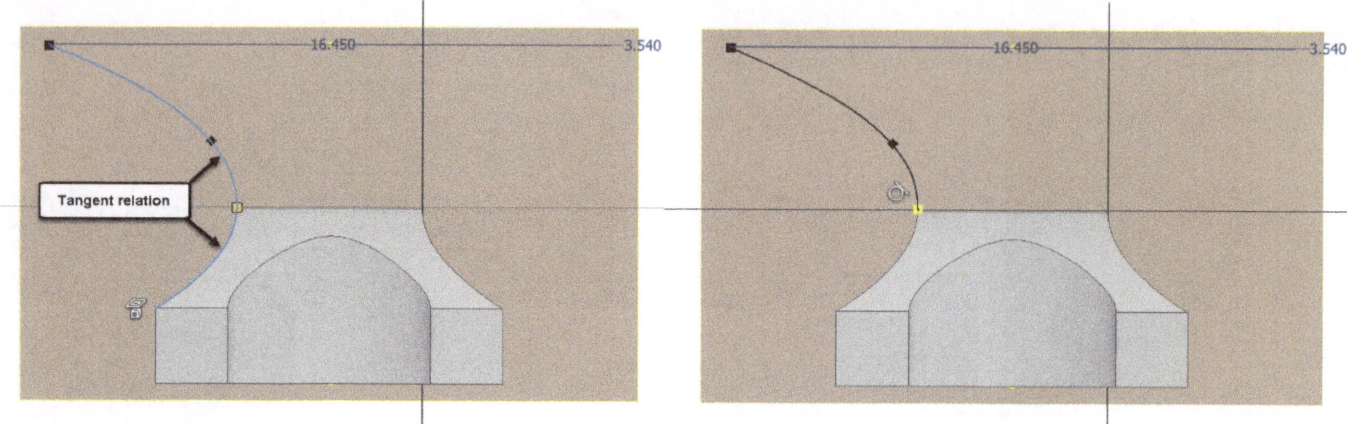

57. Zoom-in to the top rectangular sketch and select it. Click **Sketch > Create > Project Geometry** on the ribbon to project the line, as shown.
58. Click **Sketch > Constrain > Coincident Constraint** on the ribbon. Next, select the endpoint of the projected line and the top-end point of the spline.

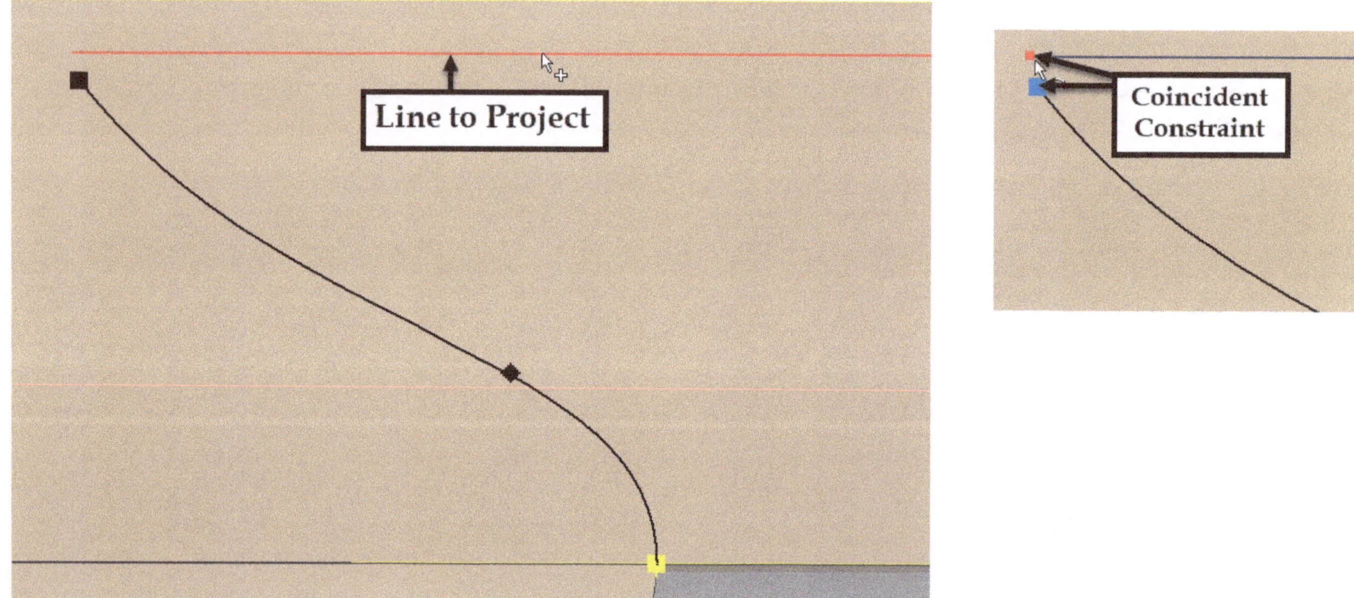

59. On the ribbon, click **Sketch > Constrain > Dimension** and then apply the linear dimensions to the middle point of the spline, as shown.

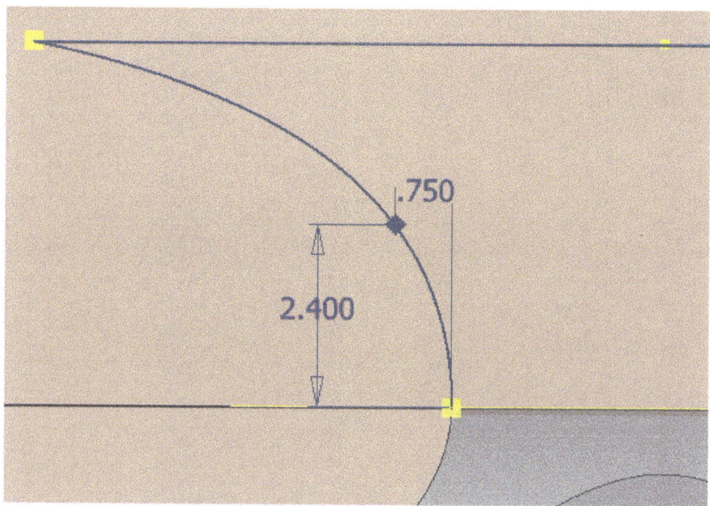

60. Click **Finish Sketch** on the ribbon.
61. Click **3D Model > Sketch > Start 2D Sketch** on the ribbon and select the plane created on the front side.
62. Likewise, convert the right edge, and then draw a spline connected to it.

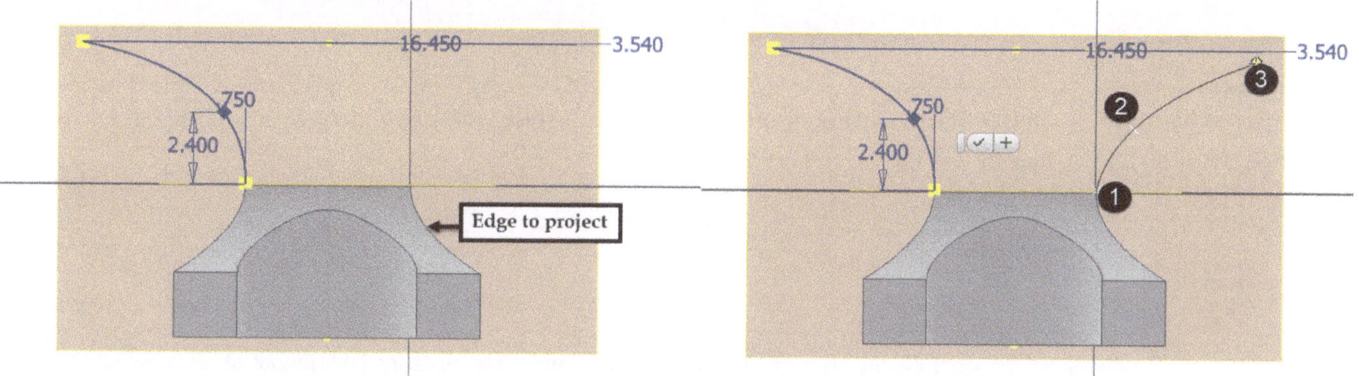

63. Next, apply the **Tangent** constraint between the converted entity and the spline. In addition to that, create the **Coincident** constraint between the endpoint of the spline and the endpoint of the projected line.

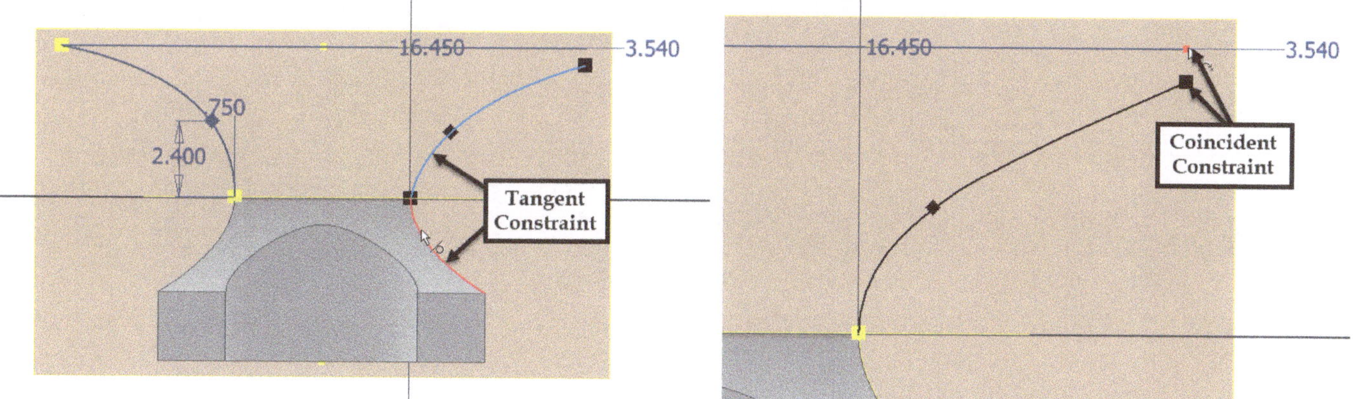

64. Apply linear dimensions to the middle point of the spline, as shown. Click **Finish Sketch** on the ribbon.

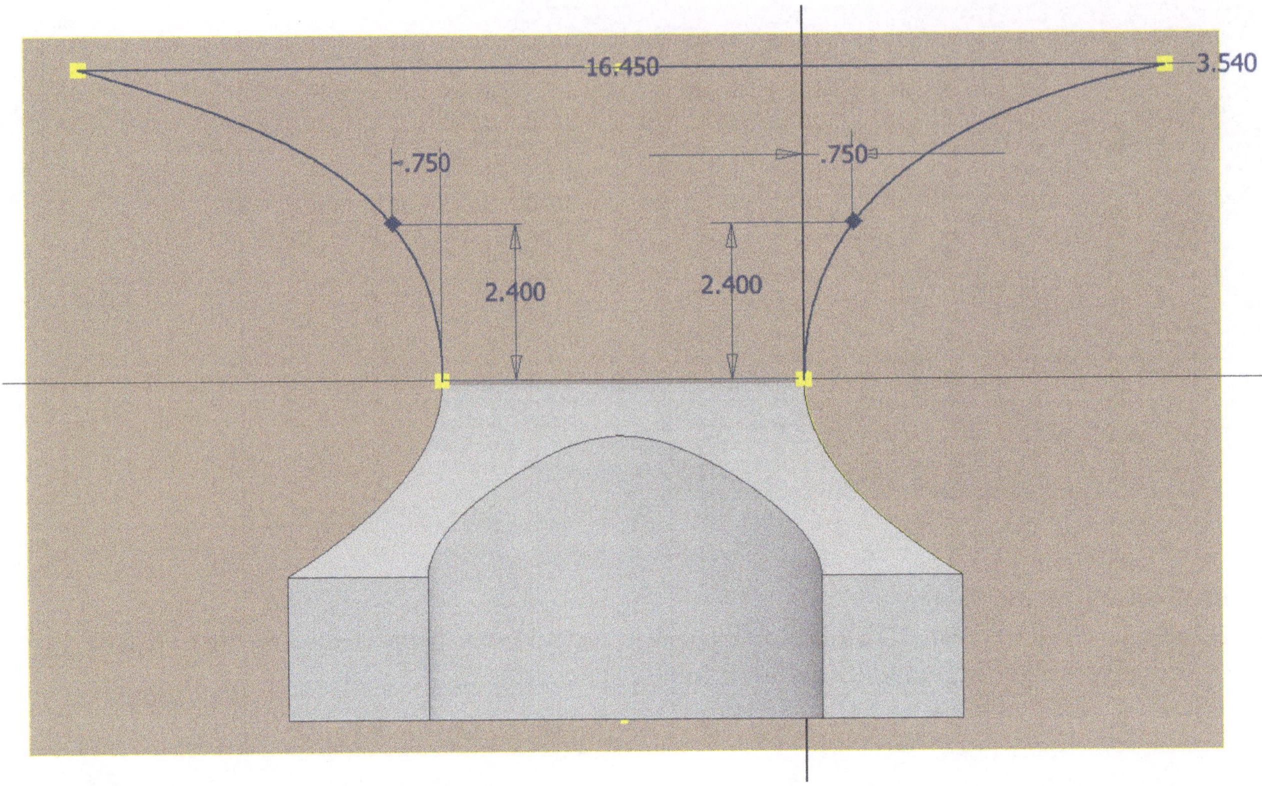

65. Click **3D Model > Sketch > Start 2D Sketch** on the ribbon and select the plane displayed on the backside.
66. Click the top right corner of the ViewCube, as shown.

67. Click **Sketch > Create > Project Geometry** on the ribbon and select the entities of the last sketch, as shown. Click **Finish Sketch** on the ribbon.

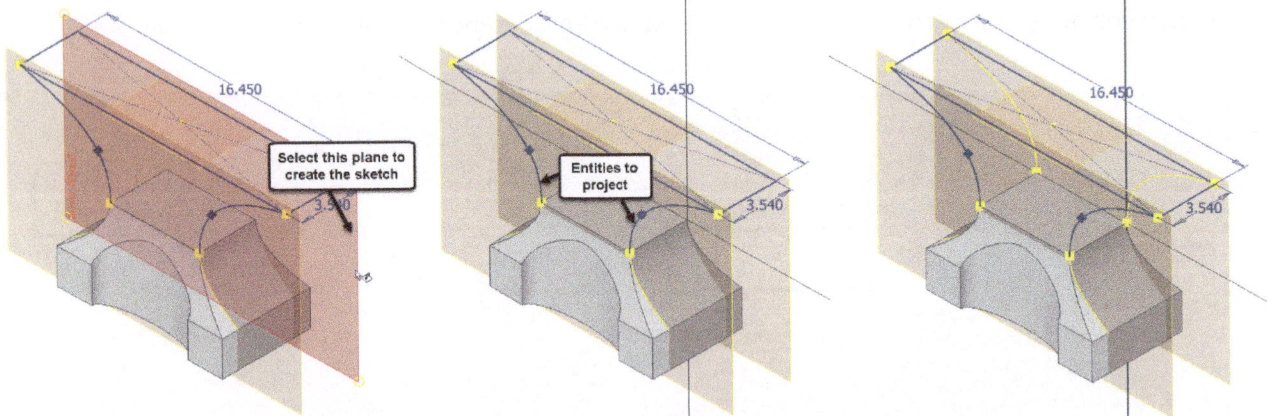

68. Click **3D Model > Create > Loft** on the ribbon; the **Loft** dialog appears on the screen.
69. On the dialog, click **Curves > Sections > Click to add** and select the first section by clicking on the top face of the model at the location, as shown.
70. Select the second section by clicking on the corner point of the rectangle, as shown.

71. On the **Loft** dialog, click in the **Rails** selection box and select the first spline.

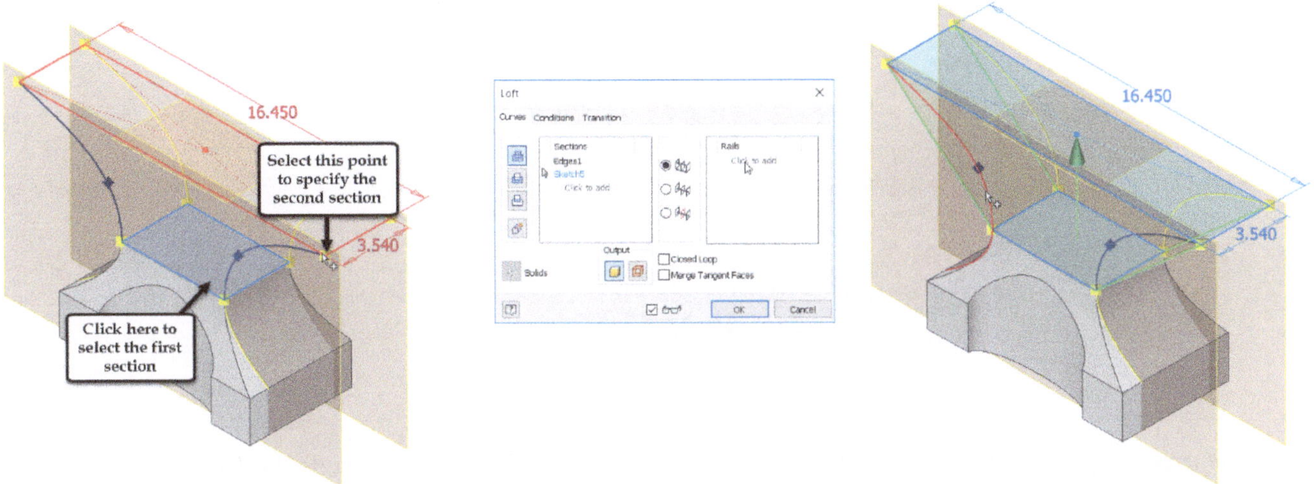

72. Likewise, select the other splines and check the **Merge Tangent Faces** option at the bottom of the dialog.
73. Make sure that the **Closed Loop** option is unchecked,
74. Click **OK** on the **Loft** dialog to create the *Loft* feature.

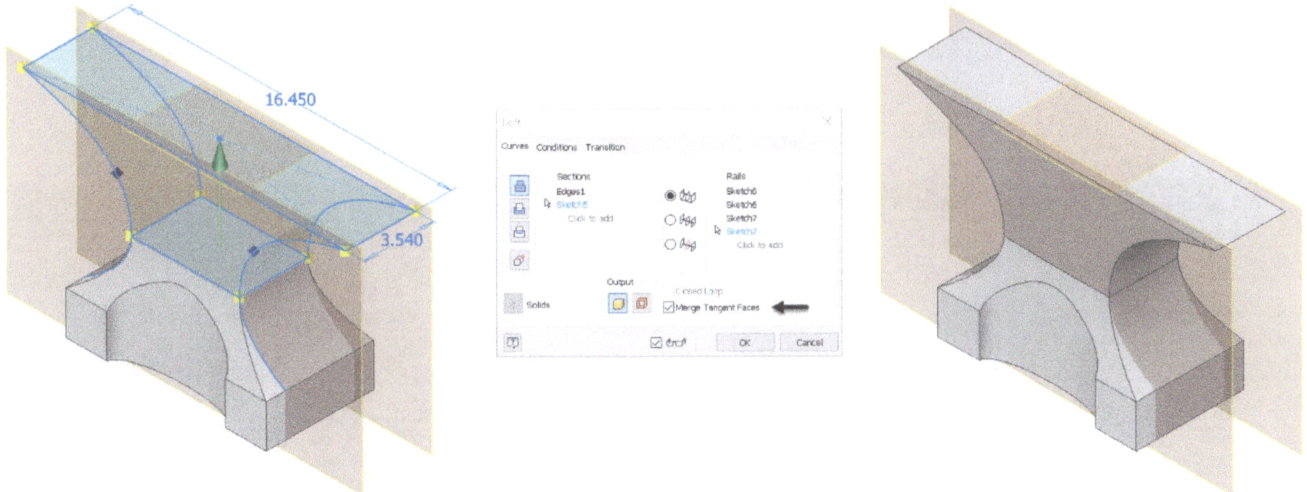

75. Click **Sketch > Create > Rectangle Two Point** on the ribbon and click on the top face of the model.
76. Specify the two corner points of the rectangle, as shown.
77. On the ribbon, click **Sketch > Constrain > Collinear Constraint**. Next, select the left vertical line of the rectangle.
78. Select the vertical edge of the model, as shown.
79. Likewise, create two more Collinear Constraints, as shown.

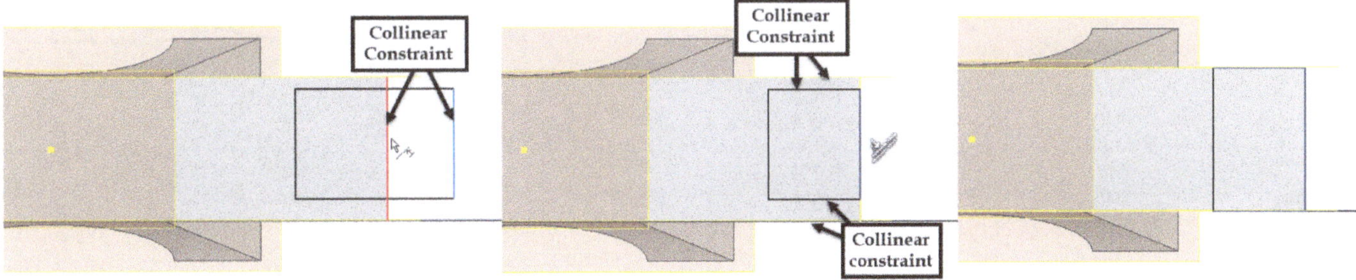

80. Activate the **Dimension** command and apply the dimension to the rectangle, as shown.
81. Click **Finish Sketch** on the ribbon.

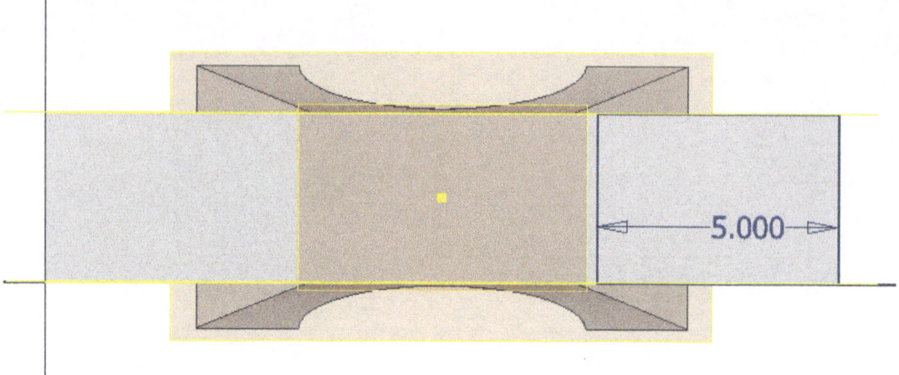

82. Activate the **Extrude** command (on the ribbon, click **3D Model > Create > Extrude**) and select the sketch (if not already selected).
83. On the **Extrude Properties** panel, click the **Cut** icon under the **Output** section.
84. Type-in 3.5 in the **Distance A** box and click **OK** to create the extruded cut feature.

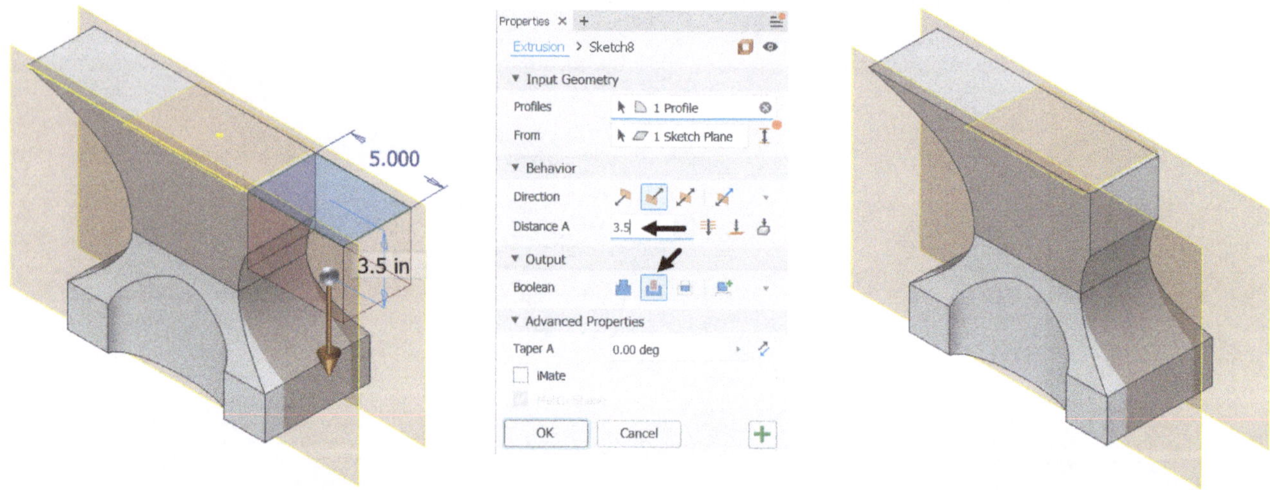

85. On the ribbon, click **Sketch > Create > Rectangle Two point**, and then click on the top face of the model.
86. On the ribbon, click **Sketch > Create > Rectangle Two point**.
87. Specify the first and second corners of the rectangle, as shown.
88. Apply the Collinear constraints, as shown. Next, click **Finish Sketch**.

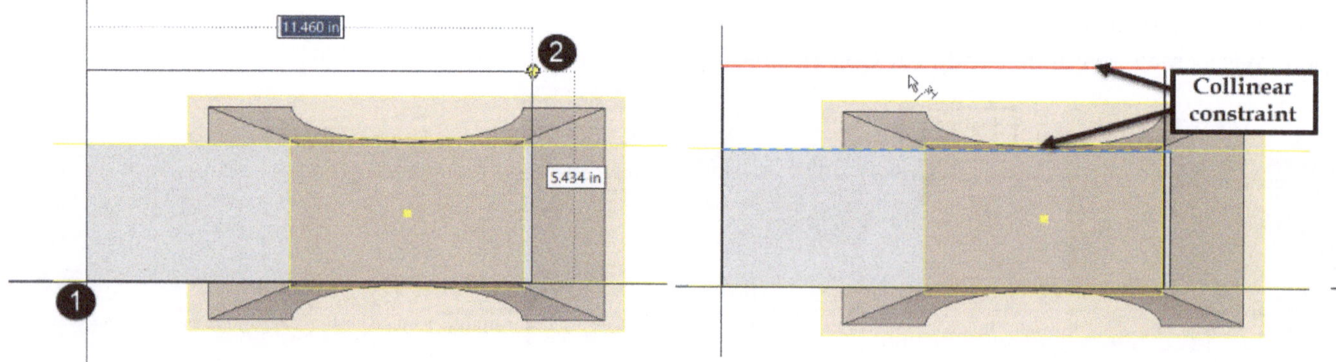

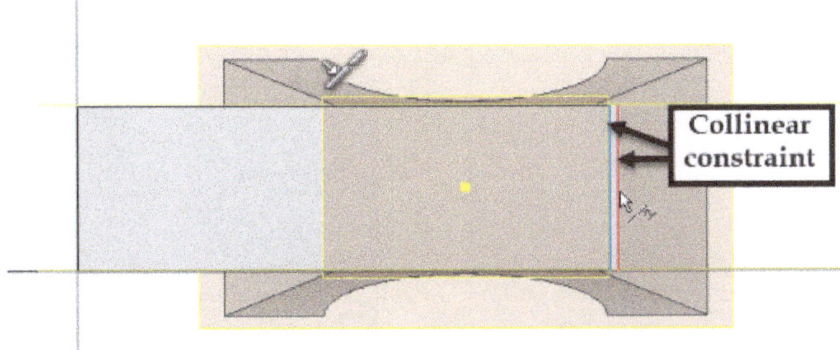

89. Click **3D Model > Create > Extrude** command on the ribbon, and select the rectangular sketch.
90. On the **Extrude Properties** panel, type 1 in the **Distance A** box, and click **OK**.

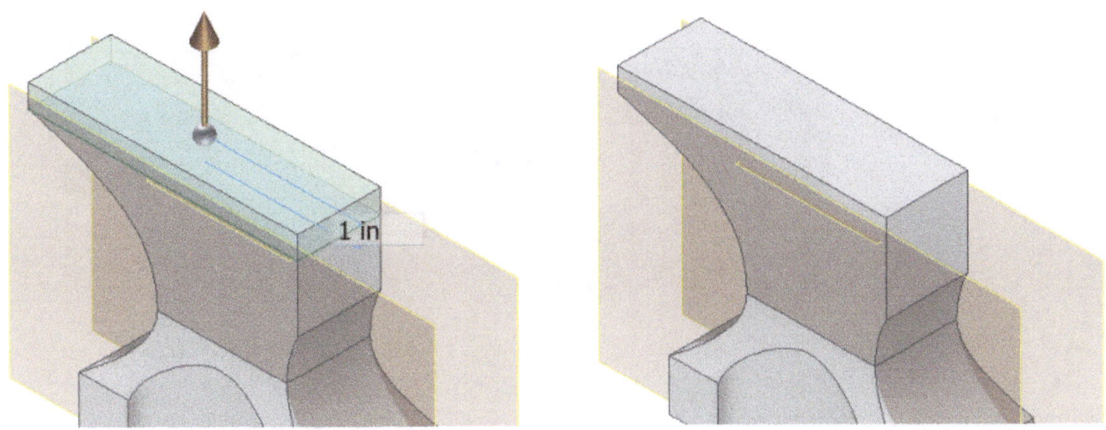

91. In the **Model** window, right-click on the **Extrusion4** feature and select **Suppress Features**.

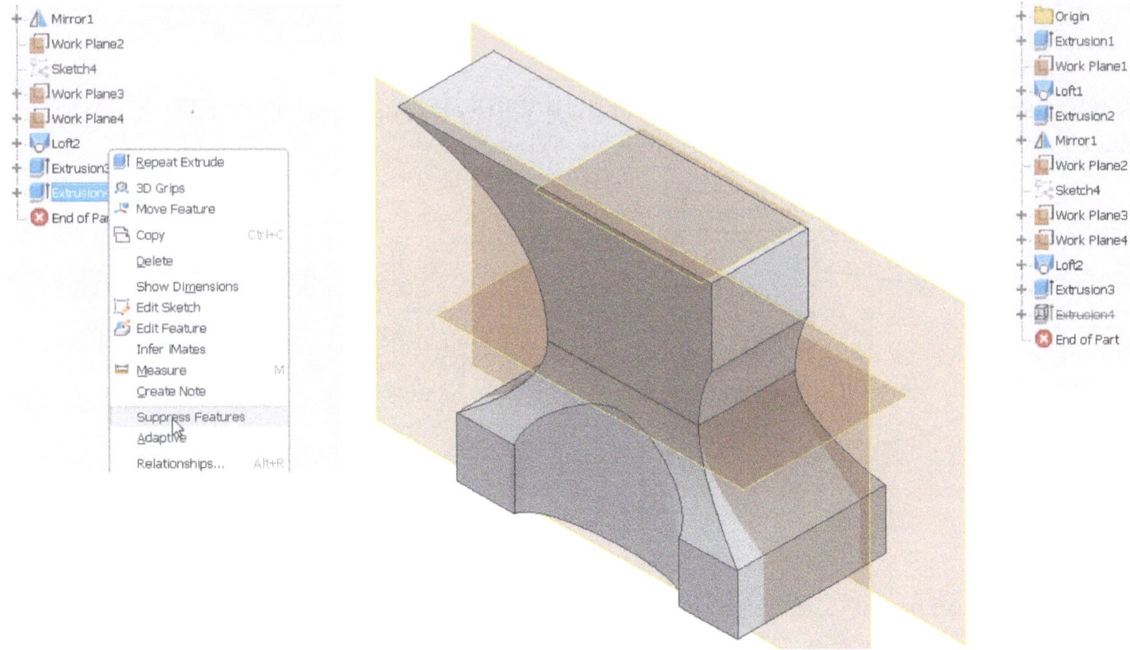

92. Click **Sketch > Circle > Ellipse** on the ribbon and click on the right face, as shown.

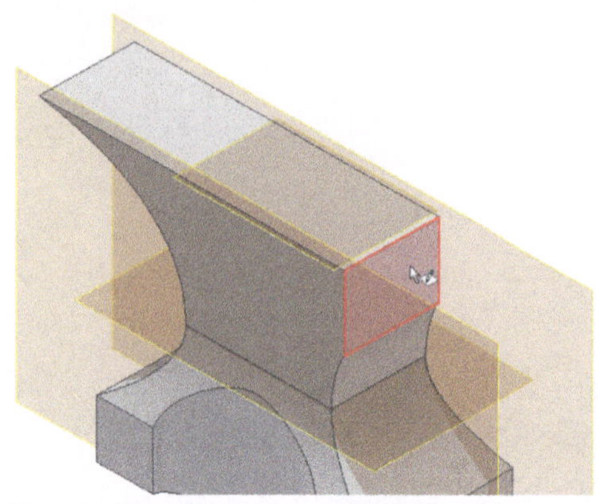

93. Create the ellipse by specifying it's center and axis points, as shown.

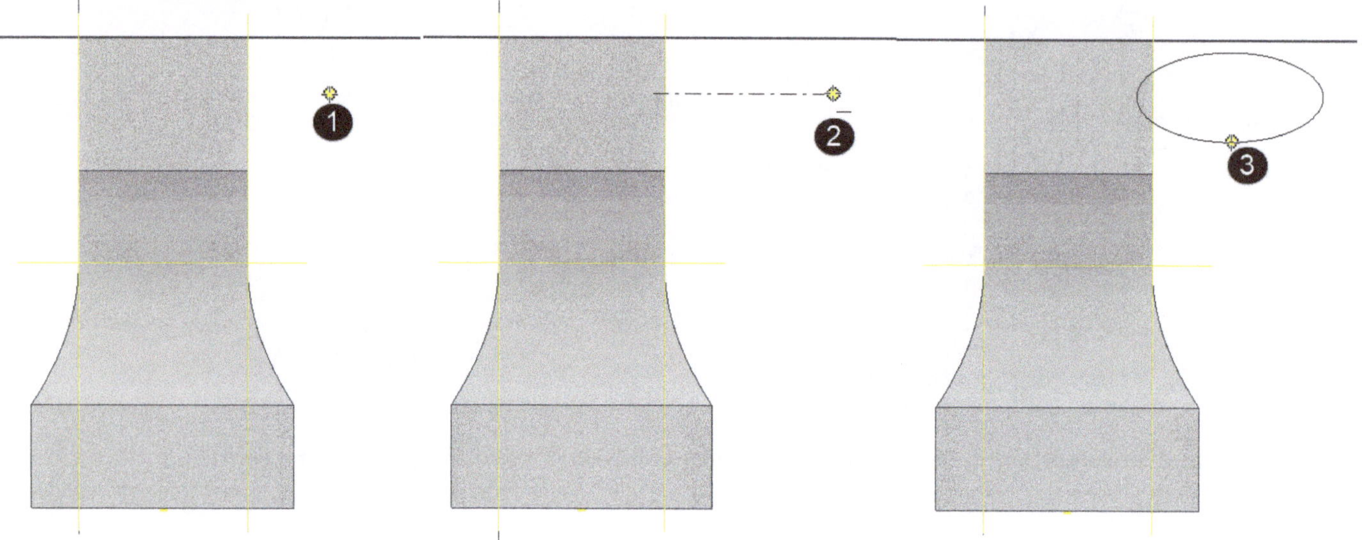

94. Apply the **Vertical Constraint** (by clicking **Sketch > Constrain > Vertical Constraint** on the ribbon) to the center point of the ellipse and the midpoint of the top edge, as shown.

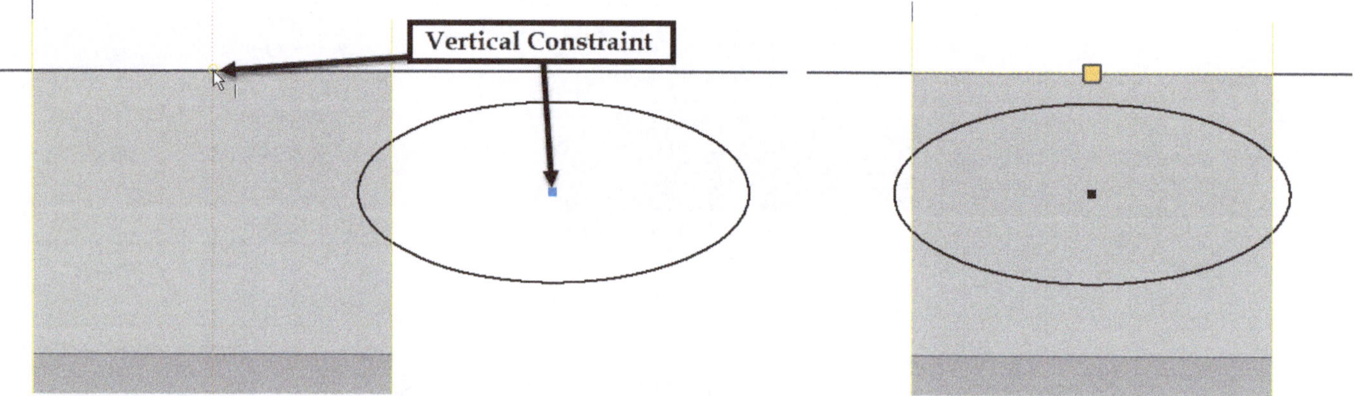

95. Click **Sketch > Constrain > Horizontal Constraint** on the ribbon and select the center point of the ellipse and the midpoint of the right edge, as shown.

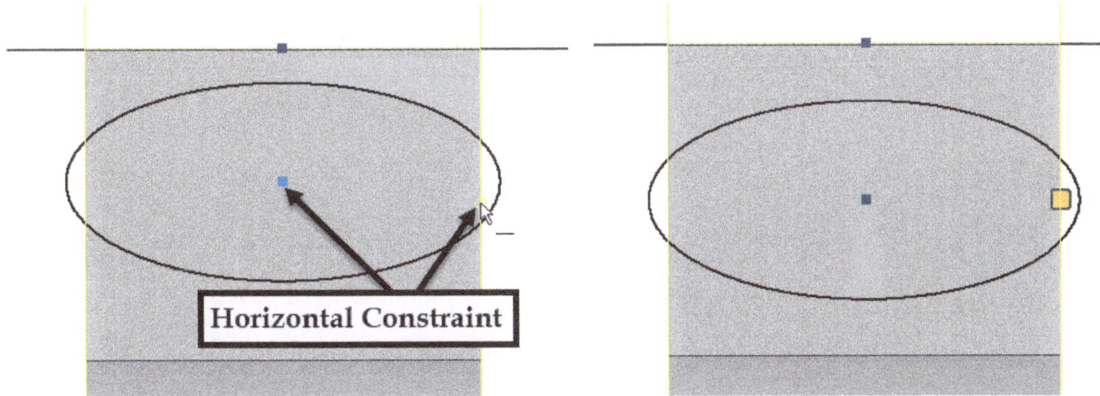

96. Apply the **Coincident Constraint** between the ellipse and midpoint of the top horizontal edge, as shown.

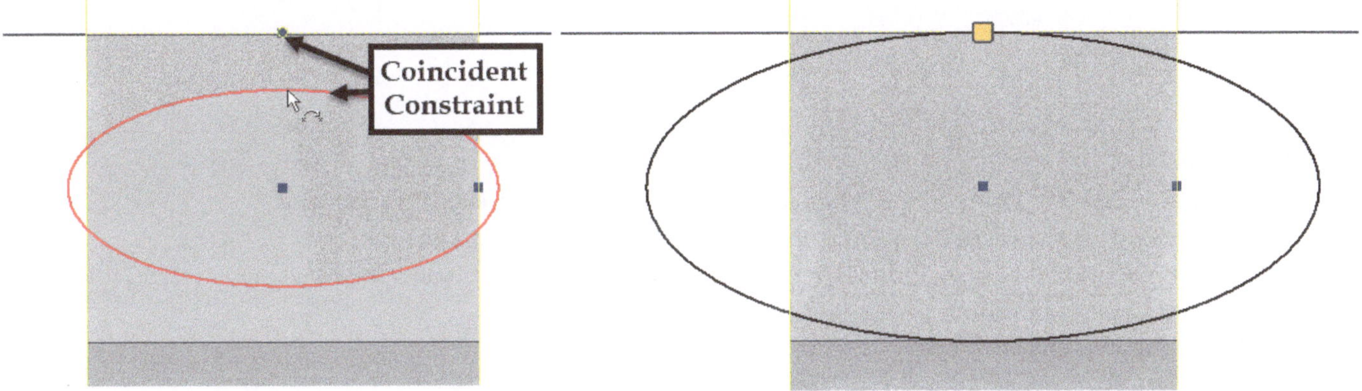

97. Apply the **Coincident Constraint** between the ellipse and the midpoint of the right vertical edge. Next, right-click and then click **OK**.

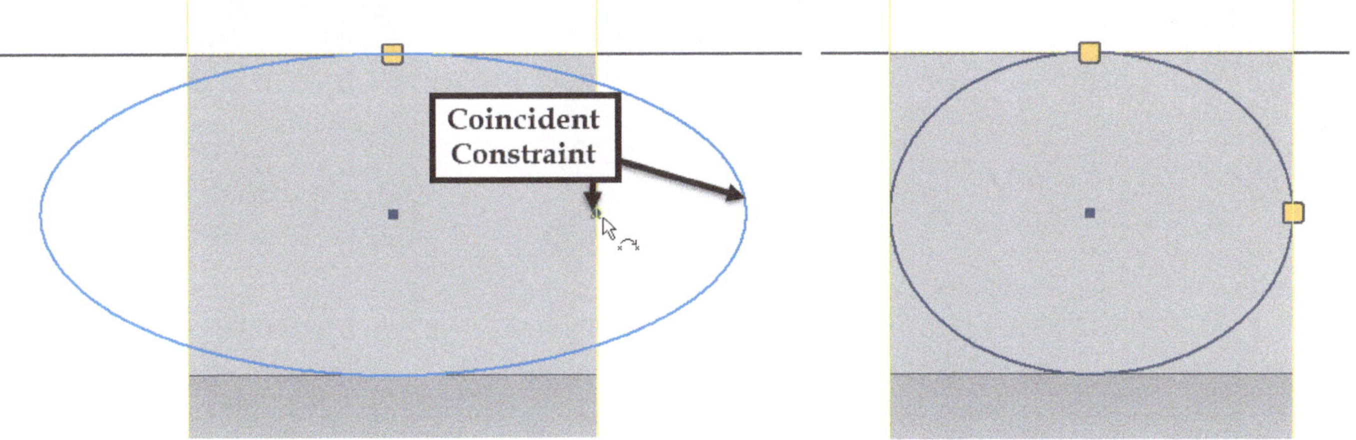

98. Click **Finish Sketch** on the ribbon.
99. Create a new plane offset to the right flat face. The offset distance is 8.22.

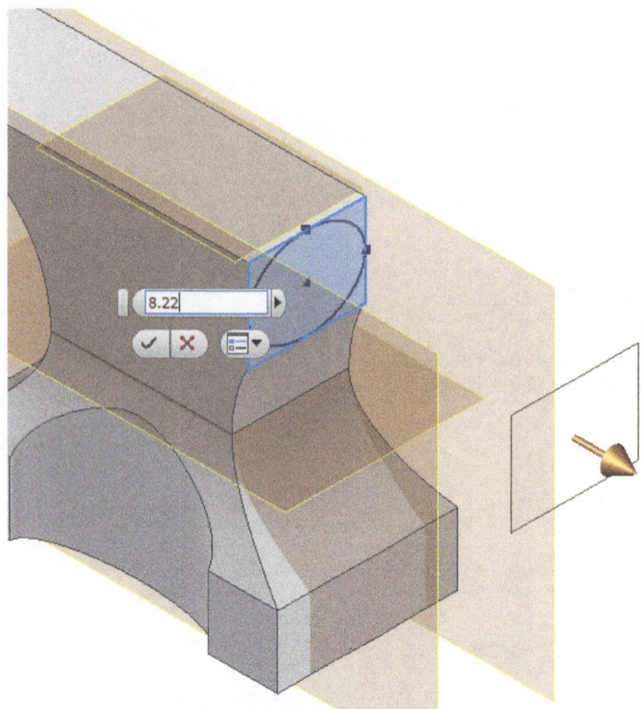

100.Click **Sketch > Create > Point** on the ribbon and click on the newly created plane.
101.Click to specify the location of the point, and then press Esc to deactivate the tool.
102.Click **Sketch > Constrain > Coincident Constraint** on the ribbon. Next, select the newly created point and the top quadrant point of the ellipse.
103.Click **Finish Sketch** on the ribbon.

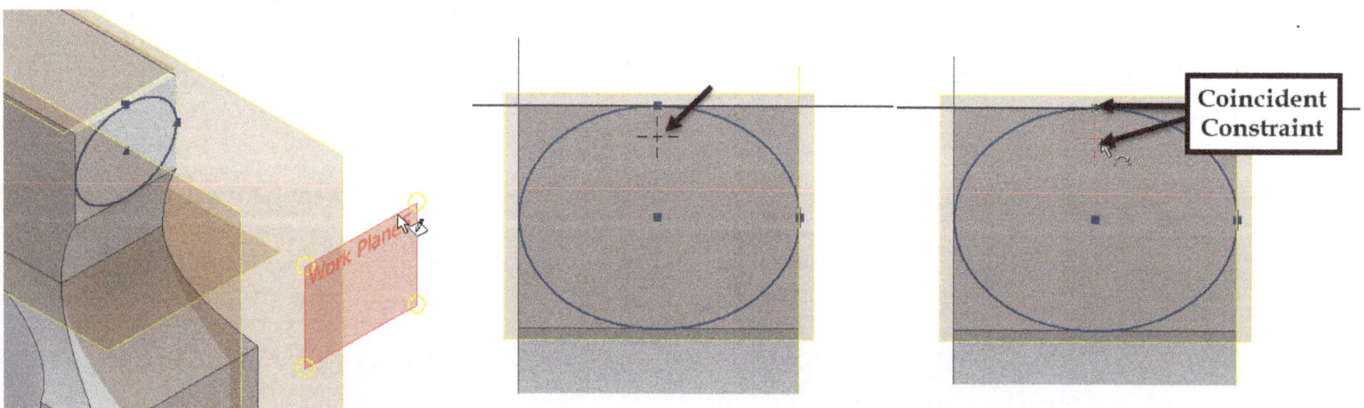

104.Click **3D Model > Sketch > Start 2D Sketch** on the ribbon and click on the XY plane, as shown.

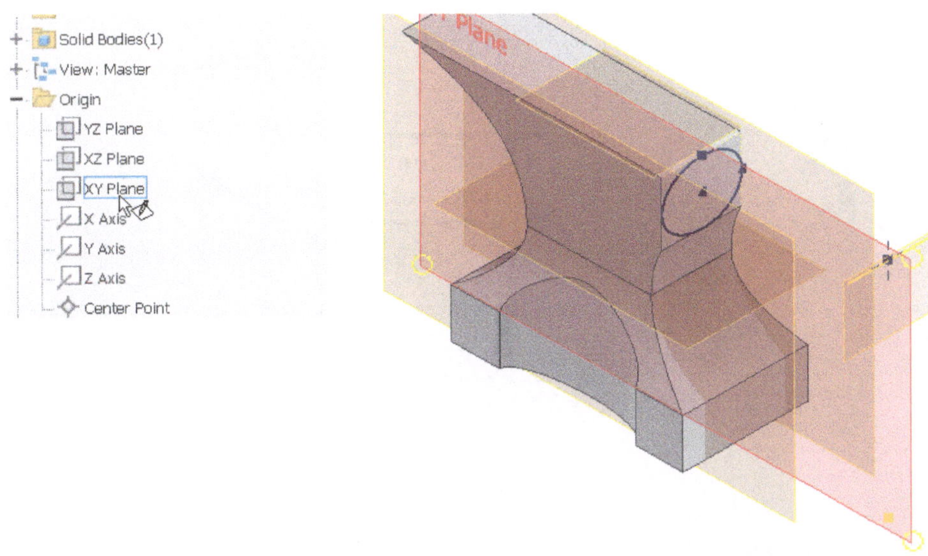

105.Click **Sketch > Create > Line > Spline (interpolation)** on the ribbon.
106.Specify the three points of the spline, as shown. Right-click and select **Create** to create the spline.

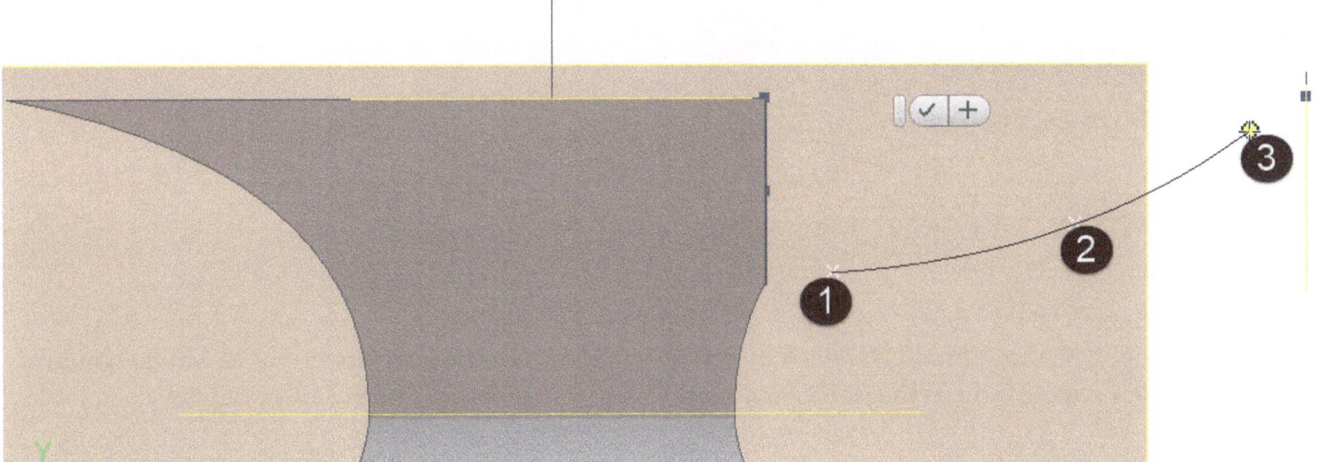

107. On the ribbon, click **Sketch > Create > Project Geometry**. Next, select the point, as shown.

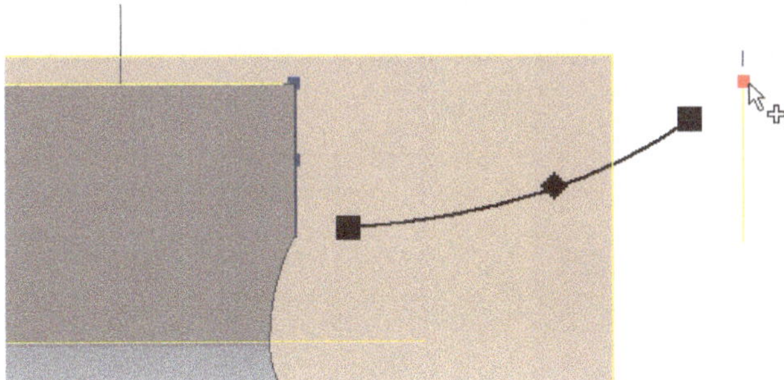

108. Click **Sketch > Constrain > Coincident Constraint** on the ribbon and select the third point of the spline and the projected point.
109. Likewise, apply the coincident constraint to the first point and vertex, as shown. Press Esc to deactivate the tool.

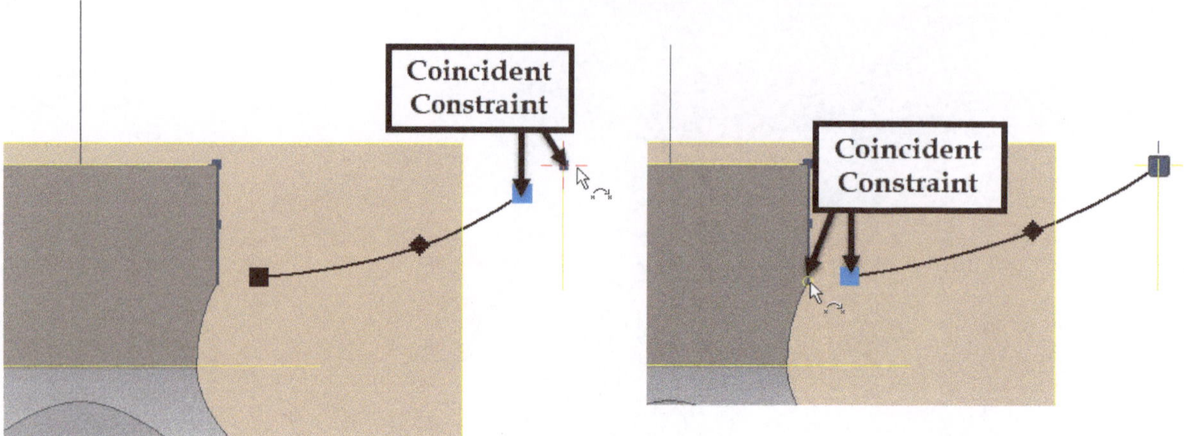

110. Activate the **Dimension** command (click **Sketch > Constrain > Dimension** on the ribbon) and apply dimensions to the midpoint of the spline, as shown.

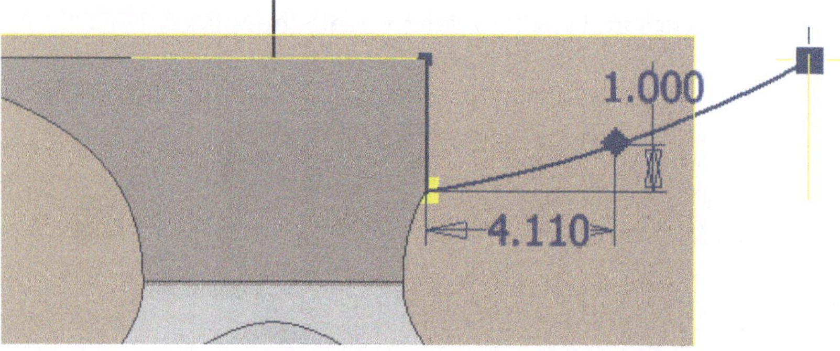

111. Click **Finish Sketch** on the ribbon.
112. Click **3D Model > Sketch > Start 2D Sketch** on the ribbon and select the **XY** plane from the **Model** window.
113. Click **Sketch > Create > Line** on the ribbon and create a horizontal line, as shown. Next, right-click and select **OK**.
114. On the ribbon, click **Sketch > Create > Project Geometry**. Next, select the point, as shown.

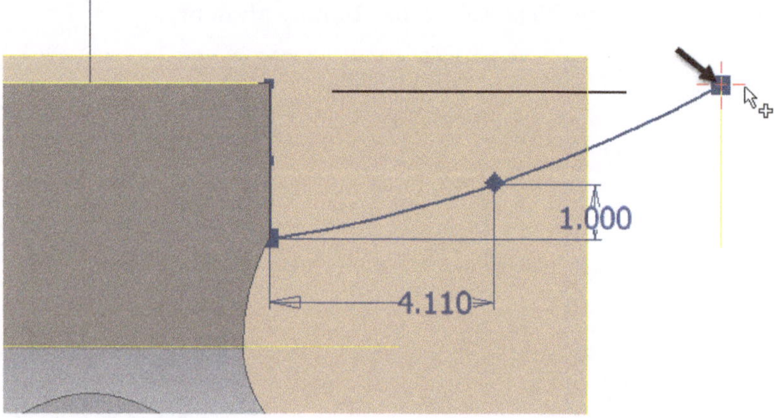

115. Apply the **Coincident Constraint** between the endpoint of the line and the third point of the spline.
116. Apply the **Coincident Constraint** between the start point of the line and vertex of the model, as shown

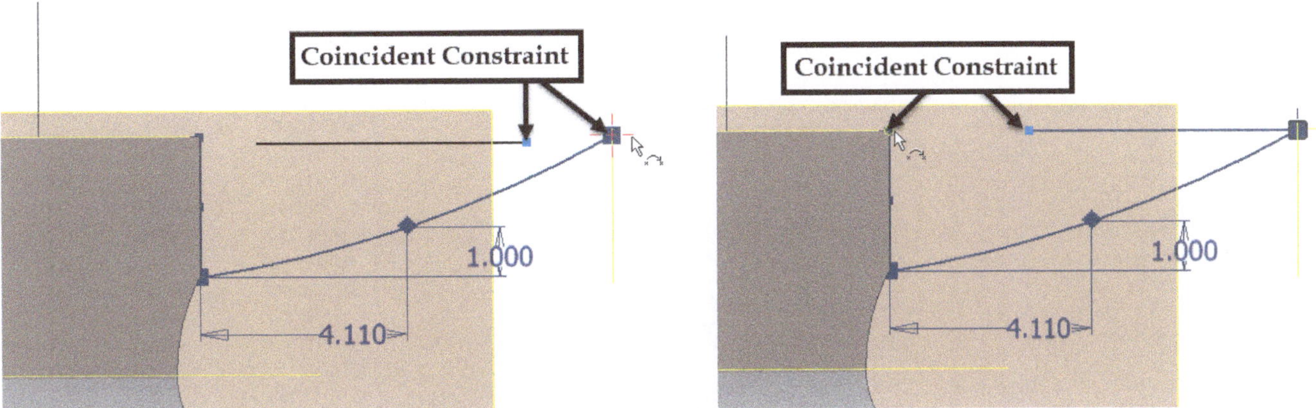

117. Click **Finish Sketch** on the ribbon.
118. Click **3D Model > Create > Loft** on the ribbon. Select the ellipse and the sketch point.
119. On the **Loft** dialog, click in the **Rails** selection box and select the spline (rail1) and line (rail2), as shown. Next, click **OK** to create the loft feature.

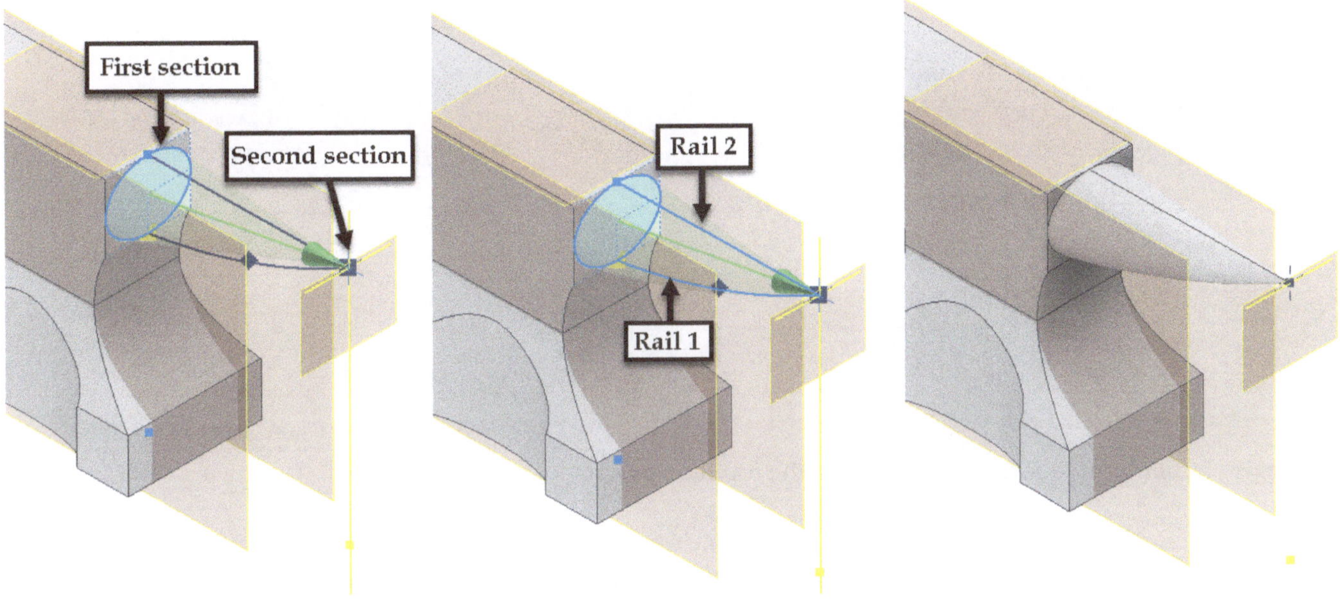

120. In the **Model** window, right-click on the **Extrusion 4 feature** and select **Unsuppress Features**.

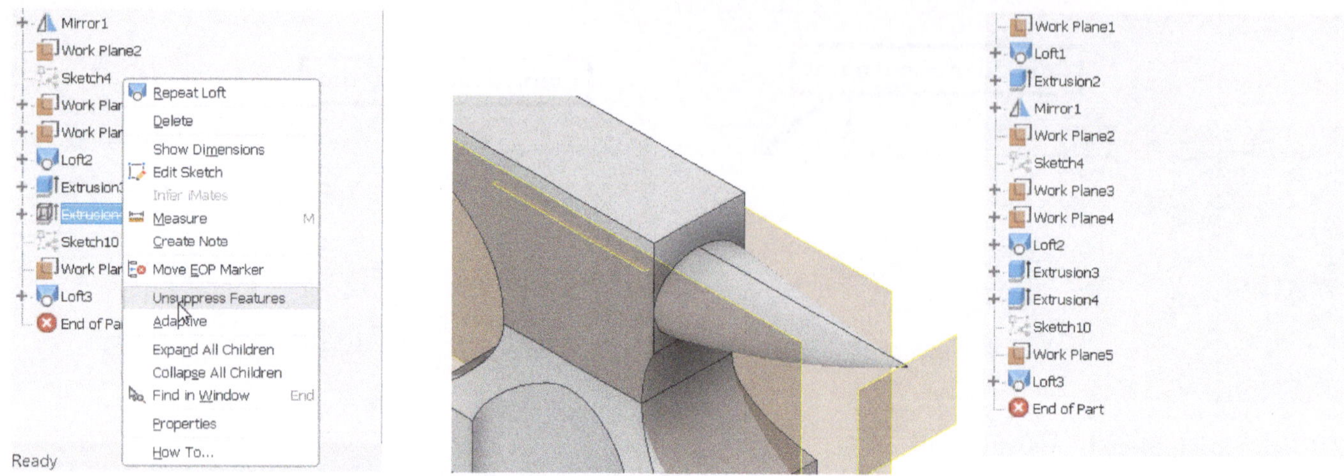

121. Create an extruded cut feature on the side face, as shown.

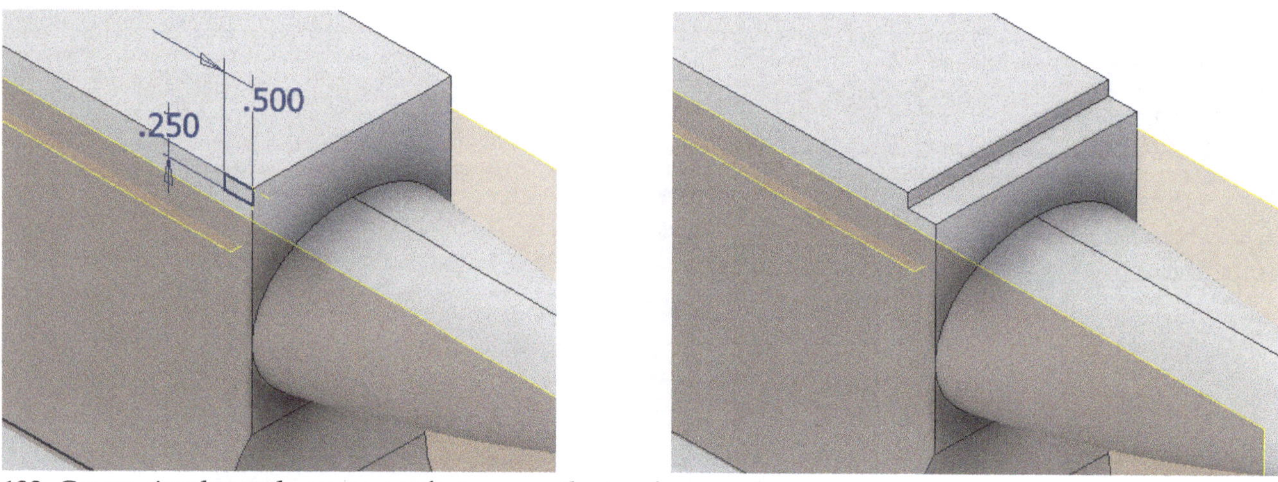

122. Create circular and square-cut features on the top face, as shown.

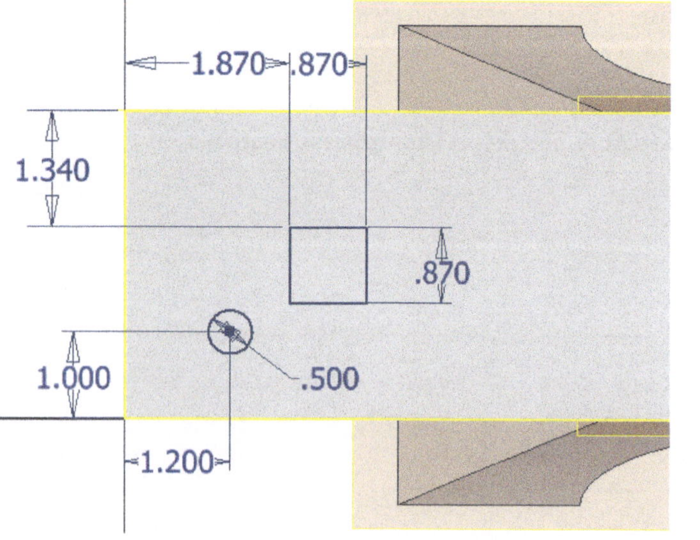

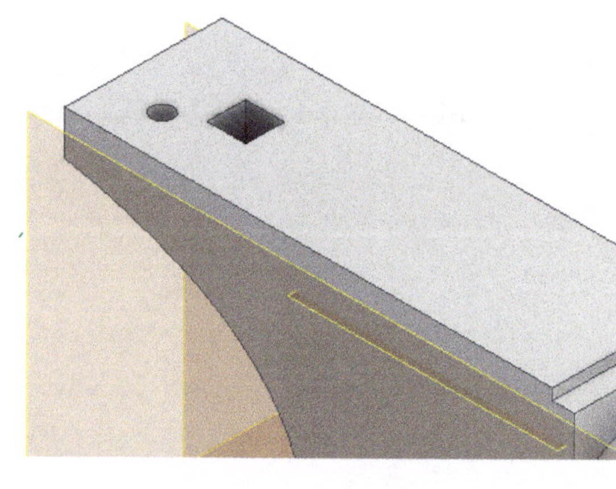

123. Save and close the file.

Questions

1. Describe the procedure to create a *Loft* feature.
2. List any two options in the **Conditions** tab.
3. List the type of elements that can be selected to create a *Loft* feature.
4. What is the use of the **Area Loft** option?

Exercises

Exercise 1

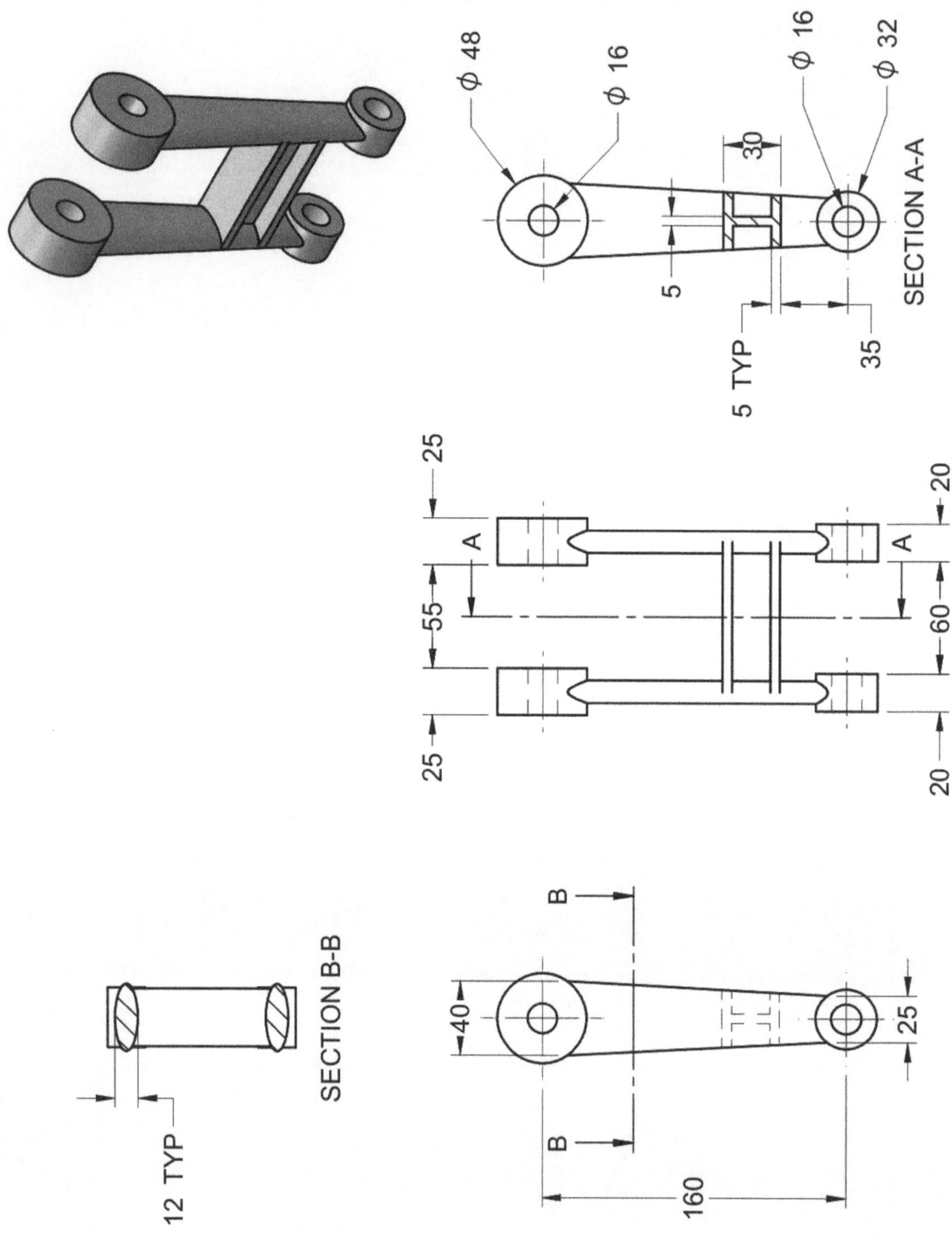

Chapter 8: Additional Features and Multibody Parts

Inventor offers you some additional commands and features which will help you to create complex models. These commands are explained in this chapter.

The topics covered in this chapter are:

- *Ribs*
- *Bend Part*
- *Multi-body parts*
- *Split bodies*
- *Combine bodies, and*
- *Emboss features*

Rib

This command creates rib features to add structural stability, strength, and support to your designs. Just like any other sketch-based feature, a rib requires a two-dimensional sketch. Create a sketch, as shown in the figure, and activate the **Rib** command (click **3D Model > Create > Rib** on the ribbon). Select the sketch; the preview of the geometry appears. You can add the rib material to either side of the sketch line or evenly to both sides. Click the **Symmetric** icon under the **Thickness** section to add material to both sides of the sketch line. Type-in the thickness value of the rib feature in the **Thickness** box. You can also set the depth of the rib; there are two options: **To Next** and **Finite**. The **To Next** option terminates the rib on the next face, and the **Finite** option creates the rib up to the specified distance. Note that you need to check the **Extend Profile** option while using the **Finite** option.

You can define the direction of the rib feature by using the **Normal to Sketch Plane** or **Parallel to Sketch Plane** option.

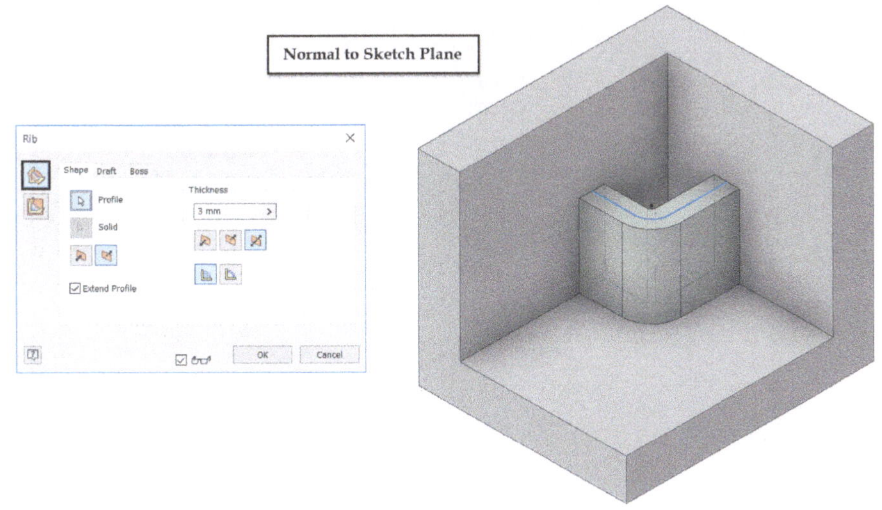

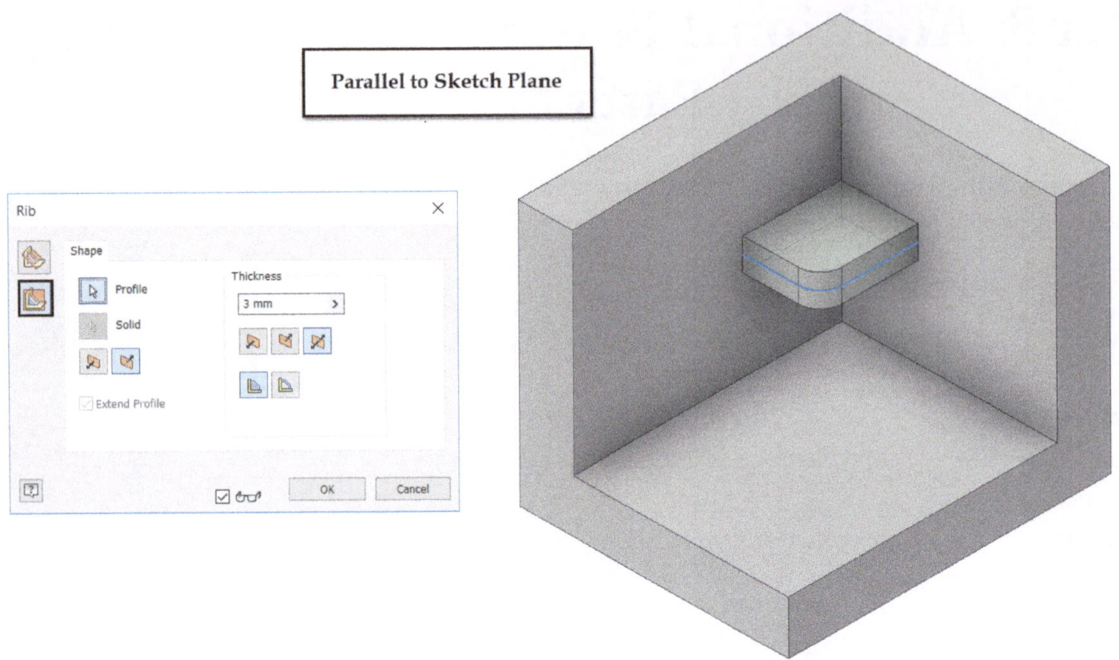

Applying Draft to the Rib Feature

Inventor allows you to apply a draft to the rib features, which is normal to sketch plane. To draft to the rib feature, click the **Draft** tab and select **Hold Thickness** > **At Top.** Next, type in a value in the **Draft Angle** box; the draft is applied to the side faces of the rib feature. The thickness of the rib feature will remain the same at the top face.

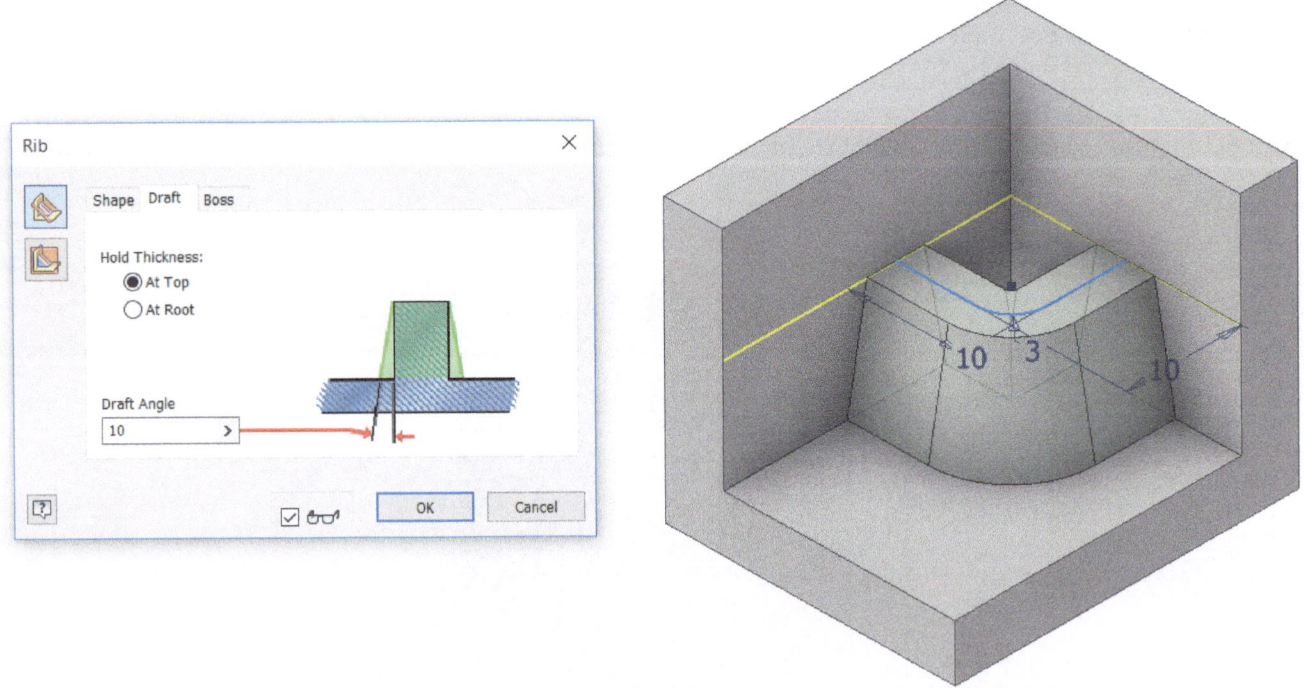

If you select **Hold Thickness > At Root**, the thickness of the rib feature will remain the same at the bottom.

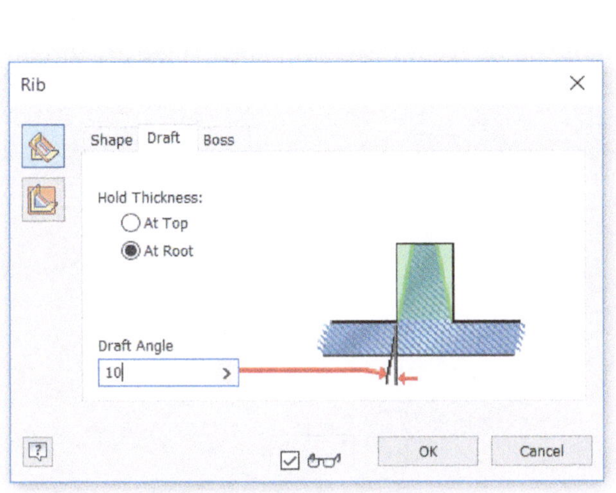

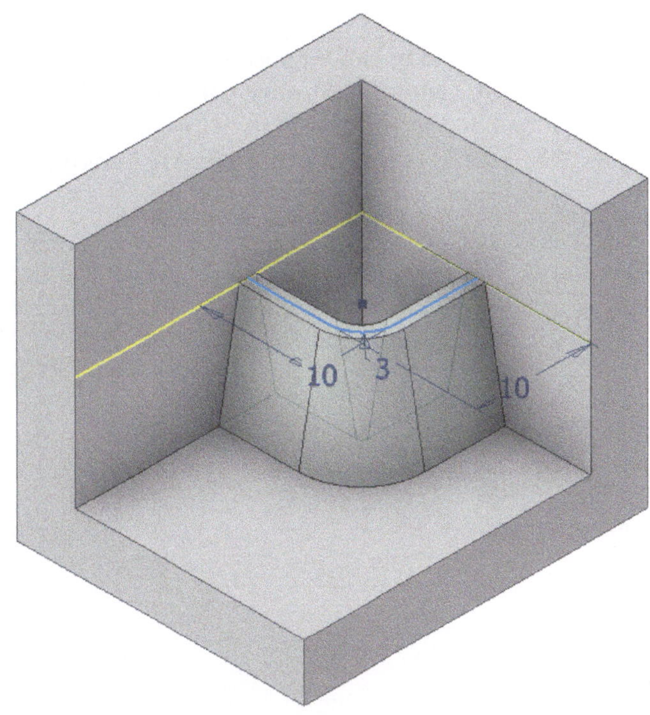

Adding a Boss to the Rib feature

Create a sketch for the rib feature and add a point to it. Make sure that the point is coincident with the sketch. Next, activate the **Rib** command and select the sketch; the preview of the rib feature appears along with the bosses. Click the **Boss** tab and notice that the **Select All** option is checked. As a result, all the points in the sketch are selected. If you want to select the points individually, then uncheck the **Select All** option, and click on the sketch points. After selecting the points, you need to specify the settings on the **Boss** tab. These settings are explained next.

Offset

This box is used to specify the height of the boss from the sketch plane of the rib feature.

Diameter

This box is used to specify the diameter of the boss feature.

Draft Angle

This box is used to add the draft to the boss feature.

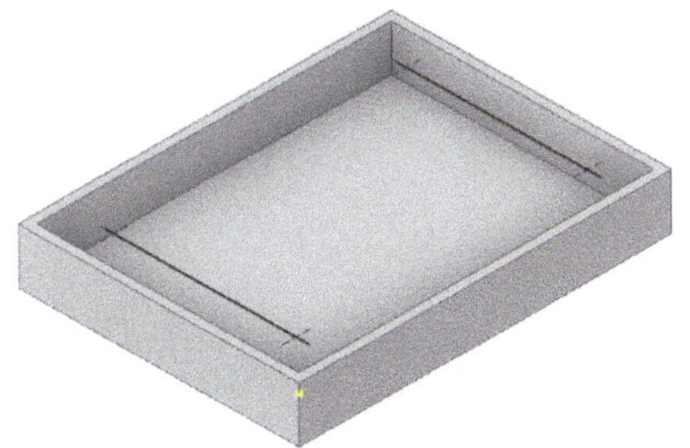

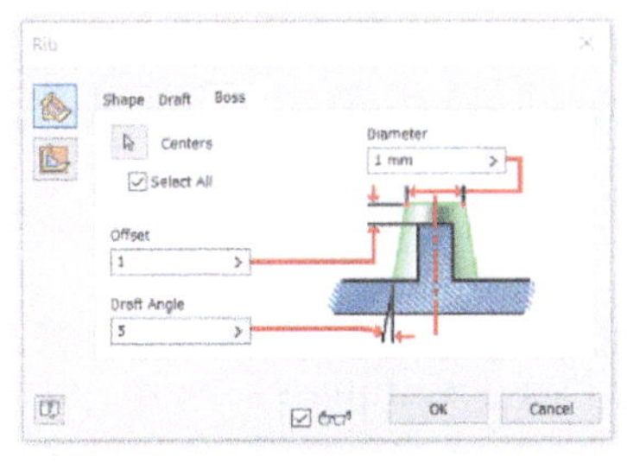

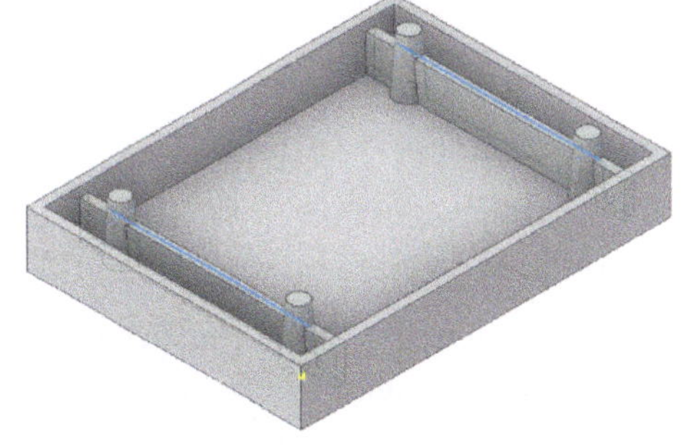

Bend Part

This command is used to bend a portion of the part geometry using a sketched line. Activate this command (on the ribbon, click **3D Model > Modify** panel **> Bend Part**) and click on the sketch line in the graphics window. Next, select the bend method from the drop-down available on the **Bend Part** Properties panel. There are three methods: **Radius and Angle**, **Radius and Arc Length**, and **Arc Length and Angle**.

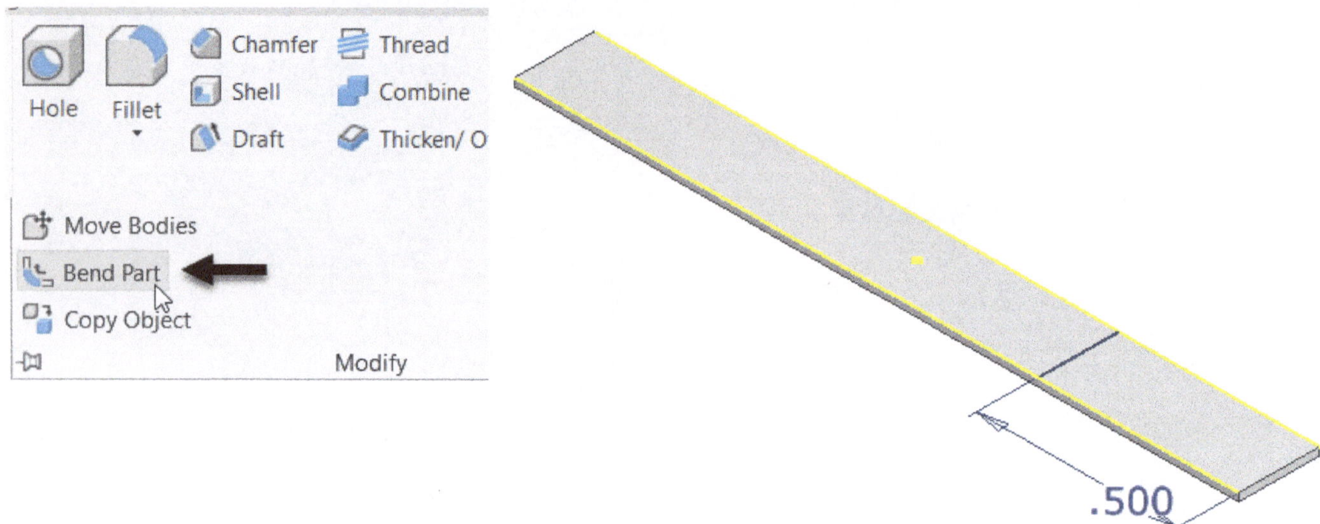

The **Radius and Angle** method creates a bend using the bend radius and angle values.

The **Radius and Arc Length** method creates a bend using the bend radius and arc length values.

The **Arc Length and Angle** method creates a bend using the arc length and bend angle values.

Next, specify the side of the part to be bend using the **Bend Side A** or **Bend Side B** or **Bend Both Sides** icons. If you want to flip the direction, then click the **Flipped direction** icon and click **OK**.

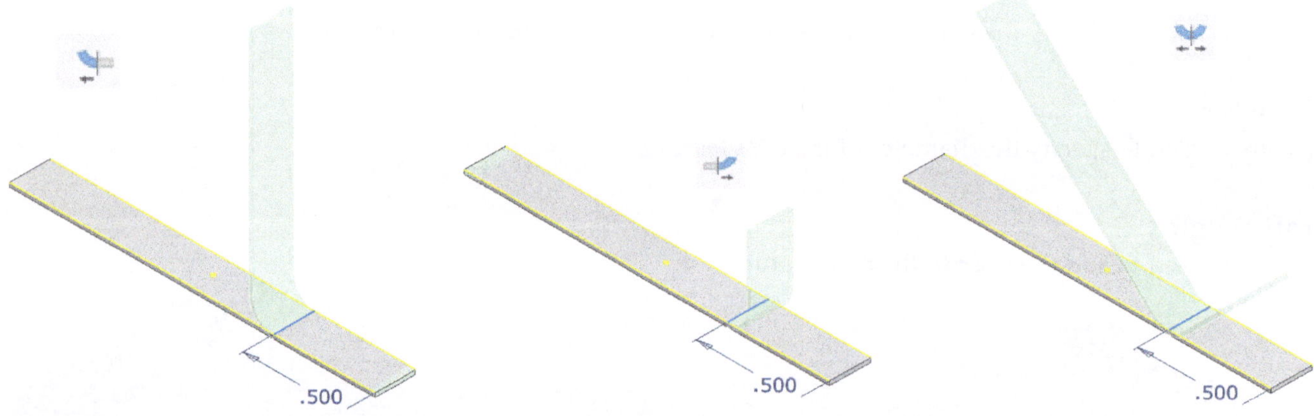

Multi-body Parts

Inventor allows the use of multiple bodies when designing parts. It opens the door to several design techniques that would otherwise not be possible. In this section, you will learn some of these techniques.

Creating Multibody Parts

The number of bodies in a part can change throughout the design process. Inventor makes it easy to create separate bodies inside a part geometry. Also, you can combine multiple bodies into a single body. In order to create multiple bodies in a part, first, create a solid body, and then create any sketch-based feature such as extruded, revolved, swept, or loft feature. While creating the feature, ensure that the **New Solid** icon is selected on the **Extrude Properties** panel. Next, expand the **Solid Bodies** folder in the **Model** Window and notice the multiple solids.

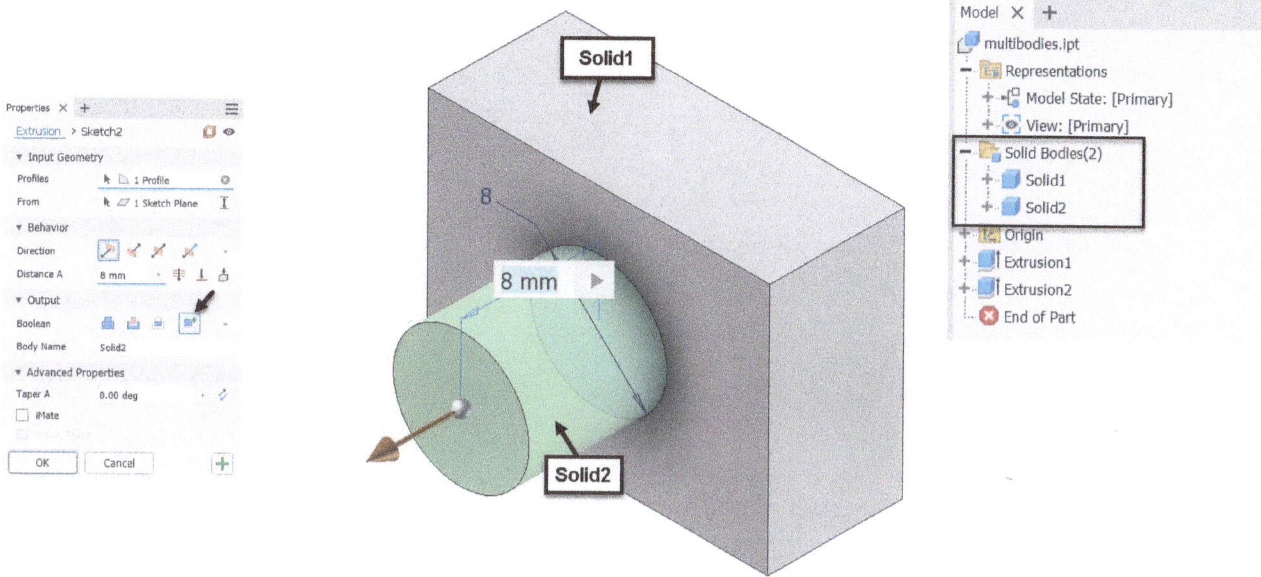

The Split command

The **Split** command can be used to separate single bodies into multiple bodies. This command can be used to perform local operations. For example, if you apply the shell feature to the front portion of the model shown in the figure, the whole model will be shelled. To solve this problem, you must split the solid body into multiple bodies (In this case, separate the front portion of the model from the rest).

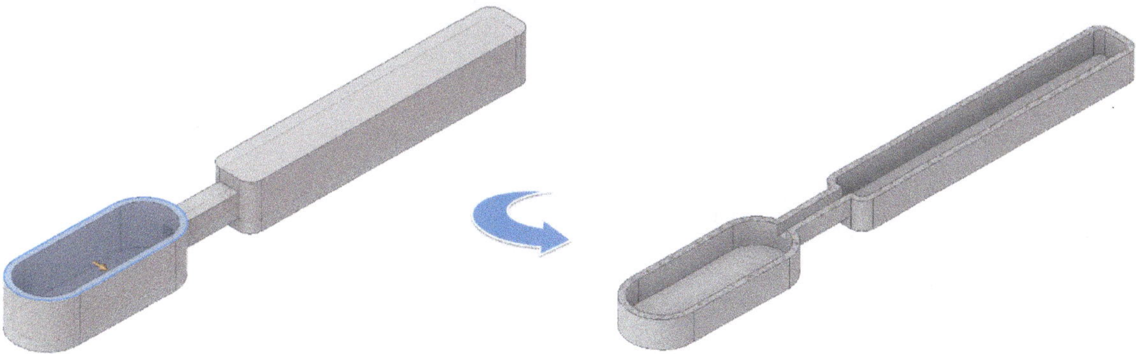

To split a body, you must have a splitting tool such as planes, sketch elements, surfaces, or bodies. In this case, a surface can be used as a splitting tool. To create a surface, click **3D Model > Surface > Ruled Surface** on the ribbon and click the **Normal** icon on the **Ruled Surface** dialog. Next, click on the edge of the split body. Specify the distance under the **Extend** section and click the **Flip** icon to reverse the direction. Click **OK** to create the ruled surface. You can use this ruled surface as a split tool to split the solid body.

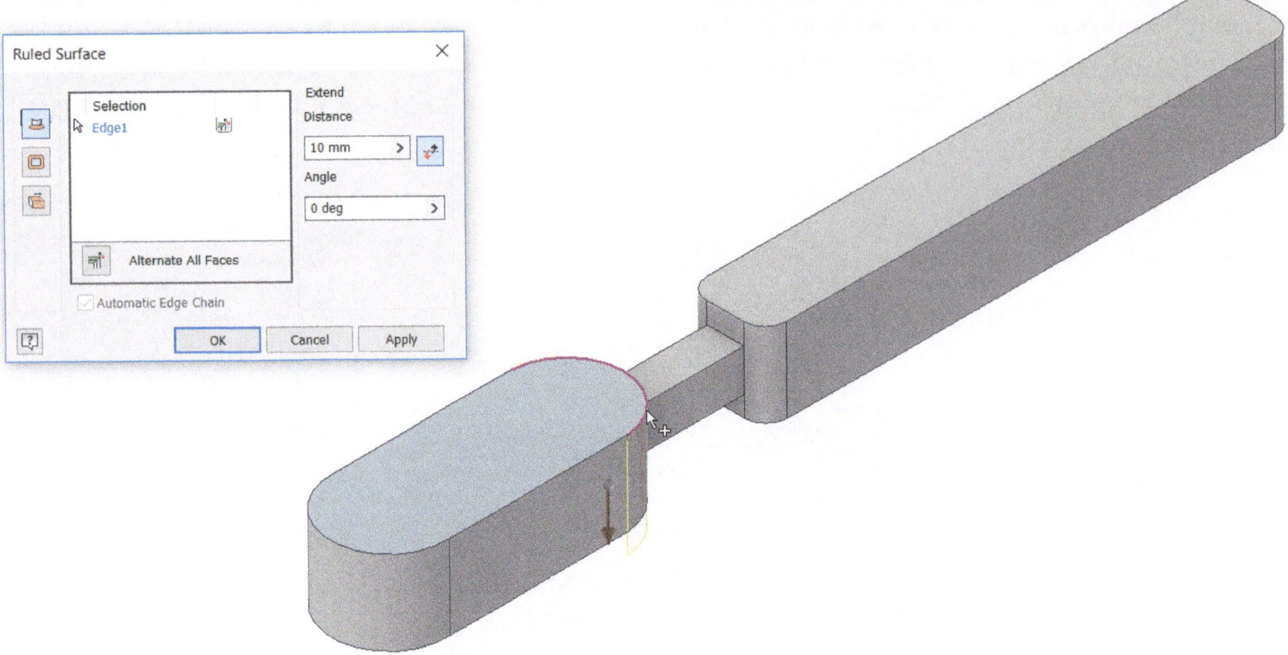

Activate the **Split** command (click **3D Model > Modify > Split** on the ribbon). On the **Split** Properties panel, click the **Solid Selection** icon next to the **Faces** selection box; the solid body gets selected automatically. Select the ruled surface from the graphics window. Click **OK**; the solid body is split into two separate bodies.

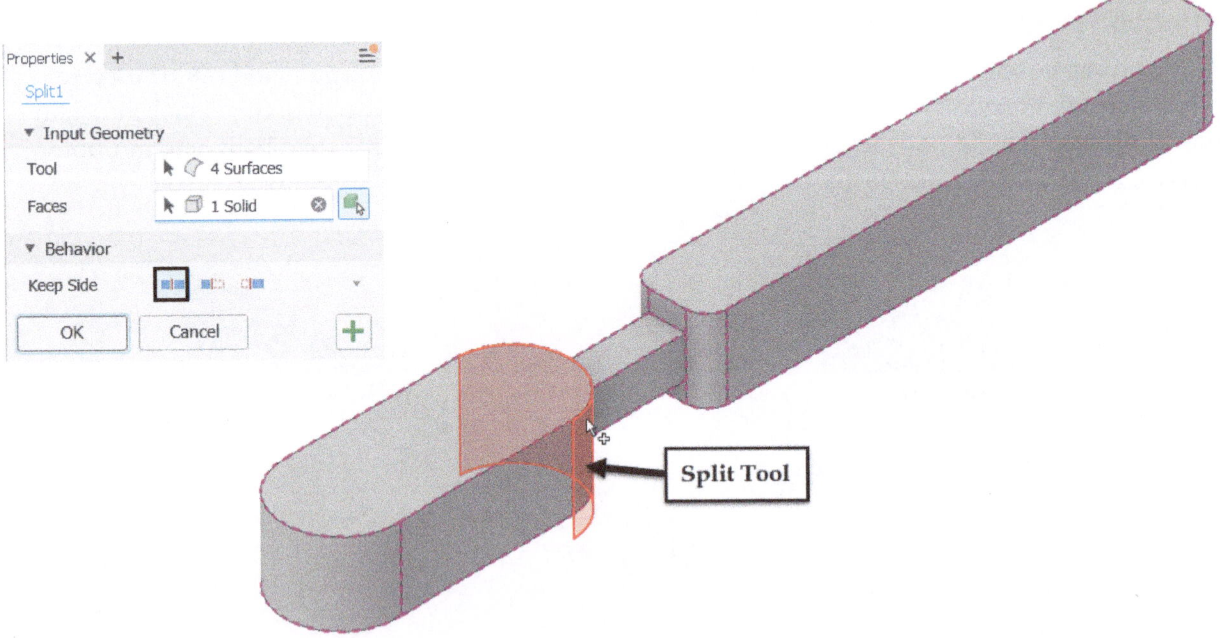

Now, create the shell feature on the split body.

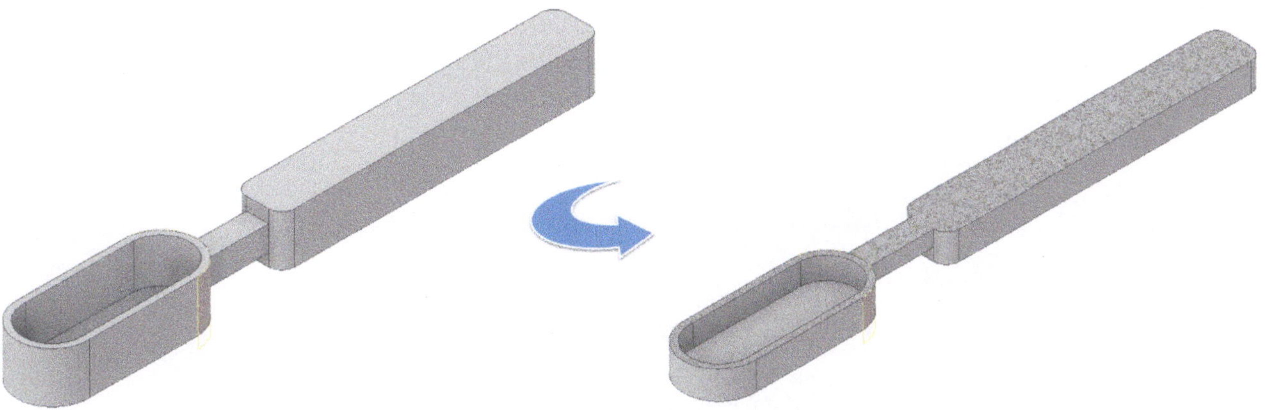

Join

If you apply fillets to the edges between two bodies, it will show a different result, as shown in the figure. In order to solve this problem, you must combine the two bodies.

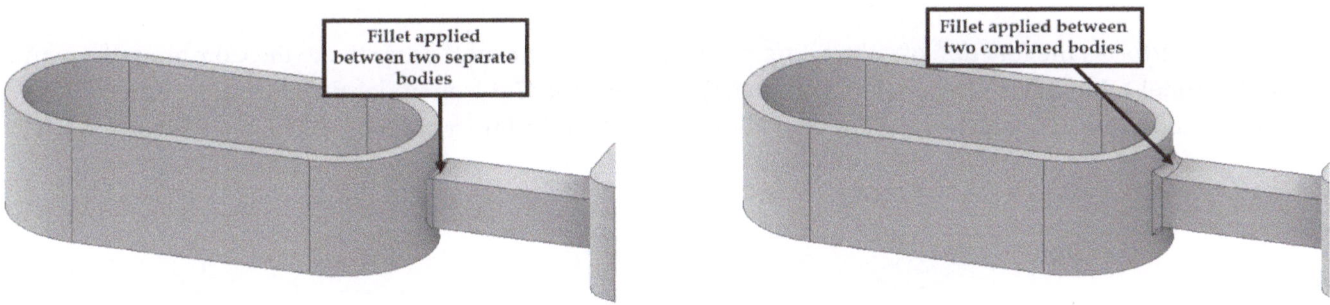

Activate the **Combine** command (on the ribbon, click **3D Model > Modify > Combine**) and click the **Join** icon on the **Combine** dialog. Next, select the two bodies. Click **OK** on the dialog to join the bodies. Now, apply fillets to the edges.

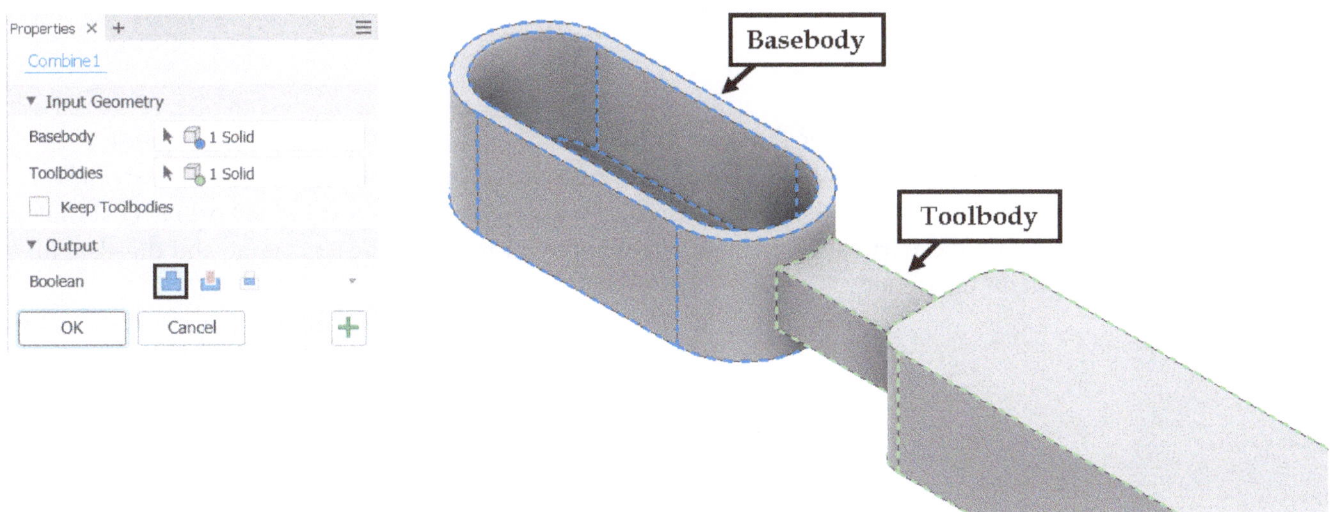

Intersect

By using the **Intersect** option, you can generate bodies defined by the intersecting volume of two bodies. Activate **Combine** command (click **3D Model > Modify > Combine** on the ribbon). On the **Combine** dialog, click the **Intersect** icon under the **Output** section and select two bodies. Click **OK** to see the resultant single solid body.

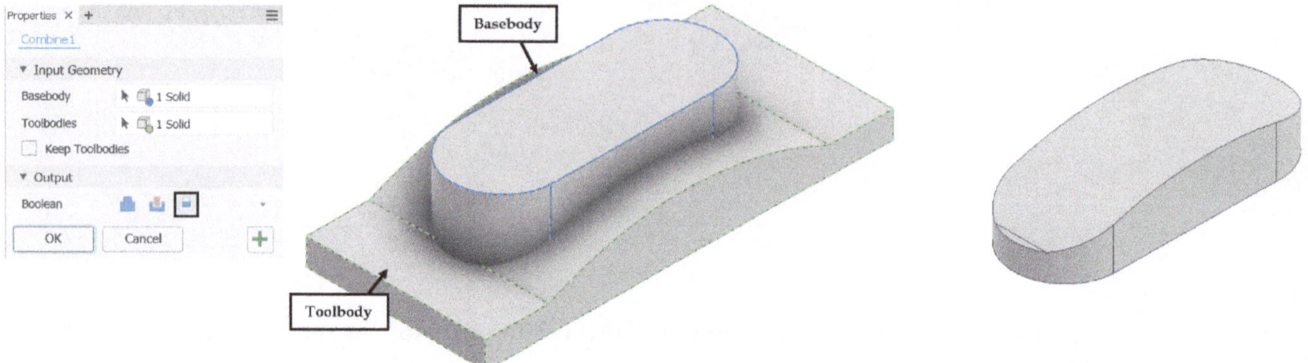

Cut

This option performs the function of subtracting one solid body from another. Activate the **Combine** command (click **3D Model > Modify > Combine** on the ribbon) and click the **Cut** icon under the **Output** section on the **Combine** dialog. Next, select the base and tool body. Click **OK** to subtract the tool body from the base.

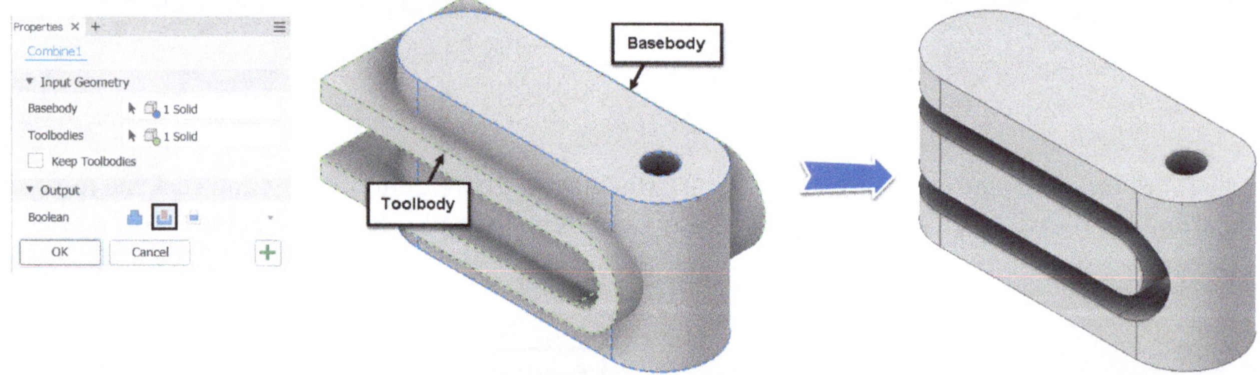

Emboss

This command embosses or engraves a text or shape on to the model geometry. For example, to engrave or emboss a sketch on to the cylindrical face of the model, first start a sketch on the plane, as shown. Next, click **Sketch > Create > Text** on the ribbon) and click in the graphics window. Type the text in the **Format Text** dialog, and then click **OK**. Next, apply the **Vertical** Constraint between the midpoint of the text frame and the sketch origin. Click **Finish Sketch** on the ribbon.

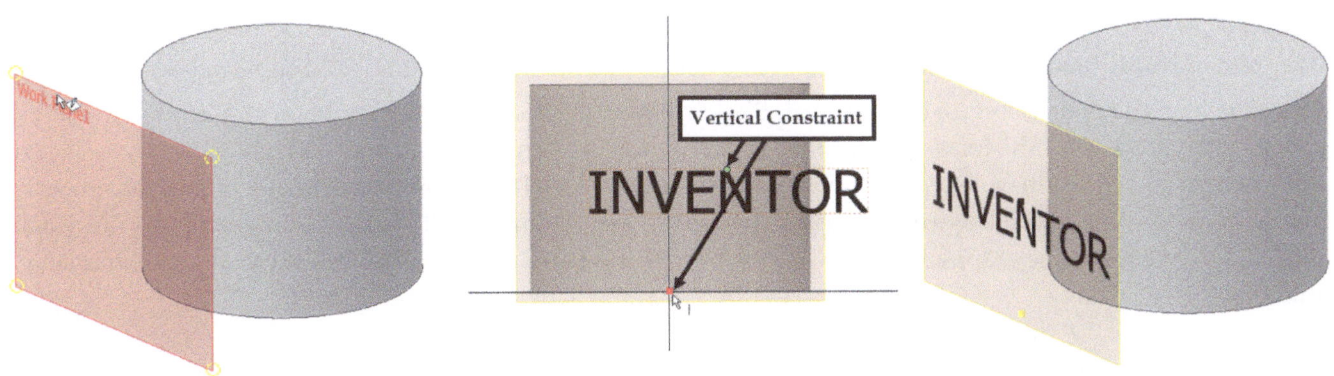

Activate the **Emboss** command (click **3D Model > Create > Emboss** on the ribbon) and click the **Emboss From Face** icon on the **Emboss** dialog. Click the **Profile** selection button and select the sketch. Next, type a value in the **Depth** box, and then click the **Top Face Appearance** swatch located below the **Depth** box. On the **Appearance** dialog, select **Steel Blue** from the drop-down and click **OK**. Check the **Wrap on Face** option and select the cylindrical face. Click the **Direction 2** icon so that the arrow on the sketch points towards the model. Click **OK** to emboss the text. If you want to engrave the text, right click on the **Emboss** feature in the **Model** window and select the **Edit Feature**. Next, click the **Engrave From Face** icon, specify the **Depth** value, and click **OK**.

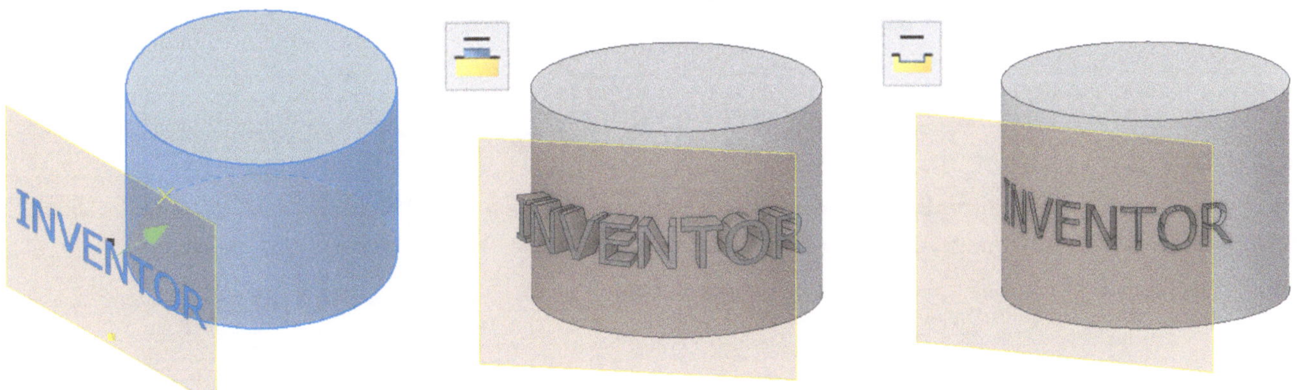

The **Emboss/Engrave from Plane** option embosses or engraves the sketch based on the position of the sketch plane.

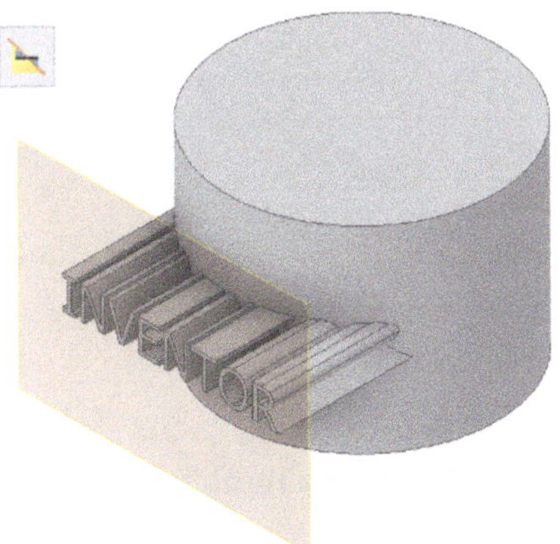

Decal

This command adds images to the model faces. For example, to add an image to the round face of a model, first start a sketch on the plane, as shown. Next, click **Sketch > Insert > Image** on the ribbon and browse to the location of the image file. The format of the image file can be GIF, Bitmap, JPEG, and PNG. You can also select an Excel or Word file. Select the image file and notice the **Link** option. This option, if checked, will link the image file with the Inventor part. If you leave it unchecked, the image will be embedded inside the Inventor part file. Click **Open**, and then click in the graphics window to position the sketch. Right click and select **OK** to exit the **Image** command.

To resize the image, click on the lower right corner point of the image, press and hold the left mouse button, and then drag. To move the image, press and hold the left mouse button on it, and then drag; the image is moved. Apply constraints between the image and model edges to position the image correctly. Click **Finish Sketch** on the ribbon to complete the sketch.

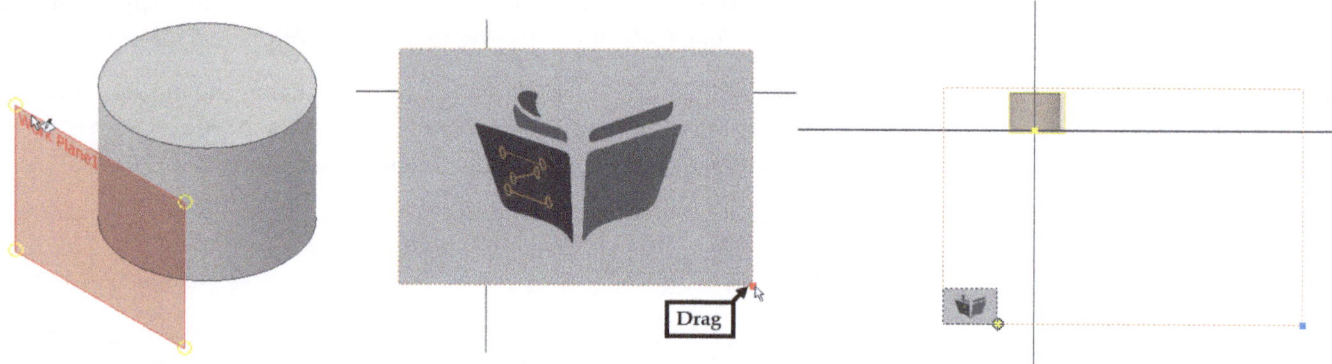

Activate the **Decal** command (on the ribbon, click **3D Model > Create > Decal**) and select the image. Next, click on the face to add the image, and then click **OK**.

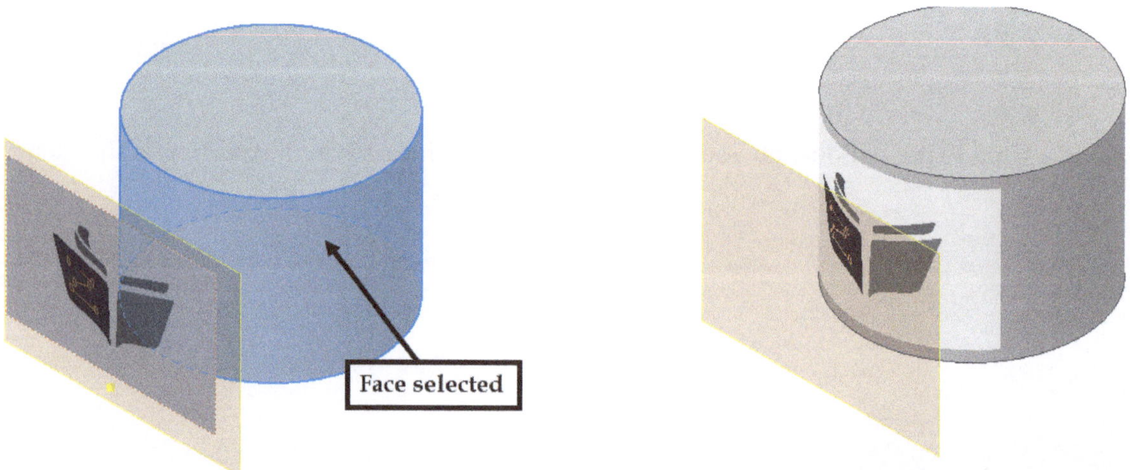

Mark

The **Mark** tool allows you to add custom text or graphics to their designs for machining tasks. It can be used to mark a wide range of objects, such as vehicle engines, printed circuit boards, surgical instruments, and jewelry. It's also useful when exporting features for laser marking, etching, or engraving to DXF or DWG files.

Using sketch text or geometry, the tool helps create precise features for these marking processes. To work correctly, the Mark sketch geometry must lie on the same plane and be placed directly on a model face.

Marking a Sketch using the Project Method

To use the **Mark** tool, open the model you want to mark. Click the **Mark** command on the **Modify** panel in the **3D Model** tab of the **Ribbon**. Select the sketch displayed on the planar face of the model. On the **Properties** panel, select **Mark through** from the drop-down located **Selection Sets** section. In the **Behavior** section, select **Method > Project** . Select **Direction > Default** . Click **OK**. Notice that the sketch is marked through the 3D geometry. As a result, the marking is created on both sides of the 3D geometry.

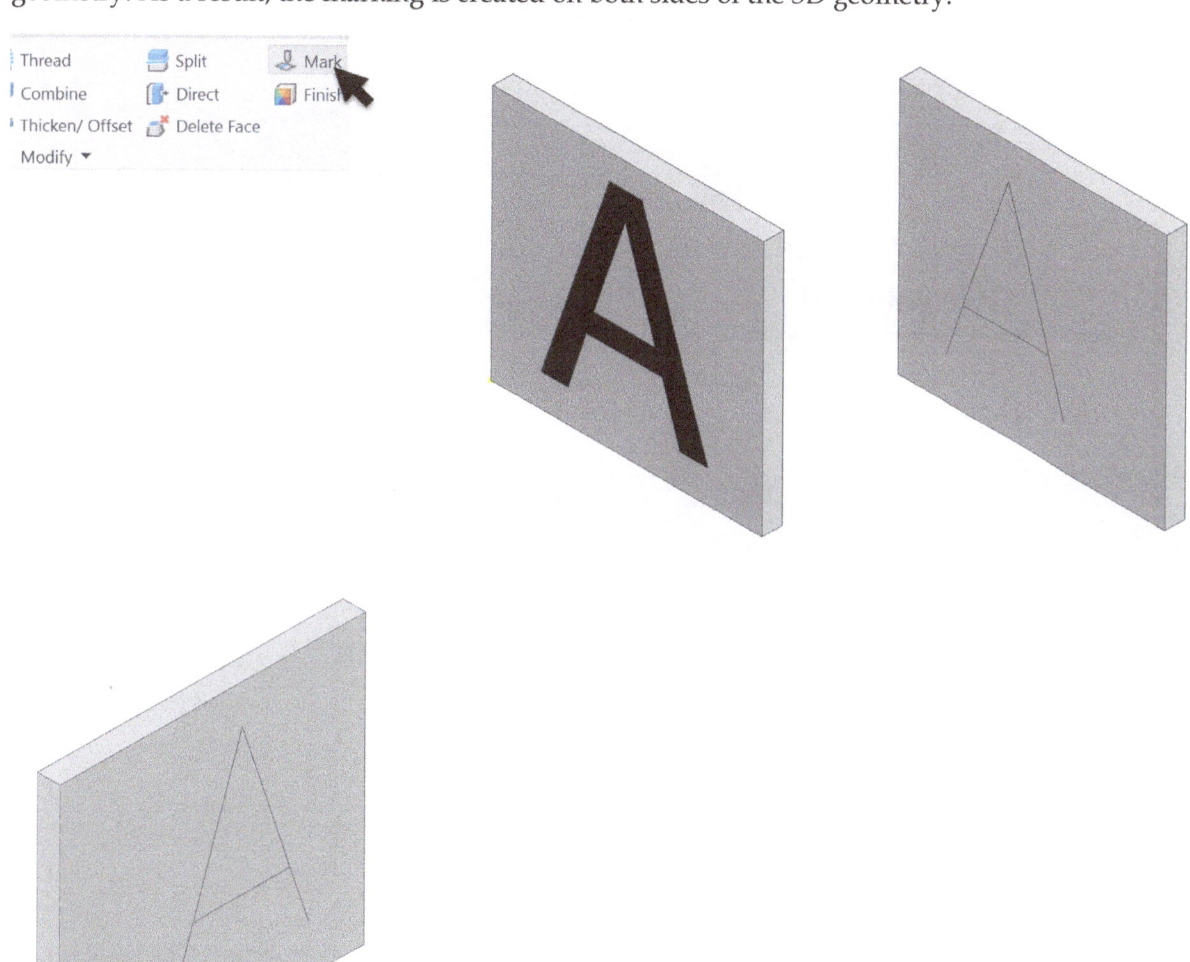

Marking a Sketch using the Wrap Method

On **3D Model** tab of the ribbon, in the **Modify** panel, click the **Mark** button. Select the sketch displayed on the curved face of the model. On the **Properties** panel, select **Mark Surface** from the drop-down located **Selection**

Sets section. In the **Behavior** section, select **Method > Wrap** . Select the curved face of the model; the text is wrapped around it. Select **Direction > Default** . Click **OK** to mark the sketch on the curved face.

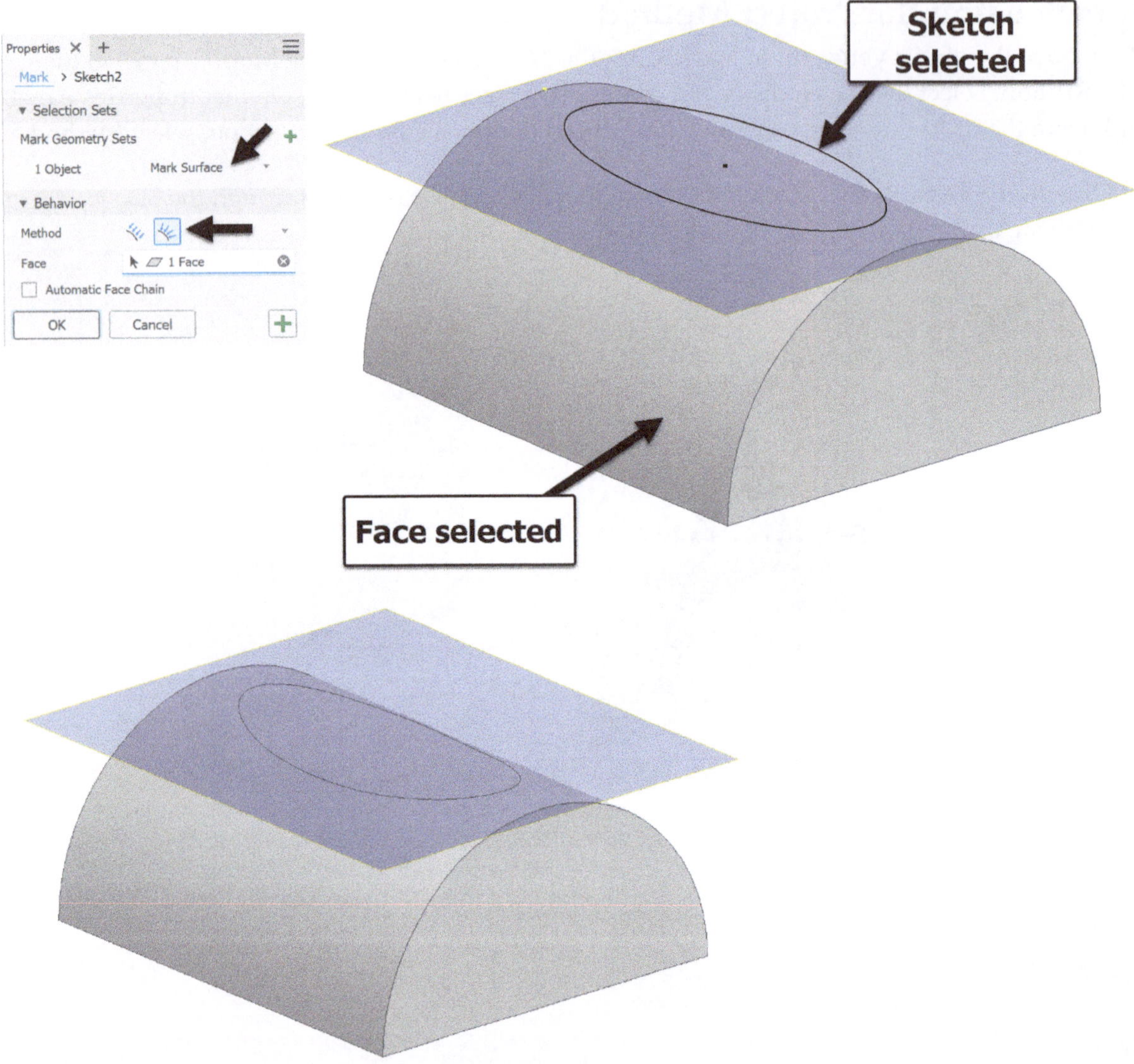

Using the Derive tool

The **Derive** tool allows you to create a derived component. A derived component is a new part or assembly that is created by referencing an existing part or assembly. This allows the new component to copy bodies, sketches, work features, and parameters from the original component. To create a derived component in Inventor, first create a new part file or assembly file. On the ribbon, click the **Manage** tab, then click the Insert panel, and select **Derive** (or) click click the **3D Model** tab, then click the **Create** panel, and select **Derive**.

In the **Open** dialog box, browse to the location of the part file or assembly file to use as the base component. Select it and click **Open**. Next, select the **Derive style**. In the **Derive Part** dialog box, there are four buttons that allow you to change the derive style. Each button performs a specific task.

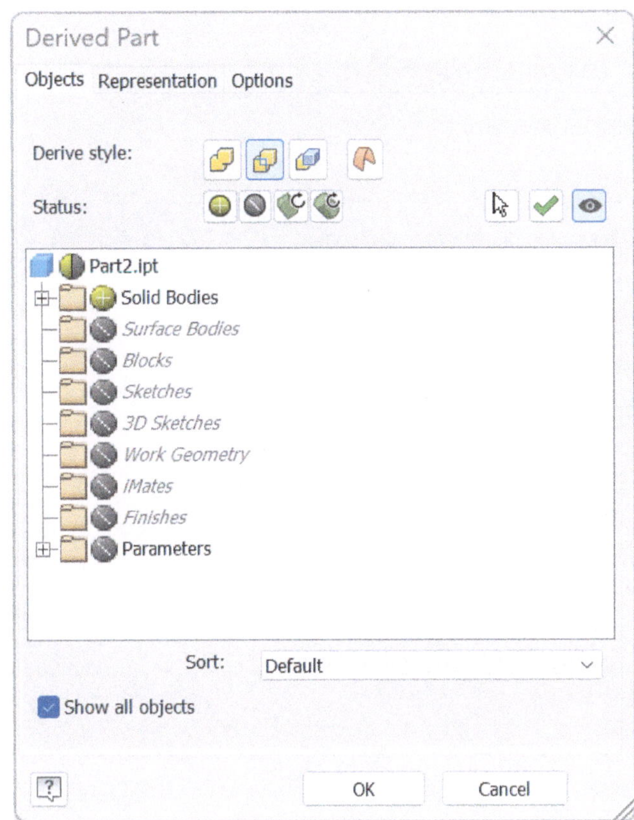

The **Single solid body merging out seams between planar faces** button merges out seams between planar faces to create a single solid body.

The **Solid body keep seams between planar faces** button keeps seams between planar faces while creating a solid body.

The **Maintain each solid as a solid body** button maintains each solid as a solid body.

The **Body as Work Surface** button treats the body as a work surface.

In the **Derived Part** dialog box, select the model elements from the tree view. Next, clicking on the status buttons displayed in the **Status** section. There are four status buttons: **Derives the selected objects**, **Excludes the selected objects**, **Includes the bounding boxes of the selected bodies**, **Includes the bounding cylinders of the selected bodies**.

To resize a component by proportion when creating a derived part or assembly, you can set the scale factor in the **Scale factor** edit box from the **Options** tab. By default, the scale factor is set to 1.0, but you can enter any positive number to adjust the size of the derived component.

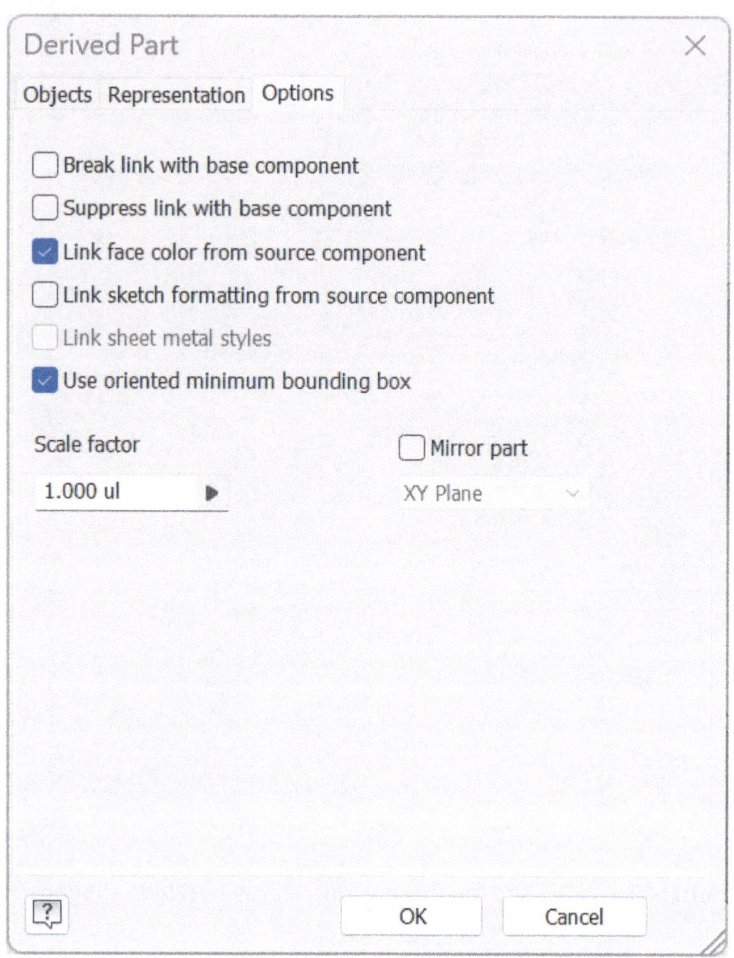

If you want to create a mirror copy of the derived part, you can select the **Mirror part** check box from the **Options** tab and choose the desired mirror plane from the drop-down menu below it. This will create a mirrored version of the derived component, which can be useful when you need to create symmetrical designs or parts. Click **OK** to create the derived component.

Using the Finish tool

The **Finish** tool helps you to add texture and material appearances to a model in the graphics area. Click **Finish** on the **Modify** panel on the **3D Model** tab of the Ribbon. On The **Finish** Properties panel, click the **Bodies** button on the right side, and then select the solid body from the graphics window; preview of appearance appears in graphics area. Click the **Exclude** selection button in **Input Geometry** section and then select the faces to be excluded from the selected body. Also, the total **Area** of selected faces appears in the **Include Geometry** section of **Properties** panel. Select finish **Type** from the **Behavior** section. You can select the **Appearance**, **Material Coating, Heat Treatment**, **Surface Texture**, or **Paint** option. Specify properties of the selected finish type in the **Behavior** section. The properties vary for each selection. Next, click on the **OK** button from the **Properties** panel.

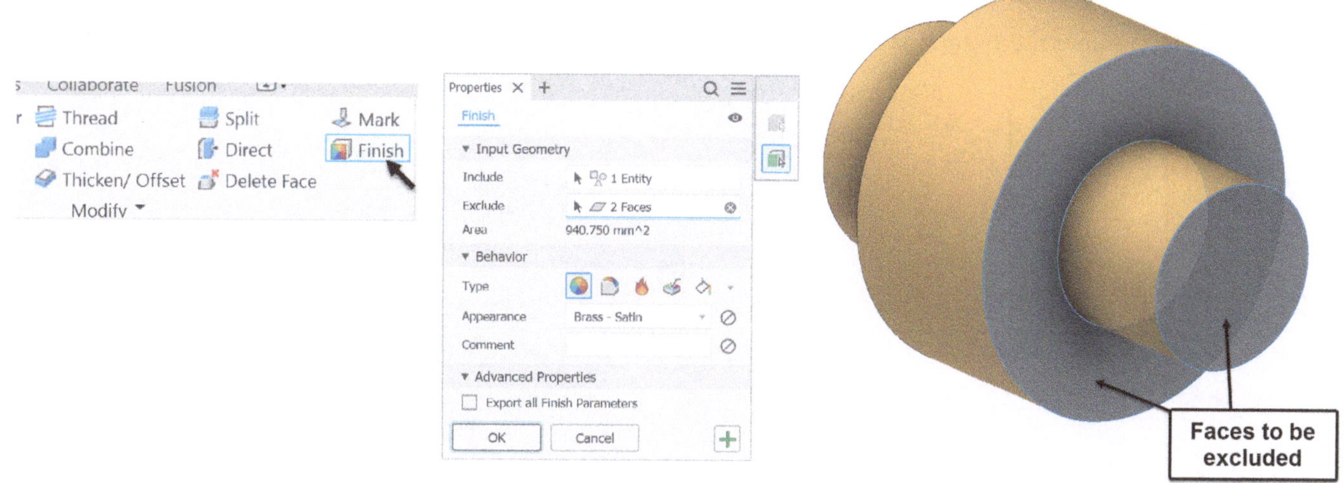

Examples

Example 1 (Inches)

In this example, you will create the part shown next.

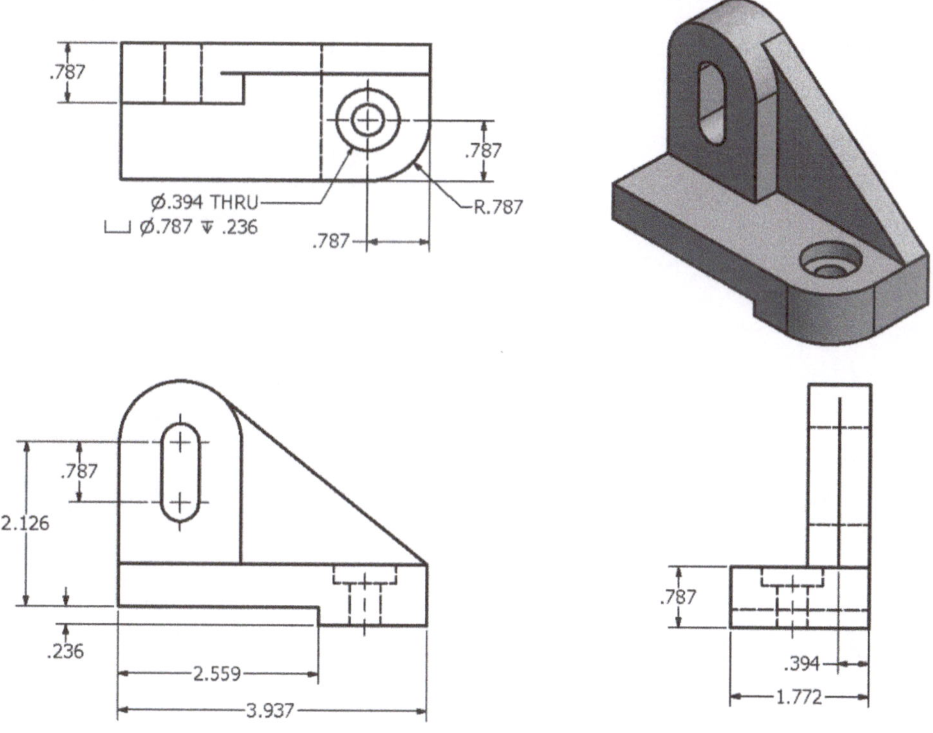

1. Start **Autodesk Inventor 2026.**
2. On the **Quick Access Toolbar**, click **New**; the **Create New File** dialog pops up.
3. On this dialog, click **Templates > en-US**. Select the **Standard.ipt** template and click **Create**.
4. On the ribbon, click **3D Model > Sketch > Start 2D Sketch** and draw the sketch on the **XZ** plane, as shown below. Next, click **Finish Sketch** on the ribbon.

5. On the ribbon, click **3D Model > Create > Extrude**. On the **Extrude Properties** panel, click the **Direction > Default** icon under the **Behavior** section and enter **0.787** in the **Distance A** box. Click **OK** to create the *Extrude* feature.

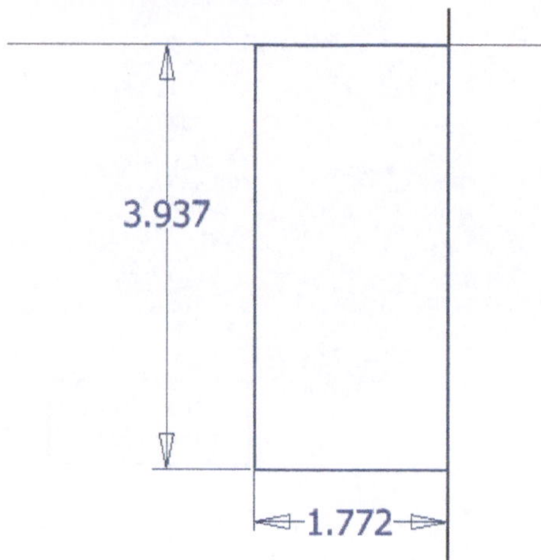

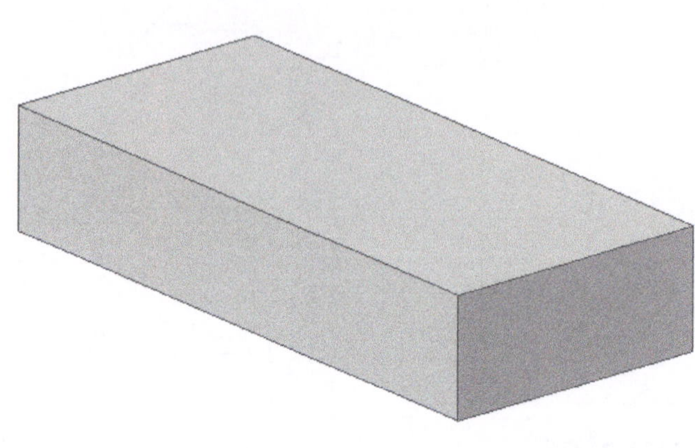

6. Activate the **Start 2D Sketch** command and click on the **XY** plane in the **Model** window by expanding the **Origin** folder.
7. Draw the sketch and add dimensions to it, as shown. Click **Finish Sketch** on the ribbon.
8. Activate the **Extrude** command and select the sketch. On the **Extrude Properties** panel, click the **Direction > Default** icon and enter **0.787** in the **Distance A** box under the **Behavior** section. Click **OK** to complete the *Extrude* feature.

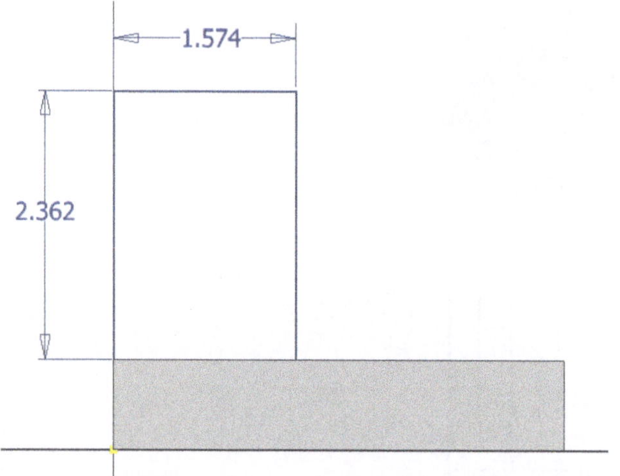

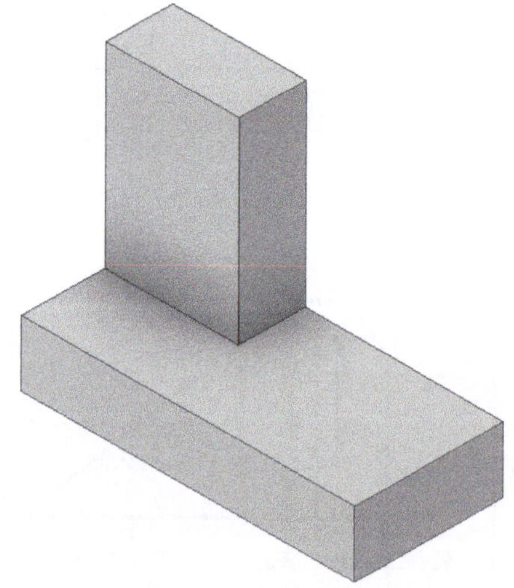

9. On the ribbon, click **3D Model > Modify > Fillet drop-down > Full Round Fillet** on the ribbon.
10. Select the faces of the second feature in the sequence, as shown. Click **OK** to create the full round fillet.

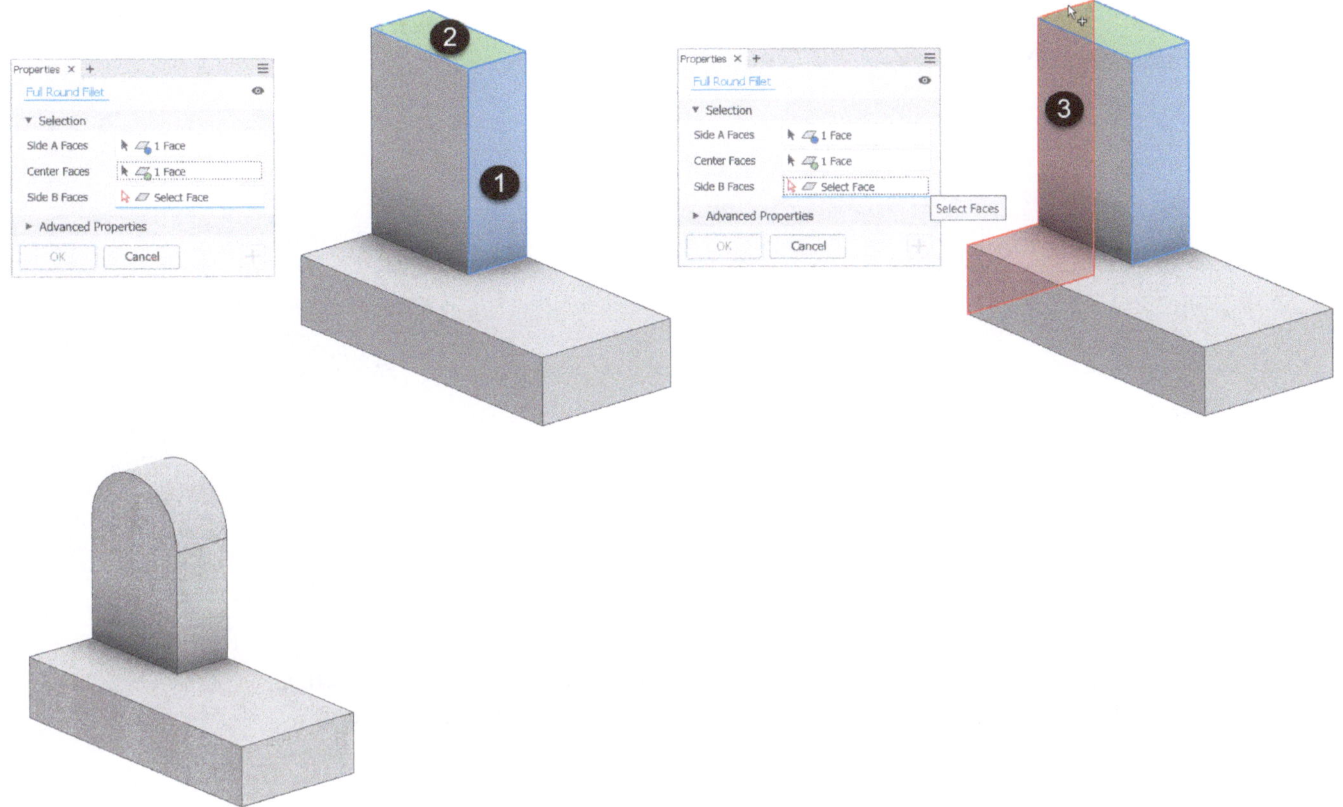

11. Activate the **Start 2D Sketch** command and click on the **XY** plane in the **Model** window. Draw an inclined line, as shown.
12. On the ribbon, click **Sketch > Constrain > Tangent**, and then select the inclined line and the curved edge; the line is made tangent to the edge.
13. On the ribbon, click **Sketch > Constrain > Coincident Constraint**, and then select the endpoint of the inclined line and the curved edge; the endpoint of the line is made coincident to the edge.
14. Likewise, make the other endpoint of the line coincident with the vertex point, as shown. Click **Finish Sketch** on the ribbon.

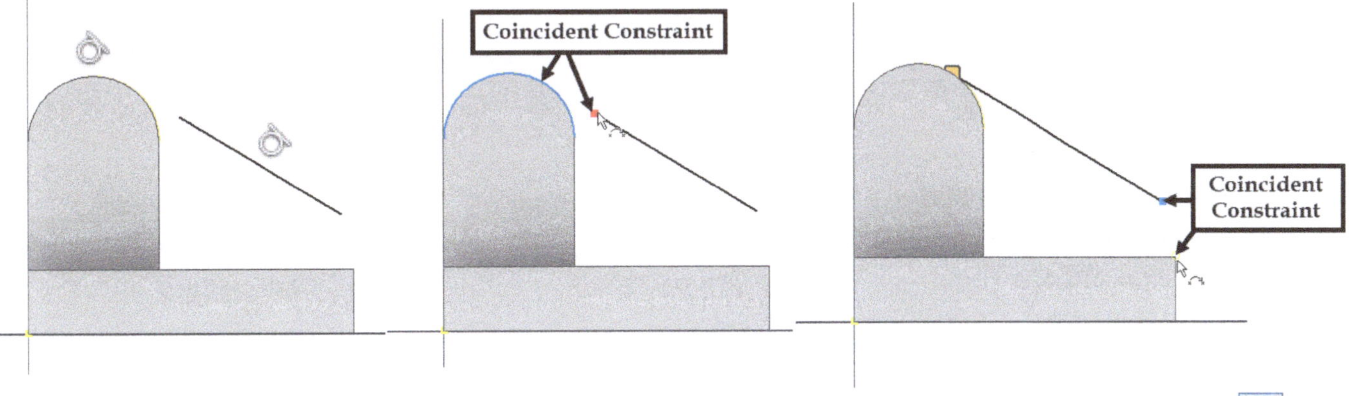

15. Click **3D Model > Create > Rib**, on the ribbon. On the **Rib** dialog, click the **Parallel to Sketch Plane** icon.
16. Click the **Profile** button and select the sketch (if not already selected). Click the **Direction 1** icon.

17. Type-in **0.394** in the **Thickness** box and click the **To Next** icon. Next, click the **Direction 1** icon in the **Thickness** area. Click **OK** to create the *Rib* feature.

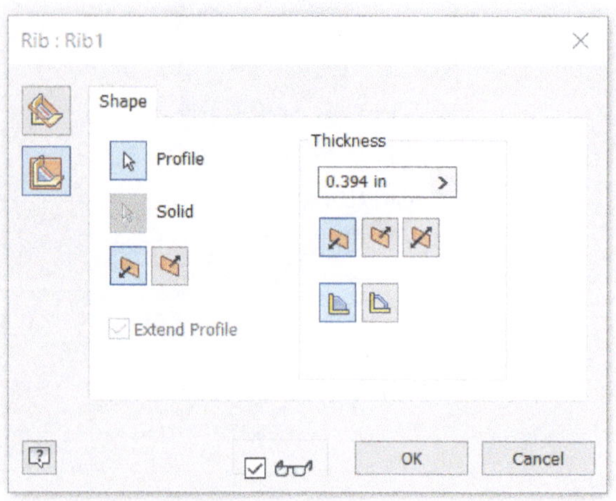

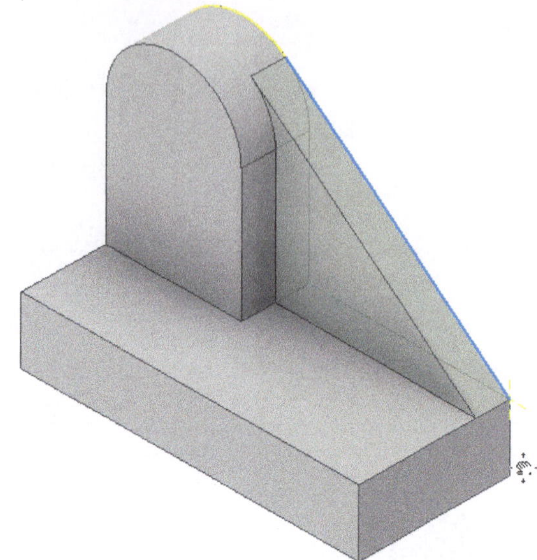

18. Activate the **Start 2D Sketch** command and click on the front face of the second feature, as shown.
19. On the ribbon, click **Sketch > Create > Rectangle** drop-down **> Slot Center to Center**.
20. Draw a slot and add dimensions to it, as shown. Click **Finish Sketch** on the ribbon.

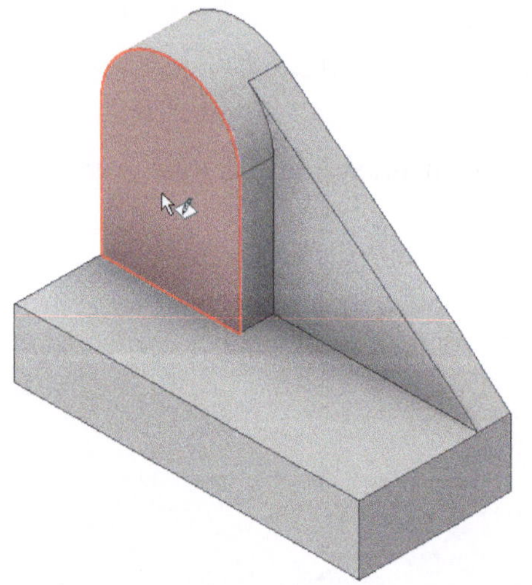

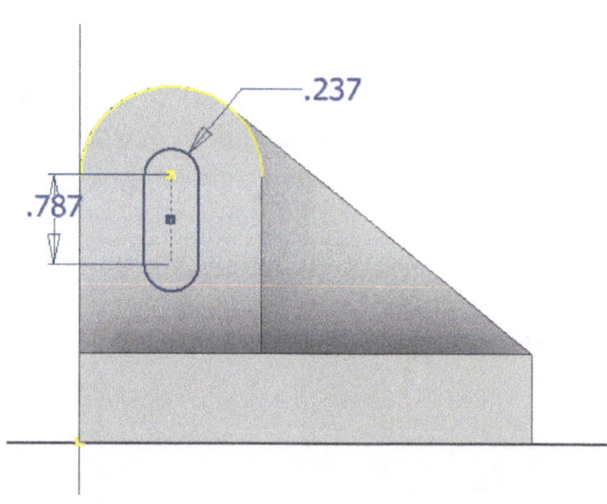

21. Activate the **Extrude** command and select the sketch. On the **Extrude Properties** panel, click the **Boolean >** **Cut** icon under the **Output** section and click the **Through All** icon under the **Behavior** section. Next, click **OK** to create the *Cutout* feature.

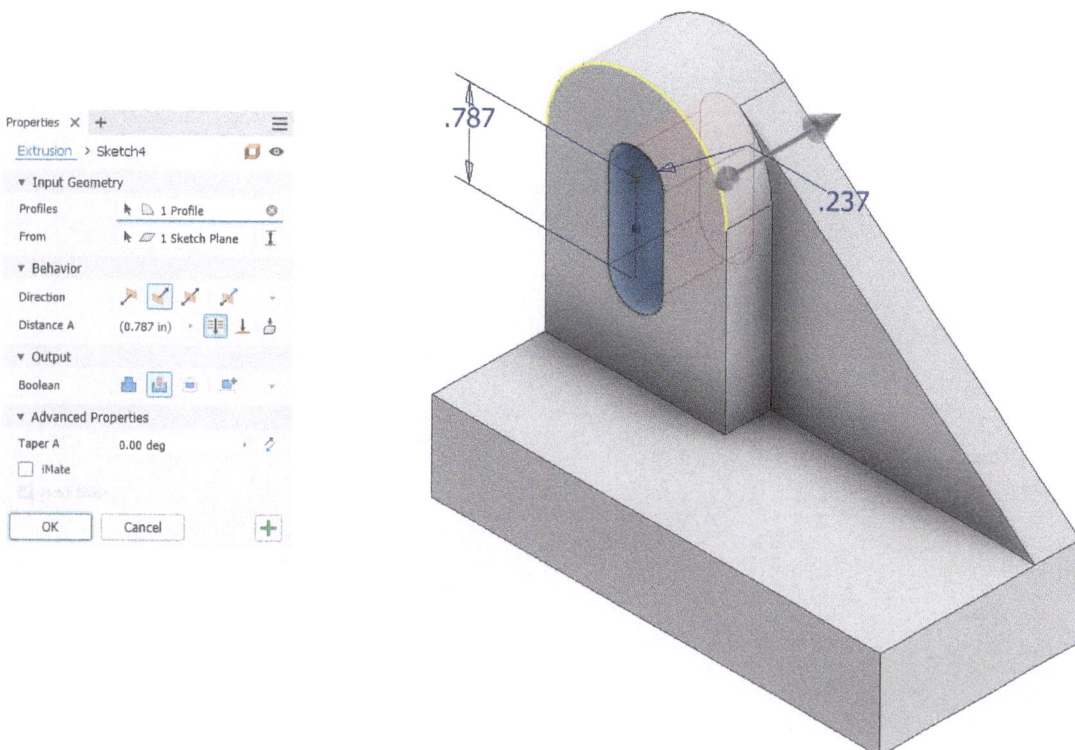

22. Add a fillet of **0.787** in radius to the right vertical edge of the rectangular base.

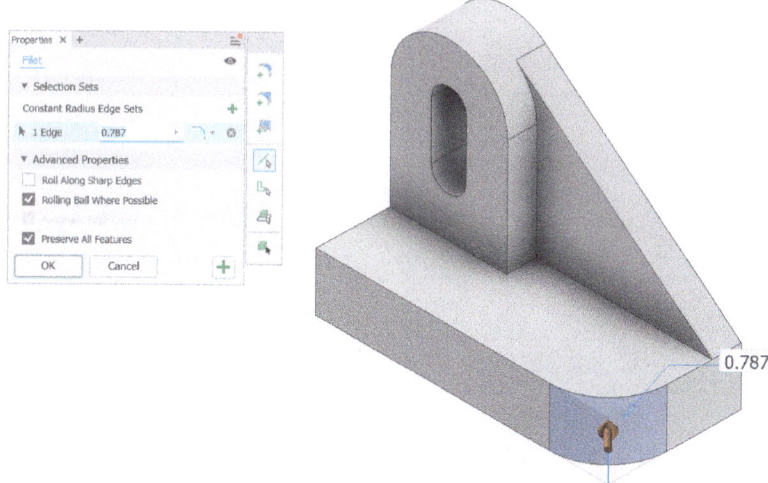

23. Activate the **Hole** command and click on the top face of the first feature. Next, select the curved edge of the fillet; the hole is made concentric to the fillet.
24. On the **Properties** panel, specify the settings, as shown. Next, click **OK** to create the hole.

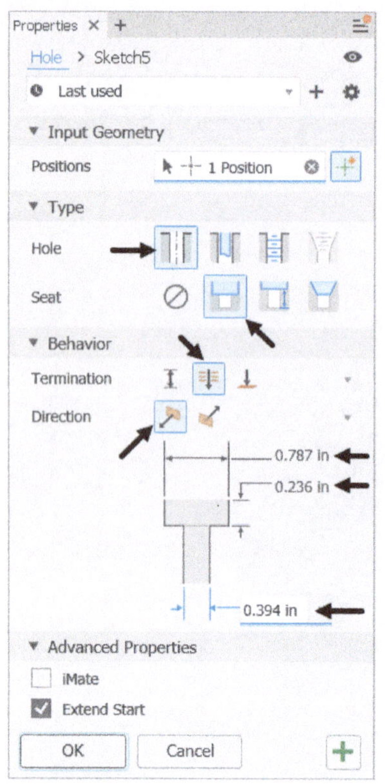

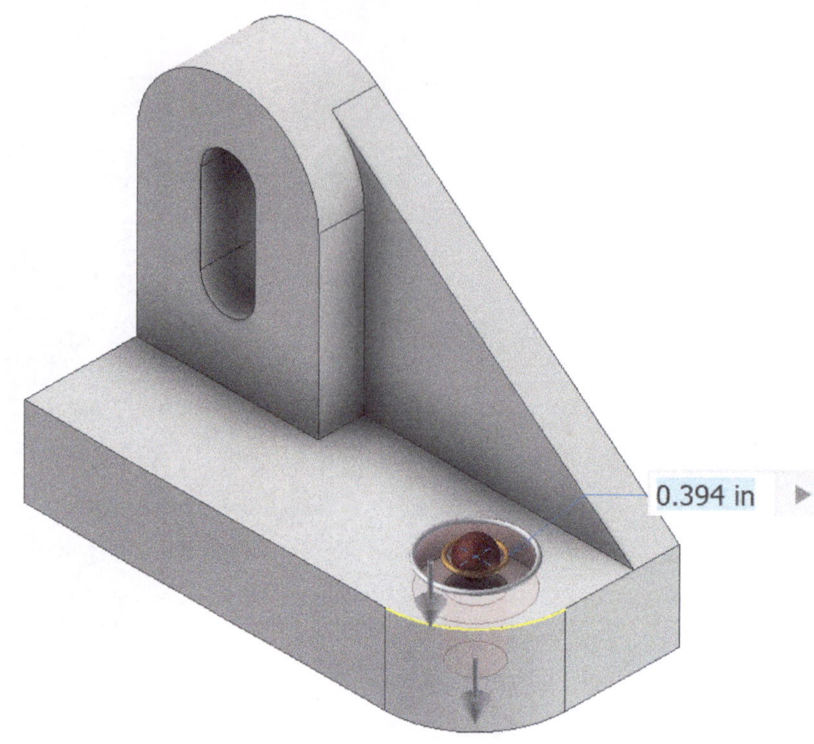

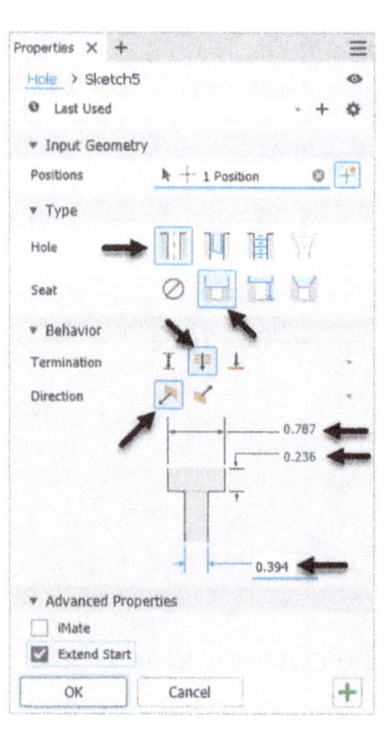

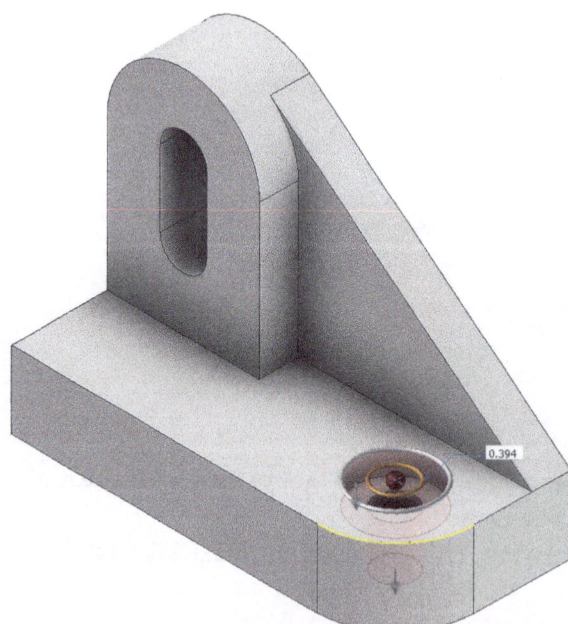

25. Activate the **Start 2D Sketch** command and select the front face of the rectangular base.
26. Draw a sketch and add dimensions to it. Click **Finish Sketch** on the ribbon.
27. Create an *Extruded Cutout* feature using the sketch.

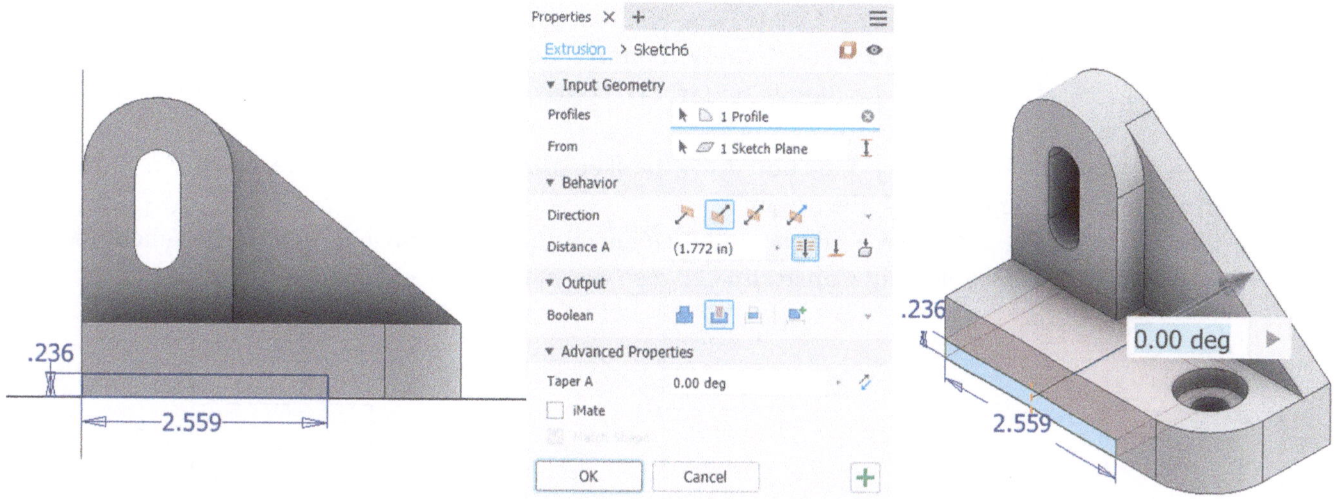

28. Save and close the part file.

Example 2 (Millimetres)

In this example, you will create the part shown next.

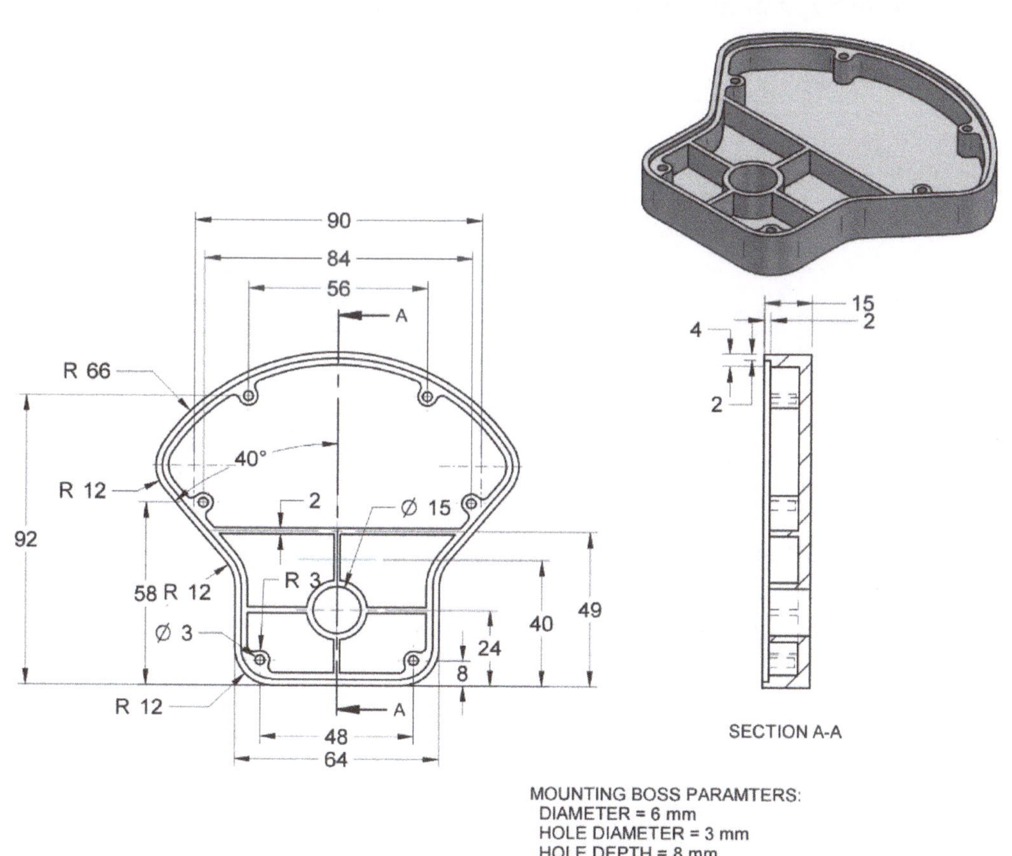

1. Start **Autodesk Inventor 2026.**

2. On the File menu, click the **New** icon; the **Create New File** dialog appears. On this dialog, click **Templates > en-US > Metric**, and then double-click on the **Standard (mm).ipt** template; a new part file is opened.
3. To start a new sketch, click **3D Model > Sketch > Start 2D Sketch** on the ribbon, and then select the **XZ Plane**.
4. On the ribbon, click **Sketch > Create > Line** and draw the sketch, as shown in the figure below. Also, create a horizontal centerline passing through the origin.
5. On the ribbon, click **Sketch > Pattern > Mirror**, and then mirror the horizontal and inclined line about the centerline. Next, apply the **Coincident Constraint** between the endpoints, as shown.

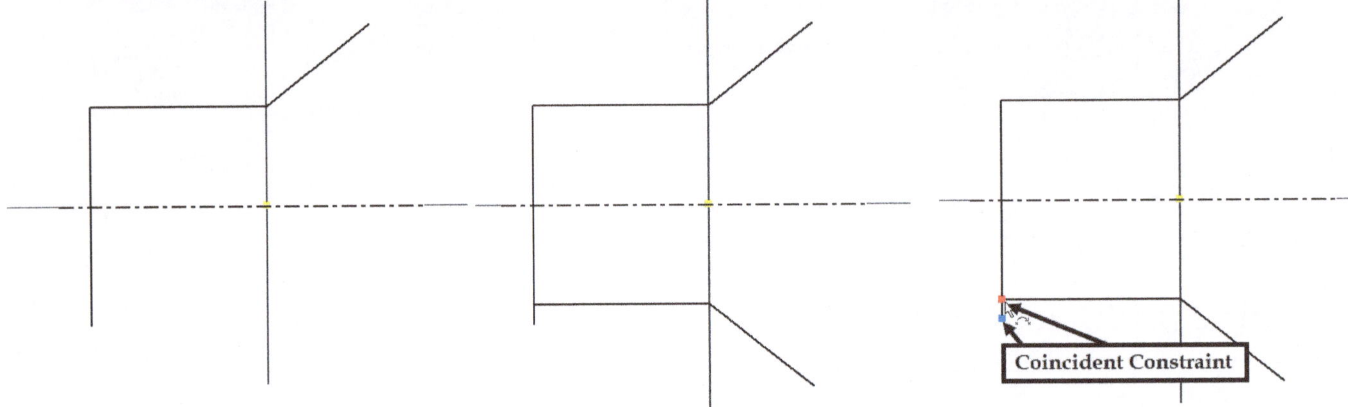

6. On the ribbon, click **Sketch > Create > Arc** drop-down **> Arc Three Point**, and then create an arc by specifying the points in the sequence, as shown.
7. Apply dimensions to the sketch. Also, apply the **Coincident Constraint** between the center point of the arc and the sketch origin.

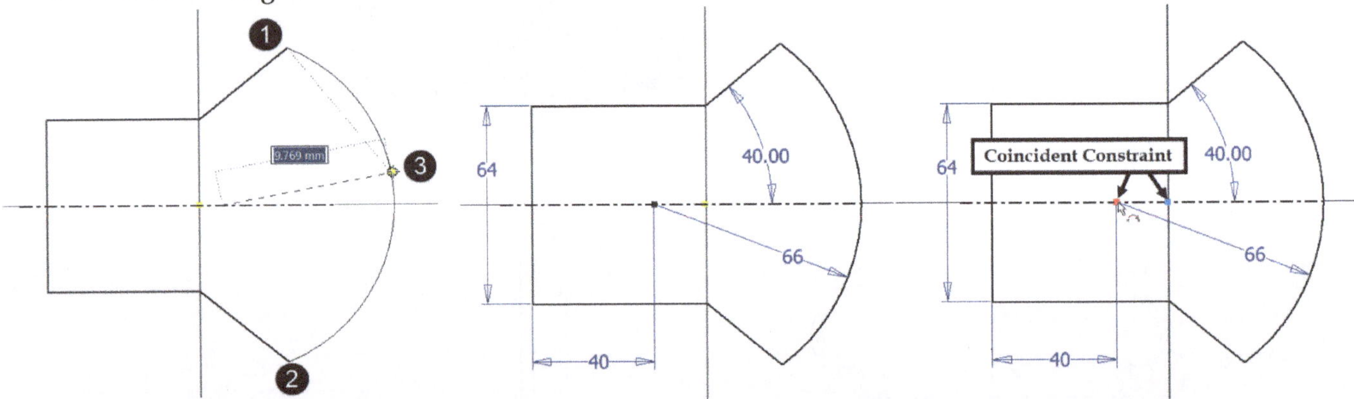

8. On the ribbon, click **Sketch > Create > Fillet** drop-down **> Fillet**, and then type **12** in the **Fillet** dialog. Create the fillet at the sharp corners, as shown.
9. On the ribbon, click **Sketch > Constrain > Dimension**. Add a linear dimension between the center points of the fillets, as shown.

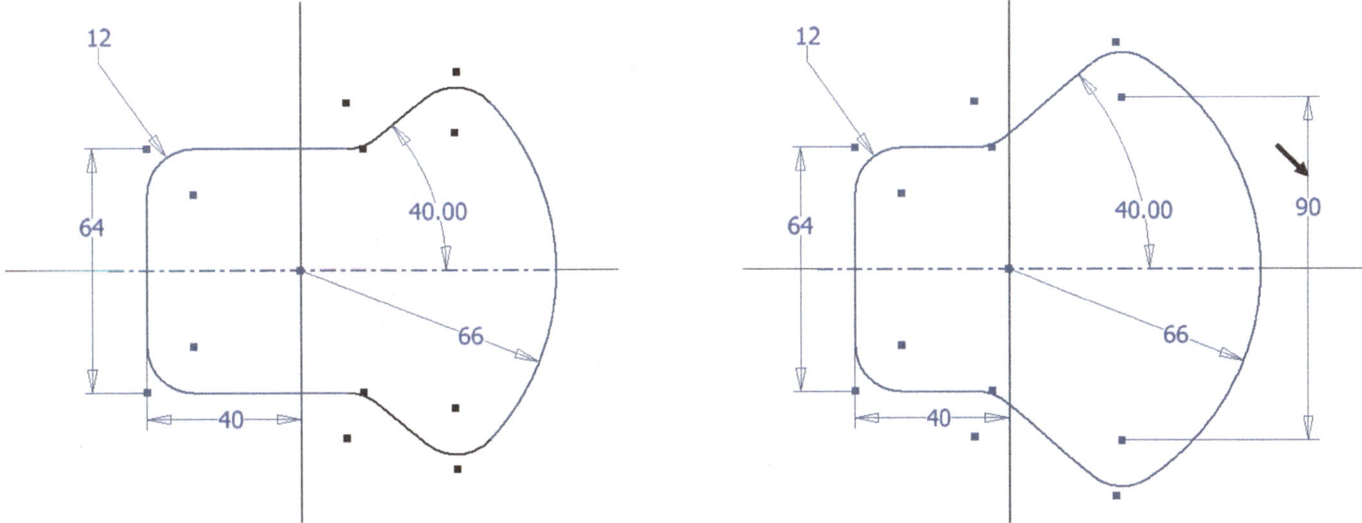

10. Click **Finish Sketch** on the ribbon, and then create the *Extrude* feature of **15 mm** depth.
11. Create the *Shell* feature of **4 mm** depth.

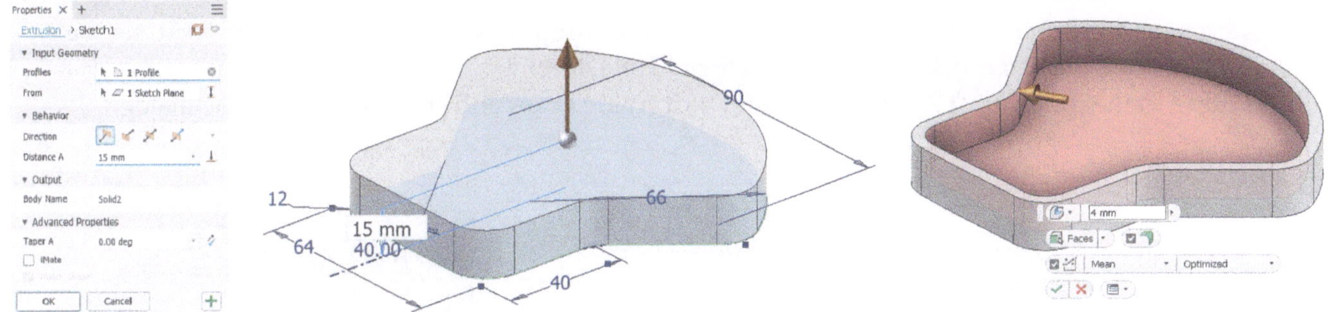

12. On the ribbon, click **3D Model > Plastic Part > Lip**. On the **Lip** dialog, click the **Groove** icon.
13. Click on the inner edge of the *Shell* feature to specify the path edges. Next, click the **Guide Face** icon and select the top face of the model.
14. Click the **Groove** tab on the **Lip** dialog and select the **Height** and **Width** values to **2**. Click **OK** to create the groove feature.

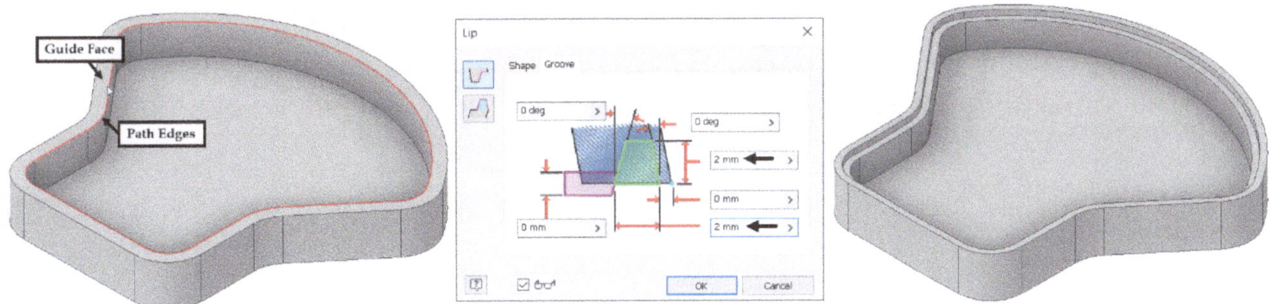

15. On the ribbon, click **3D Model > Sketch > Start 2D Sketch**, and then click on the top face of the groove feature.
16. Create sketch points and add dimensions to them. Click **Finish Sketch** on the ribbon.

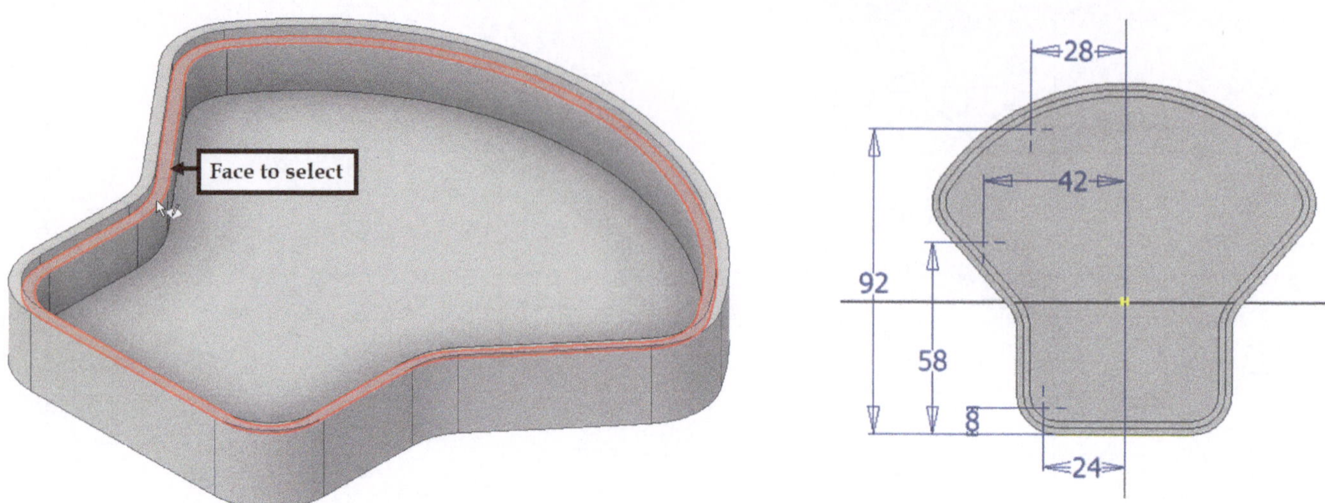

17. On the ribbon, click **3D Model > Plastic Parts > Boss**. On the **Boss** dialog, click the **Thread** icon. Next, select **Placement > From Sketch**; the points are selected, and the preview of the bosses is displayed.
18. Click the **Thread** tab on the **Boss** dialog. Next, set the **Thread diameter** to **6**.
19. Check the **Hole** option, and then select **Depth** from the drop-down displayed under it. Next, set the **Thread Hole diameter** to **3**. Enter **8** in the **Thread Hole depth** box.
20. Enter **1** in the **Inner Draft Angle** and **Outer Draft Angle** boxes and click **OK** to close the dialog.

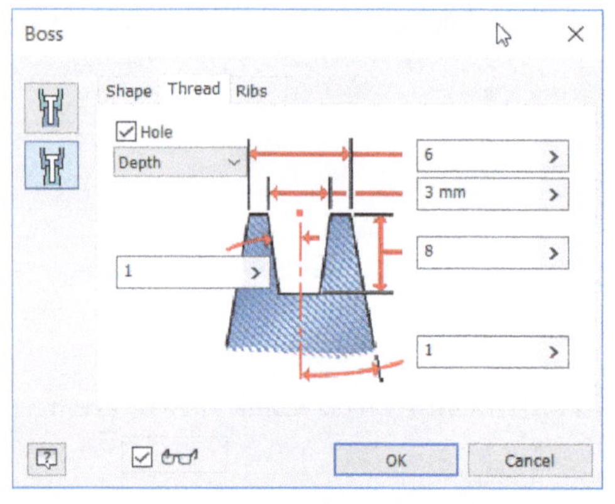

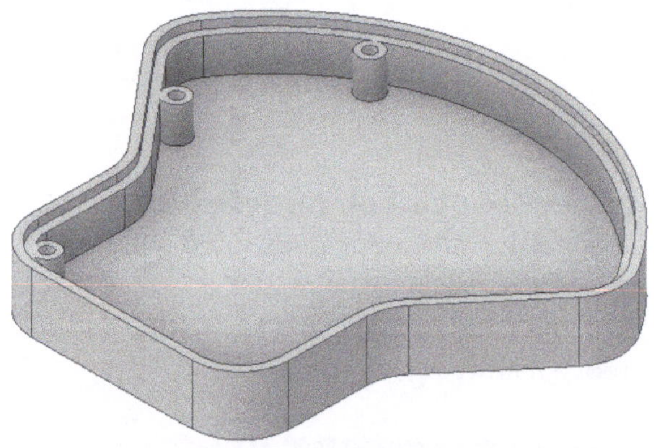

21. On the ribbon, click **3D Model > Pattern > Mirror** and select the **Boss** feature from the **Model** window.
22. On the **Mirror** dialog, click the **Origin YZ Plane** icon. Click **OK** to mirror the bosses.

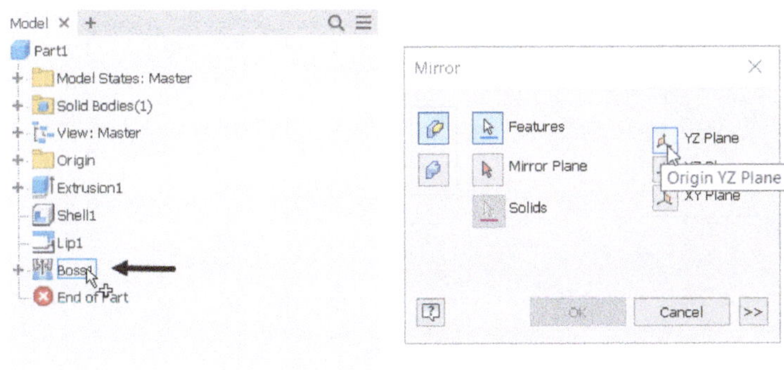

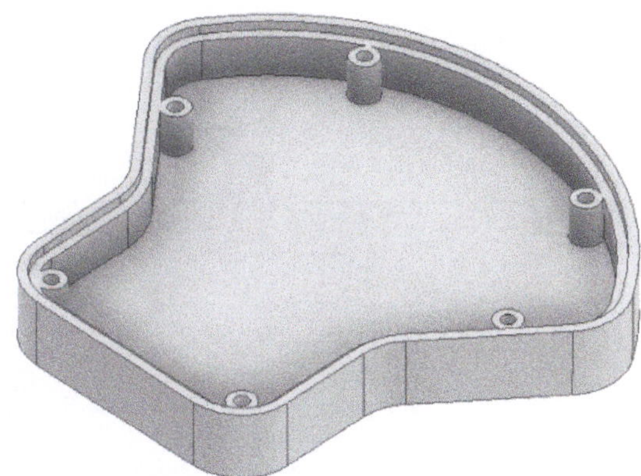

23. On the ribbon, click **3D Model > Modify > Fillet** and select the edges where the mounting bosses meet the walls of the geometry.

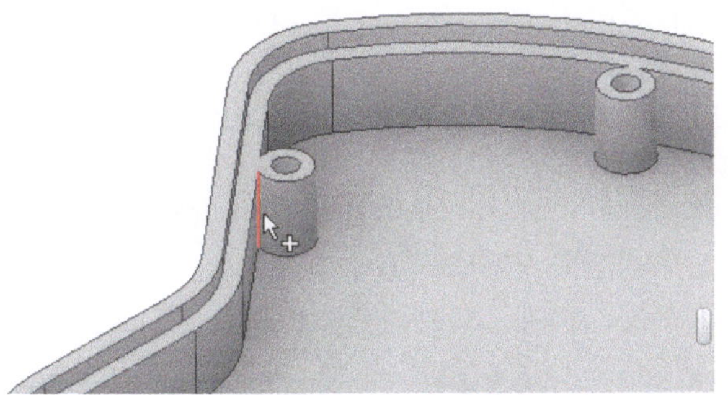

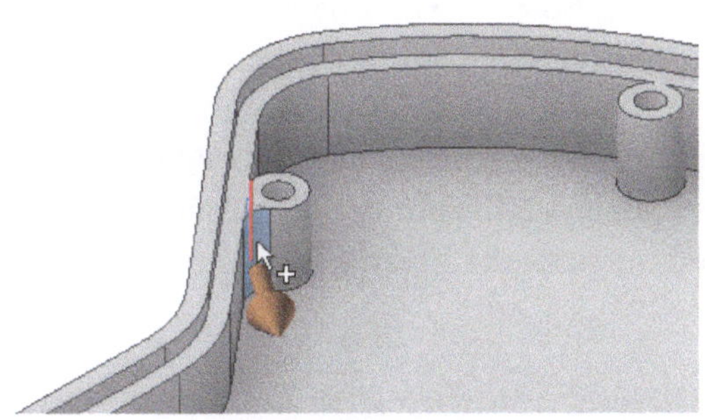

24. Type **2** in the **Radius** box on the Mini toolbar. Click the **OK** button to fillet the selected edges.

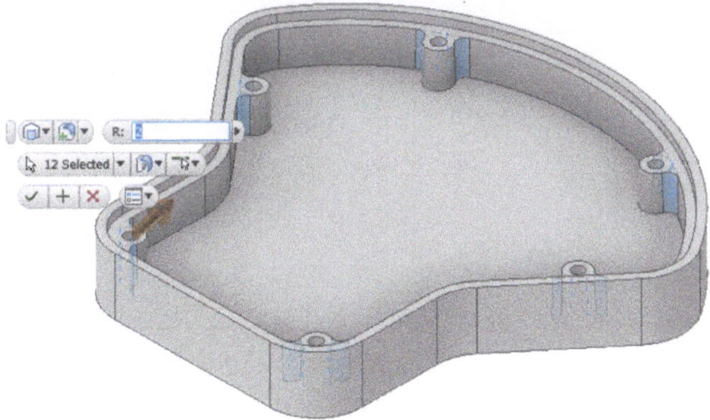

25. On the ribbon, click **3D Model > Sketch > Start 2D Sketch** and select the top face of the groove.
26. Create a sketch using the **Line** command and add dimensions to it.
27. On the ribbon, click **Sketch > Create >Point** and select the intersection point between the vertical and horizontal lines, as shown. Click **Finish Sketch** on the ribbon.

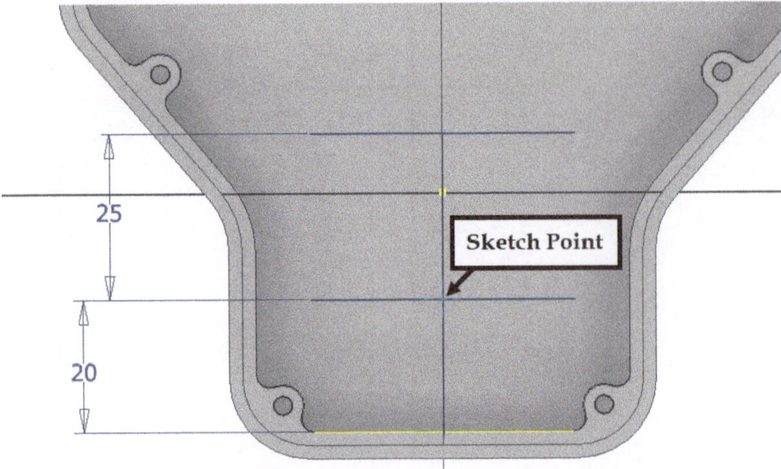

28. On the ribbon, click **3D Model > Create > Rib** and select the horizontal lines of the sketch.
29. On the **Rib** dialog, type **1** in the **Thickness** box and click the **Symmetric** icon.
30. Click the **Boss** tab and enter **17** in the **Diameter** box. Next, enter **0** in the **Offset** and **Draft Angle** boxes. Click **OK** to create the rib feature along with a boss.
31. In the **Model** window, expand the **Rib** feature and right click on the Sketch. Next, select **Visibility** from the shortcut menu; the sketch used for the rib feature is visible.
32. Activate the **Rib** command and select the vertical line of the sketch. Enter **1** in the **Thickness** box, and then uncheck the **Extend Profile** option. Click **OK** to complete the rib feature.

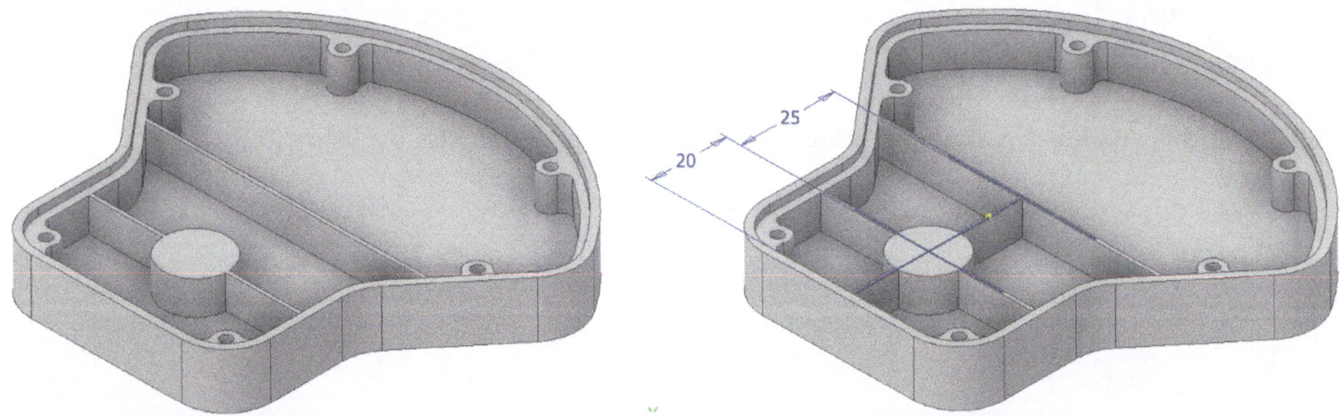

33. Activate the **Hole** command and notice that the sketch point is selected, automatically.
34. On the **Properties** panel, set the **Hole** type to **Simple Hole** and **Seat** type to **None**. Next, type **15** in the **Hole diameter** box and click **OK**.
35. In the **Model** window, expand the **Rib** feature, right-click on the sketch, and then deselect the **Visibility** option.

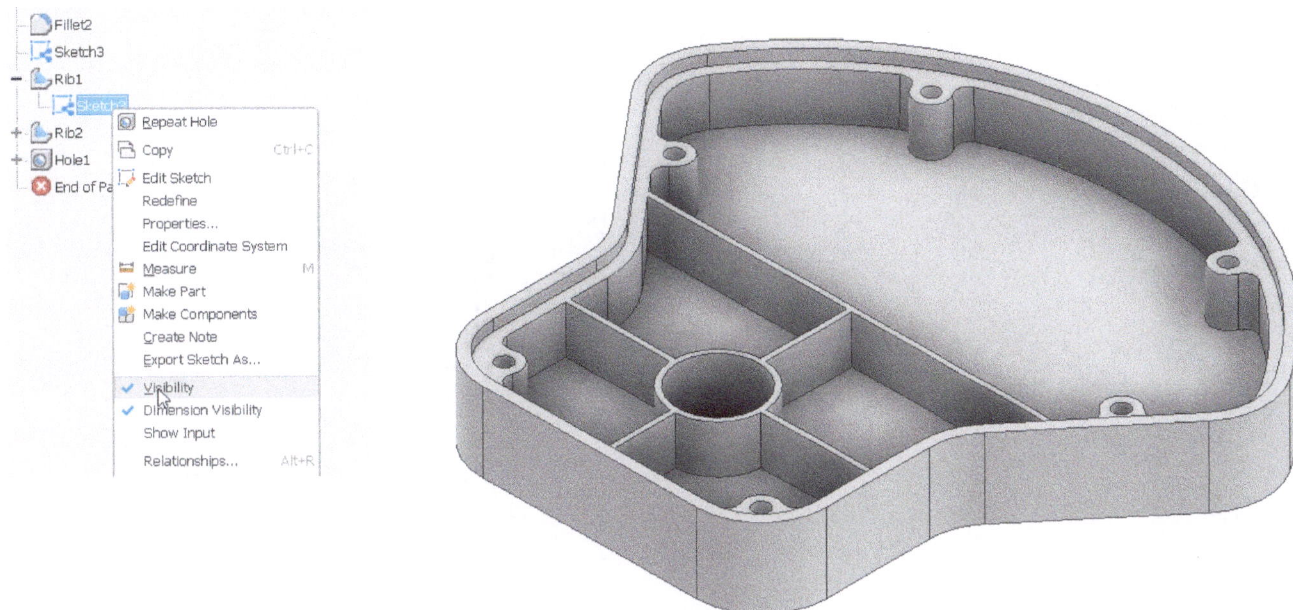

36. Save and close the file.

Questions

1. How to add a boss to a rib feature?
2. How many types of ribs can be created in Inventor?
3. Why do we create multi-body parts?
4. What are the three emboss types available on the **Emboss** dialog?

Exercises

Exercise 1 (Millimeters)

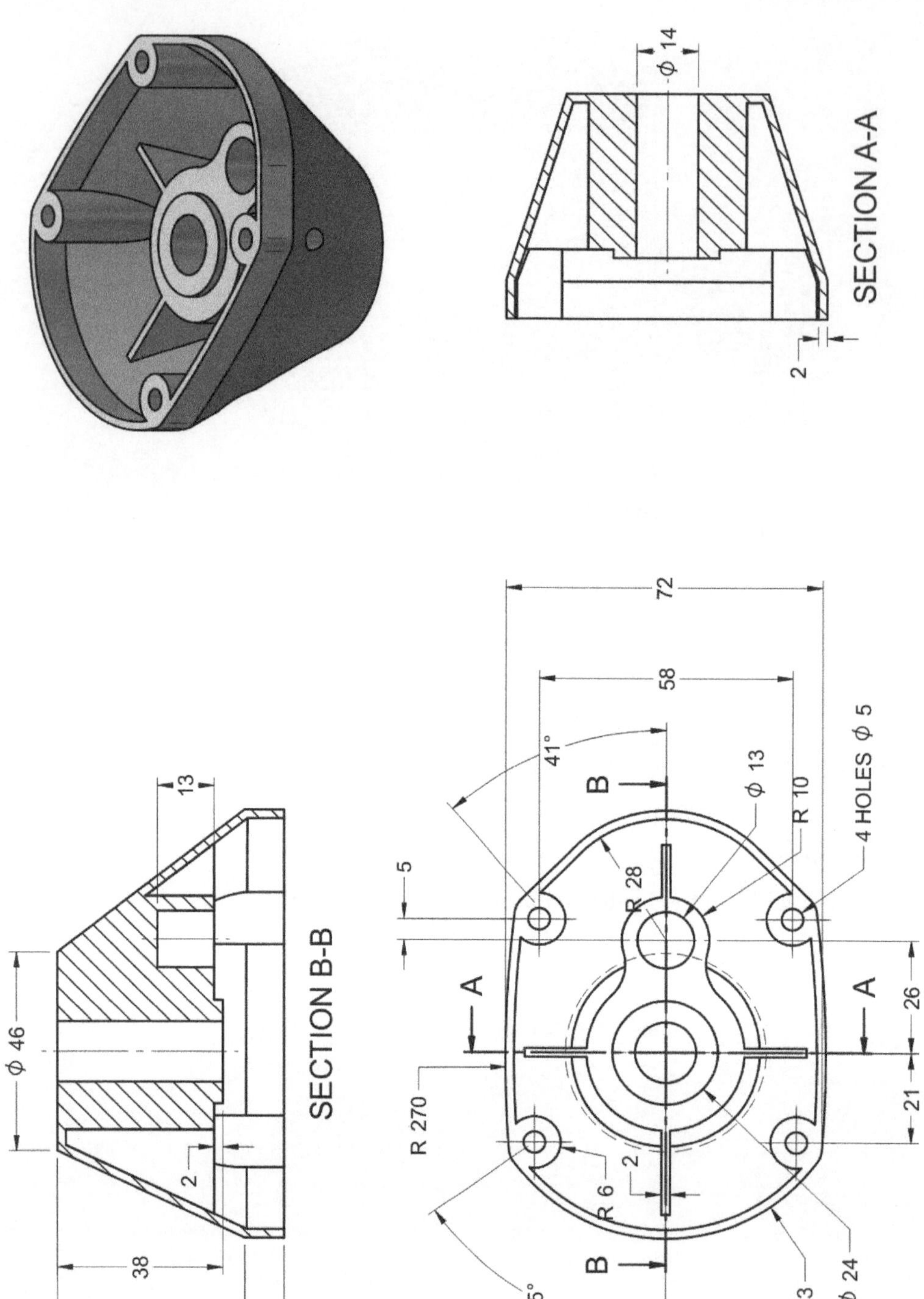
ϕ 14
SECTION A-A
2
ϕ 46
13
2
38
43
9
SECTION B-B
72
58
41°
B
ϕ 13
R 10
4 HOLES ϕ 5
5
R 28
A
A
R 270
26
21
R 6
2
55°
B
R 43
ϕ 24

Exercise 2 (Millimeters)

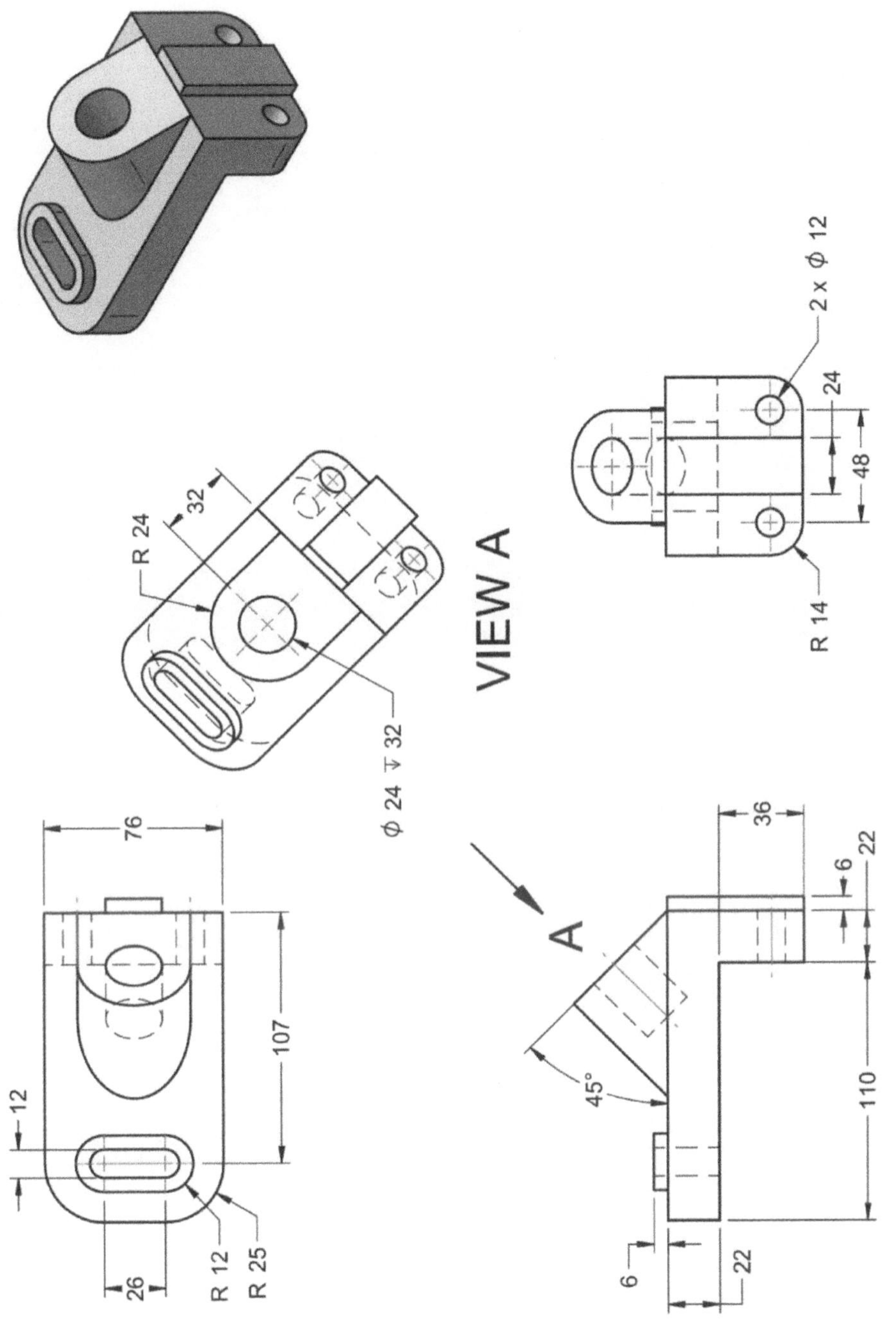

Exercise 3 (Inches)

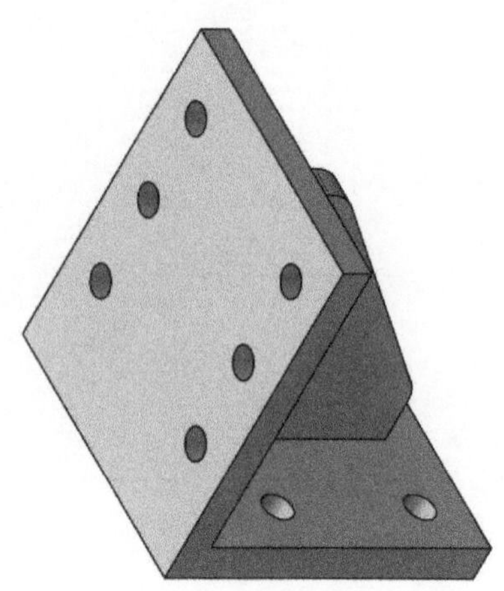

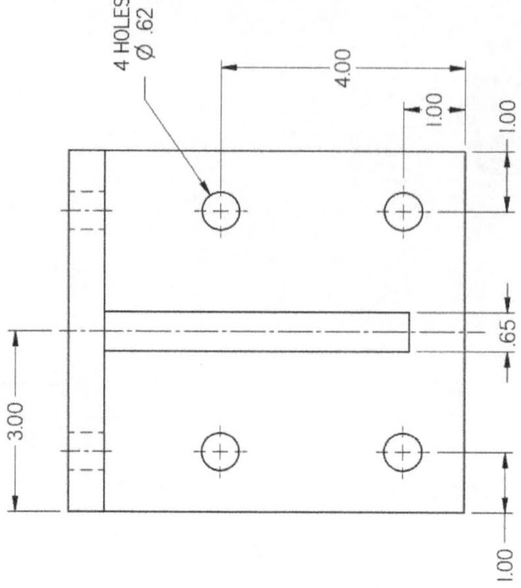

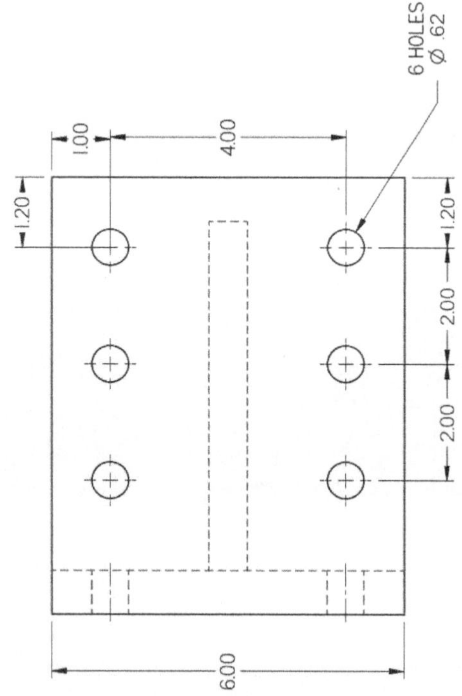

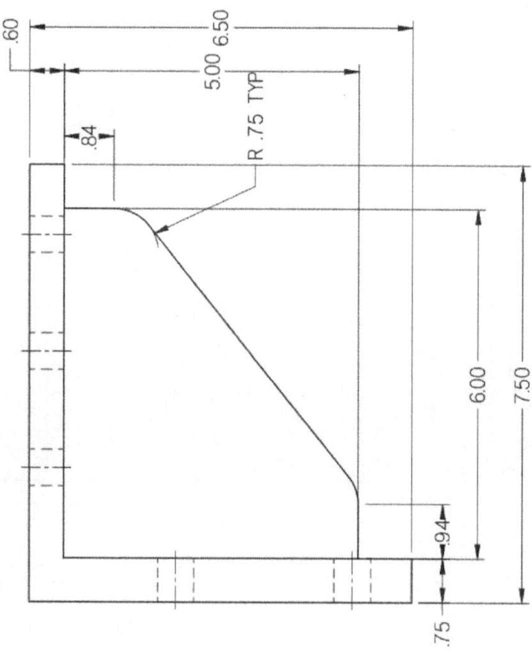

Chapter 9: Modifying Parts

In the design process, it is not required to achieve the final model in the first attempt. There is always a need to modify the existing parts to get the desired part geometry. In this chapter, you will learn various commands and techniques to make changes to a part.

The topics covered in this chapter are:

- *Edit Sketches*
- *Edit Features*
- *Suppress Features*

Edit Sketches

Sketches form the base of a 3D geometry. They control the size and shape of the geometry. If you want to modify the 3D geometry, most of the time, you are required to edit sketches. To do this, click on the feature and select **Edit Sketch**. Now, modify the sketch and click **Finish Sketch** on the ribbon. You will notice that the part geometry updates immediately.

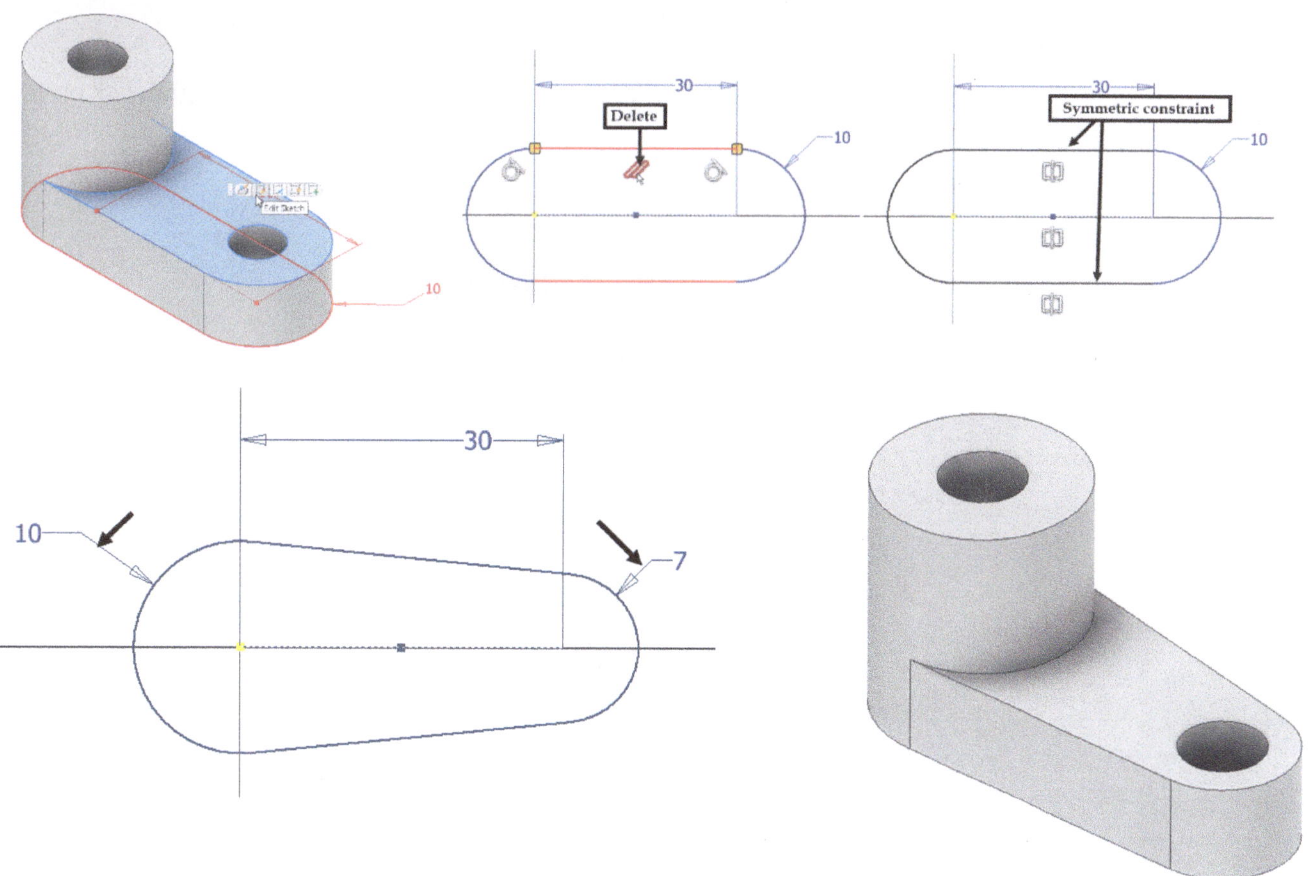

Edit Feature

Features are the building blocks of model geometry. To modify a feature, click the right mouse button on it and select **Edit Feature**. The dialog or panel related to the feature appears. On this dialog or panel, modify the parameters of the feature and click **OK**. The changes take place immediately.

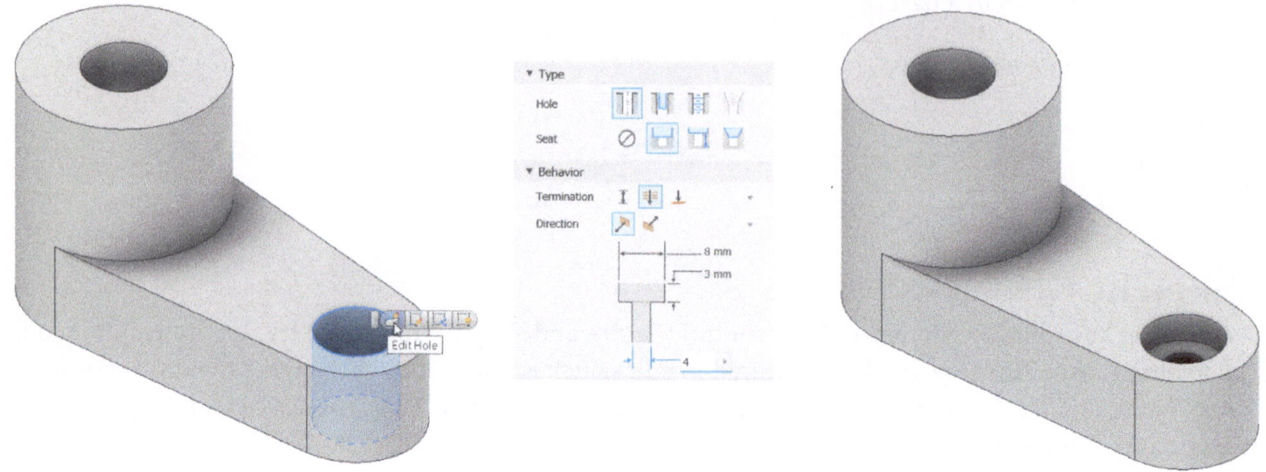

Suppress Features

Sometimes you may need to suppress some features of model geometry. In the Model window, right-click on the feature to suppress, and then select **Suppress Features**.

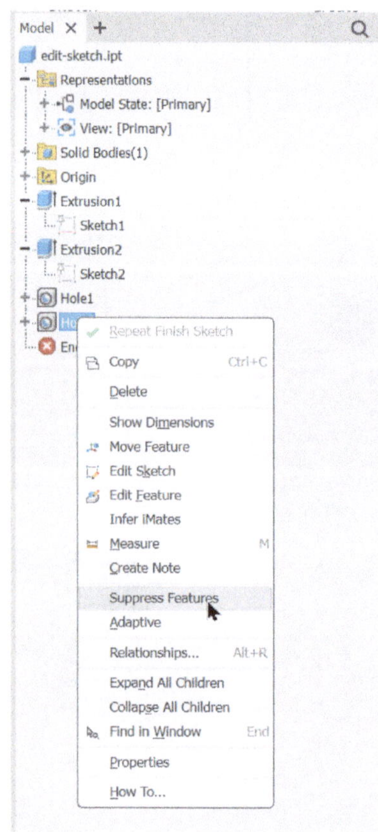

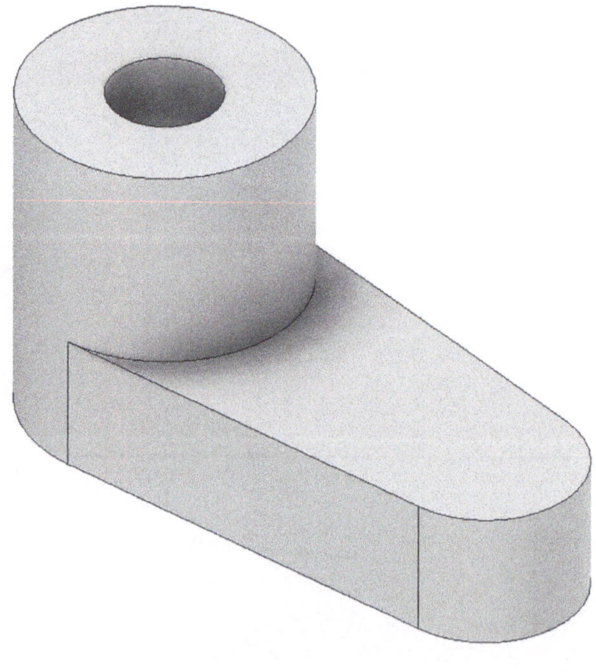

Resume Suppressed Features

If you want to resume the suppressed features, then right click on the suppressed feature in the **Model** window and select **Unsuppress Features**; the feature is resumed.

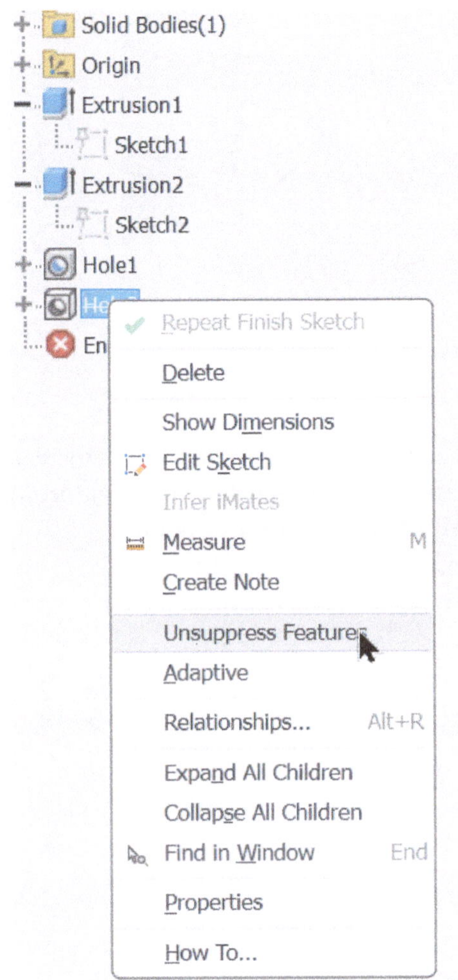

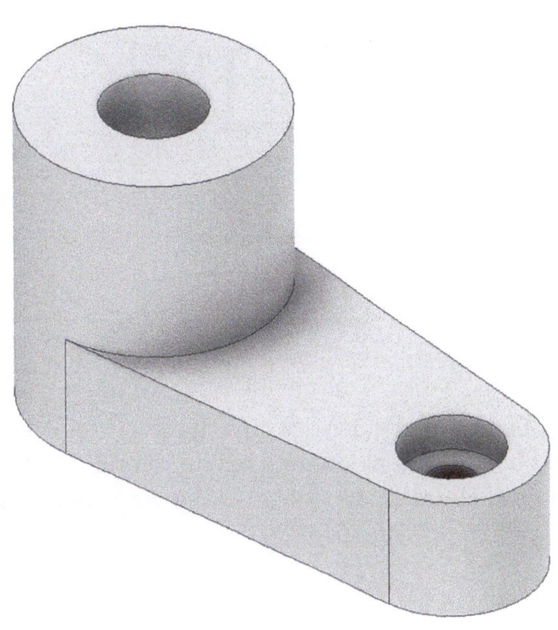

Parent-Child Relation

Parent-child relationships define dependencies between features in parametric modeling, ensuring that certain elements rely on others to exist. For example, a sketch serves as the foundational "Parent" for an extruded feature, which becomes its "Child." If the parent is suppressed or removed, dependent child features automatically lose their reference and are suppressed as well. This hierarchical structure prevents features from existing without their required references, such as sketch planes or geometric dependencies.

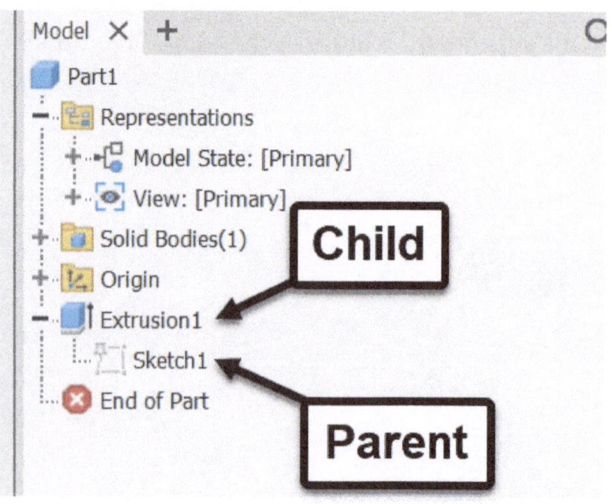

To manage feature dependencies effectively, Autodesk Inventor offers the **Relationships** tool. This tool helps you understand how different features in your model are connected. You can access it by right-clicking on a feature (as shown with **Hole1** in the image) in the browser and selecting **Relationships** from the context menu.

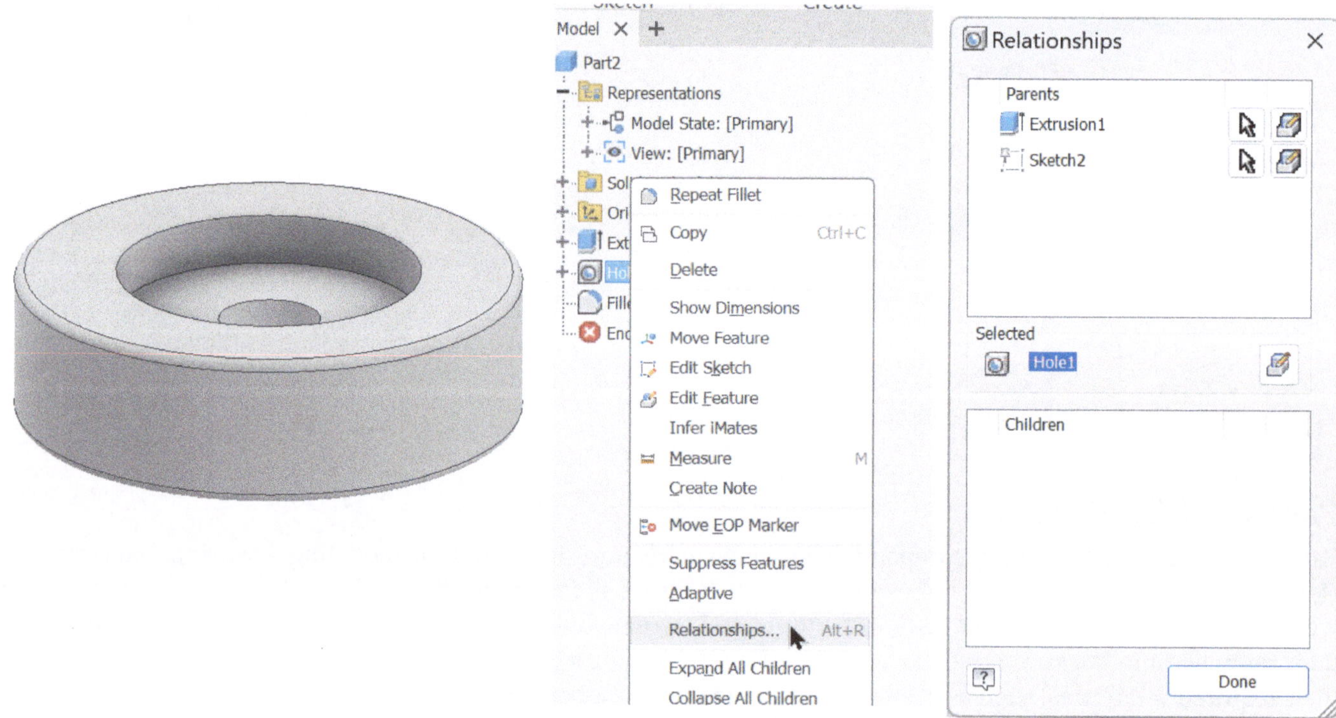

In the **Relationships** dialog, the **Parents** section lists all the features that the selected element depends on. For example, in the image, Hole1 depends on Extrusion1 and Sketch2, meaning the hole feature uses the surface created by the extrusion and the sketch that defines its position or size.

The **Children** section would list any features that depend on the selected one. If another feature had been built based on Hole1, it would appear here.

These relationships are crucial when editing complex models because they show how changes to one feature may impact others. For example, modifying or deleting Extrusion1 could directly affect Hole1 and lead to model errors if not handled properly.

The Direct Edit command

Autodesk Inventor includes a **Direct Edit** tool (on the ribbon, click **3D Model** > **Modify** > **Direct Edit**) that allows you to make flexible modifications to part geometry without editing sketches or features. This is particularly useful for quick changes in imported geometry (such as from STEP or IGES files) or when direct manipulation is faster than parametric edits. You can perform five operations using this tool: **Move**, **Size**, **Scale**, **Rotate**, and **Delete** faces.

Move

The **Move** option allows you to move the selected face or body along X, Y, or Z directions. To translate faces in a particular direction, select the **Move** option from the mini toolbar. Next, click on the face to move, and then select any of the arrows that appear on the screen. Press and hold the mouse button, and then drag the pointer. You can specify the translation distance using the arrows or the **Distance** box displayed in the graphics window.

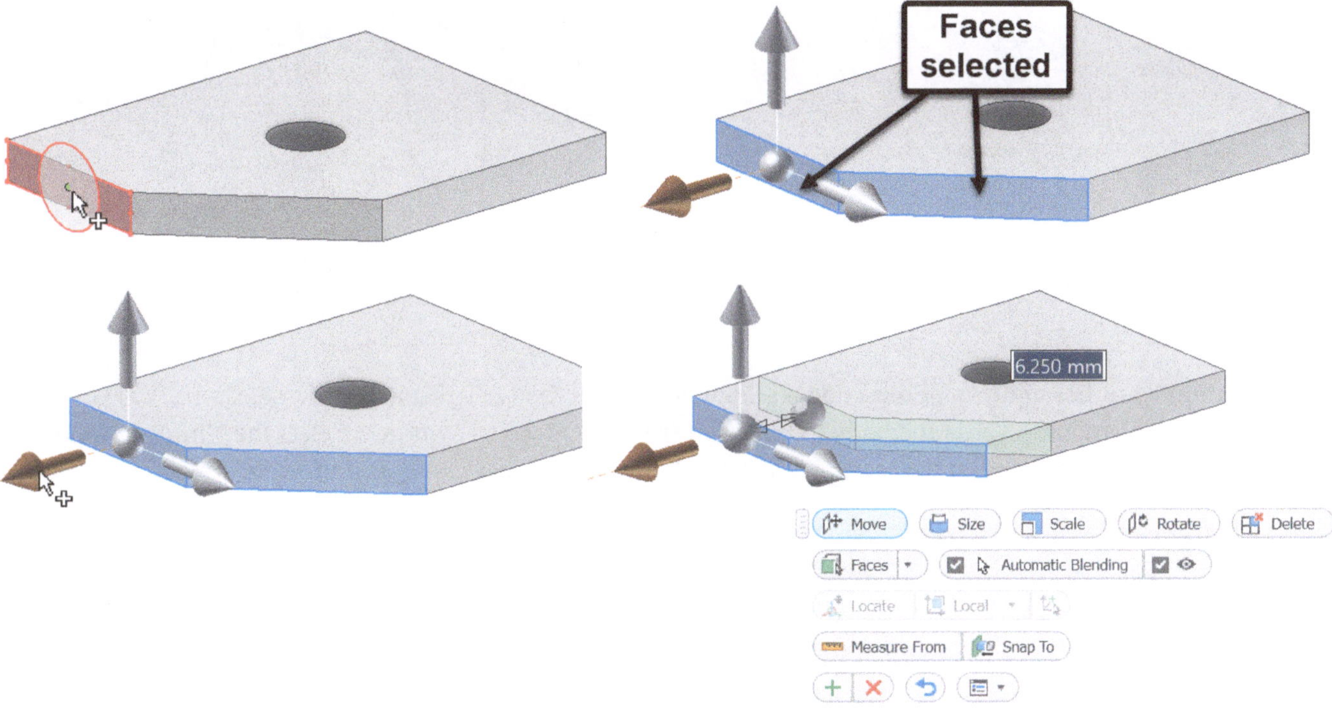

Size

The **Size** option allows you to resize faces to adjust the length, width, or depth of features. To resize a face, select the **Size** option from the mini toolbar. Next, click on the face to resize, and then drag the manipulator to adjust the size. You can also type in a value in the **Distance** box displayed in the graphics window. Click the **Apply** icon on the mini toolbar to apply the changes.

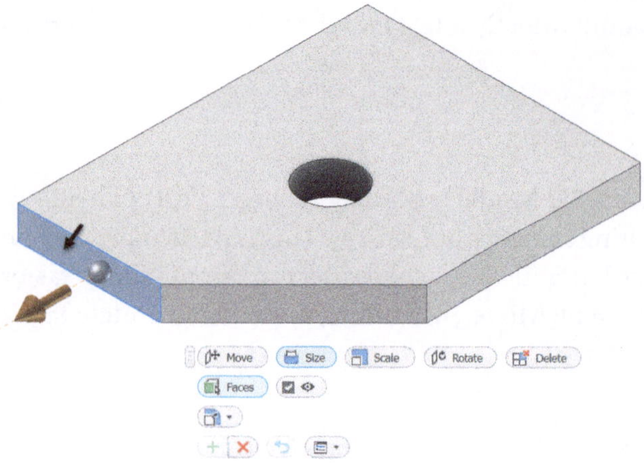

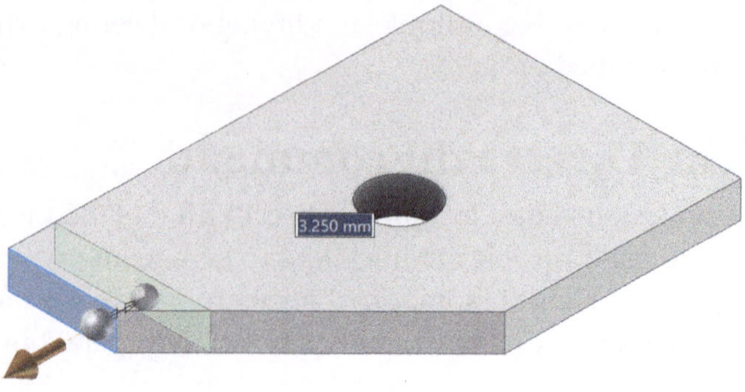

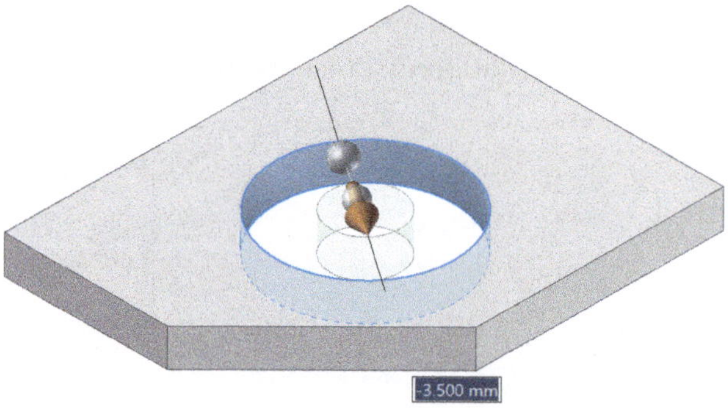

Scale

The **Scale** option applies uniform or directional scaling to selected body. To scale a body, select the Scale option from the mini toolbar. Next, select the body to be scaled from the graphics window. Select the Uniform option from the mini toolbar and type-in the scale factor in the X box; the selected body is uniformly scaled.

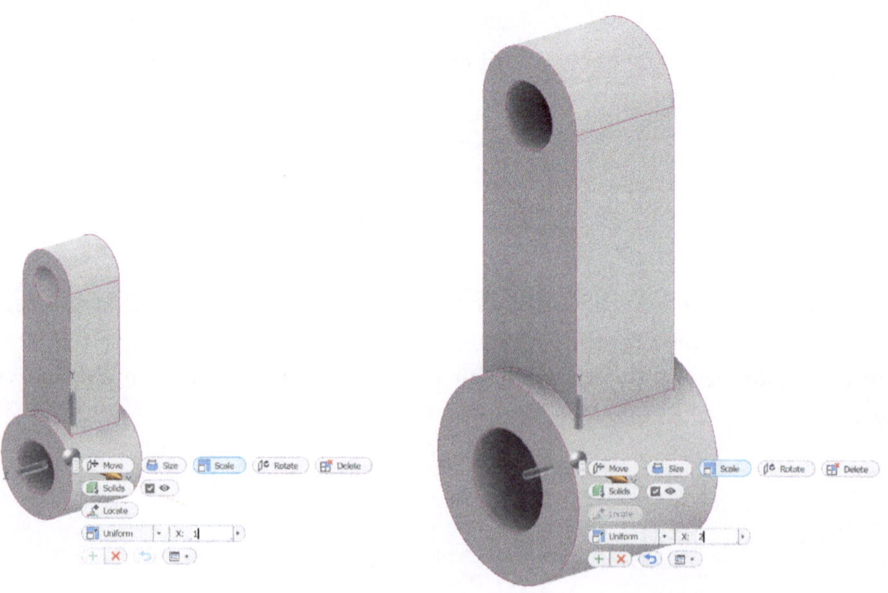

Select the **Non Uniform** option and type-in values in the **X**, **Y**, **Z** boxes; the part geometry is scaled along three directions using the coordinate values.

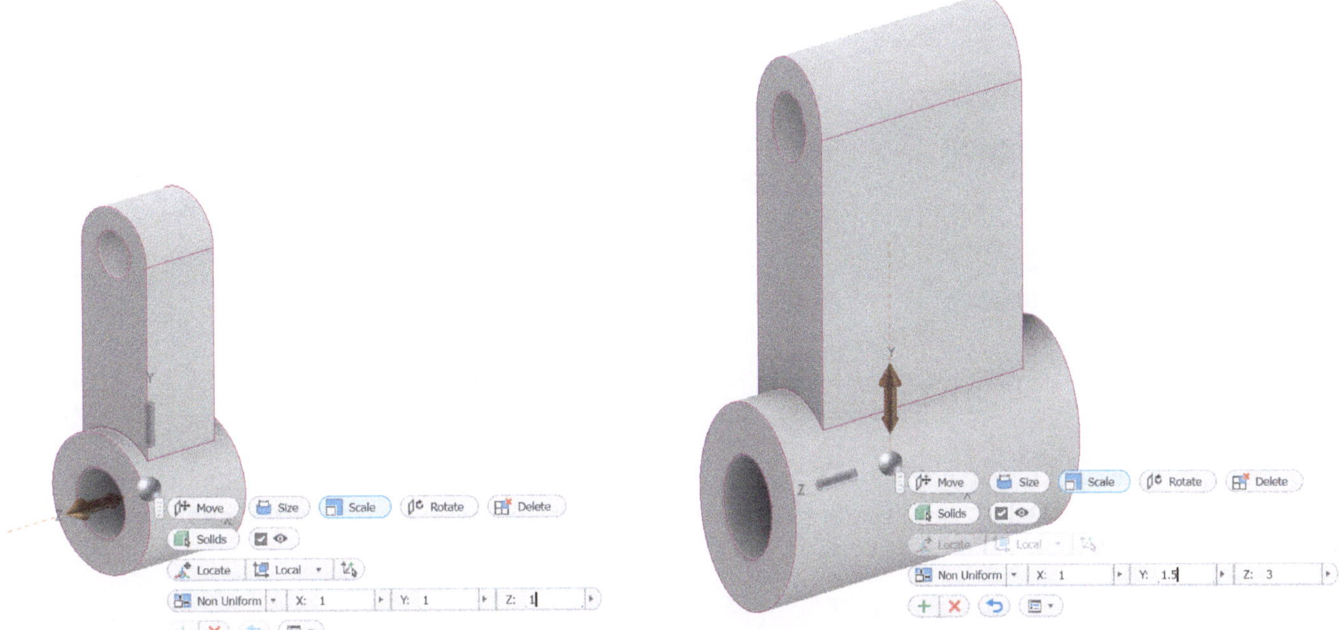

Rotate

The **Rotate** option helps you to rotate the selected faces about an axis. To rotate a face, select the **Rotate** option from the mini toolbar. Next, click on the face to rotate; the manipulator is displayed. Click the **Locate** button on the mini toolbar, and then select an edge. This defines the location of the manipulator. Next, select an axis from the manipulator and drag the sphere-shaped manipulator; the selected face is rotated. You can also type in a value in the **Angle** box displayed in the graphics window. Click **Apply** on the mini toolbar.

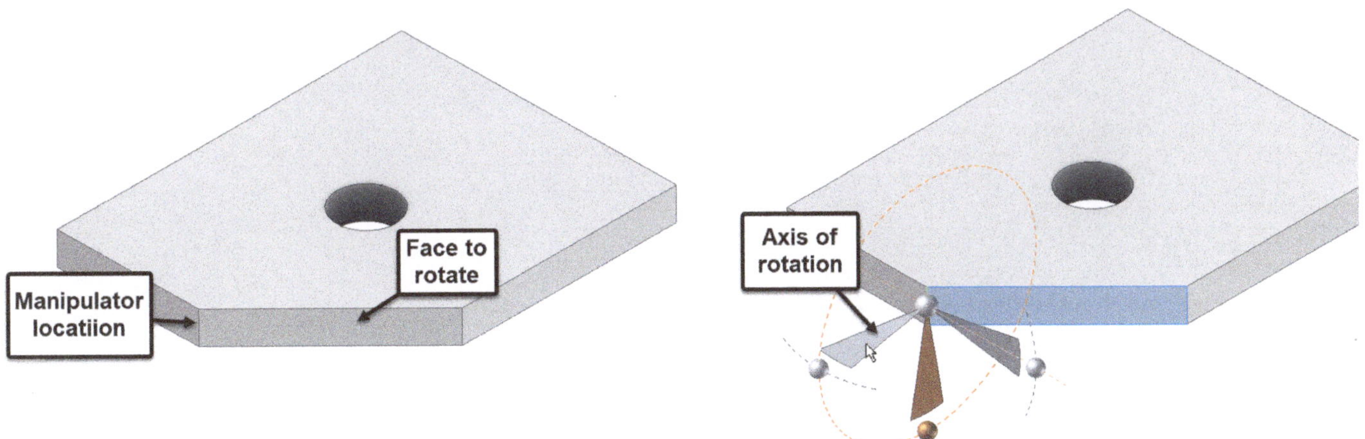

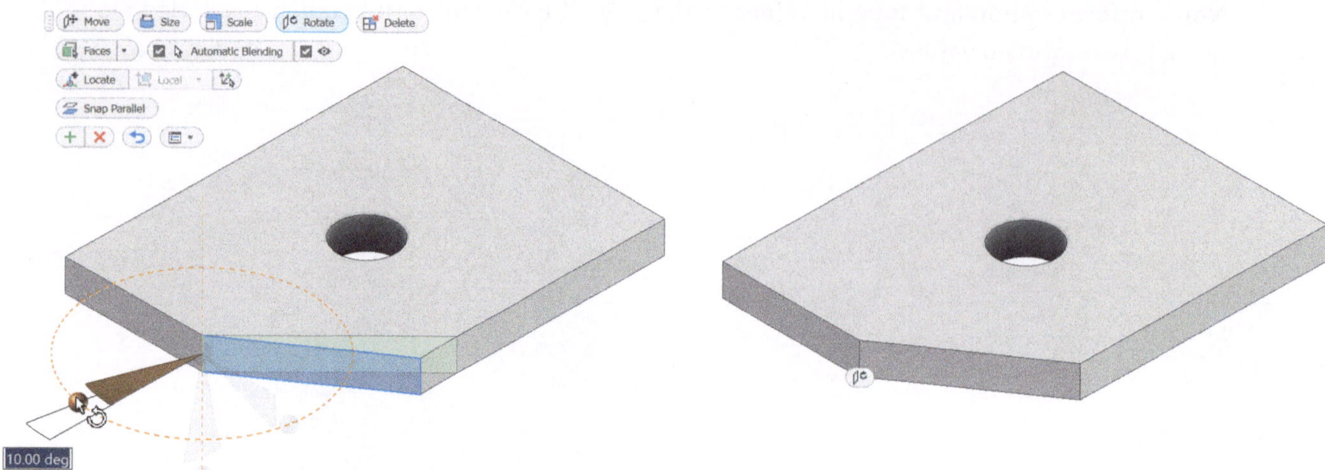

Delete

The **Delete** option helps you to remove faces from the geometry while attempting to heal surrounding surfaces. To delete a face, select the **Delete** option from the mini toolbar. Next, click on the face to delete and then click **Apply**.

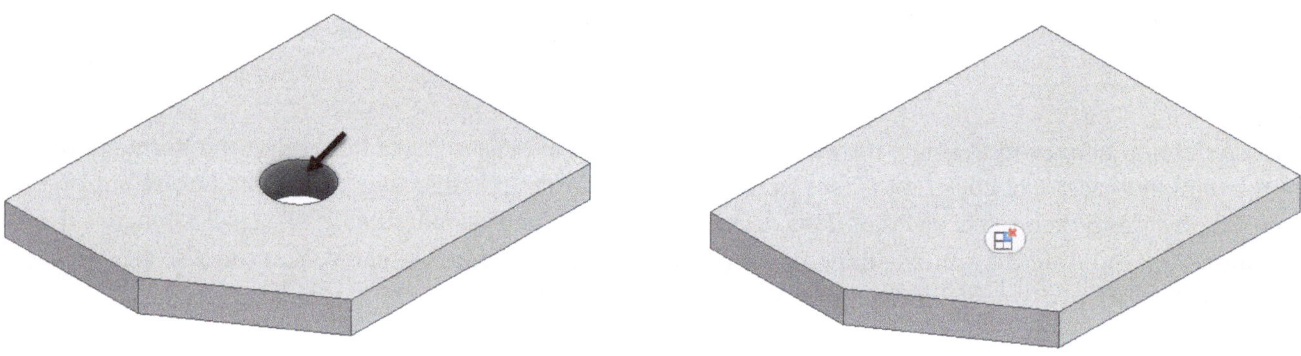

Examples

Example 1 (Inches)

In this example, you will create the part shown below and then modify it.

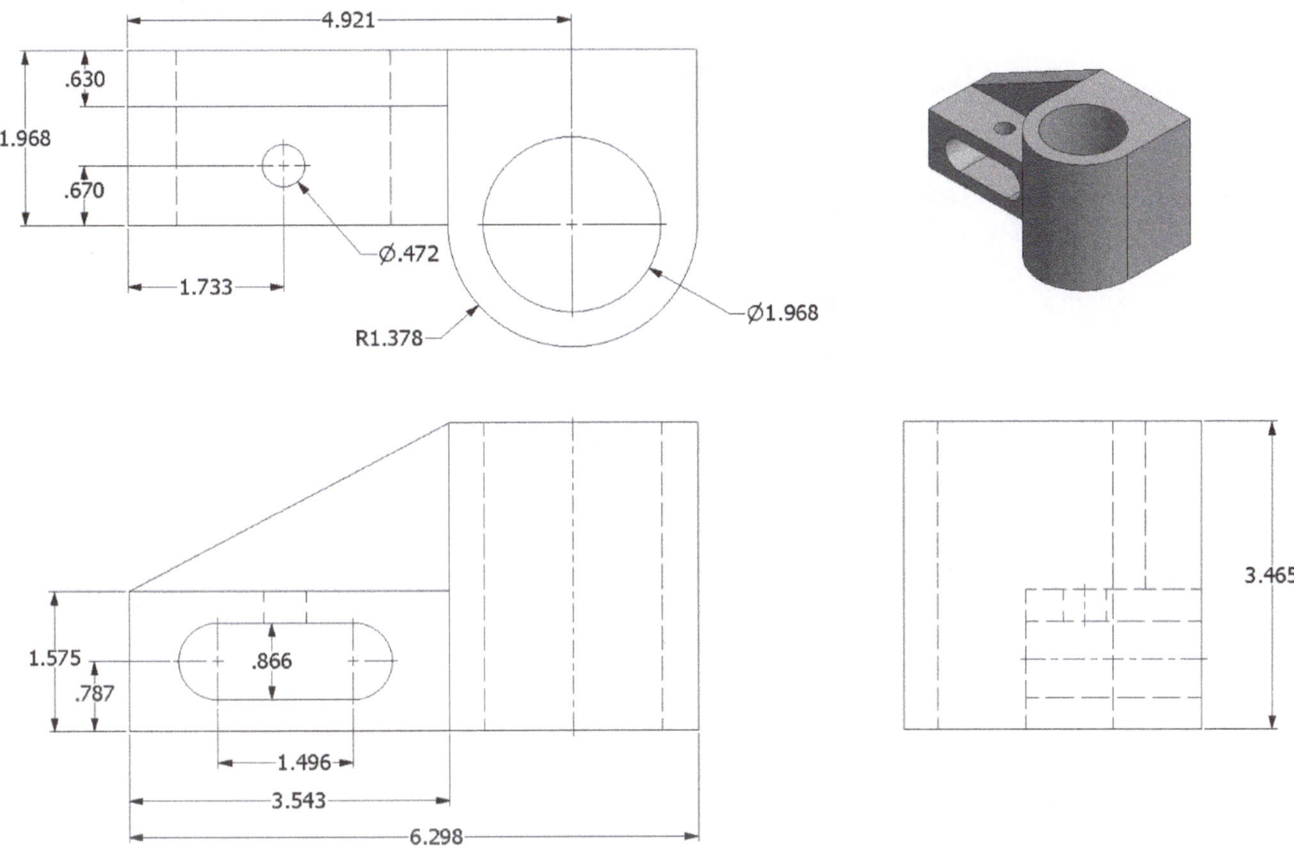

1. Start **Autodesk Inventor 2026** and open a part file and create the part using the tools and commands available in Inventor.

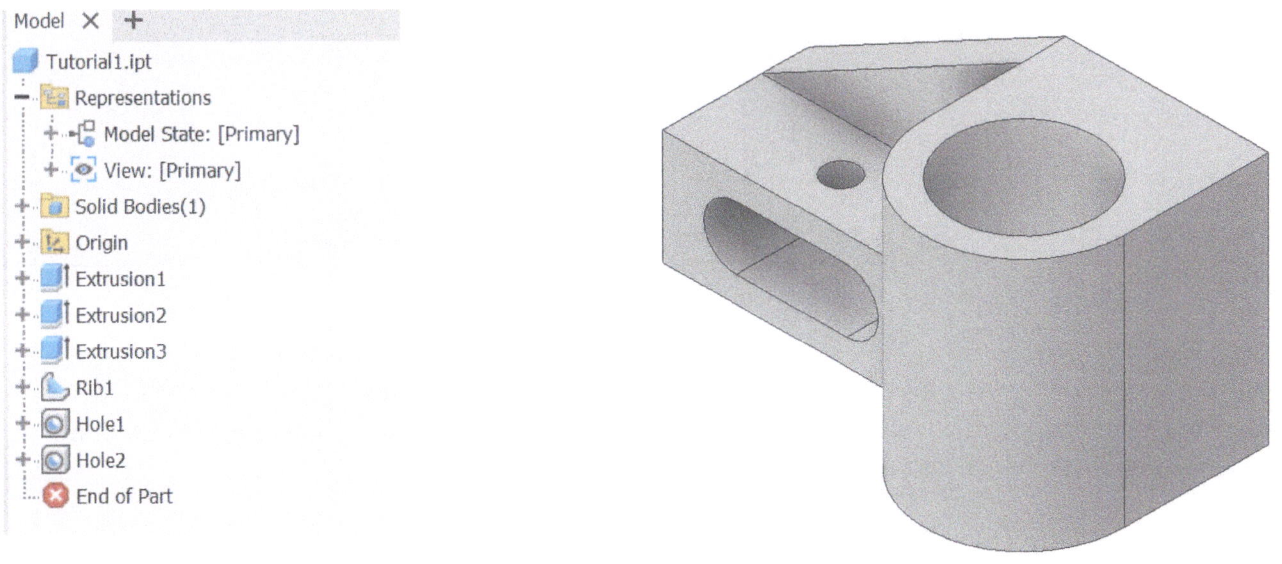

2. Click on the large hole and select **Edit Hole**; the **Properties** panel appears. On the **Properties** panel, select **Seat > Counterbore**.
3. Enter **1.378**, **1.968**, and **0.787** in the **Diameter**, **Counterbore Diameter**, and **Counterbore Depth** boxes, respectively. Click **OK**.

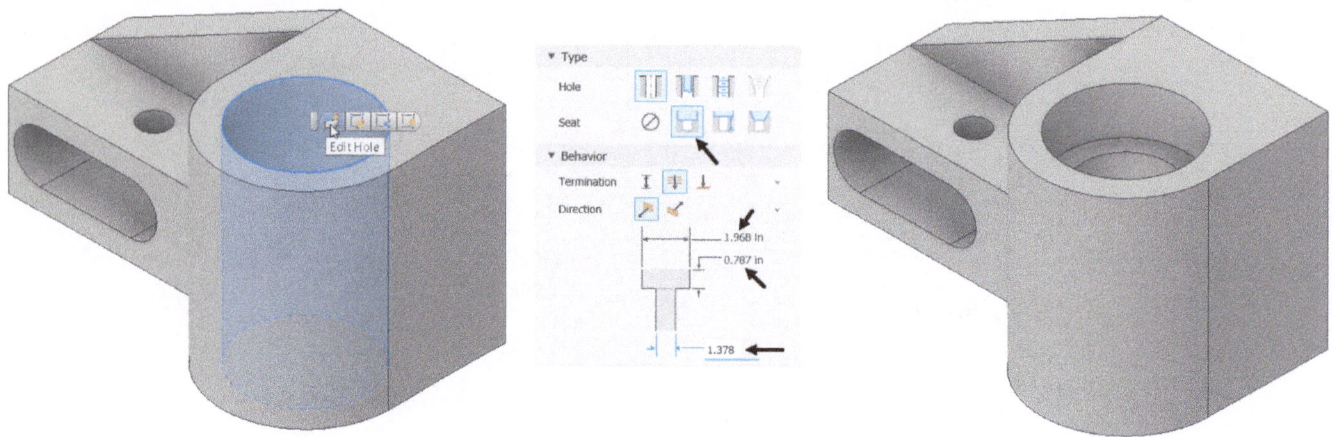

4. Click on the rectangular *Extrude* feature and select **Edit Sketch**. Modify the sketch, as shown. Click **Finish Sketch**.

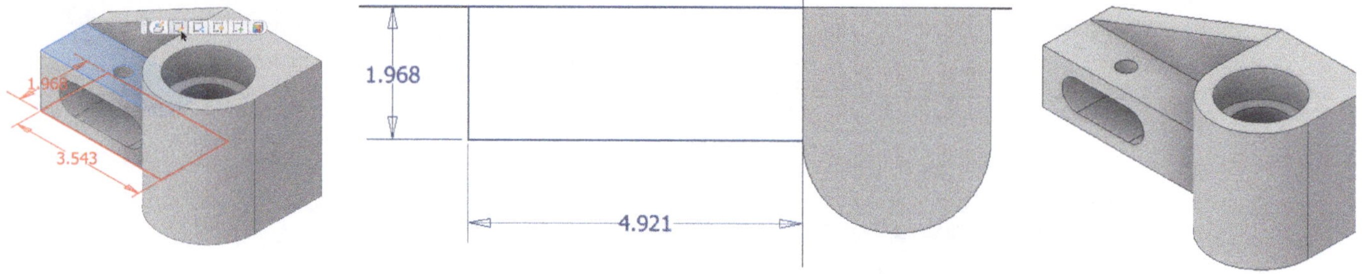

5. Click on the slot and select **Edit Sketch**.
6. Delete the length dimension of the slot, and then add a new dimension between the right-side arc and right vertical edge.

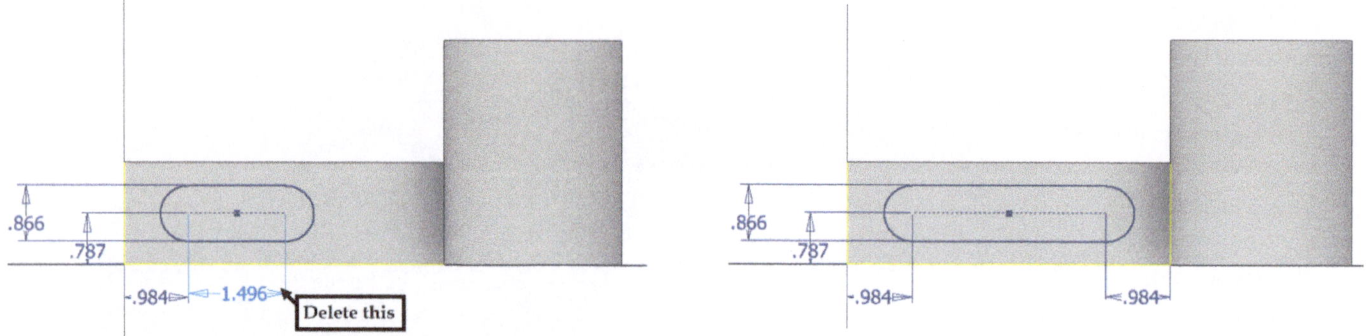

7. Delete the dimension between the centerline of the slot and the horizontal edge.
8. Apply the **Horizontal** constraint between the centerpoint of the slot and the midpoint of the left vertical edge. Click **Finish Sketch** on the ribbon.

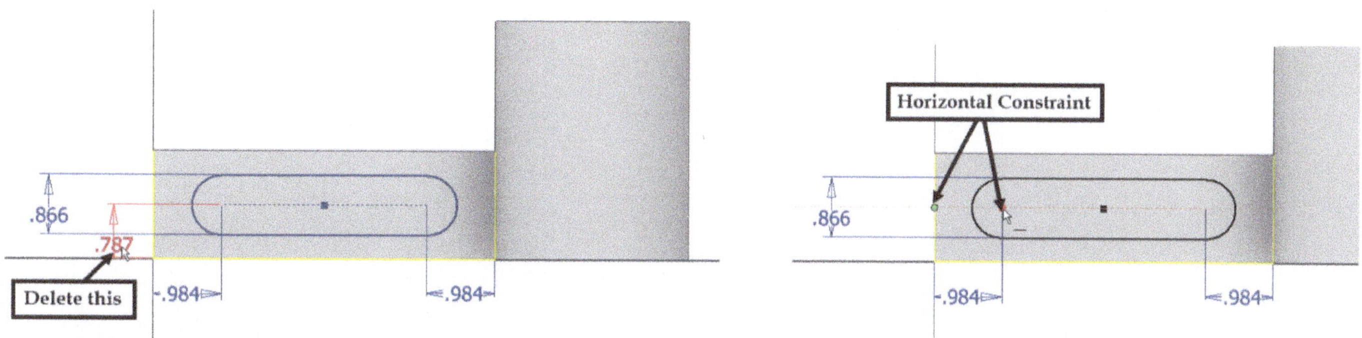

9. Click on the small hole, and then click **Edit Sketch**. Next, delete the positioning dimensions.

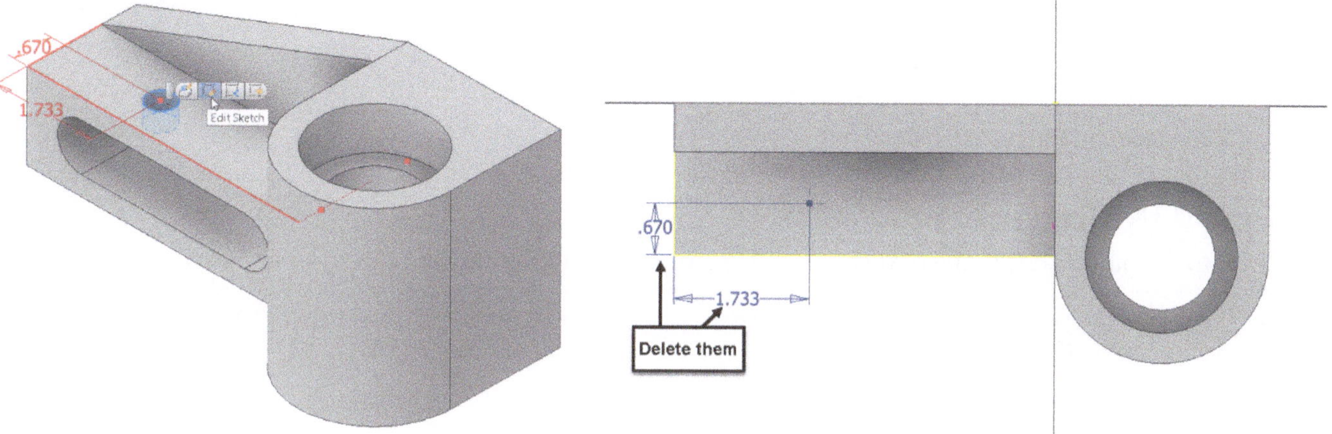

10. Create a construction line and make its ends coincident with the corners, as shown below.
11. On the ribbon, click **Sketch > Constrain > Coincident** and select the hole point. Next, select the midpoint of the construction line. Click **Finish Sketch** on the ribbon.

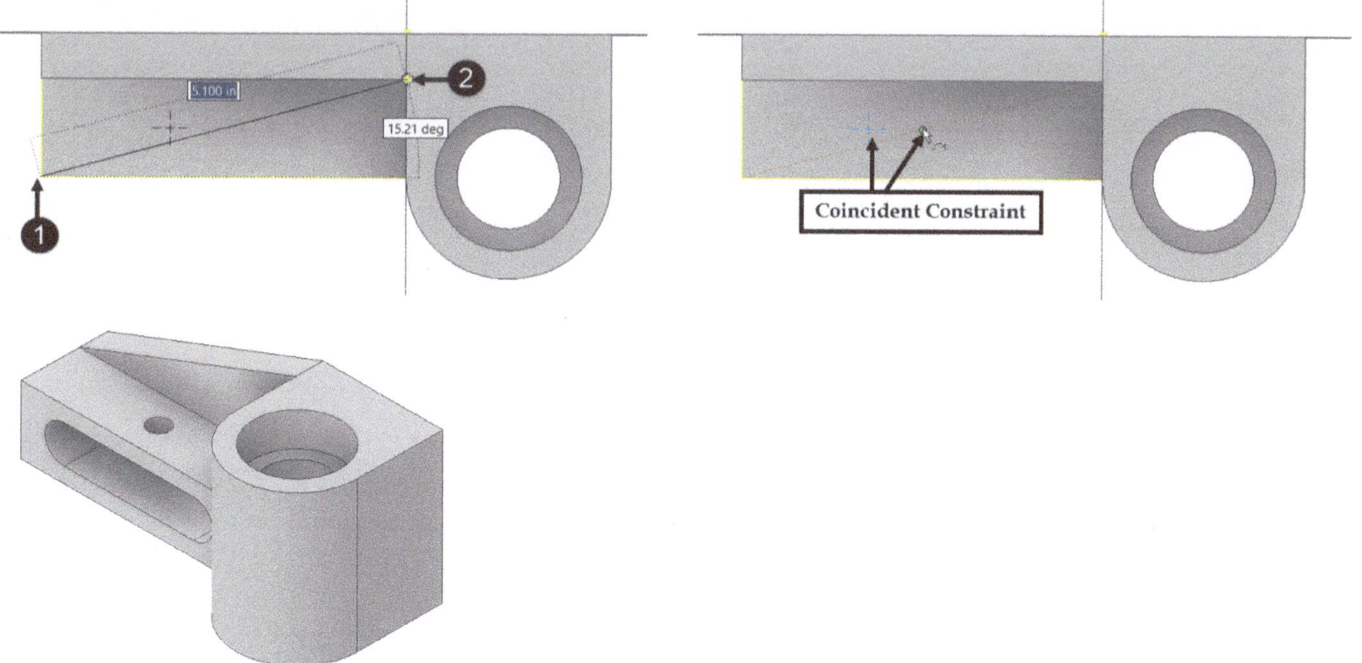

12. Now, change the size of the rectangular extrude feature. You will notice that the slot and hole are adjusted automatically.

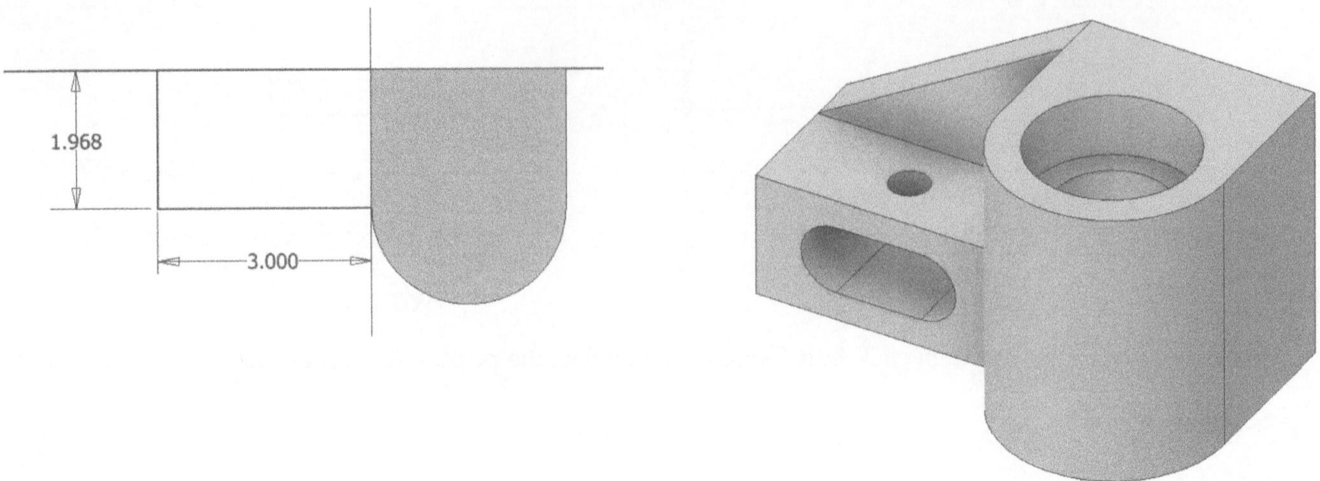

13. Save and close the file.

Example 2 (Millimetres)

In this example, you will create the part shown below, and then modify it using the editing tools.

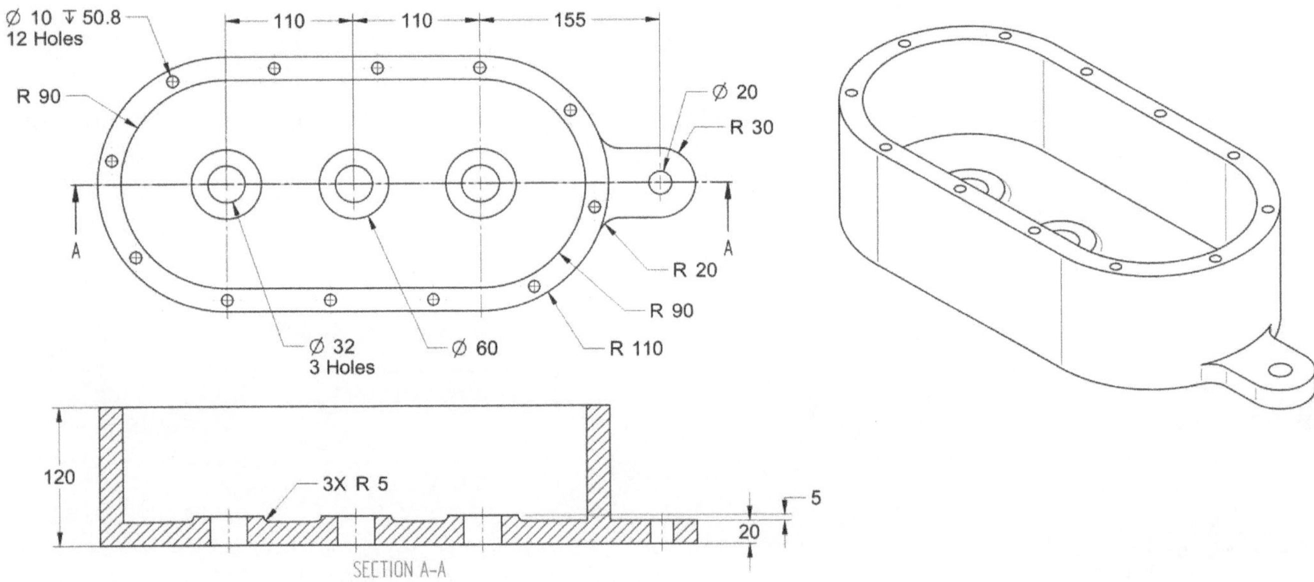

1. Start **Autodesk Inventor 2026.**
2. Click the **File** menu button located at the top left corner. On the **File** menu, click **New.** On the **Create New File** dialog, click **Templates > en-US > Metric**, and then double-click on the **Standard (mm).ipt** template; a new part file is opened.
3. Create the part using the tools and commands in Inventor.
4. Click on the **20** mm diameter hole, and then click **Edit Hole**; the **Properties** panel appears.
5. On the **Properties** panel, select **Seat > Counterbore**.
6. Set the **Counterbore Diameter** to **30** and **Counterbore Depth** to **10**. Click **OK** to close the panel.

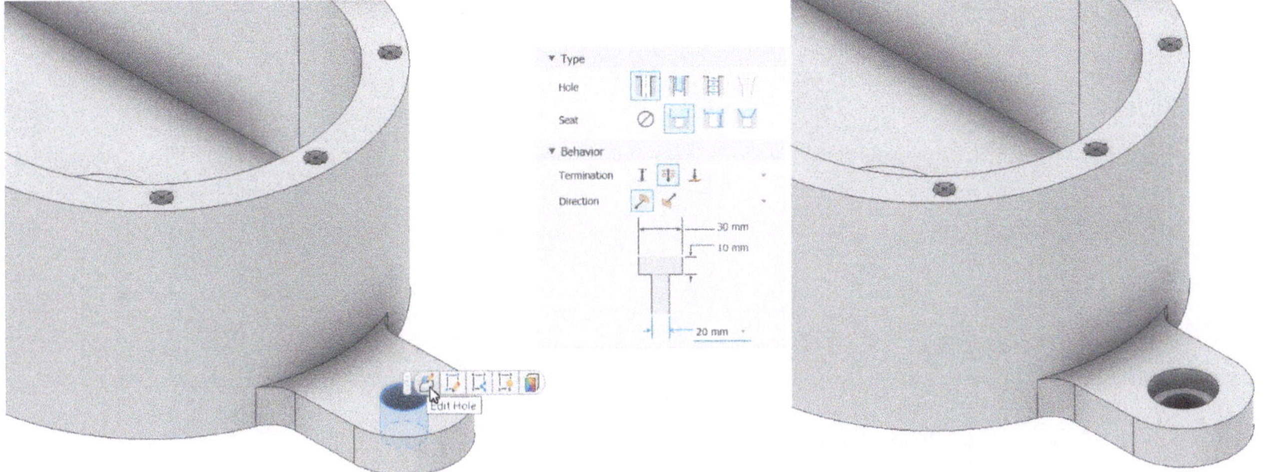

7. On the ribbon, click **3D Model > Modify > Direct**, and then click **Move** on the Mini toolbar.
8. Click on the counterbore hole and the cylindrical face concentric to it. Next, select the arrow pointing toward the right.
9. Press and hold the left mouse button on the selected arrow, drag, and then release it.
10. Type **20** in the value box that appears in the graphics window, and press Enter.

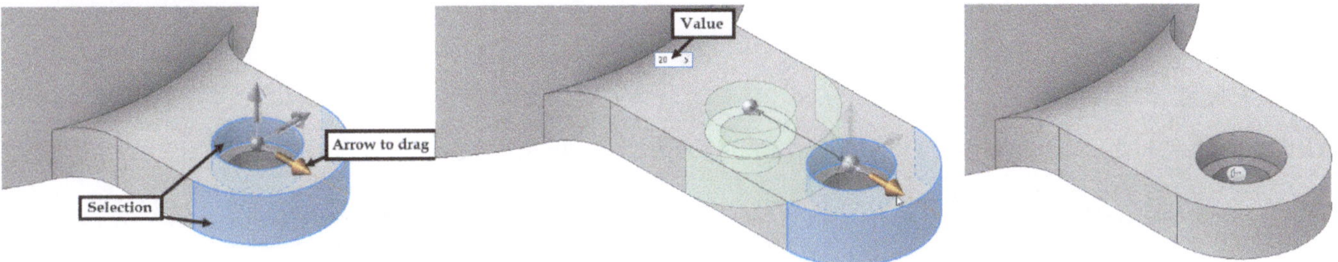

11. Click on any one of the holes of the curve driven pattern, and then select **Edit Rectangular Pattern**.
12. Type **14** in the **Occurrence Count** box and click **OK** to update the pattern.

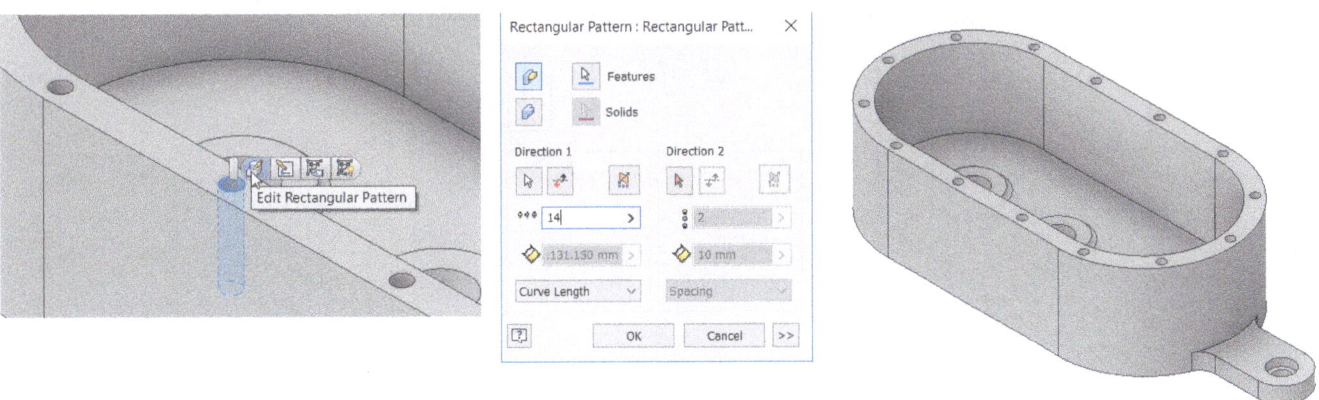

13. On the ribbon, click **3D Model > Modify > Direct**, and then select all the holes of the curve driven pattern.
14. Click on the top face of the geometry and select the **Move** option from the Mini toolbar.
15. Click on the arrow pointing upwards. Press and hold the left mouse button and drag the mouse pointer down. Type **-40** in dimension box and press Enter to update the model.

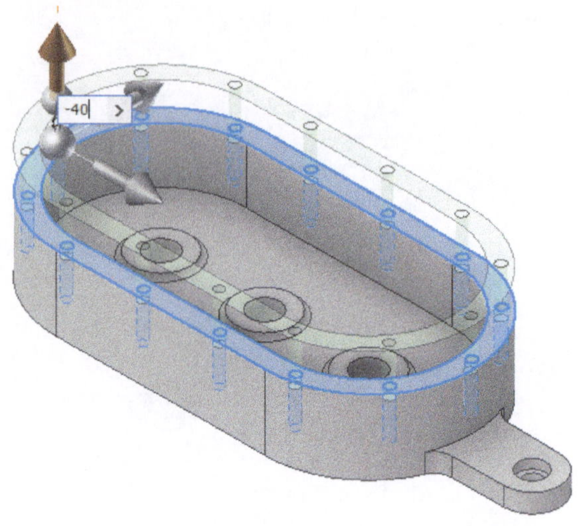

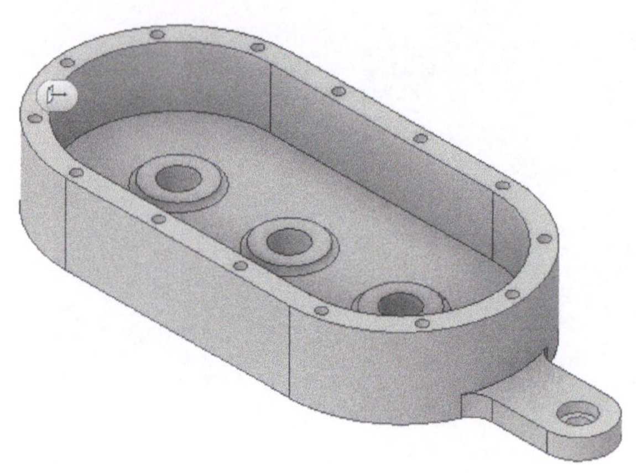

16. Save and close the file.

Questions

1. How to modify the sketch of a feature?
2. How to modify a feature directly?
3. How can you suppress a feature?

Exercises

Exercise 1

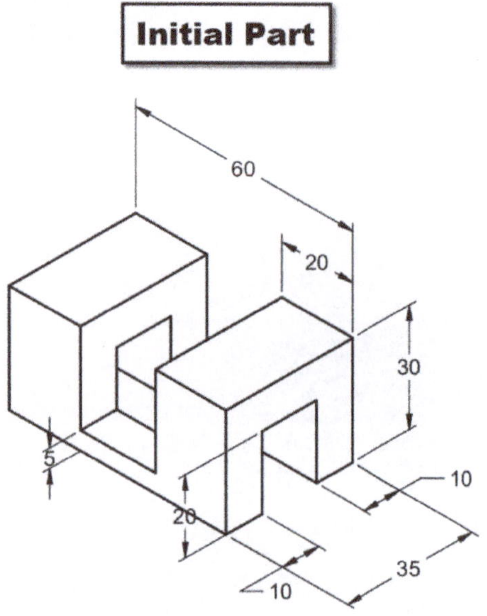

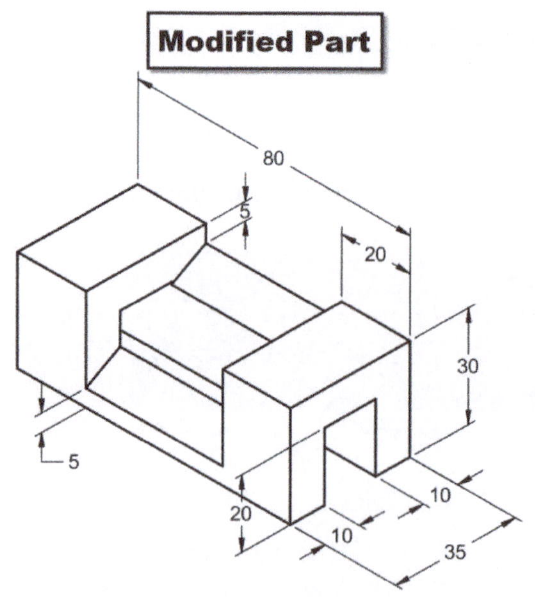

Chapter 10: Assemblies

After creating individual parts, you can bring them together into an assembly. By doing so, it is possible to identify incorrect design problems that may not have been noticeable at the part level. In this chapter, you will learn how to bring parts into the assembly environment and position them.

The topics covered in this chapter are:

- *Starting an assembly*
- *Inserting Parts*
- *Adding Constraints*
- *Dragging Parts*
- *Check Interference*
- *iMates*
- *Editing Assemblies*
- *Replace Parts*
- *Pattern and Mirror Parts*
- *Create Subassemblies*
- *Demote and Promote Parts*
- *Assembly Features*
- *Top-down Assembly Design*
- *Create Exploded Views*

Starting an Assembly

To begin an assembly file, you can select the **Assembly** option from the **New** drop-down on the **Home** Screen (or) click the **New** icon on the **Quick Access Toolbar** and select **Standard(mm).iam** from the **Create New File** dialog.

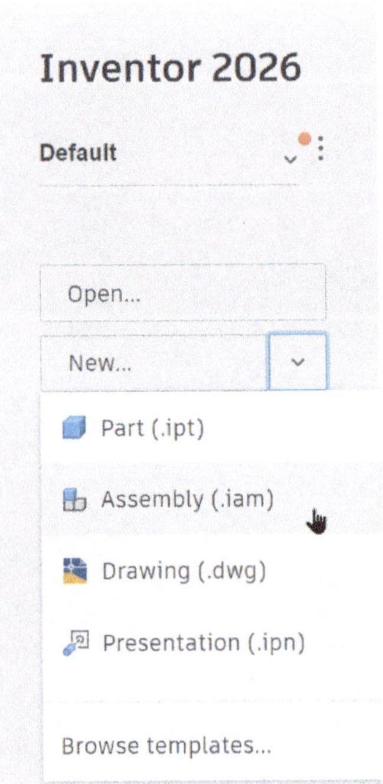

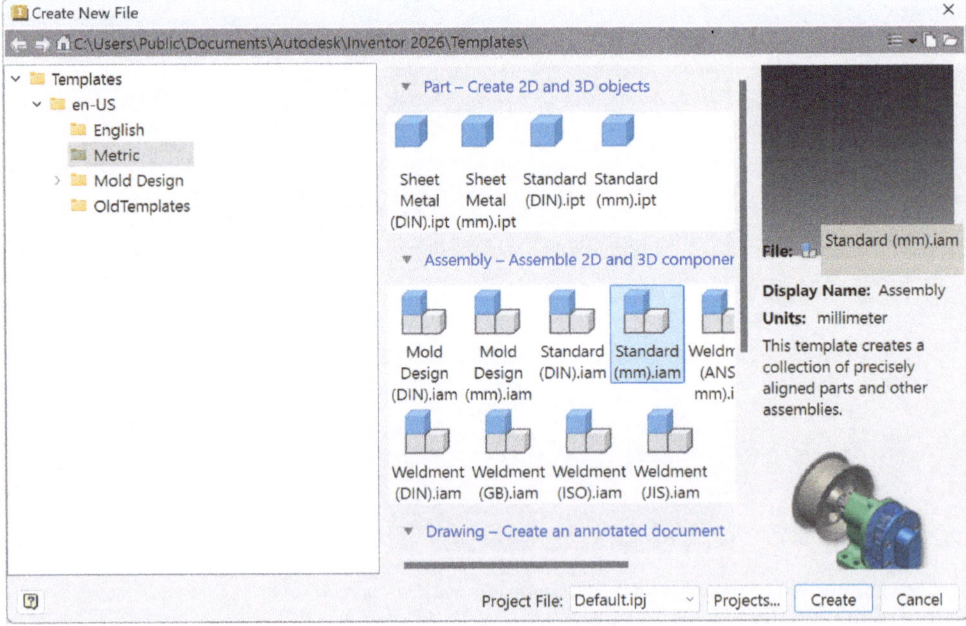

Another way to start an assembly is by using the File menu. Click on the **File menu > New > Assembly**; the assembly file is created. Now, you can insert the part file or subassembly file.

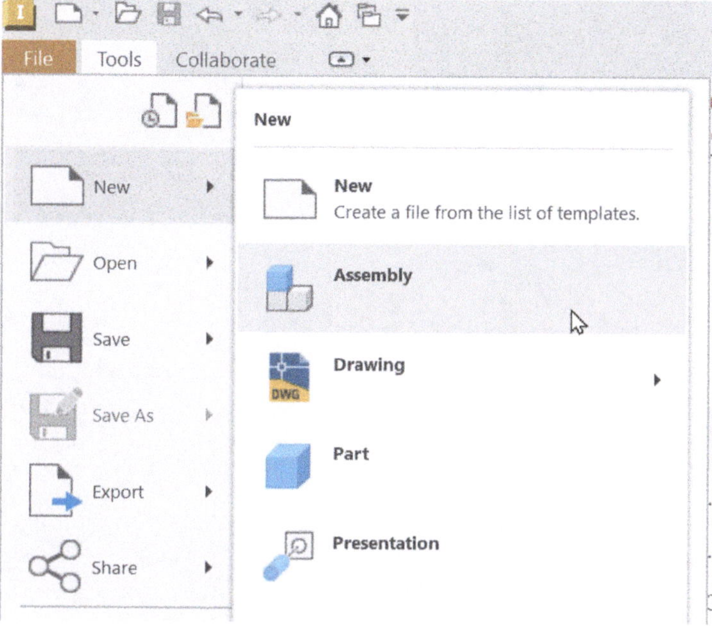

Inserting Parts

Now, you can insert parts into the assembly by using the **Place** command. On the ribbon, click **Assembly > Component > Place** to open the **Place Component** dialog. Go to the location of the parts on the **Place Component** dialog and select the component. As you select a component from the dialog, you can see a preview of the part in the **Preview** box on the left. Now, click **Open** or double-click on the part to insert.

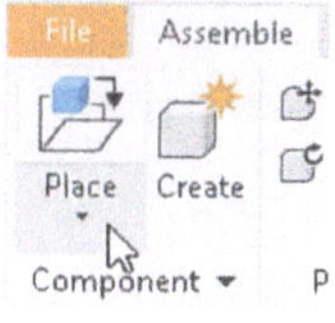

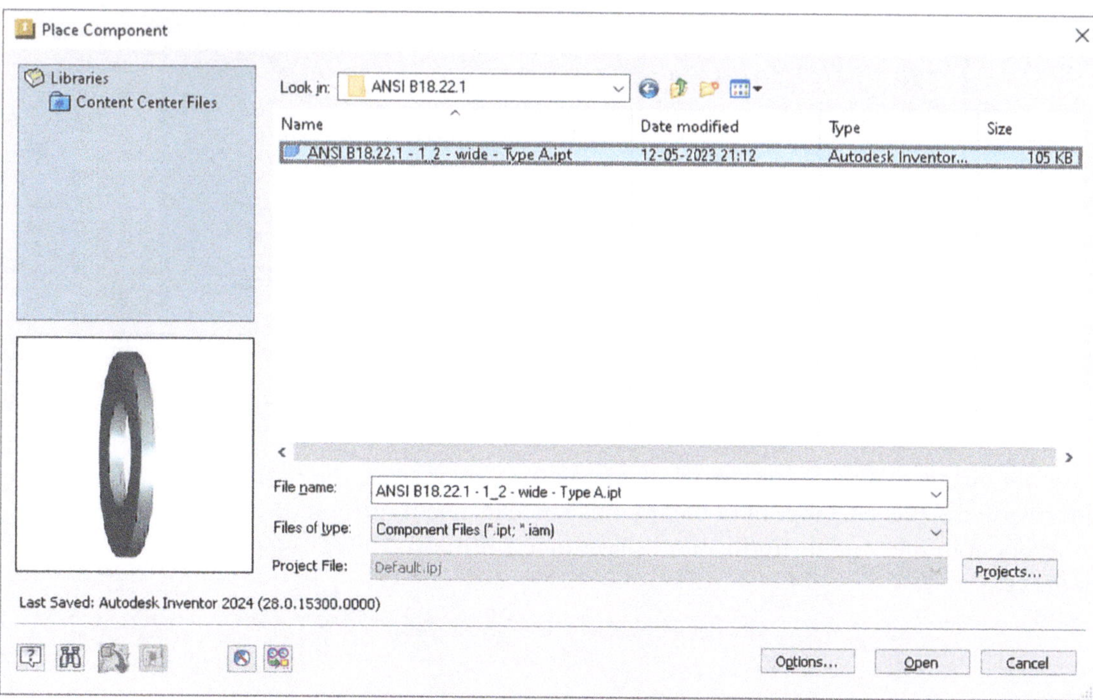

Assemblies

You can also drag a component directly from the **File Explorer**, and then place it into the graphics window.

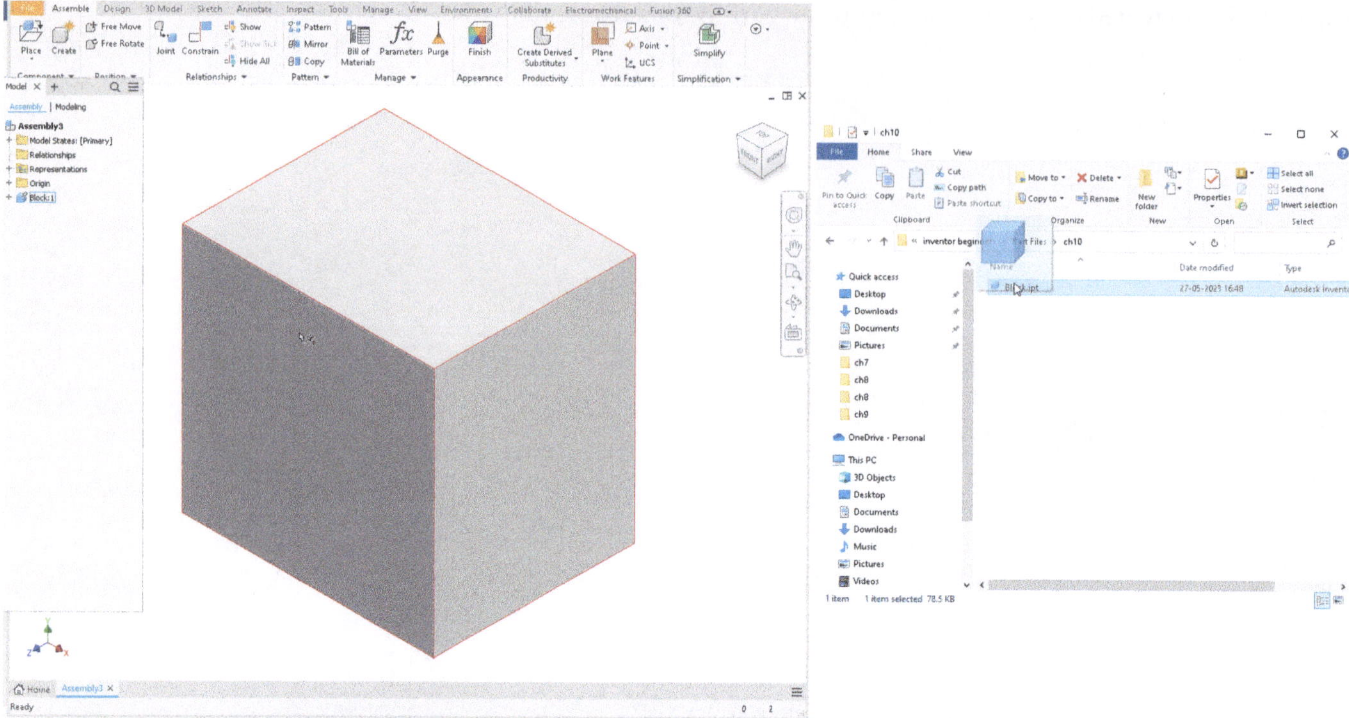

After inserting the first component, right-click and select the **Place Grounded at Origin** option to fix the component at the origin. As a result, all degrees of freedom of the part will be eliminated.

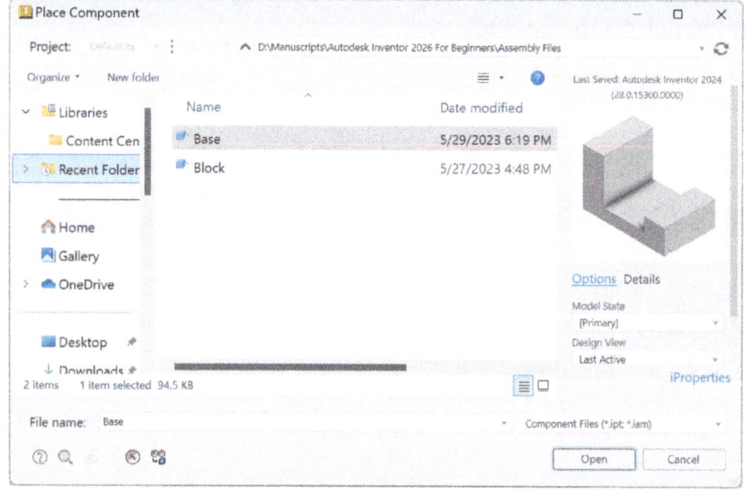

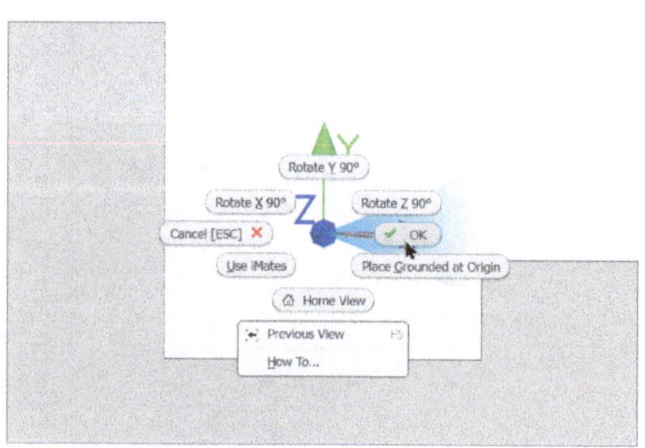

Another instance of the part is attached to pointer after placing the first part. Right click and select **OK** to deactivate the **Place Component** command. You can also unground the component by right-clicking on the component in the Model window and selecting **Grounded**. The selected component will be ungrounded and free to move.

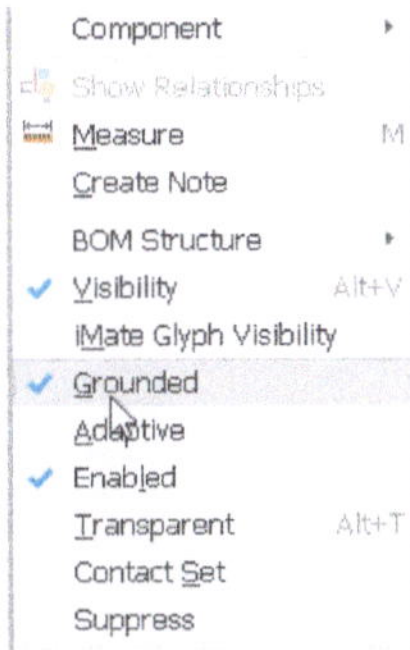

Likewise, insert the second component into the assembly window. On the graphics window, right-click and select **Rotate X 90°** to rotate the component about the X axis by 90 degrees. You can also select **Rotate Y 90°** to rotate the component about the Y axis by 90 degrees. Select **Rotate Z 90°** to rotate the component about the Z-axis by 90 degrees.

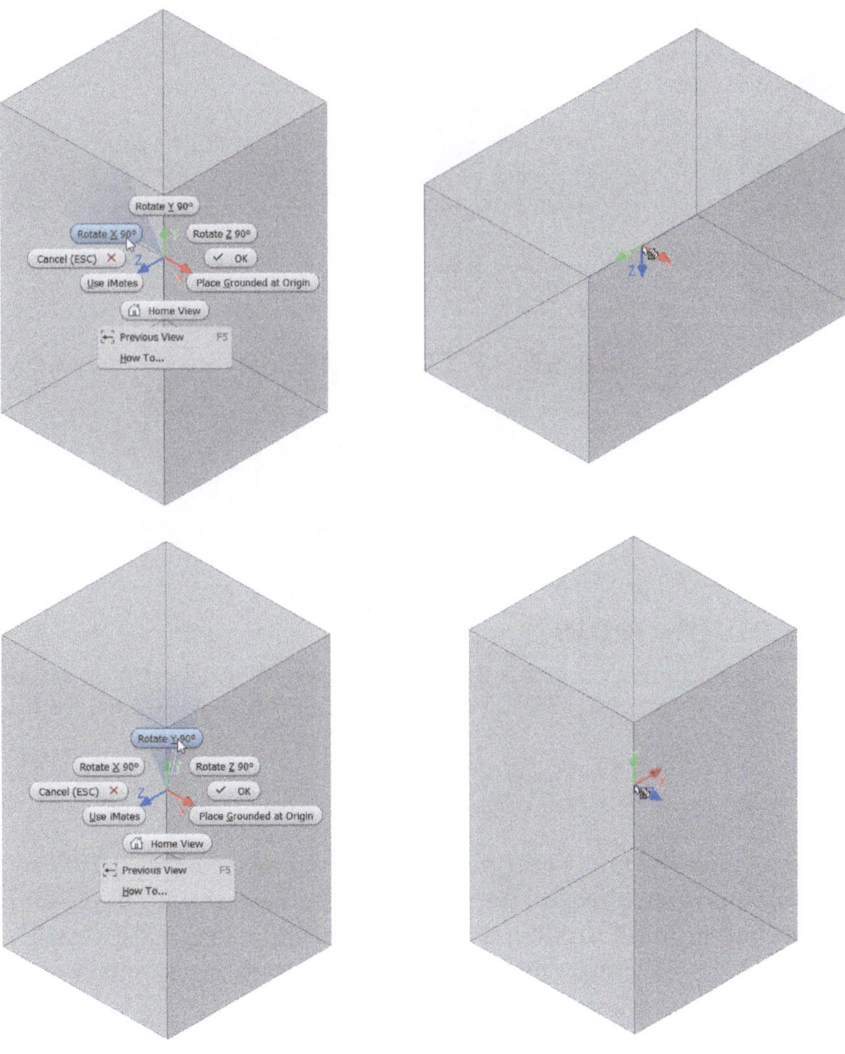

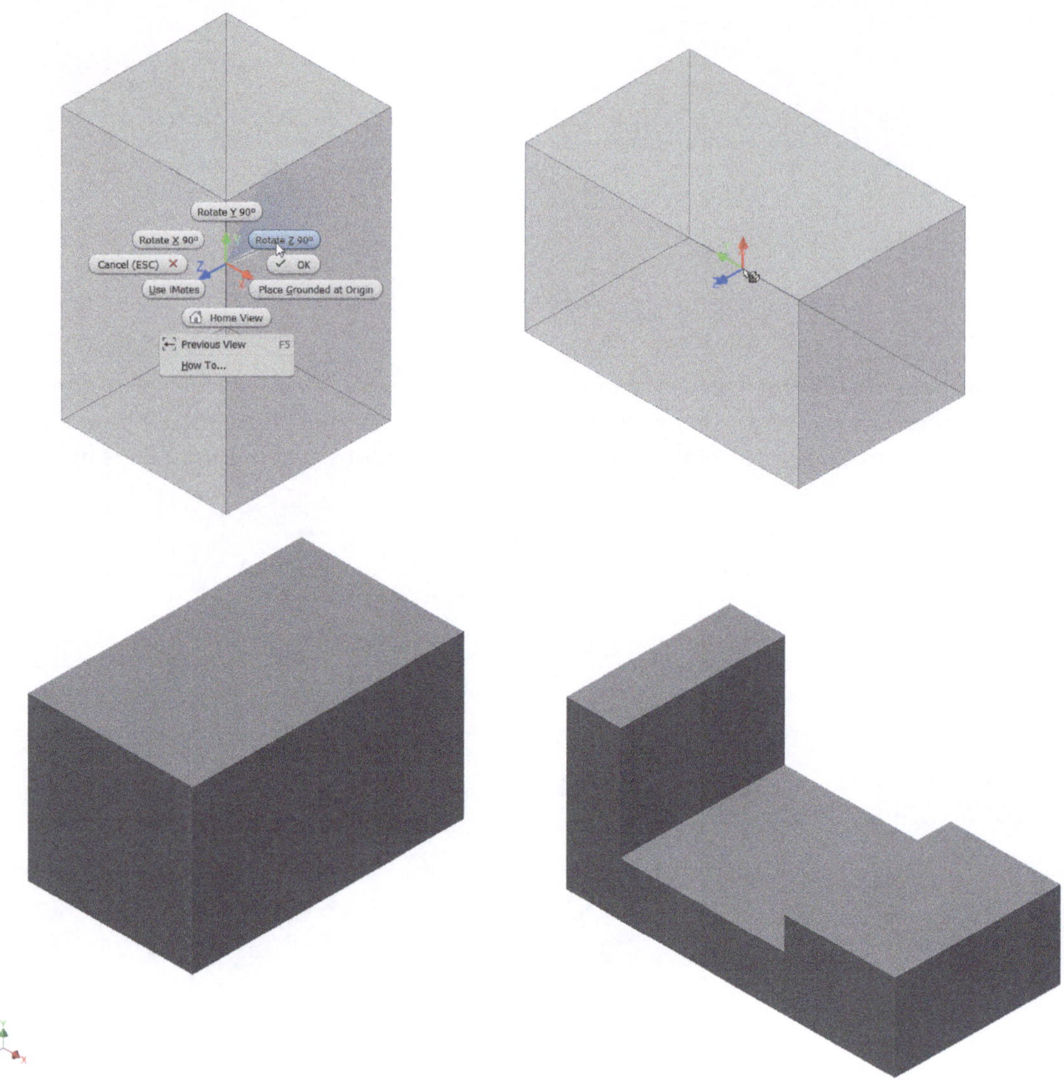

Moving and Rotating Components

Inventor allows you to drag or rotate the selected components if they are under-constrained. You can use **Free Move,** or **Free Rotate** commands to move or rotate the under-constrained parts in the assembly window. These commands are explained next.

Free Move

You can use the **Free Move** command to move the under-constrained parts in the assembly window. Activate this command by clicking **Assemble > Position > Free Move** on the ribbon. Select the part from the assembly window, press and hold the left mouse button, and then drag it to a new location. You can also drag a part without activating the **Free Move** command. To do this, press and hold the left mouse button on the part, and then drag the cursor.

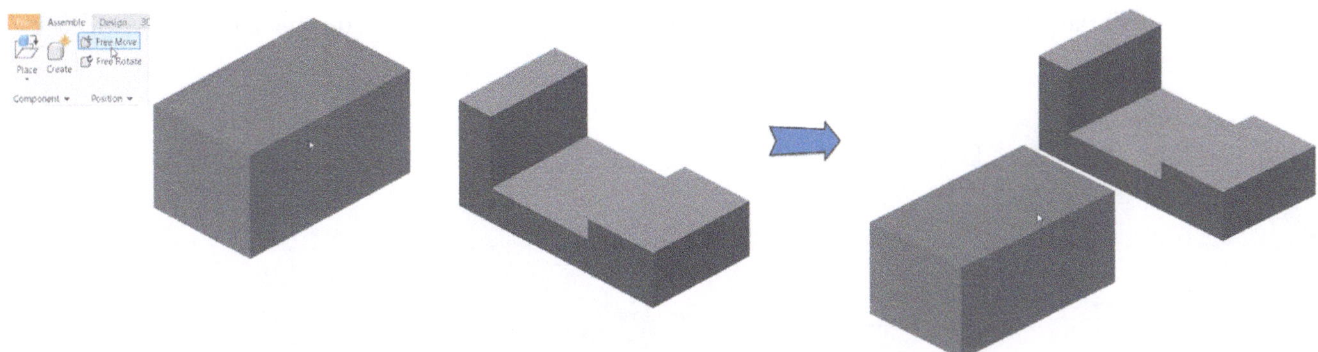

Free Rotate

You can use the **Free Rotate** command to rotate the under-constrained parts in the assembly window. Activate this command by clicking **Assemble > Position > Free Rotate** on the ribbon. Select the part from the assembly window, press and hold the left mouse button, and then drag the cursor; the part is rotated.

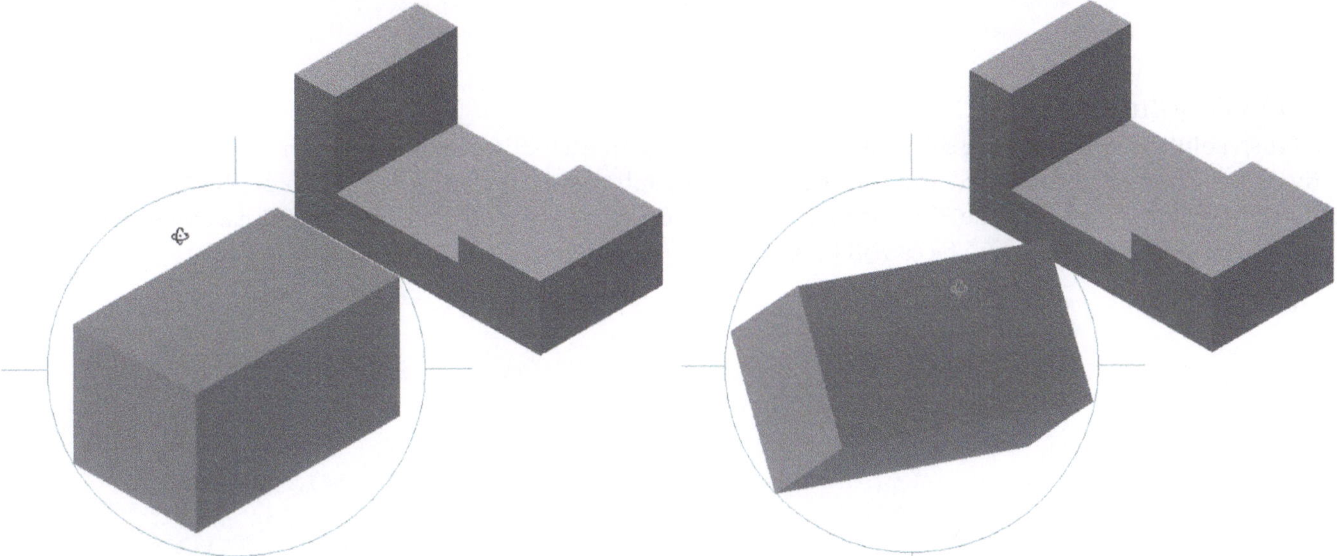

Applying Constraints

After inserting parts into an assembly, you have to apply constraints between them. By applying constraints, you can make parts to flush with each other or make two round faces concentric with each other. As you add constraints between parts, the degrees of freedom will be removed from them. By default, there are six degrees of freedom for a part (three linear and three rotational). Eliminating the degrees of freedom will make parts attached and interact with each other as in real life. Now, you will learn to add constraints between parts.

Mate Constraint

The **Mate** constraint makes two faces coincident with each other. The orientation of the two mated faces depends on the type of Solution that you select: **Mate** or **Flush**.

The Mate Solution

The **Mate** solution will make the selected faces coincident with each other. In addition to that, the orientation of the faces will be opposite to each other. To apply this mate solution, first activate the **Constraint** command (on the ribbon, click **Assemble > Relationships > Constraint**). On the **Place Constraint** dialog, click the **Assembly** tab > **Type** > **Mate** icon. Next, click the **Mate** icon in the **Solution** section of the **Place Constraint** dialog. Select the face of the placement part, and then click on a face of the target part. The two selected faces will mate with each other.

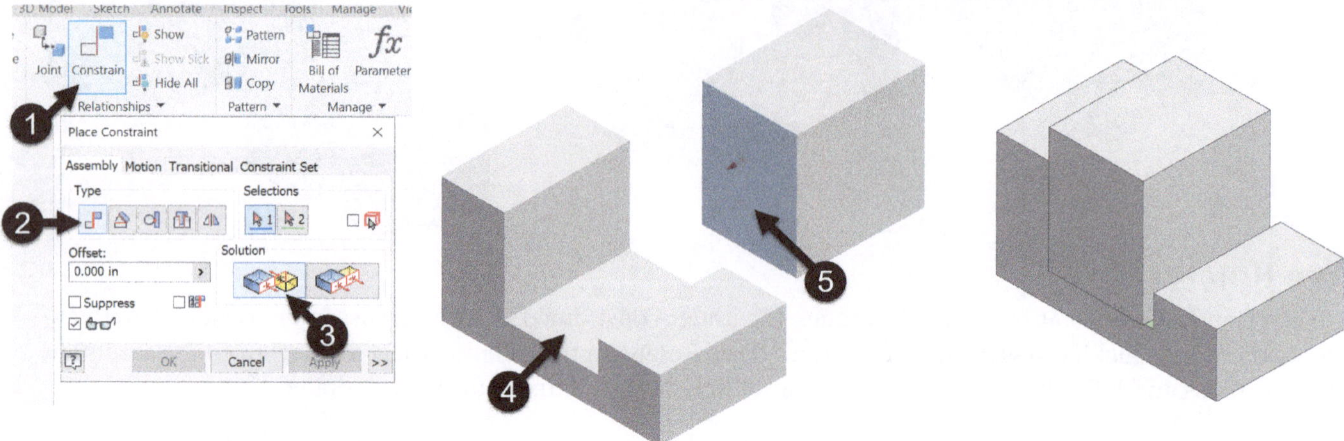

The Flush Solution

The **Flush** solution will make the selected faces coincident with each other and oriented in the same direction. Activate the **Constraint** command and click the **Assembly** tab **>** **Type** section **>** **Mate** icon on the **Place Constraint** dialog. Next, click the **Flush** icon in the **Solution** section and select a face on the placement part. Select a face on the target part. The two faces will be aligned in the same direction.

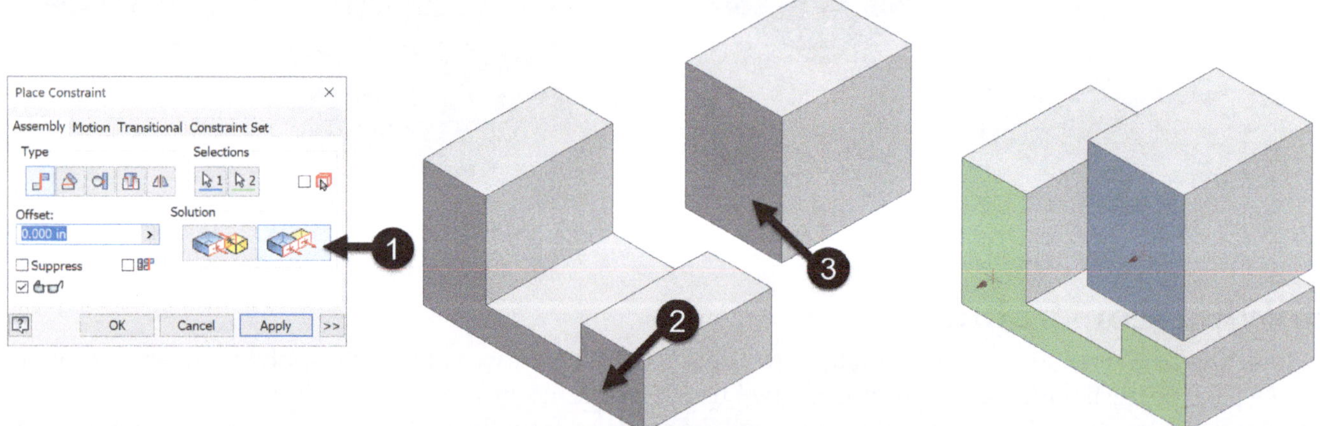

You can also enter an offset value in the **Offset** box on the **Place Constraint** dialog. The constrained components are offset from each other.

Aligning Axes or Edges using the Mate Constraint

By using the **Mate** constraint, you can make the axes of two cylindrical faces coincide with each other. Activate the **Constraint** command and click the **Assembly** tab **>** **Type** section **>** **Mate** icon on the **Place Constraint** dialog. Next, click on the round faces of the placement and target parts; the two cylindrical axes will coincide with each other. You can notice that there are options under the **Solution** section: **Opposed, Aligned**, and **Undirected**.

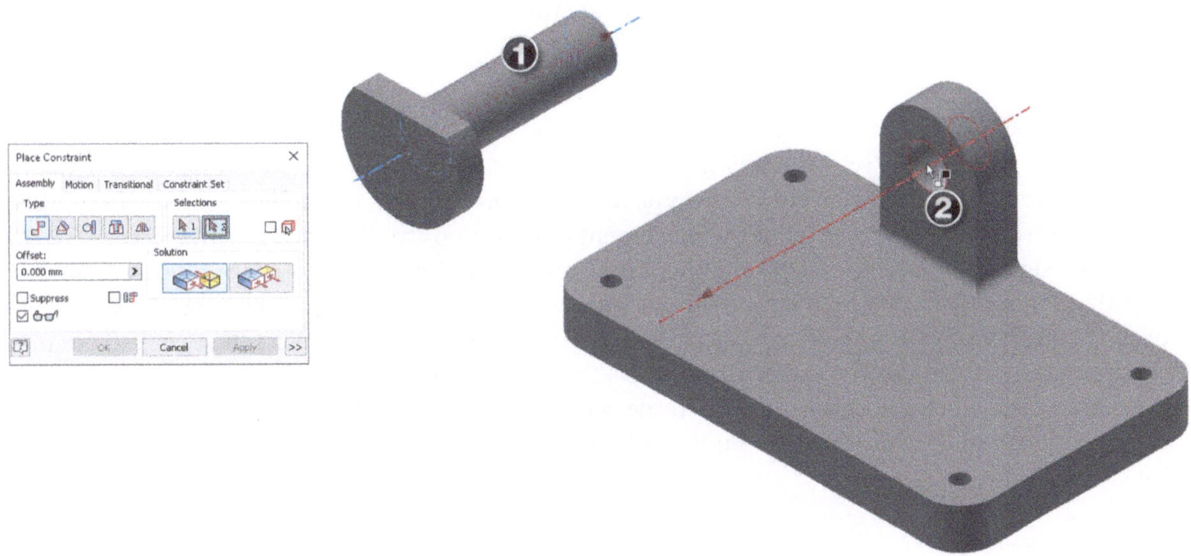

The **Opposed** option positions the two selected axes or edges in the direction opposite to each other.

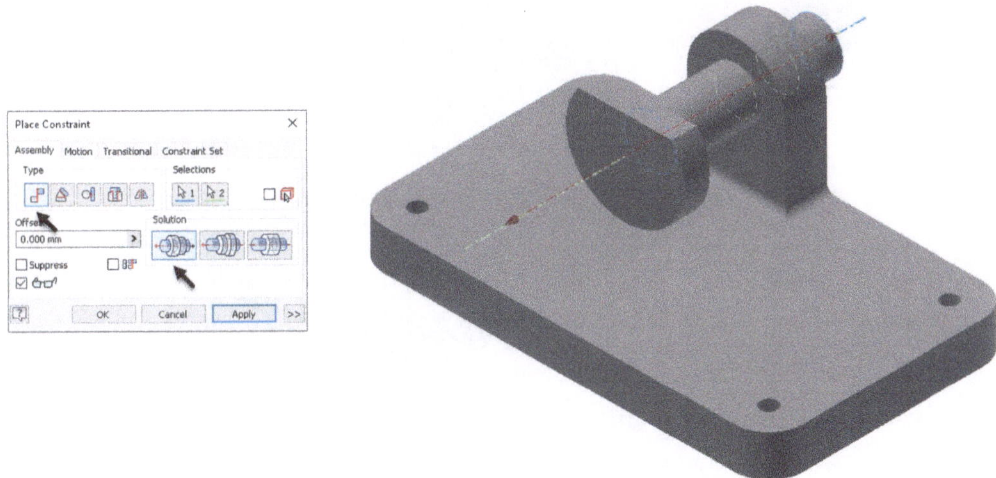

The **Aligned** option will align the parts' axes in the same direction.

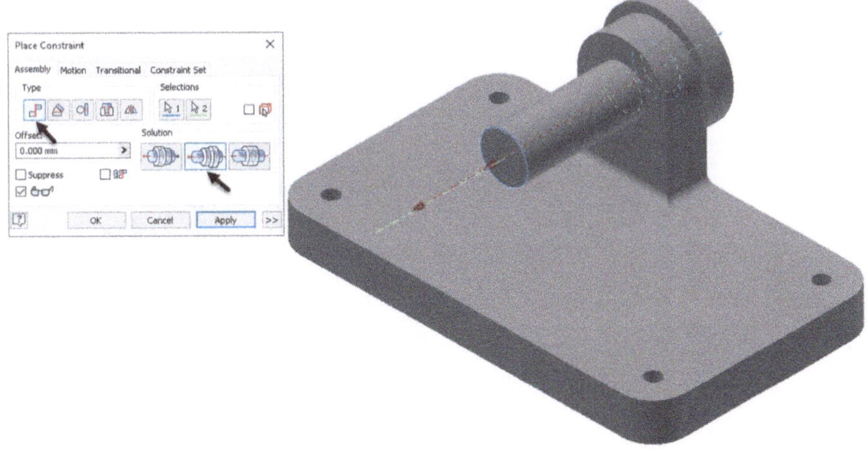

The **Undirected** option will align the two selected axes in the default direction.

Insert Constraint

The **Insert** constraint helps you to position cylindrical parts into holes. This constraint is used to apply two constraints at a time. First, it aligns the two cylindrical axes, and then it mates the adjacent flat faces. Activate the **Constraint** command, and then click **Assembly** tab > **Type** section > **Insert** icon on the **Place Constraint** dialog. Next, place the pointer on a cylindrical feature of the placement part and notice that its axis is highlighted. Also, notice that the circular edge of the circular face is highlighted. Move the pointer to the other end of the cylindrical feature and notice that the circular edge on the other end is highlighted. Click on the circular face at any one of its ends; the axis of the cylindrical face is selected along with its circular edge. Likewise, select the axis and circular edge on the target part; the two selected cylindrical axes are aligned. Also, the circular edges of the cylindrical features are made coincident. Click the **Opposed** icon in the **Solution** section to position the axes opposite to each other. Click the **Aligned** icon in the **Solution** section to position the axes in the same direction. Click **OK** on the **Place Constraint** dialog.

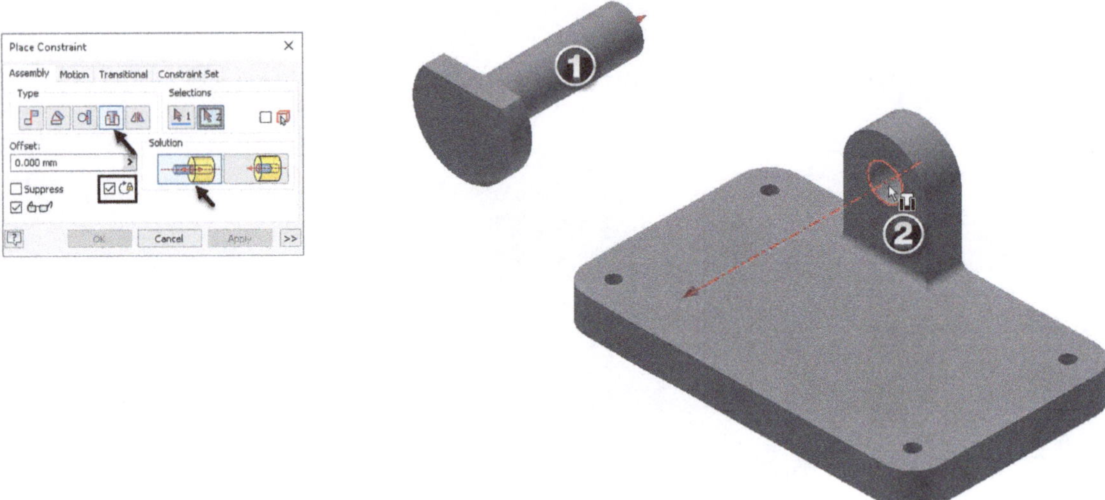

Check the **Lock Rotation** option, if you want to lock the rotation of the placement part. Click **OK** to create the constraint.

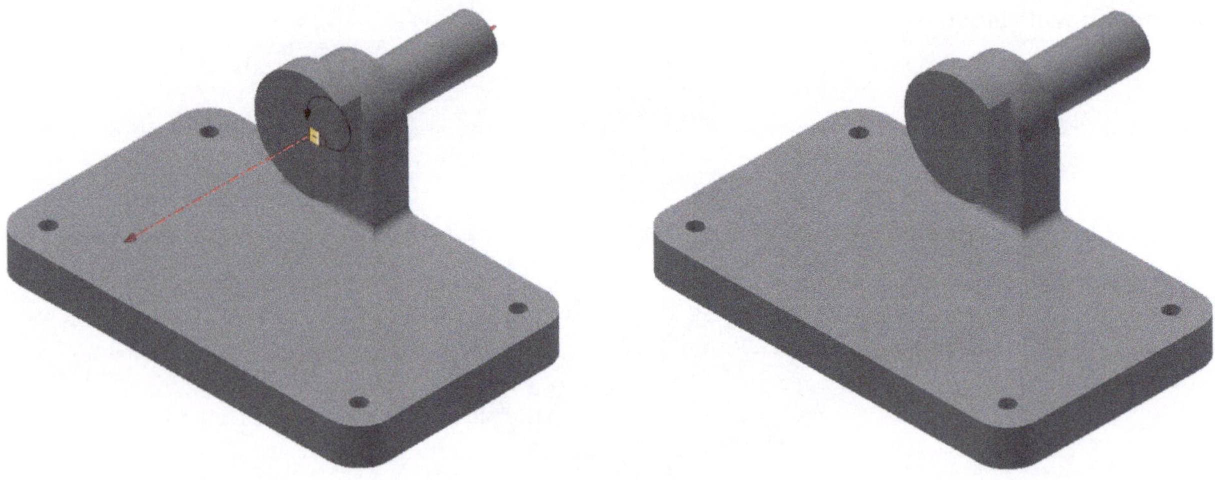

Angle Constraint

The **Angle** constraint is used to position faces at a specified angle. Activate the **Constraint** command (click **Assembly > Relationships > Constraint).** On the **Place Constraint** dialog, click the **Angle** icon under the **Type** section. Next, type in a value in the **Angle** box on the dialog and click the **Directed Angle** option in the **Solution** section.

Click on a plane or linear element of the first part. Next, click on a plane or linear element of the second part. The first part will be positioned at the specified angle.

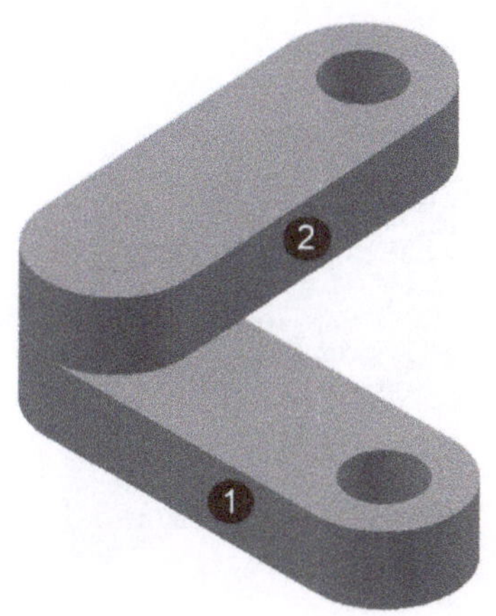

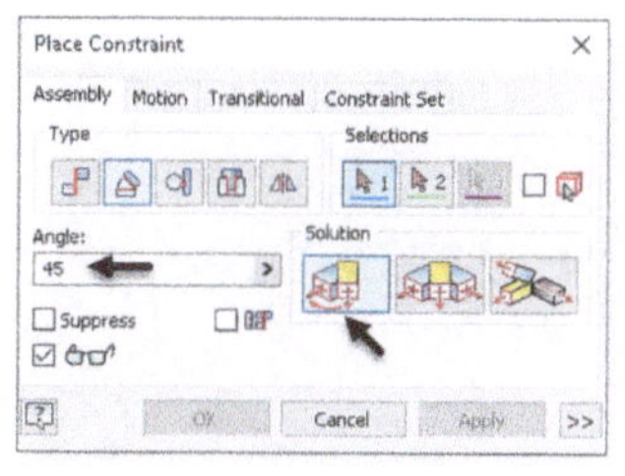

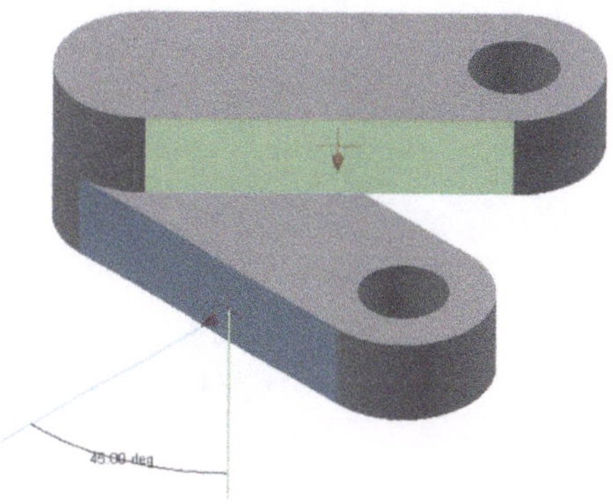

Tangent Constraint

The **Tangent** constraint is often used when working with cylinders and spears. It causes the geometry to maintain contact at a point of tangency. Activate the **Constraint** command and click the **Tangent** icon on the **Place Constraint** dialog. After activating this command, click on the face to be made tangent. Next, click on the tangent face on the target part. The first part will be made tangent to the target part. This constraint has two solutions: **Inside** and **Outside**. Inside tangency places the first selected face inside the target part at a point of tangency. Outside tangency places the first selected face outside the target part at a point of tangency.

Outside

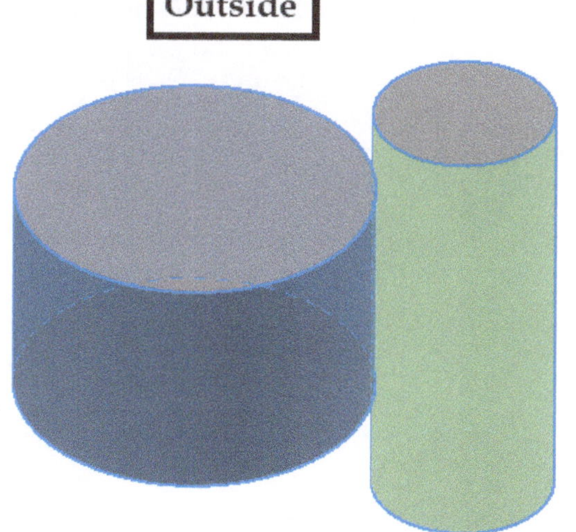

Inside

Symmetry Constraint

The **Symmetry** constraint allows you to make two parts about a plane. Activate the **Constrain** command (click **Assemble** > **Relationships** > **Constrain** on the ribbon). On the **Place Constraint** dialog, click the **Symmetry** icon in the **Type** section. Next, click on a planar face, edge, axis, vertex, or plane on the first part. Click on the same type of entity on the second part. Now, select the plane about which the parts are to be made symmetric. Click **Apply** on the **Place Constraint** dialog.

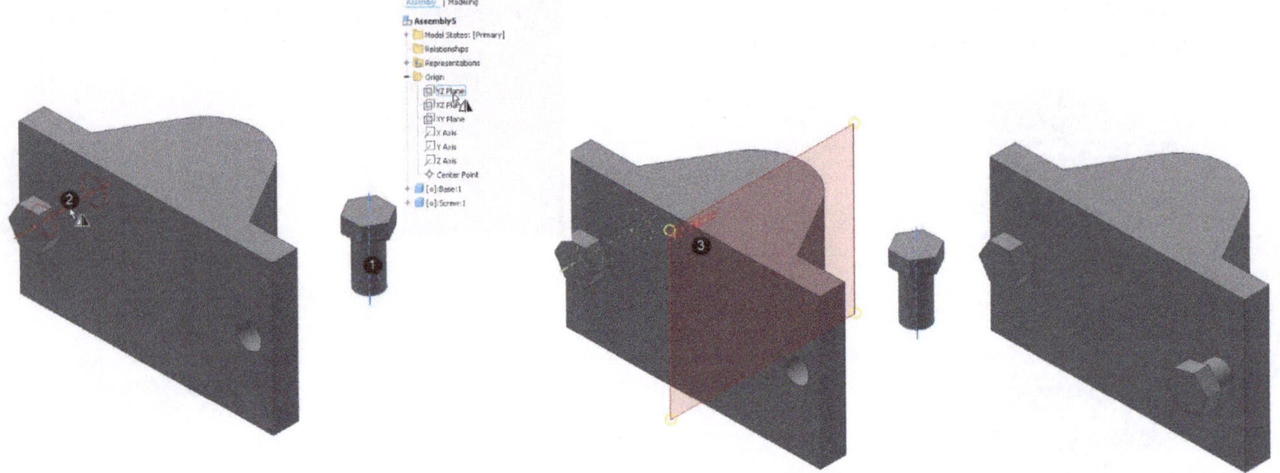

Joints

The **Joint** command is used to create joints between the parts which control the position and movement. To activate this command, click **Assemble > Relationships > Joint** on the ribbon. On the **Place Joint** dialog, there are many types of joints available in the **Type** drop-down: **Automatic**, **Rigid**, **Rotational**, **Slider**, **Cylindrical**, **Planar**, and **Ball**. These joints are explained next:

Ball Joint

The **Ball** joint creates a ball joint between two round-shaped faces. Activate the **Joint** command (on the ribbon, click **Assemble > Relationships > Joint**). On the **Place Joint** dialog, select **Type** drop-down > **Ball**. Next, select the round face of the first part. Likewise, select the round face of the second part; the ball joint is created between the selected faces.

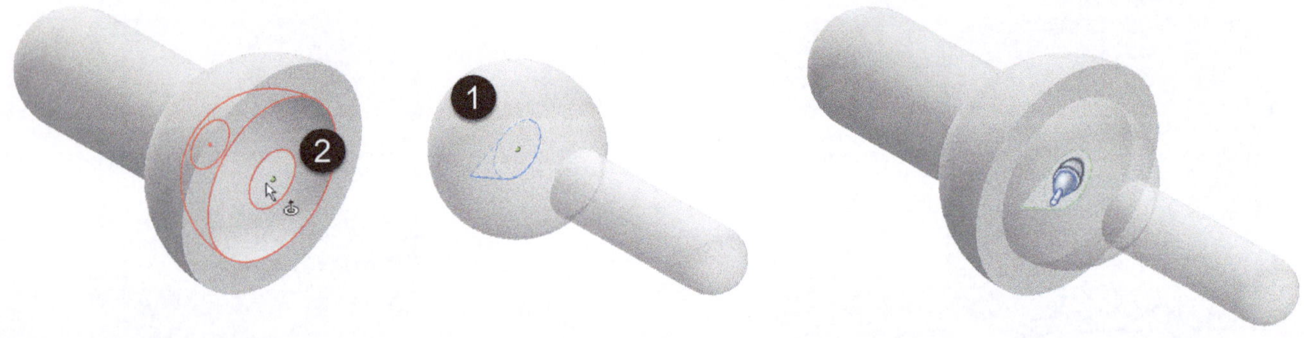

You can click the **Flip component** icon under the **Connect** section on the **Place Joint** dialog to flip the second component. To change the alignment direction, click the **Invert alignment** icon under the **Align** section. Click **OK** to create the ball joint.

Rotational Joint

The **Rotational** option creates a rotational joint between two cylindrical faces. On creating this joint, all the degrees of the freedom of the component are constrained except the rotational movement. First, activate the **Joint** command and select **Type > Rotational** option from the **Place Joint** dialog. Next, move the pointer of the circular face of the first component and notice that there are three pivot points highlighted on the component. One at the midpoint and two at both ends. Select any one of the origin points from the first component. Likewise, select an origin point from the cylindrical face of the second component; the two selected origin points are made coincident, and animation of the rotational joint is played. Now, you can use the **Flip Component** and **Invert Alignment** icons to reverse the component and its alignment, respectively. If you type any value in the **Gap** box, a gap will be created between the two pivot points. Click **OK** to create the rotational joint.

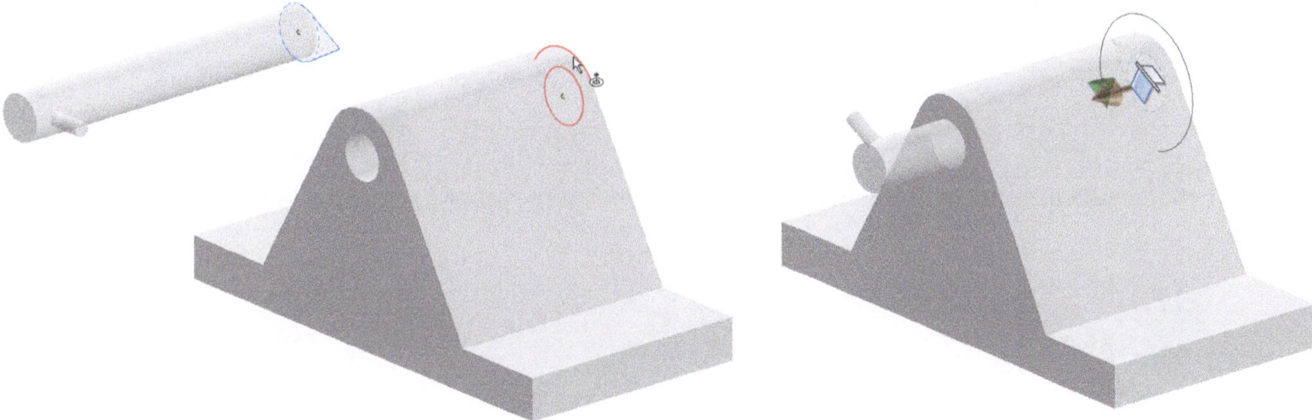

Rigid Joint

The **Rigid** joint makes the selected parts to form a rigid set. As you move a single part of a rigid set, all the other parts will also be moved. Activate the **Joint** command and select **Type > Rigid** from the **Place Joint** dialog. Select an origin point from the first part. Likewise, select the origin point from the target part.

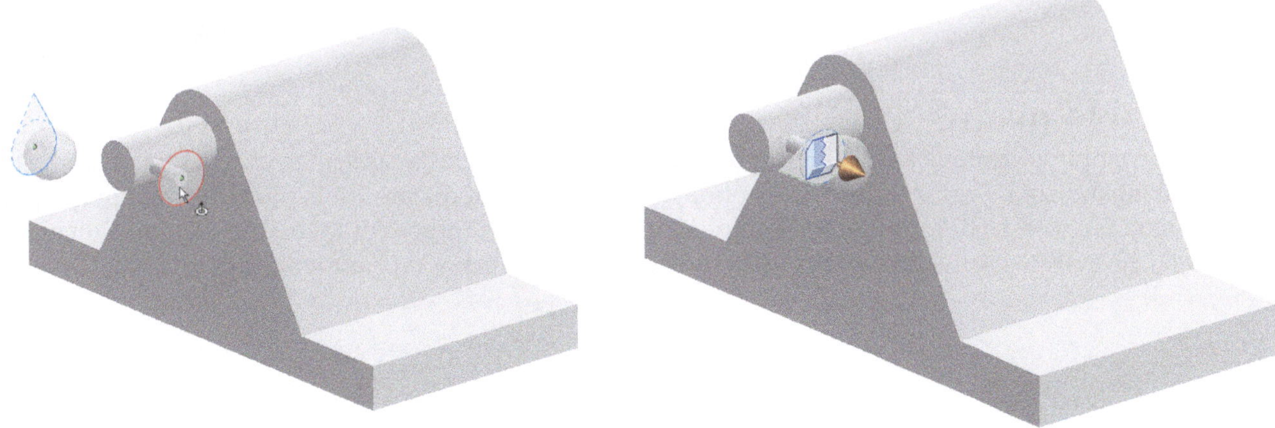

Click the **Flip Component** icon to reverse the direction of the component. Click **OK** to create the rigid set. The selected parts will form a rigid set.

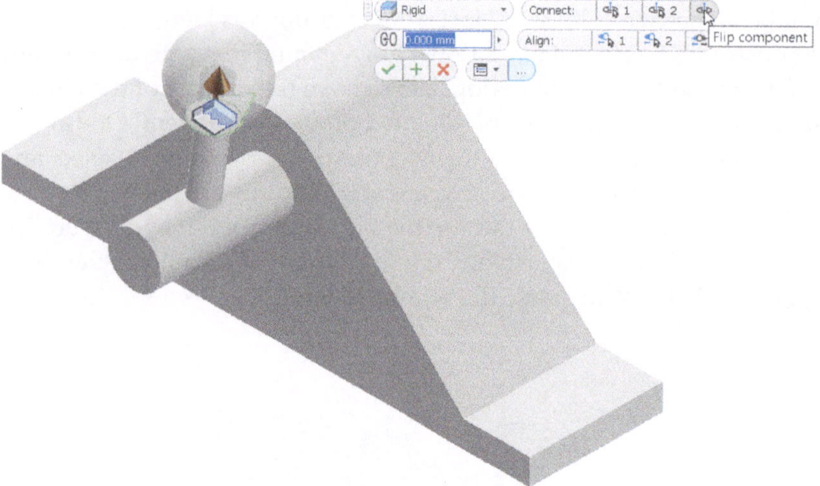

Now, if you change the position or orientation of one part, then all the other parts of the rigid set will also be affected.

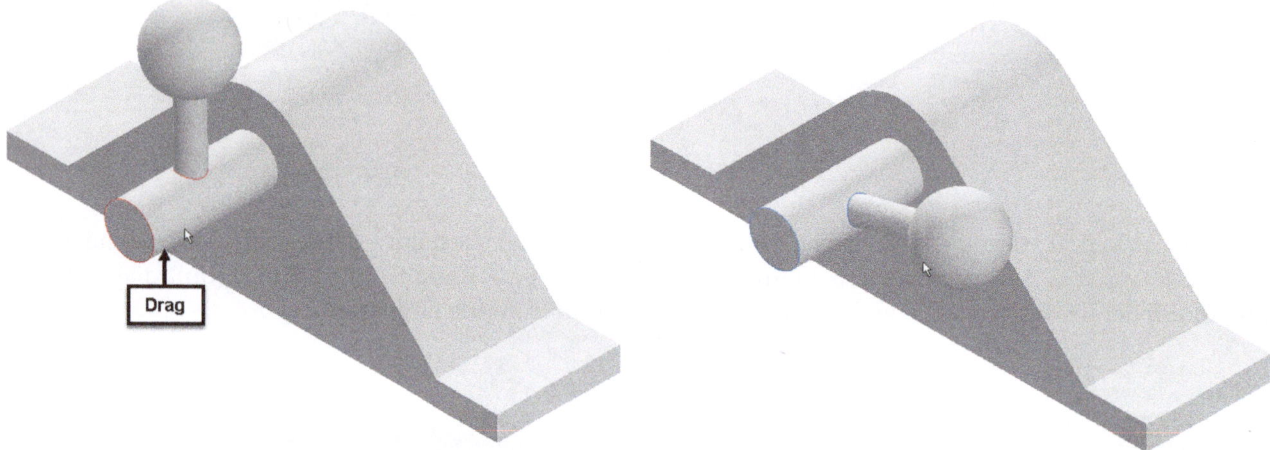

Cylindrical Joint

The **Cylindrical** option creates a joint with one translational and one rotational degree of freedom. Activate the **Joint** command and click **Type > Cylindrical** option on the **Place Joint** dialog. Next, select the joint origin points from the round faces of the first and second components. Click **Flip Component** to reverse the direction of the component. Click **OK** to create the cylindrical joint. The component can rotate and translate.

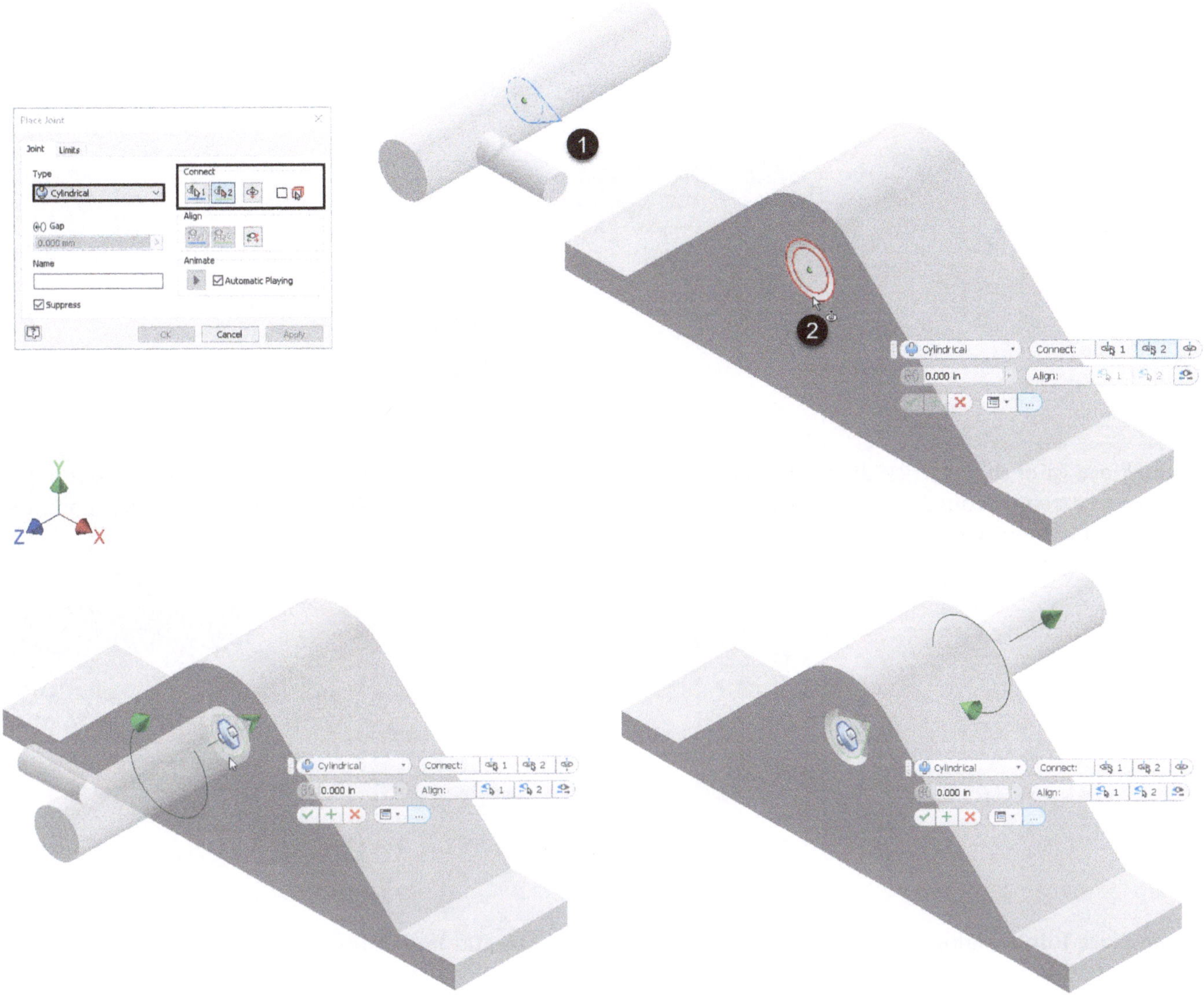

Planar Joint

The **Planar** option creates a joint with two translational and one rotational movement. Activate the **Joint** command and click **Type > Planar** on the **Place Joint** dialog. Select the joint origin points on the planar faces of the first part and target part, respectively. Click **OK** to create the planar joint.

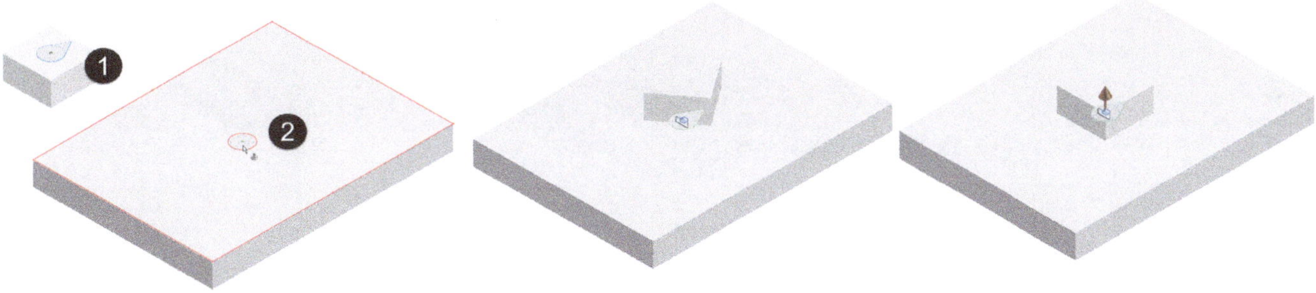

Slider Joint

The **Slider** option creates a slider joint between two components. The inserted component will slide on the target part. The sliding direction can be specified using the alignment options. To create this joint, activate the Joint command and click **Type > Slider** on the **Place Joint** dialog. Specify the pivot points on the placement and target parts, as shown.

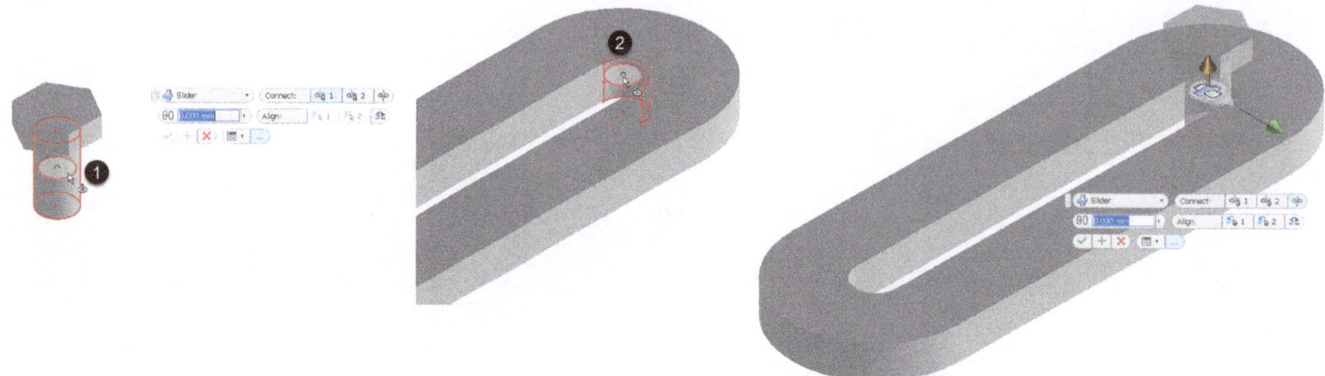

On the **Place Joint** dialog, click the **First alignment** icon in the **Align** section and select an edge from the first part. Next, select an edge from the second part; the two selected edges are aligned. Now, the first part slides along the alignment direction. The arrow indicates the sliding direction.

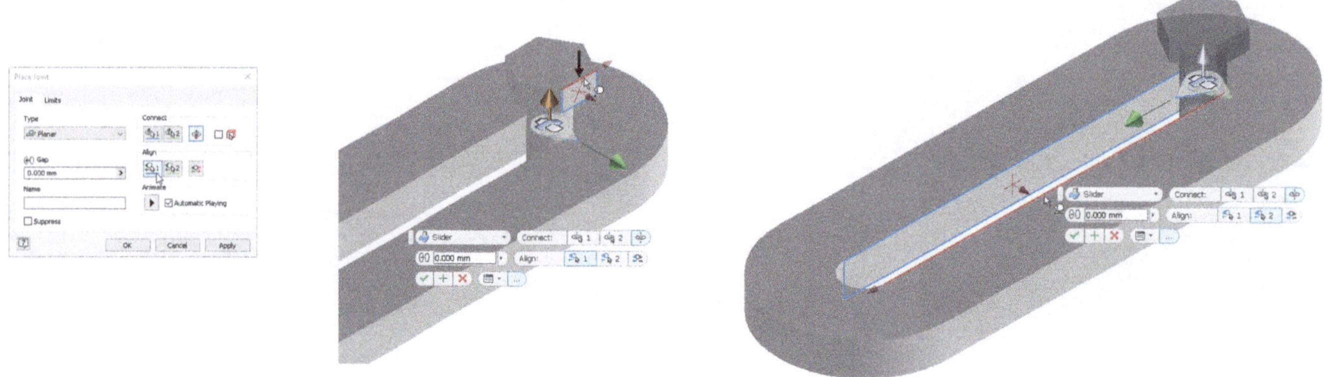

On the **Place Joints** dialog, click the **Limits** tab and check the **Start** and **End** options in the **Linear** section. Next, type-in values in the **Start** and **End** boxes, respectively. You can also use the **Measure** option to specify the start and end limits. To do this, click the arrow in the **Start** or **End** box, and then select **Measure**. Next, select the edge along which the component will slide. Click **OK** to create the slide joint.

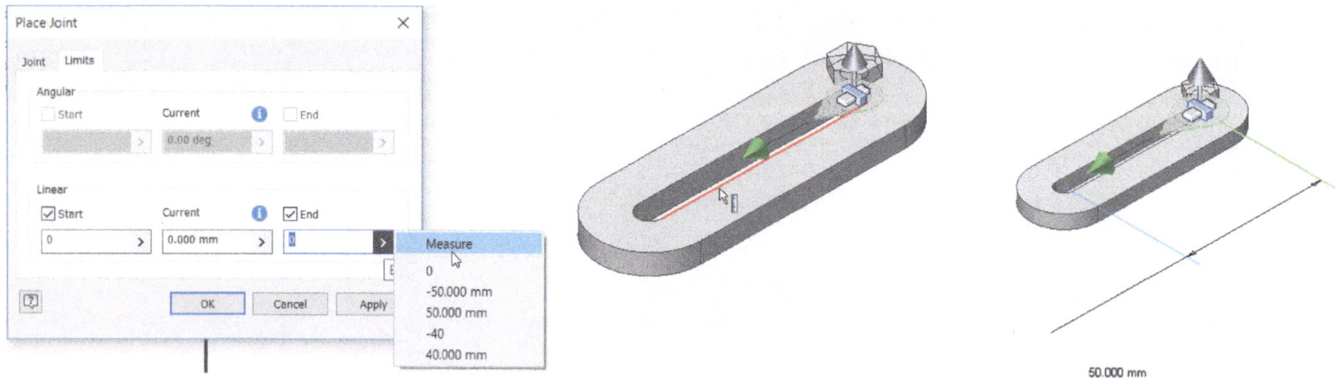

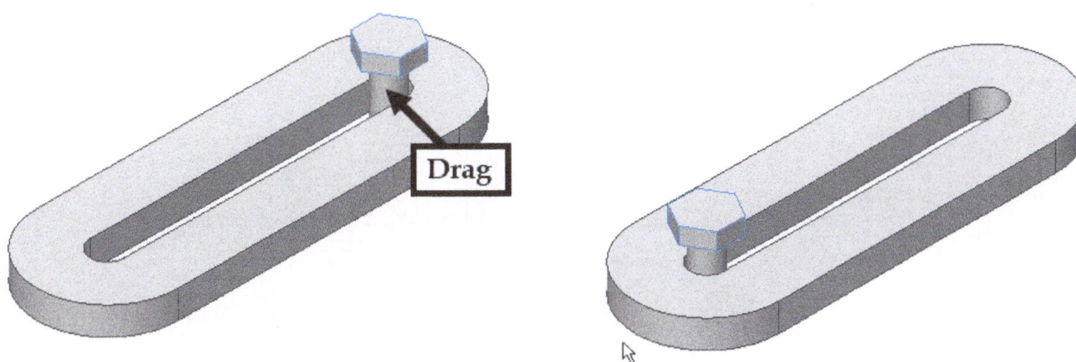

Analyze Interference

In an assembly, two or more parts may overlap or occupy the same space. However, this would be physically impossible in the real world. When you add relations between parts, Inventor develops real-world contacts and movements between them. However, sometimes, interferences can occur. To check such errors, Inventor provides you with a command called **Analyze Interference**. Activate this command (click **Inspect > Interference > Analyze Interference** on the ribbon) and select the first set. Next, click **Define set #2** on the **Interference Analysis** dialog and select the second set. Click **OK** to show the interference. A message box appears, showing that the number of interferences detected. Click **OK** on the **Interference Detected** dialog. If there is no interference, it shows that there are no interferences in the assembly.

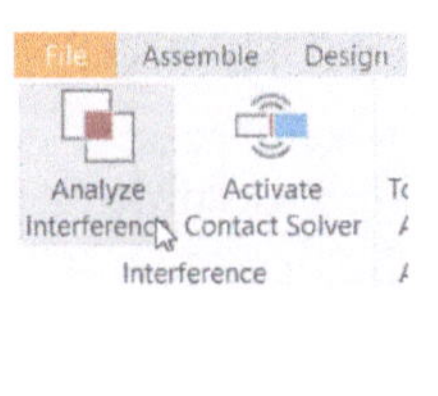

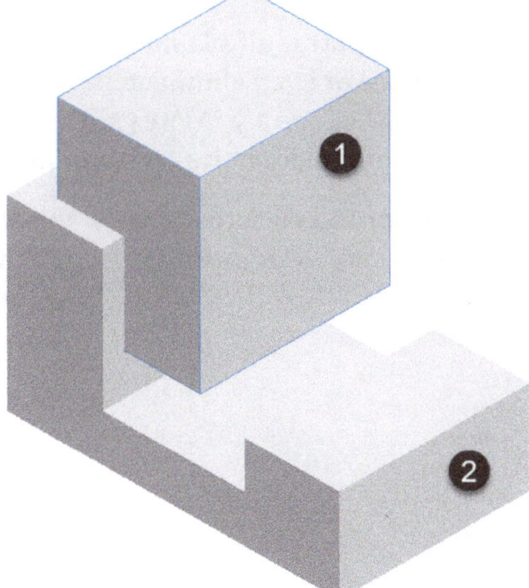

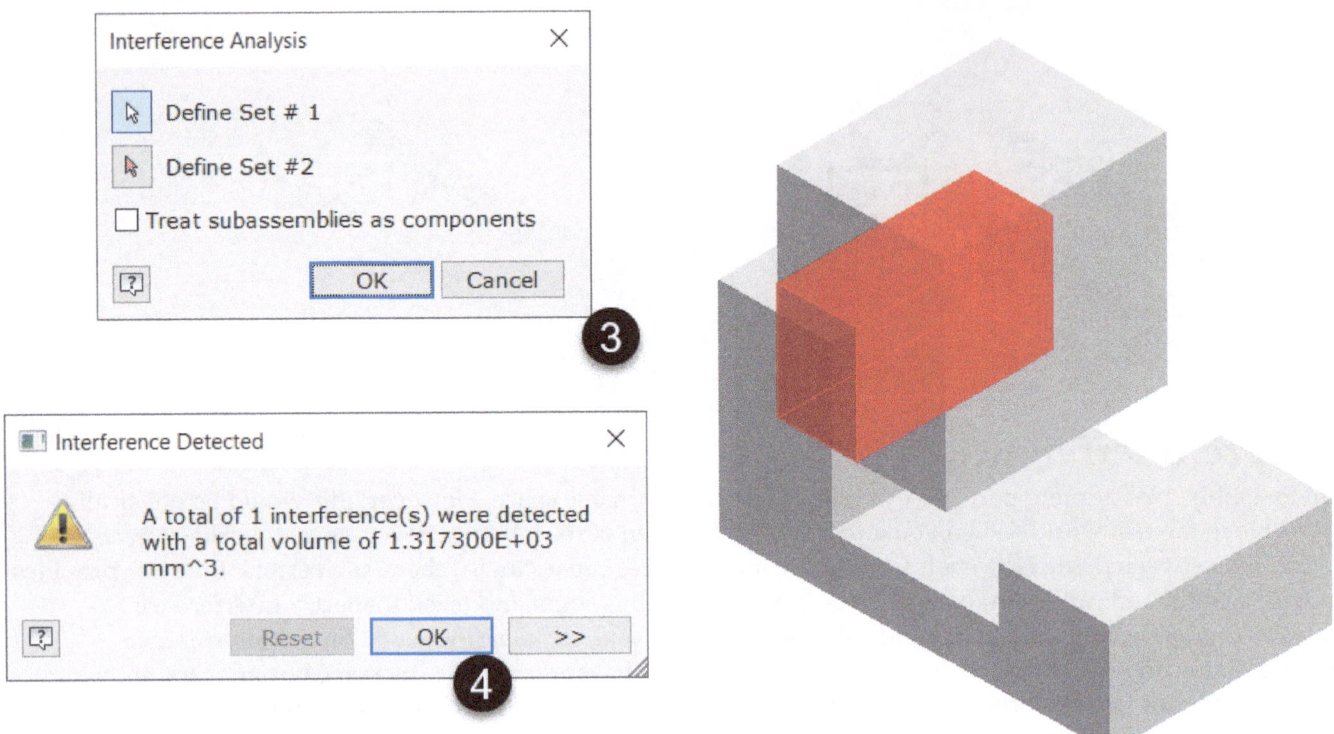

iMates

If you have an assembly in which you need to assemble the same part multiple times, it would be a tedious process. In such cases, the **iMate** command will drastically reduce or even eliminate the time used to assemble commonly used parts. To use this command, first, open the parts and apply **iMates** to the faces to be used for applying constraints. For example, create the Base component along with holes on it, as shown. Next, activate the **iMate** command (on the ribbon, click **Manage > Author > iMate**) and click the **Insert** icon in the **Type** section of the **Create iMate** dialog. Next, select the circular edge of the hole, as shown. Click **Apply** to create the **Insert** iMate. Likewise, apply the **Insert** iMate to the remaining holes, and then click **OK** to close the dialog. Save and close the part file.

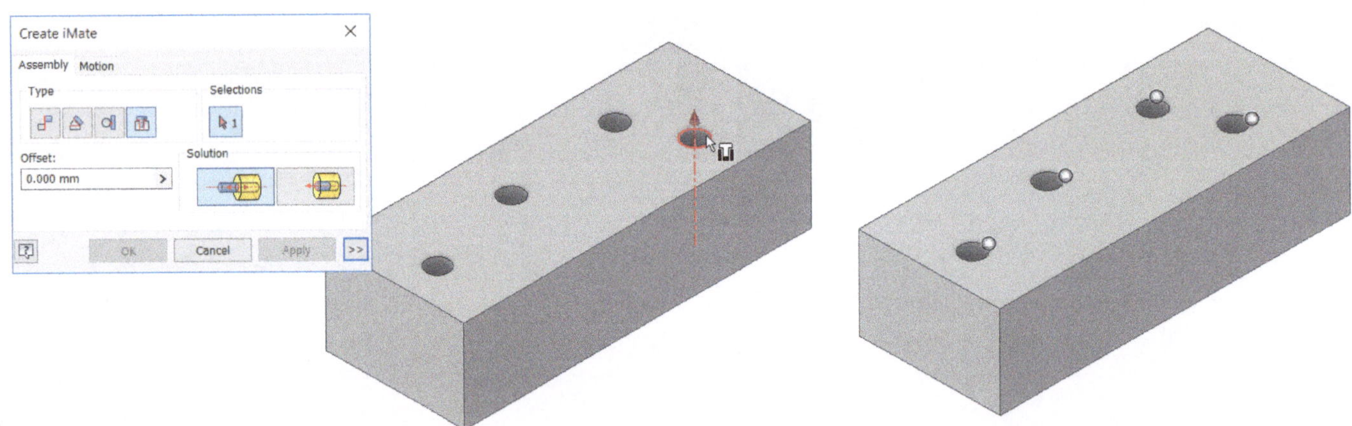

Next, create the Screw.ipt file and activate the **iMate** command and click **Type > Insert**. Next, select the circular edge of the screw, as shown. Click **OK** to apply the **Insert** iMate. Next, save and close the part file.

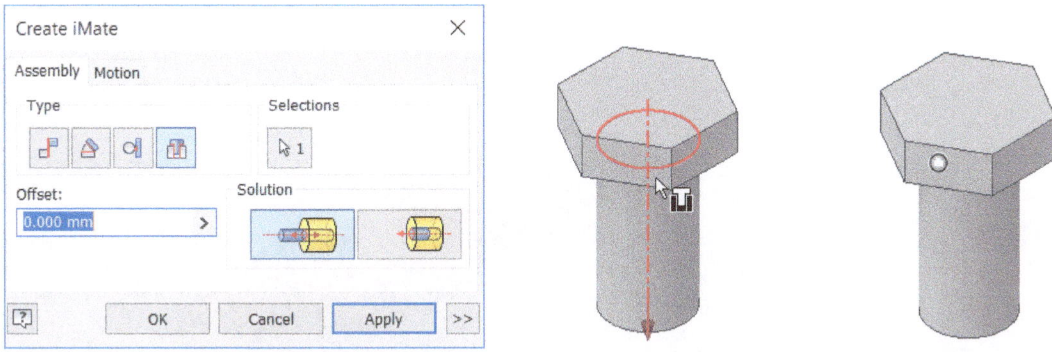

Start an assembly file and place the Base component. Next, click **Assembly > Component > Place** on the ribbon and select the Screw.ipt file. On the **Place Component** dialog, click the **Interactively place with iMates** icon located at the bottom. Click **Open** on the dialog; the screw is inserted into the hole automatically. Right click and select **Place at all matching iMates**; the screw is inserted into all the remaining holes.

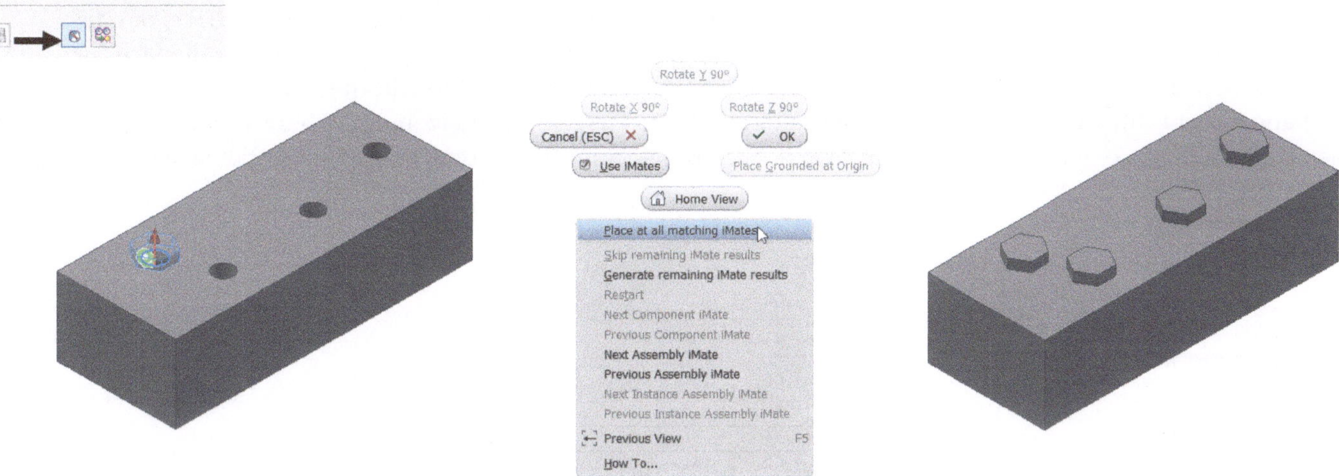

Editing and Updating Assemblies

During the design process, the correct design is not achieved on the first attempt. There is always a need to go back and make modifications. Inventor allows you to accomplish this process very quickly. To modify a part in an assembly, right-click on it and click **Edit**; the part environment will be activated. Make changes to the part and click **Return** on the ribbon; the assembly environment will be activated.

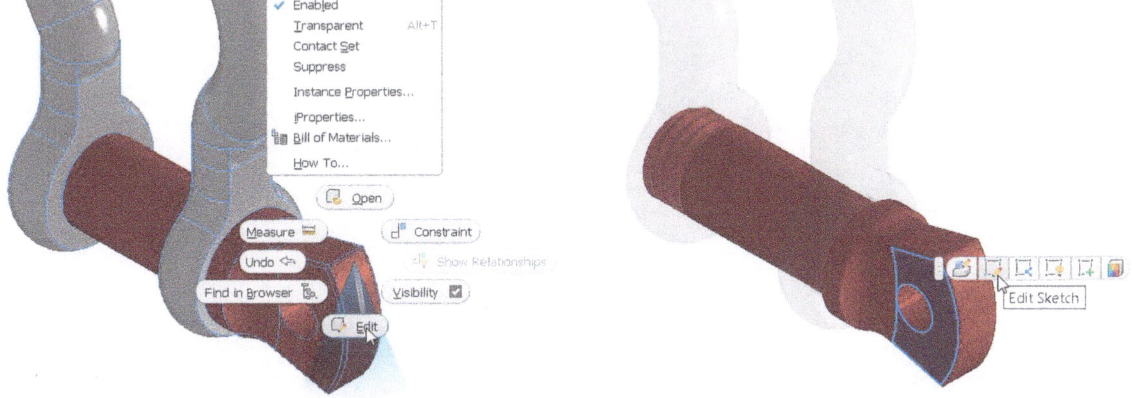

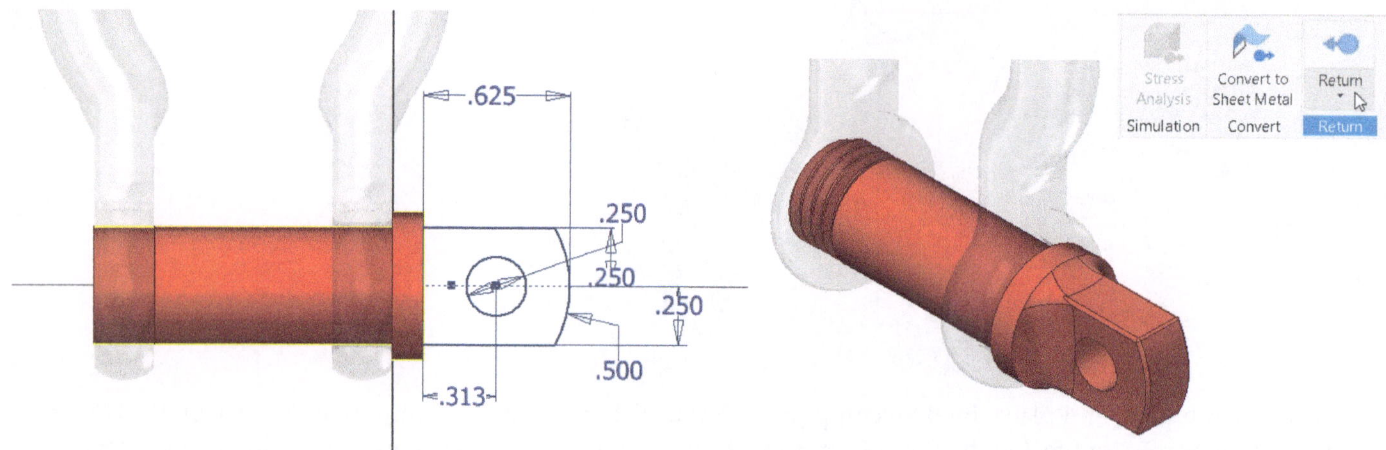

Editing Constraints

You can also edit constraints in an assembly. Select a part from the **Model** window. Next, right click and select **Show relationships**; the constraints applied to the part appear on the assembly. Click the right mouse button on a particular constraint to display the Marking menu. You can use this menu to delete, suppress, drive, or edit constraint. If you select **Edit**, the **Edit Constraint** dialog appears on the screen. You can redefine the faces or elements between which the constraint is applied. For example, if you want to edit the **Mate** constraint, right-click on it and select **Edit**. On the **Edit Constraint** dialog, click the **First Selection** icon in the **Selections** section and then click on the face of the placement part. Next, click the **Second Selection** icon and select the face of the target part. Click **OK** to apply the constraint.

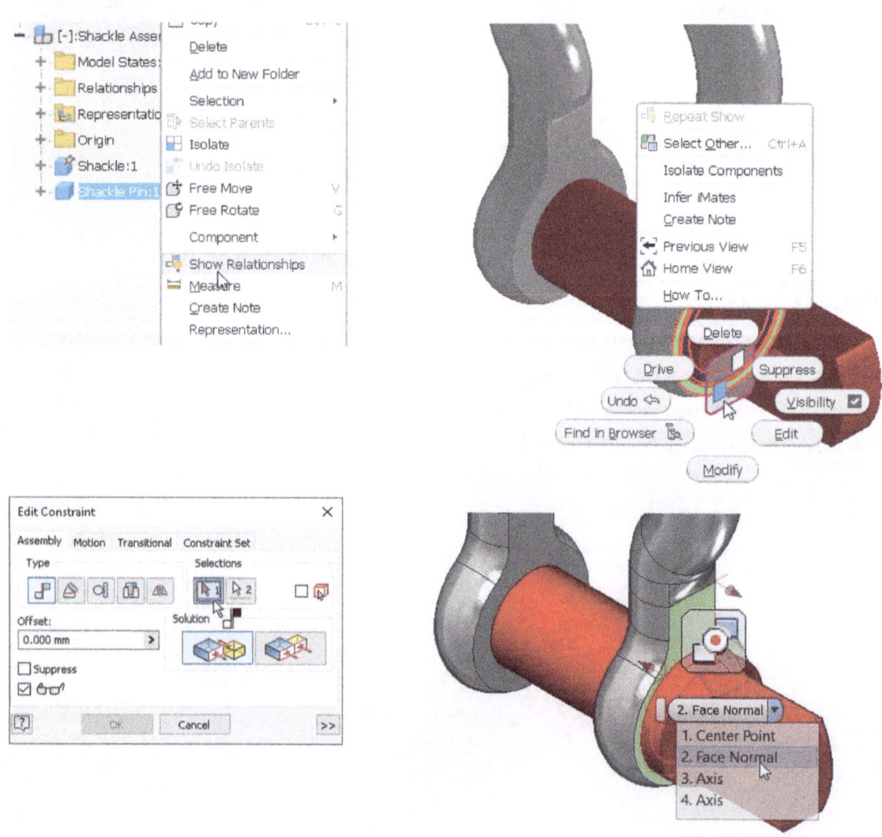

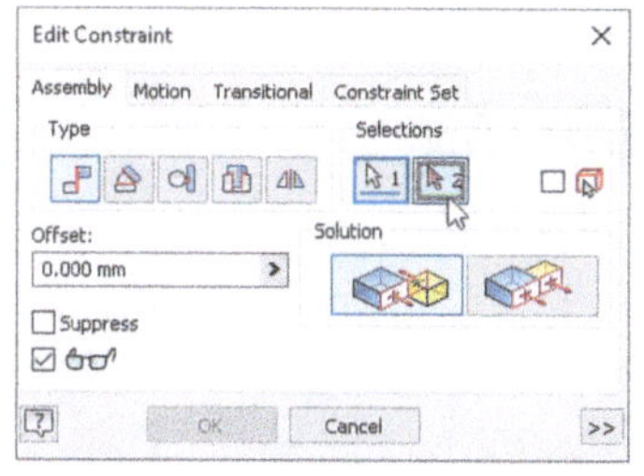

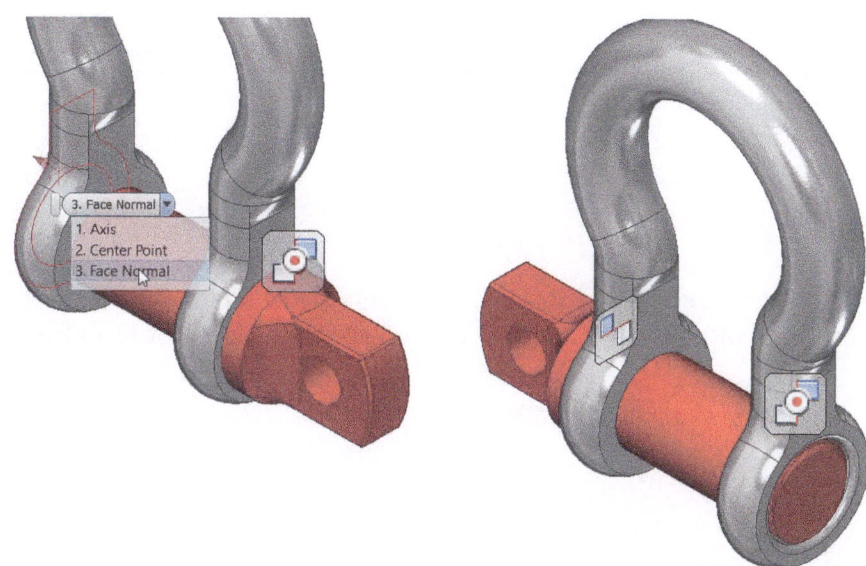

Replace Components

Autodesk Inventor allows you to replace any component in an assembly. To do this, go to the **Model** window and click the right mouse button on the component to replace. Select **Component** > **Replace** to open the **Place Component** dialog. On this dialog, click the **Browse** button and go to the location of the replacement part. Select the component and click **OK**. If the new component is not similar to the old component, then a message appears showing that the relationships may be lost. Click **OK**, and then click **Accept**. Now, you can redefine the existing constraints or delete them and define new constraints.

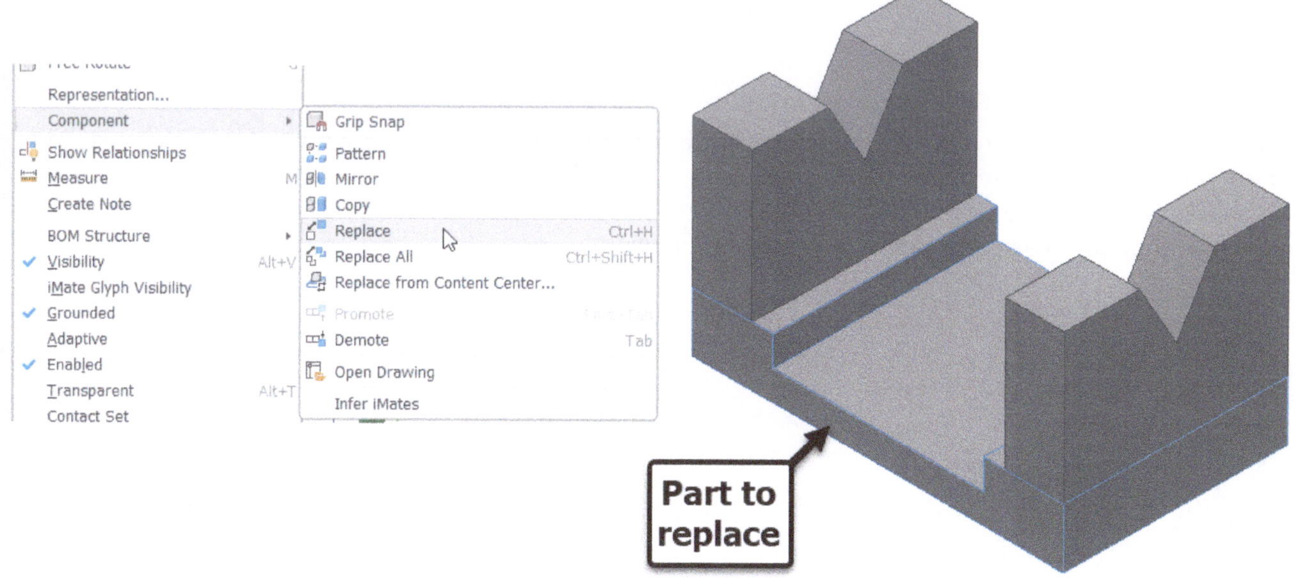

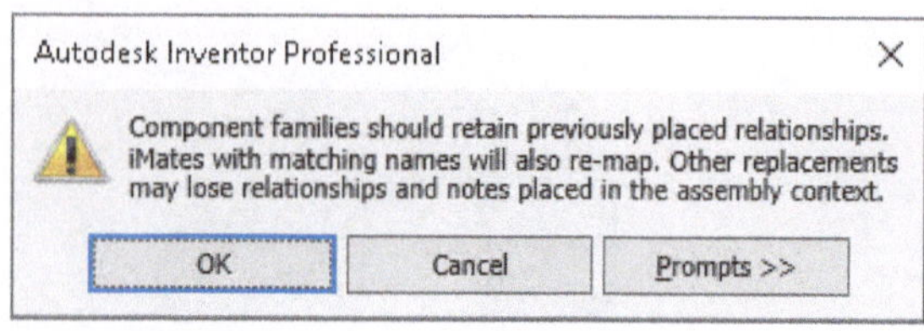

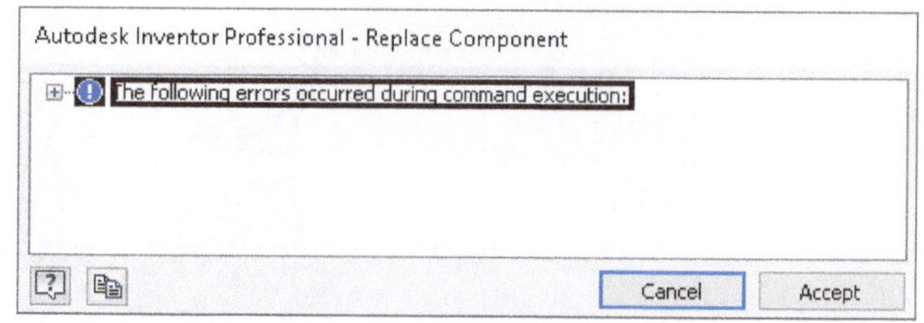

To redefine the constraints, right click on the replacement part and select **Show all relationships**. Next, right click on constraints with error symbol, and then select **Edit**. Select new faces from the model and click **OK**.

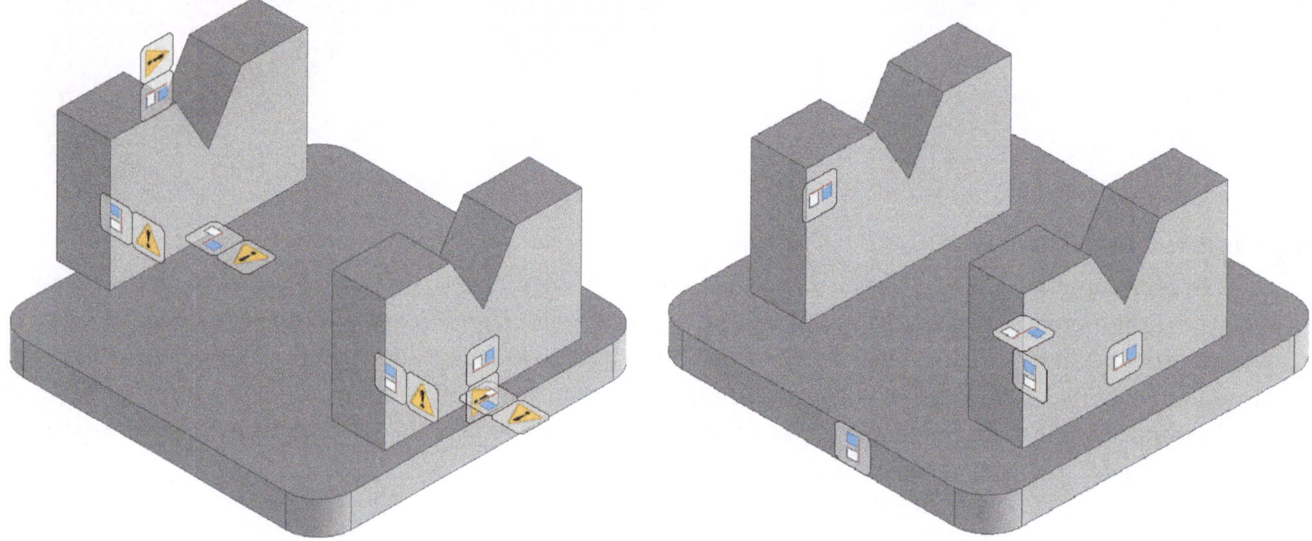

Pattern Component

The **Pattern Component** command allows you to replicate individual parts in an assembly. However, instead of defining layouts of rectangular or circular patterns, you can select an existing pattern as a reference. For example, in the assembly shown in the figure, you can position one screw using constraints, and then use the **Pattern Component** command to place screws in the remaining holes.

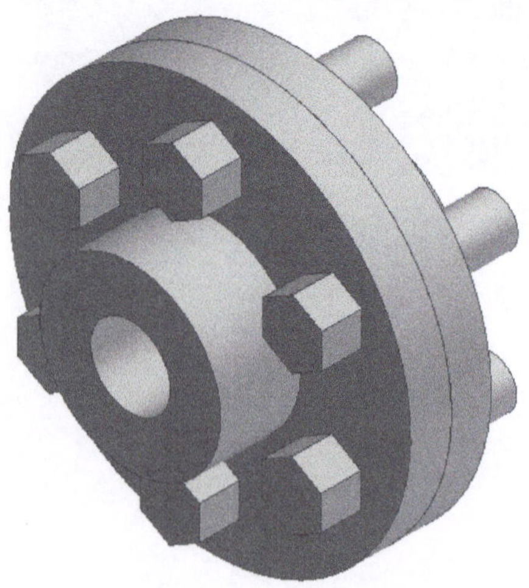

First, position the screw in one hole using the **Insert** constraint. Next, activate the **Pattern Component** command (click **Assemble > Pattern > Pattern Component** on the ribbon) and click on the part (In this case, screw) to include in the pattern. On the **Pattern Component** dialog, click the **Associative** tab, and then click the **Feature Pattern Select** button. Next, select the pattern feature from the assembly, and then click **OK**. The screw will be replicated using the existing pattern.

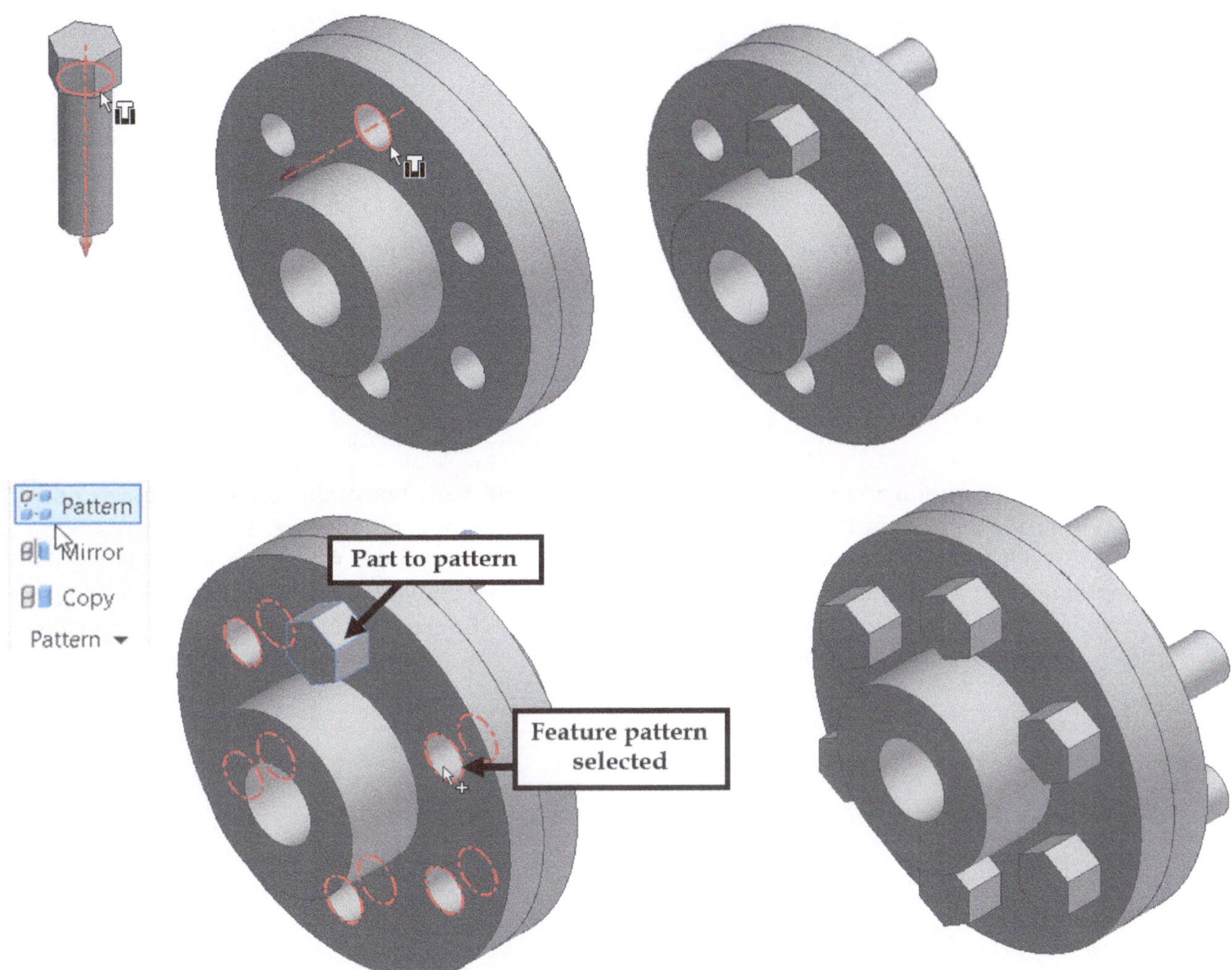

Mirror Components

When designing symmetric assemblies, the **Mirror Components** command will help you in saving time and capture the design intent. Activate this command (click **Assemble > Pattern > Mirror Components** on the ribbon) and click on the parts to be mirrored; the **Mirror Components: Status** dialog pops up on the screen. In this dialog, the status of the selected components is displayed in green. It indicates that a mirror copy of the component will be created. Click on the green dots to change the status to yellow. The yellow dots indicate that the component will be reused instead of creating a mirrored copy. For example, change the status of **Part3** to green.

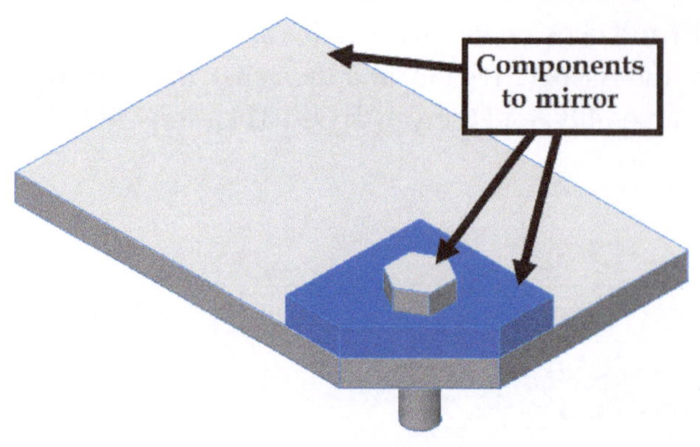

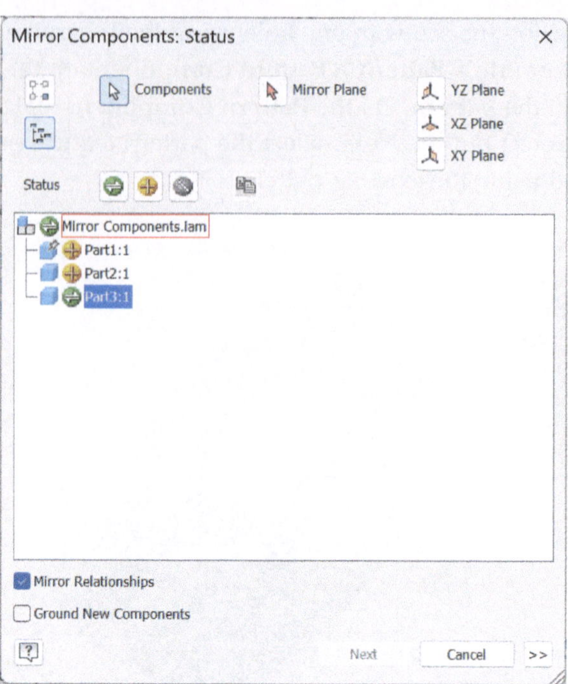

Next, click the **Mirror Plane** button and select the mirror plane (or) select any one of the reference planes (**YZ Plane, XZ Plane,** or XY plane) to mirror; the preview of the mirrored components appears. The mirrored component is displayed in green color, whereas the reused component is in yellow. Check the **Mirror Relationships** option, if you want to mirror the relationships. Click **Next** to display the **Mirror Components: File Names** dialog. On this dialog, you can view the **Source Display Name, Source File Name, Display Name, File Name, Location,** and **Status** columns. The **Source File Name** column lists all the components that are to be mirrored.

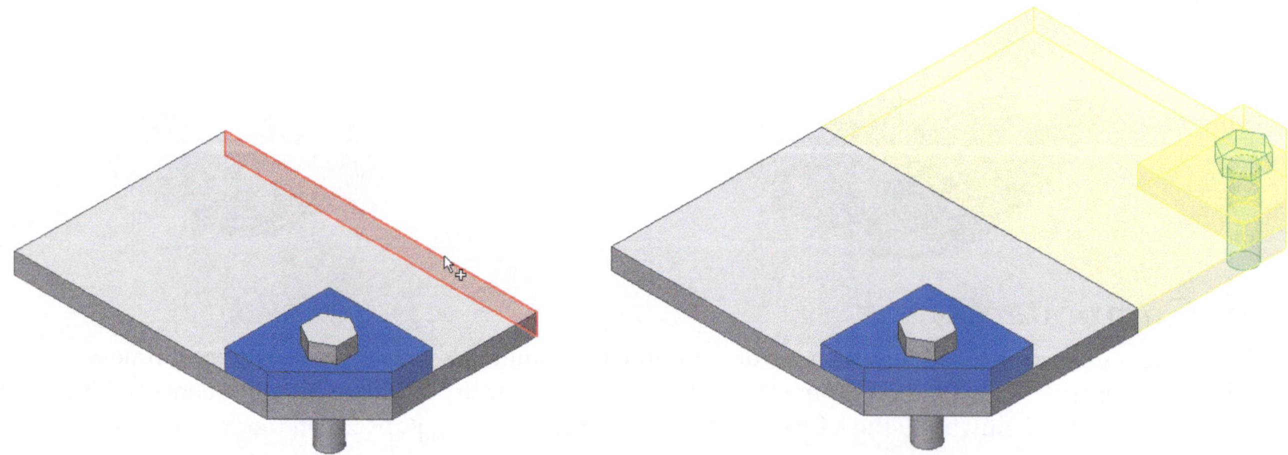

The **File Name** column lists the names of new files. The names are created automatically using the **File Name** box. By default, the mirror components suffix is **_MIR**. You can also give a prefix to the mirror component. To do this, click before the **<Source File name>** and type-in a prefix. You can also add **Assembly Name, Date Day DD, Date Month MM, Date Year YY, Project Name**, or **Unique Number** to the file name of the mirrored component. To do this, click the plus button next to the **File Name** box and select the required option.

The **Location** box specifies the location where the mirrored copy file is saved. By default, the **Source Path** option is displayed in this box. It saves the mirror copy at the same location as the original component. You can specify your own file location by clicking the plus button next to the **Location** box and selecting the **User Path**.

The **Return to Selection** button will return to the previous dialog, where you can select the components.

Select an option from the top-left corner of the dialog. When you select the **Create Flat Structure** option, only mirrored geometry is generated without maintaining any parametric link between the original and mirrored components. There is no associativity between the source and target documents. Additionally, this method does not generate a new browser node for the mirrored components.

The **Create Mirror Pattern** option replicates both geometry and orientation of source components, maintaining associativity with the mirrored versions. Mirrored components appear under a new Mirror node in the browser.

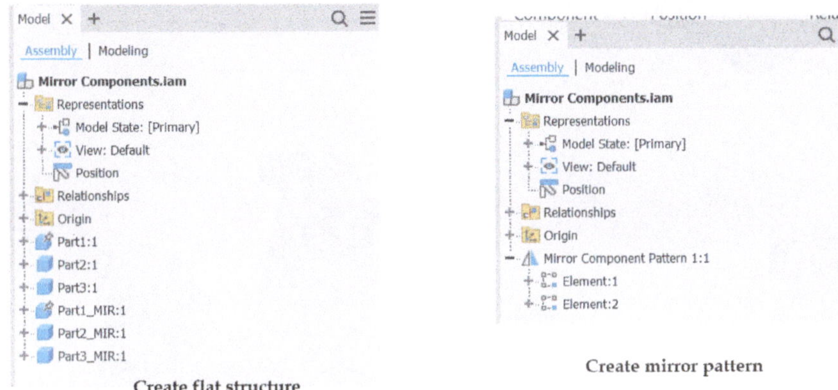

Create flat structure

Create mirror pattern

Click **OK** to complete the mirroring.

Copy Components

The **Copy Components** command allows you to copy a part. Activate this command (click the **Assemble** tab > **Pattern** panel > **Copy** on the ribbon), and then select the part to be copied. On the **Copy Components: Status** dialog, the status of the selected components is displayed in blue. It indicates that a copy of the component will be created. Click on the blue dots to change the status to yellow. The yellow dots indicate that the component will be reused instead of creating a copy. Click **Next** on the **Copy Components: Status** dialog; the **Copy Components: File Names** dialog appears. Specify the settings on this dialog and click **OK**. Next, place the copied component in the assembly.

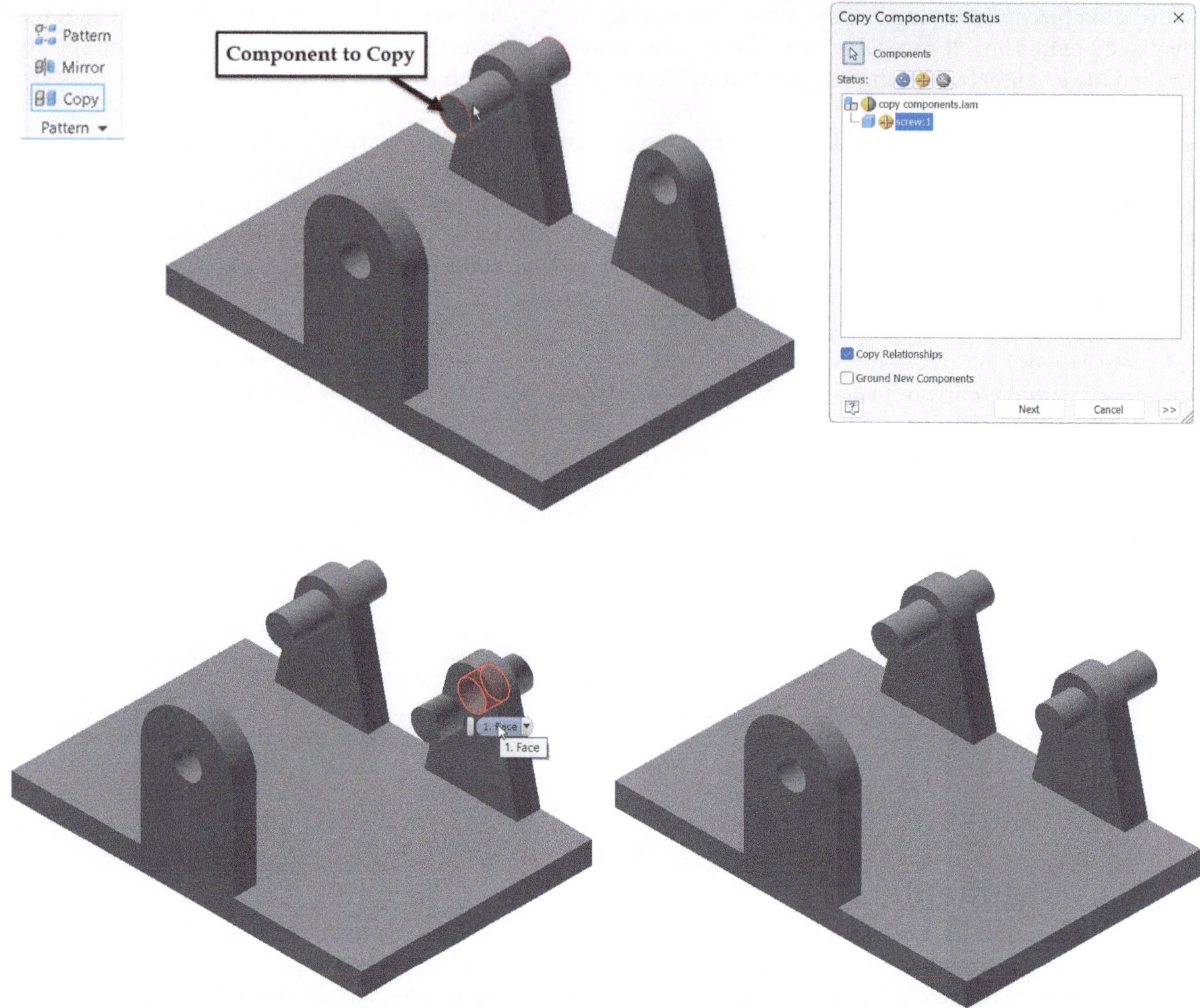

After copying the components, you can define the constraints and create the desired assembly.

Sub-assemblies

The use of sub-assemblies has many advantages in Inventor. Sub-assemblies make large assemblies easier to manage. They make it easy for multiple users to collaborate on a single large assembly design. They can also affect the way you document a large assembly design in 2D drawings. For these reasons, you need to create sub-assemblies in a variety of ways. The easiest way to create a sub-assembly is to insert an existing assembly into another assembly. You need to simply use the Place Component command to insert the subassembly into an existing assembly. Next, apply constraints to constraint the assembly. The process of applying constraints is straightforward. You are required to apply constraints between only one part of a sub-assembly and a part of the main assembly. In addition to that, you can easily hide or suppress a group of parts with the help of sub-assemblies.

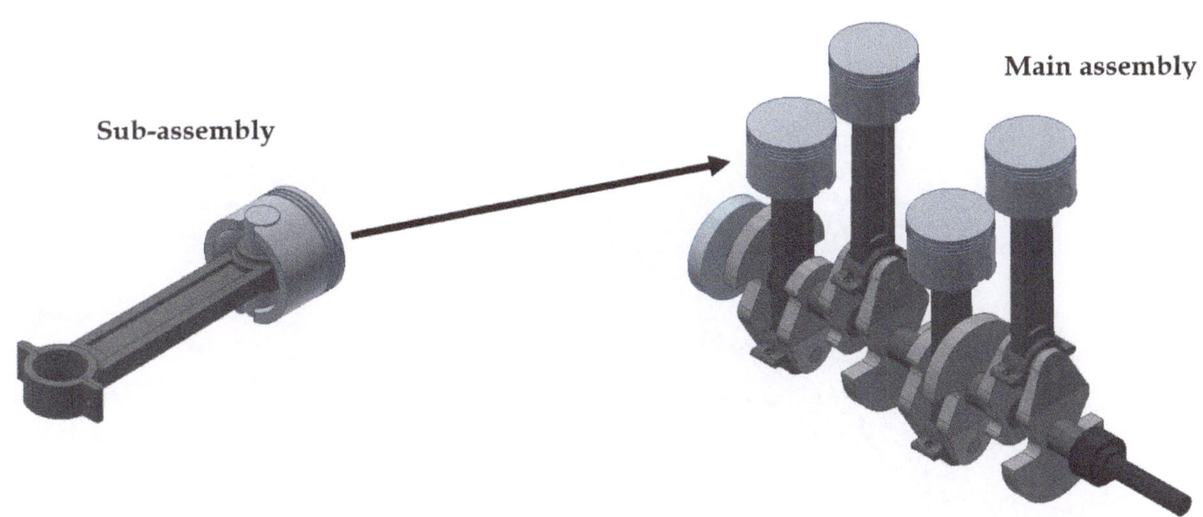

Rigid and Flexible Sub-Assemblies

By default, Inventor makes a sub-assembly as a rigid body. When you move a single part of a sub-assembly, the entire sub-assembly will be moved. If you want the individual parts of a sub-assembly to be moved, you must define the sub-assembly as flexible. Click the right mouse button on the sub-assembly in the **Model** window and select **Flexible**. Now, you can move the individual under-constrained parts of a sub-assembly. In case, if you have multiple occurrences of a sub-assembly, each occurrence can be defined as rigid or flexible, separately. To help you recognize the difference between the rigid and flexible assemblies, Inventor displays a different icon for each of them in the **Model** window.

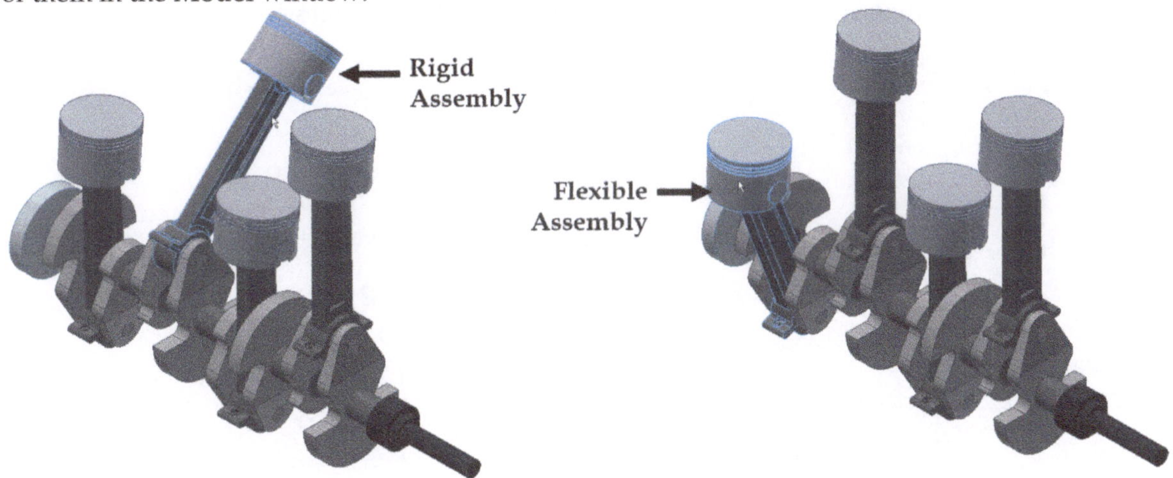

Demote

In addition to creating sub-assemblies and inserting them into another assembly, you can also take individual parts that already exist in an assembly and make them into a sub-assembly. For example, press and hold the **Shift** key and select the parts from the assembly. Next, right click and select **Component > Demote**; the **Create In-Place Component** dialog pops up on the screen.

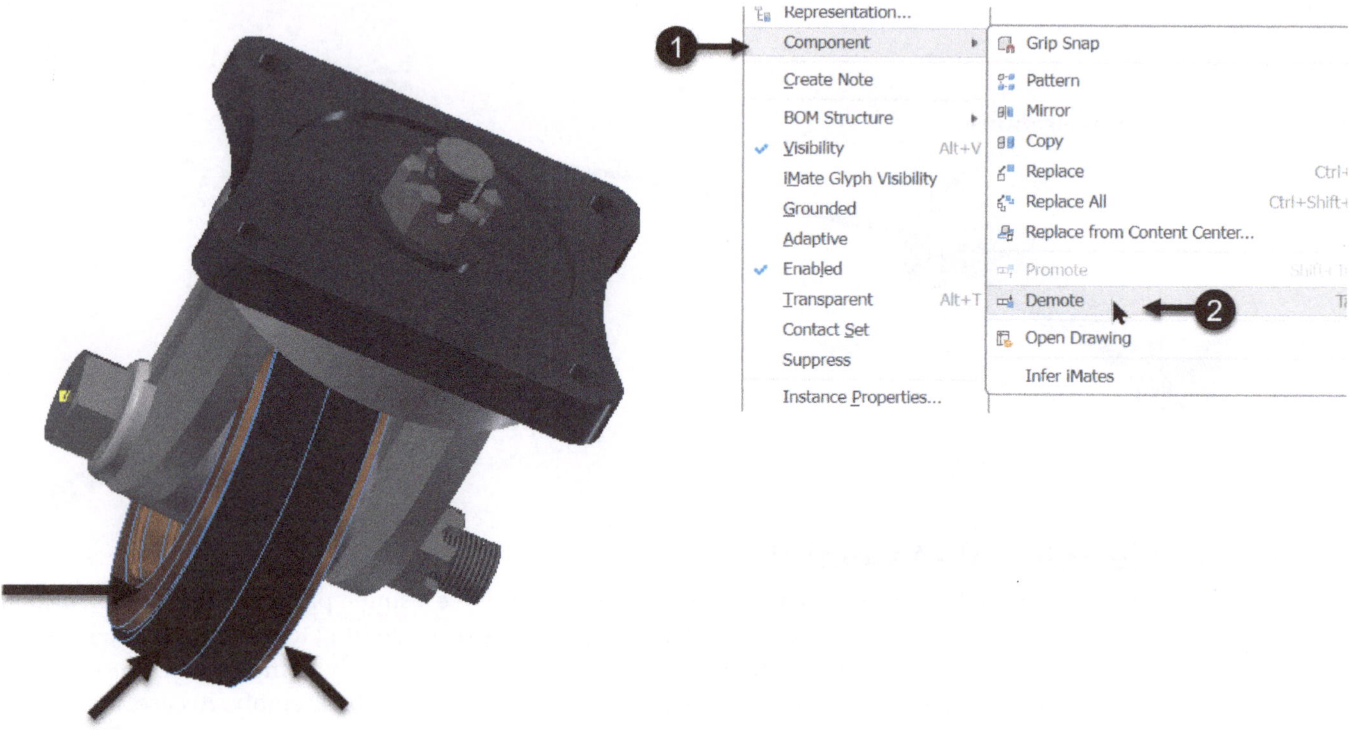

On this dialog, select the assembly template, enter the component name, specify the location, and specify the positioning method. Click **OK**; the subassembly is created and listed in the **Model** window.

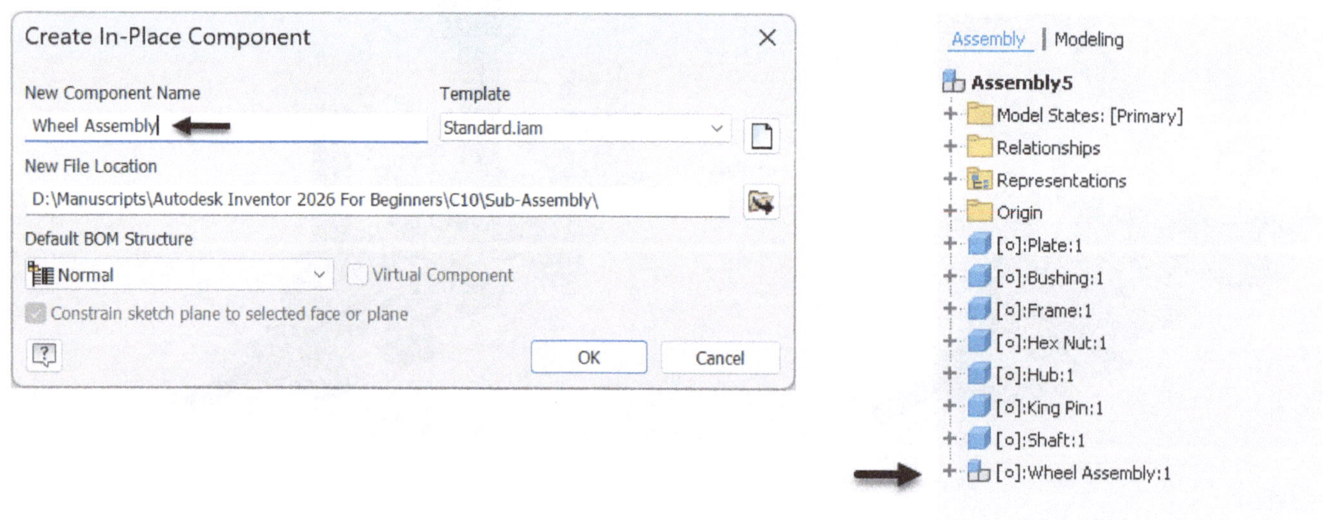

Promote

After inserting subassemblies, you may require to disperse them into individual parts. Inventor provides you with the **Promote** command to break a subassembly into individual parts. In the **Model** window, expand the subassembly and select the parts to be dispersed. Next, right-click and select **Component > Promote**; a message box pops up, showing, "The restructure operation may result in lost features due to missing references. Do you want to proceed?". Click **Yes** to transfer the parts to the main assembly.

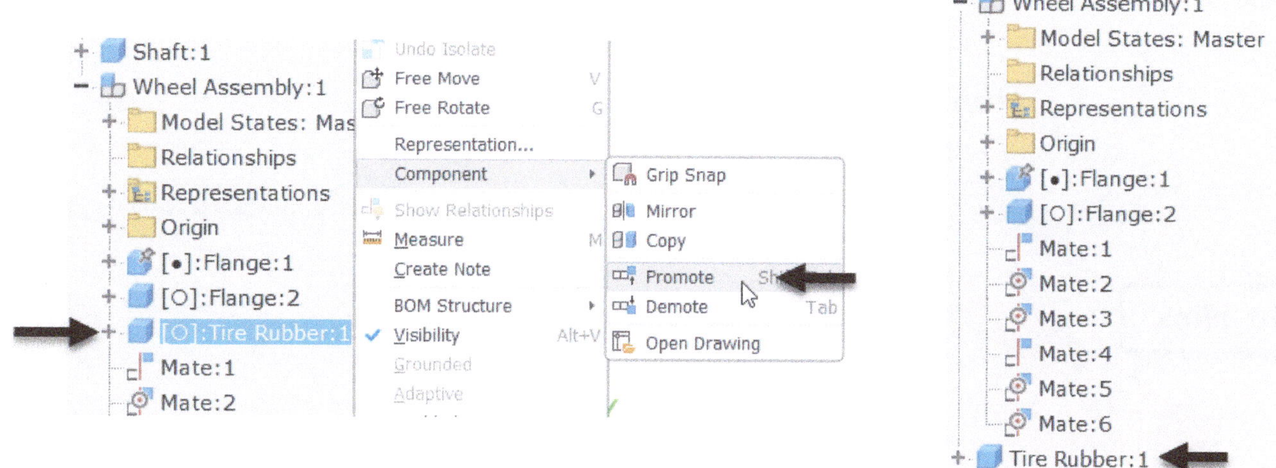

Assembly Features

Assembly features are the features that exist only in assemblies, i.e., instead of creating them at the part level; they are created at the assembly level. Most often, the features created at the assembly level are cuts, revolved cuts, holes, and welds. These features are commonly created at the assembly level to represent post assembly machining. For example, to add a cut feature to the assembly shown in the figure, create a sketch for the cut feature. For this, click **3D Model** tab **> Sketch > Start 2D Sketch** on the ribbon. Draw the sketch and click **Finish Sketch**. Next, activate the **Extrude** command (click **3D Model > Modify Assembly > Extrude** on the ribbon); the **Extrude Properties** panel pops up on the screen. On this panel, click the **OK** button to create an extruded cut.

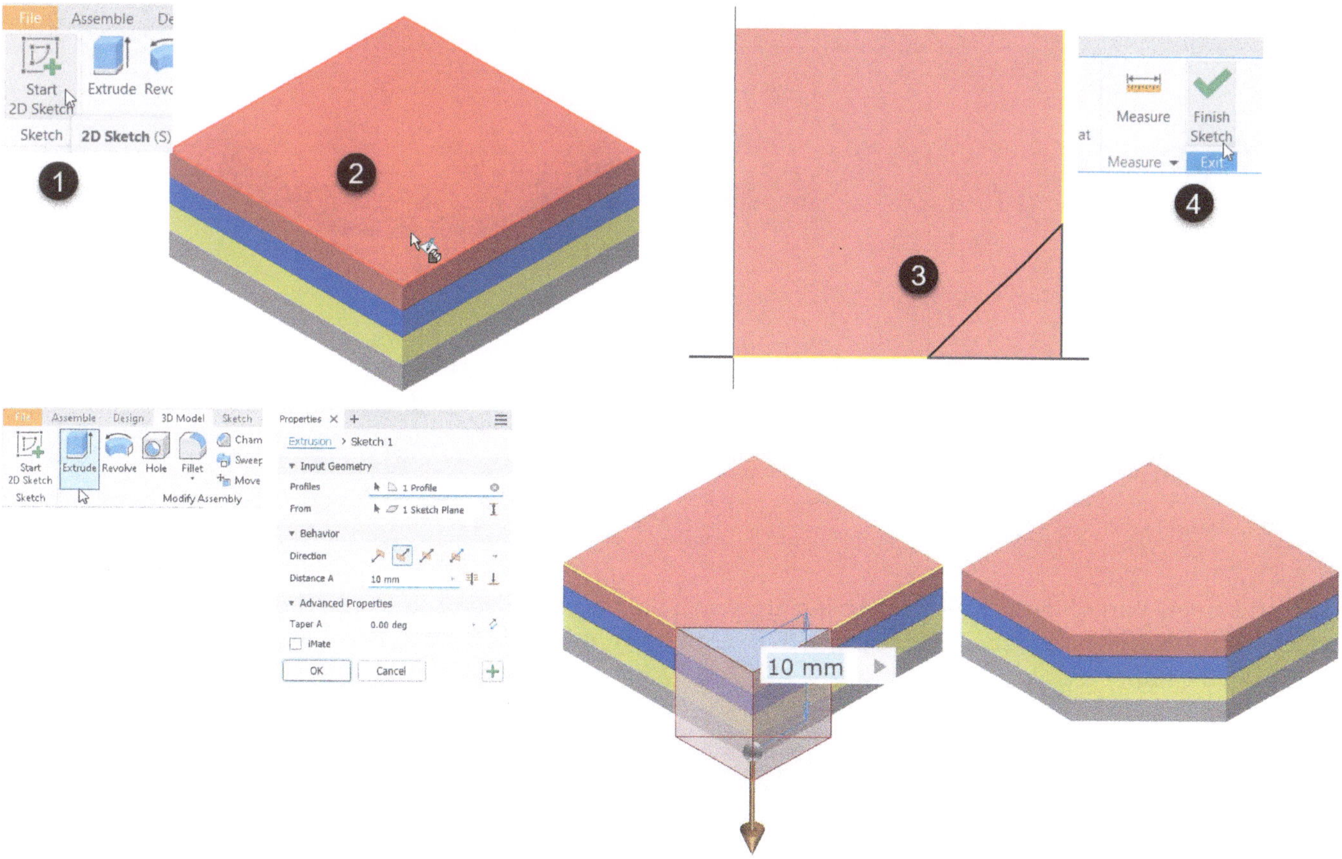

Now, open the individual part in another window. You will notice that the cut feature does not affect the part.

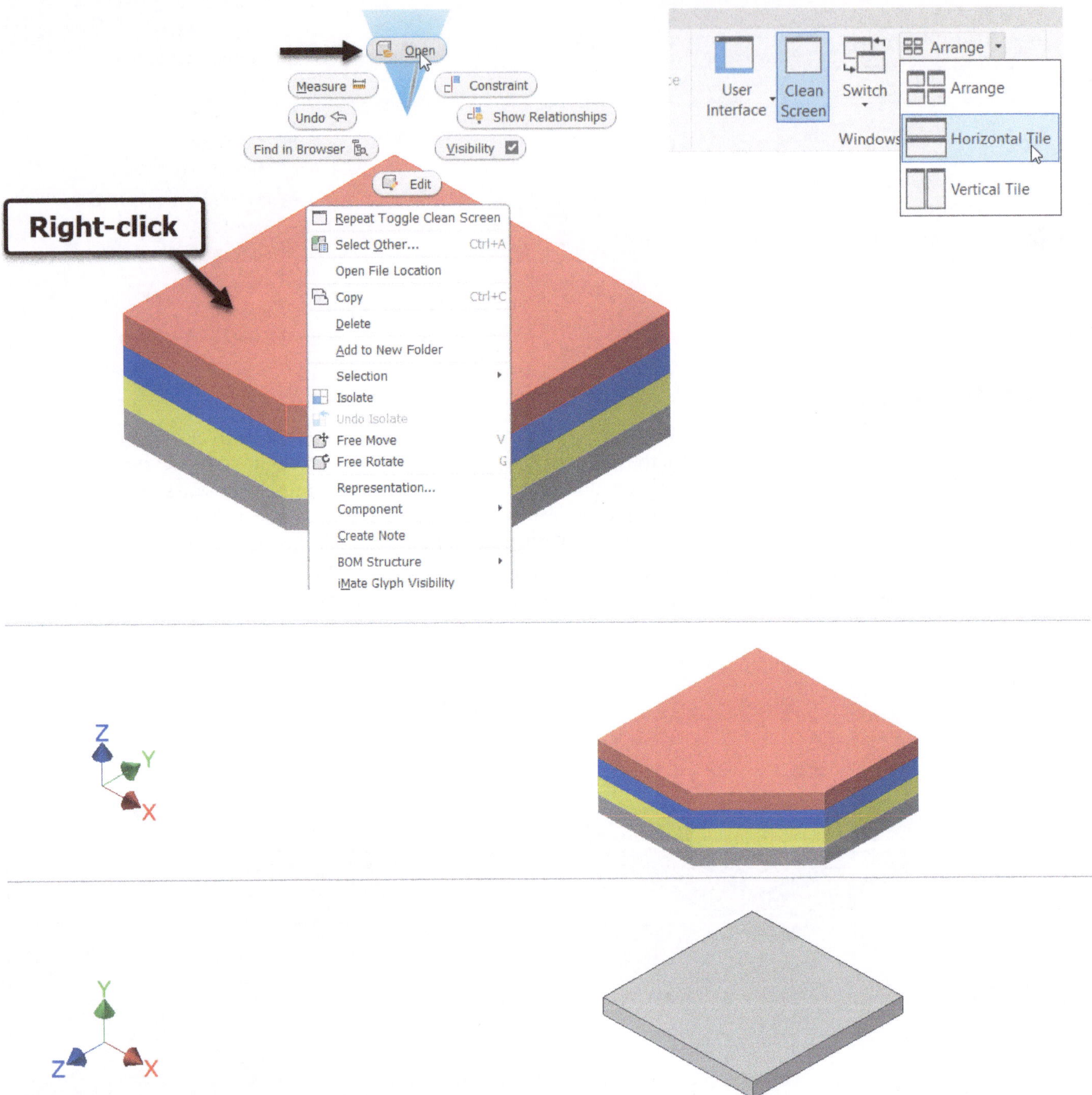

If you add a new part to the assembly, the cut feature will not affect it. You need to add the part to the extruded feature. To do this, right-click on the **Extrusion** in the **Model Window** and select **Add Participant**. Next, select the newly added component.

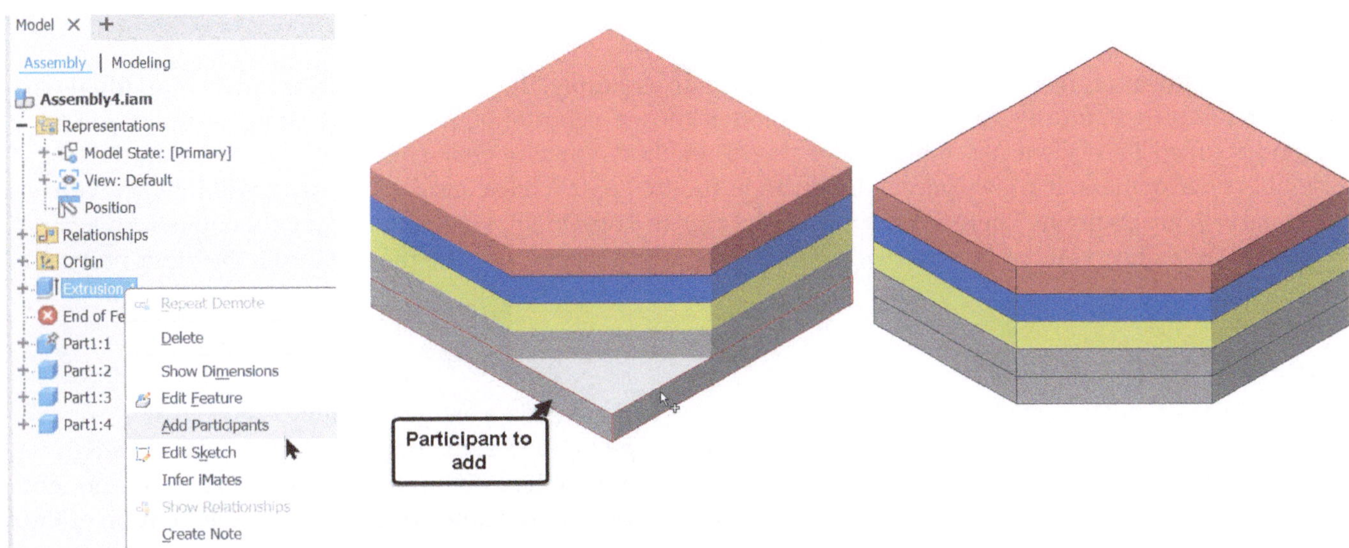

If you want to remove a participant from the assembly extrusion, then expand the **Extrusion** feature in the Model Window. Next, right click on the part, and then select **Remove Participant**.

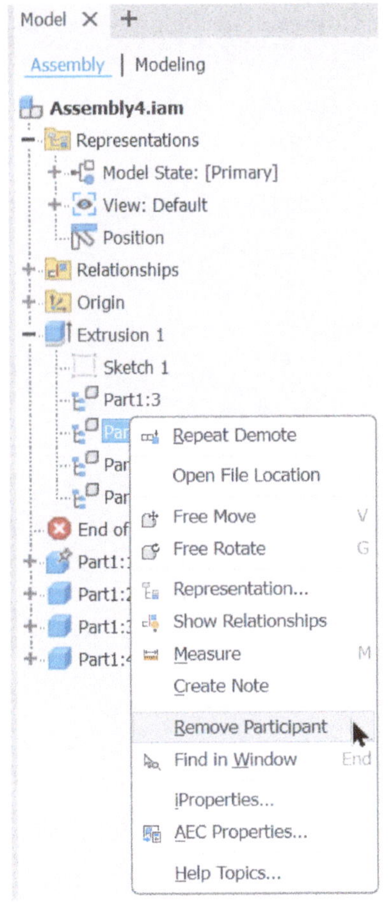

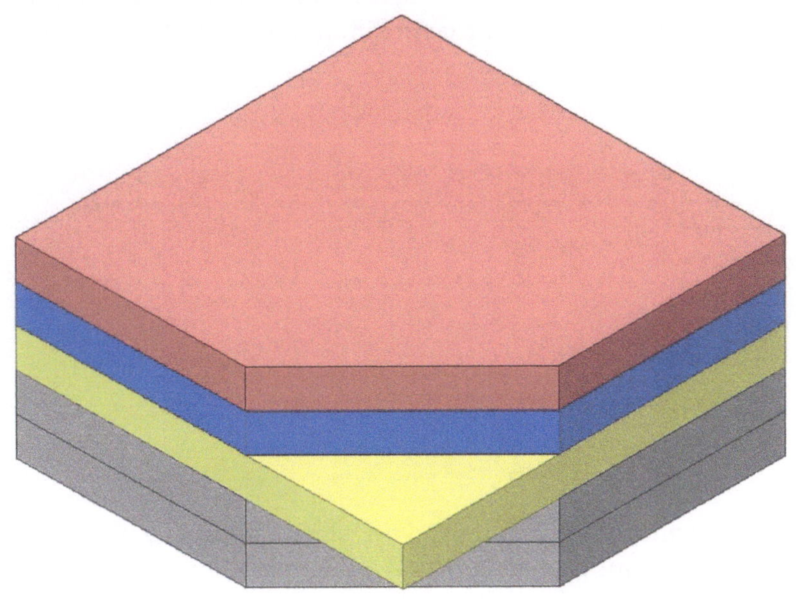

Top-Down Assembly Design

In Autodesk Inventor, there are two methods to create an assembly. The first method is to create individual parts and then insert them into an assembly. This method is known as Bottom-Up Assembly Design. The second method is called Top-Down Assembly Design. In this method, you will create individual parts within the assembly environment. It allows you to design an individual part while considering how it will interact with other parts in an assembly. There are several advantages to Top-Down Assembly Design. As you design a part within the assembly, you can be sure that it will fit properly. You can also use the edge from the other parts as a reference.

Create Component

Top-down assembly design can be used to add new parts to an already existing assembly. You can also use it to create entirely new assemblies. To create a part using the Top-Down Design approach, activate the **Create Component** command (click **Assemble > Component > Create** on the ribbon); the **Create In-Place Component** dialog pops up on the screen. Enter the name in the **New Component Name** box and specify the location of the new component. You can click the **Browse to New File Location** icon to specify the new location for the new component. Select the part template from the **Template** drop-down. If you want to access more templates, click the **Browse Template** icon to display the **Open Template** dialog. Next, select the required tab, and then select the template. Click **OK** to close the **Open Template** dialog. On the **Create In-Place Component** dialog, select an option from the **Default BOM Structure** drop-down, and then click **OK**.

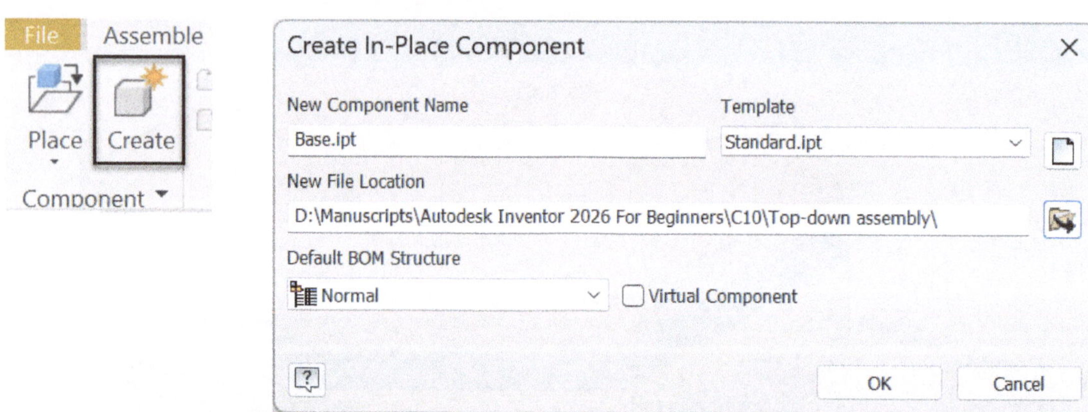

In the **Model** window, expand the **Origin** folder and select a plane; the Part environment is activated. Now, create the part features, and then click **Return** on the ribbon; the assembly environment is activated.

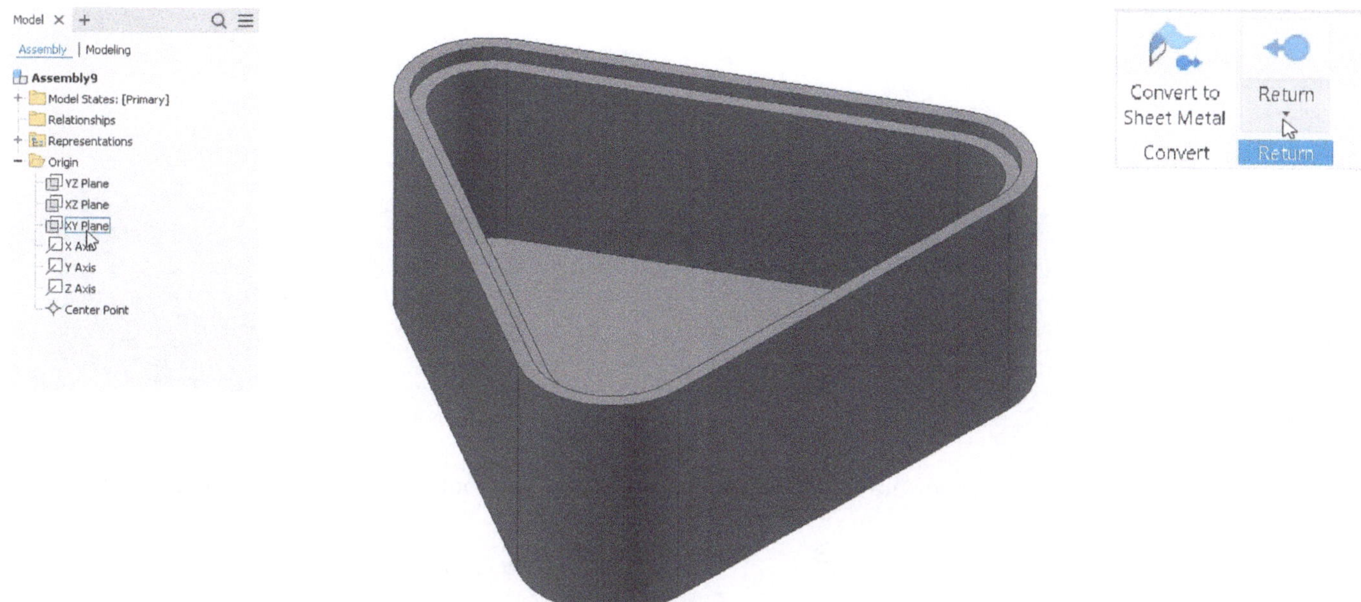

Again, activate the **Create Component** command and specify the settings on the **Create In-Place Component** dialog. Next, select a face on the first part; the part is created and opened in the Part environment. Now, create the features of the part, and then close and return to the assembly. In the example given in the figure, the **Project Geometry** command is used to project the edges of the existing part to create a sketch. The projected sketch is then extruded. It makes it easy to create a part using the edges of the existing part.

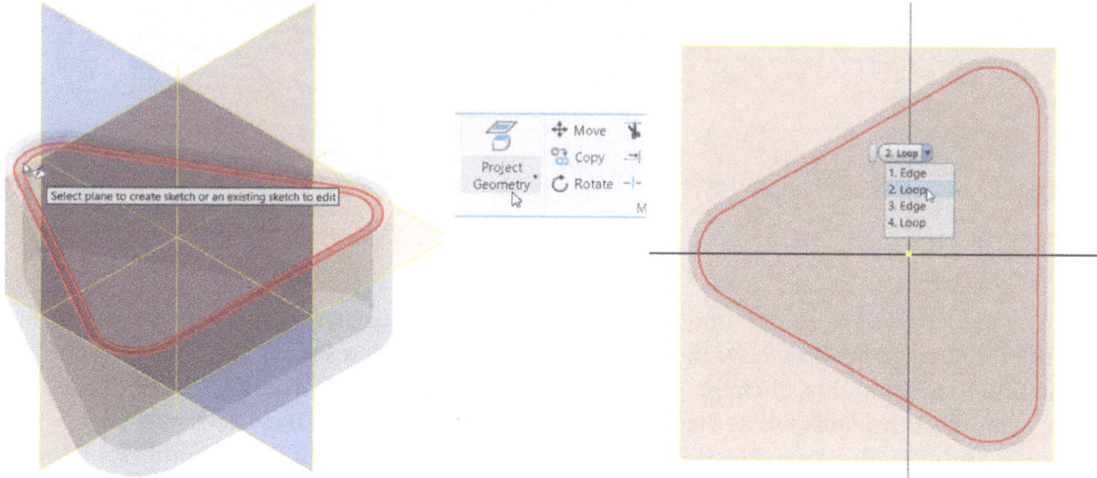

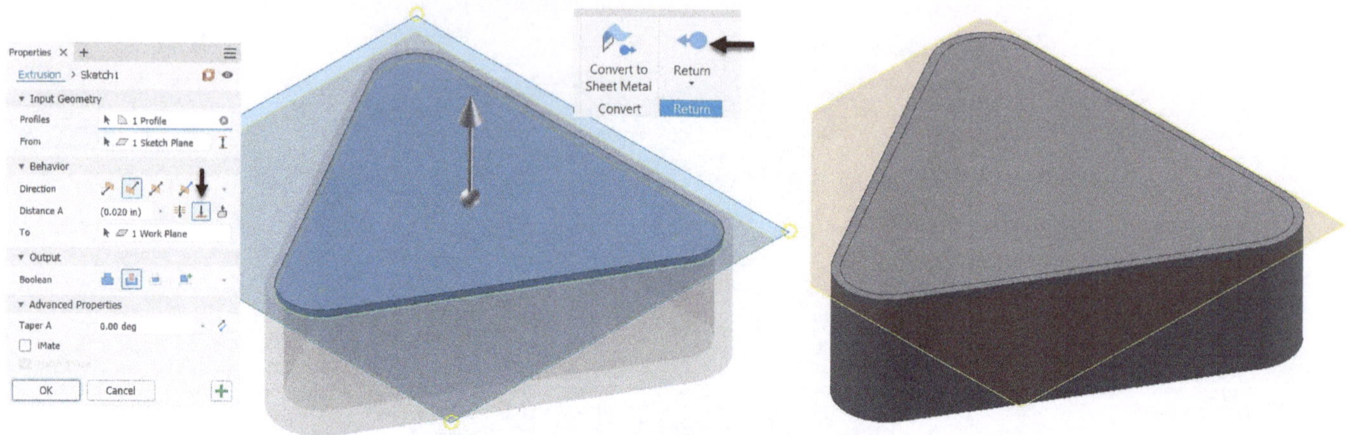

Now, if you change the parameters of the base component, the linked component will also change automatically.

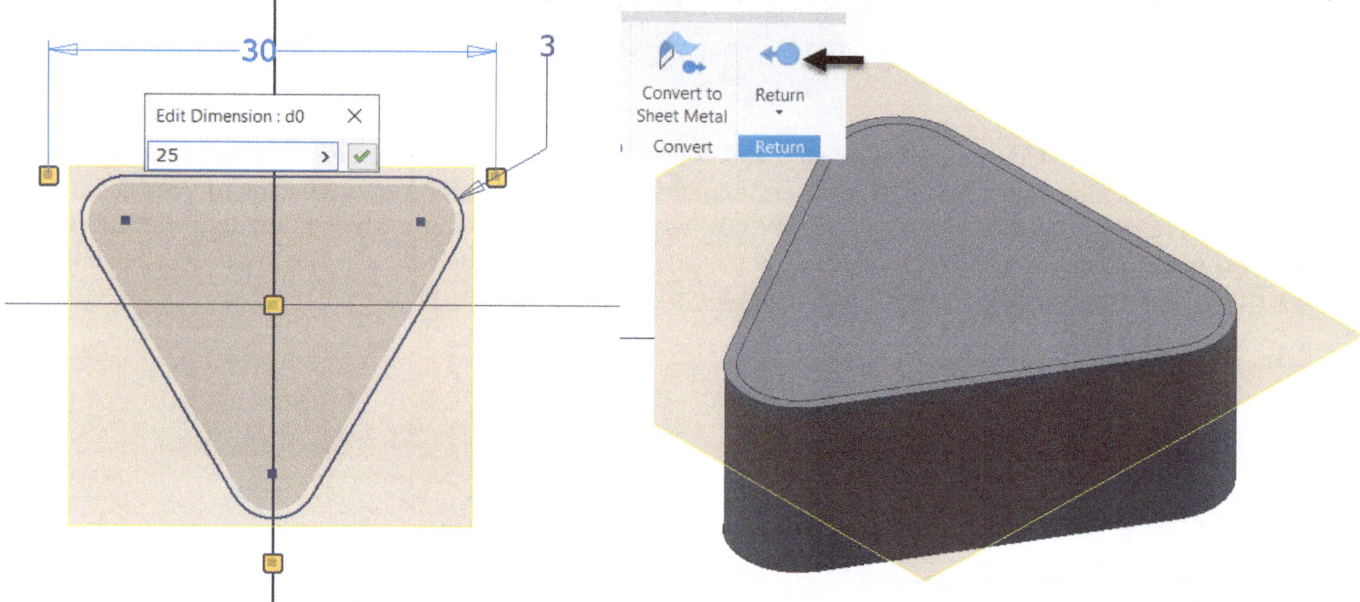

Exploding Assemblies

It is very common to create an exploded view to document an assembly design properly. In an exploded view, the parts of an assembly are pulled apart to show how they were assembled. To create an exploded view, you need to start a new presentation file. To do this, click the **New** icon on the **Quick Access Toolbar**. Next, select any one of the standard folders from the Templates list. It displays the templates available in the select standard. Scroll to the **Presentation – Create an exploded projection of an assembly** section, and then double click on the .ipn file; the Presentation environment is activated. In addition to that, the **Insert** dialog pops up on the screen. Go to the location of the assembly (.iam) file and double-click on it; the assembly file is loaded in the presentation file.

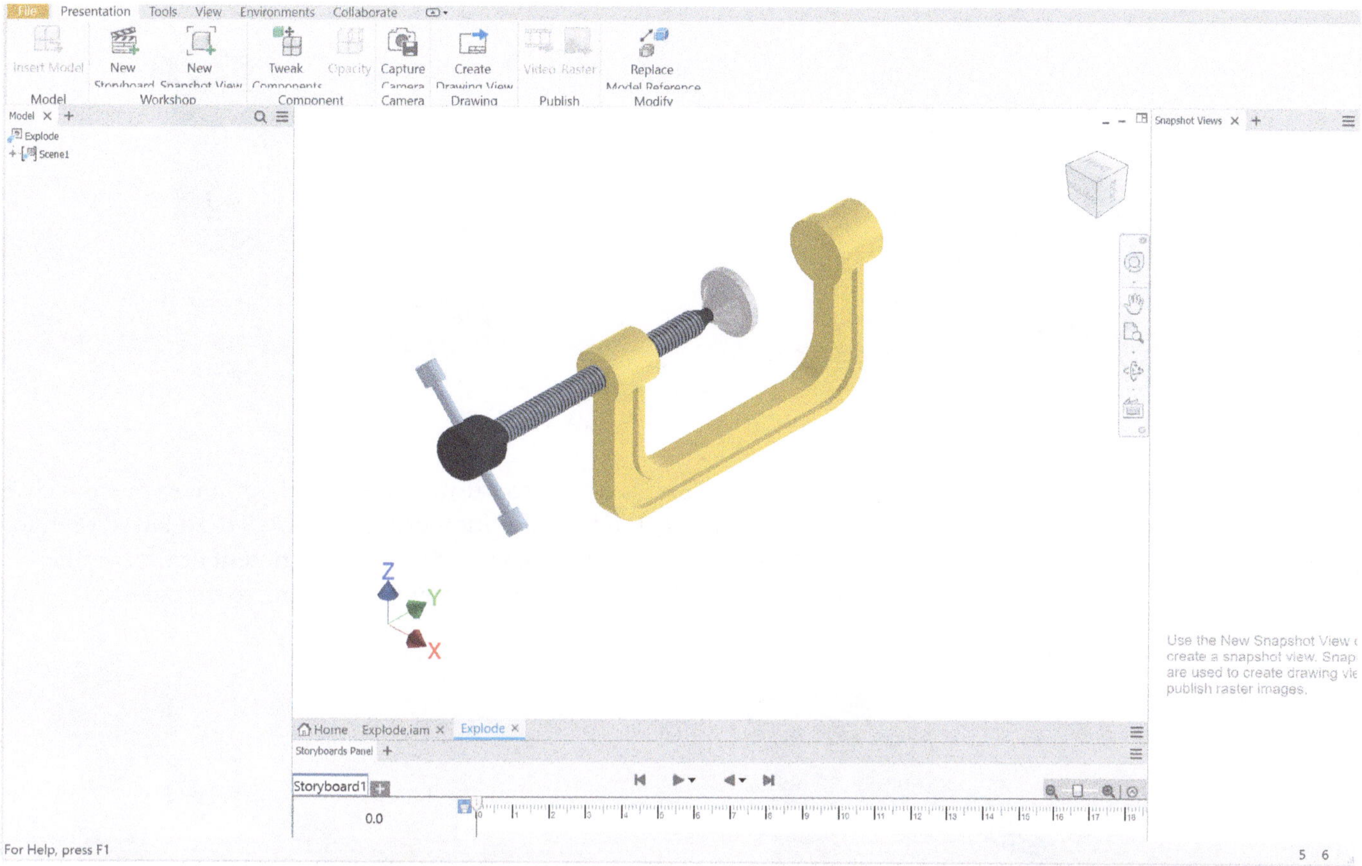

To explode an assembly, activate the **Tweak Components** command (on the ribbon, click **Presentation > Component > Tweak Components**); the mini toolbar pops up. On the Mini toolbar, select the **Part** or **Component** option from the selection type drop-down located at the top. The **Part** option allows you to select individual parts of a subassembly. Whereas, the **Component** option allows you to select the entire subassembly.

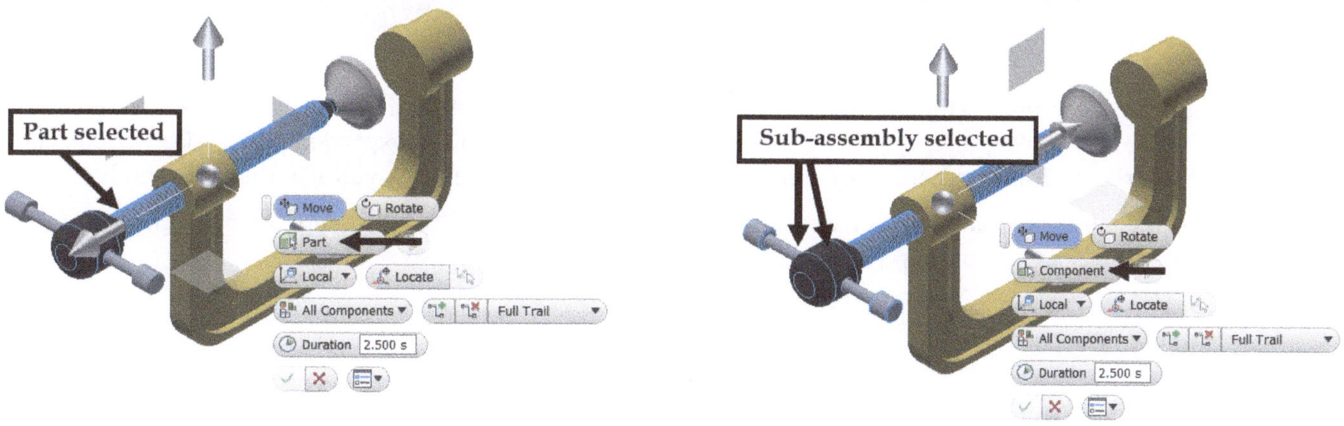

Click on the part to be exploded. If you want to select multiple parts, then press and hold the Shift key and select multiple parts; the UCS triad appears on the selected parts. On the Mini toolbar, click the **Locate** option and select a point from the assembly to define the location of the UCS triad.

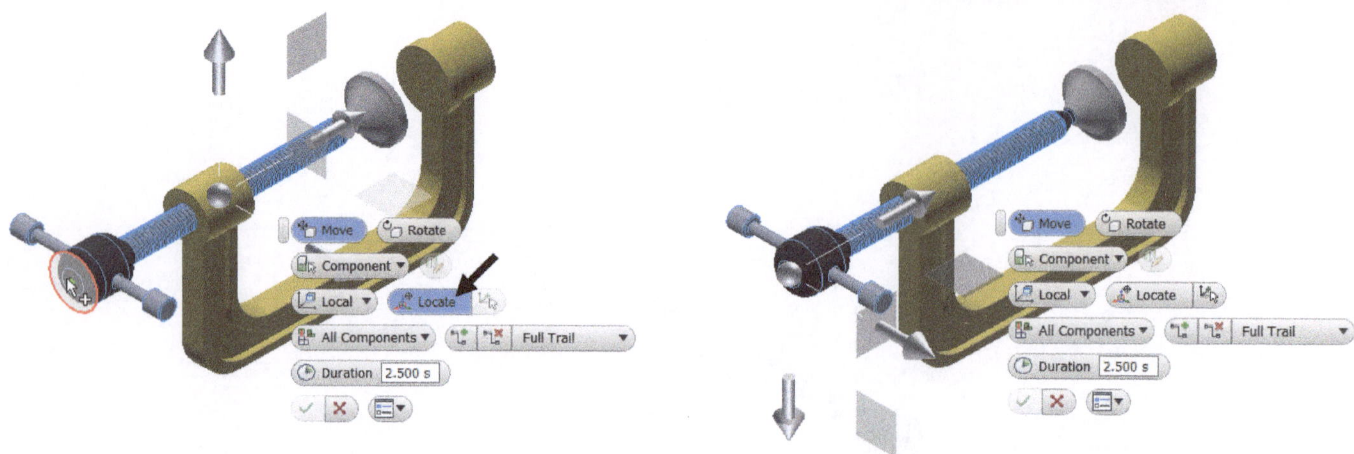

On the Mini toolbar, select the **Local** or **World** option from the UCS drop-down. The **Local** option orients the UCS triad based on the orientation of the selected part. Whereas, the **World** option orients the UCS triad based on the World Coordinate System. If you want to specify a custom orientation, then click the **Alignment** option on the Mini toolbar and select an edge or point from the assembly. The UCS triad orients according to the selected element.

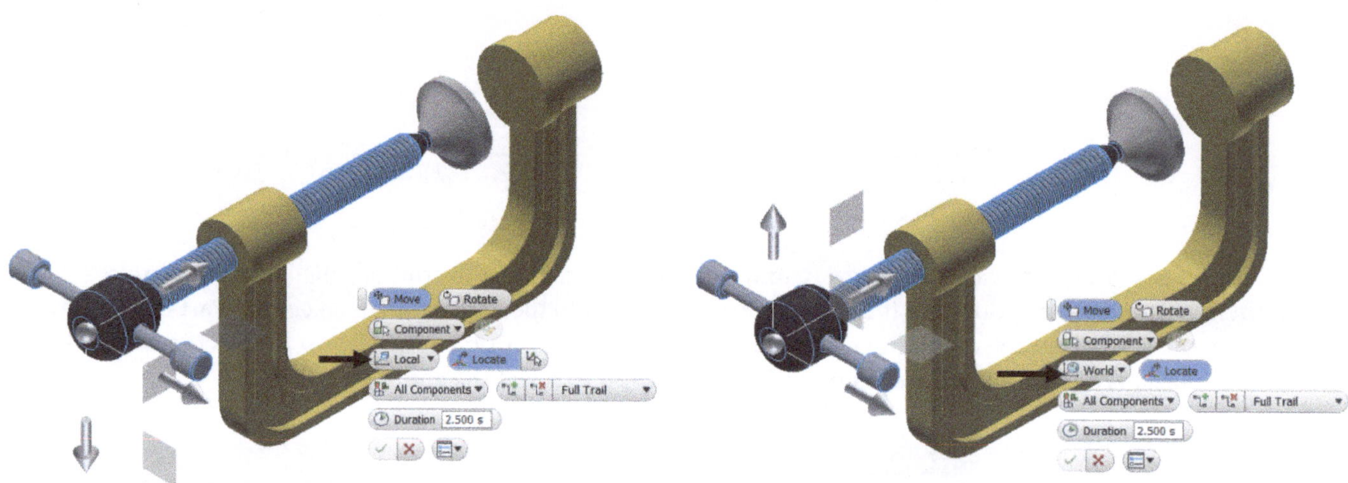

Click on any one of the manipulators of the UCS triad to define the direction of the explosion. Type a value in the box attached to the manipulator. Next, specify the option to create trials for the exploded parts. Also, specify the type of trial: Full trial or Trail Segments. After specifying the trial options, enter a value in the Duration box. It defines the distance the play marker will move on the timeline. Click **OK** on the Mini toolbar. Likewise, explode the remaining parts of the assembly.

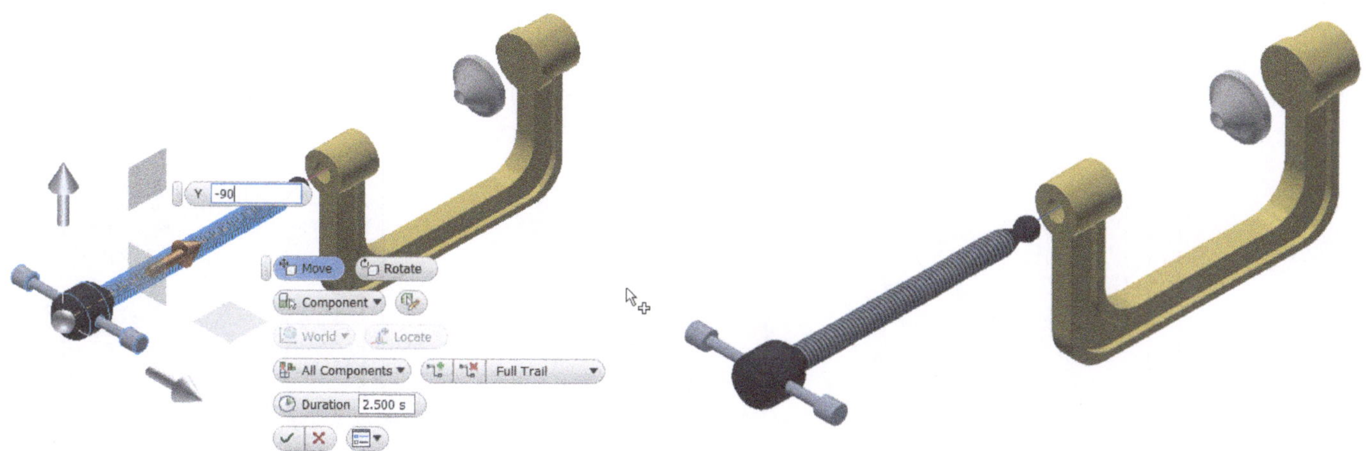

Taking a Snapshot

Adjust the position of the play marker on the timeline and notice that the positions of the components in the graphics window change. You can create a snapshot view if you want to capture a particular position of the assembly. To do this, click **Presentation** tab > **Workshop** panel > **New Snapshot View**; the snapshot is displayed in the Snapshot Views window. Double-click on the snapshot view to activate the view. Click **Finish Edit View** to exit the snapshot view. Next, save and close the presentation file.

Examples

Example 1 (Bottom-Up Assembly)

In this example, you will create the assembly shown below.

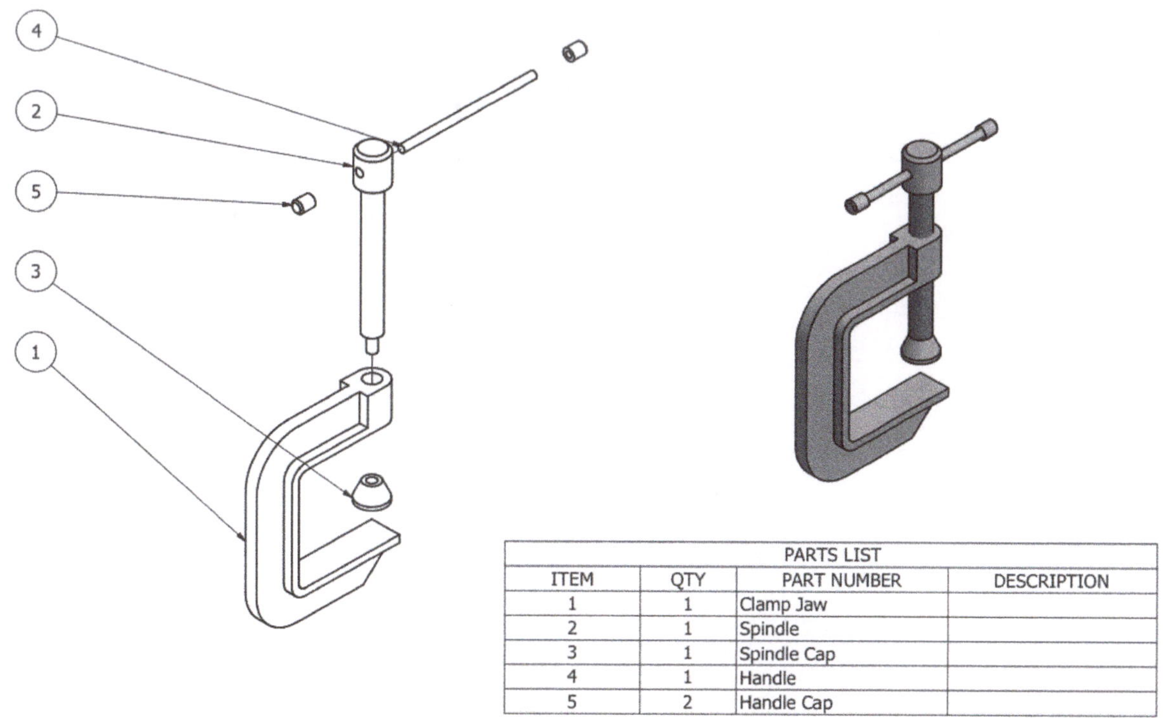

PARTS LIST			
ITEM	QTY	PART NUMBER	DESCRIPTION
1	1	Clamp Jaw	
2	1	Spindle	
3	1	Spindle Cap	
4	1	Handle	
5	2	Handle Cap	

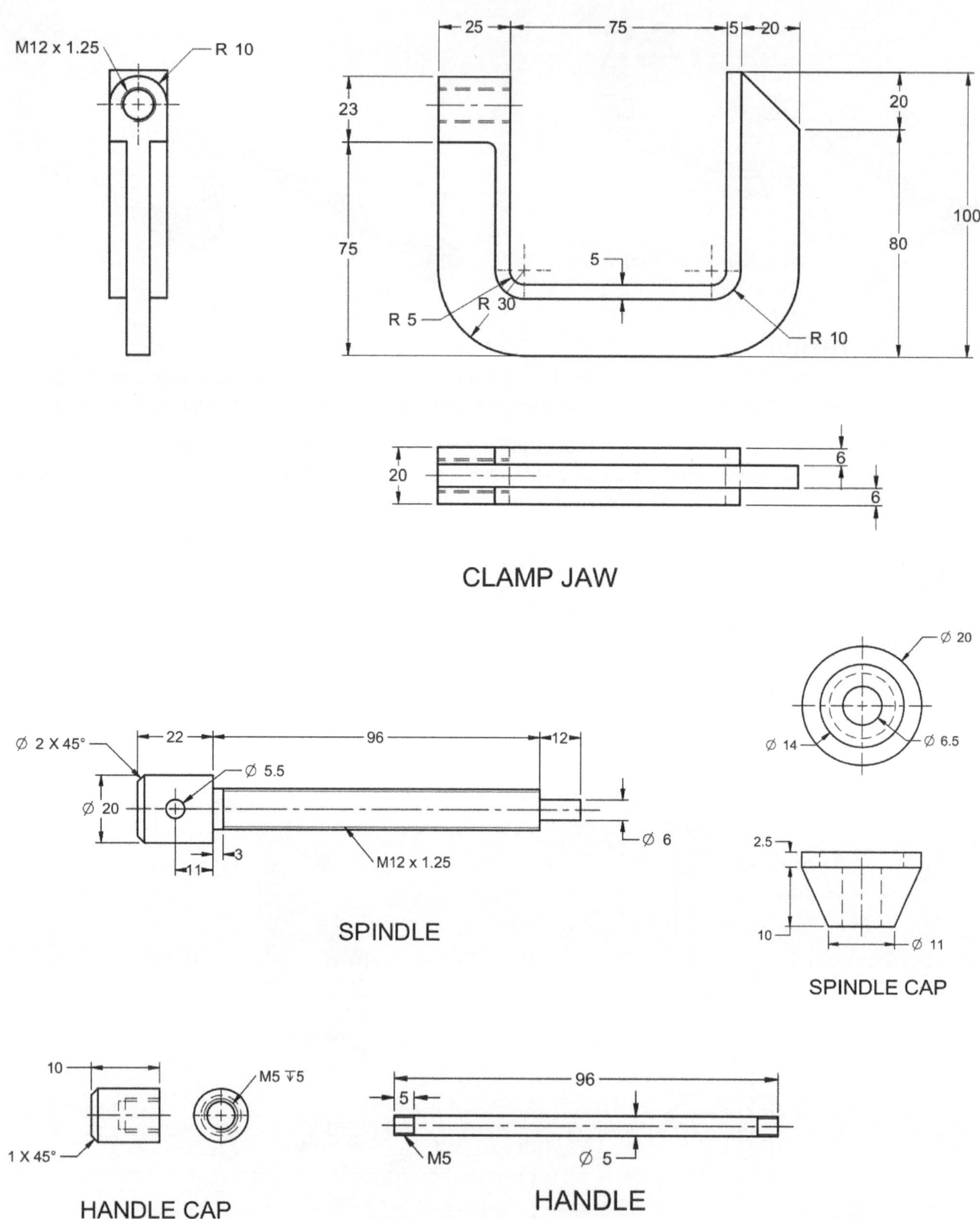

1. Start **Autodesk Inventor 2026**.

2. Create and save all the parts of the assembly in a single folder. Name this folder as *G-Clamp*.
3. On the ribbon, click **Get Started > New**. Next, select **Templates > en-US > Metric**, and then click **Standard(mm).iam**. Click **Create** to start a new assembly file.
4. On the ribbon, click **Assemble > Component > Place** drop-down **> Place**.
5. On the **Place Component** dialog, use the **Look in** drop-down menu and go to the *G-Clamp* folder.
6. On the **Place Component** dialog, click *Clamp Jaw*, and then click **Open**.
7. Right click and select **Placed Grounded at Origin**; the component is placed and fixed at the origin. Right click and select **OK**.

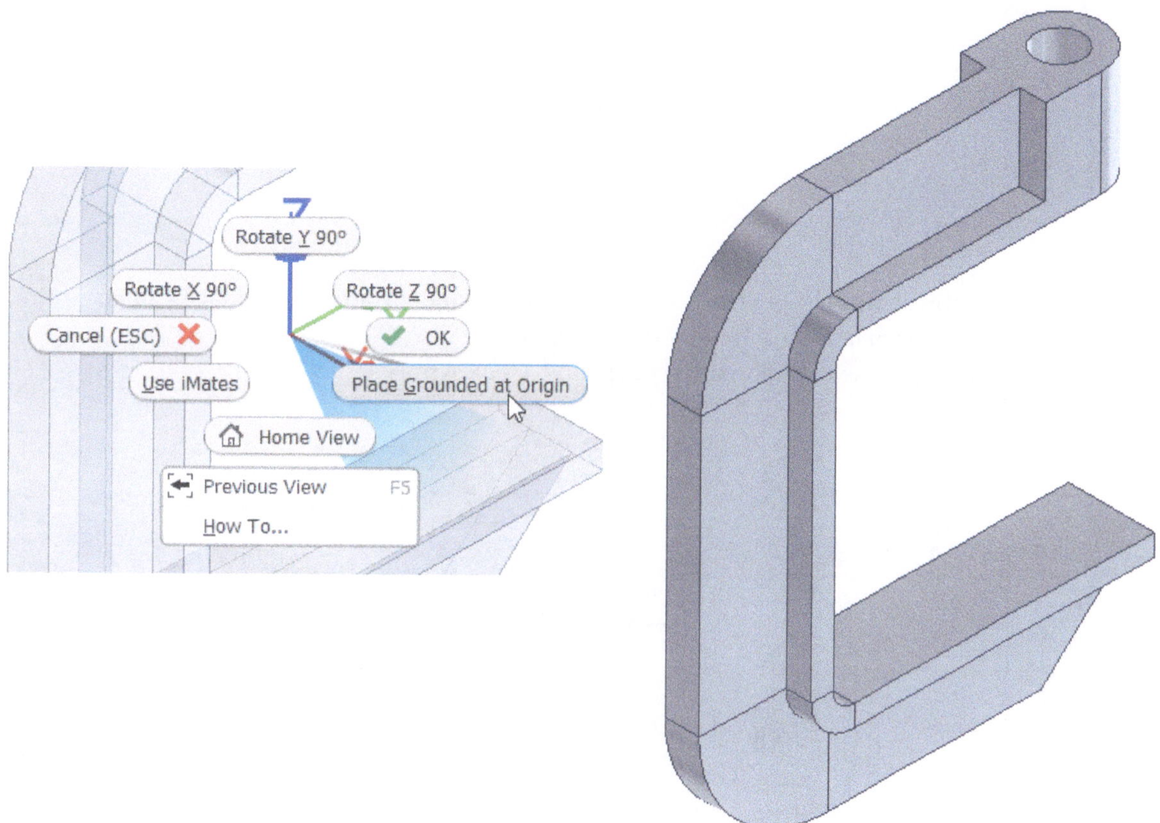

8. On the ribbon, click **Assemble > Component > Place**.
9. In the **Place Component** dialog, click *Spindle*, and then click **Open**. Click in the graphics window to place the component. Right click and select **OK** to deactivate the **Place Component** command.

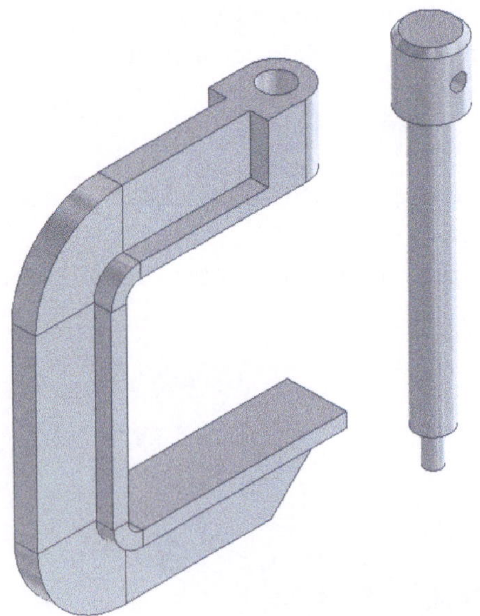

10. On the ribbon, click **Relationships > Constrain** . Next, select **Type > Mate** on the **Place Constraint** dialog.
11. Click on the round face of the *Spindle* and hole of the *Clamp Jaw*.
12. On the **Place Constraint** dialog, select **Solution > Opposed**. Click **Apply**.

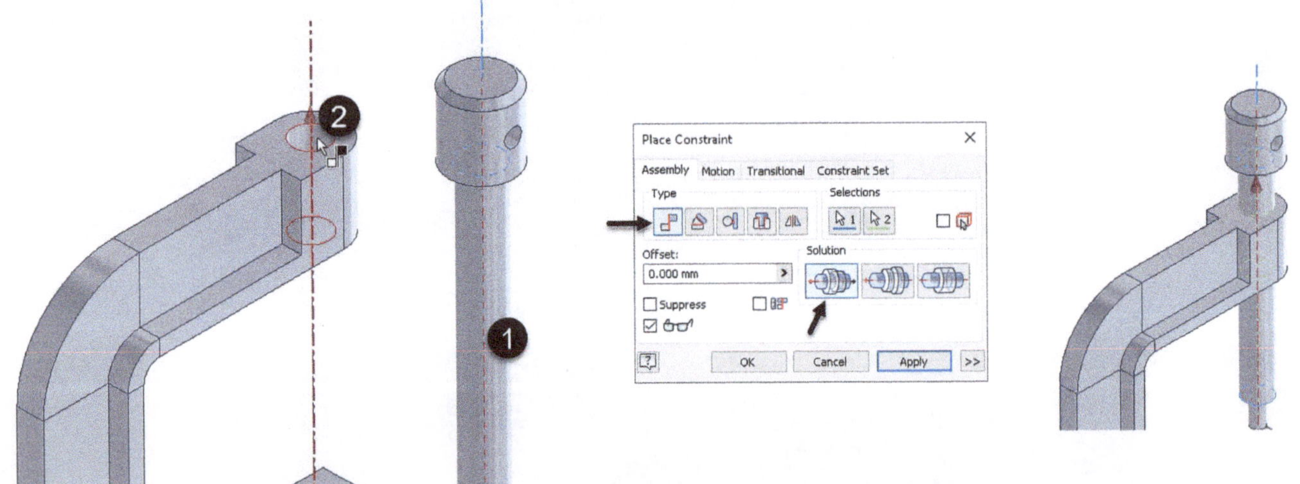

13. On the **Place Constraint** dialog, click **Type > Mate**, and then type **31** in the **Offset Value** box.
14. Click on the flat face of the *Clamp Jaw*, as shown in the figure.
15. Place the pointer on the lower circular edge of the front portion of the *Spindle*; a selection drop-down appears. Click on the drop-down and select **Face Normal**.
16. On the **Place Constraint** dialog, select **Solution > Mate**, and then click **OK**.

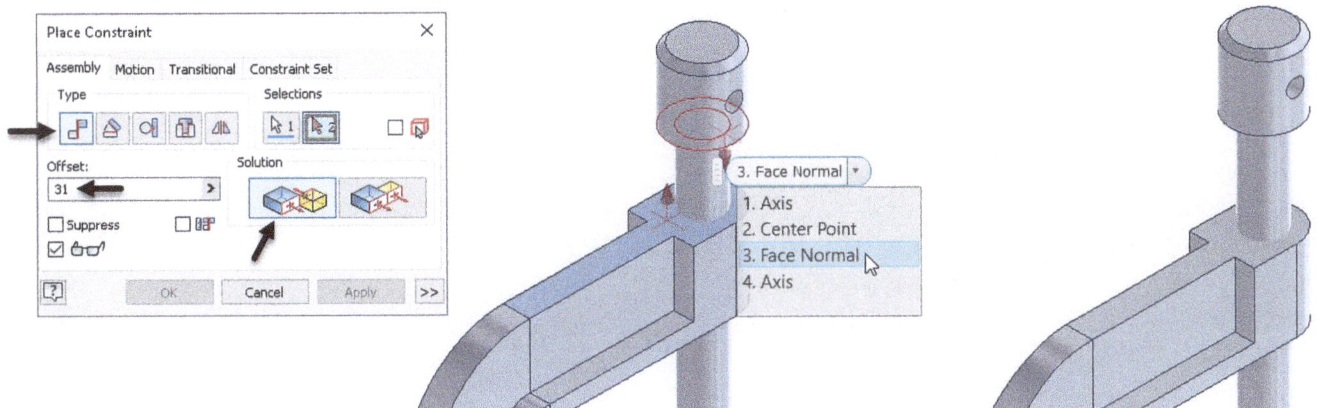

17. On the ribbon, click **View > Visibility > Degrees of Freedom**; the degrees of freedom of the spindle are displayed. The spindle is free to rotate about its axis.

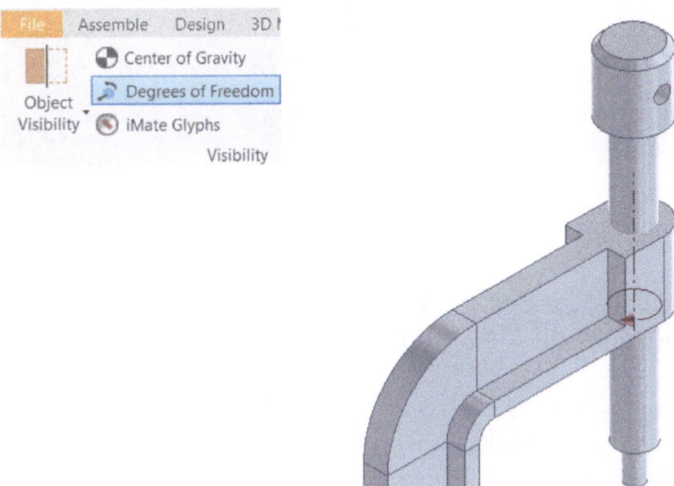

18. On the ribbon, click **Assemble > Relationships > Constrain**. Next, select **Type > Mate** on the **Place Constraint** dialog.
19. In the **Model** Window, expand **Spindle > Origin**, and then select the **XZ Plane**.
20. In the **Model** Window, expand **Assembly > Origin**, and then select the **XZ** Plane. Click **OK** on the Place **Constraint** dialog.

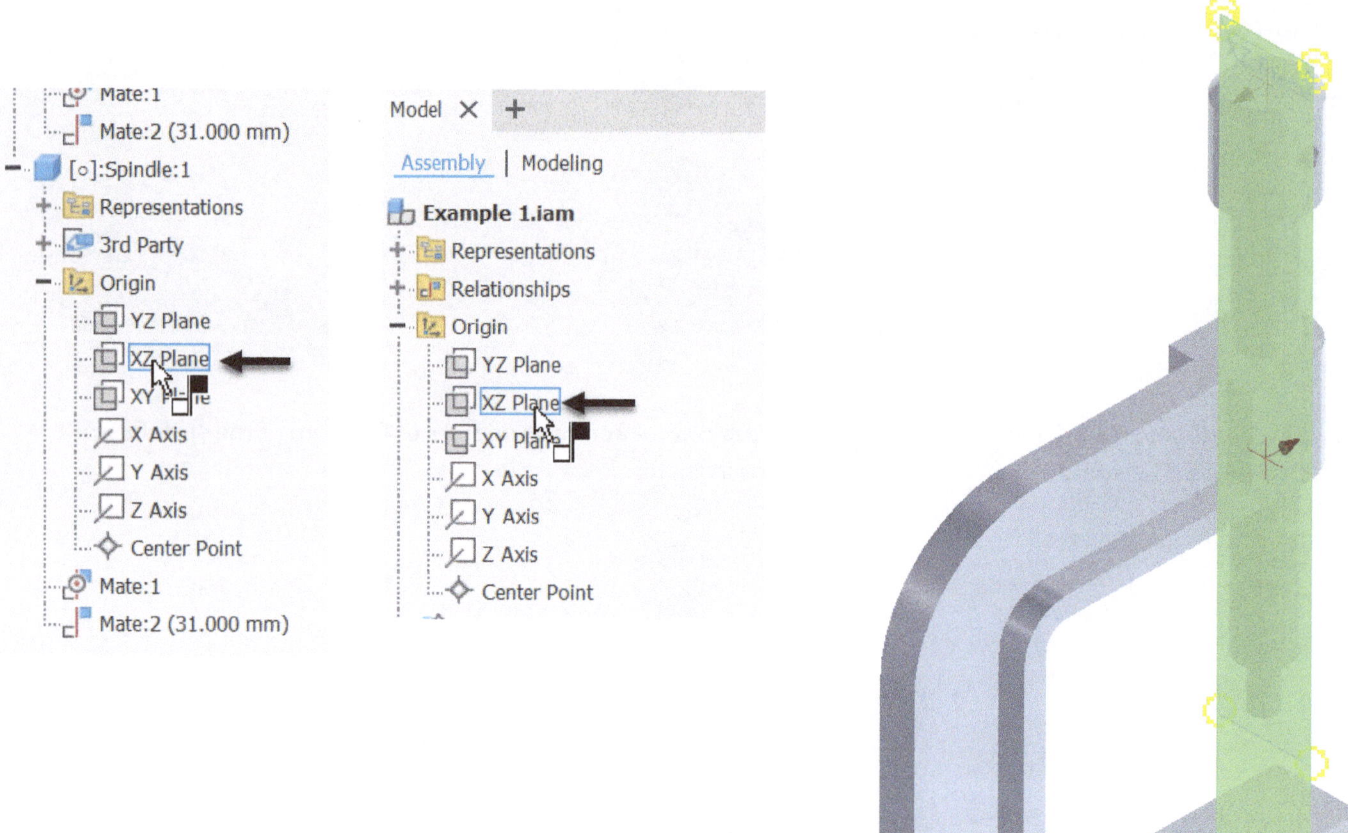

21. On the ribbon, click **Assemble > Component > Place**. On the **Place Component** dialog, click *Spindle Cap*, and then click **Open**.
22. Click in the graphics window to place the component. Next, right click and select **OK**.
23. On the ribbon, click **Relationships > Constrain**. Next, select **Type > Insert** on the **Place Constraint** dialog.
24. Click on the circular edge of the *Spindle Cap* hole, as shown.
25. Click on the circular edge of the *Spindle*, as shown.
26. Select **Solution > Opposed** on the **Place Constraint** dialog; the *Spindle* and *Spindle Cap* are axially aligned and positioned opposite to each other.
27. Check the **Lock Rotation** option on the **Place Constraint** dialog, and then click **OK**.

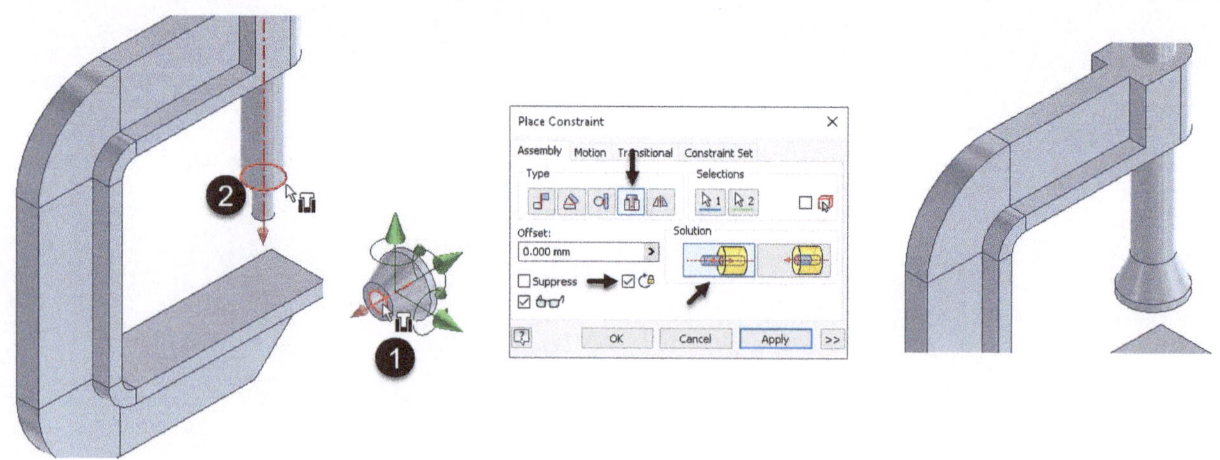

28. On the ribbon, click **Assemble > Component > Place**. On the **Place Component** dialog, click *Handle*, and then click **Open**.
29. Click in the graphics window to place the component. Next, right click and select **OK**.
30. On the ribbon, click **Relationships > Constrain**, and then select **Type > Mate** on the **Place Constraint** dialog.
31. Select the axis of the *Handle*, and then select the axis of the hole located on the *Spindle*.
32. Select **Solution > Aligned** on the **Place Constraint** dialog, and then click **Apply**.

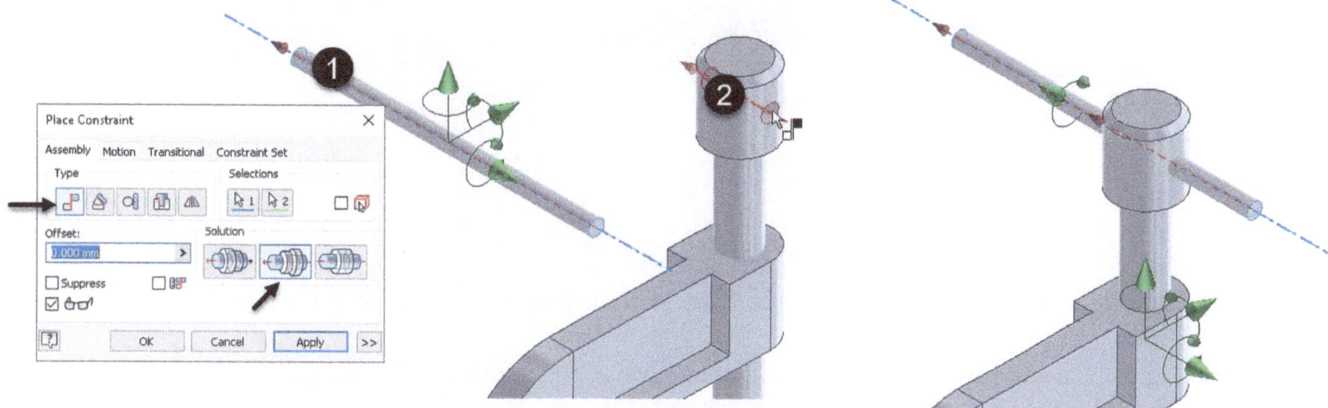

33. Select the end face of the handle and the side face of the Clamp Jaw, as shown.
34. Type -38 in the **Offset** box. Next, select **Solution > Flush** on the **Place Constraint** dialog, and then click **Apply.**

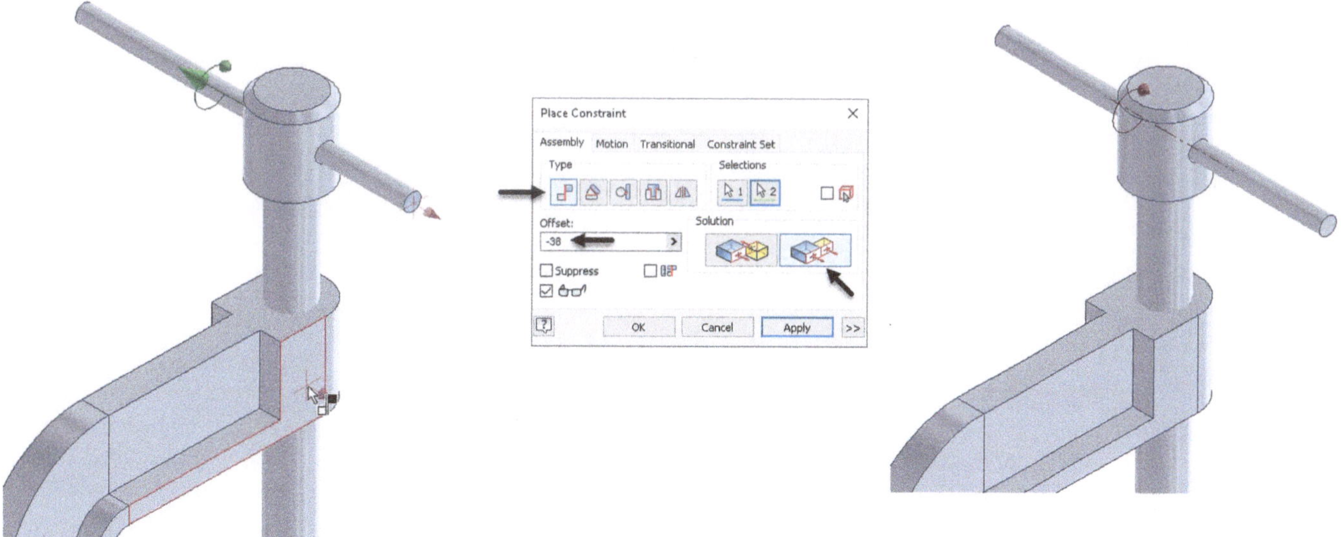

35. Select **Type > Angle** on the **Place Constraint** dialog, and then select **Solution > Directed Angle**.
36. In the **Model** Window, expand **Handle > Origin**, and then select the **XY Plane**.
37. Select the flat end face of the spindle, as shown.
38. On the **Place Constraint** dialog, enter **0** in the **Angle** box and click **OK**.

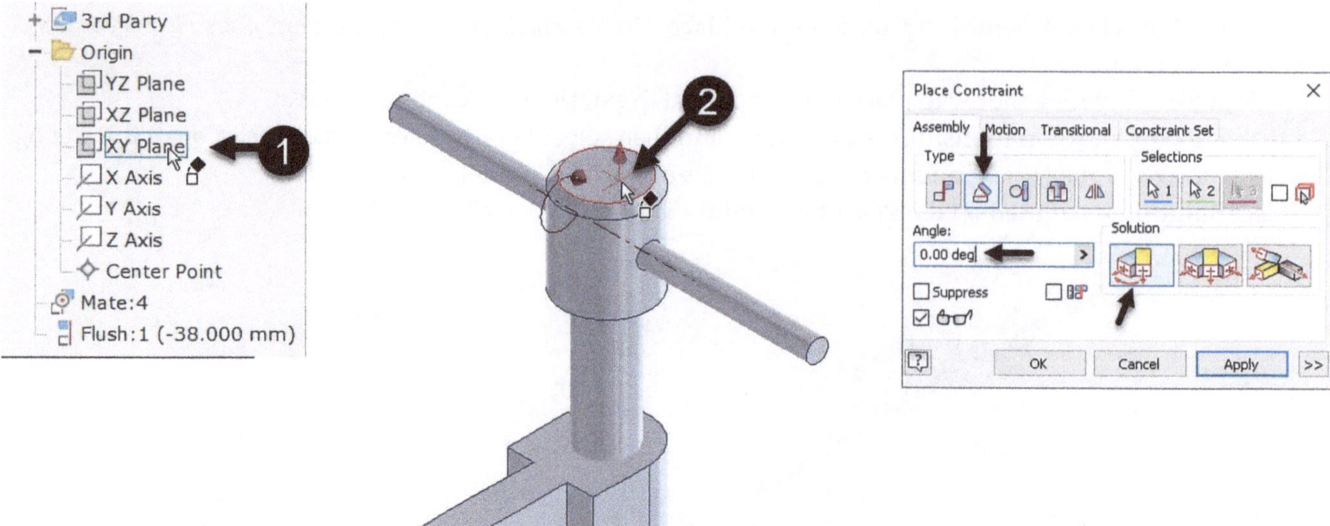

39. On the ribbon, click **Assemble > Component > Place**. On the **Place Component** dialog, click *Handle Cap*, and then click **Open**.
40. Click in the graphics window to place the component. Move the pointer and click again to place the second instance of the *Handle Cap*. Next, right click and select **OK**.
41. On the ribbon, click **View > Appearance > Visual Style** drop-down **> Wireframe**.
42. On the ribbon, click **Assemble** > **Relationships > Constrain**, and then select **Type > Insert** on the **Place Constraint** dialog.
43. Zoom to the *Handle Cap* and place the pointer near the hidden edge of the hole, as shown.
44. Select the Edge Axis Vector of the hidden edge from the **Select Other** drop-down, as shown.

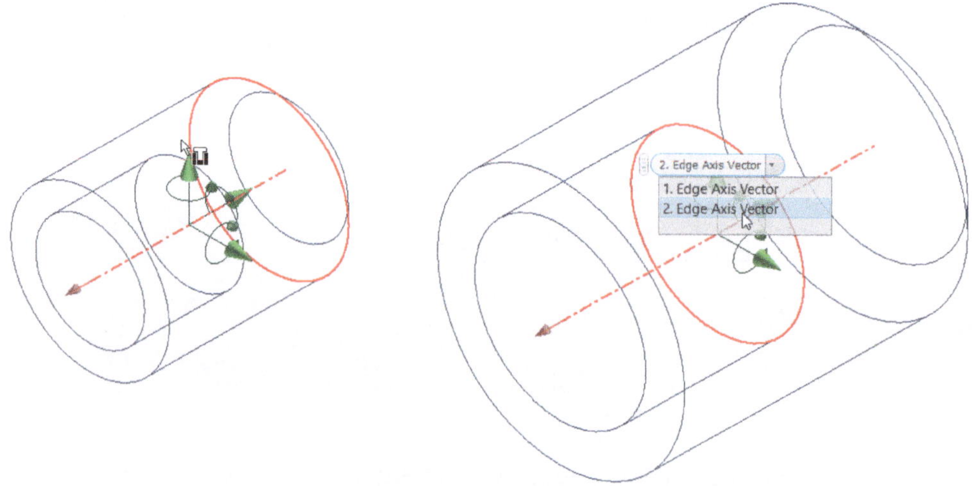

45. Select the Edge Axis Vector of the *Handle*, as shown.
46. On the **Place Constraint** dialog, select **Solution > Opposed**. Make sure that the **Lock Rotation** option is checked. Click **Apply** to constrain the *Handle Cap*.

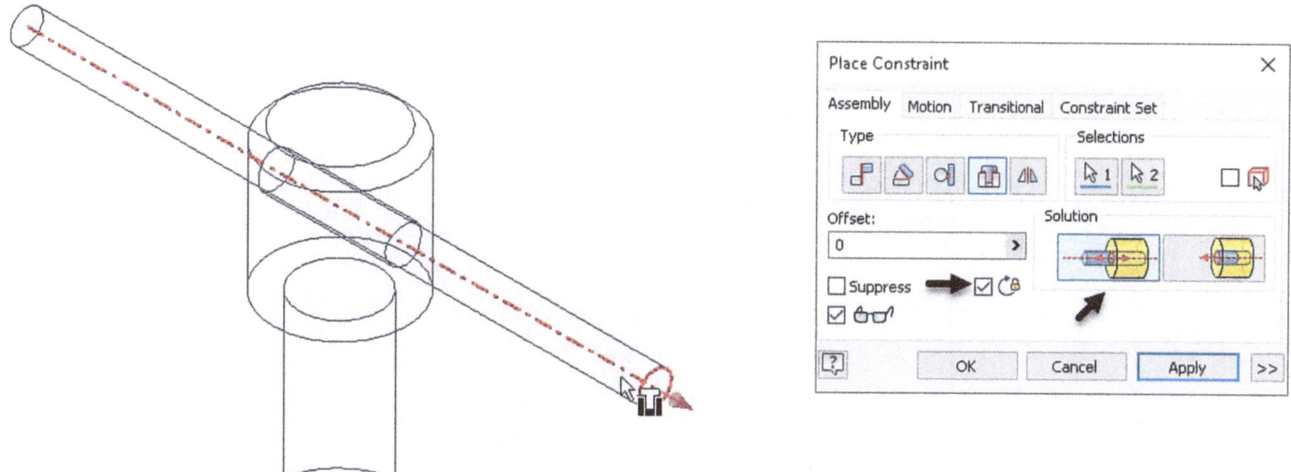

47. Likewise, apply the **Insert** constraint between the second *Handle Cap* and the other edge of the *Handle*.
48. Click **OK** on the **Place Constraint** dialog.
49. On the ribbon, click **View > Appearance > Visual Style** drop-down **> Shaded with Edges**.

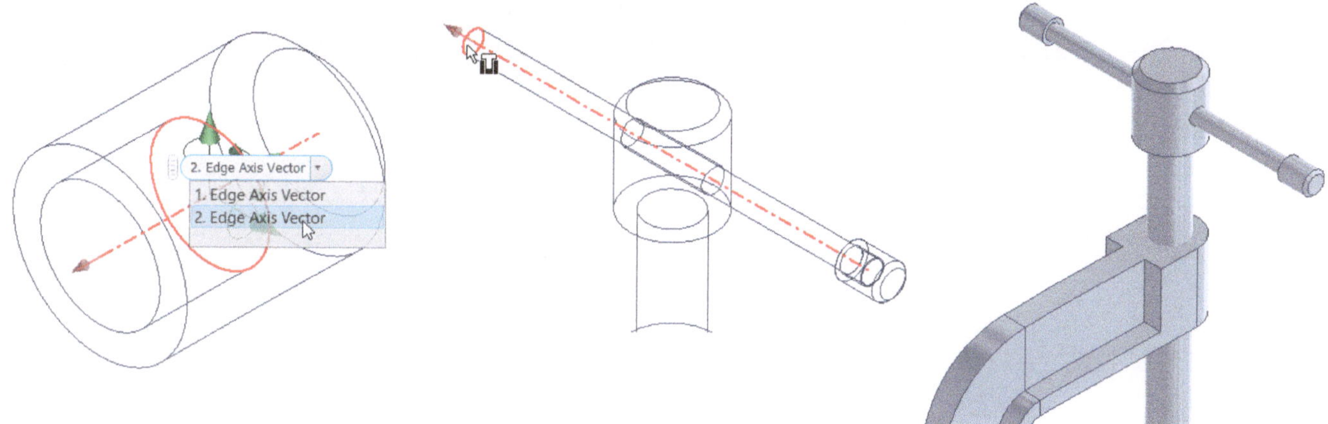

50. Save and close the assembly.

Example 2 (Top-Down Assembly)

In this example, you will create the assembly shown below.

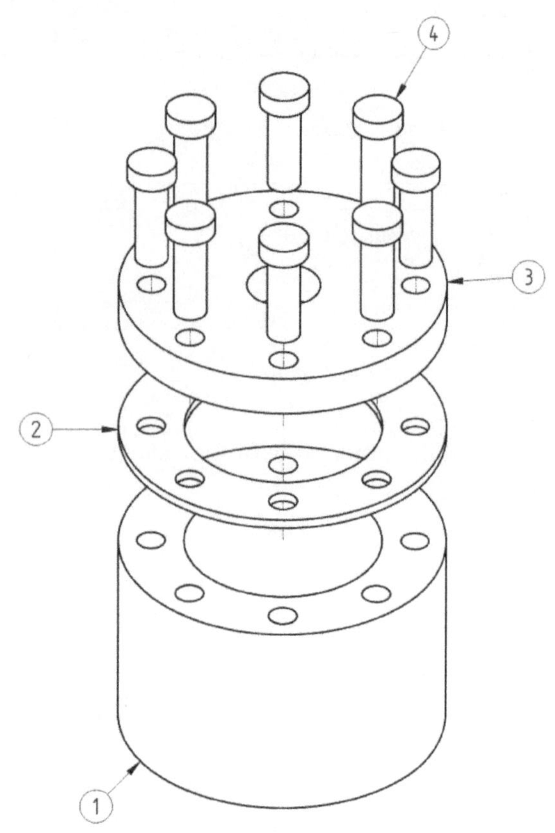

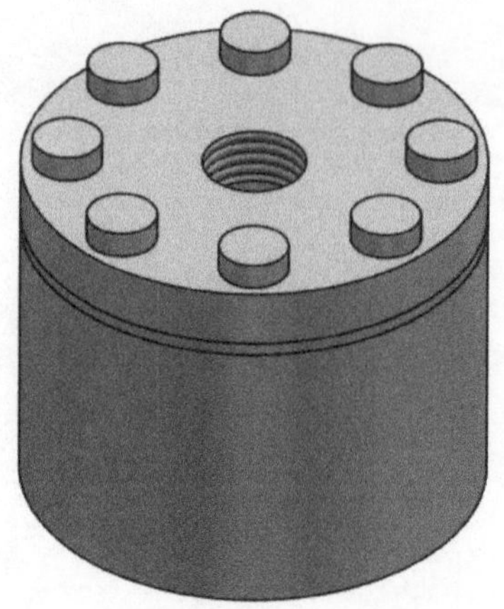

Item Number	File Name (no extension)	Quantity
1	Cylinder base	1
2	Gasket	1
3	Cover plate	1
4	Screw	8

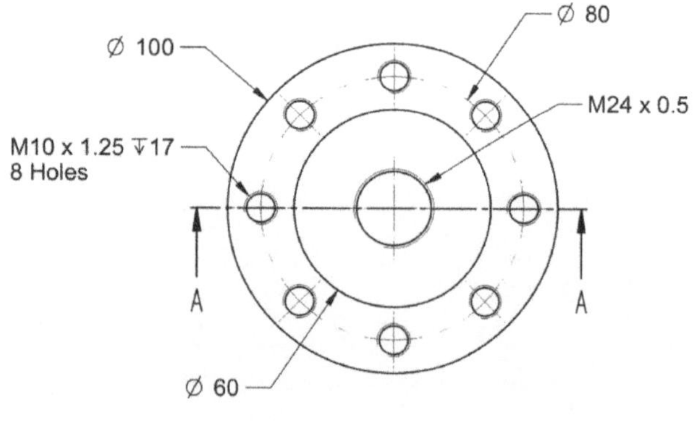

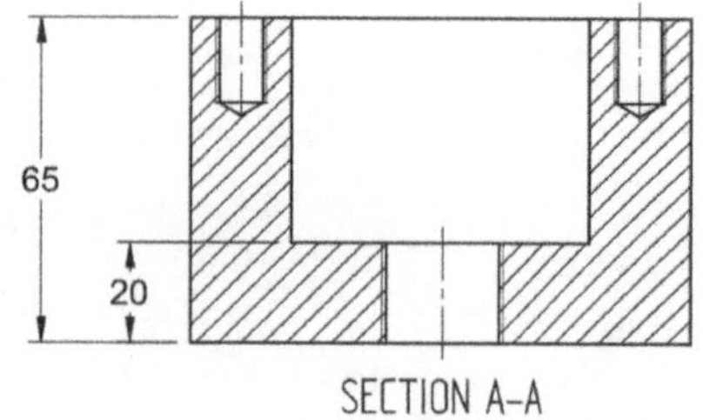

Cylinder Base

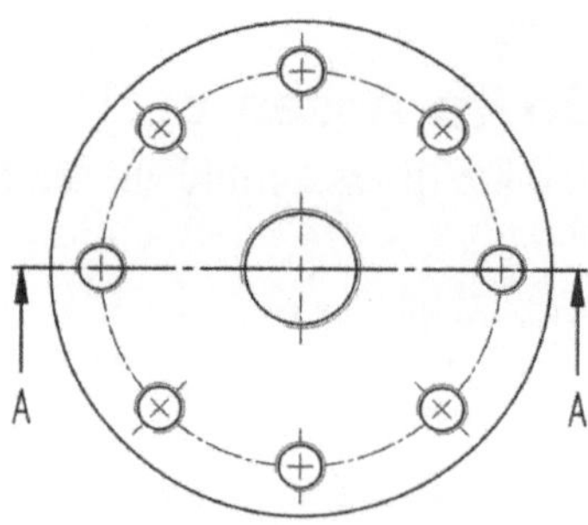

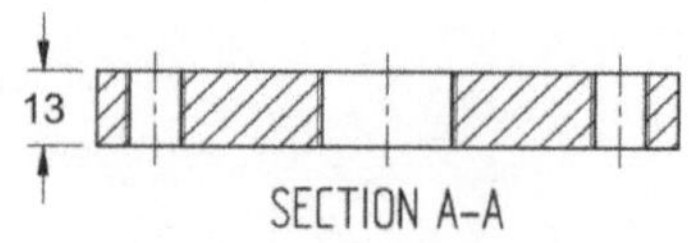

Cover Plate

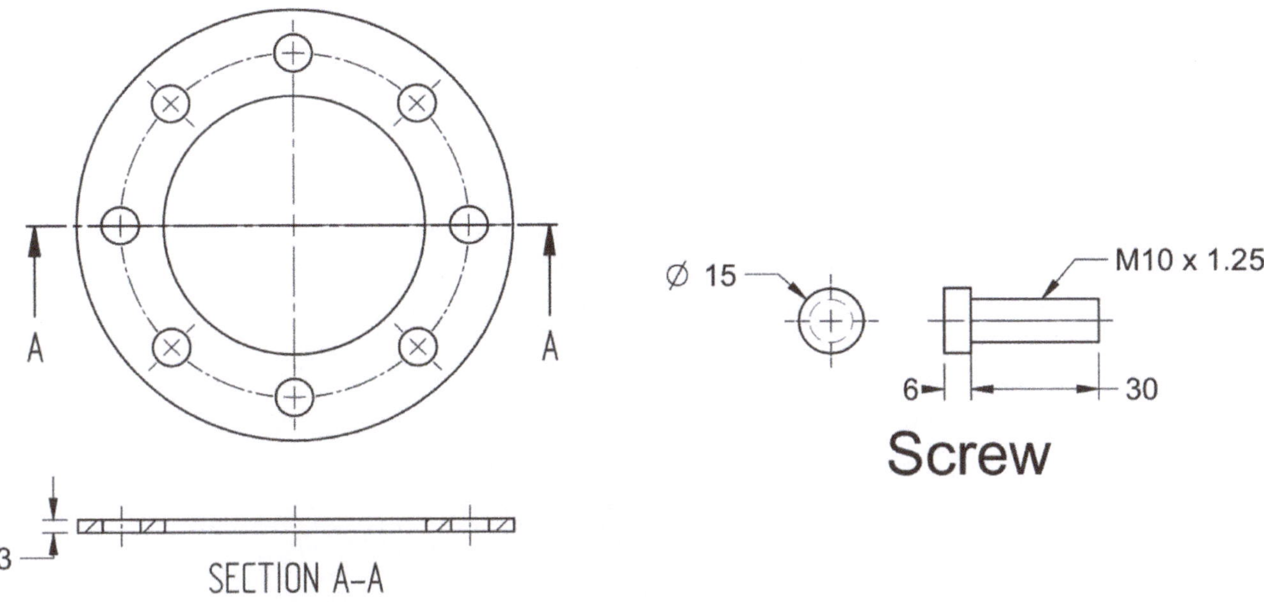

1. Start **Autodesk Inventor 2026.**
2. Start a new part file using the Standard(mm).ipt template and create the Cylinder base. Do not create the center hole.

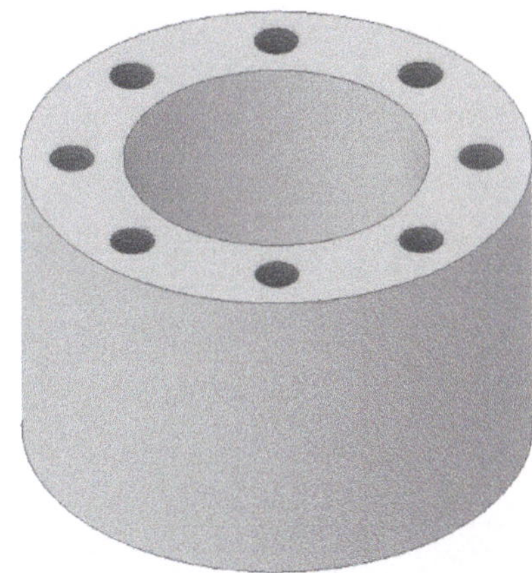

3. Create a new folder with the name *Pressure Cylinder*. Save the file with the name *Cylinder base*.
4. On the **File menu**, click **New > Assembly**. It opens a new assembly file.
5. Click **Assembly > Component > Place** on the ribbon; it opens a **Place Component** dialog.
6. On this dialog, browse to the *Cylinder base* file and click **Open**.
7. In the graphics window, right-click and click **Place Grounded at Origin**. The *Cylinder base* is grounded at the origin. Press **Esc** to deactivate the **Place Component** command after the part is placed.
8. Save the assembly file in the *Pressure Cylinder* folder.
9. On the ribbon, click **Assemble > Component > Create Component**. The **Create In-Place Component** dialog pops up on the screen. On this dialog, type-in *Gasket* in the **New Component Name** box.
10. Click on the **Browse Templates** icon; it displays the **Open Template** dialog.
11. On this dialog, click **Metric tab > Standard(mm). ipt** and click **OK**.

12. Click the **Browse to New File Location** icon and specify the location of the file in the *Pressure Cylinder* folder. Next, click **Save** on the **Save As** dialog.
13. Click **OK** on the **Create In-Place Component** dialog. Next, click on the top face of the *Cylinder base*; the part environment is activated.

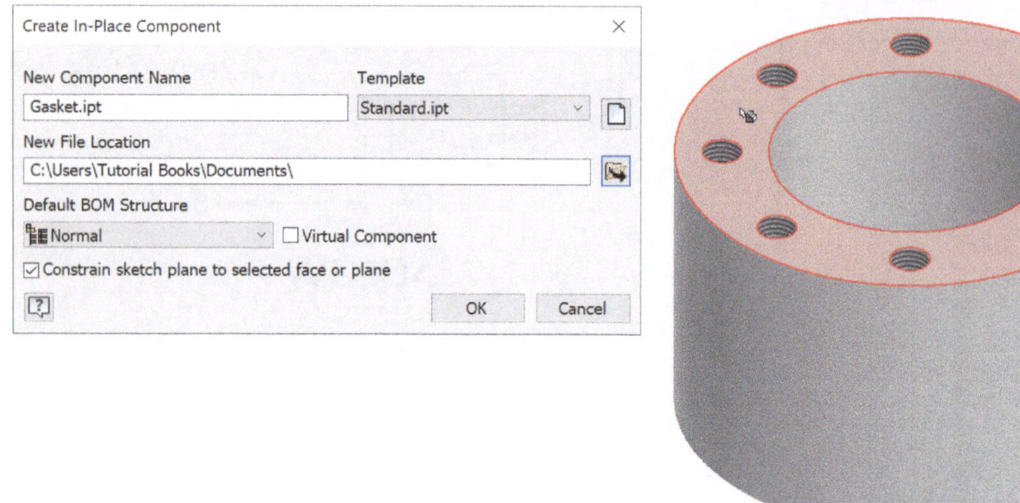

14. Click the **3D Model** tab > **Sketch** panel > **Start 2D Sketch** on the ribbon.
15. Select the top face of the *Cylinder base* from the graphics window to start a new sketch.

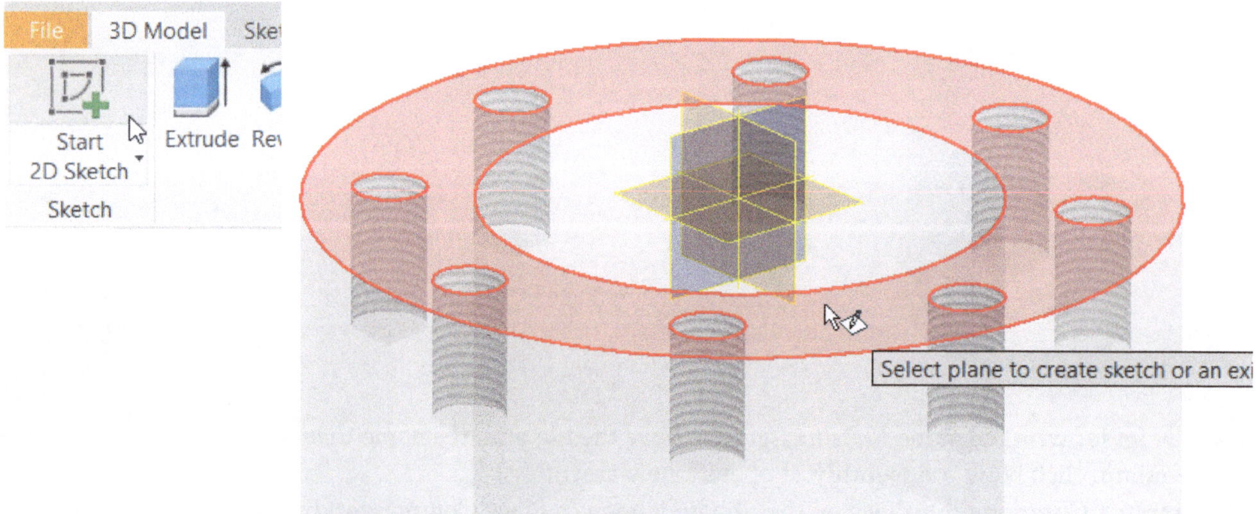

16. Click the **Sketch** tab > **Create** panel > **Project Geometry** on the ribbon.
17. Click on the circular edges on the top face of the Cylinder base. The edges are projected to the sketch plane. Click **Finish Sketch**.

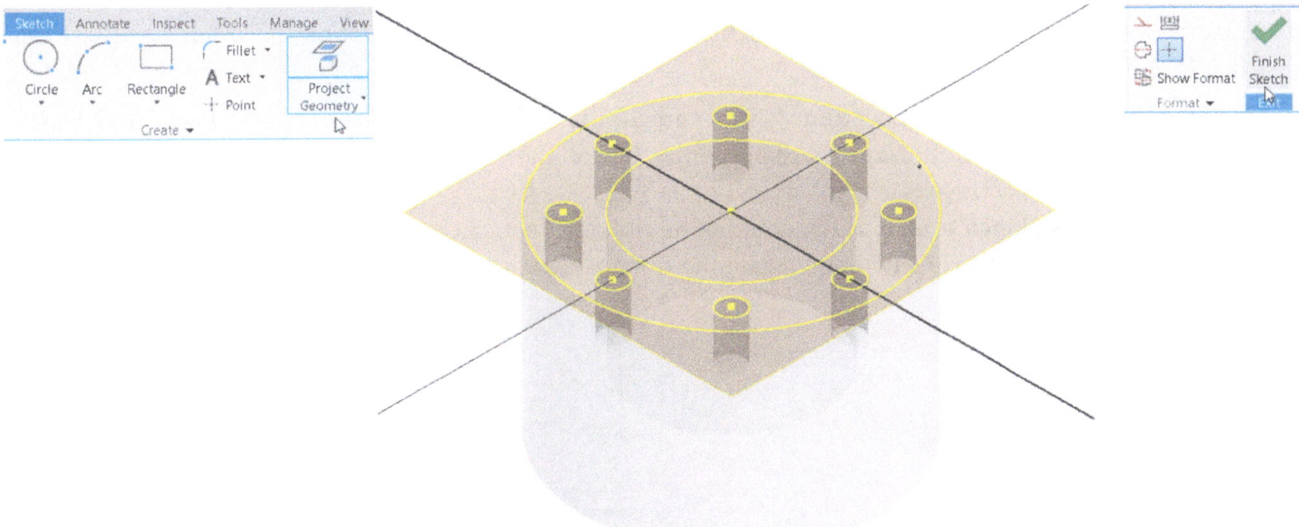

18. Activate the **Extrude** command and click in the region enclosed by the sketch. On the **Extrude Properties** panel, click the **Default** icon under the **Behavior** section to extrude upward.
19. Type **3** in the **Distance A** box and click **OK** to create the *Extrude* feature.

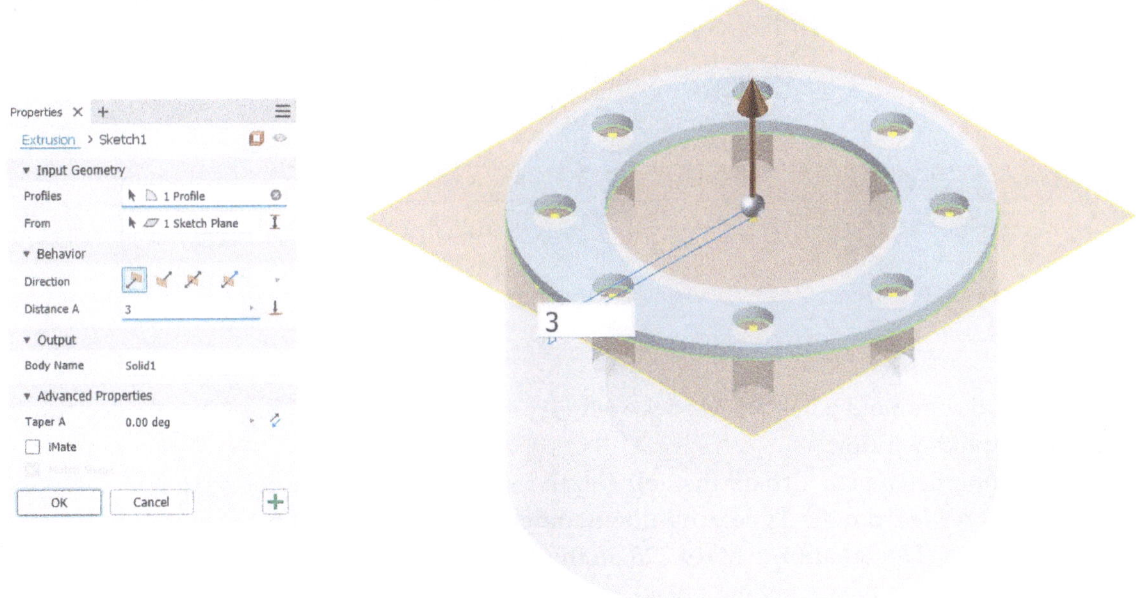

20. On the ribbon, click **Return > Return** to return to the assembly session.

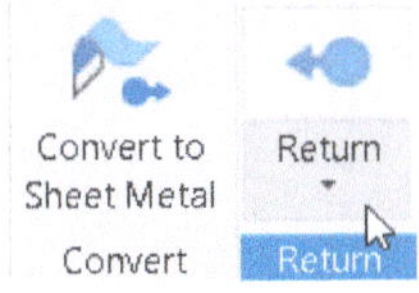

21. Click **Assemble > Component > Create Component** on the ribbon. The **Create In-Place Component** dialog pops up on the screen.
22. On the dialog, type-in *Cover Plate* in the **New Component Name** box.

23. Click the **Browse Templates** icon and click **Metric** tab > **Standard(mm).ipt** on the **Open Template** dialog. Click **OK** on the **Open Template** dialog.
24. Click the **Browse to New File Location** icon and specify the location of the file in the *Pressure Cylinder* folder. Next, click **Save** on the **Save As** dialog. Click **OK** on the **Create In-Place Component** dialog.
25. Click on the top face of the *Gasket.*
26. Click **3D Model > Sketch > Start 2D Sketch** on the ribbon. Next, click on the top circular face of the *Gasket.*
27. Click **Sketch > Create > Project Geometry** on the ribbon. Next, select the outer and small circular edges of the *Gasket*.

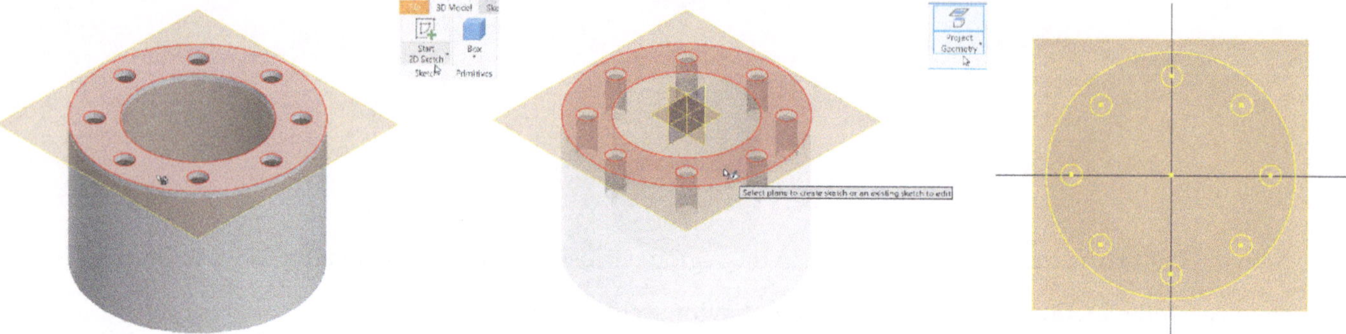

28. Click **Finish Sketch**. Next, use the sketch and create an *Extrude* feature. The depth of the extrusion is **13** mm.

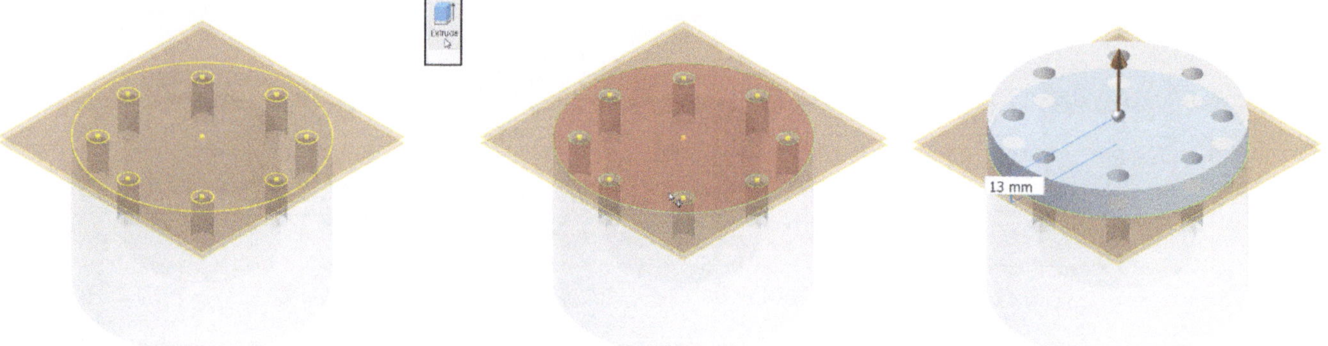

29. Activate the **Thread** command (click **3D Model > Modify > Thread** on the ribbon). Next, select any one of the holes from the graphics window.
30. On the **Thread Properties** panel, turn off the **Full Depth** icon under the **Behavior** section.
31. Select **ISO Metric Profil**e from the **Type** drop-down under the **Threads** section.
32. Select **Size > 10** and the **Designation > M10x1.25** on the **Thread Properties** panel. Next, click **OK** to apply.
33. Likewise, create threads on the remaining holes.

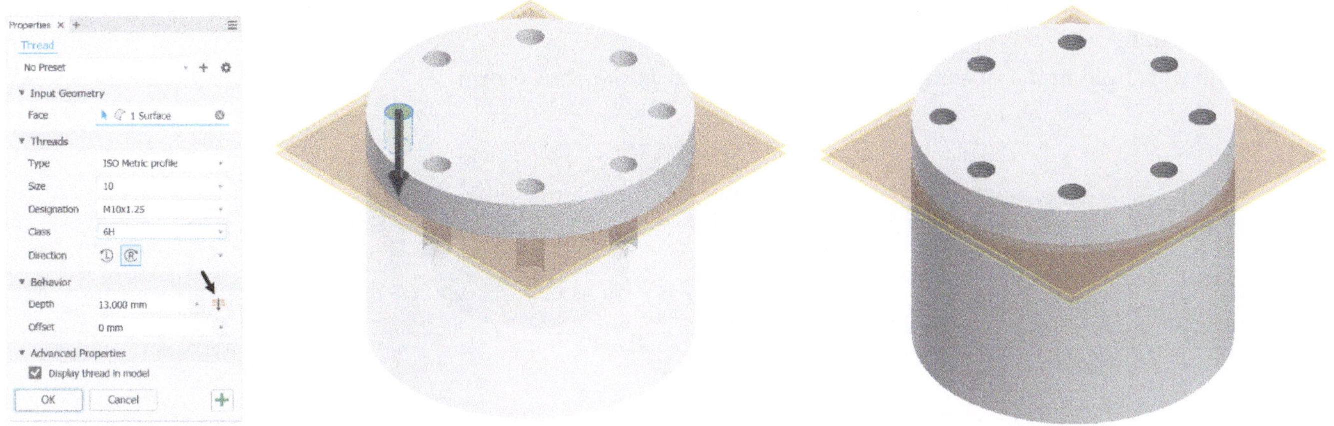

34. On the ribbon, click **Return > Return** to switch to the assembly window.
35. Activate the **Create Component** command and create the *Screw.ipt* file on the top face of the *Cover Plate*.
36. In the Part environment, activate the **Start 2D Sketch** command and select the top face of the *Cover Plate*.
37. Activate the **Project Geometry** command and select any one of the circular edges of the holes. Click **Finish Sketch**.

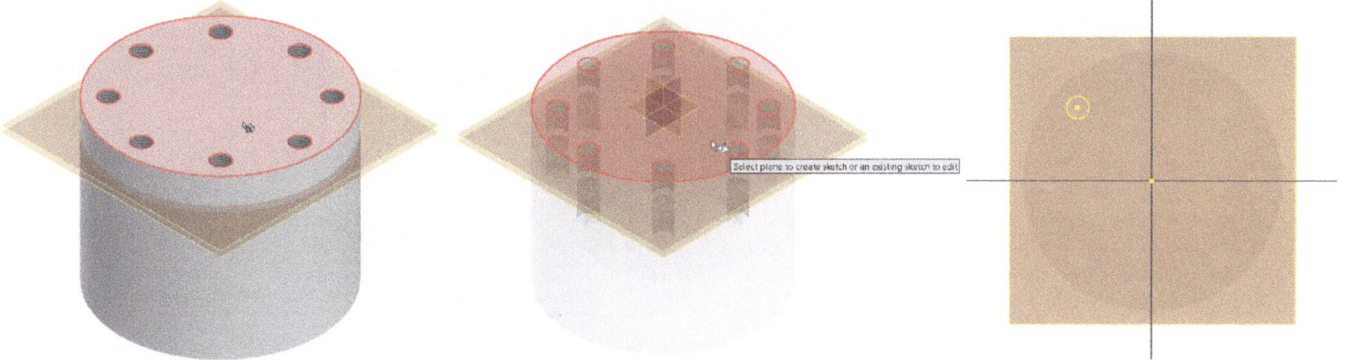

38. Use the sketch and create an *Extrude* feature of **30** mm depth. The direction of extrusion should be downward.

39. Activate the **Start 2D Sketch** command and select the top face of the last *Extrude* feature.

40. Draw a circle of **15 mm** diameter and make it concentric to the circular edge of the *Extrude* feature. Click **Finish Sketch**.
41. Extrude the circle in the upward direction. The extrude depth is **6 mm**.

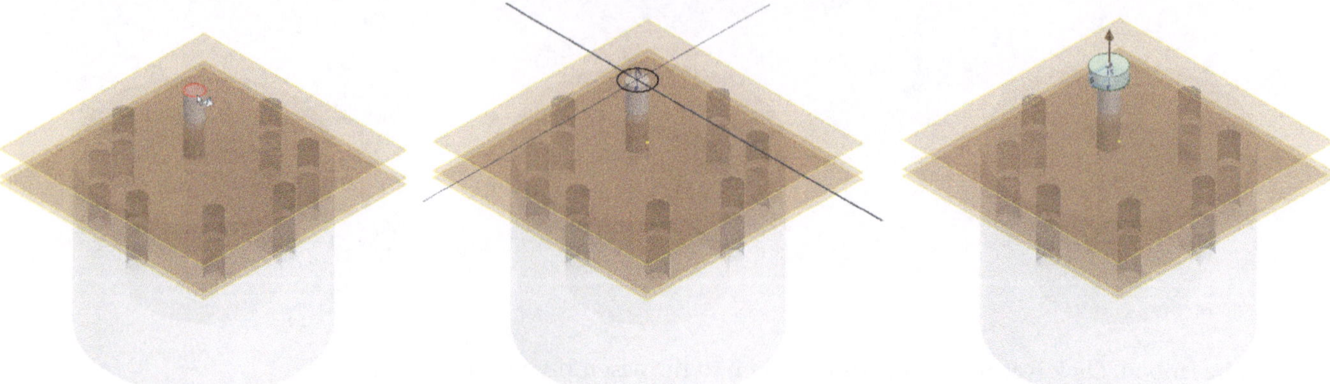

42. Activate the **Thread** command (click **3D Model > Modify > Thread** on the ribbon) and add a thread to the lower circular face of the part. The thread size is **M10 x 1.25**; Make sure that the **Full Depth** icon is turned **ON** under the **Behavior** section on the **Thread Properties** panel.

43. On the ribbon, click **Return > Return** to switch to the assembly environment.
44. On the ribbon, click **View > Visibility > Object Visibility**, and then uncheck the **User Work Planes** option; the work planes are hidden.
45. On the ribbon, click **Assemble > Pattern > Pattern**, and then click on the *Screw* component.
46. On the **Pattern Component** dialog, click the **Associated Feature Pattern** icon. Next, select the circular pattern of the holes of the *Cylinder Base*.
47. Click **OK** to create an associative pattern of the Screws.

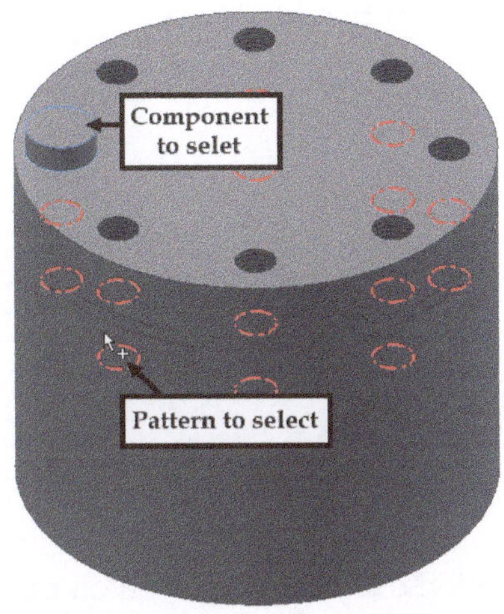

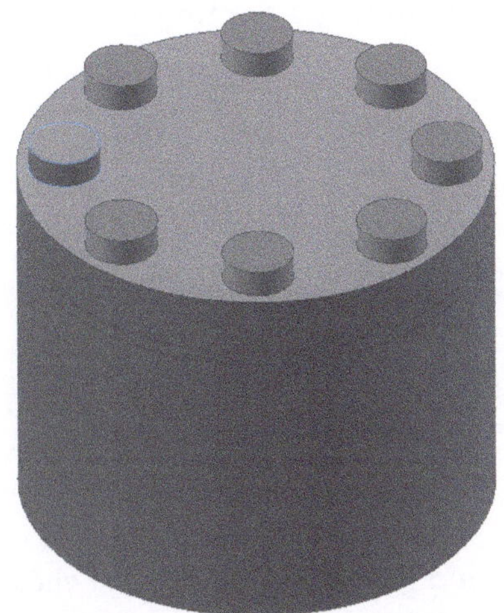

48. On the ribbon, click **3D Model > Sketch > Start 2D Sketch**, and then click on the top face of the *Cover Plate*.
49. On the ribbon, click **Sketch > Create > Point**, and then place a point at the sketch origin. Next, click **Finish Sketch** on the ribbon.
50. On the ribbon, click **3D Model > Modify Assembly > Hole**. The **Properties** panel pops up on the screen.
51. On this panel, click **Type > Hole > Tapped Hole** and set the hole options, as shown below. Click **OK** to create the hole throughout the assembly.

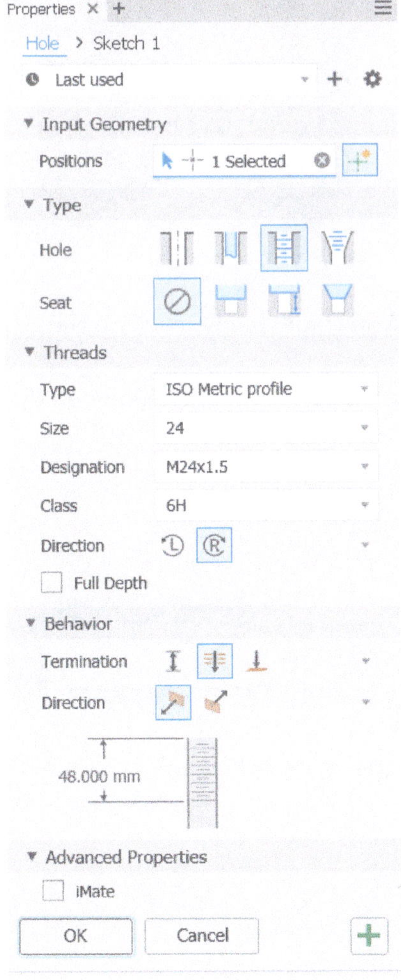

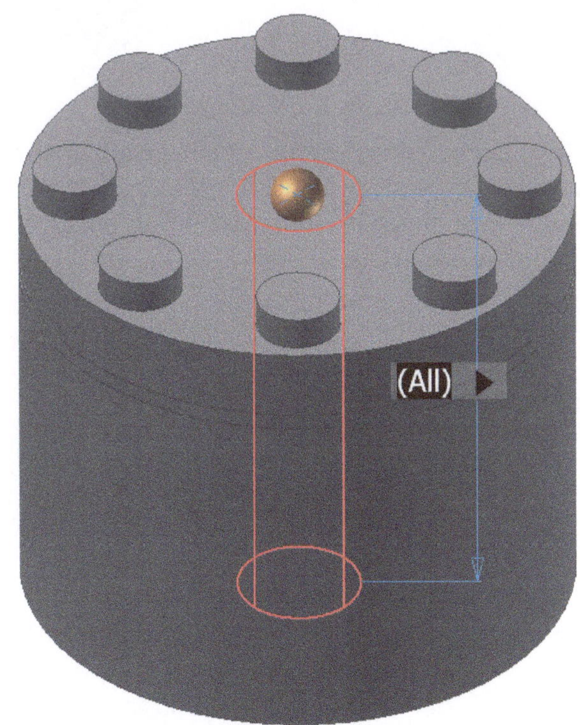

52. On the ribbon, click **View > Visibility > Section View** drop-down **> Three Quarter Section View**.

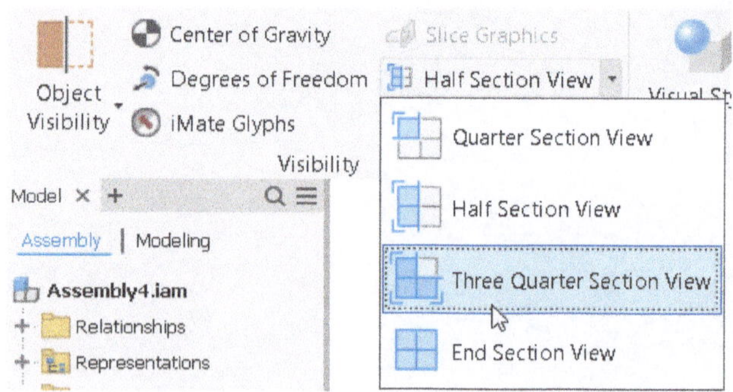

53. In the **Model** window, expand the **Origin** folder and click **YZ Plane**. Next, click the **Continue** button on the graphics window.
54. Click the **XY Plane** in the **Model** Window. Click the **OK** button to create the quarter section view.

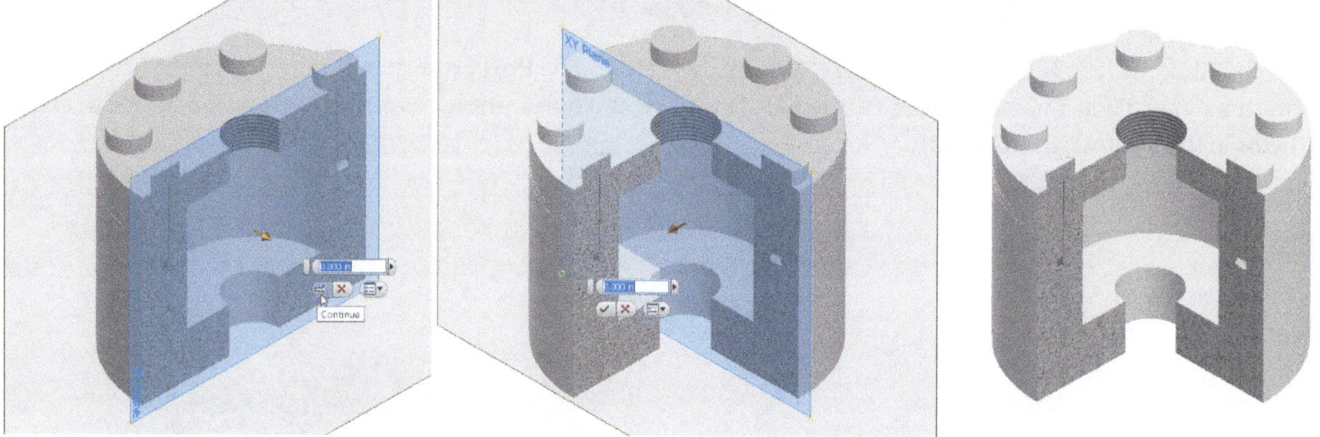

55. On the ribbon, click **Assemble > Manage > Bill of Materials**. On the **Bill of Materials** dialog, click on the **Structured** tab. Next, right click on it and select **Enable BOM View**.
56. Likewise, click on the **Parts Only** tab. Next, right click on it and select **Enable BOM View**. Click **Done** on the **Bill of Materials** dialog.

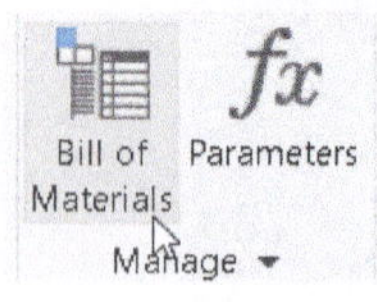

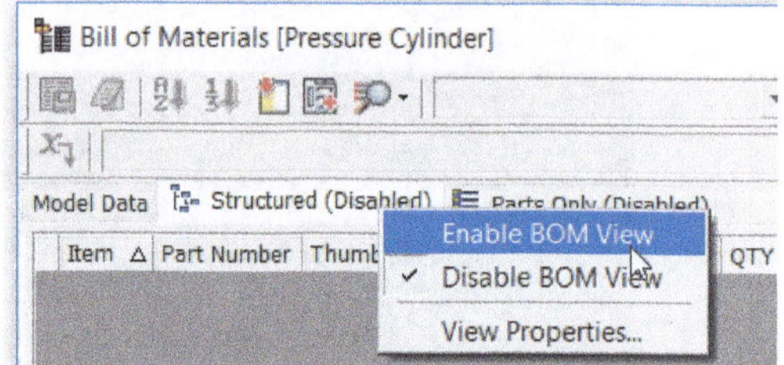

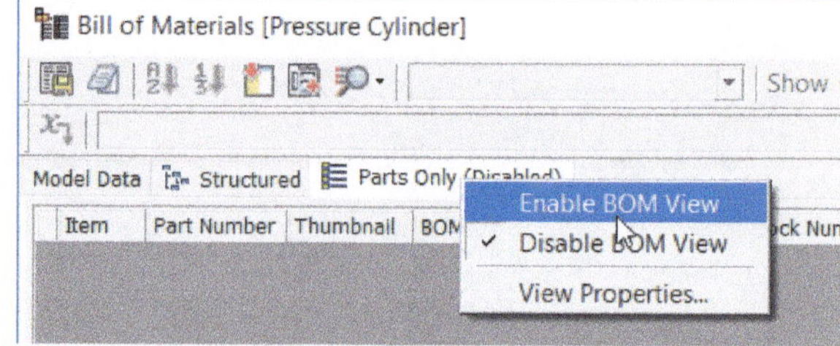

57. On the ribbon, click the **File** tab, and then click the **Save** icon. Type-in the file name and click **Save**.
58. On the **Save** dialog, click the **Yes to All** button, and then click **OK**.
59. Click **File** tab > **Close**.

Example 3 (Presentations)

In this example, you will create the presentation of the assembly created in Example 2.

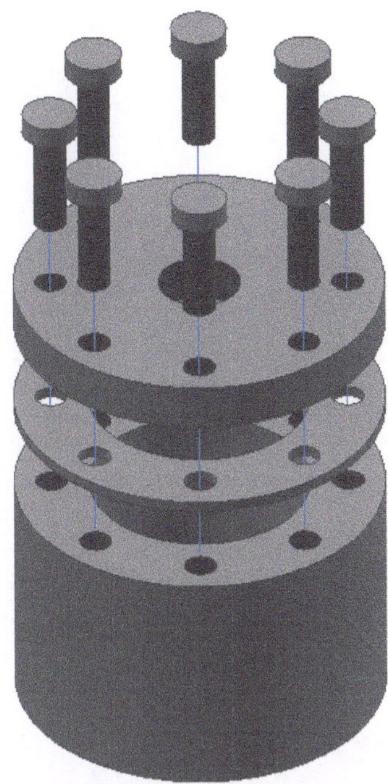

Starting a New Presentation File

1. On the ribbon, click **File menu > New.** On the **Create New File** dialog, click **Templates > en-US > Metric**.
2. Select the **Standard(mm).ipn** template from the **Presentation – Create an exploded projection of an assembly** section. Click **Create** on the **Create New File** dialog; the **Insert** dialog appears.
3. On the **Insert** dialog, go to the *Pressure Cylinder* folder and double-click on the **Pressure Cylinder.iam** file.

Creating a Storyboard Animation

1. In the Model tree, double-click on Scene1 and type Explosion.

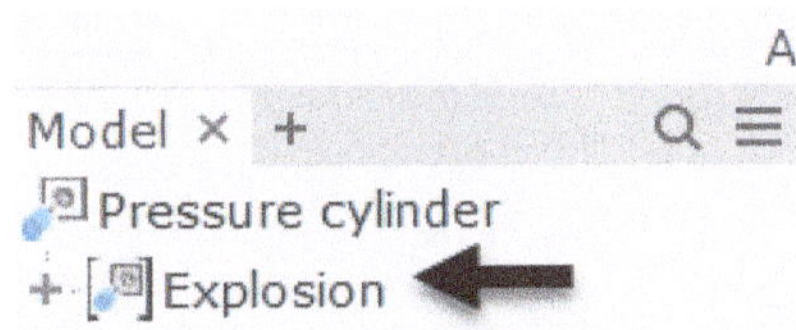

2. Click the **Tweak Components** button on the **Component** panel of the **Presentation** ribbon tab. Next, select **Part** from the **Selection Filter** drop-down of the Mini toolbar.
3. Select the **All Components** from the **Tracelines** drop-down.
4. Press and hold the SHIFT key, and then select all the screws from the graphics window. The manipulator appears on any one of the screws.

   Now, you must specify the direction along which the screws will be exploded.

5. On the Mini toolbar, select Local > World. Click the Y axis of the manipulator.
6. Type 100 mm in the Y box attached to the manipulator. Click OK on the Mini toolbar.

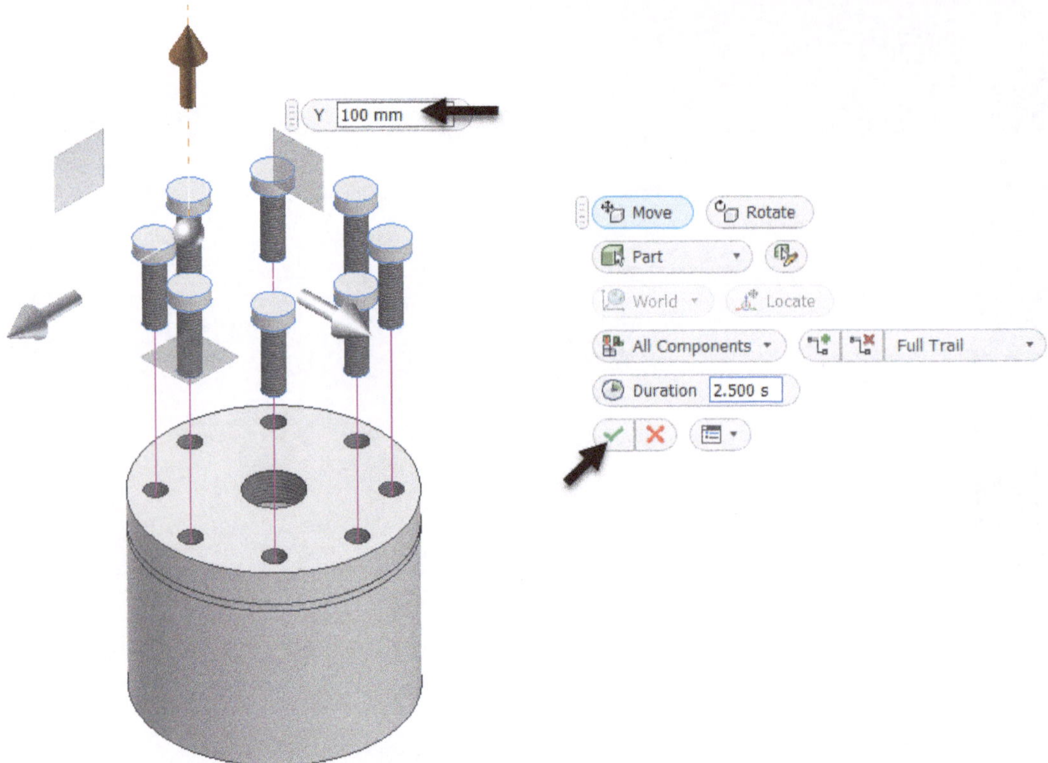

7. Right click in the graphics window and select **Tweak Components** from the Marking Menu.
8. Select **Part** from the **Selection filter** drop-down on the Mini toolbar. Select the *Cover Plate*.
9. On the Mini toolbar, select **Local > World**. Click the Y axis of the manipulator.
10. Type 50 mm in the Y box attached to the manipulator. Click **OK** on the Mini toolbar.

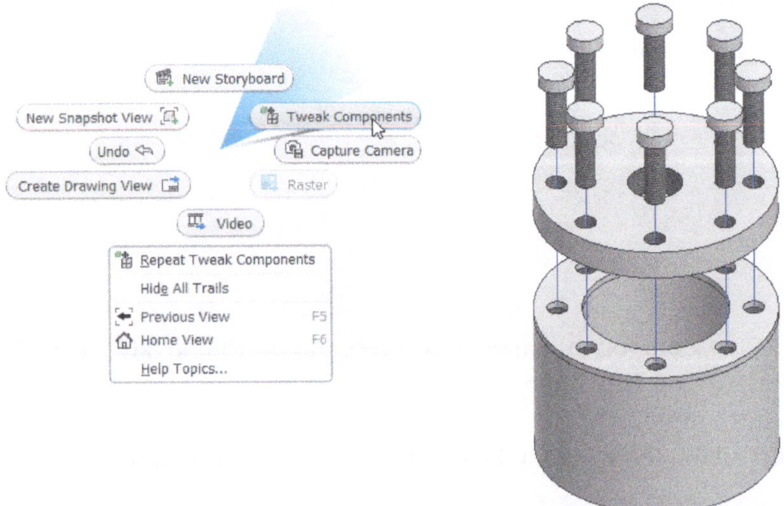

11. Likewise, explode the *Gasket* up to 25 mm distance along the Y-direction.

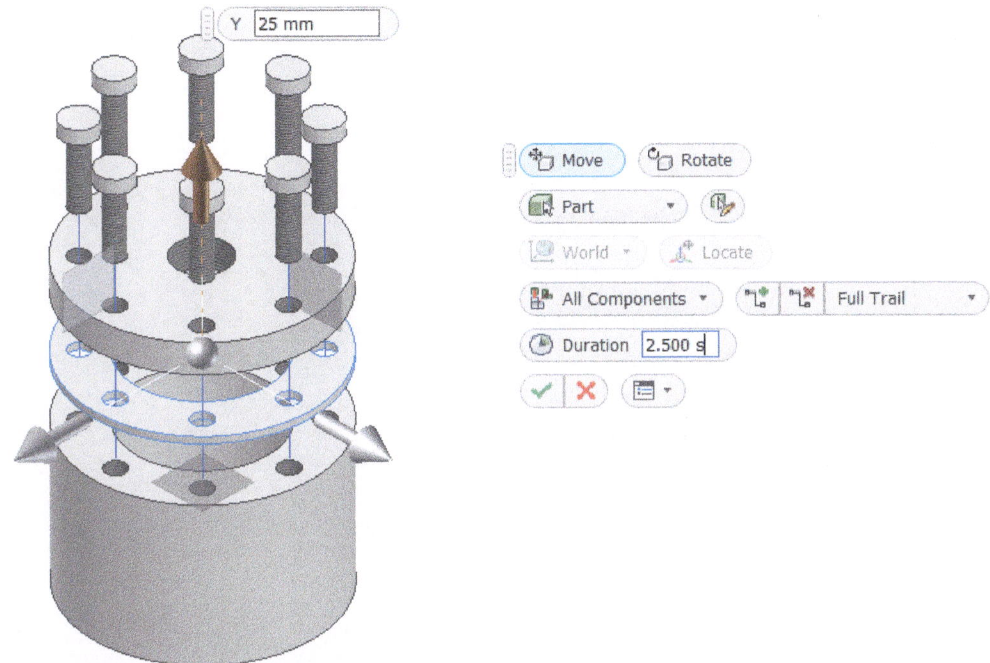

Taking the Snapshot of the Explosion

1. Click and drag the play marker on the timeline to 7.5 seconds.

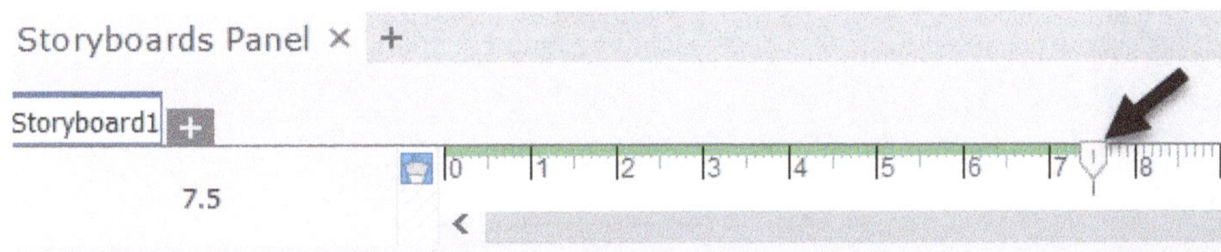

2. On the ribbon, click **Presentation** tab > **Workshop** panel > **New Snapshot View** .

The snapshot appears in the Snapshot Views window. Notice that playmarker on the snapshot. It indicates that the snapshot is dependent on the storyboard.

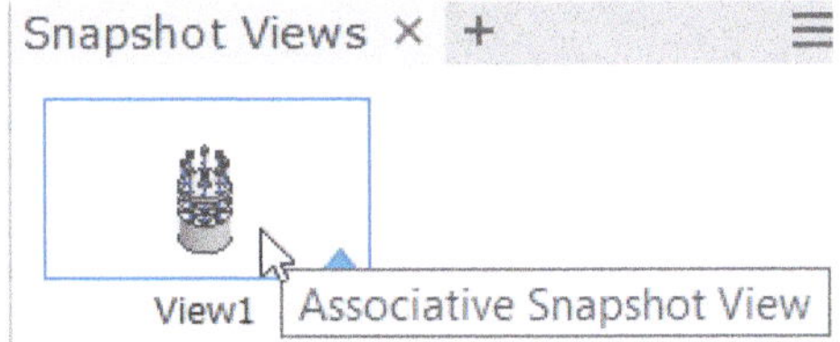

3. Click **Save** on the **Quick Access Toolbar**; the **Save As** dialog appears. Type-in **Pressure_cylinder** in the **File name box.** Go to the *Pressure Cylinder* folder, and then click **Save** to save the file. Next, click **File Menu > Close.**

Questions

1. How do you start an assembly from the **My Home** page?
2. What is the use of the **iMates** command?
3. List the advantages of Top-down assembly approach.
4. What is a grounded part?
5. What is the use of the **Constrain** command?
6. How do you create a sub-assembly in the assembly environment?
7. Briefly explain the **Create** command.
8. How to detect any interference between the parts?
9. What is the difference between rigid and flexible subassemblies?
10. How to reuse and mirror a component?

Exercise 1

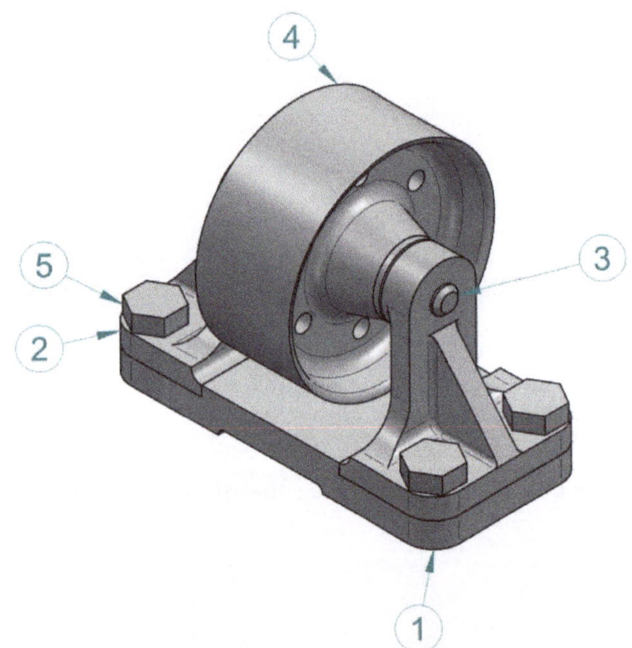

Item Number	File Name (no extension)	Quantity
1	Base	1
2	Bracket	2
3	Spindle	1
4	Roller-Bush assembly	1
5	Bolt	4

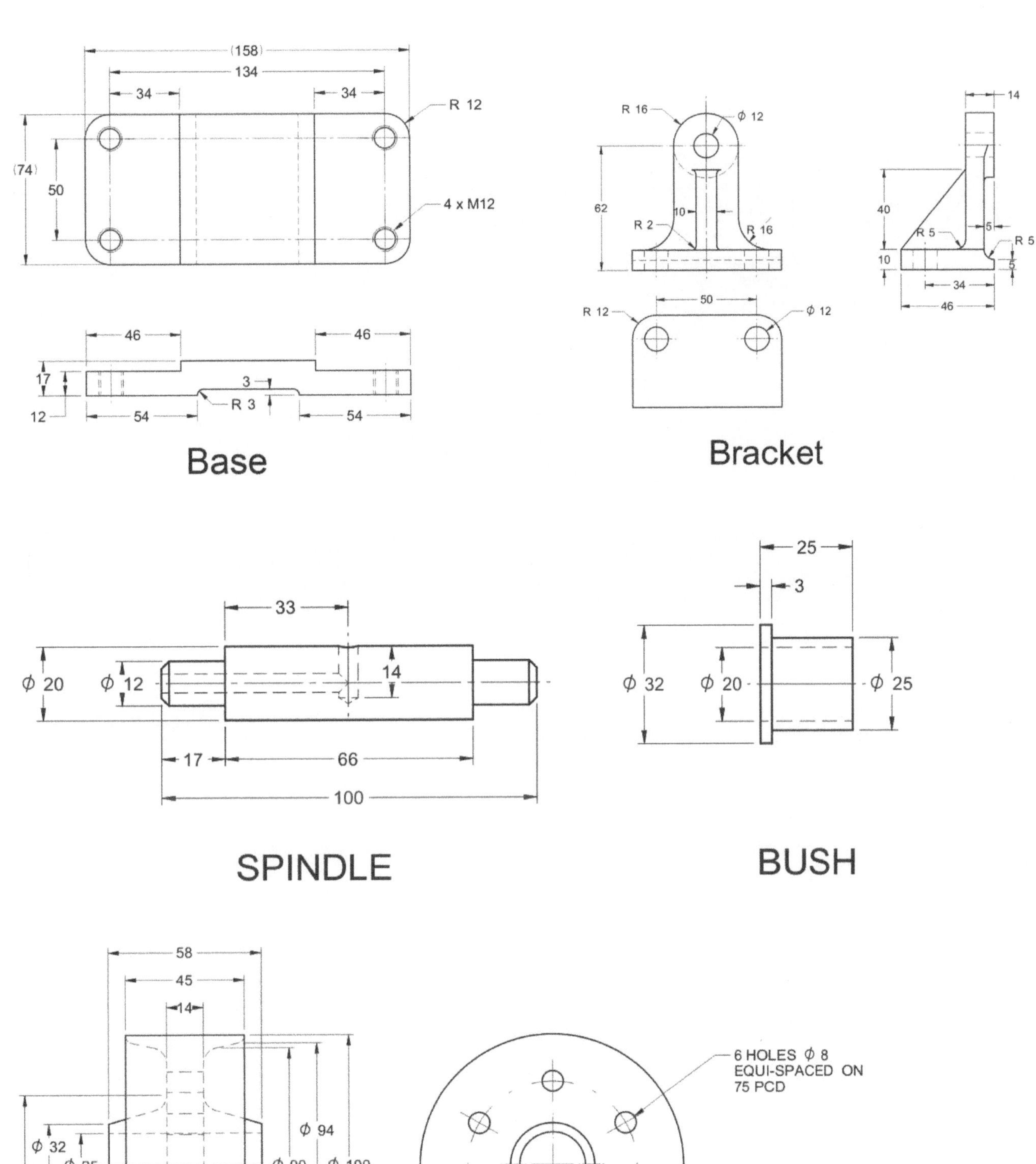
(158)
134
34
34
R 12
(74)
50
4 x M12
46
46
17
3
R 3
12
54
54
Base
R 16
Φ 12
62
10
R 2
R 16
R 12
50
Φ 12
14
40
R 5
5
R 5
10
5
34
46
Bracket
33
Φ 20
Φ 12
14
17
66
100
SPINDLE
25
3
Φ 32
Φ 20
Φ 25
BUSH
58
45
14
Φ 32
Φ 25
Φ 54
Φ 94
Φ 90
Φ 100
R 6
R 3
6 HOLES Φ 8
EQUI-SPACED ON
75 PCD
Roller

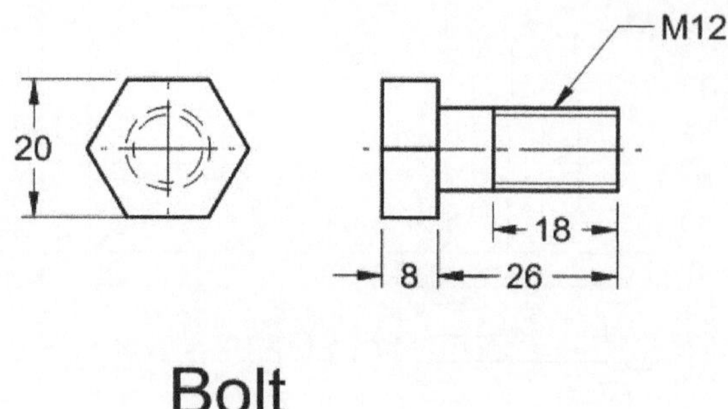

Chapter 11: Drawings

Drawings are used to document your 3D models in the traditional 2D format, including dimensions and other instructions useful for manufacturing purposes. In Autodesk Inventor 2026, you first create 3D models and assemblies and then use them to generate drawings. There is a direct association between the 3D model and the drawing. When changes are made to the model, every view in the drawing will be updated. This relationship between the 3D model and the drawing makes the drawing process fast and accurate. Because the 2D drawings are widely used in the mechanical industry, drawings are one of the three main file types you can create in Autodesk Inventor.

The topics covered in this chapter are:

- *Create Base Views*
- *Projected views*
- *Auxiliary views*
- *Section views*
- *Detail views*
- *Break-Out views*
- *Break a View*
- *Display Options*
- *View Alignment*
- *Parts List and Balloons*
- *Retrieve Dimensions*
- *Arrange Dimensions*
- *Ordinate Dimensions*
- *Center Marks*
- *Centerlines*
- *Centered Pattern*
- *Hole and Thread Notes*
- *Chamfer Notes*

Starting a Drawing

To start a new drawing, select the **Drawing** option from the **New** drop-down of the **Home** screen; the drawing file will be opened. By default, the templates available in the **New** section are of ANSI standard with their units as Inches.

Another way to start a new drawing is by using the **Create New File** dialog. Click **File menu > New** on the ribbon (or) click the **New** icon on the **Quick Access Toolbar** (or) click **File menu > New**; the **Create New File** dialog appears. On this dialog, select the required standard folder from the **Templates** tree. Next, go to the **Drawing - Create an annotated document** section, and then select the .dwg or .idw template. Click **Create** to start a new drawing.

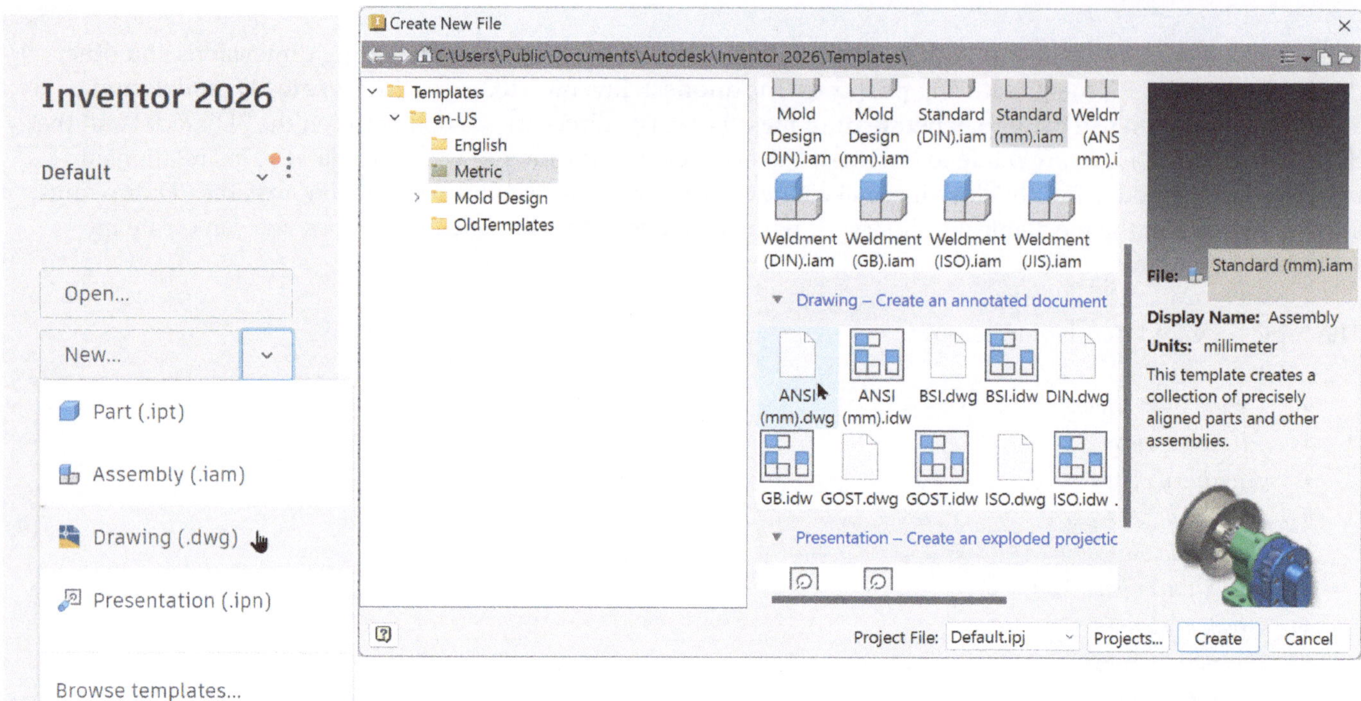

Create a drawing from an already opened Part or Assembly file

If you already have a part or assembly opened, you can create a drawing from it directly. To do this, right click on the Part or assembly name in the Model window, and then select **Create Drawing View**; the **Create Drawing** dialog appears. On this dialog, click the sub-folders under the **Templates** folder to access different sheet templates. Select any one of the sheet templates and click **OK**.

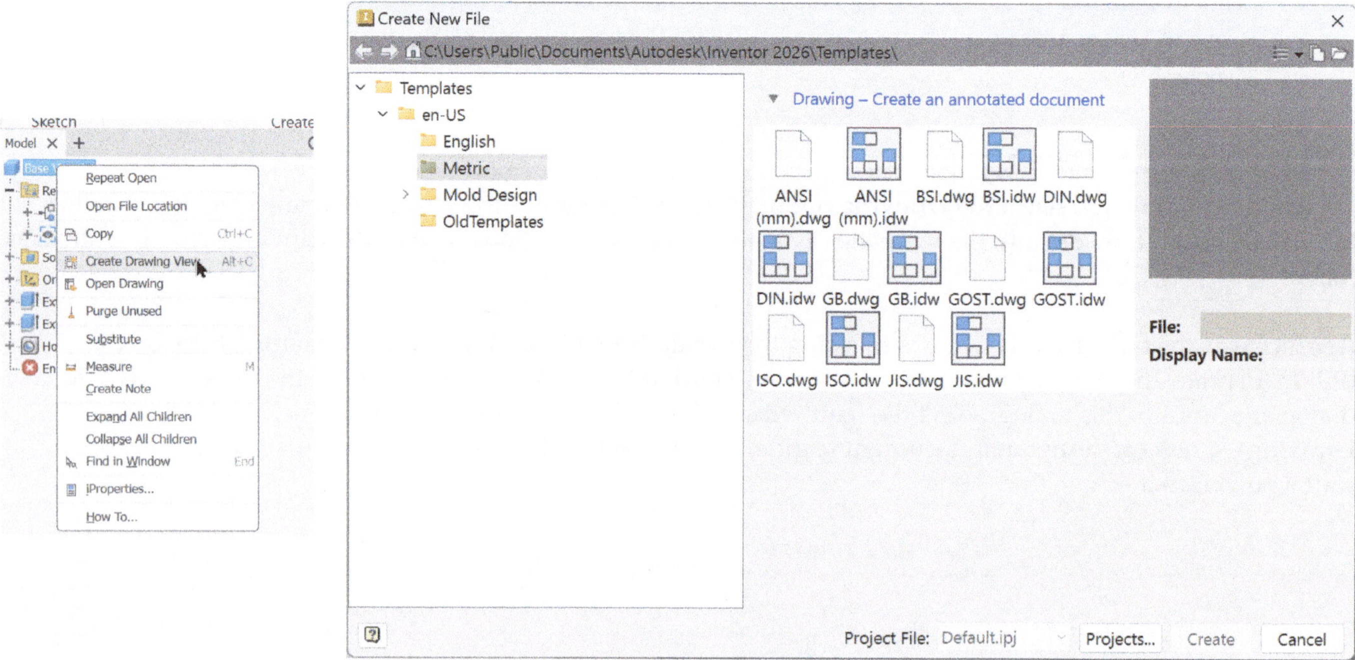

Creating a Base View

There are different standard views available in a 3D part: front, right, top, and isometric. In Autodesk Inventor, you can create these views using the **Base View** command. This command gets activated if you start a drawing from an already opened part. If it is not activated, click **Place Views > Create > Base** on the ribbon; the **Drawing View** dialog appears. Click the **Open an existing file** icon and browse to the location of the part or assembly and double-click on it; a model view will be displayed on the sheet.

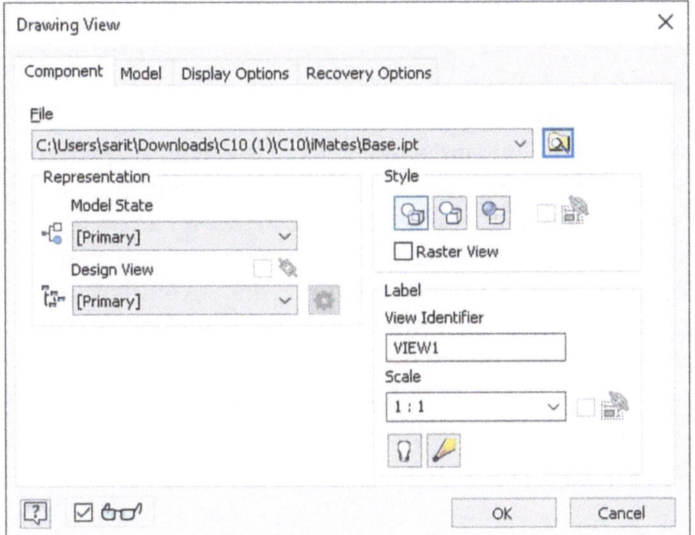

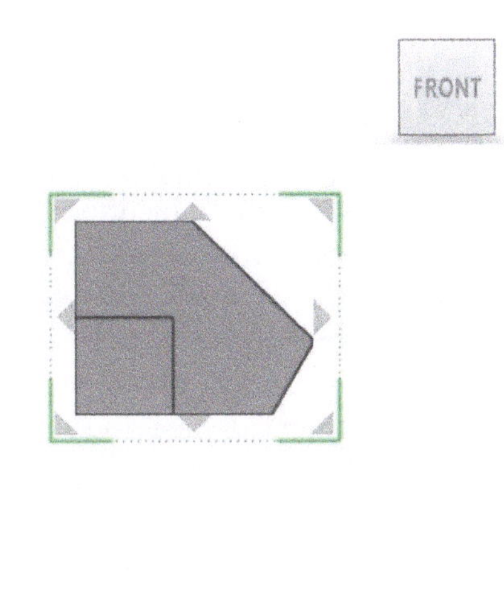

In addition to that, the ViewCube appears. Use the **ViewCube** to change the orientation of the first view, if required (refer to Chapter 1 to know how to use the ViewCube).

Change the scale factor in the **Scale** drop-down to adjust the size of the view.

Next, press and hold the left mouse button on the view and drag it to the desired location. Now, you can create other views by projecting the base view. Click **OK** on the **Drawing View** dialog or create the projected views. The **Projected View** command is explained in the next section.

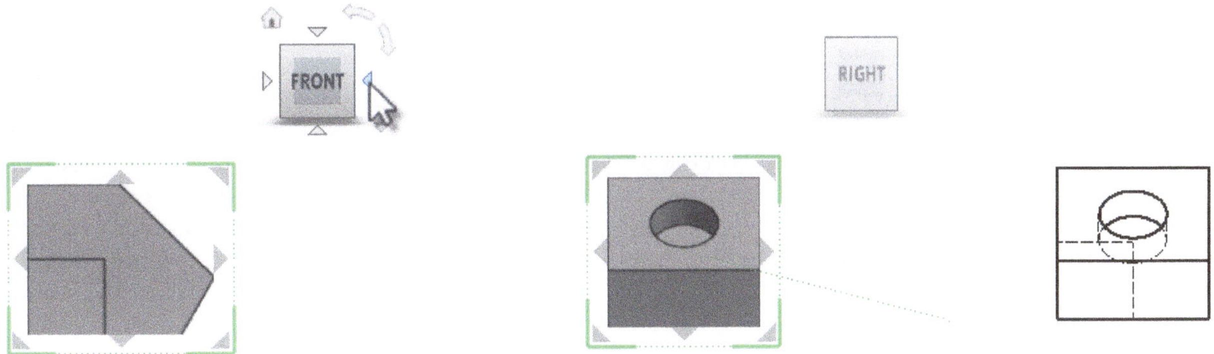

Projected View

After you have created the first view in your drawing, a projected view is one of the most straightforward views to create. Activate the **Projected View** command (click **Place Views > Create > Projected View** on the ribbon). After activating the command, select a view you wish to project from. Next, move the pointer in the direction you wish to have the view to be projected. Next, click on the sheet to specify the location. Click the right mouse button and select **Create**; the projected view will be created.

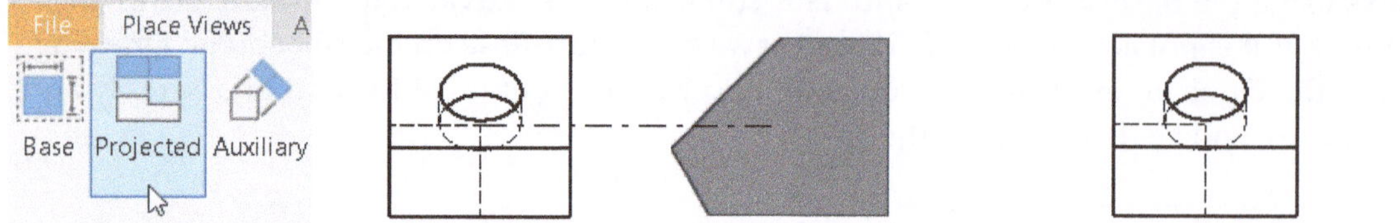

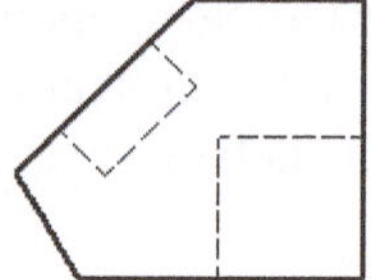

Auxiliary View

Most of the parts are represented by using orthographic views (front, top, and side views). However, many parts have features located on inclined faces. You cannot get the right shape and size for these features by using the orthographic views. To see an accurate size and shape of the inclined features, you need to create an auxiliary view. An auxiliary view is created by projecting the part onto a plane other than horizontal, front, or side planes. To create an auxiliary view, activate the **Auxiliary View** command (click **Place Views > Create > Auxiliary** on the ribbon). Next, select the view from which you want to create the auxiliary view. Click the angled edge of the model to establish the direction of the auxiliary view. Next, move the pointer to the desired location and click to locate the view.

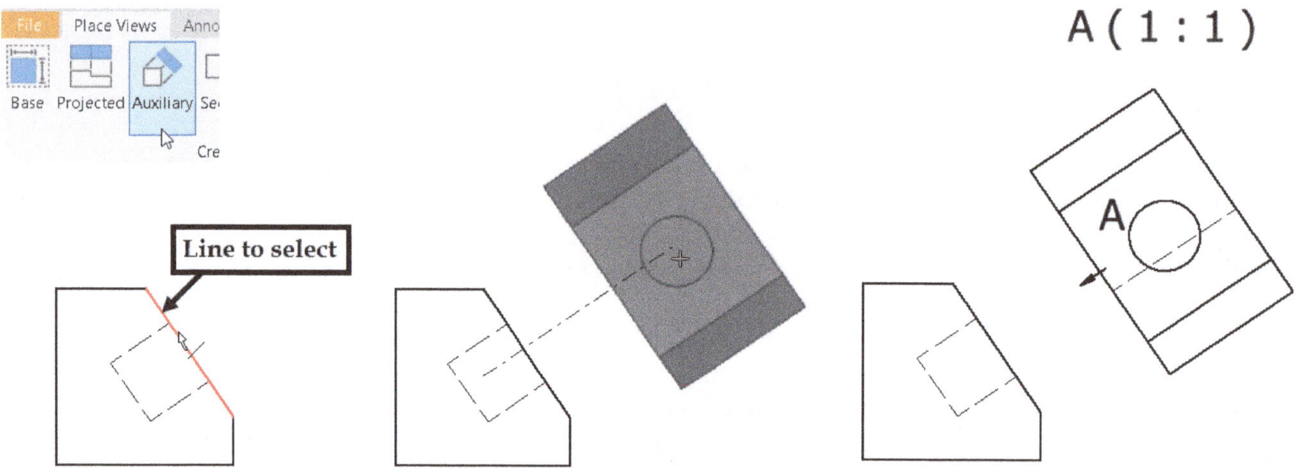

Section View

One of the most common views used in 2D drawings is the section view. Creating a section view in Autodesk Inventor is very simple. Once a view is placed on the drawing sheet, you need to draw a line where you want to section the drawing view. Activate the **Section View** command (click **Place Views > Create > Section View** on the ribbon) and click on a drawing view. Now, you have to draw a line to define the cutting plane. You can use the geometry of the drawing view to draw the line. After drawing a line, right click and select **Continue.**

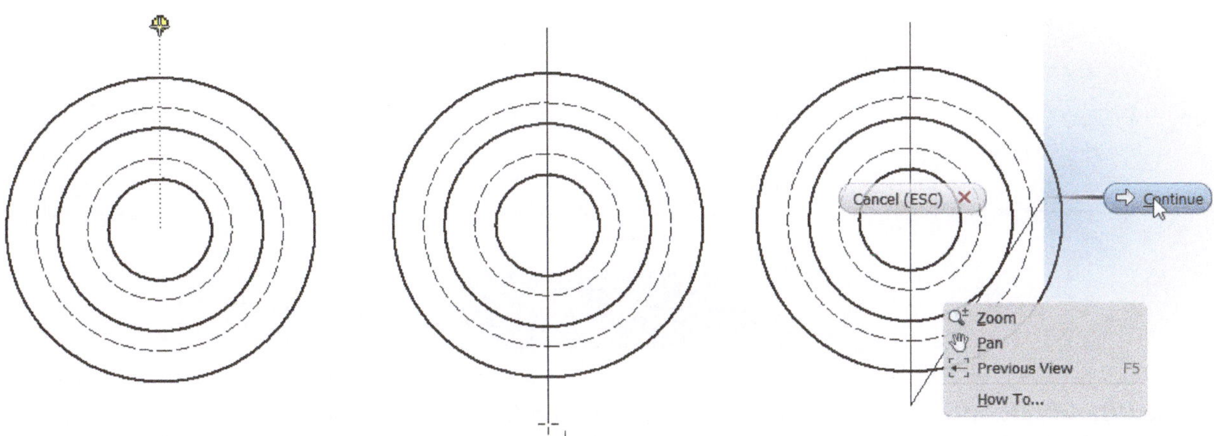

Move the pointer on either side of the cutting plane to indicate the view direction. Next, click to position the section view.

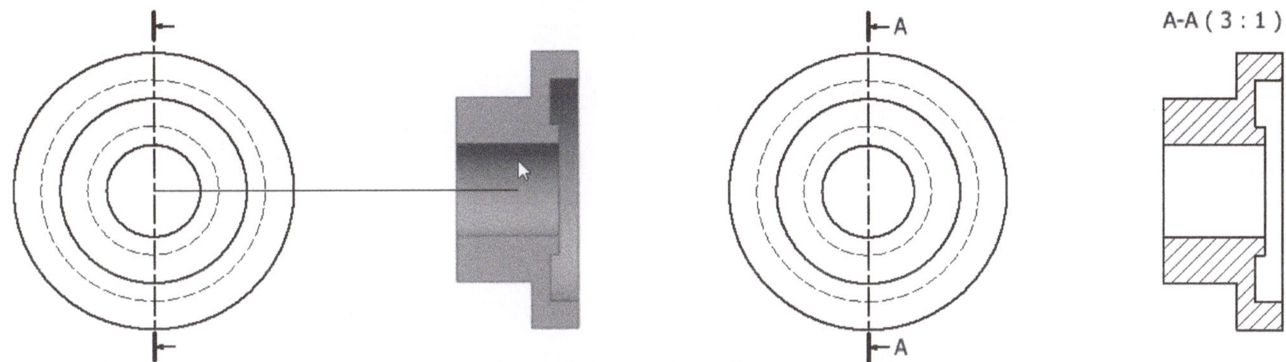

You can also use a multi-segment cutting line to create a section view.

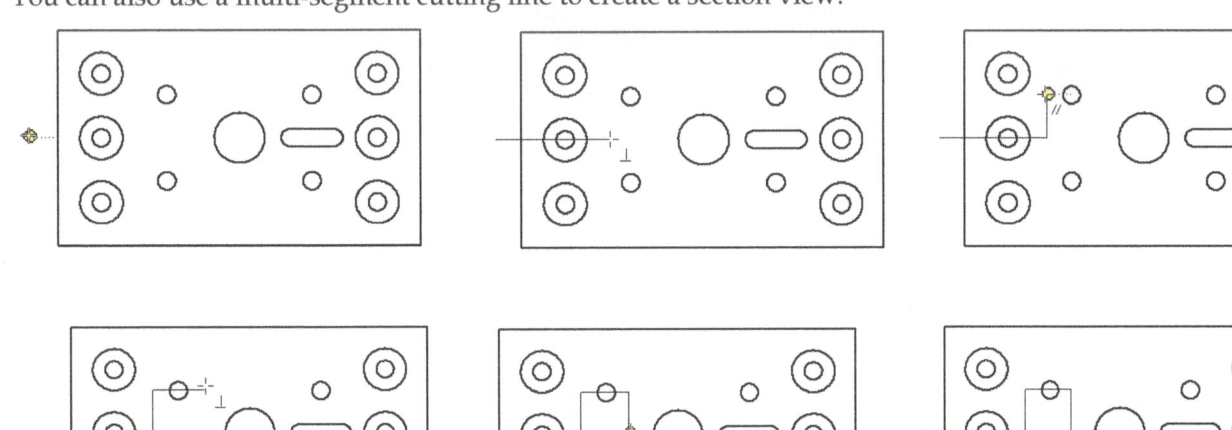

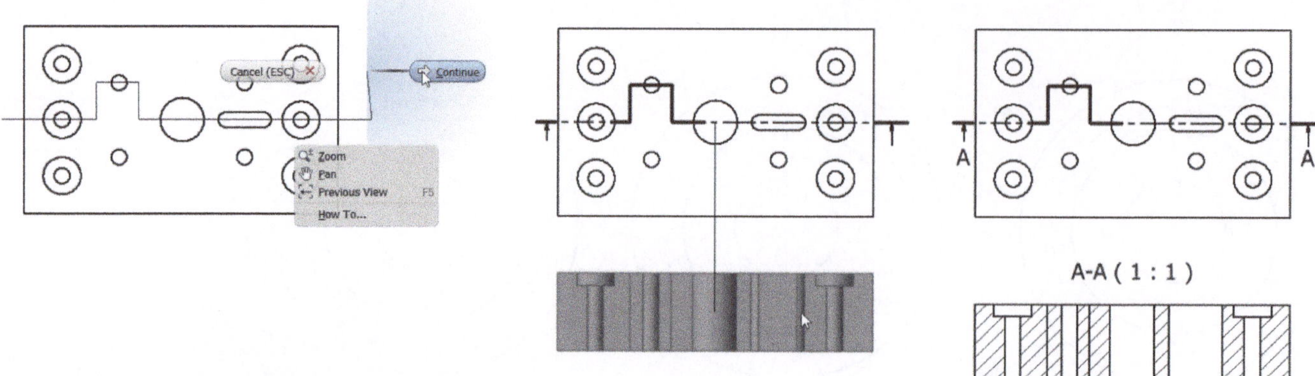

Use the **Slice the Whole part** option to display only the geometry on the cutting plane. To do this, check the **Include Slice** option in the **Slice** section of the **Section View** dialog. Next, check the **Slice the Whole part** option.

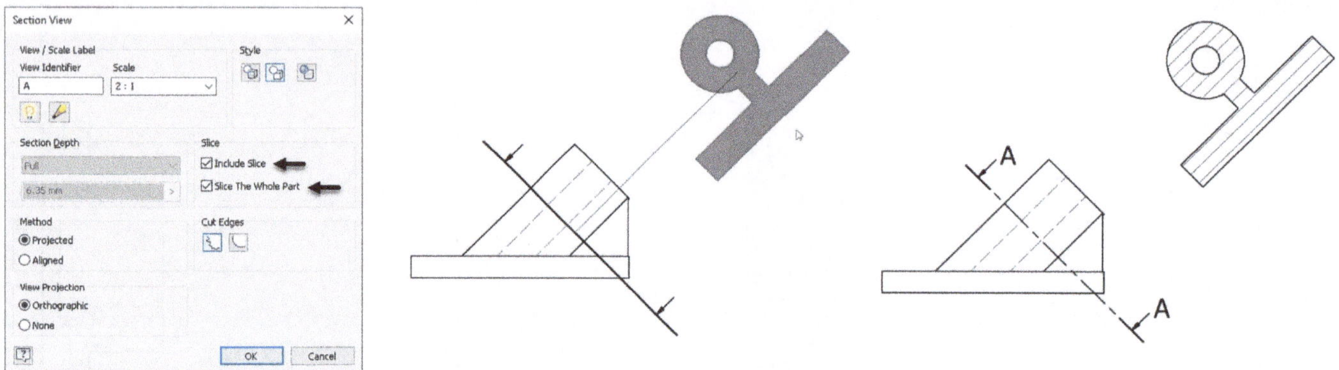

Use the **Aligned** option to create an aligned section view. First, activate the **Section View** command and draw a multiple segment cutting plane. On the **Section View** dialog, select the **Aligned** option from the **Method** section. Move the pointer in the direction perpendicular to any one of the segments of the cutting plane; this defines the direction of the aligned section view. Next, click to position the aligned section view.

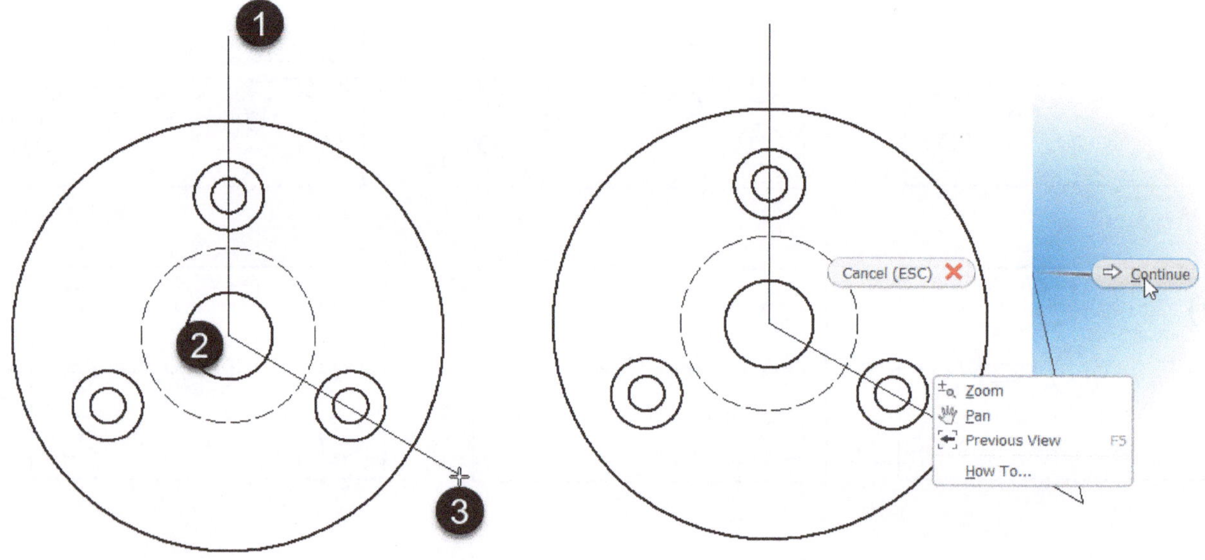

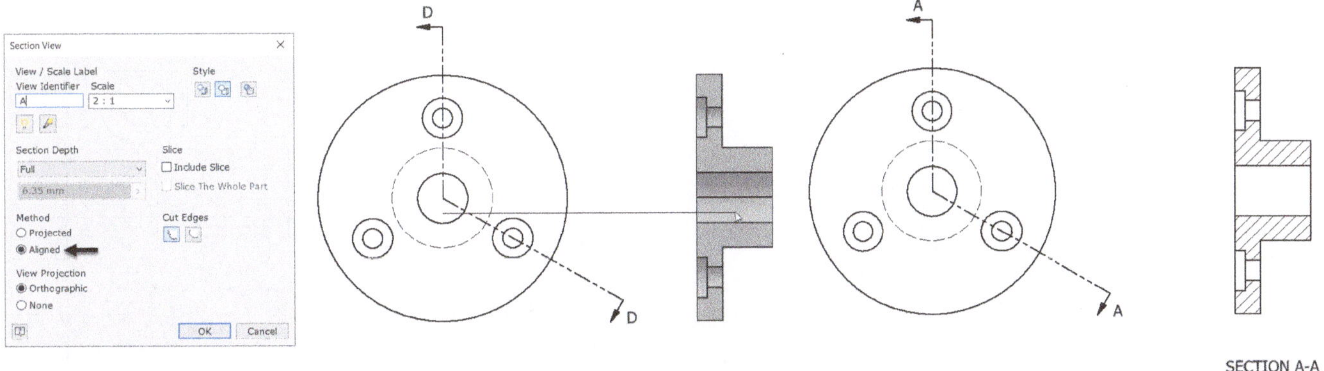

SECTION A-A
SCALE 2 : 1

When creating a section view of an assembly, you can choose to exclude one or more components from the section view. For example, to exclude the piston of a pneumatic cylinder, first create the section of it. Next, go to the Model window and expand **VIEW1: Cylinder_assembly.iam > A:Cylinder_assembly.iam > Cylinder_assembly.iam**. Next, right click on **Piston:1** and select **Section Participation > None**. You will notice that the piston is not cut.

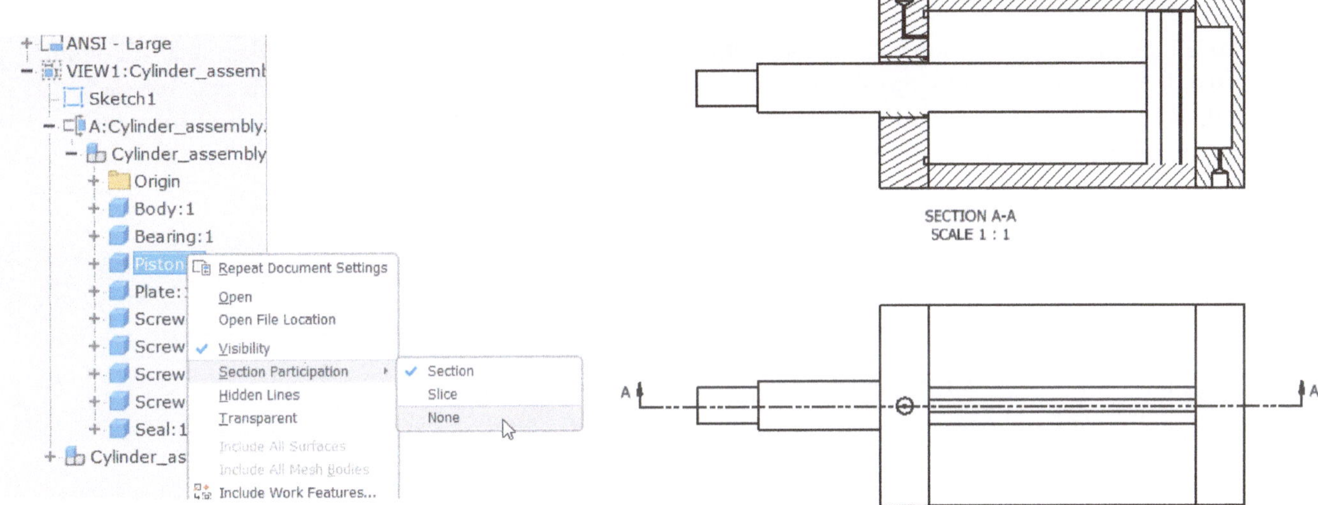

Detail View

If a drawing view contains small features that are difficult to see, a detailed view can be used to zoom in and make things clear. To create a detailed view, activate the **Detail View** command (click **Place Views > Create > Detail** on the ribbon). Next, select the base view; this automatically activates the circle tool. If you want a rectangular fence, then click the **Rectangular** icon under the **Fence Shape** section. Draw a circle or rectangle to identify the area that you wish to zoom into. Once the fence shape is drawn, select a value from the **Scale** drop-down available on the **Detail View** dialog; the scale factor scales the detail view.

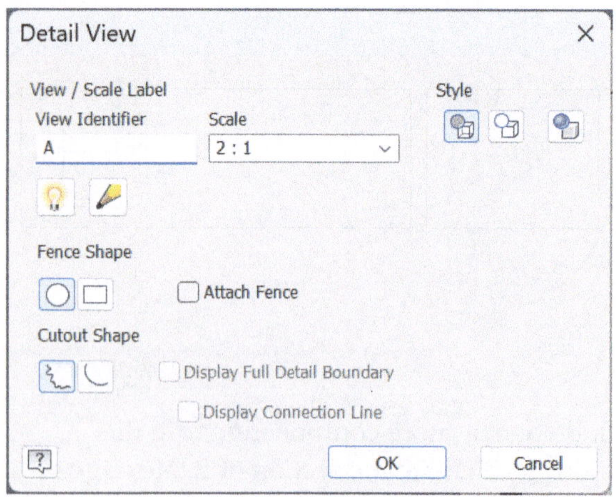

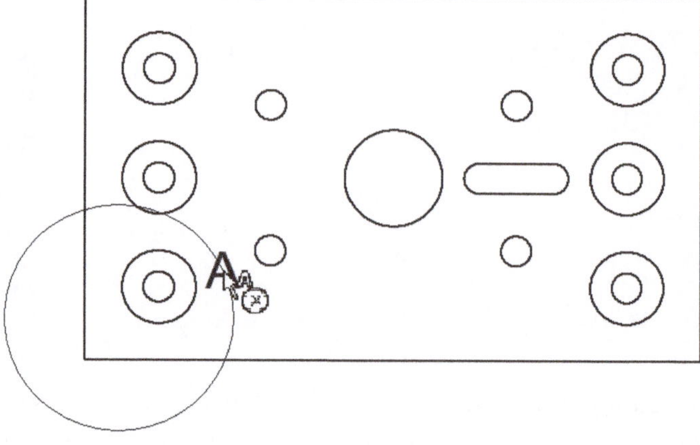

Next, click on any one of the icons available in the **Cutout Shape** section. You can select the **Set Cut Edges to Jagged** or **Set Cut Edges to Smooth** icon. The **Set Cut Edges to Jagged** option creates a jagged cut edge.

The **Set Cut Edges to Smooth** option creates a smooth cut edge. This option allows you to display a full detail boundary. To do this, check the **Display full detail boundary** option. In addition to that, you can show a connection line between the detail view and the base view by checking the **Display Connection Line** option. Next, move the pointer and click to locate the view; the detail view will appear with a label.

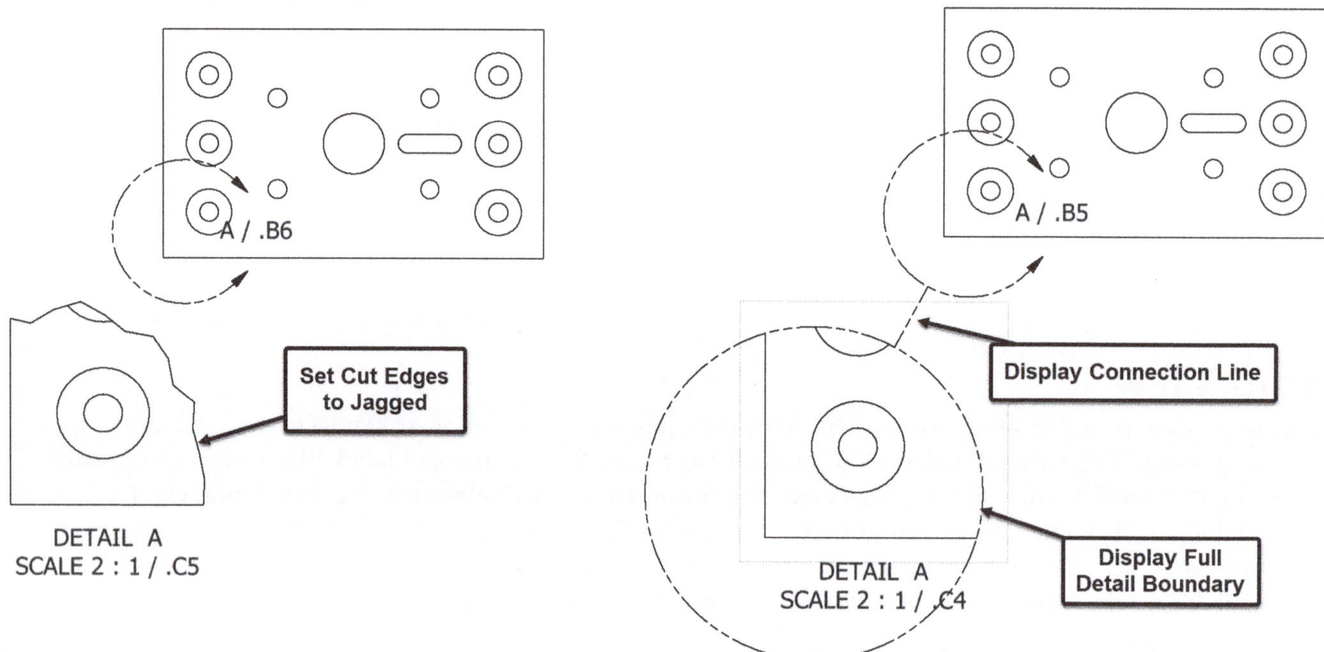

Inventor allows you to change the fence and cutout shapes even after creating the detail view. To do this, click on the detail view boundary. Next, right click and select **Edit Detail Properties**; the **Detail View** dialog is displayed. Next, select the different options from the **Fence shape** and **Cutout shapes** section, and then click **OK**.

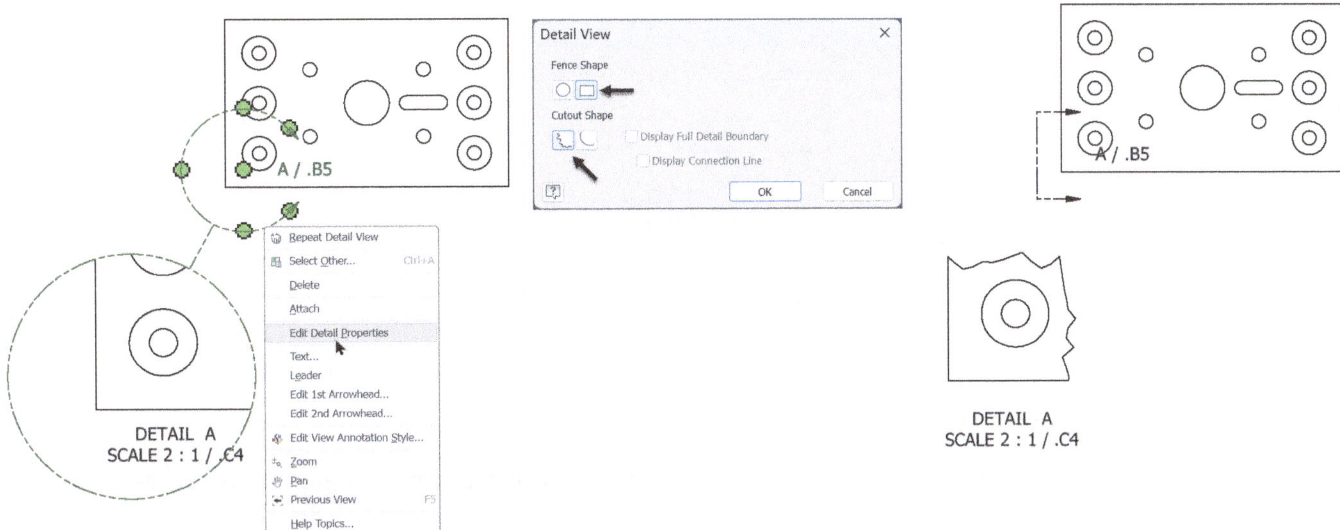

To edit the detail view label, double-click on it. The **Format Text** dialog will appear. In this dialog, you can change the font, font size, and other formatting options. You can also click on individual property tags and press **Delete** to remove them.

To add a new property, select it from the **Property** drop-down list and click the **Add Parameter** button. Then, click **OK**.

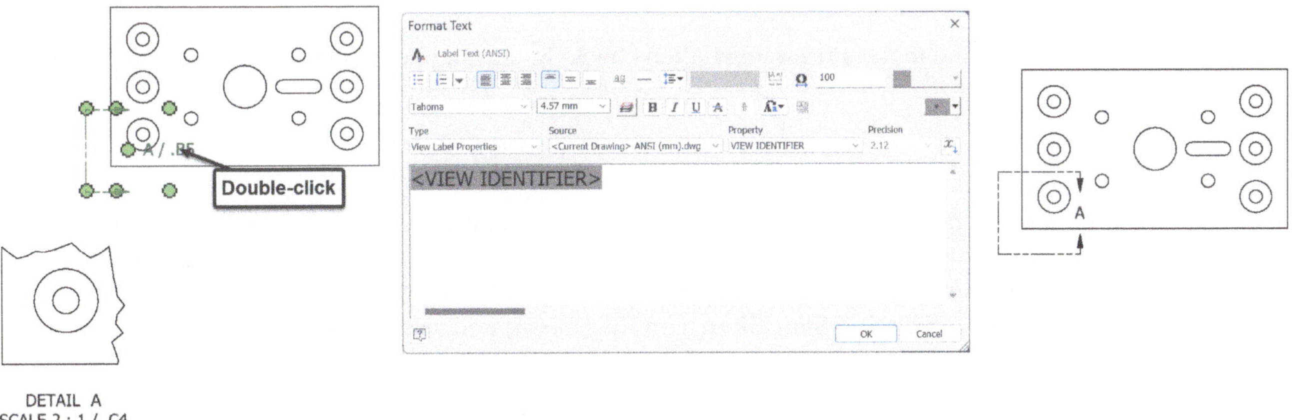

Break a View

Break lines are added to a drawing view, which is too large to fit on the drawing sheet. They break the view so that only essential details are shown. To break a view, activate the **Break** command (click **Place Views > Modify > Break** on the ribbon) and select the view; the **Break** dialog pops up. On this dialog, click the **Vertical Orientation** or **Horizontal Orientation** icon from the **Orientation** section.

Select an option from the **Style** section: **Rectangular Style** or **Structural Style** to define the break line style. Type in the desired value in the **Gap** box to specify the gap between the break lines. Specify the number of symbols to be displayed on the break lines (only for the Structural Style). Next, click and drag the dragger to adjust the size of the break lines.

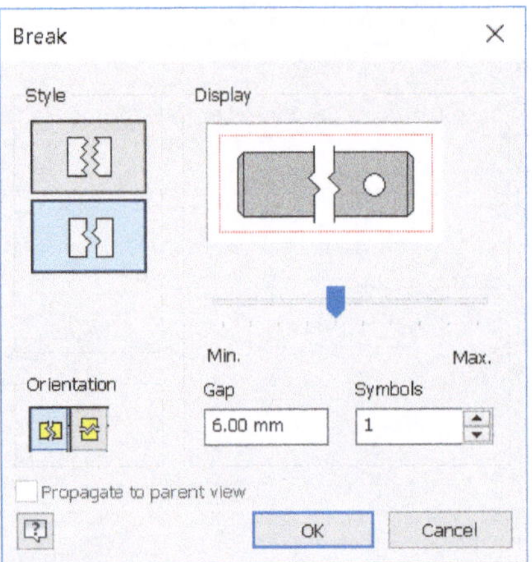

Click once to locate the beginning of the break. Move the pointer and click again to locate the end of the break; the view is automatically broken.

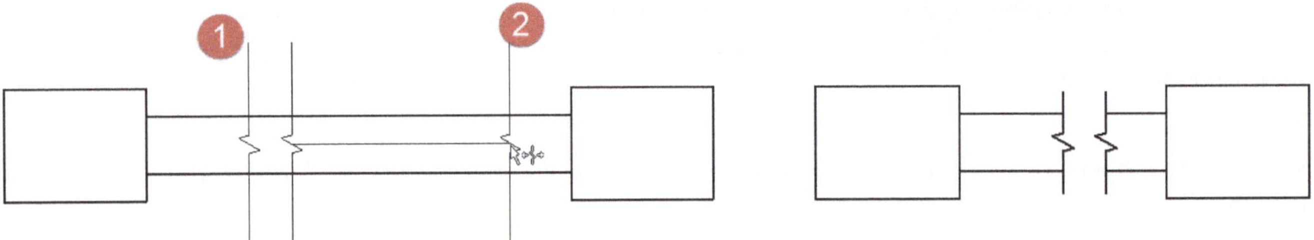

If you want to add a broken line to the parent view, then check the **Propagate to parent view** option on the **Break** dialog.

Break Out

The **Break Out** command alters an existing view to show the hidden portion of a part or assembly. This command is handy to show the parts which are hidden inside an assembly view. You need to have a closed profile to break-out a view. For example, if you want to show the piston inside a pneumatic cylinder, activate the **Start Sketch** command (click **Place Views > Sketch > Start Sketch** on the ribbon) and select a drawing view to draw the profile. Draw a closed profile on the selected drawing view and click **Finish Sketch** on the ribbon.

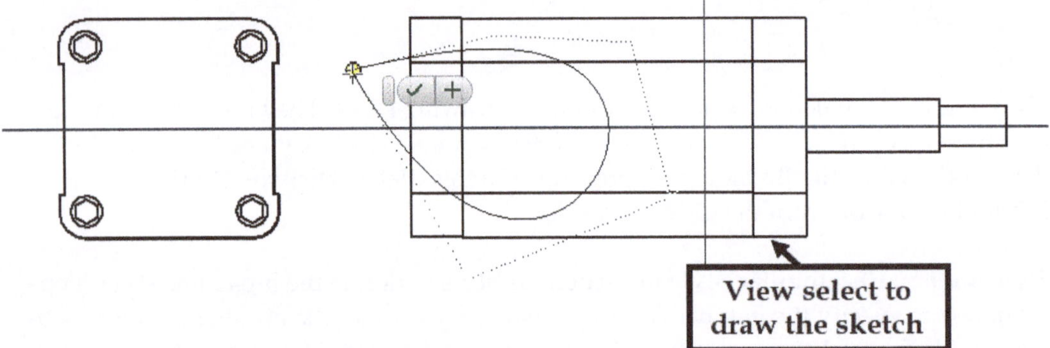

Activate the **Break Out** command (click **Place Views > Modify > Break Out** on the ribbon) and select the drawing view that is having a sketch. Now, you need to specify the depth of the breakout. You can specify the depth using four options available in the **Depth** drop-down: **From Point**, **To Sketch**, **To Hole**, **Through Part**.

Select the **From Point** option from the **Depth** drop-down, and then specify the start point of the depth on the adjacent view. Next, you can specify the depth by entering a value in the value box available in the **Depth** section (or) by selecting the endpoint of the depth. In this case, select the point shown in the figure to define the depth of the breakout. Next, click **OK** to create the break out view.

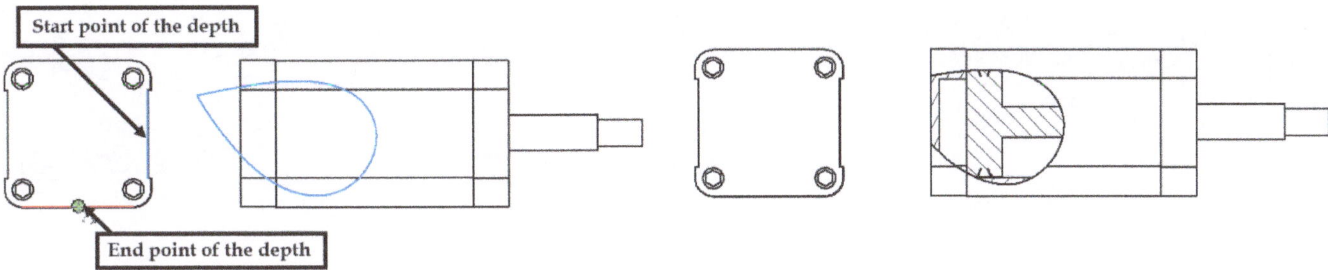

Exploded View

You can display an assembly in an exploded state as long as the assembly already has an exploded view defined in the presentation file. In addition to that, a snapshot is needed to be created in the presentation file. If you want to add an exploded view to the drawing, activate the **Base** command and click the **Open existing file** icon. Next, select the presentation file from the **Open** dialog, and then click **Open**. Click and drag the view to the desired location on your drawing sheet, and then click **OK**.

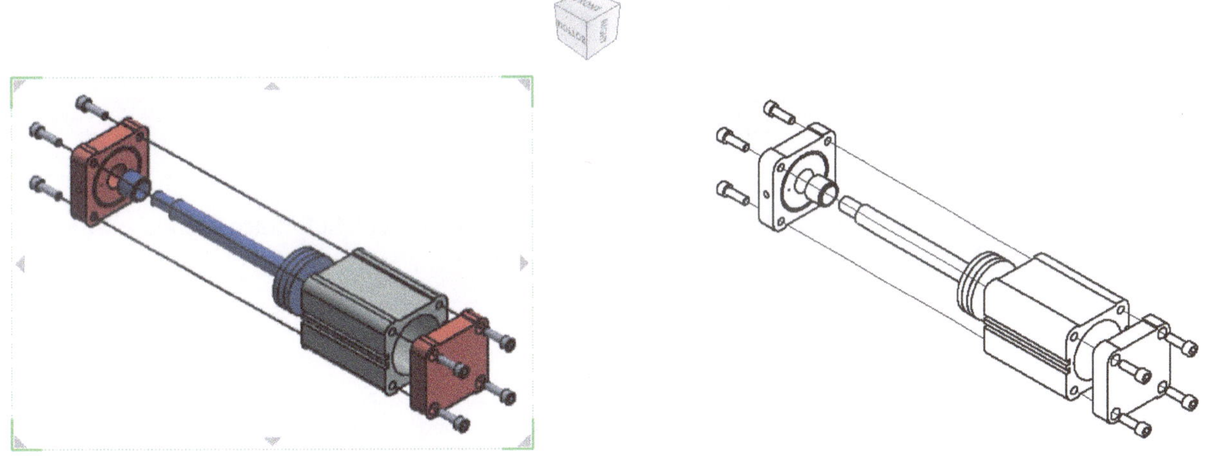

View Style

When working with Inventor drawings, you can control the way a model view is displayed by using the **Style** options. Select a view from the drawing sheet, and then select the **Edit View** option; the **Drawing View** dialog appears. On this dialog, select the desired **Style** (Hidden Line, Hidden Lines Removed, or Shaded) and click **OK**. The style of the view will be changed.

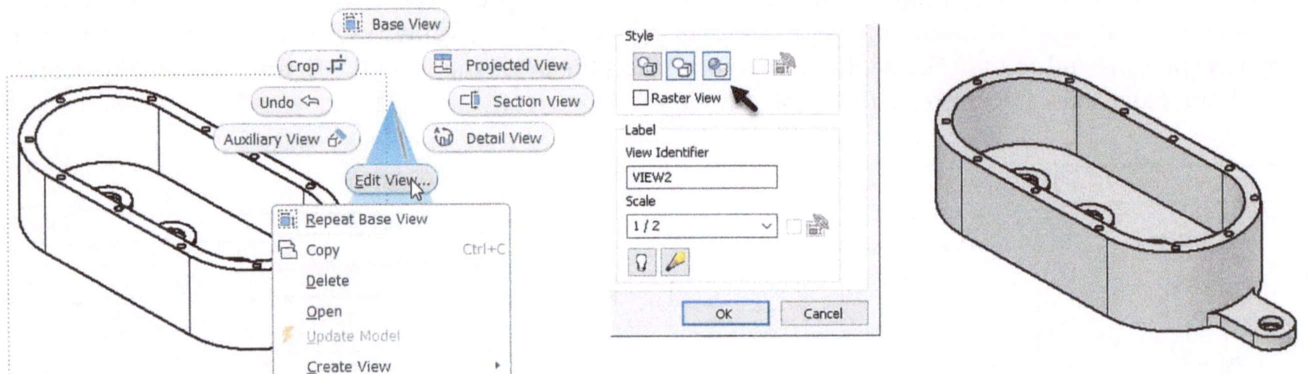

View Alignment

Several types of views are automatically aligned to a parent view. These include section views, auxiliary views, and projected views. If you move down a view, the parent view associated with it will also move.

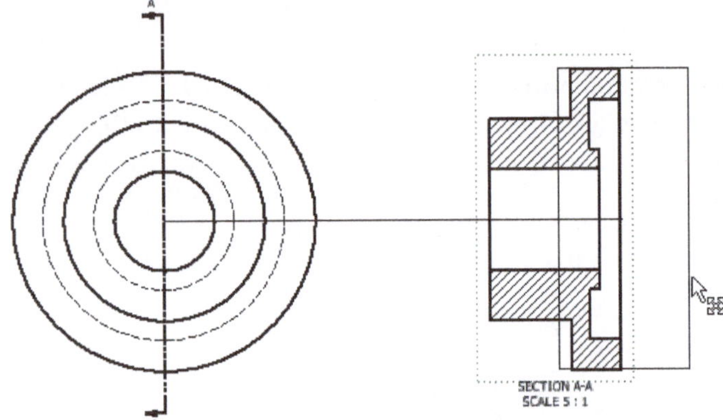

You need to break the alignment between them to move the view separately. Click **Place Views > Modify > Horizontal > Break Alignment** on the ribbon, and then select the view.

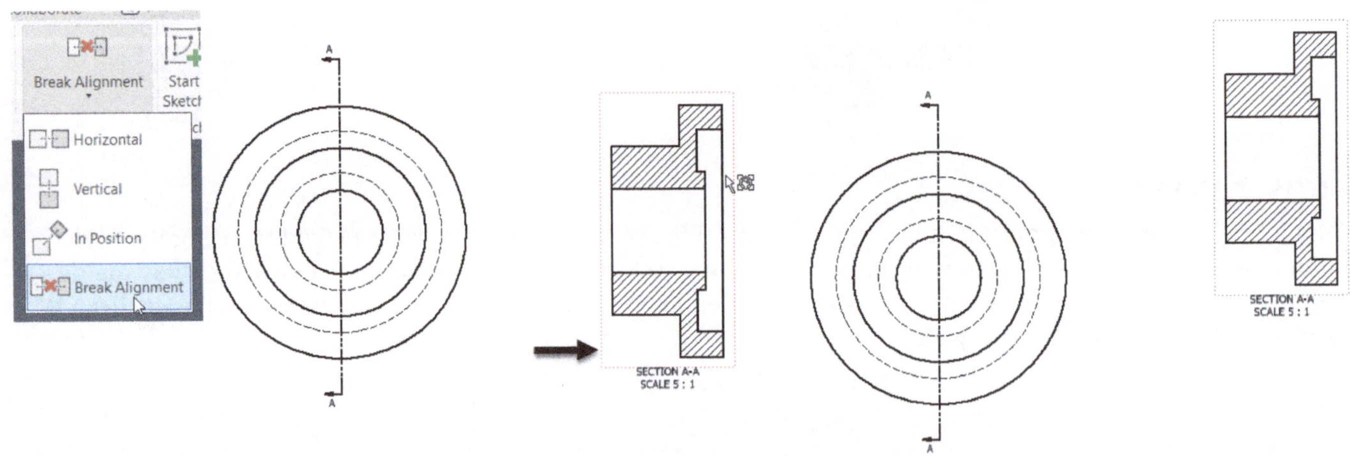

There are three commands to create alignment between the two views: **In Position**, **Vertical**, and **Horizontal**.

The **In Position** command (on the ribbon, click **Place Views > Modify > Break Alignment > In Position**) aligns the selected view with the base view at the current position.

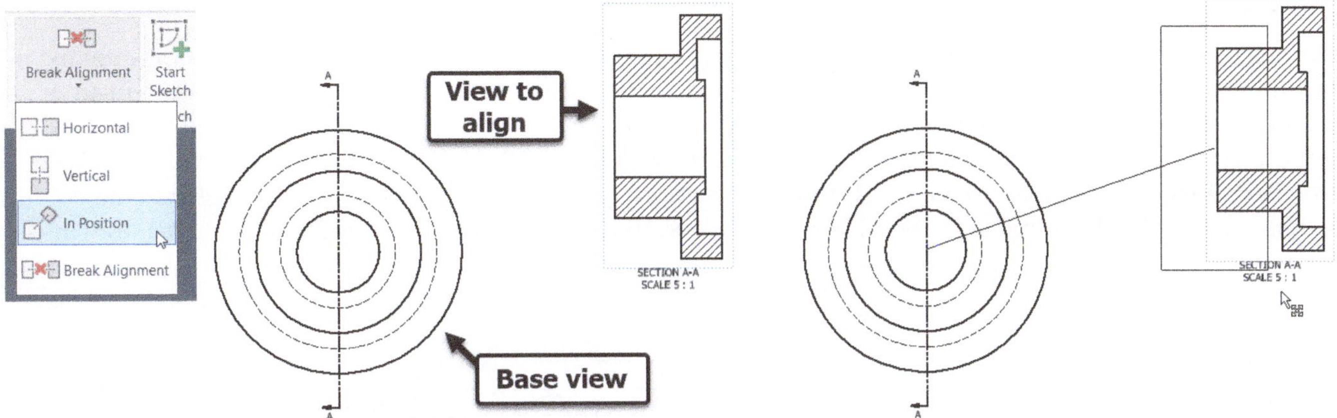

The **Vertical** command (on the ribbon, click **Place Views > Modify > Break Alignment > Vertical**) aligns the selected view with the base view vertically.

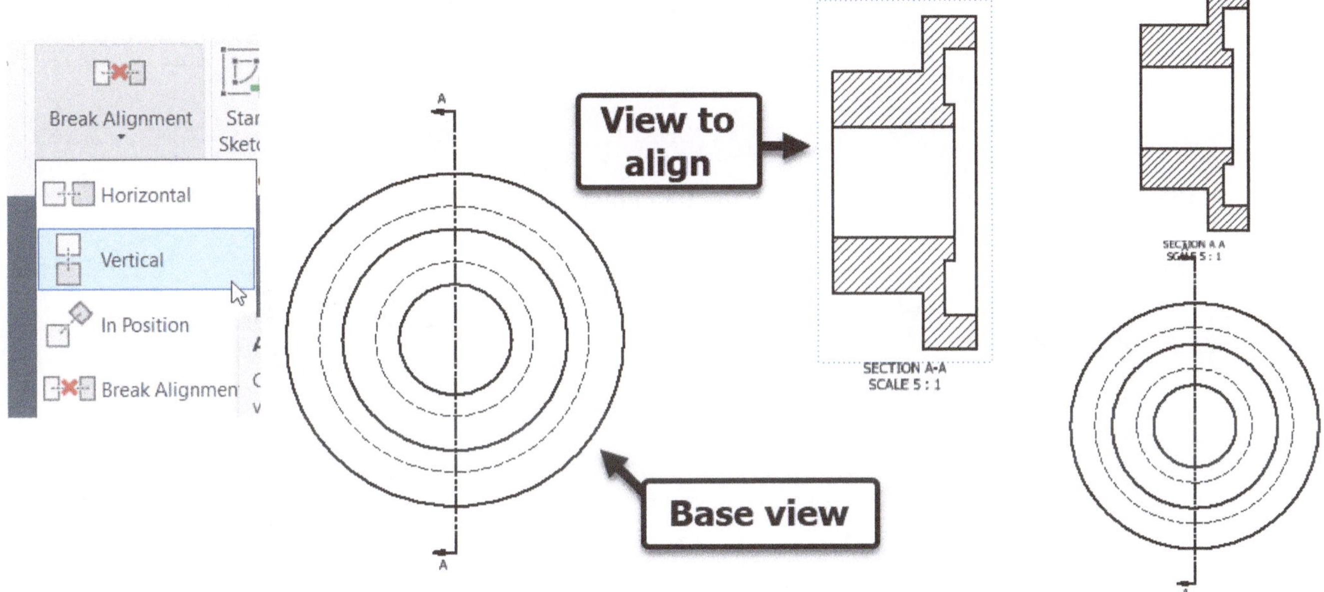

The **Horizontal** command (on the ribbon, click **Place Views > Modify > Break Alignment > Horizontal**) aligns the selected view with the base view horizontally.

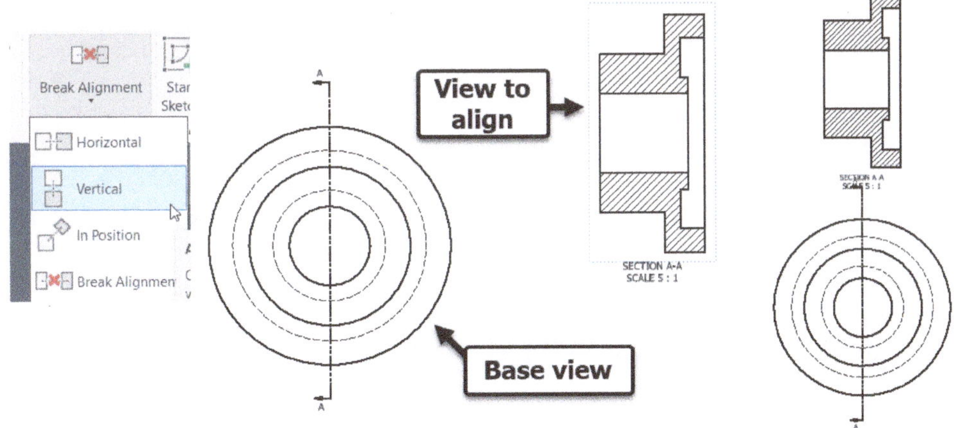

Parts List

Creating an assembly drawing is very similar to creating a part drawing. However, there are few things unique in an assembly drawing. One of them is creating parts list. A parts list identifies the different components in an assembly. Generating a parts list is very easy in Autodesk Inventor. First, you need to have a view of the assembly. Next, click **Annotate > Table > Parts List** on the ribbon, and then click on the drawing view. Click **OK** on the **Parts List** dialog; the **BOM View Disabled** message box appears if the BOM View is disabled in the assembly file. Click **OK** to enable the BOM View in the assembly. Next, place the parts list table on the drawing sheet.

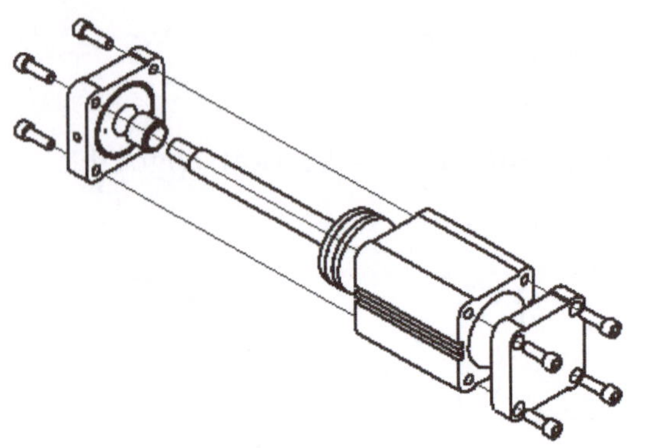

PARTS LIST			
ITEM	QTY	PART NUMBER	DESCRIPTION
1	1	Body	
2	1	Bearing	
3	1	Piston	
4	1	Plate	
5	8	Screw	
13	1	Seal	

Right click on the parts list and select **Edit Parts list**; the **Parts List** dialog appears.

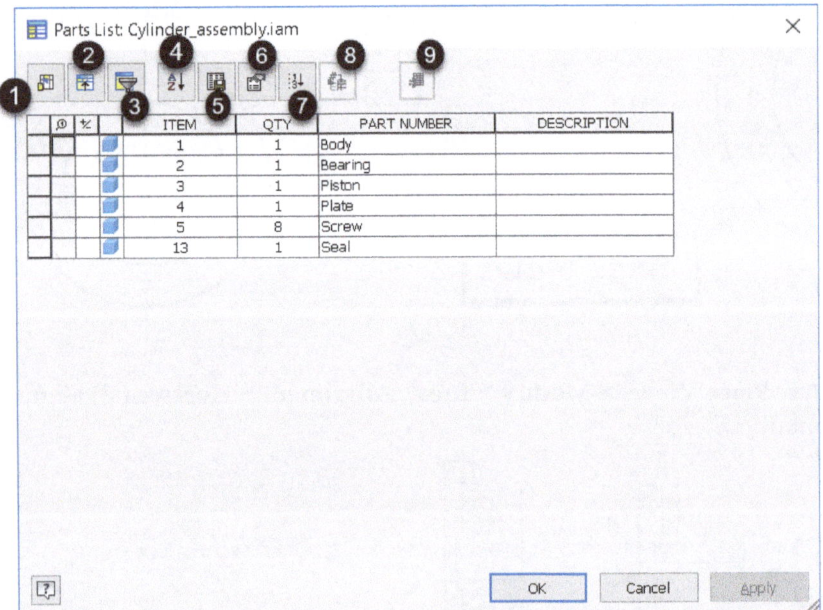

1 Column Chooser
2 Group Settings
3 Filter Settings
4 Sort
5 Export
6 Table Layout
7 Renumber Items
8 Save Item Overrides to BOM
9 Member Selection

On the **Parts List** dialog, click the **Column Chooser** icon to display the **Parts List Column Chooser** dialog. On this dialog, select the column names from the **Selected Properties** list and arrange them using the **Move Up** and **Move Down** buttons. To add a new column, select the column name from the **Available Properties** section and click **Add**. To remove a column, select the column name from the **Selected Properties** section and click **Remove**. Click **OK** to apply the changes and close the dialog. Click **OK** on the **Parts List** dialog.

Adding Balloons

To add balloons, click **Annotate > Table > Balloon** and select the part to add a balloon. Move the pointer and click to locate the balloon; notice that another line segment is attached to the pointer. Right click and select **Continue**; the balloon is added.

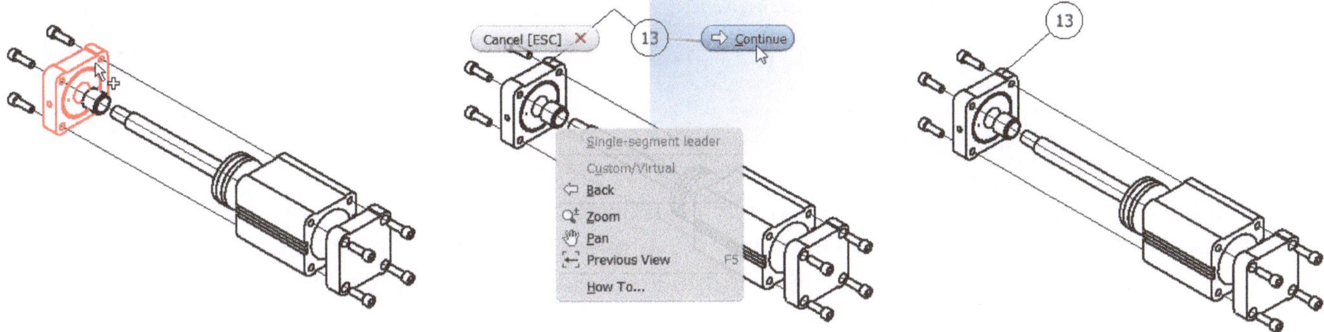

Right click and notice that the **Single Line Segment** option is displayed. This option helps you to create a single line segment balloon without prompting for multiple clicks.

Using the Auto Balloon command

The **Auto Balloon** command adds balloons to the multiple parts of an assembly at a time. Activate this command (**Annotate > Table** > **Balloon** drop-down > **Auto Balloon**) and select the assembly view. Next, drag a selection window across the assembly view; the parts in the assembly view are selected. Also, notice that the part with a balloon is not selected.

Select any one of the placement options from the **Placement** section: **Horizontal**, **Vertical**, and **Around**. Next, type in a value in the **Offset Spacing** box. Click the **Select Placement** button on the dialog and position the balloons on the drawing sheet.

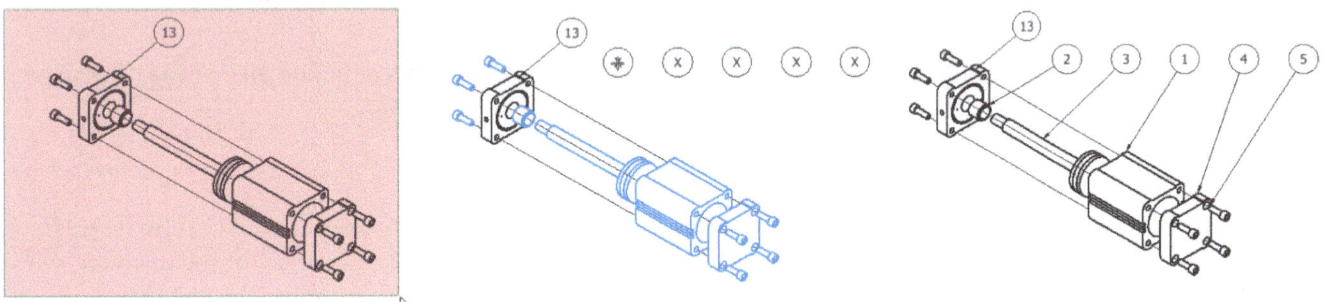

Dimensions

Inventor provides you with different ways to add dimensions to the drawing. One of the methods is to retrieve the dimensions that are already contained in the 3D part file. Click **Annotate > Retrieve > Retrieve Model Annotations** on the ribbon, and then select the view. You may notice that there are some unwanted dimensions. Select only the dimensions that are to be retrieved from the model. Next, click **OK**.

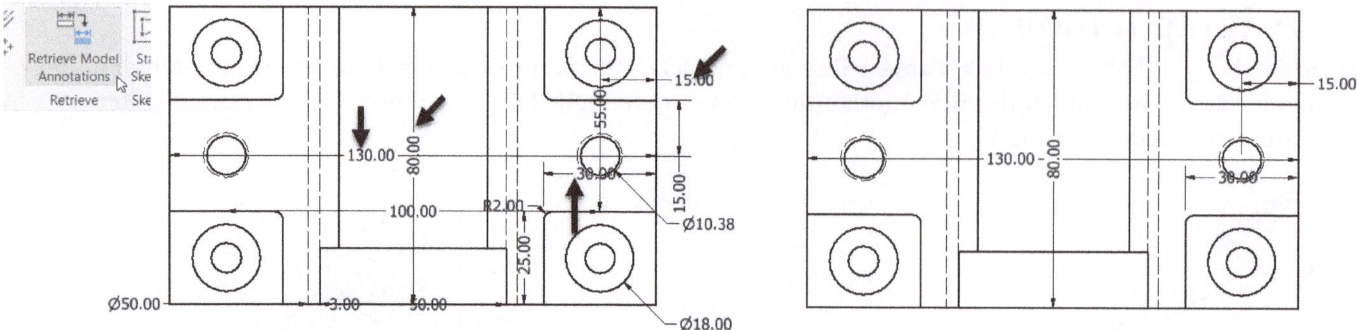

Notice that the dimensions may not be appropriately positioned. To arrange them rightly, activate the **Arrange Dimensions** command (click **Annotate > Dimension > Arrange Dimension** on the ribbon). Click on the dimensions, and then right click and select **OK**. The dimensionts will be appropriately arranged.

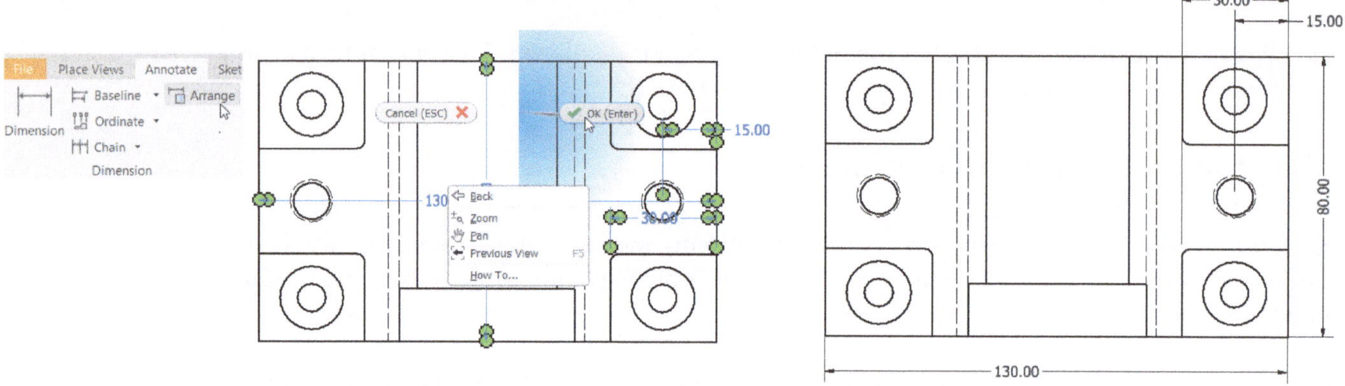

If you want to add some more dimensions, which are necessary to manufacture a part, activate the **General Dimension** command and add them to the view.

Tip: You can use the dimension handles to modify the position of the dimension and size of the dimension and extension lines. The dimension handles are displayed on selecting a dimension.

Baseline Dimension

The **Baseline Dimension** command allows you to create and arrange dimensions very quickly. Activate this command (on the ribbon, click **Annotate > Dimension > Baseline**), and then select an edge of the drawing view; this defines the origin of the baseline dimension. Next, select the remaining edges from the drawing view. Right click and select **Continue**, and then move the pointer vertically or horizontally; the dimensions are displayed based on the movement. Click to position the baseline dimensions.

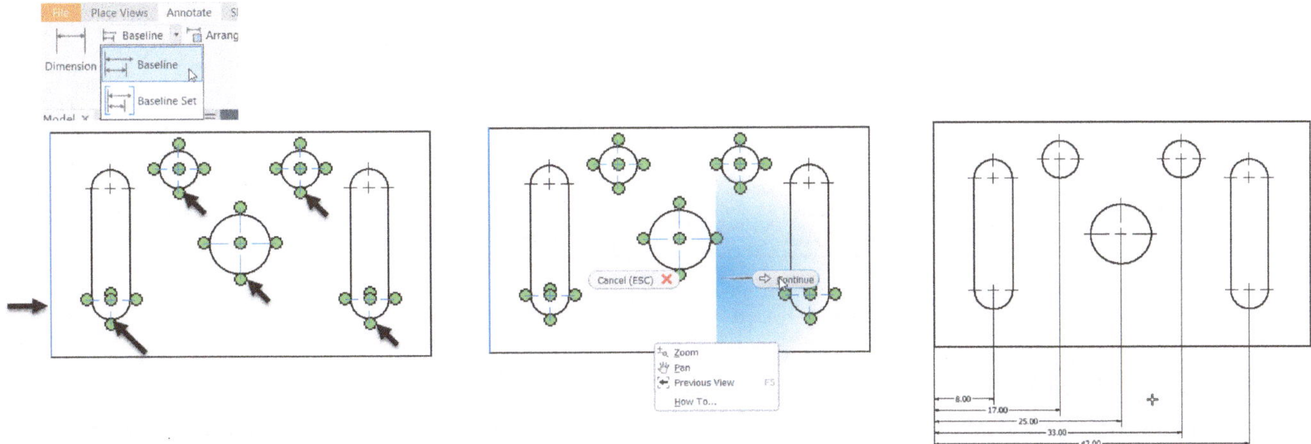

You can continue to select edges to add more dimensions. Right click and select **Create** to finish creating the baseline dimensions.

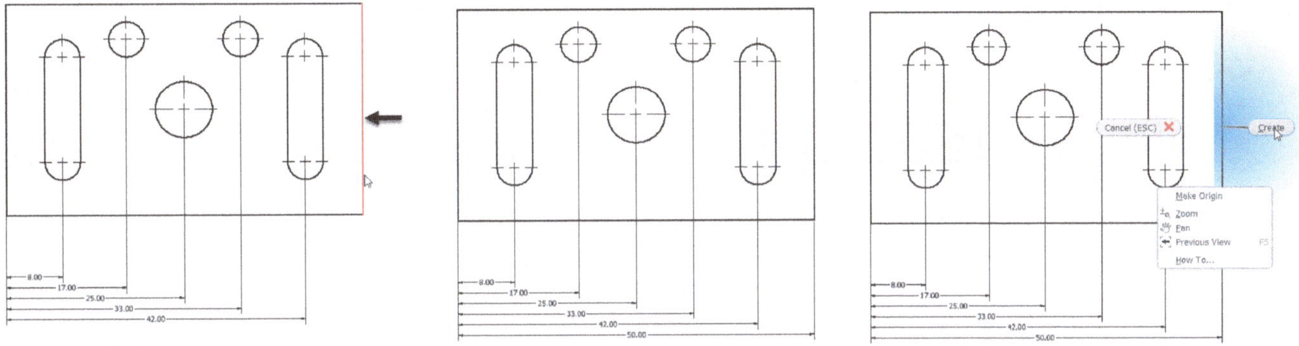

Place the pointer on the individual dimensions and notice that they are selectable individually. You can edit, drag, or delete them individually.

Baseline Dimension Set

The **Baseline Dimension Set** command creates baseline dimensions and groups them as a single set. Activate the **Baseline Dimension Set** command (on the ribbon, click **Annotate > Dimension > Baseline Set**), and then select the edges from the drawing view. Right click and select **Continue** and then place the dimensions. Next, right click and select **Create**.

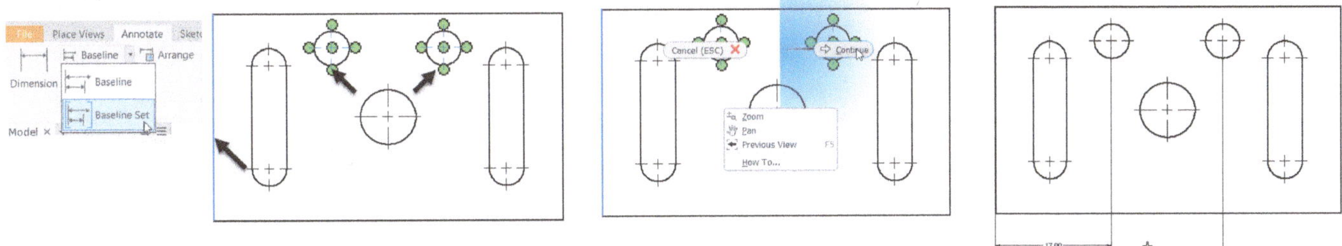

Select any one of the dimensions and notice that the entire set is selected. Right click on the dimensions and notice that a list of options is displayed (**Arrange, Make Origin, Add Member, Detach Member, Delete Member**). These options allow you to modify the baseline dimensions. For example, if you want to add a new dimension to the set, then select the **Add Member** option. Next, select an edge from the drawing view; a new dimension is added to the baseline dimension set. Press Esc.

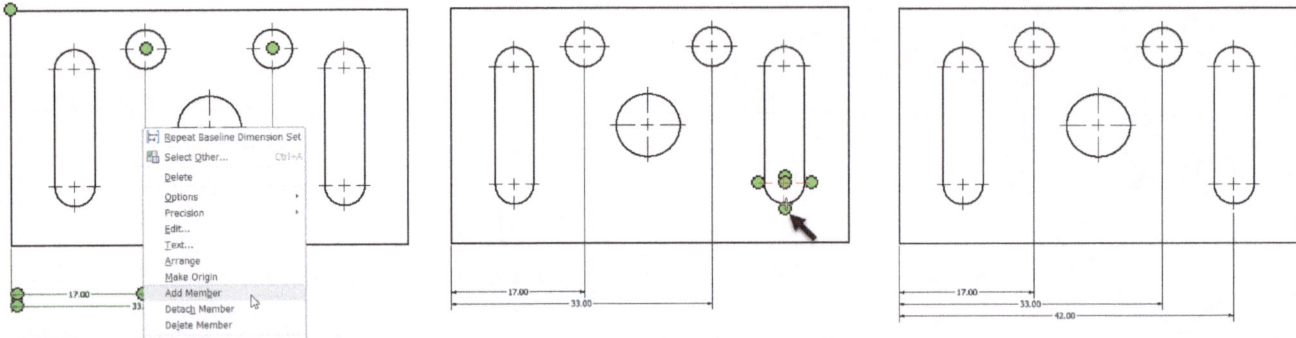

Ordinate Dimensions

Ordinate dimensions are another type of dimension that can be added to a drawing. To create them, activate the **Ordinate Dimension** command (click **Annotate > Dimension > Ordinate Dimensions** drop-down **> Ordinate** on the ribbon), and then select the view. Next, click on any edge of the drawing view to define the ordinate or zero references. Now, click on the point or edge of the drawing view. Right click and select **Continue.** Move the pointer in the vertical or horizontal direction, and then place the ordinate dimension.

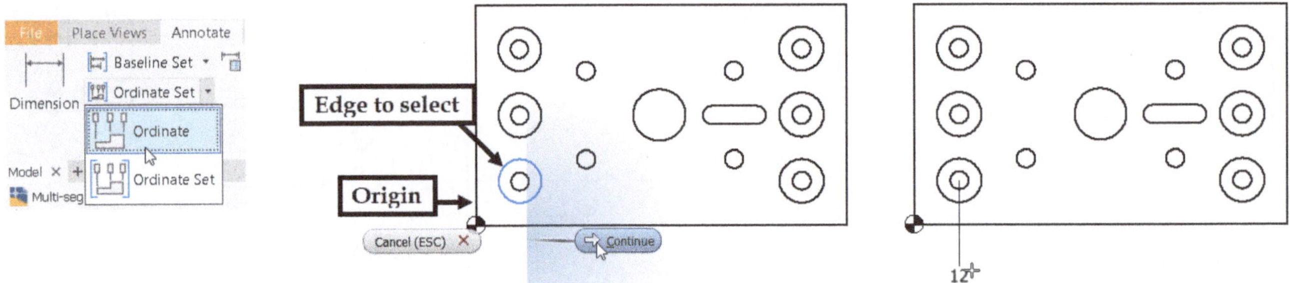

Likewise, select the remaining edges or points to create ordinate dimensions. Right click and select OK after you have finished creating the ordinate dimensions.

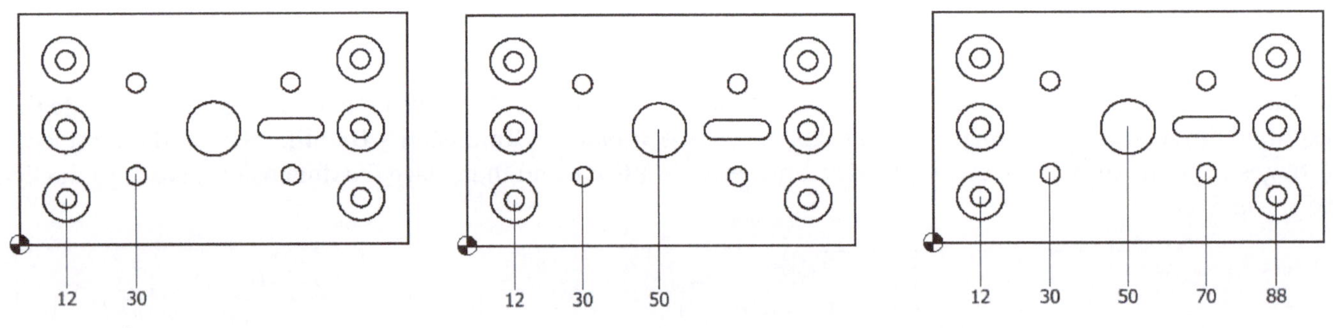

Ordinate Set

The **Ordinate Set** command creates continuous ordinate dimensions in a single set. On the ribbon, click **Annotate > Dimension > Ordinate Dimensions** drop-down **> Ordinate Set**, and select a point or edge on the drawing view to define the origin. Next, select the multiple edges or points from the drawing view. Right click and select **Continue**. Move the pointer vertically or horizontally and click to position the ordinate dimensions. Now, you can select addition points or edges from the drawing view; the new ordinate dimensions are added to the ordinate set. Right click and select **Create** to complete the ordinate set.

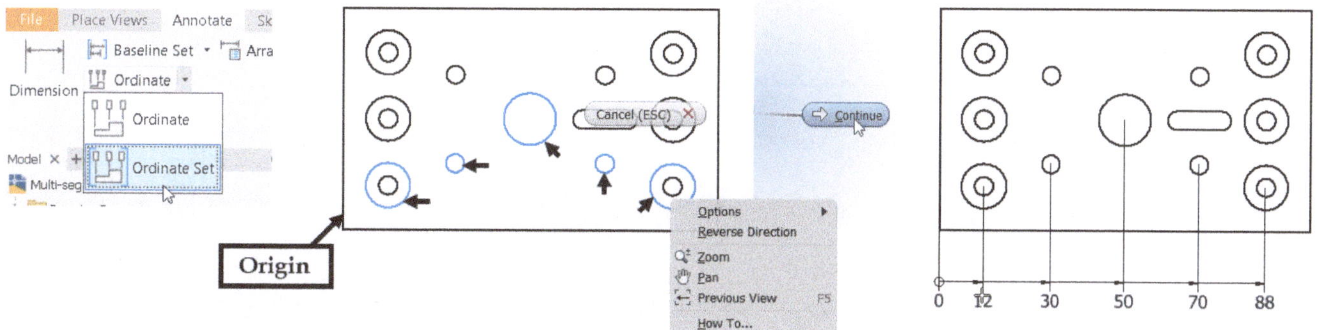

Changing the Origin

You can change the origin of the ordinate dimension set even after creating it. To do this, click the right mouse button on the ordinate dimension that you want to define as the origin. Next, select **Make origin** from the shortcut menu.

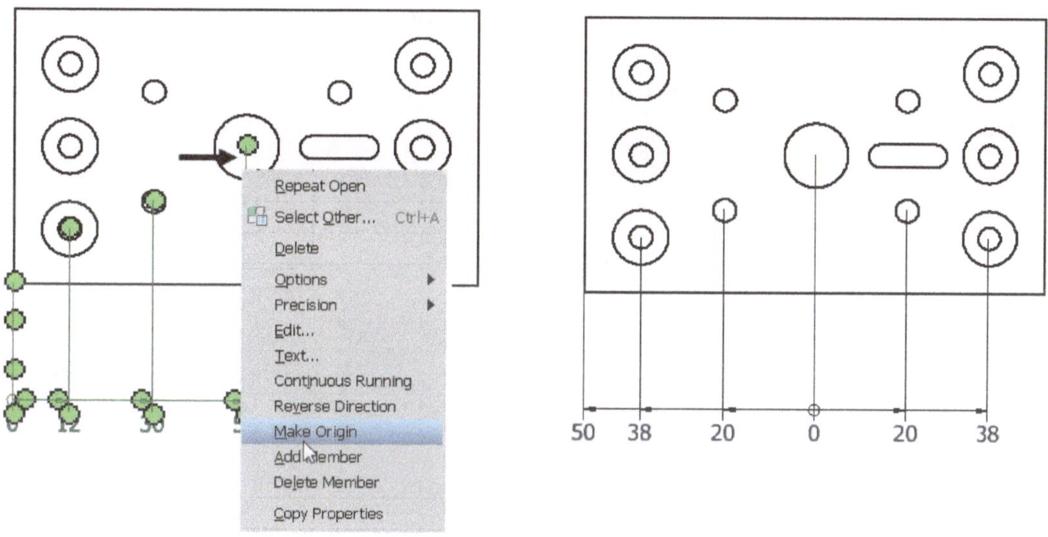

Hole Table

The hole table displays the X and Y coordinates, holes, sizes, and other properties. You can define the style of the hole table and choose the properties that you want to display in the hole table using the **Styles Editor** dialog. On the ribbon, click **Manage > Styles and Standards > Styles Editor**. On the **Styles and Standard Editor** dialog, expand the **Hole Table** node, and then select the **Hole Table (ISO)** or any other **Hole Table** standard. On the **Hole table Style** page, go to the **Default column settings** section and click the **Column Chooser** button; the **Hole Table Column Chooser** dialog appears. On this dialog, you can select the required properties from the **Available Properties** list and click the **Add** button to add them to the **Selected Properties** section. You can also adjust the position of the properties using the **Move Down** and **Move Up** buttons. Click **OK** to close the dialog.

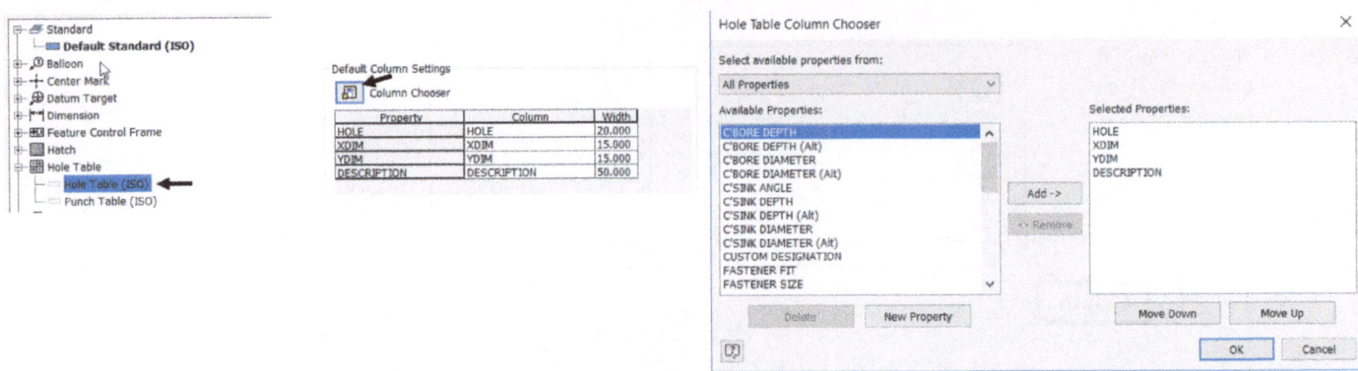

Next, select the position of the heading using the **Heading** drop-down. Specify the text styles using the options available in the **Text Styles** section. Click the **Save and Close** button on the **Style and Standard Editor** dialog.

Hole Table - Selection

Activate the **Hole Table - Selection** command (on the ribbon, click **Annotate** tab > **Table** panel > **Hole Table** drop-down > **Hole Selection**), and then select the drawing view. Next, select a point on the view to define the origin of the coordinate system. Select the holes to be displayed in the hole table. Right click and select **Create**, and then position the hole table.

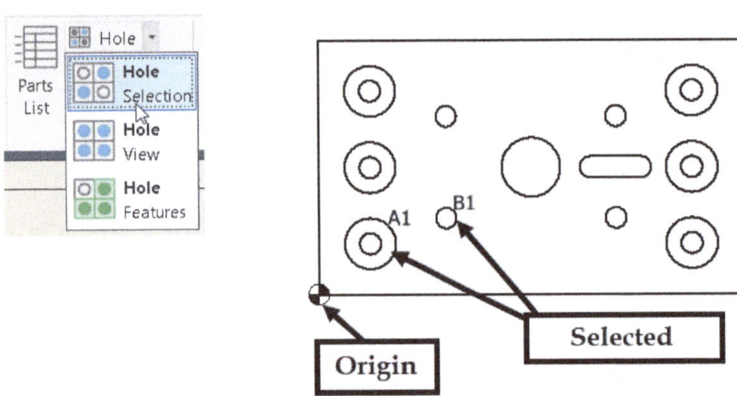

HOLE TABLE			
HOLE	XDIM	YDIM	DESCRIPTION
A1	12,00	12,00	Ø5,00 THRU ⌴ Ø12,00 ↧ 4,00
B1	30,00	18,00	Ø5,00 THRU

Hole Table - View

Activate the **Hole Table - View** command (on the ribbon, click **Annotate** tab > **Table** panel > **Hole Table** drop-down > **Hole View**), and then select the drawing view. Next, select a point on the view to define the origin of the coordinate system. Position the hole table on the drawing sheet.

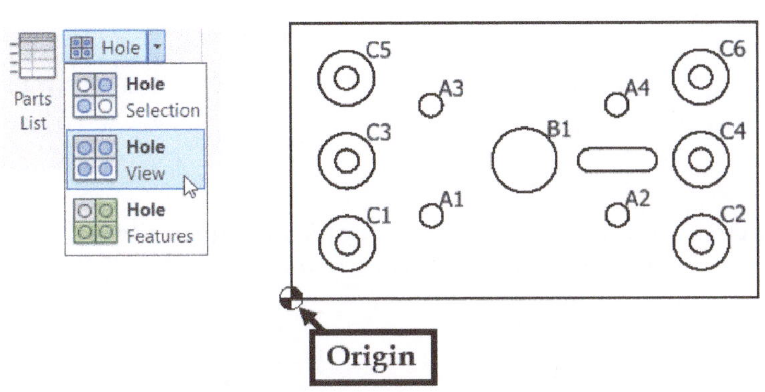

HOLE TABLE			
HOLE	XDIM	YDIM	DESCRIPTION
A1	30,00	18,00	Ø5,00 THRU
A2	70,00	18,00	Ø5,00 THRU
A3	30,00	42,00	Ø5,00 THRU
A4	70,00	42,00	Ø5,00 THRU
B1	50,00	30,00	Ø14,00 THRU
C1	12,00	12,00	Ø5,00 THRU ⌴ Ø12,00 ↧ 4,00
C2	88,00	12,00	Ø5,00 THRU ⌴ Ø12,00 ↧ 4,00
C3	12,00	30,00	Ø5,00 THRU ⌴ Ø12,00 ↧ 4,00
C4	88,00	30,00	Ø5,00 THRU ⌴ Ø12,00 ↧ 4,00
C5	12,00	48,00	Ø5,00 THRU ⌴ Ø12,00 ↧ 4,00
C6	88,00	48,00	Ø5,00 THRU ⌴ Ø12,00 ↧ 4,00

Hole Table - Feature

Activate the **Hole Table - Feature** command (on the ribbon, click Annotate tab > **Table** panel > **Hole Table** drop-down **> Hole Feature**), and then select the drawing view. Next, select a point on the view to define the origin of the coordinate system. Select the hole features to be included in the hole table. Right click and select **Create**, and then position the hole table.

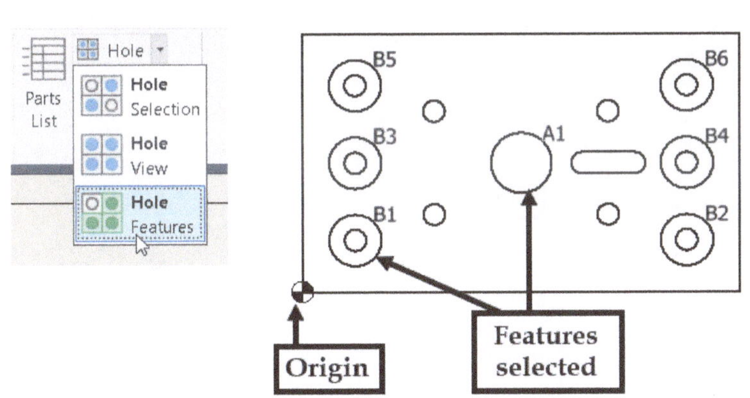

HOLE TABLE			
HOLE	XDIM	YDIM	DESCRIPTION
A1	50,00	30,00	Ø14,00 THRU
B1	12,00	12,00	Ø5,00 THRU ⌴ Ø12,00 ↧ 4,00
B2	88,00	12,00	Ø5,00 THRU ⌴ Ø12,00 ↧ 4,00
B3	12,00	30,00	Ø5,00 THRU ⌴ Ø12,00 ↧ 4,00
B4	88,00	30,00	Ø5,00 THRU ⌴ Ø12,00 ↧ 4,00
B5	12,00	48,00	Ø5,00 THRU ⌴ Ø12,00 ↧ 4,00
B6	88,00	48,00	Ø5,00 THRU ⌴ Ø12,00 ↧ 4,00

Center Marks and Centerlines

Centerlines and Centermarks are used in engineering drawings to denote hole centers and lines. To add center marks to the drawing, activate the **Center Mark** command (click **Annotate > Symbols > Center Mark** on the ribbon) and click on the hole circles. Right click and select **OK**.

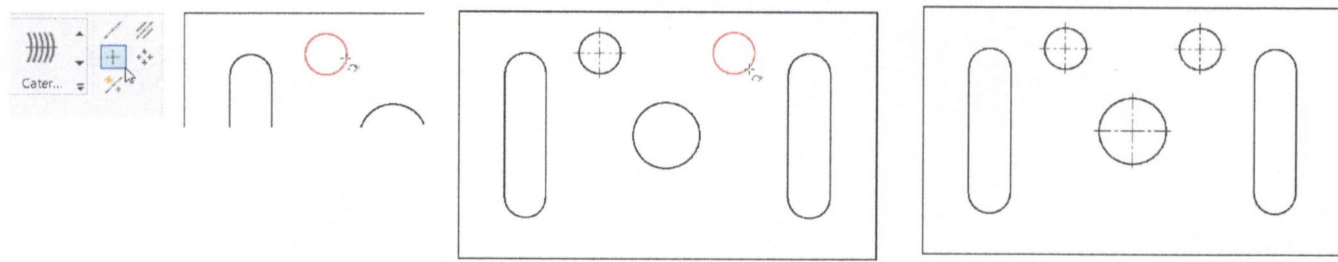

Centerlines

To add centerlines, activate the **Centerline** command (click **Annotate > Symbols > Centerline** on the ribbon). Select the start and endpoints of the centerline, as shown. Next, right click and select **Create**.

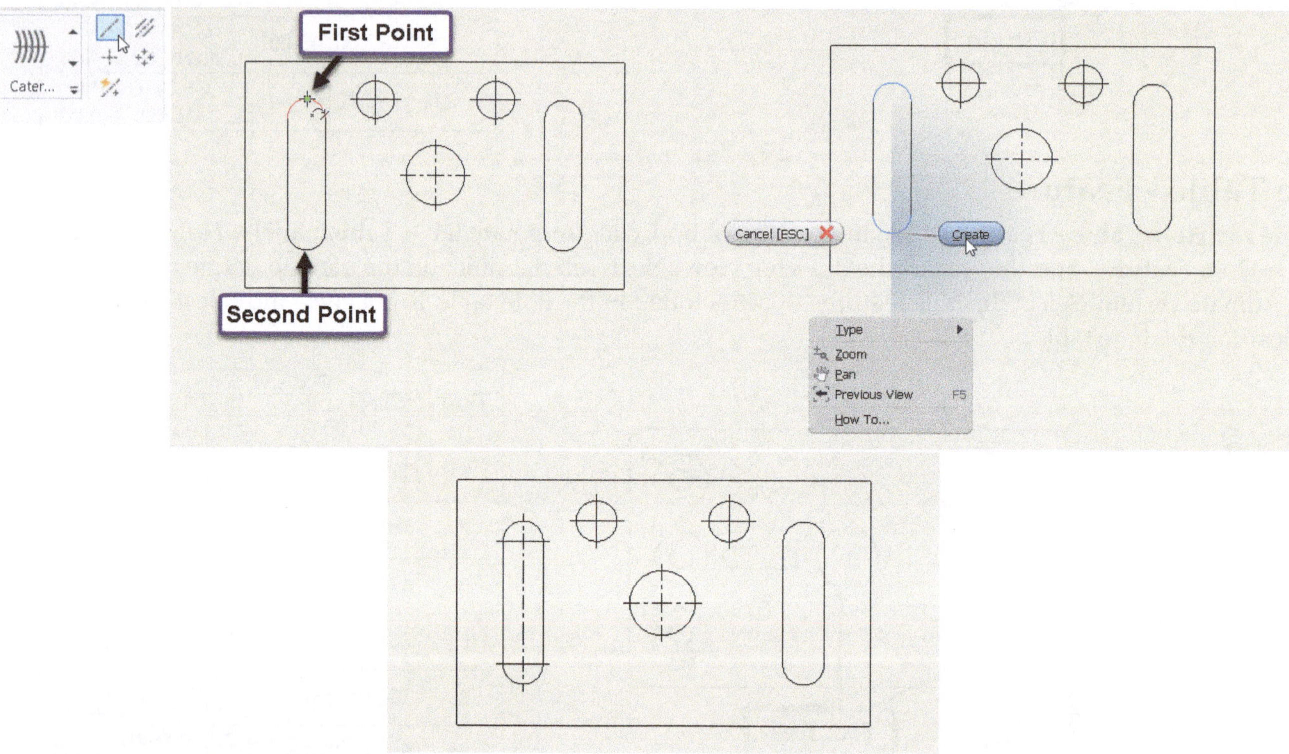

Centerline Bisector

The **Centerline Bisector** command is used to create a centerline bisecting two lines. This command is beneficial while creating a centerline on the section view or projected views. On the ribbon, click **Annotate > Symbols > Centerline Bisector**, and then click on two edges of the drawing view. A centerline will be created between the two lines.

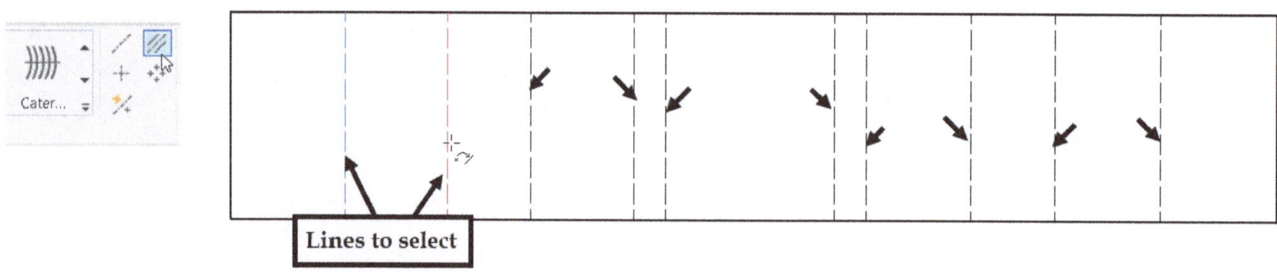

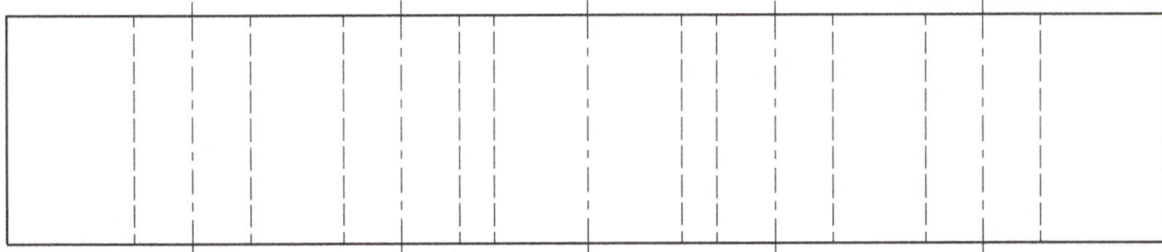

Automated Centerlines

If you want to add centrelines automatically, click **Annotate** > **Symbols** > **Automated Centerlines** and click on the drawing view; the **Automated Centerlines** dialog pops up. On this dialog, select the elements to which the centerlines and center marks are to be applied. Next, select the projection type (**Axis Normal** or **Axis Parallel**) from the **Projection** section. The **Axis Normal** option applies the centerlines to the objects whose axes are normal to the drawing view. Whereas, the **Axis Parallel** option applies the centerlines for objects whose axes are parallel to the drawing view. You can select both options from the **Projection** section if the drawing view contains both types of objects. Click **OK** to add centerlines and center marks to the drawing view.

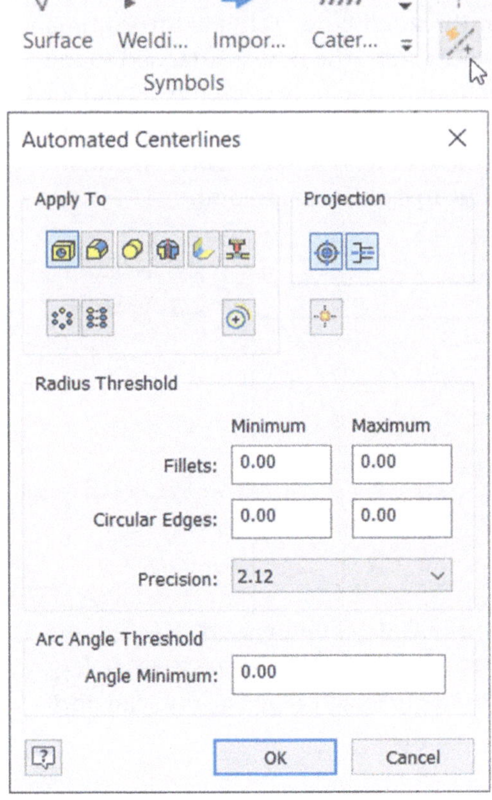

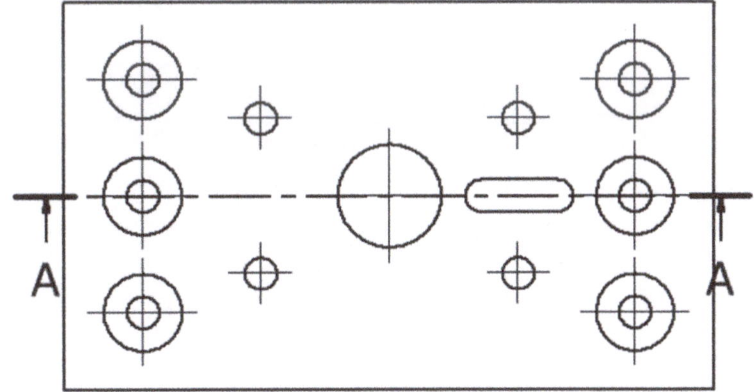

Centered Pattern

The **Centered Pattern** command (click **Annotate > Symbol > Centered Pattern** on the ribbon) allows you to add center marks to the holes arranged circularly. Activate this command and click for the center of the circular hole pattern. Next, select any one of the holes of the circular pattern. Select the remaining holes of the circular pattern; a centered pattern is created passing through the selected holes. Now, select the firstly selected hole. Right click and select **Create** to complete the centered pattern.

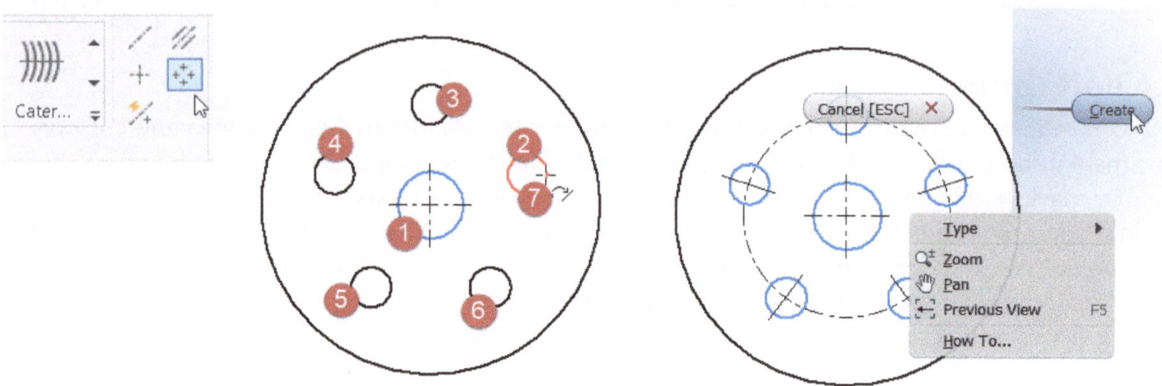

Creating Hole and Thread Notes

The **Hole/ Thread Notes** command allows you to add a note to a simple or threaded hole. Activate this command (click **Annotate > Feature Notes > Hole and Thread** on the ribbon) and select a hole; the note is attached to the pointer. Notice that the **Hole/ Thread Notes** command captures the information of the hole from the 3D model. It displays detailed information of the hole only when you have created the hole using the **Hole** command rather than the **Extrude** or **Revolve** command. Move the pointer and position the hole note. Likewise, you can add a thread note to the threaded hole or external thread. Right click and select **OK** to exit the command.

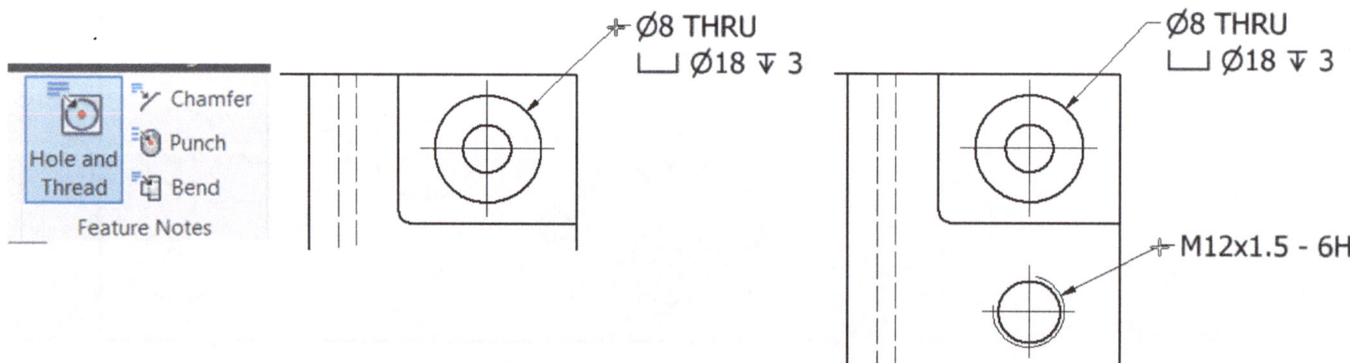

After adding a hole or thread note, you can add more information to it. For example, if you want to display the quantity of the holes in the hole note, right click on it and select **Edit Hole Note**. On the **Edit Hole Note** dialog, place the cursor in front of the diameter symbol, and then click the **Quantity Note** icon. Likewise, you can add any other symbol from the **Values and Symbols** section. Click **OK** to close the dialog.

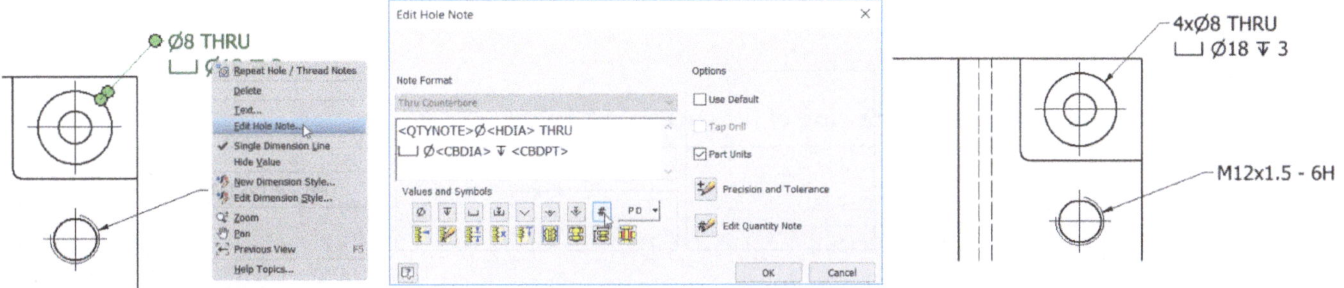

Chamfer Notes

The **Chamfer Notes** command identifies the information of the beveled edges created using the **Chamfer** command in the 3D modeling environment. Activate this command (click **Annotate > Feature Notes > Chamfer**) and select the chamfered edge. Next, select the reference edge, move the pointer, and click to position the chamfer note. Right click and select **OK**.

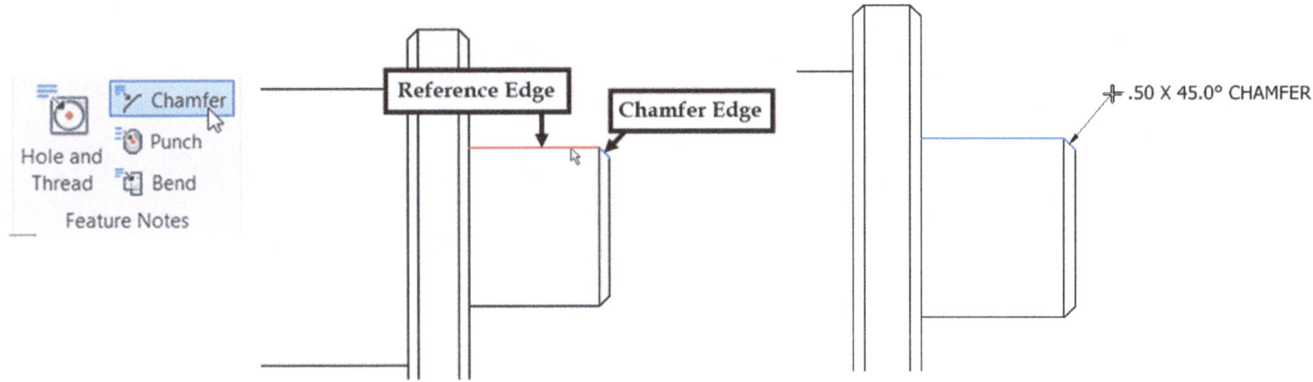

To edit a chamfer note, right click on it and select **Edit Chamfer Note**. On the **Edit Chamfer Note** dialog, you can add values or symbols to the note using the options in the **Values and Symbols** section. You can also edit the precision of the values displayed in the chamfer note using the **Precision and Tolerance** icon. The **Precision and Tolerance** dialog appears on clicking this icon. On this dialog, uncheck the **Use Global Precision** option, and then change the values in the **Unit Precision** section. You can also access the tolerance options by expanding this dialog. Click **OK** to close the **Precision and Tolerance** dialog. Next, click **OK** on the **Edit Chamfer Note** dialog to accept the changes.

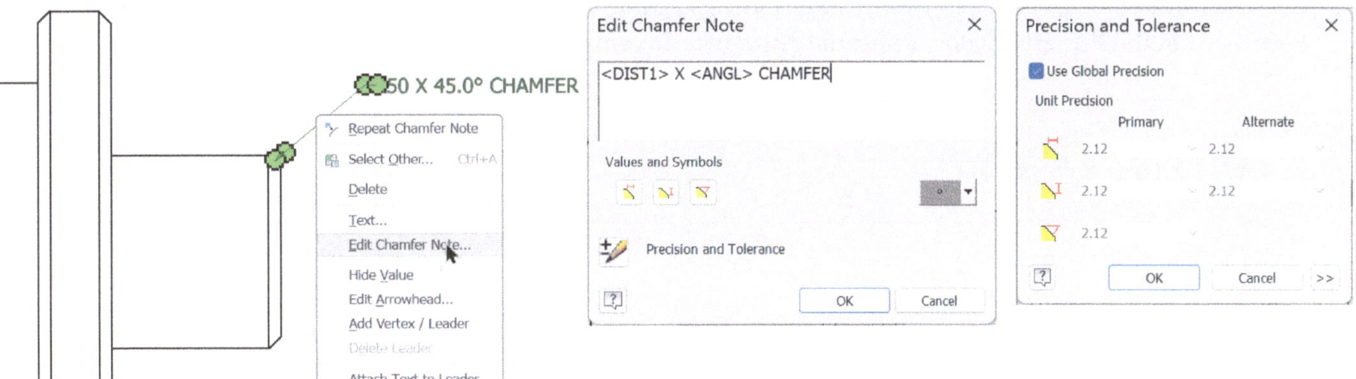

Examples

Example 1

In this example, you will create the 2D drawing of the part shown below.

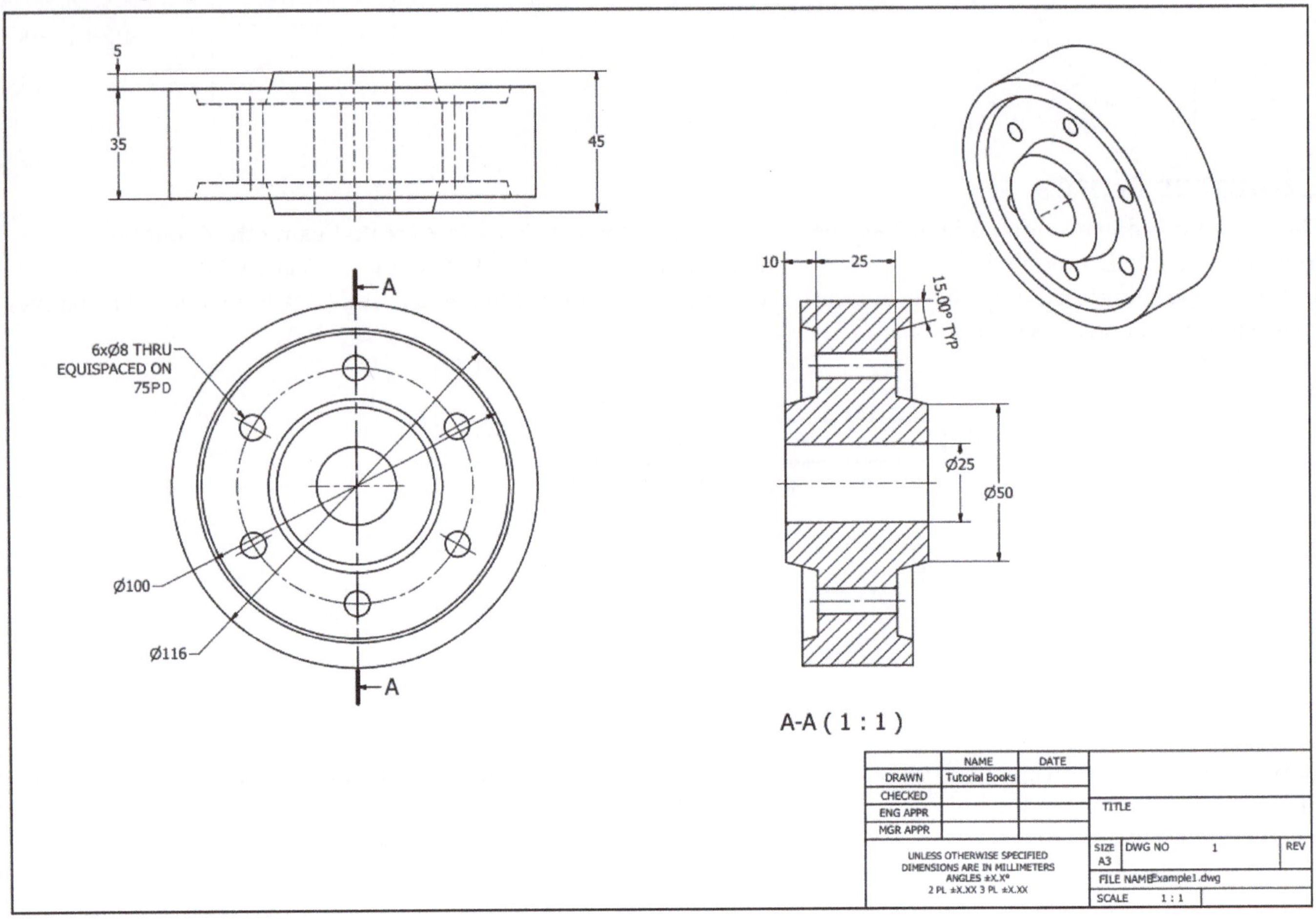

Making the Styles Library Editable

1. Start **Autodesk Inventor 2026.**
2. On the **Home** screen, click the **Projects and Settings** icon next to the **Projects** drop-down, and then select **Settings**. On the **Projects** dialog, select the **Autodesk Inventor For Beginners** project from the **Project** list.

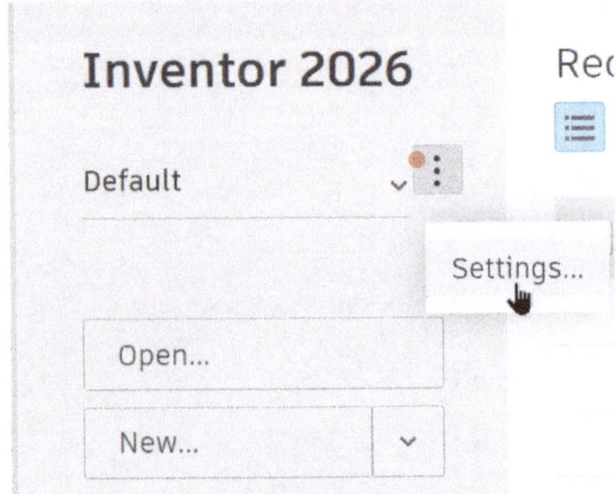

3. On the **Project** dialog, under the lower section, right click on the **Use Style Library** option, and then select **Read-Write**.

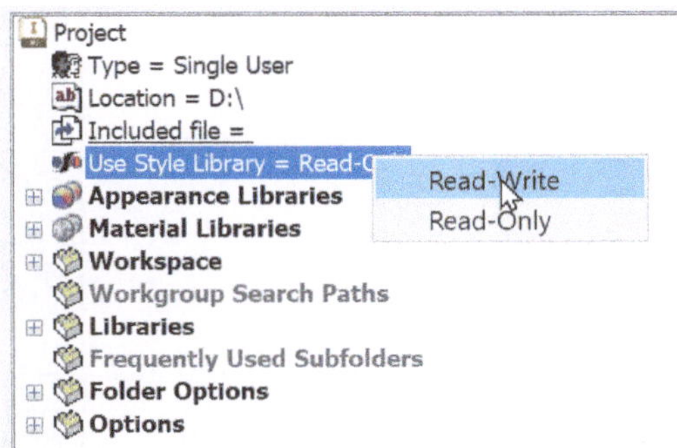

4. Click **Save** and **Done**.

Starting a New Drawing File

1. On the **Home** screen, click **New**. On the **Create New File** dialog, click **Templates > en-US > Metric**.
2. Scroll to the **Drawing – Create an annotated document** section and select the **ISO.dwg** template. Next, click **Create** to start a new drawing file.

Editing the Title Block and Borders

1. In the **Model** window, expand the **Sheet 1** node, click the right mouse button on **Default Border**, and then select **Delete**.
2. Right click on the **ISO** title block, and then select **Delete**.

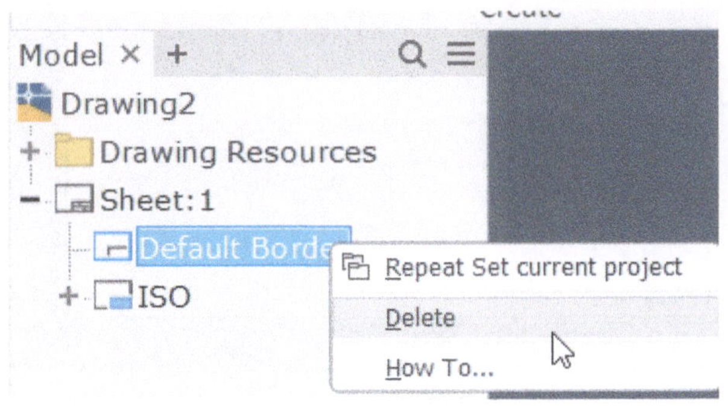

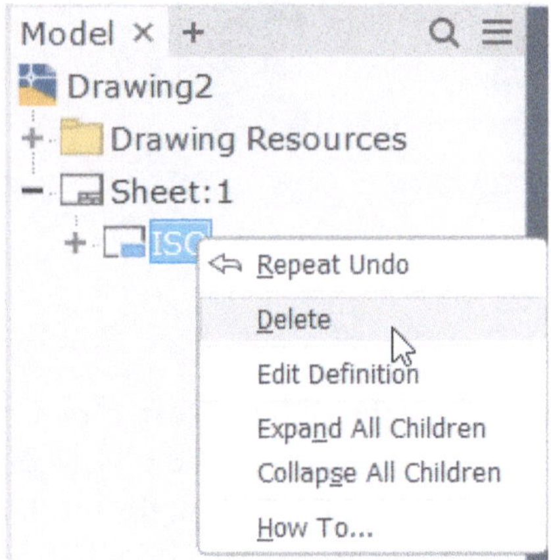

3. In the **Model** window, expand the **Drawing Resources** folder, click the right mouse button on the **Borders** sub-folder, and then select **Define New Border**.
4. On the ribbon, click **Sketch > Create > Rectangle**, and then create a rectangle, as shown.

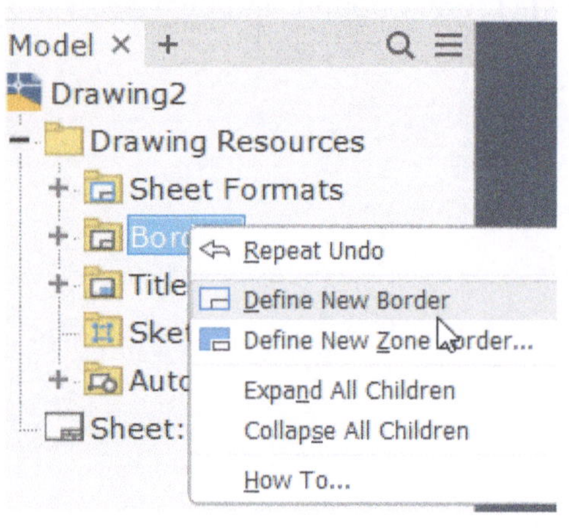

5. On the ribbon, click **Sketch > Constrain > Dimension**, and then select the left vertical line of the rectangle. Next, select the top left corner point of the sheet. Place the dimension, and then change its value to **5**.
6. Likewise, create dimensions between the remaining corner points and the rectangle, as shown.

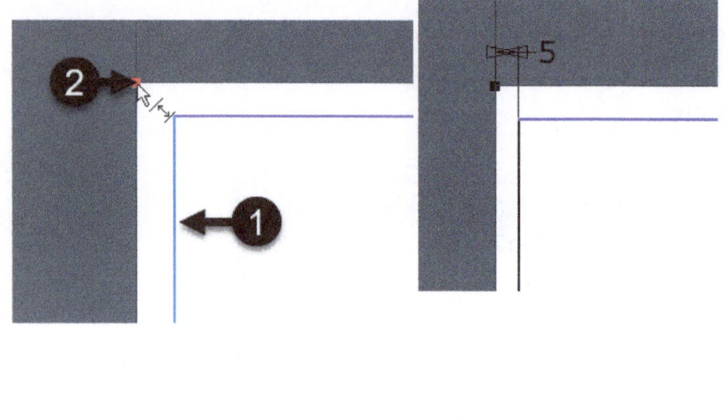

7. Click **Finish Sketch** on the ribbon. Next, type **Custom Border**, and then click **Save**.
8. In the **Model** window, right click on the **Title Blocks** folder and select **Define New Title Block**.
9. Create the title block using the **Rectangle** and **Line** commands, as shown.

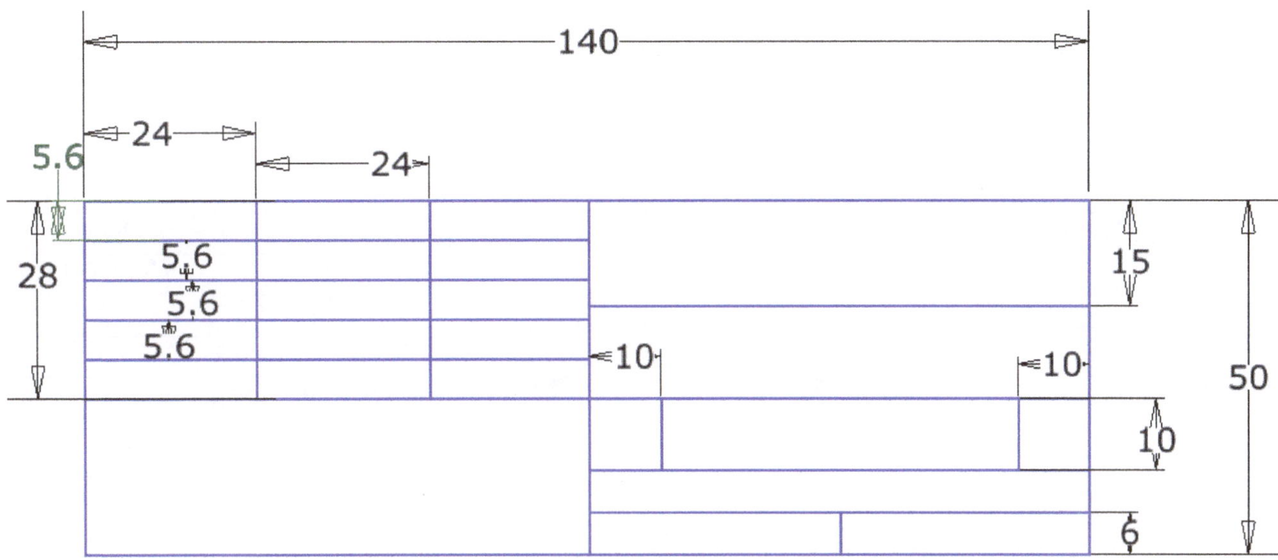

10. On the ribbon, click **Sketch > Create > Text**, and then click in the box, as shown.
11. Specify the settings on the **Format Text** dialog, as shown. Next, type DRAWN in the text box, and then click **OK**.

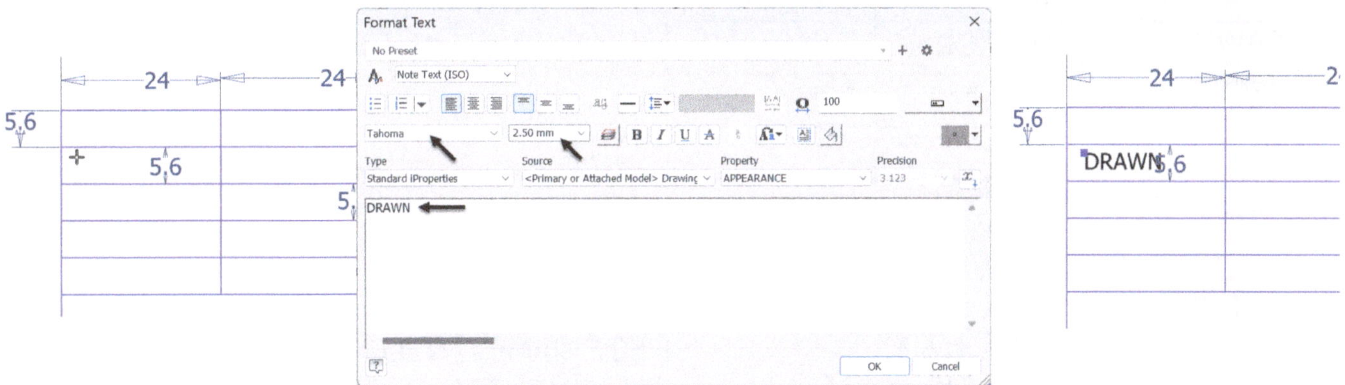

12. Likewise, insert text in other cells, as shown. You can also add **Constraints** to align them properly.

NAME
DATE
DRAWN
CHECKED
END APPR
MGR APPR
TITLE
10
10
UNLESS OTHERWISE SPECIFIED
DIMENSIONS ARE IN MILLIMETERS
ANGLES ± X.X°
2 PL ±X.XX 3 PL ±X.XX
SIZE
DWG NO.
REV
FILE NAME
SCALE

13. On the ribbon, click **Sketch > Create > Text** and then click in the box, as shown.
14. On the **Format Text** dialog, select **Standard iProperties** from the **Type** drop-down. Next, select **AUTHOR** from the **Property** drop-down.
15. Specify the **Font**, **Size**, and **Justification**, as shown. Next, click the **Add Text Parameter** icon, and then click **OK** to insert the text parameter.

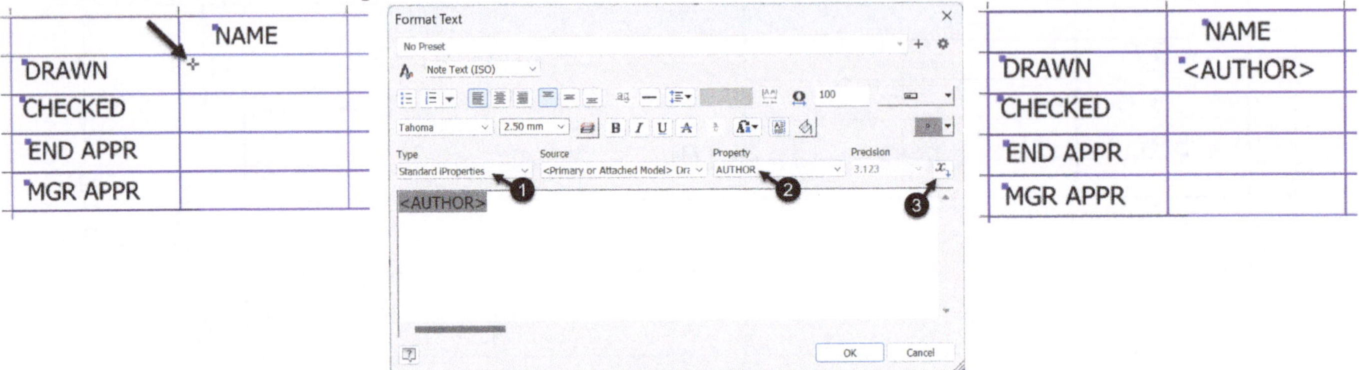

16. Likewise, insert other text parameters in the title block, as shown.

NAME DATE
DRAWN <AUTHOR>
CHECKED <CHECKED BY> <CHECKED DATE>
END APPR <ENG APPROVED BY>
MGR APPR <MANAGER>
<COMPANY>
TITLE
10 10
UNLESS OTHERWISE SPECIFIED
DIMENSIONS ARE IN MILLIMETERS
ANGLES + X.X°
2 PL +X.XX 3 PL +X.XX
SIZE <Sheet Size>
DWG NO. <Sheet Number>
REV <REVISION NUMBER>
FILE NAME <FILENAME>
SCALE <Initial View Scale>

17. Click **Finish Sketch** on the ribbon. Next, type **Custom Title Block**, and then click **Save**.
18. In the **Model** Window, expand the **Border** folder, right click on the **Custom Border**, and then select **Insert**.
19. Expand the **Title Block** folder, right click on the **Custom Title Block**, and then select **Insert**.

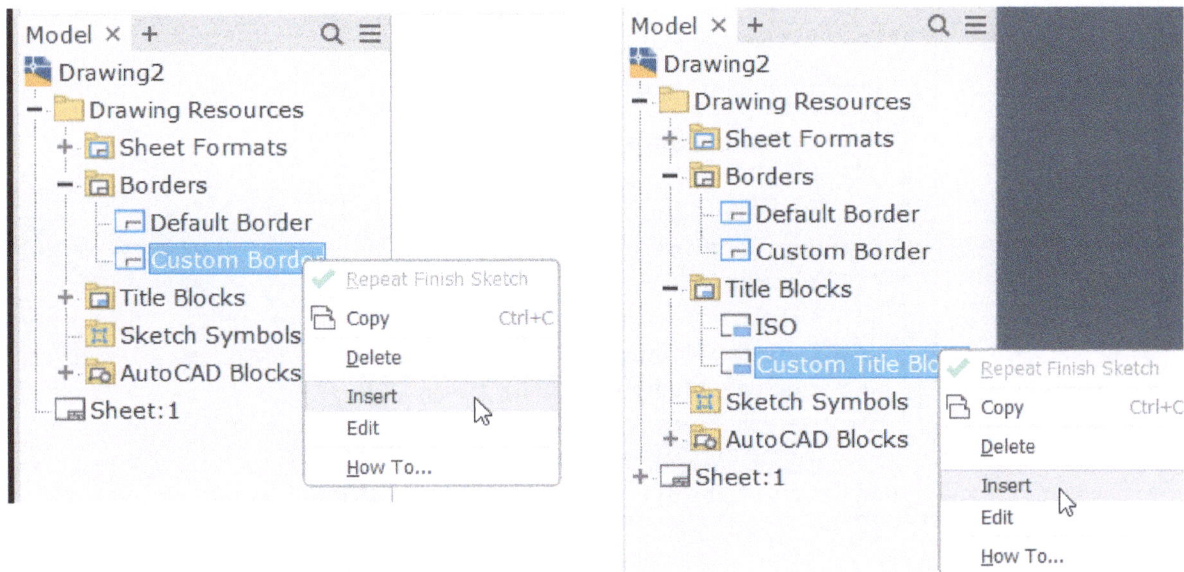

20. Right-click on **Sheet:1** and select **Edit Sheet**.
21. On the **Edit Sheet** dialog, click the **Size** drop-down and select the **A3** option. Click **OK** to close the dialog.

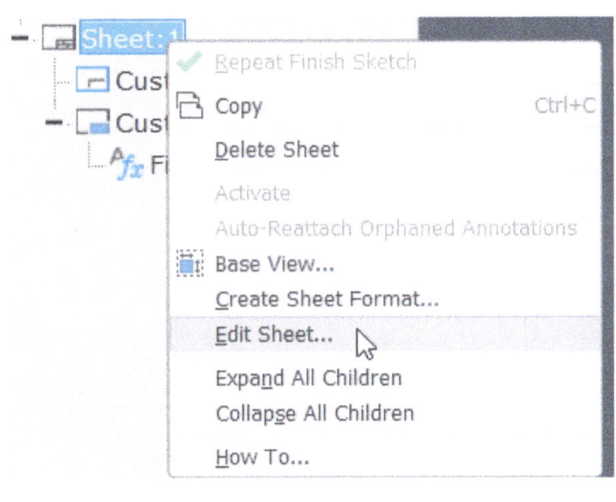

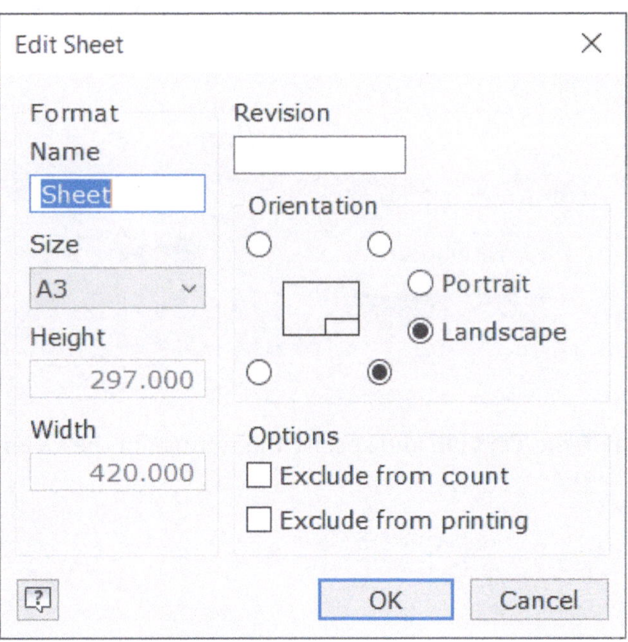

Editing the Styles and Standards

1. On the ribbon, click **Manage > Styles and Standards > Styles Editor**. On the **Style and Standard Editor** dialog, select **Dimension > Default (ISO)**.

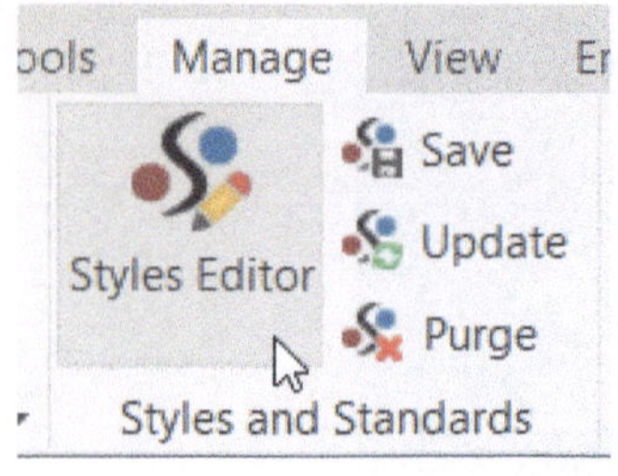

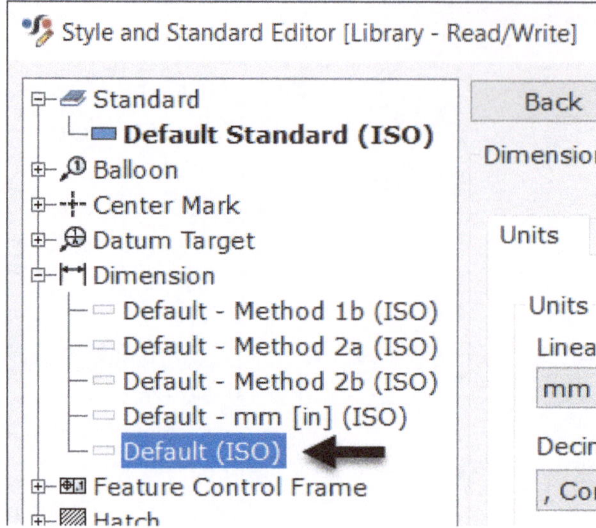

2. Click the **New** button located at the top of the dialog. Type-in **Custom Standard** in the **New Local Style** dialog, and then click **OK**.
3. Click the **Units** tab and set **Precision** to **0** in the **Linear** section. Select **Decimal Marker > . Period**.

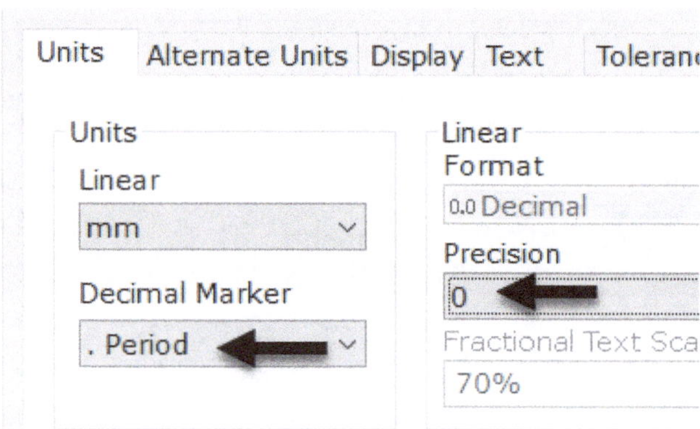

4. Click the **Text** tab and specify the settings in the **Orientation** section, as shown.

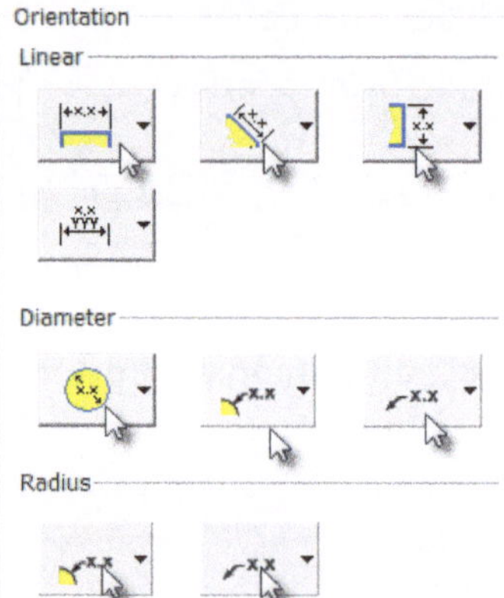

5. Click the **Notes and Leaders** tab and select the **Hole Note Settings** option. Under the **General Settings** section, select **Leader Text Orientation > Horizontal**. Next, select **Leader Text Alignment > First Line Centered**.

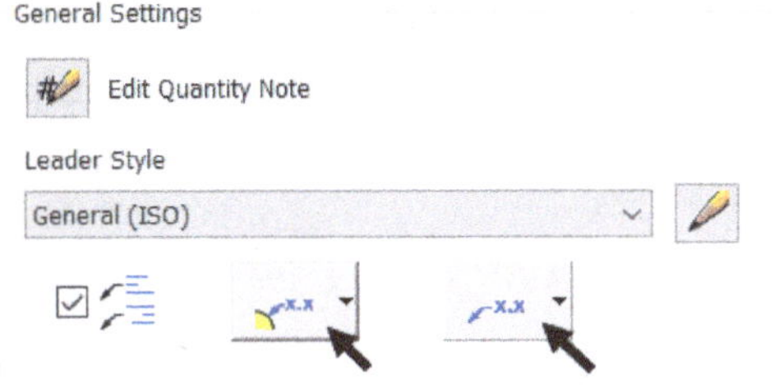

6. Click the **Save** button located at the top.
7. Select **Standard > Default Standard (ISO)**, and then click the **New** button. Type **Custom Standard** in the **New Local Style** dialog, and then click **OK**.
8. Click the **View Preferences** tab and select **Third Angle** from the **Projection Type** section.
9. Click the **Object Defaults** tab and click the **Edit Object Defaults Style** icon.
10. Select the **Dimension Objects** from the **Filter** drop-down, and then change all the **Object Styles** to **Custom Standard**. Click the **Save** button located at the top.

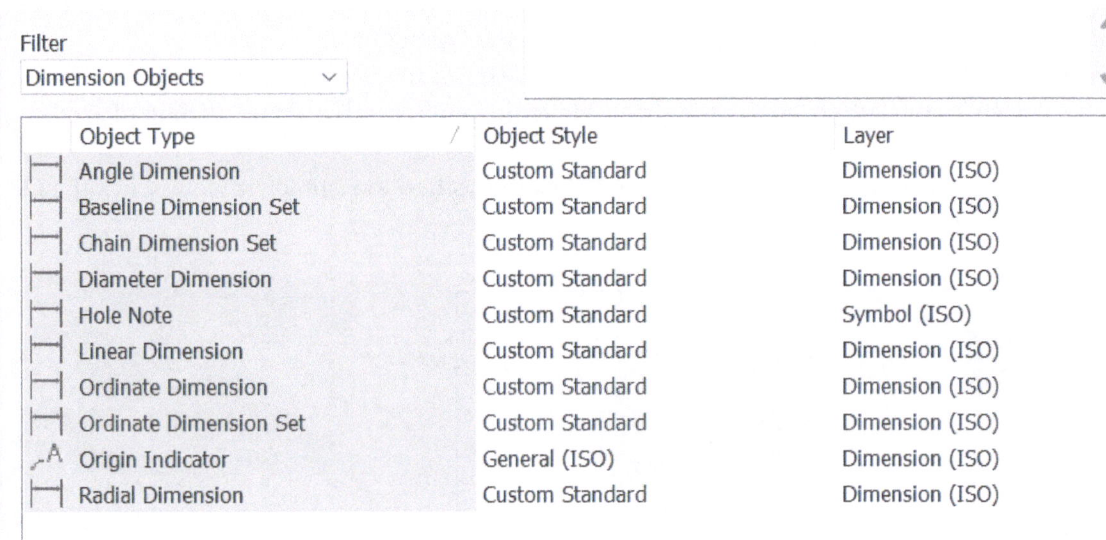
Filter
Dimension Objects

Object Type	Object Style	Layer
Angle Dimension	Custom Standard	Dimension (ISO)
Baseline Dimension Set	Custom Standard	Dimension (ISO)
Chain Dimension Set	Custom Standard	Dimension (ISO)
Diameter Dimension	Custom Standard	Dimension (ISO)
Hole Note	Custom Standard	Symbol (ISO)
Linear Dimension	Custom Standard	Dimension (ISO)
Ordinate Dimension	Custom Standard	Dimension (ISO)
Ordinate Dimension Set	Custom Standard	Dimension (ISO)
Origin Indicator	General (ISO)	Dimension (ISO)
Radial Dimension	Custom Standard	Dimension (ISO)

11. Click **Save and Close** on the dialog.
12. On the ribbon, click **Manage > Styles and Standards > Save**. Next, click **Yes to All**, and then click **OK** on the **Overwrite styles library information** dialog. Click **Yes**.
13. On the ribbon, click **Tools > Options > Document Settings**. Next, select **Active Standard > Custom Standard**, and then click **OK**.
14. On the ribbon, click **File Menu > Save As > Save Copy As Template**. Next, type **Custom Standard** in the **File name** box and click **Save**.
15. Close the drawing file.
16. On the **Home** screen, click the **Projects and Settings** button next to the **Projects** drop-down and select the **Settings** option. On the **Projects** dialog, select the **Autodesk Inventor 2026 For Beginners** project from the **Project** list.
17. On the **Project** dialog, under the lower section, right click on the **Use Style Library** option, and then select **Read Only**.
18. Click **Save** and **Done**.

Starting a New File using Custom Template

1. On the **File Menu**, click the **New** icon to open the **Create New File** dialog. On this dialog, click the **Templates > en-US** folder and select **Custom Standard.dwg**. Click **Create** to start a new drawing file.

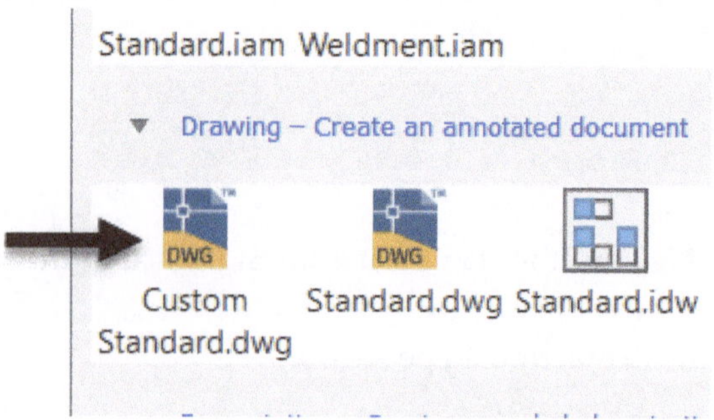

2. Activate the **Base** command (click **Place Views > Create > Base** on the ribbon). On the **Drawing View** dialog, click the **Open existing file** icon next to the **File** drop-down.
3. Browse to the location of **Example 1** of **Drawings** chapter and click on the part file (you can get the part files by sending us an email to online.books999@gmail.com). Click the **Open** button.
4. On the **Drawing View** dialog, set the **Style** to **Hidden Line**. Next, set the **Scale** to **1:1**.
5. Click and drag the view to the left portion of the sheet. Move the pointer upward and click to place the projected view.
6. Move the pointer diagonally to the top right corner and click to position the isometric view. Click the **OK** button to close the dialog.

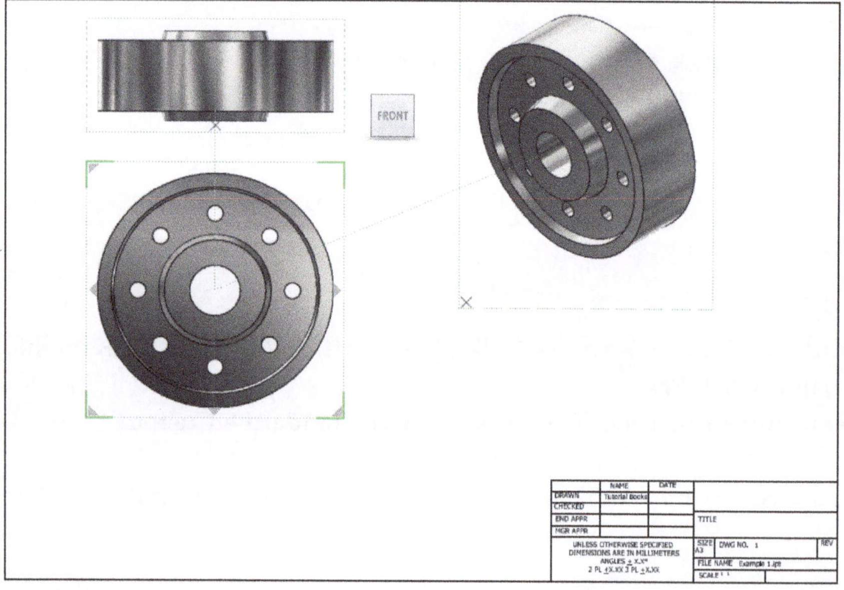

7. Right click on the isometric view and select **Edit View**. On the **Drawing View** dialog, type-in **0.75** in the **Scale** box and press Enter.
8. Click and drag the isometric view to the top right corner of the drawing sheet.

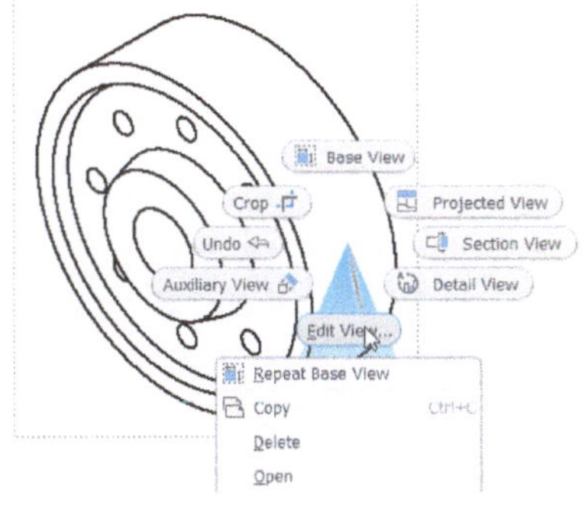

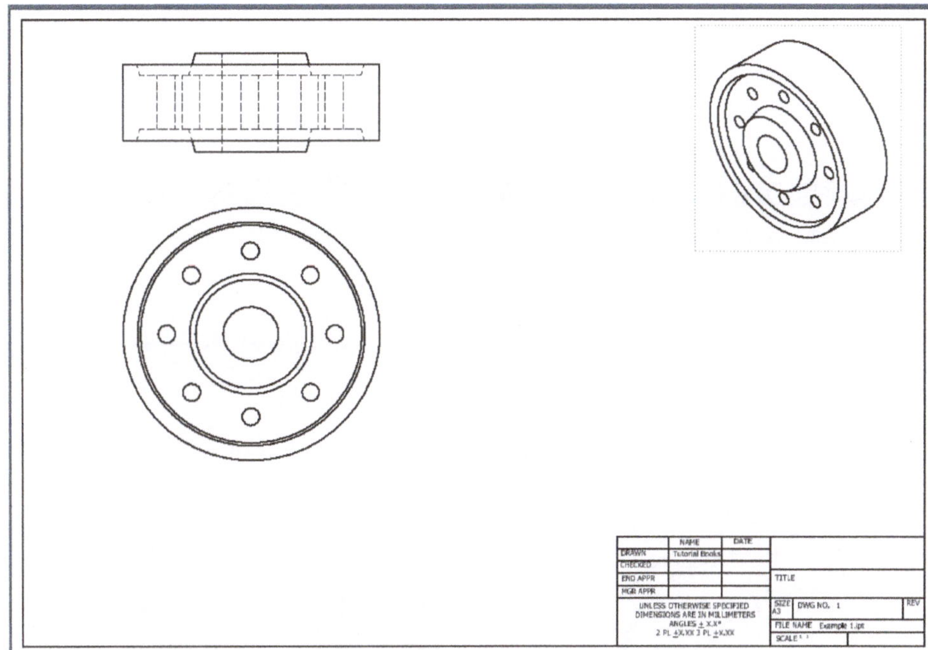

9. Activate the **Section** command (click **Place Views > Create > Section** on the ribbon) and select the front view. Create a cutting plane passing through the center of the front view.

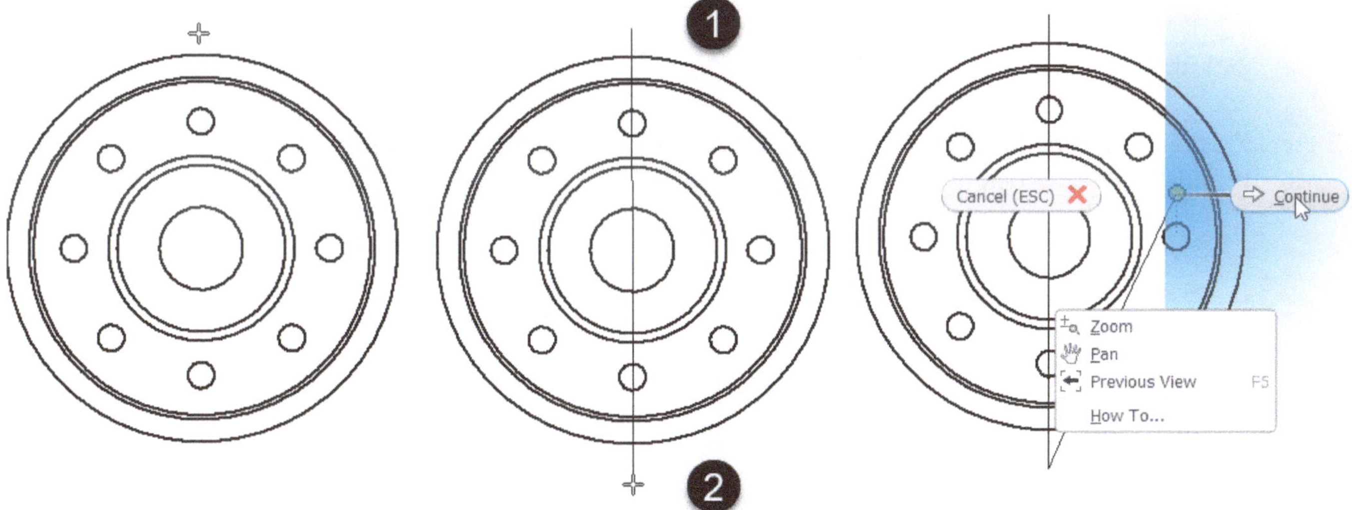

10. On the **Section View** dialog, click the **Hidden Line Removed** icon under the **Style** section.

11. Click the **Edit View Label** icon. On the **Format Text** dialog, delete the three properties using the DELETE key, as shown. Also, delete the slash (/) and click **OK**.

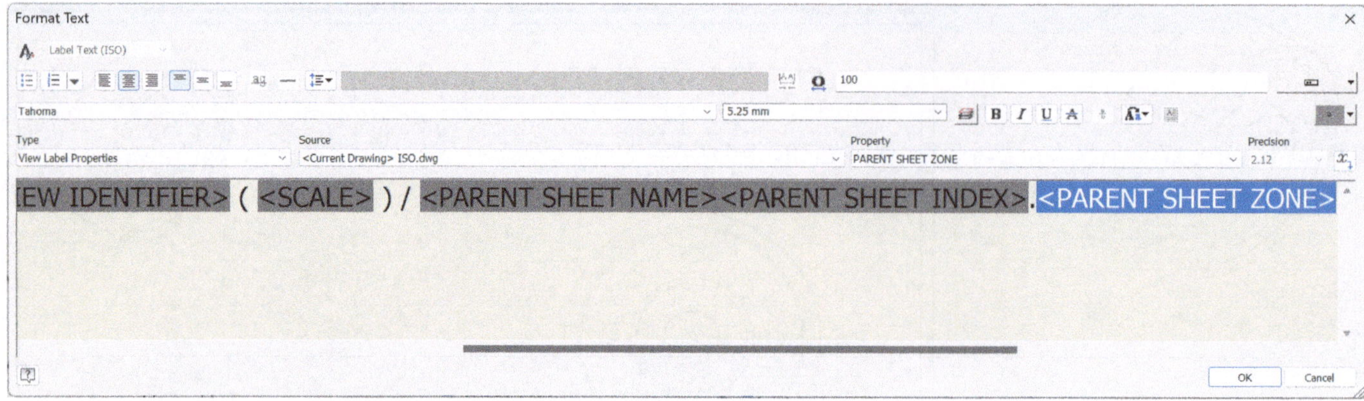

12. Move the mouse pointer toward the right and click to position the view.

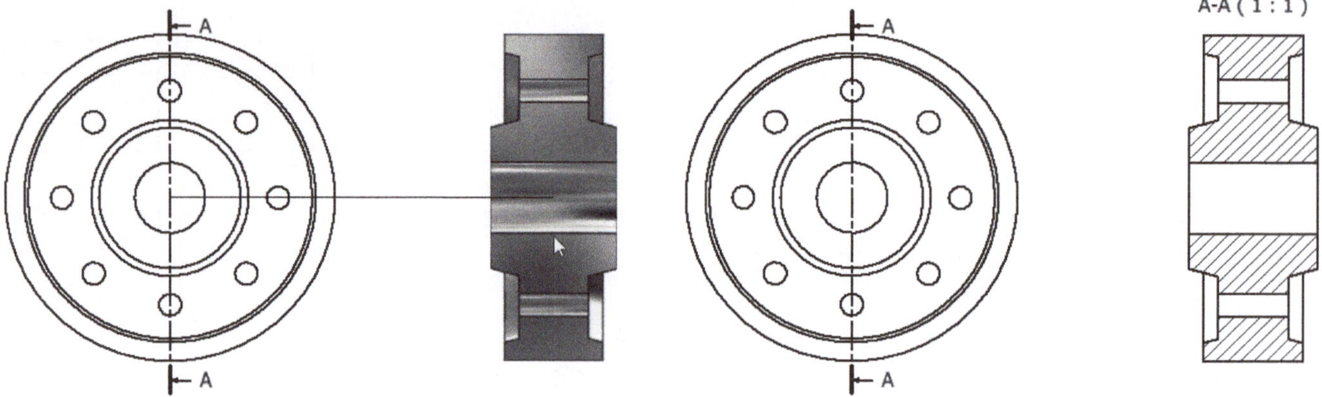

13. Activate the **Centerline Bisector** command (click **Annotate > Symbols > Centerline Bisector** on the ribbon). Click on the hidden hole edges of the top view.

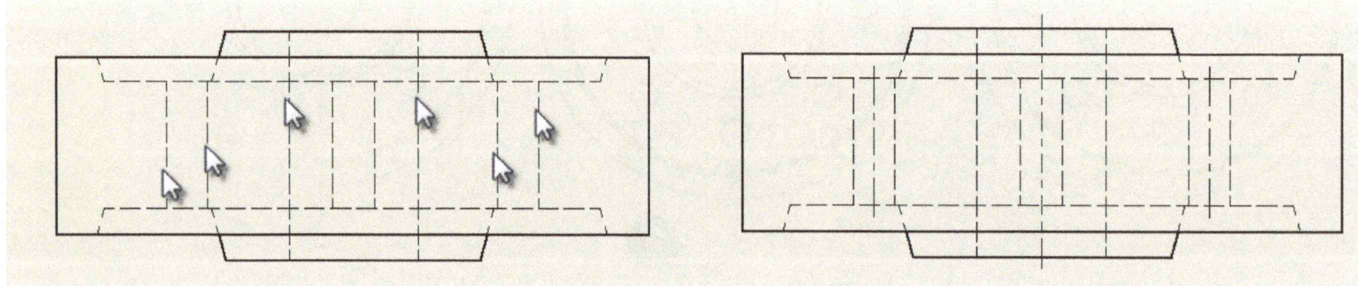

14. Activate the **Centerline** command (click **Annotate > Symbols > Centerline** on the ribbon).
15. Select the midpoints of the two edges on the section view, as shown. Right click and select **Create**; a centreline is created between the two selected points.

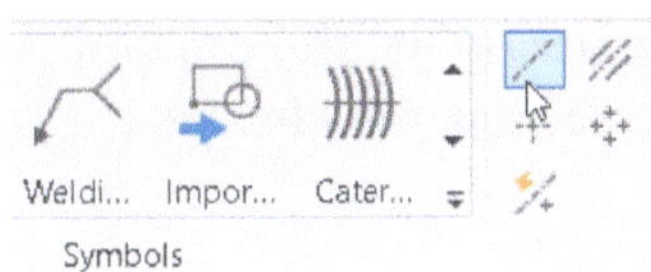

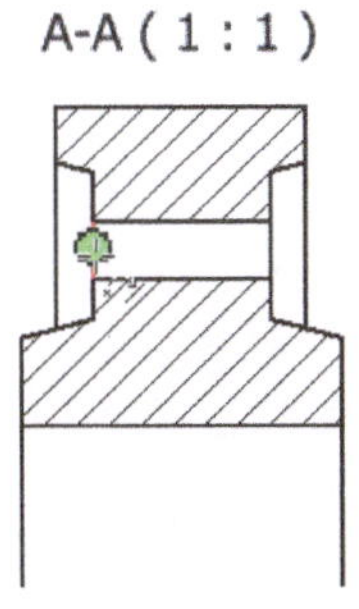

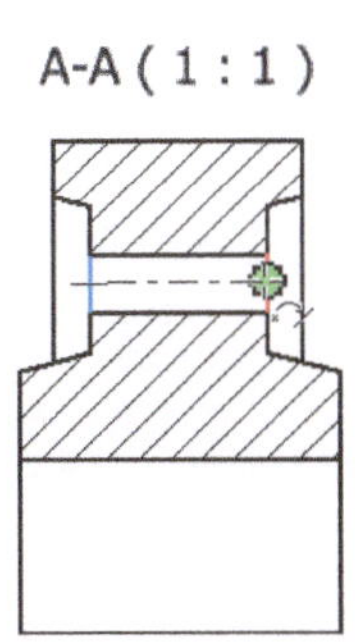

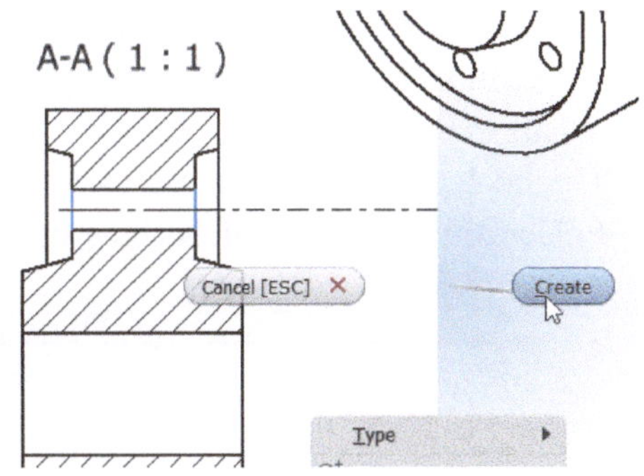

16. Likewise, create two more centerlines, as shown.

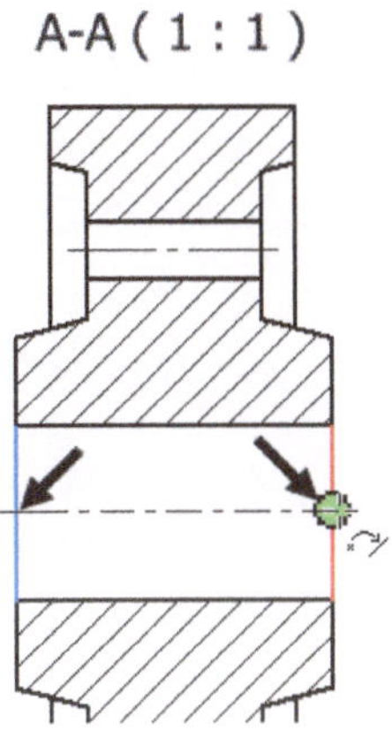

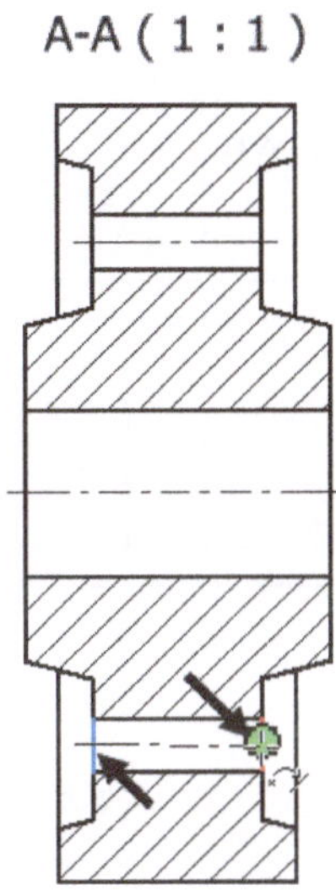

17. Activate the **Centered Pattern** command (click **Annotate > Symbols > Centered Pattern** on the ribbon) and click on the hole located at the center of the front view. Drag the mouse pointer and click on any one of the small holes; the start point of the bolt hole circle is defined.
18. Select the remaining small holes. Again, select the first small hole to complete the bolt hole circle. Right click and select **Create**.

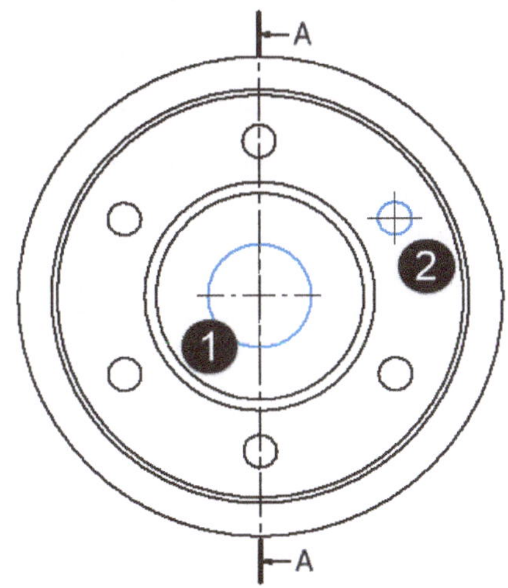

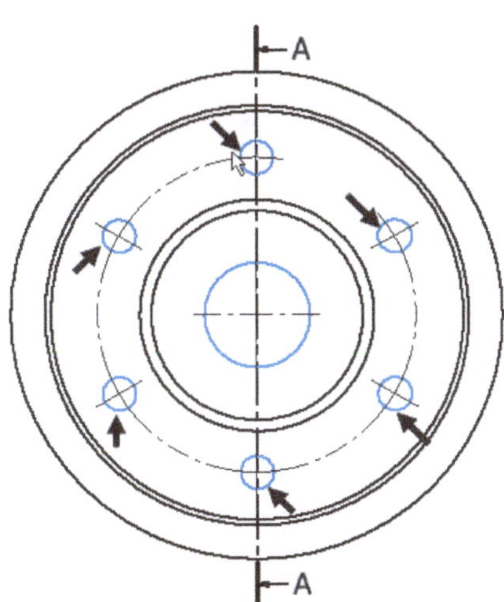

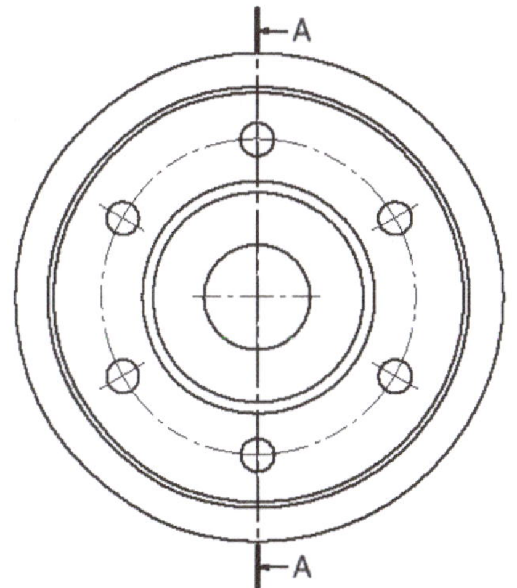

19. Activate the **General Dimension** command (click **Annotate > Dimension > Dimension** on the ribbon) and select the left vertical edge of the top view, a shown. Next, move the pointer toward the left and click to position the dimension.
20. Uncheck the **Edit dimension when created** option and click **OK**.
21. Select the two horizontal edges, as shown. Next, move the pointer and click to place the dimension.

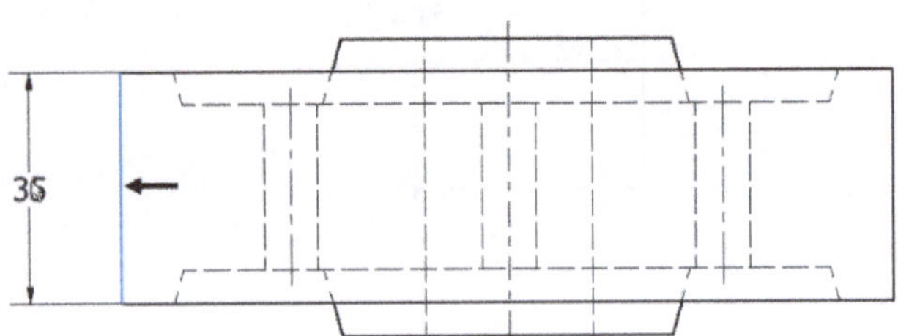

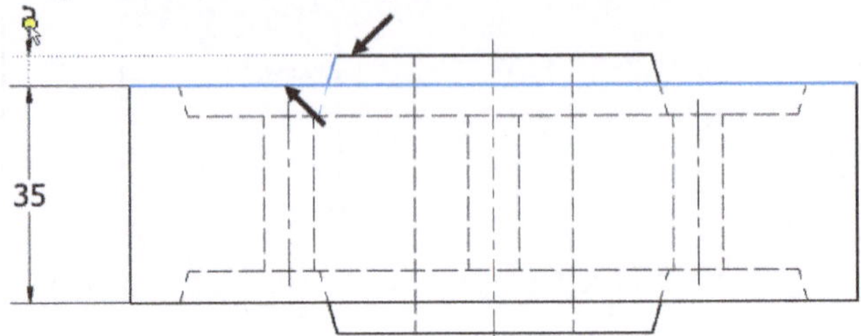

22. Likewise, create another dimension, as shown.

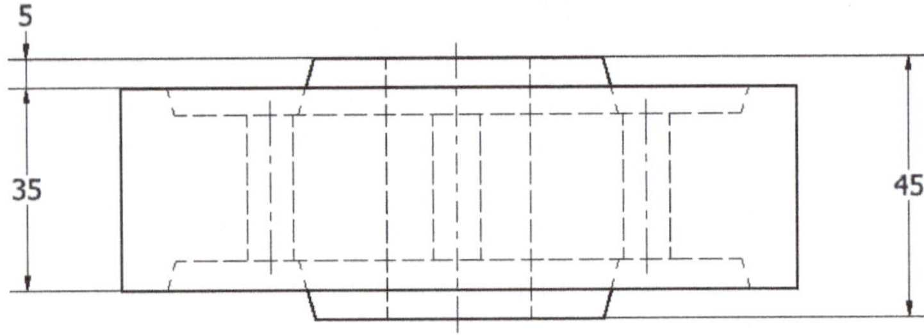

Retrieving Dimensions

Now, you will retrieve the dimensions that were applied to the model while creating it.

1. To retrieve dimensions, click **Annotate > Retrieve > Retrieve Model Annotations** on the ribbon.
2. Select the section view from the drawing sheet.

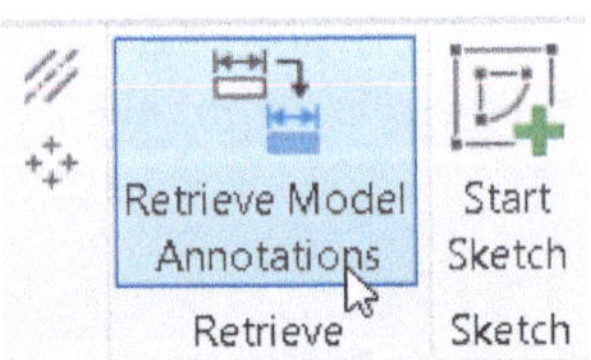

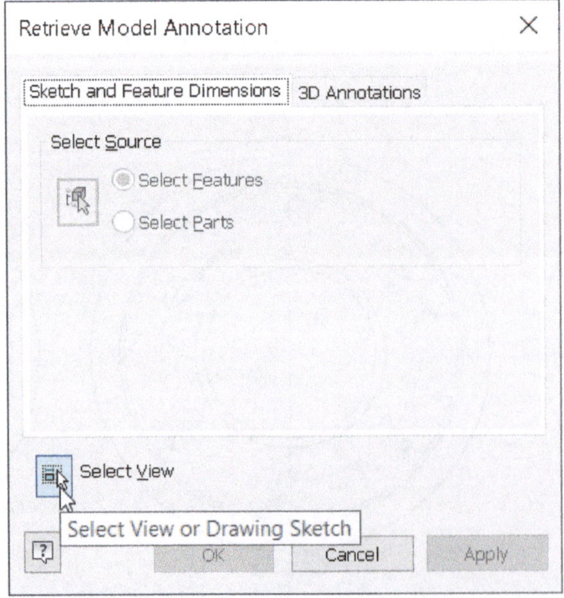

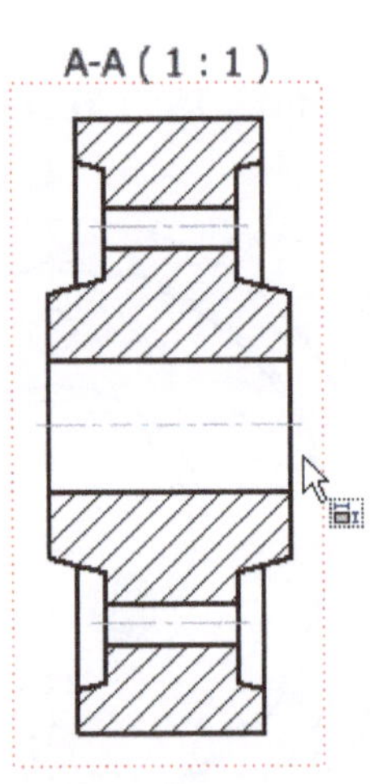

Now, you must select the dimensions to retrieve.

3. Select the dimensions of the section view and click **OK** on the **Retrieve Model Annotation** dialog.

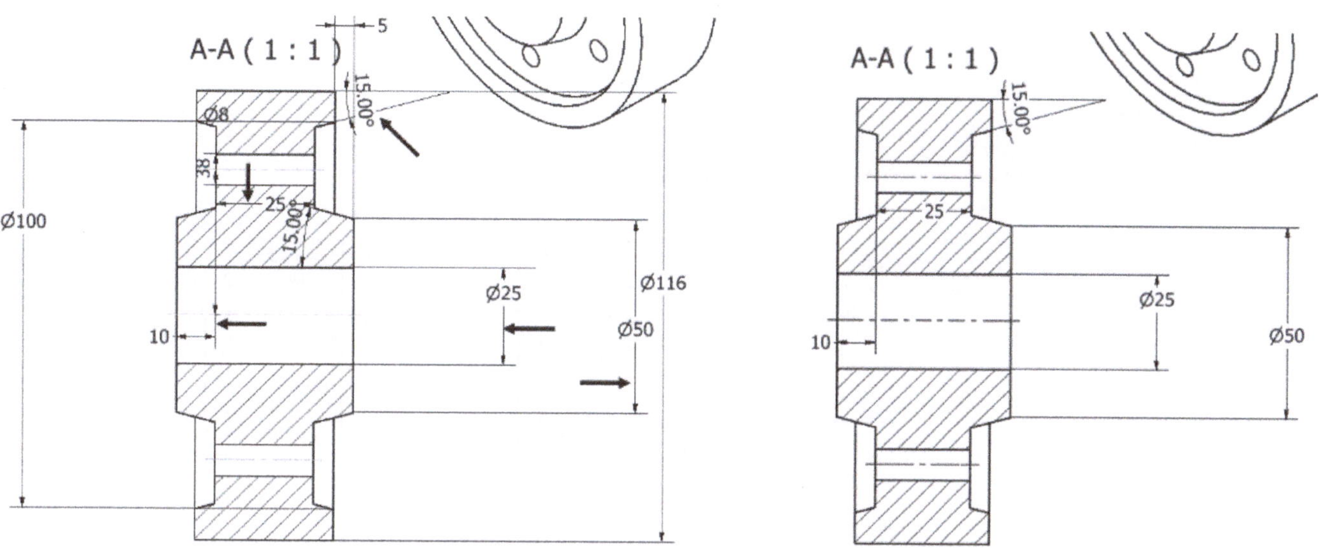

4. Click **Annotate > Dimension > Arrange** on the ribbon. Select the dimensions of the section view and press Enter.

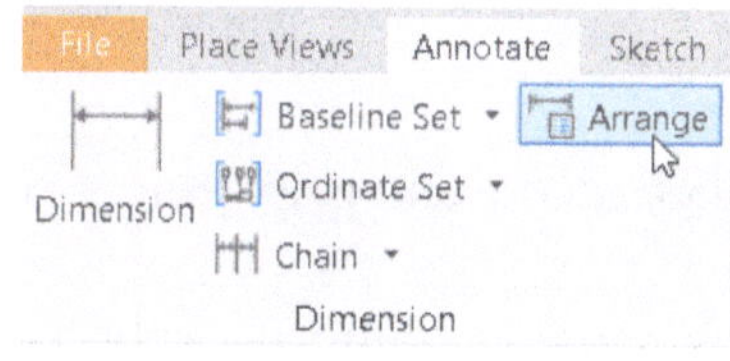

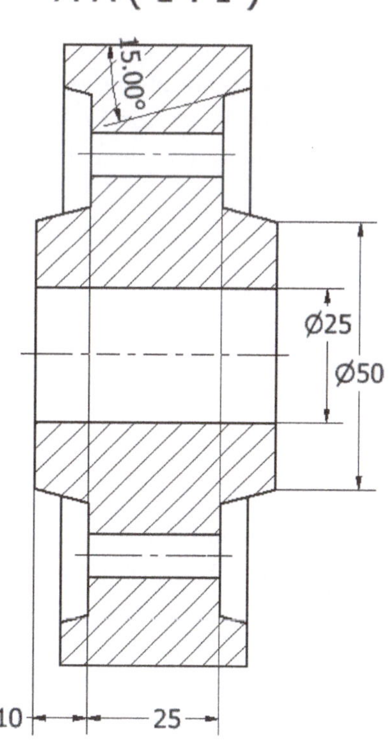

5. Drag the label of the section view and place it at the bottom.

6. Drag the dimensions one-by-one to arrange them correctly.

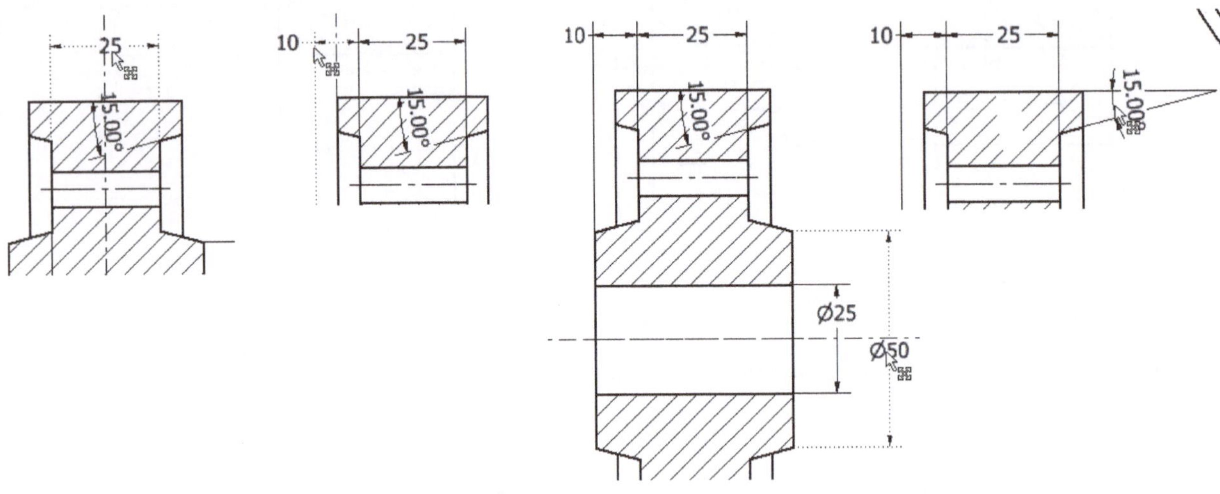

7. Select the angular dimension of the section view; the grips are displayed. Click on the end grip, drag it, and then release it on the corner point of the section view, as shown.
8. Double click on the angular dimension to display the **Edit Dimension** dialog. On this dialog, click the **Text** tab and type SPACE Bar on your keyboard. Next, type TYP in the text box, and then click **OK.**

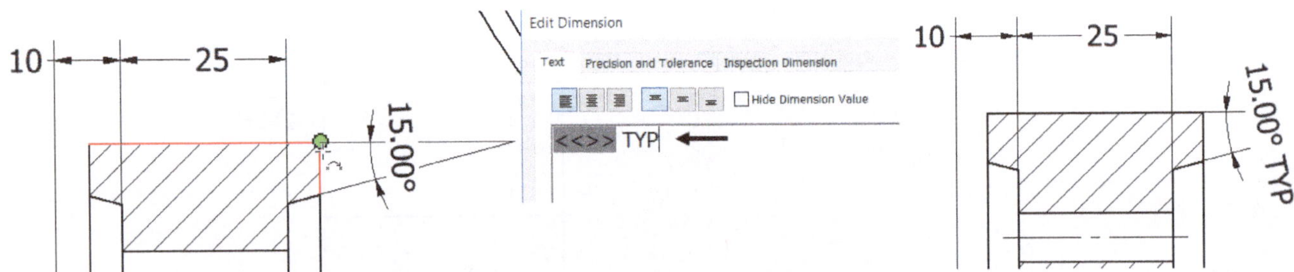

9. Activate the **Hole/Thread Notes** command (on the ribbon, click **Annotate > Feature Notes >Hole and Thread)** and click on the small hole of the front view.
10. Move the pointer diagonally and click to place the hole note. Right click and select the **OK**.
11. Double click on the hole note to display the **Edit Hole Note** dialog. On this dialog, click before the diameter symbol, and then click the **Quantity Note** icon.

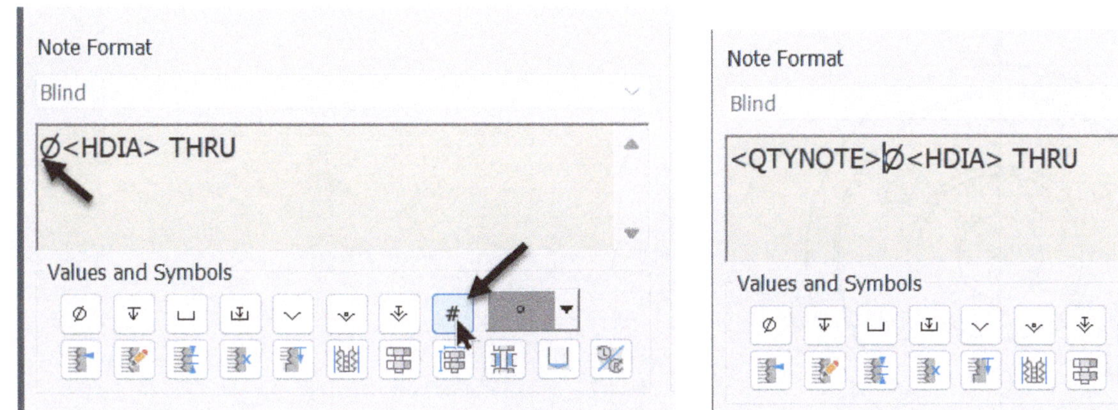

12. Click next to the THRU text, and then press ENTER. Next, type EQUISPACED ON, and then press ENTER.

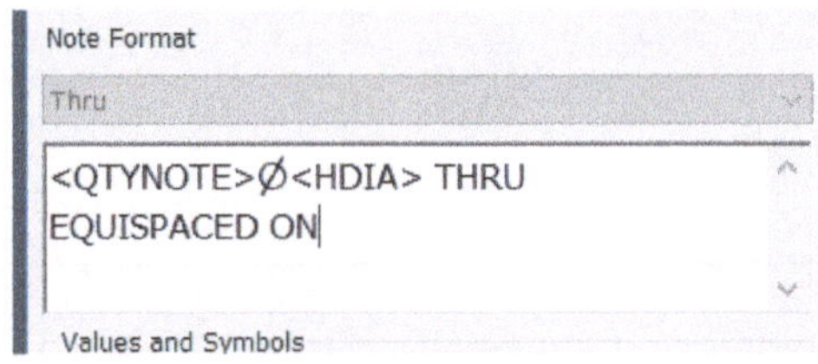

13. Type **75** and click the **Insert Symbol** drop-down. Next, select the **PD** (Pitch Diameter) option from the drop-down. Click **OK**.

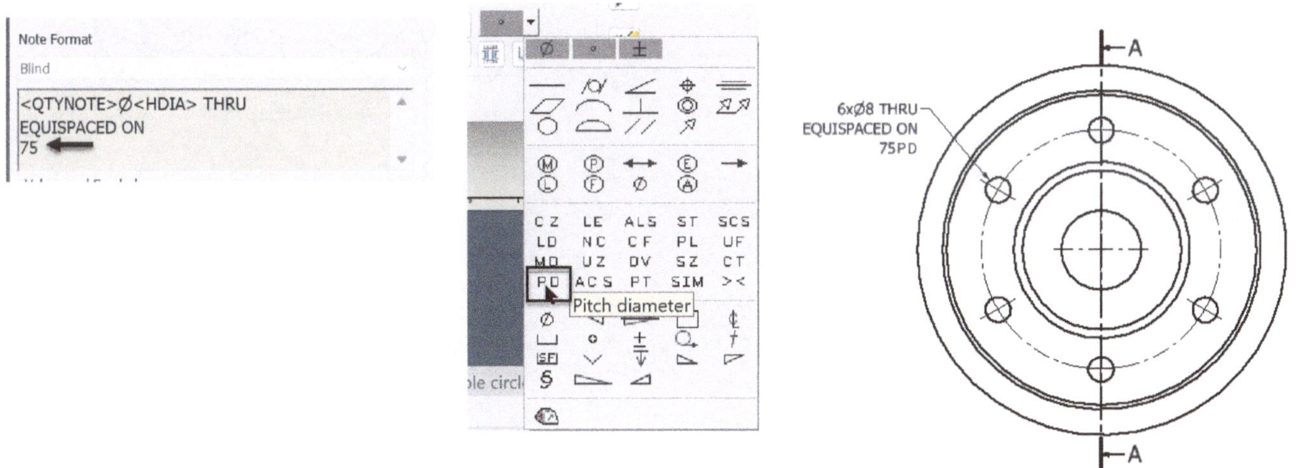

14. Create other dimensions in the drawing.

A
6xØ8 THRU
EQUISPACED ON
75P D
Ø100
Ø116
A

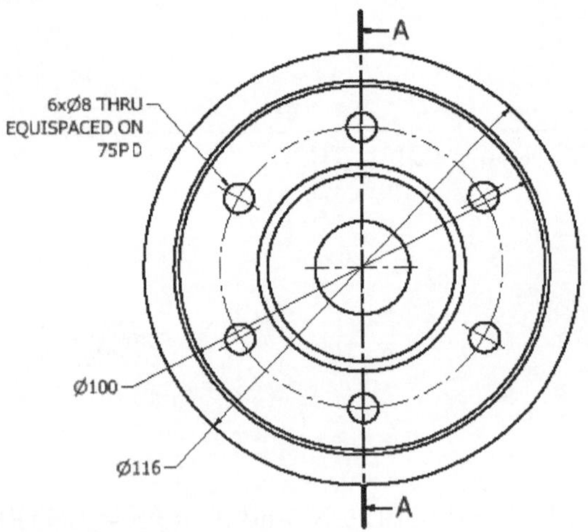

15. Save and close the drawing.

Example 2

In this example, you will create an assembly drawing shown below.

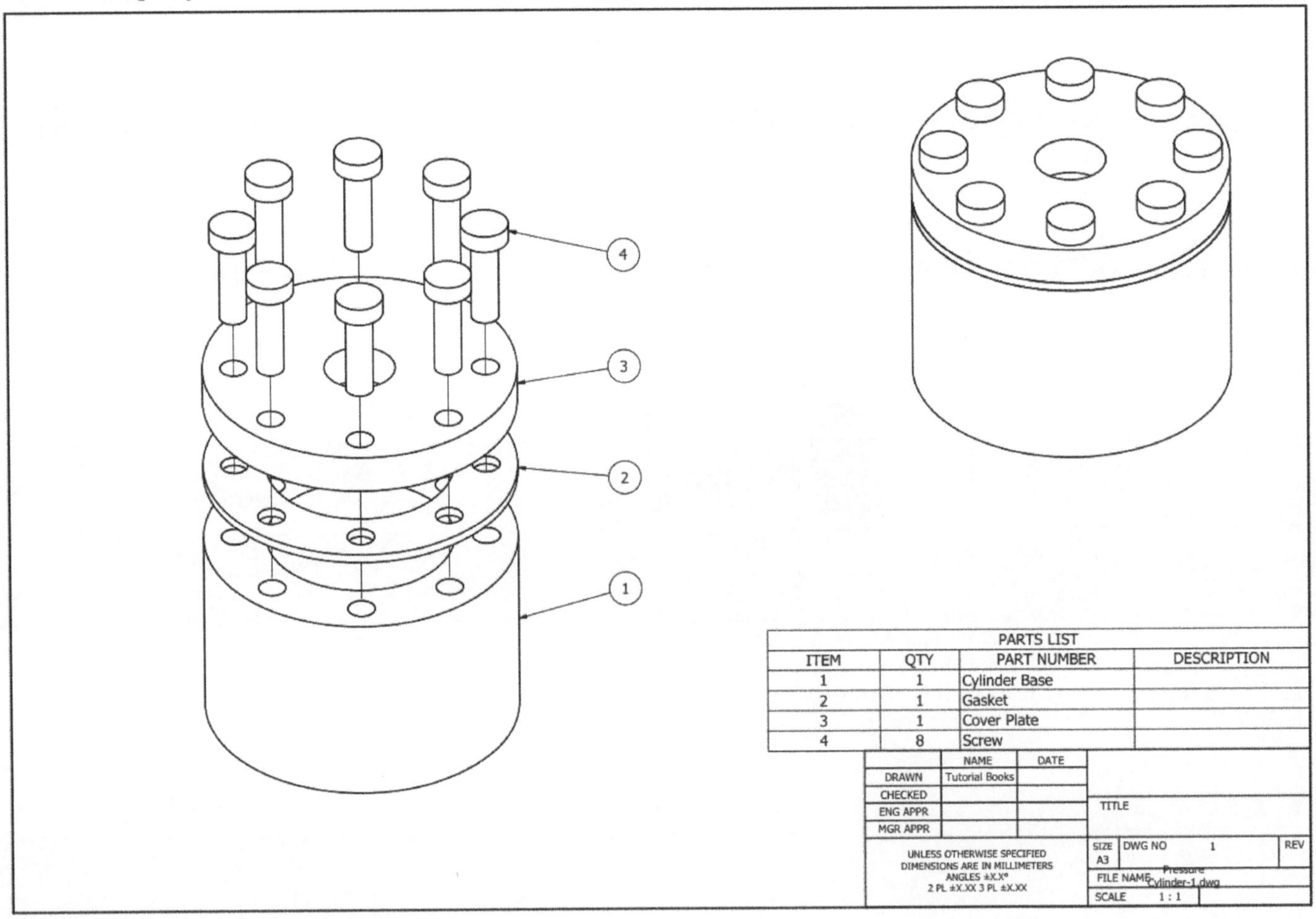

4
3
2
1
PARTS LIST
ITEM | QTY | PART NUMBER | DESCRIPTION
1 | 1 | Cylinder Base
2 | 1 | Gasket
3 | 1 | Cover Plate
4 | 8 | Screw
NAME
DATE
DRAWN
Tutorial Books
CHECKED
ENG APPR
MGR APPR
TITLE
UNLESS OTHERWISE SPECIFIED
DIMENSIONS ARE IN MILLIMETERS
ANGLES ±X.X°
2 PL ±X.XX 3 PL ±X.XX
SIZE
A3
DWG NO
1
REV
FILE NAME
Pressure Cylinder-1.dwg
SCALE
1 : 1

1. Start **Autodesk Inventor 2026.**
2. On the **Quick Access Toolbar**, click the **New** icon. On the **Create New File** dialog, double-click on the **Custom Standard.dwg** template, and then click **OK**.

3. Activate the **Base** command (click **Place Views > Create > Base** on the ribbon). Click the **Open an existing file** icon next to the **File** drop-down.
4. Browse to the location of **Example 3** of **Chapter 10** and click on the *Pressure Cylinder.iam* file. Click the **Open** button.
5. In the drawing sheet, click the **Home** icon displayed next to the ViewCube; the drawing view orientation is changed to Isometric.

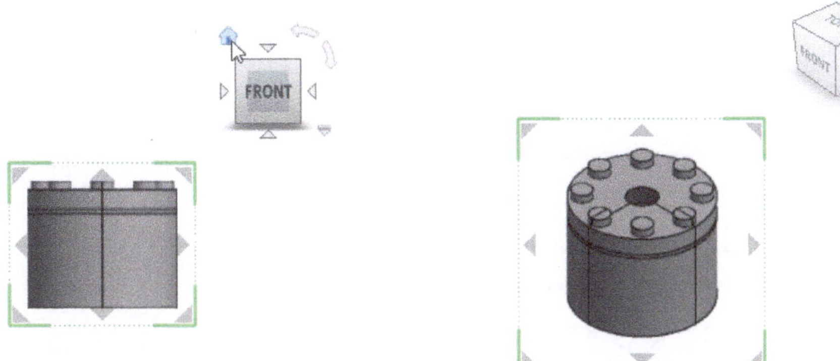

6. On the **Drawing View** dialog, select **Scale > 1:1**. Next, click and drag the drawing view to the top right corner of the drawing sheet. Click **OK** to create the Isometric view.

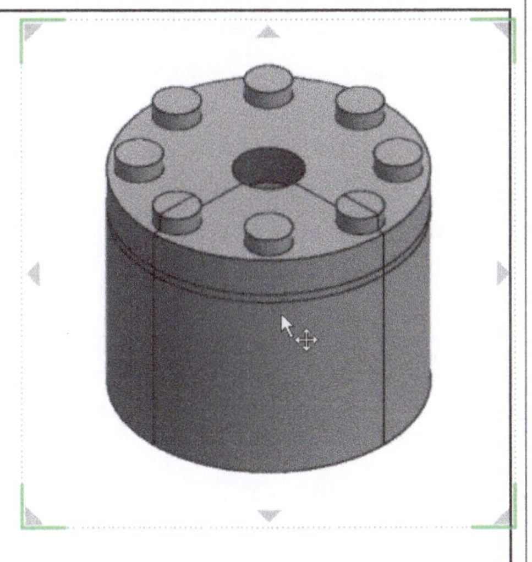

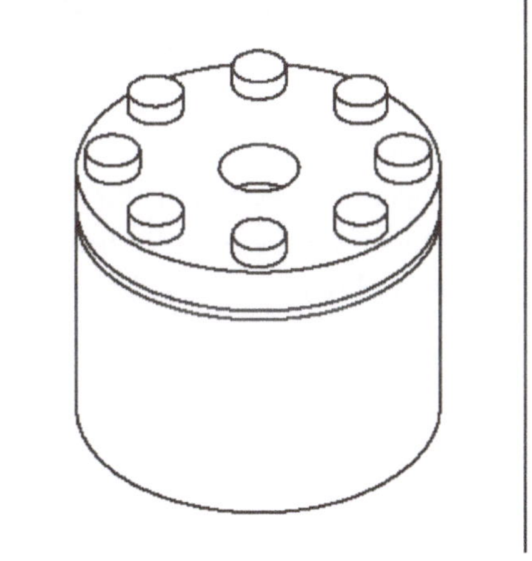

7. Again, activate the **Base** command. On the **Drawing View** dialog, click the **Open an existing file** icon and select the *Pressure Cylinder.ipn* file. Click **Open**.
8. On the **Drawing View** dialog, set the **Scale** to **1:1**. Position the exploded view at the location, as shown. Click **OK**.

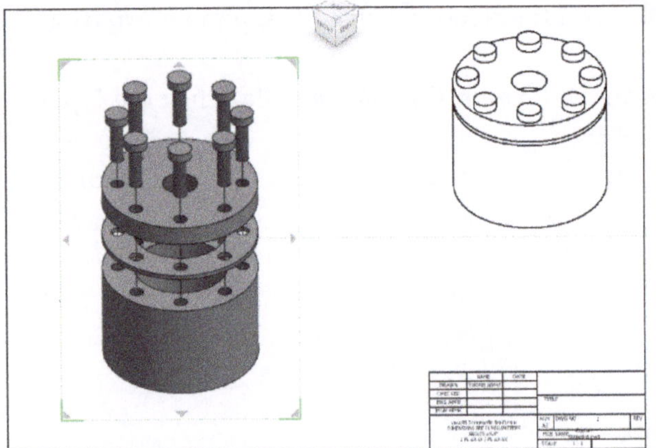

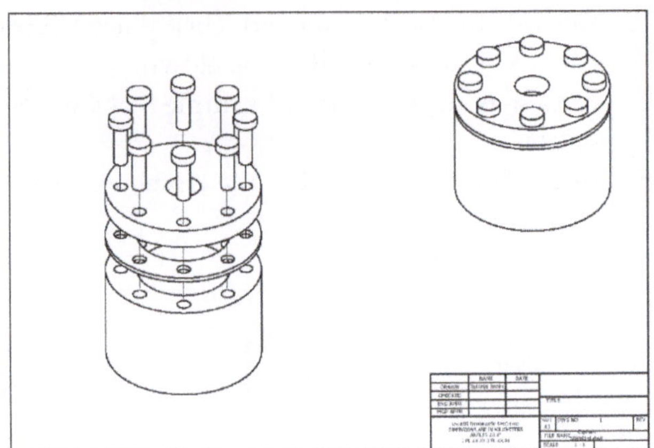

9. Activate the **Parts List** command (click **Annotate > Table > Parts List** on the ribbon) and click on the exploded view. Next, click **OK**. Place the parts list above the title block.

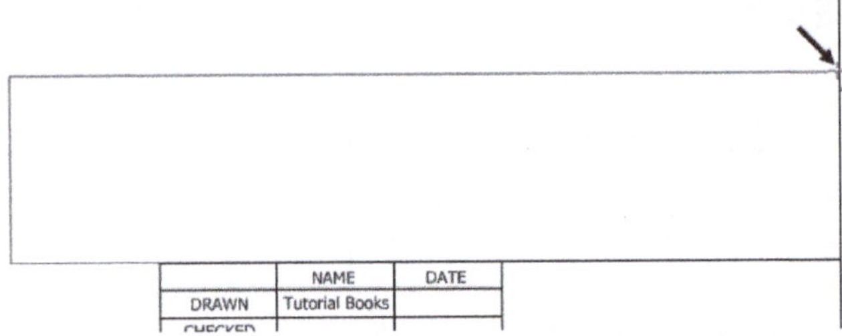

PARTS LIST			
ITEM	QTY	PART NUMBER	DESCRIPTION
1	1	Cylinder Base	
2	1	Gasket	
3	1	Cover Plate	
4	8	Screw	

10. On the ribbon, click **Annotate > Table > Balloon** drop-down **> Auto Balloon**.
11. Select the exploded view, and then drag a selection window across all the components of the view.
12. Select **Vertical** from the **Placement** section of the **Auto Balloon** dialog.
13. Click the **Select Placement** icon on the **Auto Balloon** dialog, and then specify the location of the balloons.
14. Type **25** in the **Offset Spacing** box, and then click **OK**.

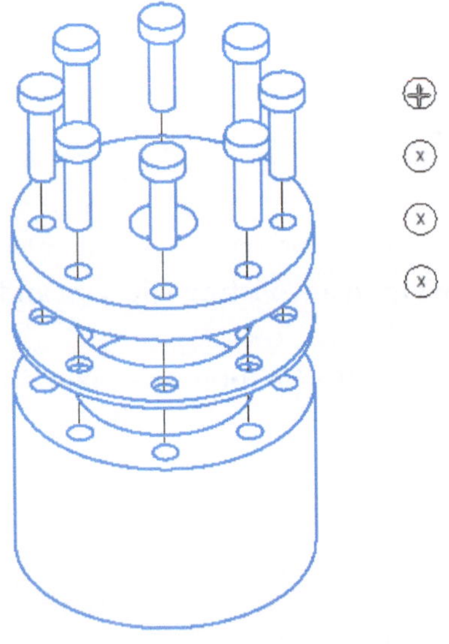

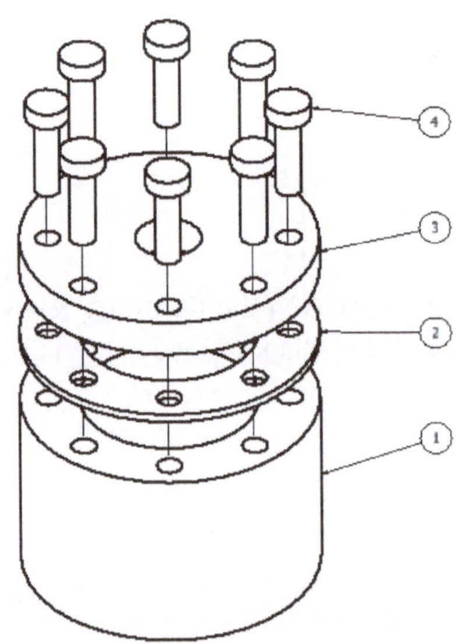

15. Save and close the drawing.

Questions

1. How to create drawing views from an existing part or assembly file?
2. How to change the display style of a drawing view?
3. List the commands used to create centerlines and center marks.
4. How to add symbols and texts to a dimension?
5. How to add break lines to a drawing view?
6. How to create revolved section views?
7. How to create an exploded view of an assembly?
8. How to change the origin of a baseline dimension set?
9. List the commands used to create hole tables.
10. List the types of section views that can be created using the **Section View** command.

Exercises

Exercise 1

Create orthographic views of the part model shown below. Add dimensions and annotations to the drawing.

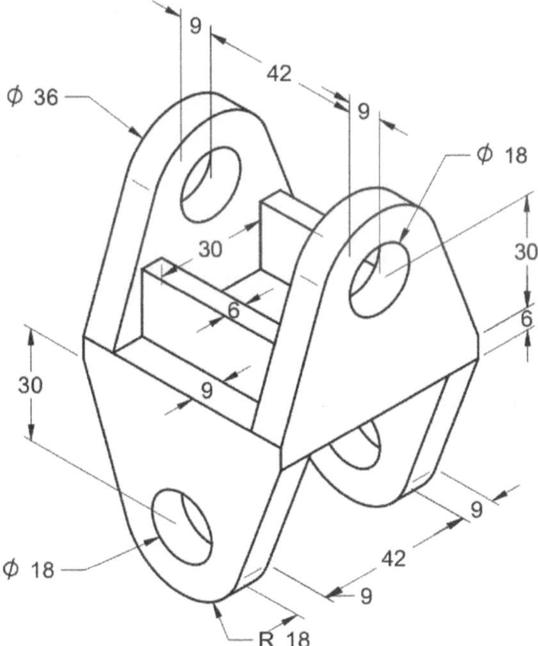

Exercise 2

Create orthographic views and an auxiliary view of the part model shown below. Add dimensions and annotations to the drawing.

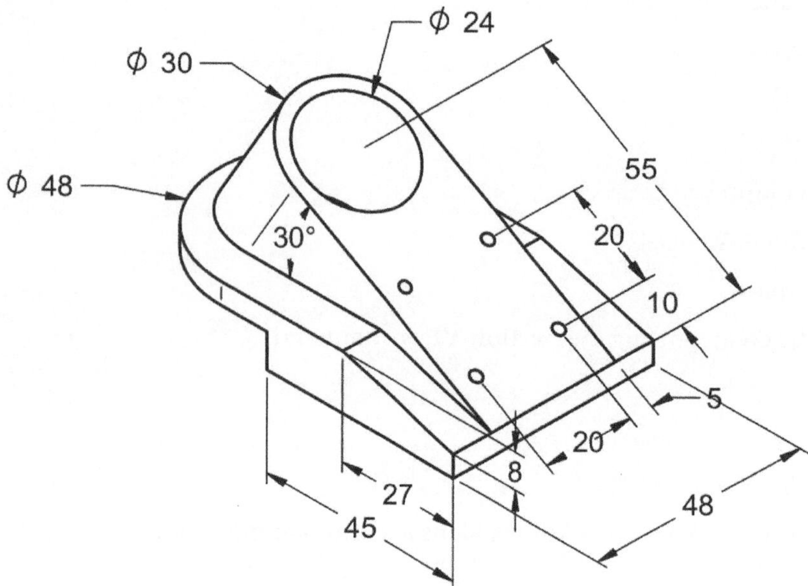

Chapter 12: Surface Design

The topics covered in this chapter are:

- *Extruded Surfaces*
- *Revolved surfaces*
- *Lofted surfaces*
- *Patch surfaces*
- *Swept surfaces*
- *Offset surfaces*
- *Stitch Surfaces*
- *Trim Surfaces*
- *Extend Surfaces*

Autodesk Inventor Surfacing commands can be used to create complex geometries that are very difficult to create using standard extruded features and revolve features. Surface modeling can also be used to edit and fix the broken imported parts. In this chapter, you learn the basics of surfacing commands that are mostly used. The surfacing commands are available in the **Surface** panel of the **3D Model** ribbon tab.

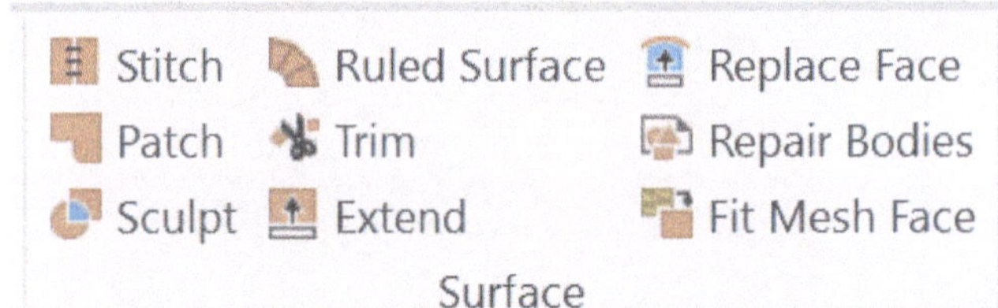

Autodesk Inventor offers a rich set of surface design commands. A surface is an infinitely thin piece of geometry. For example, consider a cube shown in the figure. It has six faces. Each of these faces is a surface, an infinitely thin piece of geometry that acts as a boundary in 3D space. Surfaces can be simple or complex shapes. The advantage of using the surfacing commands is that you can design a model with more flexibility.

Extruded Surface

To create an extruded surface, first, create an open or closed sketch and click **3D Model > Create > Extrude** on the ribbon. Next, type-in a value in the **Distance A** box. Activate the **Surface Mode** icon on the top right corner of the **Properties** panel and click **OK** to create the extruded surface. You will notice that the extrusion is not capped at the ends.

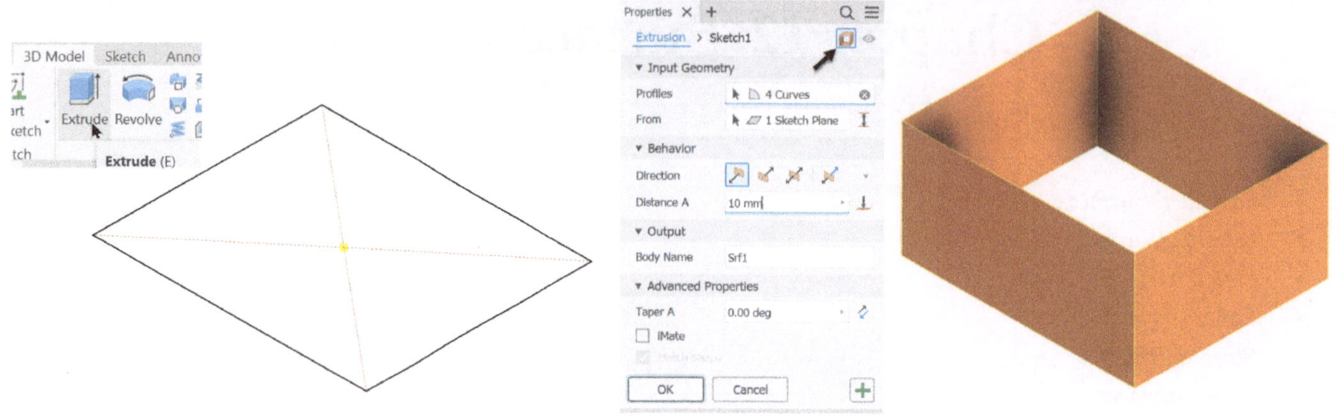

Revolved Surface

To create a revolved surface, first, create an open or closed section and the axis of revolution. Next, click **3D Model > Create > Revolve** on the ribbon. On the **Properties** panel, activate the **Surface Mode** icon located at the top-right corner. Type-in the angle of revolution in the **Angle** box and click **OK**.

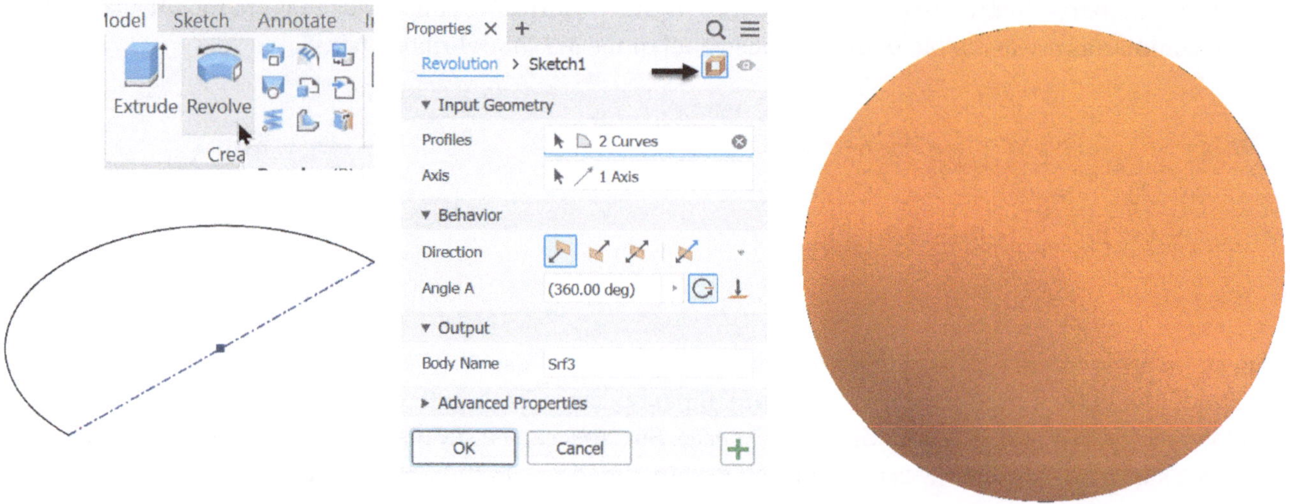

Even if you create an enclosed surface, Autodesk Inventor will not recognize it as a solid body. You can examine this by clicking the File tab, and then selecting the **iProperties** option. On the **iProperties** dialog, click the **Physical** tab and click the **Update** button. Notice that the **Mass** and **Volume** values are displayed as zero. It means that there exists no solid body. You will learn to convert a surface body into a solid later in this chapter.

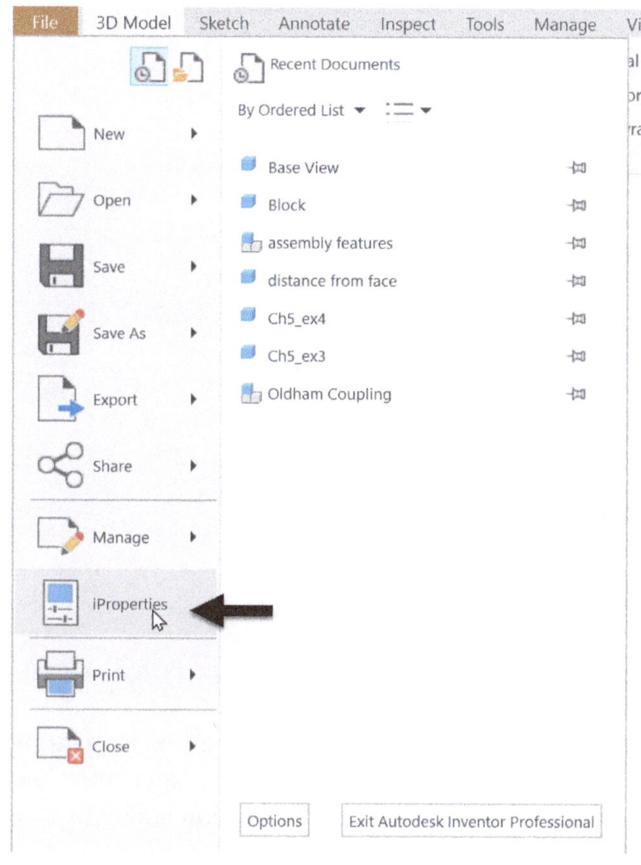

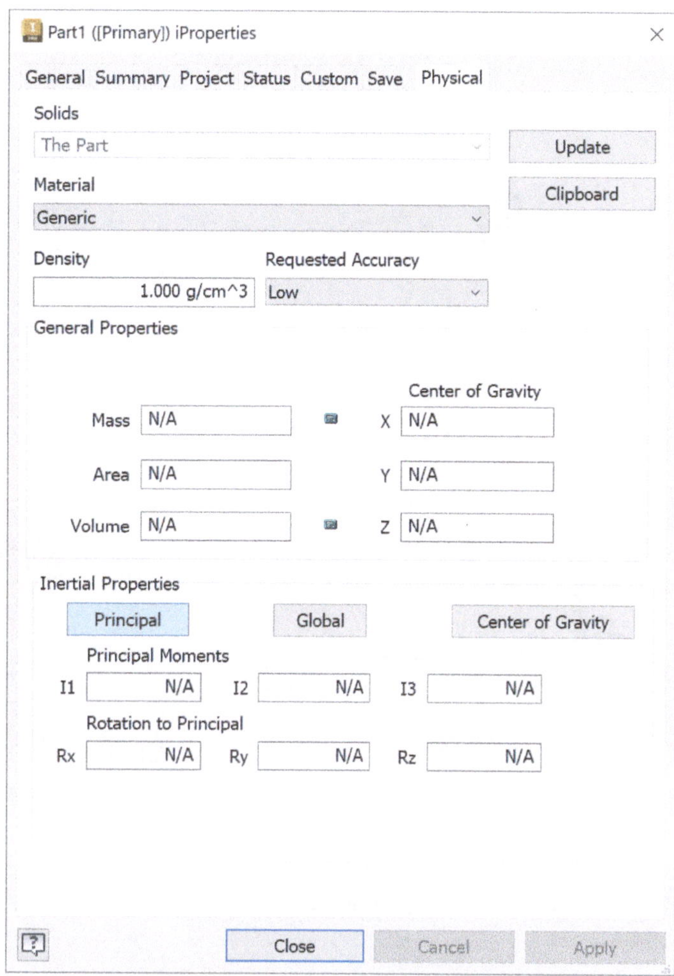

Loft

This command creates a solid or surface body through multiple sections. The shape of the geometry adjusts automatically to pass through the sections. First, create a section on different planes. Next, activate the **Loft** command (on the ribbon, click **3D Model > Create > Loft**). On the **Loft** dialog, click the **Surface** icon in the **Output** section. Select the first and second sections. Likewise, select the remaining sections. Next, click **OK**.

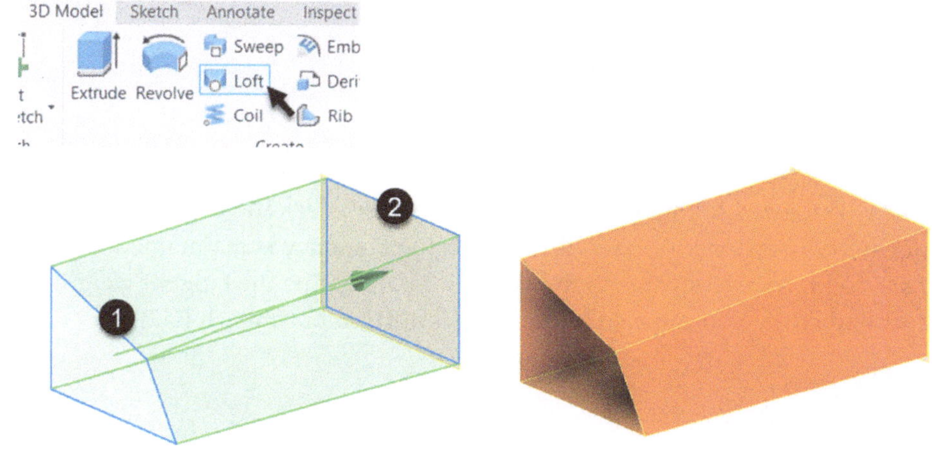

The sections can be closed, or open curves, or points, and they are not required to be on parallel planes.

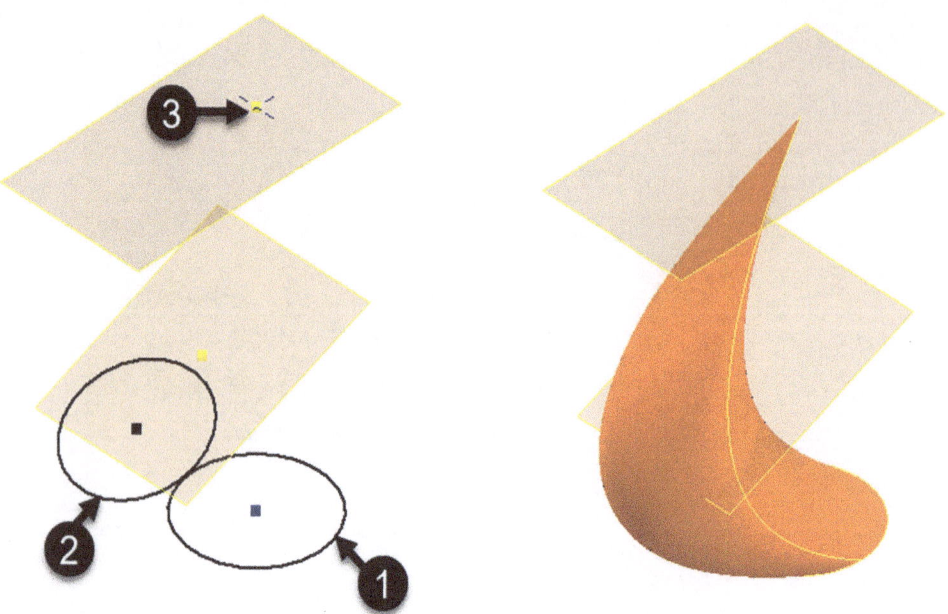

Creating a Transition Surface using the Loft command

The **Loft** command can be used to create a surface bridging the gap between two surfaces. It can be tangent or curvature, continuous in both directions. To create a transition surface, activate the **Loft** command, and select the first edge. Next, click in the **Sections** section, and then select the second section. Click the **Transition** tab to display the preview of the transition surface.

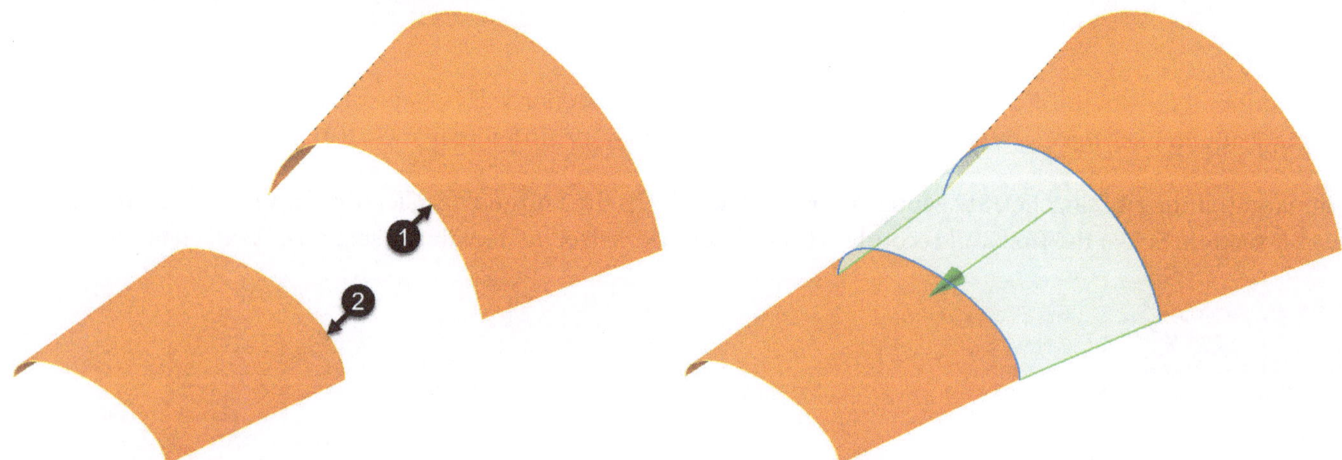

You can specify how the loft surface will be connected to the selected edges. To do this, click the **Conditions** tab and select **Tangent Condition** from **Continuity** drop-down next to the **Edge 1;** the tangency is maintained between the first edge and the loft surface. Next, type-in a value in the **Weight** box to define the tangent weight. Likewise, set the continuity type of the second edge. You can also select **Free Condition** or **Smooth (G2) Condition**.

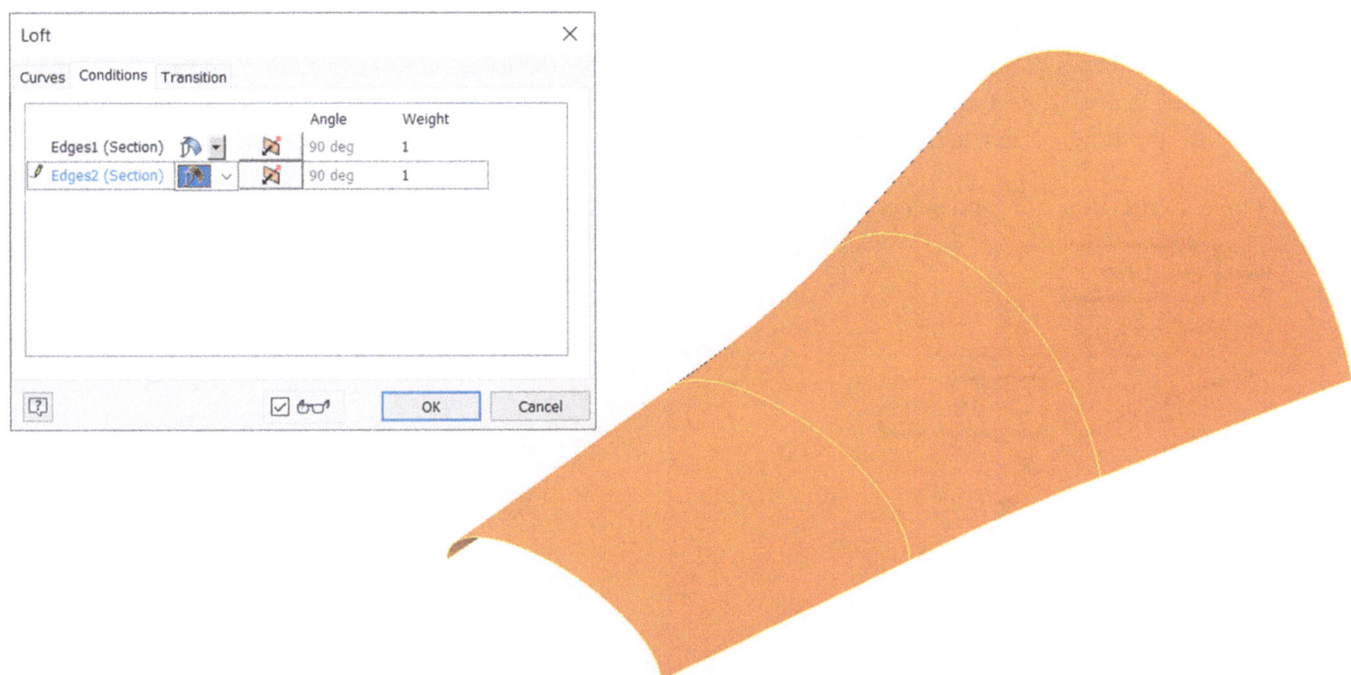

Creating the lofts using Guide Rails

The **Loft** command allows you to create a surface by lofting one or more sections along the guide rails. It also provides various options to control the shape along the guide rails. To create a loft surface using sections and guide rails, first, create the sections and guide rails. You must ensure that the guide rails and sections are well connected. Activate the **Loft** command and click the **Surface** icon in the **Output** section. Select the first and second sections. Next, select the **Rails** option from the **Guide Type** section. Click in the **Rails** section and one or more guide rails from the graphics window. Click **OK** to complete the loft surface.

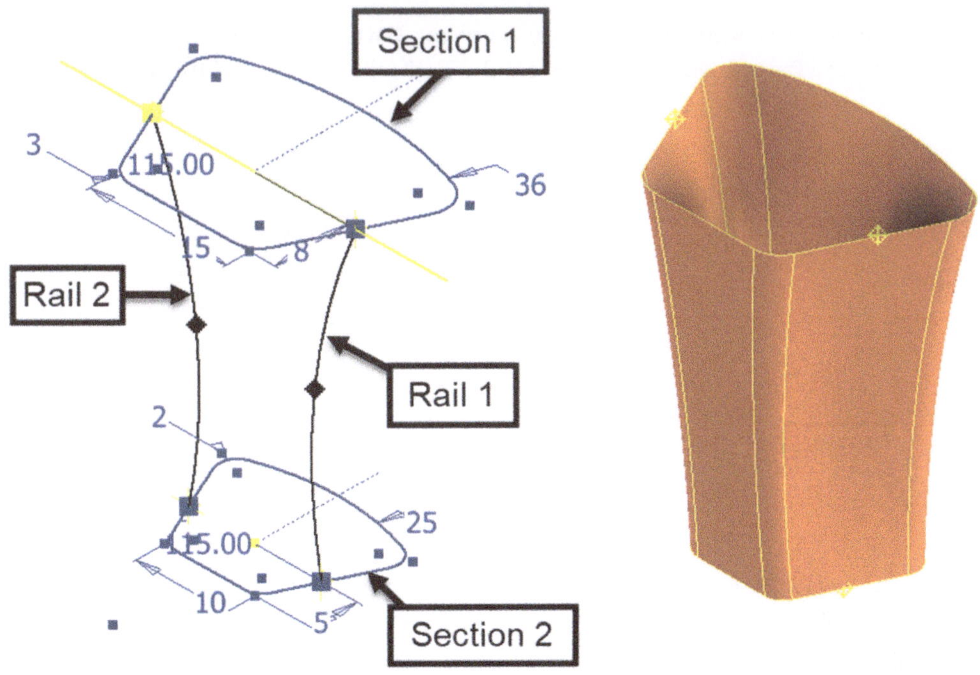

Creating a Centerline Loft

The **Loft** command allows you to create a centerline loft. The centerline loft is similar to a Guide Rail loft, except that the centerline is not needed to touch any of the sections. To create a centerline loft, first create two sections and a centerline, as shown. Next, activate the **Loft** command and select the two sections. On the **Loft** dialog, select **Guide Type > Centerline** and select the centerline. Click **OK** on the **Loft** dialog.

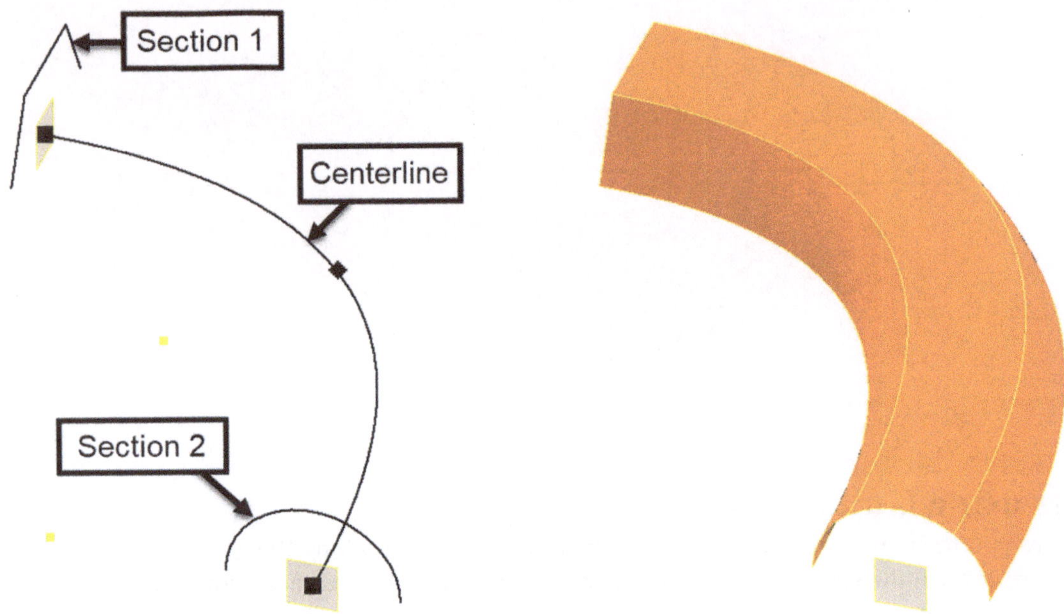

Sweep

This command creates a surface or solid body by sweeping a section along a path. First, create a sweep section and a path, and then activate the **Sweep** command (on the ribbon, click **3D Model > Create > Sweep**). Click the **Surface Mode** icon on the **Properties** panel. Next, select **Orientation > Follow Path** from the **Properties** panel. Select the profile, and then click in the **Path** selection box. Select the path; the preview of the swept surface appears.

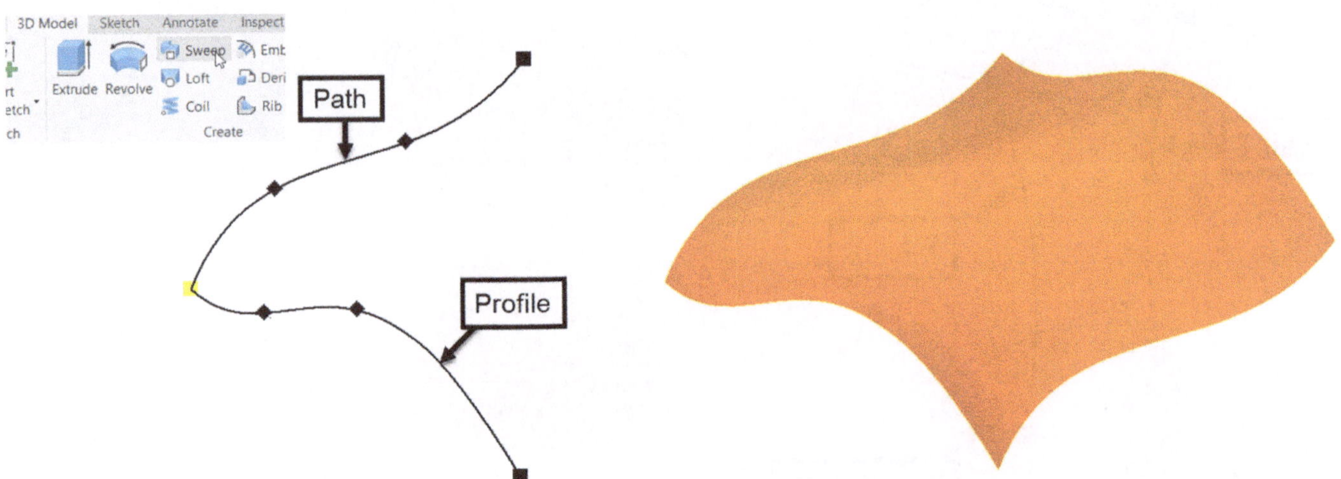

Use the **Orientation** options to specify the orientation of the section along the path. The **Follow Path** option sweeps the section perpendicular to the path. The **Fixed** option sweeps the section parallel to the section plane.

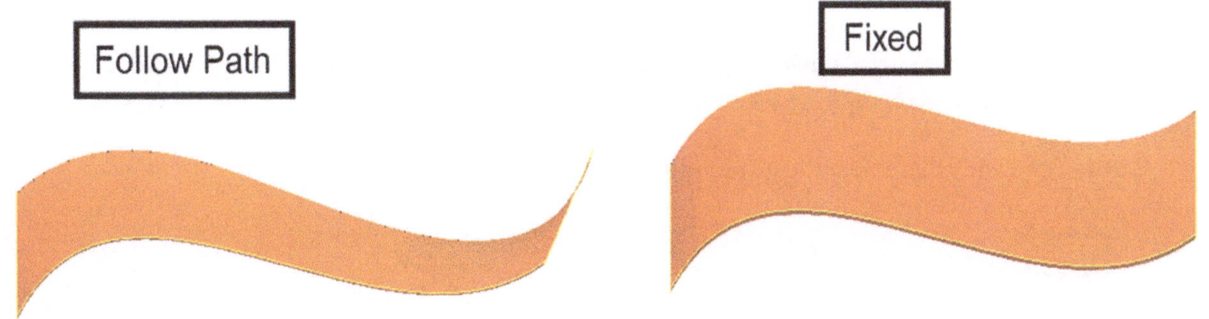

Enter a value in the **Taper** box to taper the section along the path.

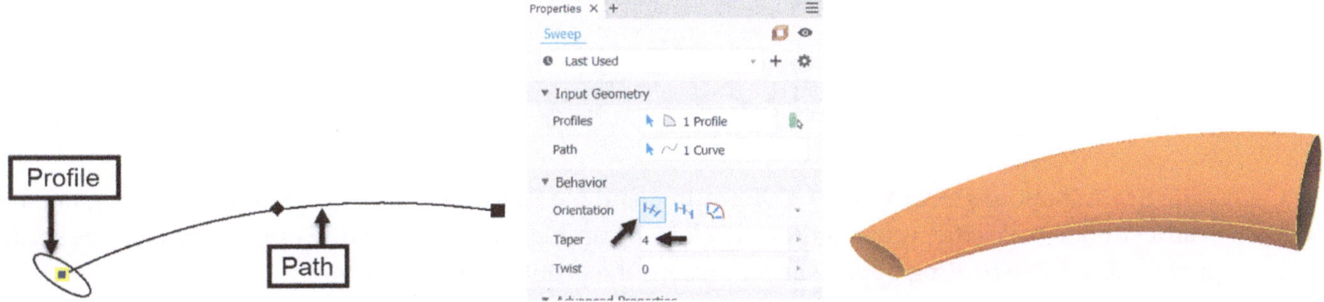

Enter a value in the **Twist** box to twist the section along the path.

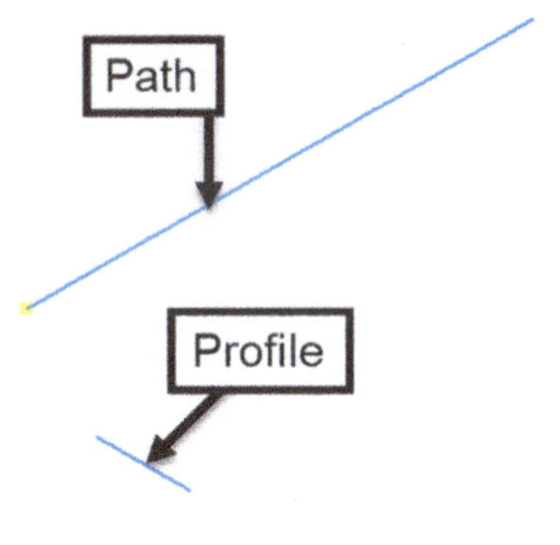

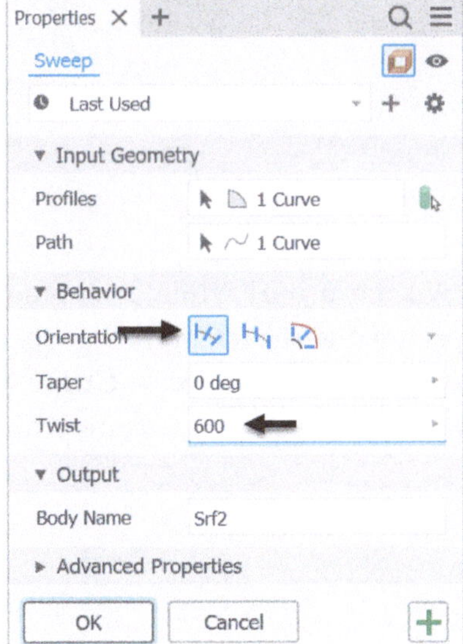

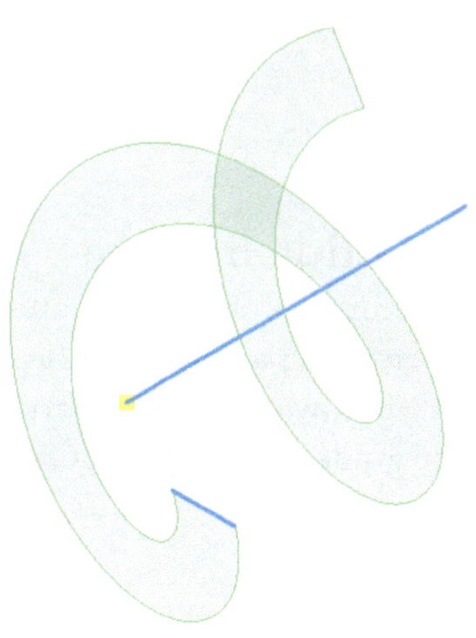

Path + Guide

The **Guide** option creates a swept surface using a path and guide. To create this type of swept surface, first create a profile, path, and guide. Next, activate the **Sweep** command and select the profile and path. Next, select **Orientation > Guide**, and then select the guide rail.

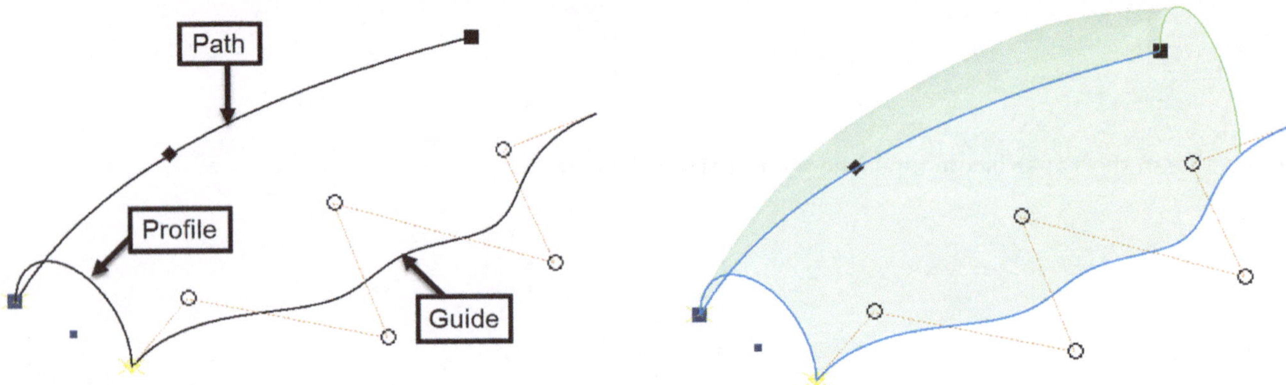

Use the **Profile Scaling** options (**X & Y Scaling**, **X Scaling**, and **No Scaling**) to scale the section long the guide rail. The **X&Y Scaling** option scales the section uniformly along the guide rail. The **X Scaling** option stretches the section along the guide rail. The **No Scaling** option simply sweeps the profile along the path.

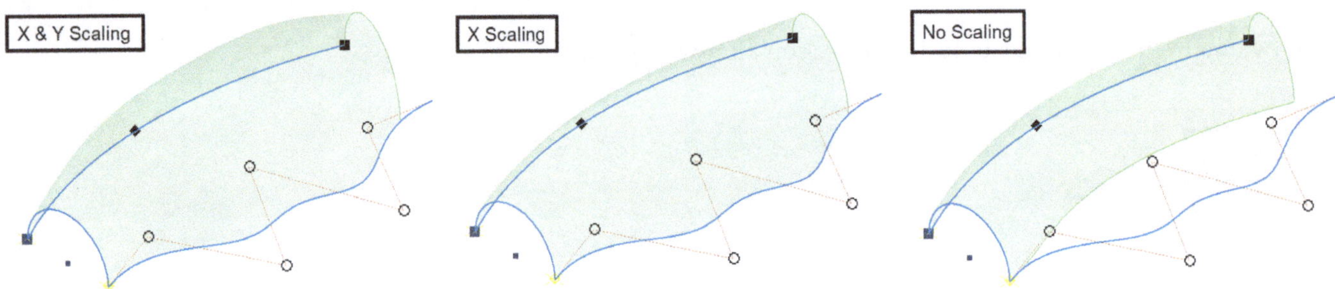

Path + Guide Surface

The **Guide** option on the **Sweep** dialog will be useful while sweeping a profile along a non-planar path. For example, create a path and section similar to the one shown in the figure. Next, select the profile and path from the graphics window. On the **Properties** panel, select **Orientation > Guide**, and then select the cylindrical surface to define the guide surface. Click **OK** and notice that the sweep feature is attached to the surface.

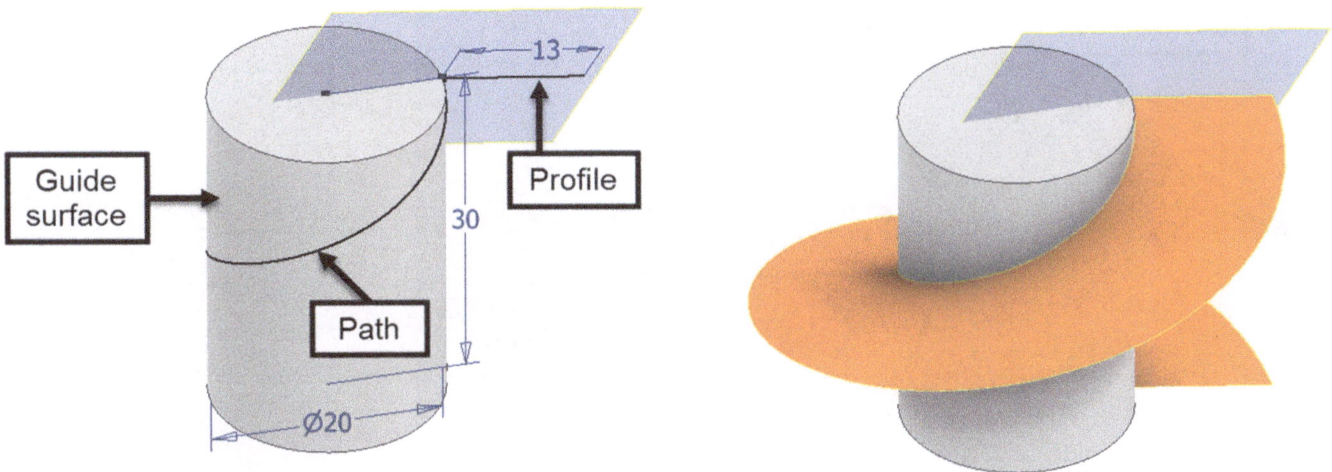

Patch

To create a patch surface, Activate the **Patch** command (on the ribbon, click **3D Model > Surface> Patch**) and select a closed sketch or closed loop of edges. Click **OK** to create the patch surface.

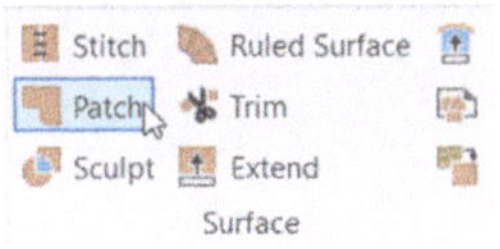

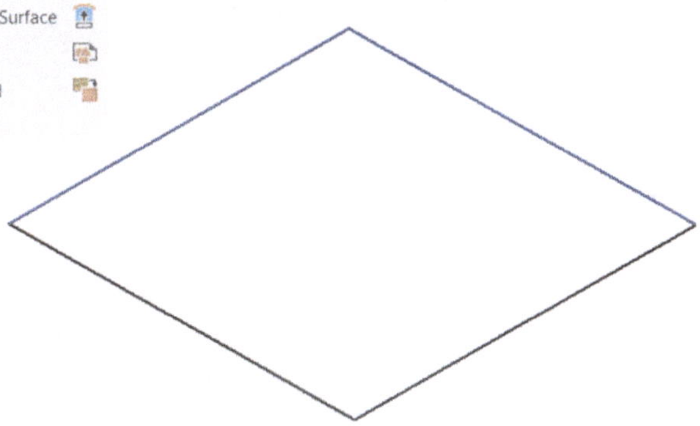

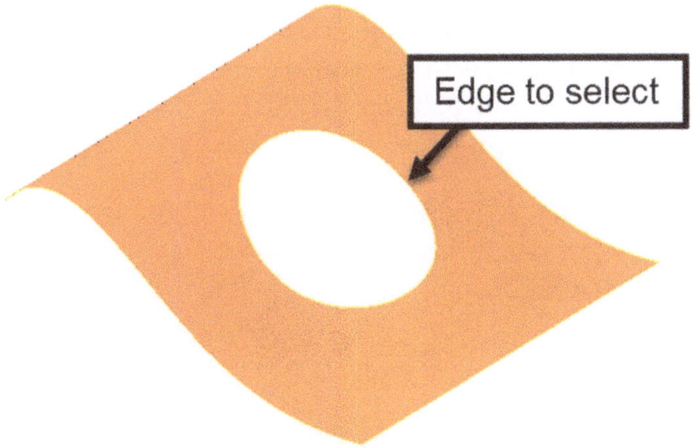

You can also use the guide rails to control the shape of the patch surface. To do this, click the **Guide Rails** selection button, and then select the guide rails. Next, click **OK**.

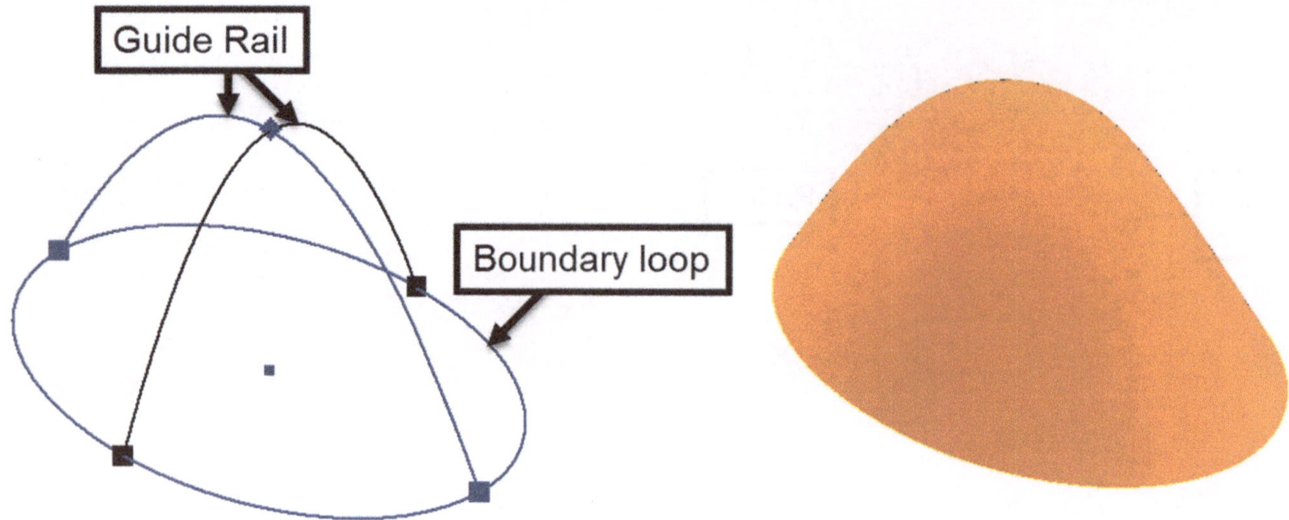

Trim

This command trims a portion of a surface using a trimming tool. The trimming tool can be a surface, plane, or a sketched entity. Activate this command (click **3D Model > Surface > Trim** on the ribbon) and select the cutting tool. Next, select the portion of the surface to be removed. Click **OK** to trim the surface.

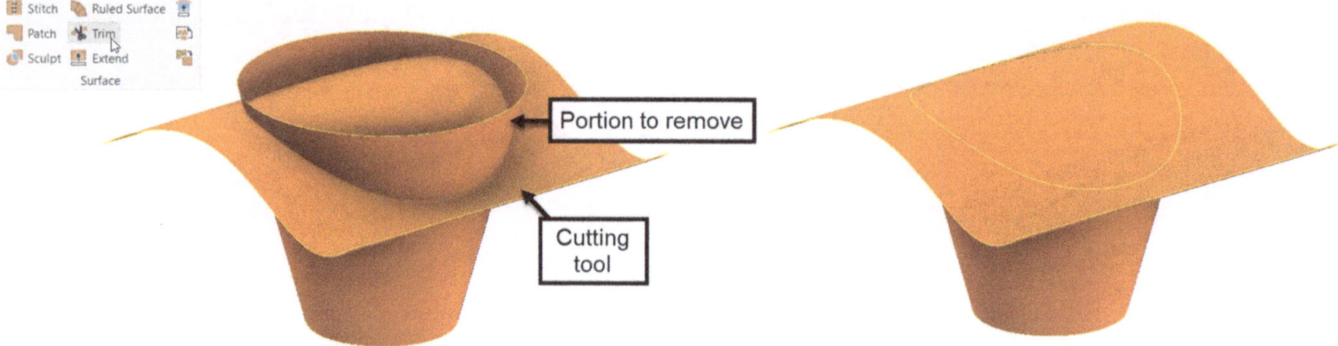

You can also trim a surface using a sketch. Activate the **Trim** command and select the sketch. You will notice that the trimming boundary is created normal to the surface. Also, the trim boundary is created throughout the model. If you want to trim only the front portion of the surface, click inside the trim boundary at the front side. Now, click **OK** to trim the surface.

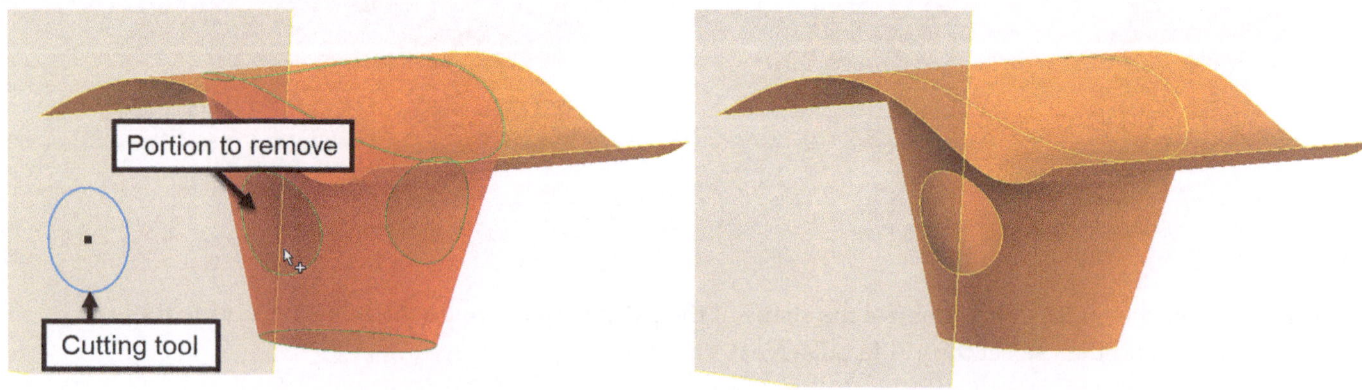

Creating Ruled Surfaces

The **Ruled Surface** tool allows you to create surfaces attached to the edges of an existing surface. You can find the **Ruled Surface** tool on the **Surface** panel. You can create three types of ruled surfaces using the options in the **Ruled Surface** dialog. These three types of ruled surfaces are discussed next.

Normal to Surface

To create this type of ruled surface, activate the **Ruled Surface** tool and select the **Normal** option from the **Ruled Surface** dialog. Select an edge from the model. Enter a distance value in the **Distance** box of the **Extend** section. Click the **Flip** button in the **Extend** section to reverse the direction, if required. Click **OK** to create the ruled surface normal to the surface on which the selected edge lies.

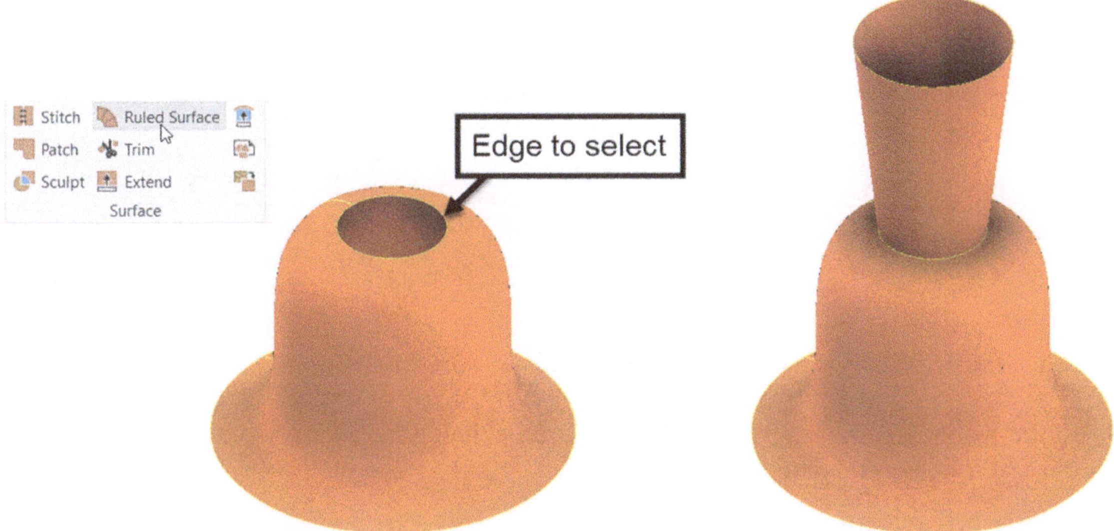

Tangent to Surface

To create a ruled surface tangent to a surface, click the **Ruled Surface** button on the **Surfaces** panel. To create this type of ruled surface, select the **Tangent** option from the **Ruled Surface** dialog. Select an edge from the model. Notice the preview of the ruled surface. The resultant surface will be tangent to the selected edge. In this case, the selected edge is associated with two reference surfaces (the vertical and the top surfaces). As a result, there will be two solutions created from the selected edge.

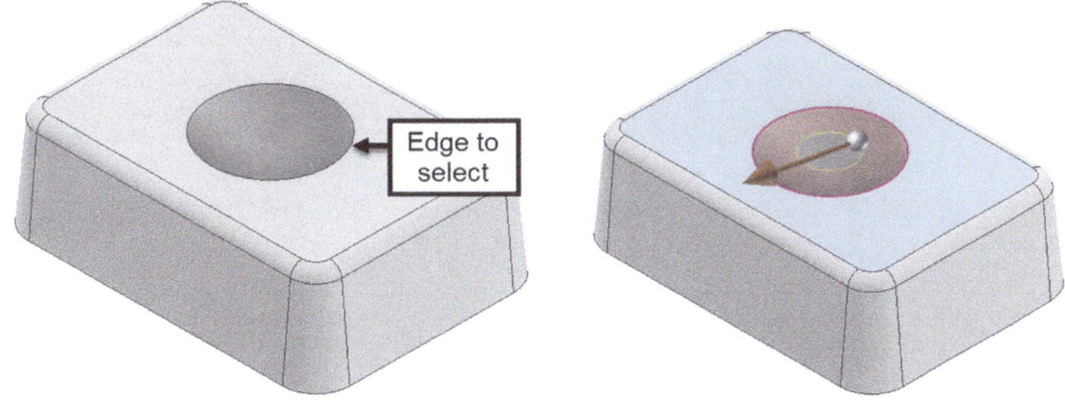

Click the **Alternate All Faces** button in the **Selection** section to view the alternate solution. Enter a distance value in the **Distance** box of the **Extend** section. You can also reverse the direction of the ruled surface using the **Flip** button next to the **Distance** box. Click **OK** to create the ruled surface.

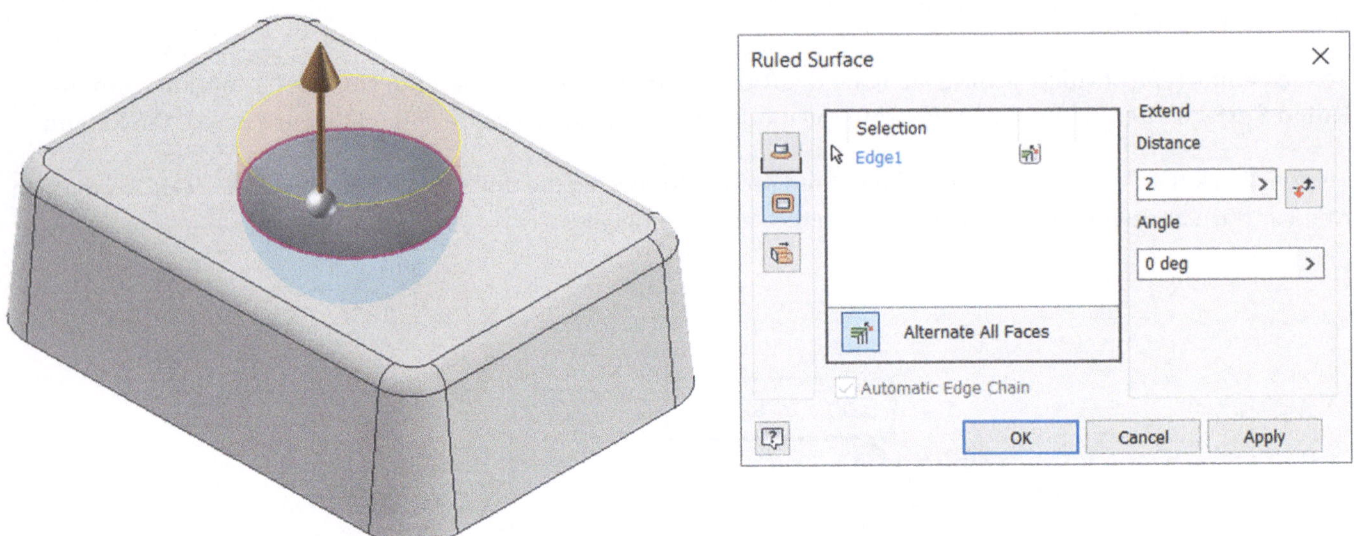

Ruled Surface along a Vector

To create this type of ruled surface, activate the **Ruled Surface** command (On the ribbon, **3D Model > Surfaces > Ruled surface**) and select the **Vector** option from the **Ruled Surface** dialog. Select an edge from the model. Click on the **Vector** button and select a face, plane, edge, or axis.

Specify the distance of the ruled surface in the **Distance** box. Specify the taper angle of the ruled surface in the **Angle** box available in the **Extend** section. Click the **Flip** button, if required. Next, click **OK**.

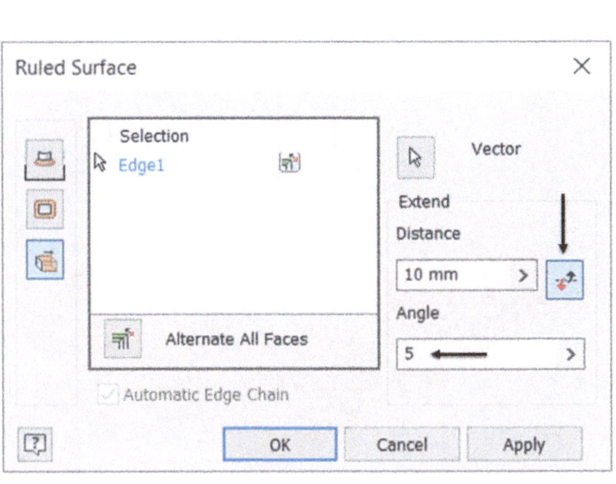

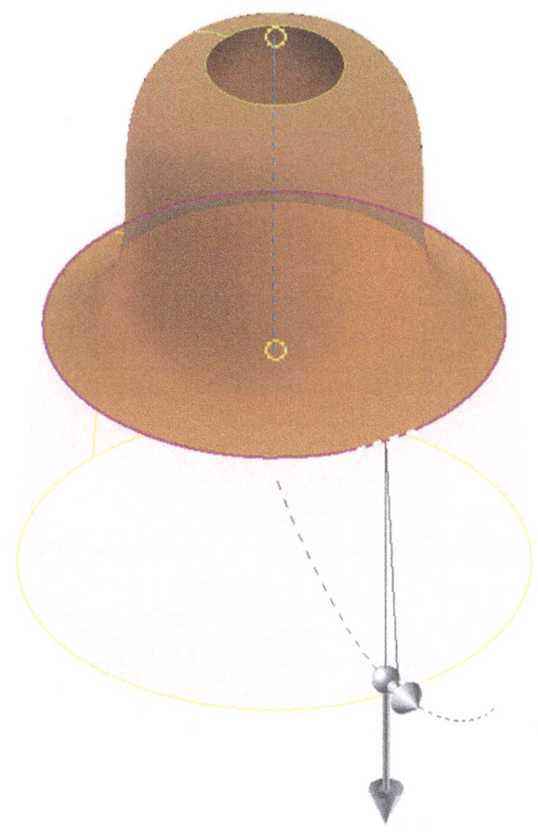

Replacing Face

The **Replace Face** tool replaces a face or group of faces with another face or group of faces. To replace a face, click the **Replace Face** button on the **Surface** panel of the **3D Model** ribbon tab. Select the existing faces for replacement. Click the **New Face** button and select the replacement surface. Click **OK** to replace the surface.

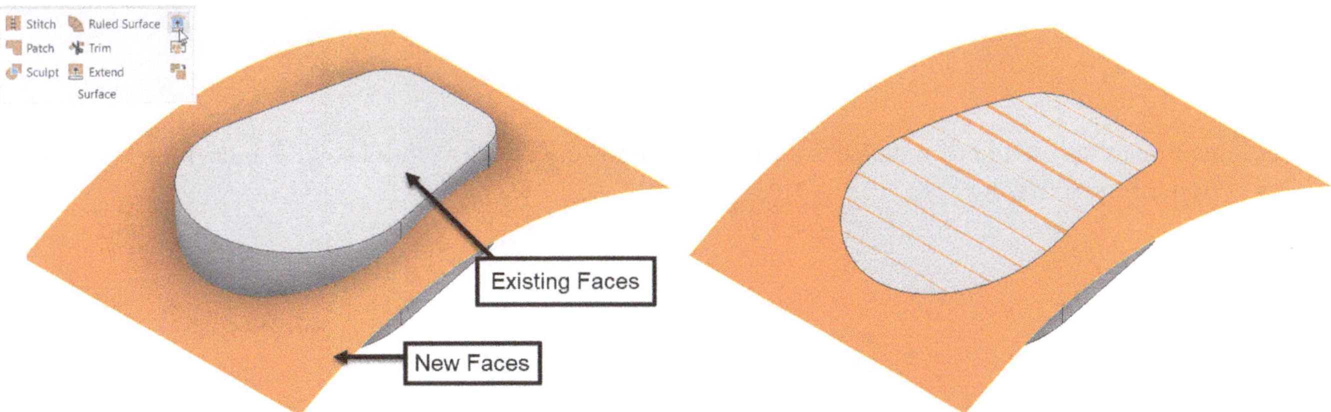

Extend

During the design process, you may sometimes need to extend a surface. You can extend a surface using the **Extend** command. Activate this command (On the ribbon, click **3D Model > Surface > Extend**) and select the edge of the surface to be extended. Next, select **Extents > Distance** and enter a value in the **Distance** box.

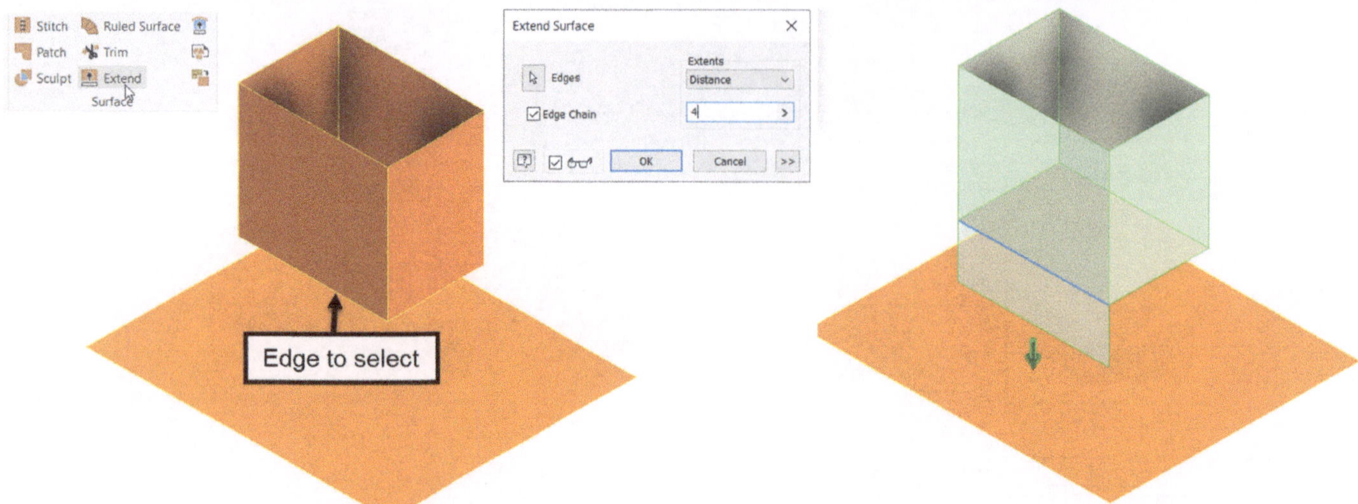

Select **Extents > To**, and then select a termination face; the edge will be extended up to the selected face.

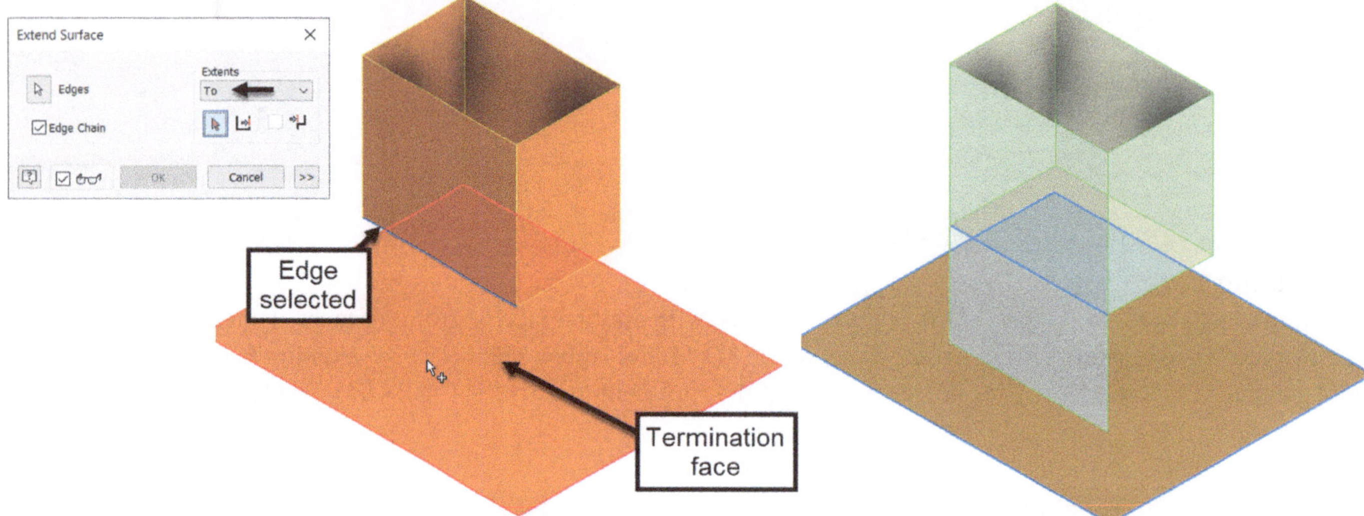

Sculpt

The **Sculpt** command is used to trim multiple surfaces at a time and create a closed solid. For example, you can use this option for the following case.

Activate the **Sculpt** command (on the ribbon, click **3D Model > Surface > Sculpt**). Select the required surfaces from the model (All surfaces in this case). Click **OK** to trim the surfaces and create a closed solid.

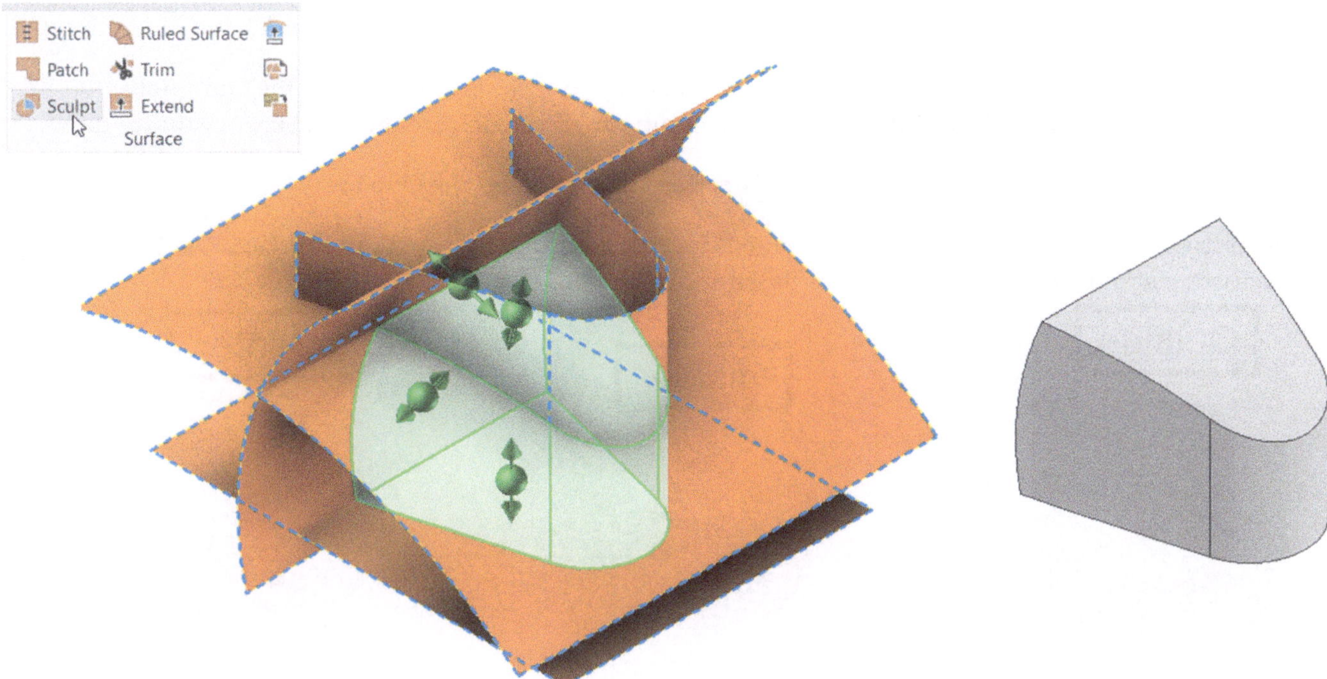

Stitch Surfaces

The surfaces that are created act as individual surfaces unless they are sewed together. The **Stitch** command lets you combine two or more surfaces to form a single surface. To stitch surfaces, activate the **Stitch** command (click **3D Model > Surface > Stitch** on the ribbon) and select the surfaces to stitch.

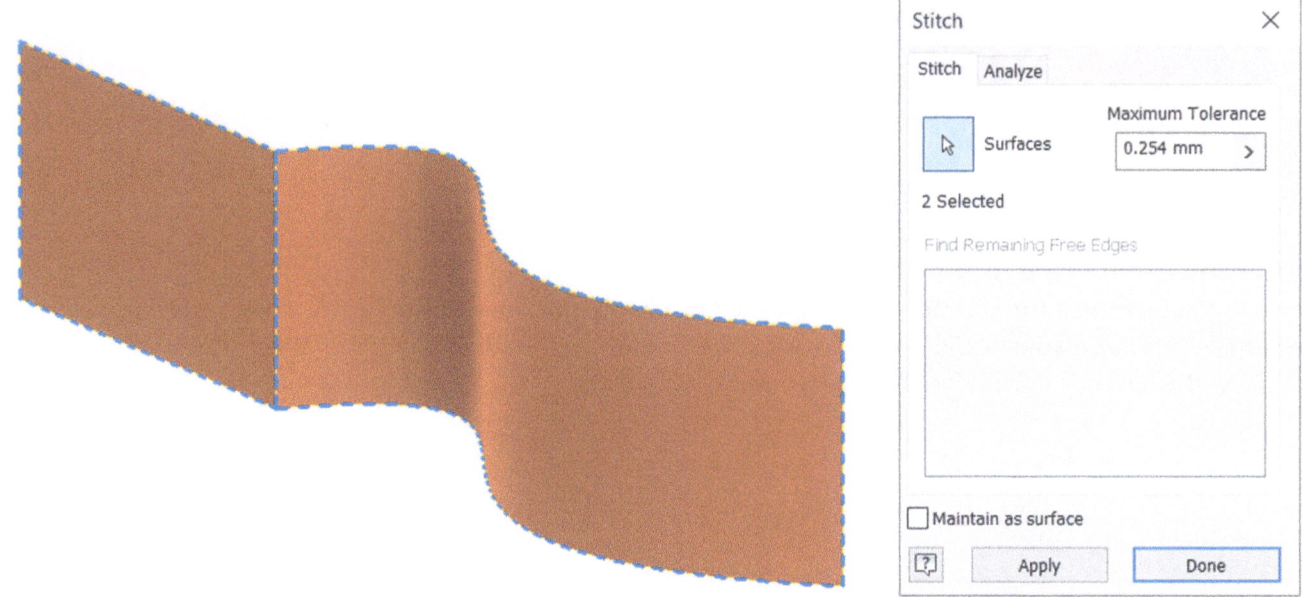

The value you type in the **Maximum Tolerance** box of the **Stitch** dialog defines the tolerance gap. All the surfaces within the tolerance gap will be stitched. Click the **Apply** button to stitch the surfaces. Click **Done** to close the **Stitch** dialog.

Thicken/Offset

Creating a solid from a surface can be accomplished by simply thickening a surface. To add thickness to a surface, activate the **Thicken/Offset** command (on the ribbon, click **3D Model > Modify > Thicken/Offset**) and select the surfaces to be thickened. You can also select the surfaces in a single click. To do this, click the **Quilt Selection** icon next to the **Faces** selection box, and then select the entire surface model. Enter the thickness value in the **Distance** box. Define the thickness side using the **Direction** buttons. Select the **Outside** button to add thickness outside the surface. The **Inside** button is used to add thickness inside the surface. The **Center** button is used to add thickness to both sides of the surface. Click **OK**.

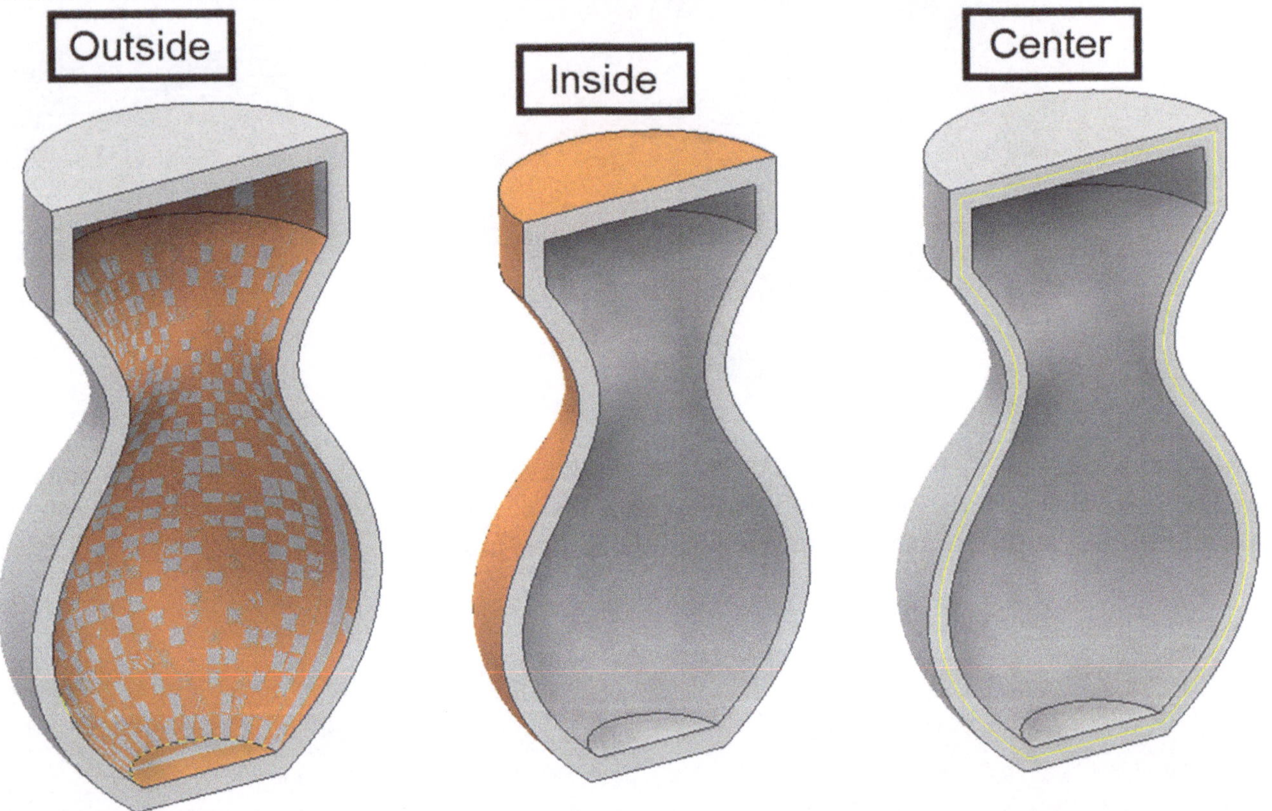

Converting a Surface to Solid

Creating a solid from a surface can be accomplished by simply thickening a surface. You can also create a solid if the surface encloses a volume. For example, consider the surface shown in the figure. It encloses a volume. However, there is only one surface body listed in the Model Tree.

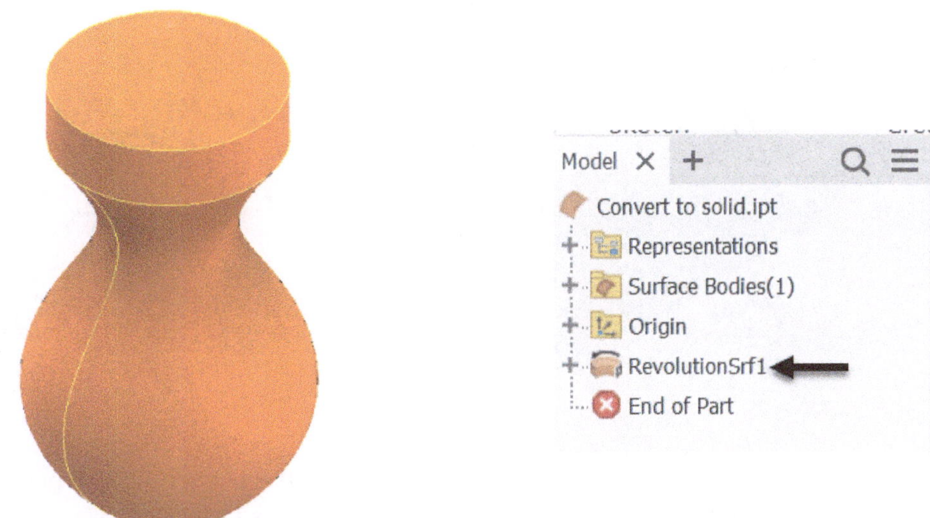

To make this surface into a solid, click the **Stitch** button on the **Surfaces** panel. Select the enclosed surface. Click **Apply** and **Done** to create a solid. You can use the **iProperties** dialog (click **File > iProperties**) to check whether the surface is converted into a solid or not. You can also use the **Half Section View** tool available on the **Visibility** panel of the **View** ribbon tab.

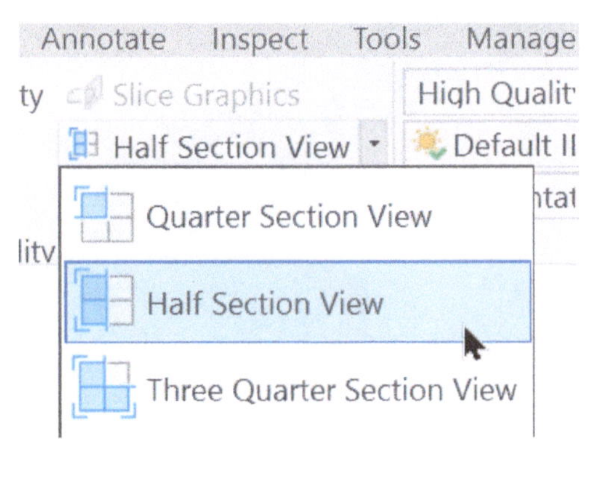

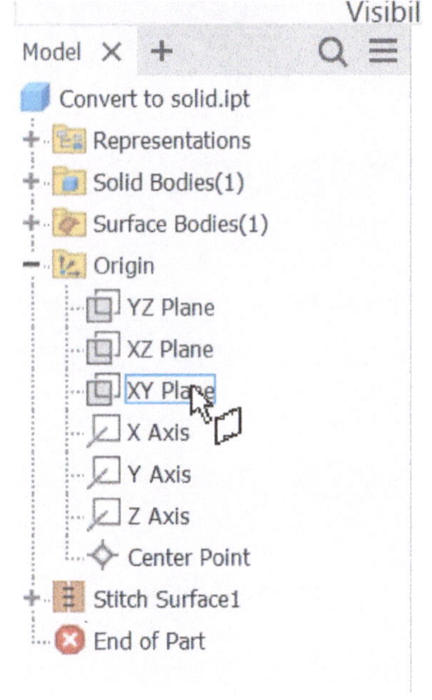

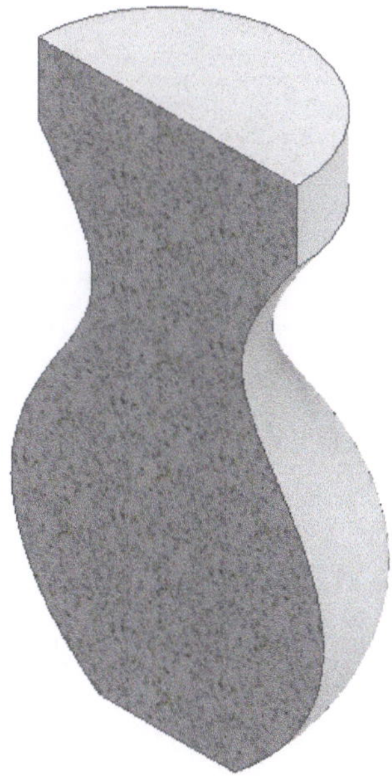

Deleting Faces

You can delete unwanted faces from a model. In the case of a solid, you can delete a face and make it a surface model. To delete a face, click the **Delete Face** button on the **Modify** panel of the **3D Model** ribbon tab. Select the face to be deleted. Select the **Heal Remaining Faces** option from the **Behavior** group, and click **OK**; the faces adjacent to the deleted faces will be healed.

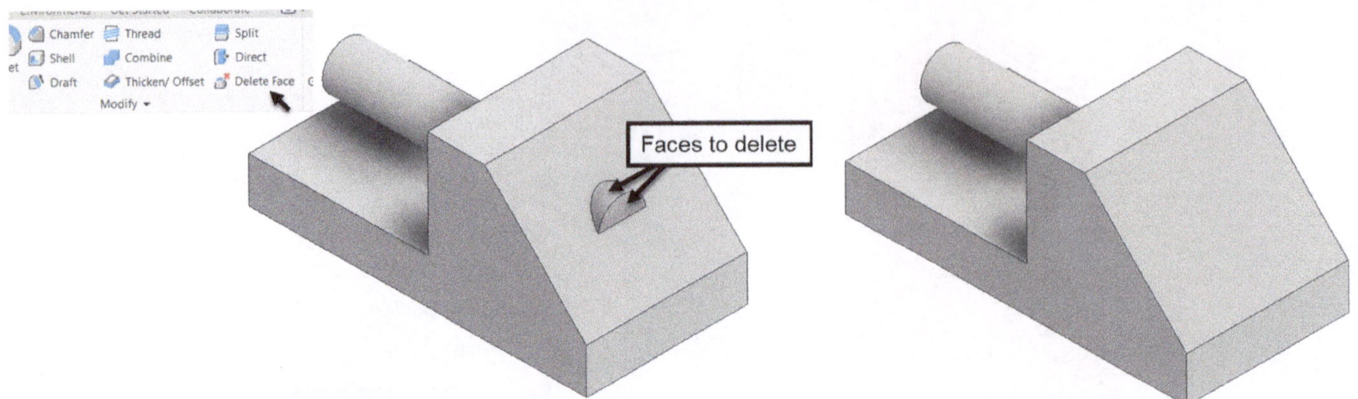

Unwrap

The **Unwrap** tool (on the ribbon, click **3D Model > Create > Unwrap**) flattens the surface body. Select the surface model, as shown. Select **Alignment > Align to Model** to align the flattened surface to the surface body. Next, click **OK**.

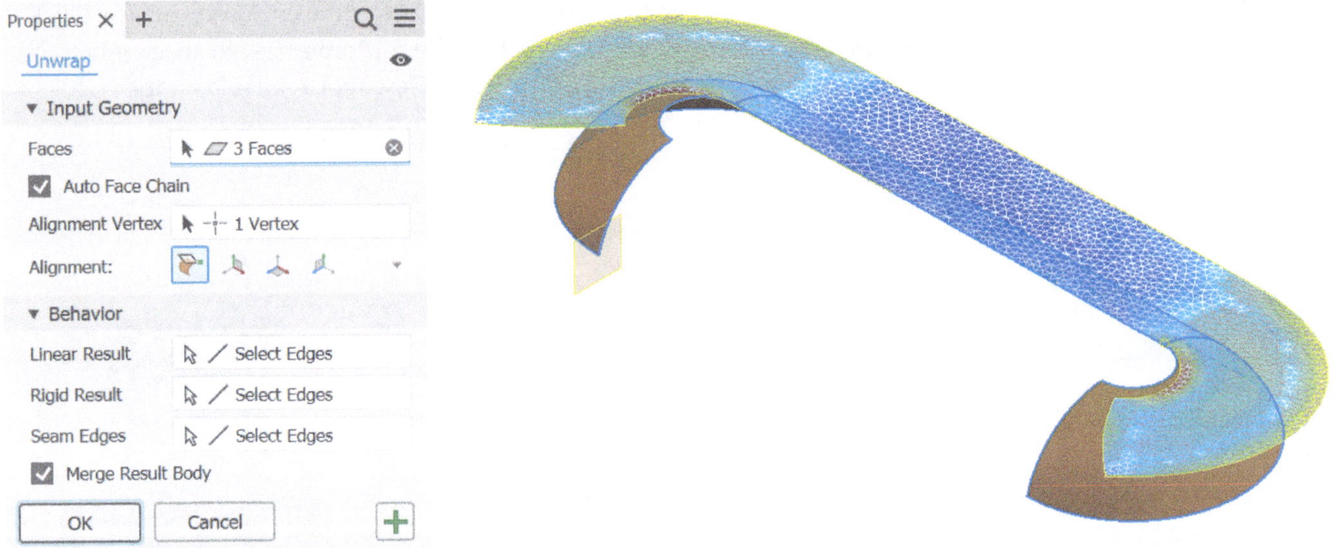

Example 1

In this example, you will construct the model shown below.

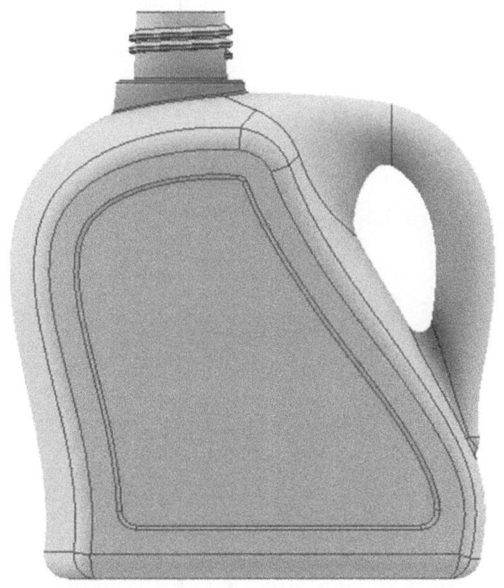

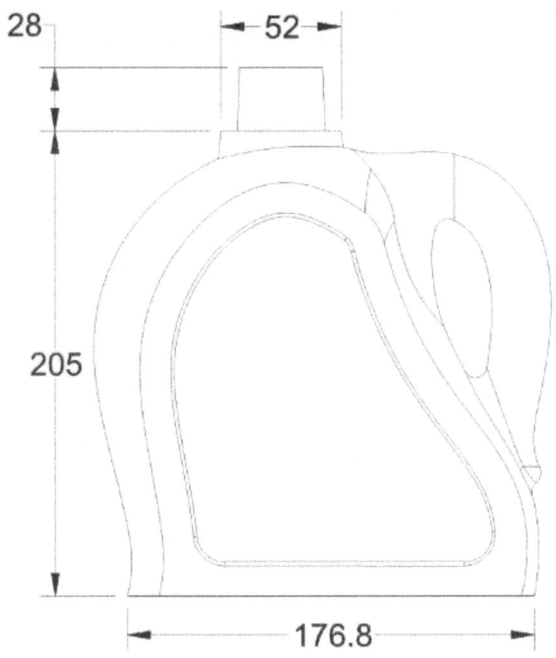

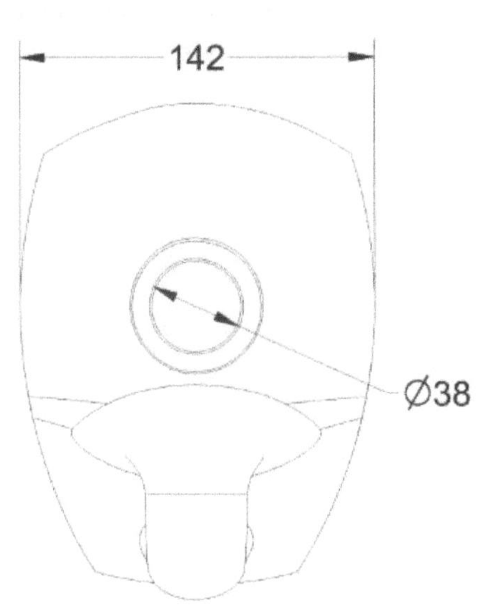

Drawing the layout sketch

1. Start **Autodesk Inventor 2026.**
2. Click **File Menu > New** on the ribbon.
3. On the **Create New File** dialog, click the **Templates > en-US > Metric** folder located in the top right corner.
4. Click the **Standard(mm).ipt** icon located under the **Part – Create 2D and 3D Objects** section.
5. Click the **Create** button on the **Create New File** dialog.
6. On the **3D Model** tab of the ribbon, and click the **Start 2D Sketch** icon on the **Sketch** panel.
7. Start a sketch on the XY plane.
8. On the ribbon, click **Sketch > Create> Line** drop-down **> Spline Control Vertex.**

9. Specify the points, as shown. Next, right-click and select **Create**.

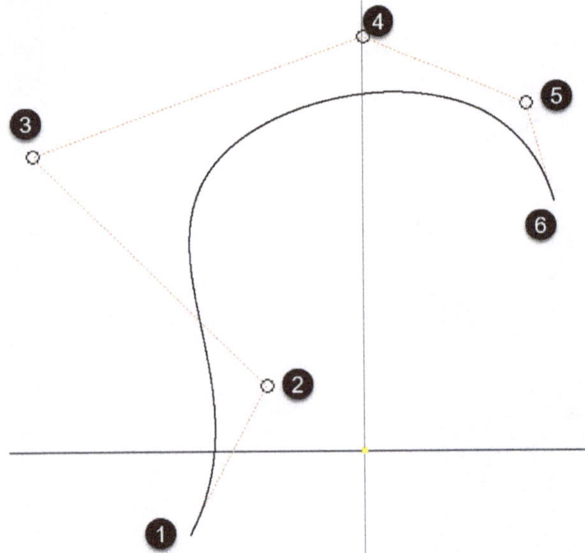

10. Activate the **Line** command (on the ribbon, click **Sketch > Create > Line**)
11. Select the sketch origin, move the pointer upward and click. Right-click and select **OK**.
12. Select the vertical line and click the **Construction** button on the **Format** panel.
13. Activate the **General Dimension** command (on the ribbon, click **Sketch > Constrain > General Dimension**).
14. Add dimensions to the sketch, as shown.

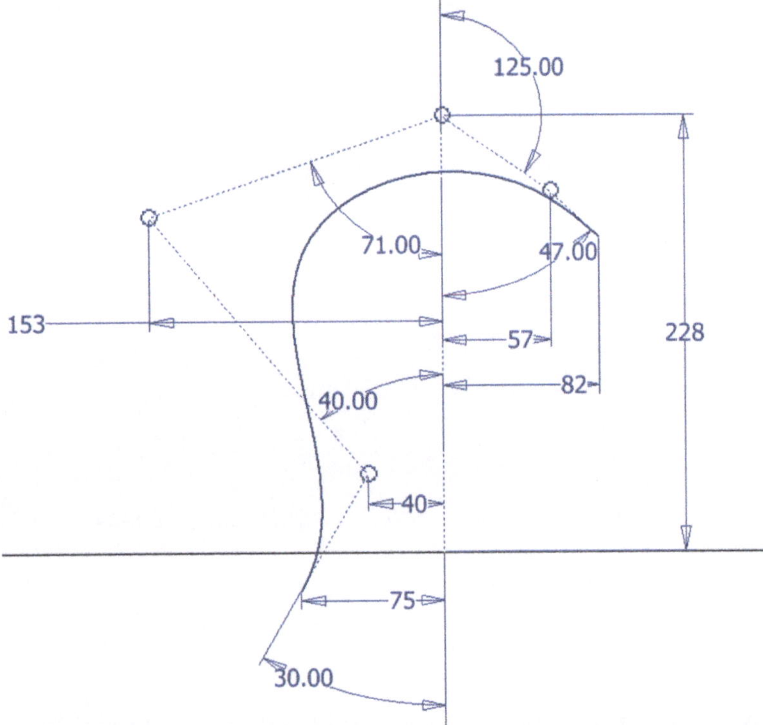

15. Click **Sketch > Exit > Finish Sketch** on the ribbon. Next, right-click on the sketch and uncheck the **Visibility** option.
16. Start a new sketch on the XY-Plane.
17. Activate the **Spline Control Vertex** command and draw another spline curve similar to the one shown in the figure.

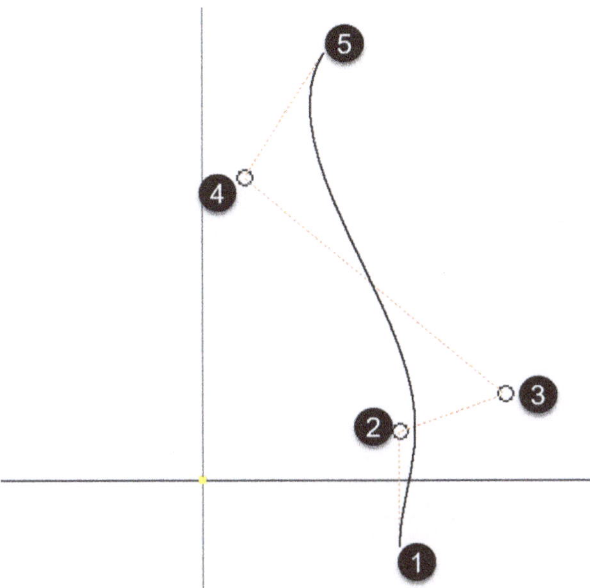

18. Add dimensions to the spline.

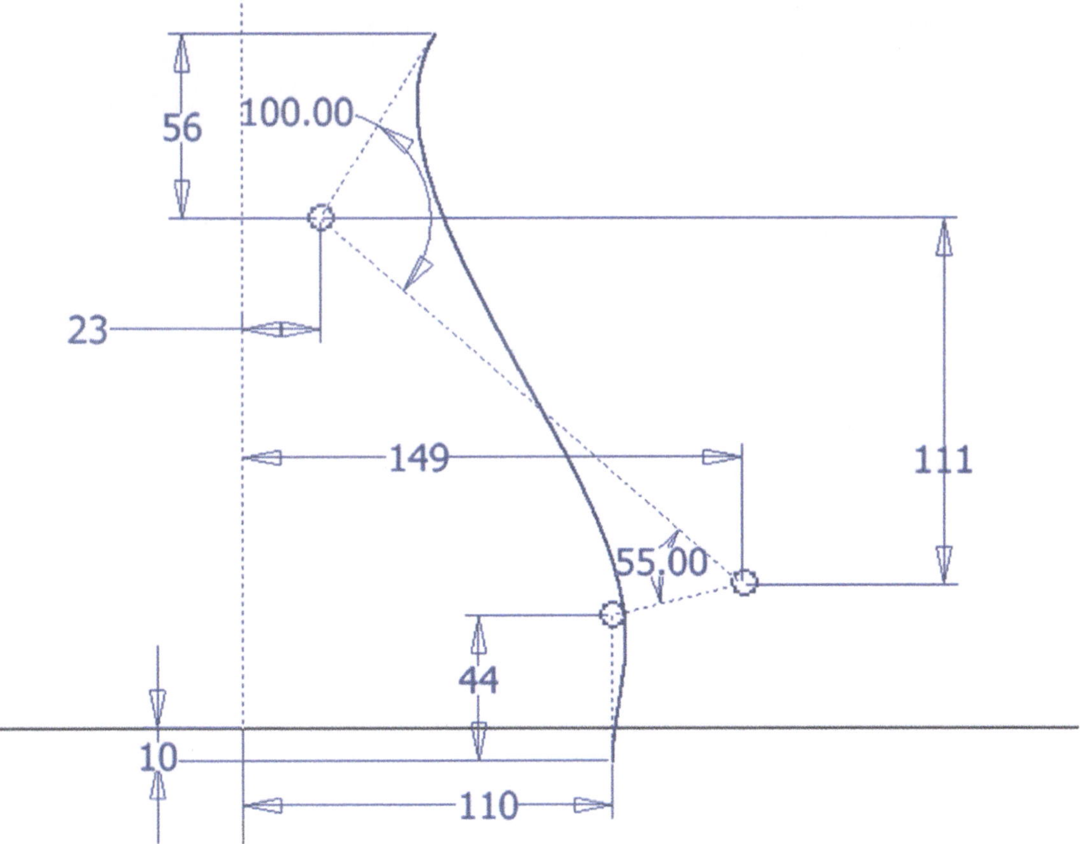

19. Click **Sketch > Exit > Finish Sketch** on the ribbon. Next, right-click on the sketch and uncheck the **Visibility** option.
20. Start a new sketch on the XY-Plane. Next, create another spline similar to the one shown below.

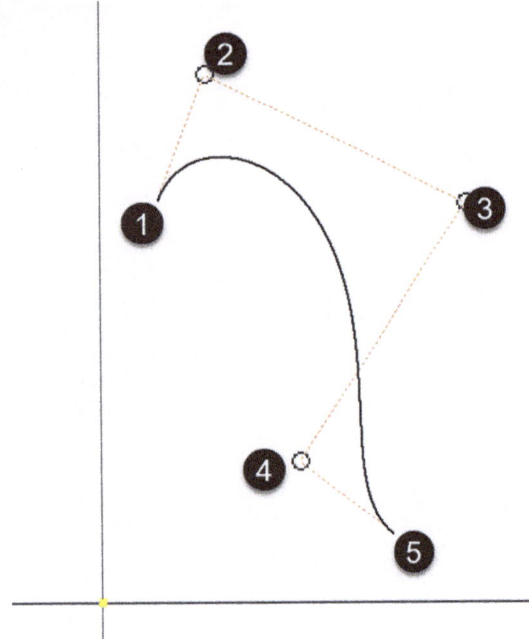

21. Add dimensions to the spline.

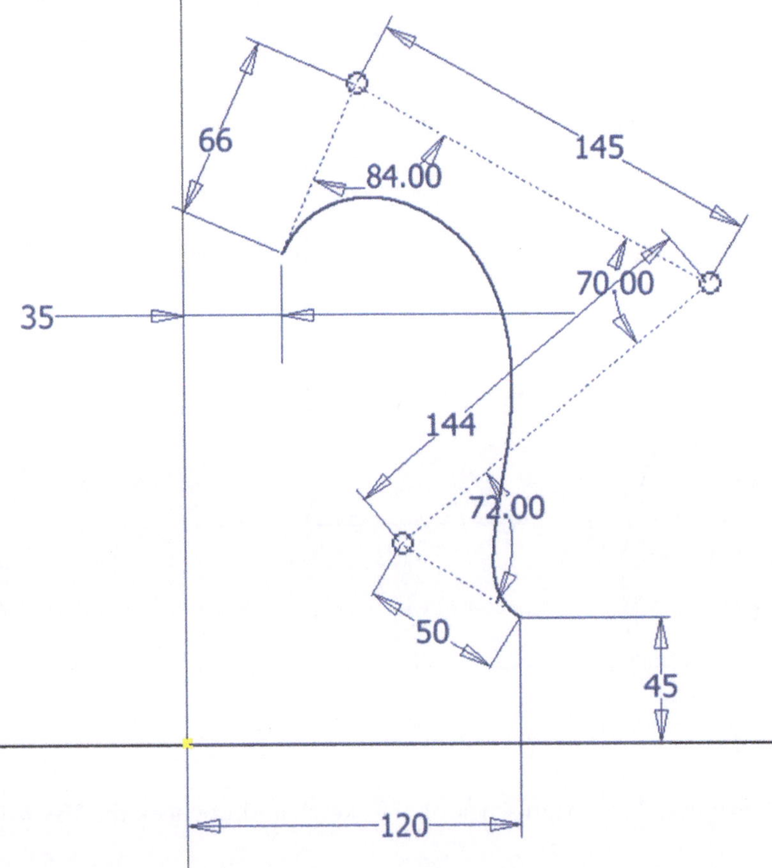

22. Finish the sketch. Next, right-click on the sketch and uncheck the **Visibility** option.

If you find it difficult to create the layout sketches, then you can download the part file from our website.

Creating the Front Surface

1. Create an arc on the XZ Plane and add dimensions to it. Note that you need to make the endpoints of the arc vertically constrained. Also, make the centerpoint of the arc constrained horizontally to the sketch origin. Finish the sketch. Next, right-click on the sketch and uncheck the **Visibility** option.

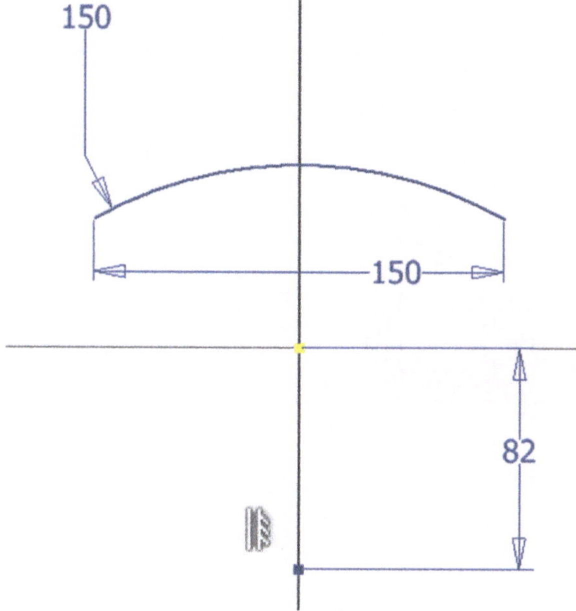

2. In the **Model** tree, press and hold the CTRL key and select the first and last sketch. Next, right-click and select the **Visibility** option.
3. Activate the **Sweep** command (on the ribbon, click **3D Model > Create > Sweep**).
4. Select the arc to define the profile. Next, select the spline to define the path.
5. Select **Orientation > Follow Path** and then click **OK**.

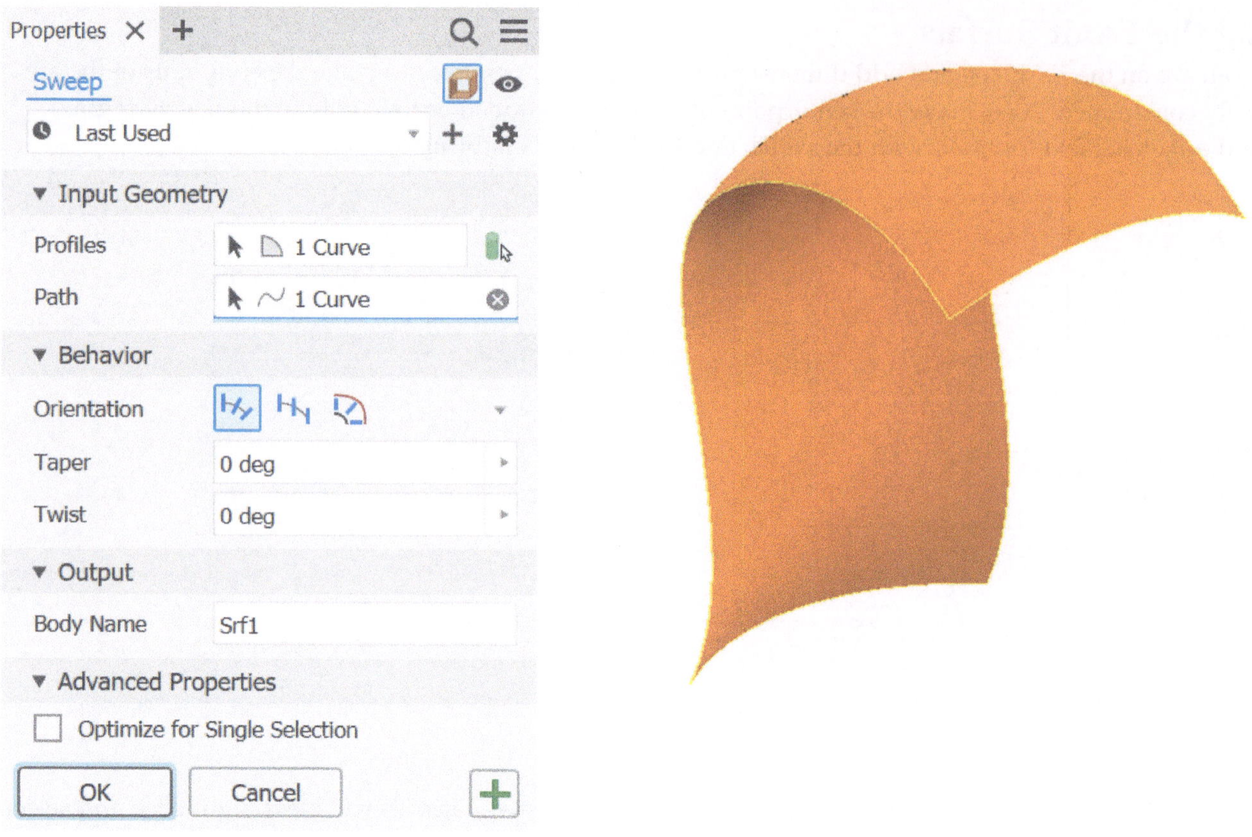

6. Save the file. As you are creating a complex geometry, you should save the model after each operation.

Creating the Label surface

1. Start a sketch on the XZ plane, and then draw a horizontal arc.
2. Click the **Slice graphics** icon at the bottom of the graphics window.
3. Draw a vertical line coincident with the sketch origin. Next, convert it into a construction line.
4. Draw a horizontal construction line coincident with the sketch origin.
5. Make the lower endpoint of the construction line coincident with the arc.

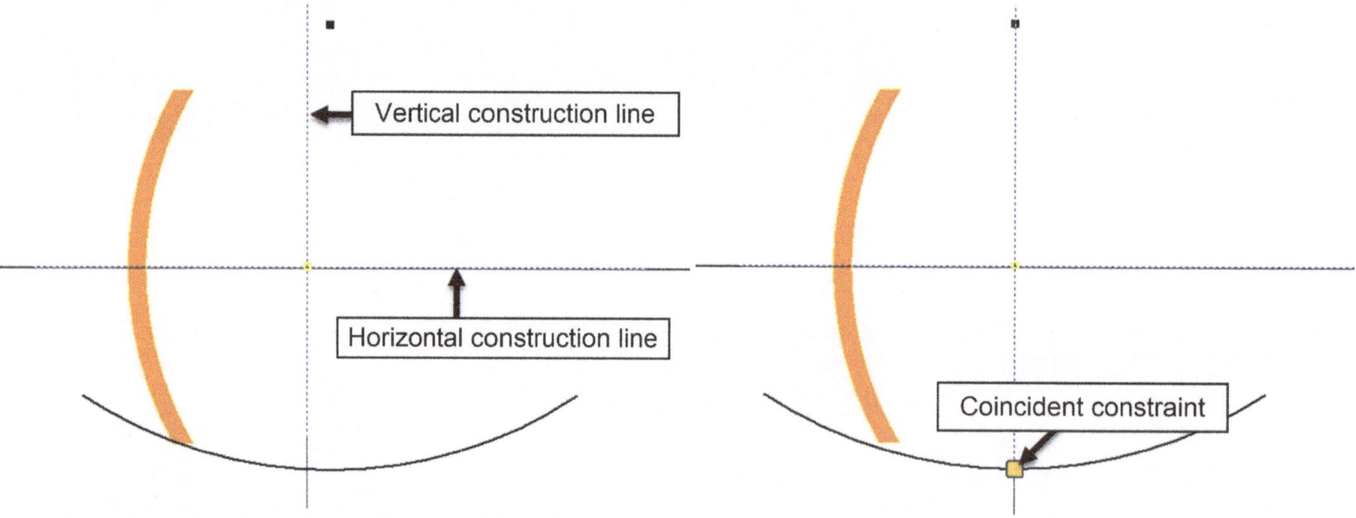

6. Make the endpoints of the arc symmetric about the vertical construction line.

7. Make the endpoints of the vertical construction line symmetric about the horizontal construction line.
8. Add dimensions to the sketch, as shown below.
9. Click **Sketch > Exit > Finish Sketch** on the ribbon.

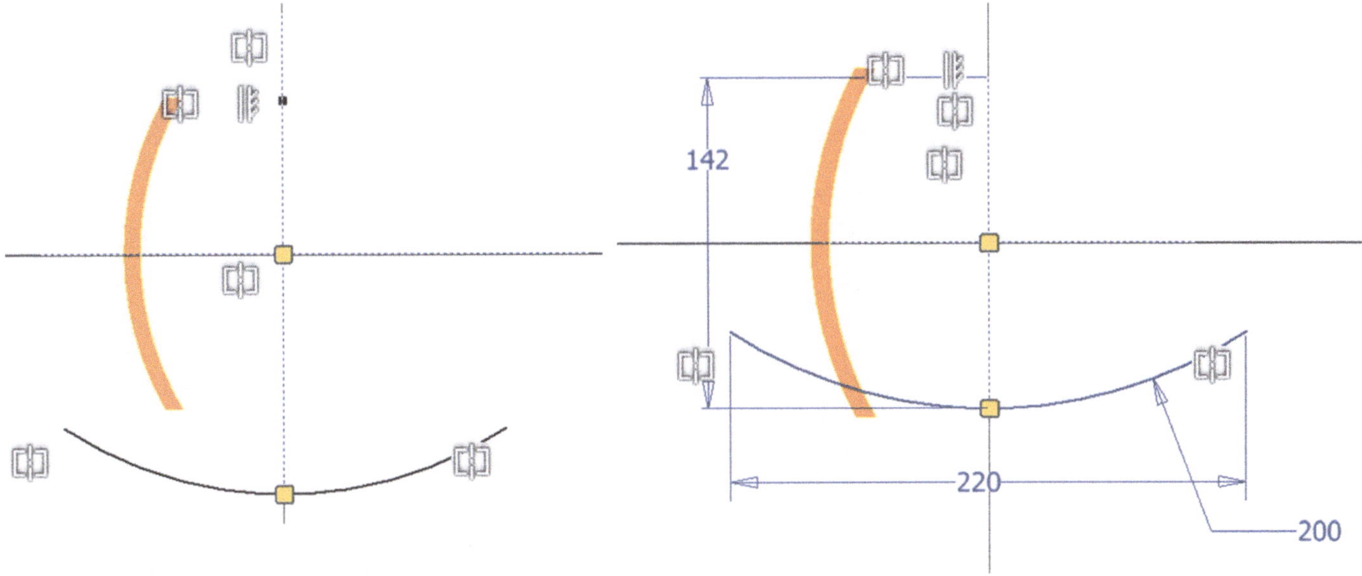

10. Activate the **Extrude** command (on the ribbon, click **3D Model > Create > Extrude**).
11. Type **220** in the **Distance A** box. Click **OK**.
12. On the ribbon, click **3D Model > Pattern > Mirror**, and then mirror the extruded surface about the XY plane.

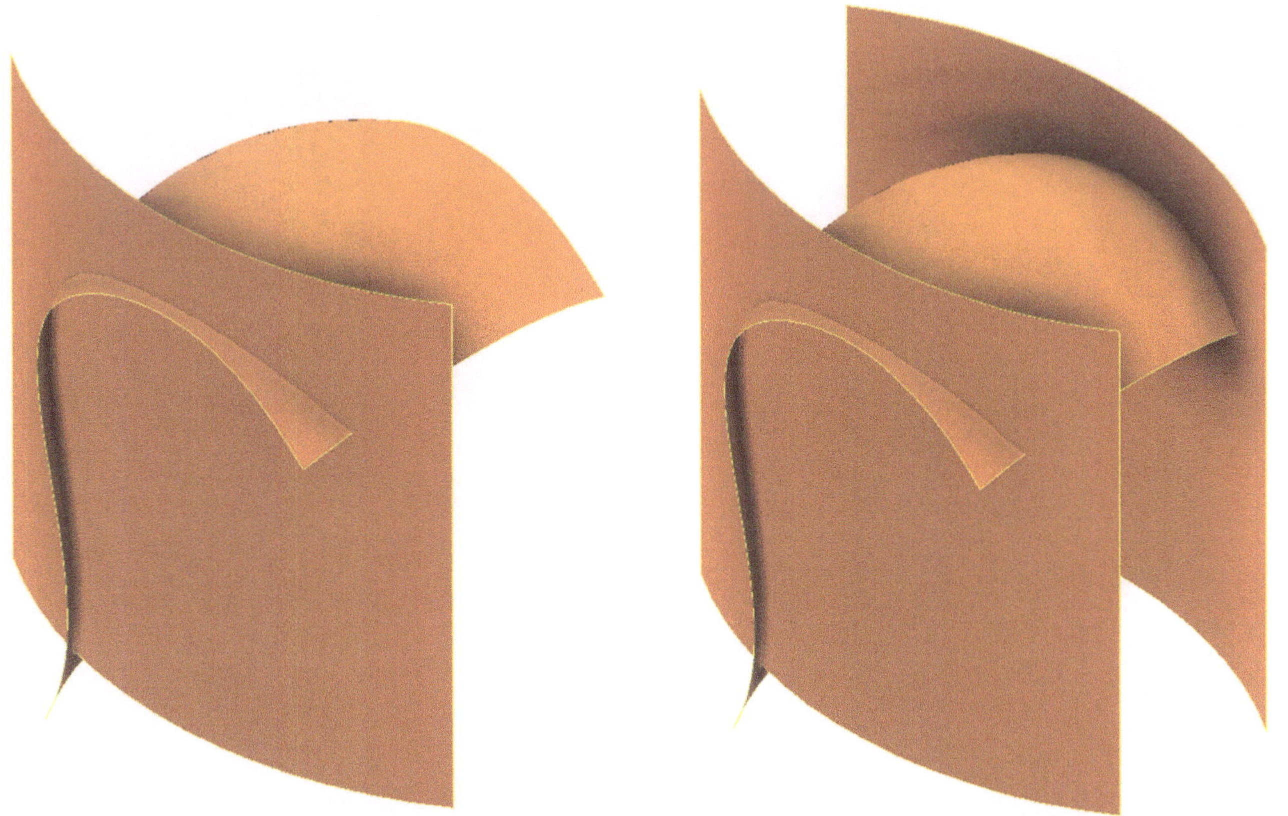

Creating the Back surface

1. Create an arc on the XZ plane. Finish the sketch.

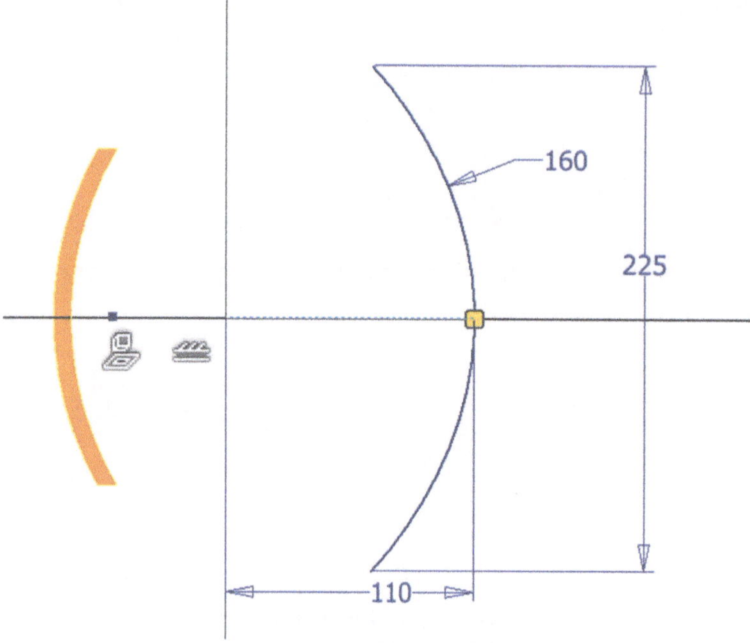

2. In the **Model** tree, right-click on the second sketch and select **Visibility**.
3. On the ribbon, click **3D Model > Create > Sweep**. Next, select **Orientation > Follow Path**.
4. Select the arc to define the profile. Next, select the path and click **OK** to create the sweep surface.

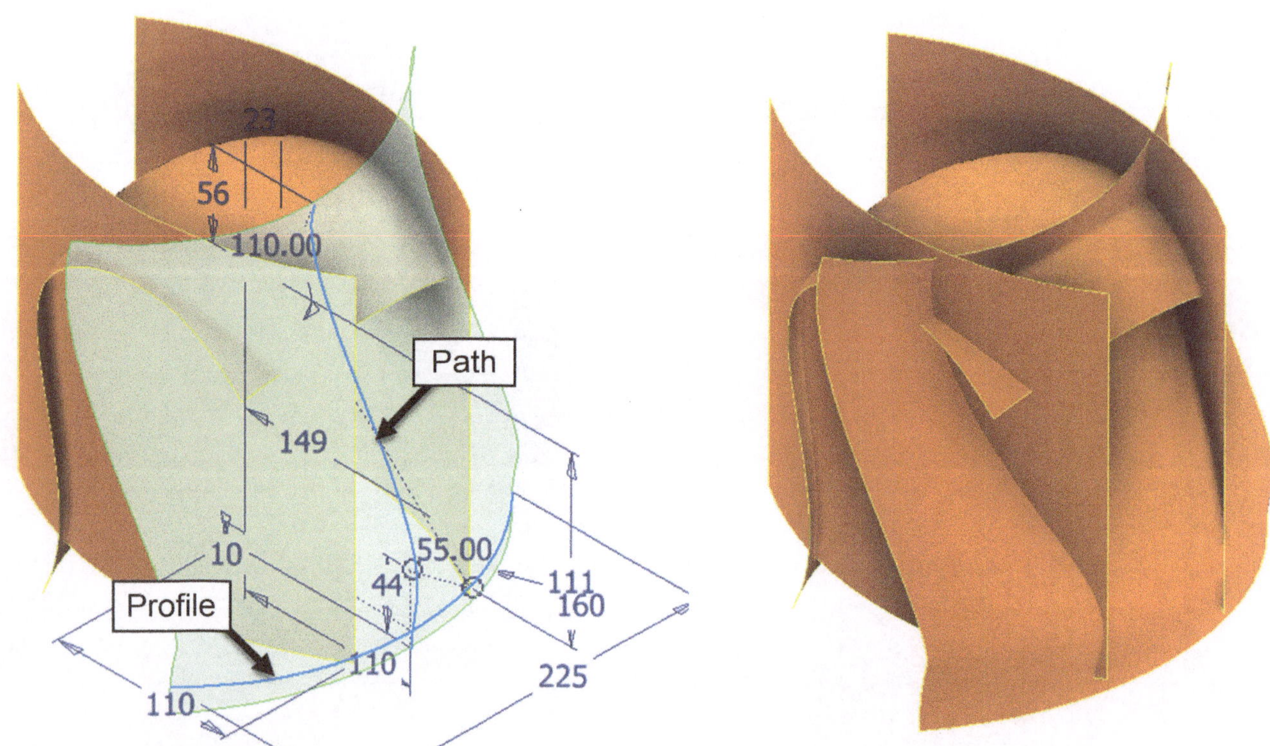

Sculpting the Surfaces

1. Start a new sketch on the XZ Plane and create a rectangle, as shown. Next, click **Finish Sketch**.
2. Activate the **Patch** command (on the ribbon, click **3D Model > Surface > Patch**).

3. Select the rectangle and click **OK**.

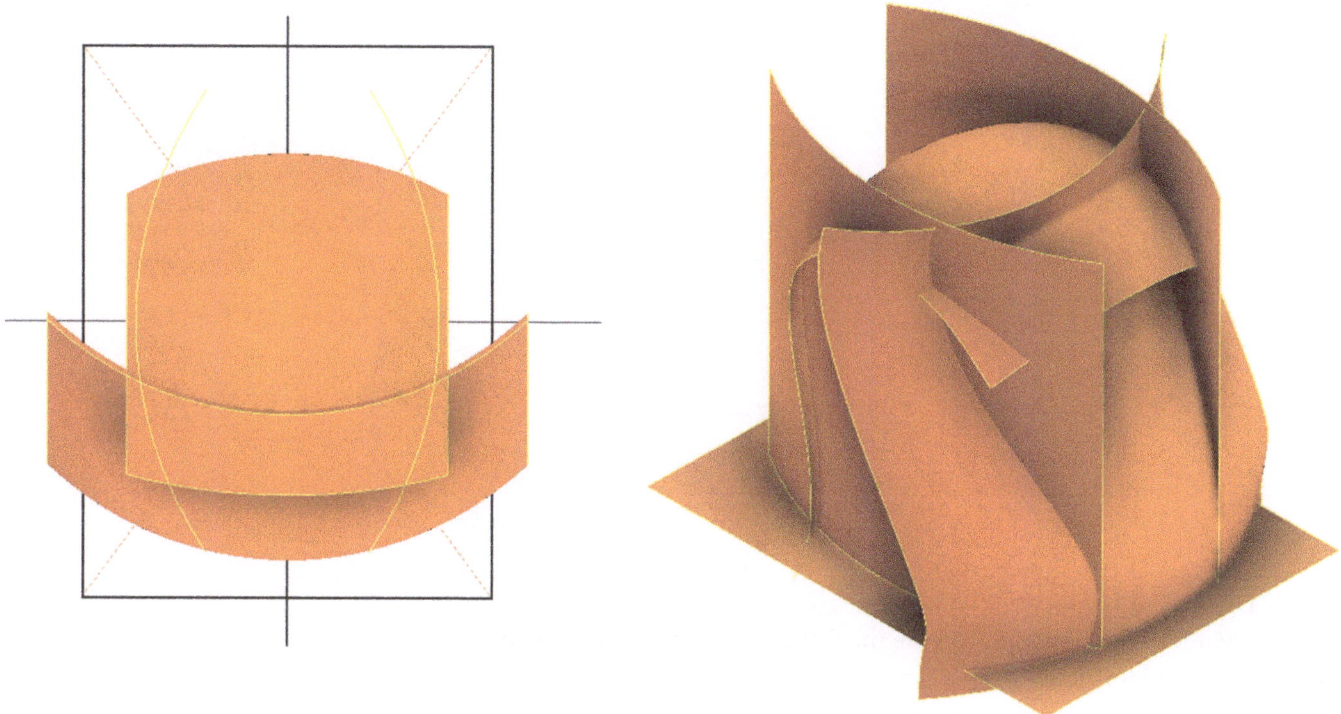

4. On the ribbon, click **3D Model > Surface > Sculpt**.
5. Select all the surfaces and click **OK**; the selected surfaces will be sculpted into a closed solid.

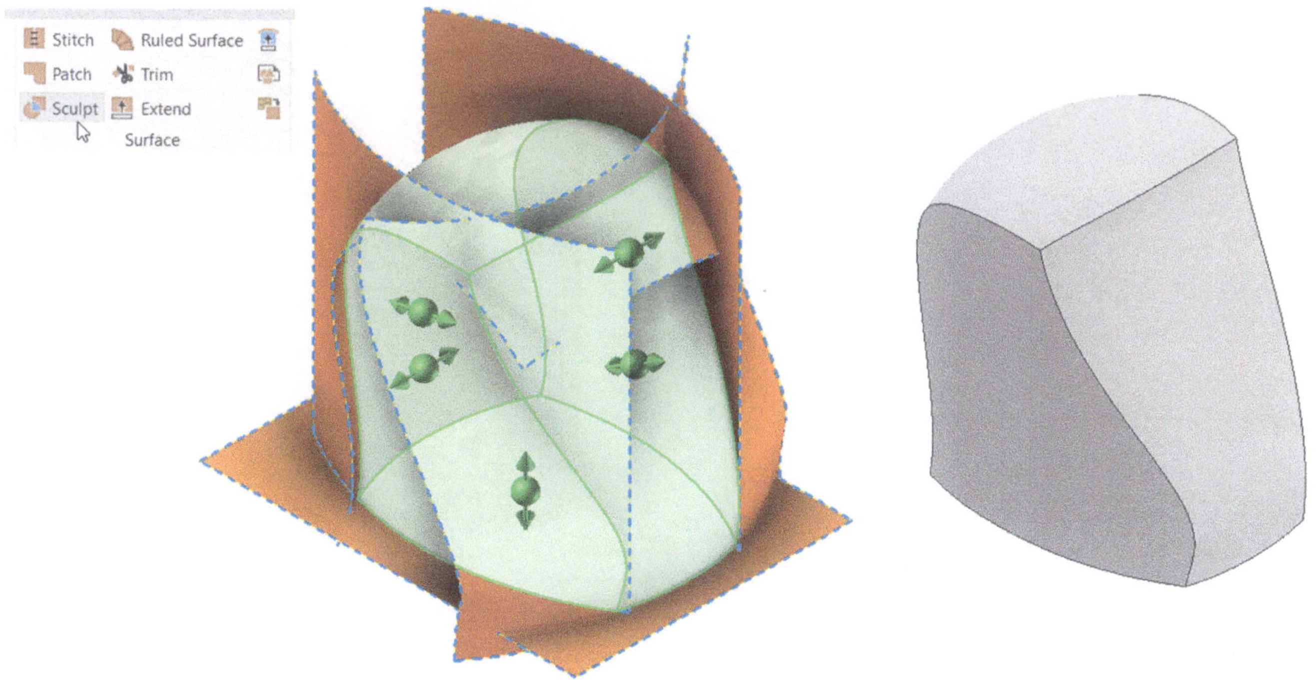

6. On the ribbon, click **3D Model > Modify > Copy Object.** Next, select all the faces of the solid body.
7. On the Properties panel, select **Method > Create Object**. Next, select **Object > Surface** and click **OK**.
8. In the **Model** tree, right-click on the Sculpt feature and select Suppress Features.

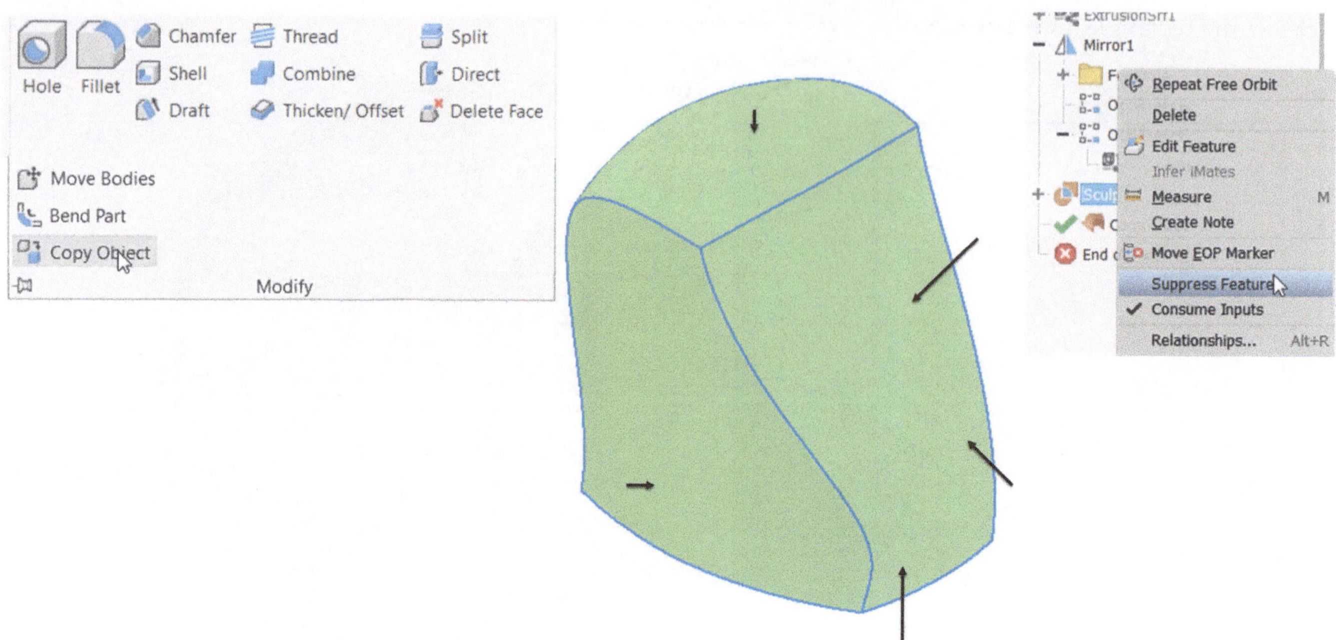

Creating the Handle Surface

1. In the **Model** tree, right-click on the third sketch and select **Visibility**.
2. On the **3D Model** ribbon, expand the **Work features** panel and click the **Normal to Curve at Point** icon.
3. Select the spline. Next, select the lower endpoint of the spline to create the plane normal to the spline.
4. Start a sketch on the plane normal to the spline.
5. Click **Sketch** > **Create** panel > **Circle** drop-down > **Ellipse** on the ribbon.
6. Click in the lower portion of the horizontal axis. Next, move the pointer horizontally toward the right and click.
7. Move the pointer upward click.

8. Next, add dimensions to the ellipse.
9. In the **Model** tree, right-click on the third sketch and uncheck the **Dimension Visibility** option.
10. On the ribbon, click **Sketch > Create > Project Geometry**. Next, select the endpoint of the spline, as shown.
11. On the ribbon, click **Sketch > Constrain > Coincident**. Next, select the top quadrant point of the ellipse and the projected point of the spline.
12. On the ribbon, click **Sketch > Constrain > Horizontal**. Next, select the center point of the ellipse and the projected point of the spline. Click **Finish Sketch**.

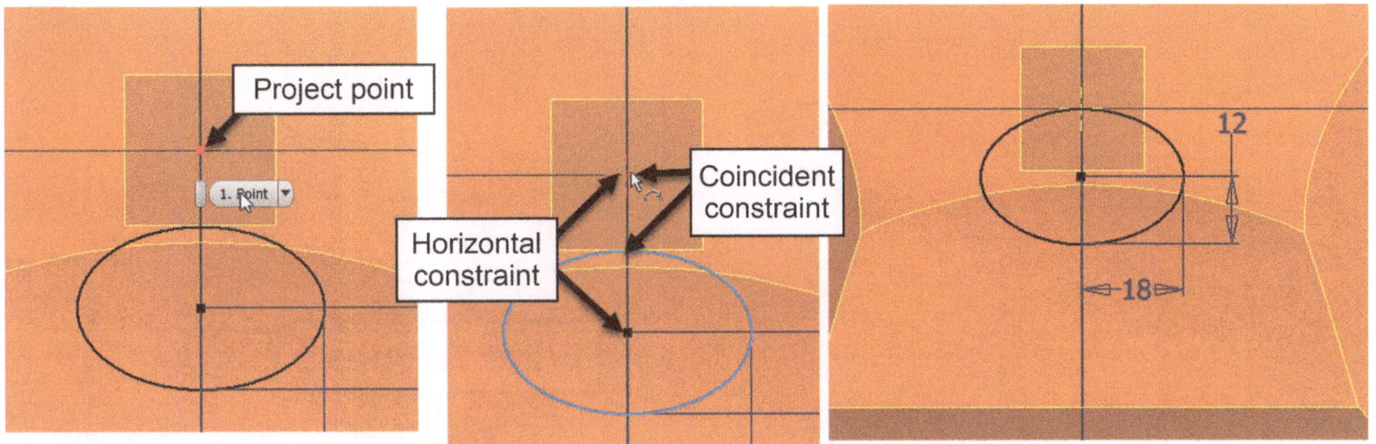

13. On the ribbon, click **Surface > Create > Sweep**. Next, select **Orientation > Follow Path**.
14. Activate the **Surface Mode** icon on the top-right corner of the **Properties** panel. Next, click **OK** to create the handle surface.

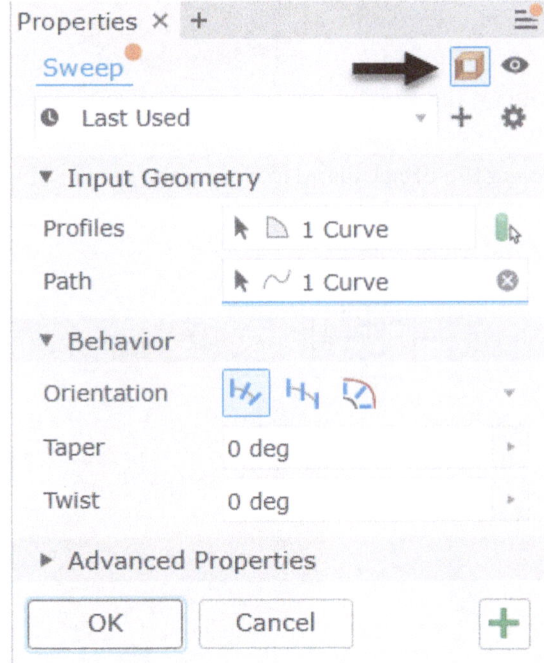

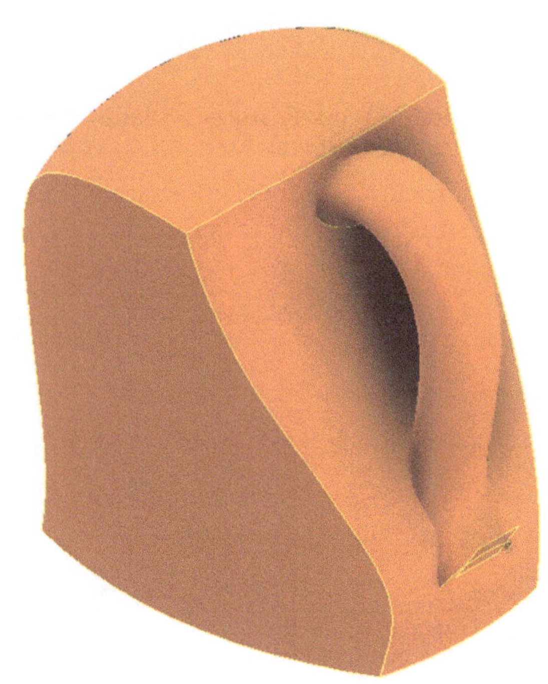

Blending the Handle with Surface Model

1. On the ribbon, click **3D Model > Modify > Fillet**.
2. Select the edge between the swept surfaces, as shown.
3. Type-in 25 in the **Fillet Constant Radius** box. Leave the default settings on the Properties panel and click **OK**.

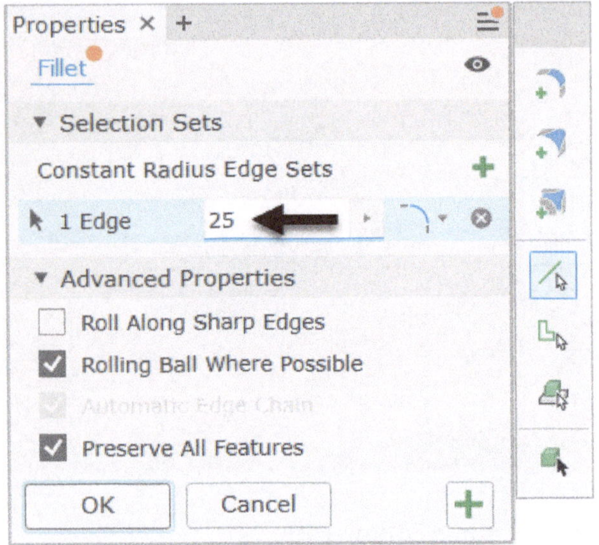

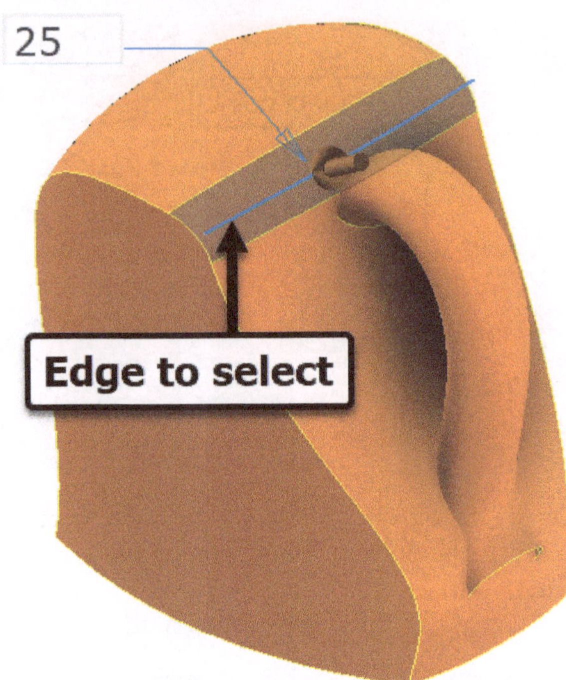

4. Click **3D Model > Work Features > Plane > Offset from Plane** on the ribbon.
5. Select the YZ Plane from the **Model** tree. Type 75 and click the green check.
6. On the ribbon, click **3D Model > Surface > Trim**. Next, select the offset plane to define the trim tool.
7. Select the left portion of the swept surface, and then click **OK**.

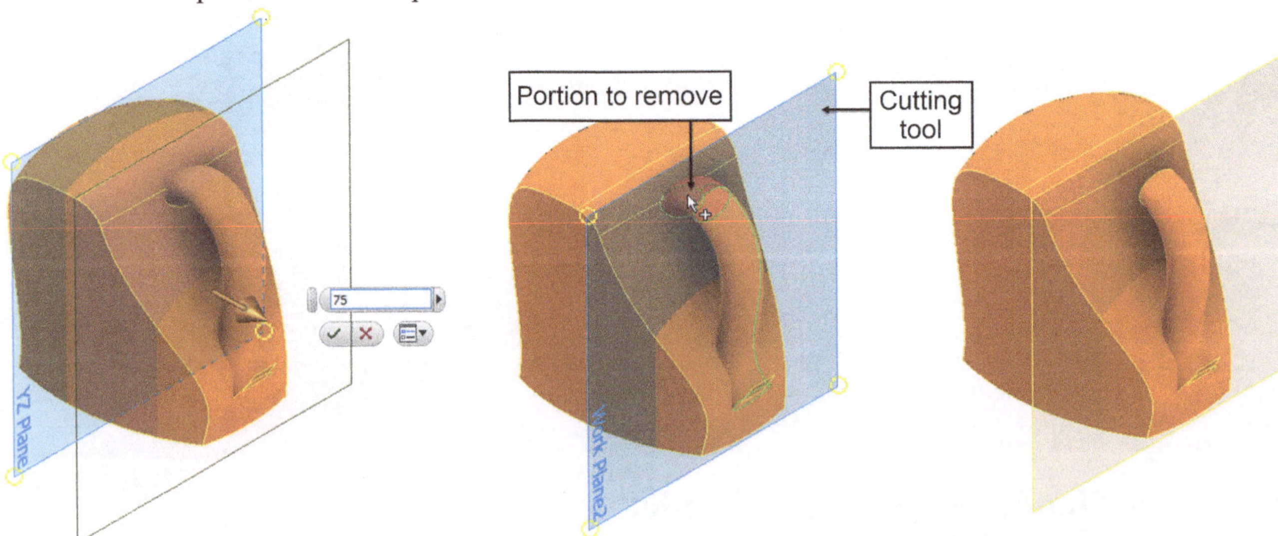

7. In the **Model** tree, right-click on the third sketch and select the **Visibility** option.
8. On the **3D Model** ribbon, expand the **Work features** panel and click the **Normal to Curve at Point** icon.
9. Select the spline. Next, select the upper endpoint of the spline to create the plane normal to the spline.
10. Start a sketch on the plane normal to the spline.

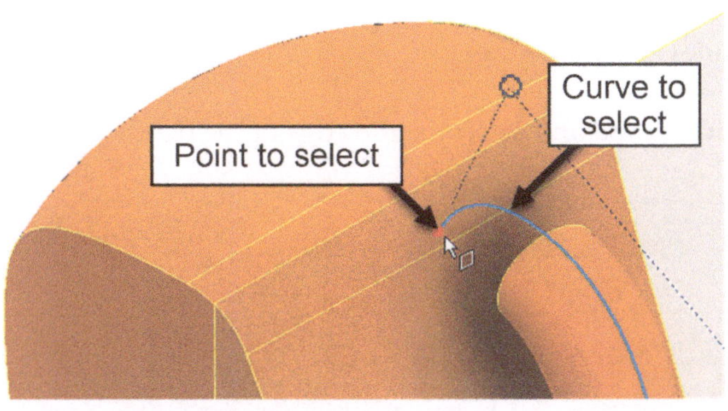

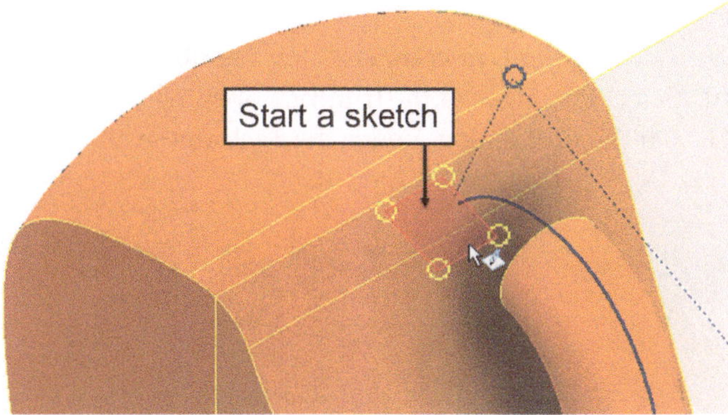

11. Click the **Slice Graphics** icon located at the bottom of the graphics window.
12. Click **Sketch** > **Create** panel > **Circle** drop-down > **Ellipse** on the ribbon.
13. Create an ellipse and add dimensions to it, as shown. Click **Finish Sketch**.

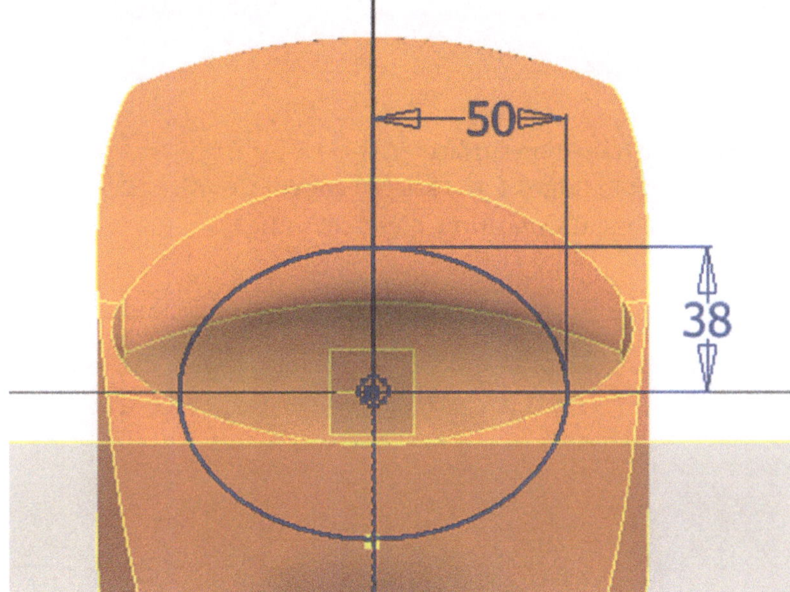

14. Activate the **Trim** command (on the ribbon, click **3D Model > Surface > Trim**), and click on the ellipse.
8. Select the portion of the surface, as shown. Next, click **OK**.

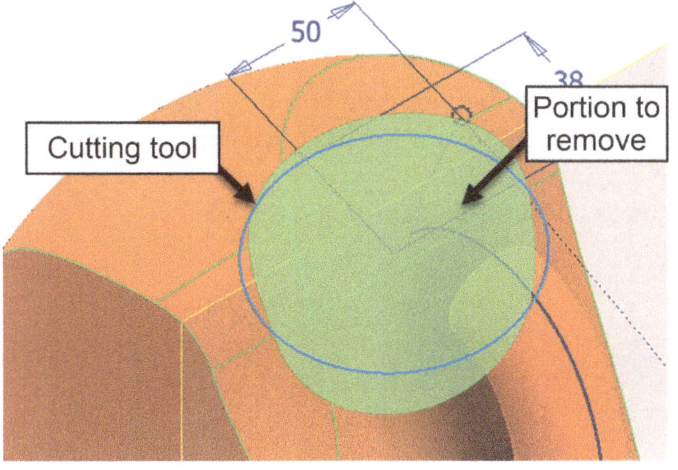

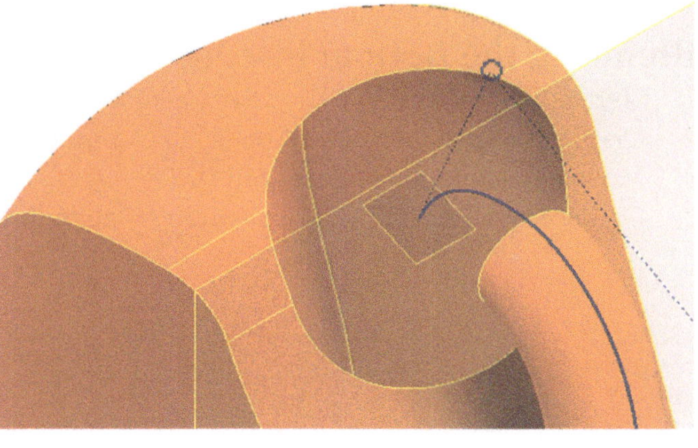

9. Activate the **Loft** command (on the ribbon, click **3D Model > Create > Loft**).
10. Select the edges of the trimmed opening.
11. On the **Loft** dialog, under the **Sections** section, click **Click to add** and select the top edge of the handle.

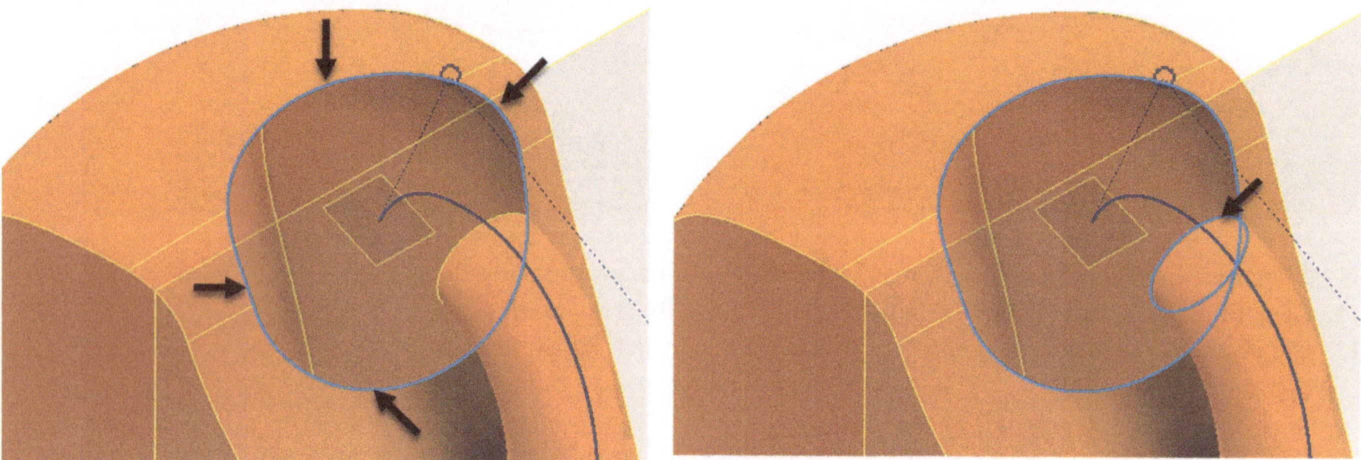

12. Click the **Transition** tab to display the preview of the transition surface.
13. Click the **Conditions** tab, click on the drop-down next to **Edges 1** and select **Tangent Condition**.
14. Click on the drop-down next to **Edges2** and select **Tangent Condition**. Next, click **OK**.

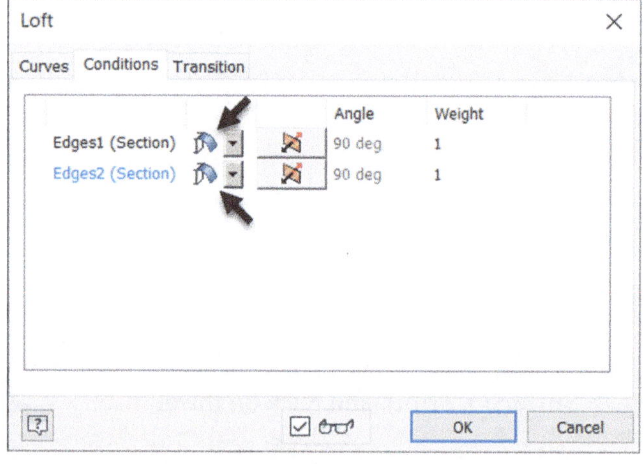

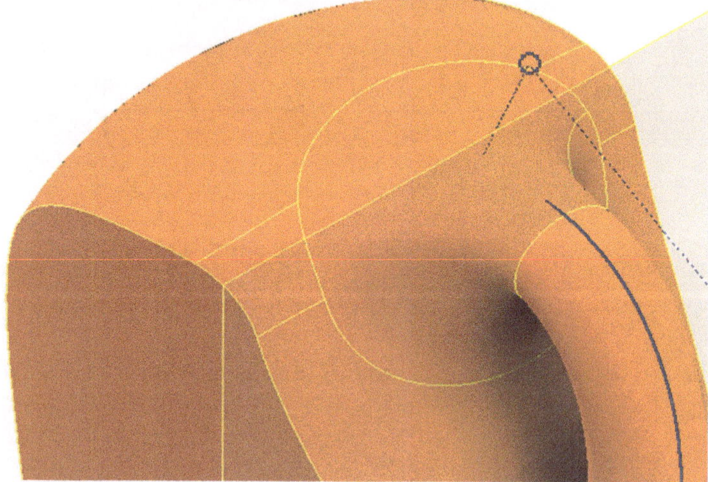

Blending the Bottom handle

1. Start a sketch on the XY Plane. Next, click **Sketch > Create** panel > **Project** drop-down > **Project Cutting Edges**.
2. On the **Sketch** ribbon, click **Create** panel > **Line**. Next, select the endpoint of the projected curve.
3. Move the pointer downward and click.
4. On the **Sketch** ribbon, click **Constrain > Tangent**. Next, select the projected curve and the line.

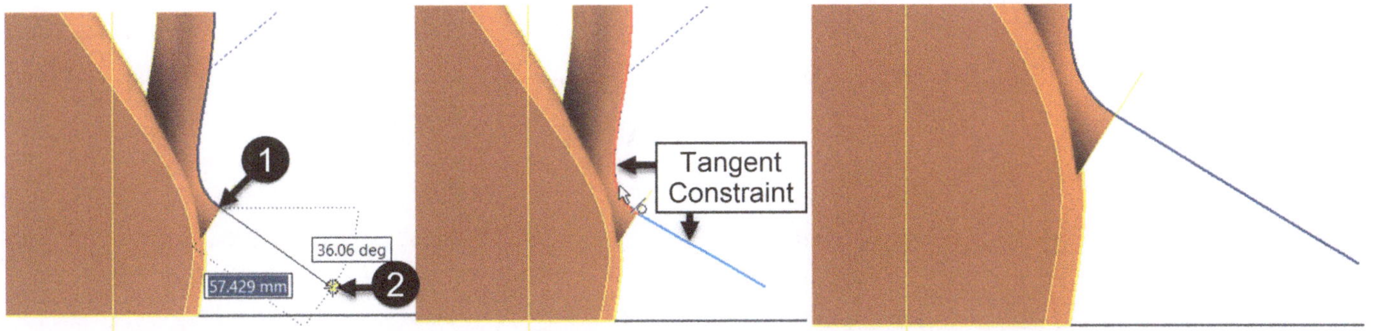

5. Click the **Finish Sketch** button on the ribbon.
6. On the **3D Model** ribbon, click **Work Features > Planes** drop-down > **Angle to Plane around Edge**.
7. In the **Model** tree, expand the Origin folder and select the XY Plane.
8. Select the sketch line tangent to the projected edge. Click **OK** to create the work plane.

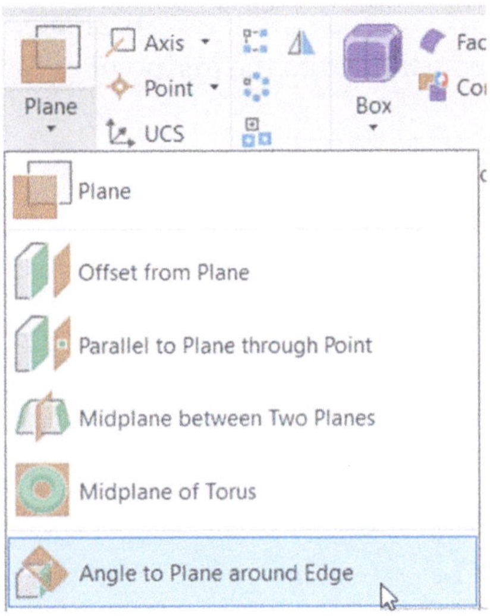

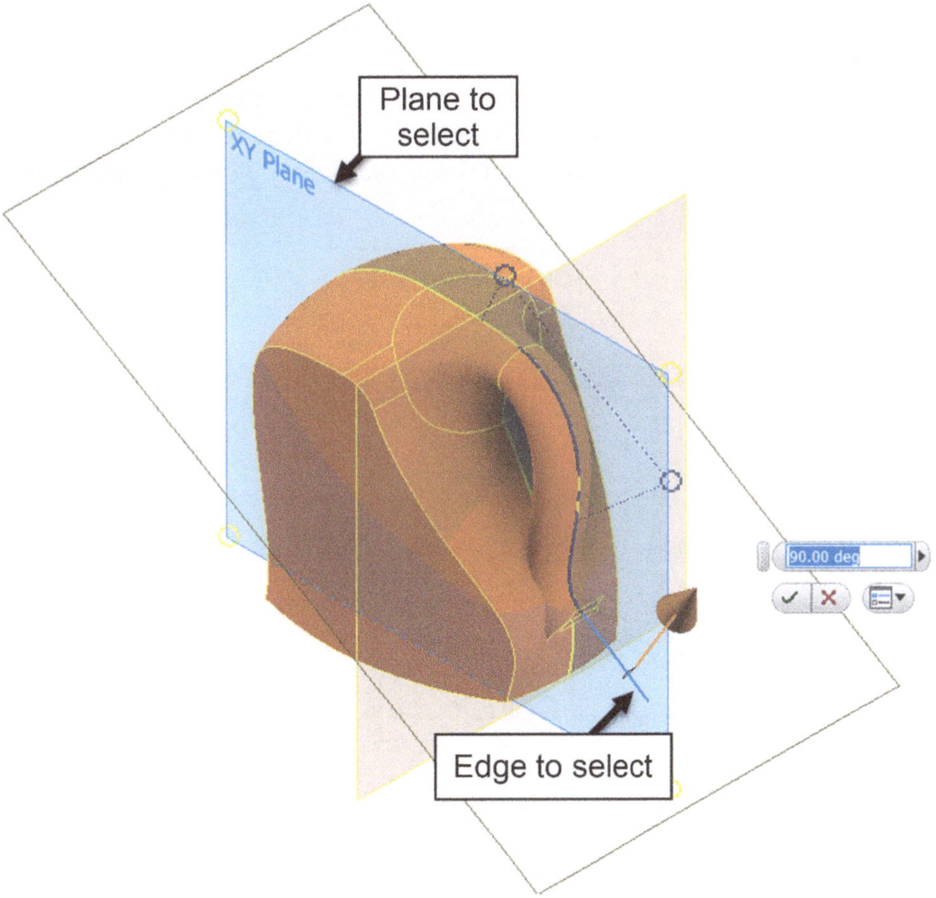

9. On the ribbon, click **3D Model > Sketch > Start 2D Sketch**. Next, select the newly created plane.
10. Create an ellipse in the space. Next, create a vertical and horizontal construction line passing through the centerpoint of the ellipse.
11. On the **Sketch** ribbon, click **Modify > Trim**, and then trim the upper portion of the ellipse.

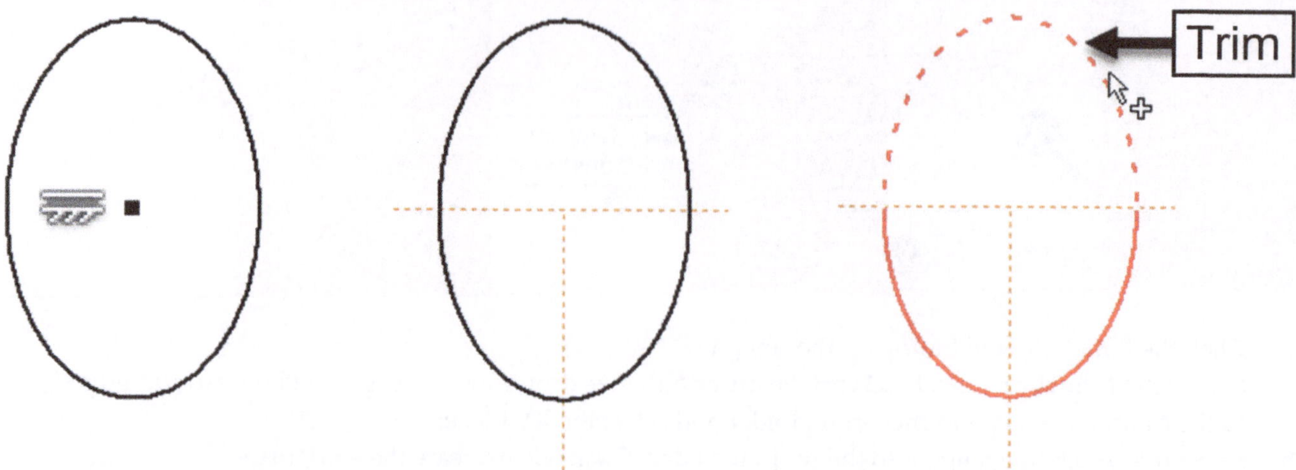

12. On the **Sketch** ribbon, click **Constraints > Coincident**. Next, select the endpoints of the horizontal line and the ellipse.
13. Likewise, create coincident constraints between the other endpoints of the lines and the ellipse.
14. On the **Sketch** ribbon, click **Constraints > Coincident**, and then select the upper endpoint of the vertical line.
15. Select the midpoint of the horizontal line; the endpoint of the vertical line is constrained to the midpoint of the horizontal line.

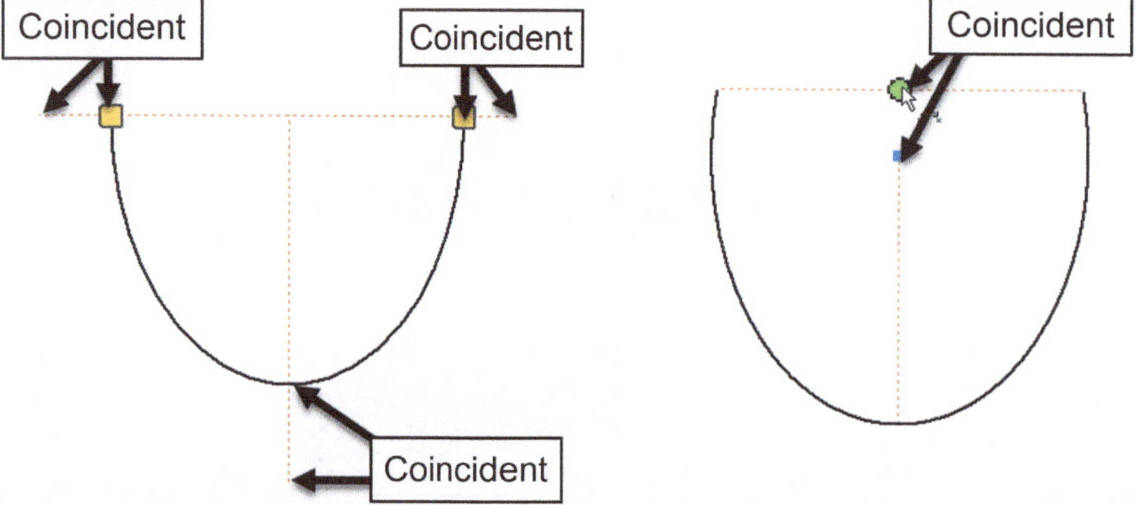

16. On the **Sketch** ribbon, click **Create > Project** drop-down > **Project Geometry**. Next, select the endpoint of the spline, as shown.
17. Constraint the centerpoint of the ellipse horizontal to the projected point.

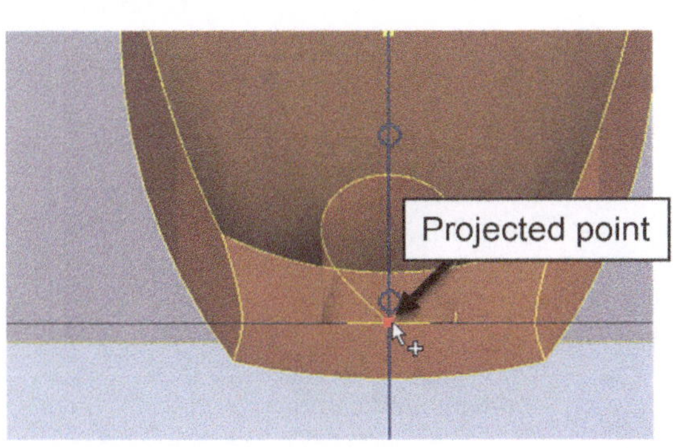

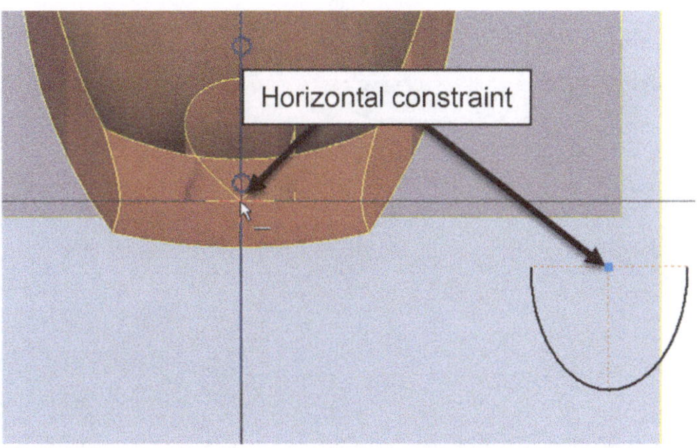

18. On the **Sketch** ribbon, click **Constrain > Dimension.** Next, add dimensions to the ellipse, as shown.

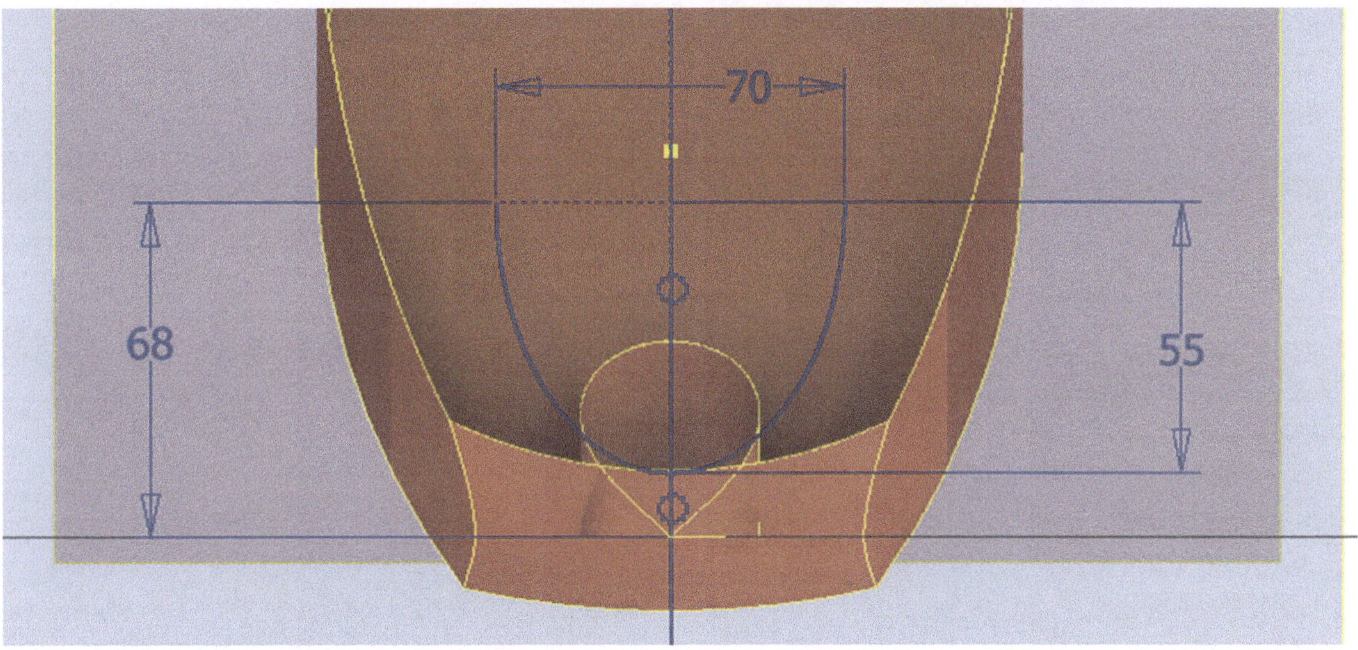

19. Click **Finish Sketch** on the ribbon.
20. On the **3D Model** ribbon, click **Create > Extrude**. Next, activate the **Surface Mode** icon on the **top-right** corner of the **Properties** panel.
21. Select the newly created sketch. Next, select **Direction** and type **60** in the **Distance A** box.
22. Click the **Direction** > **Symmetric** icon and click **OK**.

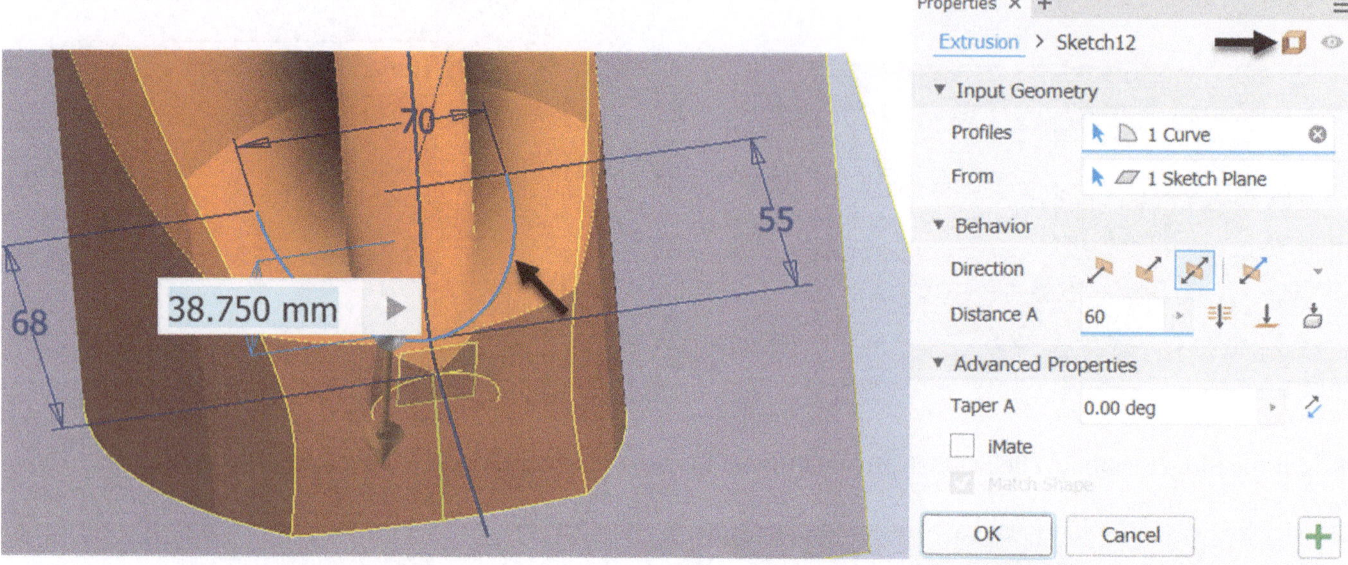

23. Activate the **Trim** command and select the extruded surface to define the cutting tool.
24. Select the lower portion of the handle surface, as shown. Next, click **Apply**.

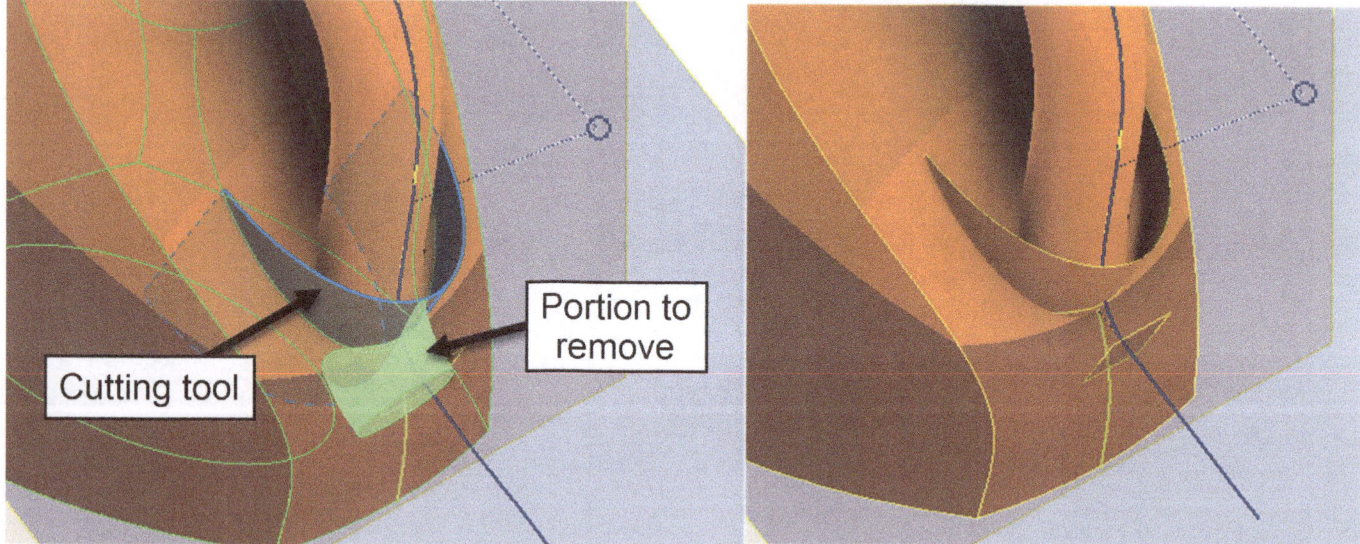

25. Select the handle surface to define the cutting tool.
26. Select the extruded surface, as shown. Next, click **Apply**.

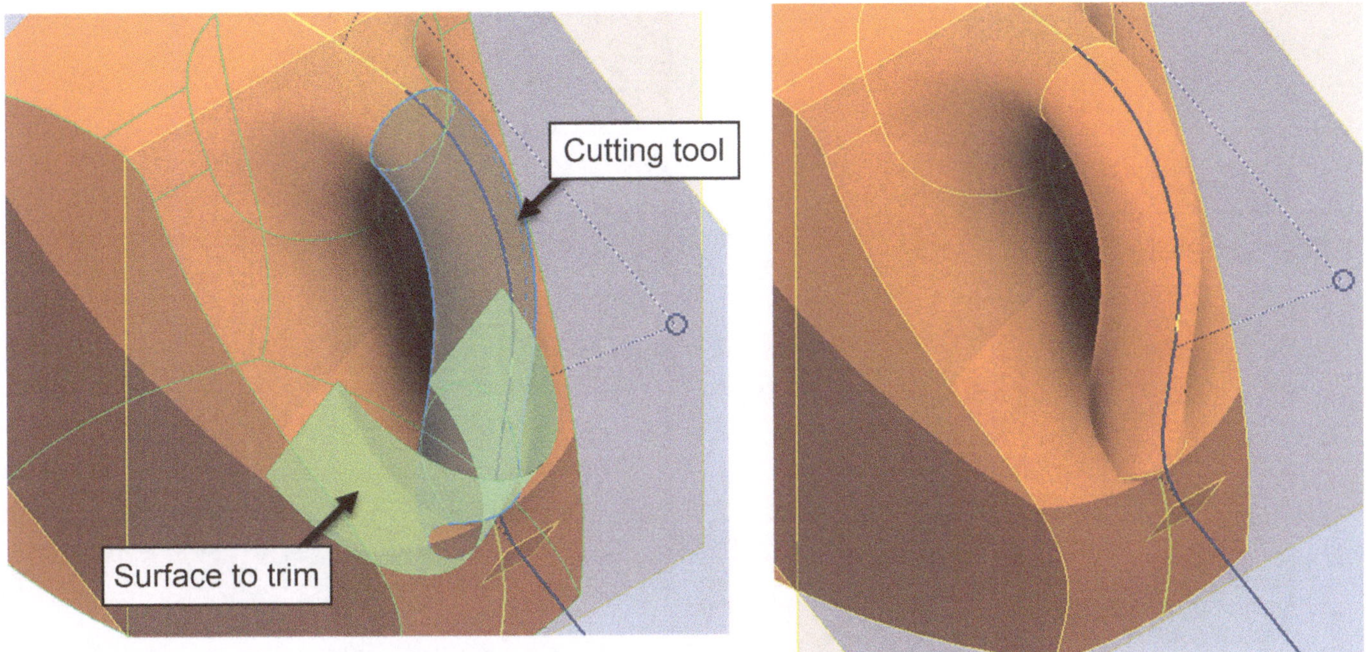

27. On the ribbon, click **View > Visibility > Section View** drop-down > **Half Section View**.
28. Select the XY Plane from the graphics window and click the green check.
29. On the ribbon, click **3D Model > Modify > Split**. Next, select the handle surface to define the tool.
30. Select the back surface to define the target. Next, click **Apply** + to split the surface.
31. Rotate the model and select the trimmed extruded surface, as shown.
32. Select the back surface to define the target. Next, click **OK** to split the surface.

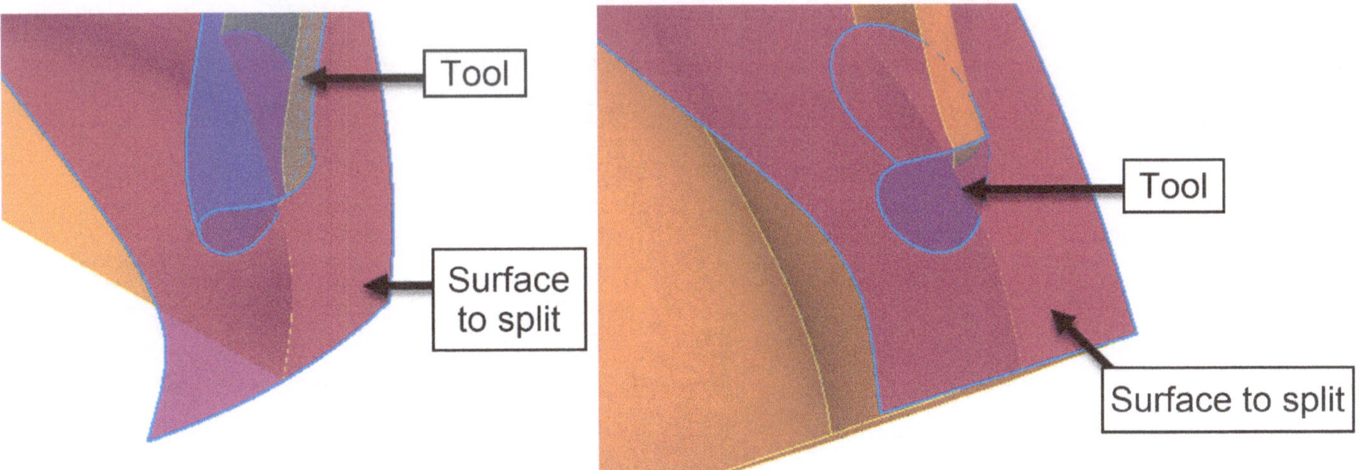

33. On the ribbon, click **3D Model > Modify > Delete Face**. Next, select the split surface, as shown.
34. Click **OK** to delete the selected face.

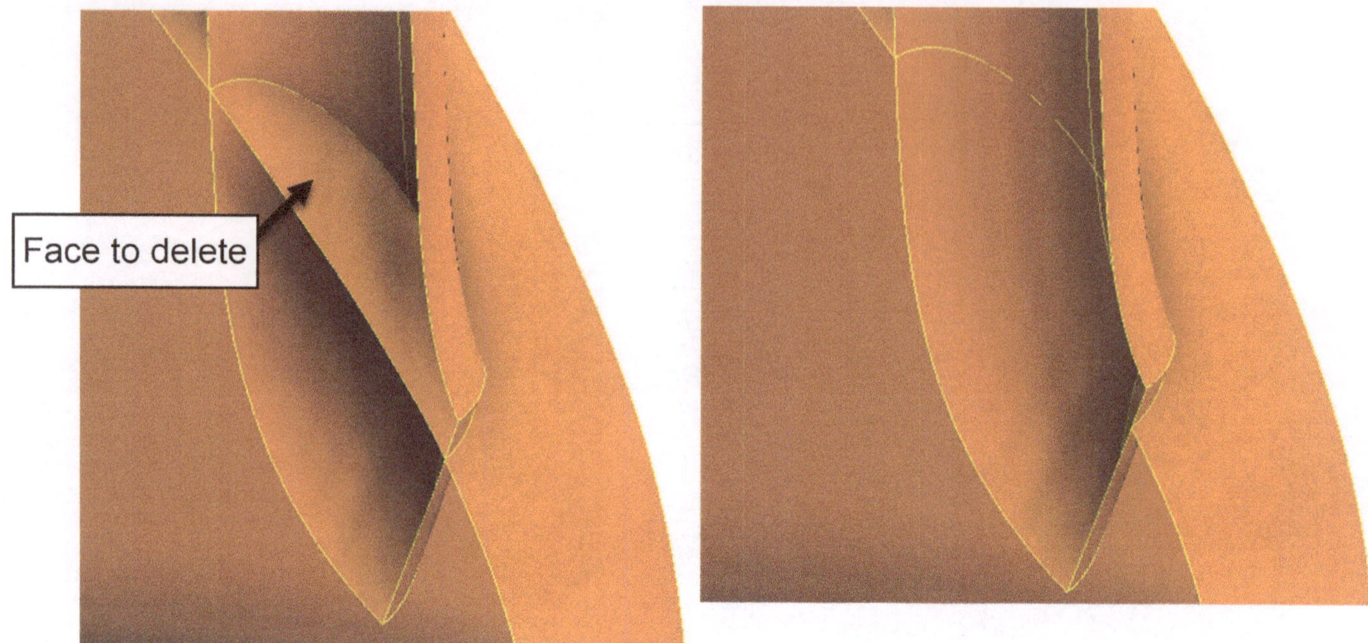

35. Activate the **Trim** command and select the copied surface to define the cutting tool.
36. Select the portion of the handle surface, as shown. Next, click **Apply**.
37. Select the copied surface to define the cutting tool.
38. Select the portion of the handle surface, as shown. Next, click **OK**.

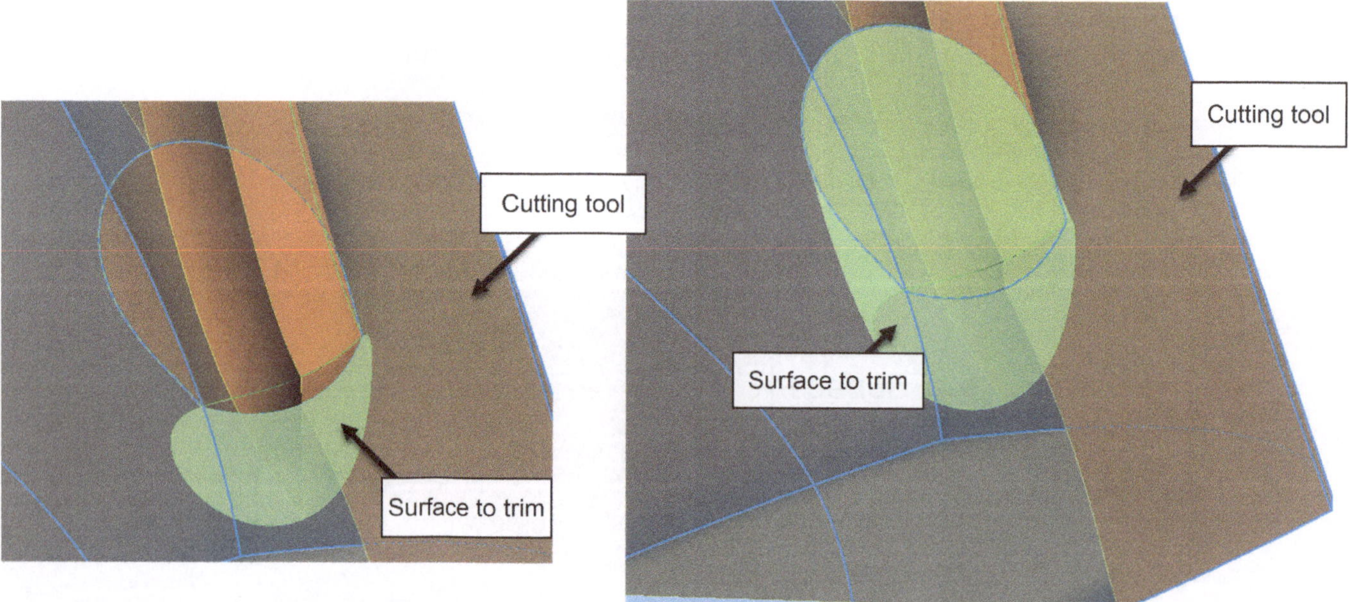

39. On the ribbon, click **View > Visibility > Section View** drop-down > **End Section View**.
40. On the **3D Model** ribbon, click **Surface > Stitch.** Next, create a selection window across the entire surface model.
41. Check the **Maintain as Surface** option. Next, click **Apply** and **Done** to stitch the surfaces.

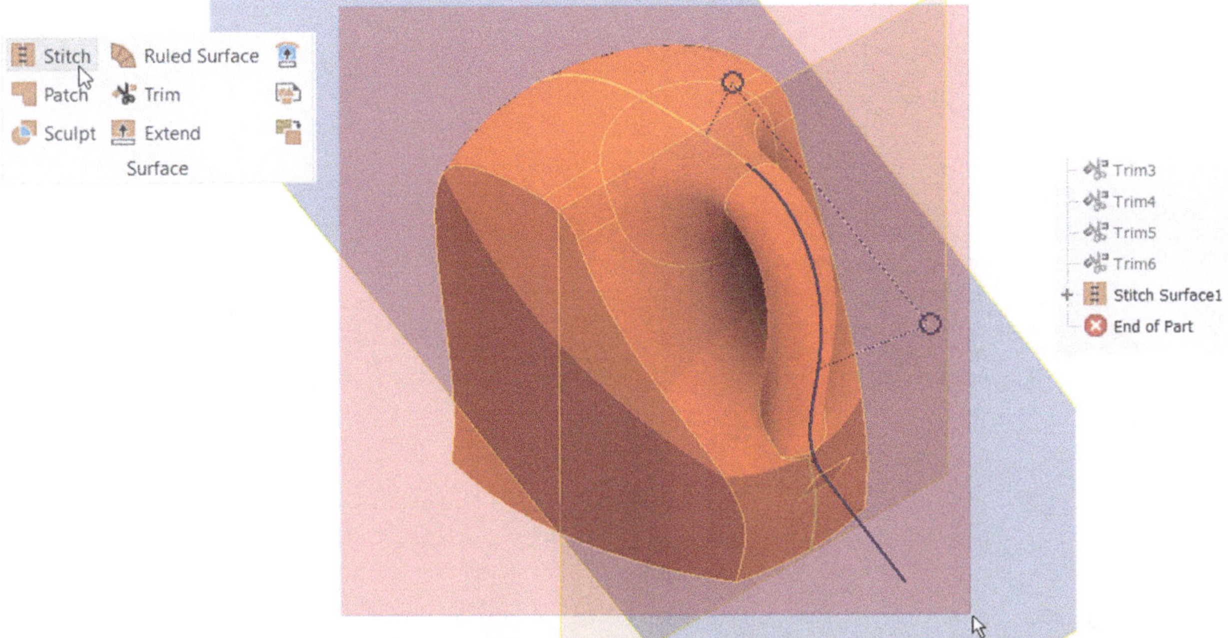

42. On the ribbon, click **3D Model > Modify > Fillet**. Next, select the edge of the handle, as shown.
43. Type **6** in the **Fillet Constant Radius** box and click the **Apply** button.
44. Select the edge between the handle and surface body, as shown.
45. Type **5** in the **Fillet Constant Radius** box and click the **OK** button.

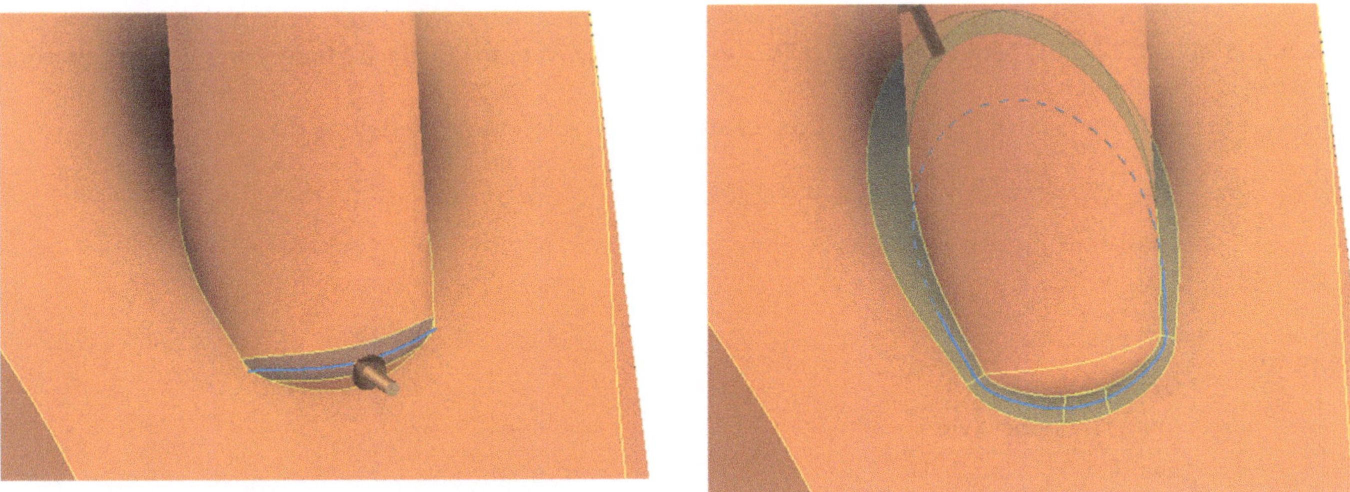

Creating the Neck and Spout

1. Start a sketch on the XY Plane and sketch the revolved surface. Next, click **Finish Sketch**.

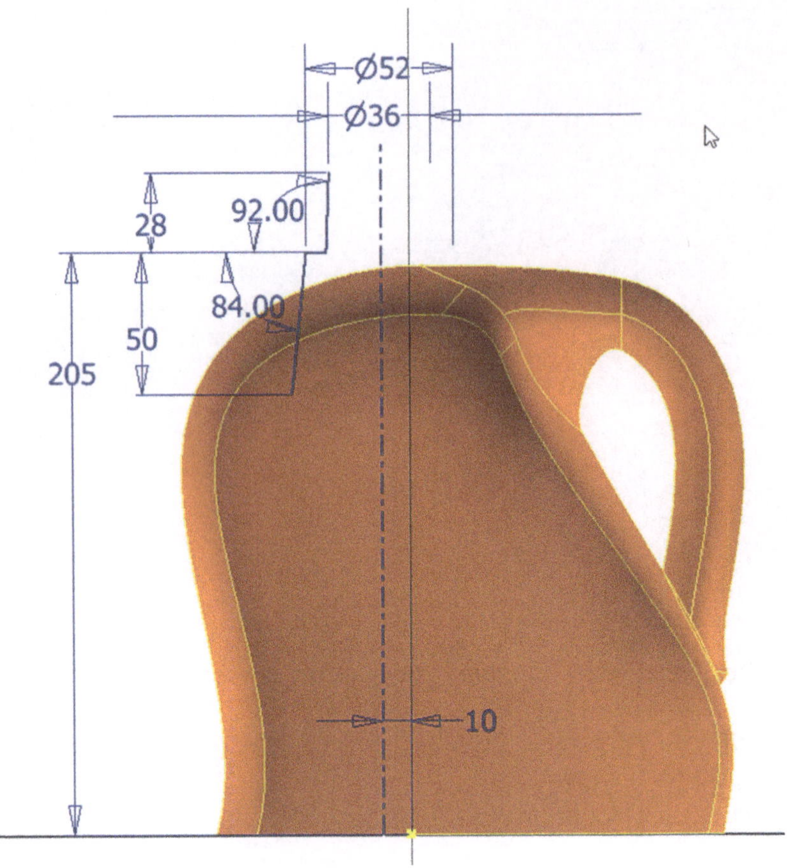

2. On the ribbon, click **3D Model > Create > Revolve**. Next, activate the **Surface Mode** icon on the **Properties** panel.
3. Select the profile, as shown. Click in the **Axis** selection box to select the centerline as the axis. Click **OK**.

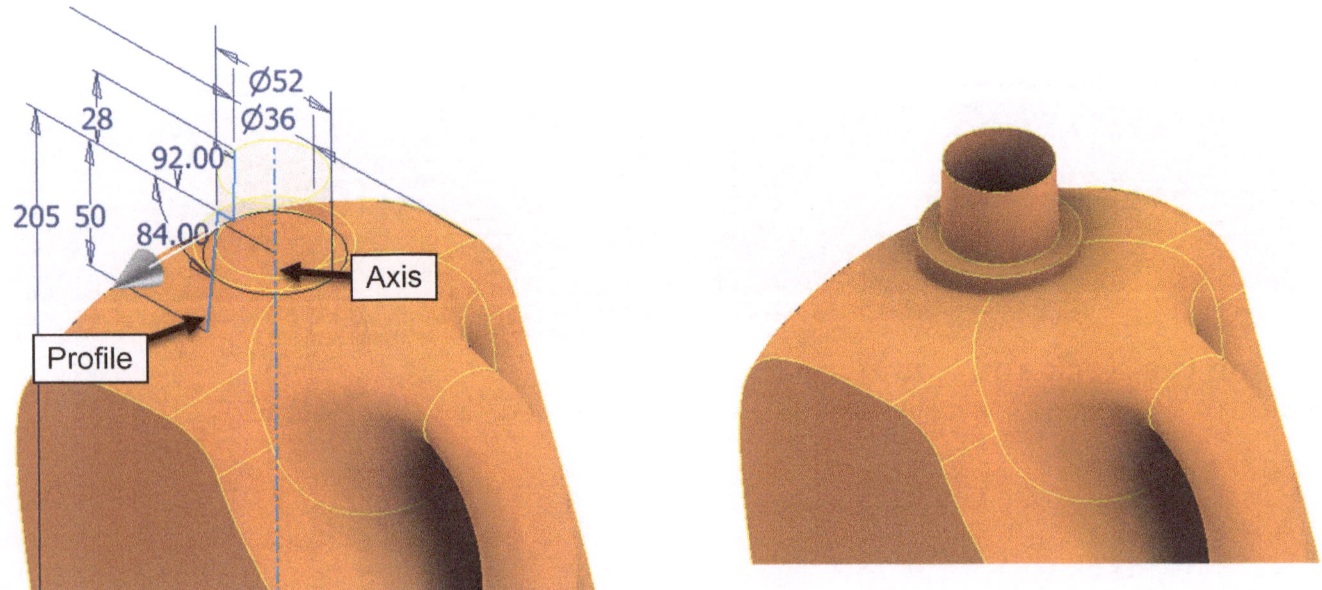

4. Activate the **Trim** command and select the revolved surface to define the cutting tool.
5. Click in the region enclosed by the revolved surface, as shown. Next, click **Apply**.

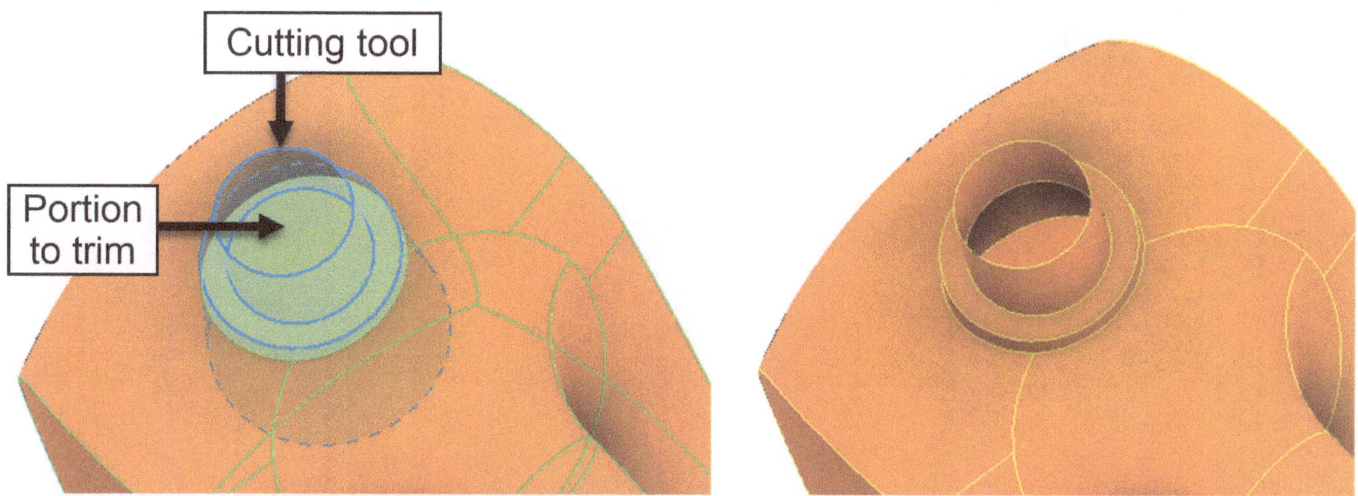

6. Select the stitched surface to define the cutting tool.
7. Select the lower portion of the revolved surface, as shown. Next, click **OK**.

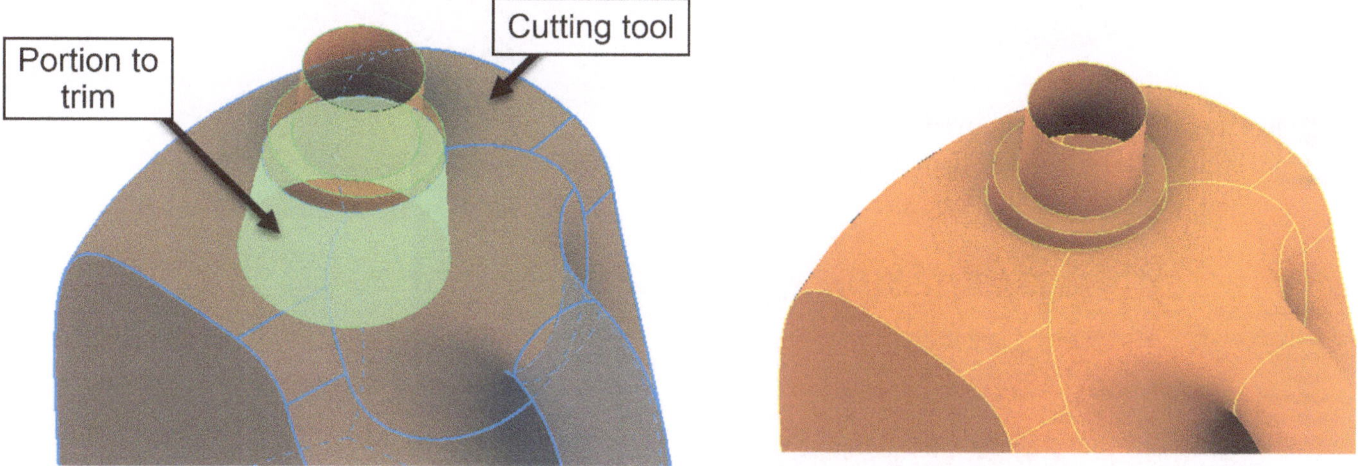

8. On the **3D Model** ribbon, click **Surface > Stitch.** Next, select the revolved surface and the remaining body.
9. Click **Apply** and **Done** to stitch the surfaces.

Filleting the Label and Bottom Surfaces

1. Activate the **Fillet** command and select the edges of both the label faces
2. On the **Fillet** Properties panel, type-in **10** in the **Fillet Constant Radius** box, and click **Apply** + .

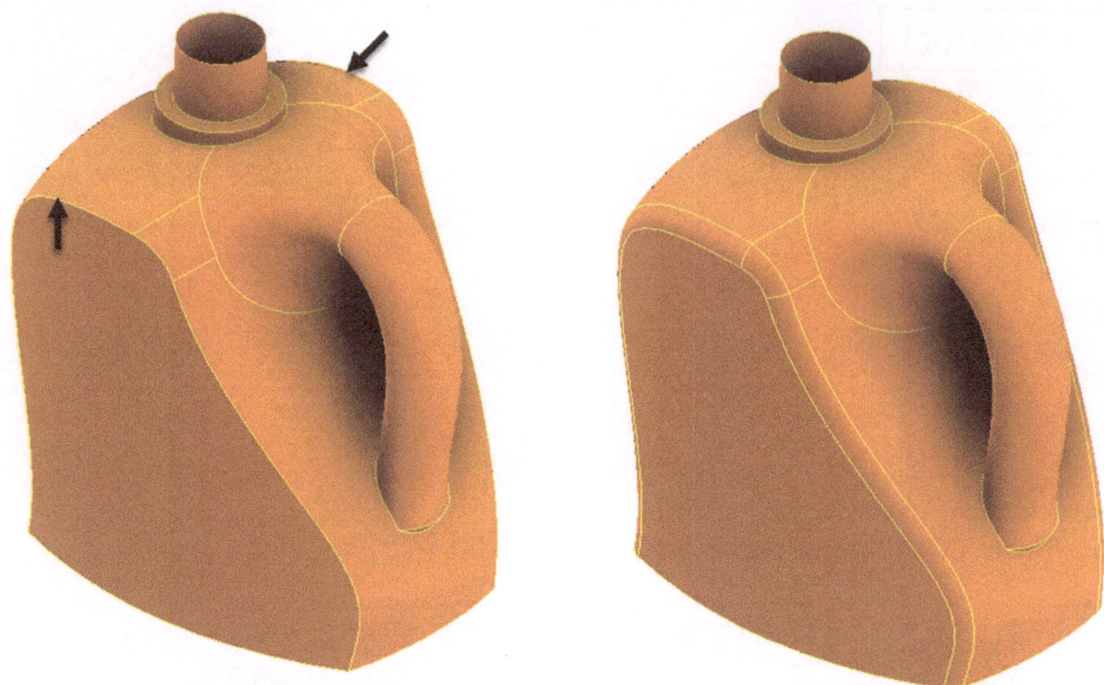

3. Select the edges of the bottom surface, as shown.
4. On the **Fillet** dialog, type-in **10** in the **Radius** box, and click **OK**.

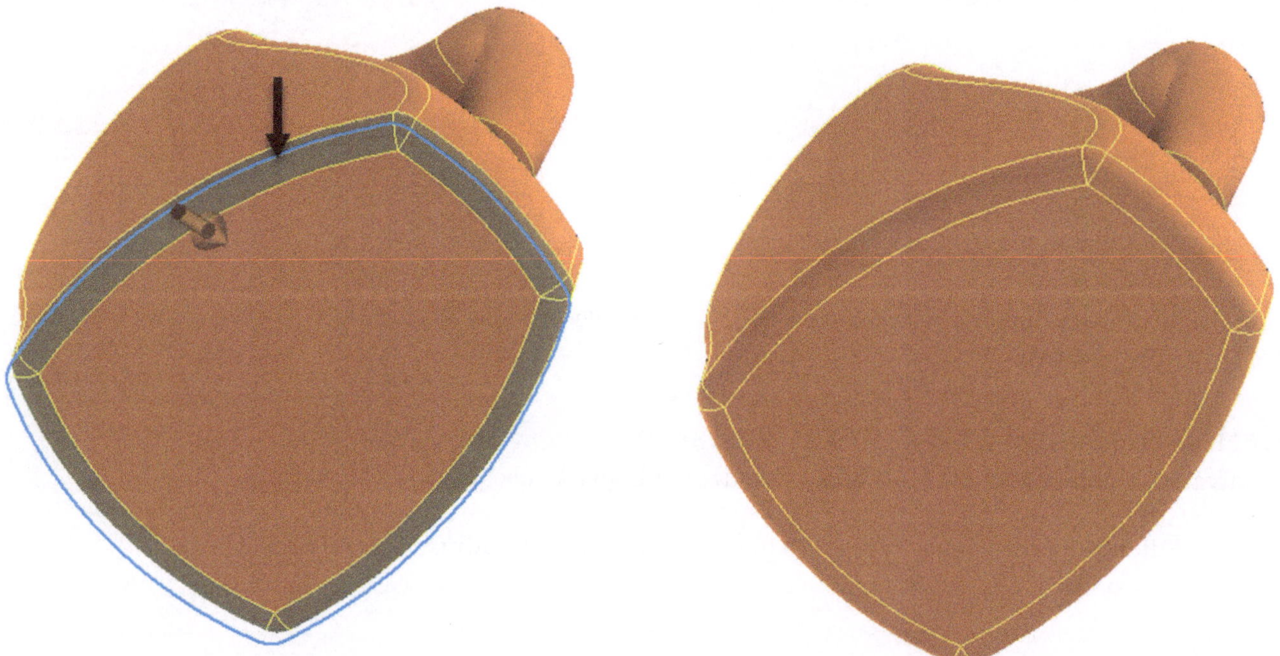

Adding thickness to the model

1. On the ribbon, click **View > Visibility > Section View** drop-down > **Half Section View**.
2. Select the XY Plane from the graphics window and click the green check.

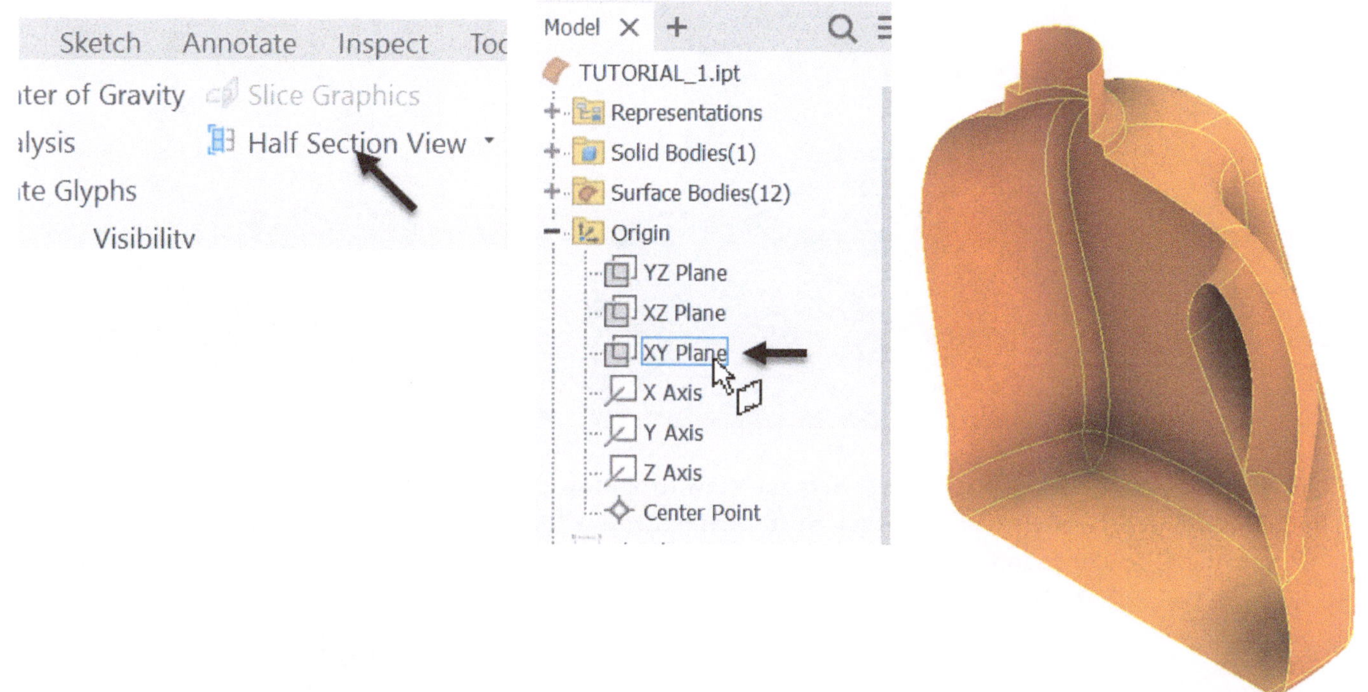

3. On the ribbon, click **3D Model > Modify > Thicken/Offset** and click the **Quilt Selection On** icon next to the **Faces** selection box.
4. Click on the surface body.
5. Type-in 1.5 in the **Distance** box. Next, click **Direction > Inside**. and then **OK**.

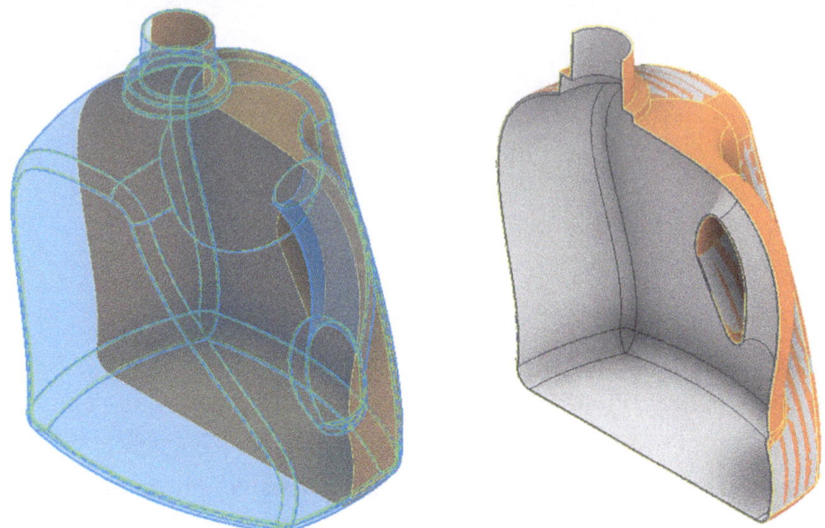

6. Activate the **Thicken/Offset** and deactivate the **Quilt Selection On** icon.
7. Select the inner faces of the spout and check the **Automatic Bending** option.
8. Click **Direction > Outside** and type 1 in the **Distance** box. Next, click **OK**.

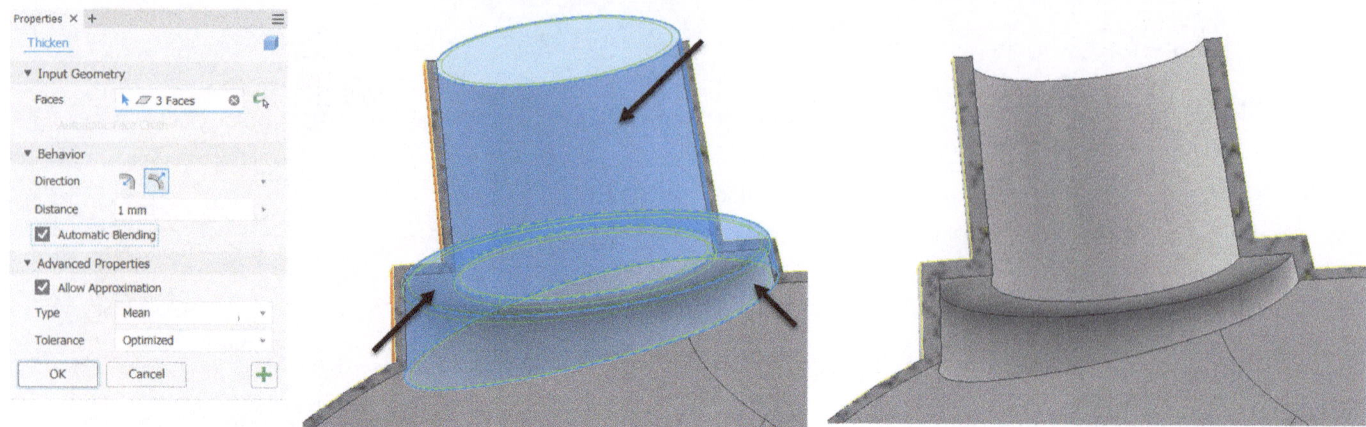

9. On the ribbon, click **View > Visibility > Section View** drop-down > **End Section View**.
10. In the **Model** tree, right-click on the **Stitch Surface** and uncheck the **Visibility**.
11. Activate the **Fillet** command, and then fillet the sharp edges of the neck and spout.

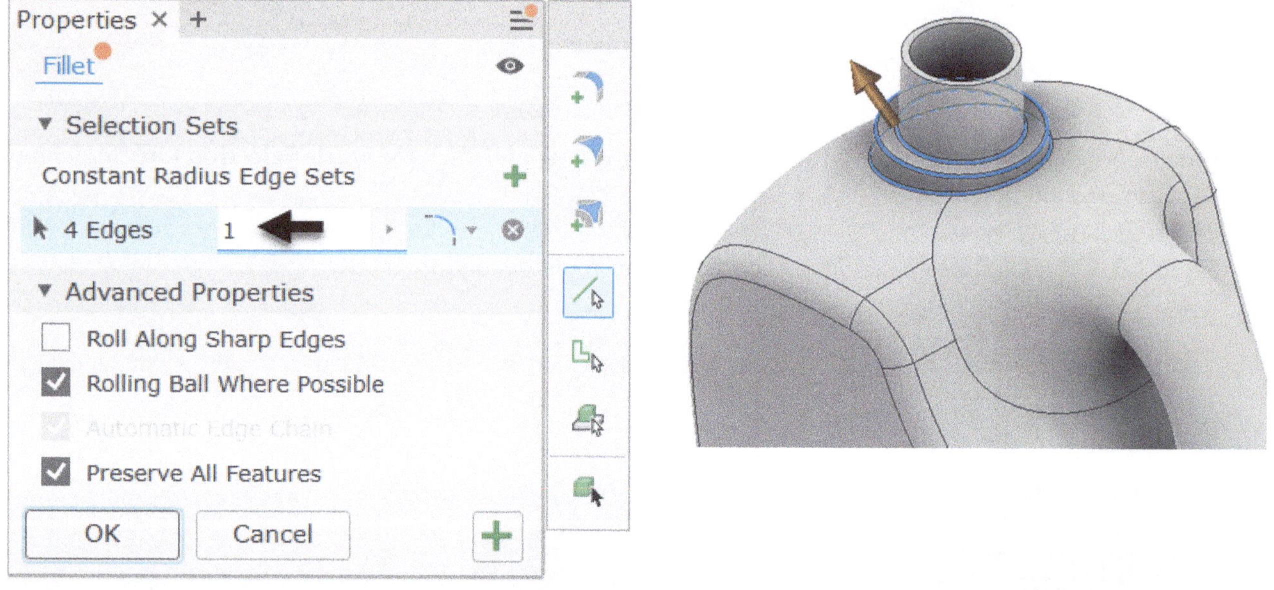

Creating the Emboss on the Label Face

1. On the **3D Model** ribbon, click **Work Features** panel > **Plane** > **Offset from Plane**.
2. Select the XY plane from the Browser window. Next, enter **125** in the **Distance** box and click **OK**.
3. Click **3D Model > Sketch > Start 2D Sketch** on the ribbon. Next, select the newly created datum plane
4. Click **Sketch** > **Create** panel > **Project** drop-down > **Project Geometry**.
5. Select the boundary edges of the label surface, as shown.
6. On the ribbon, click **Sketch > Modify > Offset**. Next, select the projected edges.
7. Move the pointer inward and click. Next, add a 12 mm dimension between the offset and projected entities.
8. Click **Finish Sketch**.

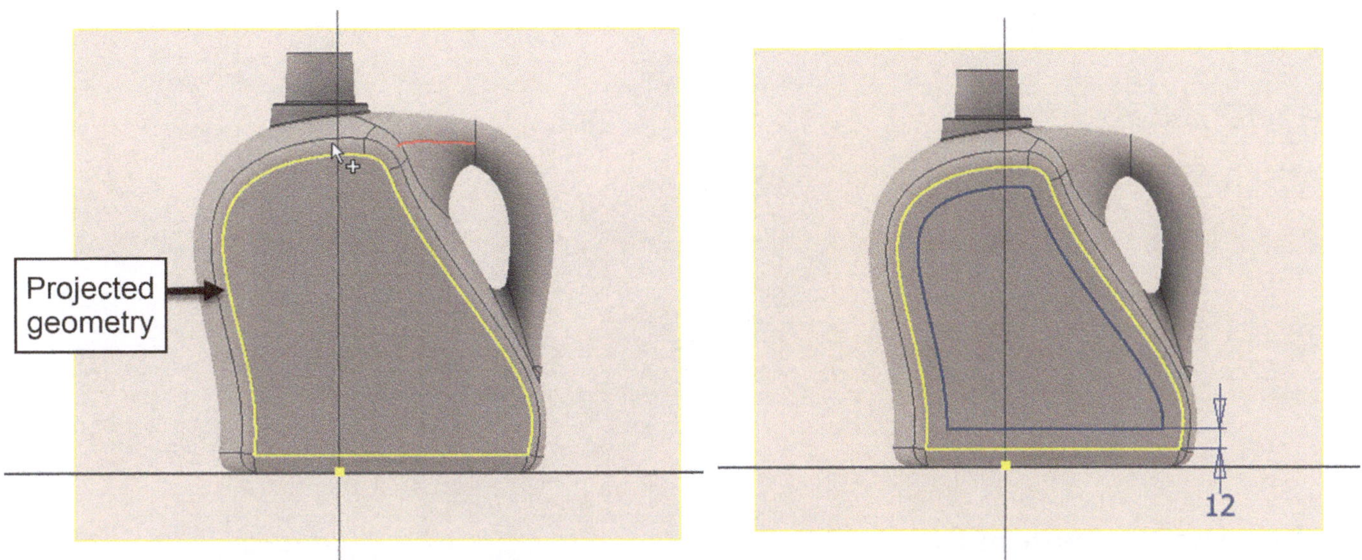

9. Click **3D Model > Create > Emboss** on the ribbon; the **Emboss** dialog appears.
10. Click in the region enclosed by the sketch. Next, click the **Engrave from Face** button on the dialog.
11. Set the **Depth** to 1. Click **OK** to create the embossed feature.

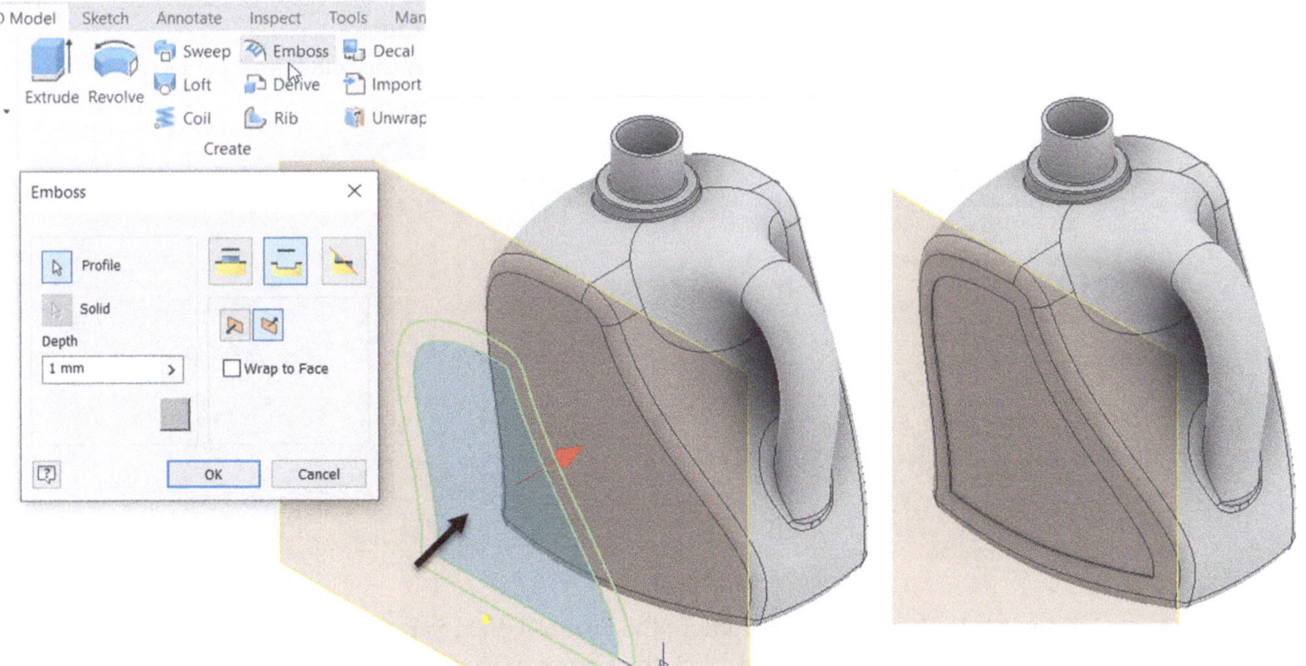

Mirroring the Emboss feature

1. Click **3D Model > Pattern > Mirror** on the ribbon. Select the emboss feature from the model geometry.
2. On the **Mirror** dialog, click the **XY Plane** button. Next, click **OK** to mirror the emboss feature.

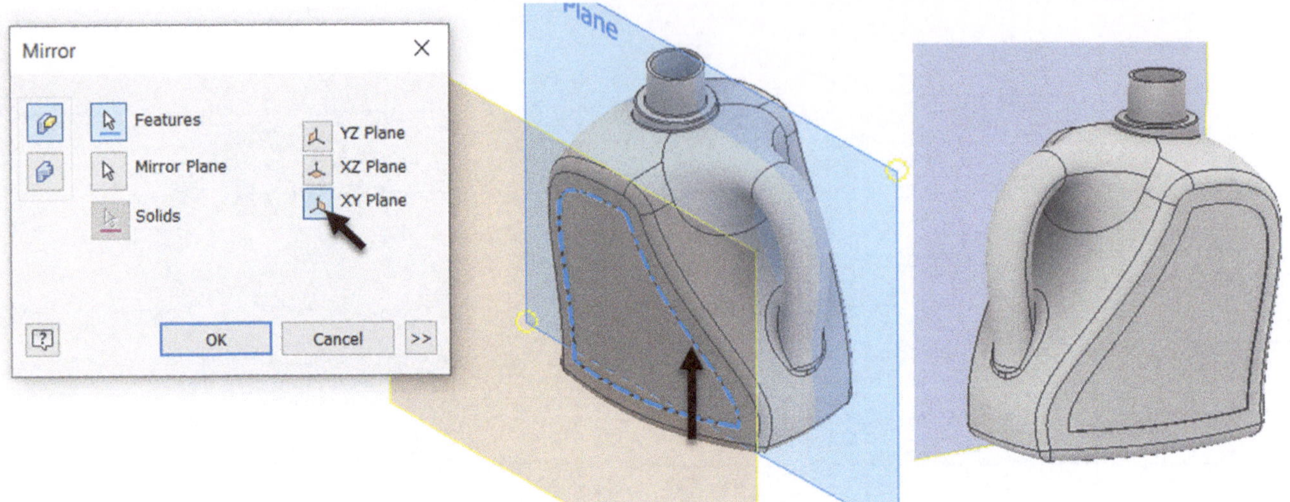

Embossing the bottom face

1. On the **3D Model** ribbon, click **Work Features** panel > **Plane** > **Offset from Plane**.
2. Select the XZ plane from the Browser window. Next, enter **-15** in the **Distance** box and click **OK**.
3. Start a new sketch on the newly created plane.
4. On the **Sketch** ribbon, expand the **Create** panel and click **Project** drop-down > **Project Geometry**.
5. Select the inner edges of the fillets, as shown.
6. On the ribbon, click **Sketch > Modify > Offset**. Next, select the projected edges.
7. Move the pointer inward and click. Next, add a 12 mm dimension between the offset and projected entities.
8. Click **Finish Sketch**.

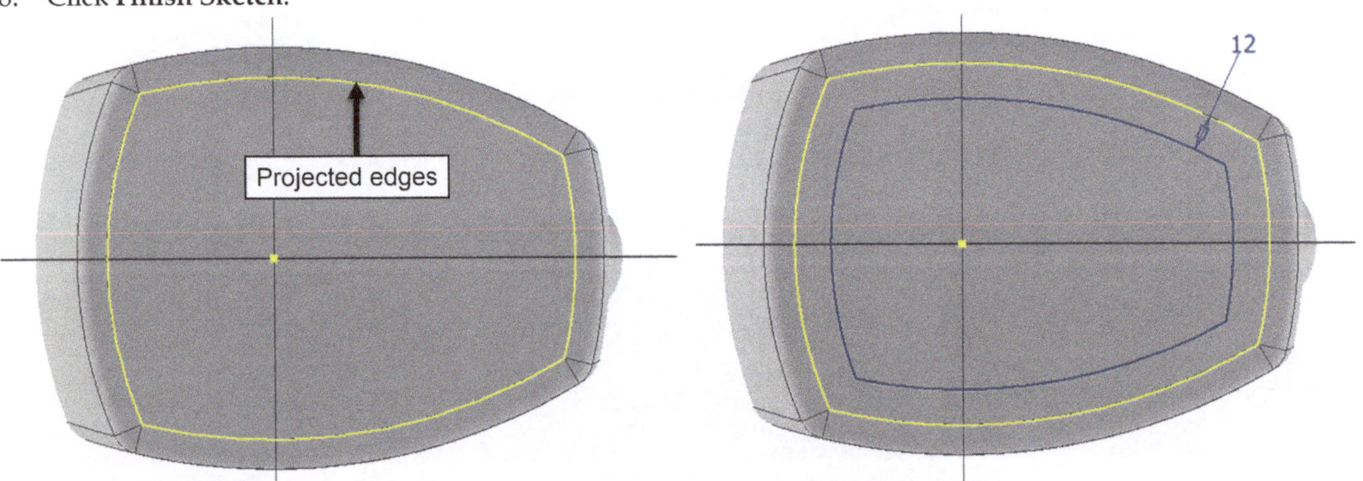

9. Click **3D Model > Create > Emboss** on the ribbon; the **Emboss** dialog appears.
10. Click in the region enclosed by the sketch. Next, click the **Engrave from Face** button on the dialog.
3. Set the **Depth** to 1. Click **OK** to create the embossed feature.

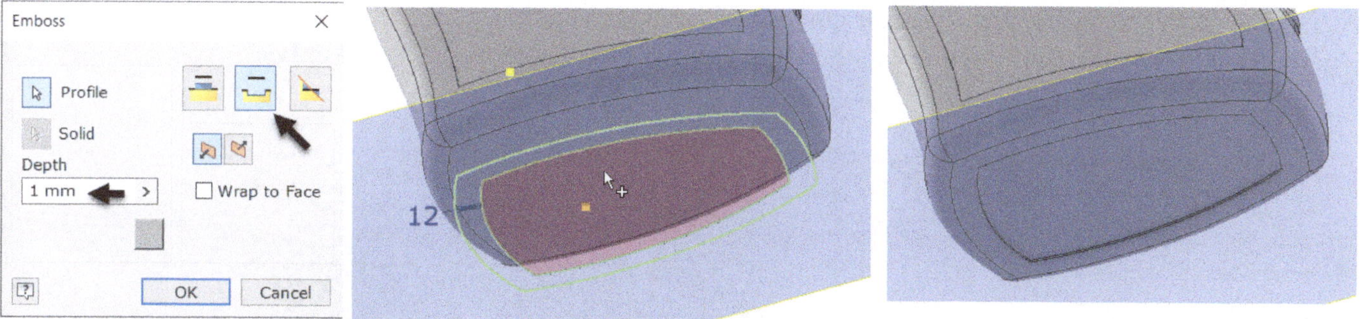

Filleting the Embosses

1. Activate the **Fillet** command and select the corner edges of the emboss feature, as shown.
2. On the **Fillet** Properties panel, type-in **6** in the **Fillet Constant Radius** box, and click **Apply** +.

3. Likewise, fillet the corner edges of the emboss feature on the backside.

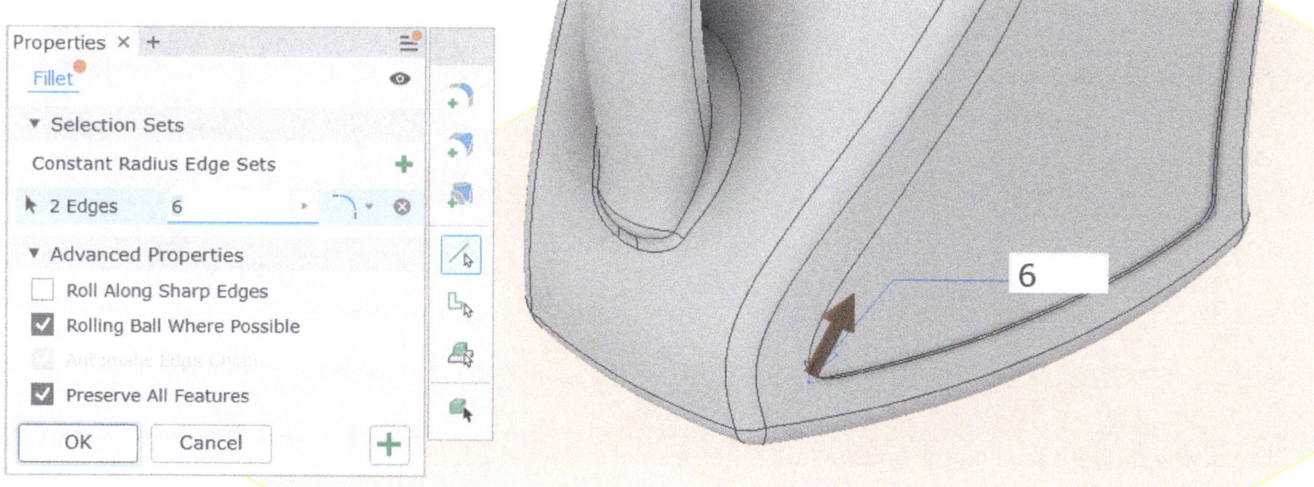

4. Activate the **Fillet** command and select the emboss edges, as shown.
5. On the **Fillet** Properties panel, type-in **2** in the **Fillet Constant Radius** box, and click **Apply**.

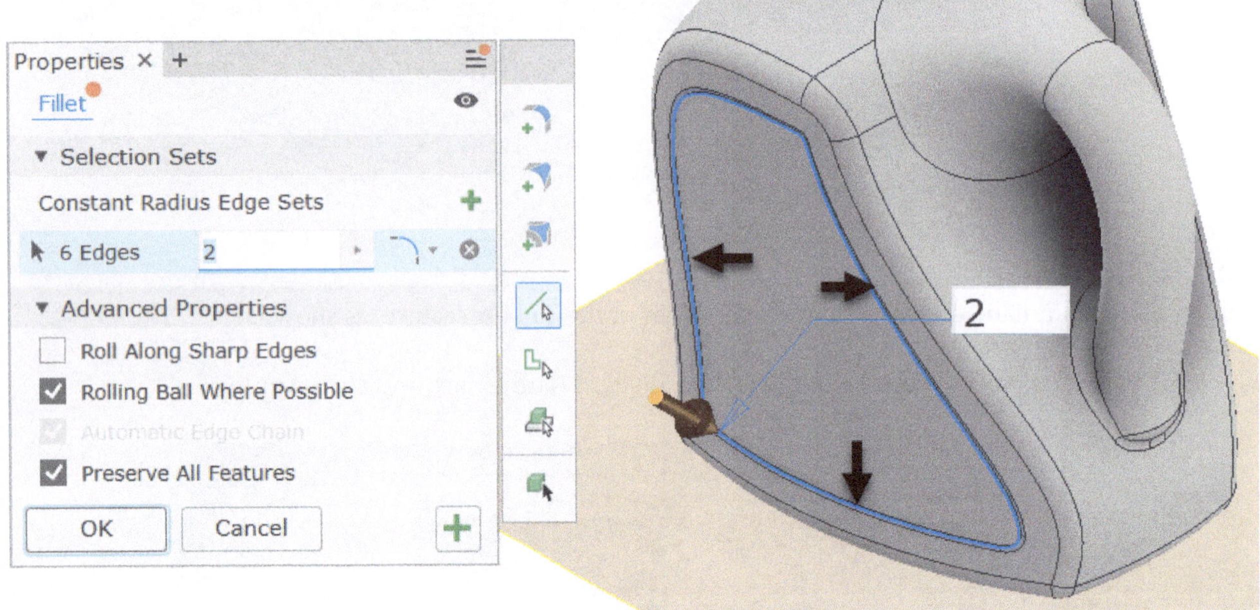

6. Likewise, fillet the trim and extend surface edges on the backside.

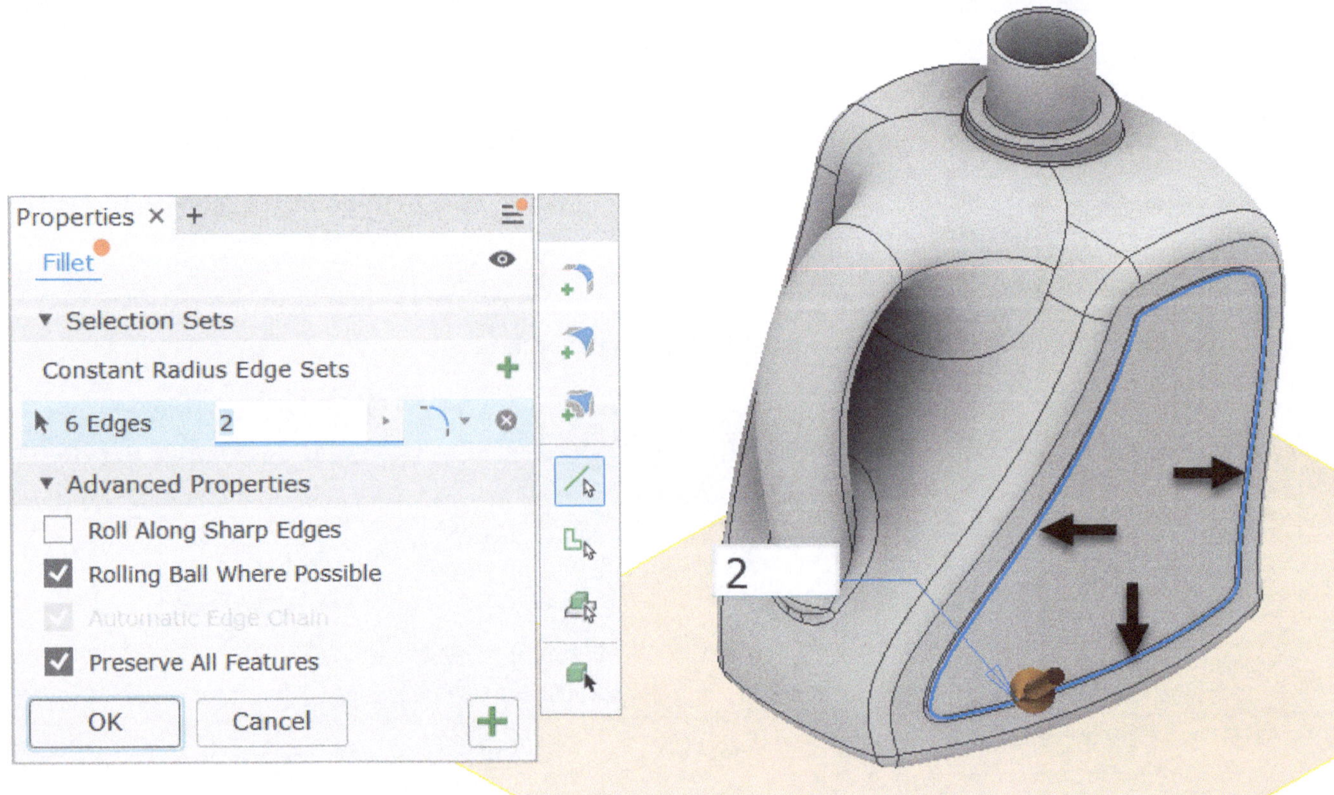

7. Rotate the model such that the bottom face of the model is displayed.
8. Activate the **Fillet** command and select the corner edges of the emboss feature, as shown.

9. On the **Fillet** Properties panel, type-in **6** in the **Fillet Constant Radius** box, and click **Apply**.

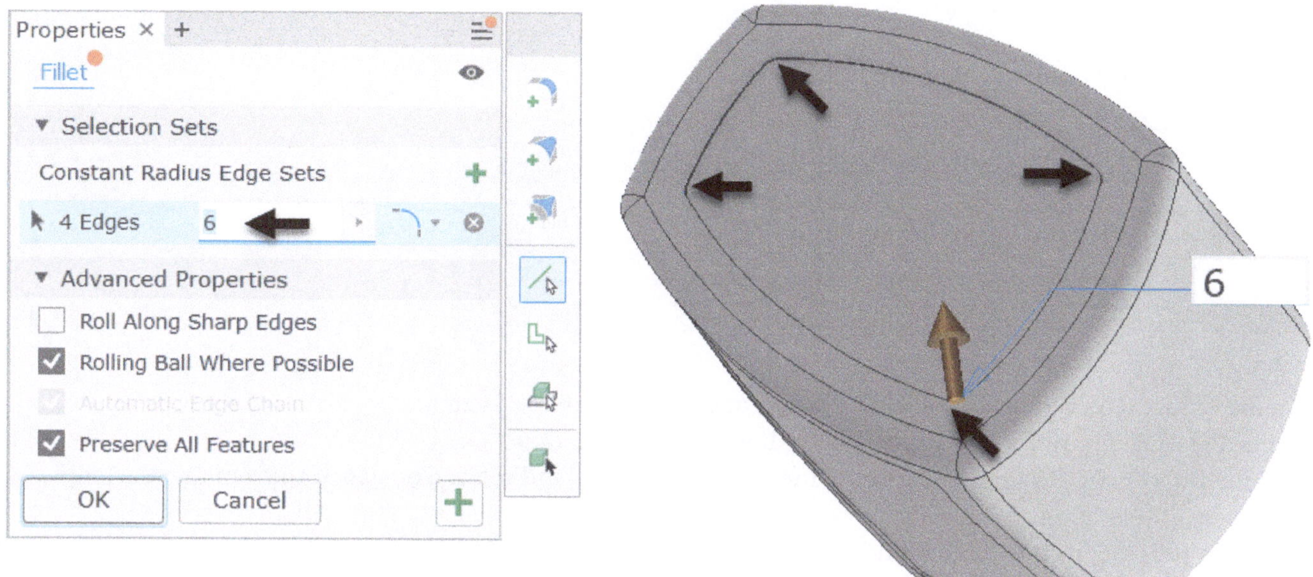

10. Select the edge loop of the emboss feature, as shown.
11. On the **Fillet** Properties panel, type-in **2** in the **Fillet Constant Radius** box, and click **OK**.

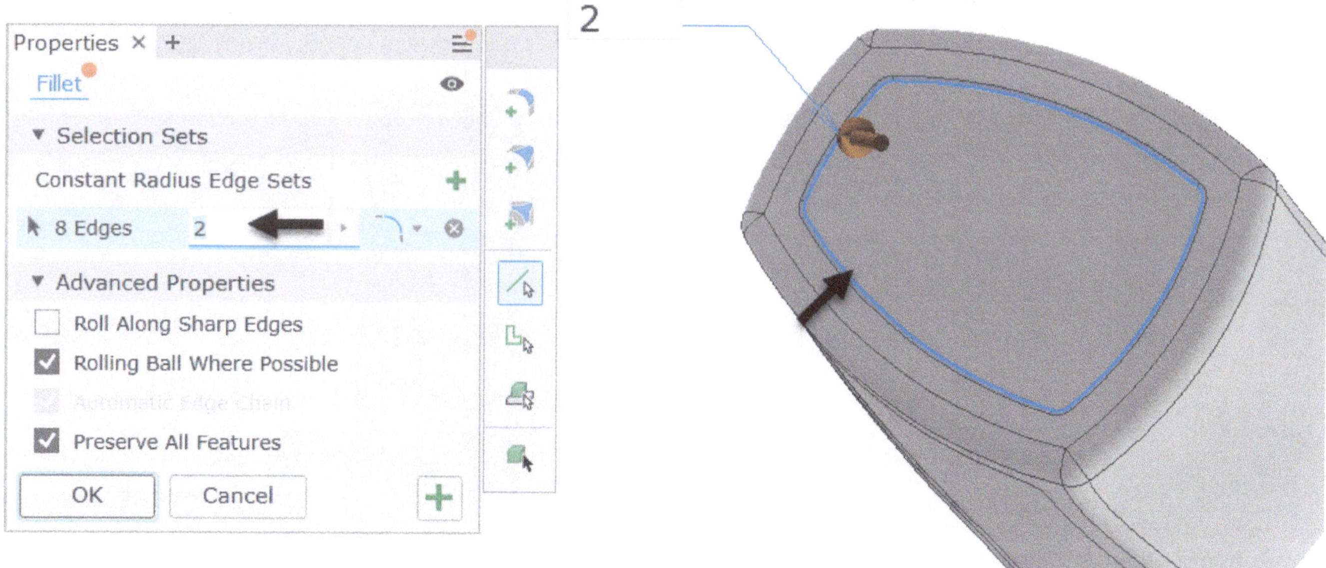

Adding Threads

1. On the ribbon, click **3D Model > Work Features > Axis**. Next, select the inner face of the spout.

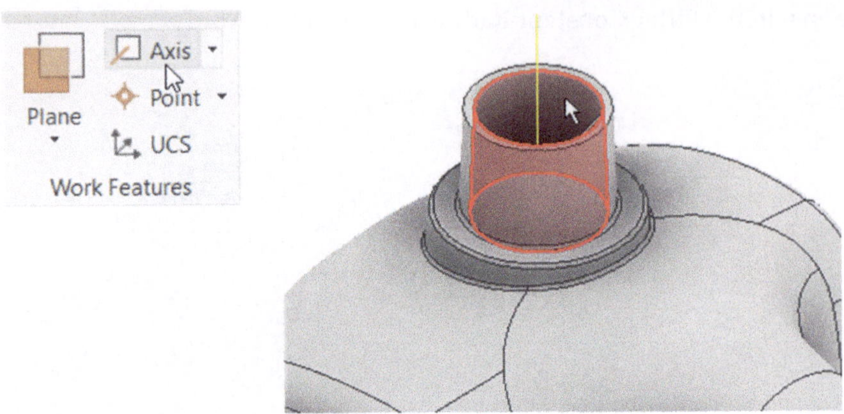

2. In the Model tree, right-click on the XY Plane, and then click **New Sketch**.
3. Click the **Slice Graphics** icon located at the bottom of the window.
4. On the ribbon, click **Sketch > Create > Line**. Next, right click and select **Construction** from the Marking Menu.
5. Create a horizontal construction line, as shown.
6. Deactivate the **Construction** icon on the **Format** panel of the **Sketch** ribbon tab.
7. On the ribbon, click **Sketch > Create > Line**. Create a closed profile, as shown.
8. On the ribbon, click the **Sketch** tab > **Modify** panel > **Fillet**.
9. Select the two corners of the sketch, as shown. Type 0.5 in the Fillet radius box and press Enter.

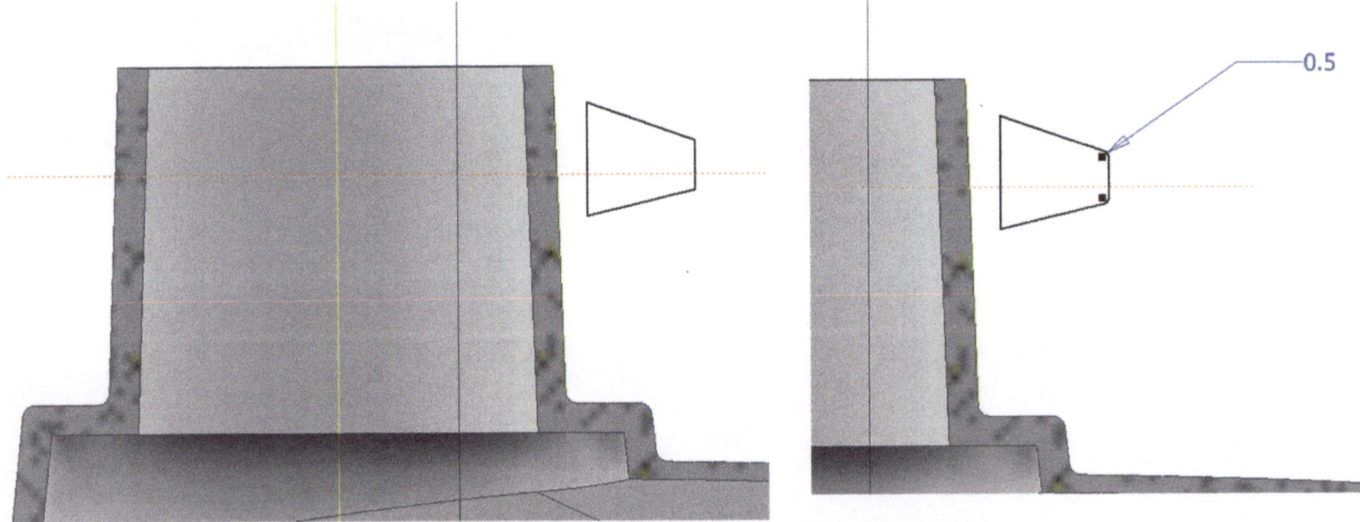

10. Activate the **Dimension** tool and apply dimensions to the sketch, as shown.

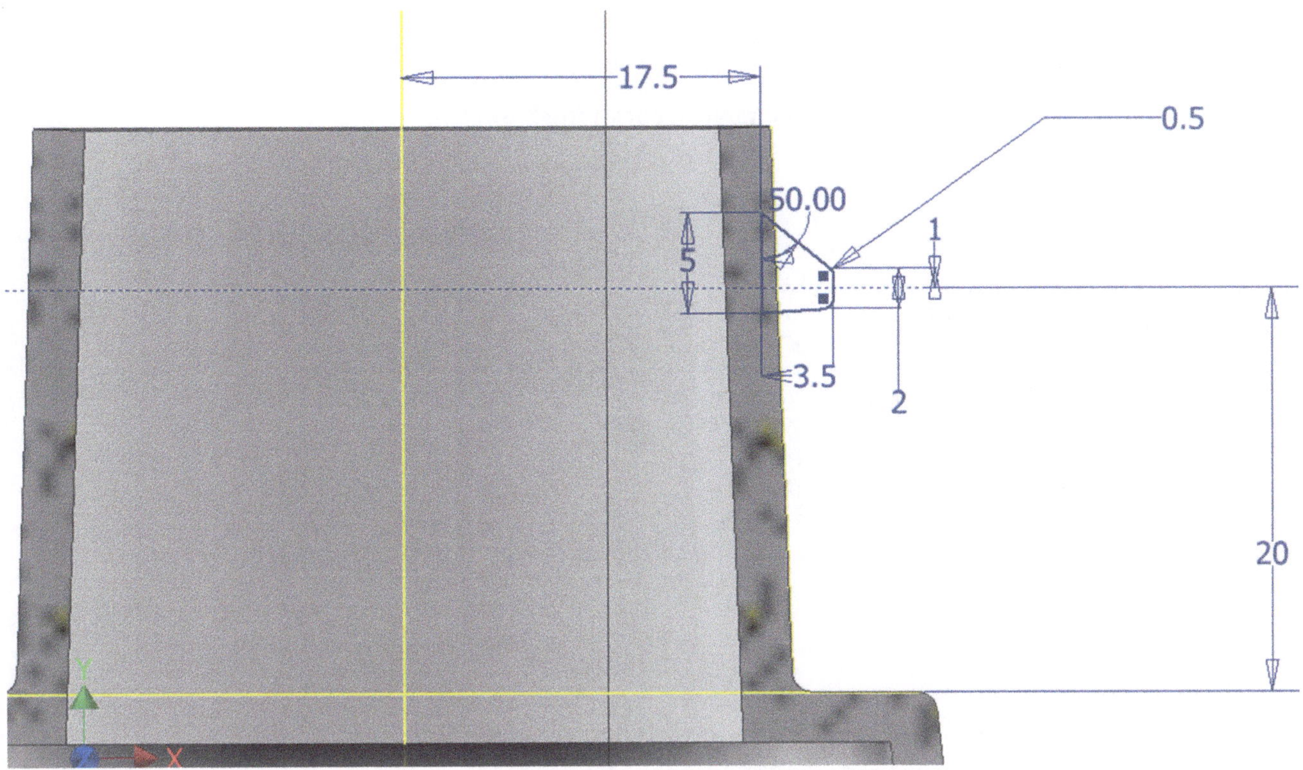

11. Click **Finish Sketch**.
12. On the ribbon, click **3D Model > Create > Coil** ; the closed profile of the sketch is selected automatically.
13. Select the axis of the coil. Click the **Reverse pitch direction along axis** icon, if the preview is displayed in the upward direction.
14. On the **Properties** panel, select **Method > Pitch and Revolution**.
15. Type-in **5** and **2** in the **Pitch** and **Revolution** boxes, respectively.
16. Uncheck the **Close Start** and **Close End** options. Next, click **OK**.

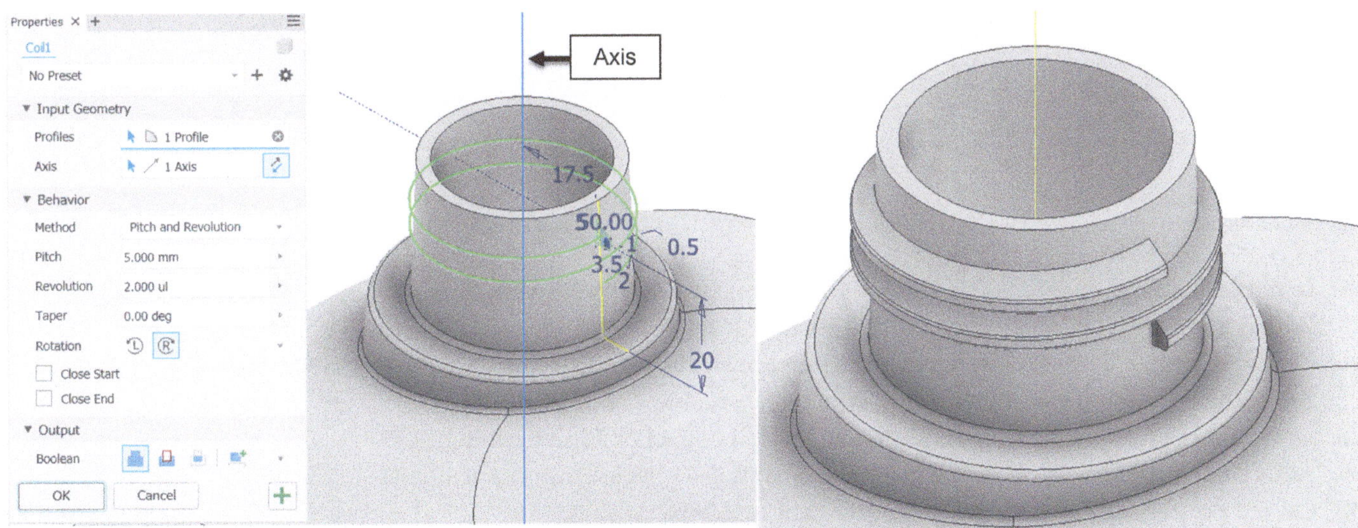

17. In the Model tree, right click on the XY Plane, and then select **New Sketch**.

18. On the ribbon, click **Sketch > Create > Project** drop-down **> Project Geometry** .
19. Select the edges of the end face of the thread.
20. Draw a straight centerline line and dimension it. Next, click **Finish Sketch**.

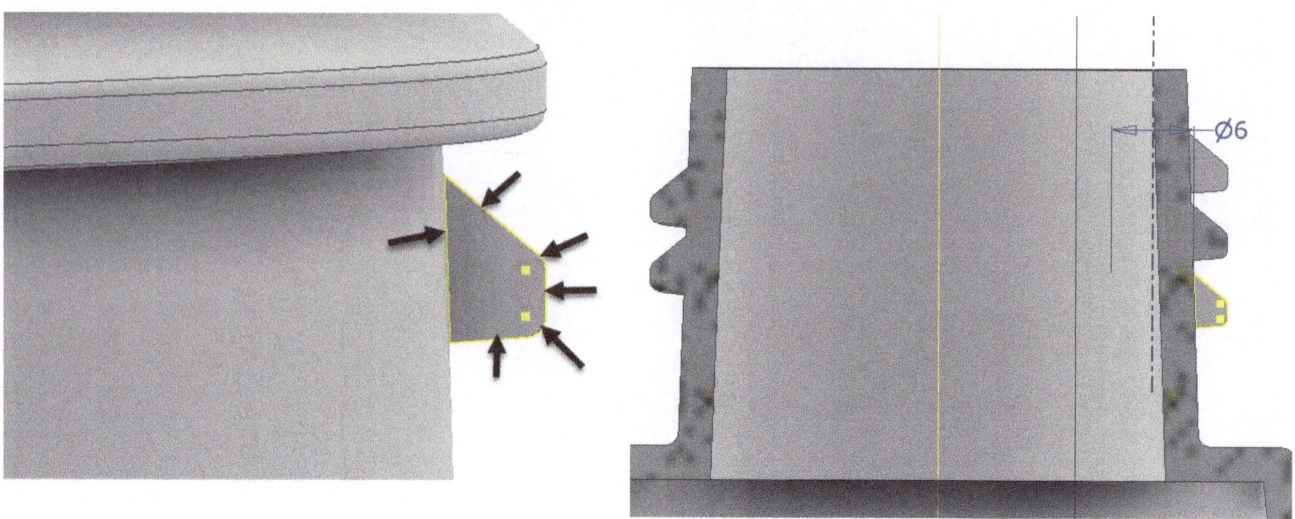

21. Activate the **Revolve** tool; the profile and the axis are selected automatically.
22. On the **Properties** panel, type-in 65 in the **Angle A** box.
23. Next, select **Boolean > Join** and click **OK**.

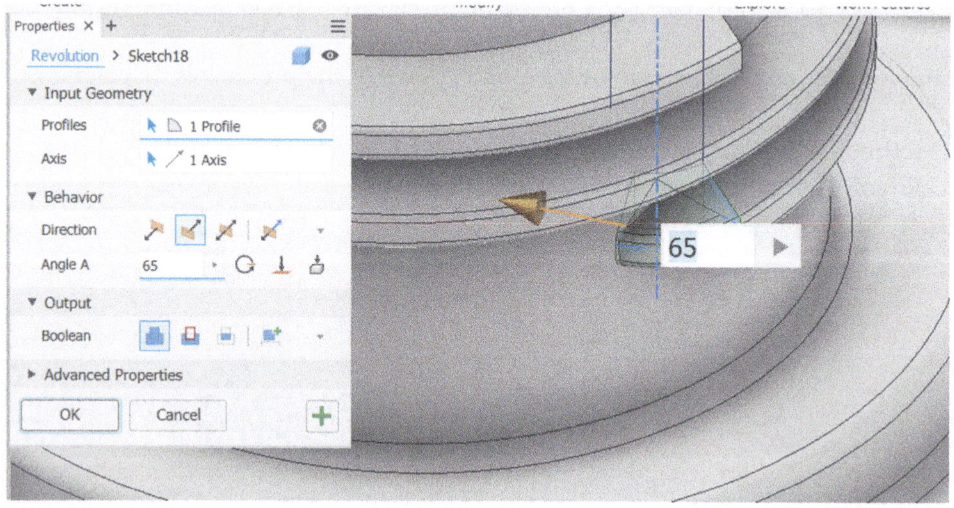

24. In the Model tree, right click on the XY plane. Next, select the **New Sketch**.
25. Rotate the ViewCube to display its Back face.
26. On the ribbon, click the **Sketch** tab **> Create** panel **> Project** drop-down **> Project Geometry.**
27. Select the edges of the end face of the sweep feature. Next, click **OK**.
28. Draw a straight centerline line and dimension it. Next, click **Finish Sketch**.
29. Activate the **Revolve** tool; the profile and the axis are selected automatically.
30. On the **Properties** panel, type-in 65 in the **Angle A** box.
31. Select **Direction > Flipped**. Next, select **Boolean > Join** and click **OK**.

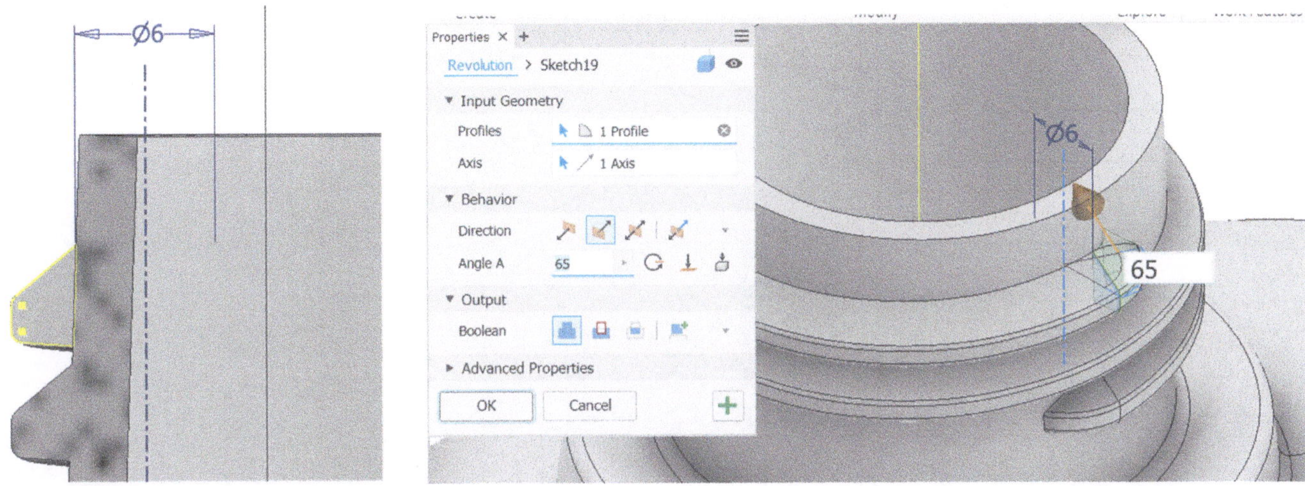

32. Save the model and close it.

Example 2

In this example, you will create a headphone surface model.

1. Start **Autodesk Inventor 2026**.
2. Click **New** drop-down **> New** on the Home screen.
3. On the **Create New File** dialog, click the **Templates > en-US > Metric** folder located in the top right corner.
4. Click the **Standard(mm).ipt** icon located under the **Part - Create 2D and 3D Objects** section.
5. Click the **Create** button on the **Create New File** dialog.
6. On the **3D Model** tab of the ribbon, and click the **Start 2D Sketch** icon on the **Sketch** panel.
7. Start a sketch on the XY plane. Next, create a rectangle and convert it into a construction element, as shown.
8. On the ribbon, click **Sketch > Create> Line** drop-down **> Spline Control Vertex**.
9. Specify the points, as shown. Next, right-click and select **Create**.

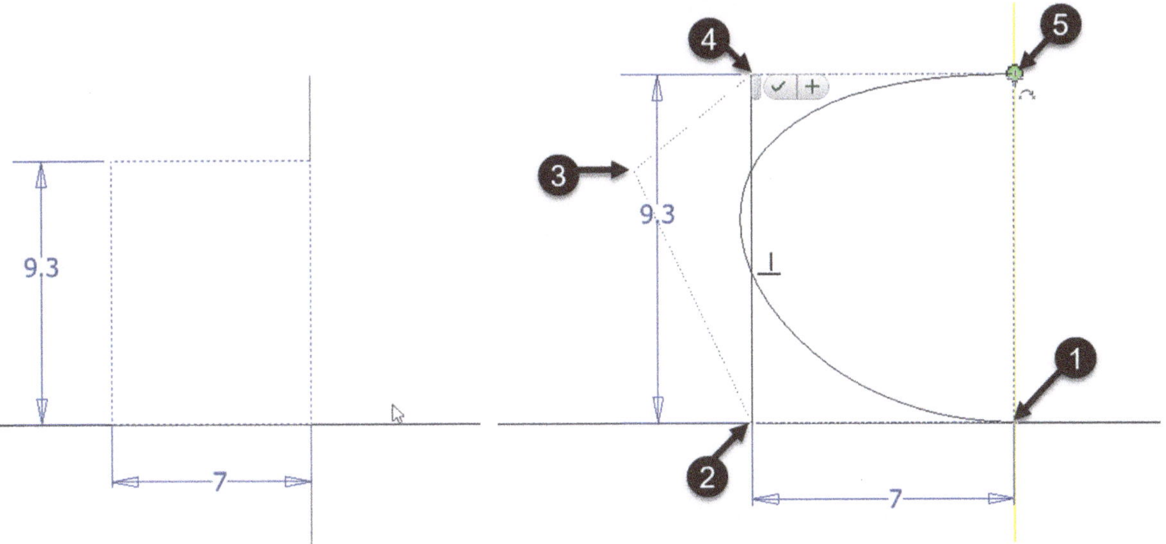

10. Add dimensions to the control vertices of the spline, as shown. Next, click **Finish Sketch**.

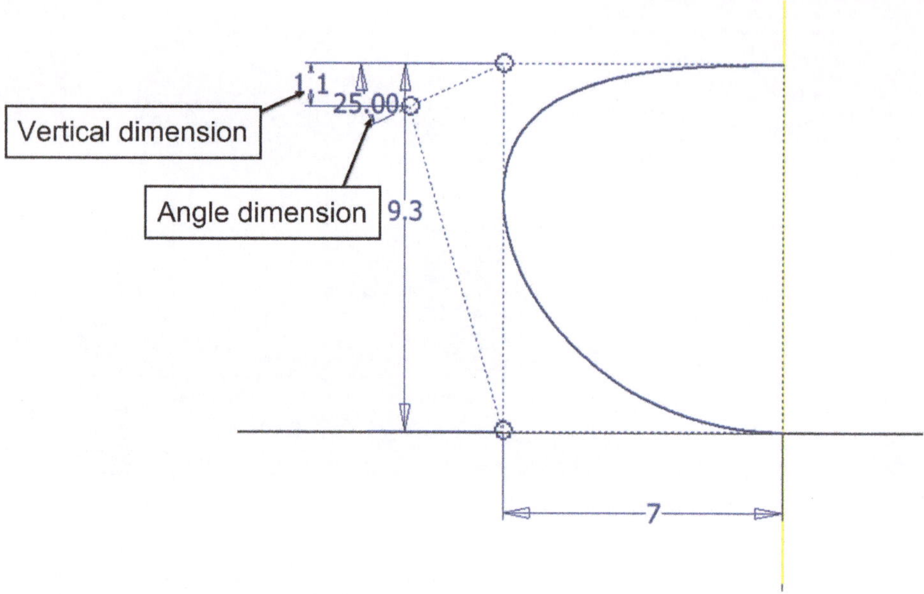

11. On the ribbon, click **3D Model > Create > Revolve**. Select the spline to define the profile.
12. In the **Model** tree, expand the **Origin** folder and select the Y-axis to define the axis of revolution.
13. Click **OK** to create the revolved surface.

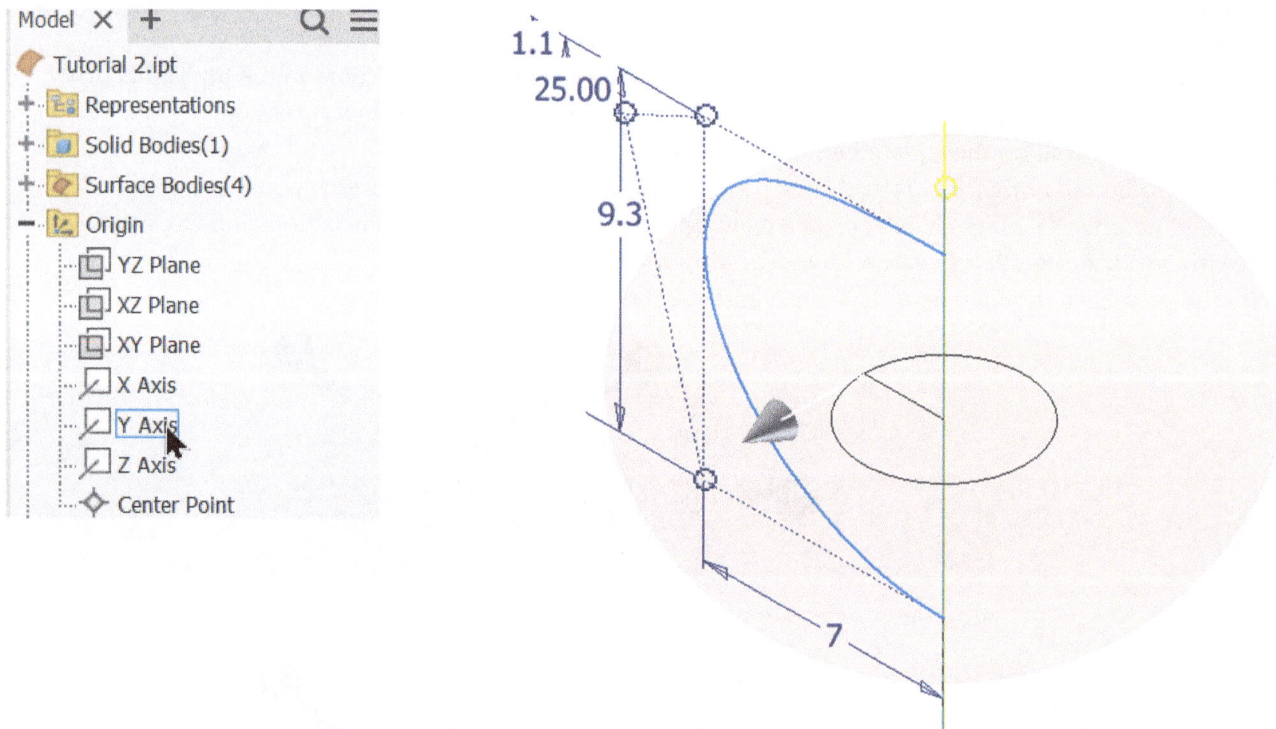

14. In the **Model** tree, right-click on the **Revolution** feature and uncheck the **Translucent** option.
15. Click **3D Model** > **Sketch** panel> **Start 2D Sketch** on the ribbon. Next, select the XY plane.
16. Create an inclined line and add dimensions to it, as shown. Next, click **Finish Sketch**.
17. Click **3D Model > Surface > Trim** on the ribbon. Next, select the inclined line to define the cutting tool.
18. Select the portion of the surface, as shown. Next, click **OK**.

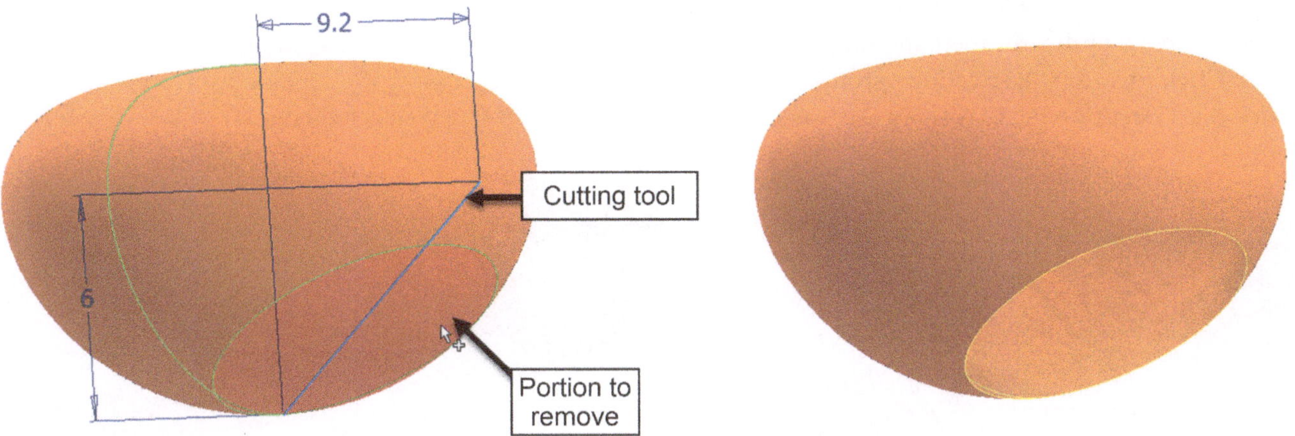

19. Click **3D Model** > **Sketch** panel> **Start 2D Sketch** on the ribbon. Next, select the XY plane.
20. Right-click and select **Create Line** from the Marking Menu. Next, create a horizontal line in the first quadrant.
21. On the ribbon, click **Sketch > Format > Centerline**. Next, create a horizontal centerline.
22. Add dimensions to the sketch, as shown. Next, click **Finish Sketch**.

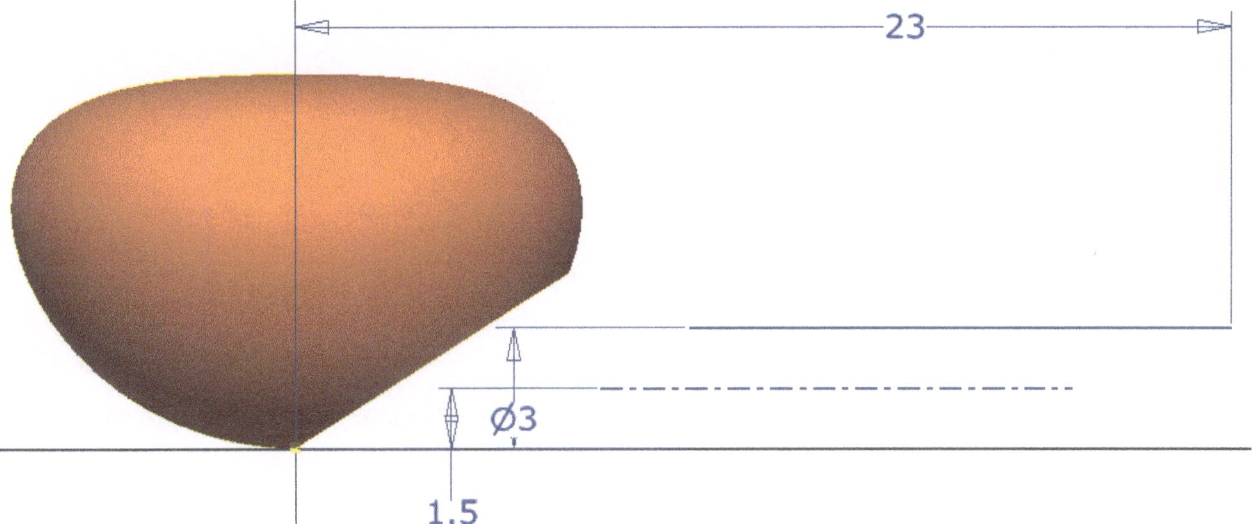

23. On the ribbon, click **3D Model > Create> Revolve**. Select the horizontal line to define the profile.
24. On the **Properties** panel, click in the Axis selection box; the centerline is selected automatically.
25. Click **OK** to create the revolved surface.

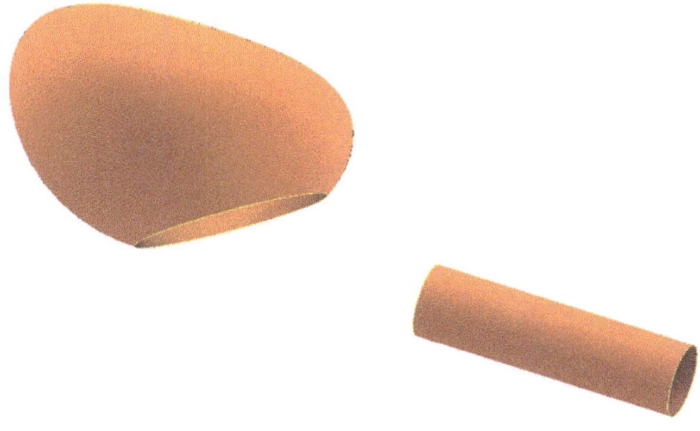

26. On the ribbon, click **3D Model > Create> Loft**. Next, click the **Surface** icon in the **Output** section.
27. Select the edge of the trimmed opening of the revolved surface to define the first section.
28. Click **Click to add** in the **Sections** group, and then select the circular edge of the revolved surface, as shown.
29. Click the **Transition** tab to display the transition surface between the two selected edges.

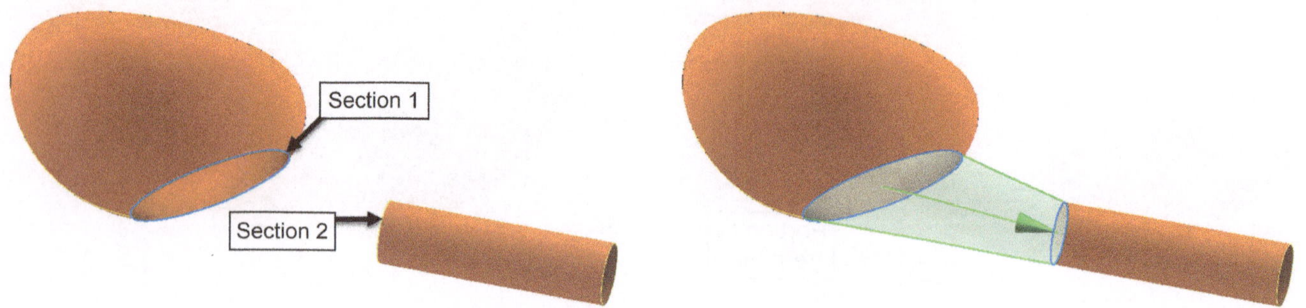

30. Click the **Conditions** tab and select **Tangent Condition** from the **Continuity** drop-down of the two sections.
31. Click the **Flip Takeoff Direction** icon next to the **Continuity** drop-down of the first section.
32. Click **OK** to create the transition surface between the two selected edges.

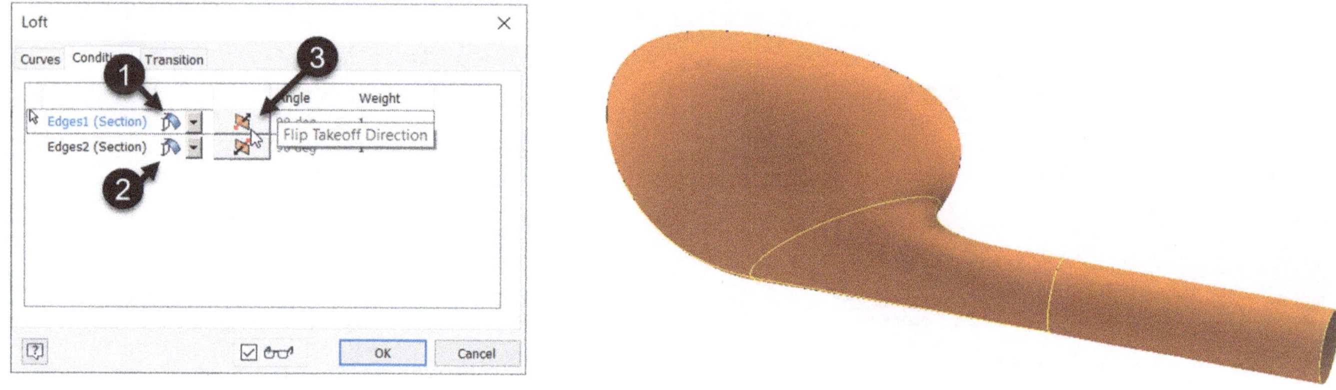

33. Click **3D Model > Surface > Stitch** on the ribbon. Next, select all the surfaces, and then click **Apply** and **Done**.
34. Click **3D Model > Modify > Thicken/Offset** on the ribbon. Next, click the **Quilt selection** icon next to the Faces selection box.
35. Click **Direction > Inward** and type **0.2** in the **Distance** box. Next, select the stitched surface and click **OK**.

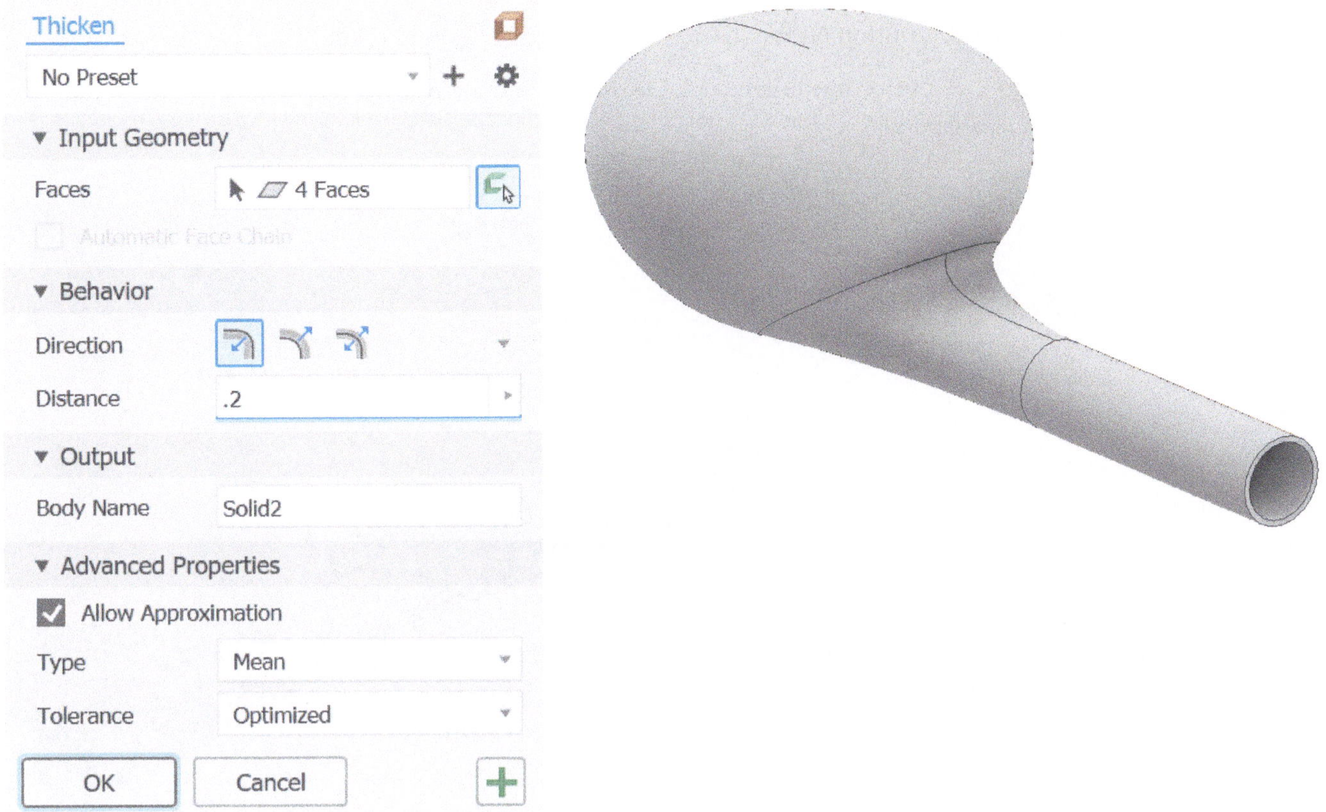

36. On the ribbon, click **3D Model > Work Features > Plane** drop-down **> Offset Plane**.
37. Select the XZ Plane from the Model tree. Next, type **15** in the **Distance** box and click **OK**.
38. Start a sketch on the offset plane, and then create a circle of 11.4 mm diameter, as shown. Next, click **Finish Sketch**.

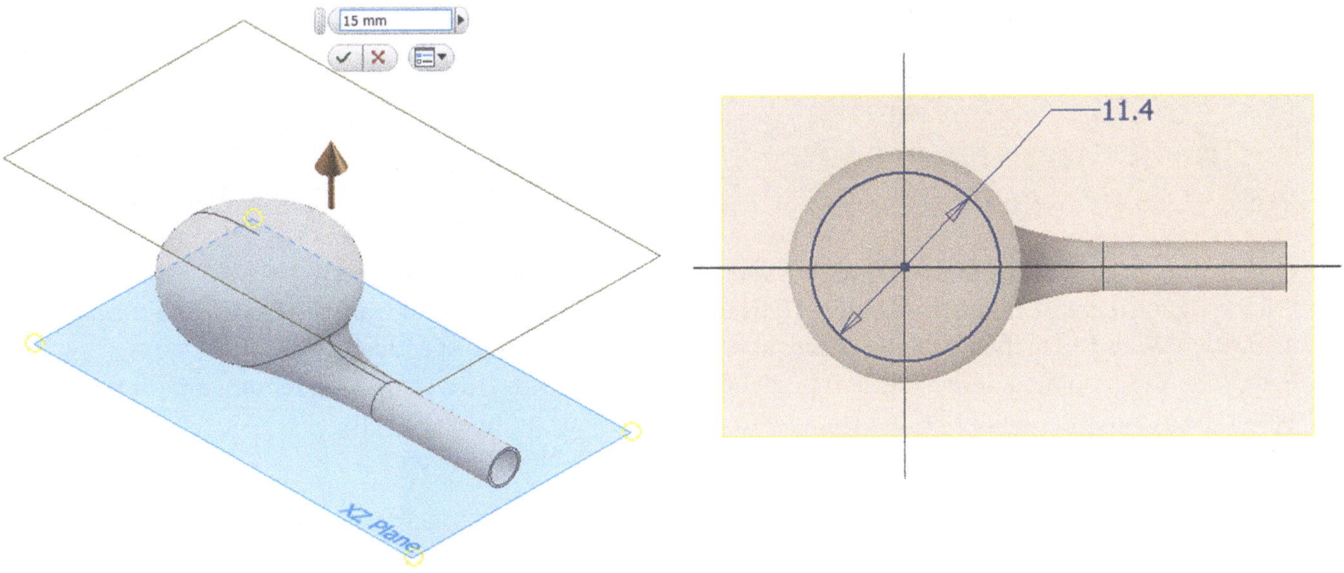

39. Click **3D Model > Create > Emboss** on the ribbon; the **Emboss** dialog appears.
40. Select the sketch, if not already selected.

41. Click the **Engrave from Face** button on the dialog. Next, set the **Depth** to 0.125.
42. Click the **Reverse Direction** button, and then click **OK** to create the embossed feature.
43. Hide the Stitched surface, if displayed.

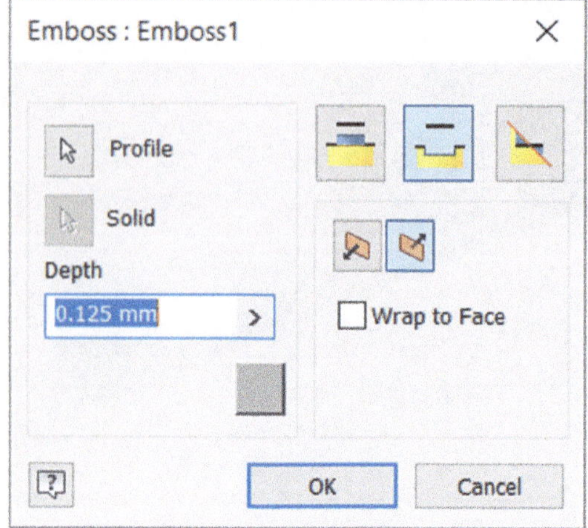

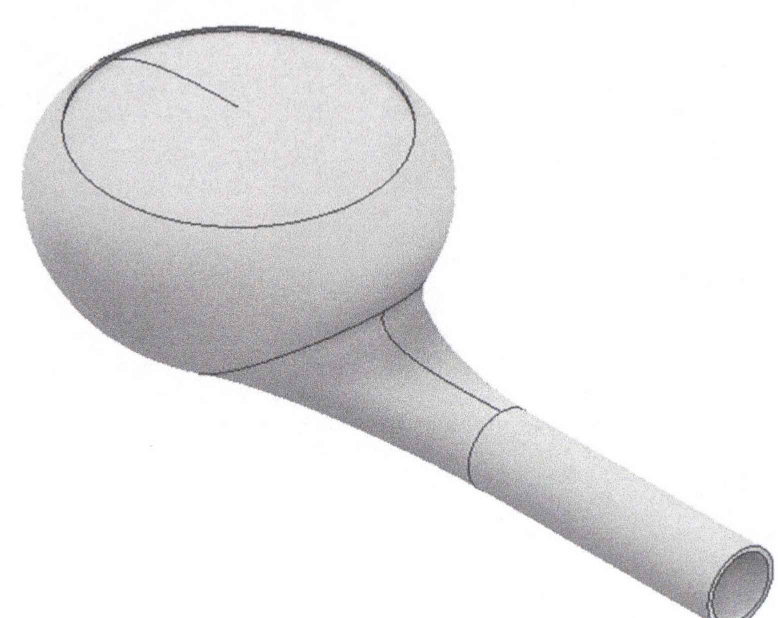

44. Click **3D Model > Modify > Fillet** on the ribbon. Next, type 0.05 in the **Fillet Constant Radius** box.
45. Select the inner and outer edges of the emboss feature, as shown. Next, click **OK** to fillet the edges.

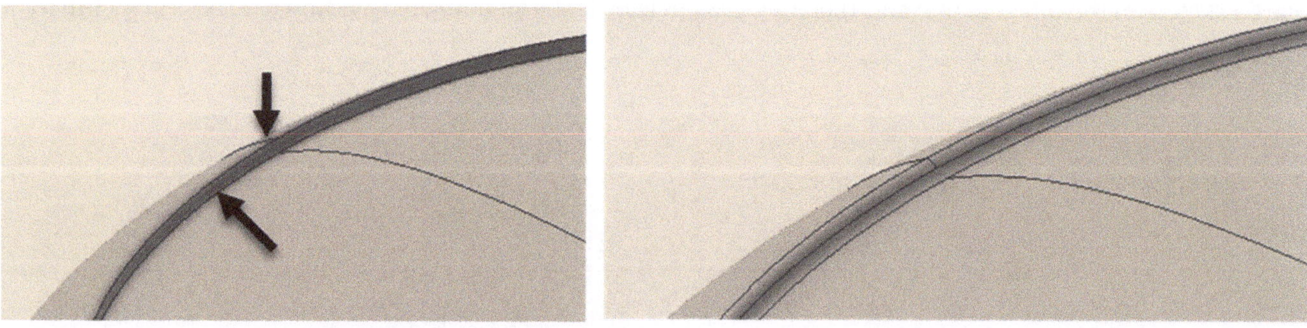

46. On the ribbon, click **3D Model > Sketch > Sketch** drop-down > **Start 3D Sketch**.
47. On the ribbon, click **3D Sketch > Draw > Helical Curve**. Next, select **Spiral** from the **Definition** drop-down.
48. Type **0.5**, **0.5**, and **10** in the **Diameter**, **Pitch**, and **Revolutions** boxes, respectively.
49. Select the origin point to define the start point of the helix axis. Next, move the pointer upward and click.
50. Select the quadrant point of the circular edge to define the start point of the helix.
51. Click **OK** to create the spiral curve. Next, click **Finish Sketch** on the ribbon.

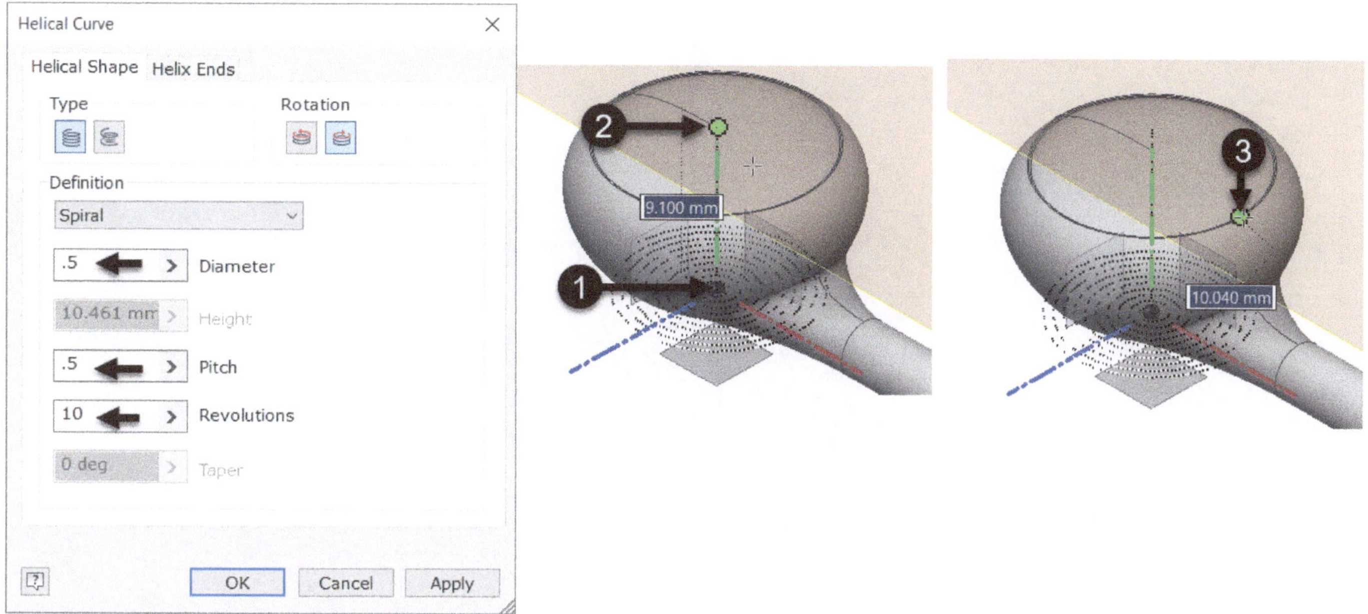

52. Start a 2D sketch on the XZ plane, and then create a circle of 0.3 mm diameter, as shown. Next, click **Finish Sketch**.

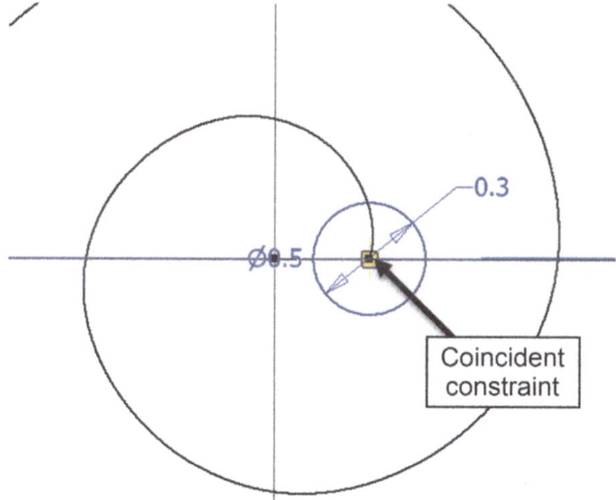

53. On the ribbon, click **3D Model > Sketch > Extrude**; the circle is selected automatically.
54. Click in the **From** selection box, and then select the embossed face. Next, click the **Cut** icon under the **Output** section, and then type 1 in the **Distance** box. Click **OK** to create the extruded cut feature.

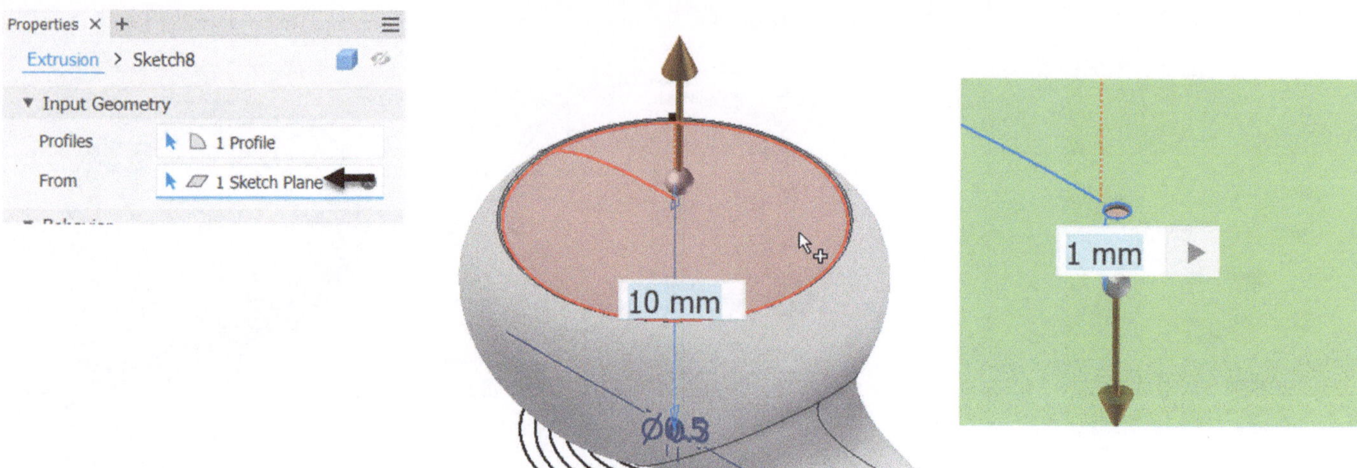

55. On the ribbon, click **3D Model > Pattern > Rectangular Pattern**. Next, select the extruded cut feature created in the last step.
56. Click the cursor icon in the **Direction A** section and select the spiral curve.
57. Select Distribution > Fitted.
58. Click the **Curve Length** icon next to the Distance box available in the **Direction A** section.
59. Type **150** in the **Number** box and click **OK** to create the pattern.

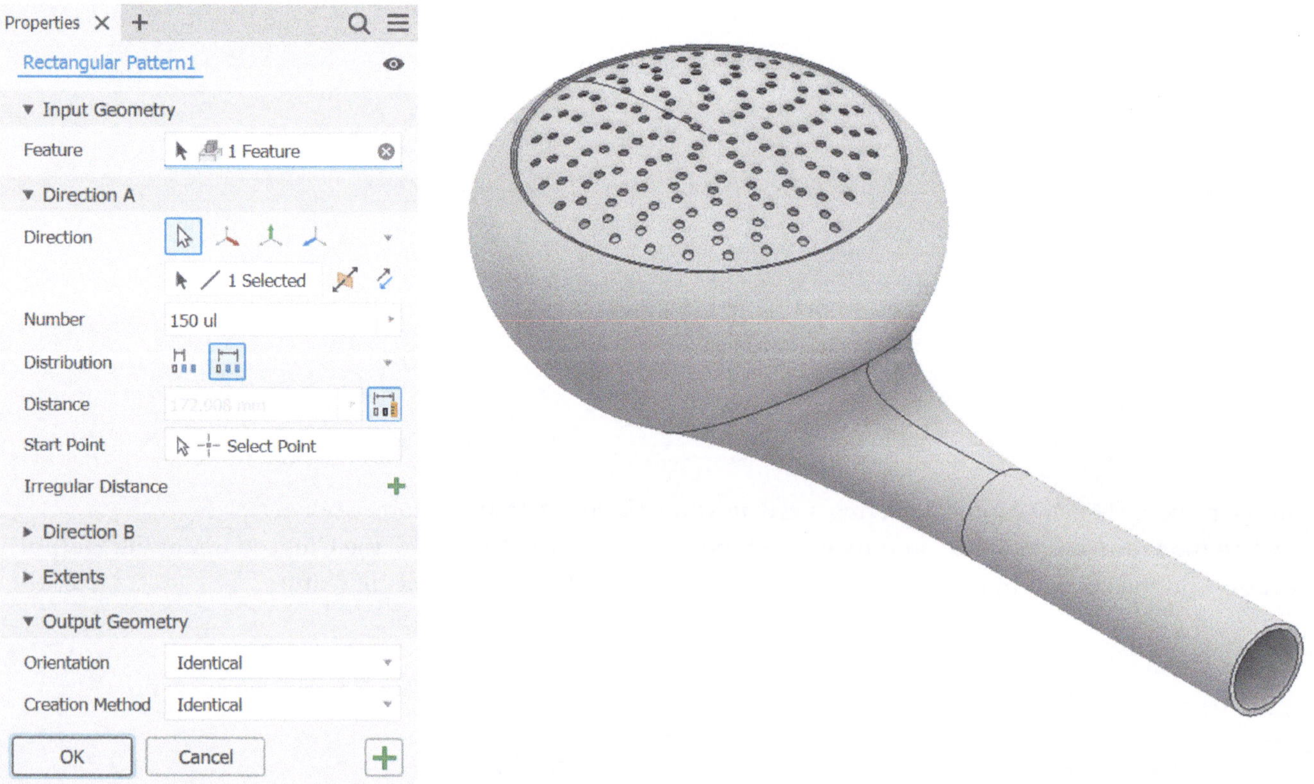

60. Save and close the part file.

Questions

1. What is the use of the **Trim** command?
2. How many types of swept surfaces can be created in Autodesk Inventor 2026?
3. Why do we use the **Patch** command?
4. Which command can be used to bridge the gap between two surfaces?
5. List the **Extend type** options that can be used to extend surfaces from an edge.

Index

Add Participant, 300
Aligned, 279
aligned section view, 336
All, 84
Analyze Interference, 287
Angle, 281
Angle to Plane around Edge, 76
Angular Dimensions, 30
Application Options, 14
Arc Tangent, 20
Arc Three Point, 20
Area Loft, 198
Arrange Dimension, 346
Assembly environment, 5
Assembly Features, 299
associativity, 2
Asymmetric, 82
At Root, 228
At Top, 228
Auto Balloon, 345
Autodesk Inventor Help, 15
Automatic Centerlines, 353
Automatic Dimensions and Constraints, 38
Auxiliary View, 334
Ball, 282
Balloon, 345
Base View, 333
Baseline Dimension, 346
Baseline Dimension Set, 347
Bend Part, 230
Break, 339
Break Alignment, 342
Break Out, 340
Center Line Loft, 197
Center Mark, 351
Center Point Arc, 22
Center Point Arc Slot, 26
Center Point Circle, 22
Center Point Slot, 26
Center to Center Slot, 25
Centered Pattern, 354
Centerline, 39, 352
Centerline Bisector, 352
Chamfer, 40, 123
Chamfer Notes, 355
Circular Pattern, 45, 148
Closed Loop, 196
Coil, 179
Coincident, 32
Collinear, 35
Color scheme, 14
Combine, 233
Concentric, 34
Constraint Settings, 37
Constraints, 32
Construction, 39
Control Vertex Spline, 47
Copy, 43
Copy Components, 295
Corner Setback, 121
Counterbored Hole, 111
Countersink Hole, 112
Create Component, 302, 303
Create Drawing View, 332
Create New dialog, 12
Create new preset, 111
Creating Multibodies, 231
Customize, 10
Cut, 81, 234
Cylindrical, 284
Decal, 236
Delete Face, 393
Demote, 297
Detail View, 337
Dialogs, 9
Dimension, 29
Dimensions, 345
Direction Condition, 193
Display Connection Line, 338
Distance, 82
Distance and Angle chamfer, 124
Drawing environment, 6
Edit Constraint, 290
Edit Feature, 258
Edit Sketches, 257
Ellipse, 28
Emboss, 234
Equal, 34

Exploded View, 341
Exploding Assemblies, 304
Extend, 41, 389
Extend Start, 110
Extents, 82
Extrude, 377
Extrude Features, 71
Extruded Surface
Face Draft, 125
Face Fillet, 122
File Menu, 6
File Types, 4
Fillet, 40, 115
Fixed Plane, 125
Flexible, 297
Flush, 278
Free Move, 276
Free Rotate, 277
Full Round Fillet, 123
Helical Cutout, 184
Hole, 107
Hole and Thread, 354
Hole Table - Feature, 351
Hole Table - Selection, 350
Hole Table - View, 350
Horizontal, 33, 343
iMate, 288
In Position, 342
Inference, 37
Insert, 280
Interpolation Spline, 48
Intersect, 81, 234
Inverted Fillet, 117
iProperties, 393
Join, 81, 233
Joint, 282
Line, 19
Linear Dimensions, 29
Loft, 192, 379, 381
Loft Cutout, 200
Loft sections, 192
Look At, 88
Marking Menus, 12
Match Shape, 85
Mate, 277, 278
Midplane between Two Planes, 75
Midplane of Torus, 76
Mirror, 47, 141
Mirror Components, 293
Mirror Solids, 142
Model window, 8
Move, 42
My Home, 331
Navigation wheel, 88
New Snapshot View, 307
New Solid, 81
Normal to Axis through Point, 79
Normal to Curve at a Point, 80
Offset, 42
Offset Faces, 261
Offset from Plane, 74
Opposed, 279
Orbit, 88
Ordinate Dimension, 348
Ordinate Set, 348
Orientation, 175
Overall Slot, 25
Over-constrained Sketch, 32
Pan, 88
Parallel, 36
Parallel to Plane through Point, 74
Part environment, 5
Parts List, 344
Patch, 385
Path & Guide Rail, 176
Path sweeps, 173
Pattern Component, 292, 293
Patterning the entire geometry, 147
Pitch and Height, 180
Pitch and Revolution, 181
Place Component, 273
Planar, 285
Planes, 74
Polygon, 27
Profile scaling, 177
Project Geometry, 73
Projected View, 333
Promote, 298
Quick Access Toolbar, 7
Rails, 194
Rectangle Two Point Center, 24
Rectangular Pattern, 46, 143
Replace, 291
Replace Face, 389
Resume Suppressed Features, 259
Retrieve Dimensions, 345

Revolution and Height, 181
Revolve, 72
Revolve Features, 72
Revolved Surface
Rib, 227
Rigid, 283
Rigid and Flexible Sub-Assemblies, 297
Rotate, 43
Rotate faces, 262, 263
Rotational, 283
Ruled Surface, 231, 387
Scale, 44
Sculpt, 391
Search Help & Commands, 8
Section View, 334
Set Cut Edges to Smooth, 338
Shaded, 89
Shaded with Edges, 88
Sheet Metal environment, 6
Shell, 126
Shortcut Menus, 12
Show All Constraints, 38
Show all relationships, 292
Simple Hole, 108
Sketch Driven Pattern, 150
Slice the Whole part, 336
Slider Joint, 285
Smooth (G2) Condition, 194
Smooth G2 Fillet, 116
Spiral, 182
Split, 231
Start 2D Sketch, 18, 49, 159
Starting an Assembly, 272
Status Bar, 8
Stitch, 391
Stretch, 44
Styles Editor, 349
Sub-assemblies, 296
Suppress, 147
Suppress Features, 258
Sweep, 172
Swept Cutout, 178
Symmetric, 36
Symmetry, 282
Tangent, 35, 281
Tangent Circle, 22
Tangent Condition, 194
Tangent to Surface through Edge, 78
Taper, 85, 175
Taper Tapped Hole, 113
Tapped Hole, 113
Thicken/Offset, 392
Thread, 114
Three Point Arc, 26
Three Point Center Rectangle, 24
Three Point Rectangle, 23
Three Points, 76
To, 83
Translate, 261
Trim, 42, 386
Tweak Components, 305
Twist, 176
Two Coplanar Edges, 77
Two Distances chamfer, 124
Two Point Rectangle, 23
UCS, 80
Undirected, 280
Unwrap, 394
User Interface, 4
Variable Radius Fillet, 120
Vertical, 33, 343
View Alignment, 342
View Cube, 8
Wireframe, 89
Wireframe with hidden edges, 89
Wireframe with Visible edges only, 89
Zoom, 88
Zoom All, 87
Zoom Selected, 88
Zoom window, 88

Printed at Repro India Ltd.